MW01711742

VOYAGE OF DISCOVERY

Fifty Years of Marine Research at Canada's Bedford Institute of Oceanography

A COMMEMORATIVE VOLUME IN CELEBRATION OF THE 50th ANNIVERSARY OF THE BEDFORD INSTITUTE OF OCEANOGRAPHY DARTMOUTH, NOVA SCOTIA, CANADA, 1962 - 2012

EDITED BY

David N. Nettleship
Donald C. Gordon, C.F. Michael Lewis
and Michel P. Latremouille

Graphics and Layout Design
Francis G. Kelly

Published by
The BIO–Oceans Association
Dartmouth, Nova Scotia

2014

Published by:

The BIO–Oceans Association
c/o Bedford Institute of Oceanography
1 Challenger Drive, P.O. Box 1006
Dartmouth, Nova Scotia
Canada B2Y 4A2

BIO-OA website: www.bio-oa.ca

EDITORIAL BOARD
Donald C. Gordon, Michel P. Latremouille, C.F. Michael Lewis,
David N. Nettleship, and Michael M. Sinclair

GRAPHICS & LAYOUT DESIGNER
Francis G. Kelly

COVER DESIGN & LAYOUT
David N. Nettleship and Francis G. Kelly

PHOTOGRAPHY & ARCHIVES
Kelly Bentham

Printed and bound in Canada
by Friesens, Altona, Manitoba, using
FSC certified paper: 100 lb. Sterling Ultra Gloss.
Printed on paper that does not contain any materials
from trees of old growth forests.

Copyright © 2014 by the BIO-Oceans Association (BIO-OA)

All rights reserved. No part of the publication may be reproduced, stored in a retrieval system other than BIO-OA, or transmitted, in any form or by any means – electronic, mechanical, photocopying, recording, or otherwise – without the prior written permission of the publisher BIO-OA.

ISBN: 978-0-9936443-0-6 hardcover
ISBN: 978-0-9936443-1-3 electronic

Suggested citation of individual papers:

Author(s). 2014. (title of paper). Pages xxx-yyy *in*: Voyage of Discovery: Fifty Years of Marine Research at Canada's Bedford Institute of Oceanography (D.N. Nettleship, D.C. Gordon, C.F.M. Lewis, and M.P. Latremouille, Eds.). BIO-Oceans Association, Dartmouth, Nova Scotia, Canada

Front cover: *CSS Hudson* on oceanographic survey, east Baffin Island - Oil on canvas (30" x 40") by C. Anthony Law
Back cover: Bedford Institute of Oceanography (2012), Dartmouth, Nova Scotia, Canada (photo: Kelly Bentham)

To The Blue Planet
and those who wish to
understand the oceans

DEDICATION

This book is dedicated to those federal elected officials and senior managers who had the wisdom and foresight to establish the Bedford Institute of Oceanography and who provided it with the resources in the early years to develop into one of the world's major oceanographic institutions and make important contributions to Canada and to ensure a better understanding of the three oceans that surround us.

OBJECTIVE & PURPOSE:

The Need to Know and Understand

"There are no applied sciences ... There are only applications of science and this is a very different matter ... The application of science is very easy to anyone who is the master of the theory of it."

Louis Pasteur
Revue Scientifique 1871

CONTENTS OVERVIEW

CONTENTS

PREFACE

The sea is everything. It covers seven-tenths of the terrestrial globe. Its breath is pure and healthy. It is an immense desert where man is never alone, for he feels life quivering around him on every side. The sea is only the medium of a preternatural and wonderful existence; it is only movement and love; it is the infinite with life breathed into it. And in reality, nature is manifested in it by her three kingdoms – mineral, vegetable, and animal. This last is largely represented by the four groups of zoophytes, by three classes of vertebrates, mammals, reptiles, and those innumerable legions of fish, an infinite order of animals that counts more than 13,000 species, of which a tenth only belongs to fresh water. The sea is the vast reservoir of Nature. It is by the sea that the globe has, so to speak, commenced, and who knows if it will not end by it?

Jules Verne (1864)
Twenty Thousand Leagues Under the Sea
Chapter 10

And so was the global ocean as viewed mid-nineteenth century. Oceanography! What is it? What are oceanographers? What are the marine sciences they practice and pursue, and why do they do it? All of these questions and uncertainties 'jump out' to anyone who has opened the covers of this volume entitled '*Voyage of Discovery*'. Efforts to answer these and related questions since the 1950s have produced a myriad of publications – popular articles and books – and spectacular television documentaries and films, but what progress has really been achieved in appreciating the importance of the oceans? Does a literate bystander understand more about the earth and its oceans today than fifty or a hundred years ago? Perhaps to a slight degree this bystander might be able to discuss certain marine topics such as fisheries (living resources), oil and gas (non-living resources), transportation, pollution, and climate change (ocean-atmosphere relations, sea-level rises), but the importance of oceanography to our society today is still not widely recognized. Part of the *raison d'être* for this book is to improve general understanding of the oceans and emphasize the critical role they play in the future welfare of humankind.

The history of oceanography as a discipline is young. Students of the history of science often place the date of birth of modern oceanography as 21 December 1872, the day when the HMS *Challenger* set sail from Plymouth, England, on her memorable voyage (1872-76) to study the deep ocean. The study approach adopted – large-scale, inter-disciplinary cooperation – set the stage for the many major research efforts that followed. Great advances in knowledge of the oceans were made in the last thirty years of the nineteenth century, so much so, that historians of science state that more was learned about the sea during that time period than had been during the previous three thousand years! With the twentieth century, came two world wars in the first half along with the consolidation of oceanography as a discipline, followed by an era of outstanding scientific and technical accomplishments. Oceanography went from a loosely defined 'science of the seas' during the first few decades to a more complex and integrated multidisciplinary science encompassing all sciences – physics, chemistry, biology, and geology – as applied to the marine world and expanding more recently to include such areas as atmospheric and climate science. The twentieth century was also a time when the value of forming conglomerates of marine scientists was realized, with multidisciplinary ocean research institutions established by many nations, especially in Europe and North America.

The first such institution in North America was the Scripps Institution of Oceanography at La Jolla, California, founded in 1903, at a time before there was a clear professional definition of 'oceanography'. In fact, it began as a marine laboratory, under the umbrella of the University of California, only receiving an official name in 1912 – Institution for Biological Research – and renamed in 1924 as Scripps Institution of Oceanography, as the subject of 'oceanography' solidified. Soon after this, in 1930, the first sister institution to Scripps was founded on the northeast coast of United States, the Woods Hole Oceanographic Institution, at Woods Hole, Massachusetts. With the maturation of the marine sciences into a unified whole, the establishment of ocean research centres in United States, and the increasing demand for oceanographic information, the Canadian government took note and began to evaluate its own role in ocean research and exploration. Building upon existing efforts, a plan was conceived by a small group of wise Canadian government science entrepreneurs that led to the birth of the Bedford Institute of Oceanography (BIO) in 1962. The experience gained in operating Scripps and Woods Hole played a significant role in the establishment of BIO.

On 25 October 2012, BIO celebrated its 50th anniversary. Since 1962, this Institute, Canada's premier marine research facility, has contributed greatly to a better understanding of the oceans that surround us and the life they hold at every depth, the valuable living and non-living resources they contain and cover, the story of the planet's history they reveal, and their importance to people everywhere. As the 50th anniversary approached, thought was given to what could be done to celebrate this milestone, and enshrine the Institute's oceanographic accomplishments, including the role that BIO researchers have played in the transformation of the formerly disparate marine sciences into a discipline called 'Oceanography'. In time, the idea of a commemorative volume appeared and with it, the task of deciding the form it should take. And so, here's the short story of the creation of '*Voyage of Discovery: Fifty Years of Marine Research at Canada's Bedford Institute of Oceanography*'.

The idea of a commemorative volume began in 2009, initiated by a small number of BIO scientists. This nucleus quickly grew into a formal 'steering committee' in 2010 comprising Allyn Clarke, Donald Gordon, Glen Harrison, Erica Head, Bosko Loncarevic, David McKeown, Eric Mills, Michael Parsons, Marilyn Rudi, Michael Sinclair, and Peter Wells. From this beginning, a larger Editorial Advisory Committee was formed with the addition of Ross Claytor, Gerald Costello, Charles Hannah, David Nettleship, and Betty Sutherland. An initial proposal and call for contributions was circulated to the BIO community in December 2010 and the response was most positive. Much discussion and debate ensued on the structure and content the book should take. Its form took shape in late January 2011, a skeleton on which layers of subjects and topics could be built along with names of potential candidates to take on the associated writing challenges. A second call for contributors was then issued together with a book rationale, structured outline, guidelines for authors, and options for publication. Once the book project was formerly launched, an Editorial Board was established composed of Donald Gordon, Michel Latremouille, Michael Lewis, David Nettleship, and Michael Sinclair, all retired BIO staff. The final team of editors for the book comprised Donald Gordon, Michel Latremouille, Michael Lewis, and David Nettleship. Then came the task to solicit contributors to fill the obvious gaps in coverage, followed later by a rigorous system of manuscript review and editing, culminating in graphics design and layout of the papers. The process took considerable effort and time, with illness taking its toll on two of the editors, and it was not possible to complete the book by October 2012 as originally intended. In March 2013, David Nettleship assumed the chief editor's role from Michel Latremouille. As well as continuing the review and editing of contributions, considerable time was spent in formulating the layout and graphics design of the volume, along with the selection of Friesens

Corporation (Altona, Manitoba) for printing and binding following evaluation of several book construction companies. The 'home stretch' from March 2013 to May 2014 has been demanding yet enjoyable and satisfying for editors and authors alike. Mission accomplished!

'*Voyage of Discovery*' summarizes a representative sample of BIO research projects on the oceanography of Arctic and Eastern Canada. In a series of 48 papers by past and present research staff from all oceanographic disciplines at BIO, the history of Canadian oceanography before BIO and a broad cross section of the Institute's work spanning five decades is featured with particular emphasis on contributions to Canadian and global understanding and management of the marine environment and resources. Divided into 12 sections with a Preface, Epilogue, and Appendices, *Voyage of Discovery* is the most extensive overview of the history and scientific accomplishments of the Bedford Institute of Oceanography under one cover: Historical Roots (papers 1-3), Arctic Studies (papers 4-9), Ocean Life (papers 10-15), Ocean Circulation and Chemistry (papers 16-18), Hydrography and Seabed Mapping (papers 19-22), Geological Oceanography (papers 23-29), Fisheries-Ecosystems-Aquaculture (papers 30-35), Marine Contamination (papers 36-37), Technology and Instrument Development (papers 38-43), Energy Developments (papers 44-46), BIO and the Law of the Sea (papers 47-48), and The BIO Experience (Epilogue: past, present, future). The papers presented in the book can be read alone by subject and category or scanned for content by viewing the 'Summary' at the start of each contribution. The intent is to allow the reader to leaf through the pages, and by doing so, discover stimulating and exciting descriptions of new findings and the role that BIO researchers have played in building the foundation of knowledge of Canada's oceans and in enhancing ocean science worldwide. The references provided serve as an introduction into the scientific literature for those readers wishing to dig deeper.

Now dip in, go on the '*Voyage of Discovery*' and enjoy (reap the rewards), learn and contemplate where BIO has been, the waters travelled, and where the future lies! Let fair winds and calm seas prevail through the next half-century of Canadian exploration and travel on, over, and under/within the wondrous oceans of the blue planet called Earth.

David N. Nettleship
Editor-in-Chief

22 May 2014

Acknowledgements

The editors and authors thank the following individuals who served as referees and copyedit readers of manuscripts submitted for publication in the commemorative 50th Anniversary volume '*Voyage of Discovery*'. It is only through their considerable efforts and care that we have succeeded in achieving a high scientific standard for papers presented in this volume (individuals who reviewed two or more manuscripts are indicated by an asterisk):

Dr. John Anderson, Dr. Robin Anderson, Dr. Komiko Azetsu-Scott*, Dr. Vaughn Barrie, Dr. Steve Bates, Dr. Donald Bowen, Dale Buckley, Robert Burke, Gordon D.M. Cameron, Dr. Allyn Clarke*, Dr. Robert H. Cook*, Dr. Peter Cranford, Dr. Graham Daborn, Dr. Ken Denman, Dr. Lloyd Dickie, Dr. Jim Elliott*, Gordon Fader, Dr. Donald Forbes*, Steve Forbes, Dr. Robert Fournier, Dr. Kent Gilkinson, Steve Grant*, Dr. Charles Hannah, Dr. Barry Hargrave, Dr. Glen Harrison, Dr. Erica Head, Dr. John Hughes Clarke, Dr. Jeff Hutchings, Paul Keizer*, Dr. Vladimir Kostylev, Dr. John Lazier, Dr. Michael Li, Dr. William Li, Dr. John Loder, Dr. Bosko Loncarevic*, Dr. Alan Longhurst*, Dr. Ron Loucks, Ruth Loucks, Richard MacDougall*, Kevin MacIsaac, Brian Maclean, Dr. David McKeown, Mark McLean*, Timothy Milligan*, Dr. Eric Mills*, Dr. Robert Miller, Dr. David Mosher, Michael Murphy*, Brian Nicholls*, Dr. Richard Pickrill, Dr. David Piper*, Gary Rockwell, Dr. Helmuth Sandstrom*, Dr. Charles Schafer*, Dr. John Shaw*, Gary Sonnichsen, Dr. James Stewart, Betty Sutherland*, Robert Taylor*, Dr. Brian Todd, Herb Vandermeulen, Dr. Alain Vezina*, Dr. Peter Wells, Dr. Harold Welsh, Dr. Graham Williams, Gary Wohlgechaffen, Dr. Melisa Wong, and Dr. Boris Worm.

We are also very grateful to numerous other individuals who have provided invaluable assistance in the preparation of this book. First and foremost was the effort of the authors (Appendix 10) to take time from their normal schedules to prepare expert syntheses and summaries of past and present researches to produce a series of reviews that collectively represent and span the breadth of work performed at BIO. As editors, we are appreciative of their patience through the lengthy editing/review process and the delays that prevented the publication of the book by its originally scheduled date. We are particularly indebted to the staff of the BIO Library for their unwavering assistance in finding and verifying references throughout the lengthy preparation of the book, in particular Houman Behzadi, Rhonda Coll, Carly Currie, Marilyn Rudi, and Heather Zinn. We are also particularly grateful to Francis Kelly, our graphics designer, whose volunteer work after a change of position within DFO at the end of 2013 kept the project alive, and to Kelly Bentham in locating and preparing photographs. Also, we extend thanks to Angela Nettleship for her careful proofreading and checking references from beginning to end of production of this volume. And lastly, our thanks to Friesens representative Ron Such for his guidance in selection of paper and bindery, and patience through the completion stage of book manuscript delivery.

From the outset, this book undertaking has been a project of the BIO-Oceans Association, and we thank members of the Executive Council for their strong support under leadership of several presidents: Robert O'Boyle, Betty Sutherland, Paul Keizer, and Michael Hughes. We also acknowledge the support of the BIO Science Management Committee with members from Fisheries and Oceans Canada (DFO), Natural Resources Canada (NRCan), Environment Canada, and Department of Defence. Both DFO and NRCan provided in-kind support including office and meeting space, printers, and various supplies as required.

We are grateful to everyone for their support and assistance in making the idea of a commemorative volume in celebration of BIO's 50th anniversary a reality. And finally, we must express our grateful thanks to our spouses for their support, and understanding our dedication and determination in seeing this ambitious '*Voyage of Discovery*' project through to completion.

The Editors

VOYAGE OF DISCOVERY

Fifty Years of Marine Research at Canada's Bedford Institute of Oceanography

Historical Roots

A map of the British Empire in North America (Samuel Dunn, 1776)

Historical Roots

1. CANADIAN MARINE SCIENCE FROM BEFORE *TITANIC* TO THE ESTABLISHMENT OF THE BEDFORD INSTITUTE OF OCEANOGRAPHY IN 1962

Eric L. Mills

SUMMARY

Beginning in the early 1960s, the Bedford Institute of Oceanography (BIO) consolidated marine sciences and technologies that had developed separately, some of them since the late 19th century. Marine laboratories, devoted mainly to marine biology, were established in 1908 in St. Andrews, New Brunswick, and Nanaimo, British Columbia, and it was in them that Canada's first studies in physical oceanography began in the early 1930s and became fully established after World War II. Charting and tidal observation developed separately in post-Confederation Canada, beginning in the last two decades of the 19th century, and becoming united in the Canadian Hydrographic Service in 1924. For a number of scientific and political reasons, Canadian marine sciences developed most rapidly after World War II (post-1945), including work in the Arctic, the founding of graduate programs in oceanography on both Atlantic and Pacific coasts, the reorientation of physical oceanography from the federal Fisheries Research Board to the federal Department of Mines and Technical Surveys, increased work on marine geology and geophysics, and eventually the founding of the BIO, which brought all these fields together.

Key words: Canadian marine science, Atlantic and Pacific biological stations, charting, tides, hydrography, post-World War II developments, origin of BIO.

E-mail: E.Mills@dal.ca

The Bedford Institute of Oceanography (BIO) opened formally in 1962 (Fig. 1), bringing together scientists and technologists who had worked in fields as diverse as physical oceanography, hydrographic charting, marine geology, and marine ecology. They became members of an institution that developed into one of the largest and most influential oceanographic laboratories in the world.

Figure 1. Bedford Institute of Oceanography in 1986: the ships at the finger pier are the CSS *Baffin* (rear) and CSS *Hudson*, and the CSS *Alfred Needler* (top) and CSS *Dawson* at the wharf (photo: Roger Belanger, BIO).

BIO grew out of marine science and technology specialties that were separate in post-World War II Canada and that had developed largely in piecemeal fashion since the beginning of the 20th century. It was the product of several unconnected or tenuously-connected strands that were brought together purposefully by scientific and institutional empire builders during a short but important time, the first decade and a half after the war, when financial and political factors were favourable. This introductory paper explores these developments, following some of the important strands from the late 19th century into the early 1960s, but concentrating on the 20th century.

THE BEGINNINGS

When Edward E. Prince (1858-1936; Fig. 2) arrived in Canada as the newly appointed Dominion Commissioner of Fisheries in 1893, he soon began to plan a way of providing scientific information on the fisheries, with the aim of establishing a marine station like those pioneered in Europe decades before. The result, achieved with the help of university biologists, was an organizational structure, the Board of Management of the Biological Station (became the Biological Board of Canada in 1912), which from 1899 to 1907 operated a mobile floating laboratory. The floating laboratory was replaced by two biological stations in 1908, one in St. Andrews, New Brunswick, the other in Nanaimo, British Columbia, that operated only seasonally for many years.

Figure 2. Edward E. Prince, Dominion Commissioner of Fisheries (right) with A.G. Huntsman (left) at the Biological Station, St. Andrews, New Brunswick, about 1920 (photo: courtesy of St. Andrews Biological Station, DFO).

The background, development, and accomplishments of the biological stations have been examined historically (e.g., Johnstone 1977, Hubbard 2006) and fêted retrospectively by scientists and historians during their centenaries (see J. Hubbard et al. in press), and so only two points need to be made about their significance. First, for many years the stations were staffed, mainly in summer, by biologists, who contributed information on many commercially-exploited marine animals, and even more that were not; there was very little physical science of any description. Second, the new biological stations attracted the attention of A.G. Huntsman (1883-1972; Fig. 2), a young biologist from the University of Toronto (Toronto, ON), who began a long association with the St. Andrews station in 1911. Huntsman soon fell under the spell of the distinguished Norwegian fishery biologist Johan Hjort (Fig. 3), who, at Prince's urging, came to Canada in 1914-15 as the organizer of the Canadian Fisheries Expedition (CFE) of 1915 (Hubbard 2006: chapter 3, Mills 2009: chapter 4). The CFE had as its ostensible aim the search for new fisheries, particularly for herring, in the Gulf of St. Lawrence. But in the hands of Hjort, fisheries science incorporated new chemical and physical techniques from Europe, notably the use of the dynamic method (Sandström and Helland-Hansen 1903), which had been developed in Scandinavia (see Hjort 1919, Sandström 1919, Mills 2009: chapter 3).

Hjort's influence on Huntsman was immense. Huntsman's immediate response to the CFE was to begin a series of summer expeditions to east coast locations which were far more comprehensive than anything done before anywhere else in Canada. These ended in 1923 with a summer-long investigation of the cod fishery of the Strait of Belle Isle region that involved physical measurements as well as biological work. But Huntsman's reach exceeded his grasp, for he was too busy to finish the analysis, and there was no one in the early 1920s who could handle the physical studies (these were only completed and published in the 1950s - see Huntsman et al. 1954). His was a lonely voice in an oceanographic wilderness in the early 1920s, and in fact for a further decade.

Figure 3. Johan Hjort (left), with an officer, probably of the CSS *Acadia* during the Canadian Fisheries Expedition of 1915 (photo: probably by A.G. Huntsman, courtesy of St. Andrews Biological Station, DFO).

CHARTING AND THE TIDES

Charting of Canadian waters started very early, during the French regime along the St. Lawrence River and in Acadia, centred on the main navigable waterways. This was true also after the British conquest of New France in the middle of the 18th century - it was the well-travelled routes and the sites of military activity that got attention, notably by outstanding cartographers like Samuel Holland, J.F.W. Des Barres, and James Cook (Thomson 1966 , Fillmore and Sandilands 1983). And in fact, British marine surveyors were active in Canadian waters until well after Confederation, among them the redoubtable H.W. Bayfield (1795-1885), who between 1816 and 1856 carried out surveys from Lake Superior to Newfoundland, and surveyors for the Board of Works who carried out surveys inland (starting in 1841) for an era of canal-building.

After Confederation, charting had to be increased in the rapidly expanding nation. In 1882, the Department of Marine and Fisheries asked the British Admiralty for help in setting up a Canadian hydrographic survey, based in part on the reaction to a disastrous steamship sinking in Georgian Bay, Ontario, that year. Staff Commander J.G. Boulton, RN (1843-1929), arrived in 1883 as head of a Georgian Bay survey, and for a time thereafter most of the charting activity was in the Great Lakes region. But gradually work on the coasts increased; the first Canadian surveys of the sea were W.J. Stewart's (1863-1925) charting of Burrard Inlet at Vancouver, British Columbia, in 1891 and work in the lower St. Lawrence River in 1905. By that time, the Royal Navy was beginning to withdraw its ships from Canadian waters in response to a perceived threat on the oceans from Germany, but British surveys continued on the West Coast until 1910 and on the East Coast until 1913 (and sporadically thereafter, especially in Newfoundland and Labrador waters).

The Hydrographic Survey of Canada evolved from the Georgian Bay Survey in 1904 (Thomson 1967, de Vecchi 1982, Meehan 2006), at first carrying out inshore surveys from small vessels. On the east coast, the Hydrographic Survey's work was put on a new footing when the new purpose-built survey vessel CSS *Acadia* came into service in 1913, and immediately went to Hudson Bay to survey potential sites for ocean shipping to meet a projected railway from the south. The Survey's world expanded during the next decade, and in 1928 it was renamed the Canadian Hydrographic Service (CHS), remaining independent of other aspects of work on the oceans except the tides until the founding of BIO in the early 1960s (for details, see MacDougall 2014).

Despite the importance of the tides to navigation, John A. Macdonald's governments resisted many requests to begin tidal surveys of Canadian waters, believing that they were unimportant, and that there was, in any case, a hydrographic survey in Georgian Bay (de Vecchi 1982, 1984). By 1884, the only systematic tidal observations that had been made in Canadian waters were on Baffin and Ellesmere islands during the First International Polar Year of 1882-83. But in 1884 the British Association for the Advancement of Science met in Montreal, Quebec, and two committees were formed to deal with the tides, the first to gather data and produce tables worldwide, the other to lobby the Canadian government for money to set up tide-monitoring stations. Year after year there was no response to the second committee's entreaties, until late in 1889 a delegation, now including influential businessmen from the shipping community in Montreal, went to the Minister of Marine and Fisheries with a new proposal. They were granted a small appropriation for 1890.

Figure 4. The CSS *Acadia*, flagship of the Canadian Hydrographic Service, shown here at Souris, Prince Edward Island, during the Canadian Fisheries Expedition of 1915 (photo: probably by A.G. Huntsman, courtesy of St. Andrews Biological Station, DFO).

Very quickly, tidal observation stations were set up at crucial locations along east coast shipping lanes, beginning at Point-au-Père, the Magdalen Islands, and Anticosti Island in Quebec, St. Paul Island, Nova Scotia, and Saint John, New Brunswick. From 1893 onward, these and an expanding network of tide-recording stations came under the control of the Canadian Tidal and Current Survey, under W. Bell Dawson (1854-1944), its superintendent until his retirement in 1924 (Fillmore and Sandilands 1983, Meehan 2006). Upon Dawson's retirement from what had in effect been his fiefdom, the Tidal Survey was incorporated as a division into the Hydrographic Survey; the united Surveys were then renamed the Canadian Hydrographic Service, a name retained through the following eight decades.

RMS *TITANIC* AND THE OCEANOGRAPHY OF CANADIAN WATERS BEFORE BIO

The new White Star liner, RMS *Titanic* hit floating ice and sank on the night of 14-15 April 1912, with great loss of life. The scientific response to the danger of icebergs in the shipping lanes was rapid, but not by Canada, which had nothing to offer by way of ships or scientific capability. Britain responded first, by sending out W.S. Bruce's auxiliary steam barque *Scotia*, with the Plymouth Laboratory's physical oceanographer D.J. Matthews (1873-1956) aboard, to do an oceanographic survey in the track of the ice across the Grand Banks of Newfoundland and off southeastern Labrador. Basing his calculations on the distribution of density in the water column, Matthews (1914) used what was then called "Bjerknes's Theorem", as simplified by J.W. Sandström and Bjørn Helland-Hansen (1903), to do a dynamic analysis of velocities and directions in the Labrador Current and a portion of the West Greenland Current. The results, overall, indicated a sluggish southward movement of the Labrador Current during the summer of 1913, and rather limited movement of the ice. This was the first, and for many years the only, systematic oceanographic study and dynamic analysis of Canadian waters, with the exception of some descriptive studies in the Bay of Fundy and Passamaquoddy region centred in St. Andrews and carried out by Huntsman's colleagues G.G. Copeland (Copeland 1912), E.H. Craigie (Craigie 1916a,b) and James Mavor (Mavor 1922, 1923) that began just before the CFE and were maintained sporadically into the 1920s.

As a result of the sinking of the *Titanic*, ice observations had been carried out during the summer of 1912 by two United States Navy cruisers and in 1913 by two United States Coast Guard cutters. Matthews' work in 1913 barely preceded a meeting held by the United States Coast Guard (then called the Revenue Cutter Service) and others in London, England, in November 1913. This was the prelude to a full-blown international treaty on the ice problem, the International Convention for the Safety of Life at Sea (SOLAS) of 1914, which stipulated that there should be an annual international patrol of ice-infested waters impinging on the North Atlantic shipping lanes. And the only organization with the willingness and capability to carry out such a patrol was the United States Coast Guard, which began its International Service of Ice Observation and Ice Patrol (soon shortened to the International Ice Patrol) that summer, using radio to transmit the location of dangerous ice and plotting its distribution during each ice season. This early start, given impetus by the example of *Titanic,* led to the next major – and non-Canadian – study of the Western North Atlantic adjacent to Canada.

The United States Coast Guard's Ice Patrol cruises centred on the southeastern Grand Banks of Newfoundland area and collected temperature (T) and salinity (S) data in a relatively hit and miss way at first. This changed with the appointment of a young Coast Guard officer, Edward H. Smith (1889-1961; Fig. 5), about 1920. Smith soon came under the influence of the Harvard biologist/oceanographer H.B. Bigelow (1879-1967) who was a technical adviser to the Ice Patrol. After completing a Master's degree under Bigelow, Smith began Ph.D. studies on arctic ice, and increasingly began to apply mathematical analysis to the growing body of oceanographic data collected on the Ice Patrol cruises. To refine his skills, he went to Norway in 1924-25 to learn mathematical physical oceanography from Bjørn Helland-Hansen (1877-1957) in the Geophysical Institute in Bergen, Norway. This resulted in charts of the circulation around the Grand Banks of Newfoundland, and also in a major publication – 'A practical method for determining ocean currents' (Smith 1926), that served as a how-to manual for the dynamic analysis of currents for many years (see Mills 2009).

The Ice Patrol cruises had surveyed only the southern part of the ice-infested area, the edges of the Grand Banks of Newfoundland primarily, but under Smith interest shifted north, and in 1928 the United States Coast Guard cutter *Marion* (Fig. 6) was sent north to the calving grounds of North Atlantic icebergs, the coast of West Greenland (Ricketts 1932).

Between July and September 1928, *Marion's* crew, under Smith's direction, made more than 190 oceanographic stations along 16 transects between the Labrador coast and Disko Island, West Greenland, at 70°N. Coincidentally, a Danish study was underway during the same summer using the Royal Danish Navy's schooner-rigged vessel *Godthaab* (Fig. 7). The two vessels coordinated their surveys and shared data, with the Danes working from Disko Island to the entrances to Lancaster and Smith sounds (the latter at about 78.5°N). Out of that busy summer came the first systematic dynamic analysis of Labrador Current waters, which, when combined with data from further Greenland cruises by the United States Coast Guard into the mid 1930s, led in 1935 to the first major monograph on the area, by Smith et al. (1937). The Danish results were also published (Kiillerich 1939), making West Greenland, Baffin Bay, and the Labrador Current areas the best known of Western North Atlantic waters, although without a single Canadian contribution.

Although the *Marion* cruise had the most significant effect on knowledge of the oceanography of northern waters adjacent to Canada, the United States Coast Guard was not alone in its attention to the area (see Smith et al. 1937 for a list of work to mid-1930s). John Murray and Johan Hjort had traversed the Grand Banks of Newfoundland in 1910 on their Norwegian North Atlantic Expedition (Murray and Hjort 1912). Helland-Hansen's analysis of the physical results appeared in 1930, as part of a synoptic monograph on the oceanography of the whole North Atlantic Ocean. Even after the limitation of its fishing areas around

Figure 5. Lieut. Edward H. Smith, USCG, during the United States Coast Guard's *Marion* expedition of 1928 to Baffin Bay and West Greenland (from Ricketts 1932).

Figure 6. The United States Coast Guard cutter *Marion* off West Greenland during the summer of 1928 (from Ricketts 1932).

Figure 7. A hydro station being taken in West Greenland waters from the Royal Danish Navy ship *Godthaab* during the summer of 1928 (from Riis-Carstensen 1931).

Newfoundland after the British/French Entente Cordial of 1904, France maintained its colony of St. Pierre et Miquelon, held some seasonal fishing rights along the west and north coasts of Newfoundland, and conducted fishery patrol and research cruises. The oceanographer Edouard Le Danois (1887-1968) reported on the temperature structure of the Grand Banks of Newfoundland in 1924 in the course of developing a theory of basin-wide water movement governing fish production and devoted a later monograph to the area (Le Danois 1924, 1937). And in 1926, the young Harvard oceanographer Columbus Iselin, another of Bigelow's protegés, spent July and August on his schooner *Chance* between Cape Race, Newfoundland, and Nachvak Bay, Labrador (59°N), delineating some of the characteristics of the Labrador Current in that region (Iselin 1930). His analysis was published in the same year that the first mathematical physical oceanography study by a Canadian took place.

A ROLE FOR CANADIANS

A.G. Huntsman had been convinced since his experience with Johan Hjort in 1914-15 that there must be a relationship between the physical environment and the production of marine animals, including fish. His summer expeditions had foundered, in part because of the lack of a physical oceanographer, and by the late 1920s he was increasingly concerned about being able to predict the fishery effects of a proposed tidal dam that would enclose Passamaquoddy Bay off St. Andrews, New Brunswick. The result was that Huntsman requested, and got the funds to hire, a physical oceanographer for the Biological Station at St. Andrews. This was Harry Hachey (1901-85; Fig. 8), who joined the Station staff in 1928 after teaching physics at the University of New Brunswick (Mills 2009).

Hachey very rapidly began an ambitious series of descriptive studies on the east coast, ranging from the circulation of Passamaquoddy Bay to the collection of temperature information from steamers crossing the North Atlantic. And within 18 months of his appointment, in the summer of 1930, he went north to Hudson Bay on the Canadian Hydrographic Service's steamer CSS *Acadia* as part of a group organized by Huntsman to assess the possibility of a commercial fishery there. The fishery came to nothing, but Hachey carried out the first dynamic analysis by a Canadian in Canadian waters, showing (admittedly on very scanty data) that the central waters of Hudson Bay were highly stable and thus unlikely to support much biological production (Hachey 1931). For the following ten years, Hachey worked increasingly on the oceanography of the Bay of Fundy region and especially the Scotian Shelf, until, with the outbreak of war in 1939, he joined the Canadian army and was out of oceanography for a time.

Coincidentally, only a short time after Hachey's appointment at St. Andrews, physical studies began on the West Coast, based in Nanaimo, and carried out by J.P. Tully (1906-87; Fig. 9), who was hired in 1931 as an assistant to the chemical oceanographer Neal Carter (Mills 2002). Tully was energetic, extroverted, and ambitious. He was also not averse to changing fields. Within a year he began to collect sea-surface temperatures taken for him by lighthouse keepers, accompanied

Figure 8. Harry Hachey (left), Canada's first physical oceanographer, in St. Andrews, New Brunswick, probably during the summer of 1928 (photo: courtesy of St. Andrews Biological Station, DFO).

Canadian Hydrographic Service steamers to remote parts of the British Columbia coast and the open Pacific, and began to develop a working relationship with the Royal Canadian Navy (RCN) that would allow him to use naval vessels for oceanographic work.

Like Hachey, Tully taught himself dynamic oceanography, using Sandström's (1919) classic monograph and Smith's (1926) more recent one, and applied it to a number of areas, including the west coast of Vancouver Island and the approaches to the Strait of Juan de Fuca. With the onset of the war in 1939, prevented from serving overseas by an artificial leg, he soon began to develop working ties with United States oceanographers, especially in San Diego, who were developing oceanographic work in support of anti-submarine warfare.

Hachey's and Tully's entrances into oceanography came at a time that was truly transitional. In 1919, a proposal had been put forward to dam Passamaquoddy and Cobscook bays, along the Maine-New Brunswick border, for tidal power. The proposal dragged on, was revived in the late 1920s, and eventually was placed before the North Atlantic Council on Fishery Investigations (NACFI), in which Huntsman and his friend H.B. Bigelow were major players, for an assessment of the potential effect on fisheries. Huntsman had been concerned for several years by the possibility that the tidal power project would have an adverse effect on all aspects of commercial marine animal production in Passamaquoddy Bay, and it was this in part that led to his promotion of a need for a physical oceanographer at St. Andrews - and to Harry Hachey's appointment in 1928. But when an international program to assess the effect of tidal dams was created, the International Passamaquoddy Fisheries Commission of 1931-33, at the suggestion of NACFI, Hachey, as a member of the St. Andrews staff, was not permitted to take part and, as a result, the physical results of the scientific work were truncated (for details, see Hubbard 2006). This was the last time that the Canadian government looked outside for scientific expertise on the oceans; Hachey's and Tully's increasing visibility in physical oceanography and the increasing competence of the St. Andrews and Nanaimo biological stations in other aspects of marine science put Canadians front and centre in national problems related to the oceans after the early 1930s. This was especially true after the outbreak of war in 1939.

A SCIENCE FORGED IN WAR

Before World War II, oceanography, including physical oceanography, marine biology and fishery biology, was done entirely in the two Biological Board laboratories, one on each coast (the Biological Board was renamed the Fisheries Research Board of Canada in 1937). The war made little difference to this situation initially, but it did lead, perforce, to increased attention to the physical sciences of the oceans when acoustic mines and particularly submarines became a threat to the North Atlantic shipping lanes and eventually to the whole east coast of North America. The Battle of the Atlantic, beginning in 1941, and attempts to counter submarines during the next three years, made it clear to the Canadian Navy that, although it recognized the utility of detecting submarines by sound (Asdic to the British, sonar to Americans) it did not have the scientific capability to use the early sonar gear effectively, nor to understand its use under varying oceanographic conditions (see Tunnicliffe 2010 on this problem and later events; also Campbell 1976 and Mills 1994).

To increase the effectiveness of anti-submarine measures, very early in 1941 the National Research Council of Canada became the research branch of the RCN. This grew out of a request by the British Admiralty to have the Acoustics Section of the NRC's Division of Physics and Electrical Engineering (the latter directed by R.W. Boyle) become involved in defences against acoustic mines. George S. Field (1905-2000) of the Acoustics Section visited laboratories in Britain and the United States early in 1941 and began to organize work on defence-related acoustics. During a later visit to the United States, Field returned to Canada with the first bathythermographs (BTs) seen in the country, essential tools in assessing the effectiveness of sonar in detecting submarines when the water column was stratified. By 1943, Acoustics Section scientists and RCN officers had made an extensive survey of temperature conditions off the East Coast.

During the early years of the war, of Canada's two physical oceanographers, only Tully was in Canada. At Field's request, in 1943 Tully was seconded to the RCN from his position at Nanaimo to conduct research on acoustics in seawater, particularly on submarine detection, using the calm, stratified - and also safe - inshore waters of southern British Columbia as a natural laboratory. He soon established links with United States scientists doing similar work at Woods Hole Oceanographic Institution (Woods Hole, MA), at the University of Washington (Seattle, WA), and, increasingly, in what became the U.S. Naval Electronics Laboratory (USNEL) in San Diego, California (a link that became even more important after World War II - see Leary 1999). Hachey, for his part, was with the Canadian Army in England. He returned to Canada in 1943, first to the defence laboratory in Suffield, Alberta, and then at Field's request returned to St. Andrews in 1944, where he was assigned the task of preparing acoustic transmission charts for submarine detection in east coast waters. Each became head of a research group, Tully's the Pacific Oceanographic Group (POG) in Nanaimo and Hachey's the Atlantic Oceanographic Group (AOG) in St. Andrews. Nanaimo and the POG were assigned the use of a converted seiner, CNAV *Ehkoli* for their work (Fig. 10) and this became the main centre for Canadian work on anti-submarine acoustics, particularly when submarine attacks made research at sea too dangerous on the east coast. Both rapidly gained experience in defence-related research and expanded into major research groups by the war's end in 1945. Tunnicliffe (2010) summarizes the war-end situation aptly:

> *"For the Canadians ... it meant that the oceanographers, with their fisheries background would have to explore an area of "oceanography" that was essentially new to them for military oceanography was rapidly becoming defined as the merging of classical physical oceanography, acoustics, sonar engineering and naval tactics. A new discipline was emerging."*

Figure 9. J.P. Tully (centre) and colleagues at the Pacific Biological Station, Nanaimo, British Columbia, in 1935 (photo: from J.P. Tully retirement scrapbook, courtesy of Pacific Biological Station Scientific Archives, DFO).

Figure 10. The CNAV *Ehkoli* towing an acoustic target in British Columbia waters in 1949 (photo: from J.P. Tully retirement scrapbook, courtesy of Pacific Biological Station Scientific Archives, DFO).

ORGANIZING OCEANOGRAPHY

The POG and the AOG, housed in FRBC laboratories and linked closely with the NRC, RCN, and newly-formed (1946) Defence Research Board (DRB), evolved after the war and for the next decade and a half into Canada's main oceanographic research groups. The environment in which they existed was at first a relatively unorganized one, but this did not last for long. Just before the start of the war in 1939, an attempt had been made to coordinate marine science activities by organizing a Canadian Committee on Oceanography. It lasted only a few months after the outbreak of war and was disbanded in 1940. After the war, several branches of government found themselves with interests in the oceans - or perhaps in some cases believed that they should. A Canadian Joint Committee on Oceanography (JCO) was established in 1946 involving the FRBC, RCN, NRC, and later the CHS, Meteorological Service of Canada, Department of Transport, and DRB, to promote cooperative oceanographic research and to allocate resources. Only the FRBC and the RCN brought real resources to the table - scientific expertise in the first case and ships in the second - but all of the organizations believed that they could not proceed alone because of the scarcity of resources available to each individually. The FRBC provided administration and laboratories (in Nanaimo and St. Andrews), and the RCN a ship on each coast (on the east coast HMCS *Sackville*, on the west coast CNAV *Ehkoli*, followed by HMCS *Cedarwood*), all nominally under the eye of the newly-appointed Chief Oceanographer of Canada, Harry Hachey.

By 1945, Jack Tully's links with the USNEL group were increasing and the POG was growing, especially after the Canadian and United States groups began to work together on acoustic studies in inshore British Columbian waters. This led to an extended period of collaboration, the Canadian-United States Beaufort Sea Expeditions, that moved into the open Pacific and the Western Arctic beginning in 1948, culminating in 1954 when the Canadian icebreaker HMCS *Labrador* traversed the Northwest Passage to meet a pair of United States vessels (with some Canadian oceanographers, including W.M. Cameron of the DRB and POG) at the western end of the Passage. The exploit was noteworthy, but behind it lay the first serious efforts to understand the water column structure and circulation of the Bering, Chukchi and Beaufort seas, albeit with Cold War defence considerations in mind. Tully and the POG were also involved in the routine monitoring of the Subarctic North Pacific at Ocean Station "P" that was taken on by Canada in 1950 and in providing information for the work of the International North Pacific Fisheries Commission beginning in 1955. Tully had begun a hydraulic modelling study of Alberni Inlet based on a series of surveys during the early war years; although this had to be shelved for the duration, he returned to hydraulic modelling of inshore British Columbia waters after the war.

With a capable ship regularly available, Tully and his co-workers also expanded their work closer to home, determining the circulation of the offshore waters between Cape Flattery and Dixon Entrance to 140°W, and making a Canadian contribution to the American-organized NORPAC, a multi-ship study in 1955 of the little-known central North Pacific waters north of 20°N. With limited resources but unlimited ambition and optimism, Tully and his POG colleagues took West Coast Canadian oceanography well beyond the bounds of limited national surveys. Hachey on the East Coast had fewer international links; instead he and his growing group of colleagues in the AOG expanded their earlier studies of the Bay of Fundy and Scotian Shelf and began work on the Gulf of St. Lawrence and northeastern Newfoundland waters. In 1950, these (with the exception of Newfoundland) became regular seasonal surveys in support of the St. Andrews laboratory's fisheries program. As the AOG's interests turned offshore, it also began work on the relatively little known Slope Water just inside the Gulf Stream south of Nova Scotia, and in 1950 collaborated with American oceanographers in Operation Cabot, a study of the Gulf Stream off northeastern North America.

LOOKING NORTH

Before 1948, Canadian scientific work in the Arctic was practically non-existent, although there had been sporadic contributions by other nations during the preceding century (particularly the United States, as discussed before – on other work through the 1940s – see Dunbar 1951). But the pace of activity picked up rapidly in 1947 with the beginning of the Cold War, and the strategic interests of the United States, in which Canada had to play a role, involving submarine activity in northern waters and the threat of attack by air across the North Pole. In particular, the DRB developed a close link with the United States armed forces' civilian and military research. Tully and the POG's work on the West Coast was one component of this.

Although Tully and the POG had not hesitated to move into Arctic waters when they could, Hachey, lacking the American resources available to Tully, had been reluctant to move north. But large political forces were at work, including the building of five joint United States-Canadian weather stations in the Canadian Arctic between 1947 and 1950, and by 1957 the building of several Distant Early Warning Line (DEW Line) radar stations along 70°N by United States contractors was well under way. Between then and the mid 1960s, when intercontinental missiles made the DEW Line obsolete, American interest in the Canadian Arctic was high. This was an opportunity for Canadian scientists, but at the same time a potential threat to Canadian sovereignty in the north. Both of these played a significant part in the marine research carried out in Canadian arctic waters from just after the war into the 1960s.

The pressure to do oceanographic work in the eastern Canadian arctic became very strong in 1947-48 when the USCG ships *Edisto* and *Eastwind* made forays into Canadian northern waters, making BT observations from Newfoundland to Greenland and then in Smith and Lancaster sounds. The first tentative step by Canadians into the eastern Canadian arctic took place in 1948, when a small flotilla of RCN ships, including *Magnificent, Haida,* and *Nootka* was sent north (Elliott-Meisel 1999, Campbell 2010) for strategic reasons centred mainly in the RCN's changing postwar role but certainly with concern about Canadian sovereignty as well. Only *Haida* and *Nootka* actually entered Hudson Bay, where *Haida* provided a platform for a series of temperature, salinity, and BT observations by W.B. Bailey (1924-82; who would become a member of Hachey's AOG two years later) every 100 miles from the Labrador Coast into the Bay. When the RCN's icebreaker HMCS *Labrador* came into service, it too provided the facilities for Arctic oceanography, beginning with its cruise through the Northwest Passage in 1954 (mentioned earlier, in connection with United States/Canadian cooperation in the western Arctic) accompanied by Bailey and two others from AOG, and during five further cruises through 1962. These resulted in more work on Arctic oceanic circulation by Bailey, N.J. Campbell (b. 1926), and by A.E. Collin (b. 1929) (Campbell 1958, Collin and Dunbar 1964, Mills 2001). Paradoxically, as American interest in joint operations like those in the western Arctic from 1948 through 1954 was waning, in 1954 the POG was officially designated to represent Canada in joint work there, and Hachey and the AOG were named to represent Canada in the eastern Canadian arctic. Although the POG did not work again in a significant way in the Arctic, Hachey took advantage of the opportunity to get information from the *Labrador* cruises into the 1960s, and from a cruise of the CNAV *Sackville,* which had been refitted by the RCN and the DRB for oceanographic work, to Davis Strait in July-August 1958 as a contribution to the International Geophysical Year.

In many respects, the most significant marine science work in the Canadian Arctic just after World War II was not in physical oceanography, but in biological oceanography in which physical oceanography played a part (Dunbar 1982). The stimulus came from M.J. Dunbar (1914-95), a Scot who had immigrated to Canada in 1939, becoming a graduate student at McGill and then a faculty member. In 1947 he began to develop a program of research in the eastern Canadian arctic that eventually became institutionalized as the Arctic Unit of the FRBC (1955) and later (1965) as the Arctic Biological Station in Sainte Anne de Bellevue, Quebec. The small motorized ketch *Calanus* (Fig. 11) was built in 1948 for Dunbar's FRBC work and sent north to allow open water and coastal studies throughout the eastern Canadian arctic that ended in 1979. Dunbar's work had begun in 1947 as an attempt to provide information on resources in Ungava Bay for native peoples. It expanded in the hands of his students and colleagues into broadly-based studies of plankton, fisheries, and marine mammals which almost always included the collection of physical oceanographic information. In a classic and heroic study, E.H. Grainger (1926-2012) and a colleague overwintered in Foxe Basin off Igloolik (Nunavut) during the winter of 1955-56; during their nine month stay, they gathered the first year-round information anywhere in the Canadian Arctic on water column properties and on the biological production cycle.

Although Dunbar's deep interest in the Arctic developed into a broad program of research in the hands of the FRBC, at McGill it involved his graduate students, several of whom joined the FRBC Arctic Unit. This was an early example, easiest for the biological sciences of the ocean, of training in universities that provided marine scientists for government laboratories. It was an informal arrangement at McGill (formalized in 1963 as the university's Marine Science Centre), but one that was impossible to match anywhere else, especially in the physical sciences, as senior government scientists realized early in the post-war period.

Figure 11. The MV *Calanus*, built in 1948 and the mainstay of Fisheries Research Board of Canada work in the eastern Canadian arctic under M.J. Dunbar until the late 1970s (photo: I.A. McLaren).

SUPPLY AND DEMAND – OCEANOGRAPHY IN THE CLASSROOM

Shortly after the end of World War II in 1945, the various organizations involved in the JCO found themselves with expanding programs of marine research, but with a scanty supply of trained marine scientists. The supply problem was particularly critical in physical oceanography, which had obvious links to Cold War defence concerns, the need to expand fisheries, and increasing interest in northern resources. New oceanographers were trained on the job, a situation that, as Tully noted in a memo in 1948, took time that could better be devoted to research and that was second-best anyway without a solid basis in the sciences to begin with. There were no physical oceanography training programs in Canadian universities, nor were there faculty members able to contribute to them.

Tully's concern about the supply of oceanographers was shared by George Field, who by mid 1949 was deputy director-general of the DRB. They, with president N.A.M. Mackenzie of the University of British Columbia (UBC, Vancouver, BC), had been discussing the problem for some time, and there had been a formal discussion of it, suggested by the JCO, at a meeting of the Royal Society of Canada in Vancouver in June 1948, resulting in a resolution that an institute of oceanography be formed in Canada (Mills 1994). This seems to have been only a formality, for in fact Field, concerned about the supply of oceanographers for the DRB and other governmental organizations, had already suggested to Mackenzie that UBC establish an Institute of Oceanography, and that it would be supported by the DRB. By early in 1949 there was substantial support for this proposal from within and outside UBC, including, crucially, Tully, who had agreed to coordinate and take part in the initial teaching program. Field proposed to pay from DRB funds one salary in the new institute, to pay for a UBC faculty member's retraining in oceanography, to make available for teaching the physical oceanographer W.M. Cameron (1914-2008; Scripps Institution of Oceanography trained, and at the time on the staff of the DRB's Pacific Naval Laboratory [PNL] in Esquimalt, BC). By late in August 1949 the UBC senate had approved the new program and it was underway within days, establishing a lone beachhead in the teaching of oceanography in Canada.

Taught at first by Tully commuting from Nanaimo and by Cameron from Victoria, Vancouver Island, many of the first students were government scientists looking for professional qualifications in oceanography. The curriculum was largely centred on physical and chemical oceanography, the main interest of its sponsor, the DRB. Biological oceanography took a position in the wings until 1959, when the NRC agreed to support through block grants not just the program at UBC, but a new one on the east coast at Dalhousie University (Halifax, NS), where biology bulked larger. Hachey too, by the late 1950s was providing space for trainee oceanographers with the AOG in St. Andrews, but never with a strong institutional academic base. Nonetheless, the training of oceanographers had gone from being largely an apprentice system at the end of World War II to well organized programs by 1959. The Bedford Institute of Oceanography was a legatee of this academic revolution.

OCEANOGRAPHY ON A BIG STAGE

By 1950, just after the teaching program at UBC began, World War II and its Cold War aftermath had expanded the scale of oceanographic research in Canada, but had not radically changed its direction or the way it was done in the early post-war years. Fisheries research was still in the hands of the FRBC, which fell outside the federal departmental structure, and the FRBC also maintained the two physical oceanography research groups, Tully's POG on the west coast and Hacheys' AOG on the east coast. Hydrographic charting and tidal studies were done by the CHS, and there was also a small but growing body of work on marine geology by scientists of the Geological Survey of Canada (GSC), within the federal Department of Mines and Technical Surveys (DMTS) after it came into being in January 1950. Marine geology first became a significant component of work by the GSC under J.M. Harrison (1915-90), director from 1956 to 1964. A marine geology unit was established in 1959 under B.R. Pelletier, with much of its early work done in the Arctic, including links with the Polar Continental Shelf Project (1958-62). Marine geophysics, with the exception of some magnetic and gravity surveys off the east coast, came later, with the establishment of BIO (Zaslow 1975, Keen 1990).

Immediately after the war in 1945, the JCO brought together the principal actors (with the exception of UBC and GSC), but in a way that was regarded as being increasingly unsatisfactory because it did not

Figure 12. W.E van Steenburgh, the architect of the expansion of Canadian oceanography during the post-World War II period; portrait in the Bedford Institute of Oceanography (photo: K. Bentham).

Figure 13. William M. Cameron (ca. 1963), Director of the Marine Sciences Branch, DMTS, 1962-1971, and earlier a participant in the Canada–United States Beaufort Sea Expeditions, 1949-1954, and one of the first teachers in the University of British Columbia Institute of Oceanography; he received the Order of Canada for his contributions in 2004. (photo: courtesy of Department of Mines and Technical Surveys Canada, Editorial and Information Division/ BIO Archives carton 11, April 1964 SCOR participants).

represent changing aims and organizations within the marine science communities. The dissatisfaction became focussed in 1953 when J.L. Kask (1906-98) was appointed the first full-time Chairman of the FRBC, with instructions to bring together its largely autonomous branches and to transform the FRBC into a world-class fisheries organization (Johnstone 1977). Oceanography was only one of the problems that Kask faced, but it was one that recurred in FRBC and JCO deliberations – how the FRBC could maintain and even increase its work in oceanography while attempting to increase the organization's significance in fisheries research. In Kask's eyes, the solution was to find another home for all but fisheries-related oceanographic research. This decision neatly coincided with the entry on the scene of an oceanographic program within DMTS.

W.E. van Steenburgh (1899-1974; Fig. 12) joined DMTS in 1956 as director-general of science services. He became deputy-minister in 1963. Originally an entomologist, he served as a military administrator during the war, then with the DRB, and returned to the federal Department of Agriculture in 1947, where, during nearly a decade, he supervised a remarkable expansion of Agriculture laboratories across the country. In DMTS he was to supervise the department's scientific programs and to develop new projects (Glen 1974). How his attention turned to oceanography is not clear – W.M. Cameron (Fig. 13), later a senior administrator under van Steenburgh, believed that it was at least partly due to an accident suffered by the CHS's survey ship CSS *Baffin,* which van Steenburgh credited to lack of professionalism (Mills 2004). Whatever the precipitating factor or factors, by 1957 van Steenburgh was promoting DMTS's intention of going into oceanography to the JCO – an idea that Cameron, who had worked with Tully in Nanaimo, who had inaugurated the teaching program at UBC, and who at the time was director of scientific services for the RCN (and shortly thereafter director of plans for DRB), found appalling. In his words (Mills 2004):

> *"So van Steenburgh went to the early meeting (of the JCO), went to the meeting almost immediately after this decision, he was going to get into this ... and he made this declaration: I thought, oh my God, this is the end of oceanography, and so I bitterly opposed it. I strenuously opposed it, I said, We've fragmented far enough. We've got to get some scientists into the traditional fields. There was no research tradition in Mines and Technical Surveys ... And he says, Cameron, I don't give a goddamn how you feel, but I'm going into oceanography."*

Cameron and others in the JCO tried to drum up support for an alternative to oceanography in DMTS with NRC, where they were rebuffed by its president, E.W.R. Steacie (1900-62), and with Jack Kask of the FRBC, who was intent on narrowing the Board's approach to the field, not expanding it. Within a couple of years Cameron had been won over by van Steenburgh and had joined the effort at DMTS (in 1960) as its director of oceanographic research, then (in 1962) as director of the newly-founded Marine Sciences Branch, including responsibility for a large new laboratory on the east coast (Dartmouth, NS) and a major research vessel.

Well before Cameron's conversion, van Steenburgh had been at work on the expansion of oceanography in DMTS, centred on the east coast. It was by no means an easy task to persuade west coast oceanographers (Tully, in particular) of the necessity of expanding oceanography in the east before the west. But Halifax was a natural site to start - it already housed a DRB laboratory (Defence Research Establishment Atlantic, DREA), as early as 1958 the FRBC was proposing to move the AOG to Halifax, the FRBC's and RCN's arctic oceanography was supported there by HMCS *Labrador*, and negotiations were at an advanced stage to teach oceanography at Dalhousie University. By December 1958, van Steenburgh had received approval from Treasury Board for a ship, and was attempting to recruit W.L. Ford (1913-92), at that time directing DRB's PNL in Victoria, to direct the new east coast laboratory. By June 1959, Treasury Board had approved the plans for the new laboratory (the first contract was let early in 1960), which would provide space for the AOG, the CHS, and marine geologists, and a new coordinating body was being organized for Canadian oceanography.

The idea that the JCO be reorganized and expanded originated with the NRC's president Steacie, who suggested to van Steenburgh that the JCO should be expanded by adding the universities (UBC, Toronto, and Dalhousie - the last opened its Institute of Oceanography in 1959, funded by NRC) to form a 'National Committee on Oceanography'. A press release by DMTS dated 17 December 1959 announced the organization of the Canadian Committee on Oceanography (CCO), with van Steenburgh as chairman and Hachey as secretary, to "coordinate and direct work in oceanography and to represent [the Canadian government] internationally in the field of oceanographic research" through links to SCOR (Special Committee on Oceanographic Research – now Scientific Committee on Oceanic Research), the ICSU (International Council of Scientific Unions), and the NATO Scientific Committee on Oceanographic Research. It also announced formally plans to open the Bedford Institute of Oceanography (BIO), and to provide the first of several new scientific vessels, the CSS *Hudson*, for the newly expanded Canadian oceanographic programs in Atlantic Canada.

By fall 1962, van Steenburgh's plans had materialized in the BIO, with a building, a director (not W.L Ford at first, but W.N. English (b. 1915), also of the PNL), a small scientific staff, and the prospect of a fine new ocean-going research vessel. In an address on 24 October 1962 (written by W.M. Cameron) to a convocation of Dalhousie University on the day before BIO opened, van Steenburgh expressed his hopes for the new institution:

> *"We hope that the new Institute will encourage close coordination and provide an integrated oceanographic program. If our plans and hopes materialize, this Institute will become an important national and international research establishment."*

The rest of this book is about just that!

REFERENCES

Campbell, I. 2010. The Royal Canadian Navy cruises in northern waters in 1948: A hint of global warming, or a cyclical change? Directorate of History and Heritage unpublished manuscript, Dept. of National Defence, Ottawa, ON.

Campbell, N.J. 1958. Recent oceanographic activities of the Atlantic Oceanographic Group in the Eastern Arctic. Fisheries Research Board of Canada, Progress Reports of the Atlantic Coast Stations 69: 18-21.

Campbell, N.J. 1976. An historical sketch of physical oceanography in Canada. Journal of the Fisheries Research Board of Canada 33: 2,155-2,167.

Collin, A.E. and M.J. Dunbar. 1964. Physical oceanography in Arctic Canada. Oceanography and Marine Biology Annual Reviews 2: 45-75.

Copeland, G.G. 1912. The temperature and densities and allied subjects of Passamaquoddy Bay and its environs. Their bearing on the oyster industry. Contributions to Canadian Biology 1906-1910: 281-294.

Craigie, E.H. 1916a. Hydrographic investigations in the St. Croix River and Passamaquoddy Bay in 1914. Contributions to Canadian Biology 1914-1915: 151-161.

Craigie, E.H. 1916b. A hydrographic section of the Bay of Fundy in 1914. Contributions to Canadian Biology 1914-1915: 163-167.

de Vecchi, V. 1982. The pilgrim's progress, the BAAS, and research in Canada: from Montreal to Toronto. Transactions of the Royal Society of Canada, Series IV, 20: 519-532.

de Vecchi, V. 1984. The dawning of a national scientific community in Canada, 1878-1896. Scientia Canadensis 18 (26): 32-58

Dunbar, M.J. 1951. Eastern Arctic waters. Fisheries Research Board of Canada Bulletin 88, Ottawa, ON.

Dunbar, M.J. 1982. The history of oceanographic research in the waters of the Canadian Arctic islands. Pages 141-152 *in* A Century of Canada's Arctic Islands (M. Zaslow, Ed.). Royal Society of Canada, Ottawa, ON.

Elliot-Meisel, E.B. 1999. Arctic focus: the Royal Canadian Navy in Arctic waters, 1946-1949. The Northern Mariner 9 (2): 23-39.

Fillmore, S. and R.W. Sandilands. 1983. The Chartmakers: A History of Nautical Surveying in Canada. NC Press, Toronto, ON.

Glen, R. 1974. William Elgin van Steenburgh O.C., O.B.E., E.D., B.A., M.A., Ph.D., L.L.D., 1899-1974. Bulletin of the Entomological Society of Canada 6: 84-86.

Hachey, H.B. 1931. The general hydrography and hydrodynamics of the waters of the Hudson Bay region. Contributions to Canadian Biology and Fisheries, Series D, 7: 91-118.

Helland-Hansen, B. 1930. Physical oceanography and meteorology. Results of the Michael Sars North Atlantic Deep-Sea Expedition 1910. Report on the Scientific Results 1 (2) Part 1, Text, pp.1-115 and Part II, Tables and Plates, pp. 1-102. Bergens Museum, Bergen, Norway.

Hjort, J. 1919. Introduction to the Canadian Fisheries Expedition, 1914-1915. Pages xi-xxviii *in* Canada. Department of the Naval Service, Canadian Fisheries Expedition, 1914-1915; Investigations in the Gulf of St. Lawrence and Atlantic waters of Canada under the direction of Dr. Johan Hjort, head of the expedition, director of fisheries for Norway. King's Printer, Ottawa, ON.

Hubbard, J. 2006. A Science on the Scales. The Rise of Canadian Atlantic Fisheries Biology, 1898-1939. University of Toronto Press, Toronto, ON.

Hubbard, J., D. Wildish, and R. Stephenson (Eds.). in press. A Century of Marine Science: The St. Andrews Biological Station 1908-2008. University of Toronto Press, Toronto, ON.

Huntsman, A.G., W.B. Bailey, and H.B. Hachey. 1954. The general oceanography of the Strait of Belle Isle. Journal of the Fisheries Research Board of Canada 11: 198-260.

Iselin, C. O'D. 1930. A report on the coastal waters of Labrador, based on the explorations of the 'Chance' during the summer of 1926. Proceedings of the American Academy of Arts and Sciences 66: 1-37.

Johnstone, K. 1977. The Aquatic Explorers: A History of the Fisheries Research Board of Canada. University of Toronto Press, Toronto, ON.

Keen, M.J. (compiler). 1990. The history of exploration of the continental margin of Eastern Canada. Pages 833-846 *in* Geology of the Continental Margin of Eastern Canada (M.J. Keen and G.L. Williams, Eds.). Appendix Table A1, pp. 833-846. Geological Survey of Canada, Ottawa, ON.

Kiilerich, A.B. 1939. The Godthaab Expedition of 1928: a theoretical treatment of the hydrographical observations. Meddelelser om Grønland 78 (5).

Leary, W.M. 1999. Under Ice: Waldo Lyon and the Development of the Arctic Submarine. Texas A & M University Press, College Station, TX.

Le Danois, E. 1924. Étude hydrologique de l'Atlantique-Nord. Annales de l'Institut océanographique, N.-É., 1: 1-52.

Le Danois, E. 1937. Hydrographie et hydrologie des bancs de Terre-Neuve. Annales de l'Institut océanographique, N.-É., 16: 466-479.

MacDougall, J.R. 2014. Hydrography: a foundation for multidisciplinary ocean science at BIO, 1962-2012. Pages 169-180 *in* Voyage of Discovery: Fifty Years of Marine Research at the Bedford Institute of Oceanography (D.N. Nettleship, D.C. Gordon, C.F.M. Lewis, and M.P. Latremouille, Eds.). Bedford Institute of Oceanography-Oceans Association, Dartmouth, NS.

Matthews, D.J. 1914. Report of Mr. D.J. Matthews. Pages 4-47 *in* Report on the Work Carried Out on the S.S. "*Scotia*", 1913: Ice observation, meteorology and oceanography in the North Atlantic Ocean. HMSO, London, England.

Mavor, J.W. 1922. The circulation of water in the Bay of Fundy. Part I. Introduction and drift bottle experiments. Contributions to Canadian Biology and Fisheries (New Series) 1 (8): 101-124.

Mavor, J.W. 1923. The circulation of water in the Bay of Fundy. Part II. The distribution of temperature, salinity and density in 1919 and the movements of water which they indicate in the Bay of Fundy. Contributions to Canadian Biology and Fisheries (New Series) 1 (18): 353-375.

Meehan, O.M. 2006. The Canadian Hydrographic Service. From the time of its inception until the end of the Second World War. The Northern Mariner, Special Edition, Canadian Nautical Research Society, Kingston, ON.

Mills, E.L. 1994. Bringing oceanography into the Canadian university classroom. Scientia Canadensis 18: 3-21.

Mills, E.L. 2001. Canadian marine science research in Arctic and northern waters. History of Oceanography 13: 3-6.

Mills, E.L. 2002. Pacific waters and the POG: the origin of physical oceanography on the West Coast of Canada. Pages 303-315 *in* Oceanographic History: the Pacific and Beyond (K.R. Benson and P.F. Rehbock, Eds.). University of Washington Press, Seattle, WA.

Mills, E.L. 2004. Interview with Dr. William Cameron, November 11, 1991. Edited transcript of audiotape, 28 p. Bedford Institute of Oceanography, Dartmouth, NS.

Mills, E.L. 2009. The Fluid Envelope of Our Planet: How the Study of Ocean Currents Became a Science. University of Toronto Press, Toronto, ON.

Murray, J. and J. Hjort. 1912. The Depths of the Ocean: A General Account of the Science of Oceanography Based Largely on the Scientific Researches of the Norwegian Steamer *'Michael Sars'* in the North Atlantic. Macmillan, London, England.

Ricketts, N.G. 1932. The *'Marion'* Expedition to Davis Strait and Baffin Bay. Pages 1-52 *in* The Marion Expedition to Davis Strait and Baffin Bay under direction of the United States Coast Guard, 1928. Scientific Results, Part I. The bathymetry and sediments of Davis Strait (N.G. Ricketts and P.D. Trask, Eds.). U.S. Treasury Department, United States Coast Guard Bulletin No. 19, Washington, DC.

Riis-Carstensen, E. 1931. The Godthaab Expedition 1928. Report on the expedition. Meddelelser om Grønland 78 (1): 1-105.

Sandström, J.W. 1919. The hydrodynamics of Canadian Atlantic waters. Pages 221-343 *in* Canada, Department of the Naval Service, Canadian Fisheries Expedition, 1914-1915: Investigations in the Gulf of St. Lawrence and Atlantic waters of Canada under the Direction of Dr. Johan Hjort, Leader of the Expedition, Director of Fisheries for Norway. King's Printer, Ottawa, ON.

Sandström, J.W. and B. Helland-Hansen. 1903. Über die Berechnungen von Meeresströmungen. Report on Norwegian Fishery and Marine Investigations 2 (4): 1-43.

Smith, E.H. 1926. A practical method for determining ocean currents. Bulletin of the United States Coast Guard 14, United States Treasury Department, Washington, DC.

Smith, E.H., F.M. Soule, and O. Mosby. 1937. The 'Marion' and 'General Greene' expeditions to Davis Strait and the Labrador Sea under the direction of the U.S. Coast Guard, 1928-1931-1933-1934-1935. United States Coast Guard Bulletin 19, United States Treasury Department, Washington, DC.

Thomson, D.W. 1966. Men and Meridians: the History of Mapping and Surveying in Canada. Volume 1. Prior to 1867. Supply and Services Canada, Ottawa, ON.

Thomson, D.W. 1967. Men and Meridians: the History of Mapping and Surveying in Canada. Volume 2, 1867 to 1917. Information Canada, Ottawa, ON.

Tunnicliffe, M. 2010. Ocean science and the Canadian Navy - the early years. Lecture to Canadian Nautical Research Society Annual Meeting, Halifax, N.S., 16 June 2010. Unpubl. report, CNRS, Halifax, NS.

Zaslow, M. 1975. Reading the Rocks: the Story of the Geological Survey of Canada 1842-1972. Macmillan, Toronto, ON.

2. BEDFORD INSTITUTE OF OCEANOGRAPHY: A UNIQUE EXPERIMENT IN FEDERAL SCIENCE

Donald C. Gordon*, Michael M. Sinclair, C.F. Michael Lewis, and David N. Nettleship

SUMMARY

In the early 1960s, oceanography was a national priority for Canada. The establishment of the Bedford Institute of Oceanography (BIO) in 1962 brought existing federal marine science organizations in eastern Canada together at one site on the shore of Bedford Basin in Dartmouth, Nova Scotia. Over the years, different federal government departments have shared an extensive infrastructure comprising research laboratories, a marine sciences library, support facilities, and a superb fleet of survey vessels. Today these departments are Fisheries and Oceans Canada, Natural Resources Canada, Environment Canada, and Department of National Defence. BIO has conducted research in all the major marine science disciplines including hydrography, physical oceanography, chemical oceanography, marine geophysics, marine geology, marine ecology, and fisheries. Examples of scientific accomplishments are provided in the papers that follow. Many aspects of this research have considered the impacts of human activities on the marine environment and vice versa. Research has benefited from collaborative links to other government agencies, universities, industry, and national and international scientific communities. Research results have been thoroughly documented and made publically available. Scientific advice has been provided on important marine issues to a wide variety of users including government decision makers and resource managers, marine industries, and non-governmental organizations. Most components of BIO have changed as their science matured and practical uses of their expertise were increasingly developed and applied. Research funding has shifted from stable multi-year support to short-term sources related to the needs of stakeholders in the marine environment. In recent years the mandate of BIO has expanded to include ecosystem management with an aim to conserving major ecological services in the marine environment. In addition, the Canadian Coast Guard is now located on the BIO campus, and Fisheries and Oceans Canada regional administration and operational personnel are currently being relocated to BIO. Despite declines in resource levels, BIO continues to carry out important fundamental and applied research.

Key words: Bedford Institute of Oceanography, federal marine science management, multidisciplinary marine research, hydrography, oceanography, marine geoscience, engineering, ecosystem management.
***E-mail:** Donald.Gordon@ns.sympatico.ca

The Bedford Institute of Oceanography (BIO) is a federal oceanographic research facility located on the shores of the Bedford Basin in Dartmouth, Nova Scotia, Canada. Since its establishment in 1962, it has grown to become Canada's largest centre for ocean research. The vision for the planning and establishment of BIO was expressed by Dr. William van Steenburgh in his speech at Dalhousie University the day before the official opening of BIO in October 1962 (van Steenburgh 1962). Dr. van Steenburgh was Director-General for Science in the then Department of Mines and Technical Surveys and is considered as the 'Father' of BIO. There was an extensive focus at the time on the Arctic and the need for applied research to reap the benefits of the first two United Nations Law of the Sea Conferences. His speech first noted that:

"The great federal research organizations emerging over the past century of Canadian history have developed into prominent institutions, all seeking to apply the scientific method to the improvement of Canadian life, and indeed that of mankind in general."

The lecture summarized the proposed five-year plan which called for a vast, many-sided research program with a broad focus on physical, chemical, geological and hydrographic issues (biology was then the purview of the Fisheries Research Board of Canada). He further stated:

"Government's research programs must, of necessity, be organized or planned along specific lines. Federal agencies have a responsibility to answer well-defined questions; planned research or 'oriented research' is a necessary element of their total activity....The correct balance between 'applied' and 'pure' research in an establishment such as the Bedford Institute cannot be determined in advance—it must become apparent with experience."

The Institute has performed targeted research, mandated by the Canadian government, to provide peer-reviewed advice and support to government decision-making on a broad range of ocean issues including sovereignty, safety and security, environmental protection, health of the oceans, conservation and protection of marine life, safe and accessible waterways, submarine landmass, natural resources (e.g., fisheries, minerals, oil, and gas), effective adaptation to climate change, and integrated management of large ocean areas.

The key events and players in the development of Canadian marine science leading up to the creation of BIO have been reviewed by Mills (2014). Before 1962, Canadian marine expertise was limited and fragmented throughout government and university research communities, even though programs were overseen nationally by the Canadian Committee on Oceanography. It was understood that a carefully coordinated and expanded effort was necessary to develop a strong and comprehensive national oceanographic program. The concept was to develop a new, centralized centre of oceanography in eastern Canada that would bring existing federal agencies conducting marine science and surveying together under one roof. Such a facility would improve communication, enhance the exchange of ideas and the transfer of information, and lead to a better coordination of research between and within scientific disciplines. This in turn would be highly cost-effective and facilitate a rapid development of multidisciplinary research programs required to understand the ocean and address marine issues of importance to Canada. By doing so, it would highlight Canada's creativity and credibility within the international oceanographic community. It would also allow efficient sharing of the necessary infrastructure for oceanographic research which included well-planned laboratories, a comprehensive marine science library, computing facilities, machine shops, equipment storage, research vessels capable of working on the high seas and in northern waters, and docking facilities.

By bringing different agencies together at one central location, the establishment of BIO was a unique experiment in the management and conduct of Canadian federal government science. It was carried out at a time when the federal government chose to allocate significant resources to meet the growing need for oceanographic research and developing Canadian expertise to investigate important national issues. This paper provides a brief overview of the development of BIO as a Canadian federal research organization between 1962 and 2012. It attempts to capture some important highlights and provide some perspective on the occasion of the BIO Fiftieth Anniversary. It describes the working environment under which the studies described in the subsequent 46 review papers were carried out. A selection of events in the organizational history of BIO are listed chronologically in Appendix 1. More detail on the history of BIO and its programs can be found in the annual and biennial reviews listed in Appendix 2. Additional historical aspects are contained in transcripts of interviews with senior staff deposited in the BIO Archives.

GROWTH OF RESEARCH PROGRAMS

The three federal agencies initially comprising BIO when it opened in 1962 were the Canadian Hydrographic Service, the Atlantic Oceanographic Group, and the Marine Sciences Branch. A Canadian hydrographic program was first established in 1883 with the founding of the Georgian Bay Survey which later became the Canadian Hydrographic Service in 1928 so, when BIO opened, the Canadian Hydrographic Service already had a long tradition of conducting hydrographic surveys off the east coast of Canada (Meehan 1964). These were run out of Ottawa, the nation's capital located in Ontario, until a regional office was opened in Halifax, Nova Scotia, in 1958. The Atlantic Oceanographic Group, established in 1946 under the Fisheries Research Board of Canada (Johnstone 1977), was initially based at the St. Andrews Biological Station in St. Andrews, New Brunswick, but moved to Halifax in 1960. The Marine Sciences Branch, created in 1961 within the department of Dr. van Steenburgh, was based in Ottawa and soon expanded into Atlantic Canada. It became the lead agency within BIO and as such the Department of Mines and Technical Services owned and managed the physical facilities. Hence, existing federal government hydrographers and oceanographers from different federal agencies were brought together under one roof in a new multidisciplinary institute.

The Geological Survey of Canada, Canada's oldest government scientific organization, established in 1842 (Vodden 1992, Zaslow 1975), was also a branch of the Department of Mines and Technical Services parallel with the Canadian Hydrographic Service and Marine Sciences Branch. Its marine geology group, which had already begun studies of continental shelves and channels in Arctic Canada as part of the new Polar Continental Shelf Project initiated in 1958, transferred to BIO in 1963. Lands offshore of Atlantic Canada were leased for exploration by the petroleum industry prior to the opening of BIO. After exploratory well drilling started in 1966, samples, reports, and data from the drill sites and seismic surveys were curated and managed at BIO by the Resource Management and Conservation Branch of the Department of Energy, Mines, and Resources. The Geological Survey of Canada, also aware of offshore hydrocarbon potential and of the industry leases, established the Eastern Petroleum Geology Section on the BIO campus in 1971 to investigate and assess the offshore sedimentary basins.

The growth of BIO during its first decade was rapid. The demand for scientific and technical staff was greater than the supply in Canada despite the creation of Institutes of Oceanography at the University of British Columbia (Vancouver, BC) in 1949 and Dalhousie University (Halifax, NS) in 1959 to train new oceanographers at the MSc and PhD levels. Many new personnel were recruited from the United States and Western Europe, especially the United Kingdom. Often, at this early stage of the Institute's development, new staff members were either trained on the job or took educational leave to complete graduate degrees in their speciality. As pre-existing units arrived at BIO, care was taken to integrate them into new groups which could operate efficiently in the new setting.

The initial emphasis of research programs was on hydrography and physical oceanography. However, programs in marine geology, marine geophysics, chemical oceanography and marine ecology grew rapidly. In addition, care was taken from the start to develop a strong in-house engineering program to develop oceanographic instrumentation in support of BIO programs. The scope of BIO research expanded further in the 1970s with the addition of programs on pollution, coastal geomorphology, sediment dynamics, geochemistry, marine fish, and seabird ecology.

When the federal government established the Department of Environment in 1971, all BIO units except the geosciences were transferred to the new department. The same year saw the creation of the Environmental Protection Service and the placement of a Canadian Wildlife Service research scientist at BIO to study the pelagic ecology of marine birds as part of an Arctic and Eastern Canada seabird program centred in Ottawa. The geoscience units were organized into the Atlantic Geoscience Centre in 1972 and remained part of the Geological Survey of Canada under the Department of Energy Mines and Resources. As of 1973, BIO consisted of: the Atlantic Oceanographic Laboratory, the Atlantic Geoscience Centre, and the Marine Ecology Laboratory, plus the Environmental Quality Laboratory of the Environmental Protection Service. In 1976, the entire Canadian Wildlife Service (CWS) Seabird Research Unit was relocated from Ottawa to BIO.

The scope of research activities increased further in 1977 due to the extension of national jurisdiction from 12 to 200 nautical miles. The need for fisheries research and advice increased and, to help facilitate this gap, the Marine Fish Division was created based upon core staff transferred from the St. Andrews Biological Station. The new fisheries research focus became effectively integrated with the oceanographic programs. Staff of the Atlantic Geoscience Centre was increased further when additional marine and coastal geoscientists from the Geological Survey of Canada in Ottawa arrived in 1978.

By the 1980s, the BIO research program had expanded to cover all the major disciplines of marine science. Based on staff size, disciplinary breadth, scientific output, and recognition, the Institute had developed into a major oceanographic institute, similar in stature to the Woods Hole Oceanographic Institution in Massachusetts and Scripps Institution of Oceanography in California (Vandermeulen and Loncarevic 1992). On occasion of the 1982 Scientific Committee on Oceanic Research meeting held in Halifax, Soviet scientist Konstantin Federov commented that BIO was the "most elegantly organized institute in the world with the most competent ship (CCS *Hudson*) in the western world" (A. Longhurst, pers. comm.). It was also clear that the research done at BIO was creating numerous tangible social and economic benefits for Canada, such as the successful resolution of the Gulf of Maine boundary dispute with the United States.

In the 1990s, the research program expanded yet further with the arrival of scientists studying invertebrate fisheries, marine plants, and diadromous fisheries when federal laboratories in neighbouring Halifax were consolidated at BIO. In 1993, the Department of National Defence established the Route Survey Office. Expansion of research programs was curtailed in the mid to late 1990s when the federal government initiated a 'program review' strategy to control and reduce its growing deficit.

MANAGEMENT

Four individuals played a critical role in the establishment of BIO (Mills 2014). These 'four Bills' (Loncarevic 2003) are pictured in Figure 1. Dr. William van Steenburgh, Director-General of the Department of Mines and Technical Services, was instrumental in promoting the concept of a federal oceanographic institute on the east coast of Canada and bringing it to fruition. Dr. William Cameron, Director of the Marine Sciences Branch, understood the benefits arising from interaction between all disciplines involved in marine research and the establishment of common facilities and services. He brought to the Institute a vision of how it should function which was the management model used up to the mid 1980s.

The first director (1962-64) was Dr. William English who endeavoured to establish BIO as an autonomous regional laboratory conducting fundamental oceanographic research. Dr. William Ford was at the helm during a period of unparalleled expansion (1965-78). He developed the concept of BIO being a centre of marine research agencies and strived to ensure that BIO programs were balanced among the various marine science disciplines. He instilled a spirit of good will and cooperation among the various agencies, fostered multidisciplinary research, and was instrumental in building BIO into a major oceanographic institution.

Between 1962 and 2012, a total of 39 people have served in director-level positions at BIO and they are listed in Appendix 3. At the beginning, the agencies were adequately resourced and were given a high degree of flexibility in establishing their programs within the general priorities established by their respective departments in Ottawa. Agencies were autonomous and managed their own budgets and administrative support. However, most of the infrastructure was funded and managed by the lead agency which initially was the Marine Sciences Branch but has been Fisheries and Oceans Canada since 1979. A strong and unique tradition of cooperation, sharing resources, and development of multidisciplinary research programs with strong internal horizontal linkages was established through the directors and staff of the different agencies within BIO.

Figure 1. Photos of the 'Four Bills' who were instrumental in the establishment of the Bedford Institute of Oceanography: (A) Dr. W. van Steenburgh, (B) Dr. William Cameron, (C) Dr. William English, and (D) Dr. William Ford.

Owing to the multi-agency structure of BIO, no single director was responsible for all aspects of the program but, as identified in Appendix 3, the senior manager of the lead agency has served as the nominal 'Director of BIO'. Institute-wide matters of business have always been managed by a committee of directors (Fig. 2) that met frequently and encouraged a strong sense of collegiality. At the beginning, the chair of this committee rotated among the directors of laboratories, but later it was chaired by the Director-General of Ocean and Aquatic Sciences followed by the Regional Science Director of the Fisheries and Oceans Canada. This committee became known as the 'Tuesday Club' because it met every Tuesday. With the introduction of sector management in the Fisheries and Oceans Canada (as described below), Tuesday Club membership expanded to include the administration managers and later senior managers of newly arrived agencies. In 2010, the Tuesday Club was renamed the BIO Campus Management Committee to reflect its broader membership and function. The same year a new BIO Science Management Committee was created to focus solely on science issues with membership from Fisheries and Oceans Canada, Natural Resources Canada, Environment Canada, and Department of National Defence.

Figure 2. Photo of 1972 BIO directors meeting (l-r): Dr. B. Loncarevic (AGC), Dr. L. Dickie (MEL) and Dr. W. Ford (AOL).

During the first 25 years (1962-87), most of the physical, geological, chemical, and biological oceanography and hydrography conducted by the federal departments in Atlantic Canada was managed by the Institute. The organizational structure of the relevant federal departments changed frequently and, as a consequence, the names of the research units within the Institute and their reporting relationships with regional and national headquarters in Ottawa changed as well (see Appendix 1). The research directors (Appendix 3), however, reported directly to Ottawa following 'line management' procedures. The hydrography, oceanography, and geology programs within Atlantic Canada and the eastern Canadian arctic were well-coordinated and supported at the highest levels of government.

A major change in the management of BIO occurred in 1986-87 during a nation-wide reorganization of research activities within Fisheries and Oceans Canada and other BIO member departments. The position of Director-General of Ocean and Aquatic Surveys, based at BIO, was abolished. Oceanographic, hydrographic and fisheries research within the region were integrated and directors reported to a single Regional Director-General who was responsible for the full range of Fisheries and Oceans Canada departmental responsibilities from small craft harbour facilities to the management of fisheries and aquaculture. The goal of this integration of research was to enhance focus on regional fisheries and habitat management priorities.

Soon after, 'sector management' began to be introduced within the federal government. Under this style of management, common functions such as finance, personnel, library services, computing support, and vessels are centralized and report directly to managers outside of the science programs. The positive benefits of centralization are potential increases in overall efficiency at the regional and national levels, but there can also be a loss of flexibility within an Institute such as BIO. This change also led to more complex relationships between Fisheries and Oceans Canada regional departmental management and headquarters with shared accountabilities. Another major change in the structure of BIO management occurred in 1995 when the Canadian Coast Guard was transferred from Transport Canada to Fisheries and Oceans Canada and took over the operation of the BIO research vessels from Science.

Beginning in 1997, the BIO mandate expanded further into ecosystem management. Ecosystem management is about managing human activities that impact habitats and the resources they sustain. This activity denotes an operational sector of Fisheries and Oceans Canada that relies on the results of marine research and ecosystem-based science to assist the decision-making process in managing human activities such as transportation, aquaculture, oil and gas, conservation, and tourism in relation to fisheries resources and fish habitats. The three key programs are Habitat Management, Oceans, and Species at Risk. Working in close collaboration with BIO scientists, the Ecosystem Management Branch assists the Fisheries and Oceans Canada to meet its obligations under the federal *Fisheries Act*, *Canadian Environmental Assessment Act*, *Oceans Act*, and *Species at Risk Act* to ensure sustainable use of our ocean, coastal, and freshwater resources.

In 2012, the Canadian Coast Guard Base in downtown Dartmouth was closed and all activities were moved to the BIO campus. In addition, all Fisheries and Oceans Canada Maritimes Region administrative and fisheries management staff are currently being relocated to BIO and these moves are expected to be completed in 2014.

FACILITIES

The BIO campus has gradually expanded over the years with both new buildings and extensive renovations to meet program requirements (Fig. 3, Appendix 4). At first, this was necessary to accommodate new staff as the scientific programs expanded, but more recently it has been driven by the relocation of government personnel to BIO as other regional facilities have been closed. When BIO opened in 1962, the campus consisted of the Main Building (which housed offices, laboratories, support services, library, meeting rooms, cafeteria, etc.), the Depot (which housed workshops, vessel support services, and storage for field equipment), and the Jetty for BIO research vessels (Fig. 3A). From the very beginning, all the necessary facilities for oceanographic research were conveniently located on site at BIO.

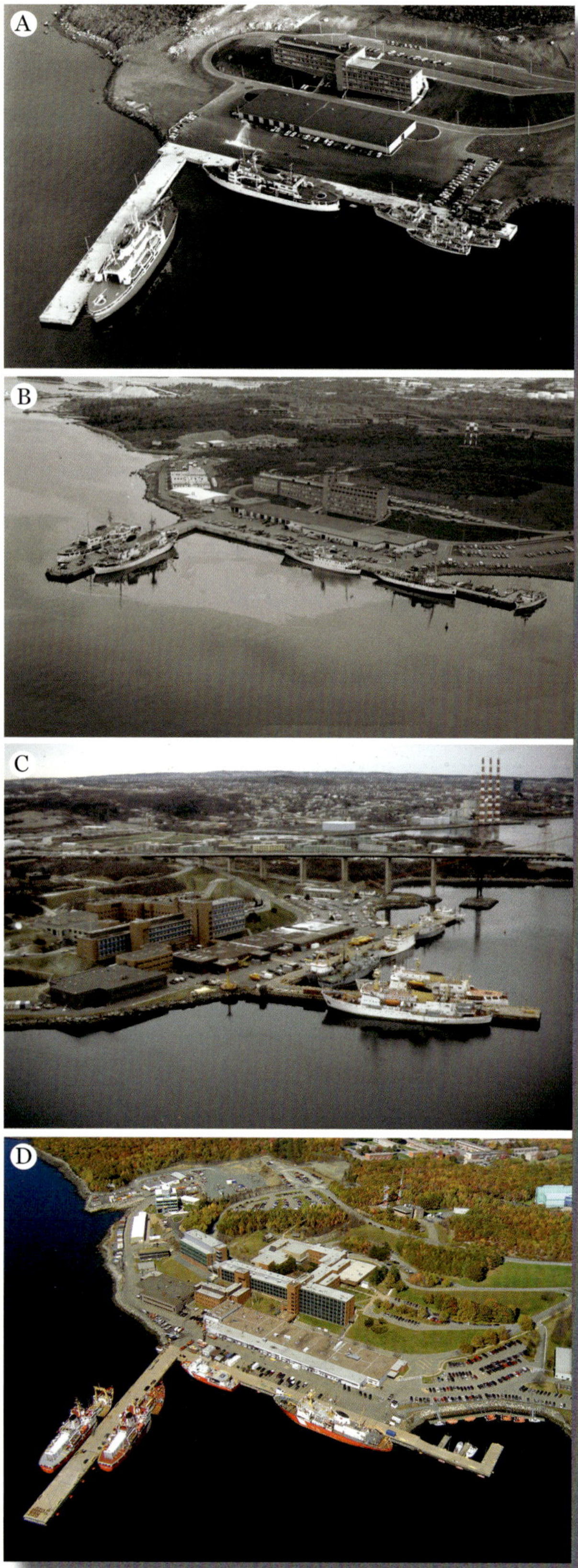

Figure 3. Aerial photos of BIO: (A) Original facilities on opening day in 1962, showing the low Depot building in front of the Main Building, and vessels (l-r) CCGS *Sir John A. MacDonald*, CSS *Baffin*, CSS *Kapuskasing*, and CSS *Maxwell*; (B) 1974 showing the Fish Laboratory, trailer complex, and a northern addition to the Main Building, and vessels (l-r) CSS *Baffin*, CSS *Hudson*, CSS *Dawson*, CSS *Acadia*, and CSS *Maxwell*; (C) 1989 showing addition of the Strickland, Murray, Holland, Coast Guard Communications buildings, the Argo Building visible under the bridge, and vessels (l-r) CSS *Hudson*, CSS *Baffin*, MV *Needler*, MV *Cygnus*, CSS *Dawson*, and MV *Chebucto*; and (D) 2012 after construction of the Ellis Building, cooling plant, and Coast Guard building. Vessels (l-r), now painted Coast Guard colours, are CCGS *William Alexander*, CCGS *Edward Cornwallis*, CGGS *Matthew* and CCGS *Hudson*.

In 1968, the Fish Laboratory was built to provide a running fresh and saltwater facility for fisheries research programs. The same year saw the start of construction of a temporary trailer complex to provide office and laboratory space for new staff until permanent facilities could be constructed. The Argo Building was constructed in 1970 and initially used to archive samples, cores and related data from offshore drilling programs. It was expanded in 1971 to accommodate scientists of the Eastern Petroleum Geology Section. Starting in 1971, the Fish Laboratory was expanded to provide facilities for pollution and applied toxicology research programs (Fig. 3B). A major expansion program began in the mid 1970s that resulted in the construction of the Strickland, Murray and Holland buildings. The Strickland Building, completed in 1978, was initially occupied by staff of the Marine Ecology Laboratory, Environmental Protection Service, and Inland Waters Directorate, many of whom had been housed in the Trailer Complex which was destroyed by fire in 1979. The Murray Building, also completed in 1978, was occupied by the Atlantic Geoscience Centre and computer centre. The Holland Building, completed in 1980, was designed to bring Institute staff together and included a large auditorium (now named the W.L. Ford Auditorium), library, and cafeteria. The two wings of the original Main Building, which housed the Canadian Hydrographic Service, Atlantic Oceanographic Laboratory, and Seabird Research Unit (CWS), were later renamed the Polaris (south wing) and van Steenburgh (north wing) buildings. In 1988, the Canadian Coast Guard constructed the Marine Communications and Traffic Services building on campus to monitor harbour traffic (Fig. 3C). In 2002, an energy-efficient cooling plant using water from Bedford Basin was constructed. The most recent laboratory building constructed, designed to safely handle toxic chemicals, was the Katherine Ellis Building which opened in 2007. And finally, in 2012 the Canadian Coast Guard headquarters moved from downtown Dartmouth, Nova Scotia, to occupy the new Maritimes Headquarters building on the BIO campus (Fig. 3D).

BIO SHIPS

A fleet of well-equipped research vessels is essential to any oceanographic institution and over fifty years BIO has been well-served by 17 vessels for hydrographic, oceanographic, geologic and fisheries studies. The ships are described in order of acquisition using their original identifier letters. For hydrographic vessels, CSS stands for 'Canadian *Survey* Ship' while for vessels used in multidisciplinary research (after 1962) it stands for 'Canadian *Scientific* Ship'. In 1995, when the Canadian Coast Guard took over the operation of the BIO fleet, these identifiers were changed to CCGS which signifies 'Canadian Coast Guard Ship'. CNAV stands for 'Canadian Navy Auxiliary Vessel' and MV stands for 'Motor Vessel'.

BIO initially had five government vessels available for use. The CSS *Acadia* (Fig. 4A) was built in 1913 in Newcastle-on-Tyne, United Kingdom, expressly for hydrographic surveying. She was retired from active duty in 1969, declared a National Historical Site in 1976, and is now on display at the Maritime Museum of the Atlantic in Halifax, Nova Scotia. The CNAV *Sackville* (Fig. 4B) was a 'Flower-class' corvette and saw extensive action on convoy duty across the North Atlantic during World War II. In 1951, she was made available to the Atlantic Oceanographic Group for oceanographic research but was still operated by the Royal Canadian Navy. Her last BIO cruise was in 1975 and she was retired by the Navy in 1982. In 1983 she was transferred to the Canadian Naval Corvette Trust (now the Canadian Naval Memorial Trust) and restored to her 1944 wartime appearance. Since 1985, she has been moored at the Maritime Museum of the Atlantic in Halifax. The CSS *Kapuskasing* (Fig. 4C), originally a minesweeper, served in World War II. Following the war, she was made available to the Canadian Hydrographic Service as a hydrographic ship with four launches and served in this function until 1972. The CSS *Baffin* (Fig. 4D), with a Lloyds Ice Class I hull, was built as a hydrographic survey vessel capable of carrying six launches and a helicopter. Soon after being commissioned, she had the misfortune of grounding on Black Rock off Lunenburg, Nova Scotia, in July 1957. Beginning in 1963, she was used to carry out general oceanographic programs. She was retired in 1991. And finally, the CSS *Maxwell* with two launches (Fig. 4E), which had been built expressly for inshore hydrographic surveys, worked out of BIO until her transfer to Fisheries and Oceans Canada Newfoundland Region in 1987.

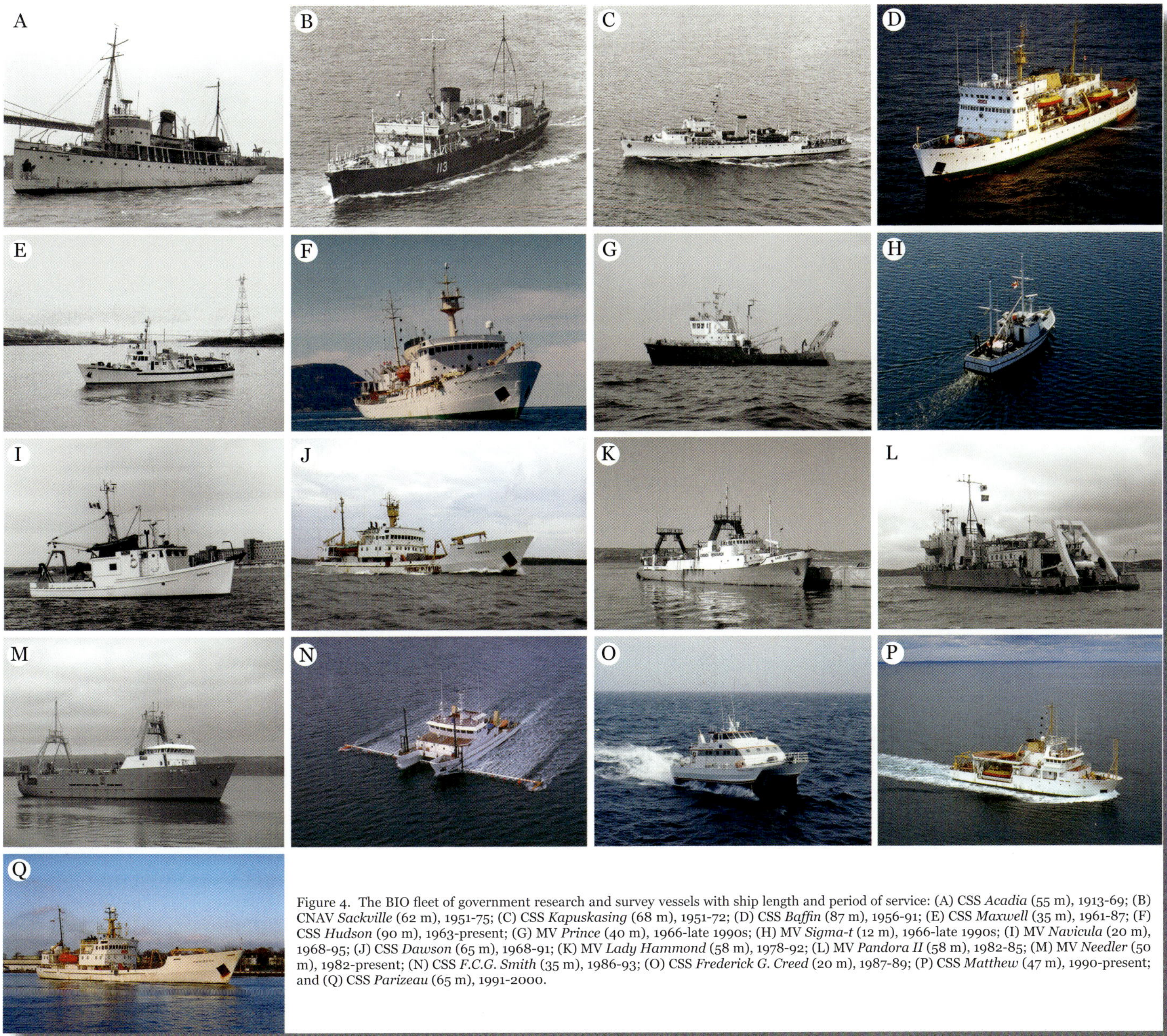

Figure 4. The BIO fleet of government research and survey vessels with ship length and period of service: (A) CSS *Acadia* (55 m), 1913-69; (B) CNAV *Sackville* (62 m), 1951-75; (C) CSS *Kapuskasing* (68 m), 1951-72; (D) CSS *Baffin* (87 m), 1956-91; (E) CSS *Maxwell* (35 m), 1961-87; (F) CSS *Hudson* (90 m), 1963-present; (G) MV *Prince* (40 m), 1966-late 1990s; (H) MV *Sigma-t* (12 m), 1966-late 1990s; (I) MV *Navicula* (20 m), 1968-95; (J) CSS *Dawson* (65 m), 1968-91; (K) MV *Lady Hammond* (58 m), 1978-92; (L) MV *Pandora II* (58 m), 1982-85; (M) MV *Needler* (50 m), 1982-present; (N) CSS *F.C.G. Smith* (35 m), 1986-93; (O) CSS *Frederick G. Creed* (20 m), 1987-89; (P) CSS *Matthew* (47 m), 1990-present; and (Q) CSS *Parizeau* (65 m), 1991-2000.

The first new vessel to join the BIO fleet was the CSS *Hudson* (Fig. 4F). She was built with a Lloyds Ice Class I hull for multidisciplinary oceanographic research and hydrographic programs. Like the CSS *Baffin,* she could carry hydrographic launches (four) and a helicopter. Well-designed for working in the North Atlantic, she soon developed an international reputation as a superb platform for working under adverse weather conditions. She became the pride of the fleet and has been used many times as an icon for BIO, including the cover of this book '*Voyage of Discovery*'. Many of her accomplishments have been summarized by Smith (2003). The most notable cruise was *Hudson*-70 in which she became the first vessel to circumnavigate the Americas (Edmonds 1973, Schafer and Smith 2012, Wadhams 2014). As testimony to her design and construction, she is still in active use in early 2014 at the age of 50 years.

The stern trawler MV *E.E. Prince* (Fig. 4G) was built for fisheries research. Although owned by the Fisheries Research Board of Canada and programmed out of their Halifax office, she was based at BIO until her retirement in the late 1990s. The *Sigma-t* (Fig. 4H) was a small inshore wooden vessel converted for biological research operated by the Fisheries Research Board of Canada but based at BIO. The Fisheries Research Board of Canada soon after took delivery of the MV *Navicula* (Fig. 4I), a wooden vessel designed for inshore biological research based at BIO. She remained active until her retirement in 1995. The programming and operation of these three vessels was transferred to BIO in 1973 when the Fisheries Research Board of Canada was dissolved.

The BIO fleet expanded further in 1968 with the arrival of the CSS *Dawson* (Fig. 4J). She was designed for general oceanographic programs and was particularly well-suited for handling moorings. She provided many years of active service, mostly on the continental shelf, before being retired in 1991. The fleet expanded further with the addition of two charter vessels. The *Lady Hammond* (Fig. 4K), a converted fishing trawler, arrived in 1978 and carried out groundfish stock assessment surveys until 1992. The *Pandora II* (Fig. 4L), a converted offshore supply vessel, was acquired from the Fisheries and Oceans Canada Pacific Region in 1982 and for three years handled the manned submersible *Pices IV* (Fig. 4L) out of BIO.

Next to join the BIO fleet, also in 1982, was the newly-built MV *Alfred Needler* (Fig. 4M). This offshore fisheries research trawler has been used to conduct groundfish surveys and various research programs and is still in operation today. The CSS *F.C.G. Smith* (Fig. 4N) was a catamaran equipped with two retractable booms containing multiple echo sounder transducers and capable of obtaining soundings across a swath of 38 m in coastal waters. She was transferred to the Fisheries and Oceans Canada Quebec Region in 1993. BIO also had the opportunity to evaluate the CSS *Frederick G. Creed* (Fig. 4O) before she too was transferred to the Quebec Region in 1989. This twin-hulled vessel was designed primarily for hydrographic surveys but also had potential for use in scientific research and fisheries patrol.

The last new vessel to join the BIO fleet was CSS *Matthew* (Fig. 4P), built to replace CSS *Maxwell*. She was designed to carry two launches for hydrographic surveys in coastal waters and is still in operation today. And finally, CSS *Parizeau* (Fig. 4Q), the sister ship of CSS *Dawson*, was transferred from the Fisheries and Oceans Canada Pacific Region in 1991 and used extensively in multipurpose oceanographic research before being retired in 2000.

Over the years, the vessels underwent annual and mid-life refits to improve their operation and bring equipment up to date. BIO hydrographers and oceanographers have also used a wide variety of other vessels for their programs. A large number of hydrographic launches and trailerable small boats has been maintained for various inshore projects. In addition, numerous vessels were chartered, especially for hydrographic surveying. These included the MV *North Star VI*, MV *Arctic Sealer*, MV *Theron*, MV *Theta*, MV *Martin Karlson*, MV *Minna*, and MV *Christmas Seal*. Ships from the Canadian Coast Guard, the St. Andrews Biological Station, and the Newfoundland Region have also been frequently used. Canadian Coast Guard vessels used have included CCGS *Griffon* and CCGS *Samuel Risley* in the Great Lakes, CCGS *Namao* in Lake Winnipeg, CCGS *Nahidik* and CCGS *Amundsen* in Beaufort Sea and the Northwest Passage, CCGS Labrador, CCGS *d'Iberville*, CCGS *Sir John A. MacDonald*, and CCGS *Louis St-Laurent* in the Arctic Ocean, and the CCGS *Edward Cornwallis* and CCGS *William Alexander* off the east coast. Icebreakers and submarines from other nations have also been used for arctic research. Additionally, BIO has used vessels belonging to industry, such as offshore oil and gas supply vessels and fishing vessels, and other oceanographic institutes. BIO scientists have also made extensive use of Canadian Coast Guard helicopters for conducting field programs.

Except for periodic seasickness, life on board was pleasant and scientific personnel looked forward to going to sea. During the first three decades, foreign ports of call were common. At the beginning, the atmosphere on board was somewhat formal. Staff dined with the ship's officers, and coats and ties were required for all meals. Staff could gather for socializing and watching movies in the officer's lounge when off duty, but socializing with the crew was discouraged. The first women went to sea on CSS *Hudson* in 1965 and skirts or dresses were required for meals. Most of the vessels had canteens that sold numerous sundry items. With time and changing social attitudes, shipboard atmosphere became more informal.

A major change in the operation of the vessels occurred with the introduction of the 'layday' system when the Canadian Coast Guard took over the operation of the BIO research fleet in 1995. Under this system, each ship has two separate crews which rotate monthly leading to much better working conditions because the crew are off duty every other month. However, double crewing each vessel increased operating costs and led to a reduction in sea time.

Despite their important role, only three vessels remain active in the BIO fleet today: the CCGS *Hudson*, the CCGS *Needler*, and the CCGS *Matthew*. Funds are allocated for the acquisition of vessels to replace CCGS *Hudson* and CCGS *Needler* which are nearing the end of their operational life. Charter and fishing vessels are frequently used to help make up for the reduction in government research ships. In addition, there has been increased use of other platforms to collect oceanographic data as new technologies have been developed. These include satellites, fixed-wing aircraft, balloons, long-term moorings, autonomous underwater vehicles (AUVs), and various floats and drifters. However, ships remain the basic means for delivery of core BIO programs.

FINANCIAL RESOURCES

Between 1962 and the early 1980s, most of the funding supporting BIO research was government A-Base (i.e., basic funding for salaries, operations and maintenance, and capital expenditures) which was relatively stable from year to year and managed by directors and their management committees which made long-term planning possible. Allocations to individual projects were determined by the directors and funding was generally adequate to attain research objectives and kept pace with increases in staff and program requirements. With time, A-Base resources began to decline due to program review, other downsizing exercises, and inadequate adjustments for inflation. At the same time, there was more demand for scientific input into ecosystem and resource management activities without corresponding resources. Also, costs for administrative activities increased.

With these reductions in A-Base funding, there was a shift toward shorter term B-Base resources and external funding sources. One of the first new funding sources was the Unsolicited Proposal Program through the federal Department of Supply and Services which was designed to transfer expertise to private industry. Later, there were numerous government B-Base funds intended for specific short-term projects overseen by managers in Ottawa. These programs included Toxic Chemicals, Green Plan, Long Range Transport of Atmospheric Pollutants, Northern Contaminants, Marine Phycotoxins, Eastern Arctic Marine Environmental Studies, Frontier Geoscience Program, Panel on Energy Research and Development, Environmental Studies Research Funds, Northern Oil and Gas Action Plan, Environmental Sciences Strategic Research Fund, and Strategic Research Fund. Continuing programs today in which BIO plays a major role include the International Governance Strategy and the Adaption to Climate Change in Aquatic Sciences. These programs have specific objectives which, in turn, influence research activities at BIO. As a consequence, goals can be directed more by the source of funds than departmental and national priorities.

Funding is also obtained from industry, in particular the oil and gas and fishery sectors, including Joint Project Agreements. Staff members with university affiliations are also able to apply for funding through the Natural Sciences and Engineering Research Council. In some cases, funding is also provided by international scientific organizations and foreign governments.

In summary, changes in the funding structure have changed the nature of research that is delivered by BIO with more focus in recent years on short-term goals. Despite this, BIO is still able to use limited A-Base funding to continue supporting important long-term core programs such as the monitoring of oceanographic and ecosystem conditions off eastern Canada.

EXTERNAL LINKS

Government Agencies

Owing to the unique management structure of BIO and the presence of different federal departments involved, there has always been a strong internal horizontal linkage through directors and staff. These linkages have had many advantages including the sharing of funding, facilities, people, and responding to requests from Ottawa. These linkages have also allowed the application of a wide range of expertise to address and solve problems, including responding to environmental emergencies. Strong links have also developed and maintained with other federal agencies involved with marine research. In the Halifax Regional Municipality area, these include the Halifax Fisheries Research Laboratory (which closed in 1997) and the Defence Research Establishment Atlantic (now Defence Research and Development Canada) of Department of National Defence. Outside the Halifax Regional Municipality but in the Maritime Provinces, these include the St. Andrews Biological Station and the Gulf Fisheries Centre, both of which have at times been managed out of BIO. Collaborative programs have also been run with staff at the Northwest Fisheries Centre in St. John's, Newfoundland. Linkages have also existed with the Maurice Lamontagne Institute in Mont-Joli, Quebec, the Institute of Ocean Sciences in Sidney, British Columbia, and numerous provincial agencies.

Universities

From the very beginning, BIO has nurtured close ties with the university oceanographic community. The early days of university oceanography programs in Canada are described succinctly by Mills (2014). Institutes of Oceanography were created at the University of British Columbia (UBC) in 1949 and Dalhousie University in 1959 while the McGill University Marine Science Centre was founded in 1963. Being right across the harbour from Halifax, especially close ties were developed with Dalhousie University. In the early years, some BIO staff taught courses at Dalhousie, especially in physical oceanography. For many years, BIO provided ship time without cost to faculty and graduate students at Dalhousie and other universities. This cooperation was initially stimulated by the personal friendship between Dr. William Ford, Director (and later Director-General) of BIO, and Dr. Gordon Riley, Director of the Dalhousie Institute of Oceanography, which dated back to when they worked together at the Woods Hole Oceanographic Institution in the 1940s.

As government oceanographic programs expanded and universities graduated an increasing number of oceanographers, many of the new positions at BIO were filled with recent graduates from Dalhousie and UBC, as well as graduates of other Canadian universities with marine science programs such as McGill, Guelph, and Memorial. Over the years, numerous BIO staff have held adjunct university positions, lectured, and supervised graduate students. Staff have also advised students and served as thesis examiners. In many cases, graduate students have been incorporated into BIO research programs to collect data for their dissertations and to help provide answers to questions considered important by BIO scientists. Government summer and work term student programs have also provided invaluable experience and encouraged many to pursue careers in marine science.

For many years, BIO was an active member of the Atlantic Provinces Council on the Sciences which has the mandate of advancing science and technology through education and public awareness and promoting scientific literacy, education, and research throughout the region. It also has participated in many joint research projects with universities such as the Ocean Production Enhancement Network at Dalhousie and the Bay of Fundy ecological studies at Acadia University (Wolfville, NS).

Industry

The fishing industry has always been a major user of BIO research and facilities. The headquarters of both the International Council for North Atlantic Fisheries followed by the North Atlantic Fisheries Organization were located at BIO in 1963-74 and 1980-89, respectively. Subsequently, the headquarters of the Canadian Atlantic Fisheries Scientific Advisory Committee was located at BIO from 1978 to 1997. These different agencies were responsible for the provision of scientific and technical advice for the management of international and Canadian commercial fisheries. BIO also provides space and support for the headquarters of the Fisherman and Scientist Research Society which it helped to create in 1994. BIO scientists have also conducted a large number of research programs in collaboration with, and for the benefit of, the fishing industry. These include stock assessment surveys, seabed mapping surveys, and experiments and assessments of the effects of fishing practices on non-target marine species and ecosystems.

BIO has also worked closely with the oil and gas industry, and, to a lesser extent, cable laying companies. The mapping of offshore bedrock geology contributed to the assessment of oil and gas reserves off eastern Canada, and information on currents, winds, waves, ice, icebergs, and geohazards has reduced the risk of failure of drilling operations and seabed installations. Collaborative programs have increased knowledge on the design and safe operation of offshore platforms and of the fate and effect of oil spills as well as operational drilling wastes around offshore drilling platforms. BIO scientists have also conducted numerous collaborative projects with tidal power proponents.

Interaction with the private sector and expansion of oceanographic industry has always been a high priority at BIO. In 1981, the Marine Advisory and Industrial Liaison Office was opened to serve the interests of Canadian industry for the benefit of Canadian citizens. BIO engineers have developed a large number of oceanographic instruments for use in both Institute programs and collaborations with industry and universities. In many cases, these have had commercial potential and have been turned over to industry for further development, commercialization and marketing. Examples of success stories include the Huntec Deep-Tow seismic system, Bedford Institute of Oceanography Net and Environmental Sampling System, Moving Vessel Profiler, Icycler, and SeaCycler which are described in the following papers. The environmental consulting industry has also benefited from BIO contracts for technical work, provisions of data and advice, and making available resources housed in the BIO Library. Over the years, BIO has also provided office and laboratory space to numerous firms in the private sector which has increased interaction with BIO scientists.

International Scientific Community

BIO staff have participated as members of a wide variety of international scientific organizations, often holding positions of high responsibility. These organizations have included the International Council for the Exploration of the Sea, Intergovernmental Oceanographic Commission, International Hydrographic Office, Scientific Committee on Oceanic Research, Group of Experts on the Scientific Aspects of Marine Pollution, International Geosphere Biosphere Program, World Climate Research Program, Global Climate Observing Program, International Ornithological Congress – Committee for the Coordination of Seabird Research, International Arctic Science Committee, and Intergovernmental Panel on Climate Change. BIO staff have also participated in and led a large number of international research programs including the World Ocean Climate Experiment, the Joint Global Ocean Flux Study, the Deep Sea Drilling and successor programs, the Engineering Committee on Oceanic Resources, and General Bathymetric Chart of the Ocean. Collaborative programs have also been carried out with foreign scientific organizations including: UK National Institute of Oceanography, Institut Français de Recherche pour l'Exploitation de la Mer, Netherlands Institute for Sea Research, US Geological Survey, Woods Hole Oceanographic Institution, Lamont-Doherty Earth Observatory, University of Rhode Island, and with scientists and ships from other nations in the Arctic Ocean (e.g., Denmark, Sweden, Germany, United States).

On many occasions, the Institute has brought the world's oceanographic community together by organizing and hosting scientific conferences and workshops. BIO staff have also been frequently requested to review scientific programs of other nations. International links have been encouraged by scientific exchange visits, including educational leave by BIO scientists. BIO has also frequently assisted other countries in dealing with environmental emergencies. These various links have been of immeasurable benefit to BIO programs and help maintain the reputation of BIO in the international oceanographic community.

In 1980, BIO established the A.G. Huntsman Award (Appendix 5). This major oceanographic award honours marine scientists of any nationality who have had and continue to have a significant influence on the course of marine scientific thought. It is presented annually by the Royal Society of Canada in one of three categories: marine geosciences, physical/chemical oceanography, and biological oceanography and fisheries science.

COMMUNICATION

The results of BIO research have always been released in a variety of scientific publications including peer-reviewed journals, government technical reports, open files, books, conference proceedings, maps, and hydrographic charts, all of which are readily available to all potential users. These are well documented in the BIO annual/biennial reports which were prepared from 1962 to 2009 (Appendix 2). Many products of BIO research can now be accessed on-line at relevant departmental websites. For example, scientific advice for decision-making is now available on the Canadian Science Advisory Secretariat website (www.dfo-mpo.gc.ca/csas-sccs/index-eng.htm). In addition, a web-based bibliography of BIO and other publications in the marine sciences has also been prepared (http://www.mar.dfo-mpo.gc.ca/libraries-bibliotheques/bibliographies/home).

In recent years, considerable effort has also been made to capture valuable data and incorporate them into accessible digital databases where they are available for use by other government and non-governmental organizations. There has been a long tradition of BIO staff presenting research results at conferences and workshops, in addition to professional journals and other publications. Staff have always provided technical scientific advice on a broad spectrum of subjects important to government resource managers, industry, and non-governmental organizations. These have included environmental assessments and the design of industry-funded environmental monitoring programs. Many of these topics have been controversial and great effort has been made to be objective and offer unbiased opinions and advice based on solid scientific findings.

BIO has also communicated extensively with the public at large through displays at its main entrance, guided tours during summer, Open Houses every five years, its Outreach program, and the media (print, radio, and television). Journalists have been taken to sea to observe and report on BIO research first hand. Numerous movies and videos of BIO research have been prepared for viewing by the general public. Canadian Wildlife Service staff have been involved in the production of numerous CBC-BBC-National Geographic television documentaries, while Geological Survey of Canada, Atlantic staff continue to support geological outreach on a volunteer basis through operation of 'EdGeo' workshops for school teachers, and other activities of the Atlantic Geoscience Society. BIO research continues to appear prominently in local and national media and in departmental outreach websites.

CONCLUSIONS

The establishment of the Bedford Institute of Oceanography was a unique experiment in the management of federal science in Canada. It recognized the critical importance of putting all marine science disciplines, including engineering, together under one roof where they could freely interact, share common facilities, and generate untold discoveries about ocean systems and how they work. The overall objective was to create a stimulating research environment for multidisciplinary investigations to study the structure and dynamics of the ocean and the seafloor, and address marine issues of long-term importance to Canada and the global community. A representative sample of the results and applications from some of the BIO research programs conducted over the Institute's first half century is now presented in the following papers. Please enjoy and appreciate how far we have come in better understanding of the three oceans that surround us. But there remains much more to learn in the next 50 years! These examples clearly illustrate the important benefits accrued to Canada by investing in marine research and creating a marine Institute of international standing.

ACKNOWLEDGEMENTS

We are grateful to the comments and corrections received from our many reviewers who willingly accepted the task of reading earlier drafts of the manuscript. These include Allyn Clarke, Lloyd Dickie, Jim Elliott, Bosko Loncarevic, Alan Longhurst, Dick MacDougall, Dave McKeown, Mark McLean, Eric Mills, Mike Murphy, Brian Nicholls, David Piper, Alain Vezina, Peter Wells, and Graham Williams. In the end, of course, all errors of omission or misinterpretation are the sole responsibility of the authors. We also feel privileged to have experienced the vision of the founders of BIO ("the four Bills") first hand and the amazing scientific achievements produced for Canada and Canadians at large over its first 50-year life span between 1962 and 2012. Long may it continue to flourish and maintain the original goals of BIO's wise founders!

REFERENCES

Edmonds, A. 1973. Voyage to the Edge of the World. McClelland and Stewart Ltd., Toronto, ON.

Johnstone, K. 1977. The Aquatic Explorers: A History of the Fisheries Research Board of Canada. University of Toronto Press, Toronto, ON.

Loncarevic, B.D. 2003. Dedication. Pages 4-5 *in* Bedford Institute of Oceanography 2002 in Review (D. Geddes, Ed.). Bedford Institute of Oceanography, Dartmouth, NS.

Meehan, O.M. 1964. The Canadian Hydrographic Service from the time of its inception in 1883 to the end of the Second World War. The Northern Mariner 15: 299-357.

Mills, E.L. 2014. Canadian marine science from before *Titanic* to the establishment of the Bedford Institute of Oceanography in 1962. Pages 3-11 *in* Voyage of Discovery: Fifty Years of Marine Research at Canada's Bedford Institute of Oceanography (D.N. Nettleship, D.C. Gordon, C.F.M. Lewis, and M.P. Latremouille, Eds.). Bedford Institute of Oceanography-Oceans Association, Dartmouth, NS.

Schafer, C.T. and R.W. Smith. 2012. Getting Around the Americas: The *Hudson* 70 Expedition. Virtualbookworm Publishing, College Station, TX.

Smith, R. 2003. CCGS *Hudson* - A snap shot of historical firsts. Pages 44-47 *in* Bedford Institute of Oceanography 2002 in Review (D. Geddes, Ed.). Bedford Institute of Oceanography, Dartmouth, NS.

van Steenburgh, W.E. 1962. Address at the Special Convocation at Dalhousie University, October 24, 1962 on the Occasion of the Official Opening of the Bedford Institute of Oceanography. BIO Library Archives, Dartmouth, NS.

Vandermeulen, J.H. and B.D. Loncarevic. 1992. The Bedford Institute of Oceanography, Nova Scotia. Pages 94-119 *in* Ocean Frontiers: Explorations by Oceanographers in Five Continents (E.M. Borgese, Ed.). Harry N. Abrams Publishers, New York, NY.

Vodden, C. 1992. No stone unturned: the first 150 years of the Geological Survey of Canada. Geological Survey of Canada, Miscellaneous Paper G12, Ottawa, ON.

Wadhams, P. 2014. The '*Hudson*-70' Voyage of Discovery: first circumnavigation of the Americas. Pages 21-28 *in* Voyage of Discovery: Fifty Years of Marine Research at Canada's Bedford Institute of Oceanography (D.N. Nettleship, D.C. Gordon, C.F.M. Lewis, and M.P. Latremouille, Eds.). Bedford Institute of Oceanography-Oceans Association, Dartmouth, NS.

Zaslow, M. 1975. Reading the Rocks: the Story of the Geological Survey of Canada, 1842-1972. Macmillan, Toronto, ON.

3. THE '*HUDSON*-70' VOYAGE OF DISCOVERY: FIRST CIRCUMNAVIGATION OF THE AMERICAS

Peter Wadhams

SUMMARY

The year 2012 was the 50th anniversary of the Bedford Institute of Oceanography, the premier marine research centre in Canada, and the forty-second anniversary of the 11-month expedition that the Institute's principal oceanographic ship CSS *Hudson* made from 19 November 1969 to 16 October 1970, the first circumnavigation of the Americas. This paper provides a short summary of events that led up to the '*Hudson*-70' ocean expedition and the research activities and accomplishments made during the nine legs of the journey. The expedition remains as a benchmark of Canada's impressive list of contributions to national and international oceanography. It has provided new understandings about the seas that surround us and their treasures of renewable and non-renewable resources.

Key words: oceanographic surveys, marine research, circumnavigation, Northwest Passage, voyages of discovery.
E-mail: PW11@hermes.cam.ac.uk

'*Hudson*-70' was one of the last of the great globe-spanning multidisciplinary oceanographic expeditions, a tradition that included the epic voyages of HMS *Challenger* (1872-76), SMS *Meteor* (1925), and the Swedish *Albatross* (1947). During an expedition lasting 11 months, the Canadian Scientific Ship CSS *Hudson*, of the Bedford Institute of Oceanography (BIO), Dartmouth, Nova Scotia, accomplished the first circumnavigation of the Americas (Fig. 1). During that voyage, she worked in the North and South Atlantic, Antarctic, Pacific, and Arctic oceans, and up to 1970 was only the sixth ship to transit the Northwest Passage (Edmonds 1973, Wadhams 2009a, Schafer and Smith 2012).

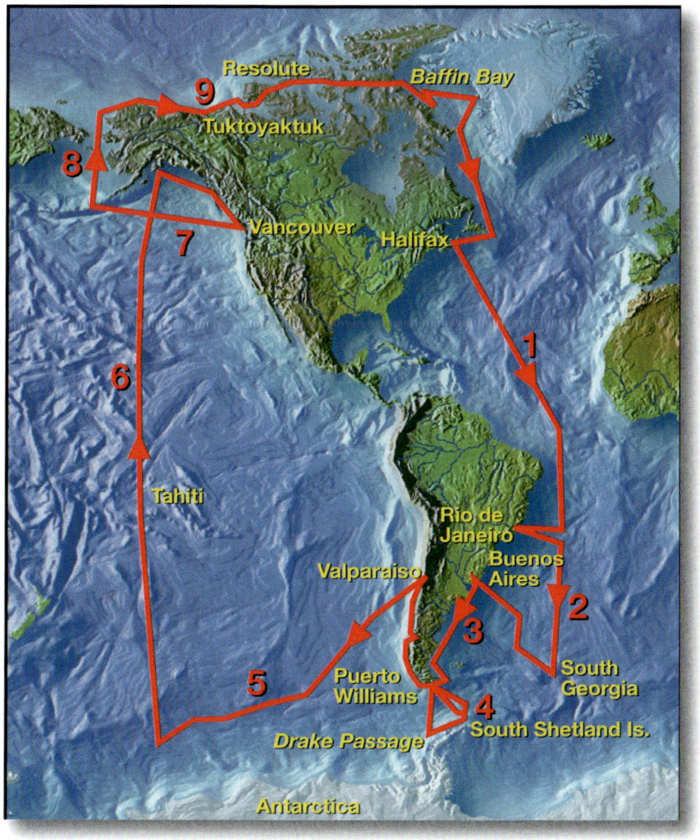

Figure 1. Sketch map showing the route of the CSS *Hudson* on its 11-month ocean science voyage and circumnavigation of the Americas, 19 November 1969 to 16 October 1970, covering 58,000 nautical miles (>100,000 km) in 330 days.

ORIGIN OF THE IDEA

BIO was founded in 1962 by the Canadian Government to investigate the waters of the North Atlantic and the eastern Canadian arctic. The Institute's fleet of research vessels worked initially in the Arctic seas of Canada, the Denmark Strait, the North Atlantic out to the mid-Atlantic Ridge, the Gulf of St. Lawrence, the Scotian Shelf, and in the warmer waters of the Gulf Stream and the Caribbean. By 1967, BIO wished to extend its horizons, and the idea was suggested by Cedric Mann, head of the Physical Oceanography Group, that it would be worthwhile to measure the great eastward flow of water through the Drake Passage between the southern tip of South America and Antarctica, which had not yet been monitored successfully.

Legend has it that this idea evolved into a circumnavigation plan in the lounge of CSS *Hudson*, BIO's newest (1963) and largest (4,600 tons) ship, while she was stormbound off the east coast of Greenland in February 1967. Cedric Mann, William Ford (Director of BIO), and the ship's Captain David Butler were wedged together against the roll of the ship. Mann introduced his Drake Passage idea; the Captain topped this by saying that he would like to take CSS *Hudson* through the Northwest Passage. Ford already knew that Canadian geophysicists wanted to work off the Queen Charlotte Islands on the Pacific coast of Canada, where there was thought to be a "triple junction", a place where three of the moving plates which make up the Earth's crust come together. He also knew that there was a need to study the unknown Beaufort Sea in the western Arctic, which even then was believed to have offshore oil potential. The Beaufort Sea is accessible from the west – round the north of Alaska – early in the summer, while the Northwest Passage is not open until later in the summer. Finally, Ford also knew that the fiord oceanographers of the University of British Columbia would love to be able to study the little-known fiords of Chile and compare them with their British Columbia counterparts. Why not combine all of these ideas in one sequential expedition? The route would be Drake Passage-Chilean fiords-Queen Charlotte Islands-Beaufort Sea-Northwest Passage, following the summer around the Americas and accomplishing a circumnavigation.

An additional boost to the idea came from William Von Arx of Woods Hole Oceanographic Institution, who pointed out how valuable it would be to do a long northward transit of the Pacific recording the gravity and magnetic fields, to serve as a calibration line for an oceanographic satellite, Seasat, due to be launched a few years later. Firm plans were in place by the autumn of 1968. Hudson would take a year to circumnavigate the Americas, working in the Southern Hemisphere from December to April and then reaching the Arctic for August and September. This would be the most ambitious single global-scale effort that Canada had ever made in the marine sciences.

The cost of the expedition, however, outstripped the resources of BIO. The shortfall was modest by today's standards – a mere $25,000 for extra fuel. Ford had to take the proposal to the Government, in fact to

J.J. Greene, Minister of the Department of Energy, Mines and Resources Canada. Greene had just rejected science proposals for a telescope and a linear accelerator, each of which would have cost $100 million, and found the CSS *Hudson* proposal an attractive and cheap alternative to support. He was due to announce approval for the project in the House of Commons in November 1968, but suffered a heart attack the day before. Planning for the '*Hudson*-70' voyage had to stop until he recovered. The vital speech was made in February 1969 and was received enthusiastically by the opposition parties as being "the sort of thing that Canada should be doing in the world". The voyage was approved (Fig.1).

Many of the seagoing scientists were still graduate students, and since CSS *Hudson* (Fig. 2) was equipped with state-of-the-art instrumentation, the combination of young and senior scientists was a memorable experience for many, and a formative influence on their careers. Two of the youngest and most junior on the scientific staff were R. Smith, then a student at Queen's University (Kingston, ON) with an interest in sediments and plankton, and myself, just graduated from University of Cambridge (Cambridge, England) and taken on as Assistant to the Senior Scientist to perform general duties. We were both on board for all or most of the voyage, and after 43 years, we were pleased to attend the BIO 50th anniversary celebrations in October 2012 as being among the few '*Hudson*-70' scientists still in full-time employment.

Figure 2. CSS *Hudson*, principal oceanographic research vessel of the Bedford Institute of Oceanography, Dartmouth, NS.

LEG 1: HALIFAX TO RIO DE JANEIRO

19 November to 14 December 1969

CSS *Hudson* sailed from BIO on 19 November 1969, and ran down to the Equator at 30°W, carrying out along-track geophysics (gravity, magnetics, and precision bathymetry) and acoustic reverberation research. Upon reaching the Equator at 30°W, she began a line of stations at 2.5° (150 nautical miles [nm]) intervals down the 30°W meridian as far as 55°S, reaching 25°S on the first leg. Each station featured a shallow and deep Knudsen bottle cast using reversing thermometers, with oxygen and nutrient analyses carried out using the Knudsen water samples (Fig. 3). Particulate organic carbon (POC) analyses were done using water from additional Niskin bottles added to the cast. The primary cast was followed by an auxiliary cast to 2,500 m using the Bathysonde, an 'STD' (salinity-temperature-depth recorder, forerunner of the modern conductivity-temperature-depth recorder or CTD), which was still too inaccurate to be used as the primary measuring device as it is today. Normal for the period, but extraordinary to remember today, was the time taken for a full station – up to 12 hours, mostly a product of having to do three casts at each station. This necessitated a large spacing of stations even though the region was almost 'virgin' as far as previous station work was concerned. There was also an assumption that oceanic conditions are stable so that the results could be entered into oceanographic atlases. An oxygen section from this and the next leg, based on analyses on board done by I. Duedall, R. Cooke and L. Atkinson, was long regarded as a standard result (Duedall and Coote 1972a).

Other work done at every station comprised: a deep scattering layer study using one-pound explosive charges, an Isaacs-Kidd mid-water trawl for an hour at 3 knots (kts), and a vertical plankton tow (Fig. 4). At night, on passage between stations, a Neusten net would be deployed

Figure 3. Bruce Carson attaching a messenger to a Knudsen bottle during a deep hydrocast.

to catch surface fish and zooplankton. Whenever whales were seen, the ship would be stopped to take acoustic recordings. Minke Whales (*Balaenoptera acutorostrata*) were common, with occasional pods of Fin Whales (*B. physalus*) and one Blue Whale (*B. musculus*).

Figure 4. Gus Vilks retrieving a plantkton net.

LEG 2: RIO DE JANEIRO TO BUENOS AIRES

20 December 1969 to 16 January 1970

During the stay in Rio de Janeiro, Brazil, the cetacean researcher on board, P. Beamish, went hunting in Guanabara Bay and brought back a *Sautelia brasiliensis*, a Brazilian dolphin, which was cut up and kept in the ship's freezer for later study. Each port call was also the occasion for a partial change of scientific personnel. In this case, C. Lalli and G. Deevey (McGill University, Montreal, QC) joined to study zooplankton, the only women scientists aboard until the Arctic legs of the voyage.

CSS *Hudson* sailed on 20 December 1969 and returned to her line of stations at 30°W. Stations from 27.5°S to 47.5°S were done at 2.5° intervals; then, as the Antarctic Convergence was approached the interval was dropped to 1.5° from 49°S to 55°S. The last station of the line was done slightly farther east, at 29°30'W, so as to be over the South Sandwich Trench in 7,900 m of water. The station routine was similar, but with a piston core sample added to each station. Christmas Day was spent at 32.5°S with suitable celebrations. New Year's Eve occurred during station 20 at 47.5°S, and thus began the International Decade of Ocean Exploration (IDOE 1970-80). In fact, probably the first sampling done in the IDOE was an expendable bathythermograph (XBT) which was launched at 00.01 GMT, and which got caught in the Bathysonde wire.

At the southern limit of the line, CSS *Hudson* encountered icebergs, albatrosses (Sooty *Phoebetria fusca*, Black-browed *Diomedea melanophris*, and Wandering *D. exulans*), Adélie Penguins (*Pygoscelis adeliae*), and the full spectrum of other Antarctic birds: Cape Pigeons (*Daption capense*), Wilson's Storm-petrels (*Oceanites oceanicus*), Sooty Shearwaters (*Puffinus griseus*), and Antarctic Fulmars (*Fulmarus glacialoides*), as well as Fin Whales and Pilot Whales (*Globicephala melaena*).

After completing the 30°W line, CSS *Hudson* sailed to 40°W to do a line of five stations between 51°30'S and 47°S, so as to investigate a gap in the Scotia Ridge which was thought to be a northward route for Antarctic Bottom Water. She then sailed for Buenos Aires, where she was opened to the public.

LEG 3: BUENOS AIRES TO PUNTA ARENAS

22 January to 23 February 1970

From Buenos Aires CSS *Hudson* sailed southward towards Magellan Strait, but was forbidden by Argentina from doing research in the areas which she claimed as her own continental shelf (200 nm from the coast). A hydrographic officer, Lt. R. Rebaudi, was put aboard to enforce the claim. Oceanographic research was therefore not carried out during the southward transit, although research on seabird populations was carried out by E. Mills (Dalhousie University, Halifax, NS), F. Cooke (Queen's University, Kingston, ON), and R. Hessler (Scripps Institution of Oceanography, La Jolla, CA). On 26 January, CSS *Hudson* entered Magellan Strait, calling at Punta Arenas to drop a steward whose brother was ill, then threaded through the Beagle Channel to reach Puerto Williams, a small Chilean port which, neglecting Antarctic bases, is the southernmost settlement in the world. Here a reception was held and CSS *Hudson* dropped off a pair of biologists, E. Bousfield (National Museum of Canada, Ottawa, ON) and J. Markham (National Research Council of Canada, Ottawa, ON), to carry out a month of independent work among the far southern islands from the ship's survey launch *Redhead*, studying coastal and beach fauna. During this survey, Bousfield discovered a new species of beach flea on a Fuegan shoreline.

CSS *Hudson* carried out bottom sled stations to collect seafloor-living species and plankton tows off Wollaston Island near Cape Horn. The ship then continued south, passing Cape Horn in very calm conditions, and started to search for areas of level seabed to deploy a line of four current meter moorings across Drake Passage, one of the original justifications for the expedition. The first mooring was 120 nm SSW of Cape Horn, at 57°49'S, 68°20'W. A bottle cast was executed at each current meter mooring site, including the use of large 30-litre Niskin bottles and a nephelometer to study particulate matter. The second and third moorings were each positioned a further 120 nm southward, and the final mooring was set at 63°26'S, 67°06'W. The taut-wire mooring chain (Fig. 5) consisted of a railway wheel at the bottom and a subsurface float at the top, with Braincon current meters at 150 m, 1,500 m, and 100 m above the bottom. Each current meter was accompanied by a thermograph and a depth gauge.

Figure 5. Deploying a current meter mooring at the northern end of the Drake Passage off the southern tip of South America.

With the moorings deployed, CSS *Hudson* began a program of stations among the South Shetland Islands off the Antarctic Peninsula. These included plankton tows, rock dredge sampling, epibenthic sled tows (Fig. 6), and Smith-McIntyre grab sampling. Work among the islands began on 5 February at South Bay, Livingston Island, and continued in Discovery Bay, Greenwich Island, then in Marion Cove, King George Island, and finally in Admiralty Bay, King George Island, where the abandoned British Base G of the Falkland Islands Dependencies Survey was visited.

Plans for further sampling were abandoned when it became necessary to return to Puerto Williams to drop off a technician whose son had just died. The two detached biologists landed earlier were also resupplied. CSS *Hudson* then headed south again to pick up the current meter

Figure 6. Bob Hessler (left) and Eric Mills (right) recovering the epibenthic sled used to collect organisms living on the sea floor.

moorings and to carry out a line of closely spaced oceanographic stations across the Drake Passage. Accompanying work included the lowering of a 2,000 litre giant bag to collect a large water sample to filter for particulate organic carbon.

We now know that the duration of the current meter measurements was too short to obtain a good average for the flow, given the very large fluctuations due to eddy activity. In fact, during the experiment the near-surface meters showed the expected strong eastward flow, but the mid-depth meters recorded little net flow, while the bottom meters recorded a net flow from east to west. The overall net water flux was negligible. One of the chief values of this surprising result was to stimulate further work, and very extensive flow measurements were made later in the 1970s during the International Southern Ocean Studies program (ISOS), yielding the more familiar large net eastward flow (150 Sv) that we use today (note: one Sverdrup equals a transport of 10^6 cubic metres per second).

Figure 7. CSS *Hudson* steaming through the Beagle Channel in Tierra del Fuego.

With all the moorings successfully recovered, CSS *Hudson* visited the crater of Deception Island on 15 February, where she did a station in Telefon Bay and the scientists visited the wreckage of the Chilean base Presidente Aguirre Cerda that had recently been destroyed in a 1969 volcanic eruption. The area was still extremely active, with fumaroles on land and hot water in the shallows of the bay. Another epibenthic sled haul was done in deep water (2,560 m) off Elephant Island, and then two additional bottle stations were completed as CSS *Hudson* steamed north, making a total of 47 so far. On 19 February, the ship re-entered Beagle Channel from the east (Fig. 7), anchored at Puerto Williams, and recovered the *Redhead* and her crew and scientists.

At this point, the presence of the Argentine hydrographer caused a problem with the Chilean authorities who insisted that he was a spy and that we could not return to Punta Arenas through Beagle Channel as he might inspect their defences. At this time, there was a boundary dispute in the Beagle Channel between Chile and Argentina, later settled by the Pope. Therefore, CSS *Hudson* sailed through Le Maire Strait, up the east coast of Tierra del Fuego, and entered Magellan Strait again at the eastern end. She took on fuel just inside the Strait entrance at Puerto Percy, with a shore excursion to sample intertidal fauna, and then docked at Punta Arenas on 23 February.

LEG 4: PUNTA ARENAS TO VALPARAISO

3 March to 7 April 1970

This leg was run by the Institute of Oceanography, University of British Columbia (Vancouver, BC), with G. Pickard as chief scientist and B. Bary as chief biologist, and with a contingent of seven Chilean scientists on board: H. Inostroza, R. Ahumada and C. Chuecas (University of Concepçion), B. Uccelletti and R. Montaner (Hydrographic Institute of Valparaiso), N. Silva (Catholic University of Valparaiso), and F. Rey (University of Chile, Valparaiso). The purpose was to study the oceanography of the Chilean fiords, a region untouched in many cases since the survey voyage of HMS *Beagle* in the 1830s (R. FitzRoy, commander; C. Darwin, naturalist). CSS *Hudson* started in the southern fiords such as Seno Almirantazgo and Whiteside Channel that lead off Magellan Strait into the mountainous interior of Tierra del Fuego. These coastal environments featured loose ice blocks from tidewater glaciers. Then CSS *Hudson* made her way through an intricate web of fiords running northwards, starting with Seno Otway. She exited the Magellan Strait at Cap Pilar and visited the small settlements of Puerto Natales and Puerto Aysen. Puerto Natales lay at the head of a complex set of inlets of which the innermost was called Estero Ultima Esperanza. It was connected to the impressive mountain scenery of the Torres del Paine National Park.

The first set of fiords, some of them fed by ice from the inland ice sheet, is terminated by a stretch of open ocean, the Gulf of Peñas, which is followed by a further set of intricate fiords. Here, many place names recall Darwin, FitzRoy and the survey ships *Beagle* and *Adventure,* and some go even further back. We encountered Canal Cheap, Wager Bay, and Bahia Anna Pink. Cheap was the captain of HMS *Wager*, a ship in Anson's British Royal Naval squadron of 1741 which was circumnavigating the world. The ship was wrecked in Wager Bay and the shipwrecked crew mutinied and sailed off to leave the captain and his officers to their own devices; the *Anna* was a supply ship in the same squadron.

CSS *Hudson* visited the small settlement of Puerto Aysen, and ended her survey at the town of Puerto Montt, the southernmost point of rail and continuous road transport in Chile. She had surveyed 32 fiords, many of which had never had oceanographic measurements made in them, and these observations led to an important paper (Pickard 1971). Most of the fiords were fully oxygenated and had a standard estuarine circulation with a two-layer water mass system.

From Puerto Montt, CSS *Hudson* sailed out westward into the open Pacific Ocean to visit Juan Fernandez Island, former home of the castaway Alexander Selkirk. She then carried out a short northward dogleg of stations before reaching Valparaiso, Chile, on 7 April.

LEG 5: VALPARAISO TO TAHITI

15 April to 12 May 1970

From Valparaiso, CSS *Hudson* sailed southwest into the high-latitude South Pacific to begin a northward line which was intended to be the longest meridional line of oceanographic stations ever completed, with the aim of providing a South-North transect of temperature-salinity structure and gravity data (using the vibrating string accelerometer of W. Von Arx) to allow calibration of a radar altimeter that was intended to be launched very shortly on the Seasat satellite. In the end, Seasat was not launched until 1978 and only lasted three months, but the long survey line remained as a validation for later altimeter-equipped satellites such as Envisat.

The start point was meant to be 65°S 150°W, but a high concentration of icebergs was encountered in the area, and so for safety reasons the line was begun at 63°S over the objections of Von Arx who pointed out the need for as long a northward line as possible. The Antarctic Convergence was crossed at 59°S. Stations were more widely spaced than in the Atlantic, carried out at 5° intervals (apart from the first at 63°S and the second at 60°S), with the same set of observations at each one as in the South Atlantic. Many of the same scientists were back on board, as well as Von Arx himself and chief scientist R. Melanson (BIO). The first South Sea island to be spotted was Tubuai, at 23°S 149°W, and the last station was done at 20°S 150°W, very close to Tahiti, although the gravity line was carried up to 16°30'S before the ship turned for Papeete.

During the voyage from Valparaiso to the far south, it was later found, by analysis of the geophysical records, that at 54° 19'S, 94° 33'W CSS *Hudson* had crossed an underwater peak which stood 1,500 m above its fellows, rising to within 2,920 m from the surface. Then, only 36 nm later, at 54°38'S, 95°12'W, she crossed a very deep trough extending down deeper than 6,103 m. These discoveries were named after our ship – Hudson Peak and Hudson Deep – and are now on the official nautical charts.

LEG 6: TAHITI TO VANCOUVER

16 May to 12 June 1970

After a visit to Tahiti, where the most junior research assistant on board and author of this account, P. Wadhams, celebrated his 22nd birthday on Moorea, CSS *Hudson* returned to the 150°W line and continued stations northward from 15°S at 5° intervals. The line was meant to extend as far as the continental shelf in the Gulf of Alaska, in order to connect with the Alaskan Geophysical Survey. The chief scientist was W. Cameron (Marine Science Branch, Ottawa, ON). The Equator was crossed on 21 May, ending six months of work in the Southern Hemisphere. Beyond 10°N station spacing was stretched to 6° to accommodate a request from BIO for two extra stations off the Queen Charlotte Islands in British Columbia. The Tropic of Cancer was crossed on 28 May, and the farthest north station was carried out at 57°30'N on 7 June. This gave Von Arx a 7,000 mile north-south gravity line, but unfortunately, owing to the need to get to Vancouver, British Columbia, for a public relations exercise, the line was finished slightly too early, while the ship was still over the Aleutian Trench. Not unexpectedly, Von Arx was very unhappy with this decision.

During the transit of this exceptionally long mid-ocean leg, marine micropaleontologists, biologists, and oceanographers continued their sampling routines to define the species diversity, abundance, biomass, and the physical characteristics that mark major Pacific Ocean water masses and subsurface ocean currents. Planktonic Foraminifera specimens were collected with a newly redesigned state-of-the-art multiple depth plankton sampler whose nets could be opened or closed at pre-programmed depths using pressure-sensitive actuator technology (Banerji et al. 1971). Those efforts facilitated the mapping of planktonic Foraminifera populations and associated water mass features at a critical time near the end of an interval of climate cooling that started just after the end of World War II and which would soon be replaced by rapid warming (Fig. 8).

Oceanographers were discovering that dissolved oxygen was one of the most useful water mass descriptors for this type of inter-regional survey because its vertical distribution varies considerably and due to the fact that it is one of the most easily measured characteristic of seawater. During the course of the leg, seawater oxygen profiles were revealing several maxima that were ascribed to a newly reported bottom current that flows between the mid-Pacific mountains and the Line Islands and then around the Hawaiian Islands Ridge (Duedall and Coote 1972b). Meanwhile, biologists from BIO's Marine Ecology Laboratory continued to pursue their study of the biomass of different size categories of marine organisms and organic particles. By the end of the leg, they had collected and processed sufficient data to be able to formulate a new hypothesis that showed, to a first approximation, roughly equal concentrations of organic material occurring at all particle sizes within a range from one micron to 10 million microns: i.e., from bacteria to whales (Sheldon et al. 1972). At each of the sampling stations occupied along the 150° W meridian, chemists and biologists were busy most of the time either collecting samples, processing or preserving them for return to their respective laboratories. The scientific survey team during this leg of the voyage consisted of 25 members representing Dalhousie University, the British Royal Navy, several BIO laboratories, the federal government's Pacific Oceanographic Group, Queens University, the Wood's Hole Oceanographic Institution, and the Defence Research Establishment-Atlantic. The ship arrived at Vancouver on 12 June.

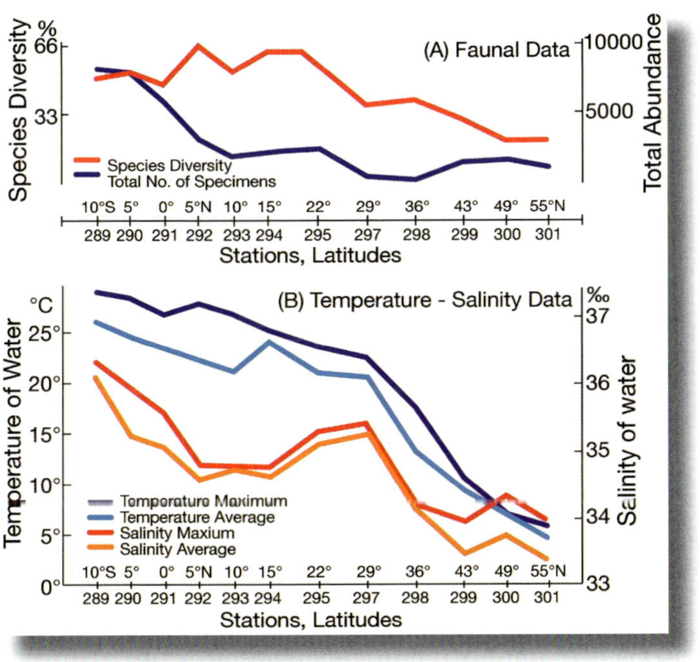

Figure 8. A plot of planktonic Foraminifera species diversity and abundance (A) in relation to water temperature and salinity (B) from the Tahiti–Vancouver leg (after Banerji et al. 1971).

LEG 7: QUEEN CHARLOTTE ISLANDS SURVEY

12 July to 5 August 1970

Upon her arrival in Vancouver, CSS *Hudson's* crew catered to the inevitable welcoming parties and open house events. The ship was then moved to the dockyard at Esquimalt for engine repairs that lasted four weeks. On 12 July she sailed for a region to the west of the Queen Charlotte Islands. Chief scientist was C. Maunsell (BIO). This coastal leg of CSS *Hudson* was designed to apply the geophysical techniques that had been developed and tested at BIO over the previous several years. Leg 7 brought a definite Canadian focus to the usual mix of 'blue water' survey programs that were dominant during the previous mid-Pacific leg. They comprised a menu of marine geological and geophysical activities that were supported by a scientific team from BIO's Atlantic Oceanographic Laboratory along with several collaborators from the Marine Sciences Branch - Victoria of the former Department of Energy, Mines and Resources, the University of Washington, and Dalhousie University. Target areas for surveys included a region west of the southern portion of the Queen Charlotte Islands, the northern termination of the Juan de Fuca Ridge and the area surrounding the Explorer Trench. Surveys aimed at confirming the existence of the Queen Charlotte Islands fault were done using a combination of bathymetric, gravity, magnetic, and reflection seismic profiling. A two-ship seismic refraction experiment was carried out in the vicinity of latitude 51 degrees 29 minutes N and longitude 133 degrees 51 minutes W in deep water seaward of the Queen Charlotte Islands. In this experiment, the CNAV *Endeavour* was used as the 'shooting ship' to deploy explosives needed to create sound waves while *Hudson* served as the 'listening ship'. Preliminary results of the experiment suggested that the mantle in this area of the seafloor exhibits a higher P-wave velocity in an east-west direction and a lower velocity (about 8.1 km/sec) in the north-south direction. Observations also indicated that the crustal structure in this area is similar to that found elsewhere in the Pacific Ocean basin. Following the completion of the seismic refraction experiment, the CNAV *Endeavour* carried out seismic profiling and rock dredging activities over the Explorer Trench and the Paul Revere Ridge.

Early publications on the Queen Charlotte Islands and Vancouver Island offshore surveys describe the presence of a sedimentary basin at the foot of the continental slope in which the sediments appeared to be progressively more intensely deformed from north to south. That observation was interpreted as evidence of the interaction of the edges of lithospheric plates that occur in this area (Srivastava et al. 1971). Important insights on plate dynamics were also gained in the area where the American, Juan de Fuca, and Pacific plates meet at a 'triple junction'. Heat flow values measured in the northern part of the Explorer Ridge taken together with the recovery of fresh basalts collected by the CNAV *Endeavour's* crew with rock dredges, showed that the Ridge was an active spreading segment of the well-known East Pacific Rise.

LEG 8: VICTORIA TO TUKTOYAKTUK

13 August to 22 September 1970

CSS *Hudson* sailed from Esquimalt Harbour on 13 August and headed for Unimak Pass in the Aleutians, which was reached on 19 August. She carried out along-track geophysical watch-keeping and daily stations. The chief scientist was B. Pelletier (BIO), and the ship was now equipped with a Bell-206 helicopter for ice reconnaissance.

The ship did her first station at 50°N, 130°W, and then, on 18 August, ran into her worst storm of the voyage, during which a bottom drill tied to the foredeck toppled over. This happened over the Aleutian Trench, just before the ship reached Unimak Pass. Entering the Bering Sea, CSS *Hudson* suffered a fire as a port-side generator exploded. This did not incapacitate the ship, but left her with only three of her four engines working. Around this time, CSS *Hudson* came across a dead Bowhead Whale (*Balaena mysticetus*) with a flag embedded in it, but we were unable to determine whether this was the work of a Japanese or Inuk whaler. Later we anchored in the shelter of St. Lawrence Island to allow the sonar transducers to be covered with protective plates against ice damage. At the time, another dead abandoned whale was sighted on the beach, this time a Humpback Whale (*Megaptera novaeangliae*).

On 22 August, the ship transited Bering Strait and crossed the Arctic Circle, encountering pack ice the next day off the northwest coast of Alaska. There was a pause while we helped search for three Inuit who had disappeared in a boat off Wainwright on a hunting trip. Then, we moved towards Point Barrow where we found heavy pack ice close in to the coast, which necessitated backing and ramming. This was the first heavy pack ice ever encountered by CSS *Hudson*, and is a contrast with recent summers in the Arctic when the sea ice has retreated almost as far as the North Pole. As we moved east, and crossed the United States-Canada boundary, we found the sea ice lying further back from the coast leaving a slot up to 150 nm wide in the southern Beaufort Sea, an exceptionally open (for 1970) situation which permitted an intensive oceanographic study of this region for the very first time (Fig. 9). The only recorded previous oceanographic work in this part of the Beaufort Sea was a few stations done from the Royal Canadian Mounted Police schooner *St. Roch* during her transit of the Northwest Passage in 1940. However, the interest of the Canadian Government had been aroused in 1969 by a successful oil find at Atkinson Point on the Beaufort Sea coast and so, the CSS *Hudson* survey was given high priority. CSS *Hudson's* program was given use of the BIO ship CSS *Baffin* (which had sailed through Panama Canal) to assist us, and also the smaller research ship CSS *Parizeau* of the Pacific Oceanographic Group. At Herschel Island, additional scientists who had been flown in by helicopter from Inuvik were taken aboard.

A survey grid was begun consisting of parallel lines, 15 miles apart, running northward from the coast. We would set out on each line from the southern end, steering at 5 knots and carrying out seismic profiling as well as recording gravity and magnetics and towing the sidescan sonar behind the ship. Every few miles a stop was made for a hydrocast and a core; one 11-m core was by far the longest yet recovered from the Arctic Ocean. The line would end when the ice edge was reached, usually more than 100 nm off the coast. The positioning was to be controlled by a Decca Hi-Fix radio navigation system set up for the summer with a line of transmitting stations along the coast. Unfortunately, the ship's Decca receiver did not work, so a satellite fix was taken at every station, which sometimes took 2-4 hours in those days before the first appearance of GPS.

Figure 9. Planning meeting on the bridge of the CSS *Hudson* in the Beaufort Sea. Left to right: Gus Vilks, Captain David Butler, Bernie Pelletier, and Navigator Roy Gould.

A fundamental discovery was made on the first survey line. Using the sidescan sonar the research team discovered seabed scouring by pressure ridges at the southern end of the line. As I wrote at the time, "we saw a complex array of long narrow troughs in the seabed, as if a drunken ploughman had been at work. It was a fascinating pattern of intersecting lines, some straight as a die and others curved round into circles and spirals" (Wadhams 2009a). Each scour mark that crossed the ship's track showed up on the ordinary echosounder as a small indentation in the seabed, only 2-4 m deep. The marks were visible out to a water depth of 100 m, deeper than the deepest contemporary pressure ridge, implying a periglacial origin for the deeper incisions at a time when relative sea level was lower (Pelletier and Shearer 1972).

Further to the east, over the shallow Mackenzie Bay, underwater pingos were discovered. Pingos on land are a well-known feature of the Mackenzie Delta, and the research team was already studying them by helicopter visits. They are basically ice-cored mounds, looking like small conical volcanoes and rising starkly from the flat muskeg landscape to a height of 70 m or more. Pingos are formed when a lake drains because of a change in the course of the streams that feed it. The deeper lakes on the muskeg do not freeze to the bottom during the winter, and their deep parts contain water at 4°C, its temperature of maximum density. This 'warm' water melts the permafrost below and around the lake. When the lake disappears, the permafrost compensates for this sudden removal of heat by rising again, pushing up the soil above it. This mechanism cannot account for a pingo forming underwater, however, and the term 'pingo-like-feature' was coined to describe them (Shearer et al. 1971). Their origin is still obscure, although their shape on the echo sounder resembles exactly that of pingos on land. These newly-discovered features were studied using bottom cameras and core sampling, and are recognized today as a seabed geohazard (Lewis et al. 2014).

At the end of the survey, the scientific personnel were exchanged by helicopter at Tuktoyaktuk, then a small Inuk settlement on Kugmallit Bay, and later to become a supply base for Beaufort Sea oil exploration. Three journalists joined the ship at this time, including D. Spurgeon of the 'Toronto Globe and Mail' and K. Palka of 'CTV' television network.

LEG 9: TUKTOYAKTUK TO DARTMOUTH

22 September to 15 October 1970

CSS *Hudson*, accompanied by CSS *Baffin*, now set off to navigate the Northwest Passage. The Captain chose the direct, northerly route through Prince of Wales Strait and into Parry Channel, the course taken by the *St. Roch* in 1940, the icebreaker CCGS *Labrador* in 1954, and the tanker *Manhattan* in 1969, but north of R. Amundsen's (1903-06) passage through Peel Sound, Franklin Strait, and Coronation Gulf.

Studies began with oceanographic stations and a seismic line in Amundsen Gulf, ending under the cliffs of Cape Lambton on Banks Island. Then Prince of Wales Strait was entered in open water, but heavy 100% pack ice was encountered near its northern end (Fig. 10). The Department of Transport Canada icebreaker CCGS *John A. Macdonald* was sent from Resolute Bay (Cornwallis Island) to assist, and broke a channel which enabled CSS *Hudson* to carry out a line of oceanographic stations through Parry Channel to Resolute at its eastern end. Hydrocasts and Van Veen bottom grabs were taken at 60 nm intervals. The ice was 100% first-year ice with pressure ridges, and populated by families of Polar Bears (*Ursus maritimus*).

Resolute Bay was reached on 30 September and a final exchange of scientists took place. The geophysical group from BIO joined for a final survey in Baffin Bay, and a plaque commemorating '*Hudson*-70', made by the bo'sun, was left behind, fastened to a rock near the Inuk settlement (Fig. 11).

The final work of *Hudson*-70 was a geophysical survey of northern Baffin Bay, involving two-ship seismic refraction work with CSS *Hudson* as listening ship and the wartime United States Wind-class icebreaker *Edisto* as shooting ship. Two seismic reflection lines were also run across the bay from west to east, and the conclusion was reached that the underlying rocks are oceanic rather than continental, a question that up to then had been in doubt (Barrett et al. 1971).

On 16 October 1970, CSS *Hudson* finally returned to Halifax and BIO from her epic scientific voyage around the Americas, to a grand welcome by fireboats (Fig. 12), a ceremony on the quay (Fig. 13), and a speech by federal Minister of the Department of Energy, Mines and Resources J.J. Greene. Hudson had steamed 58,000 nm in 330 days.

Figure 10. CSS *Hudson* left and CCGS *John A. Macdonald* ice-bound in the Northwest Passage.

Figure 11. Bo'sun Joe Avery and Bernie Pelletier installing the *Hudson*-70 plaque near Resolute Bay, Cornwallis Island, NWT.

Figure 13. Quayside ceremony officially welcoming the CSS *Hudson* home after her epic voyage. Left to right: Dr. William L. Ford (Director, BIO), The Honourable J.J. Greene (Minister of the Department of Energy Mines and Resources), and Captain David Butler.

WHY DO WE CELEBRATE '*HUDSON*-70'?

Why should we remember this expedition of 1969-70? Firstly, because it was the last of the big multidisciplinary global oceanographic expeditions that hacked out our basic knowledge of ocean structure, water masses, and currents during the 19th and 20th centuries. The year 1970 was a turning point. Before that date the ocean was still thought to be an unexplored expanse where any ship that sailed far enough afield and worked in sufficiently unfrequented waters could make fundamental discoveries about the nature of our planet. When *Hudson* started her South Atlantic section at the Equator at 30°W, she was starting a line that had never been done by another ship. From the 1970s on, it began to be accepted that the basic picture was now drawn, and new ocean expeditions tended to be short-term affairs, devoted to testing specific hypotheses about processes in a small piece of the ocean and ignoring the rest.

Figure 12. CSS *Hudson* steams up Halifax Harbour, NS, on 16 October 1970 while receiving a water-cannon salute from a local firefighting vessel.

A second reason for remembering this voyage was that the fundamental data gathering that was the rationale of the traditional big expedition was carried out by CSS *Hudson* using modern effective methods. Geophysical monitoring was done with a gravimeter, towed magnetometer, and precision depth recorder (which today would be replaced by a multibeam sonar). The only old-fashioned technique used was a continued reliance on the Knudsen bottle cast for hydrographic stations, since the CTD (then called STD) was not yet reliable enough to be used as a primary data source. In that sense *Hudson*-70 was a bridge from the classical to the modern ocean surveying world.

A third reason to celebrate this global-scale expedition was the variety of fundamental discoveries made in many different spheres and many different environments of the world's oceans. The Chilean fiord survey was the first, and still the most thorough, oceanographic survey of these fiords; the Drake Passage current meter moorings, despite their surprising results, were the first direct measurements of the Antarctic Circumpolar Current; a host of geoscience discoveries were made especially in northern waters – the structure of Baffin Bay, the existence of ice scouring along the Beaufort Sea coast, the plate structure of the North Pacific, and the water structure of the Beaufort Sea. CSS *Hudson* did the first proper multidisciplinary survey of the Beaufort Sea, and now that the sea ice is in full retreat, the results obtained so long ago gain increased value by showing us the conditions that prevailed in the era of a complete ice cover before global warming wrought its massive changes. Throughout all of the expedition's legs, the efforts of biologists, marine ornithologists, and marine micropaleontologists added new fundamental information about the distribution of species that stands as a baseline for future investigations of important problems in the realm of climate change and sustainable exploitation and development of the world's inventory of ocean resources.

For those of us who were lucky enough to take part in '*Hudson*-70', especially junior scientists like myself who stayed on for the whole voyage performing 'gofer' tasks in many spheres, it was a formative experience, the most perfect graduate-level field course that it is possible to imagine, and something that spoils a person for the rest of their life. We should celebrate '*Hudson*-70' for that too, for daring to do great things in the ocean and thus to inspire the scientists on board CSS *Hudson* to think great thoughts. It is wonderful that the ship which accomplished this outstanding work is still afloat at the advanced age of 50 years (2014) and still doing valuable work in the marine waters around Canada. BRAVO!

ACKNOWLEDGEMENTS

I thank my many friends and colleagues that shared the experience of the *Hudson*-70 expedition with me, and those that contributed ideas, diary entries, and corrections to publications produced over the years including Roger Smith, Eric Mills, Peter Wangersky, Richard Brown, and to Charles Schafer for his contribution to the Leg 6 and Leg 7 parts of the story. I am also grateful to Roger Belanger and the Bedford Institute of Oceanography for the use of photos in the BIO collection. An earlier version of this paper appeared in the journal *Oceanography* (Wadhams 2009b).

REFERENCES

Banerji, R., C. Schafer, and R. Vine. 1971. Environmental relationships and distribution of planktonic Foraminifera in the equatorial and northern Pacific waters. BIO Atlantic Oceanographic Laboratory Report 1971-7, Dartmouth, NS.

Barrett, D.L., C.E. Keen, K.S. Manchester, and D.I. Ross. 1971. Baffin Bay – an ocean. Nature 229: 551-553.

Duedall, I.W. and A.R. Coote. 1972a. Oxygen distribution in the South Atlantic. Journal of Geophysical Research 77: 496-498.

Duedall, I.W. and A.R. Coote. 1972b. Oxygen distribution in the Pacific Ocean. Journal of Geophysical Research 77: 2,201-2,203.

Edmonds, A. 1973. Voyage to the Edge of the World. McClelland and Stewart, Toronto, ON.

Lewis, C.F.M., S.M. Blasco, D.J.W. Piper, and G.V. Sonnichsen. 2014. Seabed geohazard knowledge for safe hydrocarbon development: Pages 383-394 *in* Voyage of Discovery: Fifty Years of Marine Research at Canada's Bedford Institute of Oceanography (D.N. Nettleship, D.C. Gordon, C.F.M. Lewis, and

M.P. Latremouille, Eds.). Bedford Institute of Oceanography-Oceans Association, Dartmouth, NS.
Pelletier, B.R. and J.M. Shearer, 1972. Sea bottom scouring in the Beaufort Sea of the Artic Ocean. Pages 251-261 *in* Section 8, Marine Geology and Geophysics (J.W. Murray, B.R. Pelletier, and J.R. Luternauer, Eds.). 24th International Geological Congress, Montreal Quebec. Geological Survey of Canada, Ottawa, ON.
Pickard, G.L. 1971. Some physical oceanographic features of inlets of Chile. Journal Fisheries Research Board of Canada 28: 1,077-1,106.
Schafer, C.T. and R.W. Smith. 2012. Getting Around the Americas: The *Hudson* 70 Expedition. Virtualbookworm Publishing, College Station, TX.
Shearer, J.M., R.F. Macnab, B.R. Pelletier, and T.B. Smith. 1971. Submarine pingos in the Beaufort Sea. Science 174: 816-818.
Sheldon, R.W., A. Prakash, and W.H. Sutcliffe. 1972. The size distribution of particles in the ocean. Limnology and Oceanography 17: 327-340.
Srivastava, S.P., D.L. Barrett, C.E. Keen, K.S. Manchester, K.G. Shih, D.L. Tiffin, R.L. Chase, A.G. Thomlinson, E.E. Davis, and C.R.B. Lister. 1971. Preliminary analysis of geophysical measurements north of Juan de Fuca Ridge. Canadian Journal of Earth Sciences 8: 687-703.
Wadhams, P. 2009a. The Great Ocean of Truth: Memories of "*Hudson*-70", the first circumnavigation of the Americas. Melrose Books, Ely, Cambridgeshire, England.
Wadhams, P. 2009b. *Hudson*-70: the first circumnavigation of the Americas. Oceanography 22: 226-235.

Arctic Studies

CSS *Hudson* in arctic waters

Arctic Studies

4. THE ARCTIC OCEAN: ITS WATERS AND GLOBAL SIGNIFICANCE

E. Peter Jones

SUMMARY

The Arctic Ocean is the world's smallest ocean. In spite of this, it has major roles in maintaining the fresh water balance of the Atlantic and Pacific oceans. In many ways the Arctic Ocean feeds the 'headwaters' that maintain the Global Ocean Conveyor Belt. A goal of this article is to highlight the work in the Arctic Ocean of Bedford Institute of Oceanography's (BIO) scientists in collaboration with the international Arctic Ocean research community. This article mainly focusses on the water masses, their origins, their circulation patterns within the Arctic Ocean, their changes and their global importance. In particular, it will focus on the research results and achievements of BIO's researchers with reference to those of other Canadian, Swedish, Finnish, German, and United States scientists in both describing and conceptualizing the nature and behaviour of arctic water masses, their sources, stratification, circulation patterns within the Arctic Ocean, and their global significance.

Key words: Arctic Ocean, Global Ocean Conveyor Belt, Pacific water, Atlantic water, river water, fresh water, circulation, variability, anthropogenic CO_2, climate change.

E-mail: Peter.Jones@dfo-mpo.gc.ca

The Arctic Ocean is the smallest of the Earth's oceans at 9.5×10^{12} m^2. More than half (53%) of its area consists of shelf areas (Rudels et al. 2011; Fig. 1). Nevertheless, it is central to global ocean circulation (Fig. 2) and global climate. Prior to 1975, relatively few data were available from the Arctic Ocean. Early expeditions were largely exploratory and did not provide much data of chemical constituents, which have proven to be so useful in determining origins and pathways of the different water masses. For an excellent review of a history of expeditions, and for those who wish to go deeper into the subject, see Rudels et al. (2011). Ice camp expeditions deployed on ice islands, large pieces of ice broken off landfast ice shelves, have provided excellent platforms for research – and still do. One early such camp, Fletcher's Ice Island, or T3, was occupied from 1952 to 1978 and provided much data as it circulated within the Beaufort Sea (http://www.en.wikipedia.org/wiki/Fletcher's_Ice_Island). Since about 1980, these issues have been much better addressed, mostly by ice camps and especially by recent icebreaker expeditions (Fig. 3). Typically, the work is almost always done with national and international collaborations that have contributed both scientists and logistics, all of which require a large degree of collaboration among scientists. Icebreaker expeditions typically have up to fifty researchers, almost always including investigators from different nations and all relying on each other to share in the collection and analysis of data.

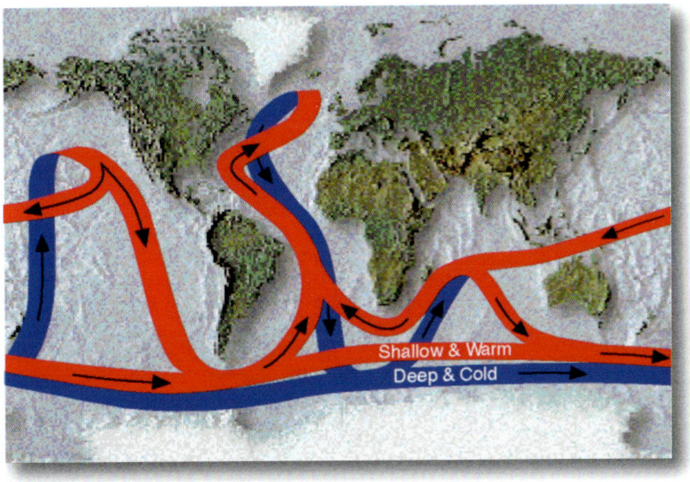

Figure 2. The Global Ocean Conveyor Belt. This is a highly schematic depiction of the much more complicated actual circulation. It does, however, summarize the relatively warm water flowing north to the Greenland Sea, where deep water is formed, then flowing south, where it circulates and upwells to become warm water in the Pacific and Indian oceans, eventually flowing north to complete the cycle.

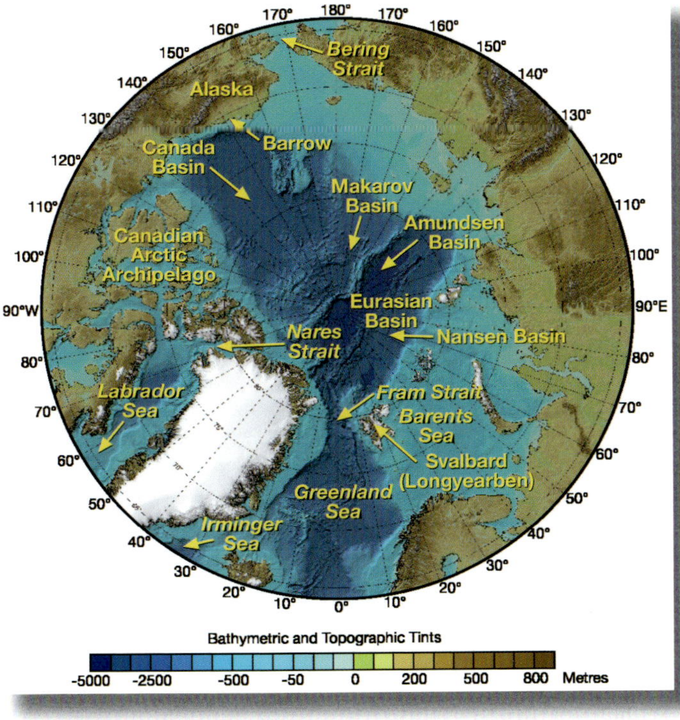

Figure 1. Map of the Arctic Ocean and adjacent seas.

Between 1980 and 2010, much was accomplished, with the impact of the Arctic Ocean on the global ocean being among the more significant findings. Bedford Institute of Oceanography (BIO) scientists contributed expertise and equipment to many of the expeditions of the Arctic Ocean (Fig. 4, Table 1). As more data became available, relatively sophisticated ocean circulation patterns throughout the Arctic Ocean were revealed by studying its water properties such as salinity, temperature, and various chemical constituents. Employed both together and separately, chemical constituents can identify (or 'fingerprint') distinct water masses to determine their origin and tell how long it takes for them to be renewed. Salinity and temperature determine the density of seawater and are fundamental in determining mixing and circulation within the oceans. Further, chemicals with very low concentrations do not affect ocean dynamics but, in addition to salinity and temperature, can be vital in tracing water masses.

The main seawater sources for the Arctic Ocean are Atlantic water and Pacific water. Atlantic water flows into the Arctic Ocean through Fram Strait and Barents Sea. Pacific water enters through Bering Strait between Alaska and Russia. Pacific water salinity is about 10% less than that of the Atlantic water and thus, along with river water, can be thought of as a source of fresh water to the Atlantic Ocean. River drainage basins contribute an amount of fresh water roughly equivalent to that of the Pacific water.

Figure 3. The icebreakers: (A) CCGS *Louis S. St-Laurent* (Canada), (B) IB *Oden* at the North Pole (Sweden), and (C) FS *Polarstern* (Germany).

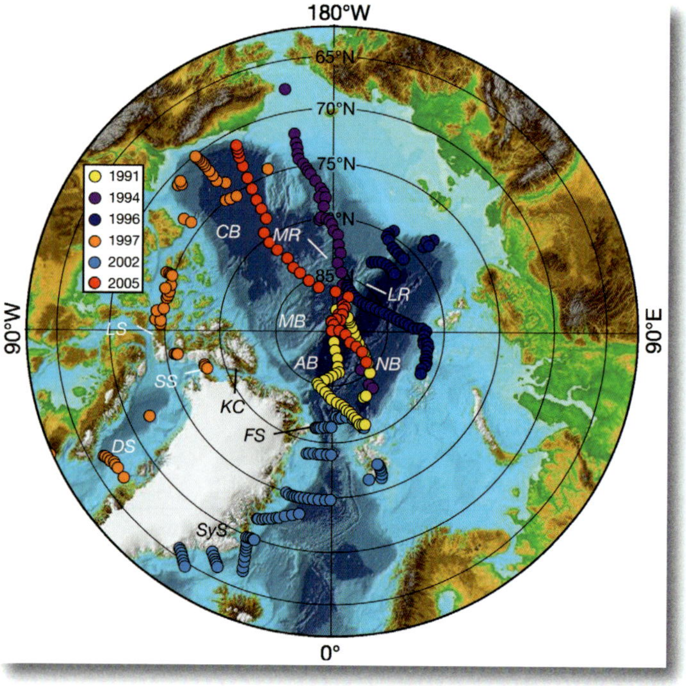

Figure 4. Icebreaker expeditions in Arctic Ocean and Greenland Sea. See Table 1 to correlate the cruise tracks to the icebreakers used. Labels indicate Canada Basin (CB), Makarov Basin (MB), Amundsen Basin (AB), Nansen Basin (NB), Mendeleyev Ridge (MR), Lomonosov Ridge (LR), Smith Sound (SS), Davis Strait (DS), Lancaster Sound (LS), Kennedy Channel (KC), Fram Strait (FS), and Scoresby Sound (SyS).

One crucial function of the Arctic Ocean is to maintain the global fresh water balance. In the Atlantic Ocean, there is more evaporation than precipitation. This evaporated water eventually falls into the Pacific Ocean, from where it flows into the Arctic Ocean as part of the Pacific water. The fresh water balance of the Atlantic Ocean is then maintained by these surface waters exiting from the Arctic Ocean back into the Atlantic Ocean via the Greenland Sea.

A pivotal question related to the fresh water budget is: "Can changes in the amount of fresh water exported from the Arctic Ocean affect the Global Ocean Conveyor Belt?" Key to maintaining the Global Ocean Conveyor Belt is the production of sufficient volumes of denser deep water within the Greenland Sea. The amount of deep water produced depends on the salinity of the surface waters exiting the Arctic Ocean. If during climate change the surface water should become too fresh, i.e., too much river water or too much Pacific water enters this region, the Global Ocean Conveyor Belt may slow down, or even cease, because of insufficient deep water formation and downwelling (Jones and Anderson 2008). If this were to occur, there could be potentially unpleasant consequences, to say the least, for the climate and peoples of Northern Europe as well as the east coast of Canada and possibly beyond. Climate change numerical models that can explore different scenarios depend critically on quality information on fresh water sources and pathways within the Arctic Ocean. Thus, both past and potential future research in this area by the BIO is of crucial importance. Canada and the world urgently need this information to be gathered, monitored over time, and interpreted with care to permit greater understanding of events and to allow time to prepare for them.

Another pivotal question is: "Does the Arctic Ocean constitute an important sink of anthropogenic carbon dioxide produced by our profligate burning of fossil fuels?" For several decades, it has been recognized that increasing carbon dioxide in the atmosphere results in climate warming. However, not all of the anthropogenic carbon dioxide stays in the atmosphere. Several studies have catalogued that a significant fraction is being sequestered in the global oceans. To help explore this issue, BIO researchers have measured, or been part of the teams performing these measurements, a wide array of dissolved inorganic carbon concentrations relevant to the anthropogenic carbon inventory (Tanhua et al. 2009, Anderson et al. 2010).

Outlined below are results from the expeditions in which BIO scientists have participated. These studies generated measurements that illuminate how the Arctic Ocean 'works' and how it fits into the global dynamic picture.

Table 1. Arctic Ocean research expeditions undertaken by BIO scientists, 1981-2005.

Arctic Ocean Ice Camps, 1981-92:	
1981	EUBEX 81 (also called *Fram* III), Yermak Plateau
1983	CESAR 83, Alpha Ridge
1985-86	Canadian Ice Island
1991-92	Ellesmere Ice Shelf
Icebreaker Expeditions in the Arctic Ocean, Greenland Sea and Canadian Archipelago (1991-2005):	
1991	IB *Oden*: Nansen, Amundsen, Makarov basins
1994	CCGS *Louis S. St-Laurent*: Trans-Arctic transect
1996	FS *Polarstern*: Amundsen, Makarov basins
1997	CCGS *Louis S. St-Laurent*: Canadian Archipelago and Canada Basin
2002	IB *Oden*: Greenland Sea
2005	IB *Oden*: Trans-Arctic transect

DETERMINING SOURCES OF WATERS IN THE ARCTIC OCEAN

Measurements reveal that Arctic Ocean waters originate from several sources. Briefly, and as mentioned earlier, water from the Atlantic Ocean enters the Arctic Ocean through Fram Strait over a deep sill (~2,500 m) and also through the Barents Sea (~300 m). Pacific water enters through Bering Strait over a shallow sill (~50 m) (Fig. 5). Water from the Atlantic

Ocean makes up much of the near surface waters in the Eurasian Basin and essentially all of the deeper water in the Arctic Ocean. Pacific water, extending to depths of about 300 m, dominates the surface waters and contributes most of the fresh water in the Canada Basin (Figs. 5 and 6). River water contributes to almost all regions of the Arctic Ocean, with sea-ice meltwater being most prominent in the central Canadian Basin. A caveat: Arctic Ocean surface waters are much affected by prevailing winds. For this reason, Figure 6 represents distributions as observed when the data were gathered.

ARCTIC OCEAN CIRCULATION

BIO scientists were part of teams that made major advances in understanding the circulation of water at all depths within the Arctic Ocean (Fig. 5; for more details, see Rudels et al. 1994, Jones et al. 1995, Rudels et al. 1996, Jones 2001, Tanhua et al. 2009). All of the waters entering the Arctic Ocean, Pacific water, Atlantic water, and river water, exit through Fram Strait and eventually flow into the Atlantic Ocean. The circulation of the near-surface waters and ice above about 100 m is determined largely by prevailing winds. Below the near-surface waters, the movement of Arctic Ocean waters is significantly influenced by the location of various undersea ridges, the highest and longest of which is the Lomonosov Ridge, with the ridge summit varying between depths of about 950 and 1,650 m and extending from the continental shelf north of Ellesmere Island to the shelf off the New Siberian Islands (International Bathymetric Chart of the Arctic Ocean: www.ngdc.noaa.gov/mgg/bathymetry/arctic). This ridge together with smaller ridges in the Eurasian and Canada basins divides the deep waters, which are made up mostly of modified Atlantic water. The circulation of waters above the ridges up to the near-surface waters follows the geometry of the bottom (Fig. 5; Rudels et al. 1994). The deepest waters are fairly isolated from those above the ridges, and their circulation was determined less precisely (Jones et al. 1995).

All waters exiting the Arctic Ocean eventually reach the Atlantic Ocean. Upper waters, mostly Pacific and river waters, exit through Fram Strait to the Greenland Sea and through the Canadian Archipelago (Fig. 5). Most Atlantic water exits through Fram Strait with a relatively small portion exiting through Nares Strait (Figs. 1 and 5).

Major contributions by BIO scientists to Arctic Ocean expeditions were to measure nutrients (phosphate, nitrate, silicate), dissolved oxygen, dissolved inorganic carbon, alkalinity, and chlorofluorocarbons (CFC-11, CFC-12, CFC-113) as well as salinity. Each of these chemicals or 'tracers' can provide unique information. In the Arctic Ocean, nitrate and phosphate are especially useful in distinguishing Atlantic and Pacific waters as they exist separately or mixed with one another. Dissolved inorganic carbon helps determine the amount of anthropogenic CO_2 absorbed by the Arctic Ocean. Alkalinity helps trace river water. Chlorofluorocarbons were first introduced into the atmosphere in the 1930s and their concentrations have been increasing in the atmosphere and thus dissolved into surface ocean waters until recently when their release was stopped. As surface waters mix and become incorporated throughout the deeper parts of the ocean, they carry their unique CFC concentrations to which they were exposed when they were last in contact with the atmosphere. They are thus especially suited to determine residence or exchange times or 'ages' of a water body. In the Canada Basin, the deepest water, about 4,000 m deep, has a residence time of about 300 years; in the Eurasian Basin it is about 200 years (Tanhua et al. 2009, Rudels et al. 2011).

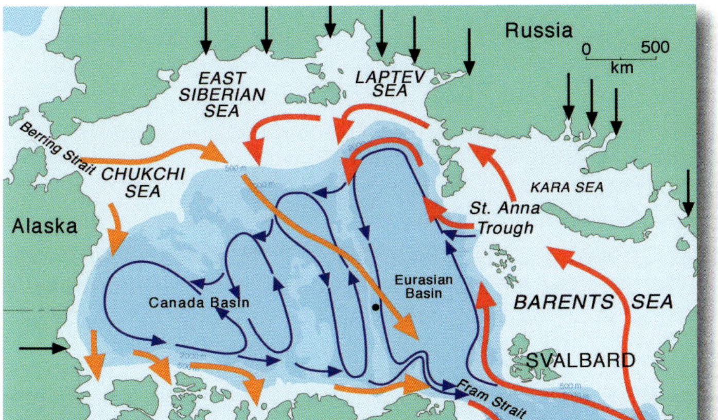

Figure 5. Near surface and deeper water circulation (from L. Anderson). Red arrows show inflowing Atlantic water, orange arrows show inflowing Pacific water, and purple arrows show mid-depth circulation of mostly Atlantic water.

ANTHROPOGENIC CARBON DIOXIDE

Global oceans are a major sink of anthropogenic carbon dioxide. The first measurements of dissolved inorganic carbon within the deep Arctic Ocean were made from CESAR (Canadian Expedition to Study the Alpha Ridge) ice camp in 1983 (Jones and Anderson 1986). Subsequent studies have much improved the estimates of the amount of sequestered anthropogenic carbon dioxide in the Arctic Ocean and have recently shown that the Arctic Ocean is not a significant anthropogenic carbon dioxide sink (Semiletov et al. 2007, Tanhua et al. 2009, Cai et al. 2010) simply because the relatively fresh surface waters are pretty well isolated from deeper waters by strong density gradients.

FRESH WATER

The inventories of fresh waters, total fresh water, Pacific water, river water, and sea-ice meltwater vary considerably throughout the Arctic Ocean (Fig. 6). River drainage basins, mostly in Eurasia, feed fresh water into the upper depths of the Arctic Ocean. Rain and snow contribute very small amounts of fresh water to the Arctic Ocean. Within the Arctic Ocean, all but sea-ice meltwater inventories are highest in the Canada Basin north of Alaska. Fresh water inventories are calculated relative to Atlantic water salinity, i.e., the amount of added fresh water that would be needed to match the observed salinity. The total fresh water inventory is more than 20 m, with river water reaching nearly 20 m in some locations and Pacific fresh water values nearly 10 m over a large region of the Canada Basin. Values for these sources are generally low in most of the Amundsen and Nansen basins. Sea-ice meltwater inventories can be as much as 4 m, though inventories are generally negative (negative sea-ice meltwater represents sea ice formation) over most of the Arctic Ocean.

In the Canadian Arctic Archipelago, Pacific and river fresh water inventories are roughly the same in Lancaster Sound and Nares Strait. In the East Greenland Current, river water inventories correspond to depths up to 10 m, typically three times greater than in the Canadian Arctic Archipelago. This is likely a reflection of significant Pacific water draining off through the Canadian Arctic Archipelago. In the near surface waters of the Arctic Ocean along the North American coast, river water tends to be farther offshore than Pacific water, likely a sign of their dominant Eurasian source. The relatively greater amounts of river water in the East Greenland Current may be reflecting this.

Fresh water exiting from the Arctic Ocean also influences the amount of denser deep water formed in the Greenland Sea. In the Greenland Sea, the warmer water from the south cools and, as salt is rejected from newly forming ice, becomes dense enough to sink and produce deep water. This deep water becomes a key part or 'driver' of the Global Ocean Conveyor Belt. The amount of deep water formation depends critically on how fresh or how dense the Greenland Sea surface waters are. If there is too much fresh water, deep water will not form and the whole climate of northeastern North America and Europe can be significantly affected if the flow north of warmer Atlantic water is reduced. It has been hypothesized that changes in the Global Ocean Conveyor Belt, perhaps originating from an excess flow of fresh water to the Greenland Sea, may have resulted in the recurrence of glacial conditions during deglaciation in previous ice ages.

The sources of fresh water flowing into the Greenland Sea from the Arctic Ocean are: river runoff, sea-ice meltwater, and Pacific water (which, as mentioned earlier, is fresher than Atlantic Ocean water). These separate sources each respond to the different circumstances of their origin. Since fresh water (mostly river water and Pacific water) in the near-surface can follow different pathways, they need to be traced separately, and it is important to note that it is inappropriate to consider fresh water only as determined solely by salinity without determining or modelling the circulation of these two main sources as well as that of sea-ice meltwater. Chemical tracers can readily do this with measurements of salinity, nitrate, phosphate, and alkalinity (Jones et al. 2008).

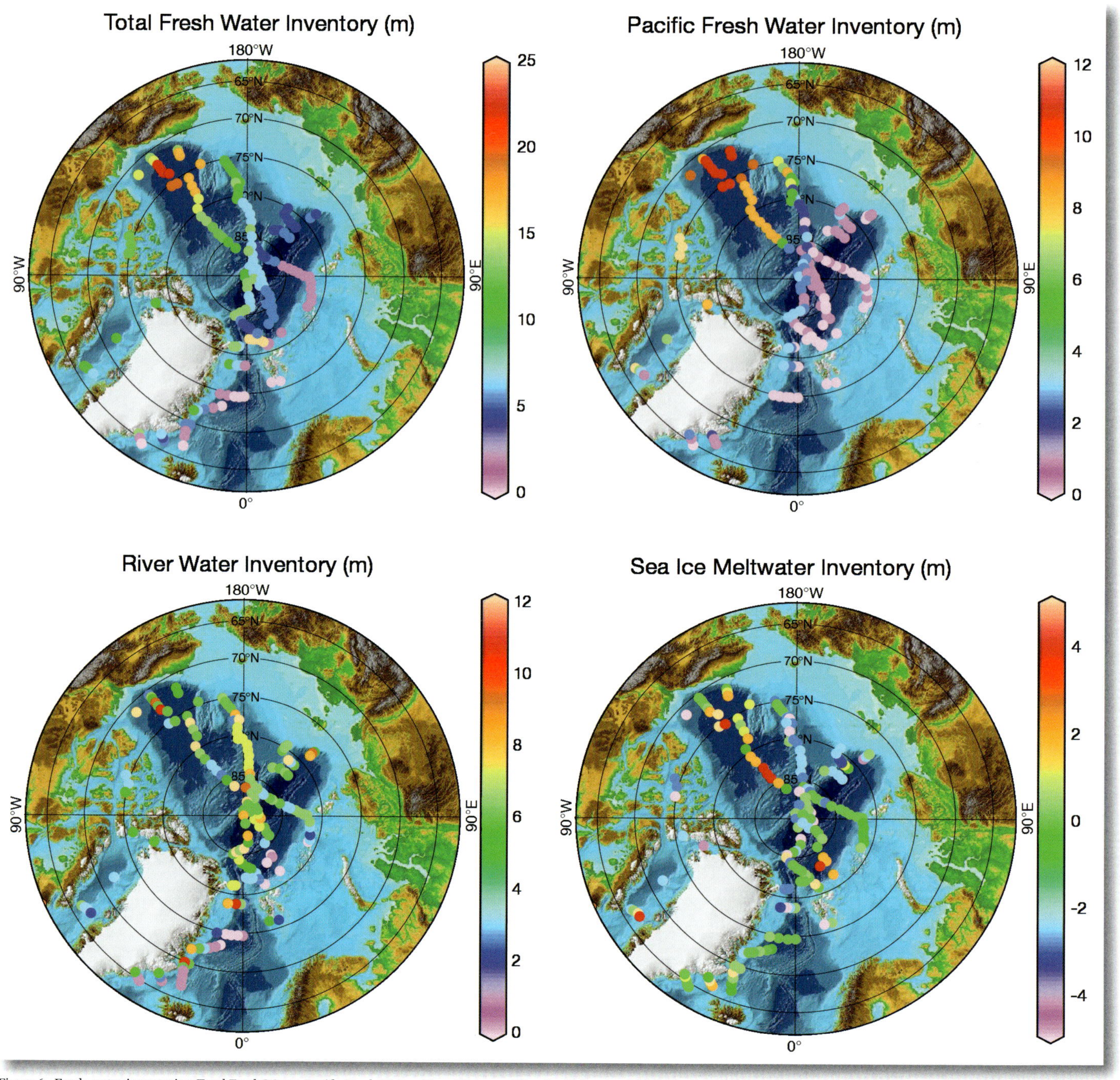

Figure 6. Fresh-water inventories: Total Fresh Water, Pacific Fresh Water, River Water, and Sea-Ice Meltwater, within the Arctic Ocean, the East Greenland Current, and the Canadian Arctic Archipelago (units of the colour bars are metres).

VARIABILITY

Since 2000, much work has been done to assess changes in circulation patterns, water mass distributions and river water distributions in the Arctic Ocean. Most of the variability has been observed in the upper waters, where these waters are strongly affected by prevailing winds. For example, major changes in the extent of the Beaufort Gyre, the near surface counter-clockwise circulation in the Canada Basin north of Alaska, are driven by changes in the prevailing wind pattern. Sometimes, the Beaufort Gyre spreads almost throughout the entire western side of the Basin; sometimes it is much more constrained close to the North American side of the Basin. The amount of fresh water stored in the Beaufort Gyre will be reflected in the changes in fresh water exiting the Arctic Ocean (Rudels et al. 2011).

Changes in the distributions of both Pacific water and river water have also been observed over the past decade (Ekwurzel et al. 2001, Schlosser et al. 2002, Anderson et al. 2004). These changes are caused primarily by changes in long-term wind patterns. These wind pattern changes can also affect the amount of Pacific water and possibly the amount of fresh water exiting the Arctic Ocean into the Greenland Sea thereby impacting the Global Ocean Conveyor Belt. Some work shows that each of the fresh water constituents (Pacific and river waters) exiting the Arctic Ocean through Fram Strait vary considerably (Falck et al. 2005). Even though the fresh water sources in Fram Strait can change, the salinity of exiting waters remains fairly constant.

IS FRESH WATER FROM THE ARCTIC OCEAN CONTROLLING THE GLOBAL OCEAN CONVEYOR BELT?

Several articles have commented on this question. Jones and Anderson (2008) suggested that a catastrophe is not imminent. As it exits the Arctic

Ocean, fresh water (not including ice) is strongly confined to near the Greenland coast and may be sufficiently removed from the region where it can have a strong influence on deep convection within the Greenland Sea. Sea-ice meltwater does not seem to be adding much to the fresh water export, though ice export remains a possible small Arctic Ocean contribution to surface freshening in the Greenland Sea.

LOOKING TOWARD THE FUTURE

Numerical models predict that the Polar Regions will warm more than the rest of the world. Climate change already has substantially impacted the Arctic Ocean ice pack with large regions formerly covered with permanent ice cover now experiencing seasonal ice cover. Ice reflects much more sunlight back into space than the open sea. Open waters are darker and absorb more heat that accelerates thawing and further increases the open water area. How this may affect the fresh water exported to the potentially vulnerable Global Ocean Conveyor Belt is a question of serious concern.

While BIO scientists' contributions to understanding Arctic Ocean processes are significant, the outlook for the future financial support is sobering. There appears to be only a slim hope that BIO scientists will be able to continue their important multi-decadal work of making measurements and interpreting data, which, in cooperation with the international science community, would yield new essential insights into the role of the Arctic Ocean in the context of global climate and global climate change.

ACKNOWLEDGEMENTS

I am especially grateful for the invaluable long term collaboration and friendships with ocean researchers of Sweden, Finland, and Germany, especially Leif Anderson, Bert Rudels, Ursula Schauer, and Peter Koltermann – good friends all. I also thank Frank Zemlyak for his technical expertise and dedicated work on the many Arctic Ocean expeditions required for this research program, as well as the numerous BIO technicians that provided essential logistic support. Funding came mainly from the Panel on Energy Research and Development (PERD), with logistic support of the ice camps provided by the Polar Continental Shelf Project. Several of the Arctic Ocean studies could not have been undertaken without support from the Swedish Polar Research Institute and the German Alfred Wegener Institute, and their provision of equipment, technical staff, and their 'state-of-the-art' icebreakers, the IB *Oden* and FS *Polarstern*, respectively. Collaboration with colleagues at the Institute of Ocean Sciences, Sidney, British Columbia, and the support of the crew of the CCGS *Louis S. St-Laurent* in 1994 are also gratefully acknowledged.

REFERENCES

Anderson, L.G., S. Jutterström, S. Kaltin, E.P. Jones, and G. Björk. 2004. Variability in river runoff distribution in the Eurasian Basin of the Arctic Ocean. Journal of Geophysical Research 109 (C01016). doi:10.1029/2003JC001773.

Anderson, L.G., T. Tanhua, G. Björk, S. Hjalmarsson, E.P. Jones, S. Jutterström, B. Rudels, J.H. Swift, and I. Wåhlstöm. 2010. Arctic Ocean shelf-basin interaction, an active continental shelf CO2 pump and its impact on the degree of calcium carbonate solubility. Deep-Sea Research I 57: 869-879.

Cai, W.-J. and 16 others. 2010. Decrease in the CO2 uptake capacity in an ice-free Arctic Ocean Basin. Science 329: 556-559.

Ekwurzel, B., P. Schlosser, R.A. Mortlock, and R.G. Fairbanks. 2001. River runoff, sea-ice meltwater, and Pacific water distribution and mean residence times in the Arctic Ocean. Journal of Geophysical Research 106: 9,075-9,092.

Falck, E., G. Kattner, and G. Budéus. 2005. Disappearance of Pacific Water in the northwestern Fram Strait. Geophysical Research Letters 32(L14619). doi:10.1029/2005GL023400.

Jones, E.P. 2001. Circulation in the Arctic Ocean. Polar Research 20: 139-146.

Jones, E.P. and L.G. Anderson. 1986. On the origin of the chemical properties of the Arctic Ocean halocline. Journal of Geophysical Research 91: 10,759-10,767.

Jones, E.P., B. Rudels, and L.G. Anderson. 1995. Deep waters of the Arctic Ocean: origins and circulation. Deep-Sea Research 42: 737-760.

Jones, E.P. and L.G. Anderson. 2008. Is the Global Conveyor Belt threatened by Arctic Ocean fresh water outflow? Pages 385-404 *in* Arctic-Subarctic Ocean Fluxes: Defining the Role of Northern Seas in Climate (R.R. Dickson, J. Meincke, and P. Rhines, Eds.). Springer, New York, NY.

Jones, E.P., L.G. Anderson, S. Jutterström, L. Mintrop, and J.H. Swift. 2008. Pacific fresh water, river water and sea ice meltwater across Arctic Ocean basins: results from the 2005 Beringia Expedition. Journal of Geophysical Research 113 (C08012). doi:10.1029/2007JC004124.

Rudels, B., E.P. Jones, L.G. Anderson, and G. Kattner. 1994. On the intermediate depth waters of the Arctic Ocean. Pages 33-46 *in* The Polar Oceans and their Role in Shaping the Global Environment: the Nansen Centennial Volume (O.M. Johannessen, R.D. Muench, and J. E. Overland, Eds.). American Geophysical Union, Washington, DC.

Rudels, B., L.G. Anderson, and E.P. Jones. 1996. Formation and evolution of the surface mixed layer and halocline of the Arctic Ocean. Journal of Geophysical Research 101: 8,807-8,821.

Rudels, B., L. Anderson, P. Eriksson, E. Fahrbach, M. Jakobsson, E.P. Jones, H. Melling, S. Prinsenberg, U. Schauer, and T. Yao. 2011. Observations in the Ocean. Pages 117-198 *in* Arctic Climate Change: the ACSYS Decade and Beyond (P. Lemke and H.-W. Jacobi, Eds.). Springer, New York, NY.

Schlosser, P., R. Newton, B. Ekwurzel, S. Khatiwala, R. Mortlock, and R. Fairbanks. 2002. Decrease of river runoff in the upper waters of the Eurasian Basin, Arctic Ocean, between 1991 and 1996: evidence from $d^{18}O$ data. Geophysical Research Letters 29: 1,289. doi:10.1029/ 2001GL013135.

Semiletov, I.P., I.I. Pipko, I. Repina, and N.E. Shakhova. 2007. Carbonate chemistry dynamics and carbon dioxide fluxes across the atmosphere-ice-water interfaces in the Arctic Ocean: Pacific sector of the Arctic. Journal of Marine Systems 66: 204-226.

Tanhua, T., E.P. Jones, E. Jeansson, S. Jutterström, W.M. Smethie, Jr., D.W.R. Wallace, and L.G. Anderson. 2009. Ventilation of the Arctic Ocean: mean ages and inventories of anthropogenic CO2 and CFC-11. Journal of Geophysical Research 114 (C01002). doi:10.1029/2008JC004868.

5. OCEANOGRAPHIC FLUXES AND SEA-ICE PROPERTIES IN LANCASTER SOUND

Ingrid K. Peterson*, Jim M. Hamilton, Simon J. Prinsenberg, and Roger G. Pettipas

SUMMARY

Between 1998 and 2011, year-long moorings were deployed across Barrow Strait to estimate volume, freshwater, and heat transport through Lancaster Sound into Baffin Bay. The principal aim of the work was to determine whether significant changes in the freshwater transport through the Canadian Arctic Archipelago (CAA) were occurring that would affect oceanographic conditions and the marine ecosystem in the North Atlantic. The freshwater and heat transports are highly correlated with the volume transport. Maximum and minimum volume transports occur during the summer and autumn, respectively. The monthly volume transport anomaly is significantly correlated with the northeastward wind anomaly in the Beaufort Sea, approximately parallel to the western side of the CAA, at monthly to inter-annual time scales. The location and wind direction, for which there is maximum correlation, are consistent with the flow being driven by a sea level difference between opposite ends of Parry Channel, the difference being determined by setup caused by alongshore winds in the Beaufort Sea. Landfast ice was present over the moorings in most years from February to May. Monthly mean ice draft measured with a moored upward-looking sonar is generally 1-2 m, and monthly maximum ice drafts vary from 2 m to 23 m, depending on the presence of ice keels.

Key words: moorings, oceanographic fluxes, sea ice, Barrow Strait, Lancaster Sound, Jones Sound.
***E-mail:** Ingrid.Peterson@dfo-mpo.gc.ca

Beginning in August 1998, Fisheries and Oceans Canada (DFO) moorings were used to monitor the volume, heat, and freshwater transports through Lancaster Sound, one of the three main passages in the Canadian Arctic Archipelago (CAA) between the Arctic Ocean and Baffin Bay (Fig. 1). The aim of the work was to determine whether significant changes in the freshwater flux through the CAA due to decreases in Arctic sea ice or other factors were occurring that would affect oceanographic conditions and the marine ecosystem in the North Atlantic. The data collected are important for validating Canadian and international numerical models used for predicting climate change. Before 2003, the international mooring program was conducted as part of the Arctic Climate System Study (ACSYS) which had two principal aims: (1) to understand the interactions of the Arctic Ocean circulation, atmosphere, ice cover, and hydrological cycle; and (2) to provide a scientific basis for more accurately representing Arctic processes in global climate models. After 2003, the mooring program was conducted as part of the Arctic-Subarctic Ocean Fluxes (ASOF) study with the principal aim of measuring and modelling the variability of fluxes between the Arctic and Atlantic oceans.

Previous work in 1981-82, when current meters were deployed in Barrow Strait, provided estimates of volume transport for nine months of the year from April to December (Prinsenberg and Bennett 1987).

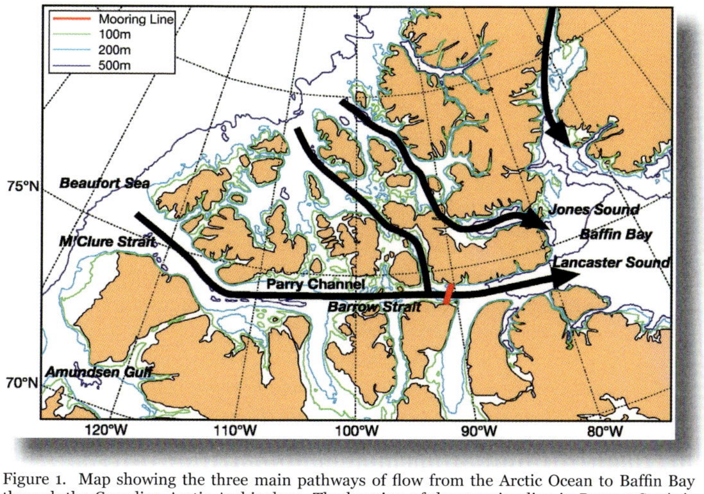

Figure 1. Map showing the three main pathways of flow from the Arctic Ocean to Baffin Bay through the Canadian Arctic Archipelago. The location of the mooring line in Barrow Strait is shown by the red line.

Monthly mean transport was highly correlated with the mean monthly pressure gradient along the Northwest Passage, estimated from long-term mean monthly water level data in the Arctic Ocean and in the mid-Passage area. This relationship was used to infer volume transport for the remaining months of the year. The estimated annual mean volume transport was 0.5 x 10^6 m^3 s^{-1} [or 0.5 Sverdrup (Sv)], with a maximum in August and minimum in January for the nine months of observations. The sea surface height variation was greater at the western end of the Northwest Passage in the Arctic Ocean than in the mid-Passage, based on the water level data. Using a diagnostic numerical ocean model, Kliem and Greenberg (2003) showed that the mean volume transport in summer through Barrow Strait is dependent on the elevation difference between the Arctic Ocean and Baffin Bay, and on the density distribution. This model was used as the basis of an early version of the Webtide tidal prediction program for the arctic region (Collins et al. 2011).

INSTRUMENTATION

Moorings were deployed from August 1998 to August 2011 across Barrow Strait, in the eastern part of Parry Channel which extends from western M'Clure Strait to eastern Lancaster Sound (Fig. 1). At the mooring line, Barrow Strait is about 69 km (37 nautical miles) wide and has a maximum depth of 285 m with a sill depth of about 125 m to the west.

The instrumentation (Fig. 2) and the first three years of processed data were described in Prinsenberg and Hamilton (2005). Currents were measured with acoustic doppler current profilers (ADCPs) (Fig. 3) with specialized compass systems for near-pole current direction measurement (Hamilton 2001, Hamilton et al. 2004) at two to four sites across the Strait. Conductivity-temperature-depth instruments (CTDs) at nominal depths of 40, 80, and 160 m provided salinity and temperature data. For shallow depths, where the lighter, fresher water is concentrated, a moored Icycler profiler (Fowler et al. 2004) was used, providing two full years and one partial year of daily salinity and temperature profiles at the southern site. Annual mean transport in Lancaster Sound in the first three years (1998-2001) was found to vary by ±0.25 Sv about a mean of 0.75 Sv, with seasonal fluxes being highest in the summer (21 June to 20 September) and lowest in the fall (21 September to 20 December), in general agreement with the earlier study. Further results described the long-term variability seen in six years of processed data (Melling et al. 2008). The ADCPs also provided ice velocity data while a moored upward-looking sonar (ULS), or ice profiler, provided ice draft data.

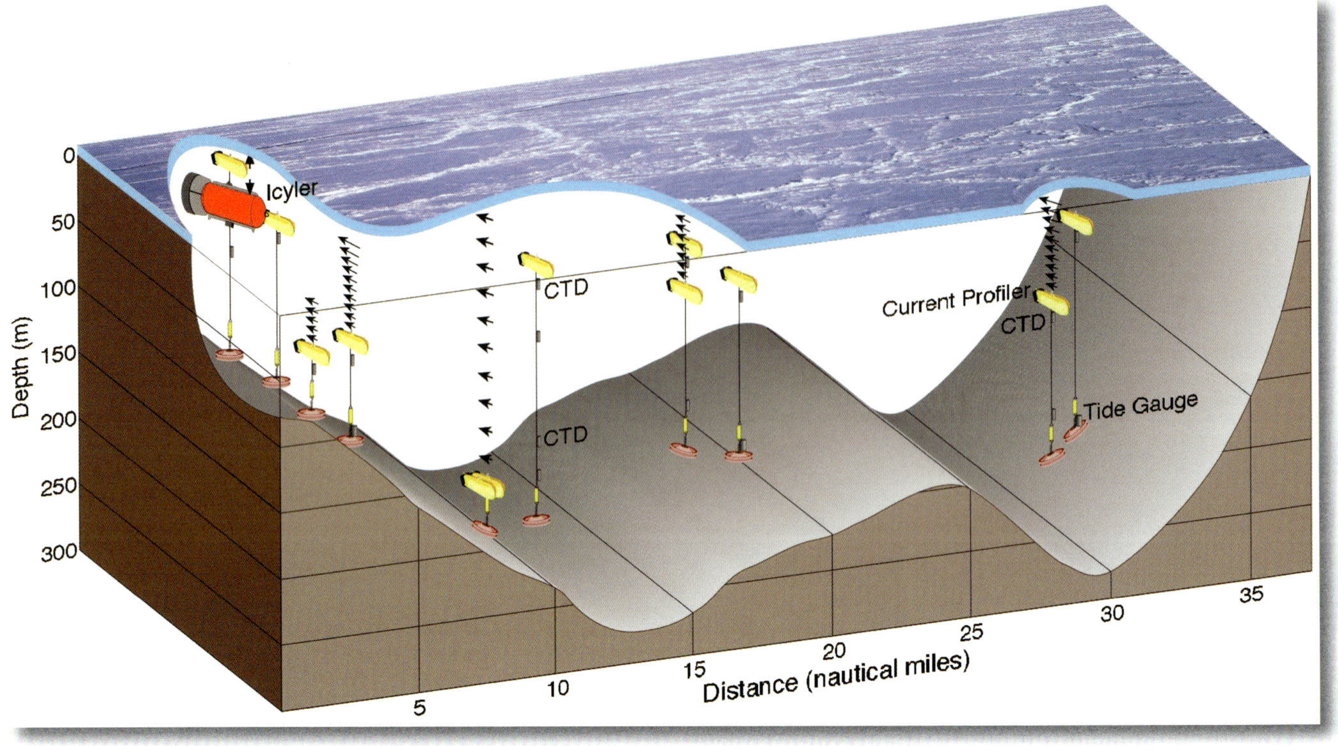

Figure 2. Illustration of the mooring array maintained across eastern Barrow Strait from August 2001 to August 2006, from south (left) to north (right).

OCEANOGRAPHIC FLUXES

The volume, freshwater, and heat transports between 1998 and 2006 are shown in Figure 4. The mean volume and freshwater transports were 0.68 Sv and 0.048 Sv, respectively. Both freshwater and heat transport are highly correlated with volume transport (Prinsenberg and Hamilton 2005). Thus, changes in the volume transport out of the Arctic Ocean

Figure 3. An acoustic doppler acoustic profiler (ADCP) being deployed from a Canadian Coast Guard ship in Barrow Strait.

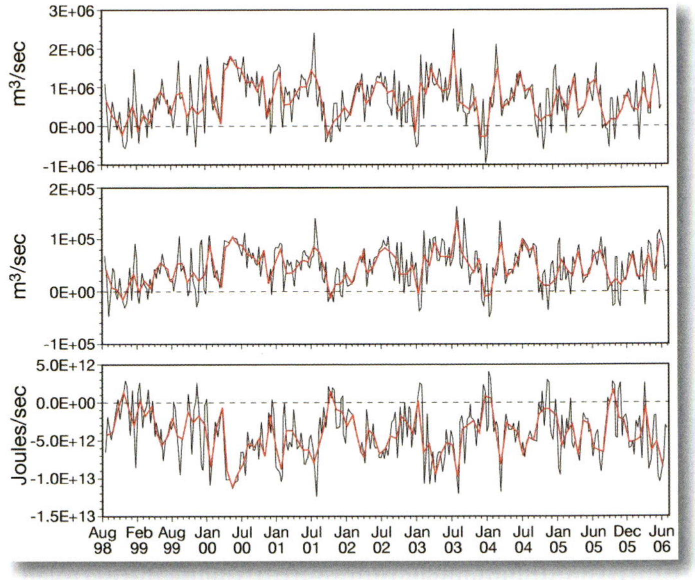

Figure 4. Weekly (black line) and monthly (red line) estimated total volume (top), freshwater volume (middle), and heat (bottom) transports through Lancaster Sound from August 1998 to August 2006.

could have a significant impact on the freshwater flux from the Arctic Ocean to Baffin Bay and thereby affect oceanographic and ecosystem properties in the Atlantic Ocean.

The value for the mean volume transport through Lancaster Sound (0.68 Sv), combined with the values of 0.3 Sv for Jones Sound (Melling et al. 2008) and 0.57 Sv for Nares Strait (Münchow and Melling 2008), implies that the relative transport values for Lancaster Sound, Jones Sound, and Nares Strait are 44%, 19%, and 37%, respectively, of the total transport through the CAA. These transport percentages are reasonably close to the values of 34%, 20%, and 46% estimated by Kliem and Greenberg (2003) using a numerical model. The annual cycle of volume transport accounts for 34% of the variance of the monthly volume transport. The transport through Lancaster Sound is generally highest in the summer (June-August) and lowest in the fall (October-December).

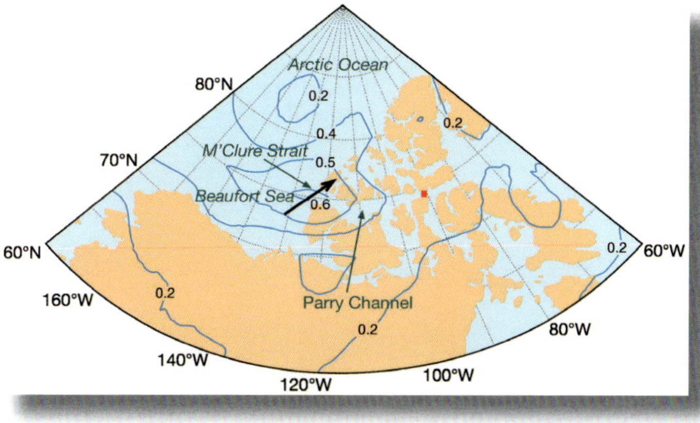

Figure 5. Map showing correlation coefficients (contour lines) between monthly anomalies of National Centers for Environmental Prediction (NCEP) surface wind and volume transport, and the wind location and direction for which there is maximum correlation (thick black arrow). The position of the Lancaster Sound mooring line is marked by a red square.

WIND FORCING

The monthly anomaly of volume transport in 1998-2006 was computed by subtracting the mean 1998-2006 values for each month from the transport for the same month within each year of the 1998-2006 period. The transport anomaly was then compared with gridded surface wind data from the National Centers for Environmental Prediction (NCEP) data set (Kalnay et al. 1996). Using a multiple regression model, Prinsenberg et al. (2009) showed that the monthly volume transport anomaly was most highly correlated ($r=0.62$, $p<0.01$) with the northeastward wind anomaly in the Beaufort Sea, just west of M'Clure Strait (Fig. 5). The location and wind direction for which there is maximum correlation are consistent with the flow being driven by a sea-level difference between opposite ends of Parry Channel, the difference being determined by setup caused by alongshore winds in the Beaufort Sea. As observed for volume transport, the annual cycle of the northeastward wind strength in the Beaufort Sea is highest in the summer (June to August) and lowest in the autumn (October to December). In autumn there is typically a strong high atmospheric pressure region over the Beaufort Sea (Beaufort High) causing strong southwestward winds west of M'Clure Strait, while in the summer winds are weak due to a weak low pressure region over the geographic North Pole.

The observed total volume transport is shown in Figure 6 (red line), along with that predicted by the Beaufort Sea wind anomaly effect, plus the annual cycle of volume transport (blue line). The wind anomaly effect plus the annual cycle accounts for 59% of the variance of the volume transport.

The observed annual mean volume transport and the predicted transport based on the mean northeastward wind anomaly (from August to July) are highly correlated ($r=0.88$), with highest values in 2000-01, and lowest values in 1998-99 (Fig. 7). The predicted transport in 1998-99 was also the lowest value over the entire 58 year NCEP time series between 1948-49 and 2005-06. If global climate models were capable of predicting changes in future wind patterns, the results from the mooring program could be used to infer future changes in freshwater transport through the CAA as a result of climate change. Unfortunately, however, present models exhibit large model-to-model differences in the response of wind indices to climate change (Solomon et al. 2007).

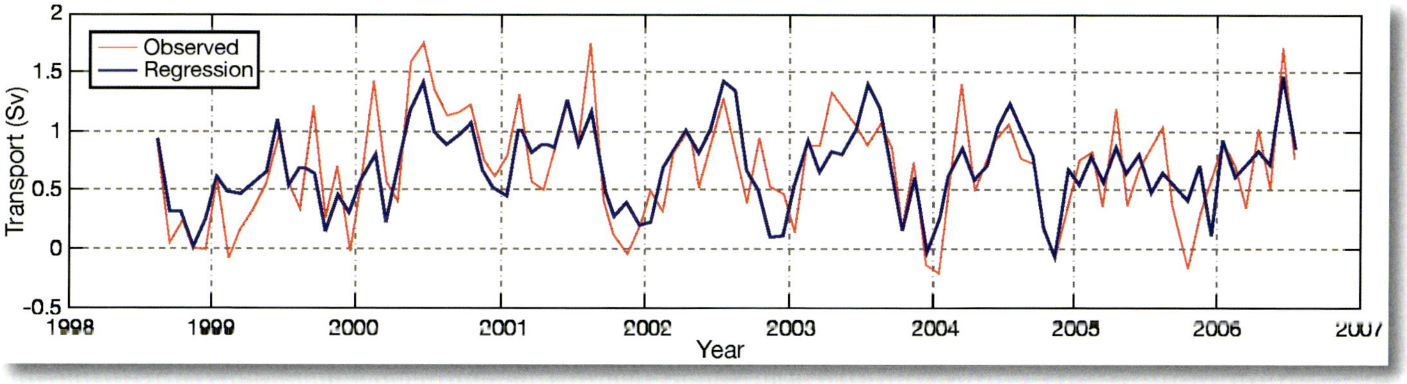

Figure 6. Monthly observed volume transport (red line), and transport estimated from regression model based on surface wind anomalies, plus annual cycle of volume transport (blue line).

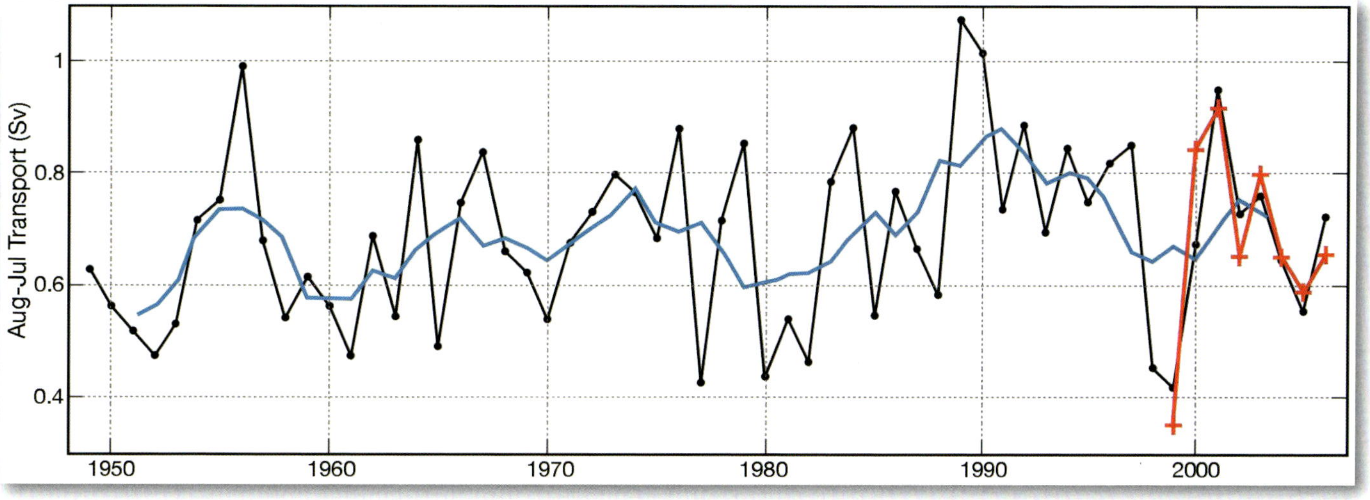

Figure 7. Annual mean transport (from August to July) estimated from alongshore winds (black line) and observed transport (red line); the blue line represents the 5-year running mean.

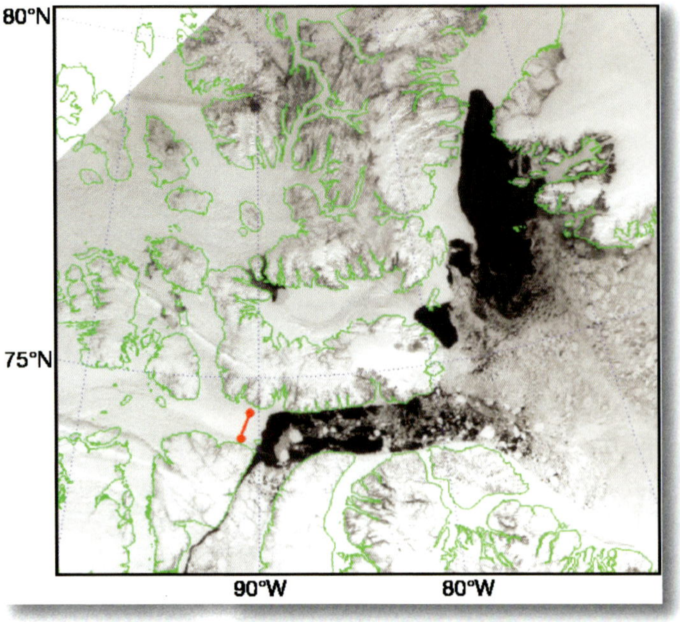

Figure 8. Visible-band Moderate Resolution Imaging Spectroradiometer (MODIS) Aqua image from 15 May 2006 (1640 Z) showing landfast ice (light grey) in Barrow Strait over the mooring line (red line), and open water (black) and mobile pack ice to the east in Lancaster Sound and Baffin Bay.

SEA-ICE PROPERTIES

Sea ice is found in Barrow Strait and Lancaster Sound throughout most of the year, either in the form of mobile pack ice or landfast ice. Both pack ice and landfast ice consist of level ice and deformed ice (i.e., ice that has been squeezed together and in places forced upwards and downwards). The easternmost position of the landfast ice-edge during the year usually occurs in February to May slightly east of the mooring line at 90°W (Fig. 8), but is found farther west or east in some years (Peterson et al. 2008).

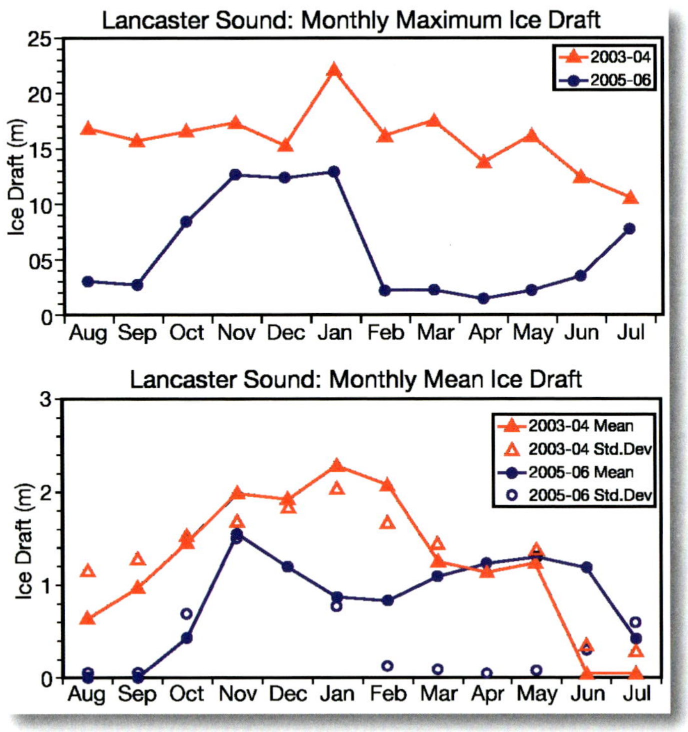

Figure 9. Two years of ice draft data from the southern site of the Lancaster Sound array: monthly maxima ice draft (top) and monthly means and standard deviations (bottom).

Monthly maximum and mean ice drafts (Fig. 9) are shown for the ice seasons of 2003-04, when the spring landfast ice edge was west of the mooring line, and 2005-06, when the spring landfast ice edge was east of the mooring line. The mean ice draft is generally about 1-2 m from November to May, with lower mean ice drafts in the summer months. In 2003-04, the ice over the moorings was mobile throughout the year, and maximum ice drafts of about 10-23 m were observed in each month due to the presence of ice keels. However in 2005-06, the maximum ice draft was only about 2 m from February to May because of undeformed landfast ice over the moorings. The mean ice draft is consistent with the expected ice growth based on observed air temperatures in the area.

PHYSICAL AND BIOLOGICAL INTERCONNECTIONS

The long time series of mooring data also provides an opportunity to study interconnections between physical and biological properties on inter-annual time scales. Analyses of the mooring data from the north side of Barrow Strait demonstrate highly correlated relationships between water properties and the formation and break-up of sea ice. Ice break-up and fall freeze-up on the north side of Barrow Strait are both highly correlated with early summer water column temperature (r^2=0.91 and r^2= 0.62, respectively). Furthermore, late summer salinity at 40 m is highly correlated with freeze-up date (r^2=0.92). These remarkably strong relationships offer the possibility of being able to predict these key events if real-time ocean observations were available.

The ADCPs used to measure current speed throughout the study also record 'echo intensity'. This is the strength of the acoustic signal reflected back to the instrument from particles being carried with the flow in the water column. Detection of the frequency shift in this reflected acoustic signal is the basis of the current measurement. However, the strength of the detected echo also provides information about the particles themselves. Since zooplankton are the principal acoustic reflectors in the water column, the strength of the detected echo can be interpreted to provide an indication of the relative biomass of zooplankton. Using this technique, we find the timing of the zooplankton growing season and the seasonally integrated relative biomass are both highly correlated with early summer water column temperature (r^2=0.78 in both cases). In years when the water in early summer is warmer than average, the growing season starts earlier, is longer, and supports a greater biomass. With real-time ocean measurements, it would be possible to predict these key features of the ecosystem for the upcoming season in this locale.

We also find that on the north side of Barrow Strait there is a trend towards warmer water in early summer (r^2=0.59). The average early summer (21 June to 1 August) water column temperature increased 0.15 °C from 1999 to 2006. This trend is consistent with the broader regional warming associated with climate change that is being observed in the Arctic. Based on the relationships identified, continued warming will result in a trend to earlier ice break-up and higher zooplankton biomass over a longer growing season in northern Barrow Strait.

DFO'S ARCTIC ICE/OCEAN OBSERVATORY

The eastward currents over the southern half of Barrow Strait transport ice from the west through most of the summer. This establishes the northern side of the strait as the principal shipping lane into the high arctic over the short summer season. Availability of up-to-date information on ice and ocean conditions is of practical value to arctic marine operators. Real-time data would also be useful for input into computer models used to forecast sea-ice conditions, as well as for the validation of those models. The predictive capability described above provides a third incentive for developing a technology that provides sea-ice and ocean conditions in real time.

With the practical value of real-time data established, a prototype ice/ocean observatory has been developed and installed at Gascoyne Inlet, Devon Island, 30 km west of the mooring line in 2011. The operational prototype (Fig. 10) consists of three components:

1. An acoustic telemetry link that passes ice drift, current, acoustic backscatter (zooplankton), and water property data from instruments on a sub-surface mooring to an underwater hub;
2. A sub-sea cable that carries data from the hub to a shore station; and
3. A two-way satellite link that transmits the data from the shore station to the distant scientist.

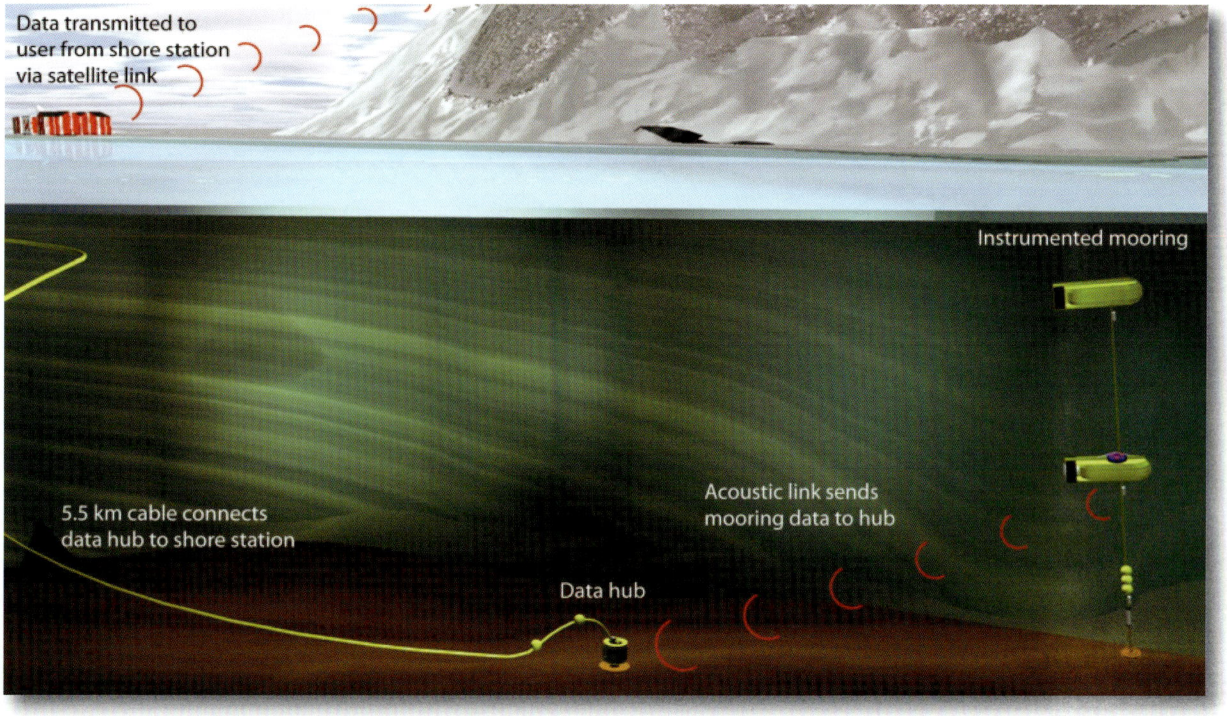

Figure 10. An illustration of the prototype real-time data system installed in Barrow Strait in 2011. Data from an instrumented mooring are acoustically transmitted to a 'data hub' at the offshore end of an underwater cable, sent through the cable, and then transmitted from the shore station by Iridium satellite to the user.

Potential expansion of the system includes the addition of ice thickness measurements, upper water column physical and biological data, and data from acoustically-linked instrumented moorings farther offshore.

CONCLUSIONS

The results described in this paper highlight the value of long-term oceanographic monitoring. Analysis of the 13-year Barrow Strait data time series has revealed the high inter-annual variability in ocean transports and connected this variability to slowly varying atmospheric patterns. The length of the data set has made it possible to establish this relationship in a statistically robust way. This result improves our understanding of the arctic climate system so that regional climate models being developed to predict climate change impacts are more reliable. The long-time series data have also made it possible to identify inter-annual relationships between the physical and biological environment in northern Barrow Strait that substantially improve our understanding of the local environment. These results offer predictive capability to enhance the practical applications of a new ice/ocean observatory. Only through long-term oceanographic monitoring can such results be obtained.

ACKNOWLEDGEMENTS

The authors thank Murray Scotney for managing the instrumentation for the collection of all the mooring data. Personnel of Canadian Coast Guard icebreakers are thanked for their continued support during field operations. This work was supported by the Canadian Program of Energy Research and Development (PERD) and the Canadian International Polar Year (IPY) Program. We acknowledge the use of data products from the Land Atmosphere Near-real time Capability for EOS (LANCE) system operated by the Goddard Space Flight Center Earth Science Data and Information System (ESDIS) funded by the National Aeronautics and Space Administration.

REFERENCES

Collins, A.K., C.G. Hannah, and D. Greenberg. 2011. Validation of a high resolution modelling system for tides in the Canadian Arctic Archipelago. Canadian Technical Report of Hydrography and Ocean Sciences 273: 1-72.

Fowler, G.A., G.R. Siddall, and S.J. Prinsenberg. 2004. An energy-conserving oceanographic profiler for use under mobile ice cover: ICYCLER. International Journal of Offshore and Polar Engineering 14: 176-181.

Hamilton, J. 2001. Accurate ocean current direction measurements near the magnetic poles. Pages 656-670 *in* Proceedings of the 11th International Offshore and Polar Engineering Conference, Stavanger, Norway, 17-22 June 2001 (Chung , J.S., M. Sayed, H. Saeki, and T. Setoguchi, Eds.). International Society of Offshore and Polar Engineers, Cupertino, CA.

Hamilton, J., S. Prinsenberg, and L. Malloch. 2004. Moored current meter and CTD observations from Barrow Strait, 2000-2001. Canadian Technical Report of Hydrography and Ocean Sciences 165. 165: 1-59

Kalnay, E. and others. 1996. The NCEP/NCAR 40-Year Reanalysis Project. Bulletin of the American Meteorological Society 77: 437-471.

Kliem, N. and D.A. Greenberg. 2003. Diagnostic simulations of the summer circulation in the Canadian Arctic Archipelago. Atmosphere-Ocean 41: 273-289.

Melling, M., T.A. Agnew, K.E. Falkner, D.A. Greenberg, C.M. Lee, A. Munchow, B. Petrie, S.J. Prinsenberg, R.M. Samelson, and R.A. Woodgate. 2008. Fresh-water fluxes via Pacific and Arctic outflows across the Canadian polar shelf. Pages 193-247 *in* Arctic-Subarctic Ocean Fluxes, Defining the Role of the Northern Seas in Climate (R.R. Dickson, J. Meinke, and P. Rhines, Eds.). Springer Verlag, Dordrecht, The Netherlands.

Münchow, A. and H. Melling. 2008. Ocean current observations from Nares Strait to the west of Greenland: Inter-annual to tidal variability and forcing. Journal of Marine Research 66: 801-833.

Peterson, I., S. Prinsenberg, J. Hamilton, and R. Pettipas. 2008. Variability of oceanographic and ice properties of the Canadian Arctic Archipelago. International Council for the Exploration of the Sea Annual Meeting, Sept 22-26, 2008, Halifax, Canada. CM 2008/B:16.

Prinsenberg, S.J. and E.B. Bennett. 1987. Mixing and transports in Barrow Strait, the central part of the Northwest Passage. Continental Shelf Research 7: 913-935.

Prinsenberg, S.J. and J. Hamilton. 2005. Monitoring the volume, freshwater and heat fluxes passing through Lancaster Sound in the Canadian Arctic Archipelago. Atmosphere-Ocean 43: 1-23.

Prinsenberg, S.J., J. Hamilton, I. Peterson, and R. Pettipas. 2009. Observing and interpreting the seasonal variability of the oceanographic fluxes passing through Lancaster Sound of the Canadian Arctic Archipelago. Pages 119-137 *in* Influence of Climate Change on the Changing Arctic and Sub-Arctic Conditions (J. Nihoul and A. Kostianoy, Eds.). Springer-Verlag, Dordrecht, The Netherlands.

Solomon, S., D. Qin, M. Manning, Z. Chen, M. Marquis, K.B. Averyt, M. Tignor, and H.L. Miller (Eds.). 2007. Contribution of Working Group I to the Fourth Assessment Report of the Intergovernmental Panel on Climate Change, 2007. Cambridge University Press, Cambridge, England.

6. OBSERVING AND UNDERSTANDING THE SEASONAL SEA-ICE VARIABILITY IN CANADIAN WATERS

Simon J. Prinsenberg*, Ingrid K. Peterson, George A. Fowler, Brian D. Beanlands, J. Scott Holladay, and Louis A. Lalumiere

SUMMARY

Sea-ice is a major component of the northern marine environment with its complex evolution controlled by the atmosphere above and the ocean below. Since the early 1970s, Bedford Institute of Oceanography personnel have studied the interaction processes of ocean, pack ice and atmosphere to isolate the different forcing mechanisms of pack ice evolution and its impact on the atmosphere, ocean and marine ecosystem. Studies have been done from ice camps on the Arctic pack ice, research ships, and with the use of fixed-wing and helicopter support. In the Canadian Arctic Archipelago, the under-ice marine ecosystem of ice algae and copepods were studied as well as the atmospheric fluxes in polynyas. Later studies have been made possible by the development of entirely new observational techniques and platforms that have often been integrated with real-time satellite communication. Specially-designed satellite-tracked ice beacons monitored pack ice pressure, and drift rate, and near-surface ocean water properties. Helicopter-borne technologies using video, laser, electromagnetic, and radar sensing techniques provided additional detailed information on the spatial variability, dynamics, and inter-annual variability of pack ice. Through the synthesis of observation and analysis, progress has been made in understanding ice-ocean processes, thereby advancing the creation and validation of models that can accurately predict aspects of the life-cycle of sea-ice that affects the marine ecosystem. With the logistic support of ships and helicopters, icebergs and pack ice along with environmental properties were monitored to enhance the safety and efficiency of oil and gas development along the Canadian east coast.

Key words: sea ice, Canadian Arctic, surveys, ice-ocean interaction processes, ice-ocean instrumentation, ice beacons, helicopter-borne sensors.

***E-mail:** Simon.Prinsenberg@dfo-mpo.gc.ca

Sea-ice has an enormous impact on many aspects of the marine environment and the human activities that occur there. The 'life-cycle' of sea-ice is complex, being influenced by many environmental factors in its growth, movement, and decay processes. Since the Arctic Ice Dynamics Joint Experiment (AIDJEX) in the Beaufort Sea (Smith 1974), these processes have been observed for over 40 years by Bedford Institute of Oceanography (BIO) personnel in an attempt to isolate the impact and interaction of different forcing mechanisms (Fig. 1). This research has been made possible by the development of entirely new observational techniques that have often been integrated with other sophisticated technologies such as remote sensing and real-time satellite communication. Through the synthesis of observation and analysis, progress has been made to understand ice-ocean-atmosphere interaction processes, and to use this knowledge to enhance operational models that can accurately predict aspects of the life-cycle of sea-ice in the marine ecosystem.

It is now generally accepted that owing to climate change, the arctic polar ice cap is melting (IPCC 2007), with arctic ice thinning (Kwok and Rothrock 2009) and decreasing in extent (Serreze et al. 2007). Large inter-year variations in pack ice properties have been observed along the coasts of eastern Canada and in the Canadian Arctic (Tivy et al. 2011). For example, in southern coastal Labrador, the decadal (10-year) variability is apparent in the early part of the time series, but this interval has been followed by a steady decline in ice extent since the early 1990s due to cli-

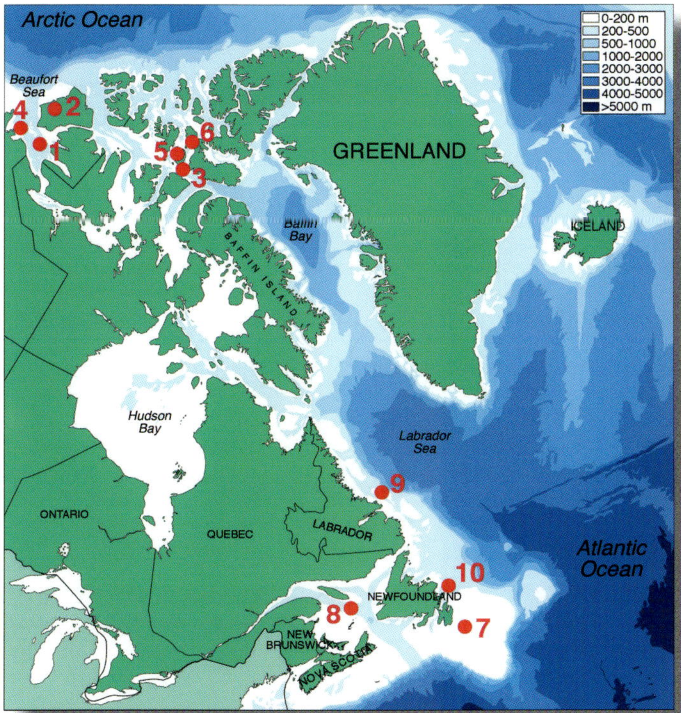

Figure 1. Map showing principal geographic features and locations for BIO sea-ice variability studies in Arctic and Eastern Canada: Amundsen Gulf (1), Banks Island (2), Barrow Strait (3), Canadian Arctic Archipelago (CAA), Cape Parry (4), Cornwallis Island (5), Dundas Island (6), Grand Banks of Newfoundland (7), Gulf of St. Lawrence (8), Labrador Shelf (9), Newfoundland Shelf (10).

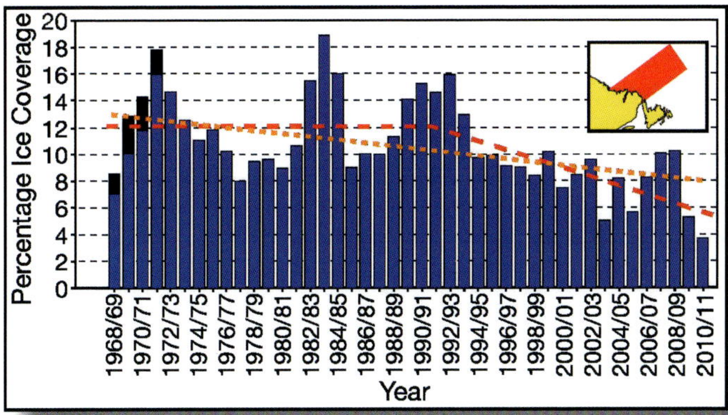

Figure 2. Forty-three year time series of ice extent along the southern Labrador Sea coast indicating a linear decline (orange line) and a trend line (red) that indicates the ice extent has declined rapidly since the early 1900s after a period of a relatively stable decadal pattern. Some estimates of ice extent (black bars) were added for areas not covered by observations in the early years of the time series.

mate change (Fig. 2; http://ice-glaces.ec.gc.ca/IceGraph103 /). Although pack ice serves as a marine habitat for species such as Ringed Seals (*Pusa hispida*) and Polar Bears (*Ursus maritimus*), it also represents a hazard to navigation and an impediment to offshore oil and gas development.

Following research in the Canadian Arctic Archipelago (CAA) on the under-ice marine ecosystem and atmospheric fluxes in polynyas (i.e., areas of open water surrounded by ice) adjacent to Dundas Island in the Queens Channel region north of Cornwallis Island (Cota et al. 1987, Smith et al. 1983), ice-related research at BIO focussed on pack ice and iceberg properties along the coasts of eastern Canada from Baffin Bay south to the Gulf of St. Lawrence and Newfoundland. Both ships and helicopters were used to monitor the environmental properties that could potentially affect the safety and efficiency of oil and gas development along the Canadian east coast. During the late 1980s, specially designed satellite-tracked ice beacons were deployed on the pack ice with helicopters to monitor pack ice and near-surface ocean water properties. The drift patterns recorded from the ice beacons verified what was observed from satellite imagery. Since the early 1990s, helicopter-borne sensors have provided additional information on the properties of the snow and ice comprising the mobile ice cover of both eastern Canada and the Beaufort Sea (Peterson et al. 2008, Prinsenberg et al. 2011). These surveys provided information for safe and efficient oil and gas developments, validated iceberg drift and pack ice forecast models, and enhanced our understanding of the processes that contribute to regional pack ice inter-year variability. Our increase in knowledge of the evolution of the pack ice in Canadian waters has contributed to marine habitat studies, development and validation of operational models, environmental inputs to international offshore regulation codes governing operations in Canadian ice-infested waters, and other national and international programs: e.g., Circumpolar Flaw Lead (CFL) project of the International Polar Year (IPY) program (Barber et al. 2010) and seal habitat studies (Bajzak et al. 2011, Iacozza and Barber 2010). All data collected, results of analyses, and conclusions drawn from them are available from the Fisheries and Oceans Canada's (DFO) 'Sea Ice' website (http://www.bio.gc.ca/science-recherche/ocean/ice-glace/index-eng.php).

UNDER-ICE MARINE ECOSYSTEM STUDIES IN THE CANADIAN ARCTIC ARCHIPELAGO (CAA): 1978-82

In the late 1970s and early 1980s, arctic research by the DFO at BIO was focussed on the effects of sea-ice on ocean and atmospheric environments. In the CAA, the atmospheric turbulence and sensible heat fluxes over pack ice and open water were studied near the recurring polynya in the area of Dundas Island and northern Queens Channel (Smith et al. 1983) and the physical and biological interaction of the under-ice ecosystem in Barrow Strait as part of the Arctic Pilot Program. The physical oceanographic observations of currents and density structures beneath the spring ice-cover (Fig. 3A) (Prinsenberg and Bennett 1987) were used by biologists to understand the temporal variability of spring under-ice biological production (Cota et al. 1987) and spring feeding habits of copepods (Conover et al. 1986).

Researchers found that large nutrient fluxes are required to produce the dense ice algae mats observed over the two-month spring bloom and that these fluxes were sustained by bi-weekly tidal mixing (Fig. 3B). When biomass levels were high in the later part of the spring bloom, ice-algae populations experienced cyclic conditions of nutrient limitation during neap tides when nutrient fluxes due to tidal mixing were minimal. These dense ice-algae mats seem to attract high aggregations of arctic copepods beneath the ice cover, and it was observed that copepod abundance and their gut pigment index corresponded with the tidal cycle (Conover et al. 1986). The results indicate that arctic copepods seem to feed opportunistically near the ice-water interface, either directly on the attached ice algae or on the algal mat as it erodes from the ice. Only a multi-disciplinary program could have determined that the variability of the spring ice algae bloom and the feeding habits of arctic copepods could be explained clearly by the bi-weekly tidal mixing that generated the required nutrient flux.

Figure 3. Measurements in Barrow Strait, March 1981: (A) Temperature, salinity, and current meter profiler used to collect physical environmental time series data for marine ecosystem studies; (B) Vacuum glass sphere used to collect nutrient samples lowered through an augured ice hole with a helicopter-portable CTD winch (photos: S. Prinsenberg).

SHIP SUPPORTED ICEBERG SURVEYS ALONG THE NEWFOUNDLAND COAST: 1983-85

In the early 1980s, with funding support from the Program of Energy Research and Development (PERD), BIO ice research focus shifted from the CAA to Atlantic Canada. Ships were used during three consecutive summers (1983-85) to document the physical and drift-track characteristics of icebergs along the eastern Newfoundland shelf and to record the regional atmospheric and oceanographic conditions that might explain the observed iceberg drift tracks. A dynamic model was developed that simulated iceberg drift trajectories forced by winds and currents using observed iceberg size and shape (Smith 1993). Employing local observed wind, oceanographic conditions, and the shape and orientation of the icebergs, the model was able to assess their drift tracks and confirm the influence of the forces and physical characteristics that govern iceberg drift. This complete data set, established from three summers of research, continues to be used in the development of operational iceberg drift models to evaluate model improvements.

During the same three-year ship surveys, visual estimates of ice concentrations and floe size distribution were made upwind from the ship. These observations, along with wind profiles collected on the ship, were used to establish the wind-drag coefficient as a function of ice type and concentration. It was found that the coefficient is highest in the marginal ice zone when the ice concentration was 8/10 cover consisting of brash ice (sea ice fragments <2 m across) and small floes (pieces of floating sea ice with diameters of 2-100 m) that effectively doubled the drag coefficient by increasing the form drag (more ice edges per unit area) and by increasing the thermodynamic ice drag due to updrafts over the numerous open water areas (Anderson 1987). Further wind-drag coefficient research was done in the southern Gulf of St. Lawrence in the winter of 1998-99; a helicopter-borne laser rangefinder/altimeter was used to determine pack ice roughness around a site where satellite-tracked ice beacons collected wind-profile data to a height of 6 m (Prinsenberg and Peterson 2001). It was found that the wind drag coefficient varied by an order of magnitude from smooth ice with above-freezing air temperatures to rough ice with below-freezing temperatures. Thus, in the same wind conditions, ice pressure against the shore or an offshore structure could also vary by an order of magnitude, as was the case with iceberg drift characteristics. The physics of the wind-drag coefficient is now well understood, and variable-drag coefficients for ice-ocean models may become available in future through inputs based on the increasing capability of remote sensing to classify ice types and ice roughness.

HELICOPTER DEPLOYMENT OF SATELLITE-TRACKING ICE BEACONS: 1983-95

Although icebergs are the main hazards for oil and gas operations in eastern Canadian coastal waters, pack ice also rates high when it is in high concentration, thick, and under pressure. Pack ice also hinders any iceberg management work. In the mid-1980s, winter pack ice and ocean properties were studied using satellite-tracked ice beacons deployed with helicopters that could quickly and cost-effectively cover the large extent of the Labrador pack ice. The surveys deployed a variety of BIO-designed and -built ice beacons that monitored ice and water temperature profiles, ice pressures, along with ice floe drift rates. All data were transmitted back in real-time to BIO via satellite transmission systems. During deployment of the beacons the ocean water structure was sampled using salinity-temperature (CTD) probes deployed through augured ice holes (Fig. 4). Additional data on ice drift patterns beyond the range of beacons was obtained by remote sensing which revealed a strong topographic steering effect on ocean currents over the Labrador shelf (Peterson 1987). Ice beacons provided data on the thermal structure and growth of shore-fast ice (Peterson et al. 1991), and showed that the rate of heat released due to new ice growth was nearly equal to the heat conducted upward through the ice, indicating that oceanic heat flux was negligible.

Several other satellite-tracked ice beacons were designed and built at BIO; some designs were transferred to the marine industry in Nova Scotia. Global Positioning System (GPS) location beacons equipped with chains of water temperature sensors and ice temperature profile staves provided data on ice and water temperatures, and on pack-ice convergence as ice moved south along the Labrador coast to the Grand Banks of Newfoundland. A total of 43 beacons were deployed during the winters of 1985 to 1989 (Peterson and Symonds 1988). The data for winter 1988-89 contributed to the international Labrador Ice Margin Experiment (LIMEX'89) that was designed to prepare for the optimal use of microwave data from new satellites. During the colder-than-normal LIMEX'89 winter, pack ice moved up to 75 km per day southwards and up to 23 km per day offshore under the influence of northwesterly winds

Figure 4. Helicopter operations in March 1988 on the Labrador shelf pack-ice showing an ice-auger hole being drilled for salinity-temperature profile sampling and deployment of an ice beacon (orange device in foreground).

where it melted in the warmer Labrador Sea. The offshore ice movement increased ice growth inshore, stimulating vertical mixing due to salt rejection from the growing sea ice (Prinsenberg et al. 1991, Prinsenberg and Peterson 1992). Ice-edge melt rates were found to increase linearly with offshore ice-drift rates perpendicular to the ice edge, and this melting required a mean heat flux of 340 watts per m^2 (Prinsenberg and Peterson 1992, Prinsenberg et al. 1991). In contrast, earlier ice-ocean models for the Atlantic seaboard used monthly mean values of only 35 watts per m^2 to predict seaward ice extent (Ikeda et al. 1988).

Besides extreme ice thicknesses, ice pressure within the pack ice represents a hazard to navigation and to iceberg management operations. Several ice beacon designs to monitor ice pressure were built and tested off eastern Canada with mixed success (Fig. 5A). To determine the ice pressure between floes as felt by ships from a single measurement in the centre of the floe is difficult, as floe shapes keep changing. For Labrador coastal land-fast ice, ice pressure was found to jointly depend linearly on wind force that was driving offshore mobile ice towards shore, and on air temperature since colder ice is stronger and more capable of transmitting larger ice pressures (Prinsenberg et al. 1997). Changes in drift rate and direction, and ice concentration can be inferred indirectly from ice convergence, as seen both by the relative movement of multiple GPS beacons and in satellite imagery (Prinsenberg et al. 1998), but so far this appears to be the only means to indicate when ice pressure events are occurring.

HELICOPTER-BORNE ICE PROPERTY SENSORS: 1991-2012

In the early 1990s, a unique Canadian-designed and -assembled suite of helicopter-borne sensors became available to monitor pack-ice properties to complement on-ice sampling and the deployment of ice beacons (Peterson et al. 2003). The suite comprises three main parts: an electromagnetic sensor (EM), a ground-penetrating radar sensor (GPR), and a video-camera system that incorporates a laser altimeter. First, a towed EM system called 'Ice Probe' was used (Fig. 5B), followed in the early 2000s by a fixed EM system called 'Ice Pic', which was mounted as a tubular projection on the front of the helicopter (Fig. 5C). The systems were first employed in co-operation with the Canadian Ice Service (CIS) to evaluate the accuracy of ice thicknesses displayed on ice charts, and ice signatures seen in satellite imagery. Data collected during ice surveys were sent directly to the CIS for incorporation into ice chart production. This work with CIS personnel enhanced the quality of sea-ice products provided to offshore marine operators. An example of helicopter-EM ice thickness data overlain on a satellite image is shown in Figure 6.

The 'Ice Pic' collects data along narrow swaths beneath the aircraft. The laser altimeter provides surface roughness profiles and the height of the EM sensor above the pack ice. Since the EM sensor measures the distance to the ocean surface water, together they provide the snow-plus-ice thickness at a sampling interval of 3-4 m. The GPR, developed during the past decade, measures snow thickness or fresh water ice thickness at a sampling interval of approximately 1.0-1.5 m (Lalumiere and Prinsenberg 2009). The video digital camera provides data on lead and ridge distributions and orientations, and on floe size distributions along the helicopter flight path.

During the Canadian Atlantic Storm Program (CASPII) in 1992, the EM sensor provided data sets off the Newfoundland coast to evaluate the accuracy of ice thickness shown on ice charts (Carrieres et al. 1996). The ice charts were found to represent well the undeformed level ice thicknesses and composite floe sizes, but lacked details about the degree of rafting, ridging, and rubble field conditions, all ice hazards to marine navigation. The data also aided in the evaluation of ice signatures seen in the National Oceanic and Atmospheric Administration's Advanced Very High Resolution Radiometer (NOAA/AVHRR) and European Remote-Sensing Satellite's Synthetic Aperture Radar (ERS-1/SAR) imagery (Prinsenberg et al. 1996). Ice thickness and surface roughness data covering several hundred kilometres of flight path were used to evaluate and confirm the change in pack-ice properties from thin, smooth, coastal ice, and open water conditions to thick, rough, consolidated offshore pack ice shown on ice charts produced with inputs from AVHRR and ERS-1 imagery and fixed-wing aircraft reconnaissance observations.

Figure 5. Variety of ice measurement equipment and study procedures: (A) Deploying ice pressure beacons off the Labrador Coast, 6 March 1993 – G. Fowler (left), B. Beanlands (right) and Canadian Coast Guard helicopter and pilot R. Moores in background (photo: S. Prinsenberg); (B) Universal helicopter towing ice property EM-laser sensor called 'Ice Probe' shown in operation during the Canadian Atlantic Storm Program CASPII off northern Newfoundland, March 1992 (photo: S. Prinsenberg); and (C) CCG helicopter with the fixed EM ice thickness probe 'Ice Pic' (tubular projection at front of helicopter) on a small ice-island fragment west of Banks Island in August 2011 – D. Barber (left) and S. Prinsenberg (right) drilling an ice hole to deploy an ice beacon (photo: D. Boisvert).

ICE-OCEAN INTERACTION PROCESSES: 2000-10

During the 2000-10 decade, ice research at BIO continued to support the evaluation of ice signatures seen in imagery of new satellites such as

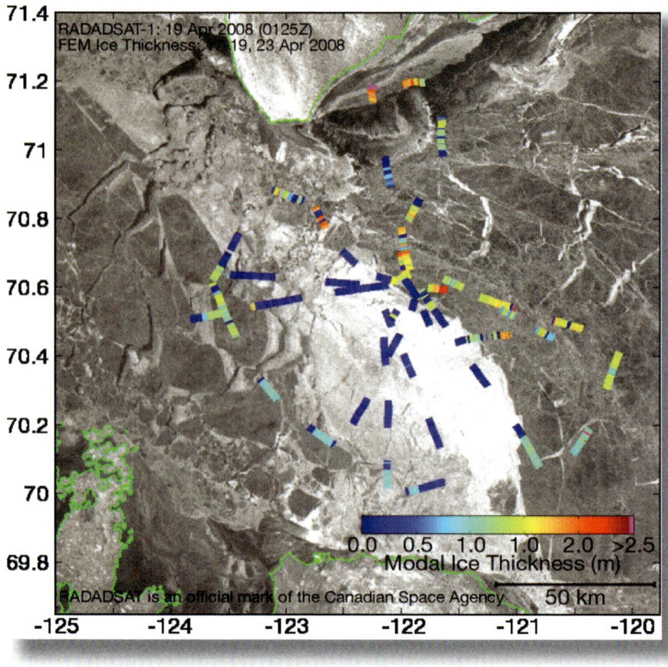

Figure 6. RADARSAT image (180 km x 180 km) of the Amundsen Gulf area from 19 April 2008 overlain with modal ice thickness observations from 19 and 22 April 2008. The modal (most frequently occurring) thickness is plotted in rectangles along the flight path according to the colour scale. Green lines show the coast lines of Banks Island (top) and of Cape Parry (bottom). The ice-rubble field sampled is adjacent to the dark land-fast ice along the southern coast of Banks Island (image courtesy of MacDonald, Dettwiler & Associates Limited).

Environmental Satellite (ENVISAT) of the European Space Agency and Synthetic Aperture Radar Satellites (RADARSAT-1 and RADARSAT-2) of the Canadian Space Agency. Ice observations, all collected by the helicopter-borne sensors 'Ice Pic' and 'Video-laser', were used to study ice-ocean interaction processes (some discussed below) that affect the evolution of pack ice and cause inter-year variability in ice extent.

The first of the process studies was the formation of an ice-rubble field when the thin ice of a flaw lead, a narrow separation zone with thinner ice between mobile pack ice and land-fast ice, is forced into land-fast ice by thicker offshore pack ice and is crushed between the two ice masses. This process was observed during the 2008 Circumpolar Flaw Lead (CFL) project in the Canadian Beaufort Sea (Barber et al. 2010). Strong northwest winds had opened an 18 km wide flaw lead south of Banks Island on which ice grew over 22 days to 60 cm in thickness. During a southeast wind storm, the thicker pack ice forced the newly frozen flaw lead into the land-fast ice of Banks Island forming a linear 1.5 km-wide, 10 m-thick ice-rubble field that was documented with helicopter-borne sensors. The RADARSAT image in Figure 6 shows that the wind had reversed during the survey flight and a new flaw lead had opened offshore in the rubble field attached to the Banks Island land-fast ice.

The EM ice-thickness profile shows two rubble-field transects towards and away from Banks Island; in the crossings the rubble fields are 1.4 km wide and 8-10 m thick on average (Fig. 7). Between these two crossings, the original land-fast ice of Banks Island (1.4-1.6 m thick) was sampled while the helicopter turned to re-cross the rubble field. Small remnants of the original 60 cm thick flaw lead can be seen in the dashed circled area of Figure 7. The closing of flaw leads by pack ice deformation results in dynamic ice thickness growth, rather than thermodynamic

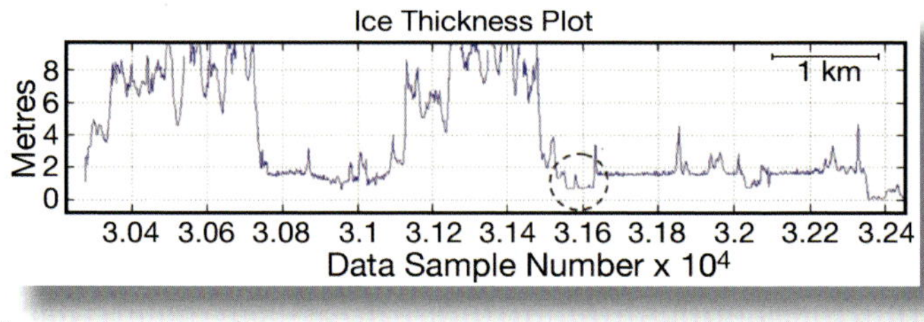

Figure 7. Ice thickness line profile data collected on 22 April 2008 traversing the rubble field twice, one acquired on a flight path towards Banks Island and one on a path leaving the island (Fig. 6). The relatively narrow band of thin ice (dashed circle) is all that remains of the 60-cm thick, 18 km-wide flaw lead.

growth by freezing. The opening and freezing of flaw leads injects dense brine into a large local area of the ocean surface layer due to salt rejection from the growing ice which promotes local vertical mixing and possibly ocean-eddy formation.

The second process was observed in the summer of 2009, when data collected by the helicopter-borne sensors documented the break-up of arctic pack-ice (large 2-3 km wide floes) into small floes by long-period waves generated by a distant storm. At noon on 6 September 2009, the icebreaker CCGS *Amundsen* was heaving very slowly due to the influence of long-period waves (13.5 sec) coming from the northwest. Video data of ice west of Banks Island from 6 September 2009 documented the start of the wave-induced break-up process (Prinsenberg and Peterson 2011). The half-wave length, inferred from observations of broken floe sizes agreed with the expected half-wave length (140 m) of an ice-deforming 13.5 s period wave (Wadhams and Boble 2009).

By 9 September 2009, after two days in which waves grew in amplitude with shorter periods and wavelengths, all the pack ice up to 300 km from the seaward boundary was broken into floes of less than 100 m diameter with most floes 50 m across (Fig. 8). This important process increases the presence of open leads within the pack ice, thereby enhancing summer heat input to the ocean and accelerating ice melt. This positive feed-back mechanism for summer pack-ice decay is enhanced further with the growth of open water areas where strong winds can generate long-period waves that are capable of penetrating great distances into the ice pack (Prinsenberg and Peterson 2011).

A third process, observed with the helicopter-borne sensors during the Labrador coast survey in March 2009, describes the decrease of snow thickness over ice in an offshore direction, as snow is increasingly blown into and trapped in leads (Prinsenberg et al. 2011). Several distinct signatures of the snow and ice cover, verified by observations, can be seen in a RADARSAT image (Fig. 9). Offshore, there is a bright homogeneous region consisting of very small floes; then inshore of this is a region with a mixture of dark areas and moderately-bright areas where larger floes and leads occurred. Farther inshore are other bright regions where small-scale ice roughness features and regions of thin ice were observed; on top of the thin ice were remnants of small-scale 'frost flowers', consisting of ice crystals extruded above the ice surface. Just offshore of the land-fast ice, several large dark areas appear representing open water and scattered frazil ice (i.e., fine plates of thin ice suspended in water).

GPR snow-depth data from the homogeneous offshore area shows that very little snow (15-20 cm mean depth) was present on these small floes. Some floes still had snow dune patterns remaining on them with thicknesses up to 40-50 cm (Fig. 10). However, much of the snow is lost to this old pack ice as it is blown into the cracks and frazil ice between the floes. On the land-fast ice, the deepest snow dunes (50 cm) were observed over the rougher ice sections as compared with the smoother land-fast ice regions which are less bright in the RADARSAT imagery.

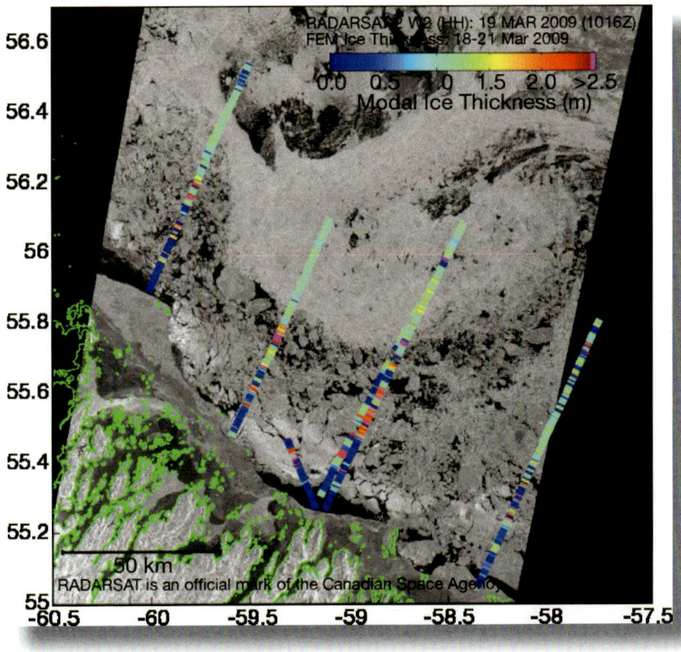

Figure 9. RADARSAT-2 image (180 km x 180 km) of 19 March 2009 covering the mid-Labrador Shelf overlain with modal ice thickness data (collected 19-20 March 2009 with the 'Ice Pic'). The modal (most frequently occurring) thickness is plotted in rectangles along the flight path according to the shown colour scale (image courtesy of MacDonald, Dettwiler and Associates Limited).

EM data from the Labrador Shelf, shown as overlain data in Figure 9, also implied that young ridges on large floes break down into their component blocks as large floes break up due to surface wave action. This process appears to occur because the cohesion between ridge blocks is apparently not strong enough to maintain ridge profiles of any significance. The onset of the ice-melt season seems to trigger the breakdown of first-year ice ridges into their component parts when rising air and water temperatures provide sufficient heat for melting (Prinsenberg and Peterson 2011).

PACK ICE VARIABILITY: 2004-11

Large inter-year pack ice variability caused by atmospheric fluctuations has been documented for two areas where repeated surveys took place: the Amundsen Gulf (eastern Canadian Beaufort Sea) for winters 2004 and 2008, and the Labrador Shelf for winters 2009 and 2011.

The 2008 Amundsen Gulf data, which revealed reduced pack ice conditions (Fig. 6), were collected during the international CFL project. The 2004 data, which represented more severe ice conditions, were acquired during the Canadian Arctic Shelf Exchange Study (CASES) (Fortier and Barber 2008). Monthly mean air temperatures from November to April were 1 to 5°C warmer during 2007-08 as compared with 2003-04. In addition, monthly mean wind directions were biased towards the west during 2007-08 which pushed ice out of Amundsen Gulf. Thus, the combined influence of warmer conditions, which reduced ice growth, and more persistent winds to the west, which increased ice transport out of the Gulf, resulted in reduced pack-ice conditions. Satellite images

Figure 8. Fractured pack ice on 9 September 2009 (1200 h), viewed from 150 m altitude west of Banks Island at 72.52°N, 136.43°W. Some of the turquoise-coloured melt ponds on the multi-year ice fragments can still be seen (photo: S. Prinsenberg).

Figure 10. Mosaic of five overlapping video frames (widths: 130 m) showing the wave-broken floes and 'grease' ice between them where blowing snow is continually trapped and lost from the offshore pack ice, March 2009.

from the Amundsen Gulf confirm these differences in the overall pack-ice conditions for the two winters. In 2008, consolidated ice was found only close to shore or in small bays in the northern and southern parts of the image, whereas in 2004, young ice was present only in the western half of the image with the pack ice in the eastern half consolidated and fixed, anchored in place by an ice arch between the southern tip of Banks Island and Cape Parry (Fig. 6).

The different winter ice conditions of 2004 and 2008 are illustrated also by variation in ice thickness distributions between the two seasons. Ice thickness histograms show a large proportion (35%) of thin ice (less than 20 cm) and open water for 2008 versus only 2% for 2004 (Fig. 11). Both histograms show a bi-modal structure representing two ice-thickness peaks: older, thicker ice and younger, thinner ice with a common separation of 40 cm. The difference from 2004 to 2008 is seen as a shift to thinner ice of both modal peaks. The lower-thickness modal peaks are interpreted as being caused by thermodynamic ice-growth, whereas most of the ice thicknesses beyond 190 cm in 2003-04 and 150 cm in 2007-08 are thought to have been caused by dynamic pack-ice deformation (rafting and ridging). The thinner ice in 2008 can be partially explained by the fact the 2008 winter was warmer, in general, and the pack ice could not have attained as great a maximum thickness in 2008 as in 2004 through thermodynamic ice growth alone. Analysis of this region showed that the intermittent removal of pack ice by export or deformation due to strong winds to the west generated large open-water regions where younger, thinner ice formed throughout the ice season. Because winds to the west were stronger and temperatures were warmer throughout the winter of 2008, ice was thinner, and more of it was exported from Amundsen Gulf, thereby explaining most of the variation between the ice thickness histograms for 2004 and 2008 (Fig. 11).

A similar data set was collected off the Labrador shelf during the winters of 2009 and 2011 (Fig. 12). The 2009 data are shown as an overlay on a RADARSAT image in Figure 9. Monthly mean air temperatures and westerly surface wind components from the Labrador Shelf are used as indicators of the difference in atmospheric forcing on ice conditions in the two winters. For the Labrador Shelf in normal winters such as 2008-09, winds from the west enhance southward ice drift and bring colder air to the region. During December and January, the early months of winter, air temperatures are still relatively warm and local ice growth is mini-

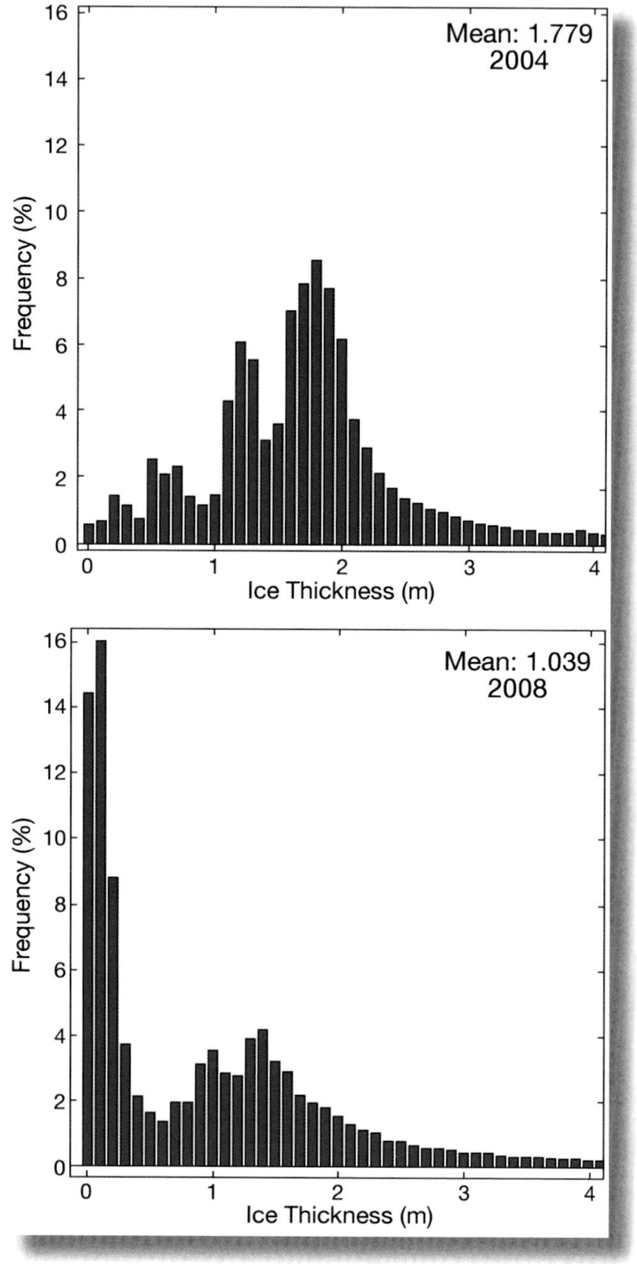

Figure 11. Ice thickness histograms of EM profile data collected in the Amundsen Gulf during the winter of 2004 (upper) and 2008 (lower).

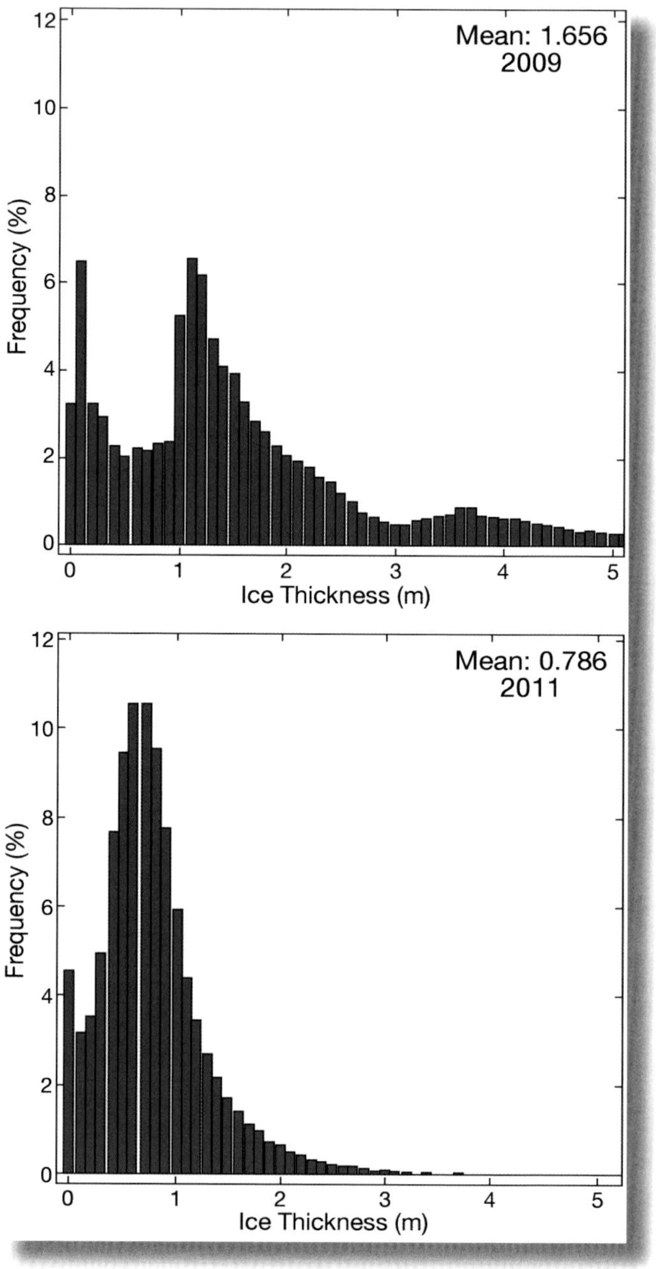

Figure 12. Ice thickness histograms of EM profile data collected off the Labrador coast over the mobile pack-ice during March 2009 (upper) and 2011 (lower).

mal, so ice thickness at this time is due mainly to ice transported into the region from more northerly latitudes. A reduced occurrence of westerly winds in December 2010 and January 2011 relative to the 2008-09 winter caused a reduction of ice transport into the Labrador Shelf area from more northern regions, leading to a marked difference in histogram distributions of ice thickness (thinner ice overall in 2011) between the two winters (Fig. 12).

The histograms show several significant differences between the 'normal' winter of 2009 and the warmer winter of 2011. Relative to 2009, the mean ice thicknesses were reduced by half. Similarly, the modal (most frequently occurring) ice thickness was reduced from 1.0-1.1 m in 2009 to 0.6-0.7 m in 2011. Another difference was the lack of any ridged ice with thicknesses greater than 3 m in 2011 compared with 2009. Very little ridging appeared to have survived the break-up of the pack ice by waves in 2011, or was even present on the larger consolidated floes. Thus, considering ice thickness alone and ignoring the reduced ice extent in 2011, the ice volume off the mid-Labrador Shelf in 2011 would have been half of that present in 2009.

The thinner and lower ice extent in 2011 resulted from the fact that the months of December 2010 and January 2011 were much warmer as winds from the southeast occurred more frequently than colder winds from the northwest. Not only was ice growth reduced during warmer southeasterly wind periods, but these winds also impeded southward ice transport along the Labrador coast. Both influences delayed and reduced ice severity in the early winter off the Labrador coast in 2011 relative to 2009; even the effect of colder temperatures in the month of February 2011 was not enough to reverse the situation.

CONCLUSIONS

The study of sea-borne ice in its various forms is much like the weather, a messy business – an unpredictable and chaotic system. Complexity hardly begins to describe the nature of the inter-relationships and processes that govern its generation, propagation, transport, accretion, disintegration, and eventual disappearance. Add to this the difficulty of actually making observations or measurements that are meaningful and practical in an environment that is both hostile and inaccessible for much of the time it is easy to appreciate why modelling the nature of sea ice is so fashionable, and because of all its intricacies, so satisfying. Fieldwork is, of course, neither. But fieldwork is absolutely essential if we are to have the validation data to enhance forecast models and to understand the ice-ocean-atmosphere interaction processes that govern their physics.

Seasonally based sea-ice research has enhanced our knowledge of the annual and inter-annual ice regimes of both Arctic and Eastern Canada. Studies have ranged from discrete biological perspectives where the examination of under-ice marine ecosystems revealed a dependence on the temporal variability of tidal mixing to wide ranging ship surveys of the Newfoundland Shelf. These latter operations resulted in a unique 3-year data set collection of environmental regional conditions, along with the physical and drift properties of icebergs. This complete data set is the only information available to test improvements in iceberg drift models. Although this dataset has proved useful in this region, there is still a need for additional studies of this kind to enhance our prediction capability, and to apply the knowledge gained to other areas of interest. Long-term studies are indispensable if we are to come to grips with the long-term challenges posed by climate change.

Wind profile data from ship surveys and similar data collected by ice beacons have shown that the wind-ice drag coefficient used in ice-ocean forecast models varies greatly with ice concentration and ice roughness (Anderson 1987, Prinsenberg and Peterson 2001). Further research is ongoing to identify the influence of ice concentration and ice roughness on the wind-ice drag coefficient, whether the coefficient can be determined through remote sensing, and how it may be assimilated into ice-ocean forecast models. Data from various types of BIO-designed ice beacons have enhanced our understanding of the interaction of ice, ocean, and atmospheric conditions that determine the inter-annual variability of ice extent and ocean mixed-layer properties along the Labrador and Newfoundland shelves. Designs of these beacons have been transferred to east coast marine industries.

Innovative helicopter-borne sensors have been developed by Canadian private industry for BIO. As a direct result of their application, validation data are available to permit insight into several ice-snow regional processes that affect the formation and development of arctic pack ice. In this paper, we have presented observations for three regional processes: the break-up of arctic pack ice by long-period waves, the rubble field formation when flaw leads are crushed, and the offshore reduction of snow depths owing to the presence of open-water regions. In addition, through repeated surveys, it was possible to show that warmer air temperatures and changes in mean wind directions are responsible for the observed large inter-year variability in sea ice properties seen over the Labrador Shelf and in the Amundsen Gulf, eastern Beaufort Sea. These data and their interpretation are enhancing our knowledge of the pack ice in Canadian waters, as are the highly-regarded observation technologies being developed. Furthermore, the data have been included as environmental inputs in international offshore regulation codes governing operations in Canadian coastal waters, and are used to validate short-term forecast, climate models, and to support national and international marine habitat studies.

ACKNOWLEDGEMENTS

The authors would like to thank Dave Barber, leader of the CFL program, and Louis Fortier, leader of the CASES program along with the ship and helicopter crews, in supporting and assisting the field programs run from the CCGS *Amundsen*. The success of the various field surveys dependent on the excellent logistic and field support the surveys received from the Polar Continental Shelf out of Resolute Bay, from the Canadian Helicopter Company out of Inuvik and Goose Bay, and from the CCGS *Hudson* and Canadian Coast Guard helicopter crew out of Charlottetown, Prince Edward Island. This work was financially supported by the Canadian Program of Energy Research Development, the Canadian Space program, and the Environmental Studies Research Funds.

REFERENCES

Anderson, R.J. 1987. Wind stress measurements over rough ice during the 1984 Marginal Ice Zone Experiment. Journal of Geophysical Research 9: 6,933-6,941.

Bajzak, C.E., M.O. Hammill, G.B. Stenson, and S. Prinsenberg. 2011. Drifting away: implication of changes in ice conditions for a pack-ice-breeding phocid, the harp seal (*Pagophilus groenlandicus*). Canadian Journal of Zoology 89: 1,050-1,062.

Barber, D.G., M.G. Asplin, Y. Gratton, J.V. Lukovich, R.J. Galley, R.L. Raddatz, and D. Leith. 2010. The International Polar Year (IPY) circumpolar flaw lead (CFL) system study: Overview and the physical system. Atmosphere-Ocean 48: 255-243.

Carrieres, T., B. Greenan, S. Prinsenberg, and I.K. Peterson. 1996. Comparison of Canadian daily ice chart with surface observations off Newfoundland, winter 1992. Atmosphere-Ocean 34: 207-226.

Cota, G.F., S.J. Prinsenberg, E.B. Bennett, J.W. Loder, M.R. Lewis, J.L. Anning, N.H.F. Watson, and L.R. Harris. 1987. Nutrient fluxes during extended blooms of Arctic ice algae. Journal Geophysical Research 92: 1,951-1,962.

Conover, R.J., A.W. Herman, S.J. Prinsenberg, and L.R. Harris. 1986. Distribution of the feeding by the copepod *Pseudocalanus* under fast ice during the arctic spring. Science 232: 1,245-1,247.

Fortier, L. and D.G. Barber. 2008. An introduction to the Canadian Arctic Shelf Exchange Study. Pages 1-11 *in* On Thin Ice: a Synthesis of the Canadian Arctic Shelf Exchange Study (D. Barber, L. Fortier, and J. Michaud, Eds.). Aboriginal Issues Press, Winnipeg, MB.

Ikeda, M., G. Symonds, and T. Yao. 1988. Simulated fluctuations in the annual Labrador sea-ice cover. Atmosphere-Ocean 26: 16-39.

Iacozza J. and D.G. Barber. 2010. An examination of snow redistribution over smooth land-fast sea ice. Hydrological Processes 24: 850-865.

IPCC (International Panel on Climate Change). 2007. Climate Change 2007: Synthesis Report. Contribution of Working Groups I, II and III to the Fourth Assessment Report of the Intergovernmental Panel on Climate Change (R.K. Pachauri and A. Reisinger, Eds.). International Panel on Climate Change, Geneva, Switzerland.

Kwok, R. and D.A. Rothrock. 2009. Decline in Arctic sea ice thickness from submarine and ICESat records: 1958-2008. Geophysical Research Letters 36, L1,15501. doi:10.1029/2009GL039035.

Lalumiere L. and S. Prinsenberg. 2009. Integration of a helicopter-based ground penetrating radar (GPR) with a laser, video and GPS system. Pages 658-665 *in* The Proceedings of the 19th International Offshore and Polar Engineering Conference, Osaka, Japan, 21-26 June 2009, Volume 1 (J.S. Chung, S. Prinsenberg, S.W. Hong, and S. Nagata, Eds.). International Society of Offshore and Polar Engineers (ISOPE), Cupertino, CA.

Peterson I.K. 1987. A snapshot of the Labrador Current inferred from ice-floe movement in NOAA satellite imagery. Atmosphere-Ocean 25: 402-415.

Peterson I.K. and G. Symonds. 1988. Ice floe trajectories off Labrador and eastern Newfoundland: 1985-1987. Canadian Technical Report of Hydrography and

Ocean Sciences 104, Dartmouth, NS.
Peterson I.K., S.D. Smith, S.J. Prinsenberg, and R.H. Orton. 1991. Remote monitoring of the thermal structure and growth of shore-fast ice off the Labrador coast. Cold Regions Science and Technology 19: 123-130.
Peterson I.K., S.J. Prinsenberg, and J.S. Holladay. 2003. Sea-ice thickness measurement: recent experiments using helicopter-borne electromagnetic systems. Recent Research Developments in Geophysics 5: 1-20.
Peterson I.K., S.J. Prinsenberg, and J.S. Holladay. 2008. Observations of sea ice thickness, surface roughness and ice motion in Amundsen Gulf. Journal of Geophysical Research 113. (C06016) doi:10.1029/JC004456.
Prinsenberg, S.J. and E.B. Bennett. 1987. Mixing and transports in Barrow Strait, the central part of the Northwest passage. Continental Shelf Research 7: 913-935.
Prinsenberg, S.J., I.K. Peterson, and G.A. Fowler. 1991. Estimates of ice edge melt rates off Labrador and Eastern Newfoundland, Canada. Annals of Glaciology 15: 163-170.
Prinsenberg, S.J. and I.K. Peterson. 1992. Sea-ice properties off Labrador and Newfoundland during LIMEX'89. Atmosphere-Ocean 30: 207-222.
Prinsenberg, S.J., I.K. Peterson, and S. Holladay. 1996. Comparison of airborne electromagnetic ice thickness data with NOAA/AVHRR and ERS-1/SAR images. Atmosphere-Ocean 34: 185-205.
Prinsenberg, S.J., G.A. Fowler, A. van der Baaren, and B. Beanlands. 1997. Ice stress measurements from land-fast ice along Canada's Labrador coast. Cold Regions Science and Technology 25: 1-15.
Prinsenberg, S.J., G.A. Fowler, and A. van der Baaren 1998. Pack ice convergence measurements by GPS-ARGOS ice beacons. Cold Regions Science and Technology 28: 59-72.
Prinsenberg, S.J. and I.K. Peterson. 2001. Variations in air-drag coefficient due to ice-surface roughness. International Journal of Offshore and Polar Engineering 12: 121-125.
Prinsenberg, S.J. and I.K. Peterson. 2011. Observing regional-scale pack-ice decay processes with helicopter-borne sensors and moored upward-looking sonars. Annals of Glaciology 52: 35-42.
Prinsenberg S.J., I.K. Peterson, S. Holladay, and L. Lalumiere. 2011. Observing the snow and ice properties over the Labrador shelf with helicopter-borne ground-penetrating radar, laser and electromagenetic sensors. POAC11-180. Pages 150-162 *in* Proceedings of the 21st International Conference on Port and Ocean Engineering under Arctic Conditions, Vol. 1, 10-14 July 2011, Montreal, Quebec. National Research Council of Canada, Ottawa, ON.
Serreze, M.C., M.M. Holland, and J. Stroeve. 2007. Perspectives on the Arctic's shrinking sea-ice cover. Science 315: 1,533-1,536.
Smith, S.D. 1974. Oceanographic investigations during the AIJEX lead experiment Bulletin 27. Division of Marine Research, University of Washington, Seattle, WA.
Smith, S.D., R.J. Anderson, G. den Hertog, D.R. Topham, and R.G. Perkin. 1983. An investigation of a polynya in the Canadian archipelago, 2. Structure of turbulence and sensible heat flux. Journal of Geophysical Research 88: 2,900-2,910.
Smith, S.D. 1993. Hind casting iceberg drift using current profiles and winds. Cold Regions Science and Technology 22: 33-45.
Tivy, A., S.E.L. Howell, B. Alt, S. Court, R. Chagnon, G. Crocker, T. Carrieres, and J.J. Yackel. 2011. Trends and variability in summer sea ice cover in the Canadian Arctic based on the Canadian Ice Service Digital Archive, 1960-2008 and 1968-2008. Journal of Geophysical Research 116 (C03007). doi:10.1029/2009JC005855.
Wadhams, P. and M.J. Boble. 2009. Sea ice thickness measurement using episodic infragravity waves from distant storms. Cold Regions Science and Technology 56: 98-101.

7. RADIOACTIVITY STUDIES IN THE ARCTIC OCEAN FROM ICE CAMPS, ICEBREAKERS, PLANES, AND SUBMARINES: 1981-2012

John N. Smith

SUMMARY

The Arctic Ocean represents a remote and potentially hostile environment in which to conduct oceanographic research and as a result has been one of the last major oceanographic regimes to undergo scientific exploration. Among other types of investigations, scientists at the Bedford Institute of Oceanography (BIO) have been carrying out radionuclide tracer measurements in the Arctic Ocean since the first baseline studies were conducted in the early 1980s. The main research objectives were to: (1) establish time scales and pathways for water circulation, (2) determine fluxes for particulate carbon and contaminant transport, and (3) study the effects of climate change on biogeochemical parameters. The history of radionuclide measurements in the Arctic Ocean parallels the much broader history of arctic oceanography in general. The first studies were carried out through ice holes carved from drifting ice stations, while more recent studies have been conducted from icebreakers, twin-otter aircraft, and submarines. This paper outlines the chronologies of BIO radionuclide studies in the Arctic Ocean with the intention of providing insight into their scope and scientific impacts.

Key words: Arctic, radionuclide, tracer, circulation, contaminants.

E-mail: John.Smith@dfo-mpo.gc.ca

During the 1980s, many scientific investigations in the Arctic Ocean were carried out from ice stations established on the arctic ice (Livingstone et al. 1984, Smith et al. 1990, Smith and Ellis 1995). Usually a hole would be cut or melted in the ice and a winch would be positioned over the hole so that water, sediment, or biological samples could be collected in the underlying water column. The water and sediment regimes that could be sampled depended entirely on the drift route of the ice field, much as in the days of early arctic exploration in the 19th century when Fridtjof Nansen's *Fram* was deliberately frozen in the arctic ice off the New Siberian Islands in September 1893 in an attempt to drift to the North Pole (Pfirman et al. 2009).

The first Bedford Institute of Oceanography (BIO) radionuclide studies in the central Arctic Ocean were water depth profiles of ^{137}Cs measured in 1981 at the FRAM III Ice Station, located north of Fram Strait (Fig. 1; Smith et al. 1990). The objective was to measure ^{137}Cs that had been discharged from European nuclear fuel reprocessing plants located in the United Kingdom (Sellafield) and France (La Hague) and subsequently transported northward through the Norwegian and Barents seas into the Arctic Ocean. Measurements of Cs isotope ratios revealed that the elevated levels of ^{137}Cs measured at a water depth of 300 m at Fram III (Fig. 1) represented water that had passed across a latitude of 60°N in the North Sea about 2 years previously (ca. 1979). It can be seen from Figure 1 (inset: ^{137}Cs input in Norwegian Coastal Current - NCC) that 1979 represented the beginning of a period of major ^{137}Cs transport into the Arctic Ocean that extended up to the time of the Chernobyl accident in 1986. This 10-year 'pulse' of ^{137}Cs passed through the Arctic Ocean along the continental margin of Russia in a cyclonic (counter clockwise) direction with return flows along the Lomonosov and Mendeleyev ridges towards Fram Strait (Fig. 1: red arrows). It was thought that measurements of the arrival of this ^{137}Cs pulse at various locations in the Arctic Ocean could be used to determine water circulation pathways and time scales in the Arctic Ocean (Livingston et al. 1984).

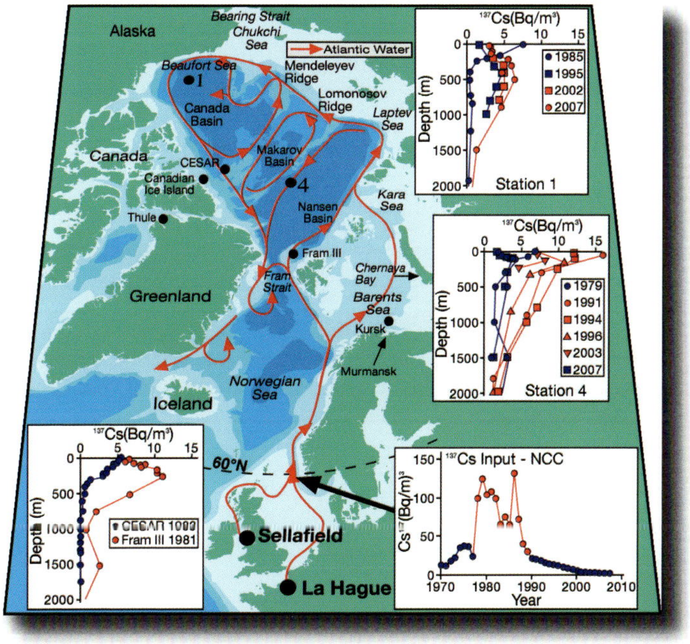

Figure 1. Time series of water depth profiles for ^{137}Cs (Smith et al. 2011) at Station 1 in the southern Canada Basin and at Station 4 at the North Pole. Pre-1990 ^{137}Cs levels at both stations (highlighted in blue) are associated mainly with fallout. The ^{137}Cs input function (bottom right hand side inset) is referenced to 60°N (shown by dashed line). The peak in ^{137}Cs inputs (1979-90: highlighted in red in inset) passed Stations 1 and 4 during the 1990s. By the 2000s ^{137}Cs levels (again, highlighted in blue) begin to decrease at both locations towards their earlier pre-1990 fallout levels. ^{137}Cs profiles in lower left inset for FRAM III (1981) and CESAR (1983) Ice Stations represent the youngest and oldest, respectively, intermediate waters in the Arctic Ocean.

This hypothesis was tested in 1983 when BIO scientists undertook further measurements of radionuclides at the CESAR Ice Station north of the Canadian Archipelago (Fig. 1; Smith and Ellis 1995). The comparatively low ^{137}Cs levels at the CESAR location were due mainly to atmospheric fallout, which indicated that the 1980s pulse from European nuclear fuel reprocessing plants had not yet arrived at this location. An even more extensive suite of radionuclides was subsequently measured in 1985, 1986, and 1989 at the Canadian Ice Island which was a large section of ice that drifted southwestward along the northern coastline of the Canadian Archipelago (Fig. 1) and afforded scientists an opportunity to study arctic oceanographic regimes not previously accessible owing to the thick, multi-year ice cover (for details, see Mudie and Jackson 2014). These various ice camp studies of ^{137}Cs distributions, including those from LOREX (Fig. 1: Station 4) and AIWEX (Fig. 1: Station 1), occupied in 1979 and 1985, respectively, provided some of the first tracer estimates of the transit times (time scales) for the flow of Atlantic Water through the Arctic Ocean (Livingston 1988, Smith and Ellis 1995). The results of additional BIO studies of Arctic Ocean chemistry and circulation are described by Jones (2014).

ARCTIC RADIOACTIVITY CONTAMINATION: ACCIDENTS AND NUCLEAR TESTS, 1984-2000

The second phase of BIO radionuclide studies was driven by international concerns about contamination of the Arctic Ocean from nuclear accidents and the dumping of radioactive wastes. The first major activity was a joint Canadian-Danish investigation in 1984 aboard the CSS *Baffin* of a large plutonium (Pu) spill at Thule, northwest Greenland (Fig. 1), resulting from a crash in 1968 of a United States B-52 bomber carrying nuclear weapons. Several weapons were destroyed upon impact and radioactivity had contaminated the underlying sediments. This study (Smith et al. 1994) identified the presence of a large quantity of plutonium (1 TBq) buried in the sediments, and found it to be largely inert, being slowly mixed downward below the biologically active sediments by natural sedimentation, with minimal impact on local ecosystems.

The experience gained during BIO investigations of the Thule accident proved valuable when environmental concerns were raised about radioactivity contamination of the Russian Arctic Ocean following the demise of the Soviet Union in the early 1990s. In 1992, it was revealed that large quantities of liquid and solid radioactive wastes, including fully fuelled nuclear reactors, had been dumped in the Kara and Barents seas (Fig. 1). In addition, there were concerns about radioactivity leakage from the large Russian nuclear submarine fleet based near Murmansk (Fig. 1), the storage of radioactive wastes on old, rusting, commercial vessels in Murmansk harbour, and the large quantities of radioactivity flowing into the Kara Sea from discharges from upstream nuclear facilities on the Ob and Yenesey rivers. BIO scientists established collaborations with Russian scientists in Murmansk and St. Petersburg that enabled them to undertake the first scientific investigations of ecosystem impacts associated with radioactivity contamination on the island of Novaya Zemlya located between the Barents and Kara seas (Fig. 1), the major Russian nuclear test site in the Arctic Ocean (Smith et al. 1995).

Oceanographic missions were carried out in 1992 and 1993 aboard the RV *Geolog Fersman* which revealed the presence of some of the highest levels of $^{239,240}Pu$ ever measured in the marine environment in the sediments of Chernaya Bay, a small fiord on the southwestern coast of Novaya Zemlya (Fig. 1). Chernaya Bay is a former Soviet Union nuclear weapons test site where underwater nuclear tests were conducted in 1955 and 1957. The low $^{240}Pu/^{239}Pu$ atom ratio (0.03) which characterizes Chernaya Bay plutonium (compared to a fallout value of 0.18) was used to track this signal over distances greater than 100 km into the Barents Sea. At least 2 TBq of $^{239,240}Pu$ had been transported from Chernaya Bay into offshore depositional basins and north-westward along the Novaya Zemlya coastline (Smith et al. 2000). It is also likely that low $^{240}Pu/^{239}Pu$ plutonium from Chernaya Bay has caused some contamination of the central basins of the Arctic Ocean. This work showed significant biological impacts on benthic organisms in Chernaya Bay associated with the high plutonium levels (Smith et al. 2000). These field investigations were led by K. Ellis, well known internationally for her arctic studies, and after whom the Katherine Ellis Laboratory Building was named on the BIO campus in 2008.

In August 2000, the Russian nuclear-powered submarine *Kursk* sank in the Barents Sea (Fig. 1). Within one month, a Canadian-Russian collaboration was initiated with Murmansk and BIO scientists collecting samples of seawater, sediment, and biota from the vicinity of the sunken vessel to assess ecosystem impacts on one of the most productive fishing areas in the world (Matishov et al. 2002). Levels of radioactivity in surface sediments and biota were within the range of values previously measured in the Barents Sea and were ascribed mainly to inputs from global fallout and the Chernobyl accident. However, levels of ^{129}I in seawater in the southern Barents Sea had increased by 500% between 1992 and 2000 owing to long range transport from European nuclear reprocessing facilities (Matishov et al. 2002). Although these results indicated that leakage from the *Kursk* had a negligible impact on the environment, they also showed that regional background levels of radioactivity were varying rapidly on annual time scales and that, somewhat ironically, Europe's nuclear reprocessing facilities were the leading contributor of anthropogenic radioactivity to Russian waters.

Figure 2. Sturgeon class nuclear submarines used in SCICEX program can surface through the ice and establish a temporary ice camp used to sample deep underlying waters and collect benthic fauna and sediments. The photos are a record of the only time the Canadian flag has reached the North Pole by nuclear submarine.

SUBMARINE MISSIONS: 1995-2003

In 1995, BIO scientists were invited to participate in the United States Navy Scientific Ice Experiment (SCICEX) program in the Arctic Ocean which represented the first deployments of warships for unclassified science since the British Royal Navy's 19th century circumnavigations and polar expeditions (Coleman 2007). Sturgeon-class submarines, built to be quiet and mobile for their Navy missions, proved to be exceptionally good science platforms for arctic operations, permitting the first systematic, synoptic oceanographic surveys ever conducted in the deep Arctic Ocean (Smith et al. 1999). BIO scientists developed a program for six SCICEX missions which involved the collection of seawater samples both through the hull of the submarine and at temporary ice camps established when the submarine surfaced through the ice (Fig. 2). These samples were analysed for the radioactive tracers, ^{129}I and ^{137}Cs, derived from European nuclear fuel reprocessing plants and represented a continuation of studies previously conducted from ice stations in the 1980s.

The SCICEX missions occurred at a time of large-scale change in arctic circulation when the Arctic Oscillation (AO) was in a strongly negative phase and Atlantic surface water had spread eastward along the Russian continental shelf into the East Siberian Sea and eastern Makarov Basin. The large pan-Arctic data set from SCICEX showed that a front between Atlantic-origin water having high ^{129}I levels and Pacific-origin water labelled mainly by fallout had shifted from its position during the 1980s when it was aligned with the Lomonosov Ridge to a position in 1995 aligned with the Mendeleyev Ridge (Smith et al. 1998, 1999). This phenomenon was subsequently reproduced in a modelling experiment in which ^{129}I transport through the Arctic Ocean was simulated using a coupled sea ice-ocean model (Karcher et al. 2012). The comparison of model and experimental results for ^{129}I in surface water in 1995 (Fig. 3) illustrates the extent to which Atlantic-origin (green data and higher) and Pacific-origin (pink data) water occupied the surfaces of the eastern and western Arctic Ocean with the front between the two approximately following the 0° to 180° longitude band along the Mendelyev Ridge.

An ^{129}I section from the 1996 USS *Pogy* mission (Fig. 4) was collected through regions of the Canada Basin inaccessible to icebreakers. It showed high levels of ^{129}I over the Lomonosov Ridge which represented the bathymetrically-steered return flow of Atlantic Water towards Fram Strait. Low ^{129}I ($<5 \times 10^7$ at/l) in surface waters of the Canada Basin represented the large pool of Pacific-origin water which had entered the Arctic Ocean through the Bering Strait and Chukchi Sea (Fig. 1) while the elevated ^{129}I levels in underlying intermediate water showed that the interior of the Canada Basin was surprisingly well ventilated owing to boundary current separation and eddy formation near the northern part of the Chukchi Plateau. The extremely low ^{129}I levels ($<1 \times 10^7$ at/l) in intermedi-

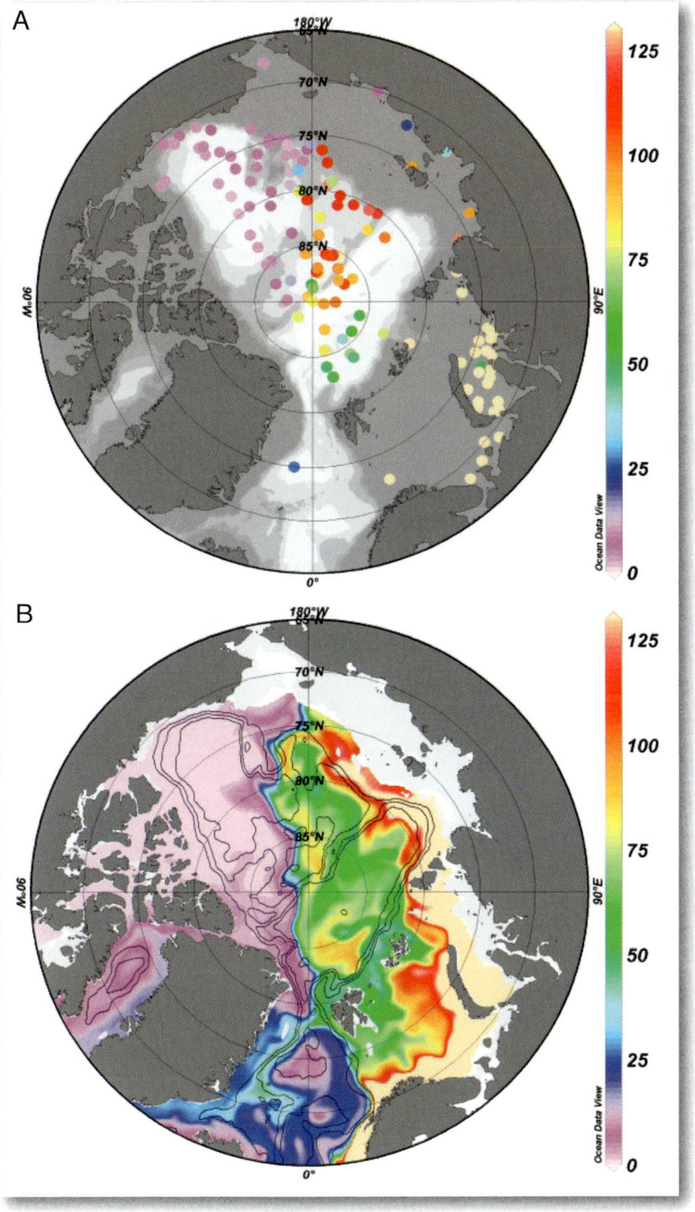

Figure 3. Comparison of observed and modelled ^{129}I concentrations in 1994-96. (A) Observed ^{129}I concentrations (10^7 at/l) for surface mixed layer depths (0 - 59 m) for 1994-96; (B) simulated ^{129}I distributions (10^7 at/l) at 59 m for September 1995 are in good agreement with 1994-96 data sets above and illustrate the eastward spread of high ^{129}I labelled, Atlantic-origin surface water across the Makarov Basin to the Chukchi Plateau under strong positive Arctic Oscillation conditions (Karcher et al. 2012).

ate waters over the northern Canada Basin and Alpha Ridge showed that these waters are extremely poorly ventilated and probably represented the oldest intermediate water in the Arctic Ocean (Smith et al. 1999). The SCICEX missions represent a unique collaboration between scientists and the United States military, and BIO scientists were fortunate to have been able to play a significant role in this innovative experiment.

ICEBREAKER MISSIONS: 1993-2012

Circulation Studies

Beginning in the early 1990s, it became more feasible to undertake scientific exploration in the Arctic Ocean using ice-breaking vessels, thereby opening up a wider range of potential studies. The most dramatic early mission involving BIO scientists was the Arctic Ocean Section (AOS) in 1994 during which two icebreakers, the CCGS *Louis S. St. Laurent* and the US *Polar Sea* together traversed the Arctic Ocean from Alaska to Fram Strait via the North Pole (Carmack et al. 1997). Subsequent missions during the 1990s and 2000s provided a large inventory of samples for $^{129}I/^{137}Cs$ analyses that permitted the determination of transit times for Atlantic Water flow for much of the Arctic Ocean (Fig. 5). The recent 'Switchyard' project has employed twin-otter aircraft which fly from northern Canada to the North Pole and land on the ice to collect seawater samples (Karcher et al. 2012).

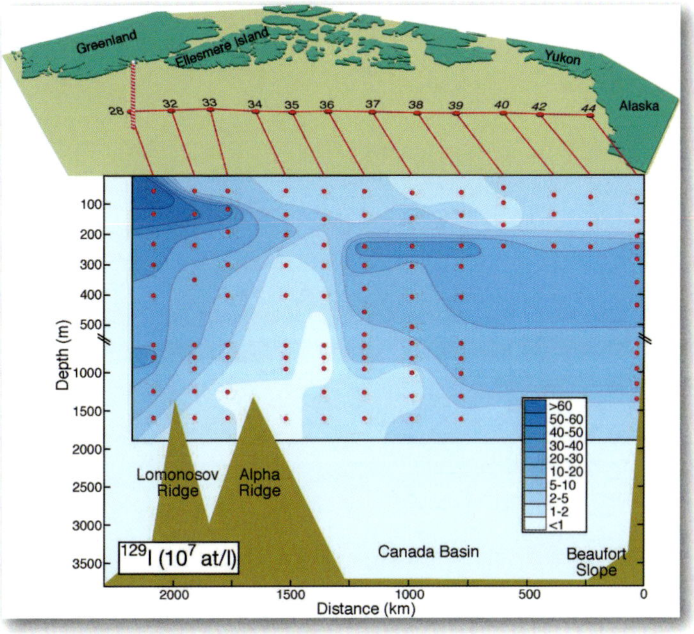

Figure 4. ^{129}I section measured from samples collected during the 1996 mission of USS *Pogy* submarine in Canada Basin. High ^{129}I over Lomonosov Ridge signifies flow of Atlantic Water from Russia towards Fram Strait; low ^{129}I in surface water shows this is Pacific Water from Bering Strait; high ^{129}I at depths of 200–400 m in Canada Basin shows ventilation of interior north of Chukchi Plateau and low ^{129}I over Alpha Ridge shows this is oldest intermediate water in the Arctic Ocean.

The flow of Atlantic surface water eastward through the Russian marginal seas during the 1990s is delineated by the geographic distribution of tracer ages in Figure 5. Tracer ages are 0.5-1 years for the Western Barents Sea, 3 years for the eastern Barents Sea, 3-6 years for the Kara Sea, 6-7 years for the Laptev Sea, and 9-12 years at the North Pole (Smith et al. 2011) referenced to transport from 60°N (Fig. 1). Tracer ages cannot be estimated for Pacific origin surface water that covers the Canada Basin because there are no nuclear facilities in the Pacific Ocean that provide a suitable radionuclide tracer signal. The distribution of tracer ages in Figure 5 also outlines the trans-polar flow of Atlantic surface water towards Fram Strait along the Mendeleyev and Lomonosov Ridges. In contrast to the surface water, transit times are somewhat greater for underlying core Atlantic Water (AW, Fig. 5) that is distinguished by a temperature maximum at depths of 250–350 m throughout the Arctic Ocean. Transit times for core AW are 5-8 years in the northern Makarov Basin, 9-15 years in the vicinity of the North Pole, and 18-21 years in the southern Canada Basin (Smith et al. 2011).

The dilution factor represents the degree to which Atlantic-origin water has been diluted by mixing during transport into the Arctic Ocean. Dilution factors of 3-4 are characteristic of surface water flowing through the Barents Sea, and values of about 5 characterize the flow from the Kara Sea into the Laptev Sea and Nansen Basin, and as far as the North Pole (Fig. 5). Most of the mixing of tracer-labelled water from the North Sea occurs during transport northward into the Barents Sea. Dilution factors for core AW have values of 5-15 across most of the central Arctic Ocean (Smith et al. 2011). Although transit times and dilution factors provide useful intuitive notions of water circulation, a more detailed understanding requires the use of transit time distributions (TTDs) that incorporate mixing into the age estimates.

Particle-reactive Radionuclides and Sediments

A significant component of the BIO radionuclide program in the Arctic Ocean has involved studies of the transport of particle-reactive ra-

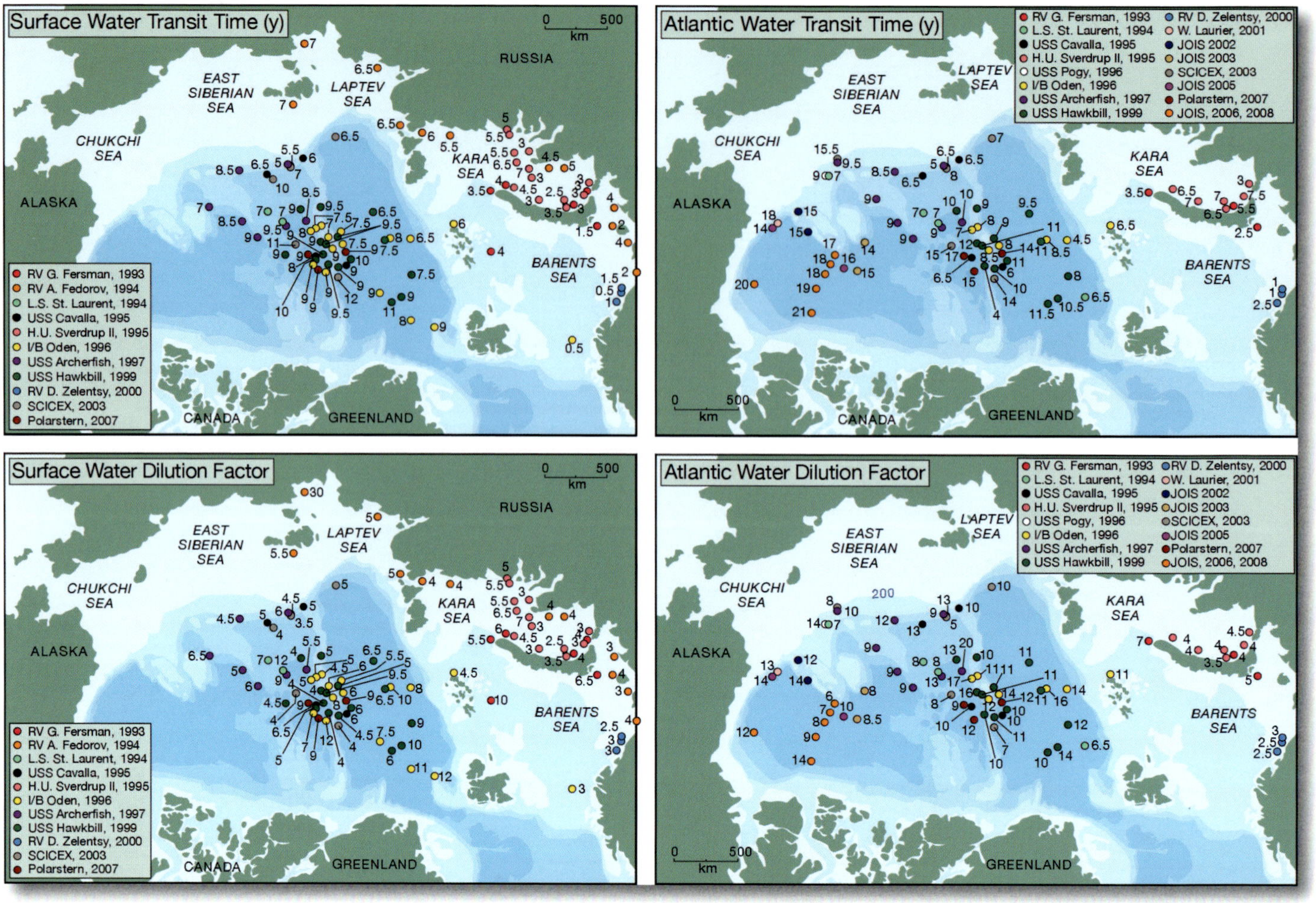

Figure 5. Transit times for Atlantic Water from the North Sea from $^{129}I/^{137}Cs$ tracer measurements for missions given in inset. Top left panel: Surface water travels mainly through the Russian shelf seas and takes about 10 years to get to the North Pole, during which (bottom left panel) it is diluted by a factor of 5. Top right panel: Deeper (200-300 m) Atlantic Water takes about 10-12 years to get to North Pole and undergoes dilution (bottom right panel) by a factor of approximately 10 (Smith et al. 2011, Karcher et al. 2012).

dionuclides and their uptake in sediments. The principles governing the transport through the Arctic Ocean of particle-associated substances, including trace metals and contaminants, differ markedly from those in more southerly latitudes. They are influenced by the long period of darkness during the winter and the constraints this imposes on primary production and the large influx of river water, which leads to pronounced stratification and varying degrees of ice cover. These factors tend to favour the removal of bio-geochemically active contaminants in the broad, highly productive, continental shelf and margin regimes compared to the deep waters of the central Arctic Ocean in a process known as 'boundary scavenging' (Smith et al. 2003). In addition to being regions for the recycling of nutrients, the shelf/margin regimes are also effective sites for the enhanced removal of surface reactive elements, either through the mediation of resuspended particles or through the provision of fresh metal oxide phases. Studies indicated that boundary currents transport water column properties cyclonically around the margins of the western Arctic Ocean, and eddies tend to carry these properties into the basin interiors. Owing to the relatively small size of the Arctic Ocean and its pronounced stratification, it appears that the influence of shelf/slope scavenging is rapidly communicated into interior waters through lateral spreading (Smith et al. 2003).

These various hypotheses were supported by the first arctic measurements of the particle-reactive radioisotope ^{210}Pb at the CESAR ice station (Fig. 1) over the Alpha Ridge in 1983 by scientists from BIO and Dalhousie University (Halifax, NS). Moore and Smith (1986) observed a deficit of ^{210}Pb (compared to its soluble precursor, ^{226}Ra) in halocline waters which they attributed to scavenging over the continental shelf and the subsequent propagation of this deficit into the interior of the Canada Basin. Smith et al. (2003) later undertook a more detailed examination

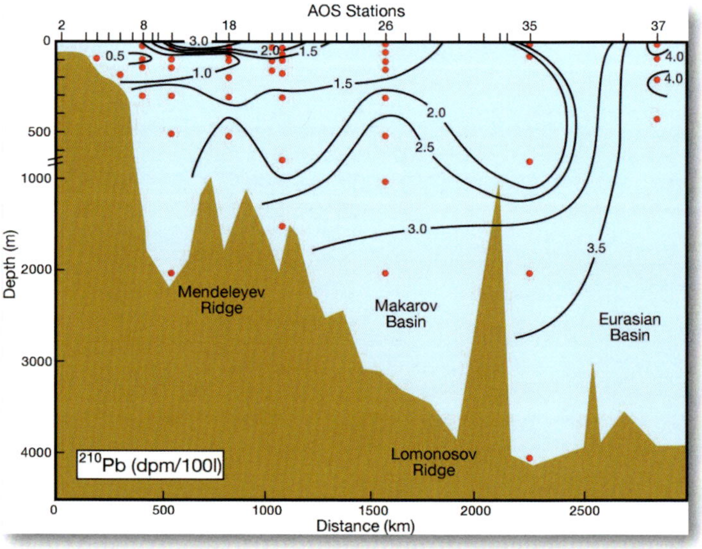

Figure 6. ^{210}Pb section for AOS-94 shows low levels in halocline waters (60–150 m depth) extending across the Makarov Basin owing to particle scavenging of ^{210}Pb from Pacific Ocean water as it flows across the highly productive, continental shelf of the Chukchi Sea (left-hand side of figure) into the Arctic Ocean.

of the distribution of ^{210}Pb in the water column using data from the 1994 AOS mission (Fig. 6). They showed that the halocline deficit in ^{210}Pb indeed extended northward from the arctic continental shelves across the Makarov Basin to the North Pole demonstrating the influence of bound-

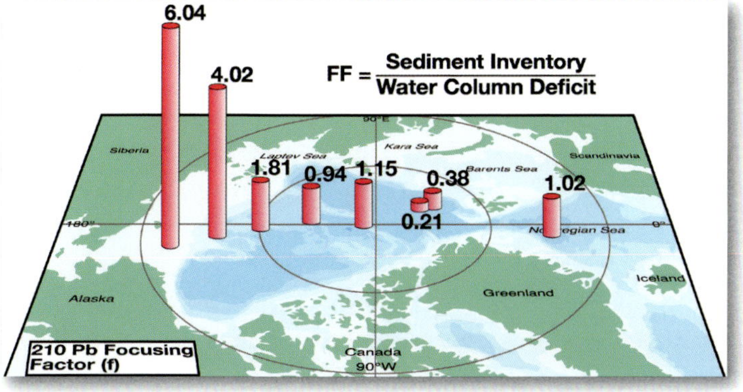

Figure 7. Focussing factors (FF) are higher in the Canada Basin compared to the Eurasian Basin and have their highest values in shelf/slope regimes of the western Arctic Ocean. This latter result is consistent with the net removal of ^{210}Pb from water flowing across the shelves and its subsequent uptake in shelf/slope sediments.

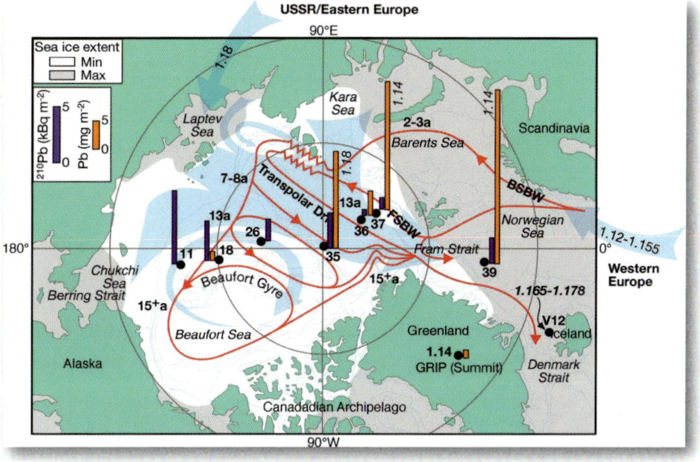

Figure 9. Anthropogenic Pb inventories determined from Pb isotope ratios are compared to ^{210}Pb inventories for sediment cores. Preferential accumulation of anthropogenic Pb in the eastern Arctic Ocean (proximal to Europe) suggests scavenging from newly arrived Atlantic Water rather than from atmospheric inputs (Gobeil et al. 2001).

ary scavenging on the properties of the basin interior. In addition, measurements of ^{210}Pb inventories in the sediments can be compared to the water column deficit of ^{210}Pb to calculate the 'focussing factor' (FF) (Fig. 7) which is a measure of the efficiency of bio-geochemical scavenging from the overlying water column and uptake in the sediments. Values of the FF in excess of 1 imply net accumulation in underlying sediments whereas those less than 1 indicate net export by lateral transport. The results for AOS-94 showed a sediment excess of ^{210}Pb in underlying shelf/slope sediment regimes (Fig. 7), which indicate that ^{210}Pb was being scavenged by particles from Pacific Ocean water as it was being transported across the Chukchi Sea into the interior of the Arctic Ocean.

These studies were supported by a BIO-University of Rhode Island (URI, Kingston, RI) collaboration which involved measurements of the long-lived, naturally occurring radionuclides, ^{231}Pa and ^{230}Th, in the water column of the Canada Basin. These results indicated that the radionuclides were being redistributed within the Arctic Ocean by horizontal mixing and preferentially removed in high productivity, marginal areas such as the Chukchi Sea slope (Edmonds et al. 1998). The influence of shelf/margin regimes on particle transport and boundary scavenging in the Arctic Ocean is important as this may exercise the dominant control over contaminant concentrations in the water column and the export of particle reactive substances to the North Atlantic (Gobeil et al. 2001).

In another BIO-URI study, Moran et al. (2005a) showed that the distribution of surface sediment ^{231}Pa/^{230}Th ratios in the Arctic Ocean can be used to establish the relative importance of scavenging removal and horizontal transport in redistributing these particle-reactive tracers between the low productivity, permanently ice-covered, interior basins and the seasonally high particle flux margins (Fig. 8). Low surface sediment ^{231}Pa/^{230}Th ratios result from chemical fractionation of ^{231}Pa and ^{230}Th in the water column and preferential export of the less particle-reactive radionuclide, ^{231}Pa, from the Arctic Ocean. The sizable export of ^{231}Pa relative to that of ^{230}Th accounts for both the low sediment ^{231}Pa/^{230}Th ratios and lack of basin-margin fractionation, despite there being significant boundary scavenging of both ^{231}Pa and ^{230}Th in the Arctic, a situation unique to this ocean basin. Measurements of particle-reactive radionuclides in water and sediments are revealing new insights into the mechanisms and time scales governing the mass flux of biogeochemically important elements through the Arctic Ocean.

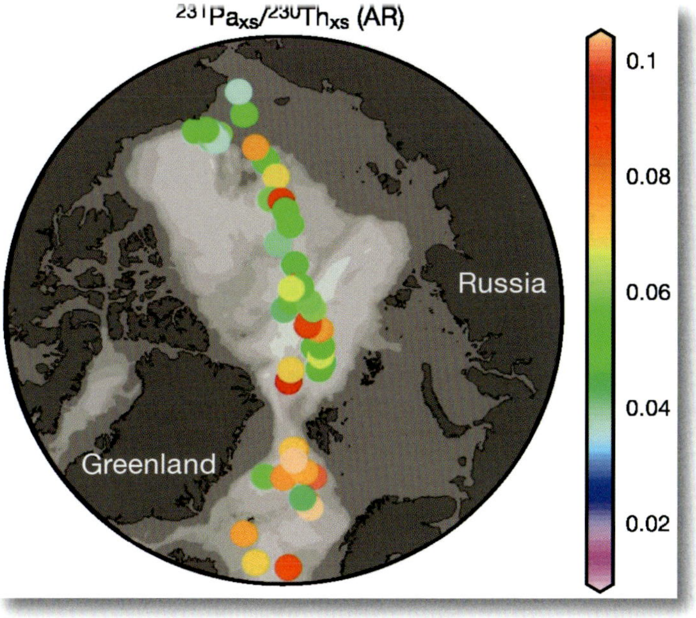

Figure 8. Distribution of ^{231}Pa/^{230}Th activity ratios (AR) in surface sediments shows low values (< 0.07) in interior basins indicating net export of ^{231}Pa from the Arctic Ocean.

The ^{231}Pa/^{230}Th studies relied on particle-reactive tracers produced within the Arctic Ocean, while another collaborative study by BIO, Institute of Ocean Sciences (IOS) and the Institut Maurice Lamontagne (IML) relied on the scavenging of anthropogenic lead (Pb) from water as it entered the Arctic Ocean from European waters. It was previously assumed that most contaminant Pb in the Arctic Ocean was derived from atmospheric emissions in Europe and Russia. However, Gobeil et al. (2001) showed that anthropogenic Pb in the sediments (estimated from Pb isotope ratios) preferentially accumulates in the Eurasian Basin where Atlantic Water initially enters the Arctic Ocean (Fig. 9). They concluded that anthropogenic Pb was being scavenged from the entering Atlantic water and that this particle-reactive contaminant had been almost totally stripped out of the water by the time this water had reached the Canada Basin. This result suggests that many of the key contaminant pathways for the Arctic Ocean are associated with water transport rather than atmospheric transport.

Particulate Organic Carbon Transport Measured by ^{234}Th/^{238}U Disequilibrium

One technique first employed in the Arctic Ocean in a BIO-URI collaboration involved estimates of the particulate organic carbon (POC) export flux determined from ^{234}Th/^{238}U disequilibrium. ^{234}Th (half-life = 24.1 days) is a particle-reactive radionuclide produced continuously in the oceans by alpha decay of soluble ^{238}U (half-life = 4.5 x 10^9 years) and is a sensitive tracer of scavenging and particle export on time-scales of days to months (Smith et al. 2006). The questions addressed in these studies were what fraction of primary production is seasonally exported downward as sinking organic matter to the benthos, and how much of this organic matter is retained in shelf and slope sediments on seasonal and decadal time-scales? These questions bear on our understanding of carbon and nutrient cycling, the efficiency of pelagic-benthic coupling, and the mechanisms for exchange of carbon and other chemicals (including contaminants) between the shelves and interior Arctic Ocean.

The first measurements of ^{234}Th in the western Arctic Ocean were made by BIO/URI scientists (Moran et al. 1998, Moran and Smith 2000) in the mid-1990s. They indicated that particle export rates over seasonally ice-free regions of the Chukchi Sea and Beaufort Sea shelves were high and comparable to those measured in shelf regions of the North Atlantic. Seasonal measurements of $^{234}Th/^{238}U$ disequilibrium in the Chukchi Sea demonstrated the importance of short-term changes in the flux of particles and associated organic C exported from the euphotic zone and the potential for exchange of particulate organic carbon (POC) between the shelf and interior slope/basin regimes. These results provided some of the first direct evidence of the strong seasonal coupling between export production and benthic respiration in continental margin regimes of the Arctic Ocean.

^{234}Th studies were also undertaken along seven shelf-basin sections in the Chukchi Sea as part of the United States Shelf Basin Interaction (SBI) program in the spring and summer of 2002 (Fig. 10) which showed enhanced scavenging and particle export in the shelf and slope waters

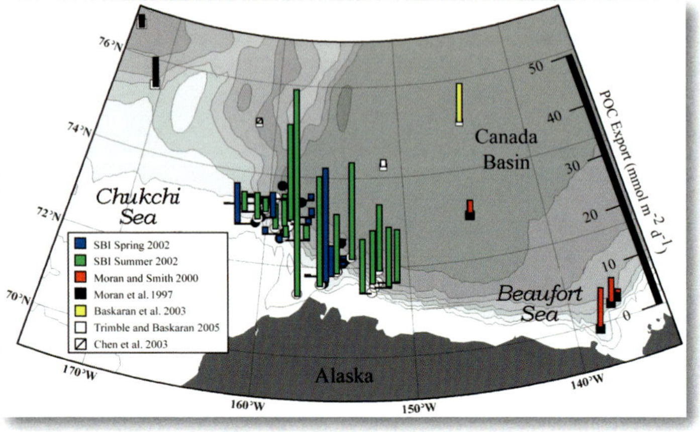

Figure 10. Particulate organic carbon (POC) export fluxes from the 2002 SBI missions, calculated from the $^{234}Th/^{238}U$ disequilibria, show significant uptake in shelf sediments and off-shelf transport into slope sediments of Beaufort and Chukchi seas.

(Moran et al. 2005b). A marked seasonal increase in POC export was clearly observed at all stations during the transition from spring to summer which was clearly associated with the seasonal increase in primary and export production. The fraction of primary production exported from the upper shelf/slope waters increased from ~15% in the spring to ~32% in the summer. The majority of shelf and slope stations indicate a good agreement between POC export and benthic C respiration in the spring and, hence, a tight coupling between primary productivity, POC export, and benthic respiration.

FUTURE EFFORTS

BIO scientists have been fortunate to have participated in the early scientific exploration of the Arctic Ocean. They have been able to make significant contributions by applying radionuclide tracers to studies of water circulation, contaminant transport, and carbon cycling. These studies began with the difficult and dangerous pioneering work undertaken at arctic ice stations in the 1970s and 1980s, and continued on through improved field methodologies associated with the progression to icebreakers, submarines, and aircraft as arctic sampling platforms. Accomplishments of this program include the use of tracers (^{129}I, ^{137}Cs) from European nuclear fuel reprocessing plants to identify arctic contaminant pathways and estimate transit times for the circulation of Atlantic Water throughout the Arctic Ocean. Particle-reactive tracers such as ^{210}Pb have provided a richer understanding of the manner in which anthropogenic contaminants can accumulate in shelf/slope regions (the 'dirty bathtub' effect), while longer lived tracers ($^{231}Pa/^{230}Th$) have been used to determine ventilation rates in the interior of the Arctic Ocean and water outflow rates on longer time scales. These studies relate to both the fate and cycling of contaminants and provide insight into the forcing mechanisms governing arctic circulation. ^{234}Th studies have been successfully applied in the Arctic Ocean to estimate carbon export fluxes to shelf and slope sediments and the associated coupling with primary production thereby enhancing our understanding of carbon cycling in arctic ecosystems.

Future efforts of this program will focus on using radioactive tracers to characterize changes in circulation and particle/carbon transport in the Arctic Ocean associated with climate change and the reduction of sea-ice cover. These changes may have far reaching impacts on ocean productivity and the composition and energetics of arctic ecosystems. BIO contributions to arctic oceanography constitute an important legacy that has contributed to the high international standing of this Institute and will help to ensure the future value of Canadian science in the Arctic.

ACKNOWLEDGEMENTS

We are indebted to the crews of the many vessels that have provided platforms for BIO studies in the Arctic Ocean and to personnel who have supported these programs in other capacities, from logistical to administrative support. The key members of the Atlantic Environmental Radioactivity Unit (AERU) at BIO who have carried out the laboratory and fieldwork described in this paper are: Richard Nelson, Grazyna Folwarczna, James Abriel, and Katherine Ellis.

REFERENCES

Baskaran, M., P.W. Swarzenski, and D. Porcelli. 2003. Role of colloidal material in the removal of ^{234}Th in the Canada Basin of the Arctic Ocean. Deep-Sea Research I 50: 1,353-1,373.

Carmack, E.C., K. Aagaard, J.H. Swift, R.W. Macdonald, F.A. McLaughlin, E.P. Jones, R.G. Perkin, J.N. Smith, K.M. Ellis, and L.R. Kilius. 1997. Changes in temperature and tracer distributions within the Arctic Ocean: results from the 1994 Arctic Ocean Section. Deep-Sea Research II 44 (8): 1,487-1,502.

Chen, M., Y. Huang, P. Cai, and L. Guo. 2003. Particulate organic carbon export fluxes in the Canada Basin and Bering Sea as derived from $^{234}Th/^{238}U$ disequilibria. Arctic 56: 32-44.

Coleman, E.C. 2007. The Royal Navy and Polar Exploration. Volume 2 - From Franklin to Scott. Tempus Publishing, Stroud, England.

Edmonds, H.N., S.B. Moran, J.A. Hoff, J.N. Smith, and R.L. Edwards. 1998. Protactinium-231 and thorium-230 abundances and high scavenging rates in the Western Arctic Ocean. Science 280: 405-407.

Gobeil, C., R.W. Macdonald, J.N. Smith, and L. Beaudin. 2001. Atlantic water flow pathways revealed by lead contamination in Arctic basins sediments. Science 293: 1,301-1,304.

Jones, E.P. 2014. The Arctic Ocean: Its waters and global significance. Pages 31-35 *in* Voyage of Discovery: Fifty Years of Marine Research at Canada's Bedford Institute of Oceanography (D.N. Nettleship, D.C. Gordon, C.F.M. Lewis, and M.P. Latremouille, Eds.). Bedford Institute of Oceanography-Oceans Association, Dartmouth, NS.

Karcher, M., J.N. Smith, F. Kauker, R. Gerdes, and W.M. Smethie, Jr. 2012. Recent changes in Arctic Ocean circulation revealed by ^{129}Iodine observations and modelling. Journal of Geophysical Research 117 doi:10.1029/2011JC007513.

Livingston, H.D. 1988. The use of Cs and Sr isotopes as tracers in the Arctic Mediterranean Seas. Philosophical Transactions of the Royal Society 325: 161-176.

Livingston, H.D., S.L. Kupferman, V.T. Bowen, and R.M. Moore. 1984. Vertical profiles of artificial redionuclide concentrations in the central Arctic Ocean. Geochimica et Cosmochimica Acta 48: 2,195-2,203.

Matishov, G.G., D.G. Matishov, A.E. Namjatov, J.N. Smith, J. Carroll, and S. Daahle. 2002. Radioactivity near the sunken submarine 'Kursk' in the Southern Barents Sea. Environmental Science and Technology 36: 1,919-1,922.

Moore, R.M. and J.N. Smith. 1986. Disequilibria between Ra-226,Pb-210 and Po-210 in the Arctic Ocean and the implications for chemical modification of the Pacific water inflow. Earth and Planetary Science Letters 77: 285-292.

Moran, S.B. and J.N. Smith. 2000. ^{234}Th as a tracer of scavenging and particle export in the Beaufort Sea. Continental Shelf Research 20: 153-167.

Moran, S.B., K.M. Ellis, and J.N. Smith. 1998. $^{234}Th/^{238}U$ disequilibrium in the central Arctic Ocean: implications for particulate organic carbon export. Deep-Sea Research II 44: 1,593-1,606.

Moran, S.B., C.-C. Shen, R.L. Edwards, H.N. Edmonds, J.C. Scholten, J.N. Smith, and T.-L. Ku. 2005a. ^{231}Pa and ^{230}Th in surface sediments of the Arctic Ocean: implications for $^{231}Pa/^{230}Th$ fractionation, boundary scavenging, and advective export. Earth and Planetary Science Letters 234: 235-248.

Moran, S.B., R.P. Kelly, K. Hagstrom, J.N. Smith, J.M. Grebmeier, L.W. Cooper, G.F. Cota, J.J. Walsh, N.R. Bates, D.A. Hansell, W. Maslowski, R.P. Nelson, and S. Mulsow. 2005b. Seasonal changes in POC export flux in the Chukchi Sea and implications for water column-benthic coupling in arctic shelves. Deep-Sea Research II 52/24-26: 3,427-3,451.

Mudie, P.J. and H.R. Jackson. 2014. The Canadian Ice Island Program: discoveries from a ship of ice. Pages 59-67 *in* Voyage of Discovery: Fifty Years of Marine Research at Canada's Bedford Institute of Oceanography (D.N. Nettleship, D.C. Gordon, C.F.M. Lewis, and M.P. Latremouille, Eds.). Bedford Institute of Oceanography-Oceans Association, Dartmouth, NS.

Pfirman, S., B. Tremblay, and C. Fowler. 2009. Going with the floe? An analysis of luck versus skill in the epic polar expeditions of Fridtjof Nansen and Sir Ernest Shackleton. American Scientist 97: 484-493. (doi: 10.1511/2009.81.484)

Smith, J.N. and K.M. Ellis. 1995. Radionuclide tracer profiles at the CESAR Ice Station and Canadian Ice Island in the Western Arctic Ocean. Deep-Sea Research II 42: 1,447-1,470.

Smith, J.N., K.M. Ellis, and E.P. Jones. 1990. Cesium-137 transport into the Arctic

Ocean through Fram Strait. Journal of Geophysical Research 95 (C2): 1,693-1,701.
Smith, J.N., K.M. Ellis, A. Aarkrog, H. Dahlgaard, and E. Holm. 1994. Sediment mixing and burial of the Pu-239,240 pulse from the 1968 Thule, Greenland, nuclear weapons accident. Journal of Environmental Radioactivity 25: 135-159.
Smith, J.N., K.M. Ellis, K. Naes, S. Dahle, and D. Matishov. 1995. Sedimentation and mixing rates of fallout radionuclides in Barents Sea sediments off Novaya Zemlya. Deep-Sea Research II 42: 1,471-1,493.
Smith, J.N., K.M. Ellis, and L.R. Kilius. 1998. ^{129}I and ^{137}Cs tracer measurements in the Arctic Ocean. Deep-Sea Research I 45: 959-984.
Smith, J.N., K.M. Ellis, and T.M. Boyd. 1999. Circulation features in the Central Arctic Ocean revealed by nuclear fuel reprocessing tracers from SCICEX 95 and 96. Journal of Geophysical Research 104 (C12): 29,663-29,677.
Smith, J.N., K.M. Ellis, L. Polyak, G. Ivanov, S.L. Forman, and S.B. Moran. 2000. $^{239,240}Pu$ transport into the Arctic Ocean from underwater nuclear tests in Chernaya Bay, Novaya Zemlya. Continental Shelf Research 20: 255-279.
Smith, J.N., S.B. Moran, and R.W. Macdonald. 2003. Shelf-basin interactions in the Arctic Ocean based on ^{210}Pb and Ra isotope tracer distributions. Deep-Sea Research I, 50: 397-416.
Smith, J.N., S.B. Moran, and E.A. Speicher. 2006. On the accuracy of upper ocean particulate organic carbon export fluxes estimated from $^{234}Th/^{238}U$ disequilibrium. Deep-Sea Research I 53: 860-868.
Smith, J.N., F.A. McLaughlin, W.M. Smethie, Jr., S.B. Moran, and K. Lepore. 2011. Iodine-129, ^{137}Cs, and CFC-11 tracer transit time distributions in the Arctic Ocean. Journal of Geophysical Research 116. doi:10.1029/2010JC006471.
Trimble, S.M. and M. Baskaran. 2005. The role of suspended particulate matter in ^{234}Th scavenging and ^{234}Th-derived export fluxes of POC in the Canada Basin of the Arctic Ocean. Marine Chemistry, 96, 1-19.

8. THE CANADIAN ICE ISLAND PROGRAM: DISCOVERIES FROM A SHIP OF ICE

Peta J. Mudie* and H. Ruth Jackson

SUMMARY

The goal of the 1980s Canadian Ice Island program was to occupy a large semi-permanent ice island as a platform for oceanographic and geoscientific studies of Canada's unmapped, pack ice-covered polar margin between Ellesmere Island and the Beaufort Sea. From 1984 to 1989, 40 people in joint government-university funded programs documented oceanographic and ice conditions, mapped the seafloor, and studied the evolution of Canada's northernmost continental margins. A permanent camp was built to conduct multidisciplinary programs including seismic surveying, seabed sampling, heat flow measurement, plankton and benthos surveys, physical and chemical oceanography, meteorology, atmospheric sampling, and ice strength studies. The camp was also used as an operations base for hydrographic surveying, and sediment and heat flow sampling. Achievements included construction of on-ice laboratories, melting of large 44 m deep holes through the ice for piston coring, dredging and water sampling, collection of >200 km of seismic reflection and bathymetric data, and recovery of the first sediment and biological samples from this unexplored part of Canada's margin – and coldest sector of the arctic continental shelves. Scientific highlights include discovery of previously unknown arctic glass sponge reefs, records of recent Canadian Arctic Ocean warming, and tracing of radioactivity and pesticide fallout to the Canadian polar margin. The hands-on training and engineering experience in this pack-ice region placed Canada in the forefront of United Nations Law of the Sea (UNCLOS) survey work, and the ice strength data are used to design hulls of Canadian Coast Guard and commercial arctic icebreakers.

Key words: multi-year pack ice, arctic warming, Law of the Sea, seismic refraction, pollution, polar production, polar shelf map.
***E-mail:** Peta.Mudie@NRCan.gc.ca

It is probably true to say that the Canadian Ice Island Program (1984–89) was the most extraordinary voyage of discovery ever undertaken by the Bedford Institute of Oceanography (BIO). For this 5-year program, a giant tabular iceberg (an ice island) was used as a platform from which to probe the secrets of the least known part of Canada's polar margin – where few people had ever gone before. Why was an ice island used instead of a research ship? The answer is that the perennial multi-year pack ice north of the Canadian Arctic Archipelago (CAA) is so thick (6-9 m on average, with chunks up to 40 m) that it cannot be sailed by vessels of any kind (Barry and Gan 2011). This formidable seascape of multi-year sea ice is made of millions of mobile ice blocks, with knife-edge crests and steep blue sides that plunge into crevasses of freezing sea water. The floating pack ice forms a jagged, moving blanket covering the polar margin north of the Queen Elizabeth Islands (QEI), stretching about 1,000 km from Ellesmere Island to the Beaufort Sea (Fig. 1). The land bordering this frozen polar margin includes Ellesmere Island, the Sverdrup Island group of Axel Heiberg, Meighen, and Ellef Ringnes islands, and the Parry Islands (Prince Patrick, Mackenzie King, Brock, Borden, and Lougheed islands).

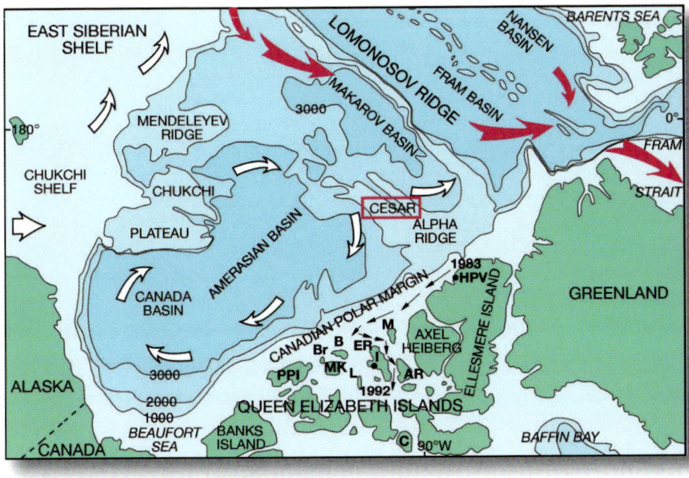

Figure 1. Map of the Arctic Ocean showing surface circulation of mainly Pacific (white arrows) and Atlantic (red arrows) waters, the location of Canadian polar margin, and the Queen Elizabeth Islands. Small arrows show the route of the Canadian Ice Island from 1983 to 1992. Islands are: M = Meighen, ER and AR = Ellef and Amund Ringnes; L = Lougheed, PPI = Prince Patrick; MK = Mackenzie King; B = Borden, Br = Brock, C = Cornwallis. I = Isachsen field station. HPV=Hansen Point volcanics. The rectangle on Alpha Ridge is the CESAR study area.

This remote region was the last of Canada's arctic marine frontiers to be explored because of its inaccessibility by land and sea, its frigid high arctic climate (average −19°C; Orvig 1981), and the dense sea fog that enshrouds the area during the two months of summer at latitude 79-83°N. Most of this polar margin was unknown when Canada was founded and was still a blank on the map when the nation accepted the gift of British claims to the islands north of mainland Canada in 1880. Not even the Inuit or their predecessors occupied this harsh environment (McGhee 1990). No archaeological sites have been found on the QEI west of Ellesmere Island except for one southern Axel Heiberg site, and today Ellesmere Island remains the only discontinuously inhabited island on the Canadian polar margin.

The Norwegian explorer Otto Sverdrup discovered Axel Heiberg Island by land on 29 April 1899. From 1900 to 1902, he and companions explored by dog-sledge from Axel Heiberg to Amund Ringnes Island, making soundings and taking samples through the sea ice (Sverdrup 1904). In 1906, American Robert Peary crossed the Canadian polar margin and said there was territory northwest of Axel Heiberg Island called Croker Land (Peary 1907). Concerned that the pack ice might hide land across the Alaska-Canada offshore boundary at longitude 141°W, the Canadian government sponsored the Canadian Arctic Expedition from 1913–18 led by Vilhjalmur Stefansson and Rudolph Anderson. Stefansson's main objective was geographical discovery, and he found Brock, Borden, Lougheed, and Meighen islands (LeBourdais 1963). It was not until 1930 that Canada officially took possession of this Norwegian territory (the Sverdrup Islands) and paid Sverdrup $67,000 for his scientific maps and journals (Cook 1981). Subsequently, advances in aviation technology revolutionized arctic surveying. After 1956, lighter aircraft on large tires and helicopters allowed geological mapping of the polar margin islands and stimulated oil and mineral exploration (Christie and Kerr 1981). During post-war surveys, the final shape was given to the coastline of arctic Canada as we now know it, although the offshore area was still unexplored until the Polar Continental Shelf Project (PCSP) began making hydrographic and geophysical measurements through the pack-ice of the polar margin in 1959 (Roots and Hobson 1986).

The first attempt to use an ice island for Arctic Ocean exploration began in 1952 when the United States Air Force occupied a flat 11 x 5 km kidney-shaped piece of ice, named 'Fletcher's Ice Island', about 40 m thick, that moved around the Amerasian Basin for more than 20 years before drifting into the Atlantic and melting in about 1985 (Sackinger et al. 1991). This 'floating island' was used for meteorological, oceanographic, and geophysical studies until 1974 when cracking of the ice made it too dangerous for continuous occupation. Temporary floating ice camps (e.g., ARLIS I and II, LOREX, CESAR, and AIDJEX) were established on large ice floes (~3 km long, 3 m thick) in spring, but these platforms could be used only until the summer melt commenced. Between 1937 and 2004, Russian scientists occupied 33 successive drifting ice floes travelling over the North Pole at speeds of up to 7.5 km per day (Frolov et al. 2005). The 1983 Canadian Expedition to Study the Alpha Ridge (CESAR) was an extremely important Canadian scientific survey: 40 researchers mapped the Canadian sector of the Alpha-Mendeleev Ridge to investigate its evolution, look for mineral and petroleum resources, and possibly lay claim to part of the ridge and the 320 km (200 mile) marine jurisdiction on either side. Unfortunately, CESAR ended after three months owing to the breakup of the seasonal ice floe (Roots and Hobson 1986).

In 1983, a new large ice island was identified off Ellesmere Island by George Hobson. This was seen as a golden opportunity for establishing a Canadian permanent floating research station to collect oceanographic, geological, and geophysical data while drifting over the Canadian polar margin. The ice island was expected to move westwards into the Beaufort Sea, then drift northwards into international waters off Alaska and Russia by 1990. Thus, in August 1983, the Canadian Ice Island (CII) program was launched with the installation of a buoy on a floating block of ice from the Ward Hunt Ice Shelf that was dubbed 'Hobson's Choice'.

Why Bother About the Canadian Polar Margin: Who Cares?

The history of arctic science is essentially as old as the history of arctic travel (Orvig 1981) and the idea that no one had studied the unnavigable continental shelf off Axel Heiberg Island since Otto Sverdrup in 1902 was an exciting challenge to many Canadian scientists. Arriving on the CII in April 1985, at the start of the first scientific field season (Fig. 2A), the scenery was unimaginable – an endless expanse of pure white, framed by a cloudless sky in which the sun did not set for four months. At the edge of the white ice island surface, the landscape was a towering, jumbled mass of turquoise multi-year pack ice (Fig. 2B). This multi-year ice starts as annual ice in temporary open water areas called leads, but instead of melting away in summer, it survives to thicken and harden through several winters. Wind and currents within the Arctic Ocean drive this hardened sea ice away from warmer areas in Siberia, and the oldest and thickest ice piles up against the northern Queen Elizabeth Islands and Greenland, the coldest coastal regions of the Arctic Ocean (Rigor et al. 2000).

Figure 2. Canadian Ice Island spring and summer: (A) Camp in April 1988 with snow-encapsulated buildings and parcoll huts; (B) Compression ice at island edge, May 1985; (C) Geology lab (centre) with the Atlantic Geoscience Centre (AGC) logo on the gantry of the winch coring system, and hydrohole boiler hut on left, oceanography lab chimney at right centre with the storage parcoll in background at left, May 1986; (D) D. Forsyth detonates explosives for seismic refraction studies (from Foster and Marino 1986); (E) Camp in summer 1986 with meltwater lakes; and (F) Geophysicists in wet gear drain meltwater from a seismic shot shack.

By early 1980, there was growing concern over rapidly rising arctic temperatures and it was realized that sea ice over channels and shelves could disappear in summer. Loss of the sea ice barrier would open up Canada's remote northern coastline to possible influx of foreign vessels and demand for resources. Suddenly, for the safety of potential shipping traffic in summer-open water, there was the need to know the depth of the continental shelf. The discovery of vast gas and oil reservoirs in the Beaufort Sea further triggered interest in the hydrocarbon potential of the continental margin north of the Sverdrup Islands sedimentary basin. As long as the islands were barricaded by the protective pack ice, little thought had been given to locating Canada's northern offshore boundary – but now this safeguard was threatened by the possibility of an arctic ice melt-down.

Warming of the QEI spurred on the need to establish Canada's presence in the northeastern offshore (along the polar margin). In 1984, little was known about the continental shelf and oceanography of this region, and there was no information on the biological and economic resources. An additional incentive for oceanographic studies came from alarm over the finding of high levels of pesticide residues in marine wildlife and in breast milk of Inuk mothers even though Canadian usage of open sources of DDT stopped in 1973 and nonelectrical uses of PCBs were banned in 1977. Overall, although the building and occupation of an ice island science camp would be a multimillion dollar operation, the PCSP was authorized to locate a suitable ice island platform and to provide logistical support for a joint government-university scientific team.

The main objective of the multidisciplinary CII expedition was to conduct oceanographic and geological surveys of the continental margin from Ellesmere Island to the Beaufort Sea. To do this, researchers brought a veritable technical arsenal onto the polar ice for gathering information on the history of the ice and underlying waters, and for conducting seismic, gravimetric, and bathymetric studies to show how the evolution of the continental shelf is related to petroleum and other resource potentials.

SUPPLYING AND NAVIGATING AN ICE ISLAND

Like other ice islands in arctic waters, CII was a rare occurrence – an island of ice, 6 x 9 km long, 43-45 m thick, formed by break-up of floating ice shelves north of Greenland and Ellesmere Island. All tabular islands are solid masses of hard, fresh-water ice several kilometres long, up to 50 m thick, that do not break up seasonally like softer salt-water ice floes (Hattersley-Smith et al. 1952, Jeffries 2000). These ice islands become embedded in the pack ice as it moves over the Arctic Ocean (Hobson et al. 1989) and usually circle the western Amerasian Basin (Canada Basin) for 5-30 years in the Beaufort Gyre current before drifting south into the Atlantic through Fram Strait or grounding in channels of the QEI (Fig. 1) (Jeffries and Shaw 1993).

It is difficult to use ice islands as research platforms because celestial navigational fixes are not easy to obtain at high latitudes during continuous daylight or twilight conditions. Moreover, because ice islands rotate slowly as they drift, a zero-zero reference azimuth must first be established as a North and all compass points and directional terms then refer to the established azimuth. To complicate matters, the passage from Ellesmere Island to the Beaufort Sea is close to the rapidly shifting magnetic north pole in the CAA along the west edge of the Sverdrup Basin (Fig. 3), so that ship and aircraft compasses need frequent readjustment. Movement of ice islands is therefore difficult to determine with precision, although an estimate of about 1.6 km per day was calculated by G. Hobson from Fletcher's Ice Island drift on the Canadian margin.

In August 1983, a Système Argos satellite-positioning buoy was placed on 'Hobson's Choice' Ice Island to track its drift, and in September 1984, PCSP started building research facilities on CII. The CII research station was led by G. Hobson staffed by various chief scientists, including

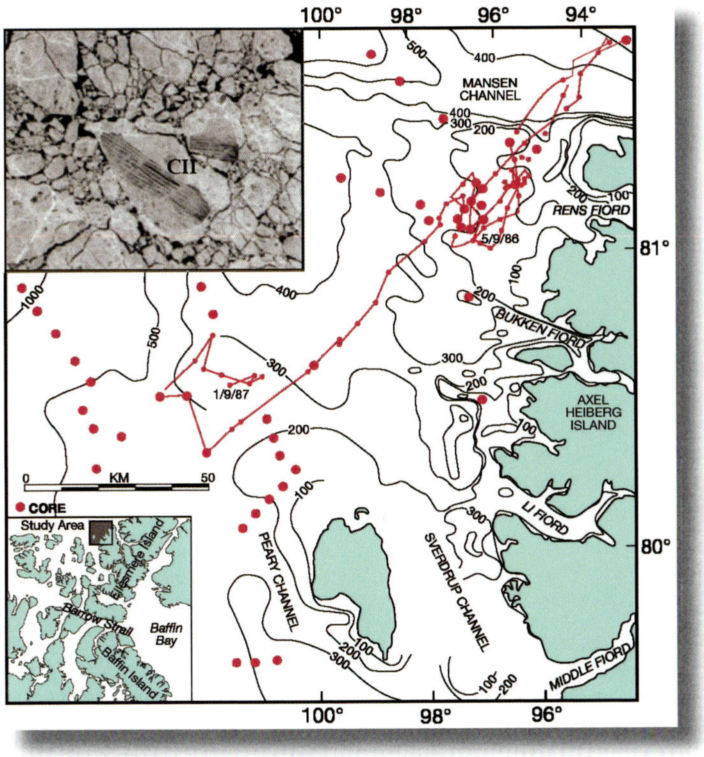

Figure 3. Map of the study area on the Canadian polar margin with upper inset (from Jeffries 2000) showing the Canadian Ice Island (CII) within a sea covered by multi-year pack ice. The drift track of CII is shown for 1985-87 in relation to the detailed bathymetry of the polar continental shelf mapped during the CII program. Large red dots indicate geological samples taken from ice-covered leads from 1987-89.

K. Ellis, B. Hargrave, R. Jackson, P. Jones, and P. Mudie from BIO, working together with university scientists from Dalhousie, Acadia, Memorial, and University of Alaska (Fairbanks) and with government scientists from Ottawa, Calgary, and Vancouver Island.

Hobson said of the CII: "You don't navigate it; you don't put a motor on it. How do you keep track of it?" (Foster and Marino 1986). Fortunately, by 1984, satellite navigation was accessible by radio when satellites were directly over the CII, and sometimes the more accurate Global Positioning System (GPS) was available. Magnetic storms sometimes interfered with satellite signals, however, and cut-off all communication between the CII radio operator and other Canadian stations. The rotational orientation was recorded by detectors placed at each end of the CII. From 1983 to 1989, no ice island had ever been so closely watched.

Aerial views of the CII showed a series of undulating ridges and troughs that distinguish arctic ice islands from icebergs and from large sea ice floes (Fig. 3; Jeffries 2000). The first task to establish a science camp on CII was the construction of a 1-km long runway to allow DC-3 aircraft to land with heavy equipment including building materials, tractor, 300-kg generator, 1-ton winch, and 1.4-ton water boilers. Later, a bulldozer and 7-ton winch were delivered to the ice island by means of a LAPES (Low Altitude Parachute Escape System) drop by the Canadian Forces. The field camp was designed to support 35 people in 14 wood buildings and six parcolls (sectional, insulated, aluminum-framed shelter with wood floors). The camp generator provided up to 50 kW of power for a kitchen, mechanical and electronics workshops.

By 1988, the camp's scientific facilities (Fig. 2) included a SATNAV navigation system, seismic reflection array, explosives magazine, and geophysics instrument hut. A separate geology lab (Figs. 2C) and 50 kW power supply enclosed two winches for deployment of piston and gravity cores, dredges, and plankton nets to a water depth of 4,000 m (Figs. 4A,C). A specially designed hot water-glycol-antifreeze boiler system in an adjacent shed was used to melt a large hydrohole (ca. 1.5 m diameter), inside the geology lab, that extended down into the water beneath the ice island (Fig. 4B). A heat exchanger system prevented salt water and brine from entering the two boilers required for its operation (Gorveatt and Chin Yee 1988). The first ice island hydrohole ever constructed required a non-stop 272-hour effort to complete. This hydrohole indicated the central ice island thickness was 44 m, with sea level 4.85 m below the ice surface, and a water depth of 283 m. The hydrohole was then used to take the first water and sediment samples from this part of the Canadian Arctic margin, using modern instruments (Van Wagoner et al. 1989). A bottom camera could be lowered through the hydrohole to obtain the first photographs of the Axel Heiberg continental shelf seafloor. These photos showed a surface of soft mud patterned by animal trails and worm burrows, large, white Foraminifera (*Planispirinoides buccilentus*), and pebbles or cobbles, possibly relicts from a glacial ice sheet that once covered the margin.

In April 1985, the first scientific field season, the CII was in thick multi-year ice at about 81.7° N, 93.5° W. The weather was expected to be cold, knowing that Isachsen on Ellef Ringnes Island recorded the severest weather in Canada from 1948 to 1978 (Alt and Maxwell 2000). There had been no significant movement of CII over winter and so, after completion of the hydrohole, work concentrated on sampling island snow, ice, and water in leads along the ice edges. These samples provided records of the physical and chemical oceanography, levels, and sources of pollutants on the Canadian polar margin, and an inventory of the planktonic biota. The ice cores gave information on the history of CII, its mechanical properties, and the multi-year pack ice.

By July 1985, however, the weather on CII was completely different. Severe melting of the island surface (Fig. 2E) turned the runway to slush so that planes had to land on skis, and the air was filled with fog from the open water of widening leads. Air temperatures rose from lows of -51° C to positive values of 7-16°C. Fog frequently delayed transport of replacement teams and supplies, and trenches had to be dug around the laboratories and sleeping quarters to prevent flooding (Fig. 2F). In the unusually warm summer of 1988, meltwater formed wide lakes between the ridges, and red snow algae (*Chlamydomonas nivalis*) coloured the snow. Smaller lakes and ponds marked multi-year ice about 10 m thick attached to the sides of the island (Fig. 3). Work now could be done in shirt sleeves, but crossing melting snow became treacherous because subsurface slush ice acts like quicksand when agitated by a misplaced leg.

During the summers of 1985 to 1987, CII travelled west over the continental shelf north of Axel Heiberg for ca. 250 km (except for two reversals in 1985 and 1986). By 1987, CII was in deep water over the continental margin northwest of Meighen Island (Fig. 3). This location pro-

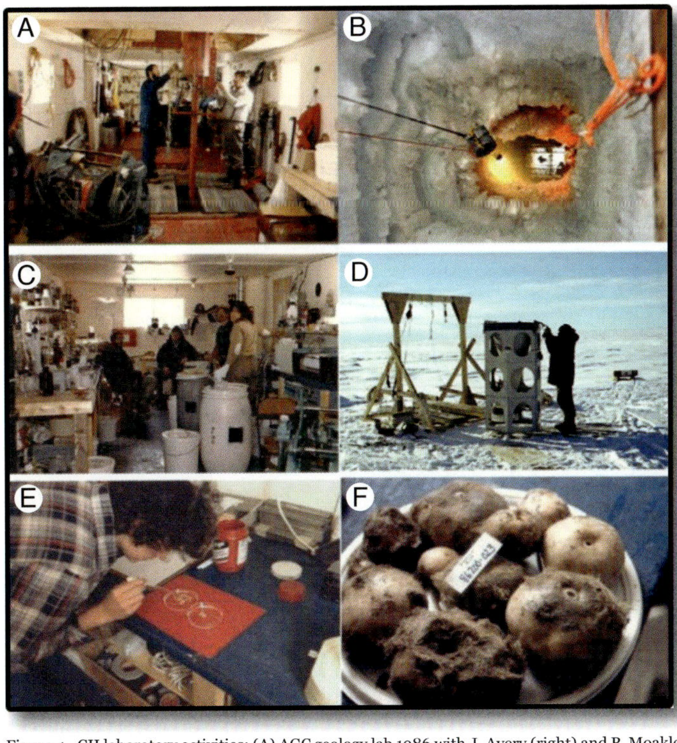

Figure 4. CII laboratory activities: (A) AGC geology lab 1986 with J. Avery (right) and P. Moakler (left) rigging Benthos piston corer; (B) The hydrohole during reaming with alternating layers of blue and white ice almost free of sediment below the surface dust layer; (C) Shared oceanography facilities, 1985: K. Ellis and F. Zemlyak analyse water from 1,000-l barrels watched by M. Gorveatt and P. Moakler in charge of bathymetric recorders (centre left); (D) P. Vass with the Kiel sediment trap; (E) A. Redden examines crustaceans from vertical plankton tow nets; and (F) *Geodia* demosponges from a dredge sample (scale bar: 2 cm).

vided opportunities for mapping shelf bathymetry and sampling both the water column and seabed. In summer 1988, however, westward movement ceased and the island drifted south from the continental slope into Peary Channel between Ellef Ringnes and Meighen islands, cutting short its circumpolar arctic journey.

RESULTS: SOME UNIMAGINABLE DISCOVERIES

How Wide and Deep is Canada's Polar Margin?

In 1958, when the United Nations held a conference on 'The Law of the Sea' to examine international policies regarding ownership and management of ocean resources, the Canadian Government did not know if it had a continental shelf east of the Beaufort Sea and Parry Islands (Roots and Hobson 1986). At the start of the CII project, there was no bathymetric map for the region between Ellef Ringnes and Ellesmere islands. The PCSP map showed a few soundings that suggested a narrow shelf c. 20 km wide dropping off steeply to the Amerasian Basin beyond depths of 200 m. However, continuous echosounder and 3.5 kHz seismic reflection profiles collected by recorders in the geology lab showed the inner shelf to be 3-6 times wider than that depicted on the 1985 chart (Van Wagoner et al. 1989). These continuous bathymetric data, combined with new regional hydrographic measurements obtained from ice floe camps (1 sounding/km^2), revealed that the continental shelf from Ellesmere to Meighen islands is about 100 km wide and mostly deeper than 300 m, with only the innermost shelf delimited by the 200 m isobath (Fig. 3). Owing to these findings, from May 1985 to November 1987, Canada's northern boundary may be expanded seawards (Verhoef 2014).

Why is the Bottom Bumpy?

The seismic reflection profiles reveal that the polar shelf floor is smooth in places but hummocky elsewhere, regardless of water depth. The most conspicuous seabed features are mounds hundreds of metres wide and up to 10 m high. In water depths deeper than 300 m, photos and grab samples showed the hummocks to be ice-rafted gravel and/or gravity-flow deposits, as expected on an ice-covered polar continental shelf (Hein et al. 1990). Totally unexpected, however, was the discovery in shallower waters of many hummocks formed by gravelly muds with living *Geodia* sponge mounds at the surface (Fig. 5). Although *Geodia* sponge colonies grow in warmer water off Russia and on the Greenland and Baffin Island shelves south of Ellesmere Island, finding them in cold water under permanent pack ice was surprising and previously unknown (Van Wagoner et al. 1989, Kenchington et al. 2011). This arctic benthic animal is a donut-shaped, spine-covered siliceous demosponge (Fig. 4F) with a hard rubbery texture, quite unlike either soft bath sponges (genus *Spongia*) or the true glass sponges (*Hexactinellida*) that grow in deeper Arctic Ocean water and off British Columbia (Van Wagoner et al. 1989).

Benthic communities are particularly important to often nutrient-impoverished polar marine ecosystems because their diversity and production feeds into higher trophic levels, and recycles nutrients for use by plankton (Wassman et al. 2011). Sponge beds provide structurally complex habitats supporting many species in arctic polynyas and areas of strong currents, but data for the polar margin north of the CAA are sparse. The CII studies show that demosponge reefs exist under the multi-year ice and support a diverse benthic community in water depths less than 130 m, supporting at least 34 species excluding the more than 100 benthic foraminiferal species that reside there (Schröder-Adams et al. 1990). The demosponge bioherms include crinoids, sea cucumbers, tunicates, three other sponges, bryozoans, two crustaceans, nine mollusc genera, and at least six ostracod genera, one of which is a new arctic genus, *Axelheibergella*, with two species on the shelf margin (Briggs 1997). Isolated sponges are usually found next to pebbles that provide a holdfast needed for seabed colonization. In the polar sub-ice environment, however, clusters of adjoining sponges support each other, which allows for vertical growth of colonies. This unique feature distinguishes the polar sponge reef communities from low-lying, hard-substrate, sponge communities at comparable depths in warmer waters (Van Wagoner et al. 1989).

Who Eats What Under Multi-year Pack Ice?

In contrast to the rich diversity of the demosponge reefs, vertical particulate matter sedimentation in the water column under the pack ice is low.

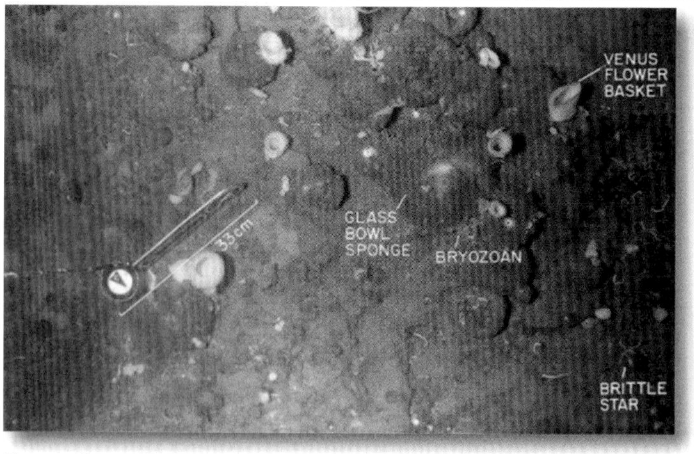

Figure 5. Photograph of the seafloor at 135 m on the Axel Heiberg Island Shelf, showing part of a demosponge reef and its biota, including glass sponges, brittle stars, and bryozoans.

This discovery came from sampling with a Kiel sediment trap (Fig. 4D) lowered 100 m below the CII in another hydrohole melted through the ice (Hargrave et al. 1989). These are the first multi-seasonal measurements of vertical sedimentation (as weight, organic carbon, and nitrogen) to be made under permanent arctic ice pack (Addison et al. 2014). Since Fridtjof Nansen's studies in 1902, it was known that Arctic Ocean waters are among the least productive in the world (Hargrave et al. 1989). Nonetheless, estimated CII annual values were less than all expectations: ten times lower than predicted from global carbon budgets. Other studies at 480 m on the outer shelf north of Ellef Ringnes Island, in near-darkness (about 0.01% of incident radiation) below 6 m of pack ice, showed that bacterial uptake of free amino acids and tritiated thymidine was almost undetectable, despite concentrations of up to 10,000 heterotrophic bacteria per millilitre (Pomeroy et al. 1990). Normally in spring, high arctic food webs are supported mainly by ice algae, but these are sparse under the permanent pack ice. The fallout of algae under the pack ice, however, escapes bacterial degradation in the water column and accumulates near the bottom, and may provide food for benthic animals such as arctic sponges.

Also unexpected were the relatively high rates of total mass flux determined from CII sediment traps on the polar margin during the dark winter period (January–March) when production of phytoplankton and under-ice (epontic) algae is usually minimal (Hargrave et al. 1994). These data showed that blooms of diatoms (mostly *Melosira arctica*) occur on the Canadian polar margin during winter darkness as well as in continuous summer light. Vertical plankton tows in August 1986 also showed that blooms of the brackish-water dinoflagellate *Peridiniella catenata* occur under multi-year pack ice, a species previously found only in arctic open water (Hargrave et al. 1989). In 1989-90, two sediment traps were designed at BIO for biweekly or monthly sampling to obtain greater resolution of seasonal variations in the vertical transport of particulate matter under permanent ice (Hargrave et al. 1994). Data from the new traps validated initial conclusions from the discontinuous 1987 Kiel trap data (Hargrave et al. 1989), and confirmed extremely low sediment fluxes.

Warming Water and Arctic Canaries

CII studies showed that there is a clear zonation of the macrobenthos on the continental shelf beneath the permanent pack-ice cover (Van Wagoner et al. 1989). In depths less than 130 m, the large living sponges support benthic communities (see above), but from 130-150 m, few living sponges exist among the extensive mats of sponge spicules, and from 150-300 m, there are only small living sponges. Radiocarbon dating of shells in the spicule mats shows that formerly extensive sponge communities have died within the past 500-2,000 years. The observed zonation characteristics indicate the possibility of a sea level deepening of 40-60 m during the past 1,000 years. However, mapping of sea-level changes in the CAA shows either no change or uplift of Axel Heiberg Island during this time period (Forbes et al. 2004). Combined evidence indicates a 20-30 m upward shift in the warm Atlantic water layer within the past 500-1,000 years, possibly in response to recent, albeit variable, warming of CAA and Arctic Ocean waters (Vincent et al. 2001, Münchow et al. 2011). Basically, the CII sponge reefs may act as 'arctic canaries' to forewarn of shifts in water temperature, polar margin food chains, and bottom sediment stability.

Hidden Dangers: Pesticides and Artificial Radionuclides

Arctic regions are particularly sensitive to pollution because food chains are short, with a rapid transfer of contaminants to higher trophic levels, and because arctic organisms are physiologically stressed from extremely low temperatures (Smith and Ellis 1993). On the cold, dry Canadian polar margin north of Axel Heiberg Island, the potential impact of pollutants on ecosystems is increased because low precipitation means longer atmospheric residence times for airborne contaminants, and volatile organic compounds persist longer in the soil and water. Northern people who depend on local wildlife for food (e.g., fish, marine mammals and birds, shellfish, seaweed) are at particular risk of accumulating high levels of toxic chemicals.

CII artificial radionuclide studies by K. Ellis and F. Zemlyak in 1985, 1986 and 1989 (Fig. 4C, Fig. 6) show that radioactive cesium (^{137}Cs) entering the Arctic Ocean from nuclear-weapon tests before 1963 was augmented by spills from the Sellafield and La Hague reprocessing facilities in England and France, respectively, in 1975-76, and the Chernobyl nuclear disaster in 1986 (Hargrave et al. 1989, Smith and Ellis 1993). Chernobyl is located in the Ukraine near the Black Sea, more than 5,000 km from the CII. Isotopes such as ^{137}Cs and ^{131}I (radioactive iodine) released during the Chernobyl accident appeared in air particle samples collected at CII less than a month after the 26 April 1986 meltdown (Fig. 6), marking the rapid atmospheric transport of radionuclides from Chernobyl to the Arctic Ocean. Higher levels of ^{131}I compared to New Brunswick for the same period show the importance of winds in the transport of industrial pollutants from Europe to the Arctic (Smith and Ellis 1993). Other evidence of long distance transport to the Canadian polar margin comes from studies of pollen grains in the dark-brown dust collected from CII meltwater pools in 1986. The dark colour of the dust indicated large amounts of fine charcoal particles (i.e., soot). The presence of Maidenhair Tree (*Ginkgo biloba*) pollen in the dust indicates a possible origin in southwestern China, as also found for soot on Hudson Bay ice (Welch et al. 1991).

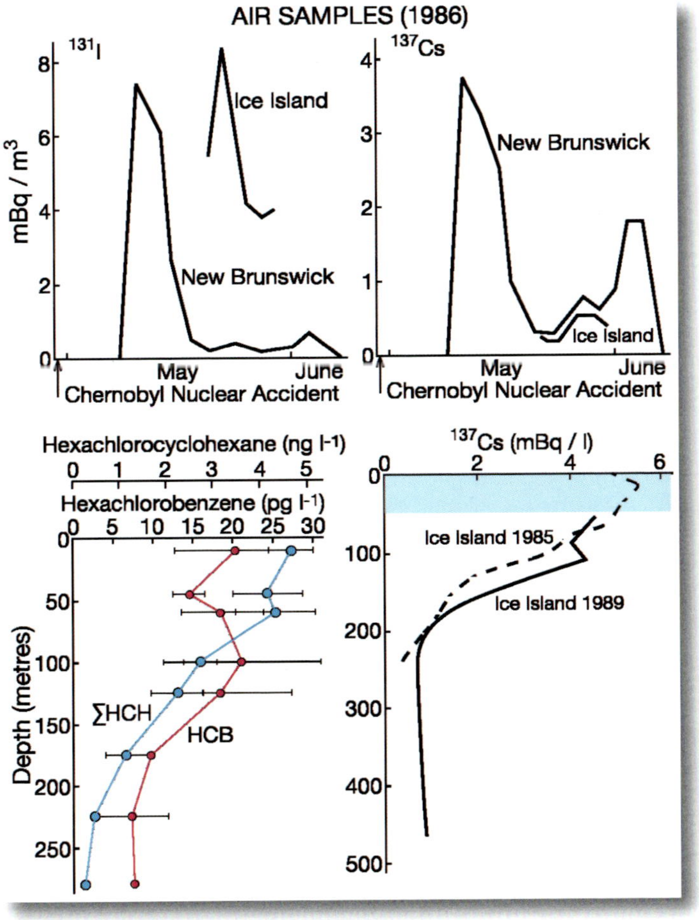

Figure 6. Profiles of arctic pollutants (from Mudie et al. 1989): upper - Comparison of levels of ^{131}I and ^{137}Cs in air on CII and in eastern Canada after the Chernobyl accident of 26 April 1986; bottom right - Distribution of ^{137}Cs in the water under CII; bottom left - Vertical profiles through the water column under CII (1986-87) showing concentrations as x ±1 SD (horizontal bars) for the most abundant organochlorine compounds in particles smaller than 1 mm.

The CII provided a sampling platform to make the first inventory of organochlorines present in the atmosphere, snow, sea ice, water, sediments, and marine organisms under the multi-year ice of the Canadian polar margin (Addison et al. 2014). These persistent organic pollutants (POPs), including DDT and PCBs, are highly nondegradable toxic chemicals that take many years to break down. The atmosphere is probably the major route of POP transfer to the Arctic Ocean after their release from southern agricultural and urban areas. CII data show that the most abundant polar margin organochlorines are HCH (hexachlorocyclohexane) and HCB (hexachlorobenzene). Surface water above 60 m depth has the highest POP levels (Fig. 6), probably entering via snow meltwater or vapour exchange over leads. Lower concentrations measured below 200 m reflect exchange with the deep North Atlantic Ocean water layer (Hargrave et al. 1988).

Movement of POPs through the marine food chain was measured from crustaceans caught with plankton net tows (Fig. 4E) and baited traps on the seabed. The CII analyses show that on the Canadian polar margin, concentrations of less water-soluble pesticides (e.g., DDT and PCBs) are 10 to 1,000 times higher in crustaceans than in the water (Mudie et al. 1989). Although arctic POP concentrations are low compared to southern regions, relatively high levels of DDT, chlordanes, PCBs, toxaphene, and polychlorinated camphenes (PCCs), occur in polar margin crustaceans and accumulate in codfish liver at roughly equivalent levels (Hargrave et al. 1988). Neither DDT nor PCCs occur in air samples previously collected at latitudes as high as CII, suggesting long-distance transport in water from Asia is their most likely pathway.

RESULTS: IMPORTANT TECHNICAL ADVANCES AND FINDINGS

How Does a Polar Margin Ice Island Move?

Previous studies of ice island movement come mainly from the central Arctic Ocean, far beyond the continental margin. From April 1985 to November 1988, Argos buoys provided the first data for Canadian polar margin ice island dynamics and, in 1986, an automatic weather station on CII recorded temperature, pressure, wind speed and direction, and peak gusts. Near Ellesmere and Axel Heiberg islands (Fig. 3), three types of movement occurred: large southwesterly movements up to 1.3 km/h, slower movements of 1-10 km/day in sequentially opposite directions along the coast, and smaller random movements of <1 km/day (Hobson et al. 1989). Synoptic surface pressure maps and the meteorological data show that larger movements are generally preceded by offshore winds with threshold surface speeds of 5-6 m/s. The Coriolis Effect caused CII to move up to 50° to the right of the surface wind direction. Pack ice was the major force impeding free motion of CII. Coastal mountain barriers can also modify regional winds and the resulting sea-surface tilt, thereby limiting ice-island motion, and at times, moving the island against the prevailing wind.

Ice islands also move in response to ocean currents. In the Amerasian Basin currents are usually weak, manifesting as a clockwise pattern of wind-driven ice drift at the surface (Fig.1), but underneath, warmer water can circulate in the opposite direction (Hobson et al. 1989). On the Canadian polar margin, however, temperature gradients are only a few millidegrees and patterns of large-scale water movement are still unknown in detail. A current meter was deployed at 48 m water depth in the CII geology hydrohole using rigid extension rods oriented to geographic north by CII navigation data (Mudie et al. 1989). Hourly surface water current records for daily periods in 1988 showed there were large seasonal variations: in spring, the current was mostly <1 cm/s, whereas in early summer with large open leads, speeds were about 5 cm/s, with semidiurnal modulations. Maximum bottom currents were estimated from sediment textures as <25 cm/s.

Testing the Water

Before the CII program, there was little knowledge of the physical properties of waters beneath the permanent ice cover off Axel Heiberg Island. In spring 1986, 1988, and 1989, CII was the base for physical oceanographic data collection by helicopter-operated conductivity-temperature-density (CTD) surveys over the polar margin. Heat flow measured with a large heat probe at five stations showed unusually cold bottom water under the pack ice at 200 m depth (Louden et al. 1990). Results showed that despite its remarkable depth (average: 400 m), shelf water is significantly different from basin water. Temperature-salinity (T-S) correlations also indicate water-mass modifications from the shelf break into shore. Surface-layer salinities were highly variable, increasing by 0.66 from 1983-87, then decreasing by 0.30 in 1988, and reversing the density difference between the shelf and offshore surface mixed layers (Hobson et al. 1989). In 1987, this difference manifested as a layer of denser shelf water 400 km from shore underneath the lighter surface layer of the Amerasian Basin. It is unlikely that local brine-formation processes could supply enough salt to create this large feature: possibly it reflects advection through the Sverdrup Basin inter-island channels. If this is correct, existing ideas regarding exclusively landward water transport through the Sverdrup Basin islands may need revision.

At the shelf break, closely spaced CTD surveys, made with a Guildline digital CTD lowered through a 23-cm hole in an ice floe (R. Perkin, unpubl. report 1988), delineated a frontal zone separating shelf and offshore regimes. Current measurements showed that shears up to 9 cm/s penetrate to >500 m, indicating a swift, narrow current which may represent much of the total regional along-shelf transport. This strong offshore current contradicts calculations made in 1983 from the Ellesmere Island Shelf expedition and CESAR, predicting a counter-clockwise basin circulation averaging <0.5 cm/s south of Alpha Ridge (Hobson et al. 1989).

Chemical measurements were made using water-bottle casts through the CII hydroholes, and from a remote camp on the shelf break off Ellef Ringnes Island. Arctic surface and deeper Atlantic water chemistry are characterized by measuring nitrate, phosphate, silicate and oxygen, stable isotopes in organic matter and water, dissolved inorganic carbon, dissolved oxygen (Hobson et al. 1989, Jones and Andersen 1990), radioactive nuclides of ^{137}Cs, ^{90}Sr, ^{210}Pb/^{210}Po, ^{226}Ra, and ^{239,240}Pu, tritium, freons, and inert gases (e.g., krypton, argon) (Moore and Spitzer 1990). Other studies show that the central Arctic Ocean and Canadian polar margin have the same three water sources: water with Siberian river content over a layer of cooled Atlantic water, water of Pacific origin modified on the Siberian continental shelves, and water of mostly Atlantic origin modified on European continental shelves (Jones 2014). Low ^{210}Pb and ^{210}Po activities in Peary Channel, along with high parent ^{226}Ra activities indicate effective particle-scavenging within the nutrient maxima near the Arctic and Atlantic water layer boundaries; however, the polar margin scavenging is much lower than in the central Arctic Ocean (Moore and Smith 1986). Peary Channel ^{239,240}Pu data for 1989 provide one of only two profiles in the western Arctic Ocean, and show that above 200 m ^{239,240}Pu/^{137}Cs ratios are lower than the expected fallout ratio of 0.0213 (Mudie et al. 1989). This low value suggests very efficient removal of plutonium by particle scavenging in the channel, in stark contrast to the shelf where scavenging rates are minimal.

Probing the Shelf Depths

The CII provided a stable platform in the pack ice to make the first seismic reflection and refraction explorations of the continental shelf north of Axel Heiberg Island (Cox et al. 1990). A seismic reflection experiment in 1984 determined that geophones operated satisfactorily on CII. In 1985, a permanent multi-channel reflection array was laid out in a cross formation 3.5 km long (107 stations, 33.3 m apart), with 13 stations 200 m apart on the cross-arm. Charges of 1 kg of 60% Geogel were fired (Fig. 2D) at a depth of 110 m through 13 narrow hydroholes with 9 geophones in a circle of 5-m radius (Hadjnal and Overton 1987). A set of 6 second common midpoint data was recorded from the 13 hydrohole shotpoints for each kilometre the island drifted, providing 87 measurement sets. The CII refraction survey covered a transition zone in an area of complex shelf bathymetry along the Canadian polar margin, including a 60-km line along the outer shelf, a 180-km parallel line along the inner shelf, and a 60-km connecting line (Fig. 7). Shotpoints offset from the line ends recorded upper mantle observations to a distance of 240 km (Asudeh et al. 1989). In 1988, charges of 1-2 kg were detonated every 20 minutes as CII moved from Meighen to Ellef Ringnes islands (Hobson et al. 1989).

What the 'Big Bangs' Tell Us About the Geology and its Significance for Canada's Jurisdiction in the Offshore

Regional gravity and magnetic surveys carried out since 1959 show that the Canadian polar margin has potential field anomalies (i.e., changes in gravity with space and time) and earthquake epicentre clusters like those of passive continental margins (Forsyth et al. 1990). The cross-shelf Peary Channel coincides with a major change in potential field anomaly pattern (Sobczak and Weber 1987). Linear magnetic lows mark areas of significant seismic activity associated with large elliptical gravity highs straddling the shelf-slope break. These gravity anomalies indicate large isostatically uncompensated (i.e., unbalanced) sediment loads that increase in average upper crust density along the coast and continental shelf from Ellesmere to Ellef Ringnes islands. This density gradient apparently reflects an eastward increase in metamorphism because borehole studies show a parallel gradient in frequency of mafic (alkaline rock) intrusions (Sobczak and Halpenny 1989). Areas of major crustal complexity are found beneath the shelf off Prince Patrick and Axel Heiberg islands. The bedding direction (strike), potential field anomalies and crustal extension across northern Sverdrup Basin indicate that polar margin rifting varied along-strike, controlled mainly by pre-existing basement features and development of the Alpha Ridge.

Data from 1985 and 1986 when CII moved slowly over the Axel Heiberg Shelf (Fig. 7: I-J) suggest a very thin (<300-700 m) layer of unconsolidated sediment covers about 4 km of high velocity (5 km/s) rock (Hobson et al. 1989). Discovery of structurally complex basement with steeply dipping reflectors supports the passive margin model, and the new outer shelf section (Fig. 7: S-T-B) reveals 15 km of sedimentary strata with a prominent unconformity at about 10 km depth, probably separating Upper Cretaceous–Tertiary strata from Lower Cretaceous and older rocks (Overton and Embry 1989). This sedimentary wedge is similar to that in Beaufort Sea and could contain significant resources (Hobson et al. 1989, Forsyth et al. 1998). Gautier et al. (2009) estimate 6 to >100 trillion cubic feet of potential gas for the region.

The final results of the CII seismic refraction program on the Canadian polar margin are summarized by Jackson (1990) and Forsyth et al. (1998). Five velocity units are mapped from Axel Heiberg to north of Meighen Island (Fig.7). Surface Unit 5 (velocity 1.9-3.4 km/s) is a few kilometres thick and apparently comprises an undeformed Neogene succession with buried Upper Cretaceous–Paleogene strata on the inner shelf. Unit 4 (velocity 4.3-5.3 km/s, up to 10 km thick) is like that of the Late Paleozoic–Late Mesozoic sequence in Sverdrup Basin. Forsyth et al. (1998) interpreted this unit as mainly mid-Jurassic–Paleogene deltaic to basinal terrigenous strata, likely deformed by folds and faults generated during the early Tertiary Eurekan Orogeny. Unit 3 (velocities 5.9-6.3 km/s), consists primarily of clastic and carbonate strata, volcanics and intrusives of the highly deformed, late Proterozoic–early Paleozoic Franklinian Basin that comprises mainly marine sedimentary rocks on the Sverdrup Basin margin. Along the shelf edge, this unit may also encompass Lower Cretaceous volcanic flows and Jurassic–Cretaceous strata extensively intruded by sills and dykes. The top of this unit is considered to be 'basement'. Velocities of 6.6-6.8 km/s for the underlying Unit 2 correlate well with the crystalline lower crust. The deepest Unit 1 represents the ultramafic, uppermost mantle (velocity 8.2 km/s). The top of the mantle, the MOHO, is about 25 km deep on the inner shelf, rising to 20 km on the outer shelf (Forsyth et al. 1998).

Of particular interest for understanding the link between onshore and offshore geology is the velocity and magnetic character of Line E-I (Fig. 7) perpendicular to the Canadian polar margin where a 5.0 km/s layer is measured near the surface. Gravity, magnetics, and onshore geology all indicate a volcanic layer. Onshore in northwestern Ellesmere Island, the Hansen Point volcanics comprise part of the high arctic Large Igneous Province while offshore the Alpha Ridge is also part of this igneous province. The seismic and other geophysical data demonstrating continuity of geological features across the polar shelf are significant because Canada is preparing a claim to the United Nations Convention on the Law of the Sea (UNCLOS) to extend our continental shelf. CII data may be used to show that the Alpha Ridge is a natural prolongation of Canada's continental margin (Verhoef et al. 2014).

The Past is All We Know About the Future

The CII was used for a marine geology sampling program to map sediments on the Canadian Polar Shelf and to study the history of pack-ice during the latest Quaternary and Holocene time (the past 15,000 years). Surficial sediments and exposed sedimentary bedrock on the polar margin were sampled by 100 grab and dredge samples, by coring with Benthos gravity or piston corers, and with a giant box corer lowered through the hydrohole. A total of 24 short (<2.3 m) cores were obtained beneath the perennial ice cover between Nansen and Peary channels (Hein et al. 1990). After 1987, regional coverage was extended by helicopter flights in a grid across the polar margin to sample the seabed from holes melted

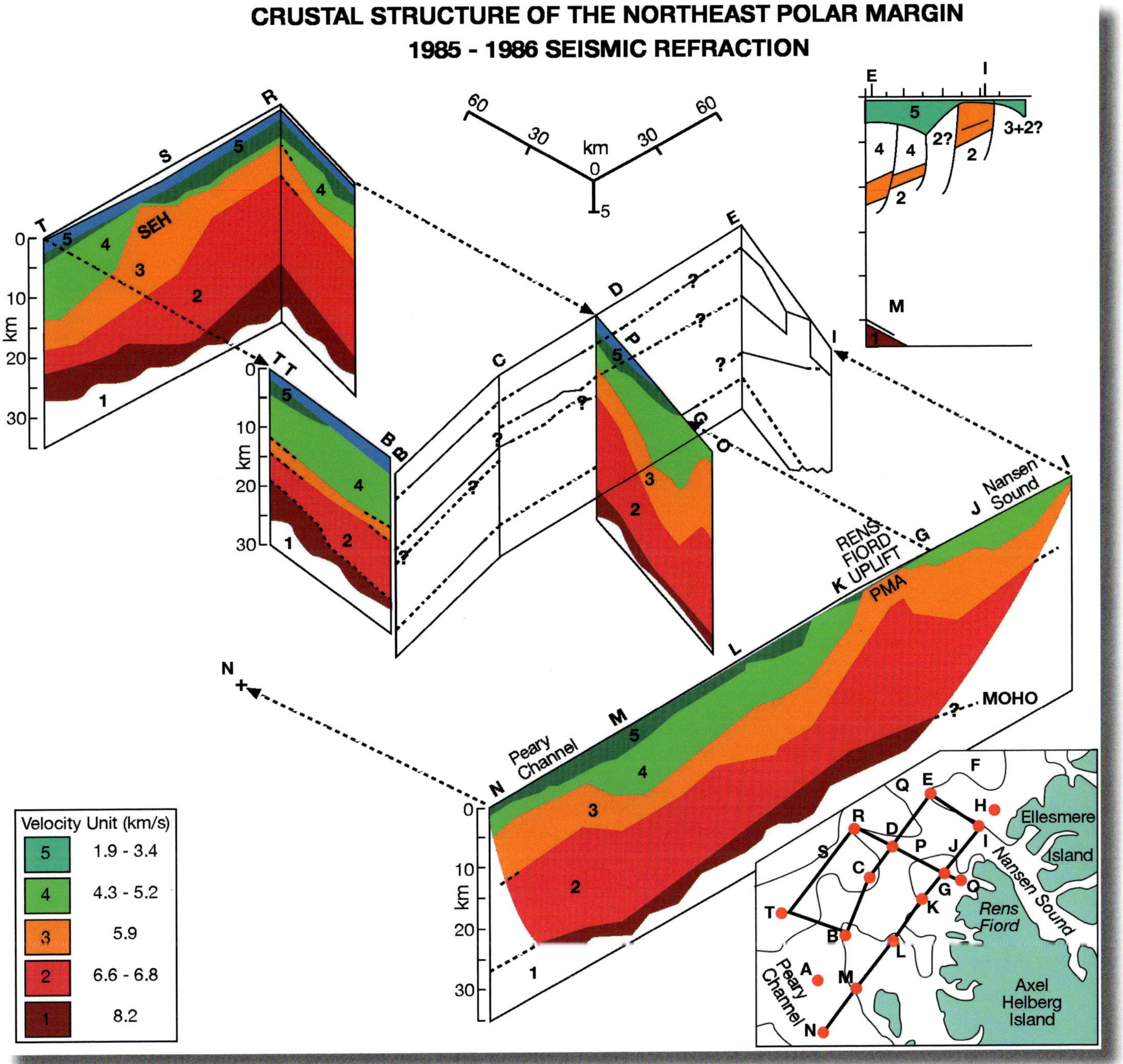

Figure 7. Refraction fence diagram showing the distribution of the five velocity units recorded on the Axel Heiberg Shelf along survey lines shown in the lower inset (from Forsyth et al. 1998). PMA = Princess Margaret Arch; SEH = Shelf Edge High. The inset shows details of Line E-I, with interpretations in terms of the crustal geology of the CAA and an assumed Moho (M) boundary marking the crust-mantle contact (from Hobson et al. 1989).

through frozen leads in the pack ice (Fig. 3). The continuous 12 kHz echograms and shallow high-resolution 3.5 kHz seismic profiles linked the core sites, allowing delimitation of sediment facies; radiocarbon ages of shells in the cores provided sediment ages and rates of deposition.

Five Late Quaternary–Holocene sediment facies are widely correlatable between 120 and 300 m water depth on the inner shelf, but the outer shelf and slope to 1200 m have <10 cm of postglacial Holocene calcareous mud above gravelly sediment of Wisconsinan Glacial Stage or older age (Hein et al. 1990, Hein and Mudie 1991). The sediments and their microfossils (benthic and planktonic foraminifera, pteropods, ostracods) and palynological data record fluctuations in ice cover over a full glacial ocean from about 10,000 to 7,000 years BP, and variations in ice-rafted detritus melted out in more open water after glacial retreat. Sediment textures and geotechnical properties do not indicate grounding of continental ice on the Axel Heiberg Shelf during the last glaciation at the core sites, but an abrupt contact between the oldest glaciomarine shelf sediments and Paleogene bedrock may indicate glacier removal of late Tertiary and older Quaternary sediments. Synsedimentary fault structures in some cores suggest recent isostatic adjustment to ice loading or tectonism on this unusually deep polar margin, and debris flows were widespread ca. 9,950 years BP when glaciers retreated during early Holocene conditions of high insolation and warmer summers (Hein and Mudie 1991).

Sediments of the youngest facies record intervals of relatively open water alternating with periods of shelf ice and multi-year pack-ice on the Axel Heiberg Shelf during the past 7,150 years. Multi-year ice cover changes are recorded by variations in amounts of coarse-grained debris (medium sand to cobble) melted out from either grounded ice, or calving of shelf ice and icebergs. Fine sand, silt and clay represent inputs from offshore winds and melted sea ice to summer open water (Hein and Mudie 1991). This geological record of alternating colder and warmer intervals corresponds to historical records of continuous shelf ice along northern Ellesmere Island at the end of the Little Ice Age (e.g., AD 1875 to 1906), followed by massive wasting during unusually warm intervals like the mid-1930s. Considerably reduced summer sea ice is reported elsewhere for the QEI from 6,500 to 4,500 years BP (Hein and Mudie 1991), coinciding with summer temperature increases of up to 4°C inferred for southern Nares Strait (Mudie et al. 2004). This increase is about the same as predictions from computer models of future arctic warming – hence, the CII cores provide pre-historical evidence of expected intervals with summer open water along the polar margin north of Axel Heiberg Island.

END PRODUCTS

By late summer 1988, despite hopes that the weather would shift and move the CII offshore into the Beaufort Gyre over the western Amerasian Basin (Fig. 1), it became clear that the island drift had shifted from the Arctic Ocean into the CAA channels. From February 1988 to August 1992, CII movements were monitored by an Argos satellite-positioning buoy and imaged by synthetic aperture radar (SAR) aboard the ERS-1 satellite. CII entered Peary Channel (Figs. 1 and 3) in late 1988, then drifted rapidly south from summer 1989 to November 1991, moving into Queens Channel 60 km north of Cornwallis Island. Over the 1990-91 seasons, all scientific equipment and installations were removed before final break-up of CII occurred. By May 1992, all traces of the CII research platform had vanished. Its rapid disintegration appears to have resulted from extensive ice break-up in the inter-island channels in above average (+2°C) summer temperatures, accompanied by atmospheric circulation and surface wind changes (Jeffries and Shaw 1993).

Despite loss of this scientific field station after only 5 years of operation, the CII left a legacy of over 50 scientific papers published by 1990, filling a void in knowledge of Canada's arctic oceanography under the multi-year pack ice where previously scientific information was sparse or absent. The discovery of *Geodia* demosponge reefs living in darkness under the multi-year pack ice where vertical particulate matter fluxes and rates of carbon use are among the lowest found in the world's oceans was both unexpected and important for interpreting the paleoecology of Paleozoic demosponge-bryozoan bioherms in rocks of the eastern CAA (Van Wagoner et al. 1989). Changes in the CII sponge reefs over the past 500-2,000 years may reflect major changes in the water column that preceded recent arctic global warming, although the thickness of multi-year ice in Nares Strait does not yet indicate this warming trend (Münchow et al. 2011). Nonetheless, the Ward Ice Shelf thickness decreased by 13 m between 1967 and 1999 (Vincent et al. 2001), and the ice shelf has now largely disintegrated. The inert gas measurements showing that arctic surface water temperature may be governed by transfer of heat directly to the sea ice has major implications for models of rapid ocean-atmosphere heat transfer in the Arctic Ocean (Moore and Spitzer 1990). CII paleoecology data also provide some analogs for possible future changes because they record changes in pack ice at known times of arctic summers up to 4°C warmer than now (Mudie et al. 2004).

CII data also show how pollutants enter the water beneath permanent pack ice and become concentrated in marine organisms. This baseline information is important for detecting long-term trends of toxic concentrations in the Arctic Ocean, particularly if ice cover continues to diminish. For example, monitoring of PCBs during the 1990s has shown that the Arctic has a slower rate of decline of PCBs than in temperate regions (Macdonald et al. 2000). Furthermore, the detailed bi-weekly/monthly measurements obtained from CII sediment traps provide crucial baseline data for monitoring changes expected to accompany continued climate warming in the pack-ice region where year-round studies are scarce and few 'footprints' of climate change are documented (Wassman et al. 2011).

Another major 'spin-off' from the CII research is the more detailed 1:500,000 scale Canadian Hydrographic Service chart now available for the polar shelf between Ellesmere and Borden islands (CHS Chart #7953). Russian icebreaker cruise ships now sail the inside passage from Amund Ringnes to eastern Ellesmere Island (Johnston 2011), although shipping along the Canadian polar margin will remain hazardous and unappealing to commercial vessels as long as heavy multi-year ice persists. Measurements of physical properties of CII and adjoining multi-year ice up to 10 m thick (Hobson et al. 1989) provide guidelines for designing stronger arctic icebreakers (Sackinger et al. 1991) and the sub-surface geophysical data point to significant gas resources that may become important when more accessible arctic reservoirs are depleted (Gautier et al. 2009).

Perhaps the most important result of all is the gaining of unrivalled technical knowledge of how to conduct scientific studies in multi-year pack ice conditions in one of the coldest parts of the Arctic Ocean. By 2009, 20 years after the CII program ended, the number of published papers providing baseline oceanographic data from this research exercise reached about 100 and continues to increase. The logistical knowledge about ice island movement and scientific operation in multi-year pack ice where ships cannot travel is now the foundation of ongoing efforts to map the continental margins north of Ellesmere Island and Greenland in order to delimit international boundaries that have yet to be firmly established. The limits of Canada's polar margin west of Ellesmere Island can now be drawn accurately, whereas previously they were 'best guesses' or unknown. Although Canada's rights to undersea resources on the Alpha Ridge have not yet been fully resolved, the outline of the western end of this submarine ridge is no longer just a dotted line on arctic bathymetric maps. If the new mapping data confirm the ridge to be an extension of the CAA volcanic province underwater north of Ellesmere Island, then Canada's northern marine frontier may expand almost to the geographic North Pole.

ACKNOWLEDGEMENTS

Space prevents listing everyone who participated in the CII program. Foremost, CII was enabled by logistical support from the Polar Continental Shelf Project (PCSP), its director George Hobson and the PCSP pilots, mechanics, and cooks. Marine geology studies depended on skills of Atlantic Geoscience Centre (AGC), now Geological Survey of Canada Atlantic (GSCA), program support engineers and the coring team led by Michael Gorveatt; oceanographers were supported mainly by BIO engineer Mark Chin Yee, and technicians Peter Vass and Frank Zemlyak. Contractor Jay Ardai designed the hydrohole drilling. Field support of AGC geologists Gary Sonnichsen and David Mosher is acknowledged – also help from Flona Cole, Jean Dabros and Shelly Thibaudeau (AGC), and university colleagues Ali Aksu, Frances Hein, Nancy Van Wagoner, and Anna Redden. We thank GSC geophysicists David Forsyth, Randall Stevenson and Ashton Embry for participation, and Michael Schmidt (PCSP) for camp operations management. Support for the CII program was provided by the Frontier Geoscience Program of Canada, Canada Departments of Energy, Mines and Resources, Fisheries and Oceans, and Atmospheric Environment Service (now Meteorological Service of Canada) of the Department of Environment.

REFERENCES

Addison, R.F., B.T. Hargrave, and G.C. Harding. 2014. Organochlorine pollutants in marine ecosystems. Pages 309-314 *in* Voyage of Discovery: Fifty Years of Marine Research at Canada's Bedford Institute of Oceanography (D.N. Nettleship, D.C. Gordon, C.F.M. Lewis, and M.P. Latremouille, Eds.). Bedford Institute of Oceanography-Oceans Association, Dartmouth, NS.

Alt, B.T. and B. Maxwell. 2000. Overview of the modern arctic climate. Pages 17-36 *in* Environmental response to climate change in the Canadian High Arctic (M. Garneau and B. Alt, Eds.). Geological Survey of Canada Bulletin 529.

Asudeh, I., D.A. Forsyth, R. Stephenson, A. Embry, and H.R. Jackson. 1989. Crustal structure of the Canadian polar margin: results of the 1985 seismic refraction survey. Canadian Journal of Earth Sciences 26: 853-866.

Barry, R.G. and T.W. Gan. 2011. The Global Cryosphere: Past, Present and Future. Cambridge University Press, Cambridge, England.

Briggs, W.M. 1997. *Axelheibergella* (Ostracoda, Crustacea), a new genus of marginally septate cladocopid ostracods from the Central Arctic Ocean. Journal of Micropaleontology 16: 109-120.

Christie, R.L. and J.W. Kerr. 1981. Geological exploration of the Canadian Arctic Islands. Pages 187-202 *in* A Century of Canada's Arctic Islands 1880-1890 (M. Zaslow, Ed.). Royal Society of Canada, Ottawa, ON.

Cook, A. 1981. A gift outright: the exploration of the Canadian arctic islands after 1880. Pages 51-60 *in* A Century of Canada's Arctic Islands 1880-1890 (M. Zaslow, Ed.). Royal Society of Canada, Ottawa, ON.

Cox, T.P., A. Overton, and R.F. Mereu. 1990. Seismic reflection results from an ice island over the Arctic continental Shelf. Marine Geology 93: 193-210.

Forbes, D.L., M. Craymer, G.K. Manson, and S.M. Solomon. 2004. Defining limits of submergence and potential for rapid coastal change in the Canadian Arctic. Berichte zur Polar und Meeresforschung 482: 196-202.

Forsyth, D.A., J. Broome, A.H. Embry, and J.F. Halpenny. 1990. Features of the Canadian polar margin. Marine Geology 93: 147-177.

Forsyth, D.A., I. Asudeh, D. White, R. Jackson, R.A. Stephenson, A.F. Embry, and M. Argyle. 1998. Sedimentary basins and basement highs beneath the Polar Shelf north of Axel Heiberg and Meighen Islands. Bulletin of Canadian Petroleum Geology 46: 12-29.

Foster, M. and C. Marino. 1986. The Polar Shelf. NC Press Limited, Toronto, ON.

Frolov, I.E., Z.M. Gudkovich, V.F. Radionov, A.V.Schirochov, and L.A. Timokhov. 2005. The Arctic Basin – results from the Russian drifting stations. Springer Publishing, Chichester, England.
Gautier, D.L., K.J. Bird, R.R. Carpentier, A. Grantz, D.W. Houseknecht, T.R. Klett, T.E. Moore, J.K. Pitman, C.J. Schenk, J.H. Schuenemeyer, K. Sorensen, M.E. Tennyson, Z.C. Valin, and C.J. Wandrey. 2009. Assessment of undiscovered oil and gas in the Arctic. Science 324: 1,175-1,179.
Gorveatt, M. and M. Chin-Yee. 1988. Arctic ice island coring facility. Pages 555-560 *in* Proceedings of Oceans '88: A Partnership of Marine Interests, Vol. 2 (S. Smith and E. Early, Chairs). Institute of Electrical and Electronics Engineers Service Center, Piscataway, NJ. Doi:10.1109/OCEANS.1988.23562.
Hadjnal, Z. and A. Overton. 1987. Reflection experiment on a floating ice platform. Geophysical Journal of the Royal Astronomical Society 89: 201-208.
Hargrave, B.T., W.P.Vass, P.E. Erickson, and B.R. Fowler. 1988. Atmospheric transport of organochlorines to the Arctic Ocean. Tellus 40B: 480-493.
Hargrave, B.T., B. von Bodungen, R.J. Conover, A.J. Fraser, G. Phillips, and W.P. Vass. 1989. Seasonal changes in sedimentation of particulate matter and lipid content of zooplankton collected by sediment trap in the Arctic Ocean off Axel Heiberg Island. Polar Biology 10: 467-475.
Hargrave, B.T., B. Von Bodungen, P. Stoffyn-Egli, and P.J. Mudie. 1994. Seasonal variability in particle sedimentation under permanent ice cover in the Arctic Ocean. Continental Shelf Research 14: 279-293.
Hattersley-Smith, G., L.S. Koenig, K.R. Greenaway, and M. Dunbar. 1952. Arctic Ice Islands. Arctic 5: 66-103.
Hein, F.J., N.A. Van Wagoner, and P.J. Mudie. 1990. Sedimentary facies and processes of deposition: ice island cores, Axel Heiberg Shelf, Canadian Polar Continental Margin. Marine Geology 93: 243-265.
Hein, F.J. and P.J. Mudie. 1991. Glacial-marine sedimentation, Canadian Polar margin, north of Axel Heiberg Island. Géographie physique et Quaternaire 45: 213-227.
Hobson, G., A. Aksu, S.A. Macko, I. Asudeh, D.A. Forsyth, M. Schmidt, L. Sobczak, M.O. Jeffries, W.M. Sackinger, A. Overton, J.R. Weber, R.G. Perkin, and N.A. Van Wagoner. 1989. Ice Island Field Station – new features of Canadian Polar margin. EOS Transactions American Geophysical Union 70: 833-839.
Jackson, H.R. 1990. Evolution and regional stratigraphy of the northeastern Canadian polar margin. Marine Geology 93: 179-192.
Jeffries, M.O. 2000. Glaciers of the Arctic Islands, Ellesmere Island ice shelves and ice islands. Pages 147-163 *in* Satellite Image Atlas of Glaciers of the World – North America (R.S.Williams, Jr. and J.G. Ferrigno, Eds.). United States Geological Survey Professional Paper 1386-J-1. US Geological Survey Information Services, Denver, CO.
Jeffries, M.O. and M.A. Shaw. 1993. The drift of ice islands from the Arctic Ocean into the channels of the Canadian Arctic Archipelago: the history of Hobson's Choice Ice Island. Polar Record 29: 305-312.
Johnston, A.E. 2011. Is Canada ready for increased arctic cruise tourism? Perspectives from the federal government. Pages 37-51 *in* Canadian Arctic Shipping: Issues and Perspectives (A.Lajeunesse, W.Russell, and A.E. Johnston, Eds.). International Centre for Northern Governance and Development Occasional Paper Series, Vol. 11-01. University of Saskatchewan, Saskatoon, SK.
Jones, E.P. 2014. The Arctic Ocean: its waters and global significance. Pages 31-35 *in* Voyage of Discovery: Fifty Years of Marine Research at Canada's Bedford Institute of Oceanography (D.N. Nettleship, D.C. Gordon, C.F.M. Lewis, and M.P. Latremouille, Eds.). Bedford Institute of Oceanography-Oceans Association, Dartmouth, NS.
Jones, E.P. and L.G. Anderson. 1990. On the origin of the properties of the Arctic Ocean halocline north of Ellesmere Island: results from the Canadian ice island. Continental Shelf Research 10: 485-498.
Kenchington, E., H. Link, V. Roy, P. Archambault, T. Siferd, M. Treble, and V. Wareham. 2011. Identification of mega- and macro-benthic ecologically and biologically significant areas (EBSAs) in the Hudson Bay Complex, the Western and Eastern Canadian Arctic. Fisheries and Oceans Canada Canadian Science Advisory Secretariat Research Document 2011/071, Ottawa, ON.
LeBourdais, D.M. 1963. Stefansson: Ambassador of the North. Harvest House, Montreal, QC.
Louden, K.E., G. Leger, and N. Hamilton. 1990. Marine heat flow observations on the Canadian Arctic continental shelf and slope. Marine Geology 93: 267-288.
Macdonald, R.W. and others. 2000. Contaminants in the Canadian Arctic: 5 years of progress in understanding sources, occurrence and pathways. The Science of the Total Environment 254: 93-234.
McGhee, R. 1990. Canadian Arctic Prehistory. Canadian Museum of Civilization, Hull, QC.
Moore, R.M. and J.N. Smith. 1986. Disequilibria between ^{226}Ra, ^{210}Pb and ^{210}Po in the Arctic Ocean and the implications for chemical modification of the Pacific water inflow. Earth and Planetary Science Letters 77: 285-292.
Moore, R.M. and W. Spitzer. 1990. Heat transfer from Atlantic Water to sea ice in the Arctic Ocean. Geophysical Research Letters 17: 2,149-2,152.
Mudie, P.J., K. Ellis, and B.T. Hargrave. 1989. Canadian Ice Island: Environmental studies of the polar margin north of Canada's arctic islands. Pages 60-67 *in* Bedford Institute of Oceanography Science Review 1988 & 1989 (T.E. Smith, Ed.). Bedford Institute of Oceanography, Dartmouth, NS.
Mudie, P.J., A. Rochon, and E. Levac. 2004. Decadal-scale sea ice changes in the Canadian Arctic and their impacts on humans during the past 4,000 years. Environmental Archaeology 10: 113-126.
Münchow, A., K.K. Falkner, H. Melling, B. Rabe, and H.L. Johnson. 2011. Ocean warming of Nares Strait bottom waters off northwest Greenland, 2003-2009. Oceanography 24: 114-123.
Overton, A. and A.F. Embry. 1989. Seismic reflection profiling from an ice island along the continental shelf of the Canadian Arctic Archipelago. Geological Survey of Canada Paper 89-1G, Ottawa, ON.
Orvig, S. 1981. A century of Arctic meteorology: from discovery to science. Pages 131-140 *in* A Century of Canada's Arctic Islands 1880-1890 (M. Zaslow, Ed.). Royal Society of Canada, Ottawa, ON.
Peary, R.E. 1907. Nearest the pole: A narrative of the polar expedition of the Peary Arctic Club in the S.S. *Roosevelt*, 1905-1906. Doubleday, Page and Co., New York, NY.
Pomeroy, L.R., S.A. Macko, H. Ostrom, and J. Dunphy. 1990. The microbial food web in Arctic seawater: concentration of dissolved free amino acids and bacterial abundance and activity in the Arctic Ocean and in Resolute Passage. Marine Ecology Progress Series 61: 31-40.
Rigor, I.G., R.L. Colony, and S. Martin. 2000. Variations in surface air temperature observations in the Arctic, 1979–97. Journal of Climate 13: 897-914.
Roots, E.F. and G.D. Hobson. 1986. The Polar Continental Shelf Project. Pages 3-23 *in* Living Explorers of the Canadian Arctic (S. Milligan and W.O. Kupsch, Eds.). Outcrop, The Northern Publishers, Yellowknife, NT.
Sackinger, W.M., M.O. Jeffries. F. Li, and M. Lu. 1991. Ice Island creation, drift, recurrences, mechanical properties, and interactions with arctic offshore oil production structures. Final Report. Contract No.: DE-FG21.88MC25027. UnitedStates Department of Energy, Office of Fossil Energy, Morgantown, WV.
Schröder-Adams, C.J., P.J. Mudie, F.E. Cole, and F.S. Medioli. 1990. Late Holocene benthic foraminifera beneath perennial sea ice on an Arctic continental shelf. Marine Geology 93: 225-242.
Smith, J.N. and K. Ellis, 1993. Radioactivity measurements in the Arctic Ocean. Pages 31-33 *in* Bedford Institute of Oceanography Science Reviews 1992-93 (A. Fiander, Ed.). Bedford Institute of Oceanography, Dartmouth, NS.
Sobczak, L. W. and J.R. Weber. 1987. Gravity and bathymetry taken along seismic refraction lines from the Canadian Ice Island during 1985 and 1986. Pages 299-304 *in* Geological Survey of Canada Current Research, Part A, Paper 87-1 A, Ottawa, ON.
Sobczak, L.W. and J.F. Halpenny. 1989. Isostatic and enhanced isostatic gravity anomaly maps of the Arctic. Geological Survey of Canada, Paper 89-16, Ottawa, ON.
Sverdrup, O. 1904. New Land: Four Years in the Arctic Regions. Volume 1. Longmans, Green and Co., London, England.
Van Wagoner, N.A., P.J. Mudie, F.E. Cole, and G. Daborn. 1989. Siliceous sponge communities, biological zonation and recent sea-level change on the Arctic margin: Ice Island results. Canadian Journal of Earth Sciences 26: 2,341-2,355.
Verhoef, J., D.C. Mosher, and S.R. Forbes. 2014. Defining Canada's extended continental shelves. Pages 407-414 *in* Voyage of Discovery: Fifty Years of Marine Research at Canada's Bedford Institute of Oceanography (D.N. Nettleship, D.C. Gordon, C.F.M. Lewis, and M.P. Latremouille, Eds.). Bedford Institute of Oceanography-Oceans Association, Dartmouth, NS.
Vincent, W.F., J.A.E.Gibson, and M.O. Jeffries. 2001. Ice-shelf collapse, climate change, and habitat loss in the Canadian high Arctic. Polar Record 37: 133-142.
Wassman, P., C.M. Duarte, S. Augusti, and M.K. Sejr. 2011. Footprints of climate change in the Arctic marine ecosystem. Global Change Biology 17: 1,235–1,249.
Welch, H.E., D.C.G. Muir, B.N. Billeck, W.L. Lockhart, G.J. Brunskill, H.J. Kling, M.P. Olson, and R.M. Lemoine. 1991. Brown snow: a long-range transport event in the Canadian Arctic. Environmental Science and Technology 25: 280-286.

9. PALEOCEANOGRAPHIC EVIDENCE OF CLIMATE CHANGE IN THE CANADIAN ARCTIC: THE PAST 10,000 YEARS

André Rochon*, Peta J. Mudie, David Ledu, and Steve M. Blasco

SUMMARY

The reduction, and ultimately the disappearance, of sea ice enhances the warming response of high latitude oceans through a positive feedback loop related to lessening of the heat reflected from ice. In theory, the more sea ice melts, the more rapidly the Arctic will warm. Computer models predict that continued global climate warming may lead to a temperature rise of 7.5°C and ice-free arctic water by 2100 AD, but they are deficient in accuracy of sea ice predictability. Paleoceanography uses fossil plankton that are tuned to modern sea-surface temperatures, salinity, and ice cover to reconstruct prehistorical changes for known times of climate conditions that were warmer and colder than now. Research using BIO vessels in the Canadian Arctic was on the forefront of the development of using sediment archives and dinoflagellate cysts to reconstruct changes in arctic temperature and sea ice over the past 10,000 years. The most recent research reveals east-west differences between Beaufort Sea and northern Baffin Bay that may allow refinement of earlier paleoclimate models for the whole Canadian arctic region.

Key words: Canadian arctic, dinoflagellate cyst, Holocene, paleoceanography, transfer functions, Northwest Passage.
***E-mail:** Andre.Rochon@uqar.ca

Climate change! Global warming! These expressions are now part of Canadian concerns, from Alert at the northern tip of Ellesmere Island, to the Canada/United States border, and the topics – climate change, global warming – have been the focus of scientists, government agencies, and the general public for over four decades. Titles such as "Is humanity occupied with influencing the climate of the world?" (Van Zuylen 1973) began appearing in the scientific literature as early as the 1970s. The scientific community is concerned with understanding the mechanisms of climate, the interactions between the many variables involved, including the role of humans in post-industrial times, while government agencies and the general population are concerned about how to adapt and eventually reduce the human impact on such changes. Thus, climate change has become as much a scientific issue as a societal issue. To this effect, the government of Canada and those of numerous countries around the world have allocated special funds to address the various issues involved, with the Bedford Institute of Oceanography (BIO) taking an early lead in studying the impacts of rising temperatures in the Arctic (Mudie and Jackson 2014). The Canadian scientific community could count on the Canadian Foundation for Climate and Atmospheric Sciences (CFCAS) and the Natural Science and Engineering Research Council of Canada (NSERC), among others, to support scientific research on various aspects of present, past, and future climate change. Vast international multi-disciplinary programs were also launched to gather data from all continents and put together a global perspective on climate change. The most recent Canadian scientific programs include the Canadian Arctic Shelf Exchange Study, ArcticNet, and the Canadian contribution to the International Polar Year, within which the Geological Survey of Canada Atlantic (GSCA) played a major role in the study of the prehistorical and geological aspects of climate change.

One of the most salient features of Earth's history is the changing state of climate since its formation 4.5 billion years ago: from glaciations as early as 2.9 billion years ago (Young et al. 1998) to warmer than present conditions (by ~4°C), such as during the Cretaceous Period, about 200 million years before the appearance of *Australopithecus afarensis*, the early ancestor of modern humans (Johanson et al. 1978). Most recently, the Quaternary Period (the last 2.6 million years) was characterized by a series of cold glacial intervals driven by the 41,000 years obliquity cycle (from 2.6 million to about 900,000 years ago) and then by the 100,000 years eccentricity cycle until today (Ruddiman 2001), alternating with warm interglacial intervals lasting 10,000 to 15,000 years. These changes are driven by slow, steady variations of the Earth's orbital parameters, eccentricity (100,000 year cycle), obliquity (41,000 year cycle) and precession (21,000 year cycle), all of which modulate the insolation (energy) received from the sun at specific sites on Earth's surface (Ruddiman 2001).

The present interglacial, the Holocene epoch, the past 10,000 years Before Present (BP), or 11,700 calibrated years BP (cal BP), also experienced these natural, slow climate changes, but it is notable for some differences that have been ascribed to the activity of modern humans (*Homo sapiens)* (Kaplan et al. 2011) who first appeared in Africa about 60,000 years ago (Brisseau and Chaline 2012). According to the astronomical theory, the Earth received maximum insolation from the sun about 9,000 years ago, and we should now be cooling down toward the next glacial period (Ruddiman 2001). Recent studies based on ice core and sediment records suggest that the next glacial inception should be within the next 1,500 years, providing that atmospheric CO2 concentrations did not exceed pre-industrial levels (Tzedakis et al. 2012). But anthropogenic production of greenhouse gases has potentially disrupted this natural cycle, and in the eastern Canadian arctic, this factor is thought to be the reason that icecaps are retreating, not expanding (Ruddiman 2003, 2007).

In addition to changes induced by orbital parameters, climate is the result of complex interactions between the atmosphere, hydrosphere, and cryosphere occurring at different timescales: annual, decadal, secular, and millennial. Instrumental records and historical archives provide some answers for the first three time scales. However, important changes take place at the millennial time scale and they cannot be addressed with the available instrumental data. This is where the climate archives preserved in ice sheet cores and marine sediments will provide long time-series and make up for the lack of instrumental data. Marine sediment cores are particularly valuable for understanding prehistorical changes in arctic sea ice and associated changes in ocean water masses.

ARCTIC PALEOENVIRONMENTAL RECONSTRUCTIONS: WHY ARE THEY SO IMPORTANT?

Instrumental data presented by the Intergovernmental Panel on Climate Change (IPCC) indicate that the global average temperature has increased by 0.74°C between 1906 and 2005, and the warming trend has nearly doubled between 1956 and 2005 (~0.13°C per decade) (IPCC 2007). In the Arctic, however, the warming trend has doubled that of the global average for the period 1906-2005. This trend is of particular concern because it is associated with thinning and shrinking of sea ice, leading to larger amounts of summer open water that allows more heat to be absorbed by the surface water, thus potentially accelerating the ice thinning. Continued greenhouse gas emissions at the current rate during the 21st century are predicted to induce changes larger than those observed during the 20th century. According to modelling experiments, the global average temperature will warm between 0.6 - 4°C within the next century, but in northern polar regions, the predicted warming can be as much as 7.5°C (IPCC 2007). Recent studies predict that the Arctic Ocean will be free of sea ice by summer 2028 (Wang and Overland 2009).

Among the many variables that are estimated in future climate scenarios, sea ice extent and thickness are among the most difficult to predict. This uncertainty is reflected in the wide range of model estimates of sea ice decrease (IPCC 2007). Sea ice measurements and satellite data for the Arctic Ocean since the late 1970s indicate a reduction in average extent of about 2.7% per decade, with a more pronounced reduction in summer (7.4% per decade on average). But sea ice is melting faster than these predictions, with the ice extent in the years 2007 and 2011 being the lowest on record (NOAA unpubl. data). Climate models are relatively inefficient at modelling sea ice, however, alternative ice indicators are necessary to verify and improve the accuracy of the results. The best alternative to that problem is the use of quantitative paleoenvironmental reconstructions to provide long time-series of various environmental variables, such as sea-surface temperature (SST) and duration of sea-ice cover (SIC). The time-series are then used in climate modelling experiments to test the accuracy of regional climate models, the assumption being that if the models can accurately reconstruct past sea ice conditions, they will accurately predict future ice conditions. Among the many paleoenvironmental proxies used in paleoceanography, very few are suitable for the reconstruction of sea ice on a quantitative basis.

FINDING THE RIGHT TOOL FOR THE JOB

Marine sediments of the Arctic contain an array of climate proxies that provide information on various parts of the water column (surface, middle, bottom), as well as global climate and continental ice volumes. These sources of proxy-oceanographic data include fossil foraminifers, diatoms, and dinoflagellates, in addition to the texture and chemistry of the sediments that enclose them. Foraminifera are unicellular organisms, often with chalky shells, some of which live in the water column, others that live on or in the sediments (Schafer 2014). Therefore, they provide information on the conditions of the entire water column. Although benthic foraminifera have a relatively high diversity in arctic environments, the planktonic ones are restricted to a single species, so they cannot provide a diversity of paleoenvironmental proxy-data. Also, arctic waters are undersaturated in calcium carbonate and the chalky shells are often corroded or completely dissolved (Azetsu-Scott et al. 2010). The information they provide is therefore limited. The same sort of problem applies to diatoms, which are unicellular planktonic algae with walls of silica. Because most arctic waters have a low silica content, the walls of most diatoms are very thin and easily break or dissolve over time (Wang et al. 2012). Some diatoms live in brine channels in sea ice and are the starting point of the spring plankton blooms that feed fish and mammals in arctic waters (Palmer et al. 2011). Both planktonic and sea-ice diatoms form highly diversified assemblages in high latitudes, but because their siliceous remains are subject to dissolution, their use as paleoenvironmental indicators in the Arctic is limited. Dinoflagellates are unicellular algae that live in the photic (sun-lit) layer of the world oceans. The vegetative stage of the dinoflagellate is composed mostly of cellulose and decomposes rapidly after the death of the cells. However, many dinoflagellates form a resting cyst as part of their life cycle in response to environmental stimuli (temperature, nutrients, light). Dinoflagellate cysts are composed of a highly resistant polymer that is acid-resistant and remains well-preserved in sediments for millions of years under most chemical conditions (Rochon et al. 1999). They form diversified assemblages throughout the Arctic Ocean and represent the environmental conditions in which they were formed. Dinoflagellate cysts are the most versatile micropaleontological proxies available in arctic environments.

Several scientific survey and coring campaigns by BIO scientists took place in the Canadian Arctic in the 1970s, 1980s, and 1990s. They provided a wealth of baseline information on sediment deposits and their microfossils throughout the eastern, central and western Arctic. Pioneer cruises by the CSS *Hudson* in the 1970s provided good sample coverage of Baffin Bay shelves and deep water basins. Although many of the deep-water sites contained long gravity-flow mud sequences and very short Holocene sections that could not provide detailed records of past climate changes (Aksu 1983, Syvitski 1983, Praeg et al. 1985), the samples established the presence of dinoflagellate cysts and pollen in arctic marine sediments and allowed initial analysis of the degree to which the surface fossils recorded the modern-day environmental conditions (Mudie 1982). In the 1980s, more samples were collected under the permanent pack-ice of the Canadian polar margin from the Canadian Ice Island (Mudie and Jackson 2014) and new collections were made in Beaufort Sea that allowed comparison of the impacts of Mackenzie River discharge versus that of Russian arctic rivers (Matthiessen et al. 2000, Richerol et al. 2008).

By the end of the 1990s, BIO, with Class-8 ice-breaker support (CCGS *Louis S. St-Laurent*), recovered samples within the ice-infested channels of the Northwest Passage during the Surface Heat Budget of the Arctic Ocean project (SHEBA), the Tundra Northwest 99 project (Mudie and Rochon 2001), and the Nares 2001 program (Mudie et al. 2005). In the Nares 2001 program, surficial sediments were surveyed and sampled in Nares Strait, from northern Baffin Bay to the Arctic Ocean (Mudie et al. 2005). A salient result of this program was the finding that Holocene climate changes in the North Water Polynya of Baffin Bay included several cycles of warmer summer SST with less ice than now (Mudie et al. 2004, Rochon et al. 2006).

Other scientific cruises or programs in which BIO participants played a role included The Joint Western Arctic Climate Study Program (JWACS), during which sampling took place in 2002 on the Mackenzie Shelf and Trough (Rochon et al. 2003), and the Canadian-led international programs Canadian Arctic Shelf Exchange Study (CASES; Bennett et al. 2008a) and ArcticNet (Bennett et al. 2008b), during which sampling took place in 2004-05 in the Beaufort Sea, Amundsen Gulf, and along the main east-west axis of the Northwest Passage.

TUNING THE KEYS

Initial studies of arctic dinoflagellate distributions and their environmental affinities were either based on empirical matching of key species with average water temperature and ice cover, or used multivariate statistical analyses for a relatively small array of samples from Eastern Canada (Mudie 1992, Mudie and Harland 1996). By 2001, however, more accurate quantitative records of changes in SST for both summer and winter, salinity, and SIC (as months per year with >50% sea ice) could be constructed from statistical fine-tuning of a large database of circum-arctic and subarctic dinoflagellate cyst assemblages. Dinoflagellate data from the tops of box-core samples at 677 arctic and subarctic sites (de Vernal et al. 2001, Mudie and Rochon 2001) were calibrated with the associated measured oceanographic data to develop paleoclimatic transfer functions using the biogeographical closest analogue method ('Best Analogue Method', now the 'Modern Analogue Technique'; Guiot and de Vernal 2011). For this study, log-transformed data for 54 dinocyst species grouped into 40 taxa were used, and the reconstructed values are the weighted average of the five best analogues. The accuracy of each parameter is estimated by using the transfer function to reconstruct the modern

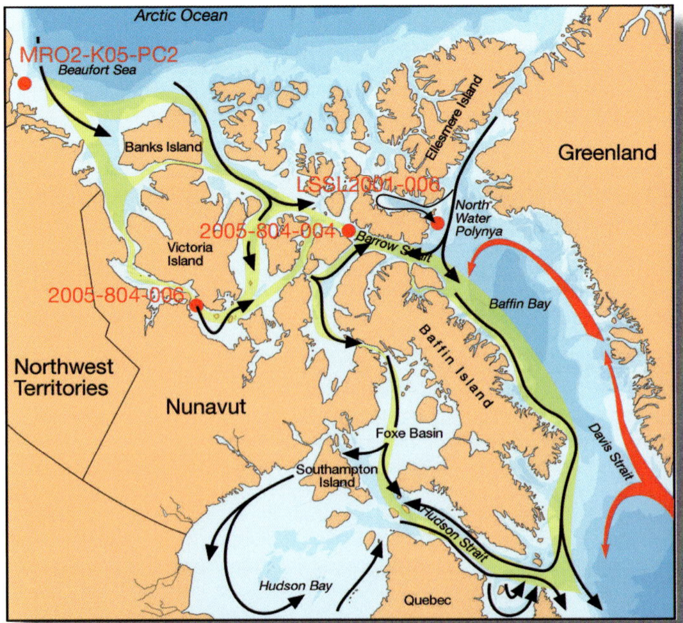

Figure 1. Map showing the physiography of the study area and surface currents: black arrows, cold water currents; red arrows, warm water currents; red dots, locations of the four marine sediment cores discussed in the text; pale yellow bands, main axis of the Northwest Passage and alternate routes (after de Vernal and Rochon 2011).

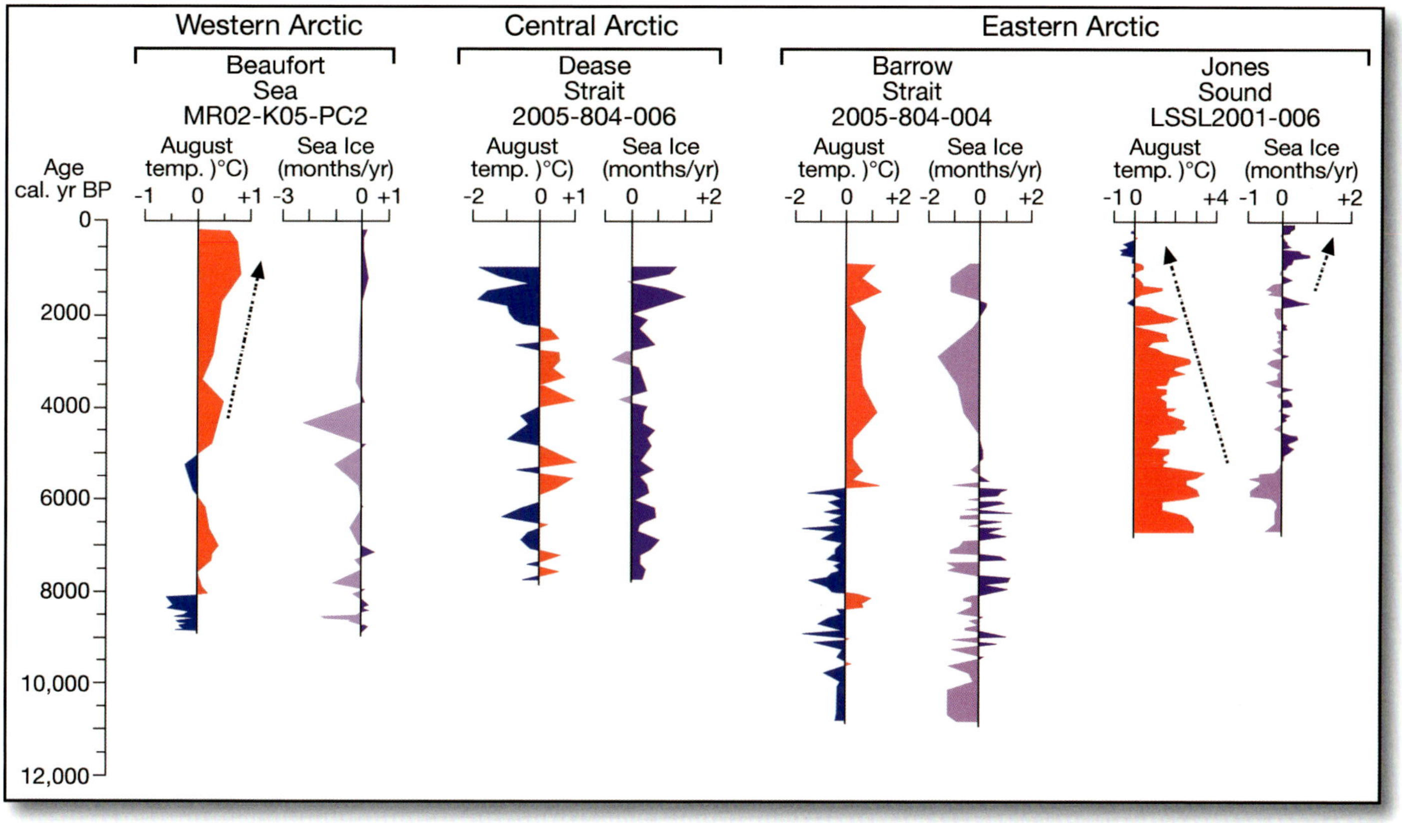

Figure 2. Diagrams showing the sea-surface temperature (SST) and duration of sea-ice cover (SIC) reconstructions for the four marine cores discussed in the text. The data are expressed as departures from the modern value of each parameter at the core site. The black arrows indicate increasing or decreasing trends (after de Vernal and Rochon 2011).

parameters and where each sample is prevented from selecting itself as an analogue. The accuracy (standard error) of the estimated SST is ± 1.3°C and 1.7°C for winter and summer, respectively, and ± 1.1 months per year for the SIC. Such uncertainties are similar to the interannual variability of the environment, which suggests that the results provided by the transfer function are reliable (Guiot and de Vernal 2011).

EAST-WEST CLIMATE CHANGE DURING THE HOLOCENE

Geological Archives for the Northwest Passage

A transect of four cores collected during various research cruises provides a glimpse of the paleoceanographic changes that took place in Arctic Canada within the last 11,700 years. These cores were collected at key locations along the Northwest Passage and approaches (Fig. 1). Holocene sediment accumulation throughout the Canadian Arctic Archipelago is heterogeneous and accumulation rates are generally in the order of 10 to 180 cm per thousand years, providing secular to millenial-scale temporal resolution (Rochon et al. 2006; Ledu et al. 2008, 2010a,b). The sediments in most marine channels consist of laminated glaciomarine silty clay of varying thickness overlaid by a relatively thin layer of recent (Holocene) sediments. The chronological framework is based on Pb^{210} measurements on sediments, Accelerator Mass Spectrometry-C^{14} ages (on mollusk shells), and on correlations with well-dated reference curves using high-resolution paleosecular variation records of the Earth's geomagnetic field. The details on the chronology are reported elsewhere (Barletta et al. 2008, 2010; Ledu et al. 2008; Lisé-Pronovost et al. 2009; Ledu et al. 2010a,b). High accumulation rates of relatively thick Holocene marine sediments were recorded only in very localized deep basins, and sedimentological analyses indicated that sedimentation was uninterrupted throughout the studied time interval (Mudie et al. 2005; Ledu et al. 2010a,b).

The marine record from the eastern Canadian arctic is represented by studies of dinoflagellate cysts in cores that were collected in Jones Sound and Barrow Strait (Fig. 2). The Jones Sound sequence covers the last 6,700 cal years, while the Barrow Strait core spans the last ~11,000 cal years. The dinoflagellate cysts show that the early Holocene (from 11,000 to ~6,000 cal BP) in Barrow Strait is characterized by relatively frigid conditions, with SST estimates as low as 2°C colder than modern conditions. Such harsh conditions are associated with the retreat of the Innuitian and Laurentide ice sheets which continued until ~8,000 and 6,800 cal BP, respectively (Dyke 1999, England et al. 2006, Carlson et al. 2008), and were important sources of cold meltwater in this area. During this interval, the estimated duration of SIC varied between +1 and -1 month per year of sea ice compared to modern conditions. Following the early Holocene maximum solar insolation, which peaked around 9,000 cal BP (Berger and Loutre 1991), arctic climate conditions improved during the middle Holocene, a period known as the Holocene thermal maximum. The Holocene thermal maximum timing and amplitude are variable in time and space (Renssen et al. 2009). In Jones Sound, dinoflagellate cysts indicate that maximum SSTs were reached around 6,000 cal BP (Fig. 2), with estimates ~2 to 3.5°C warmer than modern conditions, while in Barrow Strait, SST estimates ~1°C warmer than today were recorded around 4,500 cal BP. A cooling trend observed only in the Jones Sound area was recorded after 6,000 cal BP, when SST decreased steadily in a series of warm and cold oscillations with a periodicity of ~1,820 years (Rochon et al. 2006).

The central-western Arctic Holocene paleoceanographic record is represented by a marine sequence from Dease Strait (Fig. 2) that spans ~8,000 to 1,000 cal BP (Ledu et al. 2010a). Sea-surface conditions in Dease Strait are characterized by a series of cold and warm oscillations throughout the time period covered by the core. Temperatures 1°C warmer and 2°C colder with respect to modern conditions were inferred from dinoflagellate cyst assemblages and these warm/cold spells lasted between ~750 and 1,200 years each. The most recent cold spell, which lasted from 2,200 to 1,000 cal BP is also the coldest one with temperatures down to 2°C colder than modern conditions. The sea ice estimates indicate that most of the time period covered by the core was characterized by +1 to 1.5 month per year of sea ice longer than at present, with the exception of two very brief intervals with less sea ice at 3,800 and 3,000 cal BP (Rochon et al. 2006; Ledu et al. 2010a,b). In the western arctic, the early Holocene of the Beaufort Sea (from ~9,000 to 5,000 cal BP) was characterized by a series of temperature oscillations 0.5°C colder and 0.4°C warmer with respect to modern conditions (Fig. 2). The late

Holocene sea-surface conditions were marked by a temperature increase of ~1°C, which is well within the natural variability at this site (Rochon et al. 2006, World Ocean Atlas 2001).

Opposite East-West Climate Trends

The most salient feature of the paleoceanographic records is the presence of east-west climatic gradients expressed by opposite trends in sea-surface parameters between Baffin Bay and the Beaufort Sea. In the east, the Jones Sound record displays a cooling trend that started at ~6,000 cal BP. Such a cooling trend has been observed in several other marine and continental records from the eastern Arctic (Alley et al. 1999, Smith 2002, Kerwin et al. 2004, Kaufman et al. 2009). On the other hand, the western arctic record depicts conditions warmer than present throughout most of the Holocene with a slight warming trend and SIC decrease in the late Holocene. Another important feature is the temperature oscillations recorded in the eastern arctic. The Jones Sound core displayed a 1,820 year cycle and the central arctic records displayed a 750 to 1,200 year cycle. Climatic oscillations at various timescales are a major feature of arctic climate. The thermal regime of the Arctic Ocean was linked with the decadal variability associated with the Arctic Oscillation (Polyakov and Johnson 2006, Madhusoodanan and Bijoy 2011). The Arctic Oscillation was also identified as a mechanism responsible for changes in the wind patterns, and consequently the ice drift regime in the Arctic Ocean at multidecadal to century timescales (Darby et al. 2001, Darby and Bischof 2004). In a recent study, the variability of eastern and central arctic early Holocene sea-surface conditions was associated with a strong positive mode of the Arctic Oscillation at millennial timescales, followed by the dominance of the negative mode of the Arctic Oscillation during the late Holocene (Ledu et al. 2010b). Currently, new marine sediment core data from the Beaufort Sea suggest that the Pacific Decadal Oscillation might also contribute in part to the climate patterns (D. Ledu et al. unpubl. data, L. Durantou and A. Rochon unpubl. data) and enhanced phytoplankton productivity in the Beaufort Sea area. The temporal resolution of the sampling in most marine sediment cores was insufficient to record the modern warming trend. However, decadal-scale sea-surface condition reconstructions in three short sediment cores from the Beaufort Sea indicated that the actual warming trend started prior to the beginning of the industrial era in this region (Richerol et al. 2008). This is consistent with the millennial-scale warming trends observed in longer time series from the western arctic (McKay et al. 2008, Rochon et al. 2006), but does not allow linking the sea-surface temperature increase with anthropogenic activities.

LOOKING AT THE BIG PICTURE

Overall, it is now generally agreed that there have been climate and sea ice changes in some parts of the Canadian Arctic that have been larger and faster than those recorded previously in ice cores or marine sediments (Mudie et al. 2005, Pienkowsky et al. 2011), while other areas do not record post-industrial era changes that are larger than earlier natural cycles (Ledu et al. 2008, Rochon et al. 2006). Clearly, there is a still a lot more work to do to fully understand the complex interactions between greenhouse gas increases, short- and long-term changes in solar activity or orbital movements, and the way the ocean responds to atmospheric warming.

The role of human activities superimposed on natural climate cycles remains an important preoccupation for the scientific community and governments, as illustrated by the recent installation of a carbon stock exchange-like system based on the Western Climate Initiative regulations adopted by several Canadian provinces and states in the United States (CBC 2012). This system was implemented to reduce the production of greenhouse gases by industrial activities. In this context, documenting climate changes before and after the beginning of the industrial era (oil and gas exploration) in the Canadian arctic and quantifying the industrial contribution to such changes remains one of the scientific challenges. In order to document the climate shift associated with anthropogenic activities, the analysis of high-resolution sediment cores from the Mackenzie Trough (Canadian Beaufort Sea) are presently underway within the Malina program, which involves BIO scientists. The sampling interval represents ~4-7 years, providing a sub-decadal time resolution. Preliminary results on the last 150 years were not conclusive on identifying the human contribution to the observed changes. However, a correlation was found between the reconstructed sea-surface parameters and the Pacific Decadal Oscillation (D. Ledu et al. unpubl. data, L. Durantou et al. unpubl. data), which suggests that decadal-scale circulation oscillations may play a role in the marine variability, at least in the Beaufort Sea. High-resolution analyses of data from the last 3,000 years are currently underway and should provide clues on the anthropogenic impacts on climate change.

ACKNOWLEDGEMENTS

We wish to acknowledge support from the BIO coring team of Mike Gorveatt, Fred Jodrey, and Bob Murphy as well as the coring team during the CASES and ArcticNet sampling campaigns of Trecia M. Schell, Robbie Bennett, and David B. Scott. We also wish to thank the officers and crew of the RV *Mirai*, CCGS *Louis S. St-Laurent*, CSS *Hudson*, and CCGS *Amundsen* for their help and support during the oceanographic cruises. Sincere thanks are also due to Maryse Henry (Geotop Research Centre in Geochemistry and Geodynamics) and Etienne Faubert (Institut des sciences de la mer, Université du Québec à Rimouski) for their help with database support, sample preparations, and analyses.

REFERENCES

Aksu, A.E. 1983. Holocene and Pleistocene dissolution cycles in deep-sea cores of Baffin Bay and Davis Strait: Palaeoceanographic implications. Marine Geology 53: 331-348.

Alley, R.B., A.M. Agustsdottir, and P.J. Fawcet. 1999. Ice-core evidence of late-Holocene reduction in North Atlantic Ocean heat transport. Geophysical Monograph 112: 301-312.

Azetsu-Scott, K., A. Clarke, K. Falkner, J. Hamilton, E.P. Jones, C. Lee, B. Petrie, S. Prinsenberg, M. Starr, and P. Yeats. 2010. Calcium carbonate saturation states in the waters of the Canadian Arctic Archipelago and the Labrador Sea. Journal of Geophysical Research 115: C11021.

Barletta, F., G. St-Onge, J.E.T. Channell, A. Rochon, L. Polyak, and D.A. Darby. 2008. High-resolution paleomagnetic secular variation and relative paleointensity records from the western Canadian Arctic: implication for Holocene stratigraphy and geomagnetic field behaviour. Canadian Journal of Earth Sciences 45: 1,265-1,281.

Barletta, F., G. St-Onge, J.E.T. Channell, and A. Rochon. 2010. Paleomagnetic dating of Holocene Western Canadian Arctic sediments: combined use of the paleomagnetic secular variation and global spherical harmonic model of the geomagnetic field. Quaternary Science Reviews 29: 2,315-2,324.

Bennett, R., A. Rochon, T. Schell, J. Bartlett, S. Blasco, J. Hughes-Clarke, D. Scott, A. MacDonald, and W. Rainey. 2008a. Cruise Report *Amundsen* 2004-804: Beaufort Sea/Amundsen Gulf/Northwest Passage, June 23 - August 27, 2004. Geological Survey of Canada, Open File 5798, Ottawa, ON.

Bennett, R., A. Rochon, T. Schell, J. Beaudoin, S. Blasco, J. Hughes-Clarke, and J. Bartlett. 2008b. Cruise report *Amundsen* 2005-804: Beaufort Sea/ Amundsen Gulf/Northwest Passage, August 5 - September 15, 2005. Geological Survey of Canada, Open File 5797, Ottawa, ON.

Berger, A. and M.F. Loutre. 1991. Insolation values for the climate of the last 10 million years. Quaternary Science Reviews 10: 297-317.

Brisseau I. and J. Chaline. 2012. Fractality and migrations of *Homo sapiens*. L'Anthropologie 116: 87-97.

Carlson, A.E., A.N. LeGrande, D.W. Oppo, R.E. Came, G.A. Schmidt, F.S. Anslow, J.M. Licciardi, and E.A. Obbink. 2008. Rapid early Holocene deglaciation of the Laurentide ice sheet. Nature Geoscience 1: 620-624.

CBC (Canadian Broadcasting Corporation). 2012. Bourse du carbone: feu vert de Québec. http://www.radio-canada.ca/nouvelles/environnement/2011/12/15/001-arcand-bourse-carbone.shtml.

Darby, D.A., J. Bischof, G. Cutter, A. de Vernal, C. Hillaire-Marcel, G. Dwyer, J. McManus, L. Osterman, L. Polyak, and R. Poore. 2001. New record shows pronounced changes in Arctic Ocean circulation and climate. EOS Transactions, American Geophysical Union 82: 49.

Darby, D.A. and J.F. Bischof. 2004. A Holocene record of changing Arctic Ocean ice drift analogous to the effects of the Arctic Oscillation. Paleoceanography 19: PA1027.

de Vernal, A. and 19 others. 2001. Dinoflagellate cyst assemblages as tracers of sea-surface conditions in the northern North Atlantic, Arctic and sub-Arctic seas: the new "n=677" data base and its application for quantitative palaeoceanographic reconstruction. Journal of Quaternary Science 16: 681-698.

de Vernal, A. and A. Rochon. 2011. Dinocysts as tracers of sea-surface conditions and sea-ice cover in polar and subpolar environments. IOP Conference Series: Earth and Environmental Science 14-012007.

Dyke, A.S. 1999. Last glacial maximum and deglaciation of Devon Island, Arctic Canada: support for an Innuitian ice sheet. Quaternary Science Reviews 18: 393-420.

England, J., N. Atkinson, J. Bednarski, A.S. Dyke, D.A. Hodgson, and C.Ó. Cofaigh. 2006. The Innuitian Ice Sheet: configuration, dynamics and chronology. Quaternary Science Reviews 25: 689-703.

Guiot, J. and A. de Vernal. 2011. Is spatial autocorrelation introducing biases in

the apparent accurcy of paleoclimatic reconstructions? Quaternary Science Reviews 30: 1,965-1,972.
IPCC 2007. Climate Change 2007: The Physical Science Basis. Contribution of Working Group I to the Fourth Assessment Report of the Intergovernmental Panel on Climate Change (S.D. Solomon, M. Qin, Z. Manning, M. Chen, K.B. Marquis, M. Averyt, M. Tignor, and H.L. Miller, Eds.). Cambridge University Press, Cambridge, England.
Johanson, D.C., T.D. White, and Y. Coppens. 1978. A new species of the genus *Australopithecus* (Primates: Hominidae) from the Pliocene of eastern Africa. Kirtlandia 28: 1 -14.
Kaplan, J.O., K.M. Krumhardt, E.C. Ellis, W.F. Ruddiman, C. Lemmen, and K.K. Goldewijk. 2011. Holocene carbon emissions as a result of anthropogenic land cover change. The Holocene 21: 775-791.
Kaufman, D.S., D.P. Schneider, N.P. McKay, C.A. Ammann, R.S. Bradley, K.R. Briffa, G.H. Miller, B.L. Otto-Bliesner, J.T. Overpeck, B.M. Vinther, and Arctic Lakes 2k Project Members. 2009. Recent warming reverses long-term Arctic cooling. Science 325: 1,236-1,239.
Kerwin, M.W., J.T. Overpeck, R.S. Webb, and K.H. Anderson. 2004. Pollen-based summer temperature reconstructions for the eastern Canadian boreal forest, subarctic, and Arctic. Quaternary Science Reviews 23: 1,901-1,924.
Ledu, D., A. Rochon, A. de Vernal, and G. St-Onge. 2008. Palynological evidence of Holocene climate oscillations in the Eastern Arctic: a possible shift in the Arctic Oscillation at millennial time scale. Canadian Journal of Earth Sciences 45: 1,363-1,375.
Ledu, D., A. Rochon, A. de Vernal, F. Barletta, and G. St-Onge. 2010a. Holocene paleoceanography of the Northwest Passage, Canadian Arctic Archipelago. Quaternary Science Reviews 29: 3,468-3,488.
Ledu, D., A. Rochon, A. de Vernal, F. Barletta, and G. St-Onge. 2010b. Holocene sea-ice history and climate variability along the main axis of the Northwest Passage, Canadian Arctic. Paleoceanography 25: PA2213.
Lisé-Pronovost, A., G. St-Onge, S. Brachfeld, F. Barletta, and D.A. Darby. 2009. Paleomagnetic constraints on the Holocene stratigraphy of the Arctic Alaskan margin. Global and Planetary Changes 68: 85-99.
McKay, J., A. de Vernal, C. Hillaire-Marcel, C. Not, L. Polyak, and D. Darby. 2008. Holocene fluctuations on Arctic sea-ice cover: dinocyst-based reconstructions for the eastern Chukchi Sea. Canadian Journal of Earth Sciences 45: 1,377-1,397.
Madhusoodanan, M.S. and T. Bijoy. 2011. Decadal variability of Arctic Ocean thermal structure. Ocean Dynamics 61: 873-880.
Matthiessen, J., M. Kunz-Pirrung, and P.J. Mudie. 2000. Freshwater chlorophycean algae in Recent marine sediments of the Beaufort, Laptev and Kara Seas (Arctic Ocean) as indicators of river runoff. International Journal of Earth Sciences 89: 486-495.
Mudie, P.J. 1982. Pollen distribution in recent marine sediments, eastern Canada. Canadian Journal of Earth Sciences 19: 729-747.
Mudie, P.J. 1992. Circum-Arctic Quaternary and Neogene marine palynofloras: paleoecology and statistical analysis. Pages 347-390 *in* Neogene and Quaternary Dinoflagellate Cysts and Acritarchs (M.J. Head and J.H. Wrenn, Eds.). American Association of Stratigraphic Palynologists Foundation, Dallas, TX.
Mudie, P.J. and R. Harland. 1996. Aquatic Quaternary. Pages 843-877 *in* Palynology: Principles and Applications (J. Jansonius and D.C. McGregor, Eds.). American Association of Stratigraphic Palynologists Foundation, Dallas, TX.
Mudie, P. J. and H.R. Jackson. 2014. The Canadian Ice Island Program: discoveries from a ship of ice. Pages 59-67 *in* Voyage of Discovery: Fifty Years of Marine Research at Canada's Bedford Institute of Oceanography (D.N. Nettleship, D.C. Gordon, C.F.M. Lewis, and M.P. Latremouille, Eds.). Bedford Institute of Oceanography-Oceans Association, Dartmouth, NS.
Mudie, P.J. and A. Rochon. 2001. Distribution of dinoflagellate cysts in the Canadian Arctic marine region. Journal of Quaternary Science 16: 603-620.
Mudie P.J., A. Rochon, M.A. Prins, D. Soenarjo, S.R. Troelstra, E. Levac, D.B. Scott, L. Roncaglia, and A. Kuijpers. 2004. Late Pleistocene-Holocene marine geology of Nares Strait region: palaeoceanography from foraminifera and dinoflagellate cysts, sedimentology and stable isotopes. Polarforschung 74: 169-183.
Mudie, P.J., A. Rochon, and E. Levac. 2005. Decadal-scale sea ice changes in the Canadian Arctic and their impacts on humans during the past 4,000 years. Environmental Archaeology 10: 113-126.
Palmer, M.A., K.R. Arrigo, C.J. Mundy, J.K. Ehn, M. Gosselin, D.G. Barber, J. Martin, E. Alou, S. Roy, and J.E. Tremblay. 2011. Spatial and temporal variation of photosynthetic parameters in natural phytoplankton assemblages in the Beaufort Sea. Polar Biology 34: 1,915-1,928.
Pienkowski, A.J., P.J. Mudie, J.H. England, J.N. Smith, and M.F.A. Furze. 2011. Late Holocene environmental conditions in Coronation Gulf, southwestern Canadian Arctic Archipelago: evidence from dinoflagellate cysts, other non-pollen palynomorphs, and pollen. Journal of Quaternary Science 26: 839-853.
Polyakov, I.V. and M.A. Johnson. 2006. Arctic decadal and inter-decadal variability. Geophysical Research Letters 27: 4,097-4,100.
Praeg, D., B. Maclean, I. Hardy, and P.J. Mudie. 1985. Quaternary geology of the southeast Baffin Island continental shelf, N.W.T. Geological Survey of Canada Paper 85-14, Ottawa, ON.
Renssen, H., H. Seppä, H. Heiri, D.M. Roche, H. Goosse, and T. Fichefet. 2009. The spatial and temporal complexity of the Holocene thermal maximum. Nature Geoscience 2: 411-414.
Richerol, T., A. Rochon, S. Blasco, D.B. Scott, and R.J. Bennett. 2008. Evolution of paleo sea-surface conditions over the last 600 years in the Mackenzie Trough, Beaufort Sea (Canada). Marine Micropaleontology 68: 6-20.
Rochon, A., A. de Vernal, J.-L. Turon, J. Matthiessen, and M.J. Head. 1999. Distribution of recent dinoflagellate cysts in surface sediments from the North Atlantic Ocean and adjacent seas in relation to sea-surface parameters. American Association of Stratigraphic Palynologists Foundation Contribution Series Number 35, Dallas, TX.
Rochon, A., S. Blasco, and P. Travaglini. 2003. Cruise MR02-K05 on board the RV *Mirai*: Joint Western Arctic Climate Study (JWACS) 2002. Geoscience program LEG2 - Tuktoyaktuk (Northwest Territories) to Dutch Harbor (Alaska) September 20 - October 10, 2002. Geological Survey of Canada, Open File 1781, Ottawa, ON.
Rochon, A., D.B. Scott, T.M. Schell, S. Blasco, R. Bennett, and P.J. Mudie. 2006. Evolution of sea surface conditions during the Holocene: Comparison between Eastern (Baffin Bay and Hudson Strait) and Western (Beaufort Sea) Canadian Arctic. Abstract U43B-0867 in Eos Transactions, American Geophysical Union 87 (52), Fall Meeting Supplement, Washington, DC.
Ruddiman, W.F. 2001. Earth's Climate: Past and Future. W.H. Freeman & Company, New York, NY.
Ruddiman, W.F. 2003. The anthropogenic greenhouse era began thousands of years ago. Climatic Change 61: 261–293.
Ruddiman, W.F. 2007. Plows, Plagues, and Petroleum: How Humans Took Control of Climate. Princeton University Press, Princeton, NJ.
Schafer, C. 2014. Living and postglacial Foraminifera and their environmental applications. Pages 237-245 *in* Voyage of Discovery: Fifty Years of Marine Research at Canada's Bedford Institute of Oceanography (D.N. Nettleship, D.C. Gordon, C.F.M. Lewis, and M.P. Latremouille, Eds.). Bedford Institute of Oceanography-Oceans Association, Dartmouth, NS.
Smith, I.R. 2002. Diatom-based Holocene paleoenvironmental records from continental sites on northeastern Ellesmere Island, high Arctic, Canada. Journal of Paleolimnology 27: 9-28.
Syvitski, J. 1983. Sedimentology of arctic Fjords: cruise report CSS *Hudson* 82-031. Geological Survey of Canada, Open File 897, Ottawa, ON.
Tzedakis, P.C., J.E.T. Channell, D.A. Hoddell, H.F. Kleiven, and L.C. Skinner. 2012. Determining the natural length of the present interglacial. Nature Geoscience 5: 138-141.
Van Zuylen, G.F.A. 1973. Is humanity occupied with influencing the climate of the world? Geografie Tijdschrift (Royal Dutch Geographical Society) 7: 343-354.
Wang, M. and J.E. Overland. 2009. A sea ice free summer Arctic within 30 years? Geophysical Research Letters 36: L07502.
Wang R., W. Xiao, L. Shao, J. Chen, and A. Gao. 2012. Paleoceanographic records in the Chukchi Basin, western Arctic Ocean during the late Quaternary. Acta Oceanologica Sinica 31: 83-94.
World Ocean Atlas. 2001. World Ocean Atlas, CD-Rom Data Set. National Oceanographic Data Center, Silver Spring, MD.
Young, G.M., V. von Brumm, D.J.C. Gold, and W.E.L. Minter. 1998. Earth's oldest reported glaciation: Physical and chemical evidence from the Archean Mozaan Group (~2.9 GA) of South Africa. Journal of Geology 106: 523-538.

Ocean Life

Euphausiids: *Meganyctiphanes* Horned Krill Shrimp in the Gulf of Maine

Ocean Life

10. PLANKTON ECOLOGY AT THE BEDFORD INSTITUTE OF OCEANOGRAPHY, 1962-2012

William K.W. Li

SUMMARY

Ecological research on plankton has been conducted at Bedford Institute of Oceanography for almost 50 years. Through this time, the overarching goals have remained as originally envisioned by the founders: "to describe pathways and to measure amounts and rates of energy transfer in marine biological communities; and to study the structure and degree of organization of biological systems in the sea". Here, a scientific narrative is presented that links the initial exploration of various new oceanographic vistas, the subsequent building of conceptual and methodological foundations, the consequent reductionistic examination of processes and mechanisms, the emergent synthesis of system description, and the challenge towards ecological futures.

Key words: biogeography, biological oceanography, ecology, phytoplankton, primary production, secondary production, zooplankton.
E-mail: Bill.Li@dfo-mpo-gc.ca

"I find it interesting that this book (Longhurst 1998) and one by Mann and Lazier (1996), which together formulate modern biological oceanography, were both written by scientists who spent a significant portion of their careers at the Bedford Institute of Oceanography in Nova Scotia. What attribute of that environment stimulated these authors? Certainly not the snow, fog, and mud, I presume." (Sharon Smith, 1999)

In the pelagic ocean, plankton collectively outnumber, outweigh, and outgrow all other living creatures. Thus it is no surprise that plankton ecology has been important at the Bedford Institute of Oceanography (BIO) almost since inception. At that time, it was envisioned by the Atlantic Oceanographic Group of the Fisheries Research Board of Canada that "The proposed program will include phytoplankton and zooplankton sampling, allied physical and chemical measurements, and examining correlations between abundance of planktonic fish food organisms and concentrations of commercial fish stocks" (Prakash 1964). Over five decades, in pursuit of this deceptively straightforward goal of a mechanistic causal link from one end of the food chain to the other, plankton ecologists have come to face the complexity and perplexity of marine ecosystems. In so doing, the ethos of plankton ecology has expanded. Starting from the post-WWII modernism of the so-called endless frontier of science, the ethos now includes the postmodern worldview of sustainability underpinned by pillars that include integration of social and natural sciences, harmonization of social goals and research agenda, and public participation and judgment (Sarewitz 1996).

This article is the story of narrowly selected scientific milestones in plankton ecology at BIO. It draws from and expands upon previous personal accounts (Clarke et al. 2003, Harrison 2006), to present the contribution to knowledge and experience of biological oceanographic science at BIO. The narrative is developed from accounts in the peer-reviewed primary literature, the body of knowledge from which the milestones of science can be gleaned.

Our stories reveal a coalescence of what science philosophers recognize as distinct worldviews. One is described by the physics metanarrative of unifying the hydrosphere, atmosphere, geosphere, cryosphere, and biosphere through reductionistic approaches. The other is described by the ecology metanarrative of holistic ecosystems at risk to society (Doel 2009). With an apology to G. E. Hutchinson who can be said to have invented modern ecology (Slack 2010), we first set out the human theatre and then present the plankton ecology play. The play is in six acts, starting with a prolegomenon and ending with a post scriptum. The actors appear in segued vignettes in the dress of their scientific publications.

The 'ontogenetic escalator' or timeline of staff research investigators in plankton ecology across four major structural reorganizations, showing lateral transfers from and to different departmental units, and retirements.

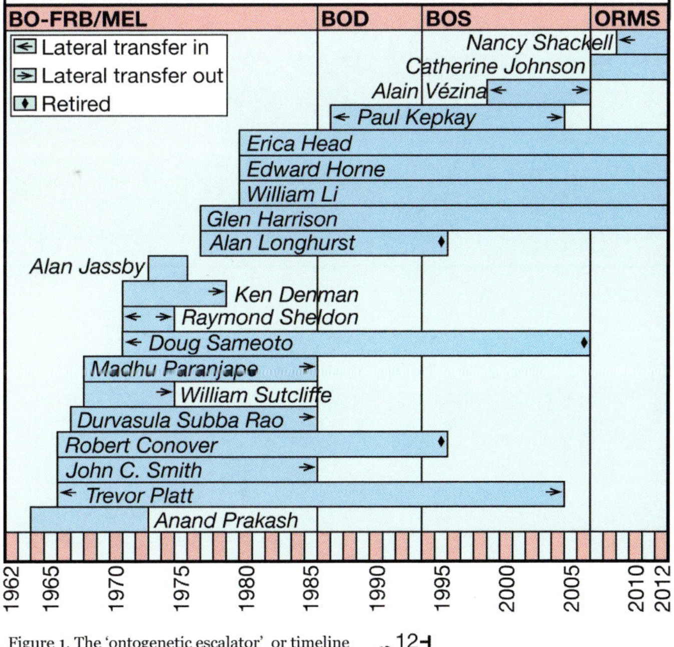

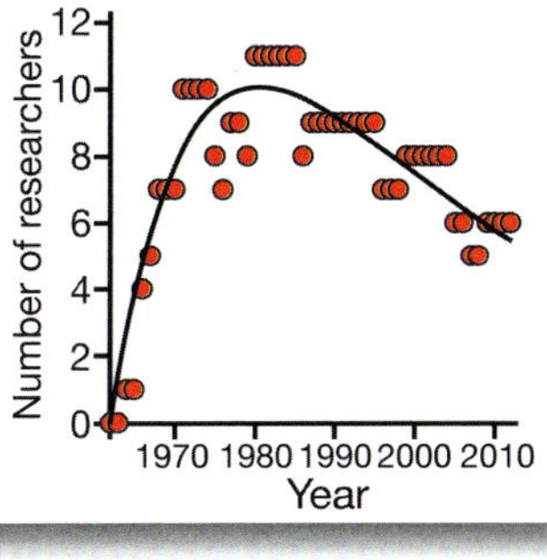

Figure 1. The 'ontogenetic escalator' or timeline of research staff in plankton ecology at BIO, 1962-2012. Abbreviations: BO-FRB/MEL (Biological Oceanogphy – Fisheries Research Board/Marine Ecology Laboratory); BOD (Biological Oceanography Division – Biological Sciences Branch); BOS (Biological Oceanography Section – Ocean Sciences Division); ORMS (Ocean Research and Monitoring Section – Ecosystem Research Division); left-pointing arrow ← (transfer into section); right-pointing arrow → (transfer out of section); Diamond ♦ (retired).

ONTOGENETIC ESCALATOR

Biological oceanography is not synonymous with plankton ecology, but the fundamental activity of observing and measuring plankton properties has been the mainstay of the progenitor BIO Biological Oceanography unit and its lineal descendants. In its early stage, this unit included research on benthic ecology, fisheries ecology, and bioacoustics, all of which were later placed into other organizational units as BIO expanded. The plankton ecology unit has been sustained by what might loosely be termed an ontogenetic escalator (Conover 1988) of successive waves of scientists who enter and exit the Biological Oceanography stage according to individual career ontogenies (Fig. 1).

The full roll-call of actors in this five decade enterprise extends very considerably beyond the 20 full-time staff research investigators appearing on the escalator. The complete list includes many technical and administrative personnel whose names appear in the collection of annual (or biennial) reviews of the Institute, and the numerous reports and documents published throughout the years. Many other scientific researchers (pre-doctoral and post-doctoral) have also stepped on and off the escalator, and some of them will be leading or supporting actors in the story to follow. It is evident that there has been a great flux of keen minds and diligent hands across the stage. The singular thread that weaves through a great length of this history is the administrative polymath M. Landry, who, like the rotating chain loop on an escalator keeps a group of people moving in perfect synchrony towards their destination.

PROLEGOMENON TO ECOLOGY AND BIOGEOGRAPHY

The desiderata for the founding studies of Biological Oceanography at BIO were "the description of pathways and measurement of amounts and rates of transfer of energy in the biological communities" and "the structure and degree of organization of the biological system in nature" for "it is these features of the system which control the availability of the energy for transfer, either as food for plants and animals or as catches for fishing vessels" (Dickie 1965). This was a prescription for seeking the 'commonplace' (in the sense of Allen et al. 2005) between disparate realities: on the one hand, rate-dependent dynamic processes of energy transfer, and on the other hand, rate-independent (but time-dependent) structures of organized communities. That is to say, this was the work needed to establish a common starting point in the discourse of ecological function and structure.

Even today, this founding challenge remains inviting and exciting, but it was early observational work in St. Margaret's Bay, Nova Scotia, that decisively led the way towards important insights. A study of the 1969 spring phytoplankton bloom in this bay (Platt and Subba Rao 1970) became a test of the hypothesis that links production and diversity over successional phases of an ecological community. For the first time at BIO, the disciplines of physics (underwater optics), chemistry (element flux), and biology (species taxonomy) were simultaneously brought to bear on a question of plankton ecology. Although some degree of empirical justification was found to support the prediction that energy flow and species diversity are related, the enduring impact of this work lay in its perceptive conclusion that a distinction needs to be drawn between short-term and long-term responses of an ecological system. Confusion of many different time scales was an important weakness of ecological theories of the day.

As goes time, so goes space. And so it was inevitable that questions arose about relevant scales in physical space. After all, if plankton are to be defined as organisms unable to maintain their distribution against the movement of water masses, how is this to be reconciled with their biological propensities for growth and motility? Are plankton no more than so-called passive scalars only to be regarded as diffusive contaminants in fluid flow? Obviously not, because at least in the vertical plane, where

Figure 2. L. Harris sampling zooplankton in Resolute Bay, Cornwallis Island, NWT.

Figure 3. R. Conover collecting ice algae in Resolute Bay, Cornwallis Island, NWT.

turbulence permits, they are arranged quite nicely. How does this happen? This problem became tractable after a method was developed at the Scripps Institution of Oceanography for the continuous measurement of fluorescence from the chlorophyll pigment in living phytoplankton cells. For the first time, it was possible to map the spatial properties of both a physical water mass characteristic and a plankton characteristic at the same level of detail. Thus in 1973, water temperature and fluorescence were simultaneously recorded at 1 s intervals from sea water pumped aboard a ship travelling at 3 m/s in the St. Lawrence estuary for tens of kilometres at a run. The quantitative nature of physical-biological interactions in the sea became immediately apparent with an elegant covariability analysis of the data (Denman 1976). At times, phytoplankton are strongly distributed by physical mechanisms such as vertical displacements associated with internal waves or other non-uniform water motions with significant vertical transport. At other times, phytoplankton appear to grow fast enough so that structure on the kilometre scale in the horizontal is relatively long-lived despite the dispersive effects of the non-steady fluid motions. A picture thus emerged of spatial complexity in phytoplankton distributions that put to rest any notion of a facile or unique explanatory mechanism.

As both time and space together go larger in scale, so goes ecology towards biogeography. And so it became clear that organism life histories are important to plankton geography at the scale of ocean basins. A solid understanding of general copepod biology extended by particular observations made from Resolute Bay, Cornwallis Island, in the arctic archipelago (Figs. 2 and 3) and elsewhere in Canada's three oceans formed the basis for a synthetic biogeography of Calanidae in high latitudes of the northern hemisphere (Conover 1988). The nine species of calanids, four of which are from the Arctic-Atlantic continuum *(Calanus helgolandicus, C. finmarchicus, C. hyperboreus, C. glacialis)*, and five of which are from the Pacific *(C. pacificus, C. marshallae, Neocalanus plumchrus, N. cristatus, N. sp.)* can be mapped onto a typology of generalized life cycles. Species have adapted to the constraints of ice, temperature, salinity, light, and food (i.e., phytoplankton) availability by having one generation per year, several generations per year, or requiring more than one year per generation. Ecological processes of abiotic and biotic interactions affecting plankton organisms, populations, and communities thus nest hierarchically towards biogeographic processes of speciation, extinction, range expansion, or contraction.

Figure 4. M. (Lewis) Kennedy deploying the BIONESS.

The space-time vista of plankton ecology and biogeography explored in these and other related studies was foundational. This conceptual seascape became the commonplace for much research within Biological Oceanography at BIO and is the leitmotif for the story in this paper. It eventually led to a seminal turning point in oceanography when we, as Smith (1999) declared, moved from the multidisciplinarity of 'The Oceans: Their Physics, Chemistry and General Biology' (Sverdrup et al. 1942) to the interdisciplinarity of 'The Ecological Geography of the Sea' (Longhurst 1998).

CATALYSTS AND ENABLERS

It is a truism that technological innovations, both hard (instruments) and soft (methods), accelerate scientific progress. In Biological Oceanography, some of these developments lowered the barrier to rapid progress by catalysing a novel solution or by improving an existing approach; other developments enabled a breakthrough into new applications.

While phytoplankton ecologists were making rapid progress at mapping chlorophyll with *in situ* fluorometers, zooplankton ecologists were likewise devising sampling systems capable of resolving the horizontal and vertical distributions of mesozooplankton and micronekton on small and intermediate scales. The requirements for such a system were met in the eponymous BIONESS (Bedford Institute of Oceanography Net and Environmental Sampling System), which is a multiple opening and closing net system equipped with environmental sensors (Sameoto et al. 1980). As BIONESS is towed, it is slowly lowered along an oblique path to the desired depth where animals are to be collected (Fig. 4). Ten nets are sequentially opened and closed at different depths to resolve vertical distribution. BIONESS can accommodate sensors for temperature, conductivity, fluorescence, depth, illumination, pitch, roll and yaw, and net closure together with internal and external flowmeters. An underwater camera and strobe flash can also be added to the top sides of the frame for the purpose of photographing the animals in front of the sampler to detect any signs of net avoidance. The successful operation of BIONESS in many studies provided the necessary depth-resolved estimates of mesozooplankton and micronekton abundance to consider questions of ecological distribution previously considered intractable. Here, a universal scientific innovation was created by in-house design and construction capacity within the BIO System Engineering and Metrology Groups.

Necessity was also the mother of the invention that led to what arguably might be considered an opening into vast new possibilities for phytoplankton field research. Faced with a problem that the characteristic time for phytoplankton acclimation is shorter than the usual time needed to measure the physiological process at sea, a device was developed to permit the measurement of the short time-scale response of phytoplankton photosynthesis to changes in available light (Lewis and Smith 1983). A temperature-controlled incubator was fabricated for measuring the amount of radioactive bicarbonate taken up by phytoplankton in a small volume of suspension (1 ml) over a short incubation period (20 min) with a sufficient number of samples (36) across a light gradient. The outcome was a plot of many data pairs showing the relationship between biological uptake of carbon-14 and available light, the so-called photosynthesis-irradiance (P-I) curve. The physical device, termed a photosynthetron, was modular in design so that later modifications (by the authors themselves and other researchers worldwide) were quite feasible. Most importantly, this innovation led to a rapid accumulation of data on the light-dependent parameters of photosynthesis that became the building block of a great deal of later work.

The photosynthetron promoted an extensive analysis of the functional dependence of photosynthesis on irradiance. The mathematical considerations required for this kind of analysis had already been established earlier (Jassby and Platt 1976), in which pragmatism dictated that the most suitable formulation ought to be based on the best fit between equation and data, and parsimony dictated that the only valid criterion for judging the relative merits of the different formulations is their ability to describe data with the minimum number of well chosen parameters. Although revealing no new significant insight on the nature of the oceans, this work endures as a great catalyst in primary production research, being the most highly cited paper to date in the individual bibliographies of the co-authors.

Going forward in the same direction, namely using observational data to solve for the parameters of a model in a parsimonious fashion, a very large step was made by the first application of inverse formalism to the estimation of fluxes in plankton food webs (Vézina and Platt 1988). Normally, starting with a compartmental model of the food web, the aim is to project state variables using known parameter values and initial conditions. However, the number of independent observations that can usually be made is far less than the number of parameters needed to describe the system. Given this fundamental limitation, the inverse method reverses that procedure by estimating parameters from observations of the state variables. Since there are more unknowns than observations, the solution is generally indeterminate. Unlike conventional curve-fitting (such as to P-I data), inverse methods offer the possibility of diagnosing model behaviour given that flow networks need to conserve mass, to satisfy basic biological constraints, and to be compatible with the observed structure of the food web. Importantly, inverse models are not meant to, and do not reveal new phenomena.

Figure 5. A laboratory technician counting phytoplankton by flow cytometry.

Figure 6. P.M. Dickie conducting at-sea measurements of bacterial production.

Discovery had to come from elsewhere – in this case from looking at plankton cells one by one with new electronic eyes. Unlike the BIONESS and the photosynthetron, the pedigree of the flow cytometer lies outside BIO. However, fluorescence-activated analysis of individual plankton cells in ocean waters using commercial off-the-shelf instruments manufactured for biomedical laboratory applications was no less a signature development at the Institute. The technique of measuring particles suspended in a very small volume of sea water utilising the principle of wavelength-specific fluorescence emission following monochromatic excitation allows for rapid, accurate, and precise analysis of plankton cells of different kinds (Fig. 5). This enabling technology led to breakthroughs in several related areas of marine microbial ecology. These include the discovery of a previously undetected phytoplankton group (Li and Wood 1988) earlier predicted as a necessary closure element (Li et al. 1983), the reconciliation of the picophytoplankton size class by reductionistic analysis of its components (Li 1994), and the semi-automation of bacterioplankton enumeration (Li et al. 1995; Fig. 6).

In these advances, we see technology exerting a transformational effect on plankton ecology, leading to a broader exploration of the oceanographic space-time vista by seeking patterns of regularity at a variety of scales (Li 2009, Li and López-Urrutia 2013). From hours to weeks to seasons to years to decades, from the Compass Buoy location in Bedford Basin (Fig. 7) to a grid of stations on the Scotian Shelf to sampling transects across other large marine ecosystems, it is possible to discern cross-scale regularity in the way that phytoplankton respond to their environment (Li et al. 2010). In earlier times, confusion of many different scales was an important weakness of ecological thinking. Only recently are we able to peer through this confusion through multifocus lenses that range through these nested scales.

PROCESSES AND MECHANISMS

With visions of the big ecosystem picture never far from mind, the devil is inescapably in the mechanistic details. The processes are anabolic (such as nutrient assimilation, photon absorption, ingestion, and growth) and catabolic (such as respiration, excretion, egestion, and autolysis), all un-

Figure 7. K. Pauley deploying the CTD assembly in Bedford Basin, NS.

Figure 8. G. Harrison conducting at-sea measurements of primary production.

Figure 9. J.C. Smith conducting at-sea measurements of phytoplankton enzyme activities.

der a strong degree of hydrodynamic control (such as mixing, turbulence, and advection), and made greatly complex by food web transfers, system feedbacks, and non-linear interactions. Storytelling and hand-waving are compelling semiotic devices; however, they fail to adequately portray the scientific groundwork that has been done by sheer tireless effort. So attention is now turned to some of those at BIO who have crafted the building blocks, but may sometimes be forgotten by those who later construct the edifice.

Primary Production

Primary production is *de novo* synthesis of living material from simple molecules using energy from light or chemicals. The biochemical process of photosynthesis can be measured by the consumption of reactant (carbon dioxide) or by the appearance of product (oxygen). The stoichiometric balance between carbon assimilation and oxygen evolution is seasonally variable in Bedford Basin (Irwin 1991), depending on several factors, including the chemical form of the inorganic nitrogen source.

Whether exogenous nitrogen is present as nitrate, ammonium, urea, or other organic form, phytoplankton have an essential need for this growth-limiting element. Although the kinetics of nutrient uptake and regeneration are complicated, they can be examined by comparative analysis of short-term isotope tracer experiments (Harrison 1983a, 1983b). These are processes underpinning a commonly observed pattern: namely the vertical separation in the water column between the depths of maximum chlorophyll and maximum primary production (Fig. 8). Phytoplankton biomass and metabolism are vertically ordered to a large extent on the balance between physically and biologically mediated supply of limiting nutrients (Harrison 1990).

In fact, biota and nutrients are vertically structured even at the centimetre scale of arctic sea-ice microbial communities. Compared to planktonic systems, vertical gradients in light and nutrients are highly intensified through sea ice, giving rise to compact distributions of ice algae at very much higher concentrations than in the underlying water. Variations in light and nutrient invoke acclimative physiological change in the cellular composition of algae. These changes are the same for epontic and planktonic algae, except that the changes are expressed over centimetres within the ice and over meters in the water column (Smith et al. 1990). But the condition of extreme low photon flux at the bottom of the ice layer has given rise to a uniquely adapted obligate shade epontic flora. Experiments conducted in Resolute Bay using a photosynthetron demonstrated that the optimal irradiance for resident ice algae is well within the dynamic range for the most energetically efficient photosynthesis (Cota 1985).

It is not surprising that algae are well adapted to their environment, whether under the ice in the epontic community, or in the phytoplankton community of the water column. Still, it is quite remarkable that for such a diverse group, the main characteristics of their photosynthetic physiology can be fairly well represented by a small number of apparently simple rules. One of the most pervasive relationships in biology is that between metabolic rate and body size. It turns out that such a relationship holds true even within a single taxonomic class. Thus, for diatoms, the relationship between photosynthesis and cell size is controlled by self-shading of chlorophyll a pigment and by the ratio of surface area to volume (Taguchi 1976).

More generally, cost-benefit analysis of the energy balance involved in algal physiology confirms the competitive advantage of small cells over large cells due to enhanced catalytic efficiencies of growth and light absorption (Geider et al. 1986). Even within a single species, different ecological types are found that possess biochemical and physiological characteristics finely tuned to environmental conditions. By experimentation on different isolates of the same species collected from waters of different oceans, it was demonstrated that the cellular light-harvesting machinery and the quantum efficiencies for converting photons to biomass differ amongst strains of *Prochlorococcus marinus* according to the light environment of their particular native habitat (Partensky et al. 1993).

The physiological response of algae to their environment can however sometimes be counter-intuitive and seemingly maladaptive. For example, although high enzyme catalytic efficiency is a general metabolic adaptation to low habitat temperature, phytoplankton in arctic waters exhibit high activation energies (low efficiencies) for Rubisco, the catalyst of the primary carbon fixation process in photosynthesis. A possible explanation lies in hydrodynamics. It seems that in the Arctic, absolute temperature may be less important than the temperature structure of the water column in relation to irradiance, the limiting factors for growth, and the exploitative strategy of the characteristic species. Indeed, the enigmatic enzyme results can be understood as an opportunistic strategy that retains an energetically inefficient carboxylating metabolism but which can confer high reproductive rates under advantageous circumstances (Smith and Platt 1985; Fig. 9).

Clearly, vertical water movement that carries phytoplankton within a well-mixed layer bears important implications for photosynthesis in the resulting fluctuating light field. Deductions can be made by knowing, first, if the light field to which the freely circulating population is exposed is substantially more variable than that experienced by a contained population; and second, if the photosynthetic performance of phytoplankton in fluctuating light is different from the response measured in constant light (Gallegos and Platt 1985). These ideas were tested experimentally using a clever analog device that simulated vertical water motions (Gallegos and Platt 1982). Under conditions of moderate forcing such as in the Arctic, vertical mixing has little quantitative effect on water column primary production because the population is uniformly adapted to near-surface conditions.

From the Arctic to the subtropical Atlantic, questions were asked at BIO about how the intrinsic growth of phytoplankton is limited in the ocean. A great deal of evidence indicates that at ecological time scales, the availability of exogenous nitrogen is often limiting to the needs of phytoplankton. However, early studies from the Bermuda Biological Station and the Woods Hole Oceanographic Institution had suggested a possibility that iron is in fact the critical element in shortest supply. Results from those studies in the Sargasso Sea were inconclusive because artifactual iron contamination of seawater by experimental manipulation could not be ruled out. These early results became even more enigmatic when others realized that iron limitation was indeed prevalent in other oceans (e.g., tropical and subarctic Pacific Ocean, Southern Ocean), but not the Atlantic Ocean because of differences in the stoichiometry of nutrient supply and phytoplankton demand. New experiments were therefore conducted in the Sargasso Sea with fastidious attention to metal-free techniques, leading to a conclusion that subtropical North Atlantic phytoplankton were indeed not limited by the supply of bioavailable iron (Subba Rao and Yeats 1984). Thus, we can now surmise that in these waters, purposeful enrichment with iron will generally not lead to enhanced fertility nor accelerated drawdown of carbon dioxide to mitigate atmospheric warming.

Nitrate supply to the upper water column is therefore of over-riding concern in North Atlantic primary production. The question then becomes economic: is the supply of nitrate from vertical flux sufficient to meet biological demand? To quantify supply, it is necessary to measure the concentration of nitrate (which is relatively easy) and the vertical eddy diffusivity (which is difficult). At BIO, shear probes that measure high-frequency fluctuations in the vertical gradient of horizontal velocity enable the dissipation rate of turbulent kinetic energy to be estimated (Oakey 1988). To quantify demand, concurrent measurements are required for primary production and nitrogen uptake. This type of study indicates the importance of turbulent mixing to new primary production, but other mechanisms such as upwelling cannot be ruled out, especially when supply does not meet demand as appears to be the case in summer on Georges Bank (Horne et al. 1996).

Supply of nitrogen can be met in another way, not from outside the system, but from within the biological community itself. This is possible because phytoplankton can use different chemical forms of nitrogen. The regeneration of ammonium by bacteria and other microheterotrophs supplies recycled nitrogen to support a significant proportion of primary production in Bedford Basin (LaRoche 1983) and the Scotian Shelf (Cochlan 1986). In fact, phytoplankton may prefer to utilize ammonium over nitrate even when the latter form is plentiful. Primary production supported by regenerated nitrogen (ammonium) tends to be packaged in small phytoplankton cells, whereas that supported by new nitrogen (nitrate) tends to packaged in large phytoplankton cells. These differences can lead to alternate secondary transformations further along the food chain.

Secondary Production

Secondary production is the assimilation of organic matter made available by primary producers to organisms that use the energy for maintenance, growth, and reproduction. By and large, a great deal of primary production is routed through the microbial food web of single-celled organisms (bacteria, archaea, protists). Much less of the primary production is transferred directly to multicellular animals, which are often portrayed in a stacked pyramid from herbivores, to carnivores, ending at an apex consumer. Indeed, it is often not realized that the largest reservoir of organic carbon in the ocean is in fact non-living. This carbon exists in various physico-chemical forms as dissolved, colloidal, or particulate entities in seawater (Kepkay 1994). To greater or lesser extents, according to their biochemical lability or recalcitrance, these entities are the organic substrates supporting secondary production of most bacteria and archaea.

In a commentary on the place of microbial ecology in marine ecosystem science at the beginning of this century, L.R. Pomeroy (2001), a BIO Hunstman Award recipient, wrote: "Old paradigms die slowly, Thomas Kuhn told us mainly through the death of their adherents. Many fisheries scientists do not yet believe it, but the marine food web consisting principally of diatoms, copepods, and fishes is now generally seen as an occasional excrescence from what is normally a microbial food web". The Kuhnian assessment of science moving ahead one funeral at a time is rather dark, but perhaps mostly true. Exceptions are notable by their vigour (e.g., Longhurst 1998).

Even in the eastern Canadian Arctic with large populations of charismatic apex consumers such as ursidaens, cetaceans, pinnipeds, and seabirds, the flow of primary production through single-celled microbes can be substantial. Experimental measurements indicated that summer communities of ciliated protists in Jones Sound and Baffin Bay have the potential to consume up to about one half of the primary production on a daily basis. The transfer of energy and the recycling of nutrients assigned to this microbial community are evidently no less at high latitudes than at lower latitudes (Paranjape 1987).

The large pool of non-living carbon in particulate form did not escape the notice of those who study the diets of multicellular zooplankton. It was reasoned that if non-selective grazing is common among small copepods such as *Pseudocalanus minutus*, unselective feeding based on available particle size should not distinguish between living and non-living particles if the sizes of the two fractions are similar. Thus, the feeding activities of such copepods should lead to maximum ingestion of those sizes of non-living particles which have the highest concentration in seawater, unless the particles are too small to be filtered. In a year-long test of this hypothesis in Bedford Basin, it was indeed shown that non-living particles cannot be considered only as a supplementary food source for small copepods, but that they are a basic food for *P. minutus* at all times (Poulet 1976).

The availability of food to zooplankton is highly variable over time. Yet, for digestion to occur, the appropriate enzymes must be active. Thus the length of time necessary to induce the enzymes may be a factor in adapting to increasing food supply. A strong test of the hypothesis that zooplankton feeding rates are associated with induction of digestive enzymes can be made during a phytoplankton bloom. Presumably, correlation between enzyme activity and food supply might be strongest during a period of accelerated primary production. In such a test carried out in Bedford Basin in the spring of 1977, this hypothesis was generally supported, but the results required careful interpretation because the structure of the zooplankton community underwent large changes (Mayzaud and Conover 1984).

A well-designed combination of experimentation and observation is the cornerstone of the scientific method. For the investigation of copepod feeding behaviour, it is important to know the state of the copepod gut at a place and time in the ocean *(in situ)*, the response of the copepod under experimental manipulation *(in vitro)*, and the rate of ingestion as measured in the gut *(in vivo)* accounting for clearance and turnover (Head 1988; Fig. 10). A mechanistic understanding of food ingestion and egestion at the level of individual animals was an important step towards a wider appreciation of the strong impact that food availability exerts on the life history and population ecology of copepods.

Macroecological characterization of the copepod-phytoplankton linkage came from large scale multidisciplinary oceanographic programs. When the animal habitat is surveyed over a geographic area sufficiently large that distinct ecological sequences can be identified, the observations then constitute results from a pseudo-experiment in which nature itself has provided the changed conditions useful for strong inference. Thus in the Labrador Sea, the relationship between food supply and copepod development can be inferred by substituting a survey over space for a sustained sequence over time, invoking the ergodic principle. In nature's pseudo-experiment, food (phytoplankton) is made available to the copepod at different levels, depending on place, but because of differences in time relative to the bloom. By measuring *Calanus finmarchicus* egg production rates and animal stage distributions in three areas of the Labrador Sea designated by the state of the phytoplankton bloom (early, mid- and late/post-bloom), it is clear that the timing of the spring bloom may have a significant impact on recruitment to the next generation (Head et al. 2000).

The importance of maintaining phase coordination between a dominant grazer such as *C. finmarchicus* and its dynamic forage is profound, especially in view of climate variability. Yet in the face of changing external conditions of temperature and phytoplankton availability, the proximate determinants of ontogenetic status remain an outcome of highly complex internal processes such as gonad maturation (Campbell and Head 2000). Mechanistic reductionism has its limits in complex adaptive systems.

Figure 10. E. Head conducting at-sea experiments on zooplankton.

ORGANIZING THE BIOLOGICAL SEASCAPE

Processes and mechanisms explain cause and effect in plankton populations based on possibilities presented by initiating conditions. No less important are the constraints imposed by boundary conditions, but these need to be sought at a higher encompassing level, which might be called the biological seascape.

The biological seascape denotes a spatial organization, but it has a broader connotation that recognizes the importance of biology to spatial architecture. A most vivid case of this is the shape of the vertical profile of chlorophyll *a* in the ocean. A typology of the deep chlorophyll maximum layer can be constructed based on the interaction between hydrography and growth, behaviour, or physiological adaptation of phytoplankton, as well as the grazing effects of zooplankton (Cullen 1982). These class types constrain known possibilities, but the actual manifestation at any particular time or place cannot be confidently predicted because idiosyncratic contingencies lead to indeterminate outcomes.

A huge step was then taken towards a global organization of the biological seascape by construction of a typology for seasonal cycles of pelagic production and consumption (Longhurst 1995). The well-known Sverdrup critical depth concept for the induction of phytoplankton growth forced by local mixing and light is the starting point for the seasonal evolution of primary production, and this is very much related to regional oceanography. However, the accumulation or loss of phytoplankton biomass is influenced by secondary processes, such as variation in the size of the herbivore population at the start of the bloom. In extending the Sverdrup model to all parts of the ocean, a typology of plankton cycles is necessary that describes a continuum from strongly seasonal regions with seasonal recharge of photic zone nutrients to weakly seasonal regions where nutrient renewal of the photic zone is slow or episodic and where productivity is largely fuelled by internal nutrient regeneration. Along this continuum, phytoplankton and zooplankton exhibit characteristic features of ecological structure and function that arise as outcomes of systemic behaviour.

A full exposition of this organizational scheme into a rational partition of the global ocean was a landmark in many respects. At its root, this ecological geography (Longhurst 1998) addresses the fundamental issues of pelagic ecology and biogeography, which distill to whether, at some level of probability, a deduction may be made about the characteristic features of any region. Here, the definition of region is crucial since it determines the scale of the biological seascape. By placing the typology of seasonal plankton cycles into the context of regional oceanography, characteristic features of ecology can be discerned at two hierarchical scales. The higher level comprises a small number of large compartments (biomes), and the lower level comprises a large number of smaller compartments (provinces).

The first application of this geographic approach was the computation of regionally and seasonally differentiated primary production in the North Atlantic using local algorthims of a light-dependent model of photosynthesis combined with satellite-derived chlorophyll data (Sathyendranath et al. 1995). In a tour de force of reductionism, whereby the whole is constructed from the sum of its parts, the total annual production for the North Atlantic basin of 10.5 gigatons of carbon per year has been computed as the sum of values from 19 separate geographic compartments. The partitioning respects the realities of regional diversity in ocean ecology, and the summation achieves an integration for the basin. Like the Cullen typology of chlorophyll profiles, the Longhurst (1998) typology of pelagic ecosystems constrains possibilities but admits indeterminacy at fine local scales.

It is possible to operationalize the Longhurst typology for ecological characterization at local time and place, but this requires a computation algorithm based on statistical analysis of geophysical and biological data to delineate irregular dynamic boundaries of the provinces in real time. Thus, instead of climate averaging into a static arrangement of provinces with rectilinear boundaries, high resolution satellite data on sea-surface temperature and ocean colour are used in an objective statistical method for accurately defining the boundaries (Devred et al. 2007). With a spatial resolution of 2.25 km^2 (1.5 × 1.5 km), this approach downscales the seascape towards what might be measured from ships at sea.

In so doing, the distinction between a partition and a continuum approach becomes increasingly blurred, emphasizing that the approaches are not mutually exclusive. On the one hand, biomes and provinces highlight ecological regularities, or in other words, the general constraints drawn by the rules of nature's necessity. On the other hand, a macroecological continuum represented by a very large ensemble of interacting biological units highlights a statistical manifestation covering the range of known possibilities allowed by nature's flexibility. The pattern of plankton diversity and water stratification revealed in ecological partitions is a motif no less evident when the biological seascape is drawn upon the shapes and boundaries of statistical distributions of phytoplankton in the North Atlantic (Li 2002).

The indicators of the structure and functioning of environmental systems at large spatial and temporal scales (i.e., macroenvironmental indicators) have potential to provide scientific insights and policy guidance, but must be carefully selected for scientific credibility to the public, for salience to decision makers, and for legitimacy to all stakeholders (Orians and Policansky 2009). All of these considerations were important in the scientific advice delivered to shape a conservation strategy for a large submarine canyon (The Gully) on the eastern Scotian Shelf (Harrison and Fenton 1998). The strategy includes environmental monitoring with regional coverage of a large number of measured variables, among which some plankton indicators serve as diagnostic clues for the status and trends of the ocean. Year-to-year changes in phytoplankton and zooplankton can be scored to indicate complex ecological processes (Harrison et al. 2009), forming the nexus between driving forces and pressures on the one hand, and impacts and responses on the other hand (Shackell 2011). At the 50-year mark of BIO, we have a 50-year record of phytoplankton and zooplankton in the Northwest Atlantic (Head and Pepin 2010), which leads us into the future.

ECOLOGICAL FUTURES

Ecological futures, that is the futures of ecological systems, are the future consequences of present choices. At this point, scientific research moves from the work station to the town hall. Here, scientists try to build an ecology of the "long now" (Carpenter 2002) for management facilitators, policy thinkers, and decision makers. In common parlance, "now" means yesterday, today, and tomorrow; "nowadays" means last year, this year, and next year. Thus, "long now" can mean last decade, this decade, and next decade, or even longer. It emphasizes that past events shaped present ecosystems, and that current actions influence future states. Nowadays, plankton ecology at BIO is an ecology of the "long now". Following a decade of Joint Global Ocean Flux Study (JGOFS) out of which ocean ecology and biogeochemistry became inextricably intertwined, the birth of systems-based observation networks to record the "long now" was realized. Thus emerged the Atlantic Zone Monitoring Program (AZMP) for the Scotian Shelf and adjoining shelf areas, the Atlantic Zone Off-shelf Monitoring Program (AZOMP) for continental slope and deeper waters of the northwest Atlantic, and the Bedford Basin Monitoring Program (BBMP) for the harbour waters that give BIO its name.

Is it possible to establish a chained link of attribution to assess whether a specified set of drivers are the cause of an observed change in a specific system? When anthropogenic radionuclides are released from nuclear reprocessing plants into the English Channel or the Irish Sea, they are carried by ocean circulation on a relentless journey. They pass through the North Sea into the Norwegian Sea, then the Barents Sea, and into the Arctic Ocean, flowing through the Kara Sea, the Laptev Sea, over the Lomonosov Ridge, the Mendeleyev Ridge, around the Beaufort Sea, out of the Arctic through the Fram Strait, around Greenland, to the Labrador Sea, and onward. The journey takes many years, but it can be documented by measuring the radionuclides at fixed stations as the water flows by as time passes (Smith et al. 2011, Smith 2014). The future of a radionuclide particle released into the English Channel many years ago can be determined with fair confidence by making measurements today.

The transit of Arctic origin water continues down the Labrador Shelf and eventually arrives on the Scotian Shelf, but not before mixing with waters from rivers, from the Gulf of St. Lawrence, and from off-shelf. Unlike salt which is conserved, other chemical constituents such as nutrients and oxygen are not conserved during transit, being consumed or produced by biochemical processes over time. The Arctic signature of non-conservative inorganic entities in waters arriving on the Scotian Shelf is modified (Yeats et al. 2010). The complex interaction between temporally variable advective and biogeochemical processes generates an ensemble of possible future outcomes for oxygen or nutrient concentrations. The challenge will be to designate the probable from the possible.

Are future states ineluctably pre-determined? Processes and mechanisms explain material, formal, and efficient causes. It is tempting to draw a deterministic future from these, but we would be wrong to do so. By this, we do not mean to tread into the teleology of final causation, although this should not be necessarily anathematic. The point we wish to make is that though ecosystem processes may not be random, they are indeterminate because organisms, unlike radionuclides or even nutrients and oxygen, are adaptive entities nested hierarchically in complex systems.

Futures cannot be observed. We can only forecast, predict, project, and explore scenarios. Empirical long-term scientific observations are the only validation that a storyline about futures is plausible, coherent, and consistent. In the Gulf of Maine, an observational time series approaching 50 years in duration records the history of the copepod community there. Changes in species diversity were greatest on interannual scales, intermediate on seasonal scales, and smallest across regions, in contrast to abundance patterns, which suggests that zooplankton diversity may be a more sensitive indicator of ecosystem response to interannual climate variation than zooplankton abundance (Johnson et al. 2011). With climate projections of a less saline more stratified surface ocean layer with possible consequent changes in the phytoplankton community, a future of a bottom-up induced change in zooplankton diversity seems plausible.

Plausible, yet uncertain, because another part of the story has yet to be considered, and that is from the top down. On the western Scotian Shelf, a decline in average body size of aggregate top predators (mainly finfish) was the dominant factor associated with the increase in prey species biomass (planktivores). In turn, declines in the abundance of larger zooplankton and increases in phytoplankton concentrations were weakly associated with the increase in prey species, suggesting that a weak trophic cascade has occurred. On the other hand, growing conditions for prey fish might have been enhanced by increased stratification (Shackell et al. 2010). Size-selective harvesting at the top of the food chain concurrent with changing climatic conditions propagating from the bottom up may lead to indeterminate ecological futures.

Scientific conjectures on ecological futures are the future of plankton ecology at BIO. Fifty years of ocean research and monitoring have prepared us well for this. As Smith (1999) presumed, it is not the snow, fog, and mud in Nova Scotia that will allow these salient conjectures to be made with credibility and legitimacy; instead it will be the creation of a reservoir of scientific knowledge that is shaped by societal norms in culture, politics, and economics. The paradox of creativity (Martin 2007) conveys a well-known ironic truth: that non-moral desires of self-fulfillment such as curiosity, truth-seeking, and appreciation of nature's beauty (all tempered by conscience) are often a more effective path to moral benefits contributing to the well-being of human society than is directed service.

POST SCRIPTUM

A contrast between the denotation and the connotation of Bedford Institute of Oceanography is important. On the one hand, the denotatum has always been immutable: BIO is an eponymous organization for the natural science of the oceans. Arguably, this denotation has been more apt for biological oceanography than for any other discipline at the Institute since there has been a continuity of plankton research in the waters of the Bedford Basin itself, from early experiments in the 1960s to the ongoing plankton monitoring program in the 2010s.

On the other hand, the connotation of BIO mutates according to what is signified by prevailing bureaucratic culture as "doing science". Science in the public interest is inherently a partially contradictory enterprise involving tensions between public goods and commercial goods, between development and conservation, between departmental mandates and political-economic imperatives, between macro and micro management policies, and between the department and its stakeholders (Doern and Kinder 2007). Viewing public sector science as an economic enterprise based on a market model of supply and demand in the community of knowledge challenges normative core science values (Hasselberg 2012) In other words, the meaning of "science" is made in ever changing contexts. Here, a semantic clarification by Day (2008) is helpful: "What we understand as science consists of three separate and distinct aspects, a dynamic body of knowledge (scientage), a process (scientody), and a profession (scientistry). This three-in-one works together in a unified manner that should be recognizable to the sufficiently educated, wherein the body of knowledge reigns supreme, the process offers the only way to the body of knowledge, and those who blaspheme against the profession will not be forgiven."

In most of 50 years, "doing the science" of plankton ecology at BIO has been a tripartite success of knowledge, process, and profession. This account has shown that the success was a result of creative work undertaken on a systematic basis to increase the stock of knowledge (that is to say, research and development, R&D), aided to some extent by complementary activities (that is to say, related science activities, RSA) that extend R&D towards socio-economic outcomes.

To prognosticate, it has not escaped our attention that ecosystem theory (Holling 2001) predicts that after growth through innovation, followed by consolidation through capitalization, any complex system becomes susceptible to catastrophic collapse due to rigidity, inflexibility, and brittleness. The complex demands of postmodern scientody on a shrinking scientistry (Fig. 1) faced with an expanding scientage may be a harbinger of Holling's omega phase. To ensure continuing perdurance of biological oceanography at BIO, it will be important to insist that science as a profession remains noble to its practitioners in the face of "narrow mandates and over-zealous accountability regimes in government" (Nicholson 2011), and that science as process is undertaken by statured professionals assiduously engaged in the changing and growing edifice of knowledge. This insistence is a necessary, but sadly insuffficent condition to ensure that in the coming years, there will always be oceanographers engaged in voyages of oceanographic discovery at the Bedford Institute of Oceanography.

ACKNOWLEDGEMENTS

This paper is dedicated to all those now passed away who were associated with the Biological Oceanography group. The Government of Canada has supported plankton ecological research at the Bedford Institute of Oceanography since its inception. I thank Glen Harrison and Erica Head for their help in the preparation of this article, and also Alan Longhurst, Ken Denman, and Charles Hannah for their comments on the draft, but all shortcomings are mine alone. The editorial advice and encouragement received from the editors is much appreciated.

REFERENCES

Allen, T.F.H., A.J. Zellmer, and C.J. Wuennenberg. 2005. The loss of narrative. Pages 333-370 *in* Ecological Paradigms Lost: Routes of Theory Change (K. Cuddington and B.E. Beisner, Eds.). Elsevier Academic Press, Burlington, MA.

Campbell, R.W. and E.J.H. Head. 2000. Egg production rates of *Calanus finmarchicus* in the western North Atlantic: effect of gonad maturity, female size, chlorophyll concentration, and temperature. Canadian Journal of Fisheries and Aquatic Science 57: 518-529.

Carpenter, S.R. 2002. Ecological futures: building an ecology of the long now. Ecology 83: 2,069-2,083.

Clarke A., J. Lazier, B. Petrie, T. Platt, P. Smith, and J. Elliot. 2003. Ocean sciences – looking back at 40 years. Pages 24-28 *in* Bedford Institute of Oceanography 2002 in Review: 40th Anniversary Edition (D. Geddes, S. Armsworthy, P. Dennis, and B. St-Laurent, Eds.). Fisheries and Oceans Canada and Natural Resources Canada, Dartmouth, NS.

Cochlan, W.P. 1986. Seasonal study of uptake and regeneration of nitrogen on the Scotian Shelf. Continental Shelf Research 5: 555-577.

Conover, R.J. 1988. Comparative life histories in the genera *Calanus* and *Neocalanus* in high latitudes of the northern hemisphere. Hydrobiologia 167/168: 127-142.

Cota, G.F. 1985. Photoadaptation of high Arctic ice algae. Nature 315: 219-222.

Cullen, J.J. 1982. The deep chlorophyll maximum: comparing vertical profiles of chlorophyll *a*. Canadian Journal of Fisheries and Aquatic Science 39: 791 -803.

Day, V. 2008. The Irrational Atheist. Benbella Books, Dallas, TX.

Denman, K.L. 1976. Covariability of chlorophyll and temperature in the sea. Deep-Sea Research 23: 539-550.

Devred, E., S. Sathyendranath, and T. Platt. 2007. Delineation of ecological provinces using ocean colour radiometry. Marine Ecology Progress Series 346: 1-13.

Dickie, L.M. 1965. Director's remarks. Pages 71-76 *in* The Annual Report for 1965 of the Atlantic Oceanographic Group. Fisheries Research Board of Canada, Bedford Institute of Oceanography, Dartmouth, NS.

Doel, R.E. 2009. What's the place of the physical environmental sciences in environmental history? Revue d'histoire moderne et contemporaine 56: 137-164.

Doern, G.B. and J.S. Kinder. 2007. Strategic Science in the Public Interest: Canada's Government Laboratories and Science-based Agencies. University of Toronto Press, Toronto, ON.

Gallegos, C.L. and T. Platt. 1982. Phytoplankton production and water motion in surface mixed layers. Deep-Sea Research 29: 65-76.

Gallegos, C.L. and T. Platt. 1985. Vertical advection of phytoplankton and productivity estimates: a dimensional analysis. Marine Ecology Progress Series 26: 125-134.

Geider, R.J., T. Platt, and J.A. Raven. 1986. Size dependence of growth and photosynthesis in diatoms: a synthesis. Marine Ecology Progress Series 30: 93-104,

Harrison, W.G. 1983a. The time-course of uptake of inorganic and organic nitrogen compounds by phytoplankton from the Eastern Canadian Arctic: A comparison with temperate and tropical populations. Limnology and Oceanography 28: 1,231-1,237.

Harrison, W.G. 1983b. Uptake and recycling of soluble reactive phosphorus by marine microplankton. Marine Ecology Progress Series 10: 127-135.

Harrison, W.G. 1990. Nitrogen utilization in chlorophyll and primary productivity maximum layers: an analysis based on the f-ratio. Marine Ecology Progress Series 60: 85-90.

Harrison, W.G. 2006. Biological oceanography in Canada (with special reference to federal government science). Proceedings of the Nova Scotian Institute of Science 43: 129-158.

Harrison, W.G. and D.G. Fenton (Eds.). 1998. The Gully: a scientific review of its environment and ecosystem. Canadian Stock Assessment Secretariat Research Document 98/83, Dartmouth, NS.

Harrison, G., C. Johnson, E. Head, J. Spry, K. Pauley, H. Maass, M. Kennedy, C. Porter, and V. Soukhovtsev. 2009. Optical, chemical, and biological oceanographic conditions in the Maritimes Region in 2008. Canadian Science Advisory Secretariat Research Document 2009/054, Dartmouth, NS.

Hasselberg, Y. 2012. Demand or discretion? The market model applied to science its core values and institutions. Ethics in Science and Environmental Politics 12: 35-51.

Head, E.J.H. 1988. Copepod feeding behavior and the measurement of grazing rates *in vivo* and *in vitro*. Hydrobiologia 167/168: 31-41.

Head, E.J.H., L.R. Harris, and R.W. Campbell. 2000. Investigations on the ecology of *Calanus* spp. in the Labrador Sea. I. Relationship between the phytoplankton bloom and reproduction and development of *Calanus finmarchicus* in spring. Marine Ecology Progress Series 193: 53-73.

Head, E.J.H. and P. Pepin. 2010. Spatial and inter-decadal variability in plankton abundance and composition in the Northwest Atlantic (1958-2006). Journal of Plankton Research 32: 1,633-1,648.

Holling, C.S. 2001. Understanding the complexity of economic, ecological, and social systems. Ecosystems 4: 390-405.

Horne, E.P.W., J.W. Loder, C.E. Naime, and N.S. Oakey. 1996. Turbulence dissipation rates and nitrate supply in the upper water column on Georges Bank. Deep-Sea Research II (43): 1,683-1,712.

Irwin, B. 1991. Coulometric measurement of primary production, with comparison against dissolved oxygen and ^{14}C methods in a seasonal study. Marine Ecology Progress Series 71: 97-102.

Jassby, A.D. and T. Platt. 1976. Mathematical formulation of the relationship between photosynthesis and light for phytoplankton. Limnology and Oceanography 21: 540-547.

Johnson, C.L., J.A. Runge, K.A. Curtis, E.G. Durbin, J.A. Hare, L.S. Incze, J.S. Link, G.D. Melvin, T.D. O'Brien, and L. Van Guelpen. 2011. Biodiversity and ecosystem function in the Gulf of Maine: Pattern and role of zooplankton and pelagic nekton. PLoS ONE 6:e16491.

Kepkay, P.E. 1994. Particle aggregation and the biological reactivity of colloids. Marine Ecology Progress Series 109: 293-304.

LaRoche, J. 1983. Ammonium regeneration: its contribution to phytoplankton nitrogen requirements in a eutrophic environment. Marine Biology 75: 231-240.

Lewis, M.R. and J.C. Smith. 1983. A small volume, short-incubation-time method for measurement of photosynthesis as a function of incident irradiance. Marine Ecology Progress Series 13: 99-102.

Li, W.K.W. 1994. Primary production of prochlorophytes, cyanobacteria, and eucaryotic ultraphytoplankton: measurements from flow cytometric sorting. Limnology and Oceanography 39: 169-175.

Li, W.K.W. 2002. Macroecological patterns of phytoplankton in the northwestern North Atlantic Ocean. Nature 419: 154-157.

Li, W.K.W. 2009. From cytometry to macroecology: a quarter century quest in microbial oceanography. Aquatic Microbial Ecology 57: 239-251.

Li, W.K.W. and A.M. Wood. 1988. Vertical distribution of North Atlantic ultraphytoplankton: analysis by flow cytometry and epifluorescence microscopy. Deep-Sea Research 35: 1,615-1,638.

Li, W.K.W., D.V. Rao, W.G. Harrison, J.C. Smith, J.J. Cullen, B. Irwin, and T. Platt. 1983. Autotrophic picoplankton in the tropical ocean. Science 219: 292-295.

Li, W.K.W., J.F. Jellett, and P.M. Dickie. 1995. DNA distributions in planktonic bacteria stained with TOTO or TO-PRO. Limnology and Oceanography 40: 1,489-1,495.

Li, W.K.W., M.R. Lewis, and W.G. Harrison. 2010. Multiscalarity of the nutrient-chlorophyll relationship in coastal phytoplankton. Estuaries and Coasts 33: 440-447.

Li, W.K.W. and A. López-Urrutia. 2013. Macroscopic patterns in marine plankton. Pages 667-680 *in* Encyclopedia of Biodiversity, 2nd Edition, Vol. 4 (S.A. Levin, Ed.). Academic Press, Waltham, MA.

Longhurst, A. 1995. Seasonal cycles of pelagic production and consumption. Progress in Oceanography 36: 77-167.

Longhurst, A. 1998. Ecological Geography of the Sea. Academic Press, San Diego, CA.

Mann, K.H. and J.R.N. Lazier. 1996. Dynamics of Marine Ecosystems. Blackwell Science, Cambridge, MA

Martin, M.W. 2007. Creativity: Ethics and Excellence in Science. Lexington Books, Bowman and Littlefield Publishers, Lanham, MD.

Mayzaud, P. and R.J. Conover. 1984. Distribution of digestive enzymes in zooplankton during the spring bloom in a Nova Scotia inlet. Canadian Journal of Fisheries and Aquatic Science 41: 245-252.

Nicholson, P.J. 2011. The value of marine research. Keynote address, Dalhousie University Oceans Week gala dinner, 2 June 2011. Dalhousie University, Halifax, NS.

Oakey, N.S. 1988. EPSONDE: An instrument to measure turbulence in the deep ocean. IEEE Journal of Oceanic Engineering 13: 124-128.

Orians, G.H. and D. Policansky. 2009. Scientific bases of macroenvironmental indicators. Annual Review of Environment and Resources 34: 375-404.

Paranjape, M.A. 1987. Grazing by microzooplankton in the eastern Canadian arctic in summer 1983. Marine Ecology Progress Series 40: 239-246.

Partensky, F.P., N. Hoepffner, W.K.W. Li, O. Ulloa, and D. Vaulot. 1993. Photoacclimation of *Prochlorococcus* sp. (Prochlorophyta) strains isolated from the North Atlantic and the Mediterranean Sea. Plant Physiology 101: 285-296.

Platt, T. and D.V. Subba Rao. 1970. Energy flow and species diversity in a marine phytoplankton bloom. Nature 227: 1,059-1,060.

Pomeroy, L.R. 2001. Book review of 'Microbial Ecology of the Oceans'. Limnology and Oceanography 46: 471–472.

Poulet, S.A. 1976. Feeding of *Pseudocalanus minutus* on living and non-living particles. Marine Biology 34: 117-125.

Prakash, A. 1964. Plankton and secondary productivity. Page 80 *in* Bedford Institute of Oceanography, Third Annual Report, Marine Sciences Branch, Department of Mines and Technical Surveys, Dartmouth, NS.

Sameoto, D.D., L.O. Jaroszynski, and W.B. Fraser. 1980. BIONESS, a new design in multiple net zooplankton samplers. Canadian Journal of Fisheries and Aquatic Sciences 37: 722-724.

Sarewitz, D. 1996. Frontiers of Illusion: Science, Technology, and the Politics of Progress. Temple University Press, Philadelphia, PA.

Sathyendranath, S., A. Longhurst, C.M. Caverhill, and T. Platt. 1995. Regionally and seasonally differentiated primary production in the North Atlantic. Deep-Sea Research I 42: 1,773-1,802.

Shackell, N.L. 2011. State of the Scotian Shelf Report: Trophic structure. Coastal and Ocean Information Network Atlantic. http://coinatlantic.ca/docs/trophic-structure.pdf

Shackell, N.L., K.T. Frank, J.A.D. Fisher, B. Petrie, and W.C. Leggett. 2010. Decline in top predator body size and changing climate alter trophic structure in an oceanic ecosystem. Proceedings of the Royal Society B 277: 1,353-1,360.

Slack, N.G. 2010. G. Evelyn Hutchinson and the Invention of Modern Ecology. Yale University Press, New Haven, CT.

Smith, J.C. and T. Platt. 1985. Temperature responses of ribulose bisphosphate carboxylase and photosynthetic capacity in arctic and tropical phytoplankton. Marine Ecology Progress Series 25: 31-37.

Smith, J.N. 2014. Radioactivity studies in the Arctic Ocean from ice camps, icebreakers, planes, and submarines: 1981-2012. Pages 51-57 *in* 'Voyage of Discovery: Fifty Years of Marine Research at Canada's Bedford Institute of Oceanography' (D.N. Nettleship, D.C. Gordon, C.F.M. Lewis, and M.P. Latremouille, Eds.). Bedford Institute of Oceanography-Oceans Association, Dartmouth, NS.

Smith, J.N., F.A. McLaughlin, W.M. Smethie, Jr., S.B. Moran, and K. Lepore. 2011. Iodine-129, ^{137}Cs, and CFC-11 tracer transit time distribtions in the Arctic Ocean. Journal of Geophysical Research 116. C04024,doi: 10.1029/2010JC006471.

Smith, R.E.H., W.G. Harrison, L.R. Harris, and A.W. Herman. 1990. Vertical fine structure of particulate matter and nutrients in sea ice of the high arctic. Canadian Journal of Fisheries and Aquatic Sciences 47: 1,348-1,355.

Smith, S.L. 1999. Organizing pelagic ecosystems. Science 283: 180-181.

Subba Rao, D.V. and P.A. Yeats. 1984. Effect of iron on phytoplankton production in the Sargasso Sea. Journal of Experimental Marine Biology and Ecology 81: 281-289.

Sverdrup, H.U., M.W. Johnson, and R.H. Fleming. 1942. The Oceans: Their Physics, Chemistry, and General Biology. Prentice Hall, Englewood Cliffs, NJ.

Taguchi, S. 1976. Relationship between photosynthesis and cell size of marine diatoms. Journal of Phycology 12: 185-189.

Vézina, A.F. and T. Platt. 1988. Food web dynamics in the ocean. I. Best-estimates of flow networks using inverse methods. Marine Ecology Progress Series 42: 269-287.

Yeats, P., S. Ryan, and G. Harrison. 2010. Temporal trends in nutrient and oxygen concentrations in the Labrador Sea and on the Scotian Shelf. AZMP Bulletin 9: 23-27.

11. LIFE AT THE BOTTOM OF THE SEA: ADVANCES IN UNDERSTANDING BENTHIC ECOSYSTEMS

Donald C. Gordon*, Ellen L.R. Kenchington, Barry T. Hargrave, and Donald L. Peer

SUMMARY

Benthic habitat and communities are important components of marine ecosystems but were poorly known in Atlantic Canada when the Bedford Institute of Oceanography (BIO) opened in 1962. Since then, BIO scientists have conducted a wide variety of programs to advance scientific understanding and provide management advice on benthic species, communities, and processes. This research evolved over the years depending on current issues and the availability of human and financial resources. Some of the work was descriptive and investigated the distribution of benthic habitat and organisms throughout Atlantic Canada in regions ranging from the nearshore to the deep sea. Other projects examined important processes such as production of key plants and animals, detritus dynamics, and pelagic/benthic exchanges. This research was heavily dependent upon the BIO fleet of research vessels as well as novel oceanographic instrumentation developed at BIO. The results have been widely published in the scientific literature and applied to numerous habitat, oceans, and fisheries management issues in Atlantic Canada.

Key words: benthic organisms (plants and invertebrates) and communities, benthic production, benthic habitat, pelagic/benthic interactions, biodiversity, seabed mapping.
***E-mail:** Donald.Gordon@ns.sympatico.ca

When the Bedford Institute of Oceanography (BIO) opened in 1962, previous studies of marine benthic ecosystems off eastern Canada had focussed on cataloguing the most common invertebrate species and their distributions, in particular intertidal and nearshore organisms which were most accessible. Few scientific studies had been conducted in offshore waters. The HMS *Challenger* expedition had collected benthic fauna off Nova Scotia in 1873, followed by additional collections made on the Scotian Shelf by the United States Fisheries Commission (Verrill 1885). Other collections of larger invertebrates had been made by various investigators in the Bay of Fundy, Gulf of Lawrence, Strait of Belle Isle, Labrador region, and Hudson Bay with the results compiled in a comprehensive catalogue of benthic invertebrates in Atlantic Canada (Whiteaves 1901). Further work on deep water benthic communities off eastern Canada was carried out in the 1950s by Russian scientists (Nesis 1965). While scientific studies had been few, a considerable amount of traditional knowledge of benthic organisms had been accumulated in the fishing community through many years of experience observing bycatch in their fishing gear. Most of the benthic information available before 1962 was qualitative (i.e., occurrence of organisms) and limited to larger species which are relatively easy to collect.

With this information, it was recognized that benthic communities were very important components of marine ecosystems and contributed significantly to fisheries production. However, the need for better understanding of benthic organisms, habitat, and processes was evident and the opportunities for innovative and exciting research in 1962 were practically unlimited. Accordingly, BIO scientists responded to this challenge and over the next fifty years conducted a wide variety of research programs covering all components of benthic ecosystems, including marine plants.

This article describes some of the major benthic programs conducted at BIO by both the Department of Fisheries and Oceans (DFO) and Natural Resources Canada (NRCan) and addresses the background for the research, some of the methods employed, important results, and how results have been applied. As will be noted, many of these projects were conducted in collaboration with other government laboratories, universities, and industry partners. This review also addresses some of the advances in sampling technology made at BIO that improved the collection of benthic data. As will become evident, BIO has made many significant contributions to improving the understanding of benthic ecosystems off Atlantic Canada, information that has advanced scientific knowledge and been applied to a wide variety of important marine management issues.

Additional aspects of BIO benthic research are described in other articles in this volume including benthic resource species such as lobster, scallop, crab and clam (Tremblay et al. 2014), benthic foraminifera (Schafer 2014), benthic impacts of aquaculture (Hargrave et al. 2014), benthic impacts of tidal power development (Gordon et al. 2014a), benthic impacts of oil spills and offshore oil and gas development (Gordon et al. 2014b), and impacts of mobile fishing gear on the seabed (Gordon and Kenchington 2014).

STUDIES IN THE 1960s

Biological oceanographic studies in Atlantic Canada began within the Atlantic Oceanographic Group (AOG) which was part of the Fisheries Research Board of Canada. Founded in 1946, AOG was initially based at the St. Andrews Biological Station (SABS), but relocated to Halifax, Nova Scotia, in 1960. In 1961, D. Peer was hired as the first benthic ecologist. He and other AOG scientists moved to BIO when the Institute opened in 1962.

Gulf of St. Lawrence

Initially, benthic projects were driven by the need to understand the relationships between benthic communities and important commercial groundfish species which feed upon them. A series of surveys to describe benthic communities was undertaken in the Gulf of St. Lawrence (Fig. 1). The major sampling device at the time was the Van Veen grab which sampled a limited bottom area (0.1 m^2) and only worked well on muddy and sandy substrates. Sampling was therefore biased towards collecting relatively small and abundant organisms. Some attempts were made to collect other organisms using a dredge and high-speed hyperbenthic sled. Benthic animals were identified to the lowest possible taxonomic level and weighed to determine biomass. The grain size distribution of sediment was also recorded to investigate the relationship of organisms to sediment type. These studies were closely coordinated with investigations of food organisms consumed by groundfish being conducted concurrently at SABS. It was believed at that time that knowing the distribution of benthic communities, as well as other oceanographic properties, would contribute to understanding the distribution and feeding of groundfish. Some of the results on community structure of benthic organisms in the Gulf of St. Lawrence were presented by Peer (1966).

Establishment of the Marine Ecology Laboratory

In 1965, AOG evolved into the Marine Ecology Laboratory (MEL) and L. Dickie arrived as Director. This was a period of rapid growth in government science and abundant funding was available for hiring new staff and expanding facilities. The new MEL program built upon the work already started by AOG with a focus on understanding the physical, chemical, and biological processes underlying marine production, especially fisheries.

Figure 1. Map of Atlantic Canada showing the location of study sites mentioned in the text. Colour codes: pink polygons represent North Atlantic Fisheries Organization (NAFO) closures to protect sensitive benthic habitats; red polygon represents The Gully Marine Protected Area; black-line arcs denote the Canadian extended economic zone (200 miles). The inset map identifies study sites near Halifax, NS.

There was a shift in the goal of benthic studies from describing the type and distribution of benthic communities to quantitative measures of production. Expanded studies in benthic ecology were seen as essential since the seafloor was known to be the site of major energy transfers and benthic organisms were important food sources for commercial fisheries. BIO was well suited to undertake such studies with its fleet of research vessels and expanding shore-based facilities.

St. Margaret's Bay

While some benthic field work continued in the Gulf of St. Lawrence, the expanding MEL benthic program initially focussed on St. Margaret's Bay, Nova Scotia (Fig. 1). Although the ultimate goal of MEL was to study all aspects of large marine ecosystems, such as the Gulf of St. Lawrence, this was impractical for logistic reasons. Instead, it was decided to conduct a detailed study of a smaller marine ecosystem that could be representative of certain features of larger systems. St. Margaret's Bay was chosen as a study site in 1966 because of its oceanographic features and proximity to BIO. It was a designated marine ecosystem area within the International Biological Program under which studies were conducted to determine the basis of different levels of production in various types of the world's ecosystems. Subsequently, several benthic projects were undertaken as part of an integrated marine production study.

Benthic surveys were carried out at numerous stations throughout the Bay using a Van Veen grab to characterize the benthic macrofauna and sediments (Fig. 2A). It was found that the large area of mud in the deeper water supported a reasonably well-defined, integrated community (Hughes et al. 1972). Detailed studies of production and predation were conducted on the polychaete *Pectinaria hyperborea* which was an important component of this muddy community (Peer 1970). To assess the relative value of benthic organisms as sources of food energy to fish, a study of the caloric content of selected benthic organisms was carried out (Brawn et al. 1968). Small scale spatial variations in the abundance of benthic organisms in St. Margaret's Bay were studied using SCUBA techniques and a start was made to describe the life histories of some of the quantitatively important organisms.

The BIO benthic program in St. Margaret's Bay expanded further when K. Mann arrived at BIO in 1967. Phytoplankton productivity studies had already begun, but nothing was known about the production of the abundant seaweeds occurring around the perimeter of the Bay. A new field program was established to determine the structure and dynamics of seaweeds using SCUBA techniques during all seasons of the year. The extent, zonation, and biomass of seaweeds were first determined (Mann 1972a) and the subtidal zone, dominated by the kelp *Laminaria*, was found to have the highest biomass. Novel methods for measuring the growth rate of kelp were then developed which demonstrated that blades behaved like moving belts of tissue, eroding at their tips and growing at their bases (Mann 1972b). This was the first year-round study of the productivity of a kelp bed conducted anywhere in the world. Surprisingly, it was observed that the growth rate was greatest in winter when water temperature was close to 0°C. Using biomass data, it was estimated that seaweed production in St. Margaret's Bay was very high, three times the production of phytoplankton averaged over the entire Bay (Mann 1973). Less than 10% of this production was grazed by herbivores while the balance was released as dissolved or particulate organic matter into the detrital food chain.

Other Benthic Surveys

Benthic surveys were also conducted in other areas, for example, just outside Boat Harbour near Pictou, Nova Scotia, before and after the discharge of wastes from a nearby bleached kraft paper mill (Peer 1972). A marked change in the composition of the benthic community was detected and attributed to the flocculated mill wastes. This was the first time at BIO that benthic communities were used to monitor effects of human activities on marine ecosystems. Benthic surveys were also conducted in Bedeque Bay, Prince Edward Island, and Ostrea Lake, Nova Scotia, to provide baseline information for the developing shellfish aquaculture industry (Hughes and Thomas 1971).

Seabed Habitat Mapping

Another important BIO initiative during this first decade was the beginning of a long-term program by geologists to map the distribution of sediments on the Scotian Shelf. Data were collected from as many locations as possible using grabs and echosounders. This early work, reviewed by Fader et al. (2014), led to the production of a series of maps showing the distribution of the major sediment units (King 1970). These maps were of great interest to the fishing community for they provided information on seabed habitat and its attractiveness to fish. This was the first large-scale benthic habitat mapping effort by BIO scientists and laid the foundation for future studies described by Pickrill et al. (2014).

STUDIES IN THE 1970s

In 1970, the Environmental Quality Division was created within MEL to address the emerging marine environmental issues of the day. This group of new scientists undertook a wide variety of research projects, many of which had a strong benthic focus. D. Gordon was hired as head in 1970 and B. Hargrave arrived the following year. In 1973, K. Mann departed to chair the Biology Department at Dalhousie University (Halifax, NS), but continued collaborative work with BIO scientists. The 1970s continued to be a period with healthy financial resources. Large federal government

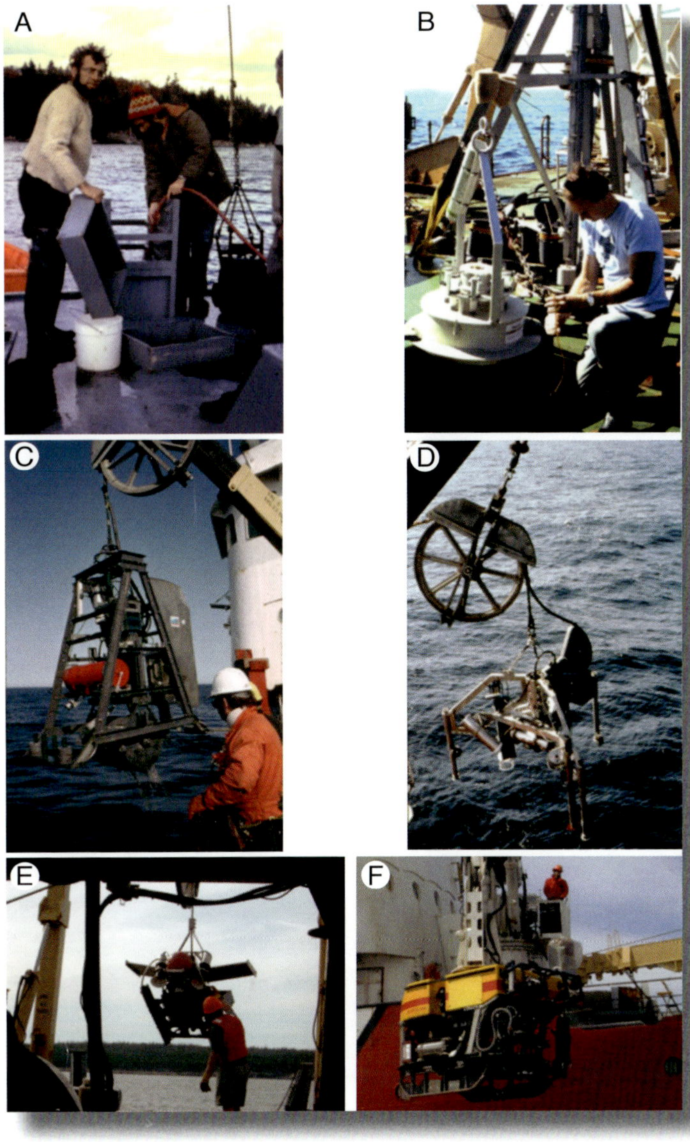

Figure 2. Different equipment types, most of which were developed by BIO (B, C, D, and E), used to sample and observe benthic habitat and communities: (A) D. Peer conducting benthic surveys with a Van Veen grab in St. Margaret's Bay; (B) B. Hargrave preparing a benthic chamber for deployment from CSS *Parizeau* on the Scotian Shelf; (C) the hydraulically-operated Videograb being recovered on CSS *Parizeau*; (D) the instrumented tripod Campod being deployed on CCGS *Hudson*; (E) the towed vehicle Towcam being recovered by D. Reimer on CCGS *Hudson*; and (F) the remotely-operated submersible ROPOS being deployed on CCGS *Hudson*.

summer student programs provided excellent training opportunities to university students and much needed support to field programs and laboratory work. Funding was also available to support a series of post-doctoral fellows (PDFs), including P. Neame, L. Cammen, F. Anderson, and C. Hawkins, all of whom made important contributions to the benthic program.

Arrow Oil Spill

In February 1970, the tanker *Arrow* ran aground in Chedabucto Bay, Nova Scotia (Fig. 1) and spilled a large volume of Bunker C fuel oil. As described by Gordon et al. (2014b), this was the first major marine oil spill in Canada and BIO became heavily involved. Much of the spilled oil washed up on the shoreline, and D. Peer and M. Thomas conducted studies of impacts on benthic communities (Thomas 1978).

St. Margaret's Bay

During the 1970s, work continued on the dynamics of the seaweed community in St. Margaret's Bay and its role in the functioning of the overall coastal ecosystem. Studies were initiated on the energetics of sea urchins, which were the dominant grazers on seaweed (Miller and Mann 1973). While they only utilized a small portion of the seaweed productivity, sea urchins were found to have a major influence on seaweed biomass. High densities of sea urchins could remove seaweeds from large areas of substrate and prevent their re-establishment. These observations led to studies of the interactions between lobster, sea urchins, and kelp beds (Breen and Mann 1976). It was demonstrated that removal of lobsters led to an increase in the abundance of sea urchins that in turn led to an overgrazing of kelp beds. This work demonstrated critical interactions between three trophic levels in a benthic ecosystem and suggested that lobster (*Homarus americanus*) was a keystone species.

Petpeswick Inlet

The discovery of the importance of seaweed production in St. Margaret's Bay led to studies of the production of other forms of coastal vegetation. This new work was initiated in Petpeswick Inlet, a shallow estuary on the Eastern Shore of Nova Scotia (Fig. 1), dominated by intertidal and subtidal sediments with extensive saltmarshes and eelgrass beds. It was found that the production of marsh grass (*Spartina alterniflora)* and eelgrass (*Zostera marina*) was quite high and, as with seaweeds, that a large amount entered the detrital food web (Hatcher and Mann 1975).

Cycling of Organic Matter

Up until this time, BIO benthic research had been concerned primarily with describing benthic invertebrate communities and studying the production of coastal macrophytes, both with links to understanding the production of marine fisheries. However, B. Hargrave's research added a new and important dimension. Its central theme was to gain more understanding of the role of sediments and benthic communities in the cycling of organic matter and dissolved nutrients. Key variables studied were the fluxes of organic carbon (both particulate and dissolved), oxygen and carbon dioxide, and dissolved nutrients. This approach was not dependent upon understanding the taxonomic identity and complexity of benthic communities but instead the chemical response of the aggregate biological community, including micro-organisms, to organic matter decomposition and nutrient cycling. Understanding the coupling and exchanges between the benthic and pelagic communities was especially important. Not only did this approach increase our understanding of the dynamics of marine ecosystems, but it also provided a foundation for assessing and understanding the fate and effects of pollutants.

It was demonstrated that the input of organic matter to sediments can be quantified by measuring oxygen uptake for decomposition across an undisturbed sediment-water interface (Hargrave 1973). Sediment core oxygen uptake was positively correlated with primary production in the water column and inversely with mixed layer depth. Hargrave and Taguchi (1978) measured sedimentation rates of particulate organic matter in Bedford Basin, Nova Scotia, and observed that just a small fraction of the material annually produced by phytoplankton reached the bottom in the deepest areas. In addition, the structure and function of the mud-water interface and metabolism of microbial communities on solid surfaces were studied. By comparing additions and losses of organic matter, an annual carbon budget was created for Bedford Basin and compared to St. Margaret's Bay. New benthic chambers developed at BIO (Fig. 2B) were used for field measurements of the flux of carbon dioxide, as well as oxygen, at the sediment-water interface (Hargrave and Phillips 1981). This new equipment made it possible to measure the consumption of organic matter by both aerobic and anaerobic processes. Changes in oxygen uptake in sediment cores isolated from organic matter supply were used to examine the utilization of labile organic carbon by benthic communities (Grant and Hargrave 1987). During this period, B. Hargrave contributed a chapter on benthic communities to a textbook on biological oceanographic processes (Parsons et al. 1977).

Bay of Fundy

In the late 1970s, BIO ecologists started a new program in the Bay of Fundy (Fig. 1) which was driven by the need to understand the potential impacts of proposed tidal power developments being considered at that time. This program had a strong benthic focus. D. Peer, B. Hargrave, and D. Gordon participated at the outset while P. Cranford and P. Schwinghamer joined the benthic team a few years later. More details on this program, which included collaboration with other organizations, are given by Gordon et al. (2014a). This program produced a wealth of new information on the composition, distribution, and production of benthic communities in the Bay of Fundy which contributed to the development of quantitative ecosystem models (Fig. 3A).

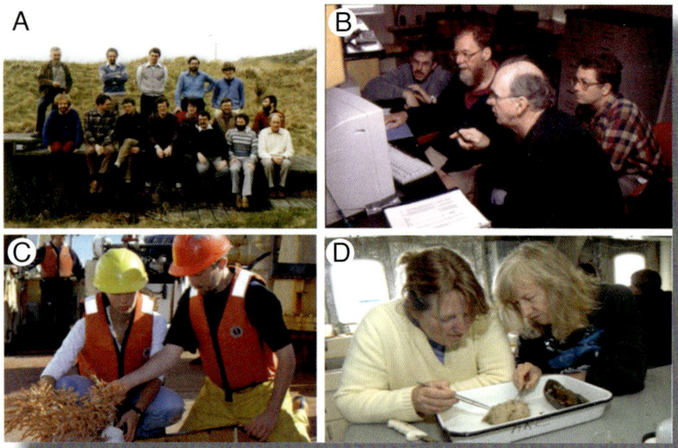

Figure 3. Some of the BIO staff who contributed to the benthic program over the years: (A) back row - P. Schwinghamer (centre), B. Silvert (second from right), front row - K. Mann (far right), D. Gordon (second from left) attending a workshop with Dutch and German colleagues at the Netherlands Institute of Sea Research; (B) left to right - G. Fader, D. McKeown, B. Hargrave, and D. Gordon planning sampling stations in The Gully; (C) L.-A. Henry and K. MacIsaac handling the first deep-water coral ever collected by Videograb on CSS *Hudson*; and (D) E. Kenchington and C. Bourbonnais-Boyce examining benthic organisms collected in Northeast Channel, Scotian Shelf, NS.

P. Schwinghamer became associated with BIO while a graduate student at Dalhousie University. His thesis was a ground-breaking study of the characteristic size distributions of organisms within benthic communities (Schwinghamer 1981). He carefully measured the biomass of organisms over the entire size spectrum from bacteria to macrofauna in sediments at Pecks Cove, New Brunswick, and Petpeswick Inlet, Nova Scotia. Three biomass peaks were observed at all locations which corresponded to bacteria, meiofauna, and macrofauna. Comparison of the data with results from other locations showed that similar size distributions characterize a wide variety of benthic communities. This was the first study to quantitatively describe the size composition of an entire marine benthic community which was an important contribution to the development of size-structure theory as described by Duplisea et al. (2014). Carrying the work on benthic biomass spectra further, Schwinghamer et al. (1986) demonstrated that it was possible to obtain reasonable estimates of annual production and its distribution among size groups. Schwinghamer et al. (1991) also examined the dynamics of saltmarsh grass (*Spartina alterniflora*) decomposition in intertidal sediments.

Ocean Dumping

Dredging and the disposal of dredged material had been practiced for many years in Atlantic Canada, with emphasis on keeping harbours safe for navigation. In time, concerns were raised about the potential environmental impacts of these practices and, in 1975, Canada passed the Ocean Dumping Control Act which made it illegal to dump any dredged material at sea without a permit from the federal Department of Environment (DOE). Requests for permits were referred to BIO by the Regional Ocean Dumping Advisory Committee (RODAC) and reviewed by experts in marine geology, marine biology, chemical oceanography, physical oceanography, and hydrography to ensure that the proposed dumping would not cause detrimental effects and was in accordance with the provisions set out under the Ocean Dumping Control Act. This advisory role continued for many years, an excellent example of how BIO expertise has been applied to address practical issues (Peer et al. 1992).

STUDIES IN THE 1980s

In 1980, K. Mann returned to BIO as Director of MEL and continued his research on the dynamics of kelp communities. He also embarked on writing a series of text books, one of which reviewed the benthic ecology of coastal waters (Mann 2000).

Abyssal Sediments

During this decade, the idea of disposal of high level radioactive waste in the deep sea became an international issue. Proposals were made by the United States and other countries for encasing nuclear waste in vitrified glass and stainless steel canisters for burial at depths up to 50 m in abyssal sediments in mid-gyre regions of the Pacific and Atlantic oceans. Stable, clay-rich deep ocean sediments were thought to have physical properties allowing for permanent containment which would prevent movement of radionuclides from waste containers into the water. There was considerable concern about the environmental implications of these proposals and, in 1980, BIO scientists were invited to join a United States-led Seabed Working Group (SWG) under the auspices of the International Maritime Organization to consider pathways by which high level radioactive waste buried in abyssal sediments might move into overlying water and ocean food webs (Hargrave 1981). These concerns prompted BIO to establish a new program investigating abyssal ecosystems, a new direction for research in both DFO and NRCan.

Models produced within the SWG predicted the behaviour of radioactive waste buried in sediments and leached from canisters. It was concluded that biological processes would be important for creating transport pathways allowing leached waste products to enter the abyssal food web and move up to shallower depths where they could be concentrated by fish, invertebrates, and seaweed potentially consumed by humans (Hargrave 1986). Three CSS *Hudson* cruises to abyssal plains in the northwest Atlantic were carried out to examine this possibility. Geological coring was conducted to establish sedimentary conditions (Buckley 1989) and benthic fauna was sampled by a box core for analysis of biomass size spectra (Schwinghamer 1985). Biomass in all size classes was lower than measured in continental shelf sediments, consistent with previous observations in abyssal sediments.

One animal identified as capable of active biological transport at abyssal depths was *Eurythenes gryllus*, a large (2-7 cm) scavenging amphipod that feeds on carcasses of mammals and fish falling to the seabed. *E. gryllus* collected during the CSS *Hudson* cruises using moored time-release baited traps built at BIO showed that food was rapidly located, consumed, and digested, common features of all scavenging marine amphipods (Sainte-Marie and Hargrave 1987). Due to the relatively large body size of the amphipods, one meal allowed survival for prolonged periods (Hargrave et al. 1995). The results confirmed that movements of megafauna such as these amphipods are at least as important to the functioning of deep sea ecosystems as physical pathways that potentially control rates of horizontal and vertical dispersal of material at abyssal depths. Measurements of stable elements and ^{210}Pb in specimens of *E. gryllus*, trapped during the abyssal plain cruises, allowed naturally occurring radioisotopes to be determined for assessment of background radiation levels. They could also be used to calculate the potential role of megafauna in redistributing elements either naturally present or added through radioactive waste disposal (Hargrave et al. 1992). Due to changing priorities, funding for these deep ocean ecology studies at BIO ended in 1987, but sample and data analysis continued for a few more years (Hargrave 1990).

St. Georges Bay

Between 1975 and 1985, BIO conducted a detailed study of the St. Georges Bay ecosystem (Lambert et al. 2014), a large embayment on the north shore of Nova Scotia (Fig. 1). This program included the determination of benthic macrofaunal production using biomass and annual turnover time data (Hargrave and Phillips 1986). It was found that production was very efficient, amounting to 20-45% of the average particulate organic carbon sedimentation. There were also very efficient predator-prey links in the benthos with demersal fish production estimated to be 1-7% of the macrofauna production.

Georges Bank

In the late 1980s, exploratory drilling on Georges Bank (Fig. 1) became a major issue to which BIO scientists responded (Gordon et al. 2014b). The Sea Scallop (*Placopecten magellanicus*), a key resource species on Georges Bank, was selected as an indicator organism for assessing potential environmental impacts of drilling wastes. Experiments were conducted to determine the relationships between food quantity and quality and absorption efficiency of this filter-feeding organism and it was found that scallops are able to maintain relatively high absorption efficiency despite high-frequency, tidally-driven variations in food supply (Cranford 1995).

Continental Shelf

At the end of this decade, a photographic atlas of the Scotian Shelf and Grand Banks of Newfoundland was compiled using seabed photographs collected over many years by BIO in support of various geological surveys (Lawrence et al. 1989). This data-mining project significantly increased understanding of the distribution of surficial sediments and benthic organisms on the continental shelf and was an important step in advancing the mapping of benthic habitat and communities.

In October 1989, BIO hosted the Canadian Continental Shelf Seabed Symposium which reviewed knowledge on the nature and stability of the seabed off the three coasts of Canada. Physical, chemical, and biological aspects were addressed, including benthic ecology, and the proceedings were published as a special issue of Continental Shelf Research (Amos and Collins 1991). One of the BIO contributions reviewed the effects of trawling, dredging, and ocean dumping on the eastern Canadian continental shelf seabed (Messieh et al. 1991).

Fish Habitat Policy

In 1986, the Fish Habitat Management Branch of DFO released its new policy for fish habitat management (Department of Fisheries and Oceans 1986). This new national policy had major implications for DFO Science, including benthic ecology. The overall objective was to increase the natural productive capacity of habitats for the nation's fisheries resources by pursuing the goals of habitat conservation, restoration, and development. The policy called for increasing cooperation between DFO Science and the Habitat Management Branch, and scientists were asked to provide advice and carry out research projects of priority to habitat managers. Further detail on this policy and how it has been implemented are given by Murphy et al. (2014).

Organizational Changes

Up until this time, BIO research was not heavily influenced by organizational changes at the national level. However, all this changed with a major DFO reorganization in 1986. The following year, MEL was dissolved and its staff reorganized. This reorganization was very disruptive and had a negative impact on staff morale. As part of the restructuring, the Habitat Ecology Division was created which became the new focus for benthic ecology at BIO. P. Schwinghamer transferred to the Northwest Atlantic Fisheries Centre in Newfoundland while S. Messieh, T. Rowell, and P. Woo moved to BIO from the Halifax Fisheries Research Laboratory. By the end of the 1980s, funding for research was reduced and scientists had to seek external financial support. The era of science-driven research in federal laboratories was largely over and scientists had to pay more attention to addressing the needs of fisheries managers, other government agencies, and industry. There also was increasing emphasis placed on developing partnerships.

STUDIES IN THE 1990s

During this decade, E. Kenchington transferred from the Halifax Fisheries Research Laboratory to join the benthic ecology group at BIO. Other new staff recruited included C. Bourbonnais, who transferred from the Marine Fish Division, K. MacIsaac, and J. Prena, a visiting scientist for several years from Germany. P. Schwinghamer transferred back to BIO, but unfortunately died soon after. Collaborative efforts between DFO and NRCan benthic scientists were further strengthened when V. Kostylev was hired by NRCan to work on benthic habitat mapping. However, the benthic ecology program was later weakened by the retirements of K. Mann, D. Peer, T. Rowell, and P. Woo. This marked the start of a gradual decline in benthic expertise at BIO as recruitment of new staff did not keep pace with retirements.

New Sampling Tools

Up until this time, knowledge of offshore benthic habitat and communities was severely limited by sampling technology. Most sampling was done 'blind' using either grabs or coring devices which worked only on soft seabed and sampled a very small area. Much information was being missed and there was a clear need for equipment that could sample on all seabed types, collect the full range of benthic organisms, and provide imagery as well as discrete samples. Therefore, new sampling tools were developed in collaboration with BIO engineers from both DFO and NRCan.

BRUTIV (Bottom Referencing Underwater Towed Instrumented Vehicle) was first developed by T. Foulkes at SABS in the 1970s as a platform with video and still cameras for examining the seabed. BRUTIV was rebuilt at BIO with numerous improvements and used successfully to collect valuable video imagery in seabed surveys carried out to determine the impacts of oil and gas development and mobile fishing gear. Numerous improvements were also made to an epibenthic sled so that it could collect quantitative samples on sandy seabeds (Rowell et al. 1997).

In addition to making improvements to existing sampling tools, BIO engineers designed and built three entirely new instruments for sampling and imaging seabed habitat and communities (Gordon et al. 2007). The first of these was Videograb, a hydraulically-actuated bucket grab equipped with video cameras (Fig. 2C). It was designed to minimize disturbance to the sampling area (0.5 m^2) and to provide the operator the ability of visually selecting the precise sampling area on the seabed, close and open the bucket remotely, and verify that the bucket closed properly prior to recovery. Videograb proved to be an excellent tool for collecting samples of sediment and associated organisms with minimal disturbance and worked well on a wide spectrum of seabed types ranging from mud to gravel.

Campod (Fig. 2D) was designed as a light-weight instrumented tripod equipped with video and still cameras. It used the same laboratory controls, slip rings, winch, cable, and block as Videograb. Campod proved to be an excellent tool for obtaining high-resolution video and photographic imagery of benthic habitat and epibenthic organisms. It could carry other sensors for benthic boundary layer studies and was able to be deployed over any kind of seabed regardless of relief, including steep walls of submarine canyons such as The Gully, Scotian Shelf.

Towcam (Fig. 2E) was developed as a more dependable replacement for BRUTIV. It was a towed body system used to collect continuous video and periodic still photos along long seabed transects. It has proven to be an excellent tool for conducting reconnaissance surveys on the scale of tens of kilometres and has the potential to carry other sensors. Towcam can be used over any seabed type as long as the relief is relatively low.

Concurrent with the development of these new tools were significant improvements to navigation. These included the development of the Atlantic Geoscience Centre navigation system (AGCNAV) by D. Heffler, the installation of differential Global Positioning System (dGPS) on BIO ships, and the availability of a Trackpoint II™ system through NRCan that allowed the tracking of gear over the side in relation to the ship. These improvements meant that the location of sampling equipment on the seabed could be determined with an accuracy of just a few metres. The application of these unique tools to study important benthic issues was made possible by having a dedicated support team that maintained the gear, prepared and operated it at sea, and looked after the details of navigation and data logging. Key members initially included P. Vass, D. Reimer, K. Bentham, and D. McKeown, and later R. Benjamin, P. Clement, and S. Roach.

Impacts of Fishing Gear

The new sampling tools were used initially in a program investigating the impacts of mobile fishing gear on benthic habitat and communities conducted in collaboration with the Northwest Atlantic Fisheries Centre (Gordon and Kenchington 2014). As well as providing new information on fishing gear impacts, this program collected detailed information on the structure of benthic communities and habitats at sites on the Grand Banks, Western Bank, and Banquereau (Fig. 1). These were the most detailed benthic surveys ever conducted in Atlantic Canada and produced some of the first data on the temporal variability of benthic communities. The study sites provide excellent baseline information for future studies of long-term variation in benthic communities.

Deep-water Corals

In the mid-1990s, deep-water corals became a major issue because of concern over how they might be damaged by fishing gear. The Ecology Action Centre (Halifax, NS) reviewed the information on distribution and status of corals off Nova Scotia and reported the occurrence of 35 species (Breeze et al. 1997). Most of the information available was anecdotal, based primarily on observations of bycatch made by fishermen. BIO scientists were called upon by environmental groups and fisheries managers for advice on this issue which was difficult to provide because of limited data and experience. Therefore, BIO scientists started collecting data on deep-water corals using Campod and Videograb which provided direct observations of corals in their natural habitat and information on associated species and community structure. The BIO benthic team was already conducting annual cruises on the Scotian Shelf as part of other programs so surveys were conducted as time allowed at key locations suspected of having corals. The first coral survey was conducted in

The Gully in 1997 (MacIsaac et al. 2001). Additional surveys were subsequently run at Haldimand Canyon, the Stone Fence, and Northeast Channel (Fig. 1). Coral data from other locations were collected by observing the bycatch in DFO annual trawl surveys. Corals were found at all areas surveyed and the results were in general agreement with the anecdotal observations reported earlier.

The Gully

Another major issue that arose during this period was the protection of The Gully (Fig. 1). In 1998, the Oceans Act Coordination Office at BIO released The Sable Gully Conservation Strategy, which identified goals for protecting The Gully ecosystem and recommended that the region be identified as an 'Area of Interest' under the newly formed DFO Marine Protected Areas (MPA) program. In 1997, a review team of BIO, university and non-governmental organization (NGO) scientists was established to review existing data, describe The Gully ecosystem, and characterize any special features (Harrison and Fenton 1998). Several new studies were carried out under a two-year DFO Maritimes Region marine science program to increase the understanding of benthic habitat and communities (Gordon and Fenton 2002; Fig. 3B). In a truly collaborative effort, BIO staff from NRCan, the Oceans and Coastal Management Division (OCMD), and the Canadian Hydrographic Service (CHS) conducted a multibeam survey of the entire Gully ecosystem with the assistance of the petroleum industry. This unique data set was interpreted from a geological perspective and the results clearly demonstrated that The Gully is morphologically and geologically unique and has a diverse number of seabed habitats within a small area. All the video and photographic imagery collected in The Gully by DFO and NRCan using Videograb and Campod was processed, and the fauna was identified to the lowest possible taxon. General remarks on sediment type and habitat were also recorded and the combined results were used to identify and map benthic assemblages (Kostylev 2002). The spatial patterns of epifaunal biomass and respiration in The Gully were also studied (Hargrave et al. 2004). These benthic data sets played an important role in the design of The Gully MPA which was officially created in 2004 (Murphy et al. 2014).

Bycatch Surveys

During this period, effort was made to expand knowledge of the distribution of benthic organisms by recording the invertebrate bycatch of DFO trawl surveys which sampled a large area of offshore waters. In addition, steps were taken to record invertebrate bycatch in the industry-funded Fisheries Observer Program on commercial fishing vessels. While limited to larger organisms caught in fishing gear, these two programs, without additional costs, provided previously missed information on the distribution of bycatch species. An identification guide with colour photos was prepared for the species most commonly caught in fishing gear. The data collected through these two programs were entered into the DFO Virtual Data Centre (VDC) where they are available to researchers. These data are selective because fishing gear is inefficient at capturing most benthic invertebrates, but they can be used to map the occurrence of large organisms such as corals, sponges, sea cucumbers, sand dollars, sea urchins, and starfish.

Seabed Habitat Mapping

Increasing collaboration between hydrographers, geologists, and benthic ecologists at BIO led to further developments in seabed habitat mapping. One example was the work done on Browns Bank (Kostylev et al. 2001) which developed a new approach based on an integrated analysis of multibeam bathymetric data and information on sediments and benthic organisms collected by Campod. This study highlighted the utility of multibeam bathymetry for interpretation of seafloor sediments and extrapolating benthic habitat characteristics across large areas of sea floor. One practical outcome of this work was the discovery that scallops were strongly associated with gravel lag deposits which are readily detected with multibeam backscatter data (Kostylev et al. 2003).

This and other examples emphasized the importance of seabed habitat mapping as an aid to managing human activities in the marine environment. However, scientific understanding of Canada's seabed bathymetry, sediments, habitat, and biological communities was woefully inadequate and the data required for new integrated ocean management plans were limited and poorly organized. Therefore, in 1999, a proposal was developed at BIO by DFO, NRCan, and DND (Department of National Defence) for a national seabed mapping program called SEAMAP (Seabed Resource Mapping Program; Pickrill et al. 2014). This ambitious program received widespread support, but unfortunately was never funded.

STUDIES IN THE 2000s

During this decade, increased attention was given by BIO benthic ecologists to addressing the needs of oceans, habitat, and fisheries managers and to participating in numerous collaborative programs with external partners, including involvement in several international projects. Regional financial resources continued to decline, but it was still possible to apply for funding from various federal sources such as the DFO Environmental Science Strategic Research Fund (ESSRF) and Science Strategic Fund (SSF), the Environmental Studies Research Funds (ESRF), the International Governance Strategy (IGS) and, through university collaboration, the Natural Sciences and Engineering Research Council (NSERC). During this decade, several more BIO benthic biologists retired including B. Hargrave, G. Phillips, C. Bourbonnais, and D. Gordon as well as key members of the technical support team including D. McKeown, P. Vass, and D. Reimer, leaving E. Kenchington as the only research scientist from the previous decade. However, as part of a staff renewal program, H. Vandermeulen relocated from Ottawa, Ontario, and M. Wong was recruited.

Regional Overviews

Considerable attention was given to collating and synthesizing existing environmental data to produce regional overviews and data bases, including benthic data where available. These 'data-mining' exercises were relatively inexpensive and yielded valuable products. For example, the Oceans and Environment Branch prepared an ecological overview of the Scotian Shelf that could be used in support of ocean planning (Breeze et al. 2002). In addition, measurements of biomass and productivity of macrobenthic and megabenthic organisms off eastern Canada were compiled into a comprehensive, georeferenced database (Stewart et al. 2001). In 2003, an assessment was made of the current state of the eastern Scotian Shelf ecosystem (Department of Fisheries and Oceans 2003) which concluded that, despite the considerable research in recent years, the benthic community was still poorly understood. Another more recent review came to the same conclusion (Zwanenburg et al. 2006).

Deep-water Corals

In 2000, BIO scientists assisted the Ecology Action Centre in organizing the First International Symposium on Deep-Sea Corals and were urged to increase research efforts on deep-water corals. Subsequently, an expanded program was funded for three years by the Environmental Studies Research Funds (ESRF) which provided support for two visiting scientists from Norway, P. Mortensen and L. Buhl-Mortensen, and a graduate student, S. Gass. During 2001-03, a large amount of new information on deep-water corals was collected using Towcam and Videograb on CCGS *Hudson* cruises targeting the Northeast Channel, the Scotian Slope, The Gully, the Stone Fence, and the southern edge of the Grand Banks (Fig. 1). Data were also obtained from DFO groundfish surveys, the Fisheries Observer Program, and interviews with fishermen, as well as laboratory work at BIO using live corals collected by Videograb (Fig. 3C). This project was conducted in collaboration with university scientists and its design was influenced by input from the oil and gas and fishing industries. Imagery and samples of coral were also collected on a cruise of the CCGS *Martha L. Black* equipped with the submersible ROPOS (Remotely Operated Platform for Ocean Sciences).

The results of this program were summarized by Mortensen et al. (2006) and Gordon and Kenchington (2007). Twenty-three coral taxa were collected or observed, including one new species. Of the areas studied, the highest abundance of corals was found in the Northeast Channel while the greatest diversity was found in The Gully (Fig. 4A, B). The results confirmed earlier suggestions of the Northeast Channel, The Gully, and the Stone Fence as prime habitats for corals. They also demonstrated that corals are abundant off Newfoundland and Labrador and extend at least as far north as Davis Strait. New information was obtained on the morphology and growth of corals. In addition, a rich associated fauna of 114 taxa was identified that use corals as a substratum or refuge against predators. Redfish (*Sebastes* spp.) were found to be particularly abundant. Of particular note was the discovery of the first

Figure 4. Representative benthic habitats and organisms in Atlantic Canada: (A) deep-water coral *Keratoisis* in The Gully, (B) deep-water coral *Paragorgia* in The Gully, (C) gravel habitat with juvenile haddock (top) and wolffish (bottom) on Emerald Bank, (D) sand habitat with juvenile haddock (lower right) and flounder (upper left) on Sable Island Bank, (E) anenomes (pink to white upstanding organisms) and coraline algae (white to grey cover) at the Rock Garden in Jordan Basin, and (F) structure-forming sponge grounds on the slope of Flemish Cap.

documented *Lophelia pertusa* reef complex in Atlantic Canada at the Stone Fence.

These results contributed to the development of coral conservation plans developed by the World Wildlife Fund (Gass 2003) and DFO (Department of Fisheries and Oceans 2006). They were also used by DFO to create three conservation areas to protect deep-water corals from human activities (Fig. 1). A 424 km^2 coral conservation area was established in the Northeast Channel in 2002, a 2,364 km^2 Marine Protected Area was formally declared in The Gully in 2004, and a 15 km^2 coral conservation area over the *Lophelia pertusa* reef complex at the Stone Fence was created in 2004.

Seabed Habitat Mapping

As part of the continuing effort to provide advice to government managers, benthic ecologists at BIO made substantial contributions to the Eastern Scotian Shelf Integrated Management (ESSIM) project, a collaborative ocean planning exercise led by the DFO Oceans and Coastal Management Division at BIO (Department of Fisheries and Oceans 2007, Murphy et al. 2014). Early on in the process it was recognized that to fulfill the objectives it was necessary to map the spatial distribution of benthic ecosystems in the ESSIM area. How best to do this was examined in a series of workshops conducted under the Regional Advisory Process (RAP) which was attended by benthic scientists, ocean managers, industry representatives, NGOs, and academia (Department of Fisheries and Oceans 2005). The first step was to review existing approaches used to classify benthic habitats and benthic habitat classification systems that had already been developed for the study area. It was then decided to construct an entirely new classification system based upon the habitat template approach which defined habitat along two axes, disturbance (physical) and adversity (scope for growth). These axes were calculated by integrating key data layers (bathymetry, stratification, chlorophyll, oxygen saturation, bottom temperature, sediment grain size, and bottom stress) and results were plotted to produce maps of disturbance and adversity (Fig. 5) (Kostylev and Hannah 2007). This approach does not predict the occurrence of a particular species, but rather the expected spatial distribution of organisms having similar life-history traits. This novel approach stimulated a lot of critical thinking and developed an

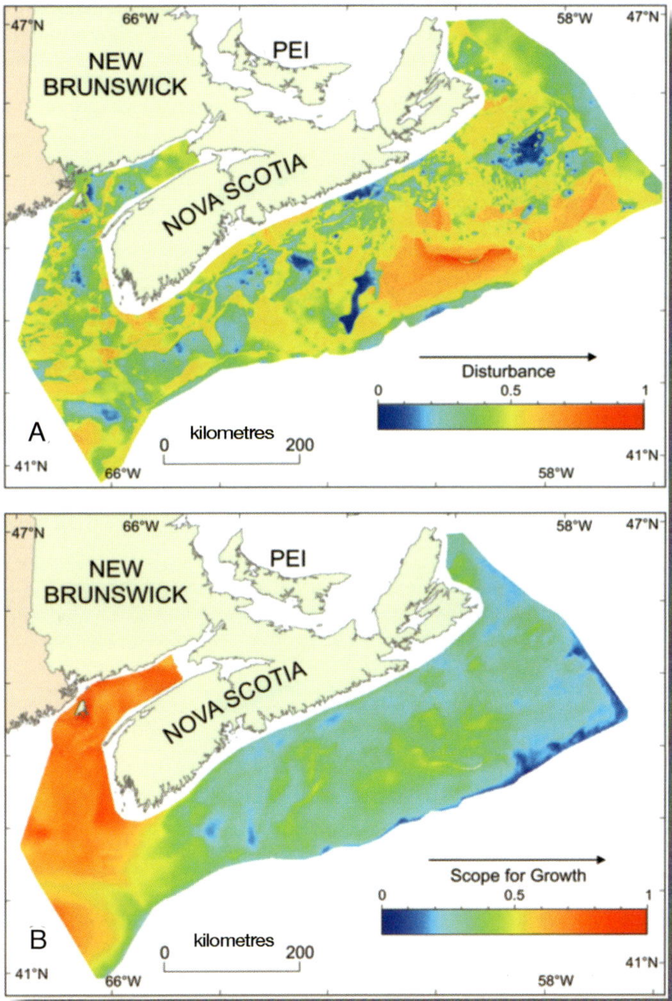

Figure 5. Maps of benthic habitat disturbance and scope for growth on the Scotian Shelf (from Kostylev and Hannah 2007).

integrated and evolving tool that can be used to address questions posed by managers. BIO benthic expertise also contributed to the identification of ecologically and biologically significant areas (EBSAs) on the Scotian Shelf (Doherty and Horsman 2007).

Utilization of Fish Habitat

As was clear from previous studies, benthic habitats and communities on the continental shelf showed considerable spatial variability due to varying environmental factors. Because of the close links between bottom-dwelling fish and the seabed, it was proposed that the spatial distribution of these demersal fish should also show considerable spatial structure, especially the juvenile stages which have the strongest fish-habitat interactions. What constituted preferred seabed habitat for fish was poorly understood, especially at small spatial scales, yet this information was needed for effective fisheries management. Therefore, in 2000, a multidisciplinary team of BIO scientists, both DFO and NRCan, came together in partnership with scientists at the Northwest Atlantic Fisheries Centre to investigate the spatial utilization of benthic habitat by demersal fish. It was a truly multidisciplinary project making full use of the unique expertise and facilities at both institutes. Funding was provided by the DFO Environmental Science Strategic Research Fund (ESSRF), the DFO Science Strategic Fund (SSF), and NRCan. The Scotian Shelf was selected as the study site because of its proximity to BIO, importance to commercial fisheries, the abundance of background scientific information, being the site of the ESSIM project, and the presence of a large (~13,000 km^2) year-round closed area created in 1987 to protect juvenile haddock. Haddock (*Melanogrammus aeglefinus*) was selected as the prime species of interest because of its dominance in the area, but data were also collected for other species, in particular Atlantic Cod (*Gadus morhua*).

Study sites were selected by analyzing the DFO summer groundfish trawl survey data collected between 1970 and 2001 to determine the areas with the highest and lowest probabilities of encountering juvenile haddock on Emerald, Western, and Sable Island banks (Fig. 1; Anderson et al. 2005). An extensive three-year field program observed seabed habitat at six sites over a wide range of spatial scales and concurrently collected data on fish, fish feeding, and benthic communities. Seabed habitat was studied using acoustic survey tools that included multibeam bathymetry, sidescan sonar, and a Biosonics DT calibrated echo sounder, as well as video and photographic imagery collected using Towcam. Fish were sampled by Campelen trawl sets (including a detailed analysis of stomach contents), the Biosonics DT calibrated echo sounder, and video imagery collected with Towcam. Benthic communities were studied using photographic imagery collected by Towcam and Videograb samples. These surveys were conducted using the CCGS *Hudson*, CCGS *Needler*, and CNAV *Quest*. Data were georeferenced to within a few metres and incorporated into a data management system. Preliminary results from this project were reviewed at a synthesis workshop held at BIO (Anderson and Gordon 2007). Juvenile fish appear to prefer gravel habitats (Fig. 4C) during the day to decrease the risk of predation, but feed over sand (Fig. 4D) at night.

Biodiversity

A major international theme emerging during this decade was biodiversity, driven by the United Nations Convention on Biological Diversity. The Centre for Marine Biodiversity (CMB) was created and E. Kenchington was appointed Director. This initiative involved partnerships among government agencies, universities, industry, and NGOs, and led to larger national and international initiatives such as the Barcode of Life program and the NSERC Canadian Healthy Ocean (CHONe) university research network.

In collaboration with SABS, the Atlantic Reference Centre, and the Gulf of Maine Census of Marine Life, the CMB created the Discovery Corridor Program. The Discovery Corridor is a large swath of ocean extending from the Fundy Isles region near St. Andrews, New Brunswick, across the northern Gulf of Maine to depths of 6,000 m. The goal was to compile an inventory of marine species within the area, and to develop projects to understand how conservation of marine biodiversity can be accommodated while sustainable utilization of marine resources occurs. In collaboration with Dalhousie and Memorial universities, benthic surveys were conducted using Campod and ROPOS on CCGS *Hudson* cruises to Jordan Basin, Georges Basin, and Northeast Channel (Fig. 2F). The findings included a significant number of new depth and location records for various species, some new species to the region, and quite possibly species new to science (Fig. 4E; Cogswell et al. 2009).

In collaboration with the Northwest Atlantic Fisheries Centre and Memorial University (St. John's, NL), ROPOS was also used on the CCGS *Hudson* in 2007 to further explore deep-water corals and associated species on the continental slope (Cogswell et al. 2009). Surveys were conducted at The Gully, the Stone Fence, Haddock Channel, and Desbarres Canyon on the southwestern Grand Banks (Fig. 1). One interesting result was the discovery of extensive areas in The Gully colonized by xenophyophores, large single-celled protozoans. Samples taken for genetic barcoding gave researchers a first look at the genetics of some of these unique species, as well as a forensic tool to assist taxonomists in making identifications. At the end of this cruise, the list of previously unreported species in Atlantic Canada or species completely new to science stood at about 40. In addition, a three-year survey of the mesopelagic fauna of The Gully was initiated and together with the benthic program will lead to a new evaluation of The Gully ecosystem from the benthos to Northern Bottlenosed Whales (*Hyperoodon ampullatus*).

Vulnerable Marine Ecosystems

In 2007, the BIO benthic ecology group, now led by E. Kenchington (Fig. 3D), created a new research program in response to the United Nations General Assembly Resolution 61/105 which called upon member states to identify vulnerable marine ecosystems (VMEs) and take steps to protect them from destructive fishing practices. This major research program was funded through the International Governance Strategy and involved K. MacIsaac, B. MacDonald, A. Cogswell, and M. Best, as well as various students from Dalhousie University. Identification of VMEs was first directed to deep water off Newfoundland under the regulation of the Northwest Atlantic Fisheries Organization (NAFO). Through international collaboration, the distribution of gorgonian corals, sea pens, and sponges down to 1,500 m were documented from research vessel bycatch data. In 2009 and 2010, the team joined an international research program led by Spain to undertake more detailed research on VMEs in the NAFO regulatory area. This multidisciplinary program utilized multibeam echosounders, seismic acoustics, box corers, rock dredges, and CTDs to collect biological, geological, and oceanographic data from the Flemish Cap region of the Newfoundland Grand Banks. Using the CCGS *Hudson*, equipped with Campod and ROPOS, surveys were conducted to depths of 3,000 m for the first time (Fig. 4F). The international dimension of this research called for close collaboration with other branches within DFO such as Policy and International Affairs.

Kenchington et al. (2009) devised a quantitative method using spatial techniques for identifying significant concentrations of corals and sponges from research vessel bycatch data. This was applied to define 13 closure areas in the NAFO regulatory region to protect these organisms (Fig. 1). The same methodology was subsequently applied to Canadian waters and identified significant concentrations of corals and sponges from the eastern Canadian arctic to the United States border, including the Gulf of St. Lawrence (Kenchington et al. 2010). This work was used by DFO Fisheries Management to assess fisheries against the Sensitive Benthic Areas policy and has prompted industry to create a voluntary closure in Emerald Basin to protect a globally unique population of glass-vase sponges. Work with NAFO on VMEs continues to be a high profile program for both DFO and NAFO, and has involved increased participation in international fora such as the Food and Agricultural Organization (FAO) and the United Nations Division for Ocean Affairs and the Law of the Sea (DOLAS).

Nearshore Studies

With the arrival of H. Vandermeulen and M. Wong, several new benthic projects were initiated in the nearshore zone, an area where BIO had been active in the 1960s and 1970s. One project has been mapping nearshore marine habitats from small boats using specialized equipment developed at BIO including a unique towfish with video, sidescan sonar, and an echosounder (Vandermeulen 2011). A related project examined the importance and sensitivity of eelgrass (*Zostera marina*) as fish habitat (Vandermeulen 2009). Observations on the habitat value of artificial reefs have also been conducted (Murphy et al. 2014). Another new activity has involved participation in the international Natural Geography In-Shore Areas (NaGISA) program as part of the Census of Marine Life (CoML; Wong and Pohle 2009) being conducted in collaboration with the Huntsman Marine Science Centre, SABS, and the Gulf Fisheries Centre. The aim of this program is to quantify the biodiversity of benthic flora and fauna in coastal habitats throughout the world. Local seagrass and rocky shore study sites in Nova Scotia have been sampled annually using a standard protocol to ensure comparability of data across all regions. In addition, food network models for various benthic habitats are being developed and used to determine the ecosystem level impacts of invasive species.

SYNTHESIS AND OUTLOOK FOR THE FUTURE

Much has been accomplished by benthic ecologists at BIO over the past fifty years. There has been an explosion of knowledge about benthic habitats, communities, and processes in Atlantic Canada ecosystems ranging from the nearshore to the deep sea. The importance and value of this research has been internationally recognized and has produced many exciting new discoveries, advanced the field of benthic ecology, and been well-published in the scientific literature. BIO benthic scientists have also played a major role in providing advice on important local, regional, national, and international marine management issues. The scientific advice has been of the highest quality reflecting results from active research projects.

Despite the extensive amount of benthic research that has been done by BIO, much more needs to be done. Significant progress has been made in mapping benthic habitat and communities but much more detail is needed to fully address the needs of habitat, ocean, and fisheries managers. Most of the research to date has focussed on larger benthic organisms which are easy to observe and collect while less attention

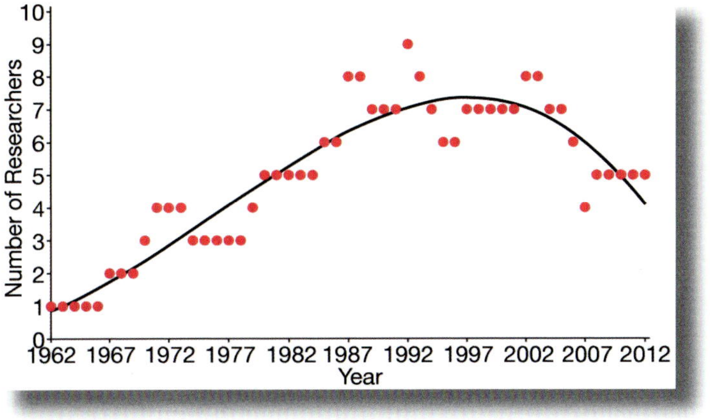

Figure 6. Changes in the number of principal scientists involved in the BIO benthic ecology program between 1962 and 2012.

has been given to the smaller micro-organisms and meiofauna which are critical to the functioning of benthic ecosystems. More information is needed to understand how benthic communities evolve and on unravelling the relative influences of natural processes and human impacts. Practically nothing is known about how benthic fauna will respond to expected changes in ocean climate that could have major impacts on the distribution and composition of benthic communities and the fisheries resources dependent upon them. There continues to be a need for new and improved models that describe how the benthos functions within the complete marine ecosystem and that can predict future changes. Such new knowledge would assist habitat, ocean, and fisheries managers in managing human activities to ensure the long term health and sustainability of Canadian marine ecosystems. There clearly is a need and justification for maintaining a strong federal program in benthic ecology.

Unfortunately, government cutbacks in recent years have seriously eroded the capacity of BIO to conduct benthic research. The recruitment of new staff has not kept up with retirements (Fig. 6). Current scientific staff members face numerous challenges that impair their productivity including the scarcity of funding, the decline and aging of the BIO research fleet, and difficulty in participating in the international research community. The ability to address new issues, respond to emergencies, and provide expert advice is now less than it was in the past. Nonetheless, the positive developments in technology, scientific discovery, and application to fisheries management that have been achieved at BIO during the last half century leave a legacy and example for meeting the future challenges of managing Canada's marine ecological resources in the presence of a changing climate and other pressures as yet unknown.

ACKNOWLEDGEMENTS

The principal scientists involved in this research are identified as authors in the selected references listed below. We thank them all, plus our many external colleagues, for their role in advancing the knowledge of benthic ecosystems in Atlantic Canada over the past fifty years. This research was also critically dependent upon the support of many other BIO staff who contributed behind the scenes by developing equipment, collecting and processing samples, processing data, and providing administrative and field support. We thank the many BIO managers and funding agencies for their support in carrying out this research. We also thank John Anderson, Paul Keizer, Kevin MacIsaac, Mark McLean, Eric Mills, Bob Miller, Brian Nicholls, Dick Pickrill, Herb Vandermeulen, and Melisa Wong for reviewing earlier drafts of this contribution; Cam Lirette kindly drafted Figure 1.

REFERENCES

Amos, C.L. and M. Collins (Eds.). 1991. The seabed of the Canadian shelf. Continental Shelf Research 11: 665-1,311.

Anderson, J.T. and D.C. Gordon, Jr. 2007. Report of the spatial utilization of benthic habitats by demersal fish on the Scotian Shelf synthesis meeting 2007. Canadian Technical Report of Fisheries and Aquatic Sciences 2770. Fisheries and Oceans Canada, St. John's, NL.

Anderson, J.T., J.E. Simon, D.C. Gordon, Jr., and P.C. Hurley. 2005. Linking fisheries to benthic habitat at multiple scales: eastern Scotian Shelf haddock. American Fisheries Society Symposium 41: 251-264.

Brawn, V.M., D.L. Peer, and R.J. Bentley. 1968. Caloric content of the standing crop of benthic and epibenthic invertebrates of St. Margaret's Bay, Nova Scotia. Journal of the Fisheries Research Board of Canada 25: 1,803-1,811.

Breen, P. A. and Mann, K.H. 1976. Destructive grazing of kelp by sea urchins in eastern Canada. Journal of the Fisheries Research Board of Canada 33: 1,278-1,283.

Breeze, H., D.S. Davis, M. Butler, and V. Kostylev. 1997. Distribution and status of deep water corals off Nova Scotia. Ecology Action Centre, Marine Issues Committee Special Publication Number 1, Halifax, NS.

Breeze, H., D.G. Fenton, R.J. Rutherford, and M.A. Silva. 2002. The Scotian Shelf: an ecological overview for ocean planning. Canadian Technical Report of Fisheries and Aquatic Sciences 2393. Fisheries and Oceans Canada, Dartmouth, NS.

Buckley, D.E. 1989. Geochemical evidence of pore-water advection along a fault in plastic sediments from the Southern Nares Abyssal Plain (western North Atlantic). Chemical Geology 75: 43-60.

Cogswell, A.T., E.L.R. Kenchington, C.G. Lirette, K. MacIsaac, M.M. Best, L.I. Beazley, and J. Vickers. 2009. The current state of knowledge concerning the distribution of coral in the Maritime Provinces. Canadian Technical Report of Fisheries and Aquatic Sciences 2855. Fisheries and Oceans Canada, Dartmouth, NS.

Cranford, P.J. 1995. Relationships between food quantity and quality and absorption efficiency in sea scallops *Placopecten magellanicus* (Gmelin). Journal of Experimental Marine Biology and Ecology 189: 123-142.

Department of Fisheries and Oceans. 1986. The Department of Fisheries and Oceans policy for the management of fish habitat. Department of Fisheries and Oceans, Ottawa, ON.

Department of Fisheries and Oceans. 2003. State of the eastern Scotian Shelf ecosystem. Maritimes Region Ecosystem Status Report 2003/004, Fisheries and Oceans Canada, Dartmouth, NS.

Department of Fisheries and Oceans. 2005. Framework for classification and characterization of Scotia-Fundy benthic habitats. Canadian Scientific Advisory Secretariat Scientific Advisory Report 2005/071, Department of Fisheries and Oceans, Dartmouth, NS.

Department of Fisheries and Oceans. 2006. Coral conservation plan: Maritimes Region (2006-2010). Oceans and Coastal Management Report 2006-01. Fisheries and Oceans Canada, Dartmouth, NS.

Department of Fisheries and Oceans. 2007. Eastern Scotian Shelf Integrated Management Plan. Report prepared by the Oceans and Coastal Management Division, Fisheries and Oceans Canada, Dartmouth, NS.

Doherty, P. and T. Horsman. 2007. Ecologically and biologically significant areas of the Scotian Shelf and environs: a compilation of scientific expert opinion. Canadian Technical Report of Fisheries and Aquatic Science 2774, Fisheries and Oceans Canada, Dartmouth, NS.

Duplisea, D.E., P.R. Boudreau, and L.M. Dickie. 2014. The size-structured view of marine ecosystems. Pages 99-103 *in* Voyage of Discovery: Fifty Years of Marine Research at Canada's Bedford Institute of Oceanography (D.N. Nettleship, D.C. Gordon, C.F.M. Lewis, and M.P. Latremouille, Eds.). Bedford Institute of Oceanography-Oceans Association, Dartmouth, NS.

Fader, G.B.J., B. MacLean, H.W. Josenhans, and S.M. Blasco. 2014. Seabed sediment mapping: from single beam to multibeam. Pages 191-199 *in* Voyage of Discovery: Fifty Years of Marine Research at Canada's Bedford Institute of Oceanography (D.N. Nettleship, D.C. Gordon, C.F.M. Lewis, and M.P. Latremouille, Eds.). Bedford Institute of Oceanography-Oceans Association, Dartmouth, NS.

Gass, S. 2003. Conservation of deep-sea corals in Atlantic Canada. World Wildlife Fund Canada, Toronto, ON.

Gordon, D.C., Jr. and D.G. Fenton (Eds.). 2002. Advances in understanding The Gully ecosystem: a summary of research projects conducted at the Bedford Institute of Oceanography (1999-2001). Canadian Technical Report of Fisheries and Aquatic Sciences 2377, Department of Fisheries and Oceans, Dartmouth, NS.

Gordon, D.C., Jr. and E.L.R. Kenchington. 2007. Deep-water corals in Atlantic Canada: a review of DFO research (2001-2003). Proceedings of the Nova Scotian Institute of Science 44: 27-50.

Gordon, D.C., Jr., D.L. McKeown, G. Steeves, W.P. Vass, K. Bentham, and M. Chin-Yee. 2007. Canadian imaging and sampling technology for studying benthic habitat and biological communities. Pages 29-37 *in* Mapping the seafloor for habitat characterization (B.J. Todd and H.G. Greene, Eds.). Geological Association of Canada Special Paper 47, St. John's, NL.

Gordon, D.C. and E.L.R. Kenchington. 2014. The impact of fishing gear on benthic habitat and communities. Pages 295-300 *in* Voyage of Discovery: Fifty Years of Marine Research at Canada's Bedford Institute of Oceanography (D.N. Nettleship, D.C. Gordon, C.F.M. Lewis, and M.P. Latremouille, Eds.). Bedford Institute of Oceanography-Oceans Association, Dartmouth, NS.

Gordon, D.C., C.L. Amos, D.A. Greenberg, P.C. Smith, and G.B.J. Fader. 2014a. Understanding the macrotidal environment of the Bay of Fundy and the impacts of tidal power development. Pages 373-382 *in* Voyage of Discovery: Fifty Years of Marine Research at Canada's Bedford Institute of Oceanography (D.N. Nettleship, D.C. Gordon, C.F.M. Lewis, and M.P. Latremouille, Eds.). Bedford Institute of Oceanography-Oceans Association, Dartmouth, NS.

Gordon, D.C., K. Lee, P.G. Wells, and P.D. Keizer. 2014b. The impacts of oil and gas activities on the marine environment. Pages 361-371 *in* Voyage of Discovery: Fifty Years of Marine Research at Canada's Bedford Institute of

Oceanography (D.N. Nettleship, D.C. Gordon, C.F.M. Lewis, and M.P. Latremouille, Eds.). Bedford Institute of Oceanography-Oceans Association, Dartmouth, NS.

Grant, J. and B.T. Hargrave. 1987. Benthic metabolism and the quality of sedimentary organic carbon. Biological Oceanography 4: 243-264.

Hargrave, B.T. 1973. Coupling carbon flow through some pelagic and benthic communities. Journal of the Fisheries Research Board of Canada 30: 1,317-1,326.

Hargrave, B.T. 1981. Sediment-water exchange processes affecting radionuclide distribution. Pages 11-12 *in* Implications of Biological Processes for Disposal of Radioactive Wastes in Abyssal Sediments (L. Gomez, Ed.). Sandia National Laboratory Publication No. 1112, Albuquerque, NM.

Hargrave, B.T. 1986. Transfer of Am-241 and Pu-237 from euphausiid moults to a carbonate-rich sediment. International Journal of Marine Radioactivity 3: 125-143.

Hargrave, B.T. 1990. Ecology of deep water zones. Pages 77-90 *in* Fundamentals of Aquatic Ecosystems (H.B. Barnes and K.H. Mann, Eds.). Blackwell Scientific Publications, Oxford, England.

Hargrave, B.T. and S. Taguchi. 1978. Origin of deposited material sedimented in a marine bay. Journal of the Fisheries Research Board of Canada 35: 1,604-1,613.

Hargrave, B.T. and G.A. Phillips. 1981. Annual *in situ* carbon dioxide and oxygen flux across a subtidal marine sediment. Estuarine and Coastal Shelf Science 12: 725-737.

Hargrave, B.T. and G.A. Phillips. 1986. Dynamics of the benthic food web in St. Georges Bay, southern Gulf of St. Lawrence. Maine Ecology Progress Series 31: 277-294.

Hargrave, B.T., P. Germain, J.-C. Philippot, G. Hemon, and J.N. Smith. 1992. Stable elements and ^{210}Pb in the deep-sea amphipod *Eurythenes gryllus*. Deep-Sea Research 39: 37-44.

Hargrave, B.T., G.A. Phillips, N.J. Prouse, and P.J. Cranford. 1995. Rapid digestion and assimilation of bait by the deep-sea amphipod *Eurythenes gryllus*. Deep-Sea Research 42: 1,905-1,921.

Hargrave, B.T., V.E. Kostylev, and C.M. Hawkins. 2004. Benthic epifaunal assemblages, biomass and respiration in The Gully region on the Scotian Shelf, NW Atlantic. Marine Ecology Progress Series 270: 725-737.

Hargrave, B.T., D. J. Wildish, and P.J. Cranford. 2014. Environmental effects of salmon and mussel aquaculture. Pages 289-294 *in* Voyage of Discovery: Fifty Years of Marine Research at Canada's Bedford Institute of Oceanography (D.N. Nettleship, D.C. Gordon, C.F.M. Lewis, and M.P. Latremouille, Eds.). Bedford Institute of Oceanography-Oceans Association, Dartmouth, NS.

Harrison, W.G. and D.G. Fenton. 1998. The Gully – a scientific review of its environment and ecosystems. DFO Canadian Stock Assessment Secretariat Research Document 98/83, Fisheries and Oceans Canada, Dartmouth, NS.

Hatcher, B.G. and K.H. Mann. 1975. Above-ground production of marsh cordgrass (*Spartina alterniflora*) near the northern end of its range. Journal of the Fisheries Research Board of Canada 32: 83-87.

Hughes, R.N. and M.L.H. Thomas. 1971. Classification and ordination of benthic samples from Bedeque Bay, an estuary in Prince Edward Island, Canada. Marine Biology 10: 227-235.

Hughes, R.N., D.L. Peer, and K.H. Mann. 1972. Use of multivariate analysis to identify functional components of the benthos in St. Margaret's Bay, Nova Scotia. Limnology and Oceanography 17: 111-121.

Kenchington, E., A. Cogswell, C. Lirette, and F.J. Murillo-Perez. 2009. The use of density analyses to delineate sponge grounds and other benthic VMEs from trawl survey data. Serial No. N562, NAFO Scientific Council Research Document 09/6. Dartmouth, NS.

Kenchington, E., C. Lirette, A. Cogswell, D. Archambault, P. Archambault, H. Benoit, D. Bernier, B. Brodie, S. Fuller, K. Gilkinson, M. Levesque, D. Power, T. Siferd, M. Treble, and V. Wareham. 2010. Delineating coral and sponge concentrations in the biogeographic regions of the east coast of Canada using spatial analyses. DFO Canadian Scientific Advisory Secretariat Research Document 2010/041, Fisheries and Oceans Canada, Dartmouth, NS.

King, L. H. 1970. Surficial geology of the Halifax - Sable Island map area. Marine Science Paper 1, Marine Sciences Branch, Department of Energy Mines and Resources, Ottawa, ON.

Kostylev, V. 2002. Benthic assemblages and habitats of The Gully. Pages 17-30 *in* Advances in understanding The Gully Ecosystem: a Summary of Research Projects Conducted at the Bedford Institute of Oceanography (1999-2001) (D.C. Gordon, Jr. and D.G. Fenton, Eds.). Canadian Technical Report of Fisheries and Aquatic Sciences 2377, Department of Fisheries and Oceans, Dartmouth, NS.

Kostylev, V. and C.G. Hannah. 2007. Process-driven characterization and mapping of seabed habitats. Pages 171-184 *in* Mapping the Seafloor for Habitat Characterization (B.J. Todd and H.G. Greene, Eds.). Geological Association of Canada Special Paper 47, St. John's, NL.

Kostylev, V., B.J. Todd, G.B.J. Fader, R.C. Courtney, G.D.M. Cameron, and R.A. Pickrill. 2001. Benthic habitat mapping on the Scotian Shelf based on multibeam bathymetry, surficial geology and sea floor photographs. Marine Ecology Progress Series 219: 121-137.

Kostylev, V., R.C. Courtney, G. Robert, and B.J. Todd. 2003. Stock evaluation of giant scallop (*Placopecten magellanicus*) using high-resolution acoustics for seabed mapping. Fisheries Research 60: 479-492.

Lambert, T.C., G.C. Harding, K.F. Drinkwater, and B.T. Hargrave. 2014. St. Georges Bay ecosystem study: an exercise in interdisciplinary science. Pages 105-112 *in* Voyage of Discovery: Fifty Years of Marine Research at Canada's Bedford Institute of Oceanography (D.N. Nettleship, D.C. Gordon, C.F.M. Lewis, and M.P. Latremouille, Eds.). Bedford Institute of Oceanography-Oceans Association, Dartmouth, NS.

Lawrence, P., K.W. Strong, P. Pocklington, P.L. Stewart, and G.B.J. Fader. 1989. A photographic atlas of the eastern Canadian continental shelf. Maritime Testing (1985), Dartmouth, NS.

MacIsaac, K, C. Bourbonnais, E. Kenchington, D.C. Gordon, Jr., and S. Gass. 2001. Observations on the occurrence and habitat preference of corals in Atlantic Canada. Pages 58-75 *in* Proceedings of the First International Symposium on deep-sea corals (J.H.M. Willison, J. Hall, S.E. Gass, E.L.R. Kenchington, M. Butler, and P. Doherty, Eds.). Ecology Action Centre and Nova Scotia Museum, Halifax, NS.

Mann, K.H. 1972a. Ecological energetics of the seaweed zone in a marine bay on the Atlantic Coast of Canada. I. Zonation and biomass of seaweeds. Marine Biology 12: 1-10.

Mann, K.H. 1972b. Ecological energetics of the seaweed zone in a marine bay on the Atlantic Coast of Canada. II. Productivity of the seaweeds. Marine Biology 14: 199-209.

Mann, K.H. 1973. Seaweeds: their productivity and strategy for growth. Science 182: 975-981.

Mann, K.H. 2000. Ecology of coastal waters. Blackwell Science Publications, Oxford, England.

Messieh, S.N., T.W. Rowell, D.L. Peer, and P.J. Cranford. 1991. The effects of trawling, dredging and ocean dumping on the eastern Canadian continental shelf seabed. Continental Shelf Research 11: 1,237-1,263.

Miller, R.J. and K.H. Mann. 1973. Ecological energetics of the seaweed zone in a marine bay on the Atlantic Coast of Canada. III. Energy transformations by sea urchins. Marine Biology 18: 99-114.

Mortensen, P.B., L. Buhl-Mortensen, S.E. Gass, D.C. Gordon Jr., E.L.R. Kenchington, C. Bourbonnais, and K. G. MacIsaac. 2006. Deep-water corals in Atlantic Canada: A summary of ESRF-funded research (2001 2003). Environmental Studies Research Funds Report 143, Calgary, AB.

Murphy, O.C., A.J. Ducharme, J.C. Naug, P.A. Macnab, and C.B. Merriman. 2014. Ecosystem Management Branch at the Bedford Institute of Oceanography: front line for ocean policy development and management. Pages 255-264 *in* Voyage of Discovery: Fifty Years of Marine Research at Canada's Bedford Institute of Oceanography (D.N. Nettleship, D.C. Gordon, C.F.M. Lewis, and M.P. Latremouille, Eds.). Bedford Institute of Oceanography-Oceans Association, Dartmouth, NS.

Nesis, K.I. 1965. Bioicoenoses and biomass of benthos of the Newfoundland-Labrador region. Fisheries Research Board of Canada Translation Series No. 1375, Ottawa, ON.

Parsons, T.R., M. Takahashi, and B.T. Hargrave. 1977. Biological oceanographic processes. Pergamon Press, Oxford, England.

Peer, D.L. 1966. A preliminary study of the composition of benthic communities in the Gulf of St. Lawrence. Fisheries Research Board of Canada Manuscript Report Series No. 145, Fisheries Research Board, Ottawa, ON.

Peer, D.L. 1970. Relation between biomass, productivity, and loss to predators in a population of a marine benthic polychaete *Pectinaria hyperborea*. Journal of the Fisheries Research Board of Canada 27: 2,143-2,153.

Peer, D.L. 1972. Effects of kraft mill effluent on a marine benthic community. Water, Air and Soil Pollution 1: 359-364.

Peer, D.L., N.J. Prouse, and G. Siebert. 1992. Concerns addressed in the ocean dumping permit process. Pages 84-86 *in* BIO Science Review 1990 & '91 (T.E. Smith and J. Cook, Eds.). Fisheries and Oceans Canada, Dartmouth, NS.

Pickrill, R.A., B.J. Todd, S.J. Smith, J.V. Barrie, and K. Conway. 2014. Marine habitat mapping in Canada's oceans. Pages 185-190 *in* Voyage of Discovery: Fifty Years of Marine Research at Canada's Bedford Institute of Oceanography (D.N. Nettleship, D.C. Gordon, C.F.M. Lewis, and M.P. Latremouille, Eds.). Bedford Institute of Oceanography-Oceans Association, Dartmouth, NS.

Rowell, T.W., P. Schwinghamer, M. Chin-Yee, K.D. Gilkinson, D.C. Gordon Jr., E. Hartgers, M. Hawryluk, D.L. McKeown, J. Prena, D.P. Reimer, G. Sonnichsen, G. Steeves, W.P. Vass, R. Vine, and P. Woo. 1997. Grand Banks otter trawling impact experiment: III. Sampling equipment, experimental design, and methodology. Canadian Technical Report of Fisheries and Aquatic Sciences 2190. Department of Fisheries and Oceans, Dartmouth, NS.

Sainte-Marie, B. and B.T. Hargrave. 1987. Estimation of scavenger abundance and distance of attraction to bait. Marine Biology 94: 431-433.

Schafer, C.T. 2014. Living and postglacial Foraminifera and their environmental applications. Pages 237-245 *in* Voyage of Discovery: Fifty Years of Marine Research at Canada's Bedford Institute of Oceanography (D.N. Nettleship, D.C. Gordon, C.F.M. Lewis, and M.P. Latremouille, Eds.). Bedford Institute of Oceanography-Oceans Association, Dartmouth, NS.

Schwinghamer, P.J. 1981. Characteristic size distributions of integral benthic communities. Canadian Journal of Fisheries and Aquatic Science 38: 1,255-1,263.

Schwinghamer, P. 1985. Observations on size-structure and pelagic coupling of some shelf and abyssal benthic communities. Pages 371-380 *in* Proceedings of the 19th European Marine Biology Symposium (P.E. Gibbs, Ed.). Cambridge University Press, Cambridge, England.

Schwinghamer, P.J., B.T. Hargrave, D.L. Peer, and C.M. Hawkins. 1986. Partitioning of production and respiration among size groups of organisms in an intertidal community. Marine Ecology Progress Series 31: 131-142.

Schwinghamer, P.J., P.E. Kepkay, and A. Foda. 1991. Oxygen flux and community biomass structure associated with benthic photosynthesis and detritus decomposition. Journal of Experimental Marine Biology and Ecology 147: 9-35.

Stewart, P.L., H.A. Levy, and B.T. Hargrave. 2001. Database of benthic macrofaunal biomass and productivity measurements for the eastern Canadian continental shelf, slope and adjacent areas. Canadian Technical Report of Fisheries and Aquatic Sciences 2336, Department of Fisheries and Oceans, Dartmouth, NS.

Thomas, M.L.H. 1978. Comparison of oiled and unoiled intertidal communities in Chedabucto Bay, Nova Scotia. Journal of the Fisheries Research Board of Canada 35: 707-716.

Tremblay, M.J., J.S. Choi, P.A. Koeller, R.J. Miller, D.L. Roddick, and S.J. Smith. 2014. Science in support of the management of invertebrate fisheries. Pages 279-288 *in* Voyage of Discovery: Fifty Years of Marine Research at Canada's Bedford Institute of Oceanography (D.N. Nettleship, D.C. Gordon, C.F.M. Lewis, and M.P. Latremouille, Eds.). Bedford Institute of Oceanography-Oceans Association, Dartmouth, NS.

Vandermeulen, H. 2009. An introduction to eelgrass (*Zostera marina* L.): the persistent ecosystem engineer. DFO Canadian Scientific Advisory Secretariat Document 2009/085.

Vandermeulen, H. 2011. Mapping the nearshore using a unique towfish. Canadian Technical Report of Fisheries and Aquatic Sciences 2959. Fisheries and Oceans Canada, Dartmouth, NS.

Verrill, A.E. 1885. Results of the explorations made by the steamer *Albatross* off the northern coast of the United States in 1883. United States Commission of Fish and Fisheries, 1883 Commissioner's Report 11: 503-699.

Whiteaves, J.F. 1901. Catalogue of the marine invertebrata of eastern Canada. Report of the Geological Survey of Canada 772, Ottawa, ON.

Wong, M.C. and G. Pohle. 2009. Monitoring nearshore benthic biodiversity: the NaGISA project. Pages 7-10 *in* Bedford Institute of Oceanography 2009 In Review (J. Ryan, Ed.). Fisheries and Oceans Canada & Natural Resources Canada, Dartmouth, NS.

Zwanenburg, K.C.T., A. Bundy, P. Strain, W.D. Bowen, H. Breeze, S.E. Campana, E. Head, D. Gordon, and B. Petrie. 2006. Implications of ecosystem dynamics for integrated management of the Eastern Scotian Shelf. Canadian Technical Report of Fisheries and Aquatic Sciences 2652, Fisheries and Oceans Canada, Dartmouth, NS.

12. THE SIZE-STRUCTURED VIEW OF MARINE ECOSYSTEMS

Daniel E. Duplisea*, Paul R. Boudreau, and Lloyd M. Dickie

SUMMARY

In the 1960s to 1970s, researchers in the Marine Ecology Laboratory (MEL) at the Bedford Institute of Oceanography (BIO), examined a series of oceanic marine plankton samples from the Atlantic and Pacific oceans using the Coulter Counter, and developed a theory of a structured particle size distribution for marine organisms which became known as the size spectrum. The discovery of an empirical size spectrum was coupled with a theory of energy flow from small to large organisms such that fish production could be determined fairly easily and robustly from plankton production. Size spectrum work at MEL then branched out to examine benthic organism size distributions and the mechanisms leading to its very different pattern from pelagic size spectra. Dynamic size spectra and work on fish community size spectra followed at MEL which had a major influence on marine ecosystem research elsewhere. Presently, size-based views of marine ecosystems are playing a major role in the development of indicators of ecosystem health, as the structural basis of ecosystem models, and as means to parameterize complex ecosystem processes in an effort to develop an ecosystem approach to human impacts on the marine environment. The work done at BIO between the 1960s and 1990s was instrumental in laying the groundwork for these approaches.

Key words: allometry, body-size, energy density, production, scaling, size spectrum, trophic level.
***E-mail:** Daniel.Duplisea@dfo-mpo.gc.ca

"Master, I marvel how the fishes live in the sea?
Why, as men do a-land—the great ones eat up the little ones."
(Shakespeare, Pericles 1608)

"Big Fish Eat Little Fish", Bruegel the Elder's classic 1556 drawing (Fig. 1), perfectly conveys a centuries-old generalization about aquatic ecosystems: they are size structured. Not until the late 1960s, however, did it become apparent that marine ecosystem structure and energy flow could be mostly accounted for by such a simple observation. It was at that time when researchers from the Marine Ecology Laboratory (MEL) at the Bedford Institute of Oceanography (BIO), began to develop and document the theory of size-based marine ecosystem structure.

Figure 1. "Big Fish Eat Little Fish" based on original by Bruegel the Elder 1556. Metropolitan Museum of Art ["Pieter van der Heyden after Pieter Bruegel the Elder: Big Fish Eat Little Fish (17.3.859)"]. In Heilbrunn Timeline of Art History, New York: The Metropolitan Museum of Art, 2000 (http://www.metmuseum.org/toah/works-of-art/17.3.859).

Elton (1927) developed a size-based view of a simple arctic island ecosystem describing the lower trophic levels having both higher production and smaller size in order to supply higher trophic levels consisting of individuals of larger size. Lindeman (1942) developed the production argument further, albeit not necessarily in a size-based context. There was little development on size-based bulk energy flows (allometry) in marine ecosystems until the work of R.W. Sheldon and colleagues in the 1960s. The new impetus for data collection and theoretical development could be largely attributed to a technological advance – the Coulter Counter. Originally a medical device used to count and size blood cells, the Coulter Counter proved useful for determining the size distribution of particles in water which for pelagic marine systems is equivalent to the plankton size spectrum (Sheldon and Parsons 1967).

In addition to the technological advance of the Coulter Counter, the BIO research vessel CSS *Hudson* completed the first circumnavigation of the Americas in 1970 (Wadhams 2014). Many pelagic water samples from areas as disparate as the Davis Strait and Tahiti collected on this cruise were analyzed with the Coulter Counter which allowed a generalization of the size distribution (Sheldon et al. 1972). In addition to the observations on plankton, Sheldon et al. (1972) developed a theory of the biomass size distribution from bacteria to whales stating that, averaged

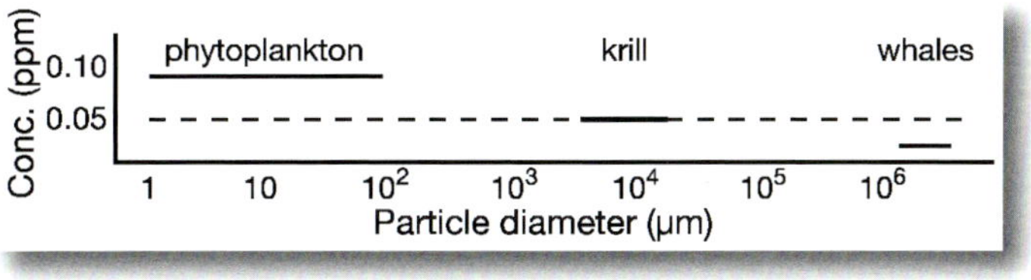

Figure 2. The potential particle-size spectrum in the world's oceans (dashed line) and the concentration of particles in different groups (solid lines). This was the first depiction in the published literature of a regular size spectrum extending through several taxonomic groups and was accompanied by empirical and theoretical considerations (after Sheldon et al. 1972).

at the proper spatial and temporal scales, it was potentially close to log-flat or that there was equal biomass of particles between 1 μm and 10 μm as there was in large organisms between 10^6 and 10^7 μm in size (Fig. 2). In reality they recognized that there was a concentration reduction going from small to large particles which would lead to latitudinal differences, and a negative slope of a line joining data points in plots of particle (organism) concentration versus size. This generality of a slope across a large range of sizes in the marine ecosystem has subsequently become known as size-spectrum theory or just the biomass spectrum (Kerr and Dickie 2001).

One of the earliest applications of size spectrum theory was to predict the biomass of larger organisms from the biomass of smaller organisms in the same system – in this case the density of 'monsters' in Loch Ness (Scotland, UK) from fish production (Sheldon and Kerr 1972). They estimated fish production in Loch Ness to be about 0.55 kg/ha/year and assumed a production to biomass ratio (i.e., ratio of average production to average standing stock of a community) of between 1 and 5 for fish, thus giving a standing stock of fish of between about 3,000 and 16,000 kg plus a seasonal migratory fish component. Assuming that monsters eating the fish would have a similar standing stock with the largest individuals in the 1,500 kg body weight or 8 m body-length class, and considering smaller juvenile monsters, they estimated monster density at 10-20 individuals.

The 'monster' example, although written clearly with tongue-in-cheek, demonstrated how one could predict standing stock of particles of different sizes in a manner similar to Lindeman's trophic arguments, but was more powerful and more easily applied because it made the simple link between body size and trophic level in aquatic systems. This meant that it was not necessary to determine 'who-eats-whom' and classify species into trophic levels in order to make the calculation. The 'generally correct' results of size-spectrum analysis elucidated 40 years ago is probably the single most important contribution of the work, though it proved to be only the beginning of size spectrum advancement at MEL and elsewhere.

REGULARITIES AND DEVELOPMENT OF SIZE SPECTRUM

The regularities of the size spectrum, including the implicit connection between body size and trophic level in marine organisms, meant that the mathematics of trophic level energy transfer could equally be applied to size. Kerr (1974) applied bioenergetic models based on individual physiology and trophic transfers, and developed a mathematical theory of size spectra. Additionally, Kerr suggested that some of the periodic deviations from a linear size-spectrum may be the result of coupling between predator and prey that had a preferred size-ratio. In other words, predators preferred prey that were a certain proportion of their own body size and the periodic deviations observed in size spectra may relate to this. Kerr's model of size spectra allowed a more sophisticated level of prediction of production in one size group from a production in smaller size groups and provided a mechanistic explanation for some of the deviations from a smooth spectrum commonly observed in empirical spectra.

In the late 1970s, further refinements in the theory and presentation of size spectra were made (Platt and Denman 1977, 1978). Platt and Denman applied a normalization to the size spectrum which essentially turned a discrete frequency distribution (i.e., number of individuals in a size category) into a continuous density distribution (i.e., expected number of individuals at any size). The normalized size spectrum was easier to treat mathematically, and its combination with allometric energetic relationships (i.e., the functional dependence of biological energy flow on body size) suggested a size spectrum slope of -0.22 (similar to the trend of an imaginary line in Fig. 2 drawn through the phytoplankton, krill, and whale groups) as opposed to a potential idealized slope of 0 (cf., dashed line in Fig. 2). That is, there is a reduction in biomass of individuals at increasing body size (i.e., higher trophic levels), because there is inefficient transfer of energy from prey body mass to predator body mass which is manifested in a negative slope. The advances of Kerr (1974), and then Platt and Denman (1977, 1978), added a level of mathematical rigour to size spectrum theory yet they remained purely steady state theories which could not account for seasonal variations in production or large and small recruitment events – they only reproduced a long-term average.

The steady state nature of idealized size spectrum slope was realized by Sheldon et al. (1972) whose empirical spectra proved to be far from flat in higher latitude systems as opposed to the equator suggesting that seasonal dynamics created energy bursts that transited the size spectrum. Clearly, the next step in the development of size spectrum mathematics and modelling was to develop a dynamic (time-varying) version of the theory (Silvert and Platt 1978, 1980). This dynamic modelling approach theoretically allowed one to predict the impact of events such as phytoplankton blooms of varying strength on upper trophic levels at some later time. The dynamic size spectrum approach held much promise, though there was not huge uptake probably resulting from a combination of the level of mathematical expertise needed to understand it and few computing resources for dynamic modelling at the time, and because the allure of size spectrum theory seemed to be in the power of its steady-state generalization given relatively simple assumptions.

Following the proof of concept example predicting Loch Ness monster density, and the mathematical advances in size-spectrum theory, a more powerful real world application of the methods and theory was developed showing how it could be used to predict fish production in the North Sea, Gulf of Maine, and the Peruvian upwelling zone (Sheldon et al. 1977).

Size-spectrum theory, although widely known and read at this time, was still very much a research topic done at MEL and thought of in terms of phytoplankton, zooplankton, fish, and mammals (Brodie 1975). With the 1980s, size spectra branched out to examine patterns in the benthos and reverted to look at the size patterns only within single trophic groups such as fish (Pope and Knights 1982).

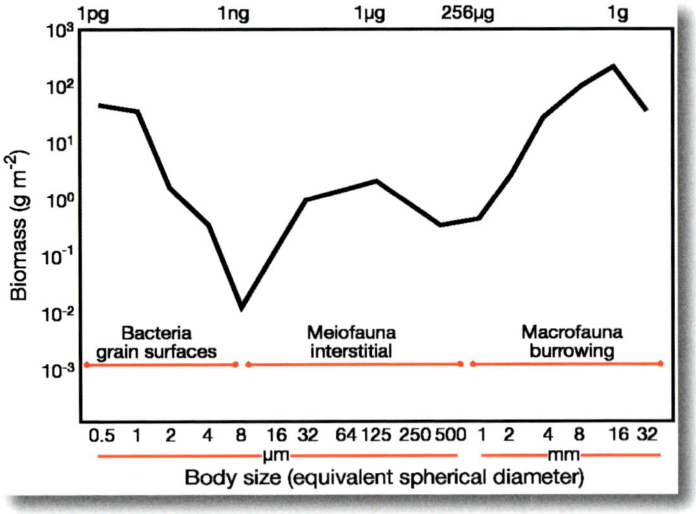

Figure 3. Benthic-size spectrum of intertidal organisms depicting the different lifestyles associated with body size modes. The main body size scaling is the diameter of a sphere of equivalent volume. An alternative scaling is shown on top of the figure in wet weight units. Biomass is expressed in relation to sediment surface area because of the two-dimensional nature of benthic communities (most organisms are in the upper 10 cm) (after Schwinghamer 1981b).

In 1978, P. Schwinghamer began doctorate work at Dalhousie University (Halifax, NS) while working at BIO to examine patterns of intertidal benthic fauna size spectra. Aside from developing techniques for the extraction of fauna from sediments (Schwinghamer 1981a), it was found that benthic size spectra were not at all as smooth as pelagic size spectra (Schwinghamer 1981b). Benthic metazoan size spectra showed two modes separated by a trough that characterized body sizes which were too large to live interstitially, and too small to be a sediment burrower. A third mode at smaller body size could also be found for bacteria living on the sediment grains themselves (Fig. 3). This size spectrum pattern and supporting theory came to be known as the 'sediment architecture hypothesis'. The metazoan biomodal pattern has been tested many times since, usually showing that neither the pattern nor its explanation are as universal as pelagic size spectra (Duplisea and Drgas 1999, Leaper et al. 2001). This suggested that although trophic forces probably dominated in pelagic systems, the physical aspects of the sediment environment were essential considerations for benthic size spectra. Schwinghamer's observations stimulated considerable work outside BIO especially by European benthic ecologists (Warwick 1984, Gerlach et al. 1985).

Equivalent Diameter (m)	FISH	ZOOPLANKTON	PHYTOPLANKTON	DETRITAL LOOP
10^0	Demersal			
10^{-1}	Pelagic			
10^{-2}	Juvenile	Carnivore		
10^{-3}		Herbivore		
10^{-4}		Microplankton	Large	
10^{-5}			Small	Microbes Detritus

Figure 4. The size-structured basis of the biological state variables in the Newfoundland Grand Banks model developed at BIO in the early 1980s which was able to capture the major dynamics of the system and permit simulation exercises to examine the potential environmental impacts of an offshore oil spill on the Newfoundland Grand Banks ecosystem (after Silvert 1985).

During the 1980s, MEL undertook a series of simulation modelling projects, even developing software to modularize the model building process called BSIM (Biological Simulation; Gordon et al. 1986). The 1980s Newfoundland Grand Banks modelling project carried out at BIO (Silvert 1985) used a size-based structure within broad groups to transfer energy from producers to consumers. The rates of energy transfers were input parameters estimated as allometric slopes and intercepts (Fig 4). This early simulation model employing size-structure was able to reproduce many of the well-known community seasonal dynamics and provide some insights into possible environmental impacts of a Newfoundland Grand Banks oil spill.

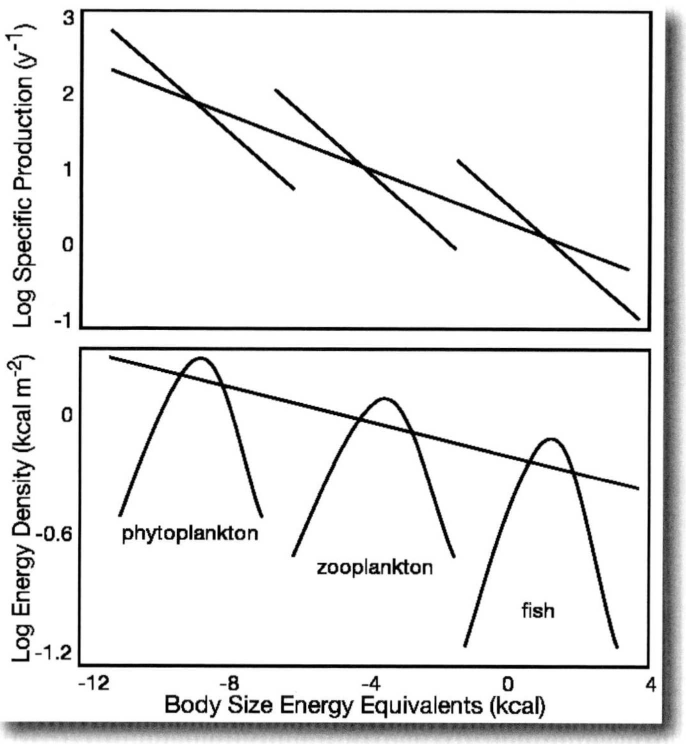

Figure 5. Biomass size spectra and specific production of the entire marine community as well as within group patterns, reflecting the overall generalization and the within group structuring mechanisms at steady state (after Boudreau et al. 1991). The straight lines spanning the full range of the x-axis are termed primary scaling, and the specific straight lines (upper) and dome-like structures (lower) are secondary scaling. Body size was expressed as energy content and biomass as energy content per unit area to better reflect the energy flow basis of size-spectrum theory. This formulation can be confusing when compared to biomass measures such as weight, body length or diameter, or densities such as ppm in earlier work, but it is conceptually equivalent.

CONCEPT OF COMMUNITY REGULARITY

In addition to size spectrum studies on benthos, fisheries scientists took an interest in the concept of regularity in community size patterns. Fisheries science is traditionally single species in focus with commonly collected survey and commercial data in the form of length-frequency distributions. It was well known that exploitation of fish populations was size selective and one of the earliest signs of over-exploitation was the loss of large fish. Thus, when fisheries biologists began to examine size spectra they tended to use length-frequency data and combined fish in length categories regardless of body form. Despite the lack of a theoretical ecological basis in energy flows, as in previous work, the fish community length-frequency distributions were still quite regular (De Aracama 1992). Change in slope of the spectrum seemed to reflect changes in management of size selective commercial fisheries such that steeper slopes equated to greater exploitation (Pope and Knights 1982, Pope et al. 1988). Although size spectra theory was not developed for just one taxonomic group, it appeared that there was utility in examining the fish length-frequency distribution for a limited number of species as an index of pressure on the entire fish community. The question then turned to what is an appropriate slope for a fish community size spectrum, and what is the influence of fishing versus other factors (e.g., climate) on the slope. These questions are still the focus of considerable research, and are discussed below.

At the same time that fisheries biologists were examining the fish-size spectrum in isolation from other system components, advances were being made to understand deviations from the linear slope size spectrum, explaining some of the deviations as within trophic-group production dynamics (Dickie et al. 1987, Boudreau et al. 1991). This new work described the well-known overall negative slope which essentially reflected the decline in biomass with increasing body size (i.e., trophic levels), and which could be derived from fitted allometric parameters. The work further described the periodic lumps in the size spectrum which roughly corresponded to the well-defined groups in a marine ecosystem: phytoplankton, zooplankton, and fish (Fig. 5). The straight line with negative slope and the periodic size-spectrum lumps were termed the primary and secondary scaling in the size spectrum, respectively.

The size-spectrum secondary scaling was said to represent the density adjustment within groups having a common food supply. Clearly, the domes (Fig. 5: lower) and secondary specific production slopes (Fig. 5: upper) are an idealized steady state balance between recruitment, growth, and mortality in individual species that have a collective community representation. Although the mechanisms behind the scaling are complex (Kerr and Dickie 2001), empirical studies clearly showed domes at the secondary scale (Sprules and Goyke 1994, Duplisea and Kerr 1995) that could not simply be written-off as the optimal catchability pattern of sampling gears at intermediate sizes. The work of Thiebaux and Dickie (1992, 1993) provides two components of the spectra, one which emphasises the straight line over several trophic levels and a second component which describes a periodic part representing the repeated parabolic domes (Kerr and Dickie 2001).

Kerr and Dickie (2001) brought together all the information on the biomass spectrum as it was available at the time, beginning with the empirical and moving into the theoretical and fisheries applications. Their book provides a comprehensive overview of all of the various pieces that were necessary to tie the empirical observations to the underlying physiology and trophic relationships to generate a theory of aquatic production on an ecological scale that is still being researched and applied today. The final chapter in the book introduces potential applications of the size spectrum to terrestrial systems. A review that encompasses much of the historical work and advances in fisheries since the Kerr and Dickie (2001) book was presented by Jennings et al. (2012).

Following the work explicating two levels of scaling in size spectra and the restructuring of BIO which resulted in the dismantling of MEL in the late 1980s, there was little new theoretical development of size-spectrum theory in BIO. However, this was not the end of size-spectrum research, as the idea had been planted deeply in many laboratories around the world, particularly in fisheries research.

SOME RECENT DEVELOPMENTS OF THE SIZE SPECTRUM

Cohen et al. (2003) examined a data-rich lake foodweb where the trophic level, body size, and abundance of all species were known. They found that body size was a better predictor of abundance than trophic level. Though the results themselves are not startling, they did provide quite solid evidence for the size-based view of aquatic energy flow. This study also unites what are sometimes considered to be different approaches to understanding community structure: i.e., the species-foodweb based approach and the size-based approach. The species-foodweb approach has previously proven to be powerful in understanding food-chain length, stability of communities as a function of interaction diversity and commonalities of community structure. Thus, to unite this approach with the simple yet powerful allometric energy flow arguments of the size-spectrum approach allows one to generalize across a broader range of communities and to understand their structures and energy flows as well as how some individual species populations contribute to the overall community structure.

Pope et al. (2006) developed a very simple community modelling approach with only modest parameter demands, but which could replicate its major predation interactions, effects of size-selective fisheries, and properties of the marine-size spectrum. Pope's model is an attempt to construct size spectra from the bottom-up in a fisheries context. The unique features of the model are that it uses the maximum body-size distribution of fish to parameterize large parts of the model. The model produces the standard negative slope biomass spectrum and shows how the slope steepens with increased fishing. The model produces similar results to an earlier model based on a similar community distribution of maximum body size of a species (L-infinity values in Duplisea and Bravington 1999) and which investigated how to best exploit a size-structured fish community to maximize value and biomass yield in the long term. Both of these approaches represent some of the new applications of size spectra to fisheries that used some simple ways to characterize different species by attributes such as maximum size and build a sensible community size spectrum out of their coupled interactions.

Trawling impacts on benthic communities became an important issue in the 1990s. It was known that there were mortality impacts of trawling on benthos, but few tools were available to determine the system-wide impacts on benthic production processes, especially in areas of repeated trawling such as the southern North Sea. Examination of the mortality impact of trawling showed that it appeared to have a size-based component where larger individuals of soft-bodied benthos were more impacted by trawling than smaller ones who were pushed out of the way of the trawling gear by the bow wave. However, for hard-shelled clams there seemed to be a refuge from the gear at large body sizes. It was assumed that this was because the larger individuals could burrow deeper. This relationship was exploited to develop a size-based model of trawling impacts on benthic biomass and production (Duplisea et al. 2002). Subsequent work modified this model so that mortality impacts of trawling were a function of both body size and habitat type (Hiddink et al. 2006). This size-based modelling approach has proven useful as a means of examining large-scale impacts of trawling on system production and biomass.

The recent European Science Foundation funded research network, Sizemic, is partially devoted to understanding how size-based indicators of exploited marine fish communities can be used as a basis for community management (Petchy and Belgrano 2010). These methods are proving useful to management even though they tend to represent just one group of the size spectrum. Further work may find added applicability as research rediscovers some of the total community energy transfer work first developed at MEL.

End-to-end models (EE), or whole ecosystem models, comprise a recently expanding approach (Fulton 2010). These are simulation approaches, often with fitted components, but usually with many speculative mechanisms. Marine EE models usually have a human component such as fishing impacts on populations. These models are seen as a way forward towards developing an ecosystem approach to marine management. What is notable about most EE approaches is that they may be partly or even largely based on a size dependent conception of marine systems and many of the dynamic processes are parameterized allometrically. The size-based view of marine ecosystem structure developed at MEL is still very important for what is considered 'cutting edge' work in marine ecology worldwide.

PERSPECTIVE

Through the groundbreaking, collaborative efforts of MEL researchers, large scale patterns in ecology were measured, modelled, and explored as a means of quantifying the dynamics of aquatic ecosystems on a level that had never been done before. The research led to the ability to empirically and mathematically capture the dynamics of predator-prey interaction that includes both the individual physiology of what organisms do to acquire and amass energy, as well as the ecology of the organisms and considerations of their density distribution through space and time, relative to their energy sources. Effectively, MEL was working on quantifying the popular, yet vague concept of ecology: i.e., the interactions of organisms with their surroundings. Since MEL ended its directed efforts, work has continued on exploring the usefulness of the size spectrum as a means of understanding and ultimately managing aquatic ecosystems. Much of the emphasis in recent years has been on the empirical delineation and comparison of ecosystems.

In summary, the size-structured view of marine ecosystems has provided an effective theoretical and empirical basis for the understanding and management of aquatic ecosystems for several decades. It can be expected to be improved with the research that is underway and continue to play a central role in future ecosystem approaches to marine management (Shin et al. 2010, Jennings et al. 2012).

ACKNOWLEDGEMENTS

We wish to thank Don Gordon for encouraging us to contribute to this volume and for important feedback on the manuscript. We would like to dedicate this chapter to our size spectrum friends and colleagues who have passed away: Steve Kerr, Peter Schwinghamer, and Bill Silvert.

REFERENCES

Boudreau, P.R., L.M. Dickie, and S.R. Kerr. 1991. Body-size spectra of production and biomass as system-level indicators of ecological dynamics. Journal of Theoretical Biology 152: 329-339.

Brodie, P. 1975. Cetacean energetics, an overview of intraspecific size variation. Ecology 56: 152-161.

Cohen, J.E., T. Jonsson, and S.R. Carpenter. 2003. Ecological community description using the food web, species abundance, and body size. Proceedings of the National Academy of Science 100: 1,781-1,786.

De Aracama, J. 1992. Length-frequency distributions of demersal fishes on the Scotian Shelf. M.Sc. thesis, Department of Biology, Dalhousie University, Halifax, NS.

Dickie, L.M., S.R. Kerr, and P.R. Boudreau. 1987. Size-dependent processes underlying regularities in ecosystem structure. Ecological Monographs 57: 233-250.

Duplisea, D.E. and M.V. Bravington. 1999. Harvesting a size-structured ecosystem. International Council for the Exploration of the Seas, CM 1999/Z:01.

Duplisea, D. and A. Drgas. 1999. Sensitivity of a metazoan benthic biomass size spectrum to differences in sediment granulometry. Marine Ecology Progress Series 177: 73-81.

Duplisea, D. and S. Kerr. 1995. Application of a biomass size spectrum model to demersal fish data from the Scotian Shelf. Journal of Theoretical Biology 177: 263-269.

Duplisea, D.E., S. Jennings, K.J. Warr, and T.A. Dinmore. 2002. A size-based model of the impacts of bottom trawling on benthic community structure. Canadian Journal of Fisheries and Aquatic Sciences 59: 1,785-1,795.

Elton, C. 1927. Animal Ecology. Macmillan, New York, NY.

Fulton, E.A. 2010. Approaches to end-to-end ecosystem models. Journal of Marine Systems 81: 171-183.

Gerlach, S.A., A.E. Hahn, and M. Schrage. 1985. Size spectra of benthic biomass and metabolism. Marine Ecology Progress Series 26: 161-173.

Gordon, D.C. Jr., P. Keizer, G. Daborn, P. Schwinghamer, and W. Silvert. 1986. Adventures in holistic ecosystem modelling: the Cumberland Basin ecosystem model. Netherlands Journal of Sea Research 20: 325-335.

Hiddink, J.G., A.M. Queirós, D.E. Duplisea, G.J. Piet, M.J. Kaiser, and S. Jennings. 2006. Cumulative impacts of a large bottom trawl fishery on the biomass and production of benthic communities in different habitats. Canadian Journal of Fisheries and Aquatic Science 63: 721-736.

Jennings, S., K. Andersen, and J.L. Blanchard. 2012. Marine ecology and fisheries. Pages 261-270 *in* Metabolic Ecology: A Scaling Approach (R.M. Sibley, J.H. Brown, and A. Kodric-Brown, Eds.). John Wiley and Sons, Chichester, England.

Kerr, S. 1974. Theory of size distribution in ecological communities. Journal of Fisheries Research Board of Canada 31: 1,859-1,862.

Kerr, S.R. and L.M. Dickie. 2001. The Biomass Spectrum: A Predator-Prey Theory of Aquatic Production. Columbia University Press, New York, NY.

Leaper, R., D. Raffaelli, C. Emes, and B. Manly. 2001. Constraints on body-size distributions: an experimental test of the habitat architecture hypothesis. Journal of Animal Ecology 70: 248-259.

Lindeman, R. 1942. The trophic-dynamic aspect of ecology. Ecology 23: 399-418.

Petchy, O.L. and A. Belgrano. 2010. Body-size distributions and size-spectra: universal indicators of ecological status? Biology Letters 6: 434-437.

Platt, T. and K. Denman. 1977. Organisation in the pelagic ecosystem. Helgolander Wissenschaftliche Meeresuntersuchungen 30: 575-581.

Platt, T. and K. Denman. 1978. The structure of pelagic marine ecosystems. Rapports et Proces-Verbaux des Reunions, Conseil International pour l'Exploration de la Mer 173: 60-65.

Pope, J. and B. Knights. 1982. Comparisons of length distributions of combined catches of all demersal fishes in surveys in the North Sea and Faroe Bank. Canadian Special Publication Fisheries and Aquatic Sciences 59: 116-118.

Pope, J., K. Stokes, S.A. Murawski, and J.S. Idoine. 1988. A comparison of fish size composition in the North Sea and on Georges Bank. Pages 146-152 *in* Ecodynamics,: Contributions to Theoretical Ecology (W. Wolff, C-J. Soeder, and F.R. Drepper, Eds.). Springer Verlag, Berlin, Germany.

Pope, J.G., J.C. Rice, N. Daan, S. Jennings, and H. Gislason. 2006. Modelling an exploited marine fish community with 15 parameters: results from a simple size-based model. ICES Journal of Marine Science 63: 1,029-1,044.

Schwinghamer, P. 1981a. Extraction of living meiofauna from sediments by centrifugation in a silica sol-sorbitol mixture. Canadian Journal of Fisheries and Aquatic Sciences 38: 476-478.

Schwinghamer, P. 1981b. Characteristic size distributions of integral benthic communities. Canadian Journal Fisheries and Aquatic Sciences 38: 1,255-1,263.

Sheldon, R. and S. Kerr. 1972. The population density of monsters in Loch Ness. Limnology and Oceanography 17: 796-798.

Sheldon, R. and T. Parsons. 1967. A continuous size spectrum for particulate matter in the sea. Journal of the Fisheries Research Board of Canada 24: 909-915.

Sheldon, R., A. Prakash, and W. Sutcliffe. 1972. The size distribution of particles in the ocean. Limnology and Oceanography 18: 719-733.

Sheldon, R.W., W.H. Sutcliffe, and M.A. Paranjape. 1977. Structure of pelagic food chain and relationship between plankton and fish production. Journal of Fisheries Research Board of Canada 34: 2,344-2,353.

Shin, Y-J. and others. 2010. Using indicators for evaluating, comparing, and communicating the ecological status of exploited marine ecosystems. 2. Setting the scene. ICES Journal of Marine Science 67: 692-716.

Silvert, W. 1985. The Grand Banks modelling project. Pages 49-53 *in* BIO Review '85 (M.P. Latremouille and B. Newman, Eds.). Bedford Institute of Oceanography, Dartmouth, NS.

Silvert, W. and T. Platt. 1978. Energy flux in the pelagic ecosystem: a time dependent equation. Limnology and Oceanography 23: 813-813.

Silvert, W. and T. Platt. 1980. Dynamic energy flow model of the particle size distributions in pelagic ecosystems. Pages 754-763 *in* Evolution and Ecology of Zooplankton Communities (W. Kerfoot, Ed.). University Press of New England, Hanover, NH.

Sprules, W. and A. Goyke. 1994. Size-based structure and production in the pelagia of Lakes Ontario and Michigan. Canadian Journal of Fisheries and Aquatic Sciences 51: 2,603-2,611.

Thiebaux, M.L. and L.M. Dickie. 1992. Models of aquatic biomass size spectra and the common structure of their solutions. Journal of Theoretical Biology 159: 147-161.

Thiebaux, M.L. and L.M. Dickie. 1993. Structure of the body-size spectrum of the biomass in aquatic ecosystems: a consequence of allometry in predator-prey interactions. Canadian Journal Fisheries and Aquatic Sciences 50: 1,308-1,317.

Wadhams, P. 2014. The '*Hudson-70*' voyage of discovery: first circumnavigation of the Americas. Pages 21-28 *in* Voyage of Discovery: Fifty Years of Marine Research at Canada's Bedford Institute of Oceanography (D.N. Nettleship, D.C. Gordon, C.F.M. Lewis, and M.P. Latremouille, Eds.). Bedford Institute of Oceanography-Oceans Association, Dartmouth, NS.

Warwick, R.M. 1984. Species size distributions in marine benthic communities. Oecologia 61: 32-41.

13. ST. GEORGES BAY ECOSYSTEM STUDY: AN EXERCISE IN INTERDISCIPLINARY SCIENCE

Timothy C. Lambert*, Gareth C. Harding, Kenneth F. Drinkwater, and Barry T. Hargrave

SUMMARY

The Marine Ecology Laboratory conducted a series of plankton surveys and experiments from April to December over a number of years in St. Georges Bay, a semi-enclosed embayment bordering on the southern Gulf of St. Lawrence in north-eastern Nova Scotia. The physical properties of the Bay were measured and a circulation model developed in support of concurrent biological studies. The main focus was the early life history of Atlantic Mackerel (*Scomber scombrus*) and American Lobster (*Homarus americanus*). Estimates of growth and mortality of these species were considered robust due to retainment of larval forms by a gyre within the Bay. Primary and secondary production were estimated to accompany measurements of the transfer of nutrients and organic matter between the benthos and overlying water column and an overall picture was developed of the seasonal dynamics of the pelagic food web. A reproductive strategy for fish is suggested, based on a spectrum of spawning tactics ranging from 'hedged bet' (i.e., sequential) to 'big bang' (i.e., all-at-once). Experimental methods were developed and apparatus designed for use in short term studies to investigate mackerel egg patch dynamics, vertical migration of zooplankton, sediment dynamics, and Langmuir circulation. The collected research supplied comprehensive baseline data for later studies and also helped address such questions as the effects of closure of the Strait of Canso by the construction of the Canso Causeway connecting Cape Breton with mainland Nova Scotia.

Key words: mackerel, lobster, herring, capelin, plankton, recruitment, growth, mortality, production dynamics, gyre.
***E-mail:** Tim.Lambert@dfo-mpo.gc.ca

Under the directorship of Dr. L. Dickie, a new Fisheries Research Board (FRB) laboratory, which officially became the Marine Ecology Laboratory (MEL), was established at the Bedford Institute of Oceanography (BIO) in 1965. Its mandate was to investigate marine ecological processes through an interdisciplinary approach by having fisheries scientists, ecologists, chemists, and physicists work together on common problems. This was a significant departure from the organizational standard of the time in which studies were separated largely along scientific disciplinary lines. The lab's first major foray into this type of study was the St. Margaret's Bay program during the late 1960s; other MEL studies employing the same approach included the Bay of Fundy project which ran concurrently.

In early 1972, a request came from FRB headquarters in Ottawa, Ontario, asking for an estimate of the size of the Atlantic Mackerel (*Scomber scombrus*) population in the Gulf of St. Lawrence (Fig. 1). Mackerel migrate from offshore waters off New England and most spawn in the warm, productive waters of the southern Gulf each summer (Sette 1950). The feasibility of expanding the mackerel fishery was under consideration in the 1970s and since there was no directed domestic fishery for mackerel, the standard stock assessment methods using commercial fishery catch data could not be used. Instead, T. Lambert chose a proxy method to estimate the population size based upon the number of eggs spawned as measured from plankton tows, female fecundity from catch samples, and the assumption of a 1:1 sex ratio. Population estimates of mackerel are still based on egg surveys today. Later that summer, Lambert and J. McRuer, assisted by four summer students, conducted an egg and larval survey in the southern Gulf of St. Lawrence using the MV *Harengus*, a wooden side-trawler belonging to the FRB, and the steam-powered CNAV *Sackville*, a World War II corvette refitted for research purposes in 1952.

During this survey, it became clear from visual inspection of the plankton catch at sea that high concentrations of mackerel eggs were present in St. Georges Bay, in the south-east corner of the Gulf of St. Lawrence (Fig. 1). At the time, mackerel were the subject of physiological studies in the laboratory at BIO. If St. Georges Bay was an important nursery ground for mackerel, it would present a great opportunity to expand these energetic studies to include the early life history of mackerel. Moreover, since recruitment studies were the primary research focus of the day in fisheries science, siting new research in the Bay seemed a worthwhile course of action. St. Georges Bay did prove to be an ideal location to study mackerel ecology because of the physical confinement of the eggs and larvae within a semi-enclosed bay. Also, its relatively small area (20 by 20 nm), enabled detailed sampling of the Bay within a day and it was within reasonable driving distance from BIO.

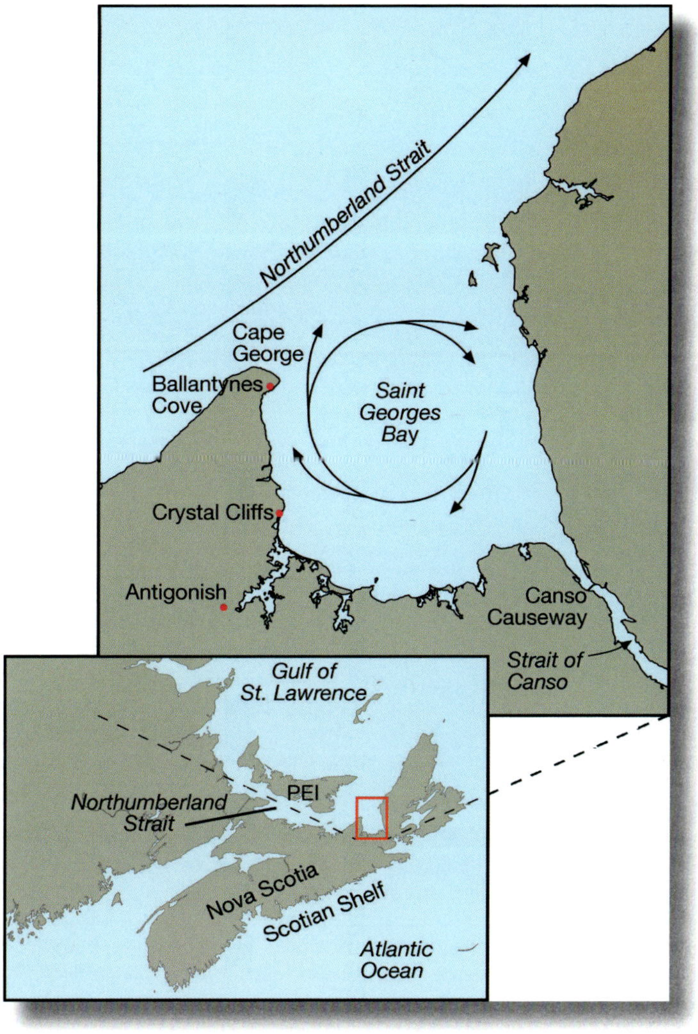

Figure 1. Map of St. Georges Bay, Nova Scotia, showing principal currents.

FIRST STEPS

Ballantynes Cove, just inside the Bay, south of Cape George (Fig. 1), was chosen as a good protected harbour for a base of operations and the MV *Navicula* (Fig. 2) was dedicated to the project from spring to winter. During 1973, the first 'pilot' year, sampling was conducted every two weeks with a neuston net and an Isaacs-Kidd mid-water trawl. The catch revealed a diverse and productive ecosystem with at least 20 species of fish larvae present, including an abundance of mackerel eggs and larvae, which guaranteed continuance of the project. Initially, living quarters were tents at the Cape George lighthouse, but by mid-summer a house trailer was moved to the site. After the first year and with an ideal sampling site confirmed, an extra trailer was added as a laboratory for on-site analysis of plankton samples that earlier had been transported to BIO.

Figure 2. MV *Navicula* at Ballantynes Cove, St. Georges Bay, Nova Scotia.

In early 1974, D. Ware, a fisheries scientist, joined the mackerel studies team. Realizing that an understanding of the physical oceanography was essential to interpreting the mackerel data, he approached R. Trites, a physical oceanographer, to become involved. Trites, head of Coastal Oceanography at the time and a member of MEL, had a long-standing interest in the Gulf of St. Lawrence (Trites 1968, 1972, Trites and Walton 1975). He fully supported Ware's idea but was already over-committed, so he successfully encouraged K. Drinkwater, a recent MSc graduate from the University of British Columbia, to provide the necessary support.

In 1975, D. Ware took over the leadership of the Fisheries Oceanography Division of MEL and, realizing the potential of a multidisciplinary approach to fisheries problems, set out to expand the St. Georges Bay program. Ware, a highly convincing and persuasive personality, enticed B. Petrie to join K. Drinkwater in examining the physical oceanography, and also convinced B. Hargrave and G. Harding to move their field research to St. Georges Bay. Hargrave studied the relationship between the water column and the bottom in terms of primary productivity and energy transfer. Harding and P. Vass saw an opportunity to expand their laboratory experiments on rate transfers of organochlorines by applying these findings to a natural ecosystem. After documenting larval lobster distribution within the Bay, Harding and Vass expanded this work, with the assistance of Drinkwater, to address lobster recruitment following a workshop on possible effects of the Canso Causeway in 1977. For this newly expanded team, working in the same bay made sense, not only from a logistic point of view, but also by allowing a greater interpretation of our results in detailed ecological terms. The enlarged program now necessitated larger accommodations and the 'Manor House' at Crystal Cliffs (Fig. 1) was provided through an agreement with St. Francis Xavier University (Antigonish, NS) from 1976 through to the mid 1980s. In 1980, R. Sheldon took over as project manager when D. Ware was transfered to the west coast. The following studies were carried out during the course of this program.

PHYSICAL OCEANOGRAPHY

Physical oceanographic studies began in 1974. D. Dobson and K. Drinkwater deployed the first current meters in the Bay from late spring to autumn. Subsequent analysis of these data revealed a mean clockwise circulation pattern (Fig. 1) and strong wind-forced current variability (Petrie and Drinkwater 1978a). The mean circulation derived from current meters reinforced visual observations made in 1972 when, following heavy rains, muddy waters were seen close to shore moving out of the Bay along the western side and joining the Northumberland Strait flow northeastward across the mouth of the Bay. The clockwise gyre in the Bay was an added bonus for the early life history studies since it meant that eggs and larvae would be retained in the Bay for some time, allowing robust estimates of growth and mortality of the mackerel larvae (Ware and Lambert 1985). Temperature and salinity data collected through the summer revealed a strong, thermally-stratified water column with temperatures ranging from approximately 20°C at the surface to 2° to 3°C at around 30 m near bottom in mid-summer (Drinkwater and Taylor 1979).

In 1975, the physical oceanographers realized that for a better understanding of hydrographic variability of the bay, more frequent measurements were needed. As a consequence, the fishing vessel, MV *Margaret and Robert*, out of Yarmouth, Nova Scotia, was chartered for four months. Several current meters were again moored around the Bay during the spring to confirm the robustness of the gyre and examine its forcing mechanism. In the fall of 1975, B. Petrie joined the physical oceanographic component of the project and began to write up the results of the first two years of data. He also developed a model of the mean circulation (Petrie and Drinkwater 1978a, 1978b) as depicted in Figure 1. In addition, the average residence time of water in the Bay was estimated to be about one month before significant exchange with Northumberland Strait water (Petrie and Drinkwater 1978a). However, it was also shown that strong winds could flush the Bay in a couple of days, as observed during the passage of tropical storm 'Blanche' in 1975 (Petrie and Drinkwater 1978a, Drinkwater 1989).

FISHERIES INVESTIGATIONS

In the 1970s, early life history studies were prominent as an approach to resolving when recruitment to a fish stock occurred. Much of the study of larval fish ecology of the day was conducted in relation to the so-called 'match/mismatch' hypothesis of D. Cushing (1975). This idea held that a critical point occurred when larval fish exhausted their internal food supply (yolk) and were obliged to begin feeding on plankton. If food was abundant (match) there would be good survival, but if food was scarce because of early or late plankton blooms, survival would be poor (mismatch). Thus, food availability at this 'critical period' was thought to be key to determining recruitment. MEL initiated early life history studies in St. Georges Bay as part of the general scientific effort to examine this larval recruitment hypothesis. The focus of these ichthyoplankton studies was mackerel, but later expanded to include Atlantic Herring (*Clupea harengus*), as new intriguing characteristics of this species became evident, and Capelin (*Mallotus villosus*). Invertebrate research centred on the American Lobster (*Homarus americanus*). Plankton surveys were conducted at varying intensities from 1973 to 1986. Sampling effort was concentrated during the first four years, after which various experimental studies were carried out along with limited monitoring of the larval fish community.

Production and survival of the eggs and larvae of the above species were estimated within the pelagic food web of St. Georges Bay (Ware 1977, Harding et al. 1982, Ware and Lambert 1985). The ultimate goal was to determine the interaction of physical, chemical, and biological factors controlling the dynamics of larval growth and survival. The residence time of water within the Bay of one month (Petrie and Drinkwater 1978a) was well within the time span of the larval life stages under study; thus, we were confident that reliable estimations of growth and mortality rates could be made.

Atlantic Mackerel

It was found that mackerel timed their migrations and spawning activity in St. Georges Bay to match narrow temperature tolerances, as reported elsewhere (Goode 1885, Sette 1950). Mean arrival in St. Georges Bay and subsequent peak spawning were predictable and correlated with sea surface temperature: the former at 6° to 8°C and the latter ~13°C (Ware and Lambert 1985). Mackerel arrived in the Bay over about a two-week period, from late May to early June. Some spawning began shortly after arrival, but most eggs were deposited over a one-week period towards the end of June. The maximum abundance of mackerel eggs in St. Georges Bay slightly precedes the abundance of their prey, thereby timing their larvae for maximum food availability (Fig. 3A). The majority of eggs were spawned within a metre of the sea surface. There was an exponential decline in abundance from the surface to 5 m and thereafter a more gradual decrease to the top of the thermocline which formed the lower boundary. Early stages of egg development were prevalent near the sea surface and later stages were deeper, resulting in newly hatched larvae being located between 5-10 m in depth. The size of mackerel eggs and resulting larvae were found to match the size of zooplankton both in time and space (Fig. 3B; Ware 1975, 1977).

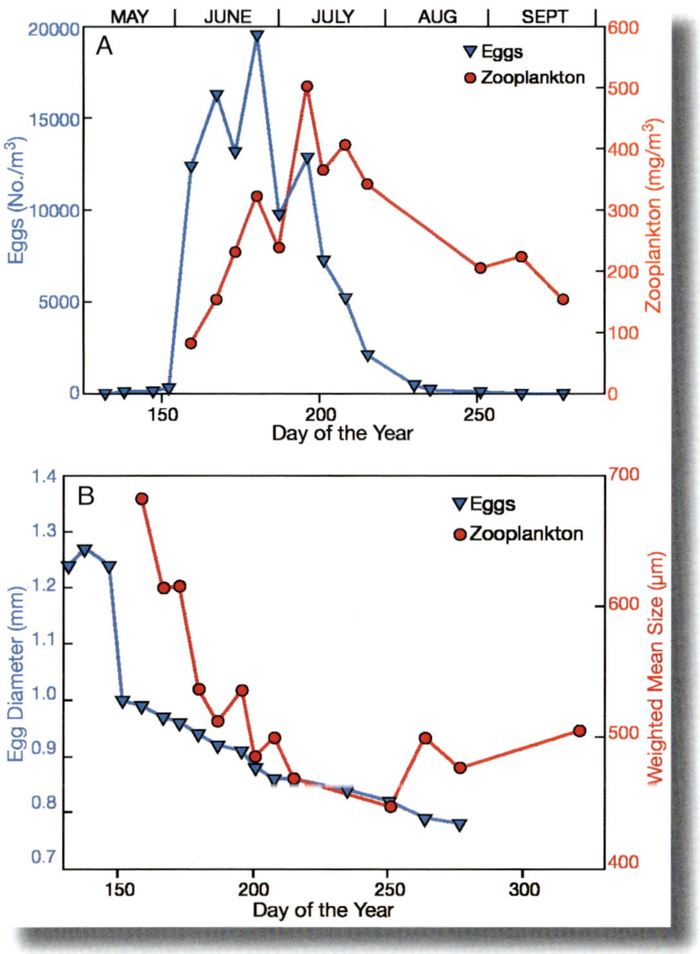

Figure 3. Mackerel eggs collected with 405 µm mesh nets and zooplankton from 80 µm mesh nets, April to October 1974: (A) egg, and zooplankton abundance, and (B) egg size and weighted mean size of zooplankton.

Egg size decreased gradually over the spawning season, as did plankton size, thus ensuring appropriately sized food for early stage larvae. Zooplankton were smaller at the depths at which hatching occurred. Furthermore, as the young mackerel grew, they gradually ascended closer to the surface where the larger copepods were distributed. Mackerel larvae undertook a daily vertical migration that followed their zooplankton prey. Larvae averaged 3 mm long at hatching and initially did not feed, depending instead on their yolk sac reserves. However, by 3.8 mm, half the young mackerel had begun to eat small zooplankters and by 4.5 mm all larvae were eating external food as their yolk sacs were now depleted. Up to a length of 8 mm all larvae ate zooplankton exclusively, but thereafter fish larvae began to appear in their diet, including those of their own species. Between 8 and 25 mm length, 58% of the guts of mackerel larvae contained fish larvae, of which 20% were mackerel (Ware and Lambert 1985). Egg mortality was high, as is the case with most fish species that disseminate their eggs broadly in the water column, particularly summer spawners. From 1973 to 1976, the egg mortality rate was on average 41% per day. Larval survival rates did not differ significantly from those at the egg stage. Mortality rate of larvae at the first feeding stage was found to be slightly higher than at later stages, which suggests some larvae have difficulties making the transition to exogenous nutrition. Nevertheless, there was no evidence that mortality was a catastrophic event at this stage. Mortality was correlated with rate of warming rather than temperature per se, which could imply abnormal development or, more likely, higher rates of predation (Fig. 4). Higher rates of warming were associated with earlier and greater stratification causing buoyant eggs to be concentrated in warmer surface water and thus presumably more susceptible to predation. Analysis of the data suggests that survival during the first growing season is determined by several factors, which include temperature and the distribution and size composition of the larvae in relation to their food supply and predators. Combined, these effects indicate that year-class strength is established during the first summer (Ware and Lambert 1985).

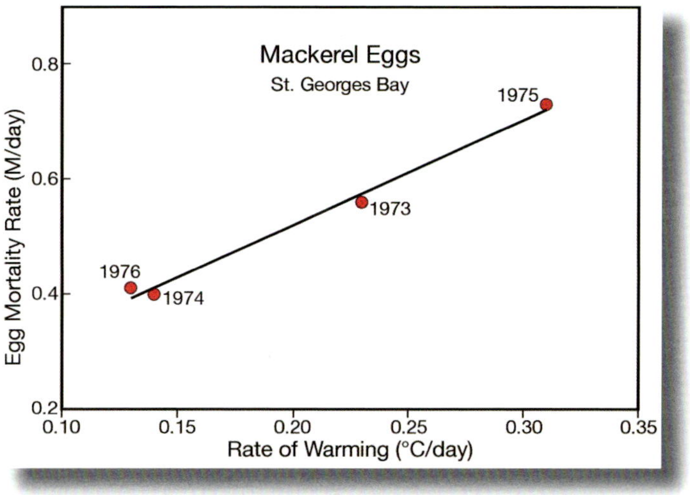

Figure 4. Relationship between mortality of mackeral eggs and rate of sea-surface warming.

Atlantic Herring

The length distributions of larval herring from St. Georges Bay exhibited a polymodal size frequency, the peaks of which could be followed over time. The larval population was composed of a number of sub-populations, or cohorts, whose growth trajectories could be tracked. Further investigation revealed that these larval cohorts stemmed from discrete spawning events (Lambert 1984, Kerr and Dickie 1985). The maturity stages of the adult herring population were monitored in the gill-net fishery during the spring spawning season in St. Georges Bay. Three peaks in the 'ripe and running' stages (immediately prior to spawning, eggs will be extruded with slight pressure to the abdomen) were evident with each of these peaks being closely followed by an increase in the 'spent' stage (immediately post spawning). As well, these three distinct groupings corresponded with three peaks in catch of herring. This was the first time this staggered spawning behaviour leading to discrete larval cohorts had been documented, and led to the concept of a 'big bang' (i.e., all-at-once) spawning tactic versus a 'hedged bet' (i.e., sequential) strategy (Lambert and Ware 1984). In the case of mackerel, all eggs were released over a short period of time in summer when conditions were optimal for growth and survival (i.e., high temperature and plentiful food). In contrast, herring released eggs over time in well-spaced batches when conditions were less favourable in the hope that at least one of the batches would encounter conditions favourable for survival. Not many species spawn before the peak in zooplankton production and the meager food supply is thus optimally exploited by distributing larval feeding pressure over time.

Capelin

Capelin, unknown to local fishermen at the time, appeared in St. Georges Bay from 1975 to 1978. A major spawning took place on the beach at Cape George (Fig. 1) in 1976, which allowed us to validate the estimated drift speed of the gyre and demonstrate its benefits. Egg-sac stage capelin larvae were prevalent at the Cape, the point source of spawning, and older and larger larvae occurred with increasing distance from the Cape. Larval growth rate was calculated by tracking changes in mean size. Then, knowing the growth rate, at any given sampling station the size of larvae and distance from the spawning beach were used to calculate the drift rate to that location. These biological estimates were found to match the modelled drift direction and speed calculated by the physical oceanographers (Lambert et al. 1982). Larvae were tracked for 2.3 circuits of the Bay before dispersal precluded further analysis. This confirmed that fish larvae were retained within the Bay.

American Lobster

St. Georges Bay supports a very stable and productive lobster fishery (Harding et al. 1983). Lobster larvae first appeared in the surface waters of St. Georges Bay in the last week of June at ~12.5 °C with maximum hatching occurring in the first weeks of July. As in the case of mackerel, this allows synchrony with the increased production of the summer small-copepod community (Harding et al. 1982, 1983). Although the larval lobster distribution extended from the surface to the thermocline, most first-stage larvae were found predominantly in the near-surface waters (Harding et al. 1987a), again analogous to the pattern seen in mackerel larvae. Under cloud cover, even more of these young lobsters rose into the upper 30 cm. During the first three moult stages, lobster larvae consumed the small copepods, *Pseudocalanus* and *Acartia*, whereas the fourth stage preferentially consumed larvae of the Rock Crab (*Cancer irroratus*), which were common in the Bay (Harding et al. 1983). The lobster settled to the bottom roughly half way through the fourth moult stage, depending on the substrate type, with settlement completed by mid-September. The long residence time of water within the Bay allowed an estimate of larval lobster survival rates, which were found to be comparable to the three highest production years in another retention area studied in the western Northumberland Strait (Fig. 1) between 1949 and 1963 (Scarratt 1964, 1973; Harding et al. 1982).

EXPERIMENTAL STUDIES

Mackerel Egg Patch Dynamics

Dense patches of newly spawned mackerel eggs were tracked over time. Combining high speed surface plankton sampling and the deployment of drogues and current meters allowed us to map areas of high concentration of newly spawned eggs over a four to five hour period (Fig. 5). Average density of these new eggs at the surface was about 440 m^{-3} decreasing to about 6 m^{-3} at a depth of 7 m (T.C. Lambert unpubl. data). The patches ranged in area from about 1 to 4 nm^2 (1.5 to 7.4 km^2) and could be tracked for at least 12 hours when winds were light. However, when winds increased, turbulence rapidly dispersed the eggs downwards in the water column and a patch could no longer be distinguished from background levels of egg density. During one six-hour patch study, the winds increased from 5 to 25 knots and the near-surface egg concentration decreased by 84% within two hours. Many predators, both vertebrate and invertebrate, feed on planktonic eggs when they are encountered in high concentrations. Furthermore, some fish, particularly mackerel, can filter feed and are often found with eggs of their own species in their stomachs. When the weather is calm and surface waters warm rapidly, the mackerel eggs are concentrated near the sea surface and are more vulnerable to predation than when winds are more frequent and eggs distributed widely throughout the mixed layer. This might explain the correlation of higher egg mortality in years of more rapid surface warming (Fig. 4) since in summers of light winds, surface waters will warm rapidly and conversely, more slowly, when there is more wind to cause wave activity which will tend to mix warm surface waters with underlying cooler water.

Juvenile mackerel have voracious appetites and use two methods of attaining food. They filter feed on copepods, as well as pursuing and ingesting large prey, including other fish. Thus, with plentiful food and warm water they attain high growth rates during their first growing season. Over about a four-month span they grow in length from 3 mm at hatching to about 20 cm before joining the migration out of the Gulf of St. Lawrence to overwinter in offshore waters off the southern Scotian Shelf (Fig. 1).

Langmuir Circulation

It has been noticed on several occasions that fish were often found in association with oceanographic phenomena such as fronts, large-scale eddies, and zones of convergence (McNaught and Hasler 1961, Malinen et al. 2001, Roman et al. 2005). Presumably, fish feed on planktonic organisms which become aggregated in these zones (see references in Barstow 1983). Our study examined the idea that zooplankton would be concentrated in convergence zones within Langmuir cells, a common phenomenon seen in oceans and lakes where counter-rotating cells of water are marked by long windrows of foam and flotsam aligned with the wind (Fig. 6). The findings were inconclusive, however, for we could detect little difference inside and outside convergence areas. We felt that the results may have been affected by inadequacies with the equipment and techniques employed: i.e., the particle counter tended to count bubbles and the computer cards marking the convergence zones interfered with the sampling process. Unfortunately, scheduling priorities precluded repeating the exercise with more sophisticated methods.

Figure 5. Dan Ware takes a break while measuring mackerel egg volumes during a patch study; a drogue for indicating surface drift is visible in the background.

In a separate experiment, neuston nets were towed on a fixed heading or in a broad circle for half-hour periods. The latter tows would be assured of capturing possible concentrations associated with Langmuir circulation, whereas a straight line tow could be 'hit or a miss'. Larval lobster catch was highest in the circular tows (Harding et al. 1982) and subsequently this protocol was used when sampling.

Figure 6. Langmuir circulation convergence zones marked by computer cards; smoke flare indicates wind direction.

PCB Contamination Within the Food Chain Using the Size Spectrum Approach

A comprehensive study of the seasonal food chain was undertaken at the same time as the productivity studies to document the biomagnification of polychlorinated biphenyls (PCBs), an industrial contaminant and one of the 'dirty dozen' banned by the Stockholm International Convention in

2001. This study was enhanced by a Canada-Germany exchange program with the introduction of seawater analysis techniques by D. Stadler and U. Ziebarth of the Deutsches Hydrographisches Institut, Hamburg, Germany. P. Vass constructed a unique apparatus that enabled contaminant-free sorting of plankton on deck by size (i.e., trophic levels). This enabled us to determine prey/predator relationships in our collections using R. Sheldon's theory on the size spectrum (Sheldon et al. 1972, Kerr and Dickie 2001, Duplisea et al. 2014). In winter, when ice precluded ship use, samples were obtained by lowering plankton nets from a Canadian Coast Guard helicopter. Although bioconcentration was most marked between seawater and phytoplankton, biomagnification only proceeded exponentially from the third trophic level of shrimps and larval fish to large fish and marine mammals (Harding et al. 1997). St. Georges Bay was revisited at ca. five-year intervals between 1976 and 1999 to record organochlorine levels in seawater, plankton, and clupeids. Contaminant levels in herring and Gaspereau (*Alosa pseudoharengus*) had decreased following the 1979 ban on the manufacture of PCBs in North America (Harding et al. 1996).

ECOSYSTEM STUDY

Overview

The core of the St. Georges Bay program was an intensive sampling program with a frequency of sampling rarely equaled in eastern Canadian studies. Between 1973 and 1977, physical and biological sampling was undertaken weekly to every two weeks, on average, from early May until late November, but as early as mid-April and as late as mid-December in some years. Dissolved nutrient and carbon-14 measurements to estimate primary production were performed by N. Prouse and G. Phillips for interpretation by G. Harrison and B. Hargrave. Sediment traps (open-ended cylinders moored upright at various depths for several days) were used to collect settling particles, which enabled us to estimate the transfer of organic matter through the water column to the sediments and benthic fauna. P. Vass and G. Harding collected plankton with nets of four mesh sizes and sorted the catch through a stacked series of geological sieves of a $\log_2$ size scale for easier trophic interpretation (Sheldon et al. 1972, Kerr and Dickie 2001). More oceanographic moorings, which included current meters and thermistor chains to record the vertical temperature structure of the water column, were deployed around the Bay. These data, together with the earlier current meter measurements, provided a thorough description of the response of the Bay to wind forcing (Drinkwater 1987, 1989, 1994). The intensity of biological sampling showed a clear succession of spawning times by fish and zooplankton species and gave great insights into the growth trajectories of marine larvae. The combined MEL studies provided a near-complete description of the structural dynamics of the St. Georges Bay ecosystem and highlighted the importance of the area as a nursery for diverse fisheries.

Production Dynamics

The presence of pack ice over the winter restricted sampling. However, samples collected by helicopter indicated that small phytoplankton blooms occurred during these months when the water column was mixed and nutrients well-distributed. The nutrient levels, particularly the various forms of nitrogen, fell following the larger spring bloom. Nevertheless, phytoplankton production and standing stock increased during the formation and deepening of a warm surface layer from late spring to late autumn. The nitrogen required to fuel this resurgence in production was estimated to have come from the gradual mixing of deeper nutrient-rich waters into the euphotic zone (7%), zooplankton excretion (23%), and microbial regeneration (70%) within the upper mixed layer (Hargrave et al. 1985). This recycling of carbon and nutrients in the surface mixed layer coincided with the reduced deposition of particulate matter during the period of strongest stratification. The origins of zooplankton cohorts coincided with peaks in phytoplankton production (as indicated by chlorophyll measurements). Despite an efficient transfer of energy from increasing primary production, zooplankton biomass, which peaked in early July, decreased rapidly thereafter. This was partially because of the replacement of the winter assemblage of large copepods by a rapidly growing small-copepod population in the warm surface waters. Secondary production mirrored primary production until mid-summer, after which zooplankton productivity remained constant while phytoplankton production continued to rise. This inability of zooplankton production to keep pace was interpreted to be caused by intensive predation on the zooplankton community. The planktivorous mackerel, herring, Gaspereau, and Rainbow Smelt (*Osmerus mordax*), plus an extensive jellyfish population, took advantage of this production. The hatching of larvae of a number of species, including mackerel, White Hake (*Urophycis tenuis*) and lobster, is also timed to take advantage of this species progression of summer production.

The overall production in St. Georges Bay was found to be similar or slightly lower than that found in the more open-ocean embayments off Canada's east coast, about one third that of the New York Bight, and an order-of-magnitude lower than that of enclosed embayments at the Hudson River mouth and Narragansett Bay. It was concluded that relatively high summer temperatures and predictable warming of surface waters in St. Georges Bay, together with the longer residence time of the small-copepod, plankton community, were more important determinants of larval fish and shellfish survival in the southern Gulf of St. Lawrence than the total amount of prey available. The predictable summer heating and resultant strong stratification of the Bay allowed for high metabolic rates of all organisms in surface waters and a rapid recycling of energy produced by the phytoplankton in the euphotic zone (Hargrave et al. 1985). The high summer growth rates of larval fish and decapods were dependent on the rapid turnover of zooplankters that are optimum food for the rapidly growing larvae. Primary production, herbivores, carnivores, and nutrient regeneration were closely coupled over the entire water column.

Daily Vertical Migration and Carbon Flux

Vass et al. (1981) designed and constructed clear plastic traps to capture zooplankton moving both up and down in the water column. Deployed from the MV *Navicula* in an open position at fixed depths, the traps were closed mechanically by a messenger, retrieved, and reset every six hours over a 24-hour period (Fig. 7). Sediment traps deployed by B. Hargrave during the same time provided an estimate of passive settlement of detritus and organisms. Two vertical flux studies were undertaken to compare the water column in spring, when it was well-mixed, to summer when highly stratified. In spring, under isothermal conditions, storms cause resuspension of bottom materials, which then gradually settle from the water column. A diatom bloom had depleted nutrients from surface layers during our experiment. Herbivorous zooplankton were scarce at this time of year and had little impact on the bloom, thereby allowing a large amount of organic material of phytoplankton origin to settle to the bottom to be utilized by the benthic community. In the summer, however, primary production increased to high levels in the highly stratified surface euphotic zone. Much of this production was consumed by a voracious small-copepod assemblage, resulting in a much-reduced transfer of organic matter to the benthic community and an efficient recycling of nutrients within the surface mixed layer. It was inferred that larval fish and decapod depredation kept the growth of the small-copepod assemblage in check (Harding et al. 1986).

Coupling of Pelagic and Benthic Production

Studies of the dynamics of pelagic and benthic food webs in St. Georges Bay between 1976 and 1981 showed that particulate matter production by phytoplankton and consumption by herbivorous and carnivorous zooplankton, and losses through nutrient regeneration and sedimentation were closely linked (Hargrave et al. 1985, Harding et al. 1987b). The resuspension of sediment during the unstratified period between October and May, particularly in the nearshore zone of the Bay, indicated the im-

Figure 7. Zooplankton trap being launched from MV *Navicula*.

portance of physical processes in redistributing organic material and nutrients. Heating of surface water during summer led to stratification and increased metabolism of pelagic organisms and bacteria. Consequently, rapid recycling of nutrients occurred above the thermocline. Approximately 90% of the organic matter produced during August, the period of maximum stratification, was estimated to be recycled in the surface stratified layer. Sedimentation of organic carbon and nitrogen below the thermocline amounted to 9% and 14%, respectively, of amounts assimilated by phytoplankton. Surface-water temperatures (>20°C) during mid-summer are about 2° to 4°C higher than average values recorded in other Atlantic embayments in coastal Nova Scotia, for example, St. Margarets Bay (Platt 1971). These elevated temperatures in surface layers lead to high turnover rates which, in combination with restricted exchange with offshore waters because of the presence of the gyre, create ideal conditions for increased growth rates of larval fish and invertebrates. Consequently, St. Georges Bay serves as an ideal nursery area for larval and juvenile fish, decapods and other invertebrates.

Sediment Dynamics

The dynamics of organic matter decomposition and nutrient regeneration within sediments were measured by mooring benthic chambers placed on the sea bottom. The equipment constructed at BIO enclosed a small area (1,452 cm^2) of undisturbed sediment with overlying water (17.1 litres) that was sampled automatically by 50-ml syringes at 6-hour intervals over 24 hours (Hargrave and Connolly 1978). The *in situ* method allowed sediment-water exchanges of dissolved gases (oxygen and carbon dioxide) and nutrients to be determined from changes in concentrations in the supernatant water above the sediment. These data were analyzed in relation to bottom water temperature, phytoplankton production, and sediment trap fluxes of particulate matter to calculate budgets for carbon and nitrogen fluxes in the water column and across the sediment-water interface.

Sediment trap deployments between April and November showed year-to-year differences in rates of sedimentation reflecting variations in stratification (Hargrave and Phillips 1986). Particle flux to the bottom was always higher in April-May and September-October when the water column was more thermally homogeneous and when the biomass of grazing plankton was low. Rates of sediment resuspension and transport, which redistribute particulate matter within the Bay, were at a maximum at these times of the year. However, the regeneration of dissolved nutrients from bottom sediments was linearly related to temperature and increased to maximum values in October-November when bottom water temperatures were maximum (9° to 11°C). Nitrogen sedimentation at 25 m (mid-water column), a depth thought to be less affected by bottom sediment resuspension than deeper depths closer to the bottom, exceeded benthic regeneration when stratification was weak. Rates were more closely balanced during the summer when stratification was strong and ca. 20% of nitrogen required for phytoplankton production could be supplied by benthic fluxes. On the other hand, carbon sedimentation and benthic respiration were approximately balanced during unstratified periods, but when the water column was stratified, sedimentation exceeded respiration by ca. 2 times. Biomass and assumed annual turnover ratios were used to estimate benthic macrofauna production, which was about 10% to 30% of the average organic carbon supply to the sediments. Demersal fish production, determined in a similar way, represented from 1% to 7% of estimated macrofauna production. The production efficiencies are within ranges observed in other highly productive coastal marine systems and indicate efficient energy transfer between the pelagic and benthic food web in the Bay.

Sediments play an important role in the Bay. They provide habitat and food resources for a diverse range of benthic and near-bottom invertebrate and fish communities, as well as bacteria responsible for organic matter decomposition and nutrient regeneration. The conversion of nutrients from particulate to soluble form in surface sediments is particularly important. Dissolved nutrients are rapidly depleted by phytoplankton in water above the thermocline during the summer and regeneration of dissolved nutrients from the bottom then becomes an important source for resupply.

APPLICATION OF FINDINGS

Canso Causeway

In the 1970s, fishermen felt that the Canso Causeway, completed in 1954, had had a detrimental effect on their industry. To address these concerns, Fisheries and Oceans Canada (DFO) organized two workshops to examine possible influences of the causeway on the local environment. The St. Georges Bay research team participated in these workshops, the first being held at BIO in 1977 and the second at St. Andrews, New Brunswick, in 1979. At the first, we presented our then current understanding of the St. Georges Bay ecosystem based on our ongoing studies, while the second workshop addressed the specific issue of whether the construction of the causeway across the Strait of Canso in 1954 had adversely affected the marine environment and the fisheries in particular (McCracken 1979).

Ware (1979) examined and analyzed the abundance and spring arrival times of herring and mackerel to the southern Gulf, pre- and post-causeway, and found no evidence for any change in catch. However, landings data for herring indicated that their arrival time in St. Georges Bay was delayed 17 days, which is their approximate swimming time around Cape Breton. There were no landings data for mackerel. However, using anecdotal information from fishermen, he estimated a one-week delay in the arrival of mackerel in St. Georges Bay. Drinkwater (1979a,b) estimated that the residual transport through the Strait of Canso before 1954 would have been south into Chedabucto Bay at 7,000 cubic metres per second, and this would have increased primary production south of the causeway by an estimated 10-20% during summer by entraining nutrient-rich deep waters into surface layers. Krank and Sheldon (1979) presented their observations on the post-causeway distribution of particulates in St. Georges Bay, Strait of Canso, and Chedabucto Bay, and demonstrated that a large amount of fine material was contributed by industry in the Strait. The lobster population on the Atlantic side of the Canso Causeway had plummeted since its construction. G. Harding, P. Wells, and K. Drinkwater re-examined the surface plankton in neuston tows from 1975 in St. Georges Bay to estimate that 100 million lobster larvae could have passed from St. Georges Bay into Chedabucto Bay through the Strait pre-causeway. It was suspected that the surface layer sampled by the neuston net was not deep enough to sample lobster larvae adequately, therefore a modified sampler was used to sample down to one meter, and St. Georges Bay was resampled during the larval season of 1978 (Harding et al. 1979). Based on these data, new estimates of the number of larvae that would have been transported into Chedabucto Bay prior to the construction of the causeway suggested that the failure of the Atlantic coast lobster fishery from Chedabucto Bay southwest may well have been initiated by a larval recruitment failure caused by the synchronous closure by the Canso Causeway and the start of a climatic cooling period (Harding et al. 1983).

Other Subsequent Research

Universities have taken advantage of the knowledge base accumulated from the various MEL studies conducted in the Bay. At Dalhousie University (Halifax, NS), K. Mann guided graduate students in studies of seagrasses (Schneider and Mann 1991), and more recently students under the supervision of A. Mataxas have undertaken a series of studies looking into small-scale distribution of planktonic and benthic organisms in St. Georges Bay. At St. Francis Xavier, our work formed the baseline for an ecological assessment of the southern Gulf waters conducted in the late 1990s (Davis et al. 1999).

Colleagues in the Atlantic Geoscience Centre at BIO studied the benthic foraminifera and pollen in St. Georges Bay (Schafer 1976, Schafer and Young 1977, Schafer and Mudie 1980, Schafer 2014). The physical oceanographic studies in the Bay were helpful in assessing environmental variability and its possible role in the domoic acid outbreak in mussels from Cardigan Bay in Prince Edward Island (Fig. 1; Drinkwater and Petrie 1988). The organochlorine studies in the Bay served a practical purpose in the 1996 risk assessment undertaken prior to the raising of the PCB-laden *Irving Whale* barge after it sank in the southern Gulf of St. Lawrence (Gilbert and Walsh 1996). Our expertise was also important in the review by the Canada-Nova Scotia Offshore Petroleum Board of the potential effects of oil and gas surveys and drilling activities prior to issuing exploration licences for the west coast of Cape Breton and Sydney Bight (Boudreau et al. 2001).

RETROSPECTIVE

The success of the research studies performed in St. Georges Bay can be attributed to a number of factors. The gyre and other physical characteristics of the Bay cannot be overemphasized. The resultant retention time for the eggs and larvae was sufficiently long to track them through these early life stages, and was key to the success of the biological program. The availability of a dedicated small research vessel was critical for the success of the studies. Studying the dynamics of larval populations becomes practical from a smaller vessel. A boat this size affords more than a single seasonal synoptic picture, which is usually the most one can achieve on a large offshore vessel shared by a number of programs. Another invaluable asset, which no longer exists, was an instrument machine shop at BIO where scientists could work hand-in-hand with engineers, electronics technicians, and master machinists to develop new instrumentation to address specific sampling requirements. Perhaps, most important was the strong scientific leadership and the dedicated interdisciplinary team of scientists and technicians, who worked closely together to gain new insights into important marine ecological processes and had fun doing it.

Sadly, this type of research program would be difficult to launch within BIO today for a number of reasons. Smaller vessels capable of carrying out such diverse work no longer exist within the BIO fleet. Rental of fishing boats can sometimes be used as an alternative, but none are suitable for the type of sampling conducted in St. Georges Bay. Specialized winches to support electronically monitored samplers, an A-frame for handling heavy gear over the stern, and a stable, regulated power supply to support electronic equipment are required. A generous summer student program also provided the staffing that enabled the comprehensive field studies which were the foundation of the project. In today's terminology this was a 'win-win' situation: students gained valuable experience during their summer employment, and science programs requiring a large workforce were possible.

The St. Georges Bay Program wound down after the creation of the Gulf Region as a separate administrative entity within the Atlantic region in 1982. At its peak, the DFO workforce involved in various studies in the Bay comprised six research scientists, four biologists, five technicians, three ships crew, up to five fishermen, and a number of summer students. Three technicians, who formed the core of the field program, also performed sample analysis and species identification, but they were laid off in later years and their expertise, particularly in taxonomy, was lost. Working hours were flexible, adjustable to weather conditions, and were determined by mutual agreement between ship's crew and science personnel. Weekend work and 24 hour at-sea stations were easily accommodated.

As well as providing an excellent research platform, the MV *Navicula* played an admirable role as a good-will ambassador. This boat and its crew provided some of the most favourable advertising BIO could hope for. She was always welcomed in the ports she visited, and many friends were made. Science questions were answered, information supplied, assistance in boat engine and equipment repair given, as well as day trips for interested fishermen and reporters to acquaint them with research activities and their goals. Today, health and safety regulations preclude on-board trips by non-government personnel and, as a result of ongoing budget reductions over the decades, field work has been reduced drastically and researchers are increasingly office-bound and obliged to rework old data. This is a worthy exercise up to a point, since often there is much more to be gleaned from old data than the purpose for which it was originally collected. However, the law of diminishing returns is real, especially in these days when the effects of climate change on global ecosystems is becoming increasing apparent.

Sixteen primary publications and eight technical reports documenting research in St. Georges Bay were published between 1973 and 1989, and publications continued to appear over the next decade. The primary publications attracted over 320 citations, with two alone garnering over 60 each (Harding et al. 1983, Harding et al. 1997). Several PhD and MSc theses were also completed. Research results were also reported at many national and international scientific conferences. Along with studies in the Bay of Fundy and St. Margarets Bay, where much of the sampling technology was pioneered, and later studies on Browns and Georges banks, the research program in St. Georges Bay remains a recognizable legacy of the success of the MEL interdisciplinary approach to understanding how physical and biological factors interact to control fisheries production systems.

ACKNOWLEDGEMENTS

A major part of the success of the St. Georges Bay program was due to the efforts of the late Captain Gordon Reyno of Sambro, Nova Scotia. His exemplary cooperation and good humour in all situations made work aboard the MV *Navicula* something to look forward to. We would like to pay special tribute to other members of the St. Georges Bay team who are no longer with us: Roger Belanger, Captain Joe Bray, Jim Hynes, Steve Kerr, Captain Neil Langille, Jeff McRuer, Madhu Paranjape, Nick Prouse, Ralph Savoury, George Taylor, Ron Trites, and Dan Ware. Thanks to all participants who made the project successful: Richard Addison, Nigel Allen, Daniel Andrews, Kathie Beall, Cynthia Bourbonnais, Paul Brodie, Maurine Butler, Bob Crawford, Rick Cunjak, Arlene Diepenbrock, Des Dobson, Annie Dupuis, Rao Durvasula, Captain C. Garrison, Ursula Grigg, Phillip Harnish, Glen Harrison, Andy Henneberry, Berit Henriksen, Mark Hodgson, Trevor Kenchington, Marthe Lanctot, Raynald LeBlanc, C. Lynch, Al MacDonald, Buddy MacEachern, Paul MacPherson, Hughie Marriott, Tim Milligan, Brian Petrie, Liam Petrie, Sifford Pearre, Jr., Don Peer, Georgina Phillips, Debbie Rutherford, Ray Sheldon, Dieter Stadler, Peter Vass, Rong Wang, Karen Watson, Peter Wells, and Udo Ziebarth. We would also like to thank the pilots, Cliff Sadler and Len Bentham, and staff of the Canadian Coast Guard helicopter group for support in Langmuir circulation studies and winter sampling. We are also grateful to the fishermen of St. Georges Bay for their support and information. Special mention is due to Alan Adams, Harold ('Himmy') Ballantyne, Carol Brown, Kimball Falkenhan and Buddy MacEachern of Ballantynes Cove. Trudy McGillivary kept us well fed, healthy, and the manor house tidy.

REFERENCES

Barstow, S. F. 1983. The ecology of Langmuir circulation: A review. Marine Environmental Research 9: 211-236.

Boudreau, P.R., G.C. Harding, K. Lee, and P.D. Keizer. 2001. The possible environmental impacts of petroleum exploration activities in the southern Gulf of St. Lawrence and Sydney Bight ecosystems. Canadian Science Advisory Secretariat Research Document 2001/112, Fisheries and Oceans Canada, Ottawa, ON.

Cushing, D.H. 1975. Marine Ecology and Fisheries. Cambridge University Press, Cambridge, England.

Davis, A., L. Kellman, G. Ruseski, J. Williams, C. Cameron, S. Mitchell, C. Edwards, and D. Spencer. 1999. St. Georges Bay Ecosystem Project (GBEP); Research Report. Department of Interdisciplinary Studies in Aquatic Resources, St. Francis Xavier University, Antigonish, NS.

Drinkwater, K. 1979a. Flow in the Strait of Canso and St. Georges Bay, Nova Scotia. Pages 11-18 *in* Canso Marine Environment Workshop, Part 4 of 4 Parts, Physical Oceanography and Environmental Effects. Fisheries and Marine Service Technical Report No. 834, Fisheries and Oceans Canada, St. Andrews, NB.

Drinkwater, K. 1979b. Nutrient entrainment in Chedabucto Bay and its possible effects on production. Pages 52-54 *in* Canso Marine Environment Workshop, Part 4 of 4 Parts, Physical Oceanography and Environmental Effects. Fisheries and Marine Service Technical Report No. 834, Fisheries and Ocean Canada, St. Andrews, NB.

Drinkwater, K.F. 1987. The response of an open stratified bay to wind forcing. PhD thesis, Dalhousie University, Halifax, NS.

Drinkwater, K.F. 1989. The response of an open embayment to near hurricane force winds. Continental Shelf Research 9: 823-839.

Drinkwater, K.F. 1994. The response of an open stratified bay to wind forcing. Atmosphere-Ocean 32: 757-781.

Drinkwater, K. and G. Taylor. 1979. Physical oceanographic measurements in St. Georges Bay, Nova Scotia, during 1976 and 1977. Fisheries and Marine Service Technical Report 869, Fisheries and Oceans Canada, Dartmouth, NS.

Drinkwater, K. and B. Petrie, 1988. Physical oceanographic observations in the Cardigan Bay region of Prince Edward Island, 1982-1987. Canadian Technical Report of Hydrography and Ocean Science 110, Fisheries and Oceans Canada, Dartmouth, NS.

Duplisea, D.E., P.R. Boudreau, and L.M. Dickie. 2014. The size-structured view of marine ecosystems. Pages 99-103 *in* Voyage of Discovery: Fifty Years of Marine Research at Canada's Bedford Institute of Oceanography (D.N. Nettleship, D.C. Gordon, C.F.M. Lewis, and M.P. Latremouille, Eds.). Bedford Institute of Oceanography-Oceans Association, Dartmouth, NS.

Gilbert, M. and G. Walsh. 1996. Potential consequences of a PCB spill from the barge *Irving Whale* on the marine environment of the Gulf of St. Lawrence. Canadian Technical Report of Fisheries and Aquatic Science 2113, Fisheries and Oceans Canada, Mont-Joli, QC.

Goode, G.B. 1885. The mackerel (*Scomber scombrus*). Pages 281-303 *in* U.S. Commission of Fisheries, Fisheries and Fishing Industry of U.S., Natural History of Useful Aquatic Animals, Section I, U.S. Government Printing Office, Washington, DC.

Harding, G.C.H., P.G. Wells, and K.F. Drinkwater. 1979. The distribution and abundance of lobster larvae (*Homarus americanus*) in St. Georges Bay, Nova Scotia, in 1975 and 1976 and the possible effect that the Canso Causeway has had on the Chedabucto Bay lobster fishery. Pages 101-111 *in* Canso Marine Environment Workshop, Part 3 of 4 Parts, Fisheries Impacts. Fisheries and Marine Service Technical Report No. 834, Fisheries and Oceans Canada, St. Andrews, NB.
Harding, G.C., W.P. Vass, and K.F. Drinkwater. 1982. Aspects of larval American lobster (*Homarus americanus*) ecology in St. Georges Bay, Nova Scotia. Canadian Journal of Fisheries and Aquatic Sciences 39: 1,117-1,129.
Harding, G.C., K.F. Drinkwater, and W.P. Vass. 1983. Factors influencing the size of American lobster (*Homarus americanus*) stocks along the Atlantic coast of Nova Scotia, Gulf of St. Lawrence, and Gulf of Maine: a new synthesis. Canadian Journal of Fisheries and Aquatic Sciences 40: 168-84.
Harding, G.C., W.P. Vass, B.T. Hargrave, and S. Pearre, Jr. 1986. Diel vertical movements and feeding activity of zooplankton in St. Georges Bay, N.S., using net tows and a newly developed passive trap. Canadian Journal of Fisheries and Aquatic Science 43: 952-967.
Harding, G.C., K.F. Drinkwater, J.D Pringle, W.P. Vass, S. Pearre, Jr., and S.J. Smith. 1987a. Vertical distribution and daily movements of larval lobsters *Homarus americanus* over Browns Bank. Marine Ecology Progress Series 41: 29-41.
Harding, G.C., B.T. Hargrave, W.P. Vass, and R.W. Sheldon. 1987b. Vertical flux of particulate matter by sedimentation and zooplankton movements in St. Georges Bay, the southern Gulf of St. Lawrence. Biological Oceanography 4: 323-357.
Harding G., P. Vass, and B. Hargrave. 1996. Organochlorine levels in the marine food web of the southern Gulf of St. Lawrence. Pages 41-44 *in* Science Review 1994 & '95 (A. Fiander, Ed.). Bedford Institute of Oceanography, Dartmouth, NS.
Harding, G.C., R.J. LeBlanc, W.P. Vass, R.F. Addison, B.T. Hargrave, S. Pearre, Jr., A. Dupuis, and P.F. Brodie. 1997. Bioaccumulation of polychlorinated biphenyls (PCBs) in the marine pelagic food web, based on a seasonal study in the southern Gulf of St. Lawrence, 1976-77. Marine Chemistry 56: 145-179.
Hargrave, B.T. and G.F. Connolly. 1978. A device to collect supernatant water for measurements of the flux of dissolved compounds across sediment surfaces. Limnology and Oceanography 23: 1,005-1,010.
Hargrave, B.T. and G.A. Phillips. 1986. Dynamics of the benthic food web in St. Georges Bay, southern Gulf of St. Lawrence. Marine Ecology Progress Series 31: 277-294.
Hargrave, B.T., G.C. Harding, K.F. Drinkwater, T.C. Lambert, and W.G. Harrison. 1985. Dynamics of the pelagic food web in St. Georges Bay, southern Gulf of St. Lawrence. Marine Ecology Progress Series 20: 221-240.
Kerr, S.R. and L.M. Dickie. 1985. Bioenergetics of 0+ Atlantic herring (*Clupea harengus harengus*). Canadian Journal of Fisheries and Aquatic Sciences 42: 105-110.
Kerr, S.R. and L.M. Dickie. 2001. The Biomass Spectrum: A Predator-Prey Theory of Aquatic Production. Columbia University Press, New York.
Kranck, K. and R. W. Sheldon. 1979. Observations on particle distribution in the Strait of Canso and vicinity. Pages 32-36 *in* Canso Marine Environment Workshop, Part 4 of 4 Parts, Physical Oceanography and Environmental Effects. Fisheries and Marine Service Technical Report No. 834, Fisheries and Oceans Canada, St. Andrews, NB.
Lambert, T.C. 1984. Larval cohort succession in herring (*Clupea harengus*) and capelin (*Mallotus villotus*). Canadian Journal of Fisheries and Aquatic Sciences 41: 1,552-1,564.
Lambert, T.C. and D.M. Ware. 1984. Reproductive strategies of demersal and pelagic spawning fish. Canadian Journal of Fisheries and Aquatic Sciences 41: 1,565-1,569.
Lambert, T.C., D.M. Ware, and J.K. McRuer. 1982. Spawning and early life history of herring and capelin in St. Georges Bay, Nova Scotia. Canadian Technical Report of Fisheries and Aquatic Sciences 1128, Fisheries and Oceans Canada, Dartmouth, NS.
Malinen, T., J. Horppila, and A. Liljendahl-Nurminen. 2001. Langmuir circulations disturb the low-oxygen refuge of phantom midge larvae. Limnology and Oceanography 46: 689-692.
McCracken, F.D. (Ed.). 1979. Canso Marine Environment Workshop, Part 3 of 4 Parts, Fisheries Impacts. Fisheries and Marine Service Technical Report 834, Fisheries and Oceans Canada, St. Andrews, NB.
McNaught, D.C. and A.D. Hasler. 1961. Surface schooling and feeding behaviour in the White Bass in Lake Mendota. Limnology and Oceanography 6: 53-60.
Petrie, B. and K. Drinkwater. 1978a. Circulation in an open bay. Journal of the Fisheries Research Board of Canada 35: 1,116-1,123.
Petrie, B. and K. Drinkwater. 1978b. Numerical model of the circulation in an open bay. Journal of the Fisheries Research Board of Canada 35: 1,631-1,635.
Platt, T . 1971. The annual production by phytoplankton in St. Margaret's Bay, Nova Scotia. Journal du conseil 33: 234-334.
Roman, M., X. Zhang, C. McGilliard, and W. Boicourt. 2005. Seasonal and annual variability in the spatial patterns of plankton biomass in Chesapeake Bay. Limnology and Oceanography 50: 480-492.
Scarratt, D.J. 1964. Abundance and distribution of lobster larvae (*Homarus americanus*) in Northumberland Strait. Journal of the Fisheries Research Board of Canada 21: 661-680.
Scarratt, D.J. 1973. Abundance, survival and vertical and diurnal distribution of lobster larvae in Northumberland Strait, 1962-1963, and their relationships with commercial stocks. Journal of the Fisheries Research Board of Canada 30: 1,819-1,824.
Schafer, C.T. 1976. *In situ* environmental responses of benthonic foraminifera. Pages 27-32 *in* Report of Activities, Part C. Geological Survey of Canada, Paper 76-1C, Ottawa, ON.
Schafer, C.T. 2014. Living and postglacial Foraminifera and their environmental applications. Pages 237-245 *in* Voyage of Discovery: Fifty Years of Marine Research at Canada's Bedford Institute of Oceanography (D.N. Nettleship, D.C. Gordon, C.F.M. Lewis, and M.P. Latremouille, Eds.). Bedford Institute of Oceanography-Oceans Association, Dartmouth, NS.
Schafer, C.T. and J.A. Young. 1977. Experiments on mobility and transportability of some nearshore benthonic foraminifera species. Pages 27-31 *in* Report of Activities, Part C. Geological Survey of Canada, Paper 77-1C, Ottawa, ON.
Schafer, C.T. and P.J. Mudie. 1980. Spatial variability of foraminifera and pollen in two nearshore sediment sites, St. Georges Bay, Nova Scotia. Canadian Journal of Earth Science 17: 313-324.
Schneider, F. and K.H. Mann. 1991. Rapid recovery of fauna following ice rafting in a Nova Scotia seagrass bed. Marine Ecology Progress Series 78: 57-70.
Sette, O.E. 1950. Biology of the Atlantic mackerel (*Scomber scombrus*) of North America. Part II. Migrations and habits. Fishery Bulletin of the Fish and Wildlife Service 51: 251-358.
Sheldon, R.W., A. Prakash, and W.H. Sutcliffe, Jr. 1972. The size distribution of particles in the ocean. Limnology and Oceanography 17: 327-340.
Trites, R.W. (Ed.). 1968. Gulf of St. Lawrence Workshop, November 28-29, 1968. Bedford Institute of Oceanography, Dartmouth, NS.
Trites, R.W. 1972. The Gulf of St. Lawrence from a pollution viewpoint. Pages 59-72 *in* Marine Pollution and Sea Life (M. Ruivo, Ed.). Fishing News, London, England.
Trites R.W. and A. Walton. 1975. A Canadian coastal sea - the Gulf of St. Lawrence. Bedford Institute of Oceanography Report Series BI-R75-10, Dartmouth, NS.
Vass, W.P., G.C.H. Harding, and S. Pearre, Jr. 1981. A bidirectional trap for quantifying the vertical migration of plankton organisms. Canadian Technical Report of Fisheries and Aquatic Science 983, Fisheries and Oceans Canada, Dartmouth, NS.
Ware, D.M. 1975. Relation between egg size, growth, and natural mortality of larval fish. Journal of the Fisheries Research Board of Canada 32: 2,503-2,512.
Ware, D.M. 1977. Spawning time and egg size of the Atlantic mackerel, *Scomber scombrus*, in relation to the plankton. Journal of the Fisheries Research Board of Canada 34: 2,308-2,315.
Ware, D.M. 1979. The possible impact of the Canso Causeway on the migration of mackerel and herring in the southern Gulf of St. Lawrence. Pages 14-25 *in* Canso Marine Environment Workshop, Part 3 of 4 Parts, Fisheries Impacts. Fisheries and Marine Service Technical Report No. 834, Fisheries and Oceans Canada, St. Andrews, NB.
Ware, D.M. and T.C. Lambert. 1985. Early life history of the Atlantic mackerel (*Scomber scombrus*) in the southern Gulf of St. Lawrence. Canadian Journal of Fisheries and Aquatic Science 3: 577-592.

14. WHALE AND SEAL RESEARCH AT THE BEDFORD INSTITUTE OF OCEANOGRAPHY THROUGH FIVE DECADES

W. Donald Bowen

SUMMARY

Marine mammal research at the Bedford Institute of Oceanography (BIO) began in the late 1960s with research on whale (Cetacea) acoustics. During the 1970s and 1980s, the focus of the research shifted toward understanding field metabolic rates, foraging energetics, and biomechanics of baleen whales. A parallel line of research aimed to determine the levels of contaminants (e.g., DDT and PCBs) in marine mammals, particularly in seals (Pinnipedia), and how contaminant levels changed over time associated with changes in the use of those chemicals. During the mid-1970s, the mandate for research on the population ecology and dynamics of Grey and Harbour seals was transferred to BIO with the twin objectives of determining population size and trends, and the impact of seals on fish stocks of commercial interest. During the 1990s and 2000s, collaborations with Dalhousie University (Halifax, NS) and other research institutions led to the development of a seal contraceptive vaccine and a new method for estimating the diets of marine mammals based on fatty acids. Those collaborations also led to a much better understanding of the energetics of reproduction, foraging behaviour and diet, and sources of variation in fitness of male and female Grey Seals and Harbour Seals. Several syntheses of information on seals and their prey with respect to the transmission of the sealworm parasite to fish and the impact of Grey Seal predation on Atlantic Cod were also undertaken.

Key words: baleen whales, Grey Seal, Harbour Seal, Atlantic Cod, organochlorines, reproduction, foraging, sealworm parasite, seal behaviour, predation.
E-mail: Don.Bowen@dfo-mpo.gc.ca

By the 1960s, many species of marine mammals around the globe had experienced dramatic declines in abundance owing to excessive commercial exploitation or predator control programs conducted to mitigate harassment of fisheries and to improve fisheries yields (Reijnders et al. 1993, Clapham et al. 1999, Bowen and Lidgard 2012). Similar declines in the abundance of many marine mammal species also occurred in eastern Canada as a result of coastal whaling, seal harvesting, and bounties. Thus, early research conducted at the Bedford Institute of Oceanography (BIO) was directed mainly toward obtaining a better understanding of the ecology of coastal species. The Scotian Shelf supports a high diversity of marine mammals, including 23 species of whales and four species of seals. However, given limited resources and time, only a small number of these species has been studied at BIO.

WHALE RESEARCH

The Order Cetacea (whales) is divided into two suborders, the Odontoceti (toothed whales) and Mysticeti (the toothless, baleen whales). Whale research got off to a slow start at BIO as federal government research on these taxa in eastern Canada was conducted at the Arctic Biological Station, Ste. Anne de Bellevue, Quebec, and the Biological Station, St. Andrews, New Brunswick. In the late 1960s, P. Beamish was hired to conduct whale research in the Marine Ecology Laboratory (MEL). During his short time at BIO, he investigated the vocal behaviour of several baleen whale species, including the Humpback Whale (*Megaptera novaeangliae*; Beamish 1978, Winn and Winn 1978) and the acoustic scattering behaviour of zooplankton (Beamish 1971). In 1972, P. Brodie joined MEL having made important contributions to age determination and growth (Brodie 1969, 1971) and population status (Sergeant and Brodie 1975) of Beluga Whales (*Delphinapterus leucas*) during his doctoral research. Determining the age of toothed whales from dentition was a relatively new field. There was debate concerning the number of light and dark bands (termed growth layer groups) deposited in dentine each year which directly affected the estimated age. This difference had to be resolved because it had significant implications for the estimation of reproductive and mortality rates and the sustainability of harvests. By comparing mandibular and tooth layers, it was clear that two growth layer groups were deposited annually. This was confirmed from counts of growth layer groups in captive Beluga Whales of known age (Goren et al. 1986, 1987).

From the mid-1970s, whale research focussed on the energetics and biomechanics of foraging. This began with an influential paper published in *Ecology* on estimates of standard metabolic rate in Fin Whales (*Balaenopters physalus*) and the implications of metabolic rate on intraspecific size variation (Brodie 1975). Estimated metabolic rates of whales varied widely depending on assumptions. Brodie (1977) observed that "so often metabolic rates are attributed to large cetaceans which appear inconsistent with the available food resources and burden the animal with a specific rate so high it would appear that their greatest source of natural mortality is spontaneous combustion." To provide a more solid foundation for such estimates, Brodie (1975) used data on the lipid content, body mass, and surface area of whales killed during commercial whaling in Antarctica. This work was important because if the energy demands of cetaceans were over-estimated, the productivity and biomass of prey supporting these species would be exaggerated.

Prey densities needed for filter-feeding whales to satisfy their daily energy requirements were unknown. Brodie et al. (1978) showed that at estimated average densities of zooplankton, Fin Whales would have to travel about 7,000 km daily to satisfy their energy requirements, an unattainable distance. Thus, average densities could not be relevant to such species.

Baleen whales use a wide range of feeding tactics, including engulfing huge volumes of water and prey, equivalent to nearly 50% of the animal's total body mass (Brodie 1977). The grooved throat wall of Fin Whales extends dramatically during feeding such that the whale's profile changes to one of "an elongated, bloated tadpole" (Orton and Brodie 1987). To determine how Fin Whales engulf such large quantities of prey-containing water, Orton and Brodie (1987) measured the mechanical properties of blubber and muscle. Coupled with some assumptions about fluid dynamics and the animal's geometry while feeding, they showed that the engulfing process in feeding could be powered solely by measured swimming speeds of 5-10 km per hour.

CONTAMINANT LEVELS IN MARINE MAMMALS

Another line of marine mammal research at MEL during the 1970s and 1980s was led by R.F. Addison, a biochemist and toxicologist. Little was known about organochlorine (OC) residue levels in marine mammals, but studies of the effects of these chemicals on terrestrial species and fish-eating birds strongly indicated a need to understand concentrations in upper-trophic level marine species. Addison conducted studies on the levels of organochlorine (OC) pesticides (e.g., DDT) and polychlorinated biphenyls (PCB) in a variety of marine mammal species, including Beluga Whales (Addison and Brodie 1973), Harp Seals (*Pagophilis groenlandicus*, now *Phoca groenlandica*; Addison et al. 1973), Ringed Seals (*Pusa hispida*, Addison and Smith 1974), Grey Seals (Addison and Brodie 1977, Addison and Brodie 1984) and Harbour Seals (*Phoca vitulina*; Addison et al. 1986a). Addison and Brodie (1977) showed that female Grey Seals

Figure 1. Adult female Grey Seal (photo: W.D. Bowen).

(Fig. 1) excreted much of their pollutant burden in milk each year, which explains why burdens increase with age in adult males but not females. Addison and Brodie (1987) subsequently studied the transfer of OC residues from Grey Seal blubber through to milk. Addison and Stobo (1993) followed up by examining OC concentrations in Grey Seal pups over the first year of life. They showed that pups have limited capacity to degrade the residue inherited from their mother.

Interest in environmental contamination by polychlorinated dibenzo-p-dioxins and furans (PCDD/Fs) and polybrominated diphenyl ethers grew during the 1990s. Like organochlorines, these chemicals were toxic, and being persistent they accumulated in the environment. Addison et al. (1999) analyzed blubber samples from Grey Seals revealing that total PCDD and PCDF concentrations were among the lowest concentrations recorded in seals, and indicated little contamination by these compounds. Ikonomou and Addison (2008) found that concentrations of polybrominated diphenyl ethers in Grey Seals were generally low and slightly lower than those found in European populations.

The biological effects of organochlorines and other pollutants on organisms are mediated by the extent to which organisms can break down and eliminate these chemicals. Addison et al. (1984, 1986a, 1988) conducted studies to determine the ability of mixed-function oxidase in Grey and Harbour seals to metabolize organochlorine residues.

An important aspect of the environmental toxicology was evaluating the effects of new regulations on the level of pollutants. Addison et al. (1984) found the concentrations of DDT-group insecticide residues in the blubber of Grey Seals in 1982 were lower than in comparable samples taken in 1974 and 1976. This trend was consistent with the availability of DDT group residues having declined. By contrast, concentrations of polychlorinated biphenyl (PCB) residues did not change over this period. Over the same 8-year time period (1974-82), a similar declining trend in DDT emerged in Harp Seals (*Pagophilus groenlandicus*) collected in the Gulf of St. Lawrence. Addison and Stobo (2001) compared OC pollutant levels in Grey Seals over the 20-year period through 1994 and found that levels of DDT in the blubber of adult female Grey Seals had declined by 95%. In 1981, PCB concentrations in the western arctic Ringed Seals were about half of those in a sample of the same population taken in 1972. This decline probably resulted from the ban on PCB manufacture and use imposed in the early 1970s (Addison et al. 1986b). Concentrations of DDT-group residues in the same population did not decline over the same interval probably due to atmospheric or water transport from the Far East, where DDT was used until at least the late 1970s (Addison et al. 1986b).

SEAL RESEARCH

MEL was the centre of marine mammal research at BIO through the mid-1970s, but this changed with the establishment of the Marine Fish Division (MFD) in 1976 and the transfer of research on Grey and Harbour seals to MFD with the move of B. Beck from the Arctic Biological Station the same year. Since the early 1960s, A. Mansfield and B. Beck had conducted research on the population biology of Grey and Harbour seals throughout eastern Canada, including Sable Island. Based on this research, Mansfield and Beck (1977) produced the first synthesis of the biology of Grey Seals in eastern Canada. This work laid the foundation for decades of research to follow.

Seal research within MFD focussed on the demography and diet of Grey and Harbour seals and their role in the transmission of the sealworm parasite, also called codworm (*Pseudoterranova decepiens*). This parasite infected the white muscle of Atlantic Cod (*Gadus morhua*) and other fish species making it necessary to remove the visible, encapsulated larvae during processing. Having to remove parasite larvae both reduced product quality and increased the cost of processing to the fish industry. In addition to the seals' role in the transmission of the parasite, both Grey and Harbour seals were considered a nuisance for damaging fishing gear such as nets for Atlantic Cod, Atlantic Salmon (*Salmo salar*), Atlantic Herring (*Clupea harengus*), and Atlantic Mackerel (*Scomber scombrus*) (Scott 1968). To attempt to reduce this damage, seal bounty programs were conducted in Nova Scotia and elsewhere in Atlantic Canada through the early 1980s (Bowen and Lidgard 2012).

The Royal Commission and Other Reviews

Seals in eastern Canada have been highly controversial both nationally and internationally for decades resulting in a series of external reviews commissioned by the Canadian Government between the mid-1980s and 2001. In June 1984, the Government of Canada created a Royal Commission to make recommendations on all aspects of seals and sealing in Canada. Although matters concerning seal hunting (mainly Harp and Hooded seals) were central for the Commission, the status of seal populations and their interactions (i.e., competition, parasite transmission, gear damage) with commercial fisheries were also considered. The Malouf Commission, as it became known, concluded that Grey Seals were a major source of parasite infection of groundfish stocks and probably contributed to losses owing to competition for fish (Malouf 1986). The Commission roughly estimated the magnitude of losses between $60 and $115 million annually. Within months of the publication of the Malouf Commission Report, the Fisheries and Oceans Research Advisory Council (FORAC) Report on seals was also published (Anon. 1988). FORAC was another independent review panel commissioned by Fisheries and Oceans Canada (DFO) and chaired by I.A. McLaren, Dalhousie University, Halifax, Nova Scotia. Based on the recommendations of the FORAC Report, the DFO Minister announced the implementation of a policy decision in 1989 not to cull Grey Seals and to undertake a five-year Grey Seal/parasite research program to investigate methods of population control of seals and parasites, interactions between Grey Seals and marine fisheries, and Grey Seal population biology.

In 1999, management of seal populations was considered also by the Fisheries Resource Conservation Council and the Standing Committee on Fisheries and Oceans, both operating under the auspices of the Government of Canada, both of whom provided recommendations on management strategies, including reducing seal populations to foster recovery of fish stocks. In response to a recommendation from the Standing Committee on Fisheries and Oceans, the DFO Minister established the 'Eminent Panel', also chaired by I.A. McLaren, to provide advice on the best strategies for management of seal populations in Atlantic Canada, including a balanced and objective review of scientific information on seal populations and predator-prey relationships, and how this information can contribute to development of management strategies (McLaren et al. 2001).

Sealworm Research

Both Grey and Harbour seals were known as definitive hosts for the sealworm parasite (i.e., the parasite matured and reproduced in seal stomachs), but details of the parasite life-cycle and its prevalence and abundance in seals were poorly understood. Working with W. Stobo at MFD, B. Beck collected seals along coastal Nova Scotia through the early

1980s. These collections provided data on sealworm prevalence and life cycle, seal population age structure, diets, and the seasonal movements and distribution of seal populations, all of which were needed to better understand what management measures might be undertaken to reduce sealworm abundance in fish species of commercial importance. The data gathered from this early research, plus those collected during the five-year study beginning in 1988, played a prominent role in the development of the first comprehensive synthesis of the population dynamics and ecology of the sealworm parasite and the role played by Grey Seals in its life cycle.

That synthesis emerged from analyses presented at two international workshops held in Halifax, Nova Scotia, in 1987 and 1988 (Bowen 1990). The workshops were initiated by J.E. Stewart, Director of Biological Sciences Branch, BIO, who recognized the need to clarify the relationship between the abundance of seals and the prevalence and abundance of the sealworm parasite in commercially important fishes. Zwanenburg and Bowen (1990) constructed an age-structured population model showing that Grey Seal population trajectories differed in the Gulf of St. Lawrence compared to Sable Island, where numbers were increasing exponentially at about 13% per year, near the maximum rate of increase for this species. Recoveries of seal tags showed that Grey Seals ranged widely throughout eastern Canada during the non-breeding season (Stobo et al. 1990a). Analysis of stomach contents showed that Grey Seals consumed a variety of fish species including Atlantic Cod, herring, and Capelin (*Mallotus villosus*), and that the diet differed seasonally and in different parts of their range (Benoit and Bowen 1990). Stobo et al. (1990b) showed how sealworm abundance and life stages varied seasonally at Sable Island, the largest Grey Seal breeding colony in eastern Canada. G. McClelland and colleagues conducted studies on the prevalence and abundance of sealworms in fish species on the Scotian Shelf and infection rates of benthic macrofauna (McClelland 1990, McClelland et al. 1990). These and other sources of data were used to construct models of sealworm dynamics (Mohn 1990).

Population Dynamics of Grey Seals

Understanding the dynamics of the Grey Seal population was needed both to understand the relationship between seal abundance and sealworm abundance in fish hosts, and to provide advice on management actions that might be taken to reduce conflicts with commercial fisheries. The first population assessment of Grey Seals in eastern Canada by D. Gray (unpubl. data) relied heavily on age-specific estimates of reproductive rates, estimates of pup production, and bounty kills taken from Mansfield and Beck (1977). A fundamental input to Grey Seal population assessments (Thomas et al. 2007) is an estimate of annual pup production on Sable Island (Fig. 2). Short trips to the island from 1963 through 1976 systematically underestimated pup production (Zwanenburg and Bowen 1990). To improve the quality of estimates, between 1977 and 1989, pup production on Sable Island was determined by tagging all pups shortly after they had been weaned (Stobo and Zwanenburg 1990). As all Sable pups carried tags during this period, and seals from Sable and other areas in the Gulf of St. Lawrence were mixing during the non-breeding season, the Sable tagging program also provided an opportunity to estimate non-Sable production using the ratio of marked to non-marked seals. Thus, total pup production of Grey Seals in eastern Canada could be estimated based on the continuing research on Sable Island (Stobo and Zwanenburg 1990, Hammill et al. 1991).

Figure 2. A portion of the Grey Seal breeding colony on Sable Island, Nova Scotia, January 2003, showing white-coated pups with adult females and the occasional male (photo: W.D. Bowen).

With over 7,000 pups born on Sable Island in 1987, and a rapidly increasing trajectory (Fig. 3), it became clear that tagging all pups would become impractical owing to limits on time and team size. Therefore, in 1989 and 1990, complete cohort tagging and an aerial photograph census were simultaneously conducted. Estimates from these independent methods showed close agreement (Bowen et al. 2003b). Since then Grey Seal pup production on Sable Island has been estimated at 3-4 year intervals using aerial photography. The method has proven accurate, and precision has increased with the use of high-resolution digital photography beginning in 2007 (Bowen et al. 2007, 2011).

Considered one of Canada's rarest sea mammals in the 1960s (e.g., Hinds 1963), DFO research over the past 50 years has documented a dramatic increase in the abundance of Grey Seals. Pup production on Sable Island increased exponentially at near 13% annually through the 1990s and by 2010 more than 62,000 pups were born on Sable Island and another 2,500 on Hay Island off the eastern coast of Cape Breton (Bowen et al. 2011). Recent estimates indicate that the rate of increase had slowed with an average annual rate of increase of only 4% between 2007 and 2010 (Fig. 3).

Estimating total population size of a seal species is usually done using a population model that is fitted to a time series of estimates of pup production. This is because, other than for newly born pups, there is no time during the year when all, or a known fraction, of the total population is available to be surveyed. The relationship between pup production and total population size is rather straightforward during a period of exponential increase, as was the case with Grey Seals at Sable Island through the 1990s. But once the rate of pup production decreases or stabilizes, additional information, such as age-specific reproductive or survival rates, is needed to estimate total population size. Age-specific reproductive or survival rates can be estimated by uniquely marking individual seals and resighting individuals over a number of years. Mark-resighting methods take longer, but provide accurate and precise estimates of both reproductive performance and survival.

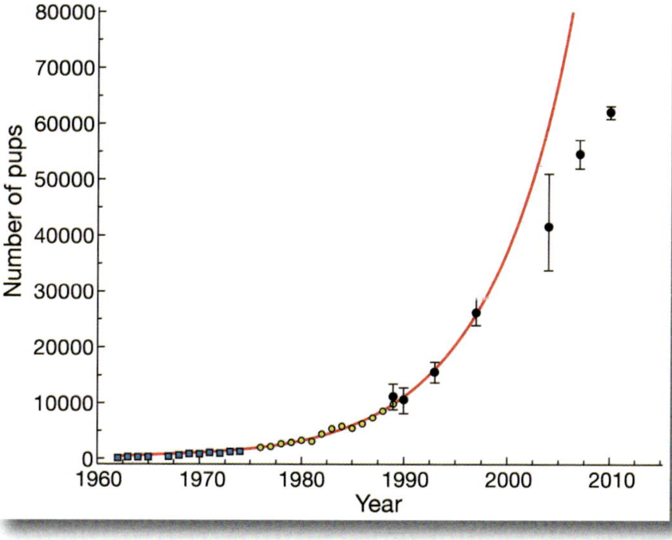

Figure 3. Estimates of number of Grey Seal pups born on Sable Island, Nova Scotia. Red curve is an exponential fit to the 1976 to 1990 data. Filled squares represent incomplete cohort tagging, open circles represent complete cohort tagging, and closed circles represent aerial photographic surveys with 95% confidence limits.

In 1963, the first group of weaned Grey Seal pups (about 100) was hot-iron branded on Sable Island, each with a single V. This was followed by the branding of 1,845 weaned pups with individual marks between 1969 and 1974 (Mansfield and Beck 1977). The motivation for this work was to study the behaviour of individuals over time. Recognizing the value of permanently marked individuals, B. Beck and colleagues from MFD uniquely branded another 2,000 weaned Grey Seal pups on Sable Island between 1985 and 1989. A further 2,300 pups were uniquely branded between 1998 and 2002, under the leadership of D. Bowen and J. McMillan of MFD, bringing the total number of uniquely-branded Grey Seals to about 6,250. Although other issues took precedence in the 1970s, by the early 1980s MFD had established a standard protocol involving weekly censuses of the entire island to record the identity and location of all branded Grey Seals. The 2012 breeding season marked the thirtieth consecutive year of this study during which about 62,000 resightings of branded adult Grey Seals have been recorded.

This rich dataset has been used to estimate survival rates and female reproductive traits, and provided a pool of known-aged individuals for a wide range of physiological and behavioural studies of reproduction and foraging ecology. Schwarz and Stobo (1997) showed that estimates of return rate were fairly insensitive to misreading of brands. Subsequently, Schwarz and Stobo (1999) demonstrated that estimates of survival are relatively unaffected by modest differences in sighting probability. Schwarz and Stobo (2000) used the resighting data through 1994 for Grey Seal cohorts branded from 1969 to 1989 to estimate juvenile and adult female survival and age-specific probabilities of giving birth. Later, Manske et al. (2002) used resighting data to estimate adult survival and mean age of recruitment of adult males to the breeding colony.

These data on resightings provided an opportunity to determine which vital rates (i.e., reproduction and survival) were responsible for the slowing of the rate of pup production observed on Sable Island. Comparison of estimates of survival rates of juvenile and adult females for seals born from 1985 to 1989 with those born from 1998 to 2002 showed that although adult survival had remained high, juvenile survival had declined from 70 to 30% (C. den Heyer et al. unpubl. data). No differences in female age at first birth were found, suggesting that the reduction in the rate of pup production was mainly due to reduced juvenile survival.

MFD conducted three other long-term programs to better understand the role of seals in continental shelf ecosystems, their impact on prey populations, and the extent to which Grey Seals might serve as indicators of ecosystem status (e.g., Bowen et al. 2006a). In addition to the pool of known-age marked individual seals, an important element in the success of seal research from the mid-1980s to the present was the long-term collaborations between MFD (D. Bowen and J. McMillan) and researchers at the National Zoological Park, Smithsonian Institution (D. Boness and O. Oftedal), Dalhousie University (S. Iverson), and the National Geographic Society. These collaborations enabled a multidisciplinary approach to the Grey and Harbour seal research, involving physiologists, behavioural and population ecologists, and geneticists. Over these decades, these researchers trained 25 graduate students and postdoctoral fellows. The value added to DFO research from these collaborations was enormous, increasing our capacity to understand the population ecology of Grey and Harbour seals.

Harbour Seals on Sable Island

MFD collaborations led to new insights into the ecology and population dynamics of Harbour Seals on Sable Island (Fig. 4). This research was initiated on the basis of observations by B. Beck of the tameness of Harbour Seals during tagging to determine annual pup production. This tameness provided the opportunity to live-capture and tag individuals for long-term studies of variation in life-history traits, such as reproductive performance. As it turned out, Beck could not have been more accurate in his assessment of the potential of Sable Island as a field laboratory, without question one of the best in the world, for physiological and ecological research on Harbour Seals. Little was known about the reproductive biology of Harbour Seals at the time largely because they mated at sea, and elsewhere within the species's breeding range, it was almost impossible to live-capture adults. Studies on Sable Island showed that, unlike Grey Seal females that fast during the lactation period, Harbour Seal females made regular foraging trips to sea, a pattern similar to that seen in Northern Fur Seals (*Callorhinus ursinus*) and Steller Sea Lions (*Eumetopias jubatus*; Boness et al. 1994). Physiological studies revealed that the need to feed during lactation was a function of the size of the female, and thus the amount of stored energy that a female had to support milk production and her own metabolic rate (Bowen et al. 2001a). Both maternal age and body size influenced the size, growth rate, and condition of offspring (Ellis et al. 2000, Bowen et al. 2001b), which in turn affected pup metabolism and food intake during the transition to post-weaning independence (Muelbert et al. 2003). Another study showed that pup survival during the lactation period was a function of pup size and genetic variability (Coltman et al. 1998a). A series of studies, using time-depth recorders, paternity analysis, and animal-borne video (Crittercam, National Geographic) on adult males, shed light on the mating system of Harbour Seals (Coltman et al. 1998b,c; Coltman et al. 1999). These studies showed the influence of body size on mating success and how behaviour changed over the course of the breeding season as more females became receptive (Coltman et al. 1997, Boness et al. 2006). Combined, these studies also shed light on the causes of a dramatic decline in the Harbour Seal population on Sable Island that occurred during

Figure 4. Adult female Harbour Seal and her dependent pup on the beach at Sable Island, Nova Scotia, June 2004 (photo: W.D. Bowen).

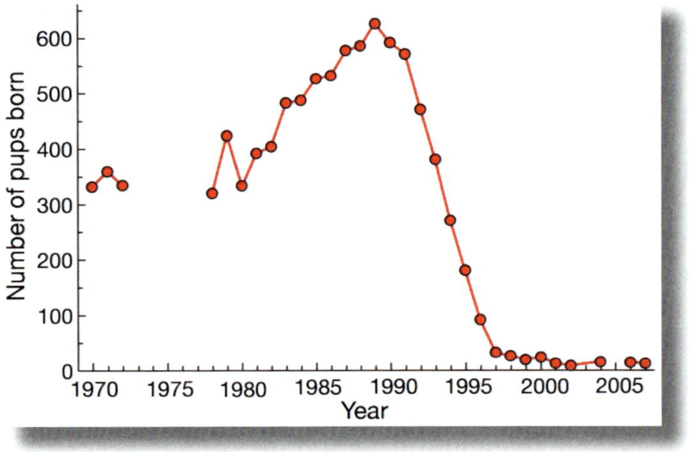

Figure 5. Trend in the number of Harbour Seal pups born on Sable Island, Nova Scotia.

the 1990s (Fig. 5). Although much of the decline could be attributed to shark predation (Lucas and Stobo 2000), declining recruitment and an increase in mean birth date (suggesting nutritional stress in females), it also pointed to greater competition from the rapidly increasing Grey Seal population on Sable Island (Bowen et al. 2003a). As of 2011, Grey Seal numbers have continued to increase and there has been no recovery of Harbour Seals on Sable Island.

Grey Seal Reproduction

Collaborative research also significantly increased DFO's capacity to learn about Grey Seal reproduction and mating system. In most species, termed 'income' breeders, the energy used to support lactation (a defining characteristic of mammals) is acquired from feeding during the period of milk production. In other species, such as Grey Seals, females fast during lactation and therefore must accumulate the nutrients needed to support milk production prior to giving birth; these species are termed 'capital' breeders. To better understand linkages between environmental change, foraging, and reproduction, researchers from MFD, Dalhousie University and the Smithsonian Institution conducted a series of physiological, behavioural, and ecological studies concerning lactation and pup development and how reproductive performance varies. These studies showed larger females produced larger pups and that daily milk energy intake was the best predictor of pup growth and body weight at weaning (Iverson et al. 1993, Mellish et al. 1999). Rapid pup growth (tripling body weight in 16 days) was associated with consumption of high energy milk (~60% fat, Iverson et al. 1993). Heritability in milk composition was high and differed by a factor of two in energy density within the Sable Island population (Lang et al. 2009). The consequence of this variation is that some females produced pups about half the size of others, and as survival is related to offspring size, the fitness of females within the population varied widely. MFD's long-term life history study also showed that reproductive performance of females differed with age (Fig. 6) and body size, increasing in young females and declining in old females, providing evidence for reproductive senescence in females older than 25-30 years of age (Bowen et al. 2006b).

Interest in the use of contraception (see below) to manage Grey Seals required a better understanding of the mating system as contraception would change the sex ratio of adults at breeding colonies, which in turn could have unintended consequences on the performance of lactating females. Females that gave birth after the peak of pupping were harassed more often by males resulting in a significant reduction in time spent suckling and a 30% decline in weight of pups at weaning (Boness et al. 1995). Lidgard et al. (2001) found that males used two main tactics to secure mates. The first was defending females at one place (known as 'tenure') and the second was intercepting females near the shoreline as they departed the colony after having weaned their pup. Genetic paternity analysis showed that males exhibiting 'tenure' had a higher probability of siring offspring than males intercepting females leaving the colony (Lidgard et al. 2004). Males of intermediate body size and age mated with the most females and achieved the highest success. Large body size provided males with an energetic advantage of greater endurance during fasting, but the largest males often were also the oldest and they were less competitive than intermediate-aged males (Lidgard et al. 2005).

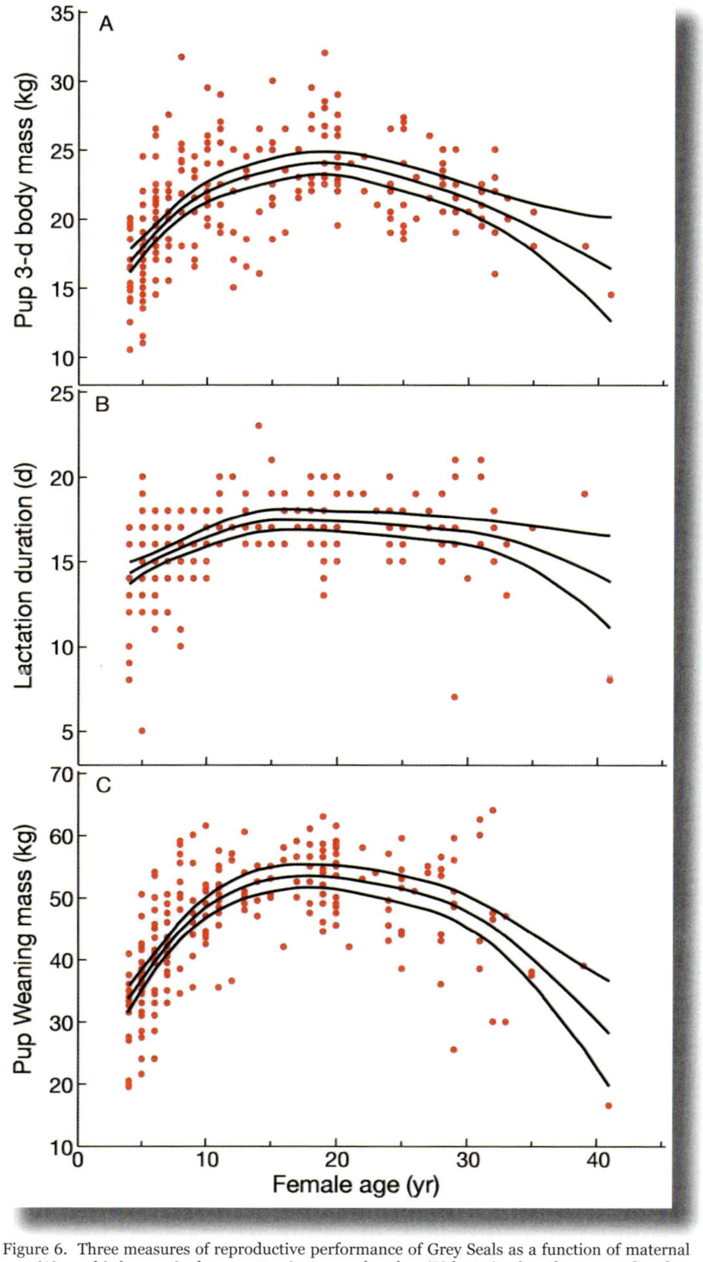

Figure 6. Three measures of reproductive performance of Grey Seals as a function of maternal age: (A) pup birth mass (3-d postpartum), n = 251 females; (B) lactation length, n = 233 females; and (C) pup weaning mass, n = 228 females. In each plot, the middle solid line is the fit of a Generalized Additive Model and the other lines represent the upper and lower 95% point-wise confidence limits of fitted values.

Seal Contraceptive Vaccine

Beginning in the late 1980s, representatives of the fishing industry in Nova Scotia approached BIO and Dalhousie University to develop tools that could be used to non-lethally manage Grey Seal population size and ameliorate damage to fish caused by the sealworm parasite. The result was a decade-long research collaboration between the MFD and Dalhousie University known as the Sealworm Intervention Project, which was initially co-funded by DFO and the fishing industry, and subsequently funded by DFO alone. Although experiments to de-worm Grey Seals were largely successful, the effect was only short lived as seals regained their parasite burden quickly once they began to feed on infected fish. As a result, this aspect of the research was abandoned and the focus was shifted to the development of a contraceptive vaccine (Anon. 1998). By 1992, the research had progressed to the point of conducting a field trial of an immunocontraceptive vaccine on female Grey Seals at Sable Island. Immunocontraceptive vaccines work by using the body's immune system to prevent penetration of the ovum by sperm, which prevents fertilization. Data collected over the following 6 years showed that the vaccine reduced birth rate by about 90% (Brown et al. 1996, Anon. 1998). An important feature of the Grey Seal vaccine is that it only required a single administration, thus making it suitable for application to wild populations (Brown et al. 1996, 1997). Although the field test showed that the vaccine was effective, it was never used as a management tool for regulating population size of Grey Seals as both the delivery system and preparation of the vaccine for large scale use require further development.

Seal Diets and Development of Quantitative Fatty Acid Signature Analysis (QFASA)

Grey and Harbour seals are upper-trophic level predators and any reasonable assessment of their impact as a predator requires an understanding of their diet. Shortly after joining MFD, B. Beck undertook a series of collections of Grey and Harbour seal stomachs from hunters in Nova Scotia and New Brunswick. Analysis of stomach contents showed that these species consumed a broad range of largely benthic fishes, and that the composition of their diets varied between species and among areas, seasons, and years within species (Bowen et al. 1993, Bowen and Harrison 1996). These studies clearly indicated that it was misleading to attempt to characterize the average diet of either seal species. Analysis of fecal samples (also known as scats) became more common during the 1990s because large samples could be collected and processed at low cost and because the estimates were less affected by differential passage of prey species from the stomach which could bias the results. From 1991 to 1998, MFD collected fecal samples to estimate seasonal and interannual variations in the diet of Grey Seals at Sable Island. Although 28 species of fish were identified, the seals' diet was dominated by American Sand Lance (*Ammodytes dubius*), followed by Atlantic Cod, Silver Hake (*Merluccius bilinearis*) and several species of flatfish. Significant seasonal and interannual variation were evident in the importance of American Sand lance and Atlantic Cod in the diet (Bowen and Harrison 1994, 2007).

Although stomach and fecal contents provided useful information on diet, it was clear that estimates of diet based on the recovery of otoliths could be seriously biased by the partial or complete digestion of fish otoliths and differential rates of prey passage from the stomach to the intestines (Bowen 2000). Fishermen also expressed concern about these methods as they claimed that seals often did not consume the head (i.e., otoliths) and, thus, estimates of diet underestimated the consumption of species such as Atlantic Cod. This meant that better methods to estimate diet were needed. S. Iverson suggested a new method based on her doctoral research on California Sea Lions (*Zalophus californianus*) at the University of Maryland, Baltimore, MD, and the National Zoological Park, Washington, DC (Iverson 1988). Although it was clear from her research that the fatty acid composition of seal blubber reflected the diet eaten, more research was needed to turn this into a quantitative tool. She agreed to come to Halifax and, with R. Ackman and D. Bowen, received NSERC and DFO financial support to conduct feeding experiments using Harp and Grey seals housed at the Dalhousie University Aquatron. Iverson subsequently took a faculty position at Dalhousie University, and for the rest of the decade continued her research on fatty acids with Bowen and several members of the faculty of mathematics and statistics (C. Smith and W. Blanchard). That research resulted in the development of a method to estimate diet known as Quantitative Fatty Acid Signature Analysis or QFASA (Iverson et al. 2004, Bowen and Iverson 2012). Funding for the QFASA application to estimate the diet of Grey Seals came from the Comparative Dynamics of Exploited Ecosystems in the Northwest Atlantic (CDEENA), a multi-year research project funded by DFO from 1999 through 2002. CDEENA provided for the collection and chemical analysis of potential prey species from the Scotian Shelf and Gulf of St. Lawrence that would comprise the prey fatty acid library used in the QFASA model (Budge et al. 2002).

The use of QFASA produced estimates of the diet of Grey Seals live-captured on Sable Island that, for the most part, contained the same species as other methods, but the proportions were often quite different (Bowen et al. 2006a, Beck et al. 2007). American Sand Lance still dominated the estimates of diet, but the percentage of Atlantic Cod in the diet was less than estimated from fecal samples collected during the same time periods. QFASA estimates confirmed both seasonal and interannual variability in the diet and also revealed large differences in the diets of males and females. In addition, conducting feeding experiments to validate the QFASA method, where the true diet is known, researchers compared characteristics of the diet within individuals derived from QFASA and stable isotope ratios, two independent methods. Both methods showed significant sex differences in diet (Tucker et al. 2007) and that the trophic level of the diet estimated from QFASA was positively correlated with that estimated from stable isotope ratios of nitrogen from the same adult Grey Seals, as expected if the two methods were estimating similar diets (Tucker et al. 2008).

Seal Foraging Behaviour

Until the late 1980s, seal research was land based and therefore focussed on those aspects of biology that could be studied while seals were hauled out on land. This limitation meant that little was known about the spatial and temporal patterns of habitat use, foraging behaviour, and geographic distribution. This all changed with the development of micro-processor data loggers, advanced telemetry (VHF and UHF), and animal-borne video (Bowen et al. 2002). D. Bowen and colleagues were among the first to study the movements, diving, and foraging behaviour of seals using these new technologies. Time-depth recorders provided detailed data on dive frequency, depth and duration, time spent at the bottom of the dive, and the overall two-dimensional shape of dives (e.g., Boness et al 1994, Bowen et al. 1999, Beck et al. 2003a). These studies revealed sex-differences in diving behaviour of Grey Seals, and thus presumably foraging behaviour, which helped explain the difference in the diets of males and females (Beck et al. 2007). Simultaneous physiological studies in the same individual seals (using stable isotope dilution methods) showed how changes in buoyancy affected diving behaviour as seals stored fat to support the energetic cost of reproduction (Beck et al. 2000), and that males and females exhibited dramatic seasonal differences in energy expenditure and gain over the course of the year (Fig. 7; Beck et al. 2003b).

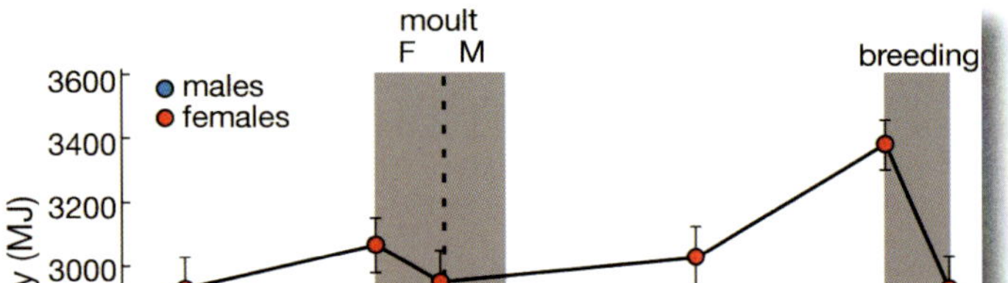

Figure 7. Seasonal changes in total body energy in adult male and female Grey Seals. Shaded areas represent the two periods of terrestrial fasting. Note that females begin and end moult about a month earlier than males. The post-breeding sample is plotted twice to better illustrate the overall annual patterns.

By the mid-1990s, tags capable of transmitting to Argos satellites were providing the opportunity to study not only diving behaviour, but movement and the geographic location of diving (Austin et al. 2004). New data loggers had also been developed to record stomach temperature in free-ranging marine mammals. In one of the first studies of its kind, Grey Seals were fitted with a satellite-linked Argos transmitter, stomach temperature recorder, and time-depth recorder to simultaneously track at-sea movements, foraging behaviour, and feeding success as indicated by a characteristic drop in stomach temperature (Austin et al. 2006a,b). Further movement studies of Grey Seals, using Argos satellite-linked telemetry and mathematical models to infer behaviour, showed strong evidence of sex-segregation in seasonal habitat use (Fig. 8; Breed et al. 2006), characteristics of foraging trips (Breed et al. 2009), and how foraging behaviour develops with age in both males and females (Breed et al. 2011).

Grey Seal Predation on Atlantic Cod

Over several decades, a principal objective of Grey Seal research was to provide scientific advice on the nature and consequences of the interactions between Grey Seals and Atlantic Cod. The first comprehensive analysis brought together our research findings on trends in Grey Seal abundance, diet, seasonal distribution, and energy requirements to estimate the total annual consumption by Grey Seals and the associated seal predation mortality on the Eastern Scotian Shelf (ESS) Atlantic Cod stock. Expressed as a fraction of the total natural mortality experienced by this cod stock, modelling results indicated that seal predation accounted for only about a quarter of the estimated natural mortality, and that other factors were likely more important than Grey Seals in preventing cod recovery (Mohn and Bowen 1996).

In October 2000, the DFO Minister commissioned an independent review to provide advice on the best strategies for managing seal populations in Atlantic Canada. The Eminent Panel report (McLaren et al. 2001) contained recommendations regarding the need to develop explicit objectives for management of seals, and research needed to fill critical gaps in knowledge. Following the Eminent Panel report, DFO received requests from the fishing industry, Newfoundland and Labrador, and the Fisheries Resource Conservation Council to establish Seal Exclusion Zones (SEZ) in various locations across Atlantic Canada to assist cod recovery. In April 2003, the Government of Canada announced the closure of three Atlantic Cod stocks in the Gulf of St. Lawrence and northeast of Newfoundland and Labrador, and that research would be conducted into the feasibility of SEZs and the types of management tools needed to keep seals away from close-to-shore waters such as St. Georges Bay and Smith Sound where cod aggregate and spawn. In addition, new research was to be conducted on seal abundance, seal co-occurrence with cod, and seal predation on cod under the two-year Atlantic Seal Research Program.

The SEZ Workshop, held in May 2004 in Halifax, Nova Scotia, and chaired by D. Bowen, was attended by 19 participants from Canada, United States, and Norway. Workshop participants concluded that excluding seals from an area would not be possible or practical in most marine environments. The ability to either exclude from or reduce the number of seals in an area would become dramatically more difficult as control sites moved seaward from rivers to more open marine environments (Bowen 2004).

Data from the Atlantic Seal Research Program were used to update estimates of Grey Seal predation mortality on the ESS Atlantic Cod stock. Results from this new analysis indicated that, since the closure of the cod fishery, Grey Seals accounted for a significant level of instantaneous mortality (21%), and along with other unknown and higher sources of natural mortality (62%), contributed to the failure of this cod stock to recover (Trzcinski et al. 2006). However, the model also indicated that, during

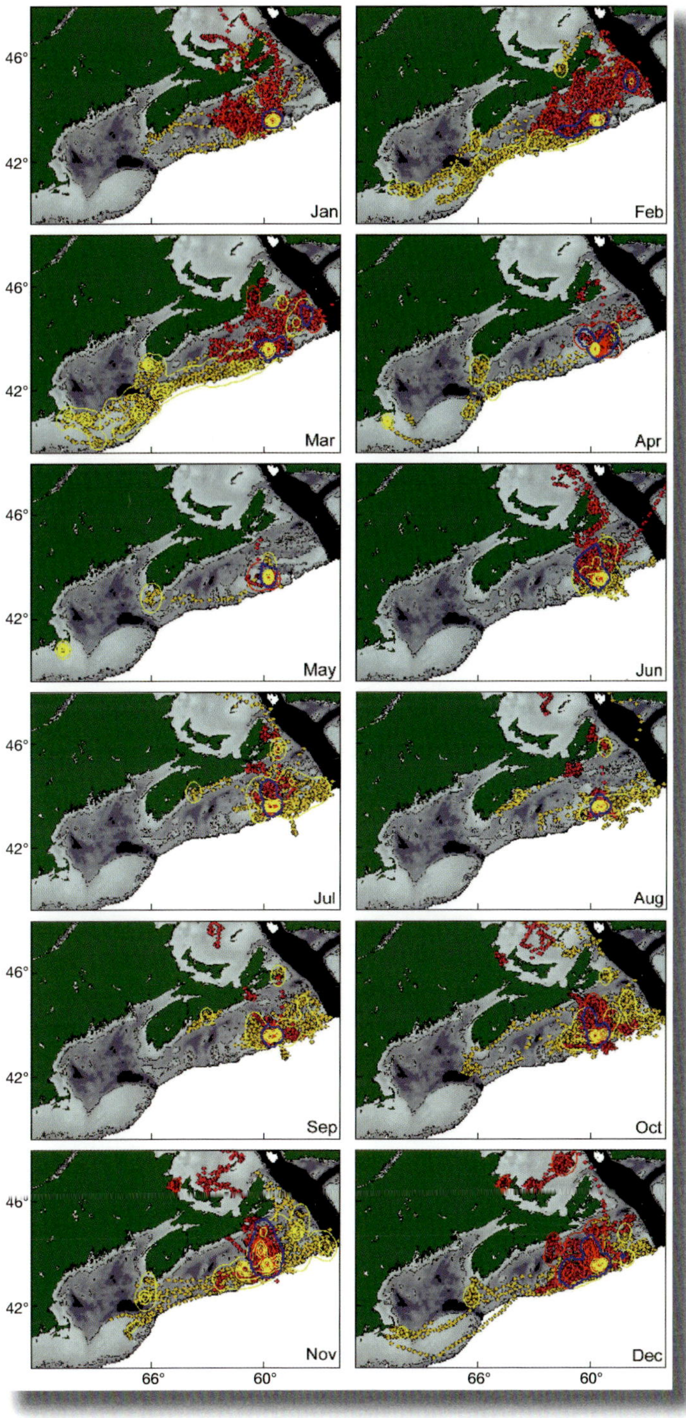

Figure 8. Monthly distributions of adult male and female Grey Seals. Yellow diamonds represent male and red diamonds female state-space estimated locations. The outer red and yellow contour lines are the 98.5% contour for female and male kernel home ranges, respectively. The blue contour is the overlap of the 98.5% contour of male and female kernels. The density of the estimated locations and the order they are rendered have caused the female (red) locations to obscure some of the male (yellow) locations, but the kernel density contour lines are visible and reflect habitat usage. The 100-m contour line has been added for reference; black areas denote shelf water depths deeper than 200 m.

the 11-year period of the fishing moratorium (i.e., 1992 to 2003), there was little evidence that Grey Seals were the principal source of natural mortality on the ESS Atlantic Cod stock. Although any mortality on a declining and depleted population is detrimental to population recovery, Trzcinski et al. (2006) concluded that even the complete removal of Grey Seal predation would not assure the recovery of the cod population, given the high levels of other sources of natural mortality. The dramatic increase in the abundance of Grey Seals not only raised questions about predation effects on single-prey species, but also was relevant to attempts to understand how continental shelf ecosystems have changed over time and the causes of those changes (e.g., Frank et al. 2005). Ecosystem modelling suggested that as a consequence of the removal of cod by fishing and a resulting trophic cascade, ESS cod abundance was kept low by predation (mainly by other fish), causing abundance to be so low that cod could not compete for prey with their abundant competitors (Bundy and Fanning 2005).

Following the completion of the Atlantic Seal Research Program, DFO sponsored a two-part international workshop to review the impacts of seals on Atlantic Cod stocks in eastern Canadian waters. Held in 2007 and 2008, the meetings were attended by about 30 participants from 5 countries and chaired by D. Bowen. Over the course of the two workshops, participants reviewed the most up-to-date analyses pertaining to predator effects on prey behaviour, sealworm effects on prey, seal ecology, mortality patterns in fish, seal diet estimation, seal prey consumption, biases and uncertainty of data, and statistical and modelling approaches (Bowen et al. 2008, 2009). In early 2010, DFO's Fisheries and Aquaculture Management (FAM) asked DFO Science to answer the following questions: How many Grey Seals would have to be removed over five years to measurably lower natural mortality on southern Gulf Atlantic Cod and other cod stocks that are experiencing high natural mortality? What might be the ecosystem responses (e.g., abundance of other predators and prey) to Grey Seal targeted removal, particularly as it may impact cod recovery? Analyses pertaining to these questions were presented at a Zonal Advisory Process in Halifax, in October 2010, which resulted in the provision of advice on the impact of Grey Seals on several Atlantic Cod stocks (Chadwick 2011).

MOVING FORWARD

Marine mammal research at BIO for more than the past 40 years has led to a better understanding of the ecology of large whales and seals on the Scotian Shelf and adjacent waters, of threats to those populations (e.g., contaminants, overfishing, habitat alteration, and disturbance), and of the ecological impacts of seal predation on prey populations. The success of marine mammal research at BIO has depended critically on long-term, continuous DFO funding and on partnerships with scientists and students from other institutions. As a result of this long-term funding, research at BIO has transformed our understanding of the energy requirements of whales and seals, the distribution, movements, and foraging behaviour of seals, and their influence on the structure and functioning of continental shelf ecosystems. Our research contributed to the development of a new method to determine the diets of marine mammals based on the composition of fatty acids stored in body fat and to new and improved instruments to remotely study the at-sea behaviour of these wide-ranging marine consumers. Integrating new information on energy requirements, diets, and population size of seals has led to a better understanding of the impacts of seals on prey populations.

Where we go from here will no doubt be guided by the development of improved scientific tools and new issues concerning marine mammals, but several areas of research would seem worthy of attention. In an era embracing ecosystem-based management, the absence of information on the distribution, abundance, and consumption of prey by whales on the Scotian Shelf is an important gap in knowledge and limits the reliability of ecosystem modelling. Uncertainties about the diets of seals and response of seal predation rate to changes in the abundance of prey remain and these uncertainties hinder evaluation of the impacts of seals on prey populations. Animal-borne video could reduce these uncertainties, but this will require the development of new or better battery technology that allows data to be collected over weeks or months, rather than the current hours or days. Integration of satellite/GPS tags with accelerometers and acoustic transceivers fitted to marine mammals, coupled with tagging of potential prey with coded acoustic tags could provide new insights into the spatial and temporal distribution of predator-prey encounters and to species interactions in the open ocean. Greater human use of the ocean has greatly increased noise levels that might compromise communication, particularly of whales. Thus, better tools are needed to evaluate the effects of human-induced noise on the behaviour and demography of these species.

Finally, looking to the future, the value of long-term studies cannot be overstated. Marine mammals are large species with longevities ranging from 9 to over 100 years. They typically have low rates of population increase and relatively high adult survival. Environmental variability acting at decadal or longer scales can have important effects on behaviour and life history traits and thus the dynamics of populations. Therefore, characterizing variability in population trends and distribution and the mechanisms underlying those dynamics requires that studies be conducted at appropriate scales. Given their longevity, we should expect marine mammal life histories to have evolved adaptations to deal with environmental variation at temporal and spatial scales ranging from months to decades and metres to hundreds of kilometres (Bowen et al. 2010). Continued long-term studies will be critical to achieving deeper insights about these intriguing mammals.

ACKNOWLEDGEMENTS

Many people have played key roles in the success of marine mammal research at BIO and of seal research on Sable Island, in particular. In fact, more than 70 people have directly contributed to DFO's Sable Island seal research alone. Brian Beck's insight and enthusiasm were key assets to the program, particularly in the early years. Jim McMillan and, more recently, Nell den Heyer, both at MFD, have played critical roles in all aspects of the work from resupplying our field camps on Sable Island to database design and data analysis. Long-term collaboration with Daryl Boness, Smithsonian Institution, and Sara Iverson, Dalhousie University, provided critical financial resources, but perhaps more importantly, it provided a broader and more intellectually stimulating environment for the research than would have otherwise been the case. Graduate students and postdoctoral fellows also contributed greatly to this stimulating intellectual environment, and Shelley Lang and Damian Lidgard deserve special recognition for their contributions over many seasons on Sable Island. DFO Science provided the long-term funding for the core population dynamics program on Grey and Harbour seals. Natural Science and Engineering Research Council grants to Bowen and Iverson provided additional general support for the field research and for graduate students and postdoctoral fellows. The Smithsonian Institution, National Zoological Park, and National Geographic Society also provided financial support for BIO seal research over many years.

REFERENCES

Addison, R.F. and P.F. Brodie. 1973. Occurrence of DDT residues in beluga whales (*Delphinapterus leucas*) from the Mackenzie Delta, N.W.T. Journal Fisheries Research Board of Canada 30: 1,733-1,736.

Addison, R.F. and T.G. Smith. 1974. Organochloride residue levels in Arctic ringed seals: variation with age and sex. Oikos 25: 335-337.

Addison, R.F. and P.F. Brodie. 1977. Organochlorine residues in maternal blubber, milk, and pup blubber from grey seals (*Halichoerus grypus*) from Sable Island, Nova Scotia. Journal of the Fisheries Research Board of Canada 34: 937-941.

Addison, R.F. and P.F. Brodie. 1984. Characterization of ethoxyresorufin o-de-ethylase in grey seal *Halichoerus grypus*. Comparative Biochemistry and Physiology 79: 261-263.

Addison, R.F. and P.F. Brodie. 1987. Transfer of organochlorine residues from blubber through the circulatory system to milk in the lactating grey seal *Halichoerus grypus*. Canadian Journal Fisheries and Aquatic Sciences 44: 782-786.

Addison, R.F. and W.T. Stobo. 1993. Organochlorine residue concentrations and burdens in gray seal (*Halichoerus grypus*) blubber during the 1st-year of life. Journal of Zoology (London) 230: 443-450.

Addison, R.F. and W.T. Stobo. 2001. Trends in organochlorine residue concentrations and burdens in grey seals (*Halichoerus grypus*) from Sable Is., NS, Canada, between 1974 and 1994. Environmental Pollution 112: 505-513.

Addison, R.F., S.R. Kerr, J. Dale, and D.E. Sergeant. 1973. Variation of organochlorine residue levels with age in Gulf of St. Lawrence harp seals (*Pagophilus groenlandicus*). Journal Fisheries Research Board of Canada 30: 595-600.

Addison, R.F., P.F. Brodie, E.M. Sergeant, and D.E. Sergeant. 1984. DDT has declined more than PCBs in eastern Canadian seals during the 1970s. Environmental Sciences Technology 18: 935-937.

Addison, R.F., P.F. Brodie, A. Edwards, and M.C. Sadler. 1986a. Mixed-function oxidase activity in the harbour seal (*Phoca vitulina*) from Sable Island, Nova Scotia. Comparative Biochemistry and Physiology C-Pharmacology, Toxicology and Endocrinology 85: 121-124.

Addison, R.F., M.E. Zinck, and T.G. Smith. 1986b. PCBs have declined more than DDT-group residues in Arctic ringed seals (*Phoca hispida*) between 1972 and 1981. Environmental Science and Technology 20: 253-256.

Addison, R.F., K.W. Renton, A.J. Edwards, and P.F. Brodie. 1988. Polychlorinated-biphenyls and mixed-function oxidase in grey seals (*Halichoerus grypus*). Marine Environmental Research 24: 111-112.

Addison, R.F., M.G. Ikonomou, and W.T. Stobo. 1999. Polychlorinated dibenzo-p-dioxins and furans and non-ortho- and mono-ortho-chlorine substituted polychlorinated biphenyls in grey seals (*Halichoerus grypus*) from Sable Island, Nova Scotia, in 1995. Marine Environmental Research 47: 225-240.

Addison, R.F., B.T. Hargrave, and G.C.Harding. 2014. Organochlorine pollutants in marine ecosystems. Pages 309-314 *in* Voyage of Discovery: Fifty Years of Marine Research at Canada's Bedford Institute of Oceanography (D.N. Nettleship, D.C. Gordon, C.F.M. Lewis, and M.P. Latremouille, Eds.). Bedford Institute of Oceanography-Oceans Association, Dartmouth, NS.)

Anon. 1988. Seal Research in Canada. Report of the Fisheries and Oceans Research Advisory Council to the Minister of Fisheries and Oceans Canada. Ottawa, ON.

Anon. 1998. Sealworm Intervention Project – Immunocontraception: Final Report. Department of Biology, Dalhousie University, Halifax, NS.

Austin, D., W.D. Bowen, and J.I. McMillan. 2004. Intraspecific variation in movement patterns: modelling individual behaviour in a large marine predator. Oikos 105: 15-30.

Austin, D., W.D. Bowen, J.I. McMillan, and D.J. Boness. 2006a. Stomach temperature telemetry reveals temporal patterns of foraging success in a free-ranging marine mammal. Journal of Animal Ecology 75: 408-420.

Austin, D., W.D. Bowen, J.I. McMillan, and S.J. Iverson. 2006b. Linking movement, diving, and habitat to foraging success in a large marine predator. Ecology 87: 3,095-3,108.

Beamish, P. 1971. Quantitative measurements of acoustic scattering from zooplanktonic organisms. Deep-Sea Research 18: 811-822.

Beamish, P. 1978. Evidence that a captive humpback whale (*Megaptera novaeangliae*) does not use sonar. Deep-Sea Research 25: 469-472.

Beck, C.A., W.D. Bowen, and S.J. Iverson. 2000. Seasonal changes in buoyancy and diving behaviour of adult grey seals. Journal of Experimental Biology 203: 2,323-2,330.

Beck, C.A., W.D. Bowen, J.I. McMillan, and S.J. Iverson. 2003a. Sex differences in the diving behaviour of a size-dimorphic capital breeder: the grey seal. Animal Behaviour 66: 777-789.

Beck, C.A., W.D. Bowen, and S.J. Iverson. 2003b. Sex differences in the seasonal patterns of energy storage and expenditure in a phocid seal. Journal of Animal Ecology 72: 280-291.

Beck, C.A., S.J. Iverson, W.D. Bowen, and W. Blanchard. 2007. Sex differences in grey seal diet reflect seasonal variation in foraging behaviour and reproductive expenditure: evidence from quantitative fatty acid signature analysis. Journal of Animal Ecology 76: 490-502.

Benoit, D. and W.D. Bowen. 1990. Seasonal and geographic variation in the diet of grey seals (*Halichoerus grypus*) in eastern Canada. Pages 215-226 *in* Population biology of sealworm (*Pseudoterranova decipiens*) in relation to its intermediate and seal hosts (W. D. Bowen, Ed.). Canadian Bulletin of Fisheries and Aquatic Sciences 222, Ottawa, ON.

Boness, D.J., W.D. Bowen, and O.T. Oftedal. 1994. Evidence of a maternal foraging cycle resembling that of otariid seals in a small phocid, the harbor seal. Behavioural Ecology and Sociobiology 34: 95-104.

Boness, D.J., W.D. Bowen, and S.J. Iverson. 1995. Does male harassment of females contribute to reproductive synchrony in the grey seal by affecting maternal performance? Behavioural Ecology and Sociobiology 36: 1-10.

Boness, D. J., W.D. Bowen, B.M. Bulheier, and G.J. Marshall. 2006. Mating tactics and mating system of an aquatic-mating pinniped: the harbor seal, *Phoca vitulina*. Behavioral Ecology and Sociobiology 61: 119-130.

Bowen, W.D. (Ed.). 1990. Population biology of sealworm (*Pseudoterranova decipiens*) in relation to its intermediate and seal hosts. Canadian Bulletin of Fisheries and Aquatic Sciences 222, Ottawa, ON.

Bowen, W. D. 2000. Reconstruction of pinniped diets: Accounting for complete digestion of otoliths and cephalopod beaks. Canadian Journal of Fisheries and Aquatic Sciences 57: 898-905.

Bowen, W.D. 2004. Report of the exclusion zone workshop. Canadian Stock Assessment Secretariat, Proceedings Series 2004/022. Fisheries and Oceans Canada, Ottawa, ON.

Bowen, W.D. and G.D. Harrison. 1994. Offshore diet of grey seals *Halichoerus grypus* near Sable Island, Canada. Marine Ecology Progress Series 112: 1-11.

Bowen, W.D. and G.D. Harrison. 1996. Comparison of harbour seal diets in two habitats in Atlantic Canada. Canadian Journal of Zoology 74: 125-135.

Bowen, W.D. and G. Harrison. 2007. Seasonal and interannual variability in grey seal diets on Sable Island, eastern Scotian Shelf. Pages 123-134 *in* Grey Seal in the North Atlantic and the Baltic (T. Haug, M.O. Hammill, and D. Olafsdottir, Eds.). North Atlantic Marine Mammal Commission, Scientific Publications, Tromso, Norway.

Bowen, W.D. and S.I. Iverson. 2012. Methods of estimating marine mammal diets: a review of validation experiments and sources of bias and uncertainty. Marine Mammal Science doi: 10.1111/j.1748-7692.2012.00604.x.

Bowen, W.D. and D.C. Lidgard. 2012. Vertebrate predator control: effects on prey populations in terrestrial and aquatic ecosystems. Mammal Review doi: 10.1111/j.1365-2907.2012.00217.x.

Bowen, W.D., J.W. Lawson, and B. Beck. 1993. Seasonal and geographic variation in the species composition and size of prey consumed by grey seals (*Halichoerus grypus*) on the Scotian shelf. Canadian Journal of Fisheries and Aquatic Sciences 50: 1,768-1,778.

Bowen, W.D., D.J. Boness, and S.J. Iverson. 1999. Diving behaviour of lactating harbour seals and their pups during maternal foraging trips. Canadian Journal of Zoology 77: 978-988.

Bowen, W.D., D.J. Boness, S.J. Iverson, and O.T. Oftedal. 2001a. Foraging effort, food intake, and lactation performance depend on maternal mass in a small phocid seal. Functional Ecology 15: 325-334.

Bowen, W.D., S.L. Ellis, S.J. Iverson, and D.J. Boness. 2001b. Maternal effects on offspring growth rate and weaning mass in harbour seals. Canadian Journal of Zoology 79: 1,088-1,101.

Bowen, W.D., D. Tully, D.J. Boness, B. Bulheier, and G. Marshall. 2002. Prey-dependent foraging tactics and prey profitability in a marine mammal. Marine Ecology Progress Series 244: 235-245.

Bowen, W.D., S.L. Ellis, S.J. Iverson, and D.J. Boness. 2003a. Maternal and newborn life-history traits during periods of contrasting population trends: implications for explaining the decline of harbour seals, *Phoca vitulina*, on Sable Island. Journal of Zoology (London) 261: 155-163.

Bowen, W.D., J.I. McMillan, and R. Mohn. 2003b. Sustained exponential population growth of the grey seal on Sable Island. ICES Journal of Marine Science 60: 1,265-1,274.

Bowen, W.D., C.A. Beck, S.J. Iverson, D. Austin, and J.I. McMillan. 2006a. Linking predator foraging behaviour and diet with variability in continental shelf ecosystems: grey seals of eastern Canada. Pages 63-81 *in* Management of Marine Ecosystems: Monitoring changes in upper trophic levels (I.L. Boyd and S. Wanless, Eds.). Zoological Society of London, London, England.

Bowen, W.D., S.J. Iverson, J.I. McMillan, and D.J. Boness. 2006b. Reproductive performance in grey seals: age-related improvement and senescence in a capital breeder. Journal of Animal Ecology 75: 1,340-1,351.

Bowen, W.D., J.I. McMillan, and W. Blanchard. 2007. Reduced population growth of gray seals at Sable Island: Evidence from pup production and age of primiparity. Marine Mammal Science 23: 48-64.

Bowen, W.D., M.O. Hammill, M. Koen-Alonso, G. Stenson, D.P. Swain, and K.M. Trzcinski. 2008. Proceedings of the National Workshop on the Impacts of Seals on Fish Populations in Eastern Canada (Part 1). Canadian Stock Assessment Secretariat, Proceedings Series, 2008/021. Fisheries and Oceans Canada, Ottawa, ON.

Bowen, W.D., M.O. Hammill, M. Koen-Alonso, G. Stenson, D.P. Swain, and K.M. Trzcinski. 2009. Proceedings of the National Workshop on the Impacts of Seals on Fish Populations in Eastern Canada (Part 2). Canadian Stock Assessment Secretariat, Proceedings Series, 2009/020. Fisheries and Oceans Canada, Ottawa, ON.

Bowen, W.D., J.D. Baker, D. Siniff, I.L. Boyd, R. Wells, J.K.B. Ford, S.D. Kraus, J.A. Estes, and I. Stirling. 2010. Long-term studies. Pages 283-305 *in* Marine Mammal Ecology and Conservation: A handbook of techniques (I.L. Boyd, W.D. Bowen, and S.J. Iverson, Eds.). Oxford University Press, Oxford, England.

Bowen, W.D., C. Den Heyer, J.I. McMillan, and M.O. Hammill. 2011. Pup production at Scotian Shelf Grey Seal (*Halichoerus grypus*) colonies in 2010. Canadian Stock Assessment Secretariat, Research Document 2011/066. Fisheries and Oceans Canada, Ottawa, ON.

Breed, G.A., W.D. Bowen, J.I. McMillan, and M.L. Leonard. 2006. Sex segregation of seasonal foraging habitats in a non-migratory marine mammal. Proceedings of Royal Society, B. 273: 2,319-2,326.

Breed, G.A., I.D. Jonsen, R.A. Myers, W.D. Bowen, and M.L. Leonard. 2009. Sex-specific, seasonal foraging tactics of adult grey seals (*Halichoerus grypus*) revealed by state-space analysis. Ecology 90: 3,209-3,221.

Breed, G.A., W.D. Bowen, and M.L. Leonard. 2011. Development of foraging strategies with age in a long-lived marine predator. Marine Ecology Progress Series 431: 267-297.

Brodie, P.F. 1969. Mandibular layering in *Delphinapterus leucas* and age determination. Nature 221: 956-958.

Brodie, P.F. 1971. Reconsideration of aspects of growth, reproduction, and behaviour of white whale (*Delphinapterus leucas*), with reference to Cumberland Sound, Baffin Island, population. Journal of the Fisheries Research Board of Canada 28: 1,309-1,318.

Brodie, P.F. 1975. Cetacean energetics: an overview of intraspecific size variation. Ecology 56: 152-161.

Brodie, P.F. 1977. Form, function and energetics of Cetacea: a discussion. Pages 45-58 *in* Functional Anatomy of Marine Mammals (R.J. Harrison, Ed.). Academic Press, London, England.

Brodie, P.F., D.D. Sameoto, and R.W. Sheldon. 1978. Population densities of euphausiids off Nova Scotia as indicated by net samples, whale stomach contents, and sonar. Limnology and Oceanography 23: 1,264-1,267.

Brown, R.G., W.C. Kimmins, M. Mezei, J. Parsons, B. Pohajdak, and W.D. Bowen. 1996. A single-administration immunocontraceptive vaccine for grey seals. Nature 379: 30-31.

Brown, R.G., W.D. Bowen, W.D. Eddington, W.C. Kimmins, M. Mezei, J.L. Parsons, and B. Pohajdak. 1997. Temporal trends in antibody production in captive grey, harp, and hooded seals to a single administration immunocontraceptive vaccine. Journal of Reproductive Immunology 35: 53-64.

Budge, S.M., S.J. Iverson, W.D. Bowen, and R.G. Ackman. 2002. Among and within species variability in fatty acid signatures of marine fish and invertebrates on the Scotian Shelf, Georges Bank, and southern Gulf of St. Lawrence. Canadian Journal of Fisheries and Aquatic Science 59: 886-898.

Bundy, A. and L.P. Fanning. 2005. Can Atlantic cod (*Gadus morhua*) recover? Exploring trophic explanations for the non-recovery of the cod stock on the eastern Scotian Shelf, Canada. Canadian Journal of Fisheries and Aquatic Sciences 62: 1,474-1,489.

Chadwick, M. 2011. Zonal advisory process on the impacts of grey seals on fish populations in Eastern Canada. Canadian Stock Assessment Secretariat, Proceedings Series, 2010/054. Fisheries and Oceans Canada, Ottawa, ON.

Clapham, P.J., S.B. Young, and R.L. Brownell, Jr. 1999. Baleen whales: conservation issues and the status of the most endangered populations. Mammal Review 29: 35-60.

Coltman, D.W., W.D. Bowen, D.J. Boness, and S.J. Iverson. 1997. Balancing foraging and reproduction in male harbour seals: an aquatically mating pinniped. Animal Behaviour 54: 663-678.

Coltman, D.W., W.D. Bowen, S.J. Iverson, and D.J. Boness. 1998a. The energetics of male reproduction in an aquatically mating pinniped, the harbour seal. Physiological Zoology 71: 387-399.

Coltman, D.W., W.D. Bowen, and J. Wright. 1998b. Male mating success in an aquatically mating pinniped, the harbour seal (*Phoca vitulina*), assessed by microsatellite DNA markers. Molecular Ecology 7: 627-638.

Coltman, D.W., W.D. Bowen, and J.M. Wright. 1998c. Birth weight and neonatal survival of harbour seal pups are positively correlated with genetic variation measured by microsatellites. Proceedings of the Royal Society of London, B. 265: 803-809.

Coltman, D.W., W.D. Bowen, and J.M. Wright. 1999. A multivariate analysis of phenotype and paternity in male harbor seals, *Phoca vitulina*, at Sable Island, Nova Scotia. Behavioral Ecology 10: 169-177.

Ellis, S.L., W.D. Bowen, D.J. Boness, and S.J. Iverson. 2000. Maternal effects on offspring mass and stage of development at birth in the harbor seal, *Phoca vitulina*. Journal of Mammalogy 81: 1,143-1,156.

Frank, K.T., B. Petrie, J.S. Choi, and W.C. Leggett. 2005. Trophic cascades in a formerly cod-dominated ecosystem. Science 308: 1,621-1,623.

Goren, A.D., P.F. Brodie, S. Spotte, H.W. Kaufman, A.J. Gwinnett, J.J. Sciubba, and G. C. Ray. 1986. Dentinal growth layer groups in an adult belukha whale of known age. Journal of Dental Research 65: 349-349.

Goren, A.D., P.F. Brodie, S. Spotte, G.C. Ray, H.W. Kaufman, A.J. Gwinnett, J.J. Sciubba, and J.D. Buck. 1987. Growth layer groups (GLGs) in the teeth of an adult belukha whale (*Delphinapterus leucus*) of known age: evidence for two annual layers. Marine Mammal Science 3: 14-21.

Hammill, M.O., G.B. Stenson, R.A. Myers, and W.T. Stobo. 1991. Mark-recapture estimates of non-Sable Island grey seal (*Halichoerus grypus*) pup production. Canadian Atlantic Fisheries Scientific Advisory Committee, Research Document 92/91. Fisheries and Oceans Canada, Ottawa, ON.

Hinds, B. 1963. Grey Seals sing, love music, but elude scientists prying into their annual migration habits. The Mail-Star (Halifax, NS) 12 February 1963: 10-11.

Ikonomou, M.G. and R.F. Addison. 2008. Polybrominated diphenyl ethers (PBDEs) in seal populations from eastern and western Canada: An assessment of the processes and factors controlling PBDE distribution in seals. Marine Environmental Research 66: 225-230.

Iverson, S.J. 1988. Composition, intake and gastric digestion of milk lipids in pinnipeds. Ph.D. thesis, University of Maryland, Baltimore, Maryland.

Iverson, S.J., W.D. Bowen, D.J. Boness, and O.T. Oftedal. 1993. The effect of maternal size and milk energy output on pup growth in grey seals (*Halichoerus grypus*). Physiological Zoology 66: 61-88.

Iverson, S.J., C. Field, W.D. Bowen, and W. Blanchard. 2004. Quantitative fatty acid signature analysis: a new method of estimating predator diets. Ecological Monographs 74: 211-235.

Lang, S.L.C., S.J. Iverson, and W.D. Bowen. 2009. Repeatability in lactation performance and the consequences for maternal reproductive success in gray seals. Ecology 90: 2,513-2,523.

Lidgard, D.C., D.J. Boness, and W.D. Bowen. 2001. A novel mobile approach to investigating mating tactics in male grey seals (*Halichoerus grypus*). Journal of Zoology (London) 255: 313-320.

Lidgard, D.C., D.J. Boness, W.D. Bowen, and J.I. McMillan. 2004. The rate of fertilization in male mating tactics of the polygynous grey seal. Molecular Ecology 13: 3,543-3,548.

Lidgard, D.C., D.J. Boness, W.D. Bowen, and J.I. McMillan. 2005. State-dependent male mating tactics in the grey seal: the importance of body size. Behavioural Ecology 16: 541–549.

Lucas, Z. and W.T. Stobo. 2000. Shark-inflicted mortality on a population of harbour seals (*Phoca vitulina*) at Sable Island, Nova Scotia. Journal of Zoology (London) 252: 405-414.

Malouf, A. 1986. Seals and Sealing in Canada. Report of the Royal Commission. Canadian Government Publication Centre, Ottawa, ON.

Mansfield, A.W. and B. Beck. 1977. The grey seal in eastern Canada. Fisheries and Marine Service, Technical Report 704: 1-81.

Manske, M., W.T. Stobo, and C.J. Schwarz. 2002. Estimation of age specific probabilities of first return and annual survival rates for the male gray seal (*Halichoerus grypus*) on Sable Island from capture-recapture data. Marine Mammal Science 18: 145-155.

McClelland, G. 1990. Larval sealworm (*Pseudoterranova decipiens*) infections in benthic macrofauna. Pages 47-65 *in* Population Biology of Sealworm (*Pseudoterranova decipiens*) in Relation to its Intermediate and Seal Hosts (W. D. Bowen, Ed.). Canadian Bulletin of Fisheries and Aquatic Sciences 222. Fisheries and Oceans Canada, Ottawa, ON.

McClelland, G., R.K. Misra, and D.J. Martell. 1990. Larval anisakine nematodes in various fish species from Sable Island Bank and vicinity. Pages 83-118 *in* Population Biology of Sealworm (*Pseudoterranova decipiens*) in Relation to its Intermediate and Seal Hosts (W. D. Bowen, Ed.). Canadian Bulletin of Fisheries and Aquatic Sciences 222. Fisheries and Oceans Canada, Ottawa, ON.

McLaren, I.A., S. Brault, J. Harwood, and D. Vardy. 2001. Report of the Eminent Panel on Seal Management. Fisheries and Oceans Canada, Catalog number Fs23-405/2001E, Ottawa, ON. (http://www.dfo-mpo.gc.ca/fm-gp/seal-phoque/reports-rapports/expert/repsm-rgegp-eng.htm)

Mellish, J.A.E., S.J. Iverson, and W.D. Bowen. 1999. Variation in milk production and lactation performance in grey seals and consequences for pup growth and weaning characteristics. Physiological and Biochemical Zoology 72: 677-690.

Mohn, R.K. 1990. A synthesis to explore internal consistency and sensitivity of sealworm dynamics. Pages 261-272 *in* Population Biology of Sealworm (*Pseudoterranova decipiens*) in Relation to its Intermediate and Seal Hosts (W. D. Bowen, Ed.). Canadian Bulletin of Fisheries and Aquatic Sciences 222. Fisheries and Oceans Canada, Ottawa, ON.

Mohn, R. and W.D. Bowen. 1996. Grey seal predation on the eastern Scotian Shelf: modelling the impact on Atlantic cod. Canadian Journal of Fisheries and Aquatic Sciences 53: 2,722-2,738.

Muelbert, M.M.C., W.D. Bowen, and S.J. Iverson. 2003. Weaning mass affects changes in body composition and food intake in harbour seal pups during the first month of independence. Physiological and Biochemical Zoology 76: 418-427.

Orton, L.S. and P.F. Brodie. 1987. Engulfing mechanics of fin whales. Canadian Journal of Zoology 65: 2,898-2,907.

Reijnders, P., S. Brasseur, J. van der Toorn, P. van der Wolf, I. Boyd, J. Harwood, D. Lavigne, and L. Lowry. 1993. Status survey and Conservation Action Plan: Seals, Fur Seals, Sea lions, and Walrus. International Union for the Conservation of Nature, Gland, Switzerland.

Schwarz, C.J. and W.T. Stobo. 1997. Estimating temporary migration using the robust design. Biometrics 53: 178-194.

Schwarz, C.J. and W.T. Stobo. 1999. Estimation and effects of tag-misread rates in capture-recapture studies. Canadian Journal of Fisheries and Aquatic Sciences 56: 551-559.

Schwarz, C.J. and W.T. Stobo. 2000. Estimation of juvenile survival, adult survival, and age-specific pupping probabilities for the female grey seal (*Halichoerus grypus*) on Sable Island from capture-recapture data. Canadian Journal of Fisheries and Aquatic Sciences 57: 247-253.

Scott, F. 1968. The seals of Nova Scotian Waters. Journal of Education 149: 16-24.

Sergeant, D.E. and P.F. Brodie. 1975. Identity, abundance, and present status of populations of white whales, *Delphinapterus leucas*, in North America. Journal of the Fisheries Research Board of Canada 32: 1,047-1,054.

Stobo, W.T. and K.C.T. Zwanenburg. 1990. Grey seal (*Halichoerus grypus*) pup production on Sable Island and estimates of recent production in the North west Atlantic. Pages 171-184 *in* Population Biology of Sealworm (*Pseudoterra nova decipiens*) in Relation to its Intermediate and Seal Hosts (W. D. Bowen, Ed.). Canadian Bulletin of Fisheries and Aquatic Sciences 222. Fisheries and Oceans Canada, Ottawa, ON.

Stobo, W.T., B. Beck, and L.P. Fanning. 1990a. Seasonal sealworm (*Pseudoterranova decipiens*) abundance in grey seals (*Halichoerus grypus*). Pages 147-162 *in* Population Biology of Sealworm (*Pseudoterranova decipiens*) in Relation to its Intermediate and Seal Hosts (W.D. Bowen, Ed.). Canadian Bulletin of Fisheries and Aquatic Sciences 222. Fisheries and Oceans Canada, Ottawa, ON.

Stobo, W.T., B. Beck, and J.K. Horne. 1990b. Seasonal movements of grey seals (*Halichoerus grypus*) in the Northwest Atlantic. Pages 199-213 *in* Population Biology of Sealworm (*Pseudoterranova decipiens*) in Relation to its Intermediate and Seal Hosts (W.D. Bowen, Ed.). Canadian Bulletin of Fisheries and Aquatic Sciences 222. Fisheries and Oceans Canada, Ottawa, ON.

Thomas, L., M.O. Hammill, and D.W. Bowen. 2007. Estimated size of the Northwest Atlantic grey seal population 1977-2007. Canadian Stock Assessment Secretariat, Research Document 2007/082. Fisheries and Oceans Canada, Ottawa, ON.

Trzcinski, M.K., R. Mohn, and W.D. Bowen. 2006. Continued decline of an Atlantic cod population: How important is grey seal predation? Ecological Applications 16: 2,276-2,292.

Tucker, S., W.D. Bowen, and S.J. Iverson. 2007. Dimensions of diet segregation in grey seals *Halichoerus grypus* through stable isotopes of carbon ($\delta^{13}C$) and nitrogen ($\delta^{15}N$). Marine Ecology Progress Series 339: 271-282.

Tucker, S., W.D. Bowen, and S.J. Iverson. 2008. Convergence of diet estimates from fatty acids and stable isotopes, support for long-term integration of natural diets within individual grey seals. Marine Ecology Progress Series 354: 267-276.

Winn, H.E. and L.K. Winn. 1978. The song of the humpback whale *Megaptera novaeangliae* in the West Indies. Marine Biology 47: 97-114.

Zwanenburg, K.C.T. and W.D. Bowen. 1990. Population trends of the grey seal (*Halichoerus grypus*) in Eastern Canada. Pages 185-197 *in* Population Biology of Sealworm (*Pseudoterranova decipiens*) in Relation to its Intermediate and Seal Hosts (W. D. Bowen, Ed.). Canadian Bulletin of Fisheries and Aquatic Sciences 222. Fisheries and Oceans Canada, Ottawa, ON.

15. 'THE SEA HAS WINGS': MARINE ORNITHOLOGY AT THE BEDFORD INSTITUTE OF OCEANOGRAPHY, 1971-2000

David N. Nettleship

SUMMARY

The Canadian Wildlife Service (CWS) seabird program was formally established in 1971 for the conservation and protection of populations of seabirds in coastal waters of eastern Canada. The aim was to provide detailed information on patterns of distribution and levels of abundance, ecological requirements, and factors contributing to changes in key population parameters of individual species occupying marine waters through the year. Long-term studies of seabirds in Canada have begun to reveal significant changes in the size and status of species populations breeding in eastern Canada. In general, highly specialized species such as petrels, terns, and alcids have tended to steadily decrease in numbers, whereas the more generalized and adaptable species like fulmars and gulls have increased dramatically over the same time interval. Details presented show both the accomplishments of the CWS seabird program centred at the Bedford Institute of Oceanography over its 30-year lifespan and what remains to be done. Critical evaluation of program structure is made to emphasize the need for better integration between monitoring changes in population sizes and the examination of primary demographic parameters of populations to elucidate cause-and-effect relationships, a goal only possible through merging avian science with oceanography. The importance of having, and maintaining, a biological monitoring program that identifies changes in population size and status, and the causal factors responsible is stressed. Only such a unified approach to population studies of seabirds will provide the information necessary to understand population dynamics and processes, knowledge essential to the future welfare of seabirds and the living systems that support them in Canadian waters.

Key words: avian distribution, biological monitoring, marine conservation, pelagic ecology, population biology, reproductive ecology, seabirds.
E-mail: DNNlundy@navnet.net

Seabirds are those species which spend long periods away from land, and obtain all or most of their food from the sea while flying, swimming or diving. They occupy all of the world's oceans and fall into four taxonomic orders-Sphenisciformes (penguins), Procellariformes (albatrosses, fulmars, prions, petrels, and shearwaters), Pelecaniformes (tropicbirds, pelicans, cormorants, and frigatebirds), and Charadriiformes (gulls, terns, noddies, skimmers, and auks) – comprising 13 families and about 280 species, all of whose evolutionary histories have been principally marine. Some secondary marine-associated birds such as loons, grebes, seaducks, and phalaropes are also sometimes referred to as seabirds. Overall, there are 'inshore' species that normally feed within sight of land, and 'offshore' species that generally forage over deep water in pelagic regions out of sight of land and are independent of it for feeding and resting.

Vast numbers of seabirds assemble in and utilize the inshore and offshore waters of Eastern Canada throughout the year. Breeding populations in the eastern Canadian arctic and Atlantic Canada are among the largest in the world, as are wintering populations in coastal regions of Newfoundland and Labrador, and the Newfoundland Grand Banks. Altogether, about 7.5 million pairs of 32 species breed in the region from Ellesmere Island, northernmost land in Canada, south to eastern Florida. The total for eastern Canada is roughly 7.0 million pairs comprising 24 species (ten not in eastern United States), whereas about 500,000 pairs of 23 species nest from the Gulf of Maine to eastern Florida. These populations are often at risk by human activity in marine regions, such as offshore oil drilling and mining, oil spills, commercial fisheries developments, unregulated hunting, use of toxic chemicals, and domestic and industrial sewage disposal and the promotion of populations of large gulls and other predatory species. Because seabirds return to a land-base to breed, their populations tend to be concentrated at the few sites that provide the three major requirements for successful reproduction: proximity to a suitable food supply, relative freedom from ground predators, and available nest sites. During the non-breeding season, the birds are usually restricted to nutrient-rich waters and/or upwellings and 'fronts' or other oceanographic mechanisms that bring food to the surface and concentrate it there. One obvious consequence of this clumped distribution throughout the year is a high risk of exposure of seabird populations to pollution and other hazardous human activities. Dense colonies make these birds easy prey for hunters, eggers and collectors – in fact, unregulated human predation resulted in the extirpation of the Great Auk (*Pinguinus impennis*) in Canada by 1800 and its extinction worldwide less than 50 years later (see Nettleship and Evans 1985).

Several other characteristics of seabirds endanger them as a group: they are long-lived, reach sexual maturity slowly, and have low reproductive rates with correspondingly slow recovery rates. These features of life-cycles among seabirds, often combined with wide variations in breeding performance from one year to the next, make it difficult to determine the factors responsible for change and to distinguish between natural fluctuations in environmental conditions and human-induced causes. Additional threats include disturbance of breeding colonies from tourism, human predation, introduction of alien predators into breeding sites, climate change (increasing the frequency of severe storms, flooding of nest sites, displacement to cooler regions), new fishing technologies (that reduce seabird survival and productivity by either depleting their prey or increasing the risk of by-catch, or both) and offshore oil developments and transport (for details, see Evans and Nettleship 1985, Nettleship 1991a, Piatt et al. 1991, Nettleship and Duffy 1992).

STATUS OF EASTERN CANADIAN SEABIRDS: A BRIEF OVERVIEW

Populations of most seabird species in Eastern Canada and northeastern United States were decimated by human predation and disturbance through the 18th and 19th centuries (e.g., Drury 1973-74, Nettleship and Birkhead 1985, Nettleship 1996). Once the worst human pressures were removed at the beginning of the 20th century by the signing of the Migratory Bird Treaty of 1916 between Canada and the United States, remnant populations began to show signs of recovery. The general increase continued until the 1930s, by which time some species such as the large gulls (Great Black-backed Gull *Larus marinus*, Herring Gull *L. argentatus*) were more numerous than they had been before the 19th century exploitation. Most species (Northern Gannet *Sula bassanus*, cormorants *Phalacrocorax* spp., terns *Sterna* spp.) showed a slow but steady growth during this period. But others, such as the alcids (Razorbill *Alca torda*, Common Murre *Uria aalge*, Atlantic Puffin *Fratercula arctica*), did not regain their former abundance and distribution, especially towards the southern limit of their breeding ranges and in the more remote and inaccessible regions (e.g., Gulf of St. Lawrence North Shore, southern Labrador) where protection could not be enforced (Nettleship 1977a, Nettleship and Birkhead 1985).

A marked change in population histories took place after 1940. By contrast to the earlier growth and expansion shown by most species, a general slowing down or reversal of population trends began. Large gulls and some other species capable of utilizing fish offal from the expanding commercial fisheries seem not to have been involved in this decrease; their population growth continued, often at a remarkably rapid rate. However, the more specialized species (particularly the terns and auks) in all parts of the North Atlantic began to experience sudden and dramatic population declines that appeared to be associated with the ever-increasing human exploitation of the marine environment (Nettleship 1977a, 1991a, 1996; Evans and Nettleship 1985; Nettleship and Evans 1985).

This increased awareness of the vulnerability of seabirds to this plethora of threats, combined with the discovery of oil on the North Slope of Alaska in 1968 and the likelihood of extensive oil drilling on Canada's continental shelf and arctic islands, led the Canadian Wildlife Service (CWS) to initiate a comprehensive investigation of seabirds in eastern Canada in 1971 under the direction of H.J. Boyd (Chief, Migratory Bird Populations – Eastern Canada) with D.N. Nettleship as program head in Ottawa and R.G.B. Brown at the Bedford Institute of Oceanography (BIO; see Nettleship 1972a, 1973a, 1977a). In 1975-76, owing to federal regionalization, it was decided to relocate the Ottawa unit (G. Calderwood, B. Dodge, D. Nettleship) to BIO to consolidate the CWS Seabird Research Unit.

CWS SEABIRD PROGRAM MAJOR CONCERNS, RESEARCH PRIORITIES AND DEVELOPMENT

At the outset (1971), emphasis was placed on Arctic and Eastern Canada, where the breeding populations of Canadian seabirds are among the largest and most at risk to proposed industrial activities, especially offshore oil drilling. The initial aims of the CWS seabird program were to:

- catalogue breeding sites (locations, species composition, population sizes) in the eastern Canadian arctic and in the Atlantic north of 40°N and west of 40°W;
- measure productivity and other primary demographic parameters of representative species of differing ecological types to allow factors responsible for observed changes in populations to be identified and assessed; and
- collect quantitative observations of the distributions of seabirds at sea in the same area to show features of water habitat usage through the annual cycle, and identify areas of importance and environmental requirements.

The overall objective was to gather and compile old and new information on seabird colonies in order to develop a seabird monitoring system sufficiently sensitive to detect real population changes in bird numbers, both at sea and at breeding colonies, and to establish a baseline from which to measure future change and to determine cause-and-effect relationships. This was to be accomplished by the establishment of a comprehensive biological monitoring system (BMS) estimated to require 20 years to put in place. The task was formidable. The geographic area is immense, and there was almost no existing information. Distribution and species composition of the major colonies in Atlantic Canada were reasonably well-known, but estimates of the sizes of those populations were restricted to orders of magnitude at best. Details of eastern Canadian arctic seabirds were very sketchy, limited to what could be gleaned from the records of 19th century arctic explorers and the more recent work done in the mid-1950s on Thick-billed Murres *Uria lomvia* by Leslie M. Tuck (see Tuck 1961). Vast lengths of coastlines in the central and eastern arctic and in the less remote regions of Atlantic Canada remained to be examined. Immediate needs were clear: statistically sensitive census techniques had to be developed and tested, species and colonies had to be identified and selected for long-term biological monitoring (changes in population size and reproductive performance), and existing procedures for recording seabirds at sea had to be refined and developed further for application in the northwest Atlantic.

By 1975, considerable progress had been made. Survey procedures for colony census work were established (see Nettleship 1972b, 1976a; Birkhead and Nettleship 1980), and for recording birds at sea (see Brown *et al.* 1975a: Appendix 1). Between 1971 and 1975, D. Nettleship and a small number of permanent (M. Channing), part-time summer (R. Kardos, A. Lock), and contract (C. Elliott) workers surveyed thousands of kilometres of coasts by air and sea and recorded several thousand seabird colonies, only a small number known previously (Fig. 1; for survey details, see Map 1i "Effort – Colony Surveys" in Brown *et al.* 1975a). Colony locations were mapped from the air, water, and land, and measures were taken to estimate breeding population sizes (see Nettleship 1974; Brown et al. 1975a; Nettleship and Smith 1975; Nettleship 1976a, 1980). Quantitative observations of seabirds at sea were collected over a set of matrices covering the study region by full-time (T. Davis, P. Germain, E. Tull) and many part-time observers under the direction of R. Brown using a system of 10-minute watches that culminated in a total of over 60,000 records by 1975 (for details of at-sea effort, see Maps 1a-h "Effort" in Brown *et al.* 1975a), and four times as large by 1984 (Brown 1986). Combined, these colony survey and pelagic distribution data allowed seabirds to be viewed as marine animals, part of marine ecosystems with their distributions linked to aspects of physical and biological oceanography, and for use in the environmental assessment of offshore hydrocarbon exploration, extraction, and transport (see Nettleship 1977a; Brown 1980, 1981; Nettleship 1991a; Piatt et al. 1991).

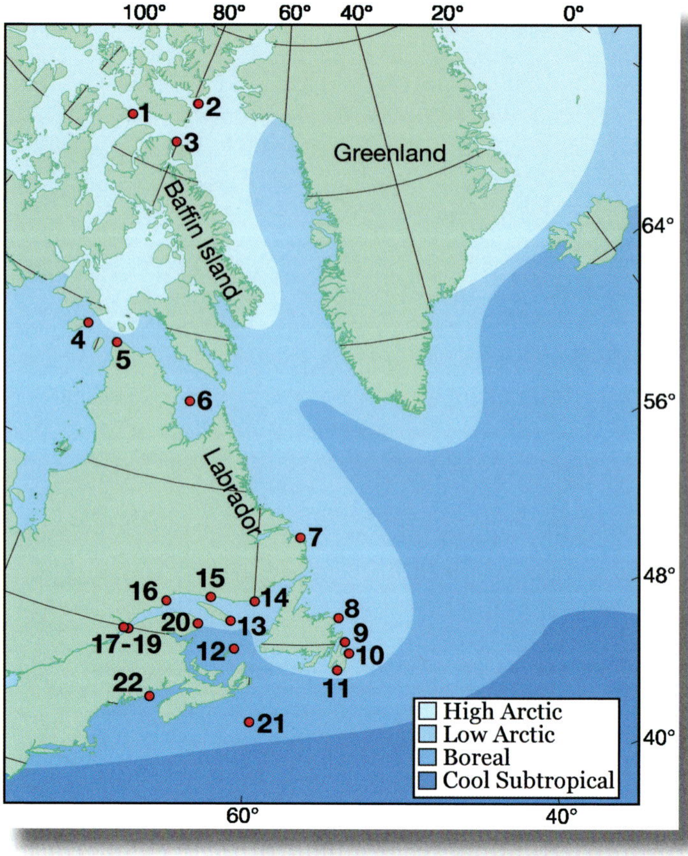

Figure 1. Locations of major seabird CWS-BMS monitoring sites in eastern Canada by oceanographic zonation where comprehensive baseline studies have been performed, 1972-2000 (see Table 2 for site names and species studied at each location). Oceanographic zonation in the northwest Atlantic and eastern Canadian arctic after Salomonsen (1965, 1972), Dunbar (1968), and Ashmole (1971).

The preliminary results of these studies were summarized in *The Atlas of Eastern Canadian Seabirds* (Brown *et al.* 1975a) and *Ecological Sites in Northern Canada* (Nettleship and Smith 1975), and a review *Seabird Resources of Eastern Canada: Status, Problems and Prospects* (Nettleship 1977a) highlighted accomplishments, identified information gaps, and focussed attention on seabird management needs and future research. Supplements and updates followed on breeding distributions and reproductive ecology (Nettleship 1980, Nettleship and Birkhead 1985, Nettleship and Hunt 1988, Nettleship 1996) and on pelagic distributions (Brown 1986, Lock et al. 1994). Together, these databases provide some of the information needed for assessing present and proposed resource developments in coastal and offshore waters in eastern Canada (Nettleship 1991a, 1991b, 1993, 1996).

Table 1. Principal factors studied in each component of the Biological Monitoring System (BMS) of the CWS Seabird Program in Arctic and Eastern Canada.

Distribution and Abundance	Demography	Causation
General breeding distribution	Phenology of breeding	Habitat needs
Patterns in distribution and abundance	Age at first breeding	Climate/ ocean change
Population size by site	Clutch size and fecundity	Mortality factors
Population change by site	Fledging success	Chick growth
	Recruitment rate	Body condition
	Survival	Diet
	Effects of age on demography	Food availability

RESEARCH AND CONSERVATION STRATEGY

Reproductive Ecology

The focus of this part of the CWS Seabird Program in eastern Canada through the 1970s and 1980s to the end of the 20th century was the Biological Monitoring System (BMS) component of the program (Nettleship 1977a, 1991a, 1993, 1997): i.e., measurement of reproductive performance and other demographic parameters of key seabird species at representative sample sites (e.g., Nettleship 1972c, 1977b; Gaston and Nettleship 1981, 1982; Nettleship et al. 1984a; Nettleship and Evans 1985; Birkhead and Nettleship 1987a, b, c; Nettleship and Chapdelaine 1988; Gaston et al. 1993). Based upon the findings of the 1972-75 colony surveys, a network of long-term biological studies was set up in Eastern and Arctic Canada that samples: (1) each oceanic zone (high arctic, low arctic, boreal); (2) species that are generalist and specialist, sedentary and migratory, low and high trophic feeders; and (3) colonies near the centre and edge of those species' breeding ranges. A list of the main features studied is given in Table 1. The populations selected for monitoring either represent a significant proportion of the species' total numbers or make up a large fraction of the avian biomass of the region. The aim was to detect long-term geographic shifts in density as well as overall change in population size and to gather demographic data that may elucidate causes of population change.

In arctic regions (north of 60°N), comprehensive baseline studies have been established at six locations since 1975 (see Fig. 1 and Table 2: sites 1-6) – Prince Leopold Island, Barrow Strait (site 1); Coburg Island, Jones Sound (site 2); Cape Hay, Bylot Island (site 3); Cape Pembroke, Coats Island (site 4), Eastern Digges Island, Hudson Bay (site 5); and Akpatok Island, Ungava Bay (site 6) – covering the four major seabird species breeding in the high and low arctic oceanic zones: Northern Fulmar *Fulmarus glacialis*, Black-legged Kittiwake *Rissa tridactyla*, Thick-billed Murre *Uria lomvia*, and Black Guillemot *Cepphus grylle* (Fig. 2). These species are supplemented by less exhaustive documentation of breeding biology for Glaucous Gull *Larus hyperboreus* and Ivory Gull *Pagophila eburnea*.

South of 60°N, there are 16 baseline sites (see Fig. 1 and Table 2: sites 7-22) for monitoring 13 principal seabird species: Leach's Storm-Petrel *Oceanodroma leucorhoa*, Northern Gannet *Sula bassanus*, Double-crested Cormorant *Phalacrocorax auritus*, Black-legged Kittiwake, Herring Gull *Larus argentatus*, Great Black-backed Gull *L. marinus*, Common Tern *Sterna hirundo*, Arctic Tern *S. paradisaea*, Razorbill *Alca torda*, Thick-billed Murre, Common Murre *Uria aalge*, Black Guillemot, and Atlantic Puffin *Fratercula arctica* (Fig. 2). These monitoring studies are supplemented by studies on Great Cormorant *Phalacrocorax carbo*, Ring-billed Gull *Larus delawarensis*, Caspian Tern *Sterna caspia*, Roseate Tern *Sterna dougalli*, and Common Eider *Somateria mollissma*.

The coastal and oceanic regions of northeastern North America can be divided into six major subdivisions based on oceanographic characteristics: (A) High Arctic region north of 68°N including Baffin Bay and Smith-Jones-Lancaster Sounds; (B) Low Arctic region comprising three parts: Davis and Hudson Straits, and Hudson Bay; (C) Labrador region extending from Cape Chidley south to the Strait of Belle Isle; (D) East Newfoundland region which encompasses the east and south shore west to Cabot Strait including St. Pierre et Miquelon; (E) Gulf of St. Lawrence region which includes the St. Lawrence River outflow and Estuary; and (F) Scotian Shelf-Bay of Fundy-Gulf of Maine region which extends from northeastern Cape Breton southwest into the Gulf of Maine including Sable Island, Grand Manan Archipelago and Machias Seal Island, areas influenced by the Gulf Stream. Each of the six regions

Table 2. Major CWS Biological Monitoring System seabird sites in Arctic and Eastern Canada where comprehensive baseline studies (Type I, see Birkhead and Nettleship 1980) of representative species populations have been conducted, 1967-2000. Numbers refer to colony locations shown on Figure 1.

Oceanic region (Location)	Monitoring species[1]
High/Low Arctic (north 60*N):	
1. Prince Leopold Island	NOFU, BLKI, GLGU, TBMU, BLGU
2. Coburg Island	BLKI, TBMU
3. Cape Hay, Bylot I.	BLKI, TBMU
4. Coats I.	TBMU
5. E. Digges I.	TBMU
6. Akpatok I.	TBMU
Low Arctic (south 60°N):	
7. Gannet Islands	NOFU, BLKI, RAZO, TBMU, COMU, ATPU
8. Funk I.	NOGA, COMU, ATPU
9. Baccalieu I.	LSPE, NOGA, ATPU
10. Witless Bay Is.	LSPE, BLKI, HEGU, GBBG, COMU, ATPU
11. Cape St. Mary's	NOGA, COMU
12. Bird Rocks, Magdalen Is.	NOGA, BLKI, RAZO, COMU, TBMU
13. Gullcliff Bay, Anticosti I.	NOGA, BLKI
14. St. Mary's Is.	RAZO, BLGU
15. Mingan	COTE, ARTE
16. Carrousel I.	BLKI
Boreal:	
17. Brandy Pot Is.	BLGU
18. Pilgrim Is.	DCCO, RAZO
19. Ile-aux-Pommes	DCCO
20. Bonaventure I.	NOGA, BLKI, COMU
21. Sable I.	HEGU, GBBG, COTE, ARTE
22. Machias Seal I.	COTE, ARTE, ATPU

[1] Species codes: NOFU, Northern Fulmar; LSPE, Leach's Storm-petrel; NOGA, Northern Gannet; DCCO, Double-crested Cormorant; HEGU, Herring Gull; GLGU, Glaucous Gull; GBBG, Great Black-backed Gull; BLKI, Black-legged Kittiwake; COTE, Common Tern; ARTE, Arctic Tern; COMU, Common Murre; TBMU, Thick-billed Murre; RAZO, Razorbill; BLGU, Black Guillemot; ATPU, Atlantic Puffin.

Figure 2. Major breeding seabird species studied in the CWS-BMS program in eastern Canada, 1972-2000, with summary details of regions of occupancy for breeding, morphometrics, mode of feeding and major foods, population status, and major threats: (A) Petrels, Gannets, Cormorants, and Gulls; and (B) Terns and Auks. All photos by Bas Teunis except Leach's Storm-petrel (by D. Jones), Double-crested Cormorant (by John Gerlach), Glaucous Gull (by David Nettleship), Dovekie (by Daniel Roby), and Thick-billed Murre (by Erick Greene).

(A) Petrels, Gannets, Cormorants, and Gulls

Northern Fulmar
Fulmarus glacialis

Zones: High & Low Arctic
Body length = 48 cm (19")
Wingspan = 107 cm (42")
Feeding: surface picking & seizing
Diet: fish, crustaceans, squid
Status: stable or decreasing (arctic)
Threats: oil spills, human predation

Herring Gull
Larus argentatus

Zones: Low Arctic & Boreal
Body length: 61 cm (24")
Wingspan: 147 cm (58")
Feeding: surface seizing & robbing
Diet: fish, invertebrates, birds
Status: increasing (offal, garbage)
Threats: oil, toxic chemicals, human disturbance

Leach's Storm- petrel
Oceanodroma leucorhoa

Zones: Low Arctic & Boreal
Body length: 20 cm (8")
Wingspan: 46 cm (18")
Feeding: surface pattering & picking
Diet: larval fish & zooplankton
Status: decreasing (NL, NB, NS)
Threats: gull & alien predation

Glaucous Gull
Larus hyperboreus

Zones: High & Low Arctic
Body length: 71 cm (28")
Wingspan: 158 cm (62")
Feeding: surface seizing & robbing
Diet: fish, invertebrates, birds
Status: decreasing or stable
Threats: oil, toxic chemicals

Northern Gannet
Sula bassanus

Zones: Low Arctic & Boreal
Body length: 93 cm (37")
Wingspan: 172 cm (68")
Feeding: deep plunge-diving
Diet: fish (herring, mackerel, capelin)
Status: increasing or stable
Threats: oil spills, human disturbance

Great Black-backed Gull
Larus marinus

Zones: Low Arctic & Boreal
Body length: 75 cm (30")
Wingspan: 160 cm (63")
Feeding: surface seizing & robbing
Diet: fish, invertebrates, birds
Status: stable or increasing
Threats: oil, toxic chemicals, human disturbance

Double-crested Cormorant
Phalacrocorax auritus

Zones: Boreal & Low Arctic
Body length: 84 cm (33")
Wingspan: 134 cm (53")
Feeding: pursuit diving (feet)
Diet: fish (sculpins, gunnels, clupeids)
Status: increasing (QC, NB, PEI, NS)
Threats: hunting, oil, toxic chemicals

Black-legged Kittiwake
Rissa tridactyla

Zones: High/Low Arctic & Boreal
Body length: 41 cm (16")
Wingspan: 91 cm (36")
Feeding: surface picking & seizing
Diet: fish, crustaceans
Status: stable or increasing
Threats: oil spills, human disturbance

(B) Terns and Auks

Common Tern
Sterna hirundo

Zones: Boreal & Low Arctic
Body length: 36 cm (14")
Wingspan: 80 cm (31")
Feeding: surface plunging
Diet: small fish, crustaceans
Status: decreasing
Threats: human disturbance

Thick-billed Murre
Uria lomvia

Zones: High & Low Arctic
Body length: 45 cm (18")
Wingspan: 76 cm (30")
Feeding: pursuit diving (wings) deep depth
Diet: small fish, crustaceans
Status: decreasing (since 1950s)
Threats: oil, human predation, and disturbances, fish nets

Arctic Tern
Sterna paradisaea

Zones: High/Low Arctic & Boreal
Body length: 36 cm (14")
Wingspan: 80 cm (31")
Feeding: surface plunging
Diet: small fish, crustaceans
Status: decreasing
Threats: human disturbance

Razorbill
Alca torda

Zones: Low Arctic & Boreal
Body length: 43 cm (17")
Wingspan: 64 cm (25")
Feeding: pursuit diving (wings) moderate depth
Diet: small fish, crustaceans
Status: decreasing (NL, QC, NB, NS)
Threats: oil, human predation, and disturbances, fish nets

Dovekie
Alle alle

Zones: High/Low Arctic & Boreal
Body length: 22 cm (9")
Wingspan: 32 cm (13")
Feeding: pursuit diving (wings) shallow
Diet: mainly crustaceans, larval fish
Status: decreasing (Greenland)
Threats: oil spills, human predation

Black Guillemot
Cepphus grylle

Zones: High/Low Arctic & Boreal
Body length: 33 cm (13")
Wingspan: 58 cm (23")
Feeding: pursuit diving (wings) shallow depth
Diet: small bottom-fish, crustaceans
Status: decreasing or stable
Threats: oil spills, alien predators

Common Murre
Uria aalge

Zones: Low Arctic & Boreal
Body length: 42 cm (17")
Wingspan: 71 cm (28")
Feeding: pursuit diving (wings) deep depth
Diet: small fish, crustaceans
Status: decreasing except east NL
Threats: oil, human predation, and disturbance fish nets

Atlantic Puffin
Fratercula arctica

Zones: Low Arctic & Boreal
Body length: 32 cm (13")
Wingspan: 55 cm (22")
Feeding: pursuit diving (wings) moderate depth
Diet: fish (capelin, sandlance), crustaceans
Status: decreasing (NL, QC, NB, NS)
Threats: oil spills, human predation, and disturbances, fish nets

are reviewed and discussed below highlighting major studies performed by the CWS Seabird Research Unit and its associates between 1971 and 2000 at BIO.

High Arctic — This region comprises Baffin Bay and associated water systems including the North Water, and outflows from the Arctic Ocean through Nares Strait, Jones and Lancaster sounds. It forms one of the most biologically productive regions in Arctic America including Greenland. The only seabird work done in the region prior to 1972 was by CWS biologist L.Tuck in 1957 at the Thick-billed Murre colony near Cape Hay, Bylot Island (Tuck 1961). In 1972 and 1973, known and suspected colonies were confirmed, discoveries of previously unknown sites made, and the first photo documentation of principal colonies in the region including the four Thick-billed Murre and six Northern Fulmar colonies (Nettleship 1973a, 1974; Brown et al. 1975a; Nettleship and Smith 1975). By 1975, BMS monitoring sites had been selected and comprehensive breeding studies planned at Prince Leopold Island, Coburg Island, and Cape Hay, Bylot Island (Nettleship 1973a, 1977b; Birkhead and Nettleship 1980, 1981; Gaston and Nettleship 1981; Nettleship et al. 1990). Sites of secondary and tertiary importance were also documented and surveyed by the SRU team, with additional sightings of small gull colonies provided by environmental consultants flying aerial surveys for the petroleum industry (oil and gas) between 1974-76 (e.g., LGL Limited for Polar Gas and Norlands Petroleums Limited). The establishment of BMS monitoring sites in the High Arctic region was complete by 1979.

Low Arctic — The region south of 68°N divides into two subareas: (1) Davis Strait from 60° to 68°N with cold polar water of the East Baffin Current running north to south along coastal Baffin Island and warmer water flowing northward along the west Greenland coast, and (2) Hudson Strait receiving the outflow of relatively warmer waters with lower salinity from Hudson Bay. These two contrasting subareas form a rich community of seabirds with concentrations of breeding birds at three colonies between Merchants Bay to Exeter Sound (Cape Searle, S. Reid Bay, Exeter Island), Ungava Bay (Akpatok), and Digges Sound (Cape Wolstenholme, Eastern Digges Island). Smaller, but important, colonies also occur at Hantzsch Island (eastern Edgell Island) off Resolution Island, SE tip of Baffin Island and Coats Island (Cape Pembroke) in Hudson Bay.

Although the Hudson Strait Thick-billed Murre colonies have been known for some time (since 1615 and earlier) and studied in the mid-1950s (Tuck 1961), only the Cape Searle colony had been described before 1972 when D. Nettleship either discovered or rediscovered the others during his extensive and intensive 1972-73 Baffin Island aerial surveys (D. Nettleship in Brown et al. 1975a, Nettleship and Smith 1975). In 1972, all Northern Fulmar and Thick-billed Murre colonies known in the Low Arctic region (Davis and Hudson Straits) were visited, locations documented and defined, and preliminary population size estimates made using aerial photography and direct observation (Nettleship and Smith 1975). Comprehensive breeding studies (BMS 'Type I' monitoring) of Thick-billed Murres followed, first at Eastern Digges Island and Coats Island by A. Gaston and team from 1980-84 (Gaston et al. 1985, 1987, 1993) and then at Akpatok Island, Ungava Bay, by G. Chapdelaine between 1982-84 (Chapdelaine et al. 1986). The establishment of BMS monitoring sites for Thick-billed Murres was complete by 1982, with Hudson Strait and northeastern Hudson Bay comprising the best documented monitoring areas for Thick-billed Murres in Arctic Canada (Gaston 1991a, Nettleship 1996). Additional baseline work remains to be done on Northern Fulmars at Cape Searle (Qaualuit Island), S. Reid Bay, and Exeter Island, and S. Reid Bay and Hantzsch Island for Thick-billed Murres.

Labrador — The Labrador Sea is bounded to the west by the coast of Labrador and to the north and east by southeast Baffin Island and Greenland respectively, and from Cape Farewell southwest to the northern edge of Strait of Belle Isle. The cold waters of coastal Labrador are formed by the East Baffin Land Current and the outflow from Hudson Strait to produce the Labrador Current which flows south along East Newfoundland and west along the north shore of the Gulf of St. Lawrence. The waters, though modified by warmer waters of the offshore Labrador Sea, are classified as low arctic (Nettleship and Evans 1985). Hydrographic features and areas of upwelling waters restrict most colonially-breeding seabirds to regions south of Nain (ca. 56°N), with the largest concentrations off Groswater Bay.

The coastal waterbirds of Labrador were first examined through the 1920s-30s (Austin 1932, Todd 1963) and 1950s (Tuck 1953, 1961), with detailed studies performed by CWS-SRU through the 1970s to the mid 1980s and early 1990s. The most complete island surveys were made by A. Lock and team in 1978-79 (by air and small boats), with comprehensive reproductive studies (BMS Type I) performed by D. Nettleship and T. Birkhead at the Gannet Islands from 1981-85 and 1992 (Nettleship and Birkhead 1981; Birkhead and Nettleship 1982a, 1982b, 1983, 1984, 1988; Nettleship and Evans 1985; Birkhead and Nettleship 1987a, b, c; Verspoor et al. 1987; Birkhead and Nettleship 1995), along with other researches (e.g., Birkhead et al. 1980, 1985a, 1985b). A detailed analysis of breeding distribution and census data from 1978 to 1992 appears in Nettleship and Glenn (1992), and reviewed in Lock et al. (1994). In summary, more than 80% of the 424 seabird colonies recorded in coastal Labrador comprised large *Larus* gulls (Herring Gull, Glaucous Gull, Great Black-backed Gull), with most other species (Northern Fulmar, Leach's Storm-petrel, Black-legged Kittiwake, Razorbill, Common Murre, Thick-billed Murre, Atlantic Puffin) concentrated at only six sites: southeast Nain, Quaker Hat, Groswater Bay, Outer Gannet Island, Gannet Islands, and Bird Islands.

East Newfoundland — The main water body of the Labrador Current flows south from Labrador along the east coast of Newfoundland and on the Grand Banks of Newfoundland where it meets and merges with the northeast moving branch of the Gulf Stream called the North Atlantic Current (see Nettleship and Evans 1985, Brown 1986). The interaction of water masses of differing densities and temperatures combined with upwellings create areas of exceptionally high primary and secondary productivity because of the concentration of nutrients. These 'hot spots' are centred from the banks immediately south of Notre Dame Bay along the coastal shelf to Cape Race and west to Placentia Bay. The locations of upwellings are readily identified by the immense concentrations of colonially-breeding seabirds.

Incidental observations of seabirds in east Newfoundland date back to the early voyages of discovery (Nettleship and Evans 1985). But accurate record keeping only began in the 1930s and 1940s with the first synthesis of existing information made by Peters and Burleigh (1951). However, it was L.Tuck, Newfoundland's first federal wildlife biologist (CWS), who initiated the first systematic surveys and breeding studies of seabirds in Newfoundland and Labrador. The work culminated in the now classic monograph entitled 'The Murres' (Tuck 1961) and numerous regional summaries including 'The Birds of Newfoundland' (Tuck 1967). Detailed studies of the reproductive ecology of seabirds began in 1967-69 with a study of the Atlantic Puffin (Nettleship 1970, 1972c), which together with exploratory pelagic seabird studies by R. Brown, set the stage for the establishment of part of the CWS Seabird Research Unit at BIO in 1971.

Systematic survey and census work using standardized methodologies began in 1972 with the development of a system of population analysis from photography for Northern Gannets and Common Murres at Funk Island and applied elsewhere (Nettleship 1976a, 1976b). In 1973, the first comprehensive aerial and ground surveys of seabird colonies in Newfoundland were conducted (designed and supervised by D. Nettleship). The entire coastline of the Island of Newfoundland was flown by L. Tuck and A. Lock in a fixed-wing single-engine aircraft to document gull colonies and uncover any major concentrations of breeding seabirds not yet known. The ground surveys at the major colonies, executed by R. Montgomerie, ranged from the Wadham Islands and Baccalieu southeast to Witless Bay and Cape St. Mary's. Repeat ground surveys were performed in 1979-80 by SRU-CWS members including T. Birkhead, D. Cairns, G. Calderwood, A. Linton, E. Greene, D. Nettleship, and E. Verspoor. In 1980, study plots (Type I) for Common Murres were established at Cape St. Mary's to allow long-term monitoring by provincial wardens stationed at the Cape each summer under the supervision of D. Minty, Newfoundland Wildlife Division (see Piatt and McLagen 1987, Piatt et al. 1991). Repeat surveys of gannets and murres took place through the 1970s and 1980s (Nettleship 1976b, Birkhead and Nettleship 1980, Nettleship and Chapdelaine 1988, Nettleship 1992b, D. Nettleship in Nelson 2002: 85-94), with emphasis on the breeding biology and population status of Leach's Storm-petrel, *Larus* gulls, Black-legged Kittiwake, and auks breeding on the Witless Bay islands, particularly at Great Island (Nettleship 1972c, Nettleship and Evans 1985). Other studies were also conducted by Memorial University of Newfoundland (MUN) scientists, particularly by W. Threlfall and his students (K. Haycock, S. Mahoney, J. Maunder, D. Snow, and others) on Gull Island and W. Montevecchi and students on Baccalieu Island. Much of the MUN research is summarized in Nettleship (1980), Brown and Nettleship (1984a), Nettleship and Birkhead (1985), and Montevecchi and Tuck (1987).

Gulf of St. Lawrence — The Gulf of St. Lawrence has two subareas: the northern and southern parts. The northern Gulf includes the St. Lawrence Estuary, North Shore, Anticosti Island, Gaspé Peninsula, and Magdalen Islands including the Bird Rocks. The southern Gulf encompasses the Gulf waters of New Brunswick, Prince Edward Island, and Nova Scotia. The area as a whole is important for breeding seabirds. Considerable survey effort occurred in the past, from the turn of the 20th century related to complaints of damage by Double-crested Cormorants to salmon fisheries of the Gaspé coast (Taverner 1915) to the 1920s along the North Shore of the Gulf where the first Canadian bird sanctuaries were established (Lewis 1925), Bonaventure Island and the Bird Rocks. A standardized method of survey and census was established in 1972 and has continued since that time (Nettleship 1973b, 1975, 1976a, 1992b; Nettleship and Lock 1973; Nettleship and Taylor 1975; Nettleship and Chapdelaine 1988). In 1976, responsibility for the seabird monitoring system set up in the Gulf was assigned to CWS biologist G. Chapdelaine, CWS Québec Region Headquarters (Québec City, QC) with assistance from P. Brousseau and others. Cooperative studies by CWS Atlantic and Québec regions continued through the 1980s and 1990s (Chapdelaine et al. 1987, Nettleship and Chapdelaine 1988, Nettleship 1992b).

Some information for the Gulf South Shore and Prince Edward Island existed prior to 1972 (e.g., Squires 1952, 1976; Godfrey 1954; Tufts 1962, 1986), but studies specific to seabirds began later (see Brown et al. 1975a) with detailed surveys performed through the 1980s by A. Lock and reported in Erskine (1992).

Scotian Shelf-Bay of Fundy-Gulf of Maine — This region divides easily into two parts: the Scotian Shelf, which extends from Cape North (Cape Breton Island) southeast to Scatarie Island and west along the Nova Scotian south shore to Freeport and the Bay of Fundy, and the Gulf of Maine including the Grand Manan archipelago and Machias Seal Island. The waters are 'boreal' and influenced by the outflow from the Gulf of St. Lawrence and to a lesser extent by eddies offshore from the Gulf Stream running northwards along the United States Atlantic seaboard (for details, see Smith et al. 2014).

Seabird monitoring in both subareas are well advanced, particularly in the New England States and regions adjacent to Grand Manan and the New Brunswick mainland (see Pettingill 1939, Palmer 1949, Drury 1973-74, Erwin 1979, Erwin and Korschgen 1979, Buckley and Buckley 1984). Colony surveys along the southern coast of Nova Scotia were largely opportunistic prior to 1971 (see Tufts 1962, 1986) when the first aerial census of the entire province was performed by A. Lock under contract to CWS's newly created Seabird Research Unit. That survey provided the first view of the pattern of distribution of colonially-breeding seabirds in Nova Scotia: mainly cormorants, *Larus* gulls, and terns (Lock and Ross 1973, Brown et al. 1975a). In 1972, detailed long-term census studies were organized by D. Nettleship at Machias Seal Island (including Leach's Storm-petrel, Arctic Tern, Atlantic Puffin), followed by reproductive ecology studies of Leach's Storm-petrel (Linton 1979), Great and Double-crested Cormorants (Ross 1973), *Larus* gulls (Lock 1973) and terns (McLaren 1981) at Sable Island, and Machias Seal Island (Newell 1985). Numerous seabird studies were also executed on Kent Island (Grand Manan) by Bowdoin College Field Station (Maine) researchers that provided major 'Type I' contributions on the breeding biology and population sizes of Leach's Storm-petrel, Herring Gull, and Black Guillemot (Gross 1935, Paynter 1949, Winn 1950, Huntington and Burtt 1972, Wheelwright 1993).

Since the early 1980s, most seabird surveys along the Nova Scotian south coast have been conducted by A. Lock. The results of these extensive colony surveys on cormorants, gulls, and terns have been summarized in Erskine (1992) and Lock et al. (1994). Considerable effort has been made to produce management plans for terns including the endangered Roseate Tern (Kirkham and Nettleship 1985, 1987; Lock et al. 1994). Additional work was performed by the Nova Scotia Department of Lands and Forests (now Natural Resources) on the distribution, breeding biology and feeding ecology of Great and Double-crested Cormorants (Milton and Austin-Smith 1983, Milton et al. 1995). Population studies continued through the 1980s and 1990s: gulls and terns at Sable Island (A. Lock), Common Loons at Kejimkujik National Park (J. Kerekes), and terns (A. Smith), Razorbills, Common Murres and Atlantic Puffins (A. Diamond, D. Nettleship, and others) on Machias Seal Island.

Conclusions — The success of the CWS Seabird Program as initiated in 1971 and the status of monitoring the major demographic characteristics of the principal seabird species breeding in Eastern and Arctic Canada was summarized briefly in the autumn 1992 issue of *Bird Trends* (Nettleship 1992a, Gaston 1992b, and others), and elaborated upon in Nettleship (1993, 1997). Perhaps the most accurate way of making the assessment is through an examination of the more comprehensive trend data on eastern Canadian seabirds that have been summarized in three groups of publications:

- Those that examine trends in populations of species that reproduce in the same geographic area (e.g., Nettleship and Lock 1973; Nettleship 1973b, 1974, 1977b; Brown and Nettleship 1981; Gaston et al. 1985; Nettleship et al. 1990; Gaston 1991a; Chapdelaine and Brousseau 1992; Lock 1992; Chapdelaine 1995);
- Those that treat populations of single species within a region or at a specific colony location (e.g., Nettleship 1975, 1976b, 1991b, 1992b, 1992c; Gaston and Nettleship 1981; Brown and Nettleship 1984a; Nettleship et al. 1984a; Nettleship and Chapdelaine 1988; Nettleship et al. 1990; Gaston 1992b; Gaston et al. 1993; Kampp et al. 1994; Chapdelaine and Bédard 1995; Nettleship and Duffy 1995); and
- Those that deal with topics critical to the welfare of seabirds and to the management of population data (e.g., Bartonek and Nettleship 1979; Brown and Nettleship 1984b; Nettleship et al. 1984b; Nettleship and Hunt 1988; Furness and Nettleship 1991; Gaston 1991b; Nettleship 1991a, 1992d, 1993, 1994, 1996; Piatt et al. 1991; Blanchard and Nettleship 1992; Chardine 1992; Nettleship and Duffy 1992, 1995; Lock et al. 1994).

Pelagic Ecology

The second part of the CWS seabird program at BIO, organized by R. Brown, provided standardized quantitative information on pelagic seabird distributions, collected from ships at sea in the western North Atlantic, north of 40° N and west of 40° W. The rapid growth in public concern over environmental issues through the 1960s caused governments to initiate studies to assess the impact of human activities on the environment. Seabirds played a significant role in this change in attitude, owing to the widespread publicity given to them about the effects of toxic chemical poisoning (gannets), oil spills (murres and other diving species), and drowning in fish nets: e.g., murres in the west Greenland salmon fishery (Tull et al. 1972) and Newfoundland-Labrador (Piatt et al. 1984, Piatt and Nettleship 1987). By the mid 1970s, numerous large scale environmental impact studies were underway to determine the side-effects of industrial expansion in the Arctic (oil and gas drilling, lead-zinc mining, etc.) where so many seabirds breed, and south along the Atlantic continental shelf to the Newfoundland Grand Banks where high numbers of North American and European seabirds spend the winter. There was a clear need to produce a quantitative, statistically meaningful database that provides information on species composition and seasonal changes in their pelagic distributions and numbers over the annual cycle. These data sets are essential to assess and minimize risks of both ongoing and proposed projects to seabirds, and to determine likely impacts on the marine environment.

For such a database, quantitative information on where the birds are and how many of them there are is required, not just for one moment in time or at one location, but throughout the geographic region of interest through the entire year. Before 1970, data on at-sea (pelagic) seabird distributions were sparse and lacked a statistical base, largely confined to a small number of established shipping lanes and poorly quantified by species or location, with no documentation of where birds were absent. The first attempts to quantify the geographical and seasonal changes of seabirds in the North Atlantic were made by P. Jespersen and V.C. Wynne-Edwards, whose pioneering studies show the importance of repeated, quantitative observation, to understand distributions and levels of abundance (Jespersen 1924, 1930; Wynne-Edwards 1935). Following these efforts, came important contributions by Moore (1941, 1951), Baker (1947), and Rankin and Duffey (1948), summarized by Bourne (1963) and Ashmole (1971). But it was not until the late 1960s and early 1970s that surveys of seabirds at sea tried to relate the observations of the birds with the oceanography of the waters they occupied. It was the CWS-SRU at BIO that led the way through its comprehensive studies in waters off Atlantic Canada and the eastern Canadian arctic (Brown et al. 1975a, Nettleship and Gaston 1978, Nettleship 1980, Gaston and Nettleship 1981, Brown 1986).

The CWS pelagic seabird program was organized and initiated in 1969 by R. Brown and P. Germain to undertake the systematic studies of the distribution of seabirds at sea in the Gulf of St. Lawrence, the western North Atlantic and Canadian Arctic waters. The program, entitled PIROP (Programme Intégré de Recherches sur les Oiseaux Pélagiques), operated completely by the CWS since early 1972, employed the relatively large oceanographic fleet of ships based at BIO and other parts of eastern Canada to collect quantitative observations in the eastern Canadian arctic and in the Atlantic north of 40°N and west of 40°W. What began as opportunistic participation by R. Brown on BIO cruises in the mid to late 1960s (e.g., Brown 1967, 1968, 1970) with oceanographers R. Pocklington (BIO) and E. Mills (Dalhousie University) became a major research project when approval for the establishment of Canada's first formal CWS seabird program was secured in early 1971 by H. Boyd, chief of migratory birds for eastern Canada. Before long, seabird data were collected from BIO research vessels all the way from Baffin Bay, Jones and Lancaster sounds (Brown 1972, 1973, 1976a, 1984, 1985a; Brown et al. 1974) south to Cape Horn (Brown et al. 1975b, Brown 1976b) and beyond (Brown 1979). These early cruises proved instrumental in the integration of bird distribution data with oceanographic characteristics of the waters they were found in, an effort to discover not only where the birds occur, but also why they are there. The simultaneous collection of physical, chemical, and biological data by BIO oceanographers on the same transects where the birds were being recorded, made for unique and ground-breaking opportunities to better understand the patterns of pelagic seabird distribution and levels of abundance.

The major task of making quantitative observations of seabirds at sea was the development of a system of data recording that allowed the data collected to be coded for computer analysis. Early on, the system used was that developed by the Smithsonian Institution Pacific Ocean Biological Survey Program (King et al. 1967, King 1970), but quickly modified owing to the greater numbers of birds in the northwest Atlantic than in the tropical Pacific. A system of 10-minute watches was adopted, recording the total numbers of each species seen during a watch along with the time, ship's position, birds' behaviour and plumage, and certain oceanographic parameters (Brown et al. 1975a: Appendix 1 – The PIROP coding scheme; summarized in Nettleship 1976a). The codes incorporated suggestions made by other investigators (Wynne-Edwards 1935, King 1970, Bailey and Bourne 1972) to control unavoidable biases such as inter-observer variability, ship-following by individual birds, counts from stationary and moving ships, and weather conditions affecting observations (e.g., fog). Tests indicated biases to be constant and known, unlikely to have a serious affect on relative changes in bird distribution and numbers, nor in analyses of year-to-year variability. The computer program, written by E. Tull, set up matrices for geographic regions with each entry corresponding to a 1°N x 2°W (Arctic region) or 1°N x 1°W (Atlantic region) block. Analyses of data for all acceptable 10-minute watches were made for each block giving average number of birds seen (by species) per 10 minutes in each block (by month) with details of mean numbers, errors, and effort. These results could be mapped and eventually printed out. The stage was set to produce atlases displaying quantitative measurements of the distributions of seabirds at sea and changes in space and time with links to differences in oceanographic conditions. In 1975, the first comprehensive Atlas of seabirds in northeastern North America appeared (Brown et al. 1975a) with considerable acclaim from the ornithological world. The usefulness of the Atlas for marine environmental management (conservation and protection) was considered to be enormous (e.g., Dunn 1976). For example, details of breeding locations of the total population of a species combined with relative abundances of its distribution at sea throughout the year allow an assessment of the likely impact that various environmental perturbations will have on that species. The methods of data collection and analysis for mapping pelagic distributions of seabirds over a large geographic region were deemed a success. However, the study approach was not yet complete.

Refinements in taking quantitative measurements of seabirds at sea continued. The push forward was to produce pelagic distribution maps that provided more than relative abundances of seabird numbers. Requirements for the conversion of the average number of birds seen per 10 minutes (by species) in each block to absolute estimates of birds present include details of ship's speed, height of observer above the sea, differential ranges that species can be seen and identified, as well as reactions to ships and other factors. After 1974, observations continued to be made in 10-min watches (in good visibility from a moving ship at not less than 4 kts or 7.4 km per h), but with adjustments for the ship's speed so that the averages presented refer to numbers of birds per linear kilometre. This allows easy comparison of our results with those from other quantitative recording systems in the North Atlantic (e.g., Powers 1982, 1983; Blake et al. 1984; Tasker et al. 1984). By 1984 the database for pelagic distributions in the northwest Atlantic was four times as large as it was in 1974, the cut-off date for the original seabird Atlas (Brown et al. 1975a). This resulted in the publication of a revised edition updating the shipboard observations of birds at sea (Brown 1986).

The revised 'at-sea' maps of seabird distributions off eastern Canada and the database from which they were created became instrumental in meeting the needs of environmental surveys commissioned by the federal government and offshore oil industry. Together with the results of supplemental studies made by petroleum consultants through the Environmental Impact Study (EIS) process, computer-generated maps with a restricted seasonal or geographical scope could be produced to show, for example, seabird distributions in the vicinity of a proposed offshore drill-site, oil tanker route, or the path of an oil slick. The long-term aim of refining techniques to allow the calculation of the absolute sizes of seabird populations at sea remains elusive and is, perhaps, unattainable. Shipboard observations, for the most part, are made on limited transects that encompass only a small fraction of a marine area, do not cover all habitats within it, and rarely survey nearshore waters. It therefore seems unrealistic to believe that we can produce estimates of absolute numbers. Nevertheless, attempts have been made to convert shipboard counts of seabirds at sea to absolute densities with limited success (e.g., Diamond et al. 1986). As expected, it seems clear that the real goal of shipboard observations is "the accurate measurement of relative variations in the numbers of birds, so that the birds' distributions may be compared with, and interpreted in terms of, the occurrence of physical and biological oceanographic phenomena" (Brown 1986). Without question, that objective has been achieved by the SRU-CWS team at BIO.

In contrast to shipboard observations, absolute estimates of bird numbers can be made from aerial surveys. If flight routes are flown along a pattern of adjacent flight-paths that covers all the marine habitats in the survey area, density values for individual species can be obtained to allow estimates to be made of total bird numbers and their distributions by species and habitat (e.g., Nettleship 1974, Johnson et al. 1976, Nettleship and Gaston 1978, MacLaren Marex 1979, McLaren 1982, Renaud et al. 1982). The major limiting factor of the aerial-survey approach is cost, which restricts surveys to largely small geographic areas spanning a short time-frame. Nonetheless, it is invaluable for short-term site-specific evaluations and monitoring.

The last phase of the 'pelagic ecology' effort addresses the question of how the quantitative seabird distribution data collected over a quarter of a century can be used to summarize and identify offshore areas where eastern Canadian seabirds and non-breeding visitors are potentially most at risk from oil pollution in the northwest Atlantic and the eastern Canadian arctic (see Figs. 3 and 4). The task began with the publication of the first Atlas (Brown et al. 1975a), continued through to the revised edition with its much stronger database for pelagic distributions (Brown 1986), and eventually culminating in an applied summation for marine birds in Atlantic Canada and their vulnerability to oil pollution (Lock et al. 1994). By the end of 1995, more than 180,000 10-minute observation records had been collected and analyzed on seabird distributions in the northwest Atlantic, most from the eastern Canadian arctic, western Greenland, and Atlantic Canada. Later, unprocessed survey data that remained (ca. 7,000 observation records) were added to the database (Hüttmann and Lock 1997) along with more than 10,000 records obtained from the Manomet Bird Observatory (MBO, Plymouth, MA), an association that began in the mid 1980s between SRU-CWS and MBO (Powers and Brown 1987). Altogether, the CWS-PIROP database developed at BIO comprises over 200,000 records in digital format that can be used for mapping pelagic distributions of seabirds in northeastern North America including western Greenland (through the year) and for

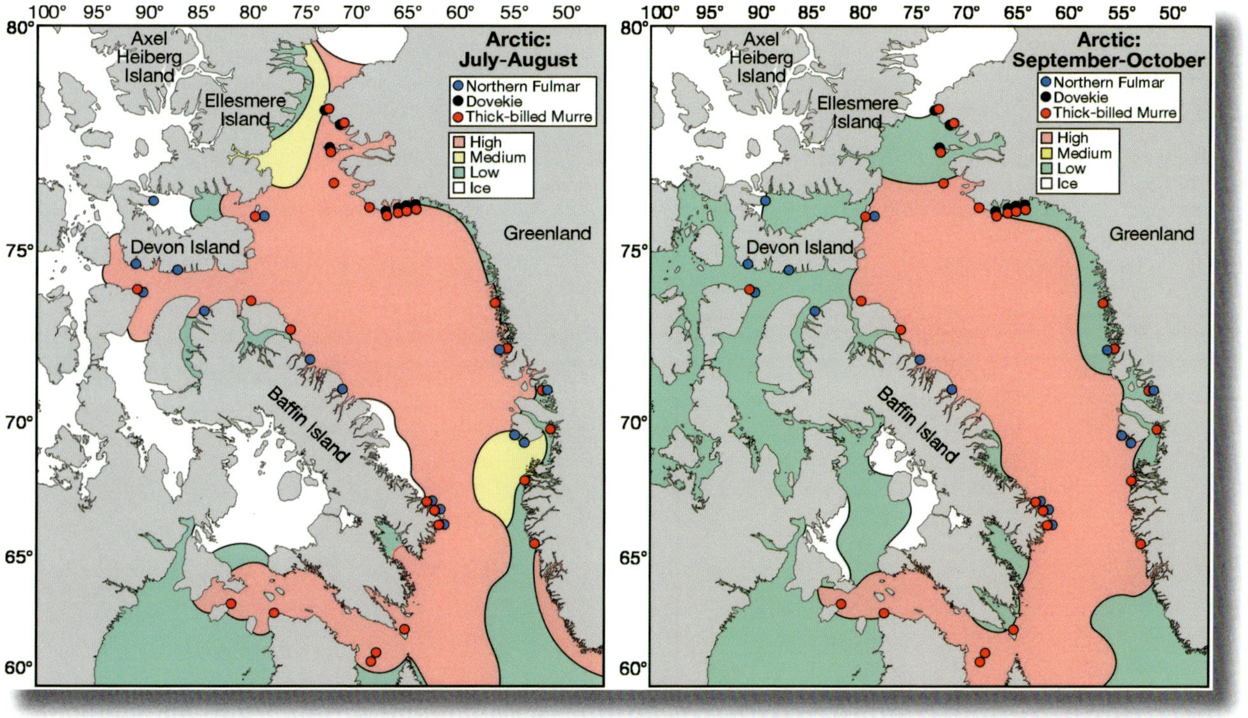

Figure 3. Vulnerabilities of seabirds at sea (low to high) in the eastern Canadian arctic and western Greenland during the peak of the breeding season (July – August) and fall exodus (September – October). Circles indicate locations of major colonies for breeding by principal species: Northern Fulmar, Dovekie, and Thick-billed Murre.

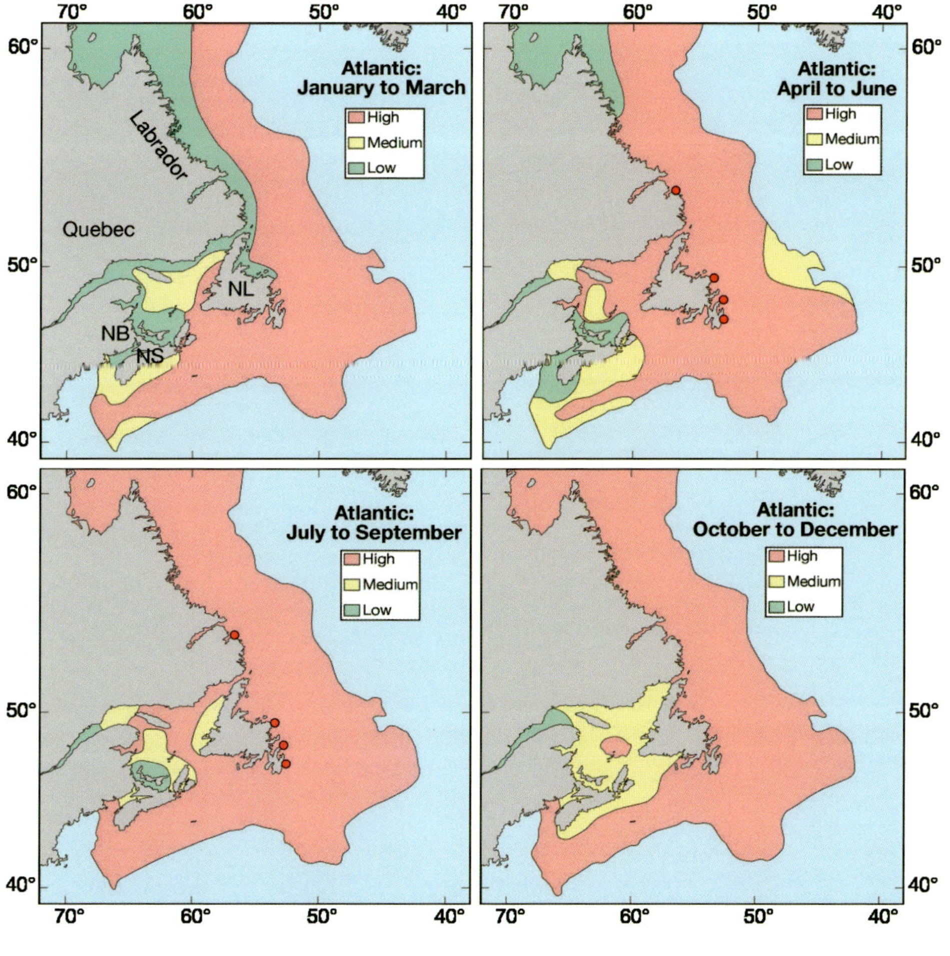

Figure 4. Vulnerabilities of seabirds at sea (low to high) in Atlantic Canada during the year. Areas of low vulnerability in January to March correspond generally with ice-covered waters. Red circles indicate locations of seabird colonies where the total breeding population exceeds 100,000 pairs comprising Leach's Storm-petrel, Common Murre, Thick-billed Murre, and Atlantic Puffin.

research and analysis of factors responsible for the distribution patterns observed.

Seabirds are most vulnerable to oil spills in the open ocean. The species most at risk in eastern Canada are those that spend much time sitting on the water, mainly diving birds such as Razorbills, Common and Thick-billed Murres, Dovekies, and Atlantic Puffins, and to a lesser extent Northern Gannets, Great and Double-crested Cormorants (Brown et al. 1973, Brown and Johnson 1980, Evans and Nettleship 1985, Piatt et al. 1991, Nettleship 1996). Other species feeding at or near the surface are also vulnerable (e.g., Northern Fulmars; Greater, Manx and Sooty Shearwaters; Black-legged Kittiwakes; *Sterna* terns and *Larus* gulls), as are other marine-associated waterbirds in coastal waters (e.g., loons, grebes, and diving ducks). Colonial seabirds are, of course, most vulnerable during the breeding season – March through September in Atlantic Canada, May through September in the Arctic – when concentrated at colony locations, and late in the season when for certain species (e.g., the murres), immense numbers of adults and flightless young cluster together in large rafts to undertake long swimming migrations to their winter quarters (Gaston 1980, Brown 1985b).

It is important to remember that one of the principal functions of the researches performed by SRU-CWS at BIO since 1971 was to provide basic information about seabird distributions in eastern Canadian waters that may be used in assessments of environmental risks. It is also critical to underline the fact that the waters off Atlantic Canada and the eastern Canadian arctic support very large populations of seabirds throughout the year. These populations comprise not only Canadian breeding birds, but also non-resident and non-breeding birds, including trans-Atlantic migrants (fulmars, shearwaters, alcids), trans-equatorial summer visitants from the South Atlantic (petrels, shearwaters), and large wintering populations. And so, an environmental mishap such as an offshore oil spill or blowout in eastern Canadian waters could adversely affect the seabirds of the entire Atlantic Ocean and beyond.

Most environmental assessments in eastern Canadian waters are concerned with the hazards presented by the offshore petroleum industry related to the discovery, extraction, and transport of oil. An assessment of the effects of an oil spill on seabirds will obviously depend on the location, time of year, and magnitude of the release. For any given situation, the SRU-CWS database can provide an immediate general picture of the distributions and numbers of the most vulnerable species in the offshore location of the spill along with their principal colonies. That information, combined with details of other species potentially at risk, goes a long way in helping to initiate the proper response and to forecast future developments.

Figures 3 and 4 summarize offshore areas off eastern Canada and west Greenland where seabirds are most concentrated (and at risk from oil pollution) at different times of the year. The figures are based on observations of birds at sea (particularly murres, Dovekies, Razorbills, and Atlantic Puffins) by SRU-CWS workers between 1969 and 1984, augmented by the results of reworking the data to 1992. Although coverage for birds in all open water areas throughout the annual cycle is incomplete, many highlights have been uncovered including the identification of 'hot-spots' for seabirds in space and time, information critical for effective management. The maps are therefore presented for quick reference only.

The distribution patterns of the species regularly occurring offshore in eastern Canada are often complex and difficult to unravel. Locations of principal colonies provide abundant information for many of the colonially-breeding species, but only for part of the year. Where the birds are outside the breeding season and away from land is often impossible to determine. Certain species are known to vacate Canadian waters during the fall exodus for southern winter quarters – e.g., Northern Gannet, Double-crested Cormorant, *Sterna* terns – where they remain until the following spring, whereas others stay through the winter often mixed with birds from the eastern Atlantic. For example, Thick-billed Murres leave their high arctic breeding colonies in Jones Sound, Lancaster Sound, Baffin Bay and Davis Strait in the first half of September and cross to west Greenland where most of them spend the winter feeding in the highly productive and late-freezing waters of the West Greenland Shelf. The remainder joins the massive movement of Thick-billed Murres from colonies in the Hudson Strait area that migrate to wintering areas off eastern Labrador and east Newfoundland. Similarly, Dovekies leave their colonies in northwest Greenland during September and reach the Labrador Sea and eastern Newfoundland in October where they remain until May. Comparable post-breeding movements by other species also take place farther south. Common Murres and Atlantic Puffins swim from eastern Newfoundland to southeast Labrador, where they remain for at least part of the winter. Most of these migrations are of large numbers of adults swimming with 'flightless' young birds of the year which are extremely vulnerable to massive casualties from oil spills at this time. Of course, a comparable risk occurs again in spring as they move back towards their breeding sites.

It is clear from this short overview that the waters off Atlantic Canada and the eastern Canadian arctic support very large populations of seabirds, many of which are at risk to environmental activities and mishaps in our waters. It is equally clear that the large database comprising quantitative information on pelagic seabird distributions, based on standardized observations made off eastern Canada by SRU-CWS shipboard observers for more than two decades, and the computer-mapping program developed at BIO summarizes offshore areas where seabirds are potentially most at risk from oil pollution both now and in the future. These pelagic data combined with information on the locations and sizes of seabird colonies (from BMS studies) will be invaluable to the success of marine conservation and management initiatives in eastern Canada.

CONCLUSIONS AND THE FUTURE

Although the original objectives of the CWS Seabird Program in eastern Canada have been realized, there are many specific gaps in our current knowledge that need to be addressed in the future. We still know little about distribution at sea in the nonbreeding season and how that changes from year to year, or the variation in reproductive performance for most individual species and how it varies within a species at different colonies in the same year. We also need to prepare for the assessment of imminent threats to seabirds from global warming and other large-scale environmental changes. More generally, we should work to expand a system similar to the Biological Monitoring System of the CWS seabird program along the Atlantic seaboard to all regions of eastern North America. Seabird researchers and managers in different regions and countries – United States, Canada, Denmark, Iceland, the Netherlands, Norway, United Kingdom, Russia – need to work together to ensure results from seabird monitoring across the North Atlantic are compatible, that duplication of effort is avoided, and that there are no large gaps in our knowledge. We must also develop standardized computerized data management systems to facilitate easy access to seabird colony data and distributions of seabirds at sea such as those developed by the Seabird Research Unit at BIO for Arctic and Atlantic Canada. And finally, we must ensure that monitoring of birds at colonies and at sea is not done in isolation, but is combined with studies of the causes of population change and is actually applied to management and conservation problems. Overall, seabird management will remain largely at the ecosystem level: i.e., protect the island or mainland site and its nearby waters, and those marine areas known to be important outside the breeding season, and one manages for seabirds (Nettleship 1991a, Duffy and Nettleship 1992, Duffy 1994, Nettleship 1998). By managing seabirds successfully, we will prevent large-scale destruction of a uniquely rich group of marine animals, and contribute to maintaining the health of the world's oceans on which most living things depend. In the future, however, the larger challenge may well be the attainment of such goals in the present climate of diminishing resources (staff and operating monies) and reduced government interest in the conservation of seabirds and the marine ecosystems they occupy.

ACKNOWLEDGEMENTS

There are many people to thank for their support and contribution to the CWS seabird program over the 29 years of its formal operation: 1971-2000. First and foremost is Mr. Hugh Boyd, a visionary senior research manager and scientist, responsible for the establishment of the CWS seabird program in 1971 and for bringing Dick Brown and me together to tackle the formidable task of creating a statistically meaningful database for seabirds in eastern Canadian marine waters. My grateful thanks also go to other managers that gave their support to the original initiative including Mr. Joe Bryant, Dr. Graham Cooch, Mr. Alan Loughrey, Dr. Andrew Macpherson, and Dr. John Tener, along with senior research scientist Dr. Leslie Tuck, and Dr. William Ford, Director of BIO between 1965 and 1978, who welcomed and encouraged a CWS seabird presence at the Bedford Institute of Oceanography. CWS managers Dr. Tony Erskine and Mr. Jim Inder provided much needed regional support from the late 1970s through the 1980s. Contributors to the seabird research program over the three decades are too numerous to list here, but they know who they are and most appear in the 'References' section of this paper. However, in addition to Dick Brown, I must give special thanks to the following for their major contributions to the SRU-CWS-BIO seabird program: Tim Birkhead, David Cairns, Gordon Calderwood, Gilles Chapdelaine, Barbara Dodge (Lock), Richard Elliot, Roderick Forbes, Tony Gaston, Gary Glenn, Erick Greene, Susan Johnson, Wayne Lidster, Anne Linton (Greene), Tony Lock, Bruce Lyon, Andrew Macfarlane, Bob Montgomerie, Philip Taylor, Stuart Tingley, Eric Tull, and Eric Verspoor. My grateful thanks to all.

REFERENCES

Ashmole, N.P. 1971. Seabird ecology and the marine environment. Pages 223-286 *in* Avian Biology (D.S. Farner and J.R. King, Eds.). Academic Press, New York, NY.

Austin, O.L., Jr. 1932. The birds of Newfoundland-Labrador. Memoirs of the Nuttall Ornithological Club No. 7: 1-229.

Bailey, R.S. and W.R.P. Bourne. 1972. Counting birds at sea. Ardea 60: 124-126.

Baker, R.H. 1947. Observations on the birds of the North Atlantic. Auk 64: 254-259.

Bartonek, J. and D.N. Nettleship (Eds.). 1979. Conservation of Marine Birds of Northern North America. United States Fish and Wildlife Service, Wildlife Research Report 11, Washington, D.C.

Birkhead, T.R. and D.N. Nettleship. 1980. Census methods for murres *Uria* species – a unified approach. Canadian Wildlife Service Occasional Paper No. 43: 1-25.

Birkhead, T.R. and D.N. Nettleship. 1981. Reproductive biology of Thick-billed Murres *Uria lomvia*: an inter-colony comparison. Auk 98: 258-269.

Birkhead, T.R. and D. N. Nettleship. 1982a. Studies of alcids breeding at the Gannet Clusters, Labrador, 1981. Canadian Wildlife Service 'Studies on northern seabirds' Report No. 125, Dartmouth, NS.

Birkhead, T.R. and D.N. Nettleship. 1982b. The adaptive significance of egg size and laying date in Thick-billed Murres *Uria lomvia*. Ecology 63: 300-306.

Birkhead, T.R. and D.N. Nettleship. 1983. Studies of alcids breeding at the Gannet Clusters, Labrador, 1982. Canadian Wildlife Service 'Studies on northern seabirds' Report No. 149, Dartmouth, NS.

Birkhead, T.R. and D.N. Nettleship. 1984. Egg size, composition and offspring quality in some Alcidae (Aves: Charadriiformes). Journal of Zoology 202: 177-194.

Birkhead, T.R. and D.N. Nettleship. 1987a. Ecological relationships between Common Murres, *Uria aalge*, and Thick-billed Murres, *Uria lomvia*, at the Gannet Islands, Labrador. I. Morphometrics and timing of breeding. Canadian Journal of Zoology 65: 1,621-1,629.

Birkhead, T.R. and D.N. Nettleship. 1987b. Ecological relationships between Common Murres, *Uria aalge*, and Thick-billed Murres, *Uria lomvia*, at the Gannet Islands, Labrador. II. Breeding success and site characteristics. Canadian Journal of Zoology 65: 1,630-1,637.

Birkhead, T.R. and D.N. Nettleship. 1987c. Ecological relationships between Common Murres, *Uria aalge*, and Thick-billed Murres, *Uria lomvia*, at the Gannet Islands, Labrador. III. Feeding ecology of the young. Canadian Journal of Zoology 65: 1,638-1,649.

Birkhead, T.R. and D.N. Nettleship. 1988. Breeding performance of Black-legged Kittiwakes, *Rissa tridactyla*, at a small, expanding colony in Labrador. Canadian Field-Naturalist 102: 20-24.

Birkhead, T.R. and D.N. Nettleship. 1995. Arctic Fox influence on a seabird community in Labrador: a natural experiment. Wilson Bulletin 107: 397-412.

Birkhead, T.R., J.D. Biggins, and D.N. Nettleship. 1980. Non-random, intra-colony distribution of bridled guillemots *Uria aalge*. Journal of Zoology 192: 9-16.

Birkhead, T.R., S.D. Johnson, and D.N. Nettleship. 1985a. Extra-pair matings and mate guarding in the Common Murre *Uria aalge*. Animal Behaviour 33: 608-619.

Birkhead, T.R., R. Kay, and D.N. Nettleship. 1985b. A new method for estimating the survival rates of the Common Murre *Uria aalge*. Journal of Wildlife Management 49: 496-502.

Blake, B.F., M.L. Tasker, P. Hope Jones, T.J. Dixon, R. Mitchell, and D.R. Langslow. 1984. Seabird distribution in the North Sea. Nature Conservancy Council, Huntingdon, England.

Blanchard, K.A. and D.N. Nettleship. 1992. Education and seabird conservation: a conceptual framework. Pages 616-632 *in* Wildlife 2001: Populations (D.R. McCullough and R.H. Barrett, Eds.). Elsevier Science Publications, London, England.

Bourne, W.R.P. 1963. A review of oceanic studies of the biology of seabirds. Proceedings of the International Ornithological Congress 13: 831-854.

Brown, R.G.B. 1967. Seabirds off Halifax, March 1967. Canadian Field-Naturalist 81: 276-278.

Brown, R.G.B. 1968. Seabirds in Newfoundland and Greenland waters, April-May 1966. Canadian Field-Naturalist 82: 88-102.

Brown, R.G.B. 1970. Fulmar distribution: a Canadian perspective. Ibis 112: 44-51.

Brown, R.G.B. 1972. Probable sightings of Little Shearwaters, *Puffinus assimilis*, on the southeastern Grand Banks. Canadian Field-Naturalist 86: 293.

Brown, R.G.B. 1973. TransAtlantic migration of dark-phase fulmars from the European Arctic. Canadian Field-Naturalist 87: 312-313.

Brown, R.G.B. 1976a. The foraging range of breeding Dovekies, *Alle alle*. Canadian Field-Naturalist 90: 166-168.

Brown, R.G.B. 1976b. Seabirds of South America and the Northwest Atlantic. Proceedings of the International Ornithological Congress 16: 716-724.

Brown, R.G.B. 1979. Seabirds of the Senegal upwelling and adjacent waters. Ibis 121: 283-292.

Brown, R.G.B. 1980. Seabirds as marine animals. Pages 1-39 *in* Behavior of Marine Animals, Vol. 4: Marine Birds (J. Burger, B.L. Olla and H.E. Winn, Eds.). Plenum Press, New York, NY.

Brown, R.G.B. 1981. Seabirds at sea. Oceanus 24(2): 31-38.

Brown, R.G.B. 1984. Seabirds in the Greenland, Barents and Norwegian Seas, February–April 1982. Polar Research 2: 1-18.

Brown, R.G.B. 1985a. The influence of ice on the ecology of Arctic and Antarctic seabirds. Proceedings of the International Ornithological Congress 18: 559-566.

Brown, R.G.B. 1985b. The Atlantic Alcidae at sea. Pages 384-426 *in* The Atlantic Alcidae: the Evolution, Distribution and Biology of the Auks Inhabiting the Atlantic Ocean and Adjacent Water Areas (D.N. Nettleship and T.R. Birkhead, Eds.). Academic Press, London, England.

Brown, R.G.B. 1986. Revised Atlas of Eastern Canadian Seabirds. I: Shipboard Surveys. Canadian Wildlife Service, Ottawa, ON.

Brown, R.G.B. and B.C. Johnson. 1980. The effects of '*Kurdistan*' oil on seabirds. Pages 184-194 *in* Proceedings of a workshop: Scientific studies during the '*Kurdistan*' tanker incident (J.H. Vandermeulen, Ed.). Bedford Institute of Oceanography Report Series BI-R-80-3, Dartmouth, NS.

Brown, R.G.B. and D.N. Nettleship. 1981. The biological significance of polynyas to Arctic colonial seabirds. Pages 59-65 *in* Polynyas in the Canadian Arctic (I. Stirling and H. Cleator, Eds.). Canadian Wildlife Service Occasional Paper45, Ottawa, ON.

Brown, R.G.B. and D.N. Nettleship. 1984a. Capelin and seabirds in the northwest Atlantic. Pages 184-194 *in* Marine Birds: Their Feeding Ecology and Commercial Fisheries Relationships (D.N. Nettleship, G.A. Sanger, and P.F. Springer, Eds.). Canadian Wildlife Service Special Publication, Ottawa, ON.

Brown, R.G.B. and D.N. Nettleship. 1984b. The seabirds of northeastern North America: their present status and conservation requirements. Pages 85-100 *in* Status and Conservation of the World's Seabirds (J.P. Croxall, P.G.H. Evans, and R. Schreiber, Eds.). International Council for Bird Preservation Technical Publication No. 2, Cambridge, England.

Brown, R.G.B., D.I. Gillespie, A.R. Lock, P.A. Pearce, and G.H. Watson. 1973. Bird mortality from oil slicks off eastern Canada, February-April 1970. Canadian Field-Naturalist 87: 225-234.

Brown, R.G.B., T. Davis, and D.N. Nettleship. 1974. Ivory Gulls, *Pagophila eburnea*, on the water. Canadian Field-Naturalist 88: 368-369.

Brown, R.G.B., D.N. Nettleship, P. Germain, C.E. Tull, and T. Davis. 1975a. Atlas of Eastern Canadian Seabirds. Canadian Wildlife Service, Environment Canada, Ottawa, ON.

Brown, R.G.B., F. Cooke, P.K. Kinnear, and E.L. Mills. 1975b. Summer seabird distributions in Drake Passage and off southern South America. Ibis 117: 339-356.

Buckley, P.A. and F.G. Buckley. 1984. Seabirds of the north and middle Atlantic coast of the United States: their status and conservation. Pages 101-133 *in* Status and Conservation of the World's Seabirds (J.P. Croxall, P.G.H. Evans, and R.W. Schreiber, Eds.). International Council for Bird Preservation Technical Pubication No. 2, Cambridge, England.

Chapdelaine, G. 1995. Fourteenth census of seabird populations in the sanctuaries of the North Shore of the Gulf of St. Lawrence, 1993. Canadian Field-Naturalist 109: 220-226.

Chapdelaine, G. and P. Brousseau. 1992. Population trends in marine birds of the St. Lawrence River, Estuary and Gulf. Bird Trends 2: 7-9.

Chapdelaine, G. and J. Bedard. 1995. Recent changes in the abundance and distribution of the Double-crested Cormorant in the St. Lawrence River, Estuary, and Gulf, Quebec, 1978-1990. Pages 70-77 *in* The Double-crested Cormorant: Biology, Conservation and Management (D.N. Nettleship and D.C. Duffy, Eds.). Colonial Waterbirds 18 (Special Publication 1), DeLeon Springs, FL.

Chapdelaine, G., A.J. Gaston, and P. Brousseau. 1986. Censusing the Thick-billed Murre colonies of Akpatok Island, Northwest Territories. Canadian Wildlife Service Progress Notes No. 163: 1-9.

Chapdelaine, G., P. Laporte, and D.N. Nettleship. 1987. Population, productivity and DDT contamination trends of Northern Gannet (*Sula bassanus*) at Bonaventure Island, Quebec, 1967-1984. Canadian Journal of Zoology 65: 2,922-2,926.

Chardine, J.W. 1992. Seabirds, oil pollution, and Operation Clean Feather. Bird Trends 2: 17-18.

Diamond, A.W., A.J. Gaston, and R.G.B. Brown. 1986. Converting PIROP counts of seabirds at sea to absolute densities. Canadian Wildlife Service Progress Notes No. 164: 1-21.

Drury, W.H. 1973-74. Population changes in New England seabirds. Bird-Banding 44: 267-313; 45: 1-15.

Duffy, D.C. 1994. Afterwards: an agenda for managing seabirds and islands. Pages

311-318 *in* Seabirds on Islands: Threats, Case Studies and Action Plans (D.N. Nettleship, J. Burger and M. Gochfeld, Eds.). BirdLife International, Cambridge, England.

Duffy, D.C. and D.N. Nettleship. 1992. Seabirds: management problems and research opportunities. Pages 525-546 *in* Wildlife 2001 (D. McCullough and R. Barrett, Eds.). Elsevier Science Publishers, London, England.

Dunbar, M.J. 1968. Ecological Developments in Polar Regions: A Study in Evolution. Prentice-Hall, Englewood Cliffs, NJ.

Dunn, E.H. 1976. Book review 30: Atlas of Eastern Canadian Seabirds. Bird-Banding 47: 378-380.

Erskine, A.J. 1992. Atlas of beeding birds of the Maritime Provinces. Nimbus and Nova Scotia Museum of Natural History, Halifax, NS.

Erwin, R.M. 1979. Coastal Waterbird Colonies: Cape Elizabeth, Maine to Virginia. United States Fish and Wildlife Service Biological Services Program, FWS/OBS/79-10: 1-212.

Erwin, R.M. and C. Korschgen. 1979. Coastal Waterbird Colonies: Maine to Virginia. United States Fish and Wildlife Service Biological Services Program, FWS/OBS/79-08: 1-647.

Evans, P.G.H. and D.N. Nettleship. 1985. Conservation of the Atlantic Alcidae. Pages 428-488 *in* The Atlantic Alcidae: the Evolution, Distribution and Biology of the Auks Inhabiting the Atlantic Ocean and Adjacent Water Areas (D.N. Nettleship and T.R. Birkhead, Eds.). Academic Press, London, England.

Furness, R.W. and D.N. Nettleship. 1991. Seabirds as monitors of changing marine environments. Proceedings of the International Ornithological Congress 20: 2,237-2,279.

Gaston, A.J. 1980. Population, movements and wintering areas of Thick-billed Murres (*Uria lomvia*) in eastern Canada. Canadian Wildlife Service Progress Note No. 110: 1-10.

Gaston, A.J. 1991a. Seabirds of Hudson Strait, Hudson Bay and adjacent waters. Pages 7-16 *in* Seabird Status and Conservation: A Supplement (J.P. Croxall, Ed.). International Council for Bird Preservation Technical Publication No. 11, Cambridge, England.

Gaston, A.J. 1991b. Conservation issues and Canadian Wildlife Service priorities for marine birds. Canadian Wildlife Service Manuscript Report, Ottawa, ON.

Gaston, A.J. 1992. Population trends of Thick-billed Murres in Hudson Strait. Bird Trends 2: 13-14.

Gaston, A.J. and D.N. Nettleship. 1981. The Thick-billed Murres of Prince Leopold Island – A Study of the Breeding Ecology of a Colonial High Arctic Seabird. Canadian Wildlife Service Monograph Series No. 6, Ottawa, ON.

Gaston, A.J. and D.N. Nettleship. 1982. Factors determining seasonal changes in attendance at colonies of the Thick-billed Murre *Uria lomvia*. Auk 99: 468-473.

Gaston, A.J., D.K. Cairns, R.D. Elliot, and D.G. Noble. 1985. A natural history of Digges Sound. Canadian Wildlife Service Report Series No. 46: 1-61.

Gaston, A.J., R.D. Elliot, and D.G. Noble. 1987. Studies of Thick-billed Murres on Coats Island, N.W.T., in 1981, 1984, 1985 and 1986. Canadian Wildlife Service Progress Notes No. 167: 1-13.

Gaston, A.J., L.N. de Forest, G. Gilchrist, and D.N. Nettleship. 1993. Monitoring Thick-billed Murre populations at colonies in northern Hudson Bay, 1972-92. Canadian Wildlife Service Occasional Paper No. 80: 1-16.

Godfrey, W.E. 1954. Birds of Prince Edward Island. National Museum of Canada Bulletin 132: 155-213.

Gross, A.O. 1935. The life history cycle of Leach's Petrel *Oceanodroma leucorhoa leucorhoa* on the outer sea islands of the Bay of Fundy. Auk 52: 382-399.

Huntington, C.E. and E.H. Burtt. 1972. Breeding age and longevity in Leach's Storm-petrel. Proceedings of the International Ornithological Congress 15: 653.

Hüttmann, F. and A.R. Lock. 1997. A new software system for the PIROP database: data flow and an approach for a seabird-depth analysis. ICES Journal of Marine Science 54: 518-523.

Jespersen, P. 1924. The frequency of birds over the high Atlantic Ocean. Nature 114: 281-283.

Jespersen, P. 1930. Ornithological observations in the North Atlantic Ocean. Oceanographic Report 'Dana' Expedition, 1920-22, No. 7: 1-36.

Johnson, S.R., W.E. Renaud, W.J. Richardson, R.A. Davis, C. Holdsworth, and P.D. Hollingdale. 1976. Aerial surveys of birds in eastern Lancaster Sound, 1976. Report by LGL Limited, Toronto, for Norlands Petroleums, Calgary, AB.

Kampp, K., D.N. Nettleship, and P. Evans. 1994. Thick-billed Murres of Greenland: status and prospects. Pages 133-154 *in* Seabirds on Islands: Threats, Case Studies and Action Plans (D.N. Nettleship, J. Burger, and M. Gochfeld, Eds.). BirdLife International, Cambridge, England.

King, W.B. 1970. The trade wind oceanography pilot study, Part VII: Observations of seabirds, March 1964 to June 1965. United States Fish and Wildlife Service Special Science Report, Fisheries No. 586: 1-136.

King, W.B., G.E. Watson, and P.J. Gould. 1967. An application of automatic data processing to the study of seabirds. I. Numerical coding. Proceedings of the United States National Museum 123, No. 3609: 1-29.

Kirkham, I.R. and D.N. Nettleship. 1985. Status of the Roseate Tern *Sterna dougallii* (Montagu) in Canada. Committee on the Status of Endangered Wildlife in Canada (COSEWIC), Canadian Wildlife Service and World Wildlife Fund Canada, Ottawa, ON.

Kirkham, I.R. and D.N. Nettleship. 1987. Status of the Roseate Tern in Canada. Journal of Field Ornithology 58: 505-515.

Lewis, H.F. 1925. The new bird sanctuaries in the Gulf of St. Lawrence. Canadian Field-Naturalist 39: 177-179.

Linton, A. 1979. The food and feeding habits of Leach's Storm-petrel (*Oceanodroma leucorhoa*) at Pearl Island, Nova Scotia, and Middle Lawn Island, Newfoundland. M.Sc. thesis, Dalhousie University, Halifax, NS.

Lock, A.R. 1973. A study of the breeding biology of two species of gulls nesting on Sable Island, Nova Scotia. Ph.D. thesis, Dalhousie University, Halifax, NS.

Lock, A.R. 1992. Tern population trends in Atlantic Canada. Bird Trends 2: 6-7.

Lock, A.R. and R.K. Ross. 1973. The nesting of the Great Cormorant (*Phalacrocorax carbo*) and Double-crested Cormorant (*Phalacrocorax auritus*) in Nova Scotia in 1971. Canadian Field-Naturalist 87: 43-49.

Lock, A.R., R.G.B. Brown, and S.H. Gerriets. 1994. Gazetteer of marine birds in Atlantic Canada: an atlas of seabird vulnerability to oil pollution. Canadian Wildlife Service – Atlantic Region, Dartmouth, NS.

MacLaren Marex. 1979. Report on aerial surveys of birds and marine mammals in the southern Davis Strait between April and December, 1978. Project No. 146 for ESSO Resources Canada, Aquitaine Canada, Canada Cities Services, and Arctic Petroleum Operators Association, Volume 1: Birds. MacLaren Marex, St. John's, NL.

McLaren, I.A. 1981. The birds of Sable Island, Nova Scotia. Proceedings of the Nova Scotian Institute of Science 31: 1-84.

McLaren, P.L. 1982. Spring migration and habitat use by seabirds in eastern Lancaster Sound and western Baffin Bay. Arctic 35: 88-111.

Milton, G.R. and P.J. Austin-Smith. 1983. Changes in the abundance and distribution of Double-crested (*Phalacrocorax auritus*) and Great (*P. carbo*) Cormorants in Nova Scotia. Colonial Waterbirds 6: 130-138.

Milton, G.R., P.J. Austin-Smith, and G.J. Farmer. 1995. Shouting at Shags: a case study of cormorant management in Nova Scotia. Pages 91-98 *in* The Double-crested Cormorant: Biology, Conservation and Management (D.N. Nettleship and D.C. Duffy, Eds.). Colonial Waterbirds 18 (Special Publication 1), DeLeon Springs, FL.

Montevecchi, W.A. and L.M. Tuck. 1987. Newfoundland Birds: Exploitation, Study, Conservation. Nuttall Ornithological Club No. 21: 1-273.

Moore, H.B. 1941. Notes on the distribution of oceanic birds in the North Atlantic. Proceedings of the Linnaean Society of New York 52: 53-62.

Moore, H.B. 1951. Seasonal distribution of oceanic birds in the western North Atlantic. Bulletin of Marine Science for the Gulf and Caribbean 1: 1-14.

Nelson, J.B. 2002. The Atlantic Gannet. Fenix Books, Great Yarmouth, Norfolk, England.

Nettleship, D.N. 1970. Breeding success of the Common Puffin (*Fratercula arctica* L.) on different habitats at Great Island, Newfoundland. Ph.D. thesis, McGill University, Montreal, QC.

Nettleship, D.N. 1972a. Inter-relationships of seabirds and the coastal zone: a summary report on seabird research. Pages 131-136 *in* Coastal Zone, Vol. 1. Environment Canada, Ottawa, ON.

Nettleship, D.N. 1972b. Seabird census techniques - preliminary draft. Canadian Wildlife Service 'Studies on northern seabirds' Manuscript Report No. 4, Ottawa, ON.

Nettleship, D.N. 1972c. Breeding success of the Common Puffin [*Fratercula arctica* (L.)] on different habitats at Great Island, Newfoundland. Ecological Monographs 42: 239-268.

Nettleship, D.N. 1973a. Canadian seabird research. Marine Pollution Bulletin 4: 62-64.

Nettleship, D.N. 1973b. Census of seabirds in the sanctuaries of the Gulf of St. Lawrence, summer 1972. Canadian Wildlife Service 'Studies on northern seabirds' Manuscript Report No. 20, Ottawa, ON.

Nettleship, D.N. 1974. Seabird colonies and distributions around Devon Island and vicinity. Arctic 27: 95-103.

Nettleship, D.N. 1975. A recent decline in gannets at Bonaventure Island, Quebec. Canadian Field-Naturalist 89: 125-133.

Nettleship, D.N. 1976a. Census techniques for seabirds of arctic and eastern Canada. Canadian Wildlife Service Occasional Paper No. 25: 1-33.

Nettleship, D.N. 1976b. Gannets in North America: present numbers and recent population changes. Wilson Bulletin 88: 303-313.

Nettleship, D.N. 1977a. Seabird resources of eastern Canada: status, problems, and prospects. Pages 96-108 *in* Canada's Endangered Species and Habitats (T. Mosquin and C. Suchal, Eds.). Canadian Nature Federation Special Publication No. 6. Ottawa, ON.

Nettleship, D.N. 1977b. Studies of seabirds at Prince Leopold Island and vicinity, Northwest Territories: Preliminary report of biological investigations. Canadian Wildlife Service Progress Notes No. 73: 1-11.

Nettleship, D.N. 1980. A guide to the major seabird colonies of eastern Canada: identity, distribution and abundance. Canadian Wildlife Service 'Studies on northern seabirds' Manuscript Report No. 97, Dartmouth, NS.

Nettleship, D.N. 1991a. Seabird management and future research. Colonial Waterbirds 14: 77-84.

Nettleship, D.N. 1991b. The diet of Atlantic Puffin chicks in Newfoundland before and after the initiation of an international capelin fishery, 1967-1984. Proceedings of the International Ornithological Congress 20: 2,263-2,271.

Nettleship, D.N. 1992a. CWS seabird program, 1972-1992. Bird Trends 2: 1-5.

Nettleship, D.N. 1992b. Gannets in North America: present status and recent changes. Bird Trends 2: 15-16.

Nettleship, D.N. 1992c. Atlantic Puffin trends at Great Island, Newfoundland, 1968-1990. Bird Trends 2: 16-17.

Nettleship, D.N. 1992d. The CWS Seabird Colony Registry: a computerized storage-retrieval system. Bird Trends 2: 18-19.

Nettleship, D.N. 1993. Seabird population monitoring program: national issues and program priorities, 1994-2004. Canadian Wildlife Service 'Studies on northern seabirds' Manuscript Report No. 265, Ottawa, ON.

Nettleship, D.N. 1994. CWS Seabird Colony Registry: a computerized data management system for access to seabird colony data. Pages 27-30 *in* Science Review 1992 and '93 (A. Fiander, Ed.). Department of Fisheries and Oceans, Dartmouth, NS.
Nettleship, D.N. 1996. Family Alcidae (Auks). Pages 678-722 *in* Handbook of the Birds of the World, Volume 3: Hoatzin to Auks (del Hoyo, J., A. Elliott and J. Sargatal, Eds.). Lynx Edicions, Barcelona, Spain.
Nettleship, D.N. 1997. Long-term monitoring of Canada's seabird populations. Pages 16-23 *in* Monitoring bird populations: the Canadian experience (Dunn, E.H., M.D. Cadman, and J.B. Falls, Eds.). Canadian Wildlife Service Occasional Paper No. 95, Ottawa, ON.
Nettleship, D.N. 1998. Ecosystem disturbance and seabirds in crisis: Eastern and Atlantic Canada. Pages 54-76 *in* Proceedings of the World Wildlife Fund Atlantic Canada Workshop on Recovery of Species at Risk (P.J. Ewins and K. Ferguson, Eds.). World Wildlife Fund Canada, Toronto, ON.
Nettleship, D.N. and A.R. Lock. 1973. Tenth census of seabirds in the sanctuaries of the north shore of the Gulf of St. Lawrence. Canadian Field-Naturalist 87: 395-402.
Nettleship, D.N. and P.A. Smith (Eds.). 1975. Ecological Sites in Northern Canada. Canadian Committee for the International Biological Programme, Conservation Terrestrial, Panel 9. Ottawa, ON.
Nettleship, D.N. and P.S. Taylor. 1975. The seabirds of Bonaventure Island, Pérce Rock and area, Quebec, summer 1974. Canadian Wildlife Service 'Studies on northern seabirds' Report No. 29, Ottawa, ON.
Nettleship, D.N. and A.J. Gaston. 1978. Patterns of pelagic distribution of seabirds in western Lancaster Sound and Barrow Strait, Northwest Territories, in August and September 1976. Canadian Wildlife Service Occasional Paper No. 39: 1-40.
Nettleship, D.N. and T.R. Birkhead. 1981. Alcid studies in Labrador: Gannet Clusters 1981. Canadian Wildlife Service 'Studies on northern seabirds' Report No. 118, Dartmouth, NS.
Nettleship, D.N. and T.R. Birkhead (Eds.). 1985. The Atlantic Alcidae: the Evolution, Distribution and Biology of the Auks Inhabiting the Atlantic Ocean and Adjacent Water Areas. Academic Press, London, England.
Nettleship, D.N. and P.G.H. Evans. 1985. Distribution and status of the Atlantic Alcidae. Pages 53-154 *in* The Atlantic Alcidae: the Evolution, Distribution and Biology of the Auks Inhabiting the Atlantic Ocean and Adjacent Water Areas. (D.N. Nettleship and T.R. Birkhead, Eds.). Academic Press, London, England.
Nettleship, D.N. and G. Chapdelaine. 1988. Population size and status of the Northern Gannet *Sula bassanus* in North America, 1984. Journal of Field Ornithology 59: 120-127.
Nettleship, D.N. and G.L. Hunt, Jr. 1988. Reproductive biology of seabirds at high latitudes in the northern and southern hemispheres. Proceedings of the International Ornithological Congress 19: 1,141-1,219.
Nettleship, D.N. and D.C. Duffy. 1992. Seabird Populations. Pages 523-632 *in* Wildlife 2001: populations (D.R. McCullough and R.H. Barrett, Eds.). Elsevier Science Publications, London, England.
Nettleship, D.N. and G.N. Glenn. 1992. Seabird colonies in Labrador. Canadian Wildlife Service 'Studies on northern seabirds' Report No. 254, Dartmouth, NS.
Nettleship, D.N. and D.C. Duffy (Eds.). 1995. The Double-crested Cormorant: Biology, Conservation and Management. Colonial Waterbirds 18 (Special Publication 1), DeLeon Springs, FL.
Nettleship, D.N., T.R. Birkhead, and A.J. Gaston. 1984a. Breeding of Arctic seabirds in unusual ice years: the Thick-billed Murre *Uria lomvia* in 1978. Pages 35-38 *in* BIO Review '84 (M.P. Latremouille, Ed.). Bedford Institute of Oceanography, Dartmouth, NS.
Nettleship, D.N., G.A. Sanger, and P.A. Springer (Eds.). 1984b. Marine Birds: Their Feeding Ecology and Commercial Fisheries Relationships. Canadian Wildlife Service Special Publication, Ottawa, ON.
Nettleship, D.N., J.W. Chardine, E.P. Huyck, and W.W. Lidster. 1990. Field investigations of seabirds at Prince Leopold Island, Lancaster Sound, Northwest Territories, 1988. Canadian Wildlife Service Technical Report Series No. 97: 1-84.
Newall, R.B. 1985. Nesting ecology of Arctic Terns *Sterna paradisea* Pontoppidan at Machias Seal Island. M.Sc. thesis, Acadia University, Wolfville, Nova Scotia.
Palmer, R.S. 1949. Maine birds. Bulletin of the Museum of Comparative Zoology 102, Cambridge, MA.
Paynter, R.A. 1949. Clutch size and the egg and chick mortality of Kent Island Herring Gulls. Ecology 30: 146-166.
Peters, H.S. and T.D. Burleigh. 1951. The birds of Newfoundland. Newfoundland Department of Natual Resources, St. John's, NL.
Pettingill, O.S. 1939. The bird life on the Grand Manan Archipelago. Proceedings of the Nova Scotian Institute of Science 19: 293-372.
Piatt, J.F. and R. McLagan. 1987. Colony attendance patterns of Common Murres (*Uria aalge*) at Cape St. Mary's, Newfoundland. Canadian Journal of Zoology 65: 1,530-1,534.
Piatt, J.F. and D.N. Nettleship. 1987. Incidental catch of marine birds and mammals in fishing nets off Newfoundland, Canada. Marine Pollution Bulletin 18: 344-349.
Piatt, J.F., D.N. Nettleship, and W. Threlfall. 1984. Net-mortality of Common Murres and Atlantic Puffins in Newfoundland, 1951-1981. Pages 196-206 *in* Marine Birds: Their Feeding Ecology and Commercial Fisheries Relationships (D.N. Nettleship, G.A. Sanger, and P.F. Springer, Eds.). Canadian Wildlife Service Special Publication, Ottawa, ON.
Piatt, J.F., H.R. Carter, and D.N. Nettleship. 1991. Effects of oil pollution on marine bird populations. Pages 125-141 *in* The effects of oil on wildlife (J. White, Ed.). Sheridan Press, Hanover, NH.
Powers, K.D. 1982. A comparison of two methods of counting birds at sea. Journal of Field Ornithology 53: 209-222.
Powers, K.D. 1983. Pelagic distributions of marine birds off the northeastern United States. NOAA Technical Memorandum NMFS-F/NEC-27: 1-201.
Powers, K.D. and R.G.B. Brown. 1987. Seabirds. Pages 359-371 *in* Georges Bank (R.H. Backus and D.W. Bourne, Eds.). Massachusetts Institute of Technology Press, Cambridge, MA.
Rankin, M.N. and E.A.G. Duffey. 1948. A study of the bird life of the North Atlantic. British Birds 41 Supplement: 1-42.
Renaud, W.E., P.L. McLaren, and S.R. Johnson. 1982. The Dovekie, *Alle alle*, as a spring migrant in eastern Lancaster Sound and western Baffin Bay. Arctic 35: 118-125.
Ross, R.K. 1973. A comparison of the feeding and nesting requirements of the Great Cormorant (*Phalacrocorax carbo* L.) and Double-crested Cormorant (*P. auritus* Lesson) in Nova Scotia. M.Sc. thesis, Dalhousie University, Halifax, NS.
Salomonsen, F. 1965. The geographical variation of the fulmar (*Fulmarus glacialis*) and the zones of marine environment in the North Atlantic. Auk 82: 327-355.
Salomonsen, F. 1972. Zoogeographical and ecological problems in arctic birds. Proceedings of the International Ornithological Congress 15: 25-77.
Smith, P.C., B.D. Petrie, J.A. Elliott, N.S. Oakley, and G. L. Bugden. 2014. Coastal ocean circulation studies. Pages 149-159 *in* Voyage of Discovery: Fifty Years of Marine Research at Canada's Bedford Institute of Oceanography (D.N. Nettleship, D.C. Gordon, C.F.M. Lewis, and M.P. Latremouille, Eds.). Bedford Institute of Oceanography-Oceans Association, Dartmouth, NS.
Squires, W.A. 1952. The birds of New Brunswick. New Brunswick Museum, Saint John, NB.
Squires, W.A. 1976. The birds of New Brunswick (second edition). New Brunswick Museum, Saint John, NB.
Tasker, M.L., P. Hope Jones, T. Dixon, and B.F. Blake. 1984. Counting birds at sea from ships: a review of methods employed and a suggestion for a standardized approach. Auk 101: 567-577.
Taverner, P.A. 1915. The Double-crested Cormorant (*Phalacrocorax auritus*) and its relation to the salmon industries on the Gulf of St. Lawrence. Geological Survey Musem Bulletin No. 13, Biological Series No. 5, Canada Department of Mines, Ottawa, ON.
Todd, W.E.C. 1963. Birds of the Labrador Peninsula and Adjacent Areas. University of Toronto Press, Toronto, ON.
Tuck, L.M. 1953. History and present populations of murre colonies in Newfoundland and Labrador. Canadan Wildlife Service Manuscript Report No. CWSC-665, Ottawa, ON.
Tuck, L.M. 1961. The Murres: Their Distribution, Populations and Biology - A Study of the Genus *Uria*. Canadian Wildlife Service Monograph Series No. 1, Ottawa, ON.
Tuck, L.M. 1967. The birds of Newfoundland. Pages 265-316 *in* The Book of Newfoundland, Volume 3 (J. Smallwood, Ed.). Newfoundland Book Publishers, St. John's, NL.
Tufts, R.W. 1962. The Birds of Nova Scotia. Nova Scotia Museum, Halifax, NS.
Tufts, R.W. 1986. The Birds of Nova Scotia (third edition). Nimbus and Nova Scotia Museum, Halifax, NS.
Tull, C.E., P. Germain, and A.W. May. 1972. Mortality of Thick-billed Murres in the west Greenland salmon fishery. Nature 237: 42-44.
Verspoor, E., T.R. Birkhead, and D.N. Nettleship. 1987. Incubation and brooding shift duration in the Common Murre *Uria aalge*. Canadian Journal of Zoology 65: 247-252.
Wheelwright, N.T. 1993. Bowdoin Scientific Station, Kent Island, 1992 Annual Report. Bowdoin College, Brunswick, ME.
Winn, H.E. 1950. The Black Guillemots of Kent Island, Bay of Fundy. Auk 67: 477-485.
Wynne-Edwards, V.C. 1935. On the habits and distribution of birds on the North Atlantic. Proceedings of the Boston Society of Natural History 40: 233-346.

Ocean Circulation & Chemistry

Principal current systems in the northwest Atlantic and eastern Canadian Arctic

Ocean Circulation and Chemistry

OCEAN CIRCULATION AND CHEMISTRY

16. STRONG WINDS AND STORMY SEAS: OCEAN CLIMATE STUDIES IN THE NORTH ATLANTIC

R. Allyn Clarke

SUMMARY

From its beginning, the Bedford Institute of Oceanography (BIO) focussed on observing, analyzing, and modelling the currents and water masses of the northwest Atlantic and eastern Arctic oceans. Throughout the past 50 years, BIO has maintained a state of the art capacity to conduct ship-based oceanographic observations in often stormy conditions. It designed deep-sea current meter moorings and successfully deployed them for up to 22 months in strong currents such as the Gulf Stream and North Atlantic Current. BIO's moorings have provided quantitative estimates of the volume and heat transport of all of the major current systems within the northwest Atlantic. Its focus on Canada's offshore waters has led to an extraordinary description of the changes of these waters over the past five decades, a history that is used by climate modellers across Canada and throughout the world. BIO's research on air-sea interactions has provided the underpinnings for the parameterizations of the momentum, heat, and water vapour fluxes used in modern weather forecast models and the coupled atmosphere-ocean climate models used to simulate climate change. BIO has also observed and analyzed ocean mixing at the smallest scale. A series of instruments capable of observing the variation of temperature, conductivity, and velocity at the scale of a few centimetres were developed and deployed in a variety of oceanographic regimes, and have provided valuable insights into how and where mixing occurs in the ocean.

Key words: water masses, currents, convection, North Atlantic circulation, Gulf Stream, North Atlantic current, air-sea interaction, microstructure, ocean mixing.
E-mail: Allyn420@aol.com

During the 1950s, for the first time, Canadian oceanographers participated in two multi-vessel oceanographic surveys of the North Atlantic organized by the international community. During 1958, the International Council for the Exploration of the Sea (ICES) co-ordinated winter and summer surveys of the sub-polar gyre of the North Atlantic (Dietrich 1969). Twenty-eight oceanographic vessels from nine countries collected more than 3,200 profiles of temperature, salinity, and oxygen over the entire North Atlantic from 40° to 70°N latitude. The Atlantic Oceanographic Group of the Fisheries Research Board of Canada, which later became part of the Bedford Institute of Oceanography (BIO), occupied 32 stations on the Scotian shelf and slope. The Fisheries Laboratory in St. John's, Newfoundland, also contributed sections across the Newfoundland Grand Banks and the Labrador Shelf. Earlier, in June 1950, the Naval Research Establishment (NRE) located in Halifax, Nova Scotia, participated in a multi-vessel survey of the Gulf Stream south of Nova Scotia (Ford et al. 1952). W. Ford, the second director of BIO, was involved in this project.

Research programs focussed on understanding the circulation and variability of the northwest Atlantic Ocean were established during BIO's first year (1962), and this focus continues to the present. From the beginning, the research was organized in three interconnected themes. The first theme was to build our knowledge of the circulation and variability of the waters of the western North Atlantic and eastern Arctic Oceans through observations. The second theme was to develop and test formulae that governed the exchanges of energy, momentum, heat, and water vapour between the ocean and atmosphere and within the ocean through mixing. The final theme was the development and testing of ocean models that could be used to predict ocean conditions. With the founding of BIO, Canada became a major contributor to oceanographic programs directed towards the North Atlantic.

OCEAN CIRCULATION AND VARIABILITY

The technology available for making oceanographic observations at sea in 1962 had not changed significantly from that used by the first large-scale oceanographic expedition by the HMS *Challenger* in 1872-76. Temperatures (and pressures) were measured by reversing mercury in glass thermometers and water samples were collected in sampling bottles that were closed mechanically at depth by dropping heavy brass messengers down the wire on which the bottles were secured. A major advance coincident with the founding of BIO was the acquisition of a laboratory instrument for measuring the conductivity of seawater samples. This instrument, developed by the National Institute of Oceanography (United Kingdom), replaced chemical titration of the chloride content as the method to determine the salinity of seawater.

During its first decade, BIO's small oceanographic group carried out an extensive series of surveys of the northwest North Atlantic. C. Mann led surveys of the Slope Water and Gulf Stream south of Nova Scotia and Newfoundland on CNAV *Sackville* in 1962. His focus then shifted to the transformation of the Gulf Stream into the North Atlantic Current in the region south and east of the Grand Banks of Newfoundland. His CSS *Baffin* surveys of this region in 1963, 1964, and 1966 led to his hypothesis that the Gulf Stream bifurcated when it encountered the Southeast Newfoundland Ridge (Mann 1967). The northern branch passing into the Newfoundland Basin became the North Atlantic Current while the southern branch continued to flow to the southeast to form the northern boundary of the Sargasso Sea. He further hypothesized that a quasi-stationary cyclonic eddy existed between these two branches. This eddy has come to be called the Mann eddy.

In addition, BIO initiated surveys of the northern regions of the North Atlantic including the Labrador Sea, Baffin Bay, and the eastern Canadian arctic. C. Ross undertook initial surveys of the eastern arctic and Baffin Bay in 1962 on the USS *Atka* and on the CCGS *Labrador* in 1963, while J. Lazier undertook a comprehensive survey of Baffin Bay and Davis Strait on CCGS *Labrador* in 1965, and the Labrador and Irminger seas on CSS *Hudson* during the winter of 1966. C. Mann completed this work from the CSS *Hudson* in the winter of 1967 with sections across the Irminger Sea and Denmark Strait as well as a section from Greenland to Ireland (Grant 1968; Fig. 1).

The following winter saw C. Ross occupying sections to observe the water properties within the deep basins of the Caribbean Sea. During the *Hudson*-70 expedition, BIO oceanographers occupied an over 6,000 km long hydrographic section along 30°W longitude down the South Atlantic from the equator to South Georgia Island at 55°S latitude, and an even longer section (13,800 km) along 150°W from 65°S to the Aleutian Trench just south of Alaska at 57°30'N, as well as a shorter section across Drake Passage south of the southern tip of South America (Mann 1971). During this period of BIO history, temperature and salinity profiles were measured using Knudsen bottles fitted with reversing thermometers which sampled at discrete and predetermined depths in the water column (Fig. 2).

BIO's first decade also saw the development of deep-sea current meter moorings. The 1967 investigation of the deep flow through Denmark Strait included a string of current meter moorings deployed

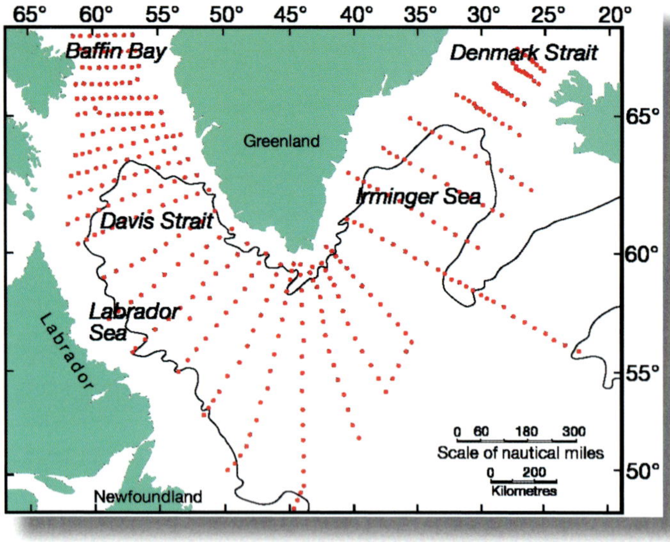

Figure 1. Oceanographic stations occupied in the Davis Strait (CCGS *Labrador*, 27 August- 27 October 1965), the Labrador Sea (CSS *Hudson*, 12 March–12 May 1966), and the Irminger Sea/ Denmark Strait (CSS *Hudson*, 16 January–5 April 1967) (after Grant 1968).

by the Woods Hole Oceanographic Institution (WHOI). Unfortunately, WHOI had underestimated the strength of the currents, and most of these moorings were lost (Worthington 1969). BIO's first attempt in 1966 to moor current meters on the continental slope south of Nova Scotia also resulted in a complete loss of instruments (Lawrence and Dobson 1966). Learning from these early failures, more robust moorings were designed and successfully deployed in three different locations in 1970: across the Drake Passage between the southern tip of Chile and the Antarctic Peninsula (Mann 1971), in the Charlie Gibbs Fracture Zone that pierces the mid-Atlantic Ridge between 52-54°N (Garner 1972), and beneath the Gulf Stream at 50°W as it passes south of the Tail of the Grand Banks of Newfoundland (Clarke and Reiniger 1973). In 1970, BIO also participated in an inter-comparison of self-recording current meters sponsored by the Scientific Committee on Oceanic Research (SCOR).

BIO's initial successes were followed by the deployment of much larger mooring arrays across the North Atlantic Current east of the Grand Banks of Newfoundland in 1972 (Clarke et al. 1980). In August-September 1973, CSS *Hudson* returned to the Denmark Strait as part of the ICES coordinated Overflow '73 project and successfully deployed an array of current meter moorings across the deep current that carries cold dense water (Fig. 3A) from the Nordic Seas into the deep North Atlantic. The month-long current meter records (Fig. 3B) showed the current transport was 2.3 x 10^6 m^3/s (Ross 1976). In all, these current meter arrays marked the world's first direct measurements of the transports of the Antarctic Circumpolar Flow, of the deep western boundary current carrying North Atlantic Deep Water southward along the Canadian continental slope, and of the cold and dense Denmark Strait Overflow water entering the North Atlantic.

The duration of the early mooring arrays were limited to a few months owing to corrosion, battery life, and data storage capacity. Unfortunately, the variability of ocean currents is such that observations

Figure 2. C. Mann secures a Knudsen sampling bottle with reversing thermometers to the hydrographic wire. This was the standard method of observing temperature and salinity profiles during BIO's first decade.

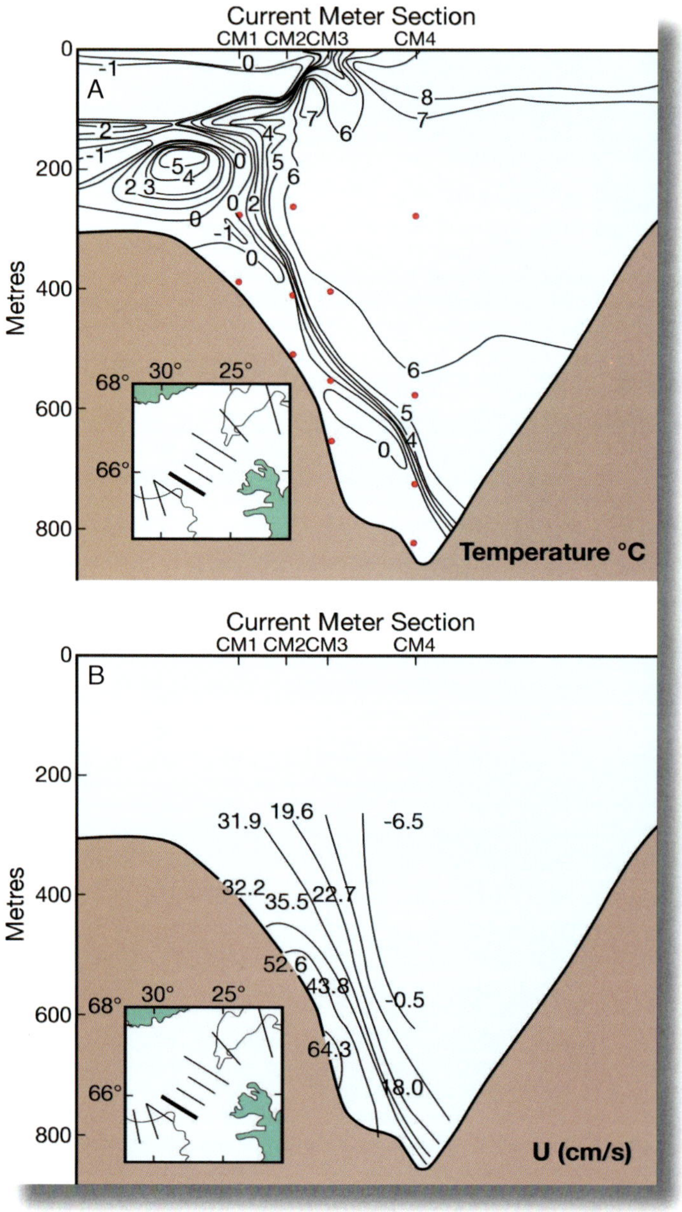

Figure 3. Temperature (A) and along-slope current (B) observed in the Denmark Strait by CSS *Hudson* in August and September 1973 as part of the BIO contribution to the ICES Overflow '73 project (U = current; southward for positive values, and northward for negative values). The currents are the average currents from mid-August to mid-September (after Ross 1976, 1978).

must be extended beyond 18 months to obtain a reasonable estimate of the mean flow. Through collaborations with mooring groups around the world, as well as with the instrument makers, these problems were gradually overcome until by the 1990s, moorings could be successfully deployed for periods of up to 2 years. Major mooring arrays were deployed across the Gulf Stream as it passes across 50°W, the North Atlantic Current east of the Grand Banks (Clarke et al. 1980), and the Labrador Current east of Hamilton Bank providing estimates of the transports of the major currents of the Northwest Atlantic.

The 1970s also saw the replacement of the mechanical

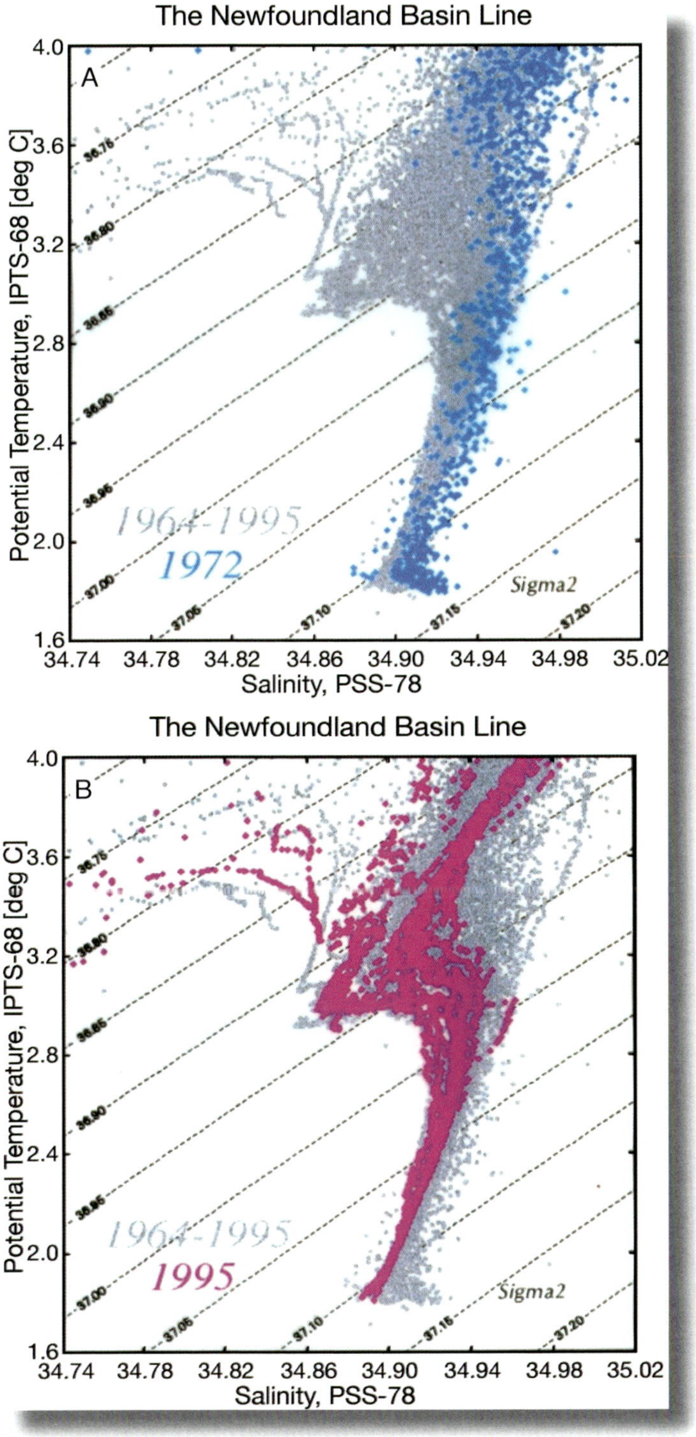

Figure 4. Changes from 1972 (A) to 1995 (B) in the temperature and salinity distributions across the deep western boundary current east of the Grand Banks of Newfoundland. The tightness of the 1995 distribution as compared to that of 1972 is a result of the order of magnitude improvement in both accuracy and precision since the 1970s. The 1995 distribution lies along the low salinity limit of the 1964 to 1995 distribution (grey points). This change reflects the freshening of the intermediate and deep waters of the northern North Atlantic over this period.

Figure 5. The CTD with its rosette of water sampling bottles as used during the WOCE cruises from 1990 to 1997. The 24 bottles collect 10-L water samples which are analyzed for a variety of chemical and biological substances.

instrumentation and laboratory procedures with electronic instruments with better precision. Sampling bottles and reversing thermometers were replaced by electronic probes that measured conductivity, temperature, and pressure as a continuous profile. By 1990, these CTD (conductivity, temperature, and depth) probes were capable of a precision in temperature of 0.001°C and in salinity of 0.001, more than 20 times the best precision achievable in the early 1970s (Fig. 4).

The mechanical Knudsen bottle only collected a litre of water so after drawing samples for salinity, oxygen, and nutrient analysis there was little volume to spare for the analysis of other substances. Separate casts using larger sample bottles were required to support interdisciplinary research at sea. This led to the development of the CTD/Rosette package which integrated the electronic probes with 24 sampling bottles, each capable of collecting more than 10 L providing samples for the analysis of several chlorofluorocarbon (CFC) compounds, tritium, total carbonate, and alkalinity as well as biological parameters (Fig. 5).

Tritium is an unstable isotope of hydrogen that was produced in large quantities through atmospheric testing of nuclear weapons in the 1950s and early 1960s. It has a half-life of 12.3 years, decaying to its daughter product, Helium-3. BIO oceanographers collected samples from the deep western boundary current in the Labrador Sea, Newfoundland Basin, and over the continental slope south of Nova Scotia for tritium/^{3}He analysis at WHOI (Jenkins and Smethie 1996). These observations are used to estimate the rate at which deep and intermediate waters are renewed from the surface. BIO also developed instrumentation to analyze the concentrations of various CFCs in the water column (Wallace and Lazier 1988). Because the rate of introduction of these compounds into the environment is known, the ratio of their concentrations provides another method of estimating the movement of water from the surface layers to the ocean depths (Azetsu-Scott et al. 2003).

Improvements were also achieved in the measurement of oxygen concentration and the concentration of the primary nutrients: nitrate, phosphate, and silicate, and new methods were developed by P. Jones and E. Levy to measure the concentration of CO_2 in sea water (Jones and Levy 1981). The CO_2 observations are conducted in order to observe the uptake of CO_2 in the intermediate and deep waters of the North Atlantic in response to its increase in the atmosphere.

At the end of the 1970s, CSS *Hudson* conducted two winter investigations of the circulation of the Labrador Sea in partnership with the Museum of Natural History in Paris, France. Winter 1976 was particularly severe with the Labrador ice-pack extending over most of the continental slope (Clarke and Gascard 1983). In mid-March, CSS *Hudson* observed evidence of deep convection extending from the surface to 2,200 m. Over the next week, the oceanographic structures associated with this event were extensively observed using neutrally buoyant floats vaned to measure vertical current, a profiling BATFISH system containing a CTD, and standard CTD profiles (Gascard and Clarke 1983). These were the first observations of the formation of Labrador Sea Water, an intermediate water mass that is associated with the observation of a salinity minimum centred at 1,500 to 2,000 m throughout the North Atlantic (Lazier 1980, Talley and McCartney 1982). CSS *Hudson* returned to the Labrador Sea in the fall of 1977 and winter (January to April) of 1978 to examine this deep convection in greater detail, but the winter was unusually mild and the convection was limited to a few hundred metres.

On 14 February 1982, CSS *Hudson* departed BIO for Reykjavik, Iceland, to pick up a team of scientists from the Scripps Institution of Oceanography (SIO) before embarking on a winter survey of the Nordic Seas. The ship was soon diverted on a search and rescue (SAR) call to proceed to the site of *Ocean Ranger*, the semi-submersible offshore drilling unit that sank in Canadian waters east of St. John's, Newfoundland, on 15 February 1982 with the loss of all 84 crew members. The crew of CSS *Hudson* spent a day at the site performing recovery operations before diverting to St. John's to land several recovered bodies.

In spite of this inauspicious beginning, a complete survey of the Nordic seas was accomplished (Fig. 6) and a high-quality data set was obtained (Clarke et al. 1990). Unfortunately, the winter was mild and the hoped for deep convection was not observed. CSS *Hudson* ended this program in Glasgow, Scotland, and a new scientific party occupied a high-density hydrographic trans-Atlantic section along 48°N as a contribution to the international Long Lines program (Hendry 1989).

BIO oceanographers returned to the Nordic seas again in February 1989 as a contribution to the Greenland Sea Project coordinated by the Arctic Ocean Sciences Board (Greenland Sea Project 1990). Since CSS

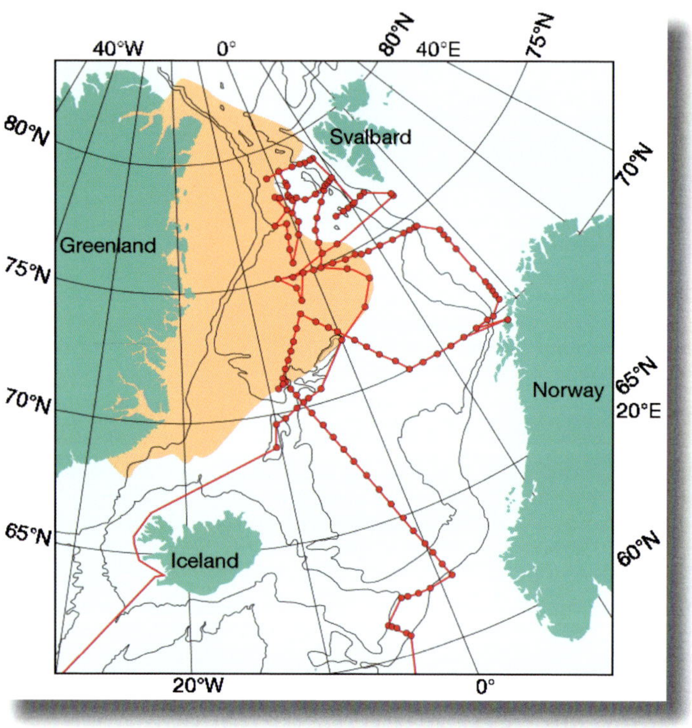

Figure 6. Cruise track and station positions for CSS *Hudson* Cruise 82-001 to the Nordic Seas (Clarke et al. 1990). Tan area on the western side marks the observed ice cover during the cruise.

Hudson was in refit, CSS *Baffin* was assigned to this project. The winter in the North Atlantic proved to be too much for CCS *Baffin*. Departing BIO on 19 January 1989, she diverted to St. John's (22-23 January), Reykjavik (30-31 January), and Glasgow (10-14 February) for repairs of storm damage encountered en route. CSS *Baffin* finally arrived in its work area on 20 February, one month after her departure date and over the next 8 days occupied 24 CTD stations. These stations were also occupied by the German RV *Valdivia* during the first week of February and during each of the first two weeks in March. The four occupations revealed that convection was taking place to depths of 1,500 m during the winter of 1988-89 (Greenland Sea Project Group 1990). CSS *Baffin's* troubles continued on her return voyage. Heavy sea ice filled Denmark Strait, forcing the longer passage to the east of Iceland, a passage slowed by three successive storms. During the third storm, the roof of the crow's nest peeled off and the top of the mast was held tethered to the side of the vessel with chain hoists. The next day, 9 March, the vessel was diverted to the east on a SAR mission to look for two small aircraft which were missing over the North Atlantic. Released from the SAR mission late on 12 March, CSS *Baffin* returned to BIO late on 18 March 1989 and was retired from service shortly afterwards.

During the 1990s, BIO was a major contributor to the World Ocean Circulation Experiment (WOCE; Clarke 1993). Under WOCE, an annual occupation of a high-density oceanographic section across the Labrador Sea was initiated: this occupation continues to the present. In addition to the physical oceanographic observations of temperature, salinity, oxygen content, and nutrients, the program collected samples that were analyzed for the chlorofluorocarbon compounds, total carbonate, and alkalinity. The physical oceanographers were joined by their biological colleagues who sampled chlorophyll, phytoplankton, and zooplankton distributions. These sections were occupied in May or June of the year in order to determine the depth of the previous winter's convection as well as to capture the strong biological productivity on both the continental shelves and the Labrador Sea. The deeper part of the section sampled the Northeast Atlantic Deep Water and the Denmark Strait Overflow Water. These waters are created through winter convection in the Nordic Seas and enter the North Atlantic through the Faero Bank Channel and Denmark Strait, respectively (Dickson et al. 2002). We were fortunate to observe the intense convection (Fig. 7) that occurred in the Labrador Sea during the winters of 1992-93 and 1993-94 (Lazier et al. 2002). This event created a large homogeneous pool of Labrador Sea Water that filled the interior of both the Labrador and Irminger Seas over the depth range of 500 to 2,200 m. A signal related to this strong convective event was still detected in the 2011 occupation of this section.

In 1996-97, WOCE coordinated an intensive survey of the entire North Atlantic (Holliday 1997). A large group of Canadian, German, and United States researchers led by Dr. R.S. Pickart of WHOI carried

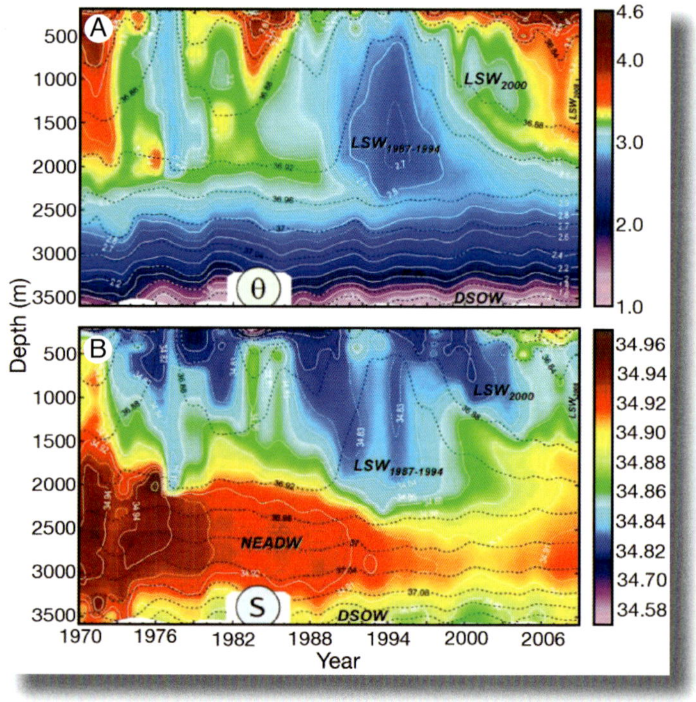

Figure 7. Time series of potential temperature (°C, A) and salinity (psu, B) in the central Labrador Sea, 1970-2009 (from I. Yashayaev). LSW is Labrador Sea Water, NEADW is North East Atlantic Deep Water, and DSOW is Denmark Strait Overflow Water. The black dashed lines represent the potential density anomaly relative to 2000 dbars.

out an intensive survey of the Labrador Sea over the fall, winter, and spring of 1996-97. BIO scientists joined this project by conducting extended surveys of the Labrador Sea from CSS *Hudson* in both the fall of 1996 and the spring of 1997 in order to establish the oceanographic conditions both before and after the winter cooling. BIO further assisted this effort by setting eleven oceanographic moorings for the University of Rhode Island (URI), University of Washington (UW), and Institut für Meereskunde, Kiel, Germany, plus 3 inverted echo sounders for URI, and deploying 39 ALACE floats for the Scripps Institution of Oceanography (SIO), 4 RAFOS floats for URI, 18 surface meteorological drifters for SIO, and three mixed layer floats for UW in the fall of 1996 (Table 1). Deep convection was observed in the western Labrador Sea during RV *Knorr's* winter survey (Pickart et al. 2002). CSS *Hudson's* spring survey confirmed the extent of the winter convection and also recovered five oceanographic moorings that had been deployed in the fall and winter cruises.

BIO's WOCE work also included intensive oceanographic surveys of the Gulf Stream-North Atlantic Current system south and east of the Grand Banks of Newfoundland in the falls of 1993 and 1994, and the spring of 1995. In addition to the oceanographic stations, a current meter array was deployed across the North Atlantic Current from 1993 to 1995 (Clarke et al. 1999). This array provided estimates of the northward transport of warm salty water by the North Atlantic Current, as well as the southward transport of the cold and fresher intermediate and deep waters in the deep western boundary current (Clarke et al. 1999).

Table 1. Number and description of floats and drifters deployed by CSS *Hudson* in the Labrador Sea, fall 1996.

Type (Number deployed)	Description
ALACE (N=39)	The ALACE (Autonomous LAgrangian Circulation Explorer) float is a deep drifter that is programmed to remain at a preset depth (up to 2,000m) for periods of 10 or more days after which it rises to the surface recording a temperature and salinity profile. It remains on the surface for several hours transferring its position and profile data to shore via satellite before diving again to a preset depth.
RAFOS (N=4)	The RAFOS float is a deep drifter that is ballasted to remain on a deep density surface. It records arrival times of low frequency acoustic signals broadcast from an array of moored sound sources. After a drift of a number of months, it releases a ballast weight, comes to the surface, and returns its recorded data via satellite link. Scientists can construct its drift pathway from the record of acoustic arrival times.
Meteorological drifters (N=18)	Meteorological drifters measure air pressure and temperature and sea surface temperature. They are drogued to track the movement of the upper 10 m of the water column. They report their data and position by satellite for use in forecasting models.

A major achievement of WOCE was the development of the ALACE profiling float (Davis and Zenk 2001; Fig. 8). Once deployed, these instruments are capable of obtaining up to 150 temperature/salinity profiles from the surface to 2,000 m over the following 4-5 years. For the first time, scientists were able to obtain subsurface oceanographic information from remote locations independent of research vessel voyages. The early prototypes of these instruments were deployed during BIO's annual transects across the Labrador Sea. Since 2000, BIO has been responsible for maintaining a fleet of profiling drifting floats over the entire western North Atlantic (Fig. 9) as part of Canada's contribution to the global fleet of 3,000 profiling drifters deployed and maintained by the international Argo program (http://www.argo.ucsd.edu).

Figure 8. Launching an ALACE profiling float from CCGS *Hudson*.

AIR-SEA INTERACTIONS

From its beginnings, BIO has also supported a strong research program directed at understanding the interactions between the atmosphere and the ocean (Smith et al. 1996). The ocean receives its energy and momentum from the sun and the atmosphere. The wind, blowing over the sea surface, transfers momentum to both the waves and to the surface currents. Heat and water vapour are also transferred between the ocean and atmosphere. At the beginning of the 1960s, our understanding of these transfers was based on measurements made in reservoirs or lakes, or occasionally over shallow near-shore banks. The instruments used for these measurements were light and delicate with observations limited to low and moderate wind speeds. The BIO Marine Engineering Group decided to rectify these deficiencies through two developments. First, they designed and constructed a thrust anemometer that would be more robust than the propeller anemometers then in use. Second, they designed and built a semi-submersible stable tower that could be moored in waters of moderate depth and serve as a scientific platform for measuring the turbulent fluxes of momentum and heat between ocean and atmosphere (Doe and Brooke 1965). These two developments were first deployed in 1964 from CSS *Baffin* in an experiment off Aruba, in the Caribbean.

A re-engineered stable tower (Fig. 10) with a much upgraded suite of instruments was maintained off the mouth of Halifax Harbour, Nova Scotia, from June 1976 until its failure during a severe winter gale in February 1978. During its 20 months of operation, momentum and heat flux data were obtained over the greatest range of wind speeds and air-sea temperature differences ever observed (Smith 1980). These data still provide the basis for the calculation of these fluxes in the ocean, weather, and climate models of today (Smith 1988).

S. Smith was a major contributor to the planning and implementation of the Humidity Exchange over the Sea (HEXOS) program carried out around a Dutch research platform in the North Sea during October-November 1986 (Smith et al. 1990). This international program deployed a variety of boundary meteorological instruments from aircraft, ships, research masts, and the Dutch research platforms in order to determine the water vapour fluxes between sea and atmosphere through evaporation and sea spray. The BIO group observed the turbulent fluxes of water vapour, heat, and momentum.

Air-sea-ice interactions were also an issue of special interest to Canada. Beginning in the winter of 1969-70, the group began a series of field programs to measure heat and momentum fluxes over a wide variety of sea-ice conditions in the Gulf of St. Lawrence, Beaufort Sea, and northern Grand Banks of Newfoundland (Banke and Smith 1973). This work revealed how these fluxes were affected by the size and roughness of the ice floes and the presence of leads in the ice pack (Smith et al. 1983). This work was then applied to the forecasting of the drift of icebergs (Smith 1993).

The group applied its expertise in the measurement of turbulent momentum, heat, and water vapour fluxes to the measurement of the air-sea flux of CO_2. An instrument was developed to measure fluctuations

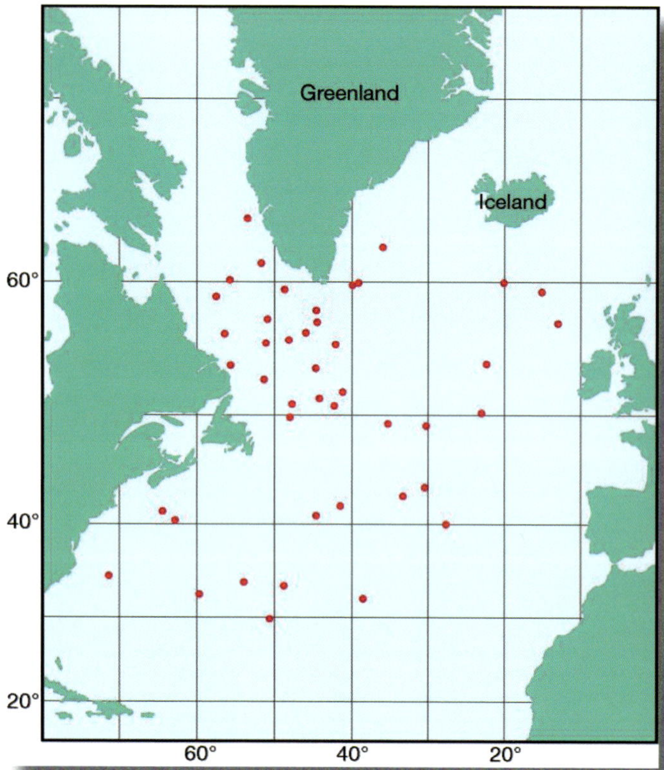

Figure 9. Locations of temperature and salinity profiles obtained by Canadian ALACE floats in the North Atlantic Ocean from 1-10 June 2012 (from USGODAE Argo GDAC Data Browser at http://www.usgodae.org/cgi-bin/argo_select.pl).

Figure 10. The stable tower with instrumentation for measuring air-sea interactions on station at the mouth of Halifax Harbour, Nova Scotia.

in CO_2 concentration in the atmosphere. This instrument, along with a three component acoustic anemometer, was mounted on a tower at the water's edge on the beach on Sable Island, Nova Scotia (Jones and Smith 1977). The turbulent flux of CO_2 between the ocean and atmosphere can be estimated by measuring the CO_2 fluctuations simultaneously with those of the vertical component of the wind. The sensitivity of the instrument was, in the end, insufficient to estimate the air-sea flux of CO_2 with sufficient accuracy; however, the sensor has gone on to be the principal tool for the observation of CO_2 fluxes over forests and croplands.

During the 1980s, the air-sea research group moved their focus from the direct observation of air-sea fluxes to the development of the climatology of winds, air and sea temperatures, clouds, and air-sea fluxes over the North Atlantic. The thrust of this research was to reconcile the estimates of the poleward ocean heat transports required by atmospheric models with those computed by ocean models. This work was an important precursor to the development of the coupled ocean–atmosphere climate models of the last decade.

OCEAN WAVES

BIO scientists were also interested in ocean waves. The years 1962 and 1963 saw the development of a wave-rider buoy that measured the vertical acceleration of the sea surface and radioed this information to a shore station several kilometres away (Gilbert 1970). This instrument was first deployed to measure waves in the Great Lakes in order to determine safe working drafts for vessels navigating the shallower areas.

Ocean waves have continued to be a focus of research at BIO. The air-sea research group participated in most of the international field and analysis programs on ocean waves through to the 1990s. These included the 1972 JOint North Sea WAve Project (JONSWAP) in the North Sea, the Bight of Abaco experiments in 1973-74, and the Joint Air Sea InteractioN (JASIN) experiment in the northeast Atlantic Ocean in 1978. The analysis of the JONSWAP wave observations provides the basis for our modern models for wave development and growth.

A particularly novel research tool, developed at BIO, was the wave follower (Harvey and Dobson 1976; Fig. 11). A bottom-mounted tower contained a hydraulic ram that was able to move up and down with the sea surface. This instrument was first deployed in the fall of 1974 in a United States/Canada wave experiment in the Bight of Abaco, Bahamas (Snyder et al. 1981). An instrument package mounted on the ram measured wind and pressure a few centimetres above the sea surface within a wave field, thus directly recording the momentum and energy transfer between the atmosphere and the wave field. These transfers are dependent on the sea state and are greater when the waves are still growing. Wave models are included in modern long-range weather models to better estimate air-sea exchanges of energy and momentum. This allows the models to improve their estimate of the development of storms as they pass over water.

Wave research continues at BIO, but observations are now obtained from satellite sensors that look at the roughness of the sea surface to estimate wind speed and wave height. These estimates are supplemented by *in situ* wind and wave observations from the moored meteorological buoy network maintained by the Meteorological Service of Canada (MSC) over Canada's offshore waters as well as pressure and air temperature measurements from a global array of drifting meteorological surface drifters maintained by meteorological agencies around the globe. Both of these meteorological buoys were originally developed through the Canadian Ocean Data Systems program by Hermes Electronics under a contract that was supervised by J. Brooke and J. Elliott at BIO and J. Garrett at the Institute of Ocean Sciences (Reid 1978).

The development of the surface drifters was a major Canadian contribution to the First GARP Global Experiment (FGGE) from December 1978 to November 1979 (Garrett 1980). The Global Atmosphere Research Program (GARP) was an intergovernmental research program sponsored by the World Meteorological Organization (WMO) during the 1970s. Its goal was to support long-range weather forecasting and hence it had particular foci on the interactions between the ocean and atmosphere. BIO scientists had also carried out a surface layer oceanographic program in the tropical Atlantic from CCGS *Quadra* in the summer of 1974 as part of the Canadian contribution to the GARP Atlantic Tropical Experiment (GATE).

In more recent years, wave research at BIO was focussed on wave models. An observer experiencing a storm at sea will notice that the dominant waves are all of about the same wavelength (i.e., the distance

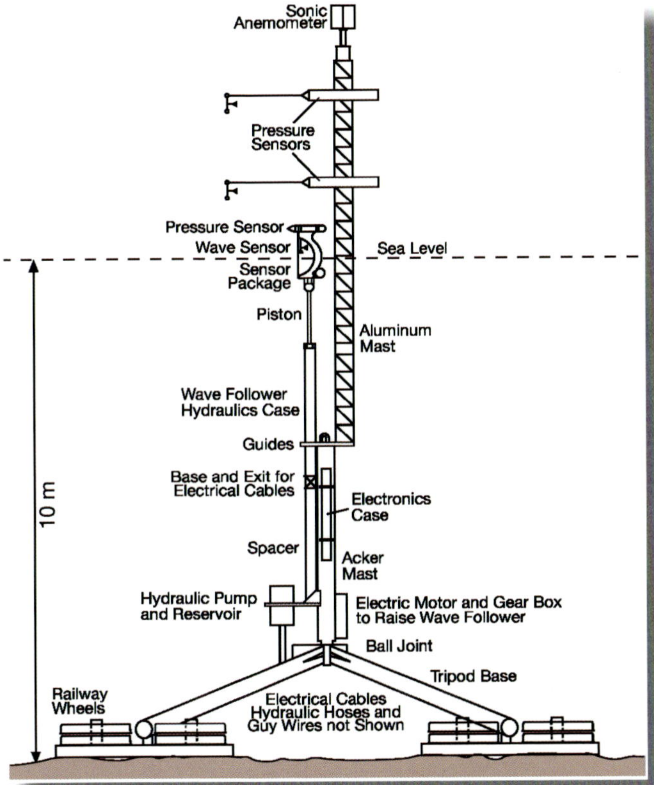

Figure 11. The wave follower assembly (from Harvey and Dobson 1976). The lower electric motor and gear box adjust the mean level of the instrument mast and wave follower for the state of the tide. The instrument is mounted on a hydraulic piston that keeps the pressure sensor a few centimetres above the sea surface.

between successive peaks), but over time will see the height and the wavelength of these dominant waves get larger. If the wind continues to blow at the same speed and direction for several hours, the waves will eventually stop growing. This phenomenon occurs because the distortion of the wind field by the dominant waves causes energy and momentum to be transferred from the wind to the waves at that dominant wavelength. However, the energy does not stay at this dominant wavelength, but is instead transferred to both longer and shorter wavelengths. The energy that is transferred to longer wavelengths causes the dominant wavelength to move to longer wavelengths as the storm continues. The height of the waves also increases. The energy that is transferred to shorter wavelengths is finally dissipated through mixing. BIO research has made important contributions to the analysis and modelling of these transfers (Perrie and Resio 2009). This research has also shown that modelling the interactions between storms and waves improves the forecast of the storm's impact (Xu et al. 2007).

OCEAN MIXING

Air-sea processes create vertical and horizontal gradients of temperature and salinity in the ocean (Clarke et al. 2001). Biological processes create similar gradients in the concentrations of nutrients (e.g., nitrates, phosphates, and silicates) and oxygen. Ocean eddies, convection, and current shear stir ocean waters, but it is ultimately processes such as molecular diffusion and mixing that operate at scales of a metre or less that smooth the vertical and horizontal gradients and return the water to a homogeneous state. The deep and bottom waters of the world oceans are created by winter cooling in the northern Atlantic Ocean and Nordic seas as well as along the coast of Antarctica (Dickson et al. 2002). These cold and dense waters fill the deep ocean basins and then, over the centuries, are slowly warmed through the diffusion of heat from above as well as geothermal heating from the seabed. This heating of the bottom waters is controlled by small-scale mixing (Toole and McDougall 2001).

During the 1970s, N. Oakey and J. Elliott developed an instrument to measure the gradients of temperature, conductivity, and velocity at centimetre scales (Oakey and Elliott 1980). The initial instrument was deployed in strong currents such as the Denmark Strait Overflow, Gulf Stream, and Equatorial Undercurrent in the Pacific Ocean. The initial instrument underwent several generations of development in which advances of electronics, data storage media, and tether were incorporated in order to improve reliability and data recording capacity (Oakey 1988).

A unique characteristic of this family of instruments was that they remained loosely tethered to the vessel while free falling through the water column. The instrument's descent was effectively decoupled from the motion of the vessel so that the observed fluctuations in temperature, conductivity, and velocity were characteristics of the water column, not artifacts of the instrument's motion. At the end of each profile, the loose tether was used to return the instrument quickly to the surface and be redeployed, which allowed multiple profiles to be recorded. Multiple profiles are required in order to obtain statistically significant estimates of turbulence levels. More recently, wings were attached to the instrument so that it would descend obliquely through the water column as a glider (Fig. 12), improving its ability to sample turbulence in the surface mixed layer (Greenan and Oakey 1999).

While these ocean turbulence instruments were used to investigate ocean mixing associated with a number of ocean processes, two studies are of particular interest. The first was an investigation of the role of mixing in the biological productivity on the Scotian Shelf. Winter cooling of the water column mixes nutrients through convective mixing. In early spring with the return of longer days, a warm surface layer forms and the growth of phytoplankton accelerates. This period of intense growth lasts for a few weeks before the nutrients in the surface layers are exhausted. Over the rest of the summer, phytoplankton continues to grow albeit at a much lower rate than in the spring. Vertical mixing of nutrients into the surface layer was estimated from observed microstructure profiles. It was shown to be sufficient to support this lower level of biological productivity (Horne et al. 1996).

A second study examined the role of mixing in the ocean interior. From the earliest oceanographic surveys, observations of the temperature and salinity fields of the North Atlantic have revealed a large tongue of warm salty water arising from the Strait of Gibraltar that spreads into the surrounding waters at depths of 800 to 1,200 m. Early theoretical studies at BIO (Needler and Heath 1975) showed that the large-scale characteristics of this tongue could be modelled by a simple balance between advection (i.e., movement of water) and diffusion (i.e., mixing of heat and salt both vertically and horizontally). The advent of continuous vertical profiles of temperature and salinity from CTD instruments revealed that this warm salinity tongue contained a number of subsurface eddies centred at about 1,000 m which contained in their cores water with the temperature and salinity of the waters entering the North Atlantic through the Strait of Gibraltar. These eddies were given the name 'meddies'. The BIO research team, in cooperation with Dalhousie University (Halifax, NS) and WHOI, observed one such meddy on four occasions during 1984 to 1986 (Armi et al. 1989). The mixing rate

Figure 12. The EPSONDE instrument in its glider configuration (photo: B. Greenan). The sensors which measure temperature, conductivity, and velocity microstructure are mounted inside the circular shields at the front of the instrument. As the instrument sinks in the water column, it traces a shallow oblique path whose angle is controlled by the short control surface at the rear of the instrument.

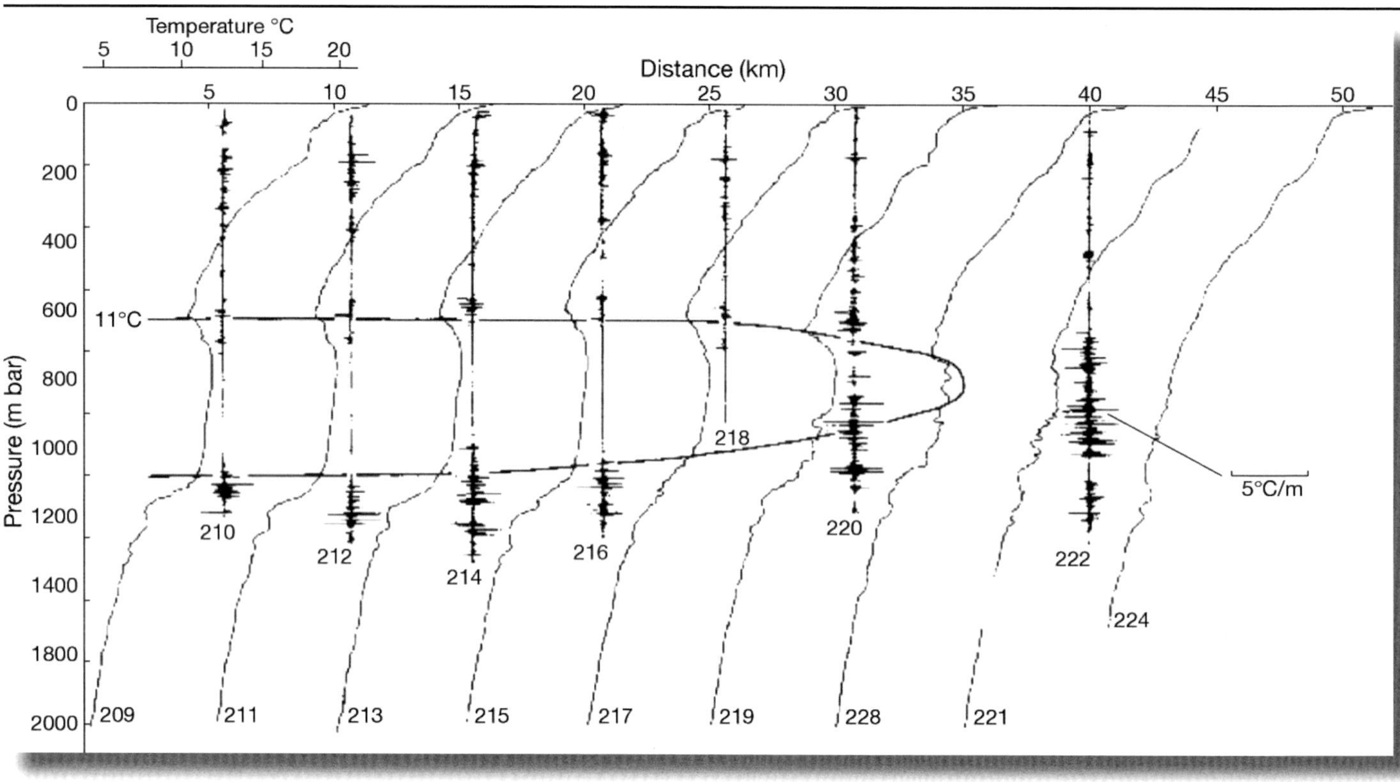

Figure 13. The temperature profiles (thin solid lines) and the corresponding temperature microstructure ('wiggly' lines) for a transit from the centre to the outer edge of the lens during the CSS *Hudson* survey of the 'meddy' (from Armi et al. 1989). The heavy 11°C isotherm marks the upper and lower boundaries of the Mediterranean Water; the temperature microstructure is greatest at these boundaries and at the outer perimeter of the 'meddy'. The vertical axis is pressure in decibars and is approximately equal to depth in metres. The horizontal axis is the position of each profile from the centre of the lens.

derived from BIO's microstructure observations showed that mixing was occurring at the upper and lower boundaries of the core as well as around its outer perimeters (Fig. 13). The rate of mixing was consistent with the observed decay of the 'meddy' over the two years that it was tracked and observed.

ACHIEVEMENTS AND THE FUTURE

Over the course of five decades, scientists at BIO have participated in all of the major international programs directed toward understanding the role of the ocean in the climate system. They not only participated in these programs, but also played leadership roles in their development and implementation. C. Mann was a member of the IOC task group that developed the oceanographic component of the FGGE (IOC 1978). F. Dobson led a study group for the Committee on Climate Change and the Ocean (CCCO) to see if the heat flux carried across the North Atlantic by both the atmosphere and the ocean could be measured (Dobson et al. 1982). S. Smith was a member of the HEXOS steering group (Smith et al. 1990). A. Clarke chaired the Scientific Steering Group (SSG) for WOCE from 1991-94 and then co-chaired the SSG for its successor program, Climate Variability (CLIVAR), from 1996-99. G. Needler was the founding Director of the International Planning Office for WOCE from 1985-89 and was then WOCE Chief Scientist from 1989 to 1992. Many other BIO scientists have served on working groups and steering committees associated with international and intergovernmental research programs. As our new generation of scientists mature, there will be opportunities for them to take similar leadership roles if they are not discouraged by restrictive travel opportunities and limited scientific resources.

Given its location, it is not surprising that BIO's deep-sea oceanographic interest focussed on the formation and circulation of the deep and intermediate waters of the North Atlantic (Yashayaev and Dickson 2008). CSS *Hudson* was particularly well-designed and was able to continue scientific operations in the northern reaches of the North Atlantic in the heart of winter, and this supported BIO's expertise in the processes of deep convection and the formation of water masses (Lazier 1980, Clarke and Gascard 1983, Clarke et al. 1990). BIO's mandate to focus on Canadian waters led to a focus on the Labrador Sea and to the collection of unique datasets describing ocean variability over the decades (Dickson et al. 2002, Lazier et al. 2002). With the reduction of BIO's research fleet to a single aging CCGS *Hudson*, the era of large-scale ship surveys extending over several months has drawn to a close. BIO is meeting this challenge through its deep-sea extensions of the Atlantic Zone Monitoring Program and its deployment of ALACE floats in the North Atlantic north of 40°N and west of 40°W. These observations will allow the Institute to continue tracking changes in the oceanic waters offshore of Canada's east coast and to form partnerships with the other scientific groups interested in the North Atlantic and its variability.

BIO's air-sea interaction group provided particular scientific leadership in the understanding of the transfers of momentum, heat, and water vapour between the sea and atmosphere. They lent their scientific and technical expertise to most of the international programs on air-sea coupling and their observations form the basis for modern weather forecasting and climate models. BIO no longer has the technical and scientific expertise needed to observe air-sea fluxes, although it continues to have expertise in the modelling of surface waves and the impact of air-sea fluxes on storm development.

ACKNOWLEDGEMENTS

Much of what has been described here has involved direct observations in the field. This work may have been inspired by the vision of BIO's research scientists; however, the work could not have been completed without the technical and engineering skills and dedication of the technical and engineering staff. BIO was also blessed with a fleet of capable research vessels with skilled officers and crews that would always seek a solution to the various operational problems that arose at sea. The BIO community is hoping that the long-awaited replacement for CCGS *Hudson* will provide that same capability to support multidisciplinary science in all parts and seasons of the North Atlantic.

REFERENCES

Armi, L., D. Hebert, N. Oakey, J. Price, P. Richardson, T. Rossby, and B. Ruddick. 1989. Two years in the life of a Mediterranean salt lens. Journal of Physical Oceanography 19: 354–370.

Azetsu-Scott, K., E.P. Jones, I. Yashayaev, and R.M. Gershey. 2003. Time series study of CFC concentrations in the Labrador Sea deep and shallow convection regimes (1991-2000). Journal of Geophysical Research 108: 3,354-3,362. doi:10.1029/2002JC001317, C11.

Banke, E.G. and A.D. Smith. 1973. Wind stress on Arctic sea ice. Journal of Geophysical Research 78(33): 7,871-7,883. doi:10.1029/JC078i033p07871.

Clarke, R.A. 1993. The World Ocean Circulation Experiment (WOCE). World Meteorological Organization Bulletin 42: 28-33.

Clarke, R.A. and R.F. Reiniger. 1973. The Gulf Stream at 49°30′W. Deep-Sea Research 20: 627-641.

Clarke, R.A. and J.-C. Gascard. 1983. The formation of Labrador Sea water, Part I - Large Scale Processes. Journal of Physical Oceanography 13: 1,764-1,778.

Clarke, R.A., H.W. Hill, R.F. Reiniger, and B.A. Warren. 1980. Current system south and east of the Grand Banks of Newfoundland. Journal of Physical Oceanography 10: 25-65.

Clarke, R.A., J.H. Swift, J.L. Reid, and K.P. Koltermann. 1990. The formation of Greenland Sea deep water: double diffusion or deep convection. Deep-Sea Research 37: 1,385-1,424.

Clarke, R.A., R.M. Hendry, I. Yashayaev, and D.R. Watts. 1999. A western boundary current meter array in the North Atlantic near 42°N. Bulletin of the Canadian Meteorological and Oceanographic Society 27: 42-44.

Clarke, R.A., J. Church, and J. Gould. 2001. Ocean processes and climate phenomena. Pages 11-30 *in* Ocean Circulation and Climate: Observing and Modelling the Global Ocean (G. Siedler, J. Church, and J. Gould, Eds.). Academic Press, International Geophysics Series 77, New York, NY.

Davis, R.E. and W. Zenk. 2001. Subsurface Lagrangian observations during the 1990s. Pages 123-139 *in* Ocean Circulation and Climate: Observing and Modelling the Global Ocean (G. Siedler, J. Church, and J. Gould, Eds.). Academic Press, International Geophysics Series 77, New York, NY.

Dickson, B., I. Yashayaev, J. Meincke, B. Turrell, S. Dye, and J. Holfort. 2002. Rapid freshening of the deep North Atlantic over the past four decades. Nature 416: 832-837.

Dietrich, G. 1969. Atlas of the hydrography of the northern North Atlantic based on the polar front survey of the International Geophysical Year winter and summer 1958. Conseil International pour l'Exploration de la Mer, Service Hydrographique, Charlottenlund Slot, Denmark.

Dobson, F.W., F.P. Bretherton, D.M. Burridge, J. Crease, E.B. Krauss, and T.H. von der Haar. 1982. The JSC/CCCO 'CAGE' experiment: A feasibility study. Report to the JSC/CCCO Liaison Committee, World Climate Programme. World Meteorological Organization, Geneva, Switzerland. http://unesdoc.unesco.org/images/0004/000489/048976eb.pdf

Doe, L.A.E. and J. Brooke. 1965. A moored stable platform for air-sea interaction studies. Alfred C. Redfield 75th Anniversary Volume, Limnology and Oceanography 10 (Supplement): 79-86.

Ford, W.L., J.R. Longard, and R.E. Banks. 1952. On the nature, occurrence and origin of cold low salinity water along the edge of the Gulf Stream. Journal of Marine Research 11: 281-293.

Garner, D.M. 1972. Flow through the Charlie-Gibbs Fracture Zone, Mid-Atlantic Ridge. Canadian Journal of Earth Sciences 9: 116-121.

Garrett, J.F. 1980. The availability of the FGGE drifting buoy system data set. Deep-Sea Research 27: 1,083-1,086.

Gascard, J.-C. and R.A. Clarke. 1983. The formation of Labrador Sea Water, Part II - Mesoscale and smaller-scale processes. Journal of Physical Oceanography 13: 1,779-1,797.

Gilbert, R.L.G. 1970. The Bedford Institute wave recorder. Journal of Geophysical Research 75 (27): 5,215-5,224. doi:10.1029/JC075i027p05215.

Grant, A.B. 1968. Atlas of Oceanographic Sections – Temperature, salinity, dissolved oxygen, silica - Davis Strait, Labrador Basin, Denmark Strait, Newfoundland Basin, 1965-1967. Atlantic Oceanographic Laboratory, Report 68-5, Bedford Institute of Oceanography, Dartmouth, NS.

Greenan, B.J.W. and N.S. Oakey. 1999. A tethered free-fall glider to measure ocean turbulence. Journal of Atmospheric and Oceanic Technology 16: 1,545-1,555.

Greenland Sea Project Group. 1990. Greenland Sea Project: a venture toward improved understanding of the ocean's role in climate. Eos 71(24): 750-751, 754-755.

Harvey, D.R. and F.W. Dobson. 1976. The Bedford Institute wave follower. Bedford Institute of Oceanography Report Series BI-R-76-13, Dartmouth, NS.

Hendry, R.M. 1989. Hydrographic measurements from CSS *Hudson* Cruise 82-002. Canadian Technical Reports of Hydrography and Ocean Sciences 118, Fisheries and Oceans Canada, Dartmouth, NS.

Holliday, P. 1997. An international survey of the North Atlantic, 1996-98N. International WOCE Newsletter 25: 42-43.

Horne, E.P.W., J.W. Loder, C.E. Naimie, and N.S. Oakey. 1996. Turbulence dissipation rates and nitrate supply in the upper water column on Georges Bank. Deep-Sea Research, Part II: Topical Studies in Oceanography 43: 1,683-1,712.

Intergovernmental Oceanographic Commission. 1978. Oceanographic components of the Global Atmospheric Research Programme (GARP). UNESCO Intergovernmental Oceanographic Commission (IOC) Technical Series 17, Paris, France.

Jenkins, W.J. and W.M. Smethie, Jr. 1996. Transient tracers track ocean climate signals. Oceanus 39: 29-32.

Jones, E. P. and S. D. Smith. 1977. A first measurement of sea-air CO_2 flux by eddy correlation. Journal of Geophysical Research 82(37): 5,990-5,992. doi:10.1029/JC082i037p05990

Jones, E.P. and E.M. Levy. 1981. Oceanic CO_2 increase in Baffin Bay. Journal of Marine Research 39: 405-416.

Lawrence, D.J. and D. Dobson. 1966. Deep Ocean Surveys. Pages 33-34 *in* Fifth Annual Report, Bedford Institute of Oceanography, Report BIO 66-10, Dartmouth, NS.

Lazier, J.R.N. 1980. Oceanographic conditions at ocean weather ship *Bravo*, 1964-1974. Atmosphere-Oceans 18: 227-238.

Lazier, J., R. Hendry, A. Clarke, I. Yashayaev, and P. Rhines. 2002. Convection and restratification in the Labrador Sea, 1990-2000. Deep-Sea Research I 49: 1,819-1,835.

Mann, C.R. 1967. The termination of the Gulf Stream and the beginning of the North Atlantic Current. Deep-Sea Research 14: 337-359.

Mann, C.R. 1971. The *Hudson*-70 Expedition. Pages 3-9 *in* Bedford Institute Biennial Review 1969/70. Bedford Institute, Dartmouth, NS.

Needler, G.T. and R.A. Heath. 1975. Diffusion coefficients calculated from the Mediterranean salinity anomaly in the North Atlantic Ocean. Journal of Physical Oceanography 5: 173-182.

Oakey, N.S. 1988. Epsonde: an instrument to measure turbulence in the ocean. *IEEE* (Institute of Electrical and Electronic Engineers) Journal of Oceanic Engineering 13: 124-128.

Oakey, N.S. and J.A. Elliott. 1980. The variability of temperature gradient microstructure observed in the Denmark Strait. Journal of Geophysical Research 85(C4): 1,933–1,944. doi:10.1029/JC085iC04p01933.

Perrie, W. and D. Resio. 2009. A two-scale approximation for efficient representation of nonlinear energy transfers in a wind wave spectrum. Part II: Application to observed wave spectra. Journal of Physical Oceanography 39: 2,451-2,476. doi: 10.1175/2009JPO3947.

Pickart, R.S., J.T. Daniel, and R.A. Clarke. 2002. Hydrography of the Labrador Sea during active convection. Journal of Physical Oceanography 32: 428-457.

Reid, F. 1978. A successful meteorological drifting buoy. Pages 18- 21 *in* Proceedings of MTS/IEEE Oceans '78 'The Ocean Challenge' Conference, Washington, DC. The Marine Technology Society, Washington, DC. doi:10.1109/OCEANS.1978.1151057.

Ross, C.K. 1976. Overflow '73 - transport of overflow water through Denmark Strait. International Council for the Exploration of the Sea (ICES), CM 1976/C 16, Copenhagen, Denmark.

Ross, C.K. 1978. Overflow variability in Denmark Strait. International Council for the Exploration of the Sea (ICES), CM 1978/C 21, Copenhagen, Denmark.

Smith, S.D. 1980. Wind Stress and heat flux over the ocean in gale force winds. Journal of Physical Oceanography 10: 709-726.

Smith, S.D. 1988. Coefficients for sea surface wind stress, heat flux and wind profiles as a function of wind speed and temperature. Journal of Geophysical Research 93: 15,467-15,472.

Smith, S.D. 1993. Hindcasting iceberg drift using current profiles and winds. Cold Regions Science and Technology 22: 33-45.

Smith, S., R. Anderson, G.D. Hartog, D. Topham, and R. Perkin. 1983. An investigation of a polynya in the Canadian Archipelago: 2, Structure of turbulence and sensible heat flux. Journal of Geophysical Research 88 (C5): 2,900-2,910. doi:10.1029/JC088iC05p02900.

Smith, S.D., K.B. Katsaros, W.A. Oost, and P.G. Mestayert. 1990. Two major experiments in the Humidity EXchange Over the Sea (HEXOS) Program. Bulletin of the American Meteorological Society 71: 161-172.

Smith, S.D., C.W. Fairall, G.L. Geernaert, and L. Hasse. 1996. Air-sea fluxes: 25 years of progress. Boundary Layer Meteorology 78: 247-290.

Snyder, R.L., F.W. Dobson, J.A. Elliott, and R.B. Long. 1981. Array measurements of atmospheric pressure fluctuations above surface gravity waves. Journal of Fluid Mechanics 102: 1-59.

Talley, L.D. and M.S. McCartney. 1982. Distribution and circulation of Labrador Sea Water. Journal of Physical Oceanography 12: 1,189-1,205.

Toole, M.J. and T.J. McDougall. 2001. Mixing and stirring in the ocean interior. Pages 337-354 *in* Ocean Circulation and Climate: Observing and Modelling the Global Ocean (G. Siedler, J. Church, and J. Gould, Eds.). Academic Press, International Geophysics Series 77, New York, NY.

Wallace, D.W.R. and J.R.N. Lazier. 1988. Anthropogenic chlorofluoromethanes in newly formed Labrador Sea Water. Nature 332: 61-63.

Worthington, L.V. 1969. An attempt to measure the volume transport of Norwegian Sea overflow water through Denmark Strait. Deep-Sea Research (Supplement) 16: 419-430.

Yashayaev, I. and R.R. Dickson. 2008. Transformation and fate of overflows in the northern North Atlantic. Pages 505-526 *in* Arctic-Subarctic Ocean Fluxes: Defining the Role of the Northern Sea in Climate (R.R. Dickson, J. Meincke, and P. Rhines, Eds.). Springer Press, New York, NY.

Xu, F., W. Perrie, B. Toulany, and P.C. Smith. 2007. Wind-generated waves in Hurricane Juan. Ocean Modelling 16: 188-205.

17. COASTAL OCEAN CIRCULATION STUDIES

Peter C. Smith*, Brian D. Petrie, James A. Elliott, Neil S. Oakey, and Gary L. Bugden

SUMMARY

Bedford Institute of Oceanography (BIO) coastal circulation studies from the early 1960s to the present are described by interweaving five main themes: (1) *climatological studies and numerical models* - including wide-ranging flow dynamics over the east coast continental shelf, connections between the deep offshore ocean and flows on the shelf, primary pathways from Baffin Bay and the Labrador Shelves in the northeast to the Gulf of Maine in the southwest with excursions through the Gulf of St. Lawrence and around the Grand Banks; (2) *air-sea interaction studies* - the focus of the Canadian Atlantic Storms Programs conducted on the Scotian Shelf and on the northern Grand Bank; (3) *early studies* - assessment of Bay of Fundy tidal power proposals, exploration of the Browns Bank ecosystem as part of The Fisheries Ecology Program, and to collaborations with United States and Canadian GLOBEC programs focussed on Georges Bank and the Northeast Channel; (4) *early contributions by BIO scientists* - the circulation in the Gulf of St. Lawrence and Estuary, and the impacts of local rivers, lakes, and coastal embayments, studies that later spurred development of high-resolution circulation models for understanding nearshore ecosystem habitats; and (5) *the present* - BIO marine science support for the assessment of and mitigation procedures for various environmental risks, tools for maintaining human safety, and forecasts for predicting important trends and events.

Key words: coastal ocean circulation, coastal climatology, turbulent mixing, air-sea interaction, tidal dynamics, nearshore studies, Gulf of Maine, Gulf of St. Lawrence, operational oceanography, air-ice-ocean modelling, and forecasting.

***E-mail:** Peter.Smith@dfo-mpo.gc.ca

Ocean science at the Bedford Institute of Oceanography (BIO) has a rich history of circulation studies in the coastal oceans, including extensive field studies, theoretical analyses, and numerical model simulations. Often these studies are part of multidisciplinary programs in which the attributes of the physical environment control or strongly impact important aspects of the marine ecosystem. In such cases, it is vital to study the physical, biological, and chemical nature of the problem jointly in order to answer the underlying research questions. Groups of related (e.g., geographically, dynamically) coastal circulation studies are reviewed following certain prominent themes. Frequently, research efforts have been revisited and expanded over the years in order to shed new light on the processes at work and to apply that knowledge to the benefit of ocean stakeholders and the public at large. Typically, trends in these research areas have moved from initial discovery and process studies to the development of operational tools and models which use the new knowledge. The latter phases of this evolution usually lead directly to significant societal benefits. In all cases, the primary motivations for these studies have been a lack of understanding (sometimes highlighted by an event, such as an oil spill or the failure of a commercial fishery), and how to use the resulting knowledge to increase our ability to deal with stresses on the marine environment and to mitigate their impacts. For present purposes, the coastal ocean will include nearshore areas (lakes, estuaries, and embayments), the continental shelf, and slope (to depths of ~1,000 m). Figure 1 depicts the full range of temporal and spatial scales for processes operating in the coastal environment.

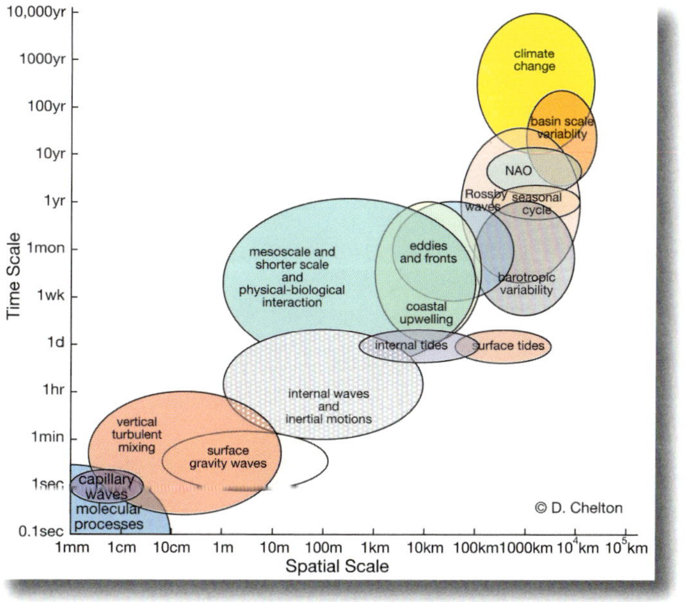

Figure 1. Depiction of the range of space and time scales which characterize the circulation of the coastal ocean (adapted from D. Chelton, Oregon State University). The largest spatial and temporal scales are associated with climate change and basin-scale variability of the mean and interdecadal currents, while the smallest scales are associated with turbulent mixing caused by air-sea interaction, breaking waves, etc. NAO is the acronym for the North Atlantic Oscillation.

COASTAL CLIMATOLOGY: MEAN FLOW, ANNUAL, INTERANNUAL, AND INTERDECADAL VARIABILITY

The continental shelf of eastern Canada has broad shelves (100-200 km) with rugged topography, separated from abyssal depths by a steep continental slope (Fig. 2). Deep basins and marginal troughs (>200 m) are typically found in the nearshore regions, whereas long chains of shallow banks in offshore regions create a partial barrier to exchanges between oceanic and coastal waters. The coastline is also very irregular and punctuated by gulfs, estuaries, and embayments at various scales. All of these physical features have important consequences for the structure and variability of the coastal circulation.

General Circulation

Over the fifty-year history of BIO, many researchers have contributed to the picture of the general circulation in the region (Fig. 2). Oxygen isotope analysis of shelf water as far south as the Middle Atlantic Bight indicates that one of its primary components is glacial meltwater and river runoff into the northern Labrador Sea which, in turn, suggests that the coastal current is driven by the buoyancy of that freshwater and extends southward for thousands of kilometres along the east coast of North America. Building on the earlier work of pioneers such as Bigelow (1927), Hachey and Bailey (1952), McLellan (1954), Trites and Banks (1958), and Bumpus and Lauzier (1965), Sutcliffe et al. (1976) summarized the major features of this circulation, based on archived data, including the two components (inshore, offshore) of the Labrador Current, exchange through the Strait of Belle Isle, flow through the Gulf of St. Lawrence, mixing of Cabot Strait outflow and offshore slope water in the Nova Scotia Current on the Scotian Shelf, and cyclonic (counterclockwise) flow through the Bay of Fundy and Gulf of Maine (Fig. 2). Using correlation analysis, they also further quantified the source of the dominant seasonal cycle in the salinity of the Scotia-Maine near-surface waters as the annual freshwater discharge of the St. Lawrence River system into the Gulf of St. Lawrence.

Figure 2. Map of Canada's east coast, including: place names, bathymetry (depth ranges for increasingly dark shades of blue are: 0-200 m, 200-500 m, 500-1,000 m, 1,000-2,000 m, and increasing intervals of 1,000 m), and major features of the mean surface circulation.

The mean annual discharge of this system (424 km^3/y) exceeds that of the sum of the entire eastern United States (353 km^3/y). Using temperature and salinity data, Drinkwater et al. (1979) estimated the resulting seasonal transports in the Nova Scotia Current off Halifax, Nova Scotia, to reach a maximum in winter of 0.60×10^6 m^3/s and a minimum in summer of 0.15×10^6 m^3/s; however, direct observation by Anderson and Smith (1989) using arrays of moored current meters indicated that the winter maximum was closer to 1.2×10^6 m^3/s. Beyond Halifax, the Nova Scotia Current appears to split, with one branch continuing southwestward toward Cape Sable at the southwestern tip of Nova Scotia, and the other heading offshore towards the shelf break. Smith (1983) reported a maximum alongshore transport into the Gulf of Maine at Cape Sable of roughly 0.3×10^6 m^3/s in December 1979. Later, as part of the United States GLOBEC program (a NOAA-sponsored effort focussed on marine ecosystems) to study the Georges Bank ecosystem, Smith et al. (2001) observed significant interannual variability in the boundary fluxes of mass, heat, and salt to the Gulf of Maine at Cape Sable and in the Northeast Channel during 1993-96. Notably, an increase in freshwater input to the Gulf over the last 2 years of observations (1995-96) was consistent with a decrease of 0.73 in the salinity of the outflow waters from the Gulf. These physical changes to the ambient water masses can have significant consequences for the structure and health of the marine ecosystem.

Labrador Current

Lazier and Wright (1993) conducted a pioneering study of the structure and variability of the Labrador Current, based on a decade (1978-88) of current meter and hydrographic (ocean temperature and salinity) observations spanning the inshore and offshore branches of the flow. Their analyses revealed two distinct regimes within the offshore branch of the Labrador Current: a strong vertically-sheared flow over the outer shelf and upper slope carrying cold freshwater southward from Baffin Island and Hudson Strait (the 'traditional' branch), and a 'deep' branch lying over the lower continental slope (~2,500 m). The latter appears to be part of the wind-driven transport in the North Atlantic's subpolar gyre. Moreover, the two components exhibit different annual cycles: southward transport in the shallow branch over the upper slope peaks in October, whereas transport in the deep branch is at a maximum in winter (January to March). Finally, it appears that the annual cycle of transport in the shallow branch of the flow is induced by the interaction between the buoyancy flux variations and bottom slope. These analyses contributed significantly to our understanding of the connectivity of various east coast ocean regions.

Other important contributions by BIO scientists to the observation and description of mean circulation on the Labrador-Newfoundland shelf and slope include Drinkwater's (1988) description of mean and tidal currents in Hudson Strait, Petrie et al.'s (1988) analysis of volumetric, heat, and salt transport through the Strait of Belle Isle, and Petrie and Buckley's (1996) work to estimate the volume and freshwater transports by the Labrador Current in Flemish Pass. K. Drinkwater's data, from just west of Ungava Bay, reveal an intense, strongly sheared jet on the Quebec side of Hudson Strait, flowing southeastward toward the Labrador Sea, a weak deeper flow toward Hudson Bay on the northern side, and cross-flow in the middle of the Strait. The net transports on the two sides are nearly equal, but the outflowing jet is much fresher. Petrie and Buckley (1996) were able to combine their data with those from other time periods and regions to constrain their estimates of the volume and freshwater transports through the Pass. Their estimates were consistent with those of Lazier and Wright (1993) in the same time frame, thereby providing an accurate picture of coastal currents through this region.

Long-term Variability

To address questions of decadal variability of the circulation and water properties on the Scotian Shelf and in the Gulf of Maine, Petrie and Drinkwater (1993) examined 45 years of hydrographic data from the entire region and concluded that the dominant low-frequency event was a cooling and subsurface freshening of the water masses from 1952 to 1967, followed by a reversal of those trends. The largest changes were subsurface, originating in the waters over the continental slope at a point south of the Grand Banks (42°N, 54°W) and decreasing westward. Horizontal exchanges with shelf waters and vertical mixing processes gave rise to surface manifestations of these anomalies. The trends were found to be pervasive in the deeper waters of the western shelves, including the Laurentian Channel (Bugden 1991), the Scotian Slope, which runs along the seaward boundary of the Scotian Shelf, and Emerald and Georges Basins, which are found in the central Scotian Shelf and Gulf of Maine, respectively. Petrie and Drinkwater (1993) attributed these trends to changes in the strength and pattern of the Labrador Current, in particular, as they affect variations in westward transport along the continental slope at the Tail of the Grand Bank. More recent work by Marsh et al. (1999) has demonstrated that periods of increased westward transport of cold, fresh Labrador Slope Water (derived from the Labrador Current) are associated with sustained periods of weak meteorological forcing over the North Atlantic, as represented by the North Atlantic Oscillation (NAO) index. Subsequent penetration of the hydrographic anomalies onto the shelf gives rise to the pervasive cooling and freshening. In describing an outstanding example of this process, Drinkwater et al. (1999) note a westward pulse of Labrador Slope Water, triggered by a single, isolated minimum of the NAO during the winter of 1996, which is then tracked along the continental slope to the Mid-Atlantic Bight over a two-year period, penetrating deeper areas of the Gulf of St. Lawrence, Scotian Shelf, and Gulf of Maine along the way. These findings give a unique insight into the driving forces for long-term changes in the properties of coastal regimes.

Numerical Modelling

Initial understanding of the nature and dynamics of the coastal ocean circulation and its variability has been derived primarily from observational studies. However, as the research has matured, a new, efficient, and practical method of study has emerged: the numerical circulation model. The primary goals of formulating and verifying such models are to provide a physical interpretation of the observations, to understand the underlying dynamics, and to extrapolate the results to a wider domain.

Early model studies, such as those of Greenberg (1983) investigating the circulation driven by the tide and steady climatological wind stress in the Gulf of Maine/Bay of Fundy, and other work studying the mean depth-averaged circulation on the Newfoundland shelf and slope, were able to reproduce some, but not all, of the observed features (Greenberg and Petrie 1988).

The rapid growth in the size and sophistication of numerical circulation modelling over the last two decades has led to much more highly-resolved, three-dimensional systems that are able to simulate not only the mean wind- and tidally-driven flows, but also density-driven effects associated with upstream sources, local rivers, etc. In the Scotia-Maine region, for instance, a new technique involving successive refinement of model results has led to accurate simulations of the seasonal and inter-decadal variability of the circulation, including the role of the intrusion of Labrador Slope Water in the cold 1960s by Hannah et al. (2001) and Loder et al. (2001).

Another modern technique for estimating annual and interannual variations in the transports of major shelf/slope currents involves remote sensing of sea-surface height distributions. Han et al. (1993) and Han and Tang (2001) and others showed that these data are most useful when combined with hydrographic data and/or a numerical model. Together, these advances have provided a means for understanding the nature of coastal circulation and forecasting its impacts.

CIRCULATION AND MIXING STUDIES AT THE SHELF EDGE

Cross-shelf Mixing

Abrupt depth changes at the edge of the continental shelf (known as the 'shelf break') lead to dynamic physical processes that significantly affect conditions on the shelves themselves. For example, water mass analysis conducted by Houghton et al. (1978) indicates that water flowing westward along the Scotian Shelf is diluted when it reaches Halifax by ~40% with off-shelf slope water as a result of cross-shelf mixing; the observed alongshore variations are consistent with measured onshore fluxes at the shelf break. Some of the processes that drive this exchange have been identified as wind-induced upwelling (Petrie 1983) and as bursts of low-frequency energy associated with offshore eddies and waves driven by the Gulf Stream (Smith 1978, Louis et al. 1982).

Upwelling

Wind-driven upwelling at the shelf break is generated most effectively by moderate, but sustained (>2 days), alongshore winds that are capable of raising water from depths in excess of 400 m on the continental slope to the shelf break (~200 m); but the source region for these deep waters is confined to within 10 km of the shelf break. The presence of the complex topography (shallow banks and troughs) on the outer shelf renders shelf-break upwelling an essentially three-dimensional process. Ikeda (1985) drew similar conclusions about the rugged Labrador and Newfoundland shelves, with the added impact of the Labrador Current front, which serves to enhance cross-shelf exchange induced by upwelling-favourable winds. These processes make significant contributions to the composition and richness (e.g., nutrients) of the shelf waters throughout the region.

Offshore Currents

On the western side of the North Atlantic basin, strong boundary currents, such as the Gulf Stream and Labrador Current, radiate low-frequency energy that impinges on, but rarely crosses, the continental margin because of constraints associated with the large depth change (Fig. 3A). Nevertheless, the associated fluxes of heat, salt, and nutrients are directed shoreward and serve to modify the shallow waters flowing along the shelf. Some of these fluxes are driven by direct interactions with powerful features of basin-scale currents (such as the Gulf Stream) and the eddies they spawn (known as 'warm-core rings'; Smith 1978), whereas others are the product of energy radiated to the shelf edge by interactions of such large scale currents with the steep topography of the continental margin (Louis et al. 1982). Such features also have a significant impact on biological productivity in the surface layers (Fig. 3B).

Tidal Mixing and Turbulence

Beginning in the early 1970s, BIO scientists commenced a multi-year investigation of the relationships between tides, turbulence, and ocean mixing at the edge of the Scotian Shelf, in order to understand the reasons for high nutrient concentration and biological productivity in the euphotic zone there (Sandstrom and Elliott 1984). The principal conclusion of these studies of tidal flow over the shelf (or bank) edge is that during off-shelf (ebb) flow, a deep depression of density surfaces develops over the upper slope. As the ebb flow weakens, the sides of the trough steepen as the feature propagates onto the shelf and evolves into a packet of short, large-amplitude internal waves, often called solitary waves or solitons (Fig. 4; Smith and Sandstrom 1988). The large amplitudes and

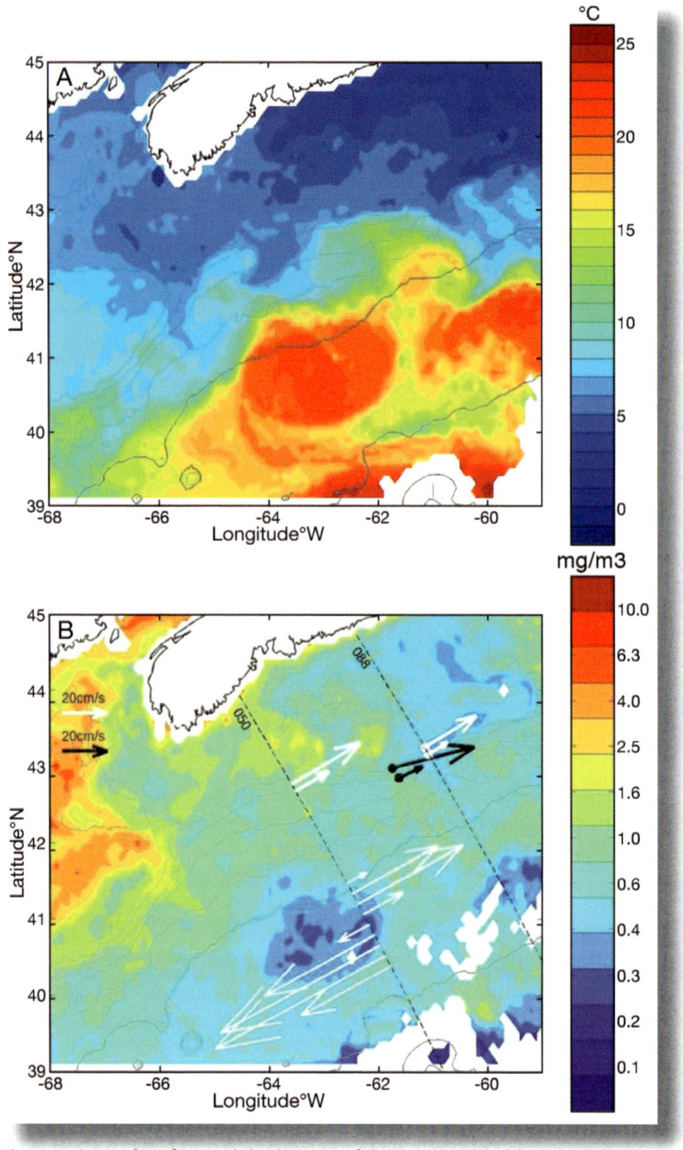

Figure 3. Sea-surface characteristics (courtesy of G. Han, NWAFC): (A) temperature map revealing a warm core ring (bright red) southeast of Nova Scotia; and (B) concurrent SeaWiFS chlorophyll concentration (mg/m³) and ring rotational speed as revealed by TOPEX/Poseidon satellite altimetry derived currents (white arrows) on 8 May 2002 and moored current meter measurements (black arrows).

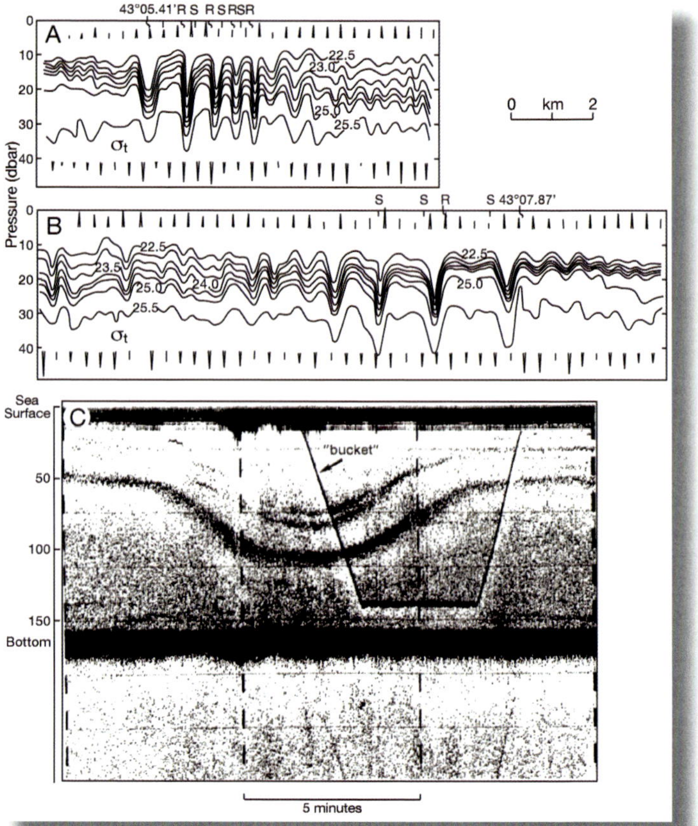

Figure 4. Ocean features near the Scotian Shelf break at 63° 30'W: top - Density anomaly (σ_t) field observed from a towed CTD (BATFISH; Smith and Sandstrom 1988) during two consecutive crossings of a short internal wave (soliton) packet near the shelf break; in panel (A), ship and waves are travelling in opposite directions, and in (B), the ship is overtaking the waves; banded surface wave pattern is marked as rough 'R' and smooth 'S'; panel (C), a single internal soliton observed by a 12 kHz acoustic sounder; the 'bucket' trace is made by a CTD cast through the soliton feature from a ship drifting near the break at 63°W.

short scales of these features are associated with strong currents and shears, which lead to instability and significant turbulent dissipation in the surface layers (Sandstrom and Oakey 1995). It is by this mechanism that the shoreward-propagating tidal energy, which is generated by offshore tides interacting with the shelf edge, is dissipated while serving to enrich the surface layers with nutrients from deeper waters. Similar packets of short internal waves have been detected as far north as Davis Strait and as far south as Florida, suggesting they are a ubiquitous feature of the shelf break circulation in the western North Atlantic. In fact, as part of their research, Sandstrom and Elliott (1984) discovered that the signatures of these solitons, consisting of alternating bands of rough and smooth surface waters, could be detected by radar, both from ships and aircraft using Side-Looking Aperture Radar (SLAR). This finding led to an extensive airborne survey of surface conditions over the outer reaches of the Scotian Shelf and Grand Banks that revealed the presence of these features, particularly during the summer season (Figs. 5A,B; Sandstrom and Elliott 2010).

Mixing rates and estimates of vertical diffusivities derived from the measurement of turbulence and microstructure rely heavily on turbulence theory. In 1996-97 during the Coastal Mixing and Optics Experiment on the continental shelf, the vertical diffusivities of heat and of density were obtained using a unique special-purpose instrument known as EPSONDE (Fig. 6), designed by Oakey (1988). When Oakey and Greenan (2004) compared these diffusivities to the direct measurement of vertical dispersion of a tracer (Ledwell et al. 2004), it was found that the two independent and very different techniques led to consistent results, giving further confidence in the indirect measurements from turbulence and microstructure profilers.

WIND-DRIVEN CIRCULATION: AIR-SEA INTERACTION

Energy Transfer

Much of the energy in the ocean is derived from its interaction with the atmosphere. Following comprehensive compilations of wave climate statistics for the Canadian Atlantic coast in the late 1960s and early 1970s by Neu (1971), early work on air-sea interaction at BIO focussed on observations both above and below the water surface. Atmospheric boundary layer measurements on Sable Island, Nova Scotia (Smith and Banke 1975) and from a stable platform off Halifax (Smith 1988) served to establish accurate drag and heat flux coefficients for the marine boundary layer on the Scotian Shelf (Smith 1988), which are vital for understanding the heat and momentum budgets of the ocean surface layers, and hence, are related to circulation and climate variability (see Clarke 2014). Furthermore, Oakey and Elliott (1982) used measurements with an early BIO-designed velocity microstructure probe (OCTOPROBE II; Oakey 1977) to establish the proportion of the turbulent atmospheric energy that flows into the surface mixed layer, where it dissipates. They also used these results to conclude that part of the mixed-layer turbulence was generated by local instabilities, rather than directly forced by surface phenomena, such as wave breaking. In a later experiment, Greenan and Oakey (1999) obtained estimates of dissipation in the ocean mixed layer using a quasi-horizontal microstructure profiler, designed and built with the assistance

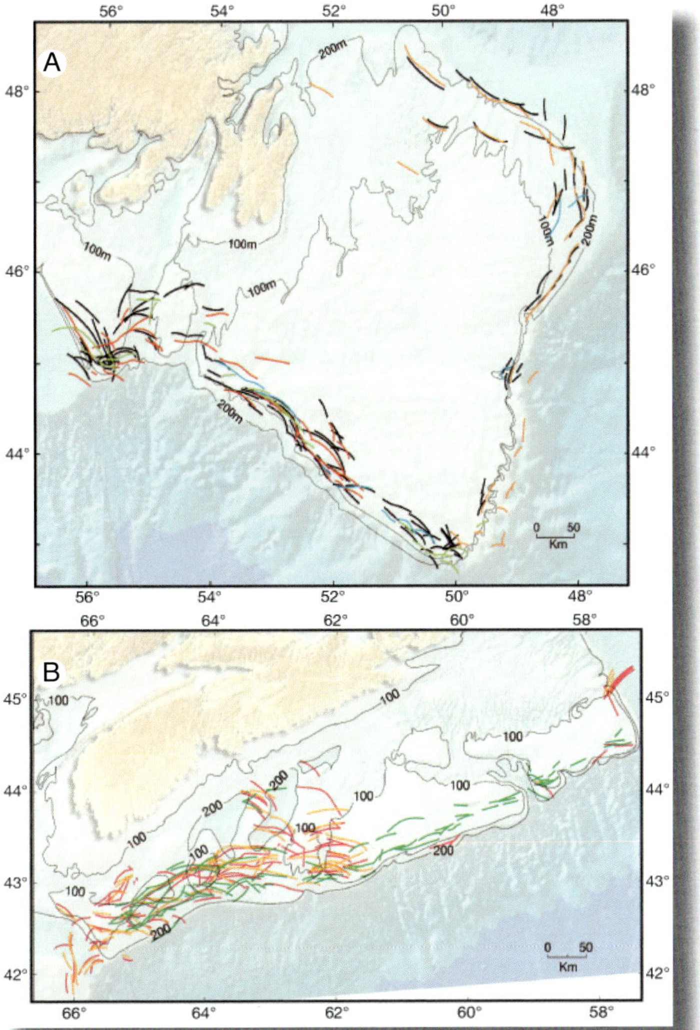

Figure 5. Composite SLAR images showing locations of the leading or dominant wave in groups of solitons propagating from their generation sites near the shelf edge onto: (A) the Newfoundland Grand Banks, and (B) the Scotian Shelf.

of others (Greenan et al. 1997). The microstructure profiler or glider is shown being deployed at sea in Figure 7. The dissipation of turbulent kinetic energy is much higher than expected from a purely shear-driven boundary layer on a flat surface (Greenan et al. 2001). The enhancement has usually been attributed to wave breaking. In this program, however, Greenan and Oakey joined F. Dobson to integrate measurements of dissipation with air-sea flux estimates and directional wave spectra to further study this issue. Dissipation rates were enhanced relative to the wind stress production and indicated that approximately 6% of the wind energy at 10 m is dissipated in the ocean mixed layer, larger than earlier estimates by Oakey and Elliott (1982). These discoveries greatly enhanced our understanding of the energetics of the surface layer.

Storm-driven Flows

The Canadian Atlantic Storms Program (CASP I, 1985-86) was a collaborative effort (with Environment Canada and the National Research Council of Canada) designed to investigate the ocean's response on the Scotian Shelf to intense winter storms. Oceanographic observations included sea level, surface waves, currents, bottom pressure, and water properties. These were complemented by meteorological buoys, a land-based network of wind measurements, and airborne surveys of the atmospheric boundary layer near the coast of Nova Scotia. The CASP I research revealed two important components of the wind-driven circulation on the shelf: (1) long, low-frequency (2-10 day periods), shoreward intensified

Figure 7. The tethered free fall GLIDER developed at BIO in the 1990s to measure ocean turbulence in the near surface (Greenan et al. 1997, Greenan and Oakey 1999) is shown near the surface at the start of a long shallow dive. Inset at the upper left shows the suite of sensors used to measure small-scale turbulence and microstructure; inset upper right shows the instrument during tests from the barge facility in Bedford Basin, Nova Scotia.

waves, and (2) energetic, but intermittent, inertial waves (natural oscillations with periods of one-half pendulum day, or ~17 h on the Scotian Shelf). Specifically, Schwing (1989) demonstrated that a significant portion of the wind-driven energy in the bottom pressure field was driven by both local wind and by waves impinging on the eastern end of the shelf. On the other hand, Smith (1989a) found that the intense inertial energy, was generated by strong, fast-moving wind shifts (i.e., fronts) associated with large storm systems. Another CASP I success was the verification of the laws of wave growth in the open ocean by Dobson et al. (1989). This work entailed synthesis of results from the land-based network, a near-shore array of nine wave buoys, and airborne surveys of wind speed and turbulence, conducted by Smith and MacPherson (1987). The CASP I results created a clear and quantitative picture of the wind-driven response of Scotian Shelf waters over the full water depth.

Figure 6. The small-scale turbulence instrument EPSONDE (Oakey 1988; instrument developed at BIO during the 1980s) being recovered from a deployment to measure turbulence and microstructure from the surface to the bottom at a site on the continental shelf. Inset (upper right) shows an early prototype , OCTUPROBE I, developed in the early 1970s, and a later prototype, OCTUPROBE II (Oakey 1977), developed in the late 1970s (lower right).

Atmosphere-ice-ocean Interactions

Following CASP I, a similar program (CASP II) was conducted on the Newfoundland Shelf in the winter of 1992-93, focussed on atmosphere-ocean interaction with sea ice. Its oceanographic component consisted of moored current meter and surface drift measurements conducted on the northern Grand Bank (Narayanan et al. 1996), an oceanographic cruise in the Marginal Ice Zone (MIZ), and more current measurements conducted by C. Tang and D. Belliveau. This was supplemented with a series of airborne surveys of the structure of the atmospheric boundary layer above the MIZ by Smith et al. (1994), and of sea-ice properties (e.g., snow-plus-ice thickness) using the 'ice probe', a newly-designed electromagnetic induction device conceived by Prinsenberg et al. (1996). The complex interaction observed between the atmospheric boundary layer, sea ice, and the open ocean shed new light on the processes at work in this harsh environment, and provided a basis for more accurate understanding and forecasting. More recently, S. Prinsenberg and colleagues have focussed their efforts on the use of helicopter-borne sensors and ice beacons to investigate interannual variability of the east coast pack ice and the processes that cause it (Prinsenberg et al. 2014).

Surface Wave Modelling

The CASP experiments spurred the growth and development of wave modelling research at BIO. Starting with an analysis of the wave-growth relationships derived from CASP I (Perrie and Toulany 1990), BIO wave modellers continued to improve and update state-of-the art wave models with new features such as air-sea coupling dynamics (Perrie and Wang 1995), ice-ocean dynamics (Perrie and Hu 1996, 1997), and new techniques for estimating wave energy transfer rates (Resio and Perrie 2008, Perrie and Resio 2009). Use of this new method has been shown to provide a significant improvement to both the speed and accuracy of wave model computations.

Summer Upwelling

Finally, it is useful to demonstrate that not all important wind-driven circulations are found in the winter. Specifically, Petrie et al. (1987) showed that the response of coastal upwelling to persistent southwesterly summer winds over the Scotian Shelf leads to the development of a band of cold water along the coast, which then evolves into trains of isolated cold-core eddies, which propagate northeastward along the coast. Alongshore wavelengths are roughly 50-75 km, similar to the cross-shore displacement amplitudes. The upwelling and subsequent eddy development are thought to play an important role in supplying nutrients to the surface waters of the shelf.

TIDAL DYNAMICS IN THE GULF OF MAINE

Fundy Tides

Theoretical and modelling studies by C. Garrett and D. Greenberg in the 1970s and early 1980s demonstrated that the Gulf of Maine and Bay of Fundy are a single ocean system with a natural resonant period slightly longer than the M2 semidiurnal period (12.42 h), giving rise to the extremely large tides recorded there (Garrett 1972, 1974; Greenberg 1979; Fig. 8A,B). As a result, much of the dynamics, mixing, and biological productivity in the Gulf of Maine is dominated by tidal processes. For example, Loder (1980) and Wright and Loder (1985) explored the dynamics of a process known as topographic rectification (the generation of a directed mean current by the interaction of tidal currents over a sloping bottom) on the flanks of Georges Bank, and Greenberg (1983) then used a numerical model to demonstrate that a large part of the mean circulation in the entire Gulf is driven by that process. Garrett et al. (1978) then showed that spatial variations in tidal mixing parameters support the summertime patterns of thermal stratification, whereas Loder and Greenberg (1986) examined means of predicting the precise locations of tidal fronts. Observations at key locations in both the Gulf (Smith 1983) and the upper Bay of Fundy (Tee 1977; Tee and Amos 1991) were used to verify the nature of tidally-induced residual currents (Tee et al. 1988) and to identify a new tidally-driven process for injecting cold, nutrient-rich water into the surface layers, dubbed 'topographic upwelling', in the waters off southwest Nova Scotia (Tee et al. 1993). Over two decades of observation, analysis, and modelling by BIO scientists and colleagues, the picture of the dynamic circulation in the Gulf of Maine became much clearer.

Bank Ecosystems

From 1982 to 1989, BIO scientists, led by K. Frank and P. Smith with F. Page, conducted an interdisciplinary study of the ecosystem on Browns Bank off southwest Nova Scotia. The particular focus of the study, known as the Fishery Ecology Program (FEP), was the Browns Bank Atlantic Haddock *(Melanogrammus aeglefinus)* stock, which supported a commercially important fishery in the area. The ultimate goal of the project was to provide sound advice for management of the fishery through increased knowledge of how the system works. Significant findings of the FEP include evidence that interannual variability in both the physical properties of the ocean and the plankton biomass are related to alongshore wind variations (Smith 1989b), that resulting temperature differences can cause variations in haddock egg stage development (Page and Frank 1989), and that stratification strongly moderates the vertical distribution of eggs and larvae with depth (Frank et al. 1989, Page et al. 1989), thereby affecting their horizontal dispersion, transport, and ultimate survival. The result of these studies was a much clearer understanding of the impact of environmental variability on the success of the haddock fishery.

In the late 1980s, the tidal dynamics and mixing processes, as well as their biological impacts, on the northern flank of Georges Bank were examined as part of the Georges Bank Frontal Study (Loder et al. 1993, Yoshida and Oakey 1996). Physical measurements were gathered from moored current meters, CTD and Batfish transects (hydrographic data), surface drifters, and a small-scale turbulence profiler, EPSONDE (Fig. 6). The tethered free fall technique used to deploy these instruments has since been copied by many other laboratories. Owing to intense vertical mixing caused by the tide on the shallow region of the Bank, a semi-permanent front exists there, separating the well-mixed Bank waters from the deeper stratified waters of the Gulf of Maine proper. Significant features of the tidal front include the strong, along-front jet on the northern flank of the Bank that spreads out and weakens somewhat over the Northeast Peak. Regular variations of frontal structure and its position over the tidal period lead to the off-bank formation of large-amplitude internal waves (similar to those observed at the Scotian Shelf break; see above), and highly variable fields of small-scale turbulence. Brickman and Loder

Figure 8. Fishing vessel alongside in Hall's Harbour, off Minas Channel, Bay of Fundy: (A) at high tide, and (B) at low tide; the tidal range in Hall's Harbour is roughly 13m.

(1993) demonstrated that this process provides a regular energy source for mixing in the frontal zone, particularly at the base of the mixed layer where the energy demands of vertical mixing are the greatest.

In the 1990s, BIO scientists continued studies of the Georges Bank/ Gulf of Maine circulation and its impacts on the sensitive ecosystems in collaboration with researchers under the United States GLOBEC Program: Phases I (1993-95), II (1996-97), and III (1998-99). The early foci of these studies were interannual and decadal variability of the regional circulation (Loder et al. 2001), and the primary inflows to the Gulf of Maine through Northeast Channel and around the tip of southwest Nova Scotia (Smith et al. 2001). Distinct interannual variations were noted in the two boundary flux components, and moreover, their strengths were largely out-of-phase, i.e., the strong deep inflow in Northeast Channel was associated with weak surface inflow from the Scotian Shelf, and vice versa. The consequences of this phenomenon are important for the heat, salt, and nutrients supplied to the Gulf, and thereby to the health of its ecosystem. Its dynamical causes and implications are a subject of active research. During Phase I, the vertical structure of turbulence was also studied on the southern flank (Burgett et al. 2001) at two sites in the spring of 1995. These data showed that the turbulent kinetic energy dissipation at both a shallow well-mixed site on the Bank and a deeper more stratified site on the flank was related to the semidiurnal M2 tide. Changes in copepod (ocean zooplankton) distribution were found to be associated with increased turbulence from wind stress (Incze et al. 2001).

Phases II and III of the GLOBEC studies dealt with exchange processes on and around Georges Bank. In particular, Phase III supported the BIO focus on 'Scotian Shelf crossovers', the direct, but intermittent, transport of surface waters from Browns Bank across the Northeast Channel to Georges Bank (Bisagni and Smith 1998, Smith et al. 2003). Using a combination of moored measurements, drogued drifters, and satellite imagery, it was estimated that 20-50% of near-surface water on Browns Bank crosses to the spawning grounds on the Northeast Peak of Georges Bank, where residence times are estimated at 3 to 4 weeks. This observation has important implications for the Georges Bank ecosystem. The most likely driving mechanism for Scotian Shelf crossovers was thought to be the incidence of small-scale, eddy-like features penetrating the Northeast Channel. Such events were found to be positively correlated with the proximity of offshore fronts over the continental slope.

Much of the scientific insight into the Gulf of Maine circulation from GLOBEC has been gained from numerical model simulations. In addition to Loder et al.'s (2001) work on interdecadal variability, Hannah et al. (1998) have explored the nature of upper ocean transport mechanisms to Georges Bank from the Gulf. Shore et al. (2000) discovered a near-surface drift pathway from Browns to Georges Bank that appears to conform to the crossover pattern; In addition, they analyzed interannual variability of the potential for particles to be retained on Browns Bank, a feature of the circulation that is very relevant to the survival of groundfish larvae in the area (Hannah et al. 2000). As the accuracy of circulation modelling grows, more operational uses are found for the results and more benefits thereby derived.

GULF OF ST. LAWRENCE

The Gulf of St. Lawrence is a highly-stratified, semi-enclosed sea connected to the North Atlantic Ocean through Cabot Strait to the southeast and the Strait of Belle Isle to the northeast. It is forced at various temporal and spatial scales by: (1) North Atlantic tides, (2) local and large-scale meteorological seasonal and transient events, (3) freshwater runoff , and (4) perturbations at the edge of the continental shelf (Koutitonsky and Bugden 1991). Early studies of the Gulf of St. Lawrence by BIO scientists sought to understand the basic character of the Gulf, both regionally and temporally. Forrester (1964), for example, described the seasonal variability of hydrographic properties at strategic cross-sections in the Gulf and demonstrated the validity of the geostrophic approximation (i.e., vertical current shear balanced by horizontal density gradients) in the narrow portion of the St. Lawrence Estuary (Forrester 1970). He also noted the presence of the internal tide in the Estuary (Forrester 1974). Lawrence (1968), made some early current measurements in Cabot Strait, and Keyte and Trites (1971) attempted to deduce the circulation patterns in the western Gulf of St. Lawrence using subsurface drogued drifters and hydrographic data. Much of this work is summarized by Trites and Walton (1975) in a comprehensive review of the physical, chemical and biological state-of-knowledge of the Gulf at that time. In particular, the physical component of the review described such elements as: (1) the freshwater input from the Gulf's extensive drainage basin, (2) the 3-layer structure of water masses, (3) winter ice, (4) tides and tidal currents, and (5) the general circulation.

Since the Trites and Walton (1975) review, BIO scientists have unravelled more mysteries of the response of Gulf circulation and mixing to physical forcing, much of which is summarized in the early 1990s review by Koutitonsky and Bugden (1991). In particular, a simple box model was used to interpret the observed seasonal variability of salt, heat and mass in the upper layers of the Gulf, balancing changes in four separate regions (Bugden 1981). Bugden (1991) also identified interdecadal temperature changes that are coherent in the deep waters of the Gulf along the Laurentian Channel from Cabot Strait to the St. Lawrence Estuary, a distance of more than 1,000 km. The physical forcing of these changes originates on the continental slope at the mouth of the Laurentian Channel as a result of varying proportions of available Labrador and North Atlantic water masses. Many other relevant studies were conducted in this time period focussed on various aspects of the circulation and mixing in the Gulf and Estuary, including: dynamics of the flow through the Strait of Belle Isle (Garrett and Petrie 1981, Toulany et al. 1987), observations of upwelling and cross-frontal mixing (Tang 1980a, 1983), frontal waves and instability in the Gaspe Current (Tang 1980b), and modelling of the annual freshwater pulse in the Estuary (Tee and Lim 1987). To this point, as in the Gulf of Maine, BIO scientists had made significant contributions to understanding the nature of the circulation in the Gulf of St. Lawrence and its implications for both local and 'downstream' marine environments and ecosystems.

Following the establishment of the Maurice Lamontagne Institute in 1987, BIO field research interests in the Gulf of St. Lawrence diminished and shifted toward modelling of the circulation. After an extensive atlas of historical hydrographic data from the Gulf was published by Petrie et al. (1996), Han et al. (1999) modelled the seasonal-mean circulation in the Gulf and surrounding shelf regions, depicting many of the well-known flow features such as the Gaspé Current and exchange through Cabot Strait. More recently, a comprehensive ocean model of the Gulf and surrounding areas has been formulated, with a focus on the southern Gulf. This model has been used extensively for both physical oceanographic and fisheries applications (Chassé and Miller 2010, Kanary et al. 2011).

NEARSHORE STUDIES: LAKES, ESTUARIES, AND EMBAYMENTS

A number of BIO research projects have focussed on smaller-scale, nearshore investigations in estuaries, lakes and embayments, such as those by Krauel (1969) in and around the Margaree and Cheticamp River estuaries in the mid-1960s, Sharaf El Din et al. (1970) in St. Margaret's Bay, Krauel (1975), Gurbutt and Petrie (1995) and Petrie (1999) in the Bras d'Or Lakes during the early 1970s, and by Seibert et al. (1979) in the Saguenay Fiord. D. Krauel's estuarine observations included currents and hydrographic properties, both inside and just outside the river mouth, sea level, and dye-tracer and drift-pole experiments. Comparison of results from the two rivers (Margaree and Cheticamp) contrasted the roles of tidal currents versus river discharge. Many of the physical oceanographic investigations provided bases for ecosystem studies with the goal of understanding both biological and physical processes that underlie marine production. For example, St. Margaret's Bay served as a model for such studies in the late 1960s.

Bras d'Or Lakes

D. Krauel's early 1970s data from the Bras d'Or Lakes formed the basis for B. Petrie's analysis of sea-level variability, which showed rapid attenuation of tidal components within the Lakes, but persistence of low-frequency fluctuations originating just outside the Lakes in the Sydney Bight. Other studies derived the mixing and exchange rates of Lakes and offshore waters, and examined the currents at critical points within the Lakes (e.g., Gurbutt and Petrie 1995, Petrie 1999, Petrie and Bugden 2002).

St. Georges Bay

With the intent to understand the dispersal of passive particles, such as fish eggs and larvae, Petrie and Drinkwater (1978) conducted a suite of field observations in St. Georges Bay, Nova Scotia, a stratified embayment opening into the Gulf of St. Lawrence. They discovered the mean circulation to be a clockwise gyre, with surface currents of order 10 cm/s, dropping to <2 cm/s near the bottom. This gyre supported long retention times for particles within the Bay, making possible studies of fish development in early life stages. Variable currents included the tides and low-frequency events, which governed the exchange rate between the Bay and the Gulf. Drinkwater (1994) refined the description of the low-frequency response of the circulation to wind, identifying two dynamically different regimes within the Bay (i.e., the region at the mouth and the interior), and concluding that wind-driven variability was more prominent in the bottom layers than near the surface. [Note: for more details on the St. Georges Bay ecosystem, see Lambert et al. 2014.]

Applied Nearshore Studies

Over the years, numerous smaller-scale reviews and/or surveys have been commissioned by interested stakeholders and supported under Fisheries and Oceans Canada's (DFO) mandate. Examples include a physical oceanographic study of St. George's Bay, Newfoundland (Seibert 1972), current statistics for the Canso Strait and Come-By-Chance Bay, Newfoundland (Lawrence et al. 1973), and a review of the physical oceanography of Sydney Harbour, Nova Scotia (Petrie et al. 2001). All of these nearshore studies, and others like them, represent an essential part of BIO's contribution to understanding and describing the state of aquatic ecosystems, and to assessing human impacts upon them. In fact, research and development of high-resolution models of nearshore zones is an essential component of DFO's operational oceanography agenda.

OPERATIONAL OCEANOGRAPHY

As BIO ocean science has matured, the number of practical applications of research results has grown dramatically. Below is a brief description of a select few of the contributions that have been made by BIO scientists and technicians over the years.

Tidal Power – Then and Now

The groundbreaking work on the tidal circulation in the Gulf of Maine by D. Greenberg and others in the 1960s and early 1970s was key to the assessment of the environmental and economic costs of the use of tidal barrages in the Bay of Fundy, and to the examination of three proposed sites for a commercial dam. The results indicated that such actions would have significant environmental consequences, a factor that played a part in the decision not to proceed with a commercial-scale barrage.

In 2013, a similar review is being conducted with respect to a proposal to generate tidal power from currents using bottom-mounted turbines (see Fig. 3B in Gordon et al. 2014) in areas of strong tidal flows, such as the Minas Passage in the Upper Bay of Fundy where currents are generally in the range of 5-7 knots. BIO oceanographers are heavily involved in the risk assessment related to two potential problems: fish mortality and the excessive erosion and/or deposition of sediment in the Upper Bay of Fundy. To help evaluate the latter, strategic current observations have been made, and sophisticated numerical models have been developed. The development of fixed fish-monitoring devices for this harsh and dynamic environment is also being explored.

Surface Layer Contaminants

Early models predicting the fate of contaminants in the ocean surface layer generally used a combination of 'rules of thumb' (e.g., surface drift = 3% wind speed), sparse historical observations, simplifying assumptions regarding dispersion of the material, and frequent updates of relevant observations during the event itself. Trites et al. (1986) used such methods to simulate the track of a spill of Bunker-C oil from the MV *Kurdistan* tanker which was grounded in Chedabucto Bay, Nova Scotia, in March 1979.

Recently, risk assessment for such questions has become more sophisticated. For example, Brickman and Smith (2007) developed a tool to evaluate the risk of invasion of shelf waters by foreign aquatic species due to ballast-water exchange practices during a typical year. The results demonstrate a preference for off-shelf versus on-shelf exchange and provide quantitative guidance to regulators for management decisions by predicting the fate of ballast water released over limited segments of east coast shipping lanes (Fig. 9). Typical consequences of these exchanges include severe alterations of domestic marine habitat, such as the smothering of benthic habitat by an invasive tunicate (sea squirt) on the northern flank of Georges Bank.

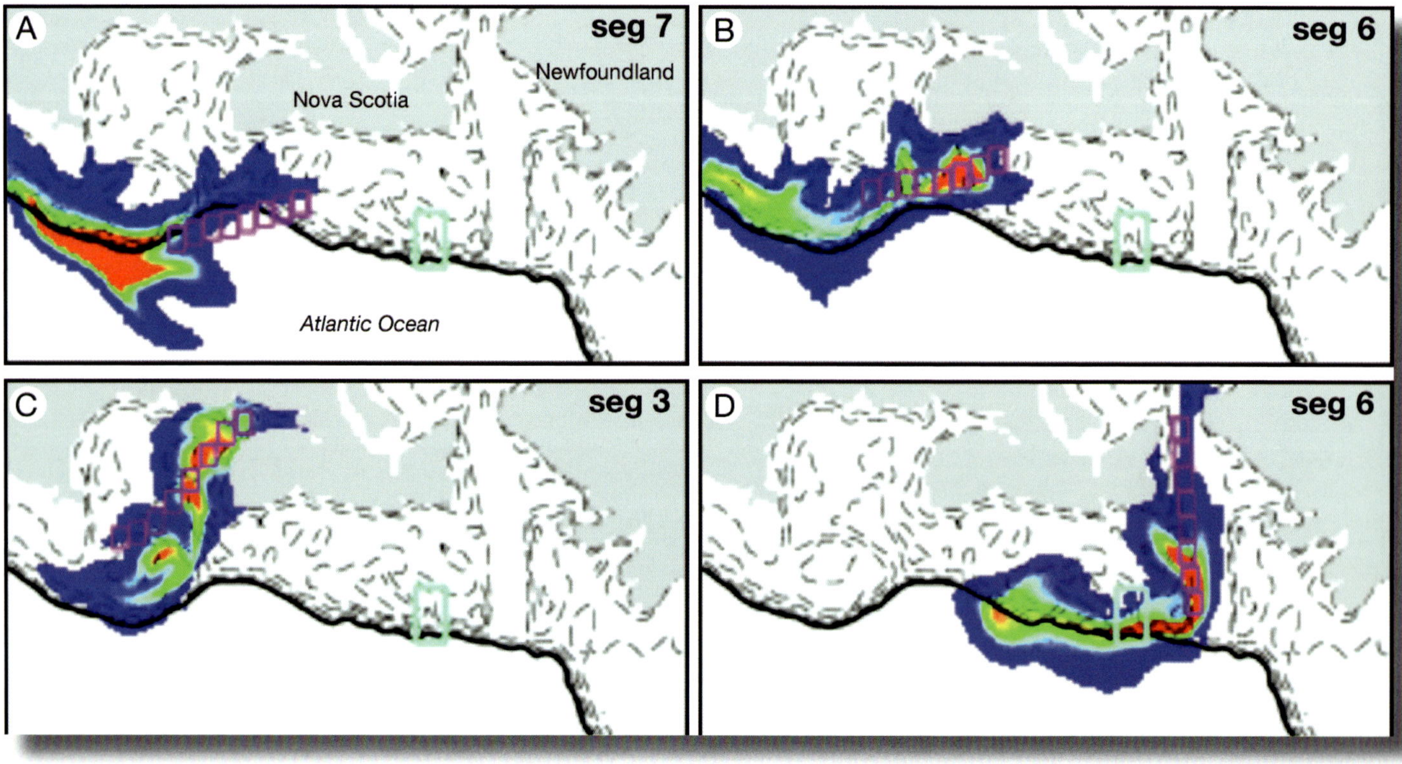

Figure 9. Model simulations for fate of ballast water exchange along various coastal shipping routes. Exchange points along the route are indicated by a succession of mauve boxes and ballast water concentrations in nearby waters are indicated by colour coding (max = red, min = blue). Dashed black lines are bathymetric contours; and solid black line is the shelf break. Turquoise rectangle in A to D encloses Sable Island and The Gully marine protected area.

Oil and Gas Research

With the advent of oil and gas exploration off Canada's east coast, Natural Resources Canada (NRCan) launched an interdepartmental research program known as the Program on Energy Research and Development (PERD), designed to ensure a sustainable energy future for Canada in the best interests of both the economy and the environment. Research funded at BIO included various aspects of offshore safety and efficiency off the East Coast (led by J. Elliott, then P. Smith, M. Lewis, D. Piper and G. Sonnichsen) and in the Arctic (led by S. Blasco), marine transportation, and offshore environmental impacts (led by D. Gordon). Outstanding examples of PERD-sponsored research include wave forecast model development (W. Perrie, B. Toulany), sea-ice studies (S. Prinsenberg, I. Peterson), and current studies (J. Loder, C. Hannah, B. Greenan). The discharge of drilling muds into the marine environment has the potential for adverse impacts on benthic organisms. With the help of PERD funding, the benthic boundary layer transport model (bblt) was developed by BIO scientists to predict the transport and dispersion of suspended particulate drill waste on offshore banks and to provide a tool to assess the fate of discharges (Hannah and Drozdowski 2005). The model has been widely used in Atlantic Canada (e.g., Georges Bank Moratorium review, Sable Offshore Energy Project, Environmental Effects Monitoring Program on Sable Island Bank, Sydney Harbour assessment, and the Hibernia platform on the Grand Bank).

Halifax Harbour Study

As part of a Task Force charged in 1989 with addressing environmental issues surrounding the discharge of raw sewage into Halifax Harbour, a practice that had endured for nearly 150 years since the first sewer pipes were installed in the 1850s, four BIO volunteers offered their time and expertise to review various options and to offer recommendations regarding regional sewage treatment practices. The Task Force, chaired by R. Fournier of Dalhousie University, Halifax, met regularly between April 1989 and June 1990, and produced a comprehensive report that offered eighteen recommendations for guiding the development of a new efficient system for the treatment of sewage from Halifax, Dartmouth, and other parts of Halifax County. Physical oceanographic and marine chemical recommendations of this report were based on work by Petrie and Yeats (1990), whereas geology and sediments were addressed by Fader (1990).

Search-and-rescue Planning

The Canadian Coast Guard's (CCG) primary planning tool for search-and-rescue, known as CANSARP, uses meteorological and ocean forecasts, along with diverse ocean observations to define the appropriate search area. BIO scientists P. Smith and D. Lawrence collaborated with Dalhousie modellers and the CCG in two sets of field trials, on the inner Scotian Shelf in February 1996 and in the southern Gulf of St. Lawrence in November and December 1999, in an attempt to improve the accuracy and efficiency of the CANSARP system (Smith et al. 1998, 2000). The drift rates of various typical search targets (e.g., life raft, person-in-water) were observed, analyzed, and used to improve model forecast skills.

Atlantic Zonal Monitoring Program (AZMP)

The AZMP was implemented in 1998 with the aim of collecting and analyzing the biological, chemical, and physical data required to detect and monitor seasonal and interannual variability in eastern Canadian waters (Therriault et al. 1998). The initial team of BIO participants included B. Petrie, D. Gregory, A. Herman, M. Mitchell, D. Sameoto, and many others. A key element of the AZMP strategy is bi-weekly (weather permitting) oceanographic sampling at fixed stations and seasonal sampling (1-3 times per year) along various strategically-located sections (e.g., Cabot Strait). Field sampling and laboratory analyses are carried out following well-established protocols. The results of the AZMP sampling are analyzed annually and interpreted in the context of historical records. Some of the many anticipated benefits of AZMP are regional quantitative measures of climate change impacts on the marine environment.

Atmosphere-ice-ocean Forecasting

One of the most practical goals of numerical model development is forecasting. The last fifteen years have witnessed the evolution of atmosphere-ice-ocean models, with BIO scientists playing a major role. Early attempts combined the coupled ice-ocean model (Tang and Gui 1996, Tang et al. 1996) with the second generation wave model (Perrie et al. 1989) to provide daily forecasts of ice, waves and currents for eastern Canadian waters. This system was replaced by a coupled multi-category sea-ice ocean model developed by Yao et al. (2000) called the Coupled Ice-Ocean Model (CIOM). In 2005-06, the model domain was extended to include Baffin Bay, the Scotian Shelf, and the Gulf of St. Lawrence with improved resolution and an advanced third generation wave model. The upgraded system continues to provide daily forecasts for the expanded domain.

CONCLUSIONS

Diverse circulation studies conducted at BIO over the last half century have provided a deep understanding of the science of the coastal ocean, as well as important applications of that science for the benefit of marine stakeholders in Canada and around the world. Leading contributions to the knowledge at all temporal and spatial scales, from the finest-scale turbulent mixing to the mapping of the general circulation in Canadian coastal and offshore waters, have established and maintained BIO's reputation for significant scientific discovery and for the practical benefits of applied research. This legacy is expected to spur even greater research and development at BIO in the next 50 years and beyond.

ACKNOWLEDGEMENTS

Implicit in all the foregoing discussions of field work in the coastal ocean is a debt of gratitude to the technical staff at BIO for their guidance and support in the required preparations and operations. In the early years, experts such as Tom Foote, Paul d'Entremont, Murray Scotney, and Bert Hartling were instrumental in obtaining the data required for the science. More recently, these tasks have been passed on to the equally competent hands of Rick Boyce, Jay Barthelotte, Adam Hartling, and many others.

REFERENCES

Anderson, C. and P.C. Smith. 1989. Oceanographic observations on the Scotian Shelf during CASP. Atmosphere-Ocean 27: 130-156.

Bigelow, H.B. 1927. Physical oceanography of the Gulf of Maine. US Government Printing Office, Bulletin of the Bureau of Fisheries XL (Part II): 511-1,027.

Bisagni, J.J. and P.C. Smith. 1998. Eddy-induced flow of Scotian Shelf water across Northeast Channel, Gulf of Maine. Continental Shelf Research 18: 515-539.

Brickman, D. and J.W. Loder. 1993. Energetics of the internal tide on northern Georges Bank. Journal of Physical Oceanography 23: 409-424.

Brickman, D. and P.C. Smith. 2007. Variability of invasion risk for ballast water exchange on the Scotian Shelf of eastern Canada. Marine Pollution Bulletin 54: 863-874.

Bugden, G.L. 1981. Salt and heat budgets for the Gulf of St. Lawrence. Canadian Journal of Fisheries and Aquatic Sciences 38: 1,153-1,167.

Bugden, G.L. 1991. Changes in the temperature-salinity characteristics of the deeper waters of the Gulf of St. Lawrence over the past several decades. Pages 139-147 *in* The Gulf of St. Lawrence: Small Ocean or Big Estuary? (J.-C. Therriault, Ed.). Canadian Special Publication of Fisheries and Aquatic Sciences 113, Ottawa, ON.

Bumpus, D.F. and L.M. Lauzier. 1965. Surface circulation on the continental shelf of eastern North America between Newfoundland and Florida. Serial Atlas of the Marine Environment. American Geographical Society, New York, NY.

Burgett, R., D. Hebert, and N. S. Oakey. 2001. The vertical structure of turbulence on the southern flank of Georges Bank. Journal of Geophysical Research 106, No. C10: 22,545-22,558.

Chassé, J. and R.J. Miller. 2010. Lobster larval transport in the southern Gulf of St. Lawrence. Fisheries Oceanography 19: 319-338.

Clarke, R.A. 2014. Strong winds and stormy seas: ocean climate studies in the North Atlantic. Pages 139-148 *in* Voyage of Discovery: Fifty Years of Marine Research at Canada's Bedford Institute of Oceanography (D.N. Nettleship, D.C. Gordon, C.F.M. Lewis, and M.P. Latremouille, Eds.). Bedford Institute of Oceanography-Oceans Association, Dartmouth, NS.

Dobson, F.W., W. Perrie, and B. Toulany. 1989. On the deep-water fetch laws for wind-generated surface gravity waves. Atmosphere-Ocean 27: 210-236.

Drinkwater, K.F. 1988. On the mean and tidal currents in Hudson Strait. Atmosphere-Ocean 26: 252-266.

Drinkwater, K.F. 1994. The response of an open stratified bay to wind forcing. Atmosphere-Ocean 32: 757-781.

Drinkwater, K.F., B. Petrie, and W.H. Sutcliffe, Jr. 1979. Seasonal geostrophic volume transports along the Scotian Shelf. Estuarine and Coastal Marine

Science 9: 17-27.
Drinkwater, K.F., D.B. Mountain, and A. Herman. 1999. Variability in the slope water properties off eastern North America and their effects on the adjacent shelves. ICES Annual Science Conference, Theme Session on Global Change Aspects, Session O: 08, Copenhagen, Denmark.
Fader, G.B.J. 1990. Geology and sediments: Appendix B, Halifax Harbour Task Force Report (R.O. Fournier, Chairman). Unpubl. report submitted to Nova Scotia Minister of the Environment, August 1990, Halifax, NS.
Forrester, W.D. 1964. A quantitative temperature-salinity study of the Gulf of St. Lawrence. Bedford Institute of Oceanography, Report Series, BI-R-64-11, Dartmouth, NS.
Forrester, W.D. 1970. Geostrophic approximation in the St. Lawrence Estuary. Tellus 22: 53-65.
Forrester, W.D. 1974. Internal tides in the St. Lawrence Estuary. Journal of Marine Research 32: 55-66.
Frank, K.T., F.H. Page, and J.K. McRuer. 1989. Hydrographic effects on the vertical distribution of haddock (*Melanogrammus aeglefinus*) eggs and larvae on the southwestern Scotian Shelf. Canadian Journal of Fisheries and Aquatic Science 46 (Suppl. 1): 82-92.
Garrett, C.J.R. 1972. Tidal resonance in the Bay of Fundy and Gulf of Maine. Nature 238: 441-443.
Garrett, C.J.R. 1974. Normal modes of the Bay of Fundy and Gulf of Maine. Canadian Journal of Earth Sciences 11: 549-556.
Garrett, C.J.R. and B. Petrie. 1981. Dynamical aspects of the flow through the Strait of Belle Isle. Journal of Physical Oceanography 11: 376-393.
Garrett, C.J.R., J.R. Keeley, and D.A. Greenberg. 1978. Tidal mixing versus thermal stratification in the Bay of Fundy and Gulf of Maine. Atmosphere-Ocean 16: 403-423.
Gordon, D.C., C.L. Amos, D.A. Greenberg, P.C. Smith, and G.B.J. Fader. 2014. Understanding the macrotidal environment of the Bay of Fundy and the impacts of tidal power development. Pages 373-382 *in* Voyage of Discovery: Fifty Years of Marine Research at Canada's Bedford Institute of Oceanography (D.N. Nettleship, D.C. Gordon, C.F.M. Lewis, and M.P. Latremouille, Eds.). Bedford Institute of Oceanography-Oceans Association, Dartmouth, NS.
Greenan, B.J.W. and N.S. Oakey. 1999. A tethered free-fall glider to measure ocean turbulence. Journal of Atmospheric and Oceanic Technology 16: 1,545-1,555.
Greenan, B.J.W., N.S. Oakey, S.W. Young, L.D. Clark, and J.-G. Dessureault. 1997. A tethered free-fall glider to measure ocean turbulence. Canadian Technical Report of Hydrography and Ocean Sciences 186, Dartmouth, NS.
Greenan, B.J.W., N.S. Oakey, and F.W. Dobson. 2001. Estimates of dissipation in the ocean mixed layer using a quasi-horizontal microstructure profiler. Journal of Physical Oceanography 31: 992-1,004.
Greenberg, D.A. 1979. A numerical model investigation of the tidal phenomena in the Bay of Fundy and Gulf of Maine. Marine Geodesy 2: 161-187.
Greenberg, D.A. 1983. Modeling the mean barotropic circulation in the Bay of Fundy and Gulf of Maine. Journal of Physical Oceanography 13: 886-904.
Greenberg, D.A. and B.D. Petrie. 1988. The mean barotropic circulation on the Newfoundland shelf and slope. Journal of Geophysical Research 93: 15,541-15,550.
Gurbutt, P.A. and B. Petrie. 1995. Circulation in the Bras d'Or Lakes. Estuarine, Coastal and Shelf Science 41: 611-630.
Hachey, H.B. and W.B. Bailey. 1952. The general hydrography of the waters of the Bay of Fundy. Fisheries Research Board of Canada, Manuscript Report (Biology) 455, Ottawa, ON.
Han, G., and C.L. Tang. 2001. Interannual variations of volume transport in the western Labrador Sea based on TOPEX/Poseidon and WOCE data. Journal of Physical Oceanography 31: 199-211.
Han, G., M. Ikeda, and P.C. Smith. 1993. Annual variation of sea-surface slopes over the Scotian Shelf and Grand Banks from Geosat altimetry. Atmosphere-Ocean 31: 591-615.
Han, G., J.W. Loder, and P.C. Smith. 1999. Seasonal-mean hydrography and circulation in the Gulf of St. Lawrence and on the eastern and southern Newfoundland shelves. Journal of Physical Oceanography 29: 1,279-1,301.
Hannah, C.G. and A. Drozdowski. 2005. Characterizing the near-bottom dispersion of drilling mud on three Canadian offshore banks. Marine Pollution Bulletin 50: 1,433-1,456.
Hannah C.G., C.E. Naimie, J.W. Loder, and F.E. Werner. 1998. Upper-ocean transport mechanisms from the Gulf of Maine to Georges Bank, with implications for *Calanus* supply. Continental Shelf Research 17: 1,887-1,911.
Hannah, C.G., J.A. Shore, and J.W. Loder. 2000. The drift-retention dichotomy on Browns Bank: a model study of interannual variability. Canadian Journal of Fisheries and Aquatic Sciences 57: 2,506-2,518.
Hannah, C.G., J.A. Shore, J.W. Loder, and C.E. Naimie. 2001. Seasonal circulation on the western and central Scotian Shelf. Journal of Physical Oceanography 31: 591-615.
Houghton, R.W., P.C. Smith, and R.O Fournier. 1978. A simple box model for cross-shelf mixing on the Scotian Shelf. Journal of the Fisheries Research Board of Canada 35: 414-421.
Ikeda, M. 1985. Wind effects on a front over the continental shelf slope. Journal of Geophysical Research 90: 9,108-9,118.
Incze, L.S., D. Hebert, N. Wolff, N. Oakey, and D. Dye. 2001. Deepening of copepod distributions in response to increased turbulence from wind stress. Marine Ecology Progress Series 213: 229-240.
Kanary, L., A. Locke, J.Watmough, J. Chasse, D. Bourque, and A. Nadeau. 2011. Predicting larval dispersal of the vase tunicate *Ciona intestinalis* in a Prince Edward Island estuary using a matrix population model. Aquatic Invasions 6: 491-506.
Keyte, F.K. and R.W. Trites. 1971. Circulation patterns in the Gulf of St. Lawrence: June 1968 and September 1969. Fisheries Research Board of Canada, Technical Report 271, Dartmouth, NS.
Koutitonsky, V.G. and G.L. Bugden. 1991. The physical oceanography of the Gulf of St. Lawrence: a review with emphasis on the synoptic variability of the motion. Pages 57-90 *in* The Gulf of St. Lawrence: Small Ocean or Big Estuary? (J.-C. Therriault, Ed.). Canadian Special Publication of Fisheries and Aquatic Sciences 113, Ottawa, ON.
Krauel, D.P. 1969. A physical oceanographic study of the Margaree and Cheticamp River Estuaries. Fisheries Research Board of Canada, Technical Report 115, Dartmouth, NS.
Krauel, D.P. 1975. The physical oceanography of the Bras d'Or Lakes, 1972-1974. Fisheries and Marine Service, Technical Report 570, Dartmouth, NS.
Lambert, T.C., G.C. Harding, K.F. Drinkwater, and B.T. Hargrave. 2014. St. Georges Bay ecosystem study: an exercise in interdisciplinary science. Pages 105-112 *in* Voyage of Discovery: Fifty Years of Marine Research at Canada's Bedford Institute of Oceanography (D.N. Nettleship, D.C. Gordon, C.F.M. Lewis, and M.P. Latremouille, Eds.). Bedford Institute of Oceanography-Oceans Association, Dartmouth, NS.
Lawrence, D.J. 1968. Current meter data from Cabot Strait, 1966. Bedford Institute of Oceanography, Data Series, BI-D-68-10, Dartmouth, NS.
Lawrence, D.J., L.A. Foster, and R.H. Loucks. 1973. Statistics of currents for navigation and dispersion in Canso Strait and Come-By-Chance Bay. Bedford Institute of Oceanography, Report Series, BI-73-6, Dartmouth, NS.
Lazier, J.R.N. and D.G. Wright. 1993. Annual velocity variations in the Labrador Current. Journal of Physical Oceanography 23: 659-678.
Ledwell, J.R., T.F. Duda, M.A. Sundermeyer, and H.E. Seim. 2004. Mixing in a coastal environment: 1. A view from dye dispersion. Journal of Geophysical Research 109 (C10013). doi:10.1029/2003JC002194.
Loder, J.W. 1980. Topographic rectification on the sides of Georges Bank. Journal of Physical Oceanography 10: 1,399-1,416.
Loder, J.W. and D.A. Greenberg. 1986. Predicted positions of tidal fronts in the Gulf of Maine region. Continental Shelf Research 6: 397-414.
Loder, J.W., K.F. Drinkwater, N.S. Oakey, and E.P.W. Horne. 1993. Circulation, hydrographic structure and mixing at tidal fronts: the view from Georges Bank. Philosophical Transactions of the Royal Society of London A (343): 447-460.
Loder, J.W., J.A. Shore, C.G. Hannah, and B.D. Petrie. 2001. Decadal-scale hydrographic and circulation variability in the Scotia-Maine region. Deep-Sea Research II (48): 3-35.
Louis, J.P., B.D. Petrie, and P.C. Smith. 1982. Observations of topographic Rossby waves on the continental margin off Nova Scotia. Journal of Physical Oceanography 12: 47-55.
McLellan, H.J. 1954. Temperature-salinity relations and mixing on the Scotian Shelf. Journal of the Fisheries Research Board of Canada 11: 419-430.
Marsh, R., B. Petrie, C.R. Weidman, R.R. Dickson, J.W. Loder, C.G. Hannah, K. Frank, and K. Drinkwater. 1999. The 1882 tilefish kill – a cold event in shelf waters off the north-eastern United States? Fisheries Oceanography 8: 39-49.
Narayanan, S., S. Prinsenberg, and P.C. Smith. 1996. Current meter observations from the Labrador and Newfoundland shelves and comparisons with barotropic model predictions and IIP surface currents. Atmosphere-Ocean 34: 227-255.
Neu, H.A. 1971. Wave climate of the Canadian Atlantic coast and continental shelf: 1970. Atlantic Oceanographic Laboratory, Report AOL 1971-10, Dartmouth, NS.
Oakey, N.S. 1977. OCTUPROBE III: An instrument to measure oceanic turbulence and microstructure. Bedford Institute of Oceanography, Report Series BI-R-77-3, Dartmouth, NS.
Oakey, N.S. 1988. EPSONDE: An instrument to measure turbulence in the deep ocean. IEEE Journal of Oceanic Engineering 13: 124-128.
Oakey, N.S. and J.A. Elliott. 1982. Dissipation within the surface mixed layer. Journal of Physical Oceanography 12: 171-185.
Oakey, N.S. and B.J.W. Greenan. 2004. Mixing in a coastal environment, Part II: a view from microstructure measurements. Journal of Geophysical Research 109 (C10014). doi:10.1029/2003JC002193.
Page, F.H. and K.T. Frank. 1989. Spawning time and egg stage duration in North west Atlantic haddock (*Melanogrammus aeglefinus*) stocks with emphasis on Georges and Browns Bank. Canadian Journal of Fisheries and Aquatic Science 46 (Suppl. 1): 68-81.
Page, F.H., K.T. Frank, and K.R. Thompson. 1989. Stage dependent vertical distribution of haddock (*Melanogrammus aeglefinus*) eggs in a stratified water column: observations and model. Canadian Journal of Fisheries and Aquatic Science 46 (Suppl. 1): 55-67.
Perrie, W. and B. Toulany. 1990. Fetch relations for wind-generated waves as a function of wind-stress scaling. Journal of Physical Oceanography 20: 1,666-1,681.
Perrie, W. and L. Wang. 1995. A coupling mechanism for wind and waves. Journal of Physical Oceanography 25: 615-630.
Perrie, W. and Y. Hu. 1996. Air-ice-ocean momentum exchange. Part I: Energy transfer between waves and ice floes. Journal of Physical Oceanography 26: 1,705-1,720.
Perrie, W. and Y. Hu. 1997. Air-ice-ocean momentum exchange. Part II: Ice drift. Journal of Physical Oceanography 27: 1,976-1,996.
Perrie, W. and D.T. Resio. 2009. A two-scale approximation for efficient representation of nonlinear energy transfers in a wind-wave spectrum. Part II: Application to observed wave spectra. Journal of Physical Oceanography

39: 2,451-2,476.
Perrie, W., H. Gunther, W. Rosenthal, and B. Toulany. 1989. Modelling wind-generated surface gravity waves using similarity. Quarterly Journal of the Royal Meteorological Society 115: 1,373-1,396.
Petrie, B.D. 1983. Current response at the shelf break to transient wind forcing. Journal of Geophysical Research 88: 9,567-9,578.
Petrie, B.D. 1999. Sea level variability in the Bras d'Or lakes. Atmosphere-Ocean 37: 221-239.
Petrie, B. and K. Drinkwater. 1978. Circulation in an open bay. Journal of the Fisheries Research Board of Canada 35: 1,116-1,123.
Petrie, B. and P. Yeats. 1990. Simple models of the circulation, dissolved metals, suspended solids and nutrients in Halifax Harbour. Water Pollution Journal of Canada 29: 325-349.
Petrie, B. and K. Drinkwater. 1993. Temperature and salinity variability on the Scotian Shelf and in the Gulf of Maine, 1945-1990. Journal of Geophysical Research 98: 20,079-20,089.
Petrie, B. and J. Buckley. 1996. Volume and freshwater transport of the Labrador Current in Flemish Pass. Journal of Geophysical Research 101: 28,335-28,342.
Petrie, B. and G. Bugden. 2002. The physical oceanography of the Bras d'Or Lakes. Proceedings of the Nova Scotian Institute of Science 42: 9-36.
Petrie B., B.J. Topliss, and D.G. Wright. 1987. Coastal upwelling and eddy development off Nova Scotia. Journal of Geophysical Research 29: 12,979-12,991.
Petrie B., B. Toulany, and C. Garrett. 1988. The transport of water, heat and salt through the Strait of Belle Isle. Atmosphere-Ocean 26: 234-251.
Petrie, B.D., K. Drinkwater, A. Sandström, R. Pettipas, D. Gregory, D. Gilbert, and P. Sekhon. 1996. Temperature, salinity, and sigma-t atlas for the Gulf of St. Lawrence. Canadian Technical Report of Hydrography and Ocean Sciences 178, Dartmouth, NS.
Petrie, B., G. Bugden, T. Tedford, Y. Geshelin, and C. Hannah. 2001. Review of the physical oceanography of Sydney Harbour. Canadian Technical Report of Hydrography and Ocean Sciences 215, Dartmouth, NS.
Prinsenberg, S.J., I.K. Peterson, and S. Holladay. 1996. Comparison of airborne electromagnetic ice thickness data with NOAA/AVHRR and ERS-1/SAR images. Atmosphere-Ocean 34: 185-205.
Prinsenberg, S.J., I.K. Peterson, G.A. Fowler, B.D. Beanlands, J.S. Holladay, and L.A. Lalumiere. 2014. Observing and understanding the seasonal sea-ice variability in Canadian waters. Pages 43-50 *in* Voyage of Discovery: Fifty Years of Marine Research at Canada's Bedford Institute of Oceanography (D.N. Nettleship, D.C. Gordon, C.F.M. Lewis, and M.P. Latremouille, Eds.). Bedford Institute of Oceanography-Oceans Association, Dartmouth, NS.
Resio, D.T. and W. Perrie. 2008. A two-scale approximation for efficient representation of nonlinear energy transfers in a wind-wave spectrum. Part I: Theoretical development. Journal of Physical Oceanography 38: 2,801-2,816.
Sandstrom, H. and J.A. Elliott. 1984. Internal tide and solitons on the Scotian Shelf: a nutrient pump at work. Journal of Geophysical Research 89: 6,415-6,426.
Sandstrom, H. and N.S. Oakey. 1995. Dissipation in internal tides and solitary waves. Journal of Physical Oceanography 25: 604-614.
Sandstrom, H. and J.A. Elliott. 2010. Current surge through a shelf internal tide. Canadian Technical Report of Hydrography and Ocean Sciences 268, Dartmouth, NS.
Schwing, F.B. 1989. Subtidal response of the Scotian Shelf bottom pressure field to meteorological forcing. Atmosphere-Ocean 27: 157-180.
Seibert, G.H. 1972. Physical oceanographic study of St. George's Bay, Newfoundland. Bedford Institute of Oceanography, Report Series, BI-72-2 Dartmouth, NS.
Seibert, G.H., R.W. Trites, and S.J. Reid. 1979. Deepwater exchange processes in the Saguenay Fjord. Journal of the Fisheries Research Board of Canada 36: 42-53.
Sharaf El Din, S.H., E.M. Hassan, and R.W. Trites. 1970. The physical oceanography of St. Margaret's Bay. Fisheries Research Board of Canada Technical Report 219, Dartmouth, NS.
Shore, J.A., C.G. Hannah, and J.W. Loder. 2000. Drift pathways on the western Scotian Shelf and its environs. Canadian Journal of Fisheries and Aquatic Sciences 57: 2,488-2,505.
Smith, P.C. 1978. Low frequency fluxes of momentum, heat, salt and nutrients at the edge of the Scotian Shelf. Journal of Geophysical Research 83: 4,079-4,096.
Smith, P.C. 1983. The mean and seasonal circulation off southwest Nova Scotia. Journal of Physical Oceanography 13: 1,034-1,054.
Smith, P.C. 1989a. Inertial oscillations near the coast of Nova Scotia during CASP. Atmosphere-Ocean 27: 181-209.
Smith, P.C. 1989b. Seasonal and interannual variability of current, temperature, and salinity off southwest Nova Scotia. Canadian Journal of Fisheries and Aquatic Science 46 (Suppl. 1): 4-20.
Smith, P.C. and J.I. MacPherson. 1987. Cross-shore variations of near-surface wind velocity and atmospheric turbulence at the land-sea boundary during CASP. Atmosphere-Ocean 25: 279-303.
Smith, P.C. and H. Sandstrom. 1988. Physical processes at the shelf edge in the Northwest Atlantic. Journal of Northwest Atlantic Fishery Science 8: 5-13.
Smith, P.C., C.L. Tang, J.I. MacPherson, and R.F. McKenna. 1994. Investigating the marginal ice zone on the Newfoundland Shelf. EOS Transactions 75: 57-62.
Smith, P.C., D.J. Lawrence, K.R Thompson, J. Sheng, G. Vernier, J. St. James, N. Bernier, and L. Feldman. 1998. Improving the skill of search-and-rescue forecasts. CMOS Bulletin 26: 119-129.
Smith, P.C., D.J. Lawrence, J. Bobanovic, and K.R Thompson. 2000. Improving the skill of the Canadian search-and-rescue planning system. Pages 17-18 *in* Bedford Institute of Oceanography 2000 in Review (D. Geddes, Ed.). Bedford Institute of Oceanography, Dartmouth, NS.
Smith, P.C., R.W. Houghton, R.G. Fairbanks, and D.G. Mountain. 2001. Interannual variability of boundary fluxes and water mass properties in the Gulf of Maine and on Georges Bank: 1993-1997. Deep-Sea Research 48 (Part II): 37-70.
Smith, P.C., C.N. Flagg, R. Limeburner, C. Fuentes-Yaco, C. Hannah, R.C. Beardsley, and J.D. Irish. 2003. Scotian Shelf crossovers during winter/spring 1999. Journal of Geophysical Research 108: 8013. doi:10-1029/2001JC001288.
Smith, S.D. 1988. Coefficients for sea surface wind stress, heat flux and wind profiles as a function of windspeed and temperature. Journal of Geophysical Research 93: 15,467-15,472.
Smith, S.D. and E. Banke. 1975. Variation of the sea surface drag coefficient with wind speed. Quarterly Journal of the Royal Meteorological Society 10: 665-673.
Sutcliffe, W.H. Jr., R.H. Loucks, and K.F. Drinkwater. 1976. Coastal circulation and physical oceanography of the Scotian Shelf and Gulf of Maine. Journal of the Fisheries Research Board of Canada 33: 98-115.
Tang, C.L. 1980a. Mixing and circulation in the northwestern Gulf of St. Lawrence: a study of a buoyancy-driven current system. Journal of Geophysical Research 85(C5): 2,787-2,796.
Tang, C.L. 1980b. Observation of wavelike motion of the Gaspe Current. Journal of Physical Oceanography 10: 853-860.
Tang, C.L. 1983. Cross-frontal mixing and frontal upwelling in a controlled quasi-permanent density front in the Gulf of St. Lawrence. Journal of Physical Oceanography 13: 1,468-1,481.
Tang, C.L. and Q. Gui. 1996. A dynamical model for wind-driven ice motion – application to ice drift on the Labrador Shelf. Journal of Geophysical Research 101: 28,343-28,364.
Tang, C.L., Q. Gui, and I. Peterson. 1996. Modeling the mean circulation of the Labrador Sea and adjacent shelves. Journal of Physical Oceanography 26: 1,989-2,010.
Tee, K.T. 1977. Tide-induced residual current – verification of a numerical model. Journal of Physical Oceanography 7: 396-402.
Tee, K.T. and T.-H. Lim. 1987. The freshwater pulse–a numerical model with application to the St. Lawrence Estuary. Journal of Marine Research 45: 871-909.
Tee, K.T. and C.L. Amos. 1991. Tidal and buoyancy-driven currents in Chignecto Bay, Bay of Fundy. Journal of Geophysical Research 96: 15,197-15,216.
Tee, K.T., P.C. Smith, and D. Lefaivre. 1988. Estimation and verification of tidally-induced residual currents. Journal of Physical Oceanography 18: 1,415-1,434.
Tee, K.T., P.C. Smith, and D. Lefaivre. 1993. Topographic upwelling off southwest Nova Scotia. Journal of Physical Oceanography 23: 1,703-1,726.
Therriault, J.-C., B. Petrie, P. Pepin, J. Gagnon, D. Gregory, J. Helbig, A. Herman, D. Lefaivre, M. Mitchell, B. Pelchat, J. Runge, and D. Sameoto. 1998. Proposal for a northwest Atlantic zonal monitoring program. Canadian Technical Report of Hydrography and Ocean Sciences 194, Dartmouth, NS.
Toulany, B., B. Petrie, and C.J.R. Garrett. 1987. The frequency-dependent structure and dynamics of flow fluctuations in the Strait of Belle Isle. Journal of Physical Oceanography 27: 185-196.
Trites, R.W. and R.E. Banks. 1958. Circulation on the Scotian Shelf as indicated by drift bottles. Journal of the Fisheries Research Board of Canada 15: 79-89.
Trites, R.W. and A. Walton. 1975. A Canadian coastal sea – The Gulf of St. Lawrence. Bedford Institute of Oceanography Report Series, BI-R-75-10, Dartmouth, NS.
Trites, R.W., D.J. Lawrence, and J.H. Vandermeulen. 1986. Modelling oil movements from Kurdistan spill in Cabot Strait, Nova Scotia. Atmosphere-Ocean 24(3): 253-264.
Wright, D.G. and J.W. Loder. 1985. A depth-dependent study of the topographic rectification of tidal currents. Geophysical and Astrophysical Fluid Dynamics 31: 169-220.
Yao, T., C.L. Tang, and I.K. Peterson. 2000. Modeling the seasonal variation of sea ice in the Labrador Sea with a coupled multi-category ice model and the Princeton Ocean Model. Journal of Geophysical Research 105: 1,153-1,165.
Yoshida, J. and N.S. Oakey. 1996. Characterization of mixing at a tidal front on Georges Bank. Deep-Sea Research II 43: 1,713-1,744.

18. TEMPORAL TRENDS IN CHEMICAL OCEANOGRAPHIC PARAMETERS OVER THE PAST 50 YEARS

Philip A. Yeats

SUMMARY

Physical, chemical and biological oceanographers at the Bedford Institute of Oceanography (BIO) have been making measurements of chemical oceanographic variables in coastal and offshore waters off eastern Canada since the opening of the Institute in 1962. Many research and monitoring projects have been conducted and data from these studies and those of outside agencies have been archived in the BioChem chemical and biological oceanographic database which was initially developed at BIO and now managed by Fisheries and Oceans Canada's Marine Environmental Data Service. BioChem is a valuable resource for investigating temporal trends in chemical concentrations that could represent environmental responses to anthropogenic carbon dioxide increases, climate change, and other chemical pollution problems. This paper documents some of the long-term trends found in pH, nutrients, oxygen, metals, and organic contaminants. Decreases in pH that usually follow the temporal trend expected from long-term changes in atmospheric carbon dioxide are observed. Trends in oxygen and nutrients in the deeper waters of the Scotian Shelf mostly reflect changes in the dominant source waters. At slightly shallower depths (50-100 m), a long-term decrease in both nutrients and oxygen is observed. On the Labrador Shelf, only silicate and phosphate concentrations are decreasing with time. Deeper waters with significant Arctic Ocean contributions in the Labrador Sea also show a parallel decrease with time in both nutrient and oxygen concentrations. Far fewer measurements have been made on heavy metal and organic contaminant concentrations. The limited observations indicate decreasing concentrations with time for several important chemical pollutants on the Scotian Shelf over the past few decades.

Key words: chemical oceanography, chemical pollution, temporal trends, climate change, BioChem database, Scotian Shelf, Gulf of St. Lawrence, Labrador Shelf and Sea, Atlantic Zone Monitoring Program.
E-mail: Philip.Yeats@dfo-mpo.gc.ca

During Bedford Institute of Oceanography's (BIO) first thirty years, chemical oceanographic measurements were made on a variety of oceanographic research cruises conducted by scientists from BIO, Dalhousie University (Halifax, NS), and other institutions. Limited amounts of earlier data were collected prior to the establishment of BIO by predecessor organizations (Mills 2014), and other oceanographic institutions. The extensive but unevenly structured data sets collected on these cruises provide the basis for investigations of temporal trends during that period. More recently, investigations of temporal trends have relied to a much greater extent on a smaller number of cruises specifically designed for collection of data to monitor trends over time. Most of the chemical data have been collected in two important monitoring programs. The more extensive of these is the Atlantic Zonal Monitoring Program (AZMP) that has collected physical, chemical, and biological oceanographic data since 1998 from the shelves and slopes of Labrador, Newfoundland, the Gulf of St. Lawrence, and the Scotian Shelf. The other important program is the annual survey conducted on an oceanographic section that extends from the Labrador Shelf across the Labrador Sea and onto the Greenland Shelf. The Labrador Sea Section was originally sampled as part of the World Ocean Circulation Experiment, but is now part of AZMP. This time series is now more than 20 years long. The continuation of the AZMP program and the archiving of the data in BioChem, a database initially developed at BIO and now managed by Fisheries and Oceans Canada's (DFO) Marine Environmental Data Service (Gregory and Narayanan 2003), will be essential for observations of chemical trends in the future.

The observations described in this paper were made in marginal seas and continental shelf and slope waters from Davis Strait in the north to the Scotian Shelf and Gulf of Maine in the south. These coastal waters are part of an extensive current system that transports water from as far northwest as the Beaufort Sea and western Arctic Ocean east into the Atlantic Ocean. Several deeper water masses in the Labrador Sea are also important components of this global transport of water from the Pacific Ocean to the Atlantic via the Arctic. A qualitative picture of this circulation and locations of oceanographic features referred to in this review are shown in Figure 1.

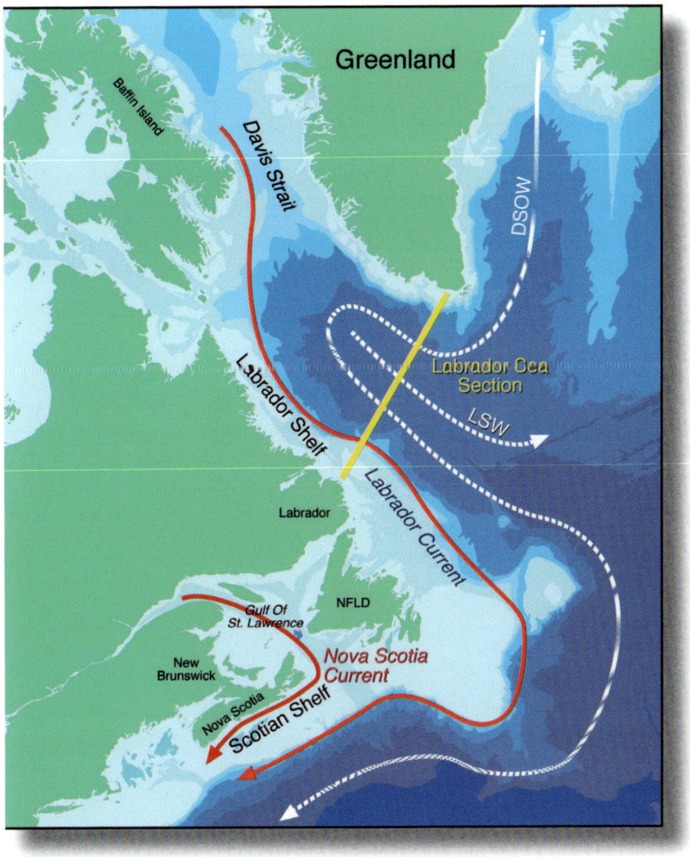

Figure 1. Map of eastern Canada showing locations of features mentioned in the text and the approximate location of the main surface currents (solid red lines) and deepwater flows (dashed white lines): LSW = Labrador Sea Water, DSOW = Denmark Strait Overflow Water.

CARBON DIOXIDE AND ALKALINITY

Measurements of total dissolved carbon dioxide (CO_2) and alkalinity have been made at BIO since the late 1960s. Early studies in the Chemical Oceanography Division focussed on physical chemistry of the carbonate system and the effects of pressure on the equilibria, but more recent studies in chemical and biological oceanography have focussed on carbonate and alkalinity as oceanographic tracers and factors in marine productivity. Measurements of CO_2 and alkalinity can be used to compute the acidity (pH) of marine waters and, given the recent interest in the effects of ocean acidification on marine ecosystems, temporal trends in pH that can be generated from the archived data are perhaps the most important legacy of years of carbonate and alkalinity measurements. The observed changes in pH are a direct consequence of changes in oceanic CO_2 concentrations.

A comparison of pH measurements on the Scotian Shelf in the 1930s by scientists from the Woods Hole Oceanographic Institution (WHOI) with recent measurements by BIO scientists collected as part of AZMP reveals a substantial reduction in coastal water pH over 75 years. This is depicted in Figure 2 which shows the expected decrease of pH with depth produced by *in situ* biological regeneration for both times and a consistently lower pH at all depths in the more recent dataset. The surface pH in 2006 was approximately 0.2 pH units lower than it was in 1934.

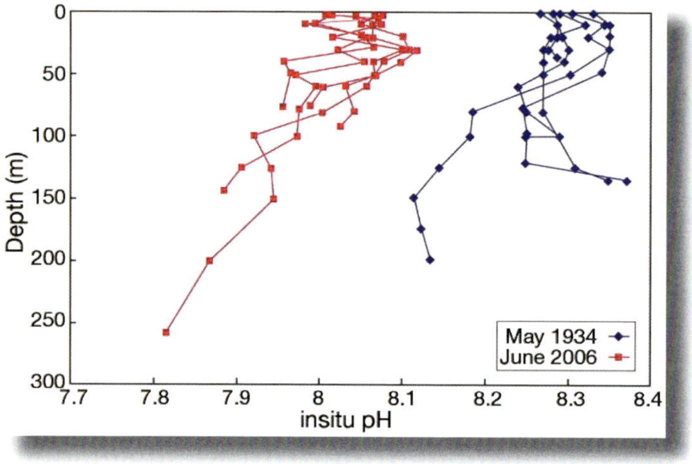

Figure 2. Vertical profiles of pH on the Scotian Shelf for May 1934 and June 2006 showing variability with depth.

An analysis of all the data in BioChem provides a picture of the trend over time on the Scotian Shelf (Fig. 3). Variability for individual datasets (cruises) is produced by short-term temporal variability (diurnal to days), spatial coverage of the cruises, and analytical uncertainties. For different cruises, data were collected at different times of the year and at very different locations across the breadth and length of the shelf. There have also been changes in methodologies, most notably the change from exclusively direct pH measurements in the first few decades to almost exclusive reliance on pH measurements calculated from alkalinity and total CO_2 measurements in the more recent ones. All of these factors contribute to the observed variability and limit the usefulness of the data to conclusively describe trends. The slight decrease in pH over the decades does correspond to the one predicted from the changes in atmospheric CO_2 concentrations (Royal Society 2005), but the data are not precise enough to permit comment on possible regional deviations from this global trend.

Labrador Shelf waters exhibit a similar trend to that recorded on the Scotian Shelf in the Cold Intermediate Water, but higher pHs and less change with time in the surface mixed-layer (Fig. 4). These data have not been corrected for depth. Variability with depth as well as the factors identified above for the Scotian Shelf contribute to the observed variability. Data from individual stations show a much more abrupt change with depth than seen on the Scotian Shelf reflecting a trend with depth that results more from changes in the physical structure of the water (low-salinity coastal water overlying Cold Intermediate Water whose source is in the Arctic Ocean) rather than from *in situ* biochemical uptake and regeneration of CO_2.

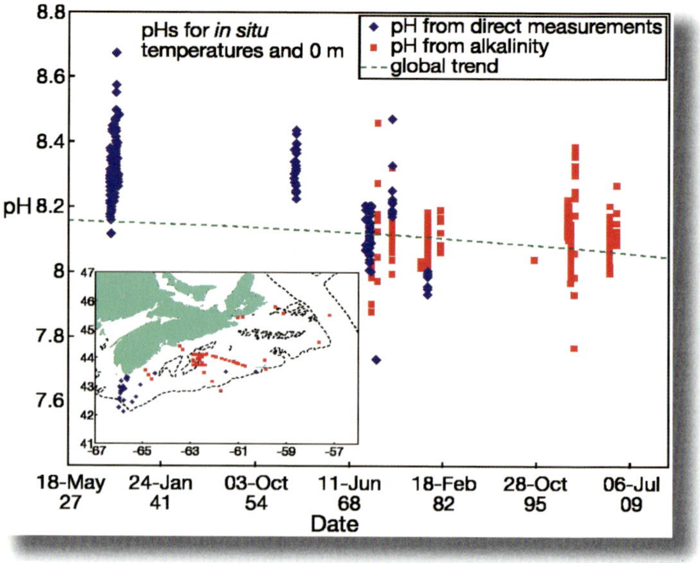

Figure 3. Temporal trend in pH in surface water (*in situ* temperature) based on all data collected on the Scotian Shelf between August 1924 and October 2006. The global trend (dashed line) is based on data from the Royal Society (2005). The inset shows the station locations.

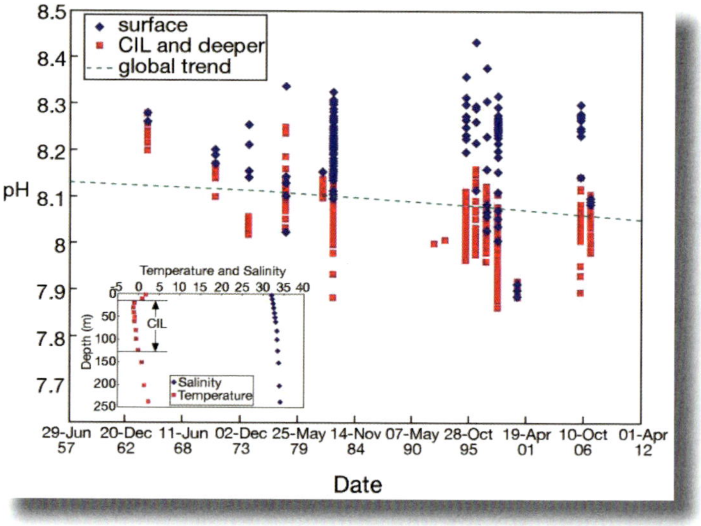

Figure 4. Temporal trend in pH in surface and deep water (*in situ* temperature) for the Labrador Shelf combining data from direct pH measurement with those calculated from total CO_2 and alkalinity. The approximate depth of the Cold Intermediate Layer (CIL) defined as waters with temperatures less than zero is indicated in the inset.

OXYGEN AND NUTRIENTS

Tens of thousands of oxygen and nutrient measurements for coastal waters of eastern Canada are archived in BioChem. Oxygen measurements have traditionally been used by physical oceanographers to characterize the oceanographic structure, but recently there has been interest in the biological impact on organisms of the reduced oxygen levels that are increasingly being seen in coastal waters as part of the global trend towards hypoxia (Gilbert et al. 2010). Nutrients have also been used as physical oceanographic tracers, but most studies have focussed on biology and the role of the nutrient salts, nitrate, phosphate and silicate, along with light, as the main drivers of primary biological productivity. Temporal trends in both coastal and deep-ocean waters that can be documented using the data in BioChem are thus of interest to both physical and biological oceanographers.

Petrie et al. (1994) documented changes in deep-water oxygen concentrations from 1961 to 1988 in Emerald Basin that were largely due to changes in the water mass structure. High oxygen concentrations prevailed when the deep water was fed largely by low temperature and low salinity water from the Labrador Current; low concentrations prevailed when it was fed by high temperature and high salinity Warm Slope Water.

The inverse relationship between oxygen saturation and temperature explained 89% of the oxygen signal. Subsequent papers (Petrie et al. 1999a, Petrie and Yeats 2000) showed that the same physical forcing produced high nutrient concentrations in Warm Slope Water years and low concentrations when the Labrador Current was dominant. Oxygen and nutrients show the expected inverse relationship. Data collected in subsequent years when the deep waters were not as clearly dominated by either of these source waters shows that another factor is causing a concurrent downward trend with time for both nutrients and oxygen. In any analysis of oxygen trends, concentrations must be expressed as either oxygen saturation (e.g., Petrie et al. 1994) or as apparent oxygen utilization (AOU: i.e., oxygen concentration for water saturated with atmospheric oxygen minus observed concentration) in order to eliminate the influence of changes in oxygen solubility with temperature and salinity on the trend.

The general downward trend with time for oxygen and nutrient concentrations on the Scotian Shelf is more easily seen in the 50 to 100 m depth range than in the deeper waters (Yeats et al. 2010). The impact of the Labrador and Warm Slope waters is still evident, but the dominant effect is the general decrease with time. Qualitatively similar trends are seen for the Eastern, Central, and Western Shelf (the polygons for shelf areas are the same as the ones used by Petrie et al. 1999b). The trends observed for nutrients for all waters from 0 to 100 m in winter (Fig. 5) are similar to the annually averaged concentrations at 50-100 m which suggests that these subsurface water concentrations are a good proxy for less commonly measured winter concentrations in the surface waters. Nutrient concentrations in these waters are thus a reasonable measure of the concentrations available for biological uptake: i.e., surface nutrient concentrations in winter that would support the spring bloom and the deeper concentrations that could fuel new productivity through the rest of the growing season. Winter nitrate concentrations indicate a decrease in concentration of the nitrate available to support new primary production in the spring of almost 50% from 1980-86 to 1999-2005, periods when winter data are available. This suggests a substantial potential decrease in new primary productivity if all other factors remained equal. The trends are illustrated here (Fig. 5) and in various papers (Petrie et al. 1999a, Petrie and Yeats 2000, Yeats et al. 2010) using plots of the temporal change in annual average concentrations for selected polygons and depth ranges but supported by multivariate statistical analysis of the variability in time and space that show downward trends with time that are highly significant ($P<0.05$) for all depths greater than 50 m.

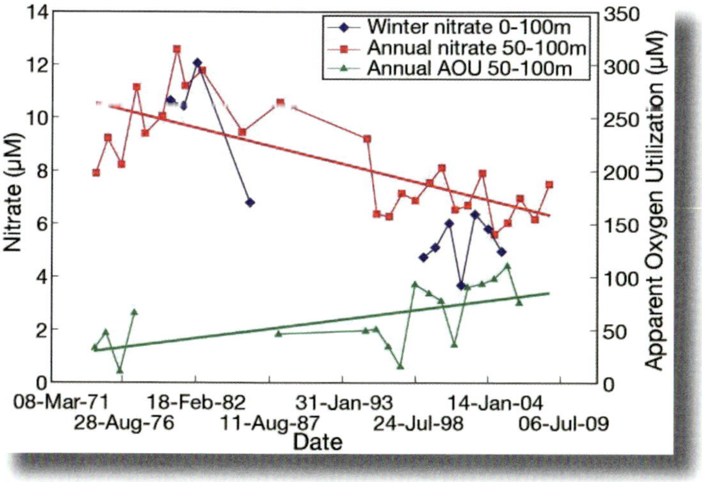

Figure 5. Temporal trends in nitrate concentrations on the Central Scotian Shelf averaging all data for the January to March period in the top 100 m, and nitrate and apparent oxygen utilization (AOU) for the complete year for the 50 to 100 m layer.

Biological regeneration of nutrients in subsurface waters is invariably accompanied by oxygen consumption. This means that changes in biological uptake and regeneration (or mixing of water masses where the oxygen and nutrient concentrations are each determined by biological processes) would generate opposing trends in oxygen and nutrients. Thus, the observed temporal decreases in the concentrations of both oxygen (inversely related to AOU) and nutrients in the subsurface waters on the Scotian Shelf (Fig. 5) cannot simply represent changes in the amount of organic matter being decomposed in the water column either locally or remotely. A more complicated mechanism incorporating changes in both physical and biological processes is required to produce a parallel decrease in both nutrients and oxygen. Recent observations of a dramatic decrease in the transport of deeper waters into the Gulf of Maine (Smith et al. 2011) suggest a potential mechanism that could lead to lower concentrations of both nutrients and oxygen. Less input of deeper offshore waters with high nutrient concentrations would lead to lower input of nutrient, and slower circulation on the Shelf would provide for longer residence times with more uptake of oxygen and more opportunity for denitrification in coastal sediments. A reduction of the relative importance of deeper offshore sources more important for nitrate compared with inshore freshwater sources more important for silicate, would also explain the relatively greater decreases observed for nitrate than silicate. The plot of excess silicate (Si-N) for the 50-100 m layer on the Central Scotian Shelf (Fig. 6) shows a strong decrease in the period from the 1960s to 1980s that is consistent with the change from dominantly Labrador Water (high Si compared to N) to Warm Slope Water (low Si). The more recent period has high Si that cannot be simply attributed to a change in the source waters. Other mechanisms such as those described above are needed to explain these observations. The importance of these changes in nutrient inputs in the adjacent Gulf of Maine has been documented by Townsend et al. (2010).

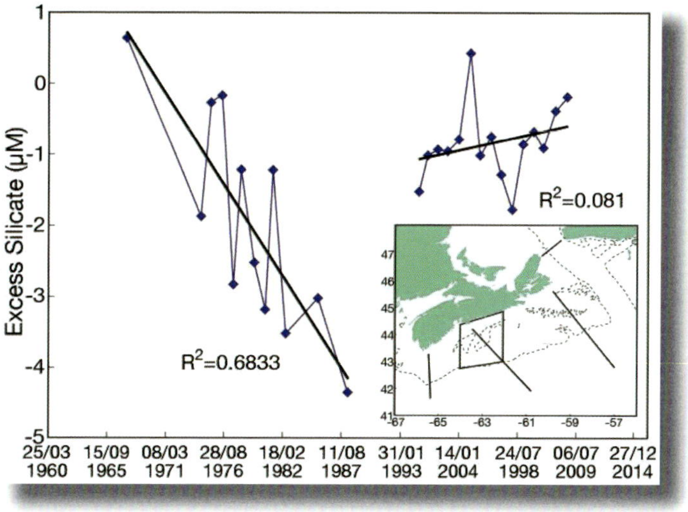

Figure 6. Temporal trends in average annual excess silicate (Si-N) in the 50-100 m layer on the Central Scotian Shelf. Inset shows the location of the main AZMP lines on the Scotian Shelf and the central shelf box used in modelling.

Gilbert et al. (2005) used BioChem and other archives to document decreases in oxygen concentrations in the deeper waters of the Gulf of St. Lawrence based on more than 70 years of data from the early 1930s to 2003. Their results account for the impact of physical oceanographic changes on the oxygen concentrations and show that a significant fraction of the decrease has to be attributed to increased biological uptake of oxygen. This is just one of many examples of decreasing concentrations at fixed stations in coastal waters that have been monitored for years (Gilbert et al. 2010). Downward trends in the oxygen on the broader Scotian Shelf (Yeats et al. 2010) are consistent with this global picture of generally decreasing oxygen concentrations at fixed monitoring stations. Long-time series are needed to establish these trends illustrating the importance of archived data in the investigation of important biogeochemical processes such as hypoxia in the coastal zone.

Multiyear trends in nutrient concentrations are also seen for waters deeper than 60 m on the Labrador Shelf (Harrison and Li 2007, Yeats et al. 2010). No changes in oxygen have been recorded for these waters. In this case, concentrations of both phosphate and silicate have been decreasing since first measurements were made in the late 1960s until the present, while nitrate concentrations have remained virtually unchanged. As a consequence, excess silicate (Si-N) and phosphate (P-N/16) have decreased. An important source for the high silicate and phosphate water seen on the Labrador Shelf is transport of arctic waters with anomalously high concentrations of both of these constituents through Baffin Bay to the Labrador Sea. Decreased input of water from the Arctic could be generating the observed trends. More limited data sets available for Baffin Bay and the Beaufort Sea (Yeats et al. 2010) indicate that excess phosphate concentrations have been decreasing in these regions and point to the importance of decreasing silicate and phosphate concentrations in the source regions and changes in the chemical composition of water escaping from the Arctic.

Most of the data used to generate the nutrient trends on the Labrador Shelf were collected as part of the ongoing monitoring of the World Ocean Circulation Experiment AR7W line across the Labrador Sea since the early 1990s. This annual time series of stations, that have been sampled at about the same time of year, provides a valuable dataset that can be used to investigate chemical trends in the deeper waters. The temporal changes in nutrients and oxygen in these waters are very small and would not have been detected without a dedicated program that provided consistent collection and analysis. The observations show that the concentrations of oxygen and all three nutrients (i.e., nitrate, phosphate, silicate) have decreased significantly ($P<0.05$ for a linear regression of components versus time, not shown here) since the early 1990s in the Labrador Sea Water and the Denmark Strait Overflow Water (Fig 1; Yeats et al. 2010). These trends were calculated using the yearly averaged concentrations for samples with densities that correspond to the characteristics of the two water masses following protocols established by Azetsu-Scott et al. (2003) in an assessment of freon data from the same series of cruises. The proposed mechanism for the parallel decreases in both oxygen and nutrient concentrations depends on decreases in near-surface Arctic waters that contribute to these deep Atlantic water masses and increases in the transit time to the Labrador Sea. A mechanism that relied on *in situ* biological processes could not explain the parallel decreases in both oxygen and nutrients. In a remnant of Labrador Sea Water that was formed by the exceptionally deep convection in 1993 and 1994, however, decreases in oxygen concentrations together with increases in nutrient concentrations attest to the importance of the biological process of oxygen consumption and nutrient regeneration in all of these water masses.

SURFACE NUTRIENTS AND CHLOROPHYLL

Chlorophyll concentration is a chemical measure that is directly related to primary productivity. Owing to the very dynamic nature of phytoplankton blooms, chlorophyll concentrations can vary greatly over very short time and space scales. It is therefore difficult to investigate temporal trends in the heterogeneously distributed data archived in BioChem. Similar problems exist for investigations of multiyear trends in surface nutrient concentrations. A comparison of average concentrations for 1974-82 and 1994-2009, two periods of relatively intense sampling, suggests that nitrate concentrations in the surface layers for spring to fall may be lower in the more recent period (0.64 versus 0.39 µM), but the large uncertainty in the estimates of the average concentrations precludes anything but the most tentative conclusions. Average chlorophyll concentrations for the two time periods are indistinguishable for both the spring bloom (April to May) and the longer spring to fall period. Plots of the seasonal cycles for nitrate versus day of the year (Fig. 7) for the two time periods illustrate how difficult it is to draw conclusions about trends from data that show substantial spatial and temporal variability. The only clear indication of a difference between the two time periods is higher winter concentrations in the earlier period (Fig. 7). The dates indicated on the plots are those computed from a polynomial fit when nitrate concentrations fall below the threshold of one micromole per litre. This threshold may have occurred about 10 days later in the earlier period. For chlorophyll (Fig. 8) there are considerably fewer data in BioChem, and the seasonal distribution is completely dominated by the strong signal during the annual spring bloom. It is not possible to derive even simple conclusions about trends from these plots, but multiple regression analysis of variability in time and space (not shown) reveals highly significant ($P<0.05$) downward trends for all three nutrients, but no trend for chlorophyll.

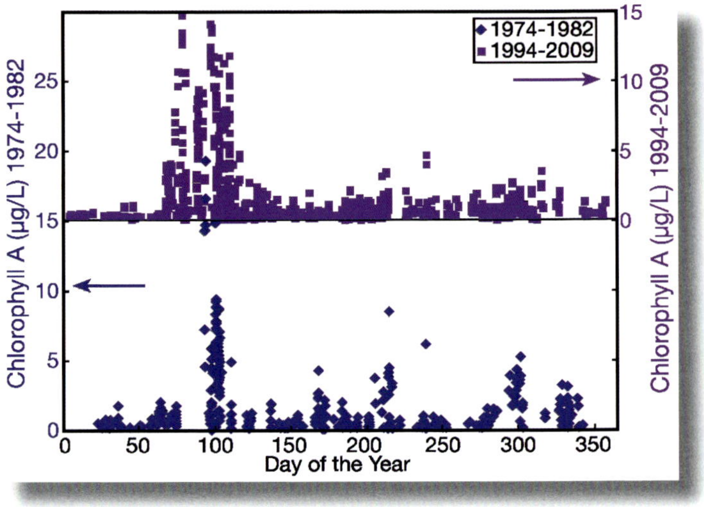

Figure 8. Annual chlorophyll a cycle for the 0-30 m layer on the Central Scotian Shelf for the two time periods with the greatest sampling density: 1994-2009 (upper) and 1974-82 (lower).

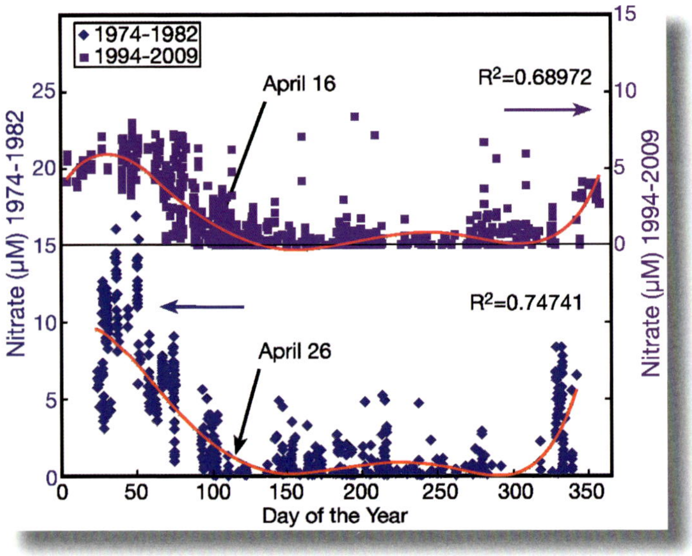

Figure 7. Annual nitrate cycle for the 0-30 m layer on the Central Scotian Shelf for the two time periods with the greatest sampling density (upper: 1994-2009, lower: 1974-82) and regression lines (5th order polynomial fits) to all the data for both periods. Note the different vertical scales for 1974-82 (left) and 1994-2009 (right). The dates are those at which the regression lines cross a threshold of 1.0 µM nitrate.

HEAVY METALS AND ORGANIC CONTAMINANTS

The archival record for measurements of potential chemical pollutants such as heavy metals or organic contaminants is shorter and many of the studies have focussed on localized environmental problems. The archived data for the Scotian Shelf indicate temporal decreases over the last few decades in concentrations of copper, zinc, and lead (Fig. 9). The trends for lead and zinc are based on averaged concentrations in surface waters for individual cruises and include samples from broad areas of the shelf. For copper, no trend is evident if the surface data are averaged, but does show a strong negative correlation with salinity; the small downward trend for copper in Figure 9 appears when the data are corrected to a common salinity ($S=32$). Trends in the concentrations of hydrocarbons in the surface waters of the Scotian Shelf and Gulf of St. Lawrence (Levy 1984, 1985), organochlorine residues in the blubber of seals at Sable Island, Nova Scotia (Addison et al. 1998), and metals and hydrocarbons in inshore sediments (e.g., Gearing et al. 1991) also show decreases in chemical contamination over recent decades that reflect, at least to some extent, an increase in public awareness to avoid environmental pollution and the effectiveness of government regulation of anthropogenic inputs of chemicals such as organochlorine pesticides, lead, and hydrocarbons.

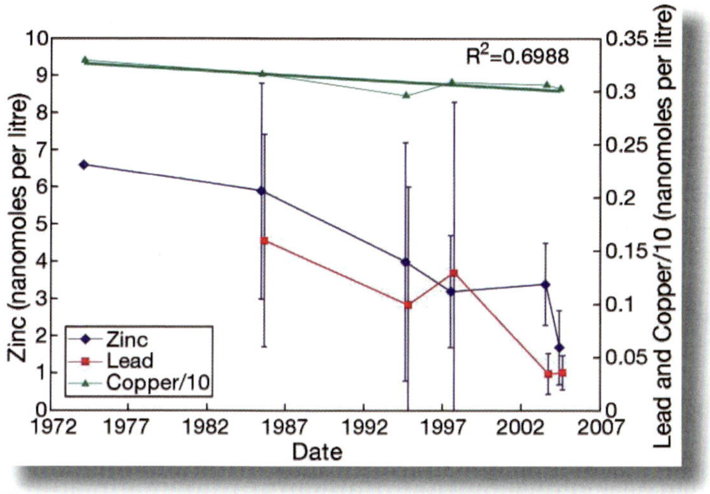

Figure 9. Temporal trends for dissolved heavy metals in the waters of the Scotian Shelf. Lead and zinc averages are based on all the observed data between the surface and 25 m; copper (Cu) results are based on salinity-normalized concentrations for samples from all depths.

CONCLUSION

This paper describes information on temporal trends in chemical variables that can be determined from data compiled in BioChem from studies conducted mostly for other purposes. Data from dedicated studies of temporal trends in chemical tracers such as radioactive contaminants or freons that are conducted in order to determine transport pathways and the time scales of physical oceanographic processes have not been considered here. Temporal trend information on both decadal and much longer scales recorded in marine sediments is also neglected. The results described in this article are based on chemical oceanographic data archived in BioChem and provide information on temporal trends in biologically important parameters such as pH and concentrations of oxygen and nutrients as well as potential chemical pollutants. Some trends such as very small changes in nutrient concentrations in deep ocean waters may only be of interest to oceanographers, but other trends in near surface and inshore waters will have relevance to ecological studies and environmental management. Observations of multiyear trends in chemical parameters are indicative of a changing marine environment, but specifying the mechanisms responsible and their biological impacts will require an understanding of concurrent changes in the physical and biological oceanographic regime. Ongoing monitoring efforts such as AZMP (Atlantic Zonal Monitoring Program) are critical for the collection of the necessary physical, chemical, and biological data sets.

ACKNOWLEDGEMENTS

This paper would not have been possible without the hard work and dedication of the people responsible for the development and maintenance of the BioChem database, and all the physical, chemical and biological oceanographers who collected and archived the data.

REFERENCES

Addison, R.F., W.T. Stobo, and M.E. Zinck. 1998. Organochlorine residue concentrations in blubber of grey seal (*Halichoerus grypus*) from Sable Island, N.S., 1974-1994: compilation of data and analysis of trends. Canadian Data Report of Fisheries and Aquatic Sciences 1043, Dartmouth, NS.

Azetsu-Scott, K., E.P. Jones, I. Yashayaev, and R.M. Gershey. 2003. Time series study of CFC concentrations in the Labrador Sea during deep and shallow convection regimes (1991-2000). Journal of Geophysical Research 108 (C11): 1,978-2,012. doi:10.1029/2002JC001317.

Gearing, J.N., D.E. Buckley, and J.N. Smith. 1991. Hydrocarbon and metal contents of a sediment core from Halifax Harbour: a chronology of contamination. Canadian Journal of Fisheries and Aquatic Sciences 48: 2,344-2,354.

Gilbert, D., B. Sundby, C. Gobeil, A. Mucci, and G.-H. Tremblay. 2005. A 72-year record of diminishing deep-water oxygen in the St. Lawrence estuary: the Northwest Atlantic connection. Limnology and Oceanography 50: 1,654-1,666.

Gilbert, D., N.N. Rabalais, R.J. Diaz, and J. Zhang. 2010. Evidence for greater oxygen decline rates in the coastal ocean than in the open ocean. Biogeosciences 7: 2,283-2,296.

Gregory, D. and S. Narayanan. 2003. BioChem: a national archive for marine biology and chemistry data. AZMP Bulletin 3: 11-13.

Harrison, W.G. and W.K.W. Li. 2007. Phytoplankton growth and regulation in the Labrador Sea: light and nutrient limitation. Journal of Northwest Atlantic Fisheries Science 39: 71-82. doi:10.2960/J.v39.m592.

Levy, E.M. 1984. Incidence and distribution of petroleum and petroleum products. Pages 70-76 *in* Health of the Northwest Atlantic; a Report to the Interdepartmental Committee on Environmental Issues (R.C.H. Wilson, and R.F. Addison, Eds.). Department of the Environment/Department of Fisheries and Oceans/Department of Energy, Mines and Resources, Ottawa, ON.

Levy, E.M. 1985. Background residues of dissolved/dispersed petroleum residues in the Gulf of St. Lawrence, 1970-1979. Canadian Journal of Fisheries and Aquatic Sciences 42: 544-555.

Mills, E.L. 2014. Canadian marine science from before *Titanic* to the establishment of the Bedford Institute of Oceanography in 1962. Pages 3-11 *in* Voyage of Discovery: Fifty Years of Marine Research at Canada's Bedford Institute of Oceanography (D.N. Nettleship, D.C. Gordon, C.F.M. Lewis, and M.P. Latremouille, Eds.). Bedford Institute of Oceanography-Oceans Association, Dartmouth, NS.

Petrie, B. and P. Yeats. 2000. Annual and interannual variability of nutrients and their estimated fluxes in the Scotian Shelf-Gulf of Maine region. Canadian Journal of Fisheries and Aquatic Sciences 57: 2,536-2,546.

Petrie, B., K. Drinkwater, and P. Yeats. 1994. Ocean climate variations for the Canadian East Coast: a simple model with an update for 1993. Atlantic Fisheries Research Document 94/17, Fisheries and Oceans Canada, Dartmouth, NS.

Petrie, B., P. Yeats, and P. Strain. 1999a. Development of a sea surface temperature index for the Canadian East Coast; nutrient and oxygen variability on the Scotian Shelf: a preliminary report from the Zonal Monitoring Program. Canadian Stock Assessment Secretariat Working Document 99/11, Dartmouth, NS.

Petrie, B., P. Yeats, and P. Strain. 1999b. Nitrate, silicate and phosphate atlas for the Scotian Shelf and Gulf of Maine. Canadian Technical Report of Hydrography and Ocean Sciences 203, Dartmouth, NS.

Royal Society. 2005. Ocean acidification due to increasing atmospheric carbon dioxide. Royal Society Policy Document 12/05, Royal Society, London, England.

Smith, P.C., N.R. Pettigrew, P. Yeats, D. Townsend, and G. Han. 2011. Regime shift in the Gulf of Maine. American Fisheries Society Symposium 79: 185-203.

Townsend, D.W., N.D. Rebuck, M.A. Thomas, L. Karp-Boss, and R.M. Gettings. 2010. A changing nutrient regime in the Gulf of Maine. Continental Shelf Research 30: 820-832.

Yeats, P., S. Ryan, and G. Harrison. 2010. Temporal trends in nutrient and oxygen concentrations in the Labrador Sea and on the Scotian Shelf. AZMP Bulletin 9: 23-27.

Hydrography & Seabed Mapping

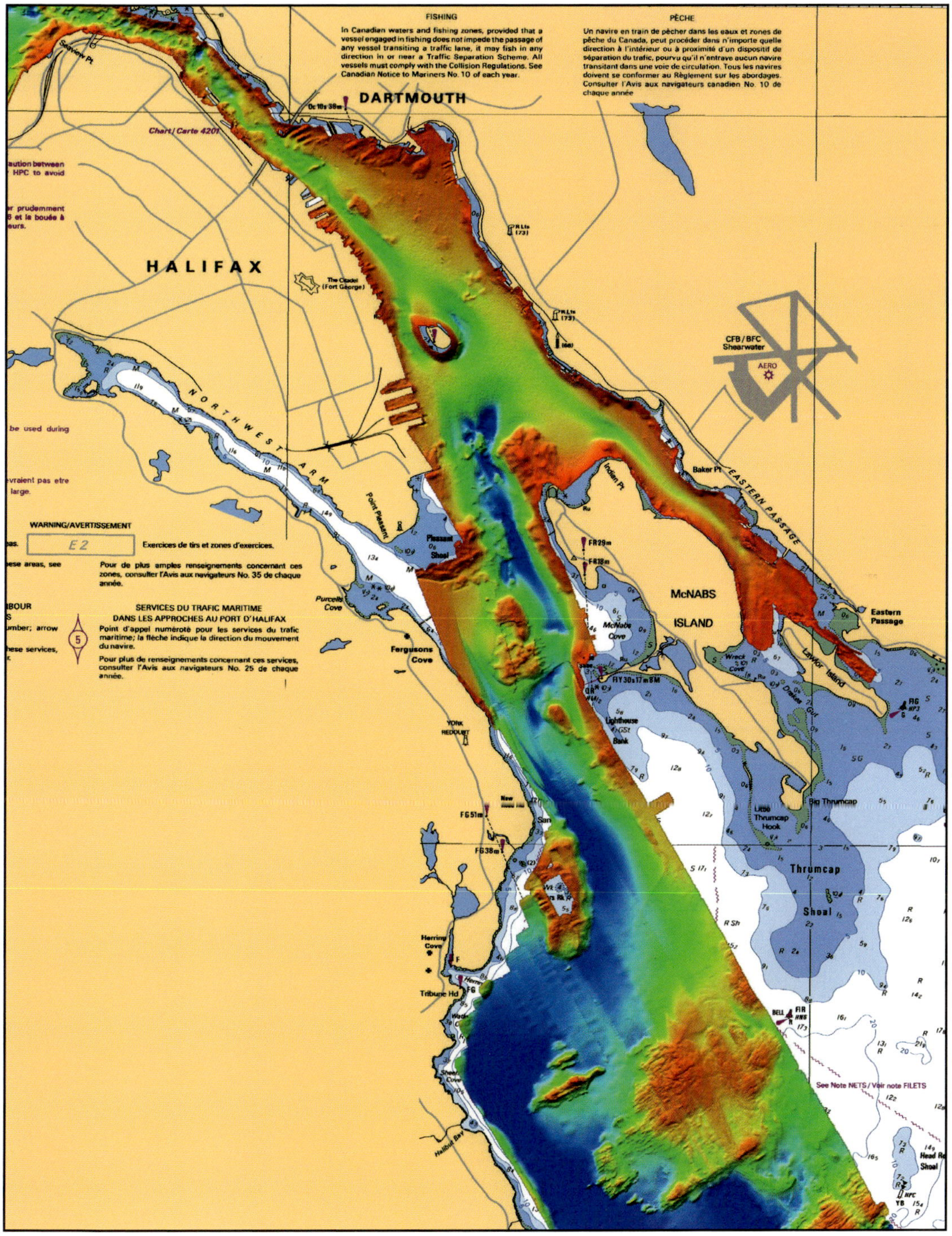

Seafloor relief of Halifax Harbour, Halifax, Nova Scotia

Hydrography and Seabed Mapping

19. HYDROGRAPHY: A FOUNDATION FOR MULTIDISCIPLINARY OCEAN SCIENCE AT THE BEDFORD INSTITUTE OF OCEANOGRAPHY, 1962-2012

J. Richard MacDougall

SUMMARY

Hydrography was one of the sciences that formed the foundation of the Bedford Institute of Oceanography (BIO) when it opened in 1962. The Canadian Hydrographic Service (CHS) brought to the Institute its fleet of survey vessels, expertise to chart the seabed, and the ability to accurately position vessels and instrumentation at sea. Over the years, CHS programs have addressed three principal service mandates: (1) navigational, (2) sovereignty and security, and (3) non-navigational. The navigational responsibility includes hydrographic surveying, charting, and studying tides, currents, and water levels in order to establish and maintain the charts and supporting publications that describe the maritime highways into and between Canadian ports. In 1962, with the exception for inshore areas, most of Atlantic Canada and the eastern Canadian arctic were considered inadequately surveyed for modern shipping. This service mandate has been on-going with legal obligations for both CHS and shipping. The sovereignty and security responsibility includes support for the Canadian Navy and Foreign Affairs when establishing maritime boundaries and expert witness support when enforcing Canadian laws offshore. The non-navigational contributions have included seabed mapping. During the last 50 years, CHS Atlantic has often been at the forefront of technological developments including offshore positioning, data logging and processing, multibeam echo sounders, and electronic chart display and information systems. However, in the half-century since BIO opened, technological changes in navigation and increased size of ships have outpaced CHS new charting requirements in Atlantic Canada.

Key words: Canadian Hydrographic Service, navigation, hydrographic surveying, charting, tides, sovereignty.
E-mail: JRMacdougall@hotmail.com

The International Hydrographic Organization (IHO) defines hydrography as:

> *"... the branch of applied sciences which deals with the measurement and description of the physical features of oceans, seas, coastal areas, lakes and rivers, as well as with the prediction of their change over time, for the primary purpose of safety of navigation and in support of all other marine activities, including economic development, security and defence, scientific research, and environmental protection." (http://www.iho.int/srvi/)*

Broadening the role of the Canadian Hydrographic Service (CHS) from the primary purpose of safety of navigation by the inclusion of hydrography among the ocean science disciplines to be housed at the Bedford Institute of Oceanography (BIO) was an integral component of the vision for the Institute when created in 1962. The appointment of Dr. W.E. van Steenburgh as Director General of the Department of Mines and Technical Surveys, then home to the CHS, marked the arrival of a scientific mind and the scientific method to the department (Fillmore and Sandilands 1983). In 1960, Dr. van Steenburgh appointed Dr. W. Cameron as the department's first oceanographer and together they were largely responsible for the development of BIO as the first federal Canadian multidisciplinary marine institute where hydrographers, oceanographers, and marine geoscientists could work together. Thus, CHS was an important piece of the foundation of BIO, bringing not only its fleet of survey vessels, but also the expertise to chart the seabed and accurately position vessels and instrumentation at sea. Decades of multidisciplinary surveys followed with survey vessels collecting both hydrographic and oceanographic data. However, the CHS service mandate to support safety of navigation has remained an on-going responsibility with legal obligations to produce and maintain navigational charts and supplementary publications critical to safe shipping in Canadian waters.

This paper provides an overview of CHS contributions to its mandates and science at BIO over the past 50 years. To provide context to the development of hydrography at BIO, the history of hydrography in Canada is reviewed briefly, as well as the national structure and mandate of CHS. Earlier reviews of CHS activities at BIO are given in Kerr (1987) and Rockwell et al. (2003).

HISTORY OF HYDROGRAPHY IN CANADA

Details of the early history of hydrography in Canada are presented in several books including Meehan (1964), Fillmore and Sandilands (1983), and Glover (2004). Historical information is also provided on the 'Friends of Hydrography' website (www.canfoh.org/Intro&Hist/history_of_hydrography.htm). While the 1867 British North America Act (BNA) vested all matters of national interest pertaining to navigation and shipping in the Minister of Marine and Fisheries, the British continued to survey Canadian waters after confederation. A Canadian hydrographic program first came into being in 1883 with the establishment of the Georgian Bay Survey within the Department of Marine and Fisheries (DMF). In 1904, this Survey was amalgamated with the hydrographic units in the Department of Public Works and Railways and Canals to form the Hydrographic Survey of Canada. The name was changed to the Canadian Hydrographic Service (CHS) in 1928 following a reorganization of the DMF. Tides and currents are closely related to hydrographic surveys and whenever hydrography was moved to another department the tidal units were transferred along with it. Thus, by 1928, the responsibility for tides also resided in CHS.

Prior to 1904, when Britain asked developed colonies to assume responsibility for surveys of their coasts, the Canadian hydrographic surveys focussed on inland waters. The first Atlantic marine survey conducted by Canadian hydrographers was in the St. Lawrence River in 1904. Surveys of Nova Scotia and New Brunswick began in 1908, Hudson Bay, Hudson Strait and Prince Edward Island in 1910, James Bay in 1912, Labrador in 1921, Newfoundland in 1939, Parry Channel and Jones Sound in 1951, and the Arctic Ocean and Queen Elizabeth Islands in 1959. While Canada carried out surveys of specific ports in Newfoundland and Labrador during World War II, the charting responsibility rested with Britain until Newfoundland joined Canada in 1949. All Atlantic coast surveys were run from Ottawa, Ontario, until a CHS regional office was established in Halifax, Nova Scotia, in 1958. This regional office moved into BIO in 1962 and has been a critical component of the Institute ever since.

STRUCTURE AND MANDATE OF THE CANADIAN HYDROGRAPHIC SERVICE

The CHS is a national organization with its headquarters in Ottawa and four regional offices: Pacific (Sidney, BC), Central and Arctic (Burlington, ON), Quebec (Ste. Flavie, QC), and Atlantic (Dartmouth, NS); the Atlantic Region also has a satellite office in St. John's, Newfoundland. Each region is led by a Director who together with the Director General/Dominion Hydrographer and two headquarters Directors make up the CHS Senior Management Committee.

CHS has three principal service mandates: (1) Navigational, (2) Sovereignty and Security, and (3) Non-navigational. Activities under the Navigational Mandate include surveying Canada's navigable waterways, producing nautical charts and related publications (e.g., sailing directions, tide and current tables), keeping these products up-to-date via Notices to Mariners, and operating the Permanent Water Level Network of tide gauges. CHS meets its Sovereignty and Security Mandate by supporting the Canadian Navy and selecting and maintaining the baseline points for Canada's Territorial Sea and Exclusive Economic Zone (EEZ). The Non-navigational Mandate of CHS changes to address current government and departmental priorities. CHS initiates, leads, and participates in development and research projects in support of all aspects of these mandates. These are also the mandates of CHS Atlantic adjusted for local demand, available budget and capabilities, and regional priorities.

The Charts and Nautical Publications Regulations of the Canada Shipping Act require all ships to carry and use up-to-date Canadian or equivalent charts and nautical publications when navigating in Canadian waters. This legal obligation of ships to use CHS products places legal liability on the Crown if an accident resulted from the use of inaccurate or out-of-date charts, an obligation that demands CHS to keep products up-to-date, and to have consistent national standards and levels of service.

The level of service provided by CHS Atlantic is governed by CHS national policies and standards. Consistency of policies, standards, and training across all regions is a key aspect of CHS and has had a direct impact on staff and organizational structure of CHS Atlantic at BIO. CHS also represents Canada at the International Hydrographic Organization (IHO) where it contributes to developing and adopting international chart standards to ensure safety of navigation globally.

After World War II, CHS recruited veterans and others with a diverse mix of skill sets. The need to train these recruits to a common level in the requirements of hydrographic surveying, marine cartography, and measurement of tides and currents led to formal training programs and career plans within CHS for both hydrographic surveyors and cartographers. The curriculum for a Hydrographic Surveyor course, which consisted of classroom and field training, was accredited by IHO and the career plan recognized by the Public Service Commission of Canada. The career plan, coupled with winter-training cruises to the Caribbean on CSS *Baffin,* was a strong recruitment/retention incentive. Hydrographic surveyors with different backgrounds from all regions were exposed to the same training program which forged lasting relationships and fostered national consistency. In the late 1960s, a University Training Program was implemented to send employees back to university to obtain degrees in fields such as mathematics, physics, computer science, and surveying engineering. In the mid-1970s, the charting aspect of CHS was moved from Ottawa to the regional offices and the duties of compilers and draftsmen were combined into a new 'cartographer' work description. A Cartographer Career Plan similar to the Hydrographic Surveyor Career Plan was subsequently developed and administered.

In 1971, CHS moved from Energy Mines and Resources Canada (EMR) to Environment Canada (DOE). Funding for vessel resources to support EMR's marine programs was transferred to DOE along with the vessels. DOE agreed to continue to provide EMR with vessel support, a key provision for maintaining multidisciplinary coherence within BIO. At the working level, BIO hydrographers, geologists, and geophysicists continued to work together irrespective of departmental affiliation. In 1976, CHS moved to the Department of Fisheries and the Environment, and in 1979 to Fisheries and Oceans Canada (DFO).

In the late 1980s and 1990s, government program review exercises to reduce federal expenditures had a major impact on CHS budgets, staff levels, and vessel time. To create flexibility in meeting staff reduction targets, CHS integrated the duties of Hydrographic Surveyors and Cartographers into a single Multidisciplinary Hydrographer work description. The associated career progression plan included a combination of hydrographic and cartographic classroom and on-the-job training over a 5-year period to progress from recruitment to working level. CHS staff levels and operating budgets (including vessels) were reduced by 30% and nearly 50%, respectively. Program adjustments included elimination of the Training Unit (recruitment ceased), reduction in number of tide gauges, helicopter use limited to special purposes (e.g., revision of sailing directions), merging DFO science and fisheries patrol fleets with Canadian Coast Guard (CCG), and decommissioning survey vessels or transferring them between regions. Offshore and arctic hydrographic surveys were no longer deemed a priority and were discontinued.

Revenue targets were established for DFO, which included CCG and CHS. The only revenue source for CHS was the sale of nautical charts, an inelastic market, and so, revenue shortfalls became an annual budget pressure. Mixing revenue generation with a 'safety of lives, property, and the maritime environment' purpose also changed the dynamics of the relationship with users of navigation products, now being asked to fund the new navigational services they requested. There were also additional challenges for CHS. The program review reductions came at a time when mariners were adopting global positioning system (GPS) navigation which was much more accurate than the survey data used to make charts at the time: e.g., nearly 200 CHS Atlantic charts were too inaccurate to be used with GPS. There was also a growing demand for electronic chart products at the same time CHS was attempting to reduce services to meet reduction targets. The years of program review, and following years, were lean ones for CHS Atlantic. DFO funding pressures were dealt with by taxing budgets of existing programs a few percent a year. New funding was primarily short-term and project-based, rather than program-based, and recruitment was limited to casual or term employees, or contractors with the skill set needed for a particular project.

In the early 2000s, CHS implemented a national quality management system and became certified to the International Organization for Standardization ISO 9001 standards. All CHS functions, administrative as well as production, were documented and staff trained in the ISO 9001 system. The philosophy was simple — "Say what you do (document processes), do what you say, and be able to prove it (audit)" — with the goal of efficiency through continuous improvement. CHS management committed to the ISO process and to respond to non-conformities and opportunities for improvement. External audits of ISO processes are also part of the ongoing process to maintain accreditation (Palmer 2002).

Throughout the last 50 years, CHS Atlantic has been proactive in embracing change and often on the leading edge of developing hydrographic policy and technology both in Canada and internationally through the IHO. Staff identify with CHS and its mission. Knowing the importance of the CHS mission and that their work directly impacts the lives of users makes finding ways to 'get the job done' second nature for CHS employees, as they strive to fulfill the three principal mandates of the organization.

NAVIGATIONAL MANDATE

The driving forces of early hydrography — surveying and charting navigable waters — were exploration and facilitation of the transportation needs of commerce between Canada and other continents, and over waterways within the country. In 2012, these CHS-defined maritime highways allowed $162 billion in cargo to move through Canadian ports (http://www.acpa-ports.net/index.html). Owing to the much lower cost per kilogram to ship by sea compared to air, water-borne transport of cargo favourably impacts what all Canadians pay for imported goods and the competitiveness of Canadian goods shipped overseas, a significant contribution to the Canadian economy. The same situation applies to the Canadian north where air cargo is the only alternative to the maritime highways that are the lifeline for supply of essential goods to remote communities.

Opening and maintaining these maritime highways as technology and user needs change (e.g., new routes, bigger ships, more accurate navigation tools, new fisheries and recreational users) remains the primary mandate of CHS, an ongoing task. When bathymetric changes occur, such as by silting and dredging, the mariners must rely on charts to determine whether the maritime highway is safe for their vessels and rely on their navigation tools to keep them on it. The charts, their companion publications, sailing directions, and tide and current tables contain relevant supplementary information, such as vessel traffic lanes, military exercise areas, and conspicuous objects, among other items.

By the 1980s, the drafts of the largest vessels in the world were more than double those in 1962 (e.g., *Seawise Giant* at 24.6 m versus USS *Enterprise* at 12 m) (http://maritime-connector.com/worlds-largest-ships/). Positioning accuracy has gone from 10 km with celestial navigation to <10 m using the differential global positioning system (DGPS). Post Panamax ships, too large for the Panama Canal, arriving in Halifax in 2012 routinely draw 15 m of water and must consider state of the tide for safe clearance under the harbour bridges. Often the profit for a voyage is in the last 30 cm of draft so there is ongoing pressure to reduce safe-under-hull clearances, use real-time water levels to gain centimetres from local tide and water level changes, and use precise navigation and near real-time 3-D survey data to manoeuvre around least depths within channels. These new conditions increase pressure on CHS to provide accurate, near real-time depth and water level information on the busiest maritime highways which leaves few resources for developing new maritime highways, improving the safety of less-travelled maritime highways, and for non-navigational mandates.

Hydrographic Surveying

When CHS Atlantic came to BIO in 1962, hydrographic surveying and charting on the Atlantic coast and eastern Arctic Canada was far from complete (Fig. 1). Surveys had been interrupted by two World Wars plus the responsibility for surveying Newfoundland and Labrador had been assumed. British charts of the 18th and 19th centuries, as well as charts of Newfoundland and Labrador produced by the United States Navy during World War II, were focussed on ports of refuge (Pietrzak 1985). Arctic charting was wholly provisional, compiled from track soundings from vessels transiting the region. Much of the continental shelf and Labrador Sea were uncharted. The areas surveyed and charted to 'modern' standards were close to shore. In addition to this being the area where the seabed was most likely to collide with ships' hulls, it was also the area where field surveys could be positioned visually by sextant relative to shore-based stations. Prior to the development of radar and early electronic positioning systems such as Decca during World War II, there was no means of accurately positioning a vessel out of sight of land.

The status of Atlantic hydrographic surveying when BIO opened is summarized succinctly by the following quote from the Dominion Hydrographer's Second Conference (1962):

> *"A resumé was given of the charting of the Atlantic seaboard of Nova Scotia. The coast from Yarmouth to Sydney, a distance of 350 miles had been surveyed by French, British and Canadian hydrographers almost continually for 110 years and is still not adequately charted. During this period eighty individual unit surveys were carried out. The coast of Labrador, also is 650 miles in length, basically uncharted and is more deeply indented. Accepting the above data as a standard for calculation, it is reckoned that 150 units of survey will be required, and the number of years involved could be in proportion. Thus, hydrographic staff could be assured that there is sufficient work for a great deal of their active careers in the area of Labrador alone."*

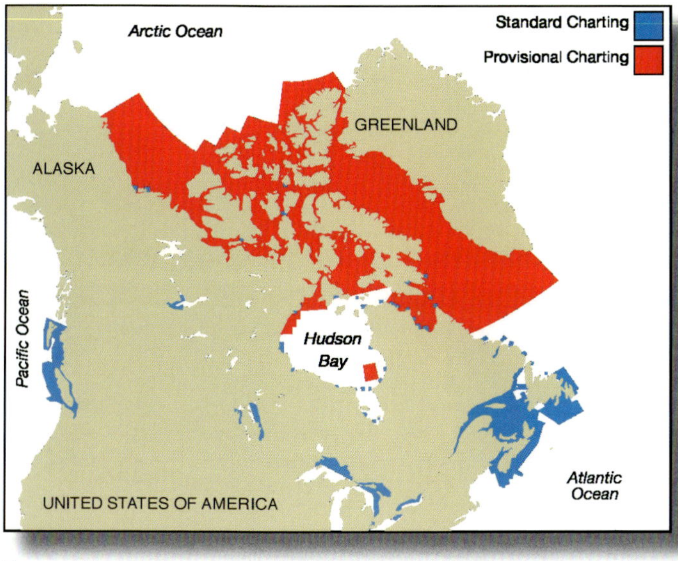

Figure 1. Status of hydrographic charting in Canada in 1958 (Canadian Hydrographic Service 1958).

The Dominion Hydrographer's Second Conference (1962) also provides insight into the status of technology employed by the CHS at that time. Maximum ranges achieved with electronic positioning systems ranged from 20 nautical miles (nm) for Hi-Fix to 450 nm with Decca Lambda. Positional accuracy ranged from ±6 m with Hi-Fix to ±60 m with Decca Lambda to ±200 m with standard Decca. The 'portable' Hi-Fix system could be transported in a 2-ton truck and the receiver could fit in a 9 m launch, but an 18 m launch was recommended. A new plotter to be installed on CSS *Baffin* weighed 1.5 tons and bulkheads needed to be strengthened prior to installation. A transducer towed from a helicopter by the Polar Continental Shelf Project (PCSP) had been 'transistorized' to reduce weight. The establishment of an electronics group and a development group was recommended.

Ships, surveys, and satellite office — The post-World War II era was a time of growth for CHS. The demand for surveys and charting was increasing. The CSS *Acadia* was back, after being seconded to the Canadian Navy during the war, decommissioned Navy minesweepers such as CSS *Kapuskasing* became available, and ice-strengthened sealing vessels were available for charter. Dominion Hydrographers F.C.G. Smith and N. Gray made the case for a new hydrographic survey ship based in Atlantic Canada which led to the launching of the CSS *Baffin* in 1956, followed by the CSS *Maxwell* in 1961. Thus, when BIO opened in 1962, there were four government vessels available for conducting hydrographic surveys. In addition, there were the hydrographic launches CHL *Anderson* and CHL *Eider* plus 18 smaller launches that were carried on the principal vessels. The MV *Arctic Sealer* and the MV *North Star VI* were also employed under charter. Furthermore, hydrographers were assigned to CCG icebreakers to collect bathymetry on an opportunity basis. Surveys typically ran from May to October each year, and this high level of effort was maintained from the 1960s through the 1980s. The offshore surveys beginning in the 1960s, collected gravity, magnetic, and at times seismic data as well as bathymetry, in co-operation with marine geoscientists at BIO.

Beginning in the mid-1970s, a government move to 'contracting for services' saw a number of hydrographic surveys performed by contractors, including the Miramichi River in New Brunswick. CHS Atlantic hydrographers monitored contracts and provided quality control. However, growing and sustaining an industry with hydrographic capability was difficult. The use of contract surveys by CHS Atlantic was sporadic, depending on the annual budget situation, so companies struggled to maintain hydrographic expertise. Inexperienced contractors underbidding experienced ones meant there was often a steep learning curve on each contract survey which negatively impacted productivity.

Over the years, the hydrographic fleet at BIO evolved. The CSS *Hudson* was built as a combined hydrographic and oceanographic vessel, and arrived soon after BIO opened. The CSS *Acadia* was retired from service after the 1969 season and in 1982 was transferred to Maritime Museum of the Atlantic in Halifax where she remains on display today. The CSS *Kapuskasing* was returned to DND for disposal in 1972. The purpose-built acoustic sweep vessel CSS *F.C.G. Smith* arrived at BIO in 1986 (Fig. 2A). She was followed by the CSS *Frederick G. Creed* that arrived in 1987 (Fig. 2B). The CSS *Frederick G. Creed* is a 19.8 m SWATH (Small Water Area Twin Hulls) vessel named after the Canadian inventor of the hull design. Both hulls are below the waterline and only a vertical plate connecting each hull to the deck passes through the air/water interface, making the vessel very stable for collection of high quality bathymetry data with a hull-mounted transducer. Following winter sea trials off Newfoundland, the CSS *Frederick G. Creed* was based in the Quebec Region but shared with CHS Atlantic.

All the systematic hydrographic surveys of the Atlantic continental shelf were done prior to the advent of MBES (Multibeam Echo Sounder Systems). Where hazards to ships were not a concern, depth data were collected at line spacing of 5 to 20 nm to get a sense of the seabed shape. In an effort to obtain more data, the concept of multiple vessels running in parallel was investigated by running the CSS *Kapuskasing* alongside CSS *Baffin*. While this approach worked, it was an expensive solution. The

Figure 2. Special-purpose hydrographic survey vessels: (A) CSS *F.C.G. Smith* sweep vessel (named after a Dominion Hydrographer) and (B) CSS *Frederick G. Creed* SWATH vessel (named after the Canadian inventor).

sea state offshore is not conducive to running crewed launches in parallel with the ship. In the 1960s, a remote controlled launch was developed and tested, but offshore it was airborne much of the time and therefore not effective. In the mid-1980s, three prototype semi-submersible vessels named DOLPHIN (Deep Ocean Platform and Hydrographic Instrumentation and Navigation) were built by International Submarine Engineering of Port Moody, British Columbia. These torpedo-shaped vessels were diesel powered and could run up to 4 m below the surface with only an air intake for the diesel engine and antenna for the remote control above the surface. This configuration obtained 'clean' data sets because the echo sounder transducer was positioned below surface aeration caused by wave action – air bubbles are avoided because they reflect sound waves, preventing acoustic resolution of the seafloor (Costello et al. 1991). Launching and retrieving DOLPHIN in rough seas using CSS *Baffin* was a challenge, especially when DOLPHIN was dead in the water. The DOLPHINs were outfitted with EM100 multibeam echo sounder (MBES) systems and transferred to industry in 1992, but the project ended in 1997 due to changing priorities and a lack of offshore work and funding.

In 1987, a CHS Atlantic satellite office was established in St. John's, Newfoundland. The CSS *Maxwell* and seven staff were transferred with a mandate of surveying Newfoundland and Labrador waters. This survey party re-introduced an old organizational model where the hydrographer-in-charge was also the captain of the vessel. The CSS *Maxwell*, with its shallow draft, was ideal for surveying the smaller ports. In 1990, the CSS *Maxwell* was decommissioned and replaced by the larger CSS *Matthew* which was transferred back to BIO the next year. In December 1990, the CSS *Baffin* was badly damaged while attempting to dock at night at the BIO jetty during a storm and was decommissioned in 1991 (Rockwell et al. 2003). The CSS *Baffin*'s survey capability was to be replaced by a combination of shore parties, the CSS *Matthew*, and hydrographic surveys on the CSS *Hudson* every second year. However, only one hydrographic survey was conducted from CSS *Hudson* before program review exercises determined that Arctic and offshore surveys were no longer priorities. In effect, CHS Atlantic's capability for conducting Arctic and offshore hydrographic surveys came to an end with CSS *Baffin*'s decommissioning. The 1993 transfer of the CSS *F.C.G. Smith* to the Quebec Region reduced the Atlantic Region's survey capability to one vessel, the CSS *Matthew* and shared survey time on CSS *Frederick G. Creed*.

Improving navigation and positioning — Navigation and positioning at sea were strengths CHS brought to BIO and were an on-going challenge prior to the satellite-based Global Positioning System (GPS). Decca was the major electronic positioning system in use in 1962. Further developments in electronic positioning systems were tested and put to work on hydrographic surveys in the Atlantic Region. The data plotter tested on the CSS *Baffin* in 1962 did not perform well due to motion and so went ashore to a more stable environment. The first general purpose minicomputer, a Digital Equipment Corporation (DEC) PDP-8 with 4 K memory, was installed on CSS *Baffin* in 1967. In 1968, the PDP-8-based Hydrographic Acquisition And Processing System (HAAPS) was developed to log depth and position data, select the depths to plot, and plot these depths while at sea (Kerr 1987).

Range ambiguity, and positional uncertainty required innovative and unique solutions and were factors behind the creation of the BIO Navigation Group in 1970 under the leadership of M. Eaton (Grant and McKeown 1987). Among the BIO Navigation Group's many contributions over the years was the introduction of Loran-C and a special ranging version called rho-rho Loran-C that eventually replaced Decca Lambda (Grant et al. 2014). Other initiatives were the development of an integrated navigation system called BIONAV (Grant and Wells 2014), early research and evaluation of GPS receivers, and extensive development and testing of early electronic chart display and information systems (Eaton 2014). In recognition of his many contributions to navigation, M. Eaton was awarded the Order of Canada in 2005.

CHS Atlantic began testing GPS receivers when only a few satellites were in orbit and used the system operationally to complement Loran-C. At this early stage of development, the satellite configuration would only provide positions for several hours twice a day (Eaton 1983). When the system became operational 24 hours a day, the United States Department of Defence degraded the accuracy by hundreds of metres for non-military receivers. To improve accuracy, CHS Atlantic placed a GPS receiver at a known position ashore, calculated the difference with the GPS position, and radioed the offsets to receivers on vessels. In time, the Canadian Coast Guard (CCG) and United States Coast Guard implemented a differential GPS (DGPS) service to provide these corrections for North American waters (with the exception of the Arctic) using Coast Guard radio stations. Later, wide area satellite-based correction services were developed. This ability to accurately position a vessel at sea 24 hours a day changed hydrographic surveying as well as navigation.

Survey challenges in arctic waterways — Surveys in Arctic Canada were an on-going challenge. When summer ice conditions were bad, little hydrographic data were collected from icebreakers that were busy escorting shipping. In the pre-GPS era, survey vessels needed to establish shore stations for navigation before beginning a survey. Often, the shore stations were no sooner deployed than the wind changed and drifting sea ice moved into the survey area ending sounding operations. The process would be repeated on the opposite side of a strait until the wind changed and the survey vessel would be forced to move elsewhere. Often little progress was made for the effort expended.

To address this challenge, the Polar Continental Shelf Project (PCSP) winter surveys, that originally mapped the Arctic Ocean continental shelf, moved south among the arctic islands after the discovery of oil in the Beaufort Sea in the late 1960s. The approach of obtaining grids of spot depths through the ice using helicopters during the winter months yielded reconnaissance bathymetric data of channels and corridors. Over the years, these winter surveys also used sounders mounted in tracked vehicles and an airborne electromagnetic system that acquired depths through the ice. CHS Atlantic led the Autonomous Remote Controlled Submersible (ARCS) Program which utilized a torpedo-like vehicle that contained an acoustic positioning system, echo sounder, data logging system, and acoustic telemetric control link for under-ice surveys (Kerr 1983b). While a prototype unit was successfully tested in southern waters, funding cuts and changing priorities prevented its arctic deployment.

Increasing the resolution of seafloor surveys — Hydrographic surveys for navigation purposes sample the water depth along vessel tracks to obtain a general shape of the seabed and further explore indications of shallower areas that might indicate hazards to vessels. The distance between vessel tracks (50 m to 20 km) was dictated by the scale of the chart, the complexity of the bottom, and the depth of the water. Line spacing was traditionally reduced in shallower water to detect indications of dangerous shoals that might be lurking between the vessel tracks (Kerr 1983a). While side scan sonar has the ability to detect indications of hazards between sounding lines, towing the fish slowed sounding operations and so the technology did not become part of the standard hydrographic survey operation.

Only important channels and harbours were 'swept' to a specified depth. Traditionally, a wire drag was suspended between two vessels at a specific depth and slowly moved along a channel. It would snag on depths shallower than the set depth. During the 1960s and 1970s, acoustic sweep systems employing a number of single beam echo sounder transducers were developed. These transducers, mounted on booms on either side of a vessel, had overlapping footprints that allowed channels to be acoustically swept more quickly than by wire drag. CHS Atlantic tested a system on the CSL *Tudlick* and then, in 1986, acquired the purpose-built sweep vessel CSS *F.C.G. Smith* (Fig. 2A; Burke 1988).

Multibeam echo sounder (MBES) systems were developed during the 1970s and 1980s. These systems transmitted multiple acoustic beams beneath and to both sides of the survey vessel. Hydrographers were now able to 'see' what was between vessel tracks and had the ability to map 100% of the bottom. Depending on the system, the swath width varied from 3 to 7 times water depth. To obtain normal hydrographic survey accuracies, line spacing was usually half the swath width so that the centre beam of one track covered the outer beams of the adjacent track (where refraction errors are greatest).

CHS acquired MBES capabilities in the late 1980s when the CSS *Louis M. Lauzier* and CSS *Frederick G. Creed* were outfitted with SIMRAD EM100 systems (Burke and Hally 1989). The CSS *Matthew* was equipped with DGPS and an EM100 system when she arrived at BIO in 1991. Considerable post-delivery testing and research took place to develop software and procedures to ensure accurate depth data were logged and processed and that the massive amounts of data generated by the system were archived. The research work, conducted in collaboration with industry and the Ocean Mapping Group at the University of New Brunswick (UNB), included measurements of vessel motion, and speed of sound along the beam path to determine vertical depths. This work led to the development of a high precision motion sensor for multibeam systems that was commercialized by Applanix (as the POS-MV), as well as adaptation of the Brooke Ocean Moving Vessel Profiler (MVP) for continuous speed-of-sound measurement. These instruments are now the world standard. The CHS development of effective ways to acquire high-resolution images of seafloor morphology and reflectivity in the wave- and swell-prone Atlantic Ocean was a boon to marine geoscientists at BIO (for details, see below under Non-navigational Mandate).

CHS Atlantic also led a national source data project to develop the data base needed to store the millions and millions of depths that MBES systems can collect. When it was determined that the design of the available relational data base systems could not handle the volume of data, H. Varma was seconded to the ORACLE Corporation to implement the hydrographic hyperspatial (HH) code (Boudreau et al. 1991) into the kernel of their data base. The commercial result of this venture was the ORACLE Geospatial data base management system.

Prior to the introduction of the echo sounder, each depth was obtained manually using a lead line and virtually every depth was added to the chart. Vessel tracks were usually obvious. The echo sounder allowed more depths than could be shown on a chart to be collected along vessel profiles, so selections of depths and contours were used to present the information on the chart. The advent of MBES collected data both along and between vessel track and allowed photograph-like images of the seabed to be created and mathematical surfaces of the seabed to be generated. While the presentation on navigation charts continue to show selected depth and contours, the underlying data is much more detailed. Changes in resolution of seafloor mapping as technology evolved are illustrated using Halifax Harbour, Nova Scotia, as an example (Fig. 3).

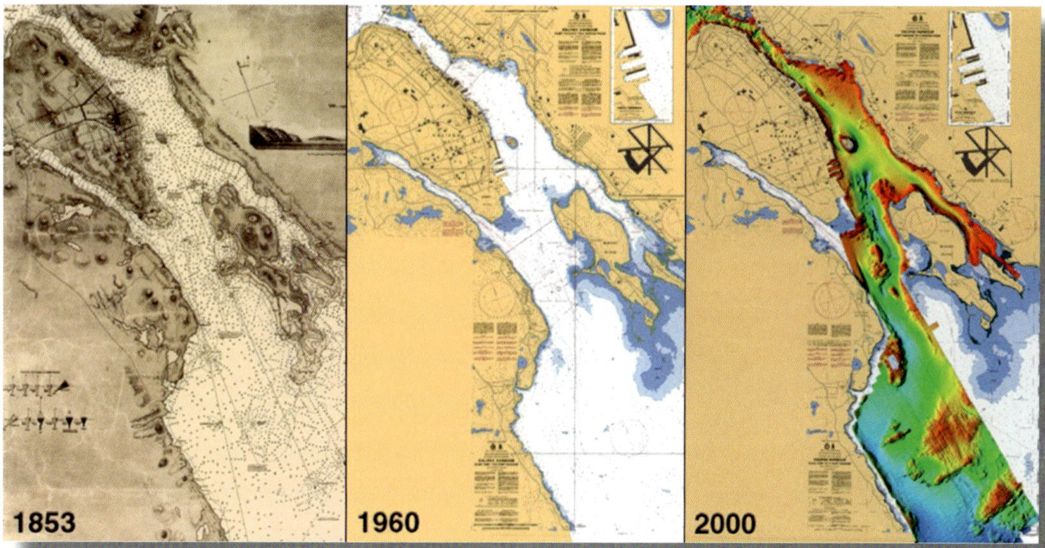

Figure 3. Development of seafloor mapping detail using Halifax Harbour as an example: 1853 – sounding lead line, 1960 – single beam echo sounder, and 2000 – multibeam echo sounder.

The challenge of surveying nearshore — The nearshore has also presented a continuing challenge for hydrography because this is the most dangerous environment for vessels and personnel. There is a foreshore area where the depth is too shallow for launches and an adjacent area where the shallow water makes 100% coverage with MBES very inefficient. The time needed to map a 1 km² area to hydrographic standards at a swath width of 5 times water depth and a speed of 10 knots is illustrated in Table 1. Extrapolating the time to map this sample area to the time to map a 1 km band in each depth range adjacent to all of Canada's >200,000 km of coastline is an indication of the magnitude of the nearshore task.

Table 1. Time required to map 1 km² with a multibeam echo sounder (MBES) at different water depths and line spacing.

Depth (m)	Line Spacing (m)	Time (hours)
100	200	0.2
50	100	0.4
20	50	1
10	25	2
5	12.5	4
2	5	10

In the late 1970s and 1980s, CHS experimented with airborne hydrography for nearshore areas. A system consisting of two cameras, mounted on a fixed boom under a helicopter, taking simultaneous pairs of photographs was tested from CSS *Baffin* at Sable Island in 1981, but depths could only be measured where there was bottom contrast. In conjunction with the Canada Centre for Remote Sensing (CCRS), CHS investigated the use of analytical stereo plotters to measure water depths from conventional aerial photographs but was unsuccessful. However,

Table 2. Comparison of the Larsen 500 and SHOALS LiDAR systems deployed from low-flying aircraft.

System	Depth Range (m)	Depth Density (m)	Depth Accuracy (m)	Swath width at 500 m altitude (m)	Area / hour (km²)
Larson 500	0.5 - 40	35	0.3	270	70
SHOALS	0 - 50	2 - 5	0.25	375	175

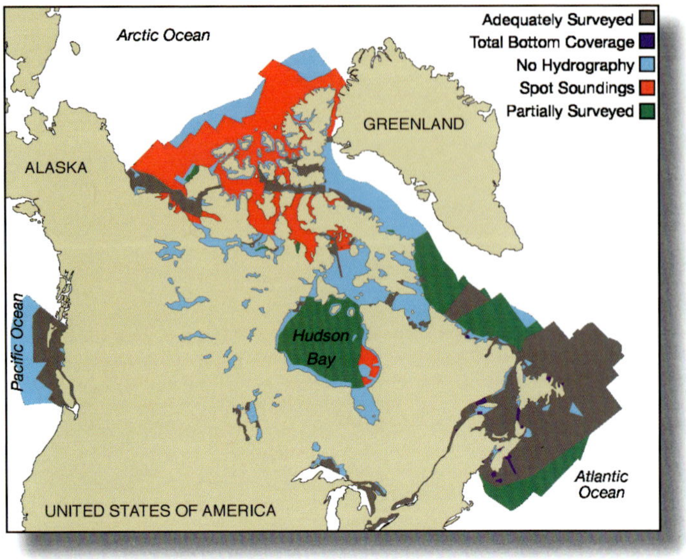

Figure 4. Status of Canadian hydrographic surveys in 1997.

depths acquired from a LiDAR (Light Detecting and Ranging) system emitting a blue green laser beam agreed with 'ground truthing' data and led to the development of a scanning LiDAR system. CHS Atlantic surveyed a ground-truth area near Sherbrooke, Nova Scotia, in 1982 for LiDAR and Multi-Spectral Scanner (MSS) evaluations. The first scanning LiDAR system in the world was built by OPTECH Ltd. of Toronto and was named LARSEN 500 after RCMP Sgt. H. Larsen, Captain of the *St. Roch*. This prototype LiDAR system was further developed and tested in-house by CHS and CCRS, and later was transferred to industry for commercialization. CHS used the commercial system operationally in the Arctic in the 1980s before funding ended and the arctic region ceased to be a priority. OPTECH Ltd. went on to develop commercial bathymetric LiDAR systems for Sweden and the United States. The United States Army Corps of Engineers LiDAR system was called SHOALS (Scanning Hydrographic Operational Airborne LiDAR Survey). In 2011, CHS Atlantic contracted the use of a SHOALS system to map 27 foreshore areas in Atlantic Canada. As with aerial photography, the depth measurement obtained with LiDAR is limited by water clarity and turbidity, and a depth range of 15-20 m was obtained in Atlantic Canada. The accuracy and coverage of the LARSEN 500 and SHOALS LiDAR systems are compared in Table 2.

The status of hydrographic surveying in Canada in 1997 is illustrated in Figure 4. It is clear that significant progress had been made since BIO was established (Fig. 1). However, hydrographic surveys in Atlantic Canada during the last two decades have been restricted to inshore areas because of the need for modern surveys in areas of highest risk to vessels. Another factor is that the only survey vessel currently available in Atlantic Canada, the CCGS *Matthew*, is restricted to 50 nm from shelter. CHS Atlantic survey capability in 2012 was limited to just 90 days on the CCGS *Matthew* which is equipped with an EM710 MBES system and carries two launches, each equipped with EM3002 MBES systems.

Charting

In the mid-1970s, the charting aspects of CHS were moved from Ottawa to the regional offices. The first eight cartographers arrived at BIO in 1977, and by 1979, the move was complete with a total of 25 staff in cartography at BIO, and responsibility for nearly 400 charts. The charts that the Atlantic Region were responsible for at that time covered the eastern Canadian arctic, Foxe Basin, Baffin Bay, the Labrador coast, the Gulf of St. Lawrence, and waters around the Atlantic Provinces to the United States border.

The move of cartographers to BIO also coincided with the introduction of digital techniques. Plotters had been introduced in the 1960s with initial uses including the drawing of borders, plotting sheets, and hyperbolic lattices. In 1977, the Graphics Online Manipulation And Drafting System (GOMADS) was developed in-house. It supported digitizing chart manuscripts, editing data on line, and plotting negatives used for printing. After GOMADS was transferred to industry it evolved into CARIS (Computer Assisted Resource Information System) which is now used in CHS, other hydrographic offices around the world, and provincial and municipal offices.

A general overview of the chart production process is given by Kerr and Macnab (1983). Chart production plans to replace old charts with modern ones are now dependent on data from many sources. While early charts were compiled by the hydrographer from observations he made during a survey, modern charts display diverse data from many sources which include CHS and Public Works surveys, port construction plans, dredging results, changes in aids to navigation, traffic separation schemes, administrative boundaries such as military exercise areas, pilot boarding stations, fishing zones, legal boundaries and limits, as well as clearances for utility cables and bridges. The agency responsible for each source provides data to CHS in different formats and standards so hydrographers must 'normalize' the information and select what to compile into a chart.

In addition, production plans are affected by national and international policy decisions that at times impact the whole suite of Canadian chart products. An example of external change includes latticing of charts for navigation systems (Decca, Loran-A, Loran-C), and removing lattices when systems were replaced. Other examples include making charts bilingual, converting to the metric system, changing black buoy symbols to green when Canada adopted international standards, and changing the horizontal and vertical reference systems. Removing the 3-nm territorial sea limit and replacing it with the 12-nm territorial sea limit, adding the 200-nm fishing zones, and later the Exclusive Economic Zone are yet other examples. When such changes affect nearly 1,000 charts nationally, scheduled chart production comes virtually to a stop.

Electronic charts — CHS was the victim of its own success with the electronic chart test bed efforts to demonstrate what an electronic chart system (ECS) could do for mariners. At the 1985 Canadian Hydrographic Conference, M. Eaton presented the electronic chart's functionality, and a future scenario of a vessel equipped with an electronic chart system arriving at Come by Chance, Newfoundland. For more than the next decade, he worked at turning that futuristic scenario into reality, both from an international standards perspective and through practical demonstration of what was possible when GPS positioning and digital chart data were combined (Eaton 2014). Electronic charting in Canada was accelerated by reaction to the *Exxon Valdez* grounding and oil spill in Alaska. The Canadian federal government appointed the Public Review Panel on Tanker Safety and Marine Spills Response Capability (the Brander-Smith Panel) and one of the recommendations in its final report was: "[to] expedite development of electronic charting technology and the required infrastructure, then introduce regulations requiring the use of electronic charts on all tankers in Canadian waters" (Grant and Goodyear 1996).

In response to this recommendation, a CHS Electronic Chart Pilot Project was funded with an objective of demonstrating the utility of ECSs and obtaining real world operational experience in supporting them. The strategy called for a number of systems to be deployed across the country in a variety of commercial vessels for extended periods of time. The pilot project was also designed to identify the stresses and strains of creation, maintenance, and day-to-day delivery of data to a broad clientele. All regions of CHS were involved in creating the digital chart files needed for the routes that the freighters, tankers and ferries, equipped with the project's ECSs, normally followed. The project was so successful that virtually every vessel equipped with a test bed system bought their own when the project's ECS was transferred to another vessel. The success of this project quickly generated demand for digital chart data to service vessels on routes not initially included.

Licensing CHS data and revenue generation — During this period, CHS Atlantic was reducing services to meet budget reduction targets. However, its workload was increasing because there were still legal obligations to maintain paper products and there was neither a suite of digital charts to meet demand, nor standards for digital chart data and ECSs. In addition, there was no distribution mechanism for digital chart data and there was no legal authority to charge for digital charts to recover costs. To help alleviate this situation, a licensing agreement for digital data distribution was signed between CHS and Nautical Data International Inc. (NDI) in 1993.

The initial CHS electronic charts were copies of information extracted from existing paper charts and were officially released in the same manner as paper charts. Priorities for production of digital chart data were jointly set by CHS and NDI based on areas where there was demand for ECSs. Demands for digital versions of survey data were handled by each CHS region on a case by case basis because, unlike digital chart files, there were no 'official' digital data products ready to be added to the NDI agreement. Once a CHS region customized a dataset to meet a user's needs, NDI licensed the digital data for commercial purposes and CHS licensed digital data for government use and partners.

These interim electronic charts met the majority of the navigation needs of Canadian mariners. When Electronic Chart Display and Information Systems (ECDIS) equipped with official Electronic Navigational Charts (ENC) were recognized as equivalent to the paper charts that vessels are required to carry by law, a significant number of vessels chose to continue to use ECSs that did not meet the paper chart equivalency. Maintaining two digital product lines plus paper charts put an additional burden on CHS. Clients not buying replacements for the interim digital charts also strained NDI's business model and viability.

Modifications to the NDI agreement to attract investment, the sale of NDI in 2000, and a different interpretation of the scope of the agreement with respect to digital survey data brought an end to the previous mode of operation and had a major impact on CHS Atlantic. Government partners who normally deposited a copy of their bathymetric data with CHS chose not to do so and risk possibly tying their digital data, and their ability to use those data as they saw fit, to the NDI agreement. This uncertainty concerning restrictions on access to, and use of digital data, if CHS was a partner in multi-departmental/joint initiatives seeking funding, was also an issue that limited CHS to a role of service provider rather than a leading or full partner in initiatives. The NDI agreement was terminated in 2007 when the Crown bought back all rights granted to NDI. CHS then licensed the use of digital chart products to value-added remarketers and used the resulting royalties to supplement shrinking budgets. However, the concept that hydrographic data as well as chart products can be used to generate revenue, and that each use must be licenced by CHS has negatively impacted the role of CHS as 'the authority' and depository for hydrographic data within the scientific community.

Making do with less — In addition to program review reductions, administrative changes within CHS has impacted CHS Atlantic. The area of responsibility of CHS Atlantic changed in the 1980s when the new Quebec Region of CHS assumed responsibility for charting and surveying the north shore of the Gulf of St Lawrence and the Magdalen Islands. The area of responsibility was further reduced in 1997 when Canadian arctic surveys and charts were assumed by CHS Central and Arctic Region. CHS Atlantic's territory of responsibility now ranged from the northern tip of Labrador to the United States border, including the waters around the four Atlantic provinces, with a responsibility for 291 charts.

With the downsizing of the 1990s, CHS as well as other government agencies were instructed to do more with less and to be innovative. In addition to partnering, CHS adopted a policy of 'single proponent pay' for new surveying and charting (similar to municipalities requiring new subdivision streets be built to a standard before assuming responsibility). While it was often difficult to identify a single proponent, the policy was successfully applied to the Voisey's Bay nickel mine in Labrador. The company contracted the hydrographic surveys of corridors into the mine site while CHS provided contract monitoring and quality control. Voisey's Bay developers then funded CHS Atlantic to produce the necessary charts to create this new maritime highway. To obtain new aerial photography for the shoreline of northern Labrador, CHS Atlantic partnered with the federal Search and Rescue Directorate, the Government of Newfoundland and Labrador, and Parks Canada (Forbes et al. 2006). CHS used the shoreline data to create base maps for a new chart series of the inside route on the Labrador coast and produced shoreline plots for the Search and Rescue Directorate for use in marine search and rescue/recovery situations.

In the late 1990s and early 2000s, there were still many areas around the coast of Newfoundland and Labrador where charts, reproduced from 18th and 19th century British charts, could not support the use of GPS because the old charts could not be directly referenced to GPS. Errors ranged from hundreds of metres to several kilometres. Mariners were required by law to use these charts but could not plot their GPS position or enter a charted position as a waypoint in their GPS. Replacing the old charts with new charts could not address the urgency of the issue. A re-survey of shoreline, rocks, docks, aids to navigation, and depths and compiling each new chart suitable for use directly with GPS would take approximately two years and cost on the order of $1 million per chart. A non-traditional approach was used to resolve this situation. Research by N. Stuifbergen showed that while shorelines changed over time, the direction or bearing of points of land, lakes, and bays retained the same orientation on old and new charts. Short-term funding from Program Integrity II was used to apply his map-matching software that used intersections of the direction of headlands and bays on old and new maps to create common virtual intersection points. The software examined the fit and residuals, allowed the rejection of outliers, and provided a statistical estimate of the positional uncertainty. Using this map-matching approach, 154 of the 187 off datum charts in Atlantic Canada were referenced for use with GPS within two years, even though the chart data were 100 to 300 years old. The charts were updated for Notices to Mariners, titles and notes bilingualized, and the charts printed using Print-On-Demand (POD) techniques (Forbes et al. 2003). Once these old charts were referenced to GPS and printed, those with areas covered by modern surveys of shipping corridors were examined and the old and new data combined in a non-traditional approach. The old depths and contour labels were converted from imperial to metric units, and the non-standard contours were stopped at a pecked line separating old data and the corridors of modern data. Area surveyed to modern standards and those not to modern standards were clearly labelled.

In the 2000s, it was recognized that using a traditional approach of surveying and compiling one chart at a time meant that it would take decades to complete a 2-nm wide inside route, and routes to ports of refuge, along the Labrador coast. Uncertainty of the annual availability of a survey vessel for decades and increased traffic were also factors in choosing an alternate approach. Consultation with commercial skippers garnered information on the routes they followed when forced to navigate close to shore (including comments that tracks crossed charted islands) and the CCGS *Matthew* was deployed to collect MBES data along these routes from Cape Mugford (just north of Nain) to Cape Chidley (Fig. 5). This field program of surveying a narrow swath over the entire route each year continued for several years. As the program progressed, the original corridor was widened and alternate routes were found around shoals and other dangers (Lamplugh 2009). By 2012, CHS Atlantic had produced new charts for the entire Labrador coast. They show a very narrow inside route as well as routes from the open sea to ports of refuge. Pecked lines distinguish the areas surveyed to modern standards from the older data and areas of no depth data. While this narrow corridor is far from ideal, because ice may force a vessel into uncharted water, and the charts are inadequate to support search and rescue operations outside the surveyed corridors, it is a start. As the surveyed corridors are widened in the future, the information will be added to the charts which are now printed using 'Print-On-Demand' technology.

In the late 2000s, CHS conducted a number of workshops with chart users across the country. A review of CHS resources led to the conclusion that only 20% of the nearly 1000 charts covering Canada could be maintained on a 5-year cycle. A risk analysis was done and priorities set on the basis of the risk of a major accident. Additional priorities were identified for remote communities dependent on maritime highways for resupply. In the Atlantic Region, 17.2% of the 291 charts were considered to cover high priority areas (Table 3). Charts in high-risk areas will be reviewed on a 5-year cycle, those in medium-risk areas on a 10-year cycle, while those in low-risk areas will be maintained by issuing Notices to Mariners when CHS learns of changes and are only reviewed when something major changes. The locations of these charts are shown in Figure 6. Overall, the user community was very understanding, accepting that only so much could be done with available budgets. The stated level of service also sets targets for other services such as issuing Notices to Mariners and responding to requests.

Figure 5. Multibeam coverage obtained by CSS *Matthew* while mapping the inside route along the northern Labrador coast between Cape Mugford (just north of Nain) and Cape Chidley. Different colours along seacoast represent different depth ranges: red is shallowest with dark blue the deepest, and yellow-green in between.

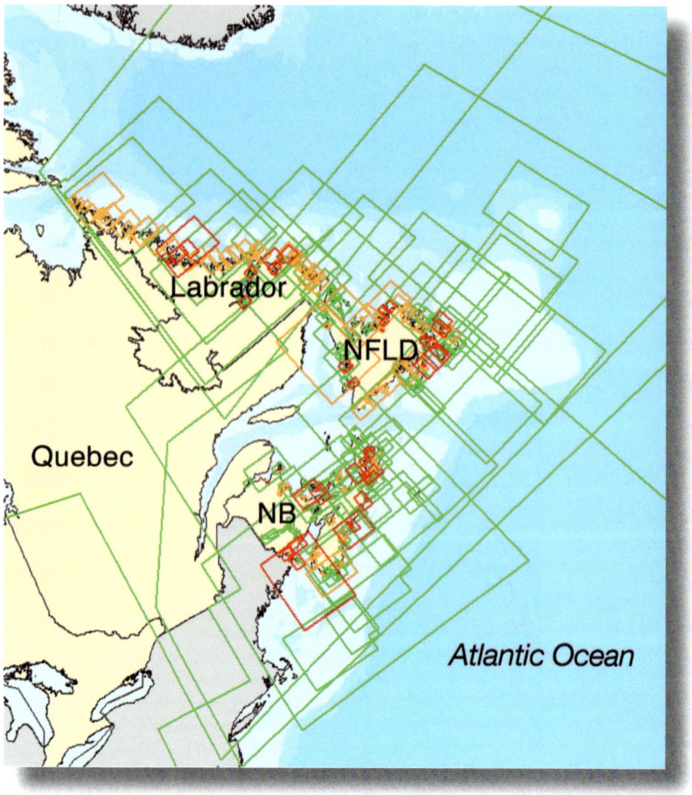

Figure 6. Priority areas in Atlantic Region as identified in the late 2000s and charts falling in each category: red = high, yellow = medium, and green = low risk / priority areas. Details on number of charts in each area are provided in Table 3.

Table 3. Atlantic Region charts in each risk level. The location of these charts is shown in Figure 6.

Risk level	Number of Charts	Percent (%)
High	50	17.2
Medium	89	30.6
Low	152	52.2
Not Assesed	0	0

Tides, Currents and Water Levels

There is a long history in the CHS of investigating tides, currents, and water levels. All automatic water gauges of Public Works on the Great Lakes and the St. Lawrence River became the responsibility of the Hydrographic Survey of Canada in 1912. Two years later, the Tidal and Current Survey Division of DMF was also transferred to the Hydrographic Survey of Canada. When the Hydrographic Survey of Canada became the Canadian Hydrographic Service in 1928, the Automatic Gauges Section was renamed the Precise Water Levels Division. Both these Divisions were amalgamated in 1956 and renamed the Tides, Currents and Water Levels Unit. In 1964, the Current Section at BIO was divided into two parts: the new Current Studies Group was headed by C. Mann, who led offshore circulation studies (Clarke 2014), while Inshore Tidal and Current Surveys section was retained within the Hydrographic Group. The Tides, Currents and Water Levels Unit focussed on operating the Permanent Water Level Network (PWLN) tide gauges to determine tidal constituent values and predict tides for mariners (Grant 1983), setting up temporary tide gauges during hydrographic surveys to collect tidal data to reduce depth data to a chart datum roughly equivalent to lowest tide levels, and measuring surface currents for inclusion in CHS navigation publications. In addition to navigation demands, the Tides, Currents and Water Levels Unit participated with national/international scientists and engineers in research projects ranging from climate change to tidal power.

In the early 1990s a Program Review Exercise (PRE) concerning the Atlantic Region tide gauges identified the gauges CHS needed to prepare the annual tide predictions for navigation and invited other science organizations to identify gauges critical to their respective mandates. CHS then removed gauges such as Nain, Labrador, as well as Arctic tide gauges which were expensive to maintain, not needed for navigation, and unfunded for non-navigational uses. Removal of these gauges interrupted continuous records at each site, which hampered the determination of long-term tidal cycles and variations in mean sea level. Long-term continuous records are important because tidal changes are the net result of multiple influences that act over varying periods of time ranging from harmonic constituents that have periods of less than half a day to long period constituents with periods such as 18.6 years. The primary constituents are the earth's rotation, the positions of the moon and the sun relative to earth, the moon's altitude above the earth's equator, and bathymetry. Observations capture the influence of local bathymetry at each gauge site over these various tidal cycles and are used to refine the values of the tidal constituents used to predict tides as well as confirm the output of tidal models. By the end of the 1990s temporary funding was found within Science Branch to re-establish four Arctic gauges including Nain. Nain is one of the Canadian gauges contributing to the Global Sea Level Observing System (GLOSS), however, these gauges remain 'temporary' gauges pursuant to annual B-based funding and the gaps in data resulting from gauge removal cannot be recovered.

Storm surges, where local atmospheric conditions increase the water level above normal predicted levels, have flooded populated areas such as Charlottetown, Prince Edward Island, in recent years. The reverse situation, a 'negative surge', where local atmospheric conditions depress the water level below predicted levels, results in reduced depths of water in channels and the risk of vessels grounding. At present, the onshore topographic maps use Mean Sea Level for shoreline while CHS bathymetric data are referenced to Lower Low Water Large Tides, leaving a considerable gap in elevations in areas of large tides such as the Bay of Fundy. The CHS Atlantic Tides, Currents and Water Level Unit has been an active partner in acquiring seamless land-water interface data and creating inundation models for specific sites, for example Truro, Nova Scotia. CHS Atlantic introduced the use of airborne LiDAR elevation mapping for coastal flooding in Canada, resulting in the first flood maps produced nationally using this technology. CHS Atlantic also initiated high precision GPS coastal surveys, occupying hundreds of tidal stations in Atlantic Canada. The goal was to determine the differences between vertical datums at these points which cumulated in accurate spatial 3-D ellipsoid separation models of seamless low and high water hydrographic datums.

Following the Indian Ocean tsunami in 2004, CHS Atlantic worked with BIO oceanographers, Public Safety and Emergency Preparedness Canada, the Canadian Meteorological Service, and provincial Emergency Measures Organizations to establish an interim Atlantic Tsunami Warning System. This proof-of-concept system linked existing tide gauges (both permanent and temporary) to a server giving weather forecasters real-time access to high-frequency water level observations. A laser tide gauge was added to each site for redundancy (MacAulay et al. 2010). However, sufficient funding has yet to be found for modelling and inundation mapping, new offshore tide gauges for earlier offshore warnings, and upgrades to existing tide gauge stations to ensure they will survive a tsunami. Critical server back-ups and operational enhancements are also still required to operate the existing gauges at a prescribed level of service above that currently in place for navigation purposes.

SOVEREIGNTY AND SECURITY MANDATE

CHS is responsible for determining the position of Canada's Territorial Sea baselines. These points were chosen from low water features on CHS charts during the 1960s and 1970s. The baseline points were declared in a series of Orders in Council (OIC) beginning in 1967 for Newfoundland and 1969 for Nova Scotia and British Columbia. The breadth of the Territorial Sea was increased from 3 nm to 12 nm in 1970. These OICs were replaced, but largely replicated, in a 1972 OIC which added a number of additional base points and described the negotiated boundary with France around the islands of St. Pierre-Miquelon. These OICs were consolidated in the Consolidated Regulations of Canada (1978) for the Atlantic and Pacific coasts. The baseline points in Newfoundland were further amended to reflect the arbitration with France. The Arctic Territorial Sea baselines were proclaimed by OIC in 1985. The baselines are a combination of straight lines between specific features where the coastline is irregular and dotted with islands and rocks while in other areas the baselines follow the low water line of the natural coastline. The OICs proclaim the baseline points relative to shoreline features on specifically identified CHS charts. These regulations were moved under the umbrella of the Oceans Act in 1996.

CHS is also responsible for determining the positions of limits drawn from the Territorial Sea baselines (such as the 12-nm Territorial Sea, the 200-nm Exclusive Economic Zone, and the 350-nm constraint line for Article 76 of the United Nations Convention on the Law of the Sea) and portraying those and other maritime limits on CHS charts. In practice, these charts are used by mariners and fishers to determine if they are within or outside fishing or other maritime zones, although the official legally valid versions of the baselines and the limits of maritime zones are those defined under the Oceans Act and regulations or OICs adopted pursuant to that Act. These charts are also used by the Department of National Defence (DND) and enforcement agencies to determine in what waters an incident has occurred and therefore which laws apply. At times CHS staff are called upon to be expert witnesses concerning the limits of maritime zones in the subsequent court proceedings. CHS Atlantic is routinely tasked with field verification of the baseline points, especially those involving low-lying offshore rocks. This involves confirming that a rock exists and determining if it dries at lowest low water. CHS staff, primarily from Ottawa, have been closely involved in maritime boundary delimitation including the Gulf of Maine (United States; Sinclair and O'Boyle 2014), St. Pierre-Miquelon (France) and most recently Greenland (Denmark).

CHS has been involved in Law of the Sea issues prior to the establishment of BIO. Following the 1958 Geneva Law of the Sea Conference confirmation that coastal states have sovereign rights over the resources of their continental shelf, CHS was an original member of the PCSP which brought together hydrographers, geologists, and geophysicists to map the Arctic Ocean continental shelf which was largely unknown at the time. This CHS involvement in Law of the Sea issues continued with multi-parameter surveys of the Atlantic continental shelf in the 1970s and 1980s.

In the two decades between the creation of the United Nations Convention on the Law of the Sea (UNCLOS) in 1982 and Canada's ratification of the Convention in December 2003, CHS Atlantic and the Geological Survey of Canada Atlantic (GSCA) were active assembling data to define the slope of the continental shelf, evaluating existing data to identify where additional information is needed, and developing plans and budget estimates for preparing Canada's submission. Following ratification, funding of $69 million for hydrographic and geological survey work to prepare Canada's UNCLOS submission was announced in the 2004 federal budget. The directors of CHS Atlantic, GSCA, and the Oceans and Environmental Law Division of Foreign Affairs and International Trade Canada formed a management board for the project and an office was established at BIO. As the project developed, both CHS and GSC created full-time director-level positions at BIO, and Foreign Affairs and International Trade created one in Ottawa. The plan called for contract multibeam and seismic survey data collection on the Atlantic coast and a greater use of government resources in the Arctic Ocean (Verhoef and MacDougall 2005). Resources for the latter consisted of CCG and United States Coast Guard icebreakers, access to Swedish and Russian icebreakers on joint projects with Denmark, ice camps supported by PCSP, and a combination of CHS, GSCA and contract staff seconded to the project as required. An additional $40 million was provided in the 2008 federal budget, primarily for arctic survey work and for Foreign Affairs and International Trade support. As in the past, the Arctic poses the greatest challenge in terms of remoteness, inhospitable climate, and needing special gear. The arctic weather has delivered a number of surprises during this project. The presence of open water in winter creates both fog that limits helicopter flying when measuring depths through the ice and makes offshore ice camps risky. The reduced ice thickness on the Arctic Ocean allowed icebreakers to collect data in areas previously not accessible. However, the ocean adjacent to the Canadian archipelago remains impenetrable even with the Russian nuclear icebreakers (Verhoef et al. 2014).

Hydrography and maritime security have always gone hand-in-hand from a maritime transportation and naval perspective. CHS participates with DND in Canada-United States committees concerning the mapping and charting needs for the defence of North America, as well as other defence committees with allies. On a day-to-day basis, DND uses CHS products for navigation of naval vessels and supplies CHS charts to allied navies for navigation in Canadian waters. Military exercise areas, as well as declassified military wrecks that are a hazard to navigation, are portrayed on CHS charts. Notices to Mariners are provided to DND in near real time and DND adds military information and forwards these to the military fleets. The CCG and RCMP fleets also obtain their folios of CHS charts through DND.

In 1993, the Canadian Navy established the Route Survey Office (RSO) at BIO. Their principal role is to provide ocean mapping information in order to identify changes on the bottom, mainly in the event of naval mining (Moody 2006). The RSO is also involved in search-and-rescue operations, collection of side scan and multibeam bathymetry data, and the location of targets of interest. The co-location of the RSO with CHS Atlantic at BIO has had many synergies. The requirements of the RSO to map specific routes for anti-terrorism, anti-mine warfare, and other defence purposes can be combined with CHS Atlantic and GSCA mapping priorities to leverage resources to obtain 100% coverage of areas using MBES. The RSO routinely uses existing CHS Atlantic and GSCA-MBES imagery in their anti-submarine and anti-terrorism warfare exercises and also when called upon to search for targets such as downed aircraft, contraband jettisoned by smugglers, the Avro Arrow test models in Lake Ontario, and the HMCS *Shawinigan* near Port aux Basques, Newfoundland. Knowing the shape and depth of the seabed permits the use of change detection analysis to identify 'unnatural' targets, thus reducing mapping time. The working relationships among individuals and familiarity with the capabilities of the co-located agencies allow CHS Atlantic, GSCA and the RSO staff to quickly assemble the needed vessels, equipment and expertise when called upon in an emergency, such as the Swiss Air crash off Peggy's Cove, St. Margaret's Bay (NS), in 1998.

NON-NAVIGATIONAL MANDATE

The synergy of co-locating the various marine science disciplines at BIO was realized from the very beginning with the integration of vessel use. In 1963, the CSS *Baffin*, which had been a purely hydrographic ship since her launch in 1956, took on oceanographic work. In addition, offshore hydrographic cruises began collecting gravity and magnetic data, and at times seismic data while oceanographic cruises began collecting bathymetric data (Loncarevic and Rockwell 1992). A more formal agreement for multi-parameter surveys was signed between CHS Atlantic and the Atlantic Geoscience Centre (AGC) in 1975 and these surveys continued until 1990. Outcomes from joint surveys included the Natural Resources Map (NRM) series, the National Earth Science Series (NESS), the 800 Series Bathymetric Maps of Canada, the AGC Open File series, as well as input to the General Bathymetric Chart of the Oceans (GEBCO). Unlike charts which are shoal-biased to highlight dangers to ships, these maps focussed on the actual shape of the seabed. Systematic surveys at various line spacing (1 to 20 nm depending on water depth) were run and contour maps prepared. These were maps not charts, schemed and named to coincide with the topographic map series on land and did not overlap adjacent sheets. The NRM series consisted of a series of map sheets (bathymetry, geology, magnetics, and gravity) on the same base map at a scale of 1:250,000. The NESS maps, at a scale of 1:1,000,000, provided a more general view of an area. The 800 Series covered all Canada at a scale of 1: 1,675,000, while the 801 and 802 series covered Atlantic Canada at a scale of 1:1,000,000. The Open File series included the NRM map sheets as well as the scientific interpretation behind each map. Finally, the GEBCO series consists of 18 bathymetric maps covering the world at a scale of 1:10,000,000. Virtually all nations supplied bathymetric data to create plotting sheets for the different maps. All vessels out of BIO contributed bathymetric data to GEBCO, and CHS produced and printed the GEBCO 5th Edition in 1984.

While the decommissioning of the CSS *Baffin* in 1991 marked the end of CHS Atlantic's offshore and Arctic surveying, her partial replacement, the CSS *Matthew*, arrived fitted with a Kongsberg EM100 MBES and thus had the ability to map 100% of the bottom area and create aerial photograph-like images of the seabed. A number of different non-navigational uses for MBES data emerged (Courtney and Fader 1994). Multibeam surveys revealed seabed morphology in unprecedented detail which led to significant advances in the quality of surficial geological and benthic habitat mapping (Shaw and Todd 2006, Fader et al. 2014, Pickrill et al. 2014), and the understanding of seabed glaciation, sedimentary processes, and hazards (Lewis et al. 2014, Shaw 2014). This MBES capability existing at BIO was also a factor that led to co-locating the RSO at BIO. CHS Atlantic acquired additional MBES systems during the 1990s, including EM100 systems for the DOLPHINs, a Kongsberg EM1000 system for the CSS *Frederick G. Creed*, and Kongsberg EM3000 shallow water systems for launches (Dinn et al. 1996).

The acquisition of MBES capability coincided with program review exercises that reduced budgets and staff levels and encouraged innovation in finding ways to do more with less. One approach used by CHS Atlantic was partnering with other branches of government, academia, and industry to stretch resources. Joint projects were in vogue and CHS Atlantic used the MBES-equipped vessels to map possible underwater pipeline and utility cable corridors, geoscience research areas, and fishing banks. These joint ventures often freed up internal funding to keep the CSS *Matthew* operating on the navigation mandate.

In the mid-1990s, P. Bellemare (Director of CHS Atlantic) chaired NACOM (National Action Committee on Ocean Mapping) which was established with funding from government and industry to develop a Canadian ocean industry with the capability to map Canada's offshore and compete worldwide. While NACOM did not result in long-term funding to map Canada's continental shelf or garner significant international interest, the seed money did allow CHS Atlantic to use the CSS *Frederick G. Creed* to map Browns Bank and demonstrate uses for the MBES data (Lamplugh et al. 2000). A follow-on project on Browns Bank with the offshore scallop industry in the late 1990s also involved GSCA and led to the mapping of not only the seabed shape, but also the bottom type and associated habitat. The scallop industry used this information to change their fishing practices, only fishing the type of bottom known to support scallops and avoiding bottom features that damaged their gear. These changes reduced the amount of fuel burned, time to catch their quotas, areas of seabed disturbed, and lost fishing gear (Robert 2001). In subsequent years when CHS Atlantic did not have available ship time to map German and Georges banks, Clearwater Fine Foods Ltd. equipped the MV *Anne S. Pierce*, a scallop dragger, with a modern MBES and entered into a Joint Project Agreement with CHS Atlantic and GSCA. Industry paid CHS Atlantic to provide hydrographers to collect and process the bathymetry and GSCA to perform the bottom and habitat classification. The intellectual property in the bathymetric data rested with the scallop industry while CHS Atlantic and GSCA could use the data for internal uses, but not share the full data sets with others.

Following the success of these projects, DFO decided to move forward towards making seabed mapping a core mandate rather than one-off projects of opportunity. A concept paper was prepared by CHS Atlantic, GSCA, DFO Science, and DND proposing that mapping of Canada's seabed was necessary for informed ocean use planning (Pickrill et al. 2014). It was proposed that this base mapping show seabed shape, bottom type and, habitat, analogous to the topography, soil, vegetation, and habitation layers on terrestrial land-use planning maps. Support for the seabed resource mapping concept was confirmed at a series of coast to coast public workshops (MacDougall et al. 2001). Estimates for the cost and timeline to map the entire Canadian continental shelf were prepared, but this proposed long-term systematic mapping program was never funded as a national priority. However, other countries did initiate national mapping programs. For example, CHS Atlantic, the Ocean Mapping Group at University of New Brunswick (Fredericton, NB), and the Canada Centre for Marine Communications (St. John's, NL) prepared the specifications for the MBES mapping of the entire Irish continental shelf, evaluated the contract proposals, and provided the contract monitoring and quality control. CHS Atlantic also provided MBES expertise to New Zealand for specific seabed mapping projects (Costello and Rowsell 2002). While the seabed resource mapping proposal was not funded, GSCA was later successful in obtaining internal funding for the Geoscience for Ocean Management (GOM) program for a number of years before departmental priorities changed. GOM built on the seabed resource mapping concept and focussed on mapping specific areas and creating the start of a map series (Shaw and Todd 2006). One area mapped in detail by multibeam was the Bay of Fundy (Todd and Shaw 2014).

CONCLUSIONS

After 50 years of surveying efforts by CHS Atlantic from BIO the question often asked is "When will all of Canada's waters be surveyed?" The short answer is "Never". What is considered modern standards for surveys will continue to evolve as ships get bigger. New demands for maritime highways will occur as natural resources are developed. Unlike terrestrial mapping where land forms can be seen from aircraft and satellites, the seabed cannot be mapped from the air or space. Airborne efforts with LiDAR only work where the water is shallow and clear. Vessels equipped with acoustic systems are needed.

An idea of the magnitude of the task of completely surveying Canada's submerged lands can be extrapolated from Table 1. A 1 km wide band around the 200,000 plus km of shoreline in 5 m of water would take 2,000,000 vessel hours. A 1 km wide band in 15 m of water (current draft of large ships), takes 300,000 vessel hours. The number of square kilometres in each depth band divided by vessel hours per year (100 days x 10 hours? 200 days at 10 hours?) yields staggering time estimates for this task.

Hydrographic surveys are normally done to meet a specific need for a new maritime highway and designed for compiling charts at specific scales. Only areas critical to navigation, such as channels, are completely sounded. Outside these areas, the seabed is sampled by profiles spaced tens of metres to tens of kilometres apart depending on chart scale and water depth. Therefore, when user needs or modern standards change, new surveys are required.

Non-navigational MBES surveys of specific areas are also done for a specific purpose (e.g., petroleum exploration, fishing, scientific studies, and sovereignty). For example, the Atlantic continental slope MBES surveys for the Canadian UNCLOS submission have profiles 30 nm apart while those in the Arctic are a nominal 50 nm apart to meet the submission requirement of a point every 60 nm (MacDougall 2008). To date, there has been no systematic MBES coverage of Canada's submerged lands

Figure 7. Areas of the seabed in Atlantic Canada mapped by multibeam as of 2012 (includes public and proprietary data collected by government, industry, and academia) shown in black: MBES swath width is a function of water depth (Table 1) so larger areas are mapped in less vessel time in deep water.

needed to create the base maps required for managing human activities in a sustainable fashion. The total area mapped by multibeam, the 'modern' standard, in Atlantic Canada as of 2012 is shown in Figure 7.

When Canada assumed responsibility for hydrographic surveying and charting the coasts of Canada in 1904, the following statement was attributed to Rear Admiral Sir W. Wharton, Hydrographer of the Royal Navy (http://www.canfoh.org/Intro&Hist/history_of_hydrography.htm): "... the surveys of the shores of the Dominion, made as a rule by Imperial officers some years ago, are inadequate to the vessels of modern navigation." Despite a century of effort by CHS in surveying and charting Canada's maritime highways, this statement remains applicable in 2012. Although the charted area of Atlantic Canada has been increased significantly, only a small dent has been made in the 1962 estimate that 150 survey seasons were required to map the Labrador coast to 1962 standards. Similar effort is required in other areas of Atlantic Canada. And like all highway systems, the existing maritime highways require on-going maintenance, with the busier highways continually needing to be upgraded, leaving CHS with few resources to upgrade less busy highways or address non-navigational needs.

The accuracy and resolution of hydrographic survey tools continue to improve. So does the accuracy of navigation tools. With more precise navigation, vessels have the confidence to pass closer to charted dangers and load deeper. Many of the surveys and charts compiled since BIO opened were not designed to meet the present navigational standards. Changes in arctic ice cover also mean more vessels are venturing into the Arctic, and drifting ice at times forces unescorted vessels out of charted corridors, which increases the risk to life, property, and the environment. This risk also applies to the narrow inside route recently surveyed adjacent to the Labrador coast. In another 50 years, the bar defining 'modern standards' will undoubtedly be moved higher and Admiral Wharton's 1904 statement about the present charts and old surveys no longer being adequate for modern navigation will still apply.

ACKNOWLEDGEMENTS

I thank Arthur Collin, Ross Douglas, and Adam Kerr for helpful discussions in outlining this paper, Sheila Acheson, Charles O'Reilly, Julian Goodyear, and Mark McCracken for providing material, and Steve Grant, Steve Forbes, Bob Burke, and Gary Rockwell for reviewing earlier drafts. In addition to the BIO Navigation Group, other CHS support groups such as Marine Electronics, Hydrographic Development, and Marine Geomatics, worked with hydrographers both at sea and on shore to develop solutions to problems. Members shared the hydrographers' objective of 'getting the job done' and 'making it work'. All were supported by the BIO boat shop, machine shop, engineers, technicians, and ships officers, and crews. Working together as a team, they found innovative solutions that over the years allowed CHS to deliver its mandates.

REFERENCES

Boudreau, H., H. Varma, and W. Prime. 1991. A new approach to spatiotemporal database management. Pages 78-80 *in* Science Review 1988 & 89 (T.E. Smith, Ed.). Bedford Institute of Oceanography, Dartmouth, NS.

Burke, R.G. 1988. Vertical acoustic sweep systems - A new capability for the Canadian Hydrographic Service. Pages 41-45 *in* Science Review 1987 (B. Bennett, Ed.). Bedford Institute of Oceanography, Dartmouth, NS.

Burke, B. and P. Hally. 1989. Multi-beam sounding systems: A new ocean-mapping tool for the Canadian Hydrographic Service. Pages 71-75 *in* Science Review 1988 & 89 (T.E. Smith, Ed.). Bedford Institute of Oceanography, Dartmouth, NS.

Canadian Hydrographic Service. 1958. Annual Report. Department of Mines and Technical Surveys, Ottawa, ON.

Clarke, R.A. 2014. Strong winds and stormy seas: ocean climate studies in the North Atlantic. Pages 139-148 *in* Voyage of Discovery: Fifty years of Marine Research at Canada's Bedford Institute of Oceanography (D.N. Nettleship, D.C. Gordon, C.F.M. Lewis, and M.P. Latremouille, Eds.). Bedford Institute of Oceanography-Oceans Association, Dartmouth, NS.

Costello, G., D. Peyton, and G. Lebans. 1991. Development of a Canadian ocean mapping system. Pages 23-32 *in* Science Review 1990 & 91 (T.E. Smith and J. Cook, Eds.). Bedford Institute of Oceanography, Dartmouth, NS.

Costello, G. and T. Rowsell. 2002. The Canadian Hydrographic Service in the international forum. Page 16 *in* Bedford Institute of Oceanography 2001 *in* Review (D. Geddes, Ed.). Bedford Institute of Oceanography, Dartmouth, NS.

Courtney, R.C. and G.B.J. Fader. 1994. A new understanding of the ocean floor through multibeam mapping. Pages 9-14 *in* Science Review 1992 & 93 (A. Fiander, Ed.). Bedford Institute of Oceanography, Dartmouth, NS.

Dinn, D.F., G. Henderson, R. Courtney, and J. Bradford. 1996. New technologies for near-shore mapping. Page 74-78 *in* Science Review 1994 & 95 (A. Fiander, Ed.). Bedford Institute of Oceanography, Dartmouth, NS.

Dominion Hydrographers Second Conference. 1962. Summary of Proceedings. Department of Mines and Technical Surveys, Ottawa, ON.

Eaton, R.M. 1983. Navstar - A global positioning system. Page 44 *in* Bedford Institute of Oceanography BIO Review '83 (M.P. Latremouille, Ed.). Bedford Institute of Oceanography, Dartmouth, NS.

Eaton, R.M. 2014. The electronic chart: development, principles, and implementation. Pages 181-183 *in* Voyage of Discovery: Fifty Years of Marine Research at Canada's Bedford Institute of Oceanography (D.N. Nettleship, D.C. Gordon, C.F.M. Lewis, and M.P. Latremouille, Eds.). Bedford Institute of Oceanography-Oceans Association, Dartmouth, NS.

Fader, G.B.J., B. MacLean, H.W. Josenhans, and S.M. Blasco. 2014. Seabed sediment mapping at the Bedford Institute of Oceanography: from single beam to multibeam. Pages 191-199 *in* Voyage of Discovery: Fifty Years of Marine Research at Canada's Bedford Institute of Oceanography (D.N. Nettleship, D.C. Gordon, C.F.M. Lewis, and M.P. Latremouille, Eds.). Bedford Institute of Oceanography-Oceans Association, Dartmouth, NS.

Fillmore, S. and R.W. Sandilands. 1983. The Chartmakers, the History of Nautical Surveying in Canada. NC Press Limited/Canadian Hydrographic Service, Fisheries and Oceans Canada, Ottawa, ON.

Forbes, S., D. Regular, C. Zeller, N. Stuifbergen, S. Grant, and A. Wickens. 2003. The CHS Atlantic 'On Datum' Project. Pages 56-57 *in* Bedford Institute of Oceanography 2002 in Review (D. Geddes, Ed.). Bedford Institute of Oceanography, Dartmouth, NS.

Forbes, S., J. Griffin, and R. Palmer. 2006. New initiatives fund search and rescue project in Labrador. Pages 20-22 *in* Bedford Institute of Oceanography, Annual Review 2005 (J. Ryan, Ed.). Bedford Institute of Oceanography, Dartmouth, NS.

Glover, W. (Ed.). 2004. Charting Northern Waters: Essays for the Centenary of the Canadian Hydrographic Service. Canadian Nautical Research Society, McGill-Queens University Press, Montreal, QC.

Grant, S.T. 1983. Canada's network of tide- and water-level gauges. Pages 7-8 *in* Bedford Institute of Oceanography BIO Review '83 (M.P. Latremouille, Ed.). Bedford Institute of Oceanography, Dartmouth, NS.

Grant, S.T. and D.L. McKeown. 1987. History of navigation research and development at BIO. Pages 58-62 *in* BIO Review '86: 25th Anniversary Edition (B. Newman and M.P. Latremouille, Eds.). Bedford Institute of Oceanography, Dartmouth, NS.

Grant, S.T. and J. Goodyear. 1996. ECDIS: Past, present and future. Pages 56-59 *in* Science Review 1994-95 (A. Fiander, Ed.). Bedford Institute of Oceanography, Dartmouth, NS.

Grant, S.T., N. Stuifbergen, and R.M. Eaton. 2014. Loran-C at the Bedford Institute of Oceanography. Pages 349-352 *in* Voyage of Discovery: Fifty Years of Marine Research at Canada's Bedford Institute of Oceanography (D.N. Nettleship, D.C. Gordon, C.F.M. Lewis, and M.P. Latremouille, Eds.). Bedford Institute of Oceanography-Oceans Association, Dartmouth, NS.

Grant, S.T. and D.E. Wells. 2014. The Bedford Institute of Oceanography integrated navigation system (BIONAV). Pages 353-357 *in* Voyage of Discovery: Fifty Years of Marine Research at Canada's Bedford Institute of Oceanography (D.N. Nettleship, D.C. Gordon, C.F.M. Lewis, and M.P. Latremouille, Eds.). Bedford Institute of Oceanography-Oceans Association, Dartmouth, NS.

Kerr, A.J. 1983a. Soundings and positioning. Pages 4-6 *in* Bedford Institute of Oceanography BIO Review '83 (M.P. Latremouille, Ed.). Bedford Institute of Oceanography, Dartmouth, NS.

Kerr, A.J. 1983b. DOLPHIN and ARCS. Pages 38-40 *in* Bedford Institute of Oceanography BIO Review '83 (M.P. Latremouille, Ed.). Bedford Institute of Oceanography, Dartmouth, NS.

Kerr, A.J. 1987. New thrusts in hydrographic technology. Pages 24-27 *in* BIO Review '86: 25th Anniversary Edition (B. Newman and M.P. Latremouille, Eds.). Bedford Institute of Oceanography, Dartmouth, NS.

Kerr, A.J. and R.F. Macnab. 1983. Nautical charts and publications. Pages 24-27 *in* Bedford Institute of Oceanography BIO Review '83 (M.P. Latremouille, Ed.). Bedford Institute of Oceanography, Dartmouth, NS.

Lamplugh, M. 2009. The Labrador Coast inshore route – finally complete, after 75 years. Pages 15-18 *in* Bedford Institute of Oceanography in Review 2008 (J. Ryan, Ed.). Bedford Institute of Oceanography, Dartmouth, NS.

Lamplugh, M.J., T.A. Kearns, and A.C. Craft. 2000. Applications of multibeam data. Pages 74-78 *in* Science Review 1996 & 97 (A. Fiander, Ed.). Bedford Institute of Oceanography, Dartmouth, NS.

Lewis, C.F.M., S.M. Blasco, D.J.W. Piper, and G.V. Sonnichsen. 2014. Seabed geohazard knowledge for safe hydrocarbon development. Pages 383-394 *in* Voyage of Discovery: Fifty Years of Marine Research at Canada's Bedford Institute of Oceanography (D.N. Nettleship, D.C. Gordon, C.F.M. Lewis, and M.P. Latremouille, Eds.). Bedford Institute of Oceanography-Oceans Association, Dartmouth, NS.

Loncarevic, B.D. and G.C. Rockwell. 1992. Gravity and magnetic surveys with CSS *Baffin*. Pages 62-67 *in* Science Review 1990 &'91 (T.E. Smith and J. Cook, Eds.). Bedford Institute of Oceanography, Dartmouth, NS.

MacAulay, P., C. Coolen, and F. Carmichael. 2010. The laser tide gauge: The Canadian Hydrographic Service Atlantic's new GLOSS water level system. Pages 17-19 *in* Bedford Institute of Oceanography 2009 in Review (J. Ryan, Ed.). Bedford Institute of Oceanography, Dartmouth, NS.

MacDougall, R. 2008. Activities toward delineating our continental shelf under Canada's UNCLOS Program. Pages 18-19 *in* Bedford Institute of Oceanography in Review 2007 (J. Ryan, Ed.). Bedford Institute of Oceanography, Dartmouth, NS.

MacDougall, R., R. Pickrill, J. Bradford, and D. Gordon. 2001. SeaMap - Discovering Canada's next frontier. Pages 41-42 *in* Bedford Institute of Oceanography 2000 (D. Geddes, Ed.). Bedford Institute of Oceanography, Dartmouth, NS.

Meehan, O.M. 1964. The Canadian Hydrographic Service from the time of its inception in 1883 to the end of the Second World War. The Northern Mariner 15: 299-357.

Moody, S. 2006. Who are those people in uniform? Pages 22-23 *in* Bedford Institute of Oceanography Annual Review 2005 (J. Ryan, Ed.). Bedford Institute of Oceanography, Dartmouth, NS.

Palmer, N.J. 2002. The sea road to ISO 9001: 2000 registration. Page 17 *in* Bedford Institute of Oceanography 2001 in Review (D. Geddes, Ed.). Bedford Institute of Oceanography, Dartmouth, NS.

Pickrill, R.A., B.J. Todd, S.J. Smith, J.V. Barrie, and K.W. Conway. 2014. Marine habitat mapping in Canada's oceans. Pages 185-190 *in* Voyage of Discovery: Fifty Years of Marine Research at Canada's Bedford Institute of Oceanography (D.N. Nettleship, D.C. Gordon, C.F.M. Lewis, and M.P. Latremouille, Eds.). Bedford Institute of Oceanography-Oceans Association, Dartmouth, NS.

Pietrzak, R. 1985. Charting the Grand Banks and adjoining areas. Pages 58-61 *in* Bedford Institute of Oceanography BIO Review '85 (M.P. Latremouille, Ed.). Bedford Institute of Oceanography, Dartmouth, NS.

Robert, G. and Canadian Offshore Scallop Industry Mapping Group. 2001. Impact of multibeam surveys on scallop fishing efficiency and stock assessment. Pages 40-41 *in* Bedford Institute of Oceanography 2001 in Review (D. Geddes, Ed.). Bedford Institute of Oceanography, Dartmouth, NS.

Rockwell, G., S. Grant, and R. Burke. 2003. The Canadian Hydrographic Service at BIO. Pages 34-37 *in* Bedford Institute of Oceanography 2002 in Review (D. Geddes, Ed.). Bedford Institute of Oceanography, Dartmouth, NS.

Shaw, J. 2014. Deglaciation and postglacial sea-level changes in Atlantic Canada: science driven by technology. Pages 325-330 *in* Voyage of Discovery: Fifty Years of Marine Research at Canada's Bedford Institute of Oceanography (D.N. Nettleship, D.C. Gordon, C.F.M. Lewis, and M.P. Latremouille, Eds.). Bedford Institute of Oceanography-Oceans Association, Dartmouth, NS.

Shaw, J. and B.J. Todd. 2006. The new marine map series: Underpinning ocean management in Canada. Pages 26-29 *in* Bedford Institute of Oceanography Annual Review 2005 (J. Ryan, Ed.). Bedford Institute of Oceanography, Dartmouth, NS.

Sinclair, M.M. and R.N. O'Boyle. 2014. The Gulf of Maine boundary dispute: the role of the Bedford Institute of Oceanography. Pages 397-405 *in* Voyage of Discovery: Fifty Years of Marine Research at Canada's Bedford Institute of Oceanography (D.N. Nettleship, D.C. Gordon, C.F.M. Lewis, and M.P. Latremouille, Eds.). Bedford Institute of Oceanography-Oceans Association, Dartmouth, NS.

Todd, B.J. and J. Shaw. 2014. Discovering the seafloor of the Bay of Fundy. Pages 231-235 *in* Voyage of Discovery: Fifty Years of Marine Research at Canada's Bedford Institute of Oceanography (D.N. Nettleship, D.C. Gordon, C.F.M. Lewis, and M.P. Latremouille, Eds.). Bedford Institute of Oceanography-Oceans Association, Dartmouth, NS.

Verhoef, J. and R. MacDougall. 2006. Delineating Canada's continental shelf under the United Nations Convention on the Law of the Sea. Pages 4-7 *in* Bedford Institute of Oceanography Annual Review 2005 (J. Ryan, Ed.). Bedford Institute of Oceanography, Dartmouth, NS.

Verhoef, J., D.C. Mosher, and S.R. Forbes. 2014. Defining Canada's extended continental shelves. Pages 407-414 *in* Voyage of Discovery: Fifty Years of Marine Research at Canada's Bedford Institute of Oceanography (D.N. Nettleship, D.C. Gordon, C.F.M. Lewis, and M.P. Latremouille, Eds.). Bedford Institute of Oceanography-Oceans Association, Dartmouth, NS.

20. THE ELECTRONIC CHART: DEVELOPMENT, PRINCIPLES, AND IMPLEMENTATION

R. Michael Eaton

SUMMARY

The electronic chart, coupled with the Global Positioning System (GPS), is the greatest advance in the safety of marine navigation since radar. More than twenty years ago, the paper chart, on its dimly lit chart table, showed the planned route with the navigator's position fixes laboriously drawn on it. Radar was on a nearby screen. Today, the planned route comes up on the screen of the chart display, with 'Own Ship' by GPS plotted continuously and radar superimposed as required. All the information the mariner needs is shown on one screen and is easy to interpret. This article describes the significant role the Bedford Institute of Oceanography (BIO) Navigation Group played in the development of the electronic chart. The Navigation Group performed the original electronic chart test-bed trials in Bedford Basin, NS, in 1984, and played an important role in the publication by the International Hydrographic Organization (IHO) of draft specifications based on trials in 1987. Then, in 1989, BIO staff led an IHO Working Group to design the display of the official electronic chart, a formidable task that was completed in 1994. Overall, this overview of the development of the electronic chart describes the process of designing the display and the general principles followed.

Key words: electronic chart, ECDIS, IHO, safety contour, presentation library, look-up table, conditional symbology procedure, colour contrast.
E-mail: MikeEaton @eastlink.ca

The Bedford Institute of Oceanography (BIO) Navigation Group was formed in 1970 under the Canadian Hydrographic Service (CHS). Through the 1980s and 1990s, a major preoccupation was the development of a mariner-friendly design for the display of the electronic chart. Over two decades of sometimes challenging and always interesting work, contracts were issued to produce the necessary software and other technical requirements, such as the colour specifications for the Commission internationale de l'éclairage (CIE). Work concentrated on developing and updating the first written display design specifications for the electronic chart which would later become the International Hydrographic Organization (IHO) SP-52 'Specifications for Chart Content and Display Aspects of Electronic Chart Display and Information System' (Buttgenbach 1994, Eaton 1994).

The electronic chart is a real-time ship-handling display used primarily for navigating ships safely in confined and heavily trafficked waters, particularly in bad weather. It is a formidable new navigation tool that takes advantage of the extraordinary accuracy of the Global Positioning System (GPS) and is probably second only to radar in significance as an advance in navigation since 1950. If the electronic chart system had been available in March 1989, the tragic *Exxon Valdez* tanker grounding and oil spill in Prince William Sound, Alaska, would probably not have happened.

In the 1920s, the Hydrographic Offices (HOs) of the developed world set up the IHO. Among other activities, the IHO published an illustrated catalogue of symbols to be used on charts (International Hydrographic Office 1992) in order to ensure that mariners saw the same clearly recognizable symbol for any given chart object, no matter which nation published the chart. When the United Nations established the International Maritime Organization (IMO) in the 1960s, the IMO required all ships to carry IHO approved charts.

This paper describes the development of the electronic chart and the creation of the colours and symbols for the new IHO electronic charts. Once fully accepted and qualified by all IHO participants, the electronic charts and symbols will be officially classified as the Electronic Chart Display and Information System (ECDIS). The IMO rules that only official ECDIS electronic charts may be carried onboard ships as an equivalent to the paper chart.

EXPLORING THE POSSIBILITIES OF ECDIS

By the early 1980s, three indications of a revolution in marine navigation charts were in sight. The Navstar GPS was on the horizon, powerful small computers were available, and, thanks to T. Evangelatos of CHS Ottawa, Canada was a leader in producing digital chart databases (Eaton et al. 1983). The potential of a flexible, computerized mariner's version of the chart with radar overlay was envisioned by the BIO Navigation Group. In 1982, an initial planning meeting was held at the Department of Surveying and Engineering, University of New Brunswick, Fredericton, New Brunswick. One participant was American physicist Mortimer Rogoff, the true 'father of the electronic chart', whose prototype electronic chart was already running onboard a fishing boat in Long Island Sound, eastern United States.

The outcome of the Fredericton meeting was that by 1984, H. Astle of CARIS (a computer cartography company in Fredericton, NB), under contract to the CHS, had a prototype electronic chart test-bed running on a small vessel in Bedford Basin, Nova Scotia. This gave an opportunity for an advisory group of local mariners, including Canadian Coast Guard officers and the Halifax Chief Harbour Pilot, to examine and evaluate the new technology. The test bed included a radar overlay and provided an insight into various aspects of ECDIS such as the need for the permanent display of essential chart objects, known as the display base, which included a safety contour, dangerous wrecks, buoys, and beacons as well the incorporation of radar.

At the international level, the earliest support for ECDIS came from the North Sea countries of Norway, Germany, and The Netherlands. The United Kingdom, with its worldwide market of excellent paper charts, was less enthusiastic. By 1988, Norway had produced a local digital database and organized a one-month demonstration of prototype electronic charts in the Baltic and North seas onboard their ship the RV *Lance*. The CHS test bed was on board, the only system interfaced to radar. RV *Lance* visited 17 countries in western Europe and hosted over 500 visitors. In response to a questionnaire, 80% of mariners saw ECDIS as a unified navigation information display rather than just a chart on a screen. Moreover, 83% wanted Automatic Radar Plotting Aid (ARPA) plots of the trajectories of other ships as well as raw radar (Stene and Kyrkjeeide 1989).

GETTING SERIOUS ABOUT ECDIS STANDARDS

In 1986, two years before the RV *Lance* cruise, the North Sea Hydrographic Commission (an organisation composed of HOs around the North Sea) started to take electronic charts seriously and considered the consequences of ECDIS. In January 1987, on behalf of the IHO, Rear Admiral and Netherlands Hydrographer H. van Opstal held a two-week working group meeting on ECDIS specifications at The Hague, Netherlands. M. Eaton served with B. Buis of the Netherlands Hydrographic Office as co-secretary for the meeting. A 30-page report of conclusions from the Canadian electronic chart test-bed project was presented. Later in 1987, both H. van Opstal and B. Buis came to BIO for further discussions. The result was a working paper that acknowledged the valuable development work of CHS (van Opstal 1987). This was followed soon after by another ECDIS report that dealt with generalities such as database structure and chart data updating, as well as with display issues such as the permanent minimum display base of essential chart objects including coastlines, safety contours selected by the mariners, and dangers to navigation (International Hydrographic Office 1988). However, at this early stage of development no work had been done on the symbols that would be used to depict the chart data. It soon became clear that the IHO needed to develop a detailed description of how to present the chart data to the mariner on the computer screen. A symbol catalogue was needed with instructions on how to use it and with clear definitions of what each symbol represented. The presentation had to be done in a standard manner, recognizing the nature of this new type of chart display and ensuring that mariners moving between ships with different makes of electronic chart would see the same standard symbols. In 1989, A. Kerr, an IHO director and previous director of CHS Atlantic at BIO, appointed M. Eaton to chair the Colours and Symbols Working Group (CSWG) to resolve this problem.

Significantly, the International Hydrographic Office (1988) stated that ECDIS must be the legal equivalent of the paper chart, thereby involving the IMO which is responsible for worldwide shipping safety. In the early 1990s, there was a blossoming of working groups which included an IHO Committee on ECDIS, an IHO-IMO Harmonization Group, an ECDIS manufacturer's liaison group, and an IHO Database Working Group. These working groups usually met annually and attendance was required in order to represent the CSWG viewpoint and to keep up-to-date with progress in allied fields.

S. Grant of the BIO Navigation Group, also an ex-mariner, was assigned to yet another important IHO working group, the Updating Working Group, which was responsible for ensuring that mariners around the world could keep their electronic chart data up-to-date. This covered details of data transfer formats and mechanisms, how to deal with a range of situations like revisions to updates, and the national and international infrastructure that would be needed. Grant was also a member of the CHS Electronic Chart Working Group, and managed and participated in a number of related research projects.

DEVELOPING COLOUR AND SYMBOL STANDARDS FOR ECDIS

The development of the ECDIS 'colour and symbol standards' was divided into two parts: a presentation library module which draws the chart display and a colours and symbols section to be used in the presentation.

Presentation Library

Through contacts made during the numerous working group meetings, ex-mariner and computer expert G. Buttgenbach at the Hamburg Sea School, Germany, was contracted by Canada and the United States to develop the presentation library, the 'brain' of ECDIS. The first draft was produced in short order and improved with experience later on (Buttgenbach 1994).

The first section of the presentation library contains look-up tables that take each chart object in the IHO database and assign a symbol to it (or a colour for a line or depth area). The process also assigns an IMO category (whether or not it is part of the mandatory display base) and whether to draw it over or under the radar. This direct look-up table procedure works except in the case of objects whose symbolization depends on decisions by the mariner. For example, the mariner's choice of safety contour affects the symbolization of wrecks. A 'dangerous wreck' is defined as a wreck which lies in safe water (water deeper than the safety contour), but whose depth is less than that of the safety contour. Such dangerous wrecks in otherwise safe waters are not symbolized by the normal wreck symbol, but instead by the 'Isolated Danger' symbol, a conspicuous magenta octagon with a white cross in the middle, intended to emphasize the wreck's danger to navigation. To handle such cases, the look-up table consigns the object – all such dangerous wrecks, rocks or other obstructions in this example – to a conditional symbology procedure, a flow chart styled according to Nassi-Schneiderman diagrams (Yoder and Schrag 1978), which specifies the appropriate symbolization. These conditional procedures can be formidable, but they work.

Colour and Symbol Specifications

While G. Buttgenbach worked on the presentation library, the BIO Navigation Group worked on colours and symbols in consultation with J. Walraven of the Netherlands TNO Perception and Ergonomics Institute, Soesterberg, and later with S. McFadden of the Canadian Defence and Civil Institute of Environmental Medicine in Toronto, Ontario (Eaton 1994).

Initially existing paper chart symbols were used where they were appropriate and new symbols were developed where necessary, such as for 'own ship', 'planned route and past track', 'radar', and 'ARPA' information. The symbolization of certain non-chart objects (e.g., radar) involved collaboration with technical bodies such as the Radio Technical Commission for Maritime Services. Colours were defined for all individual chart symbols as well as for background area fill-ins and lines. In ECDIS, the colours are carried in 'colour tokens', which are specified in five tables appropriate for bridge conditions ranging from 'Bright Sun' to 'Night', as selected by the mariner. For example, the area colour token for deep water is white by day and black by night. Similarly, the line defining a traffic separation scheme boundary is a prominent magenta-coloured token which will be a more luminescent magenta by night than by day in order to retain its prominence. A colour token is assigned to every chart object in the look-up table of the presentation library in the process of building up the chart display. Throughout, effort was made to ensure maximum clarity on the display and establish predominance among chart symbols based on their relative importance to the safety of navigation.

By day, the ECDIS colours follow the design principle of being similar to the paper chart (Fig. 1A). In doing so, a major consideration was to offset the 'wash-out' effect of bright sun on the bridge display screen. To accomplish this goal, ECDIS colours were designed to give maximum contrast between foreground features and the background. ECDIS uses saturated (deep, densely coloured) shades of magenta, red, green, yellow, and black for foreground features, contrasting against a white background for safe water deeper than the safety contour, a washed-out blue for shallow waters, and a light brown for land areas. By night, the aim to maintain clarity remains, but it is essential to protect the night vision of the mariner on the bridge so that other ships, buoys, and beacons can be seen out of the bridge windows. The ECDIS must have minimum

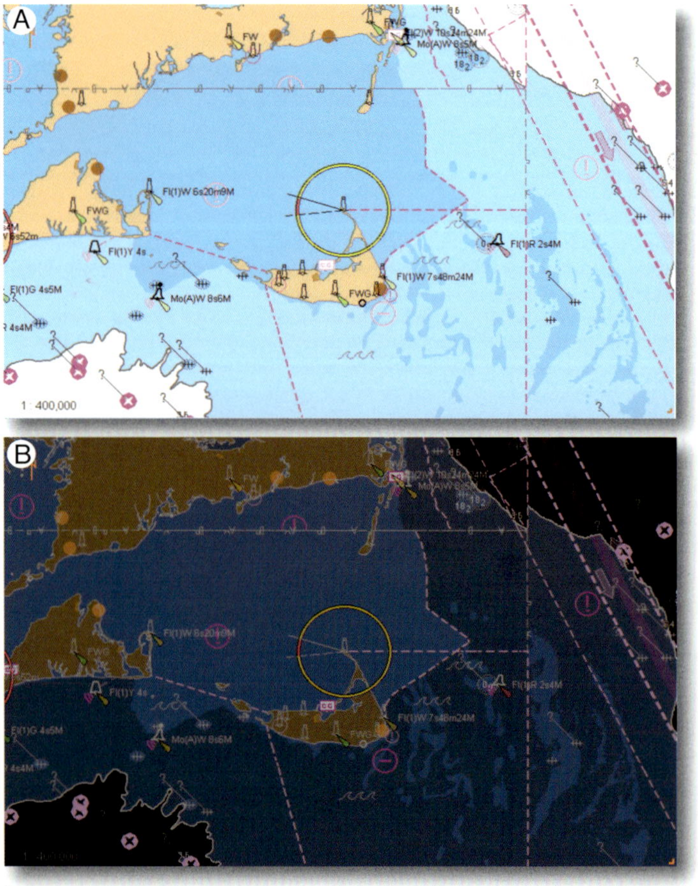

Figure 1. Two chart screen examples of an electronic navigation chart of Cape Cod, Martha's Vineyard, and Nantucket: (A) day screen and (B) night screen (courtesy United States National Oceanic and Atmospheric Administration).

luminance which is achieved by switching to black for the safe water background and shades of dark blue-gray for shallower areas (Fig. 1B). Except for features that are black by day and switch to white by night, all other foreground features use the same colours day and night, with the exact colour-values adjusted for optimum contrast against the night backgrounds.

Many examples of ECDIS symbology are illustrated in Figure 1. For instance, the safety contour is set at 20 m, and there are several examples of the conspicuous 'Isolated Danger' symbol in the bottom left window of safe water. The ECDIS user has wide choices in setting up the display. In this case, the user has chosen to display light characteristics in text. The alternative is to cursor-pick on any object of interest for further details. For example, in this case the mariner might check on the 'Isolated Dangers' symbols to see whether they are rocks or wrecks, and to check their depth.

CONTINUED DEVELOPMENT

As work on the colour and symbols standard progressed, the Hamburg (Germany)-Harwich (United Kingdom) ferry *Hamburg* was used as an advanced test bed. In 1992, a seagoing workshop was held onboard the *Hamburg* with mariners, ECDIS manufacturers, and Hydrographic Office attendees. Following this workshop, further development continued culminating in a meeting of the CSWG onboard the Helsinki (Finland)-Travemunde (Germany) ferry *Finnjet* in November 1994, after which the first operational edition of the colour and symbol specifications and presentation library, IHO SP52, was issued.

From 1994 onwards, further development was still needed to adapt the presentation library and colour and symbol specifications to sea experience, decisions of the various working groups, and to changes in both IHO Special Publication 57 and its appendix, the IHO Chart Object Catalogue. This maintenance function was carried out in Canada by M. Eaton, first with H. Astle and S. Munn at CARIS in Fredericton, New Brunswick, and later with M. Gregory at Nautical Data International in St. John's, Newfoundland. Both companies were funded by CHS and the Canadian Coast Guard. This continual updating and extension of the specifications gained considerable credit for Canada internationally.

In 1997, M. Eaton stepped down as Chair of CSWG and was replaced by J. Goodyear, also of CHS Atlantic. Then, in 2001, M. Jonas of the Bundesamt für Seeschiffahrt und Hydrographie (BSH), Germany, succeeded J. Goodyear and the German Hydrographic Office assumed the responsibility for ECDIS colours and symbols. In 2004, M. Eaton brought the colour and symbol specifications up to date, the final action by BIO in the development of ECDIS.

SOME PRACTICAL EXPERIENCES

While working on these IHO developments, M. Eaton took advantage of opportunities to check out what commercial electronic chart developers were doing. One impressive experience was seeing the effect on the electronic chart screen onboard a Norwegian freighter at Tromso, Norway, in 1993 when the low mid-summer sun shone directly on the screen and virtually wiped out the chart display. As a consequence, M. Eaton and S. McFadden spent considerable time during the summer of 1993 working on a screen set up outside the CARIS office in Fredericton, New Brunswick, adjusting colours and symbols to make sure that the last objects to remain visible in bright sun are the ship's symbol and the safety contour. However, there was no doubt that an ECDIS must have a viewing hood when the sun is shining in on the bridge. Another investigation trip took place on a vessel bound for Montreal, Quebec, from Hamilton, Ontario. As the ship approached the locks at night, thick fog closed in. The captain verified his GPS positioning by checking that the radar image of the coastline and beacons superimposed on the electronic chart exactly fitted the chart display. Once verified, the ship was allowed through the locks, whereas ships without an electronic chart had to anchor and wait until the fog lifted. A final telling experience occurred in Bedford Basin, Nova Scotia, when a captain had to berth his large ship at the much shorter gypsum wharf near BIO. He manoeuvred the ship so that the bow and midships section could be secured to the wharf while the stern carrying the bridge was still protruding into the Basin, well short of the dock. This was as intended, but not easy to do. As the captain rang off the engines, he turned and said "I don't know how I would have managed that tricky manoeuvre without an electronic chart!"

EPILOGUE

The marine navigation community is now seeing a revolutionary change. Until recently, the chart has been a sheet of paper on the bridge chart table, dimly lit at night (to preserve the mariners' night vision), showing hand-plotted positions along the pre-planned route. On the bridge, there was also a radar screen with plots of target ships from ARPA, which calculates danger of collision, and in some ports, an automatic identification system was broadcast showing a plot of all ships in the navigation channels plus their radio call signs. All of these were separate displays of information which were not easy for the captain to assimilate quickly. Now, the electronic chart allows the mariner to merge as many of these aids to safe navigation as needed, together with a real-time plot of his own ship, all on one chart display. It is a picture 'worth a thousand words' and it takes the stress out of navigation in conditions of close quarters.

Since 2004, ECDIS colour and symbol standards are being well maintained. CHS has made great progress in producing the official electronic navigation charts (ENCs) for virtually all our charted waters, including the Arctic (only 10% of which is charted). This has been accomplished while keeping the paper charts up to date, a dual responsibility because IMO requires the navigator to keep the track on a paper chart while using an electronic chart. However, it seems clear that the IMO will progressively introduce requirements for all ships to carry ECDIS. ECDIS keeps a track record and so, paper charts will eventually no longer be required.

With ECDIS, and to a lesser extent with ECS (Electronic Chart Systems), the electronic chart will improve interpretation of the situation in close quarters at sea and greatly reduce stress on the bridge, leading to fewer collisions or groundings, and a reduction in the number of oil spills.

ACKNOWLEDGEMENTS

I thank all those people mentioned by name in this review paper. They all share with me, to the same degree, the thanks of mariners who will benefit from the improved safety of navigation provided by ECDIS. I also thank Steve Grant for help in preparing this article.

REFERENCES

Buttgenbach, G. 1994. SP-52: Specifications for chart content and display aspects of ECDIS, Presentation Library (Annex A to Appendix 2). International Hydrographic Office, Monaco.

Eaton, R.M. 1994. SP-52: Specifications for chart content and display aspects of ECDIS. Appendix 2 – Colour and symbol specifications for ECDIS. International Hydrographic Office, Monaco.

Eaton, R.M., N.M. Anderson, and T.V. Evangelatos. 1983. The electronic chart. The Canadian Surveyor 37: 235-245.

International Hydrographic Office (IHO). 1988. Draft specifications for electronic chart display and information systems (ECDIS). International Hydrographic Office Special Publication 52 (SP-52), Monaco.

International Hydrographic Office (IHO). 1992. INT1, Symbols, abbreviations, and terms used on charts. International Hydrographic Office, Monaco.

Stene, O. and A. Kyrkjeeide. 1989. The North Sea Project. A test project for the electronic navigational chart – Experiences and conclusions. Norwegian Hydrographic Service, Stavanger, Norway.

van Opstal, L. H. 1987. Draft specifications for electronic chart display and information systems (ECDIS). Report by ad-hoc Group of Experts of the IHO Committee on ECDIS, International Hydrographic Office, Monaco.

Yoder, C.M. and M.L. Schrag. 1978. Nassi-Schneiderman charts: an alternative to flowcharts for design. Association for Computing Machinery Special Interest Group for Software Engineering (ACM SIGSOFT) Notes 3: 79-86.

21. MARINE HABITAT MAPPING IN CANADA'S OCEANS

Richard A. Pickrill, Brian J. Todd*, Stephen J. Smith,
J. Vaughn Barrie, and Kim W. Conway

SUMMARY

For many years researchers have been aware of the association between benthic and pelagic communities and their physical habitats. However, not until the 1990s when multibeam mapping became commonplace, was it possible to 'strip away the water column' to provide high-resolution imagery of the seabed and to accurately map the physical environment. From these foundations, teams from Natural Resources Canada, Canadian Hydrographic Service, and Fisheries and Oceans Canada Science Branch developed an interdepartmental habitat mapping program. The emergence of new capabilities was timely: both in Canada and globally there was an awakening to the need for integrated management of our offshore resources, embracing an ecosystem-based, precautionary approach. Habitat mapping provided the seafloor and ecological information needed to underpin integrated ocean management. Following several demonstration projects with the fishing industry, the federal government recognized the value of the habitat-mapping approach and provided new funding to develop a national program. Regional projects were completed in seven priority areas across the country. The Bedford Institute of Oceanography led the world in developing the new science of habitat mapping and advised several countries on implementing mapping strategies. Despite the program's success and the demonstrable benefits to environmental stewardship and economic development, the program was curtailed and habitat mapping is no longer a federal government priority.

Key words: marine habitat mapping, multibeam sonar, GeoHab, SEAMAP.
***E-mail:** Brian.Todd@NRCan-RNCan.gc.ca

From the beginning, marine ecologists at the Bedford Institute of Oceanography (BIO) have recognized the importance of seafloor habitat to the biodiversity and sustainability of marine ecosystems in Canada's oceans. From the 1960s to the early 1980s, hydrographers of the Canadian Hydrographic Service (CHS), Fisheries and Oceans Canada (DFO), and geologists of the Geological Survey of Canada (GSC), Natural Resources Canada (NRCan), systematically mapped the continental margin off Canada's Atlantic Provinces, providing a regional-scale perspective of the seafloor morphology and texture of the seafloor sediments (Fader et al. 2004). These early surficial geology studies produced a series of reports and maps useful for benthic ecosystem research.

Habitat research could not advance beyond regional-scale studies until geologists and hydrographers were able to provide more detailed maps of the seabed. The first breakthrough came in the 1970s when the GSC acquired sidescan sonar. While the power of this new seafloor imagery was quickly recognized, it was limited to providing ground truth of relatively small areas. Errors in ship and instrument positioning, combined with time-consuming manual data processing, hampered the application of the technology. Nevertheless, the power of high horizontal resolution mapping was recognized and this encouraged development of stronger collaborative links between the three principal players: DFO Science Branch, CHS, and GSC.

EMERGENCE OF HIGH-RESOLUTION SEAFLOOR MAPPING

The development of new technologies in the 1990s coincided with the emergence of new demands for fisheries management and a global shift towards ecosystem-based integrated ocean management. High resolution habitat mapping was needed to underpin these new management strategies. Unfettered access to the Global Positioning System (GPS) at that time enabled accurate positioning of ships and instruments deployed at sea. Concomitant with GPS was the development of ship-borne multibeam sonar systems designed to map swaths of underwater terrain with unprecedented accuracy (and associated data volumes). CHS quickly embraced this emerging mapping technology and by the mid-1990s relatively large areas of the continental shelf were being remapped with hitherto unheard-of positional accuracy and data density. From the outset, the GSC worked closely with CHS to improve the quality of the data and, most importantly, to develop software tools to process the backscatter strength signal to produce maps of seabed reflectivity (a proxy for seafloor roughness and sediment grain size) to accompany the multibeam sonar bathymetric imagery. For the first time, high-resolution imagery of the seabed was comparable to land images obtained from aerial photography or satellite imagery.

EMBRACING THE NEW MAPPING STRATEGY

As we entered the 21st century, all of the components were in place for BIO staff to take global leadership in the emerging new science of habitat mapping. Federal resource managers in DFO and NRCan were driving the need for information to manage both living and nonliving resources. Users in the private sector were pushing government to transfer this new knowledge and expand its application to commercial applications. The teams and the technology had been built to optimize the talents of hydrographers, geologists, benthic ecologists, and fisheries scientists required to deliver the science.

The power of GPS-based multibeam sonar mapping technology arguably provided the single most important advance in our scientific understanding of the seafloor and its associated flora and fauna since the founding of BIO in 1962. Industry was quick to recognize the benefits from applying these seafloor mapping tools. Early adopters included petroleum and telecommunications companies and, most importantly for the appreciation of habitat mapping, the fishing industry. Research partnerships established between government and industry enabled large, regional-scale multibeam sonar surveys to be conducted. These partnerships proved vital in enabling BIO to conduct some of the most extensive surveys of the continental shelf to date, but more importantly, early adoption and application demonstrated the benefits of this new systematic seafloor mapping approach to industry and to government resource managers.

In 1999-2000, staff at BIO from NRCan (GSC), DFO (Science, CHS) and Department of National Defence (DND) developed a concept paper for a national seafloor mapping strategy (Pickrill et al. 1999). This plan was supported by senior managers in the respective departments and presented to the Clerk of the Privy Council. The Privy Council requested that NRCan, DFO, and DND develop SEAMAP (Seabed Resource Mapping Program) as a national seafloor mapping program to be presented to Cabinet. Despite being approved by Cabinet, the program did not secure funding. However, a reduced national SEAMAP program was subsequently funded under Canada's Ocean Action Plan (OAP) with the result that the seven highest priority areas in Canada's oceans have been surveyed and systematically mapped, including: the Bay of Fundy, continental shelf banks off southwest Nova Scotia, Placentia Bay, and the St. Lawrence Estuary in Atlantic Canada; much of the Salish Sea, Queen Charlotte Sound, and Hecate Strait in British Columbia; and part of the Beaufort Sea in the Arctic Ocean (Figs. 1–3).

The mapping program established research partnerships with industry and academia, most notably the Nova Scotia Offshore Scallopers Association and the Ocean Mapping Group at the University of New Brunswick. The industry partnerships extended the survey coverage by many thousands of square kilometres under agreements using the government fleet (MacDougall 2014), equipping industry vessels with multibeam sonar systems, and by chartering vessels with deep-water survey capability. Academic partnerships helped solve technical challenges of processing these large data volumes.

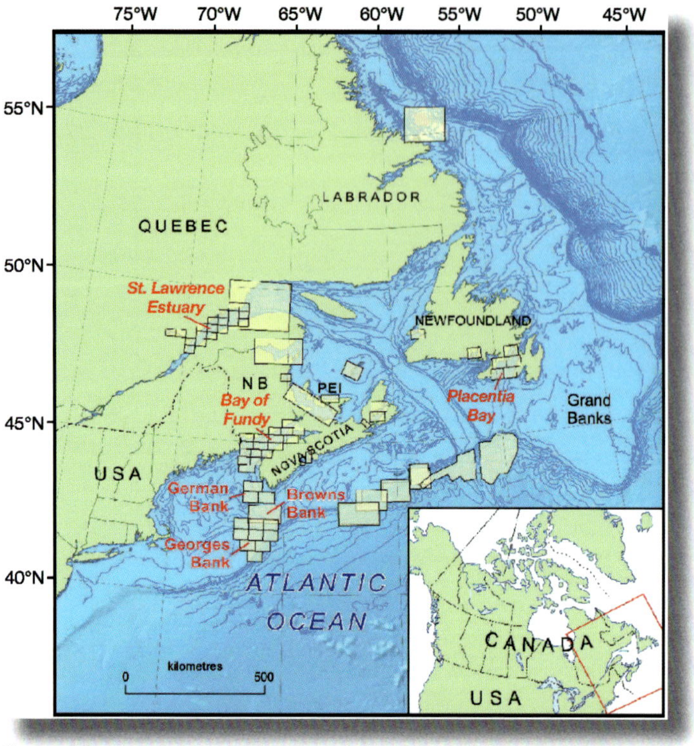

Figure 1. Atlantic coast of Canada. Marine areas in boxes show multibeam sonar seafloor mapping coverage as of 2013. Location of Browns Bank map in Figure 4 is indicated.

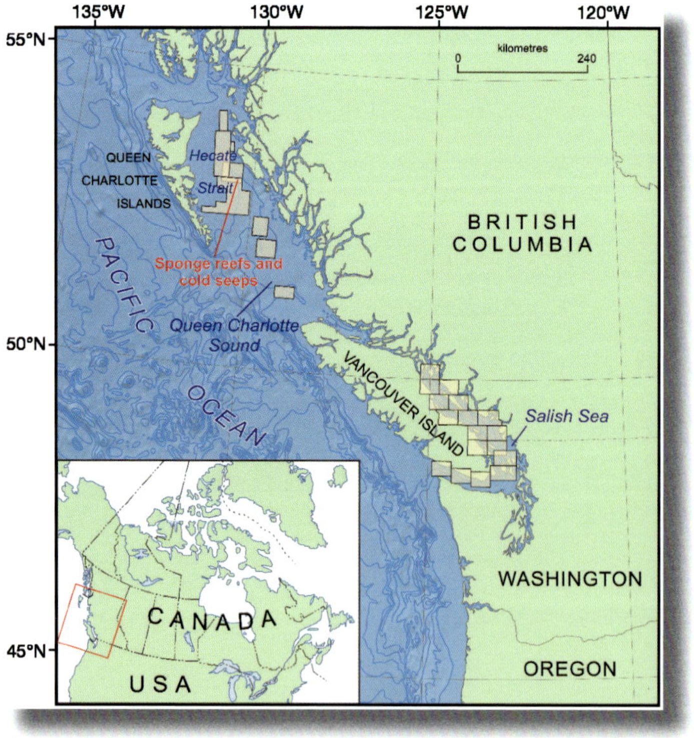

Figure 2. Pacific coast of Canada. Marine areas in boxes show multibeam sonar seafloor mapping coverage as of 2013. Location of sponge reefs and cold seeps illustrated in Figure 5 is indicated.

Figure 3. Beaufort Sea coast of Canada. Marine area in box shows multibeam sonar seafloor mapping coverage as of 2013. Location of pockmarks and ice scours illustrated in Figure 6 is indicated.

Habitat mapping emerged in response to new capabilities realized through technological developments to meet a growing need for a holistic approach to ocean resource management. It thrived because the applied benefits from the research were readily apparent, and the science sold itself to both government and industry. In this review article we highlight just one aspect – among many – of habitat mapping in each of Canada's three oceans.

ATLANTIC OCEAN: THE OFFSHORE SCALLOP FISHERY

In 1998, a chance meeting between managers at Clearwater Seafoods Limited (CSL; formerly Clearwater Fine Foods) and staff at BIO led to one of the most extensive and successful research collaborations at the Institute. At that early date, CSL staff was provided a demonstration of multibeam sonar mapping imagery. The scallop fishing industry had long been aware that scallops prefer to live on coarse gravelly substrates and, using local knowledge, had been able to optimize catch rates and minimize damage to gear. On seeing the seafloor imagery and its ability to differentiate muddy and gravelly seafloor sediments, CSL quickly realized the value in applying this technology to the fishery. The GSC and CHS established research partnerships to map Browns Bank on the Scotian Shelf (Fig. 4) where benthic sampling established direct relationships between substrate type and scallop density (Kostylev et al. 2003). The benefits to the offshore scallop fleet were immediate: charts were exported to digital navigation systems, bottom-tow times were reduced, and gear damage was minimized enabling quotas to be reached with just 25% of the pre-mapping fishing effort (Pickrill and Todd 2003). The offshore scallop industry provided the momentum to develop much broader-based models of habitat mapping, revolutionizing the discipline by using substrate as a proxy for community analysis (Kostylev et al. 2005). The new understanding of scallop habitat led fisheries management to change survey design for stock assessment. Traditionally, surveys were random and stratified by depth; they remain random, but are now stratified by habitat.

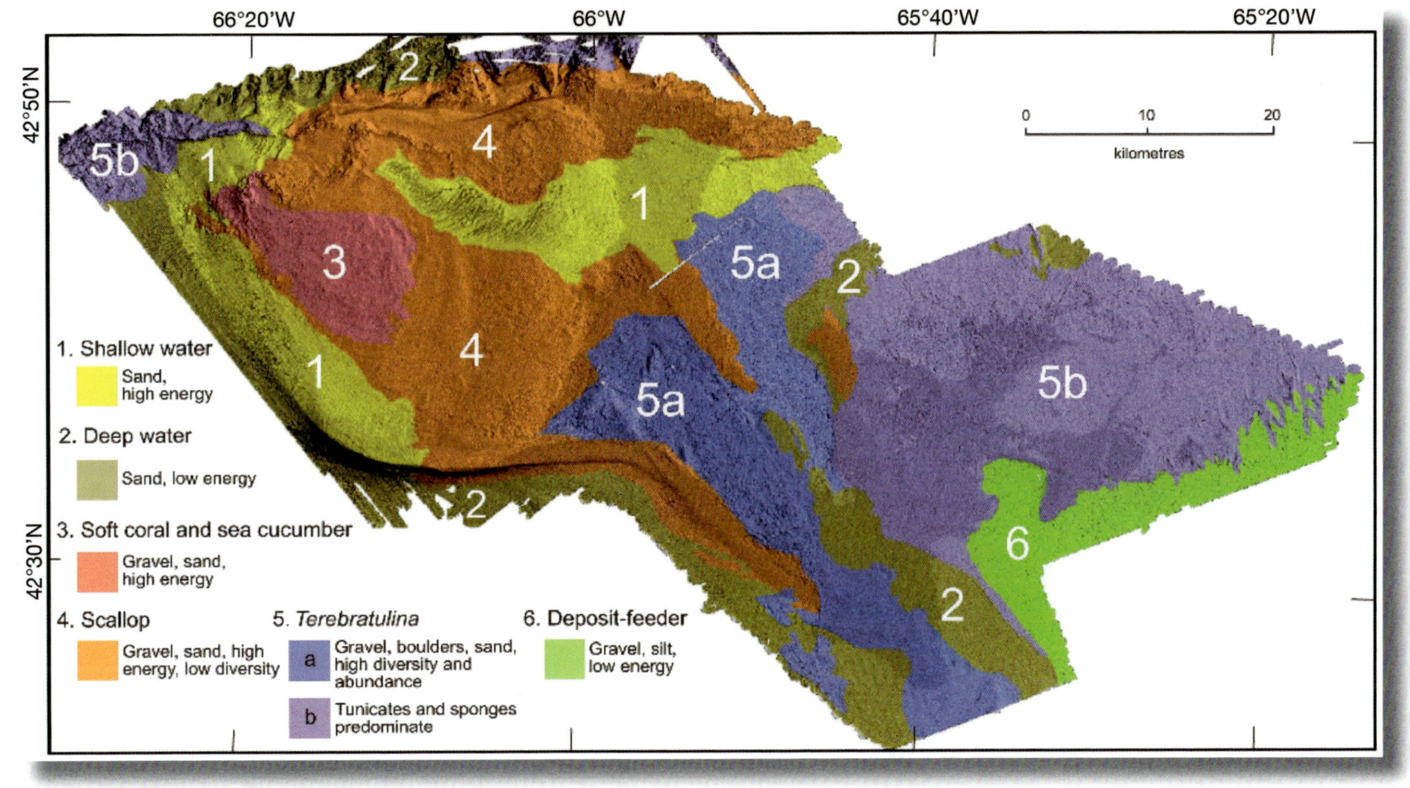

Figure 4. Benthic habitat map of Browns Bank, Scotian Shelf (from Kostylev et al. 2001). See Figure 1 for location.

The benefits to the scallop fishery enabled CSL to make the business case to invest in converting a scallop dragger into a research ship equipped with multibeam sonar and dedicated to surveys on Georges Bank and German Bank, with subsequent surveys in international waters. CSL went on to develop its own navigation and data management systems and today remains a world leader in applying modern mapping techniques to fisheries practice and fleet management.

The partnership between the offshore scallop industry and BIO provided the catalyst for much habitat research to be published in the first decade of the 2000s. Industry support provided the resources to map the most extensive areas of continental shelf with more than 200 sea-days being devoted over five years. In 2001, the mapping technology was adopted by the inshore fishery when a new scallop fishery was initiated in an area inshore of German Bank off southwestern Nova Scotia referred to as Scallop Fishing Area (SFA) 29 West. A three-year joint project agreement was signed in 2002 involving the inshore fishing fleets participating in the SFA 29 West fishery, with NRCan and DFO. All parties provided funds to map the fishing area (Fisheries and Oceans Canada 2006). At the time, the southern banks of Nova Scotia were mapped with the most extensive, publically available survey data on the world's continental shelves. The research partnerships, while extremely productive, also exposed the technical and scientific staff to frequent challenging questions from industry. For example, industry pushed NRCan to identify and automate mapping of the smallest boulders that may damage scallop rakes, while the diversity of fishermen in SFA 29 West led to the development of digital maps that could be imported into a variety of navigation systems. DFO annual monitoring surveys of scallop grounds were also designed using these maps (Smith et al. 2009), thus reducing costs and survey impacts on the bottom. As a result of this collaborative work, DFO and NRCan staff received the 2008 Federal Partners in Technology Transfer Award.

PACIFIC OCEAN: SPONGE REEFS AND COLD SEEPS

The Queen Charlotte Basin off the northern coast of British Columbia was identified by DFO as a Large Ocean Management Area (LOMA) – the Pacific North Coast Integrated Management Area (PNCIMA) – to undepin management of a region containing a UNESCO (United Nations Educational, Scientific and Cultural Organization) World Heritage Site, an area identified for its cultural heritage, unique ecosystem, and resource wealth in fisheries, hydrocarbons, renewable energy, and minerals. Government consideration of lifting the moratorium on hydrocarbon exploration heightened the need for ocean management, particularly to address the inevitable conflict between fisheries and other resource sectors. NRCan, in cooperation with CHS, with funding from several partners, undertook extensive mapping of the areas where conflict would be the greatest in an attempt to provide integrated geoscience, oceanographic, and habitat knowledge (Barrie and Conway 2007). One consequence of this integrated mapping approach was the discovery of cold seeps (ecosystems based on seafloor venting of methane, hydrogen sulphide, and other fluids) in an actively trawled region of Hecate Strait (Fig. 5). The seep sites are located as part of a linear pockmark chain, and within the largest of the pockmarks actively venting authigenic carbonate chimneys (mounds) occur that are surrounded by a wide halo of shells and shell debris (Barrie et al. 2011). The faunal assemblage found at the cold seeps is distinct from that of the surrounding soft substrate habitat and atypical of other cold-seep communities. These taxa were apparently attracted by the presence of hard substrate in an otherwise soft seabed environment and by the hydrocarbons present. The significant preservation of shell debris that surrounds the carbonate chimneys suggests that the chemistry of the water near the seabed has been altered by hydrocarbon seepage. The exposure of the carbonate chimneys is a result of discontinuous expulsion of thermogenic gas from the hydrocarbon reservoir and continued deepening of the pockmarks.

Extensive glass (*hexactinellid*) sponge reefs exist on the western Canadian continental shelf (Conway et al. 1991, Krautter et al. 2001). These reefs are unique in the modern world ocean with the closest analogous reefs having become extinct 40 million years ago in western Europe. The reefs are constructed by frame building sponges of the Order Hexactinosa which, much like coral reefs, form a framework that allows diverse reef forms to develop. The reefs can be up to 25 m high, and are normally clustered in extensive complexes up to 600 km^2 in area (Fig. 5). Detailed multibeam mapping of the main reef complexes was undertaken between 2002 and 2007 as part of the Pacific North Coast Integrated Management Area (PNCIMA) ocean mapping strategy. This was done to provide an understanding of the development of the reefs over time, and more importantly, to define precise reef boundaries that were urgently needed for fisheries management purposes (Conway et al. 2007a). Prior to the

Figure 5. Multibeam sonar bathymetric image of an area of sponge reefs and pockmarks associated with cold seeps, offshore British Columbia. See Figure 2 for location.

mapping, groundfish trawl fisheries had exacted a huge toll on these sensitive reefs with more than 50% of the known reefs destroyed by trawl vessels. Sponge biomass caught as bycatch during fishing in the reef complexes was massive, with up to 12 tonnes of sponges recovered in a single trawl tow (Conway et al. 2007b). Mandated trawl fishery closures undertaken by DFO in 2002 were reviewed and expanded following assessment of multibeam results after 2007 (Jamieson et al. 2007). The reefs are currently being designated as Marine Protected Areas to provide more comprehensive protection than simple fisheries closures.

ARCTIC OCEAN: BEAUFORT SEA IMPACTS

The Beaufort Sea in the southern Arctic Ocean was identified by DFO as a LOMA. A management plan was needed to balance the competing demands for developing the considerable hydrocarbon reserves with the unique ecosystem of this shallow sea while respecting the cultural and economic needs of the indigenous Inuvialuit population. NRCan has undertaken seabed hazard and geotechnical research programs in the Beaufort Sea since the 1970s (Lewis et al. 2014). However, with the growing interest in integrated resource management coincident with the tabling of industry proposals to move from hydrocarbon exploration to production, the research program was expanded under the Oceans Action Plan to include habitat mapping.

Unique engineering challenges to bringing hydrocarbons to market are posed by the Beaufort Sea's harsh arctic environment. These challenges make it equally difficult to conduct systematic surveys that permit identification of unique or sensitive habitats to be considered in the management plan. Mapping techniques developed for the scallop fisheries on the Atlantic coast and for sponge reefs on the Pacific coast could not be simply transferred to the Beaufort Sea. The open-water season available for ship surveys in the Beaufort Sea is very short and unpredictable, while the shallow coastal waters, combined with the large geographical area to be considered for the LOMA, made systematic surveys of the entire area impractical.

Despite its shallow depths, the Beaufort Sea seabed contains a variety of unique physical habitats evolving from local processes acting at the seabed. For example, seasonal ice scouring reworks the seafloor, disturbing the habitat, and creating special geomorphology at the macro scale; local seafloor processes, such as expulsion of shallow gas at the surface, modify the seabed geomorphology, sediments, and habitat (Fig. 6). In the 1970s and 1980s, exploration companies dredged much of the available aggregate to create artificial islands for installation of oil rigs. Dredging destroyed old habitats and created new ones, many of which are now distinctly different from the natural environment.

Mapping these different seabed physical environments with the gradation of processes across the Beaufort Sea shelf revealed a number of potential habitat types (Pickrill and Kostylev 2007). Targeted seafloor mapping and sampling surveys were conducted at representative study sites, including artificial islands, ice-scoured sea floor, gas vents, distinct geological regions, and water depths. The major physical forces structuring benthic habitats in the Beaufort Sea are the disturbance by dynamic pack-ice scouring and the presence of land-fast ice which limits scouring and biological productivity in the nearshore zone. Overall, low primary productivity in the Beaufort Sea is controlled by seasonal ice and the effect of suspended sediment load from Mackenzie River runoff (Chapman and Kostylev 2007). These major driving forces explain increasing biodiversity and biomass of benthic communities with depth, decreased biodiversity in ice scoured areas and scarcity of benthos on eroded surfaces of artificial islands. Conlan and Kvitek (2005) demonstrated that benthic communities in ice-scoured arctic environments recover from scouring impact after more than 30 years. This extreme natural disturbance was assessed by Blasco et al. (2005) who, on the basis of sidescan and multibeam surveys, produced a map of ice scouring rates thereby establishing that the highest frequency of disturbance occurred in water depths of 20 to 30 m. By developing and testing models linking benthic community associations with seafloor processes, we can extrapolate, with confidence, to the regional scale to provide a framework within which management plans and infrastructure (such as hydrocarbon installations) can be developed. This approach has provided a pragmatic and cost-effective solution to habitat mapping in extreme environments. Habitat mapping can now be conducted in all of Canada's bordering seas.

MAPPING STRATEGIES AND THE INTERNATIONAL PERSPECTIVE

Funding of the Geoscience for Ocean Management Program through Canada's Oceans Action Plan provided the platform for NRCan to develop a Canada-wide habitat mapping program. Priorities were established through stakeholder consultations (2002) and seven research projects

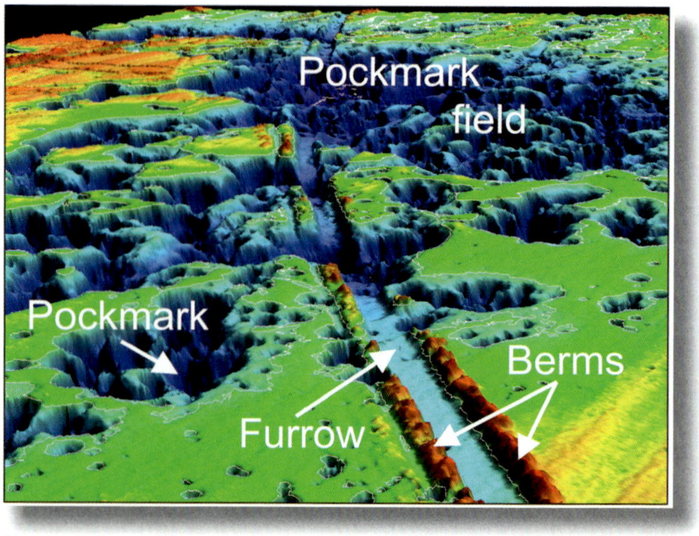

Figure 6. Oblique multibeam sonar bathymetric image of the shallow inner shelf of the Beaufort Sea. The flat seafloor has been cut by grounding ice, resulting in curvilinear furrows and flanking berms. The labelled furrow is 18 m wide. Expulsion of shallow gas from underlying sediments has left the surface pockmarked. These active seafloor processes have created unique seafloor habitats (Blasco et al. 2005). Vertical exaggeration is 10 times. See Figure 3 for location.

were completed in 2008 on all three oceans. Funding was passed to CHS to enable full-scale regional multibeam sonar surveys to be completed over a period of three years, from 2005 to 2008.

National mapping strategies and standards were implemented in 2004 and a new GSC 'A Series' map product developed incorporating interpreted multibeam sonar bathymetry, backscatter strength, and benthic habitat at scales appropriate to the data resolution and mapping extents. The vision was a simple one, namely to 'remove the water column' and extend mapping of Canada's landmass offshore to its limits of jurisdiction. The strategy proved relatively straightforward for the hydrographers and geoscientists to implement. However, the benthic habitat proved more challenging and a spectrum of approaches was proposed and tested, ranging from correlation based on detailed geological and community analysis (e.g., Browns Bank, as described by Kostylev et al. 2001), through to deterministic modelling using environmental conditions and constraints as proxies for community and habitat structure and diversity (as applied to the Scotian Shelf by Kostylev and Hannah 2007).

While the regional multibeam surveys at the core of this research were primarily conducted to advance the science of habitat mapping, advances in our understanding of the regional geology of Canada's continental shelves cannot be understated. Multibeam surveys were followed up by regional geological surveys to provide 'ground truth' of the multibeam interpretation. Targeted bottom sampling, photography, coring, and seismic reflection surveys facilitated a new understanding of the Quaternary geology of the continental shelf. Some of the results from these geological surveys are reported elsewhere in this volume (see Fader et al. 2014, Shaw 2014, Todd and Shaw 2014). Probably the most significant progress has been made in Hecate Strait (BC), St. Lawrence Estuary (QC), Placentia Bay (NL), Bay of Fundy (NB, NS), and the shallow banks off southwest Nova Scotia.

One of the most exciting developments during the formative years was the recognition that the BIO work was not done in isolation. Marine habitat mapping emerged as a new science simultaneously in many countries around the world where, as in Canada, governments were pushing science towards an ecosystem approach to integrate management of our oceans. In fact, following Canadian leadership, Australia, the European Union, Ireland, Norway, and other countries developed national seafloor mapping strategies similar to SEAMAP.

GEOHAB

The GeoHab (Geological and Biological Marine Habitat Mapping) organization was created from this synchronous convergence of policy need and technological capability. In 2001, following a Geological Association of Canada scientific meeting on marine habitat mapping in St. John's, Newfoundland, an international group of marine scientists met at BIO and founded GeoHab, which has grown over the past decade into an international scientific organization dedicated to benthic habitat mapping. In many respects, GeoHab is a specialized organization that provides a forum for benthic ecologists, geoscientists, and hydrographers to meet and share common objectives. From its founding days, scientists at BIO have played a leadership role in this evolving new organization. GeoHab's annual meeting attracts more than 100 delegates worldwide, a clear indication of the high value of the organization to the marine research community. Since 2007, GeoHab has published two books (Todd and Greene 2007, Harris and Baker 2012) and one special supplement of a scientific journal (Heap and Harris 2011) dedicated to marine habitat mapping. Perusing these publications shows that strategies to map habitat are as diverse as the number of countries now engaged in this research. The study approaches are evolving to meet the specific needs of each nation, yet the overall objective is the same: i.e., to map the seafloor resources to underpin and improve ocean management.

FUTURE OF MARINE HABITAT MAPPING IN CANADA

Since 2002, marine habitat mapping has grown into a new interdisciplinary field of marine research. Scientists and technologists at BIO are privileged to be at the forefront of this exciting development. As with many advances in science, no single event can be identified as leading to this 'breakthrough', but rather a number of coalescing circumstances that provided fertile ground for new concepts and visionary thinking to be established. It is worthwhile recapping these catalysts, as the future of habitat mapping is as inextricably bound to them as it was in the past.

Habitat mapping was enabled by the emerging new technology of multibeam sonar, a technological advance that rendered unparalleled high-resolution imagery of the seafloor. Other laboratories had this technology, but few were able to assemble the interdisciplinary teams of scientists, engineers, and data processors necessary to enhance the imagery, collect and process the data, and develop a map production routine. The institutional structure, inherent to BIO, enabled hydrographers, geologists, ecologists, and fisheries scientists to pursue new research opportunities. However, none of this would have been possible without the political will. With the passing of the Oceans Act in 1996, Canada implemented a visionary framework for integrated management of its ocean resources: i.e., habitat mapping would deliver the data, maps, and ecological knowledge to provide a solid foundation for the development of ocean management plans. Finally, the program sold itself by showing clear benefits to all sectors of the marine economy.

The technology now exists, and the last decade has shown that the science needed to support management plans, conservation, fisheries management, and ocean engineering can be delivered. Multibeam sonar mapping is most efficient in deep water. One of the challenges in the SEAMAP proposal was to complete 100% coverage of our littoral zone and estuaries. Launches are restricted by shallow water and are expensive to operate. Since SEAMAP was proposed, airborne LiDAR (light detection and ranging) technology has been used in clear water areas to provide shallow bathymetry and substrate information (Cottin et al. 2009). Furthermore, the development of small, inexpensive, easily-deployed Autonomous Underwater Vehicles (AUVs) equipped with multibeam sonar that can operate in both clear and turbid water has removed the visibility barrier completely. The use of AUVs in all ocean depths will ultimately reduce costs and increase resolution. The future of marine habitat mapping is no longer limited by technology.

The present challenge in mapping marine habitat is to convert single-point source data–be it geological or biological in nature –into spatially interpreted maps, and multibeam mapping has provided the geospatial framework to achieve this goal. The ecosystem-based approach to management has been adopted by many countries, including Canada, for the effective management of ocean resources. In the near future, the application of bottom maps will be expanded to provide the foundation for interpreting ecosystem data to deal with issues such as the mitigation and reduction of bycatch of non-target species in fisheries (Tremblay et al. 2009), the implementation of sustainable fishing practices, and the design of marine protected areas (Pickrill and Todd 2003).

Unfortunately, federal science priorities and opportunities for marine habitat mapping have changed. Ocean management is no longer a federal government priority and, as a consequence, funding has been reduced and mapping programs largely curtailed. Canada's former position at the forefront of applied seafloor mapping has declined markedly. The concept of a national seafloor mapping strategy, embodied in SEAMAP for Canada, is recognized worldwide by many countries including Australia, Baltic States, Ireland, New Zealand, and Norway. Owing to the expertise available at BIO, staff members have been asked regularly to assist in the establishment of national mapping programs in Ireland (Irish National Seabed Survey), Norway (MAREANO: Marine AREA Database for NOrwegian waters), and the European Union (BALANCE: BALtic seA Management – Nature Conservation and sustainable development of the Ecosystem through spatial planning). The hope is that decision-makers in Canada will rediscover the critical need for marine habitat research in the search for wise management of our ocean waters. Once that occurs, the methodology for mapping marine habitat, developed at BIO and augmented internationally, can be applied for the effective management of benthic ecological resources in Canada's expanded area of seafloor jurisdiction.

ACKNOWLEDGEMENTS

We acknowledge improvements in this article resulting from reviews by John Shaw and Michael Lewis of the Geological Survey of Canada and the editors of this volume. Scott Hayward and Phil O'Regan assisted with the preparation of illustrations.

REFERENCES

Barrie, J.V. and K.W. Conway. 2007. Ocean management of Queen Charlotte Basin, British Columbia, Canada. Pages 441-450 *in* Mapping the Seafloor for Habitat Characterization (B.J. Todd and H.G. Greene, Eds.). Geological Association of Canada, Special Paper 47, St. John's, NL.

Barrie, J.V., S. Cook, and K.W. Conway. 2011. Cold seeps and benthic habitat on the Pacific margin of Canada. Pages S85-S92 *in* Geological and Biological Mapping and Characterisation of Benthic Marine Environments (A.D. Heap and P.T. Harris, Eds.). Continental Shelf Research 31, Issue 2, Supplement 1. doi:10.1016/j.csr.2010.02.013.

Blasco, S.M., R. Bennett, J. Hughes Clarke, J. Bartlett, and J.M. Shearer. 2005. 3-D multibeam mapping reveals geological processes associated with fluted seabed, pockmarks, mud volcanoes, deep water ice scours and slump features in the Beaufort Sea-Amundsen Gulf. Page 13 *in* Abstracts, Vol. 30, Geological Association of Canada-Mineralogical Association of Canada-Canadian Society of Petroleum Geologists-Canadian Society of Soil Science Joint Meeting, 16-18 May 2005, Halifax, NS.

Chapman, A.S. and V.E. Kostylev. 2007. Distribution, abundance and diversity of benthic species from the Beaufort Sea and western Amundsen Gulf – a summary of data collected between 1951 and 2000. Open File Report 5498, Geological Survey of Canada, Ottawa, ON.

Conlan, K.E. and R.G. Kvitek. 2005. Recolonization of soft-sediment ice scours on an exposed arctic coast. Marine Ecology Progress Series 286: 21-42. doi:10.3354/meps286021.

Conway, K.W., J.V. Barrie, W.C. Austin, and J.L. Luternauer. 1991. Holocene sponge bioherms on the western Canadian continental shelf. Continental Shelf Research 11: 771-790. doi:10.1016/0278-4343(91)90079-L.

Conway, K.W., J.V. Barrie, and M. Krautter. 2007a. Complex deep shelf habitat: sponge reefs in the Pacific northwest. Pages 259-269 *in* Mapping the Seafloor for Habitat Characterization (B.J. Todd and H.G. Greene, Eds.). Geological Association of Canada, Special Paper 47, St. John's, NL.

Conway, K.W., J.V. Barrie, P.R. Hill, W.C. Austin, and K. Picard. 2007b. Mapping sensitive benthic habitats in the Strait of Georgia, coastal British Columbia: deep-water sponge and coral reefs. Current Research 2007-A, Geological Survey of Canada, Ottawa, ON. doi: 10.4095/223389.

Cottin, A., D.L. Forbes, and B.F. Long. 2009. Shallow seabed mapping and classification using waveform analysis and bathymetry from SHOALS LiDAR data. Canadian Journal of Remote Sensing 35: 422-434.

Fader, G.B.J., T. Lynds, R.O. Miller, D.R. Parrott, S. Hynes, and A. Sherin. 2004. Scotian Shelf regional surficial geology compilation. Open File 4671, Geological Survey of Canada, Ottawa, ON.

Fader, G.B.J., B. MacLean, H. Josenhans, and S. Blasco. 2014. Seabed sediment mapping at the Beford Institute of Oceanography: from single beam to multibeam. Pages 191-199 *in* Voyage of Discovery: Fifty Years of Marine Research at Canada's Bedford Institute of Oceanography (D.N. Nettleship, D.C. Gordon, C.F.M. Lewis, and M.P. Latremouille, Eds.). Bedford Institute of Oceanography-Oceans Association, Dartmouth, NS.

Fisheries and Oceans Canada. 2006. Presentation and review of southwest Nova Scotia benthic mapping project. Canadian Science Advisory Secretariat, Proceedings Series, 2006/047, Dartmouth, NS.

Harris, P.T. and E.K. Baker (Eds.). 2012. Seafloor Geomorphology as Benthic Habitat: GeoHAB Atlas of Seafloor Geomorphic Features and Benthic Habitats. Elsevier, London, England.

Heap, A.D. and P.T. Harris. 2011. Geological and biological habitat mapping and characterization of benthic marine environments – Introduction to the special issue. Pages S1–S3 *in* Geological and Biological Mapping and Characterisation of Benthic Marine Environments (A.D. Heap and P.T. Harris, Eds.). Continental Shelf Research 31, Issue 2, Supplement 1. doi:10.1016/j.csr.2010.09.015.

Jamieson, G.S., K.W. Conway, and J.V. Barrie. 2007. Re-evaluation of sponge reef complex occurrences and their protection in Pacific Canada. Canadian Science Advisory Secretariat, Research Document 2007/010, Sidney, BC.

Kostylev, V.E., B.J. Todd, G.B.J. Fader, R.C. Courtney, G.D.M. Cameron, and R.A. Pickrill. 2001. Benthic habitat mapping on the Scotian Shelf based on multibeam bathymetry, surficial geology and sea floor photographs. Marine Ecology Progress Series 219: 121–137. doi:10.3354/meps219121.

Kostylev, V.E., R.C. Courtney, G. Robert, and B.J. Todd. 2003. Stock evalution of giant scallop *(Placopecten magellanicus)* using high-resolution acoustics for seabed mapping. Fisheries Research 60: 479–492. doi:10.1016/S0165-7836(02)00100-5.

Kostylev, V.E., B.J. Todd, O. Longva, and P.C. Valentine. 2005. Characterization of benthic habitat on northeastern Georges Bank, Canada. Pages 141-152 *in* Benthic Habitats and the Effects of Fishing (P.W. Barnes and J.P. Thomas, Eds.). American Fisheries Society Symposium 41, American Fisheries Society, Bethesda, MD.

Kostylev, V.E. and C.G. Hannah. 2007. Process-driven characterization and mapping of seabed habitats. Pages 171-184 *in* Mapping the Seafloor for Habitat Characterization (B.J. Todd and H.G. Greene, Eds.). Geological Association of Canada, Special Paper 47, St. John's, NL.

Krautter, M., K.W. Conway, J.V. Barrie, and M. Neuweiler. 2001. Discovery of a "living dinosaur": globally unique modern hexactinellid sponge reefs off British Columbia, Canada. Facies 44: 265–282. doi:10.1007/BF02668178.

Lewis, C.F. M., S.M. Blasco, D.J.W. Piper, and G.V. Sonnichsen. 2014. Seabed geohazard knowledge for safe hydrocarbon development. Pages 383-394 *in* Voyage of Discovery: Fifty Years of Marine Research at Canada's Bedford Institute of Oceanography (D.N. Nettleship, D.C. Gordon, C.F.M. Lewis, and M.P. Latremouille, Eds.). Bedford Institute of Oceanography-Oceans Association, Dartmouth, NS.

MacDougall, J.R. 2014. Hydrography: a foundation for multidisciplinary ocean science at BIO, 1962-2012. Pages 169-180 *in* Voyage of Discovery: Fifty Years of Marine Research at Canada's Bedford Institute of Oceanography (D.N. Nettleship, D.C. Gordon, C.F.M. Lewis, and M.P. Latremouille, Eds.). Bedford Institute of Oceanography-Oceans Association, Dartmouth, NS.

Pickrill, R.A., D.C. Gordon Jr., R. MacDougall, and J. Bradford. 1999. Canadian seabed resource mapping program (SEAMAP): a knowledge base for ocean management in the 21st Century. Internal Report, Bedford Institute of Oceanography, Dartmouth, NS.

Pickrill, R.A. and B.J. Todd. 2003. The multiple roles of acoustic mapping in integrated ocean management, Canadian Atlantic continental margin. Ocean and Coastal Management 46: 601-614. doi:10.1016/S0964-5691(03)00037-1.

Pickrill, R.A. and V.E. Kostylev. 2007. Habitat mapping and national seafloor mapping strategies in Canada. Pages 483-495 *in* Mapping the Seafloor for Habitat Characterization (B.J. Todd and H.G. Greene, Eds.). Geological Association of Canada, Special Paper 47, St. Johns, NL.

Shaw, J. 2014. Deglaciation and postglacial sea-level changes in Atlantic Canada: science driven by technology. Pages 325-330 *in* Voyage of Discovery: Fifty Years of Marine Research at Canada's Bedford Institute of Oceanography (D.N. Nettleship, D.C. Gordon, C.F.M. Lewis, and M.P. Latremouille, Eds.). Bedford Institute of Oceanography-Oceans Association, Dartmouth, NS.

Smith, S.J., J. Black, B.J. Todd, V.E. Kostylev, and M.J. Lundy. 2009. The impact of commercial fishing on the determination of habitat associations for sea scallops (*Placopecten magellanicus*, Gmelin). ICES Journal of Marine Science 66: 2,043-2,051. doi:10.1093/icesjms/fsp196.

Todd, B.J. and H.G. Greene (Eds.). 2007. Mapping the Seafloor for Habitat Characterization. Geological Association of Canada Special Paper 47, St. John's, NL.

Todd, B.J. and J. Shaw. 2014. Discovering the seafloor of the Bay of Fundy. Pages 231-235 *in* Voyage of Discovery: Fifty Years of Marine Research at Canada's Bedford Institute of Oceanography (D.N. Nettleship, D.C. Gordon, C.F.M. Lewis, and M.P. Latremouille, Eds.). Bedford Institute of Oceanography-Oceans Association, Dartmouth, NS.

Tremblay, M.J., S.J. Smith, B.J. Todd, P.M. Clement, and D.L. McKeown. 2009. Associations of lobsters *(Homarus americanus)* off southwestern Nova Scotia with bottom type from images and geophysical maps. ICES Journal of Marine Science 66: 2,060–2,067. doi:10.1093/icesjms/fsp178.

22. SEABED SEDIMENT MAPPING AT THE BEDFORD INSTITUTE OF OCEANOGRAPHY: FROM SINGLE BEAM TO MULTIBEAM

Gordon B.J. Fader*, Brian MacLean, Heiner W. Josenhans, and Steve M. Blasco

SUMMARY

Mapping seabed sediments on the continental shelf of southeastern Canada was begun soon after the opening of the Bedford Institute of Oceanography in 1962. Marine geologists discovered that echograms collected by the Canadian Hydrographic Service to map water depths could also provide information on the material composition of the seabed. Echogram information combined with that from strategically positioned grab samples of the same area could then be used to construct accurate maps of sediment type and distribution. Applying this technique in a systematic manner, regional maps of sediment type were prepared and used to unravel the seabed's often complex geological history. New seabed features such as gas-escape pockmarks, offshore moraines, and sand dune fields were also discovered during the mapping. These maps were used by the fishing community to identify habitats, by engineers to choose cable routes and understand structure foundations, and by a wide user group concerned with other aspects of the seabed. During the 1980s and later, new technology was developed to map the seabed at higher resolution, and mapping moved to the northern regions of offshore Canada to cover most continental shelf and inland sea regions. Today's multibeam bathymetric systems map the seabed with decimetre resolution, and allow us to visualize it much like aerial photographs allow us to see land areas. Many offshore regions of Canada now need to be remapped using the new technologies to address developing issues of resource use and sustainability.

Key words: marine geology, sediments, continental shelf, seabed mapping, multibeam bathymetry, geological history.
***E-mail:** Gordon.Fader@ns.sympatico.ca

What could be more fundamental to a marine-oriented society than knowledge of the seabed habitat, sediments, and bedrock? Bottom fishing, the laying of electrical and communications cables, marine mining, hydrocarbon pipeline routing, seabed dredging, and offshore wind-farm and tidal-power device siting are all examples of projects and activities that occur in the offshore and that require knowledge of the shape, properties, and processes active on the seabed. A century ago, detailed hydrographic maps of ocean depths were lacking in most areas and the technology of the time to measure depth consisted largely of tallow-filled lead weights attached by rope or wire to a vessel and dropped to the seabed. As marine geology developed and advanced following World War II (1939-45), a need arose to not only determine seabed relief and topography, but also to obtain samples of materials to better understand the distribution of sediments, minerals, and dynamic conditions of sediment transport. Lead lines were replaced with echo sounders that determined water depth based on the speed and timing of sound through water (King 1967).

Early marine geologists relied on grab samplers to provide bulk samples of seabed sediments and these were normally collected in a grid pattern without any relationship to the shape of the seabed. Like all new sciences, the progress of marine geology depended largely on the development of new technology to advance investigations of the seabed and subsurface. These advances benefited greatly from acoustic research undertaken by the military that was used for the detection of submarines and underwater mines.

Bathymetric mapping was largely conducted by hydrographers of the Canadian Hydrographic Service (CHS) who produced contoured maps with minimal information on seabed material. The object of these surveys was to identify the seabed relief or topography with emphasis on shoal and shallow water areas for the safety of shipping (MacDougall 2014). However, further information was required for an understanding of deeper areas and the seafloor geology.

USE OF ECHO SOUNDERS

Very soon after the Bedford Institute of Oceanography (BIO) opened in 1962, a group of new scientists began projects to study the distribution of sediments at the seabed. Their first efforts used the accepted practice of locating sample sites based on a grid pattern so that the results would be statistically robust. L. H. King was an early pioneer who wanted to study the geochemistry of the sediments on the continental shelf off Nova Scotia, and needed to understand their distribution on the seabed. During the first surveys, echo sounders were used to measure water depths at locations where sediment samples were collected. Most of BIO's initial fleet of vessels was outfitted with Kelvin Hughes 26B echo sounders. These were simple devices that used a magnetostrictive transducer at 14.25 kHz to produce acoustic pulses. The information was graphically etched on moving rolls of paper by a stylus that actually burned the conductive paper to physically mark the time of sound arrival from the seabed and the intensity of the return signal. The smell of the burning paper was often enough to make young sailors seasick.

L.H. King and his team of marine geologists observed that the echo sounder paper rolls presented imagery that varied depending on the bottom type as evidenced from samples (Fig. 1). This was truly an 'eureka' moment in making a correlation between sediment type and the bottom as characterized on the paper tracings. Soft fine-grained mud on the seafloor was displayed as a fine line overlying a transparent subbottom, often over a subsurface high-intensity reflector from an underlying denser sediment unit, and the interval between surface and subsurface reflections thus indicated the thickness of the mud. Glaciomarine sediments (earth materials released from a glacier and deposited in the marine environment) were portrayed with limited acoustic transparency and sometimes with coherent reflections, which were interpreted as layering. Bedrock commonly produced a hard, rough, and irregular reflection; sand was imaged by a wide pulse with no sub-bottom penetration; and a till (sediment of mixed particle sizes deposited beneath a glacier) surface was displayed as a high-intensity reflection, commonly with an unusual hummocky surface, later known to represent iceberg furrows. It was quickly realized that these echo sounders and their varying return signals could be used to accurately map the distribution of sediments, and fewer samples needed to be collected. Thus, the routine grid pattern of sediment sampling was abandoned: fewer samples were collected and greater reliance was placed on the echo sounder data. This was a true turning point for marine geologists, and marks the beginnings of a discipline called 'seismostratigraphy'.

NEXT STAGES

Following a successful proof-of-concept phase of comparing echo sounder profile interpretations with grab samples, marine geologists were assigned individual regions of the southeastern Canadian continental shelf to study and map their seabed geology. One major advantage of this process was that it could use archived CHS echo sounder data that previously had been collected to produce bathymetric charts of offshore areas.

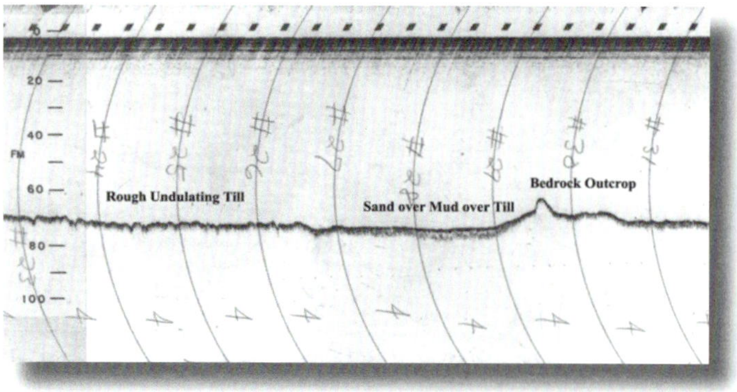

Figure 1. Echo sounder record from a Kelvin Hughes 26B system collected from the centre of the Bay of Fundy between Nova Scotia and New Brunswick (Fig. 2) along a 4-km seabed track showing interpreted sediment units. The early sediment mapping of southern areas of offshore Canada used these types of records to differentiate sediment type and, when combined with targeted seabed samples, provided a powerful tool for mapping (from Canadian Hydrographic Service).

Much of the early mapping was undertaken aboard CSS *Kapuskasing* using Decca navigation systems (Grant et al. 2014). By using the CHS data, the surficial maps benefited from the most accurate positioning available at the time.

The aim of these maps and associated reports was to systematically describe the distribution and character of offshore sediments with the ultimate goal of unravelling the geological history. As the technology for mapping the seabed improved, deeper-penetrating sounders (e.g., airgun seismic reflection systems) and sidescan sonars (to image off-track changes in sediment type and seafloor relief) were added to provide more information on the sediment cover, the morphology of the seabed, and the underlying bedrock.

That data collected could be used for both mapping sediment and bedrock was realized early on, thereby reducing both ship time and operating costs. During the late 1960s and 1970s, the surveys became more complex with the addition of a systematic bedrock mapping component that included use of rock dredges and rock core drills for obtaining samples from bedrock that was often buried at shallow depths beneath the seafloor.

The maps in the surficial geology series were published first by the CHS and later in conjunction with the Geological Survey of Canada (GSC). They were accompanied by reports that discussed the mapping approach, the data base, and each of the surficial sediment units as summarized in Fader et al. (2004). Using these approaches, the Scotian Shelf was fully mapped by the early 1980s (Fig. 2).

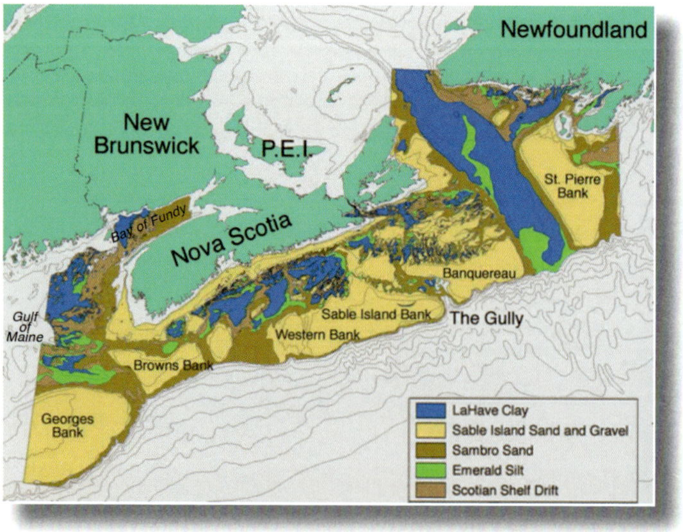

Figure 2. Compilation map of the surficial sediments of the Scotian Shelf and adjacent areas, largely based on the interpretation of many thousands of line-kilometres of echo-sounder data combined with approximately 5,000 seabed samples. Deeper areas in basins and channels are generally covered with LaHave Clay shown by blue colour (map from Fader et al. 2004).

DISCOVERY HIGHLIGHTS

The regional mapping program resulted in a number of significant seabed discoveries that stand as pioneering research of wide-ranging value: a few examples are highlighted here. V-shaped notches on the echograms from muddy seabeds of the Scotian Shelf were thought to represent channels. However, their conical shape quickly became apparent as viewed from the manned submersible *Shelfdiver* in Emerald Basin, north of Western Bank (Fig. 2). They were clearly seen, not as channels, but as circular depressions termed 'pockmarks' (Fig. 3). These features were first discovered by King and MacLean (1970) who proposed a model of their formation whereby gas or water emanating from below the seabed eroded the sediment and formed cone-shaped depressions. The features were both small and large with some over 1 km in diameter and up to 40 m in depth (King and MacLean 1970). Since this discovery, pockmarks have been found in all the world's oceans and in many lakes, and they have served as indicators of gas release in the petroleum industry's search for

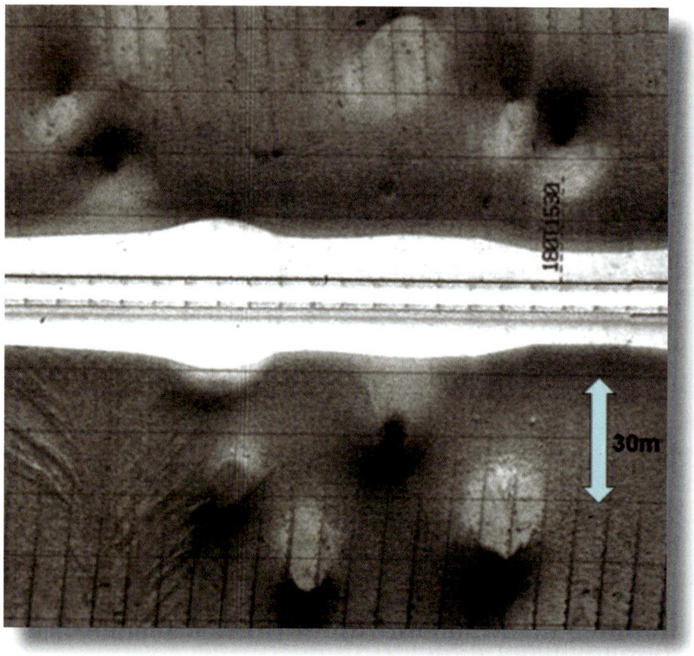

Figure 3. A sidescan sonogram of pockmarks (light-toned circular areas) on the seabed. These cone-shaped depressions were discovered during the surficial mapping and occur largely in the muddy basins of the shelf where the sediments record the venting of subsurface gas from the seabed (sonogram from 1989 MV *Navicula* cruise in Bay of Fundy).

hydrocarbons. Hundreds of papers and several books have been written on pockmarks (e.g., Hovland and Judd 1988). Research on their role in the release of greenhouse gasses and their effects on climate change continues today.

Large linear sediment ridges were found during the surficial sediment mapping. Samples collected from these features contained rocks derived from unique outcrops hundreds of kilometres onshore to the northwest. The surfaces of these features were very rough and irregular and this character could be used to assist in mapping the features from the echograms. The first use of sidescan sonars showed that these moraines were covered with many generations of ancient iceberg furrows. The features were interpreted as moraines deposited by glaciers (King et al. 1972). The discovery of the moraines proved that glaciers had extended across the continental shelf, and their shape and distribution could be used to reconstruct patterns of glacier advance and retreat in the offshore.

As the mapping progressed, sidescan sonar technology was introduced to the survey kit, and in particular a BIO-designed system was used to image the seabed (Jollymore 1974). In the Gulf of Maine and Bay of Fundy, the imagery showed large bedforms of sand and gravel, iceberg furrows, and pits, as well as bedrock outcrops, clearly revealing the dynamic nature of the seabed. To enhance the value of the surficial sediment maps, those produced for the Bay of Fundy, Gulf of Maine, and the Laurentian Channel and western Grand Banks of Newfoundland areas portrayed features in symbolized form as track-line interpretations overlying the sediment maps. This was a new advance for providing additional information on the maps.

SPIN-OFF MAP USES

The first surficial geology maps were used by the fishing community to better define sites for bottom fishing, allowing them to protect their equipment by avoiding boulder fields and hard irregular bottoms. This use later evolved into understanding the relationships between the benthic communities and bottom sediments that became useful for habitat mapping and targeted fishing. Groups of fishermen often visited the GSC laboratory at BIO to discuss the results of their fishing activities and their correlation to the surficial geology. They brought well-used paper maps marked with the best sites for a variety of fishing operations and wanted to learn where else they could go to fish based on the new surficial maps. For the marine geologists, this was a very rewarding process that showed the value of the geological mapping to the fishing industry.

As hydrocarbon exploration expanded on the Scotian Shelf, engineers were initially very concerned with the possible effects of sediment properties on the anchoring for drilling rigs. Many meetings were held on the topic, and design changes were subsequently made to the anchors and anchoring procedures for the first round of exploration.

Cable laying and route selection traditionally occurred without much knowledge of seabed conditions owing to the absence of information. This changed with the production of the surficial geological maps as routes could then be chosen to avoid hazards and to take advantage of softer sediments for cable burial and protection. Considerable consultation with the cable-laying industry occurred during the 1970s when the Canadian Transatlantic Telecommunications Cable (CANTAT) series of communication cables was planned to cross the Scotian Shelf. The maps provided options in routing, and cables that were laid during that time have never experienced a break.

TECHNOLOGY DEVELOPMENT FOR BETTER MAPPING

The development of sidescan sonars provided a giant leap forward in understanding sediment type and distribution (Fader et al. 2004). Echo sounder survey lines were always separated by considerable distances (hundreds of metres to kilometres) and maps of sediment distribution had to rely on correlation across these gaps based on bathymetry and geological experience in interpretation. With sidescan sonar, these gaps were filled with information and those correlations were accurately undertaken. To meet these needs, BIO developed a remarkable sidescan sonar for its time, capable of mapping at ranges of over 1 km at relatively high survey speeds (Jollymore 1974).

One of the major limitations of echo sounder systems was an inability to acoustically penetrate hard gravel and till seabeds. To meet this challenge, R. Hutchins of Huntec '70 Limited, with advice and assistance from government, successfully developed a broad-band acoustic boomer sub-bottom profiling system — the Huntec Deep Tow High Resolution Seismic system (Huntec DTS; for details, see McKeown et al. 2014). Acoustic data from the Huntec system allowed marine geologists to differentiate and map all of the surficial sediment units above bedrock, to develop the 'till-tongue model' that referred to a sedimentary record of ice advance and retreat (King and Fader 1986), and ultimately to unravel the history of glacier advance and retreat in offshore Canada.

ALONG COMES MULTIBEAM

In the 1980s and 1990s, a need arose for a higher resolution understanding of seabed morphologies, materials, and processes to: safely develop offshore hydrocarbon resources, understand the relationship between fish and bottom habitat, and sustainably manage the offshore using an ecosystem approach as adopted by Canada's Oceans Act. Owing to these requirements, a revolution in the technology and understanding of the seabed based on the application of multibeam bathymetric surveying has occurred over the past two decades. This revolution resulted from the merging of three technologies: large powerful computers, precision navigation systems using GPS (Global Positioning System), and the development of multibeam sonar hardware to emit precise sound signals that cover large swaths of seabed. The multibeam sonar systems for use in Canadian Atlantic waters were initially introduced by the CHS at BIO (MacDougall 2014).

Accurate ship-motion sensors were also required to remove unwanted artifacts from the data. The Ocean Mapping Group at the University of New Brunswick (OMG-UNB) pioneered the development of these systems and worked closely with GSC marine geologists and CHS hydrographers at BIO (Loncarevic et al. 1992). What resulted from the integration of these technologies is sometimes termed 'sound images of the seabed'. The multibeam bathymetric images appear as if the water was drained and one is flying over the seabed with the sun setting at a low angle. It is a marine equivalent of aerial photography: i.e., technology that has been around for more than 70 years and which has revolutionized our understanding of the earth's surface, its geology, biology, and topography. The dramatic improvement in capturing seafloor detail is shown by comparing Figure 4A, an example of early mapping of a large sand wave feature termed a banner bank in the Bay of Fundy, and Figure 4B, a modern multibeam image over the same feature providing much greater detail.

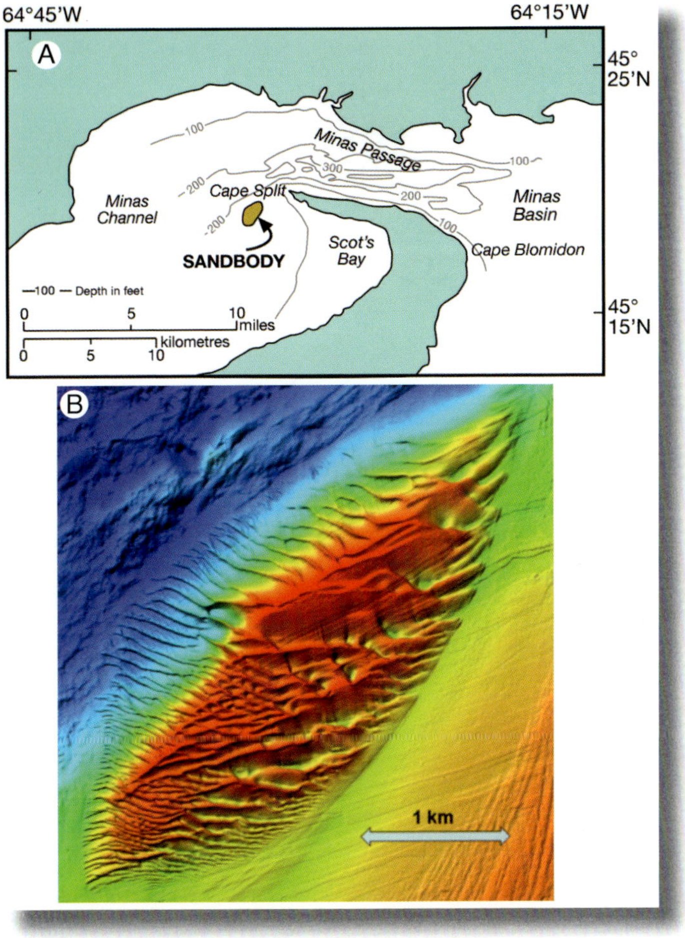

Figure 4. Comparison of early and multibeam maps of the Cape Split sand body in the Minas Channel area of Bay of Fundy: (A) areal distribution of asymmetric sand waves from eight seismic reflection profile lines in the 1960s by Huntec Ltd. (Swift et al. 1966), and (B) a multibeam bathymetric 3-D colour shaded-relief image surveyed in 2002 from CCGS *Frederick G. Creed*. The modern imagery shows many scales of sand megaripples and dunes in the feature now interpreted as a headland, gyre-controlled banner sand bank.

Presently, multibeam mapping has been conducted largely in the southern regions of Canadian waters, but the application of this technology is expanding rapidly to all regions. A multibeam imagery database, initiated in 2003 by ArcticNet (a network of universities for arctic studies, see http://www.arcticnet.ulaval.ca/index.php) and the OMG-UNB, has been steadily building on an annual basis for the Northwest Passage and other marine areas of the eastern Canadian arctic and the Beaufort Sea (MacLean et al. 2010). By 2012, 10% of the offshore had been mapped with multibeam systems and it is hoped that this coverage will rapidly expand in the future.

During the late 1970s and 1980s, as the first round of regional mapping of the southeastern Canadian continental shelf was nearing completion, marine geologists moved to more northern regions: G. Fader to the

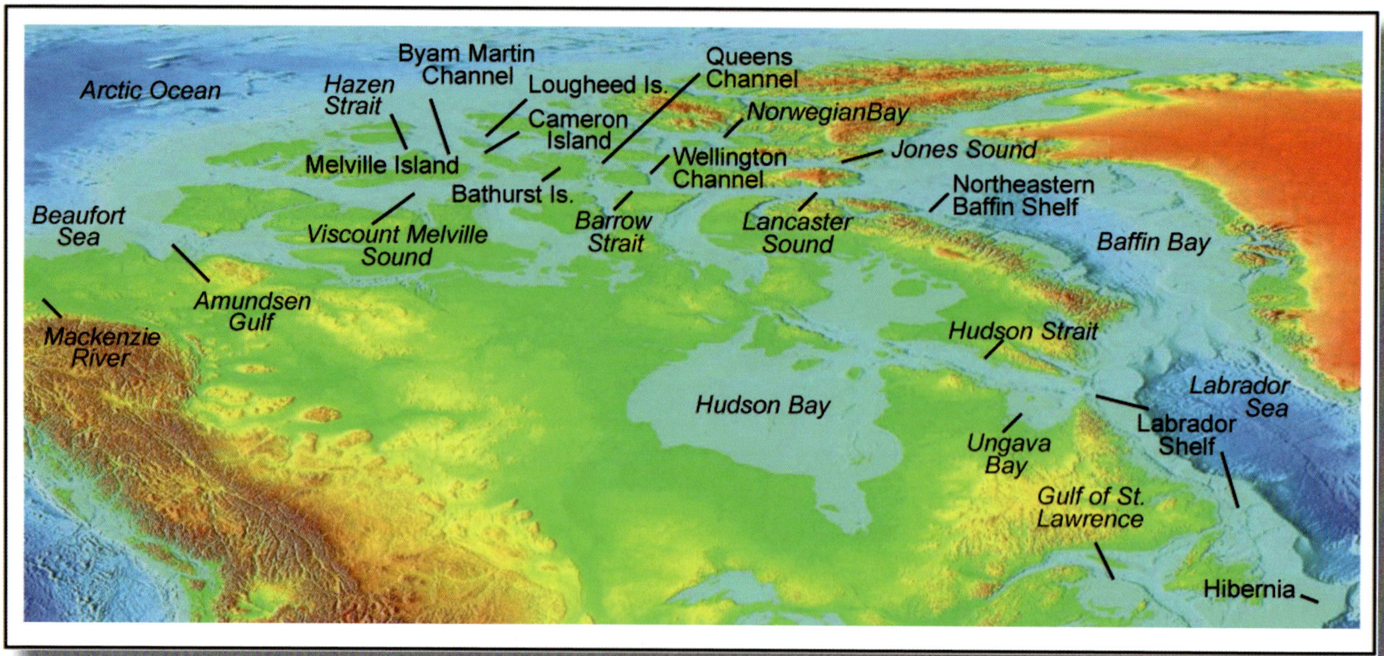

Figure 5. Oblique relief map of northern Canada illustrating locations of features named in the text (map base by J. Shaw, GSC-Atlantic, from US-NOAA 5 arc-minute global relief model: ETOPO5). Parry Channel in the Canadian Arctic Archipelago comprises Lancaster Sound, Barrow Strait, and Viscount Melville Sound as shown.

Grand Banks; B. MacLean to the Baffin Shelf, Hudson Strait, and high arctic regions; H. Josenhans to the Labrador Shelf and Hudson Bay; and S. Blasco to the Beaufort Sea and Great Lakes, where he worked in collaboration with M. Lewis (see Lewis et al. 2014a). M. Lewis and G. Sonnichsen also undertook the investigation and compilation of iceberg scouring of the seafloor, and other constraints, on a regional basis, with initial emphasis on the Grand Banks of Newfoundland where the Hibernia hydrocarbon deposits were about to be developed (Sonnichsen 1994, Lewis et al. 2014b). These mapping efforts resulted in a multi-fold increase in knowledge of continental shelf regions in northern Canada (Sonnichsen and MacLean 1988).

THE LABRADOR SHELF

Regional mapping of the unconsolidated sediments of the Labrador Shelf (Fig. 5) by H. Josenhans began in the early 1980s. Frontier oil exploration in northern areas had underscored the oil industry's need for a better understanding of the nature and thickness of the surficial sediments. The industry was obliged to carry out detailed and expensive site-specific studies of sediment character and thickness in order to determine its potential impact on rig anchors and the subsurface drilling methods to be used. These localized site surveys were often unable to clearly define the subsurface stratigraphy. Improvements in acoustic surveying tools, such as the Huntec Deep Tow Seismic system (McKeown et al. 2014), combined with the regional surveys carried out by the BIO teams, provided the essential geological framework and defined the origin of the surficial sediments and depth to bedrock. This information was published in detailed maps (Josenhans and Zevenhuizen 1989), and in scientific publications which described the geological history of the mapped units (Josenhans et al. 1986). Sediments deposited beneath a glacier (tills) containing boulders lie above the bedrock surfaces which have been intensely eroded and sculpted by multiple and extensive glacial advances. These tills were deposited beneath and in front of massive glaciers which covered the Labrador Shelf and its deep troughs, extending into water depths of 500-700 m. At least three successive deposits of till have been identified and mapped, and these are locally up to 60 m in composite thickness (Josenhans et al. 1986). As ice ages ended and conditions warmed, glaciers retreated from the shelf edge and broke into massive icebergs which dispersed in a southerly direction. Some of the largest icebergs were over 700 m thick and carved massive grooves into the till surfaces (Josenhans and Barrie 1982). These grooves can be seen at the seabed to this day as iceberg furrows. Melting of these icebergs also resulted in dropping of the glacier bedload, including large boulders (ice-rafted debris). Large volumes of fine-grained sediments suspended in meltwater were discharged from glacial ice margins. The resultant fine sediment blanket and ice-rafted debris forms stratified layers above the glacial tills that are termed glaciomarine sediments. These layered silty muds are generally confined to the deep troughs of the Labrador Shelf and locally reach a thickness of 30 m. Muddy sediments deposited after retreat of the last glacial advance overlie the glaciomarine sediment sequence, but these are confined to the deepest shelf troughs and rarely exceed 15 m in thickness (Josenhans et al. 1986).

Three prominent tills were mapped on the Labrador Shelf that confirmed glacier advances across the shelf (Josenhans et al. 1986). The lower till extended to the shelf edge, whereas the upper till is restricted to the inner shelf, marginal trough, and inter-bank saddles. The youngest Hudson Strait Till is confined to the northern part of Saglek Bank (northernmost Labrador Shelf), spilling out from Hudson Strait (Josenhans and Zevenhuizen 1989). An important component of detrital carbonate sediment occurs in the overlying Qeovik Silt, but not in the underlying tills, which suggested that this component was sourced from the north and not the region of Hudson Strait, although recent interpretation suggests the carbonate source was in Hudson Bay and was transported through Hudson Strait by catastrophic drainages of meltwater and glacial lakes (Fig. 5; Lewis et al. 2012). An ice shelf did not form on the Labrador Shelf during ice recession which is in sharp contrast to the southern offshore areas of Canada, such as the Scotian Shelf, where interbedded tills and glaciomarine sediments are common, and locally derived glaciomarine sediments are thick (Josenhans and Fader 1989).

HUDSON BAY AND GULF OF ST. LAWRENCE

Regional surficial geological and bedrock surveys of Hudson Bay followed the Labrador Shelf surveys and began in the late 1980s (Fig. 5). These surveys were aided by investigations carried out earlier by CHS which collected 11,000 line-km of near surface (3.5 kHz) seismic profiles in addition to echo-sounding data for water depth determination. This grid of parallel seismic profiles was spaced 440 m apart and used to supplement more deeply penetrating, widely-spaced regional seismic lines. The data allowed improved insight into the surface morphology, distribution, and local architecture of the surficial sediments (Zevenhuizen and Josenhans 1990).

Hudson Bay experienced multiple glacial episodes similar to the Labrador Shelf, and a similar sequence of tills, and glaciomarine stratified sediments with localized pockets of surficial muds was deposited. Generally, the unconsolidated sediment sequence is thinner in this large bay than it is on the continental shelves, possibly due to a very rapid retreat of the last glaciers which had insufficient time to deposit thick sediment sequences (Josenhans et al. 1988). Detailed sediment mapping shows subglacial erosional channels cut into the underlying limestone bedrock, well-preserved ice flow and ice retreat features such as de Geer moraines (sub-parallel, small till ridges deposited at subaqueous ice margins, possibly annually), and massive iceberg scours which must have been formed by very large tabular icebergs that calved off a rapidly retreating ice margin. Land-based studies of Quaternary sediments combined with the offshore evidence also suggested that Hudson Bay may have changed rapidly from being largely covered by grounded glacial ice to being free of ice (Josenhans and Zevenhuizen 1990, Josenhans 1997).

H. Josenhans then moved his studies to the Gulf of St. Lawrence (Fig. 5), and following on the earlier mapping by D. Loring (Loring and Nota 1973) who had concentrated on the geochemistry of sediments, unraveled the complex history of ice advance and retreat across the region. Using the high-resolution Huntec DTS and critically-positioned cores, the timing of a step-wise retreat of ice from the Laurentian Channel to the adjacent shallower shelf regions was determined (Josenhans and Lehman 1998).

BAFFIN SHELF, HUDSON STRAIT, AND THE HIGH ARCTIC

Early geophysical investigations in the southeastern Baffin Island and eastern Hudson Strait – Ungava Bay regions by A. Grant and K. Manchester, and on adjacent Labrador Sea regions by D. Ross, S. Srivastava, and others in the early 1970s, were followed in the mid-1970s through to the early 1990s by extensive investigations of the bedrock and Quaternary geology of the Baffin Shelf, Hudson Strait, and inter-island channels of the Canadian Arctic Archipelago (Fig. 5). This work was conducted primarily from CSS *Hudson* and, as was done in southern areas, each cruise collected data pertaining to both the bedrock and surficial sediment.

The emphasis from 1975 to 1985 was primarily on delineating bedrock units by means of seismic reflection and magnetometer systems, and sampling those units by core-hole drilling with the BIO underwater electric rock core drill (for details, see MacLean et al. 2014). Air gun seismic reflection and Huntec DTS systems were the main tools to locate drill sites. They, and sidescan sonar systems in conjunction with piston corers and grab samplers, were the primary tools used for investigations of the surficial geology. Results were published in geological maps and reports (e.g., MacLean et al. 1989, 2001; Praeg et al. 1986).

At the same time as the explorations were beginning off Baffin Island, investigations of glacial history were underway by the GSC at BIO and onshore by other institutions. Principal among the latter were researchers from the Institute of Arctic and Alpine Research (INSTAAR) at the University of Colorado. As both groups were involved in studies of the Quaternary record in the region, close cooperation developed and INSTAAR researchers became more involved in, and contributed to, the offshore studies. This was well illustrated during collaborative studies of Hudson Strait (Fig. 5) with scientists from INSTAAR (J. Andrews, A. Jennings, W. Manley, G. Miller, and T. Pfeffer), and by J. Gray from the University of Montreal who was studying the Quaternary record on the southern sides of Hudson Strait and Ungava Bay (Fig. 5), a partnership that produced many scientific successes (e.g., Vilks et al. 1989, MacLean et al. 2001, Andrews and MacLean 2003). Figure 6 illustrates a moraine formed by a late readvance of glacial ice in south-central Hudson Strait identified during those collaborative studies.

Superimposed glacial deposits in Hudson Strait document the former presence of at least six glacial ice streams (Fig. 5; Andrews and MacLean 2003). Some of these extended to the edge of the shelf and discharged large quantities of sediment, meltwater, and icebergs into the Labrador Sea (Fig. 5) and North Atlantic at 7,000-year intervals which

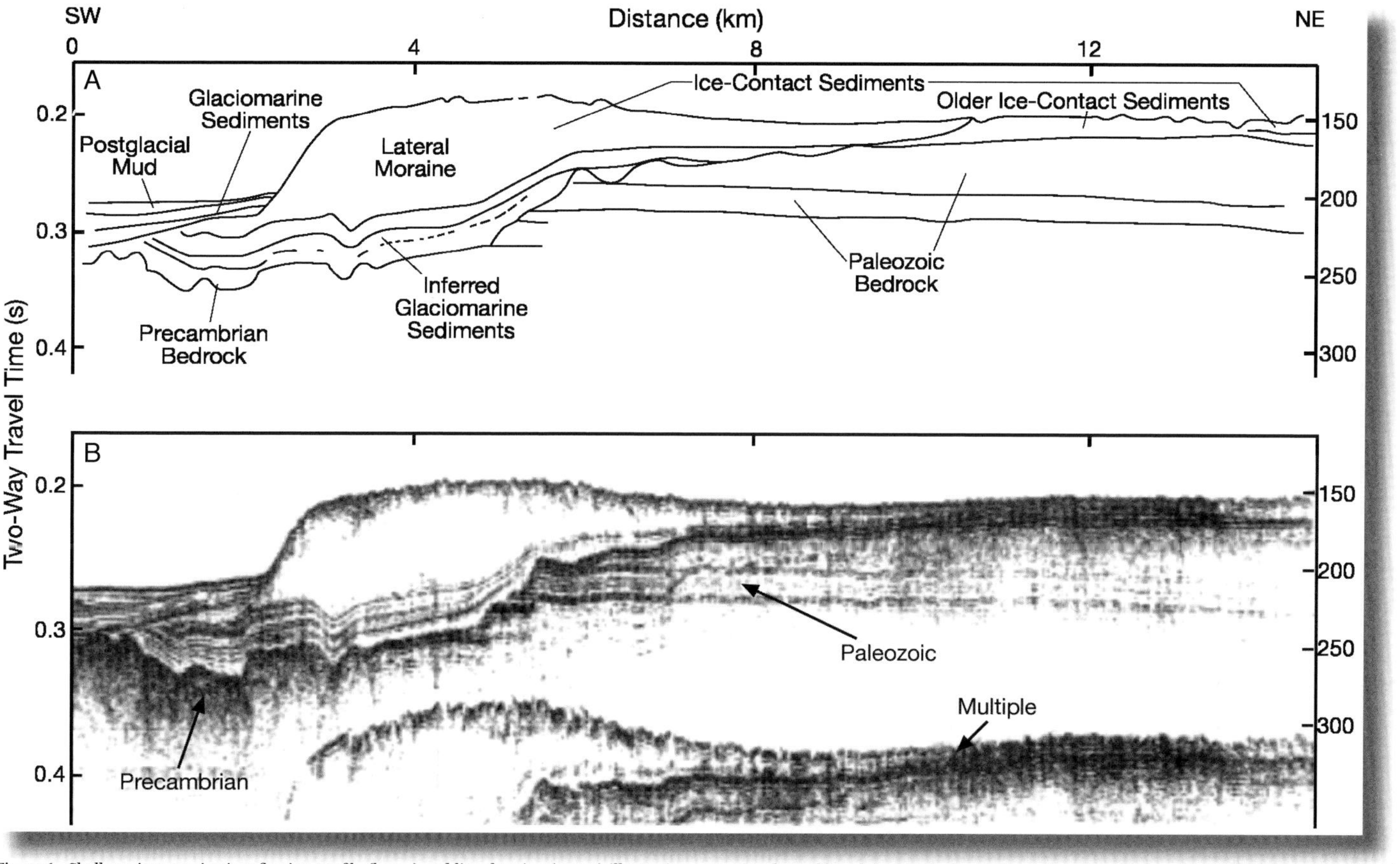

Figure 6. Shallow air gun seismic reflection profile (lower) and line drawing (upper) illustrating a moraine formed by a late glacial advance in south central Hudson Strait, depth in metres at right (from MacLean 1997).

became known as 'Heinrich Events', based on ice-rafted debris in North Atlantic sediments determined by marine geologist H. Heinrich to have come from Hudson Bay (Fig. 5; Heinrich 1988). During such events, armadas of icebergs broke off from Hudson Strait glaciers and traversed the North Atlantic. Rock fragments eroded by the glaciers were carried in the floating icebergs, and were dropped onto the seafloor as 'ice-rafted debris' as the icebergs melted. The discharges from Hudson Strait are considered to be the primary sources for six distinct carbonate-rich layers (labelled H1 to H6) in Labrador Sea and northwest North Atlantic sediments (Andrews and MacLean 2003). The volumes of meltwater discharged into the Labrador Sea and North Atlantic from the ice streams and from the later drainage of a large ice-dammed lake into Hudson Bay are considered to have affected climatic conditions (Broecker 1994, Barber et al. 1999).

In 1976, a submarine oil seep that formed a surface oil slick was discovered on the northeastern Baffin Shelf during geophysical surveys of Baffin Bay (Fig. 5; Falconer and Loncarevic 1977). It was extensively examined during subsequent years by geological and geophysical investigations in conjunction with chemical oceanographic studies at BIO (Levy and Ehrhardt 1981). Investigations also included visual examination and sampling of the seafloor in the seep area from the manned research submersible *Pisces IV*, and recently, using multibeam imagery, and an ROV (i.e., remotely operated vehicle) from CCGS *Amundsen*. The seep is continually active, and is important from a petroleum-potential perspective because it indicates that conditions favourable for the generation of hydrocarbons existed in Baffin Bay during the Upper Cretaceous (65+ million years ago; MacLean et al. 2014).

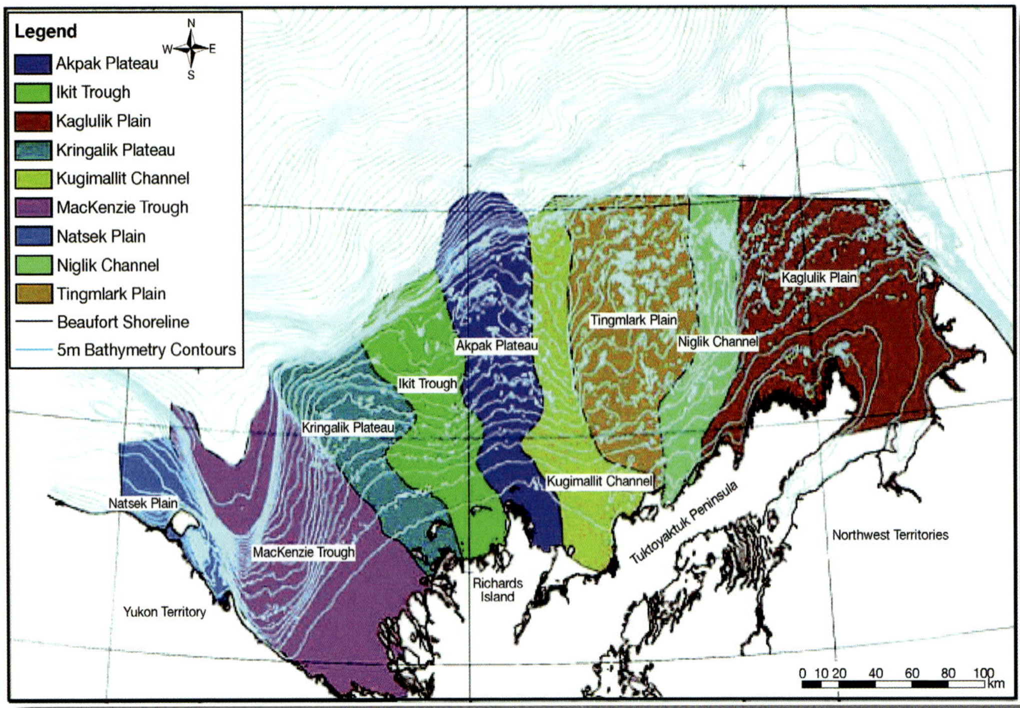

Figure 8. Bathymetric and physiographic map of the Canadian Beaufort Sea showing nine areal units differentiated by distinct geological and physical properties resulting from processes of deglacial meltwater drainage, sea-level rise, marine sedimentation, and ice-seabed interaction since the last glacial maximum about 19,000 years ago (from Blasco et al. 2013). Water depth contour intervals of 5 m on the shelf, e.g., to 120 km north of Richards Island, and 50 m north of the shelf.

Figure 7. A temporary halt during seismic surveying operations in an ice lead near Cameron Island (Fig. 5), Canadian Arctic Archipelago, July 1987; T. Atkinson is the survey team member on board the inflatable boat (photo: G. Sonnichsen).

Early studies of seafloor geology in the Canadian high arctic included investigations in Barrow Strait (Fig. 5) and parts of adjacent channels by Lewis et al. (1977), and of potential pipeline crossing sites by Polar Gas. Geological studies of Jones Sound (Fig. 5) were conducted during a CHS cruise aboard CSS *Baffin* in 1983. Ice conditions were bad throughout the six weeks CSS *Baffin* was there, but an overview of the seafloor geology was obtained (MacLean et al. 1984). The following year similar investigations of the seafloor geology were conducted in Norwegian Bay (Fig. 5), also during a CHS-led cruise aboard CSS *Baffin*.

In the mid-1980s, studies were begun of the seafloor geology in other inter-island channels of the Canadian Arctic Archipelago as part of the Northern Oil and Gas Action Plan (NOGAP). These included helicopter-supported sediment sampling through holes drilled in the ice in the northern extension of the Byam Martin Channel region from a base at the Pan Arctic Oils Limited Bent Horn oil field on Cameron Island (Fig. 5). G. Vilks had done similar work in the 1960s in the adjoining Hazen Strait region northwest of Melville Island (Fig. 5). Helicopter-supported expeditions were continued in 1985 and 1986 (Sonnichsen and MacLean 1988) using leads in the permanent ice cover to survey and sample seafloor sediments in this general region (Fig. 7). This was the first time such work had been attempted. The surveys were conducted from a small inflatable boat equipped with seismic profiling and satellite navigation systems. Crews and the inflatable boat were transported from a base camp on Lougheed Island (Fig. 5) and from lead to lead by a helicopter provided by the Polar Continental Shelf Project (PCSP). Continuous 24-hour daylight allowed the survey activities to go on without interruption. Also, as part of the Northern Oil and Gas Action Plan (NOGAP), extensive seismic surveys and sediment sampling were conducted in 1986 from CSS *Hudson* in ship-accessible areas of Barrow Strait, western Lancaster Sound, Wellington, Queens, Parry and Byam Martin channels, and northern Viscount Melville Sound (Fig. 5; MacLean et al. 1989). This work showed the ubiquitous presence of till in the channel floors and demonstrated that glaciomarine and postglacial sediments are very limited in their occurrence. R. Taylor (GSC Atlantic) and D. Hodgson (GSC Terrain Sciences Division) carried out investigations of coastal and terrestrial geology from the ship using CSS *Hudson's* helicopter. The CSS *Hudson* also served as a platform for biological and water studies by E. Head of Fisheries and Oceans Canada at BIO, and heat flow studies by A. Taylor of Energy Mines and Resources Canada, Ottawa, ON.

Multibeam and 3.5 kHz sub-bottom profiler transects were obtained by ArcticNet and the OMG-UNB from CCGC *Amundsen* from 2003 to 2011. This work, supported by the Natural Sciences and Engineering Research Council (NSERC), provided information on the regional distribution of seafloor sediments, evidence of ice keel interaction with the seabed, and on foundation conditions in many of the channels in the

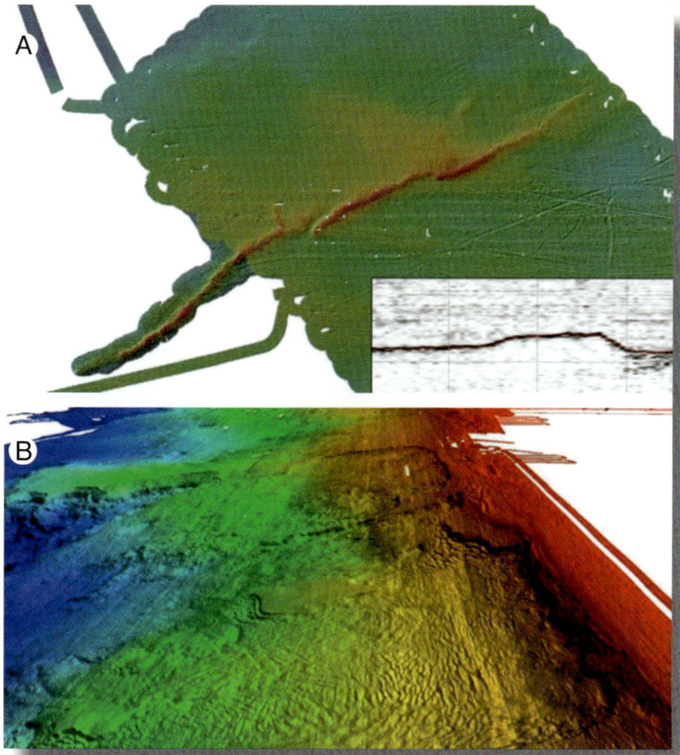

Figure 9. Multibeam sonar images of the Canadian Beaufort seabed (from Blasco et al. 2013): (A) a raised linear feature that is a possible paleo shoreline at a depth of 80 m – observed shoreline segment is 8 km long, 150 m wide, and 5 m high; the cross-section profile, lower right shows the asymmetry of the feature with its steep side facing north, towards the top of the multibeam image; and an intersecting pattern of ice scours is also evident, mainly south of the paleo shoreline. (B) upper part of the continental slope looking east, illustrating the occurrence of submarine landslides exposed on the seabed in an area of 100 km by 60 km – water depths range from 100 m at the shelf edge to the south (orange) to 1,200 m down slope (blue); seismic profiles show that the illustrated seafloor topography is repeated at depth where older submarine landslides have been infilled by successive slope failures.

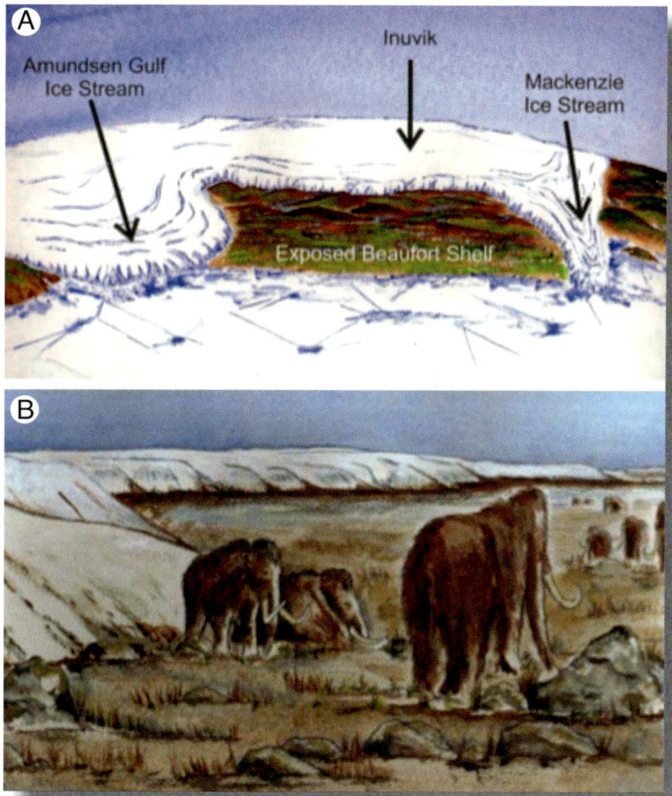

Figure 10. Paleo-reconstruction of the exposed Beaufort Sea Shelf during the Last Glacial Maximum 19,000 years ago (from Blasco et al. 2013; artwork: K. McClemment): (A) the shelf was subaerially exposed to present water depths of 100-130 m - ice streams from the Laurentide ice sheet extended down the Mackenzie Trough and Amundsen Gulf; exposed area between ice streams was ca. 400 by 100 km. (B) Beaufort Shelf ecosystem ca. 19,000 years ago illustrating the ice front and an ecological refugium populated by Woolly Mammoth (*Mammuthus primigenius*) and other animals that survived on herb tundra vegetation.

Canadian Arctic Archipelago. Parallel linear ridge and groove features preserved on the seafloor in many channels document the former presence of fast-moving glacial ice streams (MacLean et al. 2010).

CANADIAN BEAUFORT SEA

Seabed sediment mapping of the Canadian Beaufort Sea (Figs. 5 and 8) has been conducted from a variety of research vessels. BIO-directed research was initiated with the '*Hudson*-70' expedition (Wadhams 2009, 2014). CSS *Hudson* conducted bathymetric, shallow seismic, and sediment coring operations across the Beaufort Shelf and down slope under the direction of B. Pelletier. The survey was assisted by the CSS *Richardson* that conducted bathymetric and sidescan surveys under the direction of J. Shearer. CCGS *Nahidik* became the survey platform from 1976 through 1990 and again from 2001 through 2009. CCGS *Nahidik* field programs acquired single beam and multibeam bathymetric data, sidescan sonar, and subbottom and shallow seismic profiles augmented by box and gravity sediment coring operations. Since then, BIO-supported activity in the Beaufort Sea has been conducted solely from the CCGS *Amundsen* in collaboration with ArcticNet, Imperial Oil Ltd., and BP Resources. CCGS *Amundsen* field activities acquired multibeam sonar, subbottom profiles, box, and gravity and piston sediment cores. CCGS *Nahidik* field work was directed by K. Moran, P. Hill, and S. Blasco; CCGS *Amundsen* field operations were directed by S. Blasco. Two-dimensional single beam sonar mapping used since 1970 was augmented by 3-D multibeam sonar in 2001, which facilitated the interpretation of seabed topography and shelf/slope processes.

Knowledge of the geological history and processes active on the Beaufort Shelf and upper slope over the last 25,000 years started with the '*Hudson*-70' expedition. Vilks et al. (1979) published many of the scientific discoveries of this survey. The shelf is dominated by a thin layer of silty clay sediment deposited over the last 10,000 years: Mackenzie River sediment outflow is transported to the east along the coast then west along the outer shelf – an anticlockwise circulation pattern that may have been in place for the last 5,000 years. Sedimentological and faunal evidence suggested paleoshorelines may be preserved on the seabed, and recent 3-D multibeam sonar imagery of a relict shoreline has confirmed this suspicion (Fig. 9A). Paleoenvironmental evidence indicated *in situ* estuarine coastal deposits were present within deep-water sediments. These results were supported by the publication of the first sea-level curve constrained by radiocarbon data for the Beaufort Shelf by Hill et al. (1985), and updated in Hill et al. (1993). Relative sea level was discovered to be rising at an average rate of 7 m per 1,000 years for the last 6,000 years or more. The determination of absolute sea-level rise is complicated by poorly constrained Beaufort-Mackenzie basin subsidence rates, isostatic forebulge effects and global eustatic changes. Pelletier's (1984, 1987) two marine science atlases clearly illustrate the '*Hudson*-70' expedition's discoveries in a comprehensive series of maps, cross-sections, and schematic drawings.

The first comprehensive interpretation of shelf history over the last 25,000 years was published by Blasco et al. (1990), and updated in Blasco et al. (2013). The discovery that the evolution of the shelf is dominated by glacial/interglacial processes and not, as previously believed, delta-dominated fluvial processes related to Mackenzie River outflow was an unanticipated finding. The regional synthesis of geological, geophysical, and geotechnical data led to the discovery that the main shelf was subaerially exposed during the last glacial maximum 19,000 years ago. The exposed shelf was bracketed by ice streams in the Mackenzie Trough and Amundsen Gulf (Fig. 10A) and, like other arctic regions, was a mammal refugium (Fig. 10B; Harrington 2005). The shelf was subsequently flooded with glacial outwash sand as massive amounts of meltwater and sediments drained from the ablating Laurentide ice sheet. The rise of sea level overstepped these terrestrial sands and led to the deposition of thin transgressive interbedded sands and silty clays, followed by marine silty clays as the shelf became inundated by sea water from 12,000 years ago to present. Unlike other major river deltas like the Mississippi River delta, the Mackenzie River delta is not expanding seaward, but has been retreating since sea level began to rise following glaciation. Current coastal retreat rates range from 0.6 m to 22.5 m per year (Solomon 2005).

Seabed topography is dominated by four cross-shelf linear meltwater channels eroded into the outwash sands by meltwater discharge during the last phases of deglaciation about 12,000 years ago. The topography of these channels has been reduced by the subsequent differential infilling by transgressive and marine sediments, but are still evident in the present bathymetry where they are identified as troughs and channels (Fig. 8).

The major topographic feature that disrupts the continuity of the low gradient Beaufort Shelf is the Mackenzie Trough (Fig. 8). Excavated by at least two ice streams in the last 70,000 years or more (Blasco et al. 1990), the Trough has been infilled by more than 400 m of sediment. Over 125 m of this infill occurred since the retreat of the last ice stream about 13,000 years ago (Hill et al. 2001, Dyke et al. 2003.). Mackenzie River sediment discharge took almost 10,000 years to fill the Trough to the point where sediments suspended in water currents could overflow the eastern edge of the Trough and be transported eastward along the coast. The mapping of seabed sediment properties and their distribution, coupled with seabed topography, led to the subdivision of the shelf into nine physiographic regions, each with distinct characteristics (Fig. 8; Blasco et al. 2013). This map served as a base for the geological framework provided to the National Energy Board of Canada and the oil industry to guide future Beaufort Sea hydrocarbon exploration, and as a base for understanding seabed geohazards (Lewis et al. 2014b).

The recent extension of seabed mapping from outer shelf to upper slope indicates the history of the seabed over the last 25,000 years is dominated by distal submarine glacial outwash deposits, meltwater channels, and marine clays that have been spatially and temporally subjected to submarine landslide processes and the redeposition of these sediments as mass transport deposits (Fig. 9B; Blasco et al. 2013, Mosher et al. 2011).

In hindsight, BIO-driven seabed mapping in the Canadian Beaufort Sea has been the primary source of new discoveries and the scientific advancement of the knowledge of an arctic glaciated shelf. The extension of mapping into deeper waters down slope provides the opportunity for new and exciting discoveries.

THE PATH TO THE FUTURE

The early mapping and research on the seabed and sediments off southeastern Canada was truly pioneering work that led the way for both Canadian and global seabed mapping activities. The discovery of previously unknown seabed features and research on their origins helped advance the science of marine geology and provided a comprehensive understanding of the geological history of the Canadian offshore. The application of this knowledge to many offshore projects provided the fundamental underpinning for safe and environmentally responsible development. Mapping undertaken on a systematic and regional basis meant that those developing new projects or dealing with unforeseen disasters could always depend on having some degree of previous knowledge for their planning and response. The experience gained in the southern waters also helped many of the geoscientists as they moved northward in their research, and the legacy of this experience is expected to continue to support future seabed mapping in frontier and northern areas.

The development of multibeam bathymetry in the 1990s and its ability to provide continuous high resolution imagery of the seafloor heralded a revolution in seabed mapping (Courtney and Fader 1994, Pickrill et al. 2014). Most multibeam bathymetric surveys in new regions have produced new findings about the seabed and allowed marine geological science to grow to new levels of understanding. Growing interest in the offshore has demanded high-resolution imagery and understanding of the seabed for the benefit of the many sectors that operate there. The older maps and reports still have value, but they no longer answer all the needs of the biological, engineering, and fishing communities who require resolution of seafloor features as small as 10 cm. The value of the older maps lies in their regional coverage, context for local detailed surveys, and in the stratigraphic framework they provide for understanding the geological history. Now is the time to remap the entire offshore of Canada using the new high-resolution survey tools. Although multibeam bathymetric mapping has covered large areas in the southern regions, these areas represent less than 10% of the total Canadian offshore. A high-resolution image database of surficial sediments and sedimentological processes is necessary for adequate insight and understanding of the offshore seabed and its associated resources, knowledge that is essential for safe and sustainable development.

ACKNOWLEDGEMENTS

We acknowledge L.H. King and B.R. Pelletier for their pioneering contributions and leadership in the fields of seabed sediment mapping and marine geology. We recognize the Canadian Hydrographic Service at BIO and the Ocean Mapping Group at University of New Brunswick (Fredericton, NB) for their contributions in marine survey and acoustic mapping expertise which have significantly aided our progress in these fields. We are indebted to all of the individuals listed below for their contribution to this work. However, we would be remiss not to single out Gus Vilks and Bhan Deonarine for their significant paleoceanographic and biostratigraphic contributions to these investigations. Very special thanks are also extended to the following for their excellent cooperation and assistance: Captains D. Deer, F. Mauger, L. Strum, and J. Lewis, other officers and crew members of CSS *Hudson*, as well as the officers and crews of CCGS *Nahidik* and *Amundsen*; and to technical and scientific contributors: John Andrews, Tony Atkinson, Darrell Beaver, Roger Belanger, Kelly Bentham, George Bika, Austin Boyce, Bill Briggs, Borden Chapman, Vern Coady, Art Cosgrove, Tom Courtney, Claudia Currie, Guy Fenn, Norman Fenerty, Paul Girouard, Mike Gorveatt, Jim Gray, Iris Hardy, Bob Harmes, Phil Hill, Doug Hodgson, Mike Hughes, Kate Jarrett, Anne Jennings, Fred Jodrey, Larry Johnston, Francis Kelly, Bill LeBlanc, Don Locke, Bill Manley, Susan Merchant, Bob Miller, Kate Moran, Peta Mudie, Bob Murphy, Jess Nielsen, Patrick Potter, Dan Praeg, Kevin Robertson, Andy Sherin, Gary Sonnichsen, Roy Sparkes, Graham Standen, Bob Taylor, Martin Uyesugi, Nancy Weiner, and John Zevenhuizen. We also wish to thank the many students we were fortunate to have worked with over the years of seabed mapping.

REFERENCES

Andrews, J.T. and B. MacLean. 2003. Hudson Strait ice streams: a review of stratigraphy, chronology and links with North Atlantic Heinrich events. Boreas 32: 4-17.

Barber, D.C., A. Dyke, C. Hillaire-Marcel, A.E. Jennings, J.T. Andrews, M.W. Kerwin, G. Bilodeau, R. McNeely, J. Southon, M.D. Morehead, and J.-M. Gagnon. 1999. Forcing of the cold event of 8,200 years ago by catastrophic drainage of Laurentide lakes. Nature 400: 344-348.

Blasco, S.M., G. Fortin, P.R. Hill, M.J. O'Connor, and J. Brigham-Grette. 1990. The Late Quaternary stratigraphy of the Canadian Beaufort continental shelf in the Arctic Ocean Region. Pages 491-502 *in* The Geology of North America, Volume L (A. Grantz, L. Johnson, and J.F. Sweeny, Eds.). Geological Society of America, Boulder, CO.

Blasco S.M. and others. 2013. State of knowledge: Beaufort Sea seabed geohazards associated with offshore hydrocarbon development. Geological Survey of Canada, Open File 6989, Ottawa, ON.

Broecker, W.S. 1994. Massive iceberg discharges as triggers for global climate change. Nature 372: 421-424.

Courtney, R. C. and G.B.J. Fader. 1994. A new understanding of the ocean floor through multibeam mapping. Pages 9-14 *in* Science Review 1992 & '93 of the Bedford Institute of Oceanography, Halifax Fisheries Research Laboratory, and the St. Andrews Biological Station (A. Fiander, Ed.). Fisheries and Oceans Canada, Bedford Institute of Oceanography, Dartmouth, NS.

Dyke, A.S., A. Moore, and L. Robertson. 2003. Deglaciation of North America. Geological Survey of Canada, Open File 1574, Ottawa, ON.

Fader, G.B.J., T. Lynds, R.O. Miller, D.R. Parrott, S. Hynes, and A. Sherin. 2004. Scotian Shelf regional surficial geology compilation. Geological Survey of Canada, Open File 4671, Ottawa, ON.

Falconer, R.K. and B.D. Loncarevic. 1977. An oil slick occurrence off Baffin Island. Pages 523-524 *in* Report of Activities, Part A. Geological Survey of Canada, Paper 77-1A, Ottawa, ON.

Grant, S.T., N. Stuifbergen, and R.M. Eaton. 2014. Loran-C at the Bedford Institute of Oceanography. Pages 349-352 *in* Voyage of Discovery: Fifty Years of Marine Research at Canada's Bedford Institute of Oceanography (D.N. Nettleship, D.C. Gordon, C.F.M. Lewis, and M.P. Latremouille, Eds.). Bedford Institute of Oceanography-Oceans Association, Dartmouth, NS.

Harington, C.R. 2005. The eastern limit of Beringia: mammoth remains from Banks and Melville islands, Northwest Territories. Arctic 58: 361–369.

Heinrich, H. 1988. Origin and consequences of cyclic ice rafting in the Northeast Atlantic Ocean during the past 130,000 years. Quaternary Research 29: 142-152.

Hill P.R., P.J. Mudie, K. Moran, and S.M. Blasco. 1985. A sea-level curve for the Canadian Beaufort shelf. Canadian Journal of Earth Sciences 22: 1,383-1,393.

Hill, P.R., A. Héquette, and M-H. Ruz. 1993. Holocene sea-level history of the Canadian Beaufort Shelf. Canadian Journal of Earth Sciences 30: 103-108.

Hill, P.R., C.P. Lewis, S. Desmarais, V. Kauppaymuthoo, and H. Rais. 2001. The Mackenzie Delta: sedimentary processes and facies of a high-latitude, fine-grained delta. Sedimentology 48: 1,047-1,078.

Hovland, M. and A.G. Judd. 1988. Seabed Pockmarks and Seepages: Impact on Geology, Biology, and the Marine Environment. Graham and Trotman, London, England.

Jollymore, P.G. 1974. A medium range side-scan sonar for use in coastal waters; design criteria and operational experiences. Pages 108-114 *in* Oceans'74, Proceedings of the IEEE (Institute of Electrical and Electronic Engineers) International Conference on Engineering in the Ocean Environment, Volume II, Halifax, NS. IEEE, New York, NY.

Josenhans, H. 1997. Glacial sole markings on bedrock and till in Hudson Bay, Canada. Pages 46-47 *in* Glaciated Continental Margins: An Atlas of Acoustic Images (T.A. Davies, T. Bell, A.K. Cooper, H. Josenhans, L. Polyak, A. Solheim, M.S. Stoker, J.A. Stravers, Eds.). Chapman and Hall, London, England.

Josenhans, H.W. and J.V. Barrie. 1982. Preliminary results of submersible observations on the Labrador Shelf. Pages 269-276 *in* Current Research Part C. Geological Survey of Canada, Paper 82-1B, Ottawa, ON.

Josenhans, H.W. and G.B.J. Fader. 1989. A comparison of models of glacial sedimentation along the Eastern Canadian Margin. Marine Geology 85: 273-300.

Josenhans, H.W. and J. Zevenhuizen. 1989. Quaternary geology 1, Labrador Sea, Quaternary history. Page 8 *in* Labrador Sea/Mer du Labrador (J.S.Bell, R.D. Howie, N.J. McMillan, C.M. Hawkin, and J.L. Bates, Eds.). Geological Survey of Canada, East Coast Basin Atlas Series, Dartmouth, NS.

Josenhans, H.W. and J. Zevenhuizen. 1990. Dynamics of the Laurentide ice sheet in Hudson Bay, Canada. Marine Geology 92: 1-26.

Josenhans, H. and S. Lehman. 1998. Late glacial stratigraphy and history of the Gulf of St. Lawrence, Canada. Canadian Journal of Earth Sciences 36: 1,327–1,345.

Josenhans, H., J. Zevenhuizen, and R.A. Klassen. 1986. The Quaternary geology of the Labrador Shelf. Canadian Journal of Earth Sciences 23: 1,190-1,213.

Josenhans, H., S. Balzer, P. Henderson, E. Nielson, H. Thorleifson, and J. Zevenhuizen. 1988. Preliminary seismostratigraphic and geomorphic interpretations of the Quaternary sediments of Hudson Bay. Pages 271-286 *in* Current Research Part B: Eastern and Atlantic Canada. Geological Survey of Canada, Paper 88-1B, Ottawa, ON.

King, L.H. 1967. Use of a conventional echosounder and textural analyses in delineating sedimentary facies – Scotian Shelf. Canadian Journal of Earth Sciences 4: 691-708.

King, L.H. and B. MacLean. 1970. Pockmarks on the Scotian Shelf. Bulletin of the Geological Society of America 81: 3,141 – 3,148.

King, L.H. and G.B.J. Fader. 1986. Wisconsinan Glaciation of the Atlantic Continental Shelf of Southeast Canada. Geological Survey of Canada, Bulletin 363, Ottawa, ON.

King, L.H., B. MacLean, and G. Drapeau. 1972. The Scotian Shelf submarine end-moraine complex. Pages 237-249 *in* Proceedings of the 24th International Geological Congress, Section 8, Marine Geology and Geophysics, Montreal, QC (J.W. Murray, B.R. Pelletier, and J.R. Luternauer, Eds.). International Geological Congress, EMR Canada, Ottawa, ON.

Levy, E.M. and M. Ehrhardt. 1981. Natural seepage of petroleum at Buchan Gulf, Baffin Island. Marine Chemistry 10: 355-364.

Lewis, C.F.M., S.M. Blasco, B.D. Bornhold, J.A.M. Hunter, A.S. Judge, J.W. Kerr, P. McLaren, and B.R. Pelletier. 1977. Marine geological and geophysical activities in Lancaster Sound and adjacent fiords. Pages 495-506 *in* Current Research, Part A. Geological Survey of Canada, Paper 77-1A, Ottawa, ON.

Lewis, C.F.M., A.A.L. Miller, E. Levac, D.J.W. Piper, and G.V. Sonnichsen. 2012. Lake Agassiz outburst age and routing by Labrador Current and the 8.2 cal ka cold event. Quaternary International 260: 83-97.

Lewis, C.F.M., B.J. Todd, S.M. Blasco, D.L. Forbes, G.D.M. Cameron, and E.L. King. 2014a. Marine geoscience and lakes. Pages 225-230 *in* Voyage of Discovery: Fifty Years of Marine Research at Canada's Bedford Institute of Oceanography (D.N. Nettleship, D.C. Gordon, C.F.M. Lewis, and M.P. Latremouille, Eds.). Bedford Institute of Oceanography-Oceans Association, Dartmouth, NS.

Lewis, C.F.M., S.M. Blasco, D.J.W. Piper, and G.V. Sonnichsen. 2014b. Seabed geohazard knowledge for safe hydrocarbon development. Pages 383-394 *in* Voyage of Discovery: Fifty Years of Marine Research at Canada's Bedford Institute of Oceanography (D.N. Nettleship, D.C. Gordon, C.F.M. Lewis, and M.P. Latremouille, Eds.). Bedford Institute of Oceanography-Oceans Association, Dartmouth, NS.

Loncarevic, B.D., D.J.W. Piper, and G.B.J. Fader. 1992. Application of high-quality bathymetry to geological interpretation on the Scotian Shelf. Geoscience Canada 19: 5-13.

Loring, D. and D.J.G. Nota. 1973. Morphology and sediments of the Gulf of Saint Lawrence. Bulletin of the Fisheries Research Board of Canada, Vol. 182. Fisheries and Marine Service, Ottawa, ON.

MacDougall, J.R. 2014. Hydrography: a foundation for multidisciplinary ocean science at the Bedford Institute of Oceanography, 1962-2012. Pages 169-180 *in* Voyage of Discovery: Fifty Years of Marine Research at Canada's Bedford Institute of Oceanography (D.N. Nettleship, D.C. Gordon, C.F.M. Lewis, and M.P. Latremouille, Eds.). Bedford Institute of Oceanography-Oceans Association, Dartmouth, NS.

MacLean, B. 1997. Submarine lateral moraine in the south central region of Hudson Strait, Canada. Pages 86-87 *in* Glaciated Continental Margins: An Atlas of Acoustic Images (T.A. Davies, T. Bell, A.K. Cooper, H. Josenhans, L. Polyak, A. Solheim, M.S. Stoker, and J.A. Stravers, Eds.). Chapman and Hall, London, England.

MacLean, B., J.M. Woodside, and P. Girouard. 1984. Geological and geophysical investigations in Jones Sound, District of Franklin. Pages 359-365 *in* Current Research, Part A. Geological Survey of Canada, Paper 84-1A, Ottawa, ON.

MacLean, B., G. Sonnichsen, G. Vilks, C. Powell, K. Moran, A. Jennings, D. Hodgson, and B. Deonarine. 1989. Marine geological and geotechnical investigations in Wellington, Byam Martin, Austin, and adjacent channels, Canadian Arctic Archipelago. Geological Survey of Canada, Paper 89-11, Ottawa, ON.

MacLean, B., J. Andrews, J. Gray, F. Hall, I. Hardy, A. Jennings, W. Manley, W.T. Pfeffer, and G.Vilks. 2001. Hudson Strait Quaternary sediments and late glacial and deglaciation history: a discussion and summary. Pages 181-191 *in* Marine Geology of Hudson Strait and Ungava Bay, Eastern Arctic Canada: Late Quaternary Sediments, Depositional Environments, and Late Glacial-Deglacial History Derived from Marine and Terrestrial Studies (B. MacLean, Ed.). Geological Survey of Canada, Bulletin 566, Ottawa, ON.

MacLean, B., S. Blasco, R. Bennett, J. England, W. Rainey, J. Hughes Clarke, and J. Beaudoin. 2010. Ice keel seabed features in marine channels of the central Canadian Arctic Archipelago: evidence for former ice streams and iceberg scouring. Quaternary Science Reviews 29: 2,280-2,301.

MacLean, B., G.L. Williams, and G.A. Fowler. 2014. Bedrock studies of the Baffin Island Shelf and Hudson Strait: a technological and scientific adventure. Pages 331-336 *in* Voyage of Discovery: Fifty Years of Marine Research at Canada's Bedford Institute of Oceanography (D.N. Nettleship, D.C. Gordon, C.F.M. Lewis, and M.P. Latremouille, Eds.). Bedford Institute of Oceanography-Oceans Association, Dartmouth, NS.

McKeown, D.L., P.G. Simpkin, G.B.J. Fader, D.R. Parrott, and D.C. Mosher. 2014. The Huntec Deep Tow Seismic system: a revolution in high resolution profiling. Pages 337-341 *in* Voyage of Discovery: Fifty Years of Marine Research at Canada's Bedford Institute of Oceanography (D.N. Nettleship, D.C. Gordon, C.F.M. Lewis, and M.P. Latremouille, Eds.). Bedford Institute of Oceanography-Oceans Association, Dartmouth, NS.

Mosher D.C., J. Shimeld, D. Hutchinson, N. Lebedeva-Ivanova, and C.B. Chapman. 2011. Submarine landslides in Arctic sedimentation: Canada Basin. Pages 147-157 *in* Submarine Mass Movements and Their Consequences (Y. Yamada, K. Kawamura, K. Ikehara, Y. Ogawa, R. Urgeles, D. Mosher, J. Chaytor, and M. Strasser, Eds.). Springer, Dordrecht, The Netherlands.

Pelletier B.R. 1984. Marine science atlas of the Beaufort Sea: sediments. Geological Survey of Canada, Miscellaneous Report 38, Ottawa, ON.

Pelletier B.R. 1987. Marine science atlas of the Beaufort Sea: geology and geophysics, Geological Survey of Canada, Miscellaneous Report 40, Ottawa, ON.

Pickrill, R.A., B.J. Todd, S.J. Smith, J.V. Barrie, and K.W. Conway. 2014. Marine habitat mapping in Canada's oceans. Pages 185-190 *in* Voyage of Discovery: Fifty Years of Marine Research at Canada's Bedford Institute of Oceanography (D.N. Nettleship, D.C. Gordon, C.F.M. Lewis, and M.P. Latremouille, Eds.). Bedford Institute of Oceanography-Oceans Association, Dartmouth, NS.

Praeg, D.B., B. MacLean, I.A. Hardy, and P. Mudie. 1986. Quaternary geology of the Southeast Baffin Island Continental Shelf, N.W.T. Geological Survey of Canada, Paper 85 14, Ottawa, ON.

Solomon, S. M. 2005. Spatial and temporal variability of shoreline change in the Beaufort-Mackenzie Region, Northwest Territories, Canada. Geo-Marine Letters 25: 127-137.

Sonnichsen, G. and B. MacLean. 1988. A reconnaissance study of the marine geology of the Lougheed King Christian islands region, NW Arctic Islands channels. Pages 115-120 *in* Current Research Part D, Geological Survey of Canada, Paper 88 1D, Ottawa, ON.

Sonnichsen, G.V., K. Moran, C.F.M. Lewis, and G.B.J. Fader. 1994. Regional seabed geology and engineering considerations for Hibernia and surrounding areas. Energy Exploration and Exploitation 12: 325-345.

Swift, D.J.P., A.E. Cok, and A.K. Lyall. 1966. A subtidal sand body in the Minas Channel, Eastern Bay of Fundy. Maritime Sediments 2: 175-179.

Vilks G., F.J.E. Wagner, and B.R. Pelletier. 1979. The Holocene marine environment of the Beaufort Shelf. Geological Survey of Canada, Bulletin 303, Ottawa, ON.

Vilks, G., B. MacLean, B. Deonarine, C. Currie, and K. Moran. 1989. Late Quaternary paleoceanography and sedimentary environments in Hudson Strait. Géographie physique et Quaternaire 43: 161-178.

Wadhams P. 2009. The Great Ocean of Truth: Memories of "*Hudson*-70", the First Circumnavigation of the Americas. Melrose Books, Ely, Cambridgeshire, England.

Wadhams, P. 2014. The *Hudson*-70 voyage of discovery: first circumnavigation of the Americas. Pages 21-28 *in* Voyage of Discovery: Fifty Years of Marine Research at Canada's Bedford Institute of Oceanography (D.N. Nettleship, D.C. Gordon, C.F.M. Lewis, and M.P. Latremouille, Eds.). Bedford Institute of Oceanography-Oceans Association, Dartmouth, NS.

Zevenhuizen, J. and H. Josenhans. 1990. Digital maps of surficial geology of Hudson Bay. Geological Survey of Canada, Open File 2215, Ottawa, ON.

Geological Oceanography

Coastal dynamics, Hertford and Ciboux Islands (Bird Islands), Cape Breton, Nova Scotia

Geological Oceanography

23. COASTAL GEOSCIENCE STUDIES AT THE BEDFORD INSTITITE OF OCEANOGRAPHY, 1962-2012

Robert B. Taylor*, Donald L. Forbes, David Frobel, Gavin K. Manson, and John Shaw

SUMMARY

Since 1962, scientists at Bedford Institute of Oceanography have mapped large stretches of coastline, and increased our understanding of the wide diversity of Arctic and Atlantic coastal systems in Canada. Areas investigated range from the macrotidal Bay of Fundy to the microtidal sandy barrier, and dune systems of the Gulf of St. Lawrence; from the paraglacial gravel barriers of the submergent Atlantic coast and the gravel-dominated emergent coasts of the central Canadian Arctic Archipelago to the ice-bound coasts of the northwestern Archipelago; and the higher-energy, transgressive coast of the Beaufort Sea with its ice-rich tundra cliffs and the second largest delta on the Arctic Ocean. A coastal systems approach including aerial imagery of more than 20,000 km of coastline has led to greater understanding of integrated shore-zone, shoreface, and inner-shelf processes based on innovative approaches and technology for data acquisition in challenging nearshore and ice-congested waters. Monitoring was initiated at 613 sites, nearly half on arctic shores, with 67 of these surveyed repetitively over more than 20 years. These data have provided a baseline reference for analysing the risk of flooding and shoreline change in coastal communities, assessing environmental impacts of developments in the coastal zone, and predicting the potential impacts of climate change and accelerated sea-level rise. Today, with high-resolution satellite imagery and other advanced technology, larger areas of coastline can be examined remotely with suitable resolution. Nevertheless, a requirement remains for field investigations to provide an understanding of complex coastal environments, and to respond to societal needs.

Key words: coastal mapping and monitoring, coastal erosion and hazards, shore types, sediment dynamics, climate change impacts, adaptation.
***E-mail:** Bob.Taylor@NRCan-RNCan.gc.ca

Canada has the longest marine coastline in the world (Fig. 1), nominally about 243,000 km (Canada 1972), although the fractal nature of coastlines makes this a scale-dependent measure. In the early 1970s, when coastal geoscience research was initiated at the Bedford Institute of Oceanography (BIO), the field was relatively undeveloped in Canada, although centres of expertise in coastal geomorphology and engineering were emerging in several universities and at the National Research Council of Canada in Ottawa. Expertise existed elsewhere, but the length of coastline, diversity of coastal environments, and unique physical character associated with current and past glaciation and permafrost created new challenges in this country (Fig. 2). Scientists at BIO were pioneers in developing a vision for documenting and understanding the coastline of Canada.

Research at BIO has focussed mainly on the Atlantic and Arctic coasts of Canada, with occasional involvement on the Pacific coast, in Lake Winnipeg, and in other countries. The first overview of coastal characteristics and geoscience research on all three marine coasts of Canada and the Great Lakes was the focus of a meeting at BIO in 1977 (Fig. 3), a conference in Halifax, Nova Scotia, in 1978 and a subsequent publication (McCann 1980). Working with the Marine Sciences Branch of the Department of Mines and Technical Surveys (now Natural Resources Canada) and later at BIO, E.H. Owens established a framework to investigate coastal diversity in the Maritime Provinces (Owens and Bowen 1977). This was published in *Maritime Sediments*, a journal that originated at the Atlantic Geoscience Centre at BIO (now Geological Survey of Canada Atlantic; GSCA) and focussed on coastal and marine geoscience. It subsequently evolved into the e-journal *Atlantic Geology* that continues to be published today by the Atlantic Geoscience Society. Later work produced regional overviews such as those on the Sverdrup Basin in the Canadian Arctic Archipelago (Taylor 1980), the Beaufort Sea coast (Forbes and Frobel 1985), Newfoundland (Forbes 1984), Nova Scotia (Taylor et al. 1985), and Lake Winnipeg (Forbes and Frobel 1996). Long-term coastal geoscience research based at BIO has contributed over the years to several regional, national, and international syntheses including Keen and Williams (1990), Shaw et al. (1998), and Forbes (2011).

COASTAL MAPPING AND MONITORING

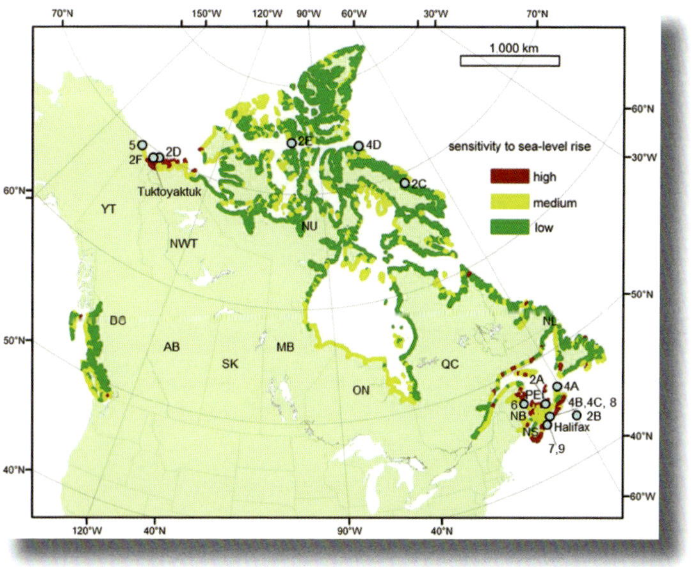

Figure 1. The coastline of Canada showing coastal sensitivity to sea-level rise (after Shaw et al. 1998). Numerals, some with letters, indicate locations of other figures.

Sovereignty issues and the lack of knowledge of Arctic Canada sparked the establishment of the Polar Continental Shelf Project (PCSP) in 1959 (Pelletier 1962). PCSP-sponsored investigations of inter-island channels and adjacent coasts in the Canadian Arctic marked some of the earliest northern research from BIO (Marlowe 1966). In 1970, the MV *Arrow* marine oil spill in Chedabucto Bay, Nova Scotia, increased awareness of our lack of knowledge on shore conditions and oil-shore interactions (Vandermeulen 1977). Much research concentrated on the Bay's oiled shorelines and on documenting oil weathering and shoreline recovery over the following decades (Owens and Rashid 1976, Gordon et al. 2014a). Arctic oil and gas exploration, hydrocarbon shipping to southern markets, and the threat of marine oil spills became important drivers

Figure 2. Examples of varied coastal settings in Canada: (A) Rooted stumps of trees killed by rising sea level and marine transgression, Poverty Beach, eastern PEI (1993 photo: R. Taylor); (B) Fences and vegetation transplants used on Sable Island to repair cuts through narrow parts of the island caused by human activity and reduce flooding during storms (1983 photo: R. Taylor); (C) Head of Itirbilung Fiord, Baffin Island, NU, with 900 m high fiord walls - helicopter deploying a string of instruments to monitor sediment fluxes off delta front as part of the SAFE program (1983 photo: R. Taylor); (D) Thermo-erosional niche undercutting cliffs with massive ground ice following severe storm in August 2000, Tuktoyaktuk Island, NT (photo: S. Solomon); (E) Flights of beach ridges emerged as relative sea level fell in the central Arctic Archipelago during the last 9,000 to 10,000 years (2007 photo: D. St-Hilaire-Gravel); and (F) Subtle levee at eroding front of Mackenzie Delta (2007 photo: D. Forbes).

Figure 3. Participants at a coastal geoscience workshop hosted by the Atlantic Geoscience Centre at BIO in 1977. Standing (l to r): Brian Bornhold, Gerry Reinson*, Dave Frobel*, Patrick McLaren, Bernard Long*, Bob Skinner, Brian McCann*, Peter Rosen*, Dale Buckley*; and seated (l to r): Peter Lewis, John Luternauer, Carl Amos*, Bob Taylor*, Michael Lewis*, Terry Day (* former, current, or future BIO-based individuals as of 1977).

of funding for coastal studies in the 1970s and early 1980s (McLaren and Barrie 1983). Knowledge and expertise acquired by BIO scientists through follow-up studies in Nova Scotia and elsewhere contributed to development of Environment Canada's Shoreline Cleanup Assessment Technique (SCAT) for assessing oil spills along shorelines, an approach now utilized in Canada and many other countries.

The logistical challenge of mapping the coastline of Canada was initially met using a combination of aerial reconnaissance with detailed investigations, often over several years, of a few representative shore types in each region (McCann 1980; Forbes and Frobel 1985, 1996; Taylor and Frobel 2006). Aerial reconnaissance mapping included oblique photo and video coverage with voice commentary and interpretation (Frobel et al. 1987). Aerial video imagery was acquired in cooperation with the Canadian Coast Guard for all three Maritime Provinces and large parts of Newfoundland, and with the PCSP for the entire Canadian Beaufort Sea coast, as well as extensive areas in the Canadian Arctic Archipelago. Coverage for Eastern Hudson Bay was acquired with academic partners at Laval University (Quebec, QC) and the entire perimeter of Lake Winnipeg was imaged as part of the Lake Winnipeg Project in 1994 (Forbes and Frobel 1996, Lewis et al. 2014a). Slightly less than 20,000 km of Canada's coastline has been imaged (8%) and archived in digital format at BIO.

Aerial video images of coastal conditions combined with visual observations provided much more detail than conventional topographic maps and air photos, yet there remained the challenge of how to capture all the data in a cartographic format. This led to the development of an in-house Coastal Information System (CIS). This system evolved from early steps prior to the introduction of off-the-shelf Geographic Information System (GIS) software to a sophisticated Arc-Oracle geospatial database system incorporating dynamic segmentation with capability for documenting alongshore and cross-shore variability in coastal geomorphology and sediments at high resolution (Sherin et al. 2003). The current CIS includes data for parts of the Maritime Provinces and the western Arctic (Beaufort Sea coast and Banks Island, NT) and has been used to explore the applicability of objective erosion hazard indices (Solomon and Gareau 2003).

Apart from its utility for in-house coastal classification and mapping, the aerial oblique video imagery was recognized as a valuable resource for teaching and research in many disciplines (Frobel et al. 1987). Since 1986, when the aerial video was first made publicly available, there have been 726 orders for copies of selected areas. Much of the imagery has been used by Environment Canada for shoreline sensitivity mapping for oil-spill response. Other external applications have included government enforcement and regulation, property tax assessment, assessment of recreational activities in the coastal zone, family history, scouting film locations, in an art installation at the Art Gallery of Nova Scotia (Halifax, NS), and in medical practice as therapeutic visuals for enhancing lucid dreams.

Figure 4. Evolution of beach survey technology over 30 years: (A) Two surveyors in surf with handheld rods and tape using natural horizon for levelling, calling numbers back to note-taker on beach, Aspy Bay, NS (1981 photo: D. Forbes); (B) Optical theodolite and staff survey on gravel barrier, Eastern Shore, NS (1989 photo: D. Forbes); (C) Total station (electronic theodolite) set up on crest of Story Head Beach, NS (1988 photo: D. Forbes); and (D) RTK GPS survey base station setup with rover receiver on rod at right, Bylot Island, NU (2007 photo: R. Taylor). Locations provided in Figure 1.

An important objective over many years has been the monitoring of long-term shoreline response to changing environmental conditions and coastal management activities. GSCA is the only federal government agency investigating long-term shoreline physical response across Canada (Taylor et al. 1995, Solomon 2005). Much of this work has been accomplished through a wide network of coastal sites at which semi-permanent markers were established to facilitate repetitive surveys (Fig. 4). By 2012, there were 613 sites in Canada. Of these, almost half were in Arctic Canada and 67 included observations spanning more than 20 years. Excluding the Yukon-Alaska border site first measured in 1912, the longest site record spans 37 years. These baseline reference surveys pay dividends when assessing the longer-term impacts of extreme storm events, maladaptive coastal activities such as sediment extraction, and the potential impacts of climate change (Taylor 2000, Forbes et al.

2004). Survey technology has evolved over the years from handheld rod-and-tape (Fig. 4A) and optical levels or theodolites (Fig. 4B) to electronic laser theodolites (total stations; Fig. 4C) and high-resolution real-time kinematic (RTK) differential global positioning system (GPS) or global navigation satellite system (GNSS) survey instruments (Fig. 4D). The development of total stations, and especially of satellite-based RTK systems, dramatically enhanced survey capacity by facilitating precise positioning of surveys for later repetition even after the loss of survey monuments. These systems also encouraged more complete site surveys, expanding from cross-shore profiles to alongshore surveys (e.g., cliff-top, barrier- or dune-crest, berm, or water-line) and maps of special features (e.g., washover channels) among others (Fig. 5). More recently, these efforts have been supplemented by new opportunities using high-resolution airborne and satellite remote sensing systems, including multispectral satellite imaging with sub-metre pixel resolution (Manson et al. 2005, James et al. 2013) and airborne laser altimetry and bathymetry (Light Detection and Ranging, LiDAR; Webster and Forbes 2006, Cottin et al. 2009, Xhardé et al. 2011). Topographic LiDAR surveys enable the creation of high-resolution digital elevation models with vertical precision of ±15 cm or less and have been used for surveys of coastal barrier-dune morphology and sand volumes (Fig. 6; O'Carroll et al. 2006), as well as for simulating future flood levels under climate-change scenarios.

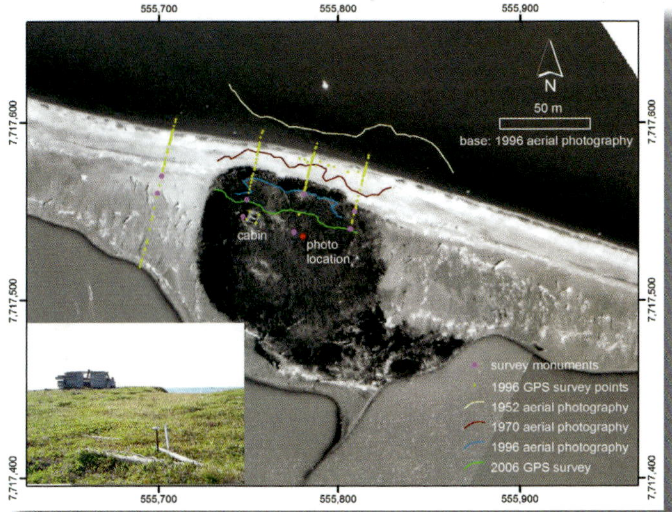

Figure 5. Eroding tundra remnant showing cliff-top positions 1952-2006 with 1930s Stefansson log cabin (inset), Nunaluk Spit, Yukon coast, 1996. RTK survey points (light green-yellow points) and survey monuments (purple circles) enable registration of airphotos to monitor bluff recession. Mean rate of cliff-top retreat over 1996-2006 ranged from 0.4 to 1.5 m/year. Red dot is camera location for inset photo (by G. Manson) showing a survey monument in foreground. Coordinates are in UTM (Universal Transverse Mercator) projection, zone 7N with a grid spacing of 100 m.

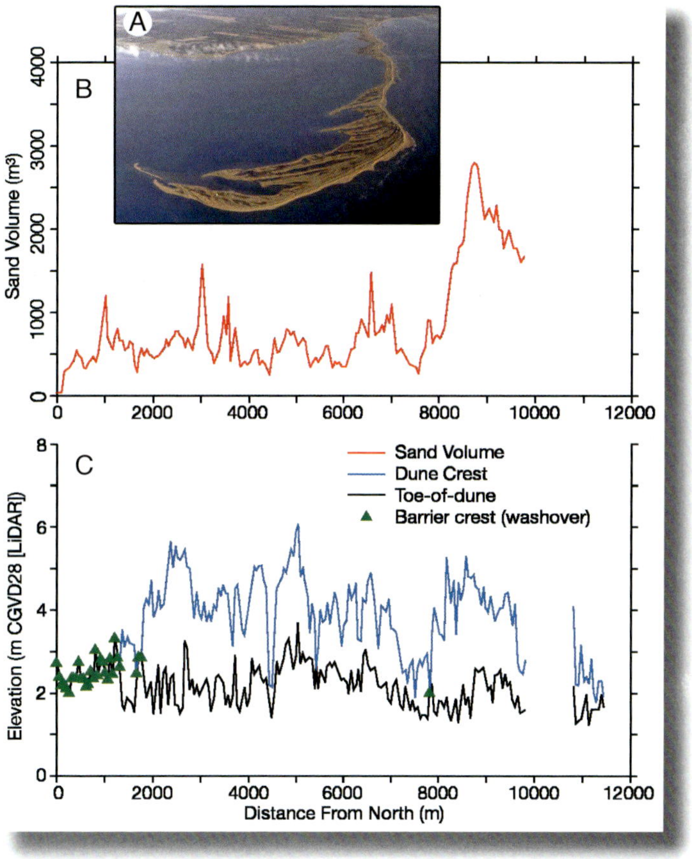

Figure 6. Sand volumes and elevations along Bouctouche Spit (la Dune de Bouctouche), NB : (A) Oblique view of spit, looking north (updrift) with distal recurved ridges in foreground and narrow neck in distance (1972 photo: E. Owens); (B) Sand volume as a function of distance along the spit from north to south; (C) Dune crest, toe-of-dune, and barrier-crest (washover) elevations relative to Canadian Geodetic Vertical Datum of 1928 (CGVD28). Dune volumes (m³/m) and elevations derived from a LiDAR DEM validated against ground surveys (O'Carroll et al. 2006).

COASTAL SYSTEMS

Some projects over the years have adopted a multidisciplinary approach to the integrated study of marine systems in coastal waters including the Strait of Canso, Miramichi Estuary, and Halifax Harbour (Fader and Miller 2008, Buckley 2014). Other multi-year programs took place in the Îles-de-la-Madeleine (Owens 1977), Cape Breton Island (Shaw et al. 2006), Baffin Island fiords (Syvitski and Schafer 1985), Barrow Strait (Taylor and Frobel 2006), and Lake Winnipeg (Lewis et al. 2014a).

In the 1970s, the potential for tidal power development and the construction of tidal barrages and causeways in a macro-tidal environment stimulated research in Chignecto Bay and the Minas Basin. Innovative approaches such as quantitative estimates of suspended particulate concentrations from Landsat multispectral imagery, mapping of bedforms using cameras in tethered blimps, and sediment tracing using radioactive glass beads greatly expanded knowledge of sediment dynamics in the Bay of Fundy (Amos and Long 1980). These studies pointed to the risk of large-scale sedimentation resulting from the construction of tidal barriers, as previously observed following construction of causeways in the Avon and Petitcodiac estuaries in Nova Scotia and New Brunswick, although the specific morphodynamic responses in individual systems varied (van Proosdij et al. 2009). Recent interest in the potential for tidal power generation using seabed turbines has once again focussed BIO research in the Bay of Fundy (Gordon et al. 2014b, Todd and Shaw 2014).

In the early years, there was a strong focus in the microtidal southern Gulf of St. Lawrence, with its extensive sandy barrier beach and dune systems (McCann 1980). Migrating tidal inlets in this region provide important access to small craft harbours utilized by the inshore fishing fleet, but inlet migration, sediment transport and evolution of tidal ebb- and flood-delta deposits create navigation hazards and occasionally plug harbour mouths, leading to a need for dredging or coastal engineering intervention. Over the decades, researchers associated with BIO have contributed to improved understanding of longshore and cross-shore sediment transport, inlet migration, and rapidly changing barrier island configuration along the Gulf coasts of New Brunswick and Prince Edward Island (Armon and McCann 1979, McCann 1980, Forbes and Solomon 1999). Detailed investigations of coastal sedimentary features also contributed to identification and understanding of coastal lithofacies (sediment types) within the rock record (Reinson 1984). From 1982 to 1984, a large multi-partner project, the Canadian Coastal Sediment Study, led to important advances in the modelling of coastal sediment transport and demonstrated the importance of understanding the entire coastal system, above and below water (Forbes 1987). Early seabed mapping in Northumberland Strait (Kranck 1971) demonstrated the discontinuous cover of sand offshore, but later work also identified large, tidal, sandy bedforms in the narrower parts of the Strait (O'Carroll et al. 2006). Results from studies of aeolian sand transport and coastal dunes were utilized by several staff involved during the 1970s and 1980s with the Sable Island Environmental Advisory Committee that directed dune restoration activities on Sable Island (Taylor 1988).

Later in the 1980s, scientists from BIO and academic partners focussed considerable attention on shoreface sediment dynamics on the inner Scotian Shelf (Fig. 7). Sidescan sonar surveys, combined with direct observation and sampling from submersibles, provided new

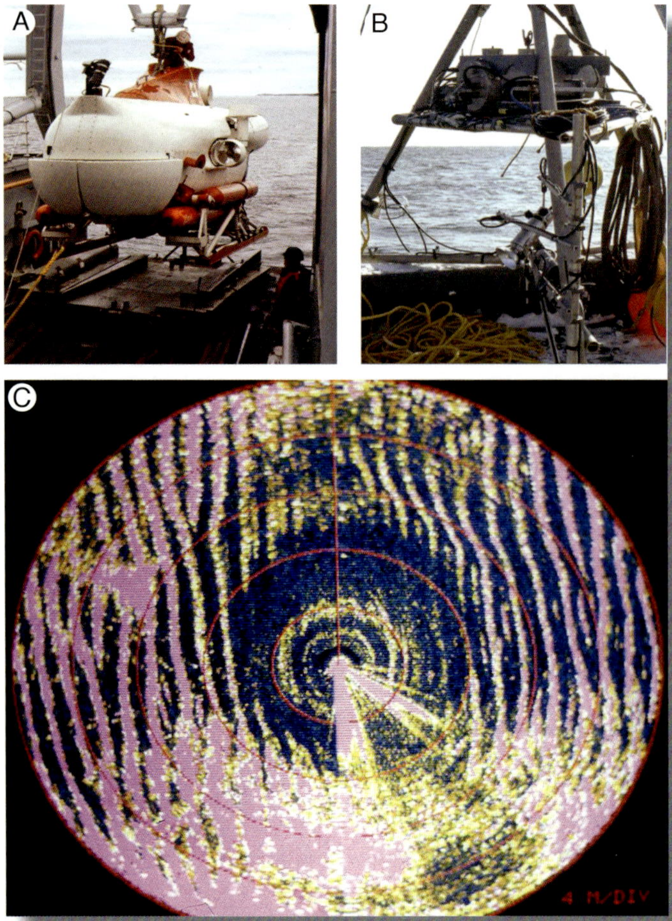

Figure 7. Shoreface studies off Eastern Shore of Nova Scotia: (A) Launching *SDL-1* submersible from HMCS *Cormorant* (1989 photo: D. Forbes); (B) Seabed lander 'Ralph' on tripod mount during Canadian Atlantic Storms Program 1987 (Forbes and Drapeau 1989); (C) Scanning sonar image of large-scale gravel ripples off the mouth of Halifax Harbour (scale 4 m per radial division; 1989 photo: D. Forbes).

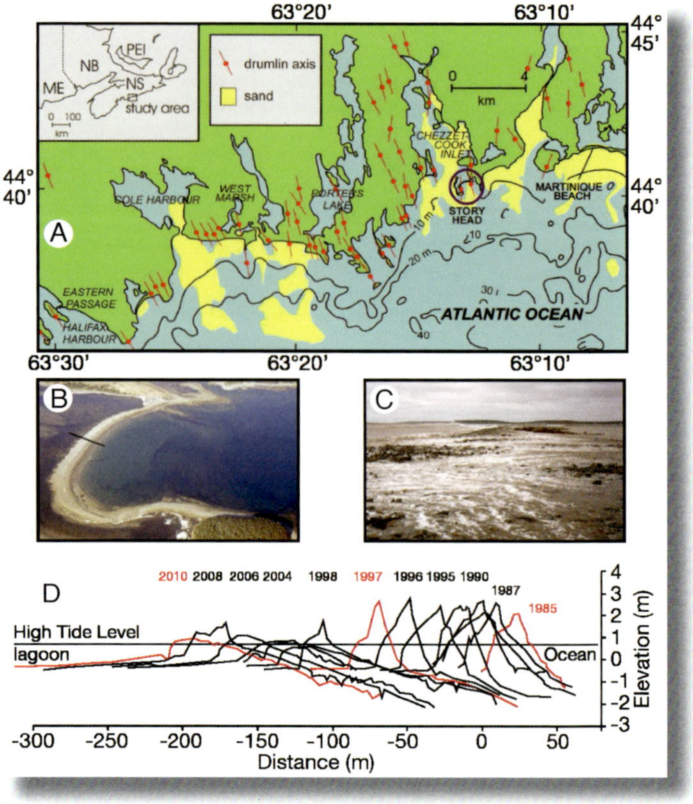

Figure 8. Coastal drumlins and nearshore sand occurrences on part of the Eastern Shore of Nova Scotia: (A) Sand distribution on the inner shelf and morphology resulting from marine transgression through a coastal drumlin field (Story Head circled); (B) Oblique view of Story Head Beach with Story Head in lower right foreground - black line shows approximate location of transect line in (D) (1990 photo: R. Taylor); (C) Waves washing over Story Head Beach (l to r) during Hurricane Hortense (1996 photo: D. Forbes); and (D) Landward migration of the barrier (r to l) at transect black line from surveyed profiles 1985-2010.

understanding of gravel entrainment and large-scale ripple formation during storms (Fig. 7A,C; Forbes and Boyd 1987, 1989). Under the Canadian Atlantic Storms Program in 1987, in-house and contracted work contributed to a better understanding of the potential for sediment transport and scour under pipelines crossing the inner shelf (Judge and Forbes 1987, Forbes and Drapeau 1989). This work made use of a prototype seabed lander named 'Ralph' (Fig. 7B; Heffler 1996) and associated development of a rotating sonar that provided images of large-scale ripple morphology (Fig. 7C), while time-lapse bottom photography provided insights on shoreface sand dynamics. This work demonstrated the sparse distribution of sand on the inner shelf (Fig. 8A), the mobility of seafloor sediments, and the occurrence of previously unknown features, including steep-walled scour pits in exposed transgressed estuarine muds (Judge and Forbes 1987). Subsequent refinement and deployment of similar equipment in areas such as Sable Bank provided critical information for the development of hydrodynamic and sediment transport models and their application to understanding seabed stability near submarine infrastructure (Li and Amos 2001, Lewis et al. 2014b).

Recognition of critical links between the visible parts of coastal systems and the adjacent underwater shoreface, forming an integrated coastal sedimentary system, prompted an extensive inshore mapping program in the late 1980s and early 1990s. This benefited from early adoption of new technologies, including multibeam bathymetric mapping and digital and interferometric sidescan sonar. Multibeam bathymetric survey technology revolutionized our ability to image and visualize the shallow seabed using GIS to produce mosaics and shaded-relief bathymetric models with varying backscatter intensity (Fader et al. 2014, Shaw 2014). Large banner banks, spit platforms, shoals with extensive spillover deposits in coastal basins, scour pits and the distribution of mobile sediments on the inner shelves were revealed. The information contributed to answering key questions related to large-scale coastal developments, such as the Confederation Bridge between New Brunswick and Prince Edward Island, and contributed to an understanding of drowned coastal features and the history of postglacial relative sea-level change in the Atlantic region.

Given the widespread glacial legacy along Canadian coasts, research at BIO has focussed extensively on gravel-dominated shores, which were poorly documented and understood prior to the 1980s. Since Forbes and Taylor (1987) first applied the term 'paraglacial' to coasts developed in areas of former glaciation, the concept has been widely adopted as a useful paradigm for understanding the role of glacial deposits as source materials for beach and barrier systems dominated by gravels and the distinctive processes operating in these settings (Forbes and Syvitski 1994, Forbes 2012). Since the late 1970s, considerable attention has been devoted by BIO researchers and external partners to the evolutionary patterns and stability of coarse-clastic beaches and barriers, in Arctic Canada (Taylor and McCann 1983, St-Hilaire-Gravel et al. 2012), Atlantic Canada (Carter et al. 1990, Shaw et al. 1993, Forbes et al. 1995, Taylor et al. 1995), and elsewhere (Taylor et al. 1986, Orford et al. 2000). Particular insight has been derived from work on the transgressive drumlin coast of the Eastern Shore of Nova Scotia, with the development of conceptual models for the cyclic growth and decay of drumlin-fed barriers as the finite sediment supply is tapped and then exhausted, leading to landward migration of the 'erosional front' (Fig. 8A; Carter et al. 1989, Forbes 2012). Much has been learned from monitoring a rapidly stretching, partially overstepped, and (since 1998) failing barrier beach fed by sediments from the eroding drumlin headland at Story Head, Nova Scotia (Fig. 8B, C; Carter et al. 1990). Repetitive surveys over 25 years have documented rapid landward migration of this low gravel barrier (and others in the region) and retreat of drumlin headlands at rates exceeding 10 m per year (Fig. 8D; Taylor et al. 1995). Detailed investigations of subaerial processes and geotechnical properties of drumlin shore cliffs provided additional knowledge of conditions affecting retreat of these critical shoreline anchor features (Manson 2002).

Coastal geoscience research in Arctic Canada has been sponsored under a succession of focussed government programs such as the Northern Oil and Gas Action Program (NOGAP) and Eastern Arctic Marine Environmental Studies (EAMES), supplemented by academic funding through ArcticNet and other sources. Substantial effort was devoted to an understanding of shore-zone ice dynamics in various Arctic and mid-latitude settings (Taylor 1978, Rosen 1979, Forbes and Taylor 1994), the stability of coastal systems in ice-bound settings (Taylor 1980, Taylor and Forbes 1987), and sediment dynamics within fiord environments. Fiords are large-scale glacially sculpted landforms dominating the coast in several regions of Canada. In the 1980s, GSCA initiated a multi-disciplinary project, the Sedimentology of Arctic Fjords Experiment (SAFE), to examine modern and late Quaternary sediment processes and fluxes within fiords of eastern Baffin Island (Fig. 2C; Syvitski and Schafer 1985). Detailed studies examined subaqueous delta-front and prodelta sedimentation processes and the distinctive morphology they produce (Syvitski and Hein 1991, Forbes and Syvitski 1994). Fiords with one or more bedrock sills are major sediment traps in the terrestrial to deep-sea sediment pathway. Results from the SAFE program contributed significantly to global understanding of the complex sedimentary and biological processes operating within fiords (Syvitski et al. 1987).

In the Beaufort Sea region, BIO researchers elucidated the role of thermokarst (thaw) processes in coastal erosion and the formation of a complex and intricate shoreline pattern through erosional breaching of thaw lakes (Ruz et al. 1992, Hill et al. 1994). More detailed studies of coastal evolution focussed on climate change, sea-level rise, and storm impacts (Héquette et al. 2001, Manson and Solomon 2007). The research was applied to erosion risks for cultural resources (Fig. 5; Forbes 1997) and site conditions for potential subsea pipeline landfalls, shore-base facilities, and communities such as Tuktoyaktuk, Northwest Territories, built on sediments containing very high proportions of ground ice (Wolfe et al. 1998, Solomon et al. 2008). Over the past decade, community- and port-related activities in the Beaufort region and across Arctic Canada have been reinvigorated under the Climate Change Geoscience Program (Natural Resources Canada), the Nunavut Climate Change Partnership, and the Beaufort Regional Environmental Assessment program (e.g., Manson et al. 2005; James et al. 2011, 2013; Forbes et al. 2014).

Substantial work on the Mackenzie Delta has been undertaken to develop the knowledge base for planning, engineering design, environmental assessment, and regulation of natural gas development and production in the outer delta region (Fig. 2F). This entailed substantial effort in support of the Mackenzie Gas Pipeline Joint Review Panel for the proposed gas pipeline to southern markets. Surveys of winter ice conditions, breakup flooding, delta subsidence, sediment transport, and scour on the inner shelf off the front of the Mackenzie River have yielded new insights. These include the distribution and importance of bottom-fast ice, the flooding and erosional effects of breakup discharge interaction with ice in the delta, and rates of delta-front recession and channel bank erosion in the outer delta (Solomon 2005, Solomon et al. 2008, Lesack et al. 2013).

CLIMATE-CHANGE IMPACTS AND ADAPTATION

Beginning in the late 1980s, concern about future impacts of climate change and the implications of accelerated sea-level rise in the coastal zone became an issue for coastal geoscience in Canada (Shaw et al. 1998). Because local sea-level rise is a combination of changing sea level (the local manifestation of global sea-level rise) and any vertical crustal motion at the site, the widespread effects of postglacial isostatic adjustment (the attenuated crustal response to loading by ice sheet formation and subsequent unloading following deglaciation) are important to understand and measure. This geophysical component of local sea-level change is one area in which collaboration between GSCA scientists at BIO and Natural Resources Canada colleagues at the Geodetic Survey Division and the Geological Survey of Canada Pacific (GSCP) has contributed to more robust projections of sea-level rise for coastal communities in Canada (Forbes et al. 2009, James et al. 2011). For a number of years, BIO hosted the national office for the coastal theme of the Canadian Climate Impacts and Adaptation Research Network (C-CIARN). Twenty major scientific studies were funded that addressed issues on all three marine coasts and the Great Lakes. The final report in April 2005 identified the most important coastal climate issues and knowledge gaps for each region in Canada.

Over the past 10-15 years, much of the focus of coastal geoscience at BIO has been on climate-change impacts and adaptation in the coastal zone. Particular emphasis was placed on the dissemination and application of scientific knowledge to reduce negative impacts on communities through appropriate planning and adaptation measures (Daigle 2006; Forbes et al. 2009, 2014). This included development of impacts visualization techniques combining high-resolution digital elevation models derived from LiDAR data in a GIS environment with water levels associated with various flood scenarios and sea-level projections (Fig. 9). BIO coastal researchers have also contributed to national and international climate-change assessments (Intergovernmental Panel on Climate Change 2007, Lemmen et al. 2008, Forbes 2011). This work has been undertaken with other federal departments, provincial and territorial governments, local governments, academic partners, and professional and community organizations such as the Canadian Institute of Planners and Ittaq, a community research and heritage centre in Clyde River, Nunavut. New insights have been developed on the factors affecting regional rates of sea-level rise and on the interplay between long-term climate, sea-level trends, and natural hazards in extreme events.

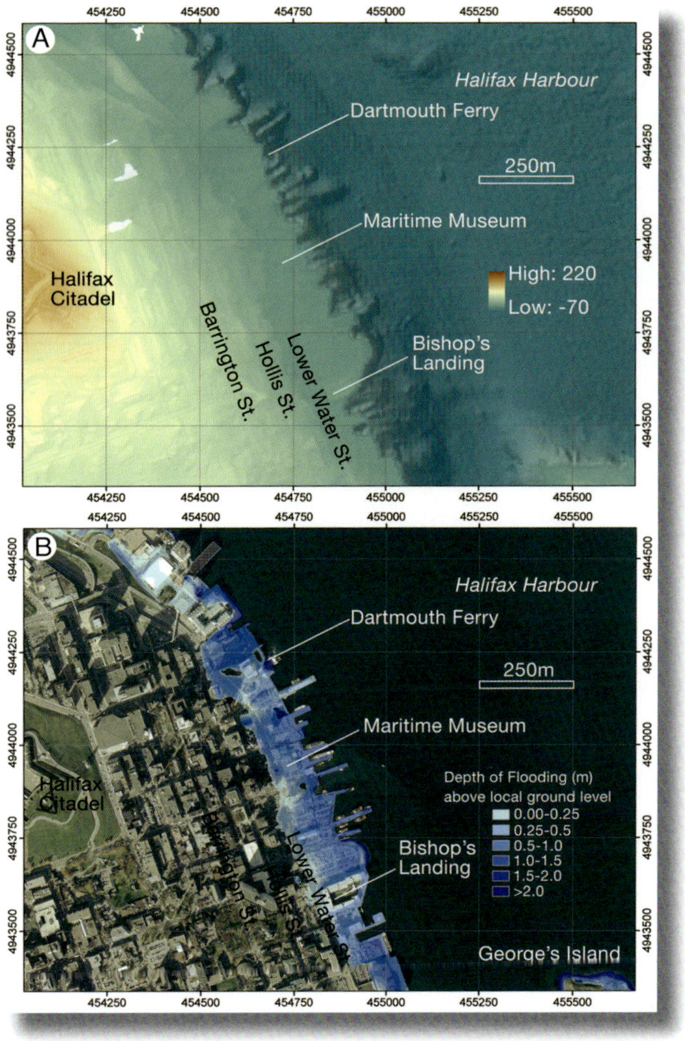

Figure 9. Flood simulation for extreme events under climate-change scenarios for the future: (A) Bare-earth LiDAR digital elevation model (DEM) for part of downtown Halifax, NS; (B) Flooding extent and depth along the Halifax waterfront for a simulated 1-in-50 year storm event on a plausible scenario of sea-level rise in the year 2100. Flood simulation was developed using the DEM in (A) and overlain on an optical image to show locations of buildings and other features familiar to residents (after Forbes et al. 2009). Coordinates are in UTM projection, zone 20N with a grid spacing of 250 m.

Figure 10. South Pacific coastal environments covered by BIO researchers seconded to SOPAC in the mid-1990s: (A) Atoll-rim island of Bairiki in South Tarawa, Kiribati, showing reef flats on seaward (far) and lagoon (near) sides of the island (1995 photo: D. Forbes); (B) Cross-reef transport through gaps in atoll rim islands, Manihiki, Northern Cook Islands (1996 photo: S. Solomon); (C) Degraded coast at Fijian village in the Rewa Delta, Viti Levu, where natural mangrove cover has been removed and seawalls have been largely ineffective (1995 photo: D. Forbes); and (D) Cliffs of the raised atoll forming the island of Niue, where tropical cyclone waves in 1990 and 2003 caused massive infrastructure damage (Solomon and Forbes 1999), including deposition of large boulders up to 100 m landward of the cliff top (1995 photo: D. Forbes).

INTERNATIONAL LINKS

In the early 1980s, collaborative research was initiated with R.W.G. Carter (University of Ulster, Northern Ireland) and J.D. Orford (Queen's University of Belfast, Northern Ireland), whose pioneering work on gravel beaches in the United Kingdom and Ireland was clearly relevant to the paraglacial coasts of Atlantic Canada (Taylor et al. 1986). This led to a highly productive partnership lasting more than 20 years, working in part on the British and Irish coasts and more extensively in Nova Scotia, including detailed work at Story Head and other sites on the Eastern Shore (Fig. 8). While most published literature at the time focussed on sandy beach systems, this collaboration contributed to numerous insights on the evolutionary development, stability, and breakdown of coarse clastic beaches and barriers typical of much of eastern Canada, with substantial implications for back-barrier habitat stability and strategies for coastal management (Carter et al. 1989, 1990; Forbes et al. 1995; Orford et al. 2000).

In the mid-1990s, two GSCA coastal researchers from BIO were seconded to the South Pacific Applied Geoscience Commission (SOPAC), with funding from the Canadian International Development Agency. Projects undertaken during this time responded to coastal management challenges facing a number of Pacific Island countries, including Fiji, Samoa, Cook Islands, Kiribati, and Niue (Fig. 10). Results highlighted the importance of El Niño-Southern Oscillation variability in prevailing winds and of reef systems as biogenic sand sources for management of sand and gravel resources and coastal erosion. They also addressed early concerns about potential vulnerability to sea-level rise (Forbes and Hosoi 1995, Solomon and Kruger 1996). This work also documented a range of coastal hazard exposure conditions affecting diverse island types, including the low-lying coastal fringes of islands with high relief, low-relief atoll rim islands, and cliffed raised atolls (Solomon and Forbes 1999, Forbes et al. 2013). A more recent GSCA contribution to hazard mitigation in tropical island settings, under the auspices of UNESCO (United Nations Educational, Scientific and Cultural Organization) and the Intergovernmental Oceanographic Commission, was a post-impact survey in the Seychelles following the 2004 Indian Ocean earthquake and tsunami (Jackson et al. 2005). It demonstrated the vulnerability of sites behind islands to tsunami wave refraction or reflection, the importance of maintaining natural buffers when coastal development is undertaken, and the relative immunity of atolls on seamounts rising from abyssal depths.

The GSCA coastal group at BIO has also played leading roles in arctic circumpolar coastal geoscience. S. Solomon was an early leader in the Arctic Coastal Dynamics (ACD) project sponsored by the International Arctic Science Committee and the International Permafrost Association (Brown and Solomon 1999). With other members of the group, he made important contributions to many later ACD workshops and initiatives, culminating in publication of a digital geospatial coastline analysis for the Arctic basin (Lantuit et al. 2012). An outgrowth of this work and collaboration with the Land-Ocean Interactions in the Coastal Zone (LOICZ) project was an assessment of the state of the coasts of Arctic Canada with substantial input from BIO researchers (Forbes 2011).

THE FUTURE

The long history of coastal geoscience at BIO has built up a unique expertise and knowledge base, particularly on polar and temperate, coarse-clastic, barrier beach systems. BIO researchers developed a framework for classifying coastal environments at regional and local scales, identifying primary shore types, and have contributed to regional and local projections of sea-level rise, including estimates of crustal motion. Extensive stretches of Canada's coastline have been examined, but there remain large gaps in our knowledge of some Arctic and sub-Arctic coastal regions. Continued monitoring of representative coastal sites is critical to confirm, for coastal management purposes, complex dynamic relationships between the ocean, land, and weather/climate systems.

Future research will involve increased use of automated observatories, numerical modelling, and remote sensing, which will increase challenges in data management. Continued miniaturization and increased hardiness of instruments, more economic satellite communications, and further efficiencies in off-grid power systems will allow automated monitoring of shorelines using multi-sensor coastal observatories. Meteorological, oceanographic, and geomorphic data collected in real-time will become publicly available through the Internet. Increased use of 2D and 3D numerical hydrodynamic and sediment transport models will elucidate processes of erosion and sedimentation in coastal waters and guide investigations of coastal change (Li and Parrott 2009). Recent availability of airborne bathymetric LiDAR will accelerate seamless mapping of large expanses of coastline including shallow water and terrestrial areas (Cottin et al. 2009), and provide a better understanding of sediment reserves and the role of shoreface adjustment to onshore changes and shoreline stability (Xhardé et al. 2011).

Remote-sensing technologies mounted on various satellites, aircraft, and watercraft will be increasingly adopted and will complement traditional ground-based field surveys. Field surveys will not cease, but their role will become targeted as remote sensing and modelling capabilities are refined. Satellite imagery combined with GPS and GIS technologies produce huge amounts of digital information. The challenge for the future, given limited coastal personnel at BIO, and indeed within Canada, is whether we have the capacity to organize, manage, validate, and make effective use of the vast amounts of new information and to make it available to decision makers in a useful and timely manner.

ACKNOWLEDGEMENTS

We acknowledge the dedication of the people who have worked over the years at the Atlantic Geoscience Centre (now GSC-Atlantic) directly investigating and contributing to our knowledge of the coastline of Canada. We also thank those within the organization who provided management, administrative, and technical support and others in BIO and elsewhere who have cooperated in these investigations. Primary coastal investigators no longer working at BIO include Carl Amos, David Atkinson, Ted Bryant, Dale Buckley, Arnaud Héquette, Phil Hill, Azharul Hoque, Bernard Long, Jim Marlowe, Brian McCann, Ed Owens, Bernie Pelletier, Gerry Reinson, Peter Rosen, James Syvitski, and Gus Vilks. We especially wish to acknowledge the contributions of Steve Solomon who passed away in August 2011. His vitality, scientific knowledge of cold coasts, and love of gadgets substantially enhanced and accelerated our adoption of innovative small-boat technology, shallow-water instrumentation, and the newest survey applications of global navigation satellite systems. Dale Buckley and Brian Todd kindly reviewed and provided helpful comments on an earlier version of the manuscript. This is contribution 20110350 of the Earth Sciences Sector of Natural Resources Canada.

REFERENCES

Amos, C.L. and B.F.N. Long. 1980. The sedimentary character of the Minas Basin, Bay of Fundy. Pages 153-180 *in* The Coastline of Canada (S.B. McCann, Ed.). Geological Survey of Canada Paper 80-10, Ottawa, ON.

Armon, J.W. and S.B. McCann. 1979. Morphology and landward sediment transfer in a transgressive barrier island system, southern Gulf of St. Lawrence, Canada. Marine Geology 31: 333-344.

Brown, J. and S. Solomon (Eds.). 1999. Arctic Coastal Dynamics: Report of an International Workshop. Geological Survey of Canada Open File 3929, Ottawa, ON.

Buckley, D.E. 2014. Discoveries in environmental marine geology. Pages 247-252 *in* Voyage of Discovery: Fifty Years of Marine Research at Canada's Bedford Institute of Oceanography (D.N. Nettleship, D.C. Gordon, C.F.M. Lewis, and M.P. Latremouille, Eds.). Bedford Institute of Oceanography-Oceans Association, Dartmouth, NS.

Canada. 1972. Facts from Canadian Maps: A Geographic Handbook. Department of Energy Mines and Resources, Surveys and Mapping Branch, Ottawa, ON.

Carter, R.W.G., D.L. Forbes, S.C. Jennings, J.D. Orford, J. Shaw, and R.B. Taylor. 1989. Barrier and lagoon coast evolution under differing relative sea-level regimes: examples from Ireland and Nova Scotia. Marine Geology 88: 221-242.

Carter, R.W.G., J.D. Orford, D.L. Forbes, and R.B. Taylor. 1990. Morphosedimentary development of drumlin-flank barriers with rapidly rising sea level, Story Head, Nova Scotia. Sedimentary Geology 69: 117-138.

Cottin, A.G., D.L. Forbes, and B.F. Long. 2009. Shallow seabed mapping and classification using waveform analysis and bathymetry from SHOALS LiDAR data. Canadian Journal of Remote Sensing 35: 422-434.

Daigle, R. (Ed.). 2006. Impacts of Sea-level Rise and Climate Change on the Coastal Zone of Southeastern New Brunswick. Environment Canada, Ottawa, ON.

Fader, G.B.J. and R.O. Miller. 2008. Surficial Geology, Halifax Harbour, Nova Scotia. Geological Survey of Canada Bulletin 590, Ottawa, ON.

Fader, G.B.J., B. MacLean, H.W. Josenhans, and S.M. Blasco. 2014. Seabed sediment mapping at the Bedford Institute of Oceanography: from single beam to multibeam. Pages 191-199 *in* Voyage of Discovery: Fifty Years of Marine Research at Canada's Bedford Institute of Oceanography (D.N. Nettleship, D.C. Gordon, C.F.M. Lewis, and M.P. Latremouille, Eds.). Bedford Institute of Oceanography-Oceans Association, Dartmouth, NS.

Forbes, D.L. 1984. Coastal geomorphology and sediments of Newfoundland. Pages 11-24 *in* Geological Survey of Canada Current Research Paper 84-1B, Ottawa, ON.

Forbes, D.L. 1987. Shoreface sediment distribution and sand supply at C^2S^2 sites in the southern Gulf of St. Lawrence. Pages 694-709 *in* Proceedings of Coastal Sediments '87, New Orleans, LA (N.C. Kraus, Ed.). American Society of Civil Engineers, New York, NY.

Forbes, D.L. 1997. Coastal erosion and nearshore profile variability in the southern Beaufort Sea, Ivvavik National Park, Yukon Territory. Geological Survey of Canada Open File 3531, Ottawa, ON.

Forbes, D.L. (Ed.). 2011. State of the Arctic Coast 2010: Scientific Review and Outlook. International Arctic Science Committee, Land-Ocean Interactions in the Coastal Zone, Arctic Monitoring and Assessment Programme, International Permafrost Association and Helmholtz-Zentrum, Geesthacht, Germany. (http://arcticcoasts.org)

Forbes, D.L. 2012. Glaciated coasts. Pages 223-243 *in* Estuarine and Coastal Geology and Geomorphology (B.W. Flemming and J.D. Hansom, Eds.), Volume 3, Treatise on Estuarine and Coastal Science (D. McLusky and E. Wolanski, Eds.). Academic Press, Waltham, MA.

Forbes, D.L. and D. Frobel. 1985. Coastal erosion and sedimentation in the Canadian Beaufort Sea. Pages 69-80 *in* Current Research. Geological Survey of Canada Paper 85-1B, Ottawa, ON.

Forbes, D.L. and R. Boyd. 1987. Gravel ripples on the inner Scotian Shelf. Journal of Sedimentary Petrology 57: 46-54.

Forbes, D.L. and R.B. Taylor. 1987. Coarse-grained beach sedimentation under paraglacial conditions, Canadian Atlantic coast. Pages 51-86 *in* Glaciated Coasts (D.M. FitzGerald and P.S. Rosen, Eds.). Academic Press, San Diego, CA.

Forbes, D.L. and R. Boyd. 1989. Submersible observations of surficial sediments and seafloor morphology on the inner Scotian Shelf. Pages 71-81 *in* Submersible Observations off the East Coast of Canada (D.J.W. Piper, Ed.). Geological Survey of Canada Paper 88-20, Ottawa, ON.

Forbes, D.L. and G. Drapeau. 1989. Near-bottom currents and sediment transport on the inner Scotian Shelf: sea-floor response to winter storms during CASP. Atmosphere-Ocean 27: 258-278.

Forbes, D.L. and J.P.M. Syvitski. 1994. Paraglacial coasts. Pages 373-424 *in* Coastal Evolution: Late Quaternary Shoreline Morphodynamics (R.W.G. Carter and C.D. Woodroffe, Eds.). Cambridge University Press, Cambridge, England.

Forbes, D.L. and R.B. Taylor. 1994. Ice in the shore zone and the geomorphology of cold coasts. Progress in Physical Geography 18: 59-89.

Forbes, D.L. and Y. Hosoi. 1995. Coastal erosion in South Tarawa, Kiribati. Technical Report 225, South Pacific Applied Geoscience Commission (SOPAC), Suva, Fiji. http://ict.sopac.org/VirLib/TR0225.pdf

Forbes, D.L. and D. Frobel. 1996. Shore-zone morphology and processes of Lake Winnipeg. Pages 355-391 *in* Lake Winnipeg Project: Cruise Report and Scientific Results (B.J. Todd, C.F.M. Lewis, L.H. Thorleifson, and E. Nielsen, Eds.). Geological Survey of Canada Open File 3113, Ottawa, ON.

Forbes, D.L. and S.M. Solomon. 1999. Inlet division and coastal instability following tidal prism diversion. Pages 1,418-1,433 *in* Proceedings of Coastal Sediments '99, Long Island, New York (N.C. Kraus, Ed.). American Society of Civil Engineers, Reston, VA.

Forbes, D.L., J.D. Orford, R.W.G. Carter, J. Shaw, and S.C. Jennings. 1995. Morphodynamic evolution, self-organisation, and instability of coarse-clastic barriers on paraglacial coasts. Marine Geology 126: 63-85.

Forbes, D.L., G.S. Parkes, G.K. Manson, and L.A. Ketch. 2004. Storms and shoreline retreat in the southern Gulf of St. Lawrence. Marine Geology 210: 169-204.

Forbes, D.L., G.K. Manson, J. Charles, K.R. Thompson, and R.B. Taylor. 2009. Halifax Harbour extreme water levels in the context of climate change: scenarios for a 100-year planning horizon. Geological Survey of Canada Open File 6346, Ottawa, ON.

Forbes, D.L., T.S. James, M. Sutherland, and S.E. Nichols. 2013. Physical basis of coastal adaptation on tropical small islands. Sustainability Science 8: 327-344.

Forbes, D.L., T. Bell, T.S. James, and K.M. Simon. 2014. Reconnaissance assessment of landscape hazards and potential impacts of future climate change in Arviat, Nunavut. Pages 183-192 *in* Summary of Activities 2013. Canada-Nunavut Geoscience Office, Iqaluit, NU.

Frobel, D., R.B. Taylor, and D.L. Forbes. 1987. Video applications in coastal research. Pages 429-436 *in* Proceedings of Canadian Coastal Conference 1987 (Y. Oullet, Ed.), Québec, QC. National Research Council, Ottawa, ON.

Gordon, D.C., K. Lee, P.G. Wells, and P.D. Keizer. 2014a. The impacts of oil and gas activities on the marine environment. Pages 361-371 *in* Voyage of Discovery: Fifty years of Marine Research at Canada's Bedford Institute of Oceanography (D.N. Nettleship, D.C. Gordon, C.F.M. Lewis, and M.P. Latremouille, Eds.). Bedford Institute of Oceanography-Oceans Association, Dartmouth, NS.

Gordon, D.C., C.L. Amos, D.A. Greenberg, P.C. Smith, and G.B.J. Fader. 2014b. Understanding the macrotidal environment of the Bay of Fundy and the impacts of tidal power development. Pages 373-382 *in* Voyage of Discovery: Fifty years of Marine Research at Canada's Bedford Institute of Oceanography (D.N. Nettleship, D.C. Gordon, C.F.M. Lewis, and M.P. Latremouille, Eds.). Bedford Institute of Oceanography-Oceans Association, Dartmouth, NS.

Heffler, D.E. 1996. RALPH – A dynamic instrument for sediment dynamics. Pages 728-732 *in* Proceedings of Oceans '96, MTS (Marine Technology Society)/ IEEE (Institute of Electrical and Electronic Engineers): The Coastal Ocean -Prospects for the 21st Century, Fort Lauderdale, FL. Institute of Electrical and Electronic Engineers, Piscataway, NJ.

Héquette, A., M. Desrosiers, P.R. Hill, and D.L. Forbes. 2001. The influence of coastal morphology on shoreface sediment transport under storm-combined flows, Canadian Beaufort Sea. Journal of Coastal Research 17: 507-516.

Hill, P.R., P.W. Barnes, A. Héquette, and M-H. Ruz. 1994. Arctic coastal plain shorelines. Pages 341-372 *in* Coastal Evolution: Late Quaternary Shoreline Morphodynamics (R.W.G. Carter and C.D. Woodroffe, Eds.). Cambridge University Press, Cambridge, England.

Intergovernmental Panel on Climate Change. 2007. Climate Change 2007: Impacts, Adaptation and Vulnerability. Contribution of Working Group II to the Fourth Assessment Report of the Intergovernmental Panel on Climate Change (M. Parry, O. Canziani, J. Palutikof, P. van der Linden, and C. Hanson, Eds.). Cambridge University Press, Cambridge, England.

Jackson, L.E., Jr., J.V. Barrie, D.L. Forbes, J. Shaw, G.K. Manson, and M. Schmidt. 2005. Effects of the 26 December 2004 Indian Ocean Tsunami in the Republic of Seychelles. Report of the Canada-UNESCO Indian Ocean Expedition. Geological Survey of Canada Open File 4539, Ottawa, ON.

James, T.S., K.M. Simon, D.L. Forbes, A.S. Dyke, and D.J. Mate. 2011. Sea-level projections for five pilot communities of the Nunavut Climate Change Partnership. Geological Survey of Canada Open File 6715, Ottawa, ON.

James, T.S., D.J.R. Whalen, K.A. Jenner, S.V. Hatcher, M. Ulmi, D.L. Forbes, G.K. Manson, J.A. Henton, and M.C. Craymer. 2013. Coastal geoscience for sustainable development in Nunavut: 2012 activities. Pages 143-150 *in* Summary of Activities 2012. Canada-Nunavut Geoscience Office, Iqaluit, NU.

Judge, J.T. and D.L. Forbes. 1987. Measurements of currents, bottom sediments and seafloor disturbance during CASP. Pages 975-980 *in* Proceedings of Oceans '87, IEEE (Institute of Electrical and Electronic Engineers) and MTS (Marine Technology Society), Halifax, NS. Institute of Electrical and Electronic Engineers, Piscataway, NJ.

Keen M.J. and G.L. Williams. 1990. Geology of the continental margin of Eastern Canada. Geology of Canada Number 2, Geological Survey of Canada, Ottawa, ON.

Kranck, K. 1971. Surficial geology of Northumberland Strait. Marine Science Paper 5 and Paper 71-53, Geological Survey of Canada, Ottawa, ON.

Lantuit, H., P.P. Overduin, N. Couture, and 21 others. 2012. The Arctic Coastal Dynamics database: a new classification scheme and statistics on Arctic permafrost coastlines. Estuaries and Coasts 35: 383-400.

Lesack, L.F.W., P. Marsh, F.E. Hicks, and D.L. Forbes. 2013. Timing, duration, and magnitude of peak annual water-levels during ice breakup in the Mackenzie Delta and the role of river discharge. Water Resources Research 49: 8,234-8,249.

Lewis, C.F.M., B.J. Todd, S.M. Blasco, D.L. Forbes, G.D.M. Cameron, and E.L. King. 2014a. Marine geoscience and lakes. Pages 225-230 *in* Voyage of Discovery: Fifty Years of Marine Research at Canada's Bedford Institute of Oceanography (D.N. Nettleship, D.C. Gordon, C.F.M. Lewis, and M.P. Latremouille, Eds.). Bedford Institute of Oceanography-Oceans Association, Dartmouth, NS.

Lewis, C.F.M., S.M. Blasco, D.J.W. Piper, and G.V. Sonnichsen 2014b. Seabed geohazard knowledge for safe hydrocarbon development. Pages 383-394 *in* Voyage of Discovery: Fifty Years of Marine Research at Canada's Bedford Institute of Oceanography (D.N. Nettleship, D.C. Gordon, C.F.M. Lewis, and

M.P. Latremouille, Eds.). Bedford Institute of Oceanography-Oceans Association, Dartmouth, NS.

Lemmen, D.S., F.J. Warren, J. Lacroix, and E. Bush (Eds.). 2008. From Impacts to Adaptation: Canada in a Changing Climate 2007. Government of Canada, Ottawa, ON.

Li, M.Z. and C.L. Amos. 2001. SEDTRANS96: the upgraded and better-calibrated sediment-transport model for continental shelves. Computers and Geoscience 27: 619-645.

Li, M.Z. and D.R. Parrott. 2009. Sediment stability and dispersion at the Black Point offshore disposal site, Saint John Harbour, New Brunswick, Canada. Journal of Coastal Research 25: 1,025-1,040.

Manson, G.K. 2002. Subannual erosion and retreat of cohesive till bluffs, McNab's Island, Halifax, Nova Scotia. Journal of Coastal Research 18: 421-432.

Manson, G.K. and S.M. Solomon. 2007. Past and future forcing of Beaufort Sea coastal change. Atmosphere-Ocean 45: 107-122.

Manson, G.K., S.M. Solomon, D.L. Forbes, D.E. Atkinson, and M. Craymer. 2005. Spatial variability of factors influencing coastal change in the western Canadian Arctic. Geo-Marine Letters 25: 138-145.

Marlowe, J.I. 1966. Sedimentology of the Prince Gustaf Adolf Sea Area, District of Franklin. Geological Survey of Canada Paper 66-29, Ottawa, ON.

McCann, S.B. (Ed.). 1980. The Coastline of Canada. Geological Survey of Canada Paper 80-10, Ottawa. ON.

McLaren, P. and W.B. Barrie. 1983. The coastal morphology and sedimentology of eastern Lancaster Sound and northeast Baffin Island: a study of shoreline sensitivity to a potential oil spill. Geological Survey of Canada Paper 83-24, Ottawa, ON.

O'Carroll, S., D. Bérubé, D.L. Forbes, A. Hanson, S. Jolicoeur, and A. Fréchette. 2006. Coastal erosion. Pages 324-401 *in* Impacts of Sea-level Rise and Climate Change on the Coastal Zone of Southeastern New Brunswick (R. Daigle, Ed.). Environment Canada, Ottawa, ON.

Orford, J.D., S.C. Jennings, and D.L. Forbes. 2000. Origin, development, reworking and breakdown of gravel-dominated coastal barriers in Atlantic Canada: future scenarios for the British coast. Pages 23-55 *in* Ecology and Geomorphology of Coastal Shingle (J.R. Packham, Ed.). Smith-Settle, Otley, England.

Owens, E.H. 1977. Temporal variations in beach and nearshore dynamics. Journal of Sedimentary Petrology 47: 168-190.

Owens, E.H. and M.A. Rashid. 1976. Coastal environments and oil spill residues in Chedabucto Bay, Nova Scotia. Canadian Journal of Earth Sciences 13: 908-928.

Owens, E.H. and A.J. Bowen. 1977. Coastal environments of the Maritime Provinces. Maritime Sediments 13: 1-31.

Pelletier, B.R. 1962. Submarine geology program, Polar Continental Shelf Project, Isachsen, District of Franklin. Geological Survey of Canada Paper 61-21, Ottawa, ON.

Reinson, G.E. 1984. Barrier island and associated strand-plain systems. Pages 119-140 *in* Facies Models, 2nd edition (R.G. Walker, Ed.). Geoscience Canada Reprint Series 1, Geological Association of Canada, St. John's, NL.

Rosen, P.S. 1979. Boulder barricades in central Labrador. Journal of Sedimentary Petrology 49: 1,113-1,123.

Ruz, M-H., A. Héquette, and P.R. Hill. 1992. A model of coastal evolution in a transgressed thermokarst topography, Canadian Beaufort Sea. Marine Geology 106: 251-278.

Shaw, J. 2014. Deglaciation and postglacial sea-level changes in Atlantic Canada: science driven by technology. Pages 325-330 *in* Voyage of Discovery: Fifty Years of Marine Research at Canada's Bedford Institute of Oceanography (D.N. Nettleship, D.C. Gordon, C.F.M. Lewis, and M.P. Latremouille, Eds.). Bedford Institute of Oceanography-Oceans Association, Dartmouth, NS.

Shaw, J., R.B. Taylor, and D.L. Forbes. 1993. Impact of the Holocene transgression on the Atlantic coastline of Nova Scotia. Géographie physique et Quaternaire 47: 221-238.

Shaw, J., R.B. Taylor, D.L. Forbes, S. Solomon, and M-H. Ruz. 1998. Sensitivity of the coasts of Canada to sea-level rise. Geological Survey of Canada Bulletin 505, Ottawa, ON.

Shaw, J, R.B. Taylor, E. Patton, D.P. Potter, G.S. Parkes, and S. Hayward. 2006. The Bras d'Or Lakes, Nova Scotia: seafloor topography, backscatter strength, coastline classification, and sensitivity of coasts to sea-level rise. Geological Survey of Canada Open File 5397, Ottawa, ON.

Sherin, A.G., P. Fraser, S. Solomon, D.L. Forbes, K.A. Jenner, S. Hynes, T. Lynds, and P. Gareau. 2003. A decade in the life of a coastal information system. Proceedings, CoastGIS 2003: 5th International Symposium on GIS and Computer Cartography for Coastal Zone Management, Genoa, Italy. (http://www.gisig.it/coastgis/papers/sherin.htm)

Solomon, S.M. 2005. Spatial and temporal variability of shoreline change in the Beaufort-Mackenzie region, Northwest Territories, Canada. Geo-Marine Letters 25: 127-137.

Solomon, S. and J. Kruger. 1996. Vulnerability and adaptation assessment, coastal impact of sea-level change, Suva and vicinity, Viti Levu, Fiji Islands. SOPAC Technical Report 242, South Pacific Applied Geoscience Commission, Suva, Fiji. http://ict.sopac.org/VirLib/TR0242.pdf

Solomon, S.M. and D.L. Forbes. 1999. Coastal hazards and associated management issues on South Pacific islands. Coastal & Ocean Management 42: 523-554.

Solomon, S. and P. Gareau. 2003. Beaufort Sea coastal mapping and the development of an erosion hazard index. Pages 1,091-1,096 *in* Permafrost, Proceedings of International Conference on Permafrost (M. Phillips, S.M. Springman, and L.U. Arenson, Eds.). Balkema, Leiden, The Netherlands.

Solomon, S.M., D.L. Forbes, P. Fraser, B.J. Moorman, C.W. Stevens, and D. Whalen. 2008. Nearshore geohazards in the southern Beaufort Sea, Canada. Pages 281-289 *in* Proceedings of the 7th International Pipeline Conference, Calgary, Alberta. American Society of Mechanical Engineers, New York, NY. (CD-ROM).

St-Hilaire-Gravel, D., D.L. Forbes, and T. Bell. 2012. Multi-temporal analysis of a gravel-dominated coastline in the central Canadian Arctic Archipelago. Journal of Coastal Research 28: 421-441.

Syvitski, J.P.M. and C.T. Schafer. 1985. Sedimentology of Arctic Fjords Experiment (SAFE): project introduction. Arctic 38: 264-270.

Syvitski, J.P.M. and F.J. Hein. 1991. Sedimentology of an Arctic Basin, Itirbilung Fiord, Baffin Island, Northwest Territories. Geological Survey of Canada Paper 91-11, Ottawa, ON.

Syvitski, J.P.M., D.C. Burrell, and J.M. Skei. 1987. Fjords: Processes and Products. Springer Verlag, New York, NY.

Taylor, R.B. 1978. The occurrence of grounded ice ridges and shore ice piling along the northern coast of Somerset Island, N.W.T. Arctic 31: 133-149.

Taylor, R.B. 1980. Coastal reconnaissance for marine terminal planning in the Sverdrup Basin, NWT. Geological Survey of Canada Open File Report 693, Ottawa, ON.

Taylor, R.B. 1988. Terrain management activities on Sable Island 1982-85. Geological Survey of Canada Open File Report 1973, Ottawa, ON.

Taylor, R.B. 2000. A re-examination of beach mining along the Gaspereaux Shore, Prince Edward Island. Geological Survey of Canada Open File Report 3864, Ottawa, ON.

Taylor, R.B. and S.B. McCann. 1983. Coastal depositional landforms in northern Canada. Pages 53-77 *in* Shorelines and Isostasy (D.E. Smith and A.G. Dawson, Eds.). Institute of British Geographers, Special Publication 16, London, England.

Taylor, R.B. and D.L. Forbes. 1987. Ice-dominated shores of Lougheed Island: type examples for the northwest Queen Elizabeth Islands, Arctic Canada. Pages 33-48 *in* Proceedings of Canadian Coastal Conference 1987 (Y. Oullet, Ed.), Québec, QC. National Research Council, Ottawa, ON.

Taylor, R.B. and D. Frobel. 2006. Cruise Report 2005-305: 2005 field survey of coastal changes along Barrow Strait, Bylot and northern Baffin islands, Nunavut. Geological Survey of Canada Open File 5395, Ottawa, ON.

Taylor, R.B., S.L. Wittmann, M.J. Milne, and S.M. Kober. 1985. Beach morphology and coastal changes at selected sites, mainland Nova Scotia. Geological Survey of Canada Paper 85-12, Ottawa, ON.

Taylor, R.B., R.W.G. Carter, D.L. Forbes, and J.D. Orford. 1986. Beach sedimentation in Ireland: contrasts and similarities with Atlantic Canada. Pages 55-64 *in* Geological Survey of Canada Current Research, Part A, Paper 86-1A, Ottawa, ON.

Taylor, R.B., D. Frobel, D.L. Forbes, and K. Parlee. 1995. Coastal stability and the monitoring of physical shoreline changes in Nova Scotia. Pages 829-843 *in* Proceedings of Canadian Coastal Conference 1995, Dartmouth NS. Canadian Coastal Science and Engineering Association, Ottawa, ON.

Todd, B.J. and J. Shaw. 2014. Discovering the seafloor of the Bay of Fundy. Pages 231-235 *in* Voyage of Discovery: Fifty Years of Marine Research at Canada's Bedford Institute of Oceanography (D.N. Nettleship, D.C. Gordon, C.F.M. Lewis, and M.P. Latremouille, Eds.). Bedford Institute of Oceanography-Oceans Association, Dartmouth, NS.

Vandermeulen, J.H. 1977. The Chedabucto Bay spill – *Arrow*, 1970. Oceanus 20: 31-39.

van Proosdij, D., T. Milligan, G. Bugden, and K. Butler. 2009. A tale of two macrotidal estuaries: differential morphodynamic response of the intertidal zone to causeway construction. Journal of Coastal Research SI 56: 772-776.

Webster, T.L. and D.L. Forbes. 2006. Airborne laser altimetry for predictive modelling of coastal storm-surge flooding. Pages 157-182 *in* Remote Sensing of Aquatic Coastal Ecosystem Processes: Science and Management Applications (L.L. Richardson and E.F. LeDrew, Eds.). Springer, Dordrecht, The Netherlands.

Wolfe, S.A., S.R. Dallimore, and S.M. Solomon. 1998. Coastal permafrost investigations along a rapidly eroding shoreline, Tuktoyaktuk, NWT. Pages 1,125-1,131 *in* Proceedings of 7th International Conference on Permafrost (A.G. Lewkowicz and M. Allard, Eds.), Yellowknife, NT. Collection Nordicana, No. 55, Université Laval, Québec, QC.

Xhardé, R., B.F. Long, and D.L. Forbes. 2011. Short-term beach and shoreface evolution on a cuspate foreland observed with airborne topographic and bathymetric LiDAR. Journal of Coastal Research SI 62: 50-61.

24. FIFTY YEARS OF SURFICIAL MARINE GEOSCIENCE FOR CANADIANS: A SCIENTIST'S VIEW

David J.W. Piper

SUMMARY

Canada's seas and oceans, once the claim under the United Nations Convention on the Law of the Sea is accepted, will make up about 42% of the Canadian territory. Canada has by far the longest coastline in the world. Mapping and understanding the geology of this vast marine area is about 100 years behind the analogous process on land. Despite 50 years of work by the Bedford Institute of Oceanography (BIO), almost all of the marine area north of 50°N off eastern and northern Canada is known only at a reconnaissance level, the way that much of the Canadian land territory was known in 1912. A six-pronged strategy for acquiring geological knowledge served BIO well over the past 50 years and with adaptations is suitable for the next 50 years. The key elements of this strategy are: (1) detailed geological mapping in relatively small important areas that serve as case studies, (2) regional reconnaissance surveys to assess variability away from the case studies, (3) monitoring and study of processes active at the sea-floor and their influence on seafloor geology, (4) development and application of scientific concepts that help to predict geological conditions in areas where data are sparse or absent, (5) continual technological development, and (6) archiving data and samples collected at great expense. Examples of how these approaches are intertwined and yielded past successes are given in this contribution and in other reviews in this volume. They also serve as a guide to the way ahead.

Key words: surficial geology, sediment, mapping, bathymetry, geohazards, environment, petroleum.
E-mail: DPiper@NRCan.gc.ca

Canada is a maritime nation. Including additional lands likely to be claimed under the United Nations Convention on the Law of the Sea (UNCLOS), about 42% of Canada is marine, versus 53% that is land and 5% freshwater (Table 1). Canada's marine waters to the limit of the Exclusive Economic Zone (EEZ) comprise 36% of pre-UNCLOS Canadian territory, and Canada is actively regulating beyond that limit through the Canada-Newfoundland and Labrador Offshore Petroleum Board, with exploration wells in Orphan Basin and Flemish Pass. Canada has 202,080 km of coastline, the longest of any country in the world, and equivalent to the next five countries in line (Table 2). Providing geoscience knowledge for such a vast area requires many skills. The survey time required for conventional geological mapping, even at a 1:250 000 scale, is staggering; it is a project for the next 50 years of the Bedford Institute of Oceanography (BIO).

Table 1. The importance of the oceans to Canada.

Measure	Area km[2]	Area %
Onshore land[1]	9,093,507	53.2
Onshore freshwater[1]	891,163	5.2
Marine areas to Exclusive Economic Zone (EEZ) limit[2]	5,600,000	32.8
Potential extended seabed under UNCLOS[3]	1,500,000	8.8
Totals	17,084,670	100.0

Data sources: [1]Statistics Canada (www.statcan.gc.ca) Search: Canada Year Book Geography; Click: Data tables for geography; Click: Table 15.7.
[2]Fisheries and Oceans Canada (www.dfo-mpo.gc.ca/oceans/canadasoceans-oceansducanada/marinezones-zonesmarines-eng.htm); marine areas = internal waters + territorial sea + exclusive economic zone.

Table 2. The importance of the Canadian coastline.

Country	Coastline length (km)[1]
Canada	202,080[2]
Indonesia	54,716
Greenland	44,087
Russia	37,653
Philippines	36,289
Japan	29,751

[1]Length of coastline depends on the fractal scale used; values presented are based on 'The World Factbook' (https://www.cia.gov/library/publications/the-world-factbook/fields/2060.html) in order to provide a consistent comparison with other countries or territories.
[2]Natural Resources Canada gives a length of 243,000 km (Canada 1972).

Providing geoscience knowledge of the seabed and immediately underlying sediments in Canada's marine realm and coastal zone has been the responsibility of the Marine Environmental Geoscience subdivision of the Geological Survey of Canada (GSC), and its predecessor organizations, since 1962. The task has been daunting. The GSC was founded in 1842, and by its fiftieth year (1892) very little was known of northern and western Canada (Zaslow 1975). Access by rail, packhorse, canoe, or on foot was certainly a little slower and physically more strenuous than working at sea in an inflatable or a large research vessel. But a 2008 research cruise to Baffin Bay required two weeks of transit time for 14 days of work! Multi-year sea ice in the eastern part of Canadian territory in the Arctic Ocean is a serious impediment to geological mapping.

As with geological investigations on land by the GSC in the nineteenth century, the overall driver of marine geoscience research can be summarized as knowledge for effective management of the many competing uses of the land surface (Pickrill and Piper 2005). To the long-standing driver of economic development, we can add today's emphasis on safe and environmentally sustainable exploitation of the oceans. We also know that the three oceans around Canada, particularly the Arctic Ocean and the Labrador Sea, are critical parts of the earth's climate system. The record of environmental change in their sediments provides important insights for predicting future climate change (Weaver and Hillaire-Marcel 2004). Work on land around the 50th anniversary of the GSC in 1892 was multidisciplinary. The sections surveyed through the Rockies for transportation routes by McConnell (1886) did not just look for suitable routes and the ease with which surficial material could be levelled: they were also concerned with the topography of the surrounding peaks, the bedrock structure of the area, and its impact on coal resources. When Robert Bell and Albert P. Low mapped the bedrock of the shores of Ungava Bay at the end of the 19th century they were concerned not only with basic geological mapping, but also topography, economic resources, and the nature of the surficial cover (Bell and Low 1900).

The paucity of geological work in Canada's marine territory in the 19th and first half of the 20th century was largely because there was neither an economic driver nor a strong perception of Canadian sovereignty over the seabed far from shore. The shape of the floor of the ocean was important to the international cable industry; submarine canyons from Venezuela to Labrador were shown in a map by Spencer (1903). The presence of sedimentary rocks offshore Nova Scotia and Newfoundland was recognised by Dahl (1925) on the basis of material recovered by fishermen in trawls. Shepard (1931) proposed an origin by glacial erosion for the Laurentian Channel. Study of sediment samples collected on the 1928 voyage of the *Marion* to the Labrador Sea and Baffin Bay led to the recognition of the importance of ice rafting as a sediment transport process (Trask 1932). Except for the paper by Spencer, a Canadian, all of these studies were by Americans. The great Grand Banks earthquake and tsunami of 18 November 1929 (Ruffman and Hann 2006) stimulated little Canadian work, and it was decades before the cause of the resulting cable breaks was understood (by the Americans, Heezen and Ewing 1952). It was also American work (Officer and Ewing 1954) that led to the recognition of a deep petroliferous sedimentary basin off Nova Scotia, leading to the first exploration drilling in 1965. Since that time, the petroleum wealth of the offshore has been an important driver for marine geological research. Canadian perception of sovereignty over its marine realm was strengthened in 1977 by the extension of fisheries jurisdiction to the 200-nautical mile limit.

OUR PARTNERS

The GSC Atlantic (GSCA, formerly called Atlantic Geoscience Centre) has been the principal group working on the geology of Canada's marine realm. Canadian universities have for many years found it difficult to obtain sufficient funding and ship time to maintain ongoing marine programs, as summarized in the 1998 Natural Sciences and Engineering Research Council (NSERC) report (Ingram 1998). Except for the support of ArcticNet of the Networks of Centres of Excellence of Canada, the funding situation has not improved significantly during the last two decades. Some provinces in Canada have a coastal geologist, and foreign nations including the United States, Russia, and Spain have done important work, particularly in deeper water areas adjacent to Canada. Only one Ocean Drilling Program long, cored borehole lies within Canada's current eastern and arctic marine realm. Most scientific publications on marine territory of Canadian waters are by the GSC.

Industry partners – petroleum, cable, or fishing industries – generally lack technical knowledge of the geology of the seabed. In the case of the petroleum industry, geotechnical groups located in Houston, TX, may have experience in the Gulf of Mexico, West Africa, and Indonesia, but rarely have experience in glacially-derived marine sediments. Similarly, other government departments, both federal and provincial, have relied on the GSCA for technical advice on issues as diverse as substrates for corals, locating bundles of drugs on the seafloor, assessing sediment transport from offshore dump sites, and numerous management issues in the coastal zone. It makes no economic sense for any of these groups to try to cover off this need by creating their own geological survey, especially since many of the issues are beyond the experience and knowledge base of private industry.

THE STRATEGY

The general strategy of the GSCA at BIO that has served Canada well over the past 50 years has used six approaches to provide the necessary knowledge and advice:

1. Detailed geological mapping in areas selected for their immediate importance, that can serve as case studies. This has included understanding not only the material on the seafloor, but also the character of sediments for hundreds of metres below the seafloor.
2. Reconnaissance surveys on a regional basis for assessing regional variability away from the case studies.
3. Studies of processes active at the seafloor and how they influence seafloor geology: the effect of waves and currents in scouring and transporting sediment, the effect of storms on beaches, how pollutants migrate in contaminated sediment, and how microfossils are indicators of marine environments in the past.
4. Development of scientific concepts that help to predict the geological framework in areas in which data are sparse or absent. For example, the controls that past glaciation and sea-level change have had on the development of offshore geology, or the manner in which gas hydrates may destabilize the seafloor and produce submarine landslides and dangerous tsunamis.
5. Continual technological development, in both the field and the laboratory, with partners in other marine institutes where appropriate.
6. Archiving and conserving data and samples collected, at great expense, at sea so that they are available for re-analysis as new questions arise or new scientific techniques become available.

These approaches are illustrated in a few case studies of successful service to Canadians over the past 50 years.

LESSONS FROM CASE STUDIES

Early mapping of the Scotian Shelf by L. King and his team provided a template for surficial mapping elsewhere on the eastern Canadian margin (King 1970, King and MacLean 1976). The emphasis was on the use of high-resolution seismic reflection profiles, collected at speeds of 5-7 knots, and 'ground-truthed' by some samples and sidescan sonar data. Widely-spaced seismic lines were interpolated using closely-spaced Kelvin Hughes MS26B sounding records collected by the Canadian Hydrographic Service – an illustration of an effective partnership that has lasted 50 years. These techniques allowed the efficient mapping of large areas from mid-sized vessels. It led to a series of maps of the near-seabed geology of the Scotian Shelf (King and MacLean 1971; Drapeau and King 1972; Fader et al. 1977, 1978, 2014), which became a regional case study that provided a template for reconnaissance work elsewhere, such as the Grand Banks and Labrador Shelf. On much of the eastern Canadian continental shelves, sedimentation rates have been low over the past 6,000 years (0.1–0.3 mm/year), but were much higher during past glacial and deglacial times (0.5–2 mm/year). The use of seismic techniques provided good information on the glacial sediments in the top metres to tens of metres of the seafloor, but was less successful in mapping variations in contemporary sediment at the seabed. The analogy on land would be that the rocks were mapped, but not the soils. Seismic-based mapping was of great value in identifying geohazards that provided constraints to oil and gas exploration and development (King 1980, Lewis et al. 2014). The first 'pockmarks' were discovered on the Scotian Shelf (King and MacLean 1970). It soon became apparent that a Sable Island gas pipeline to land would be feasible, but Hibernia oil from offshore Newfoundland would have to be transported by tanker because of iceberg scouring (King and Fader 1981). The mapping of the Scotian Shelf led to new concepts of proglacial marine sedimentation, involving an important role for floating ice shelves (King and Fader 1986). These were influential when first proposed, but subsequent developments in radiocarbon dating of small marine samples and in understanding of the flow of glaciers and ice sheets has led to a new understanding of how sediment was dispersed and deposited during glacial periods (Syvitski and Praeg 1989, Shaw et al. 2006). This modern understanding emphasizes the predominant role of ice-streams occupying the major erosional transverse troughs on the continental shelf in controlling both sediment supply and the style of deglaciation.

The important role of past glaciations in sculpting seascapes became of prime importance in the Gulf of Maine boundary dispute with the United States, one that was referred to the International Court of Justice in The Hague in the early 1980s (Sinclair and O'Boyle 2014). At that time, the concept of natural prolongation had played an important role in the considerations of the Court on the maritime boundary between Tunisia and Libya, although ultimately the Court ruled that primacy should be given to geomorphology rather than geology (Stanley 1982). Great South Channel and Northeast Channel, transverse troughs formerly occupied by ice streams that bound Georges Bank to the east and west, were of key importance to the Canadian case. In its judgement, however, the Court put aside all the natural prolongation arguments (Sinclair and O'Boyle 2014). In the later dispute with France on the St. Pierre Bank, surficial geology issues played a much lesser role.

Mapping of the 'soil' rather than the 'rocks' on the continental shelf was prohibitively demanding on ship time before the availability of multibeam bathymetry technology and only regional compilations were possible (Piper 1991). On the Grand Banks and northward, much of the 'driver' for understanding the upper metre of the seafloor came from concerns about how grounding icebergs could plough the seabed and damage petroleum infrastructure, including possible pipelines. Local case studies were based on detailed sidescan sonar mosaics, including repetitive mapping of known groundings (Lewis et al. 2014), followed up in some cases by manned submersible investigations (Piper 1989). With time, it became apparent that deep ploughing to subbottom depths of many metres by icebergs took place thousands of years ago when 'armadas of icebergs' were released during deglaciation and the impact of modern icebergs is largely on the upper metre of the seafloor. This discovery essentially made development of the oilfields of the Newfoundland Grand Banks economically feasible. Like so many important findings at sea, it depended on targeted surveys integrated with scientific concepts that were developed from both case studies and a regional understanding of geological history, glaciology, and physical oceanography. Targeted surveys alone would not have provided the confidence that interpretations were consistent with a scientific understanding of how geological processes have changed over time. That scientific understanding also provides guidance on the potential impact of rapid deglaciation of major ice streams in Greenland (Hughes et al. 2004, Holland et al. 2008, Thomas et al. 2009).

Studies of contemporary sedimentation and the nature of the 'soil' at the seabed based on older technology were possible in coastal inlets of limited geographic extent, using core and grab samples and sidescan sonar. Work in the early 1970s focussed on pollution and changes in sedimentation in the Strait of Canso, Nova Scotia, following the 1956 construction of the Canso Causeway and the consequent industrialization of the Port Hawkesbury area. This work provided methods and standards for assessing pollution levels from seabed geochemistry and microfossil faunas (Buckley et al. 1974) and became a template for studies in areas such as Halifax Harbour (Fader and Miller 2008) and the Bay of Chaleur (Buckley 2014). Such studies provided a baseline for safe and effective dredging and the installation of sewage treatment facilities (Buckley 2014). They also allowed the development of scientific models of the response of formerly glaciated coastal zones to changes in sea level (Piper et al. 1983, Boyd and Penland 1984) that could be applied to new areas.

Much of the eastern Canadian margin is indented by fiords, glacially over-deepened inlets with steep walls and commonly seaward sills of bedrock or glacial moraines. Many coastal settlements are located in fiords (Stanley 1968, Syvitski and Schafer 1996). The geological evolution of fiords is diachronous from north to south. Ice retreated from Nova Scotia and southern Newfoundland fiords 16,000 to 14,000 years ago, but is still present in some Baffin Island fiords. For this reason, the Sedimentology of Arctic Fjords Experiment (SAFE) project in the early 1980s mapped sediment distribution and investigated active sedimentation processes in Baffin Island fiords (Syvitski et al. 1987). This work provided a foundation of scientific concepts for evaluating the surficial geology of southern fiords including Halifax Harbour and, more generally, the effect of glacial conditions on sedimentation in areas such as the St. Lawrence Estuary (Syvitski and Praeg 1989). These concepts have in recent years been used to better understand geohazards in the St. Lawrence Estuary applicable to seafloor infrastructure and potential gas exploitation (Pinet et al. 2011).

But the consequences of the Baffin Island fiord work were more far reaching. Studies of the discharge of the sediment laden rivers that built deltas in the Baffin Island fiords led directly to the work of Mulder and Syvitski (1995) that defined the conditions under which direct flow of rivers into the oceans would create turbidity currents. With over 350 citations, it has been arguably the most influential geoscience paper published at BIO. But its influence has been in ways that were never imagined when the Baffin fiord project was approved in 1982. The world's conventional energy resources of oil are coming increasingly from deep-water sandstone reservoirs, many deposited by the process so clearly elucidated by Mulder and Syvitski (1995).

Oil exploration reached deep water off Nova Scotia and Newfoundland in the late 1970s when the Acadia K-62 (1978) and Blue H-28 (1979) wells were drilled at water depths of 866 m and 1,486 m, respectively. Deep-water drilling ended with the termination of National Energy Program subsidies in the mid-1980s, but resumed in the new millennium, first on the Scotian Slope, and later in Orphan Basin and Flemish Pass. Research necessary to provide the regulatory boards with necessary information on geohazards, environmental issues, and drilling constraints required new technologies, or the adaptation of existing shelf technologies to the greater pressures of deep water. The ease with which large areas of deep water can be surveyed by multibeam bathymetry, and the willingness of industry to pay for such surveys, resulted in rapid progress in understanding the geological framework and seabed stability of the steep continental slopes out to 2,500 m water depth in offshore parts of Nova Scotia and Newfoundland. Although the primary 'drivers' were safety and sustainability of deep-water petroleum exploration, the spin-off benefits from this new data acquisition were much broader. At a time when petroleum exploration was moving into deep water elsewhere in the world, the benefits of international comparisons and collaborations helped accelerate the development of scientific concepts in Canadian waters. The GSCA was able to advise university partners on where to obtain particular paleoclimate records and partners in Fisheries and Oceans Canada (DFO) and universities on the substrates for vulnerable marine ecosystems involving deep-water corals and sponges. The risk of tsunamis from proximal submarine landslides was quantified (Mosher 2009). Contributions were made to the understanding of petroleum reservoirs in various types of deep-water sands. The influx of new data for one purpose, enabled by new technology, led to a blossoming of science and knowledge in a wide range of fields.

The national marine core repository has 20,000 core, grab, and dredge samples and almost all marine seismic data collected by the GSCA is now online as jpeg 2000 scans. The data availability provides new opportunities, in a manner similar to the example of deep-water geohazard research, of supporting new work by academic or industry partners, or the GSCA itself, in directions quite different from those for which the data were originally collected. In the past, work on legacy samples by academic partners led to the recognition that Heinrich layers were sourced in Hudson Strait (Bond et al. 1992) and the discovery of the only Alleghanian age pluton in Canada (Pe-Piper et al. 2010). As the Internet makes discovery of GSC data holdings much more efficient, we can look forward to continued use of this unique archive.

Historically, the GSCA produced syntheses of regional geology, the most recent being the Decade of North American Geology (DNAG) volume for the Canadian East Coast offshore (Keen and Williams 1990). In an increasingly digital world, the hope over the two decades since that DNAG volume was that increasingly both data and interpretations would be released digitally. That dream has been only partly realized, due to the sheer volume of legacy data and organizational changes that have separated data release from scientists. As the number of focussed narrow publications and the availability of data increases throughout the world, the need for informed syntheses has never been greater. If the GSCA is to properly serve Canadians, the production of informed syntheses needs to be given higher priority, both for individual scientists or groups and for the entire organization. In marine areas of Canada, no one other than GSCA is equipped to produce such syntheses.

WHERE SHOULD WE GO FROM HERE?

In Canadian waters, it is still true that *"We know less about the ocean's bottom than about the moon's back side"* (R. Revelle *in* Nierenberg 1992). High-resolution maps are available for all of the moon's backside. In contrast, only about 10 % of Canada's Exclusive Economic Zone (EEZ) south of 60°N has multibeam bathymetry coverage (of which almost half was paid for by industry or foreign governments), with less than 3% coverage of Canada's arctic waters (including Hudson Bay) and areas beyond the EEZ. This also contrasts with smaller, but poorer, countries such as Pakistan and Ireland, which have most or all of their deep-water areas surveyed. As discussed by Fader et al. (2014), multibeam bathymetry provides the skilled interpreter with a first-order understanding of geological framework and processes in a marine area, analogous to what can be interpreted from air photographs and satellite imagery in the terrestrial realm. It has become the foundation of modern marine geoscience.

The geological knowledge base in some Canadian marine areas appears sufficient to declare that reconnaissance exploration work is no longer necessary. Our knowledge of the Bay of Fundy, Scotian Shelf and Slope, Gulf of St. Lawrence, Newfoundland Grand Banks, Flemish Pass, and southern Orphan Basin is sufficient that technical questions can be answered on the basis of existing knowledge and scientific concepts. These areas are effectively mapped at 1:250 000 scale. As a consequence, if issues arise in these areas, targeted short-term studies can be designed efficiently and executed. The knowledge base for many of the more densely inhabited coastal areas of Atlantic Canada is also sufficient to carry out future research on a short-term targeted basis, provided that basic coastal monitoring is maintained. Knowledge of these areas has reached the standard of knowledge of the remoter terrestrial areas of Canada.

The approach that has served the GSCA organization well over the past 50 years is still necessary in the remaining part of the Canadian marine realm. The knowledge base in most northern waters (north of 50°N) and beyond the 2,000 m isobath is insufficient to provide definitive advice on seafloor geology in response to most technical questions, whether they involve competing uses of the seabed, geohazards, environmental assessment, planning of targeted sampling or survey campaigns, or responding to questions not yet formulated. In 1962, when BIO was founded, who would have foreseen the way in which seafloor geology would be used to support the case for Canadian offshore sovereignty, to assess the risk of oil-well blowouts at 2,500 m depths, to use pockmarks as an exploration tool for petroleum, or to assess earthquake and tsunami hazards? Scientific concepts applicable to remote, ice-infested, or deep water are not well developed and the paucity of reconnaissance data limits the effectiveness with which existing scientific concepts can be applied. Provision of public policy advice in most of Canada's ocean waters cannot at present be organized using a short-term, land-based model, where gaps are filled by other partners. In many areas of ocean, the knowledge base is insufficient and too few partners are involved. Projects must have a multi-year duration and a broad scope. Of necessity, they will have a component of exploration and if good science is allowed to flourish, they will have unexpected benefits in the future. If Canada is to exercise sovereignty over its marine territory, that sovereignty must be based on knowledge.

ACKNOWLEDGEMENTS

I appreciate the intellectual environment at BIO that encourages scientific questioning. I thank Dave Mosher, John Hughes Clarke, Gary Sonnichsen, and Gordon Fader for providing data and advice, but I alone am responsible for the content of this paper. The opinions of the author are personal and certainly do not completely correspond with those of Natural Resources Canada.

REFERENCES

Bell, R. and A.P. Low. 1900. Map of the coasts of Hudson Strait and Ungava Bay. Geological Survey of Canada Map 699, Ottawa, ON.

Bond, G., H. Heinrich, W. Broecker, L. Labeyrie, J. McManus, J. Andrews, S. Huon, R. Jantschik, S. Clasen, and C. Simet. 1992 . Evidence for massive discharges of icebergs into the North Atlantic Ocean during the last glacial period. Nature 360: 245-249.

Boyd, R. and S. Penland. 1984. Shoreface translation and the Holocene stratigraphic record: Examples from Nova Scotia, the Mississippi Delta and eastern Australia. Marine Geology 60: 391-412.

Buckley, D.E., E.H. Owens, C.T. Schafer, G. Vilks, R.E. Cranston, M.A. Rashid, F.J.E. Wagner, and D.A. Walker. 1974. Canso Strait and Chedabucto Bay: Multidisciplinary study of the impact of man on the marine environment. Pages 133-160 *in* Offshore Geology of eastern Canada, Volume 1 - Concepts and Applications of Environmental Marine Geology (B.R. Pelletier, Ed.). Geological Survey of Canada, Paper 74-30, Ottawa, ON.

Buckley, D.E. 2014. Discoveries in environmental marine geology. Pages 247-252 *in* Voyage of Discovery: Fifty Years of Marine Research at Canada's Bedford Institute of Oceanography (D.N. Nettleship, D.C. Gordon, C.F.M. Lewis, and M.P. Latremouille, Eds.). Bedford Institute of Oceanography-Oceans Association, Dartmouth, NS.

Canada. 1972. Facts from Canadian Maps: A Geographic Handbook. Department of Energy Mines and Resources, Surveys and Mapping Branch, Ottawa, ON.

Dahl, W.H. 1925. Tertiary fossils dredged off the northeastern coast of North America. American Journal of Science, Series 5, 10: 213-218.

Drapeau, G. and L.H. King. 1972. Surficial geology of the Yarmouth-Browns Bank map area. Geological Survey of Canada, Paper 72-24, Ottawa, ON.

Fader, G.B.J. and R.O. Miller. 2008. Surficial geology, Halifax Harbour, Nova Scotia. Geological Survey of Canada, Bulletin No. 590, Ottawa, ON.

Fader, G.B., L.H. King, and B. MacLean. 1977. Surficial geology of the eastern Gulf of Maine and Bay of Fundy. Geological Survey of Canada, Paper 76-17, Ottawa, ON.

Fader, G.B., L.H. King, and B. MacLean. 1978. Surficial geology of Canso Bank and adjacent areas. Geological Survey of Canada, Paper 76-15, Ottawa, ON.

Fader, G.B.J., B. MacLean, H.W. Josenhans, and S.M. Blasco. 2014. Seabed sediment mapping at the Bedford Institute of Oceanography: from single beam to multibeam. Pages 191-199 *in* Voyage of Discovery: Fifty Years of Marine Research at Canada's Bedford Institute of Oceanography (D.N. Nettleship, D.C. Gordon, C.F.M. Lewis, and M.P. Latremouille, Eds.). Bedford Institute of Oceanography-Oceans Association, Dartmouth, NS.

Heezen, B.C. and M. Ewing 1952. Turbidity currents and submarine slumps, and the 1929 Grand Banks earthquake. American Journal of Science 250: 849-873.

Holland, D.M., R.H. Thomas, B. De Young, M.H. Ribergaard, and B. Lyberth. 2008. Acceleration of Jakobshavn Isbrae triggered by warm subsurface ocean waters. Nature Geoscience 1: 659-664.

Hughes, T., R. Thomas, E. Frederick, W. Krabill, S. Manizade, and C. Martin. 2004. Greenland ice sheet and rising sea level in a worst-case climatic change scenario. Polar Meteorology and Glaciology 18: 54-71.

Ingram, R.G. 1998. Revised Final Report: Workshop on Marine Sciences in Canada, 1997. Available at http://earthsciencescanada.com/cfes/_Archive_jan7_2011/papers and reports/marinegeo.html.

Keen, M.J. and G.L. Williams (Eds.). 1990. Geology of the continental margin of eastern Canada. Geological Survey of Canada, Geology of Canada No. 2, Ottawa, ON.

King, L.H. 1970. Surficial geology of the Halifax - Sable Island map area. Marine Science Paper 1, Marine Sciences Branch, Department of Energy Mines and Resources, Ottawa, ON.

King, L.H. 1980. Aspects of regional surficial geology related to site investigation requirements. Pages 37–60 *in* Offshore Site Investigations (D.A. Ardus, Ed.). Society for Underwater Technology, Graham and Trotman, London, England.

King, L.H. and B. MacLean. 1970. Pockmarks on the Scotian Shelf. Geological Society of America Bulletin 81: 3,141-3,148.

King, L.H. and B. MacLean. 1971. Surficial geology of the Banquereau and Misaine Bank map area. Geological Survey of Canada, Paper 71-52, Ottawa, ON.

King, L.H. and B. MacLean. 1976. Geology of the Scotian Shelf. Geological Survey of Canada, Paper 74-31, Ottawa, ON.

King, L.H. and G.B. Fader. 1981. Seabed conditions east of the Avalon Peninsula to the Virgin rocks, Newfoundland. Geological Survey of Canada, Open File 723, Ottawa, ON.

King, L.H. and G.B. Fader. 1986. Wisconsinan glaciation of the continental shelf, southeastern Atlantic Canada. Geological Survey of Canada Bulletin, No. 363, Ottawa, ON.

Lewis, C.F.M., S.M. Blasco, D.J.W. Piper, and G.V. Sonnichsen. 2014. Seabed geohazard knowledge for safe hydrocarbon development. Pages 383-394 *in* Voyage of Discovery: Fifty Years of Marine Research at Canada's Bedford Institute of Oceanography (D.N. Nettleship, D.C. Gordon, C.F.M. Lewis, and M.P. Latremouille, Eds.). Bedford Institute of Oceanography-Oceans Association, Dartmouth, NS.

McConnell, R.G. 1886. Section across the Rocky Mountains in the vicinity of the Canadian Pacific Railway. Geological and Natural History Survey of Canada, Annual Report, 1886, Part D, Ottawa, ON.

Mosher, D.C. 2009. Oceans, submarine land-slides and consequent tsunamis in Canada. Geoscience Canada 36: 179-190.

Mulder, T. and J.P.M. Syvitski. 1995. Turbidity currents generated at river mouths during exceptional discharges to the world oceans. Journal of Geology 103: 285-299.

Nierenberg, W.A. 1992. Roger Revelle. Physics Today 45: 119-120.

Officer, C.B. and M. Ewing. 1954. Geophysical investigations in the emerged and submerged Atlantic Coastal Plain. Part 7. Continental shelf, continental slope and continental rise south of Nova Scotia. Geological Society of America Bulletin 65: 653-670.

Pe-Piper, G., S.L. Kamo, and C. McCall. 2010. The German Bank pluton, offshore SW Nova Scotia: petrology, age and regional significance for Alleghanian plutonism. Geological Society of America Bulletin 122: 690-700.

Pickrill, R.A. and D.J.W. Piper. 2005. Marine geology in Atlantic Canada. Proceedings of the Nova Scotian Institute of Science 43: 91-109.

Pinet, N., V. Brake, D.C. Campbell, and M. Duchesne. 2011. Seafloor and shallow subsurface of the St. Lawrence River Estuary. Geoscience Canada 38: 31-39.

Piper, D.J.W. (Ed.). 1989. Submersible observations off the East Coast of Canada. Geological Survey of Canada, Paper 88-20, Ottawa, ON.

Piper, D.J.W. 1991. Seabed geology of the eastern Canadian continental shelf. Continental Shelf Research 11: 1,013-1,035.

Piper, D.J.W., J.R.J. Letson, A.M. de Iure, and C.Q. Barrie. 1983. Sediment accumulation in low-sedimentation, wave-dominated, glaciated inlets. Sedimentary Geology 36: 195-215.

Ruffman, A. and V. Hann. 2006. The Newfoundland Tsunami of November 18, 1929: An examination of the twenty-eight deaths of the "South Coast Disaster". Newfoundland and Labrador Studies 21: 1,719-1,726.

Shaw, J., D.J.W. Piper, G.B. Fader, E.L. King, B.J. Todd, T. Bell, M.J. Batterson, and D.J.E. Liverman. 2006. A conceptual model of the deglaciation of Atlantic Canada. Quaternary Science Reviews 25: 2,055-2,081.

Shepard, F.P. 1931. Saint Lawrence (Cabot Strait) submarine trough. Geological Society of America Bulletin 42: 853-864.

Sinclair, M.M. and R.N. O'Boyle. 2014. The Gulf of Maine boundary dispute: the role of the Bedford Institute of Oceanography. Pages 397-405 *in* Voyage of Discovery: Fifty Years of Marine Research at Canada's Bedford Institute of Oceanography (D.N. Nettleship, D.C. Gordon, C.F.M. Lewis, and M.P. Latremouille, Eds.). Bedford Institute of Oceanography-Oceans Association, Dartmouth, NS.

Spencer, J.W. 1903. Submarine valleys off the American coast and in the North Atlantic. Geological Society of America Bulletin 14: 207-226.

Stanley, D.J. 1968. Reworking of glacial sediments in the North West Arm, a fjord-like inlet on the southeast coast of Nova Scotia. Journal of Sedimentary Petrology 38: 1,224-1,241.

Stanley, D.J. 1982. Plate tectonics and offshore boundary delimitation: Tunisia-Libya case at the International Court of Justice. Geo-Marine Letters 2: 101-107.

Syvitski, J.P.M. and D.B. Praeg. 1989. Quaternary seismo-stratigraphy of the Lower St. Lawrence Estuary. Geological Survey of Canada, Open File 2230, Ottawa, ON.

Syvitski, J.P.M. and C.T. Schafer. 1996. Evidence for an earthquake-triggered basin collapse in Saguenay Fjord, Canada. Sedimentary Geology 104: 127-153.

Syvitski, J.P.M., D.C. Burrell, and J.M. Skei. 1987. Fjords: Processes and Products. Springer-Verlag, New York, NY.

Thomas, R., E. Frederick, W. Krabill, S. Manizade, and C. Martin. 2009. Recent changes on Greenland outlet glaciers. Journal of Glaciology 55: 147-162.

Trask, P.D. 1932. The sediments. Pages 62-81 *in* The "Marion" expeditions to Davis Strait and Baffin Bay, Scientific Reports, Part 1. United States Treasury Department, Coast Guard Bulletin 19, Washington, DC.

Weaver, A.J. and C. Hillaire-Marcel. 2004. Ice growth in the greenhouse: a seductive paradox but unrealistic scenario. Geoscience Canada 31 (2): 77-85.

Zaslow, M. 1975. Reading the Rocks – The Story of the Geological Survey of Canada 1842-1972. Macmillan, Toronto, ON.

25. ROCKS OF THE DEEP: THE SUBSURFACE GEOLOGY OF OFFSHORE EASTERN CANADA

Graham L. Williams*, Robert A. Fensome, and Sonya A. Dehler

SUMMARY

Basins composed of relatively young sedimentary rocks, usually not more than about 220 million years old, underlie much of eastern Canada's vast continental margin. The best-known are the Jeanne d'Arc Basin beneath the Grand Banks of Newfoundland, and the Scotian Basin off Nova Scotia. The origin of these basins dates back to the opening of the North Atlantic Ocean and the Labrador-Baffin Seaway (from the Labrador Sea to Baffin Bay) after the supercontinent Pangea split up. From the pioneering studies at the Bedford Institute of Oceanography (BIO), plus the work of industry and academic geoscientists, we now have a much better understanding of the geology of offshore eastern Canada. These efforts have included seismic studies, as well as analyses of rocks (sedimentology/lithostratigraphy) and fossils (paleontology/biostratigraphy) from offshore wells, all contributing to compilations of the regional geology. Studies of buried organic material and the thermal history of the rocks have led to an understanding of the proven and potential petroleum reserves in the offshore basins, a foundation for the continuing search for these resources. BIO scientists have added knowledge, and created comprehensive databases which are powerful tools for both ongoing and new research and exploration, showcasing a classic model in the formation and subsequent development of a geologically passive margin, and confirming the foresight shown in maintaining research capability to resolve the offshore subsurface geology. For Canadians, these studies have provided detailed knowledge of the geology of petroleum basins, valuable information for governments to manage effectively the offshore domain.

Key words: offshore eastern Canada, subsurface geology, sedimentary basins, seismic, well data.
***E-mail:** Graham.Williams@NRCan-RNCan.gc.ca

Offshore eastern Canada stretches from about 43° to 85° N, or roughly 4,660 km. The geology of this region has primarily been unravelled in the past 50 years, reflecting the refinement of geoscientific techniques and the commitment of numerous scientists, many of whom have been or are at the Bedford Institute of Oceanography (BIO). In the early to mid-twentieth century, our understanding of the geology of the offshore sedimentary basins, the continuously subsiding depressions in which sediments several kilometres thick have accumulated, was minimal. This situation changed dramatically in the 1960s, motivated by the oil companies, plus the establishment of BIO in 1962, and the creation of the Eastern Petroleum Geology Section of the Geological Survey of Canada (GSC) in 1971. This Section and its successors, plus the former Regional Geology Subdivision, now constitute the Marine Resources Geoscience Subdivision of the Geological Survey of Canada-Atlantic (GSCA) located at BIO. Research by GSCA staff has enhanced our knowledge of the offshore geology by bringing together studies of the deeper parts of the crust, what most geologists think of as 'basement', with studies of the sedimentary basins. The in-depth studies of the crust by BIO and other scientists over the last 50 years have led to major advances in our understanding of the geological evolution of offshore eastern Canada over the past 600 million years.

Thanks to the development of plate tectonics, we now know that the geological foundations of the Maritime Provinces, much of the island of Newfoundland, and the adjacent offshore were once a series of microcontinents, or terranes. These wanderers were situated in long-lost oceans, and were not part of the ancient core of what is now North America. As the supercontinent Pangea came together between 450 and 300 million years ago, several oceans closed, catching and squeezing the microcontinents between larger continents to form the Appalachian Mountain belt in what is today North America and the Caledonian Mountain belt in present-day northwestern Europe (prior to the opening of the Atlantic).

The Appalachian-Caledonian collision zone involved major structural elements and lines of weakness in the rocks that were rejuvenated in part as a rift system some 220 million years ago when the supercontinent Pangea began to break up. Initial rift basins formed in what were to become the North Atlantic borderlands, exemplified by the Fundy and Scotian basins (Fig. 1). Ultimately the North Atlantic Ocean began to develop. Oceans are born when rifting becomes drifting, or when oceanic or basaltic crust starts to form. Outpourings of basalt at mid-oceanic ridges cause widening of the ocean, a process that is ongoing today at the Mid-Atlantic Ridge and that can be seen in Iceland, where basalt is constantly being formed. Offshore eastern Canada represents a passive continental margin (continental shelf and continental slope), being in the vicinity of where oceanic crust generated at the Mid-Atlantic Ridge comes into contact with the continental crust of North America, but does not subduct beneath it; in fact no plate boundary is involved. The above scenario, based on research over the last 50 years, represents a startling advance in our understanding of how the oceans evolved.

The basins formed on the passive margin of offshore eastern Canada reflect the orientation of the original rift that led to the birth of the North Atlantic and are aligned approximately northeast from the Scotian Margin to the southeast Grand Banks of Newfoundland (Fig. 1). There they swing to the northwest along the northeast Newfoundland and Labrador coasts and, ultimately, into Baffin Bay. This change of orientation reflects changes in plate alignment. From south to north, the sedimentary basins containing primarily rocks younger than 220 million years old are: the Fundy Basin, the Scotian Basin, the adjacent Whale and Horseshoe basins which are parallel to each other, the Jeanne d'Arc Basin with the Carson Basin to the southeast and the Flemish Pass Basin to the northeast, Orphan Basin, St. Anthony Basin, Hopedale Basin, Saglek Basin, and Baffin Basin (Fig. 1). Separating the basins are basement highs that are topographically and/or structurally high-standing. Much of our understanding of the basins' geology and evolution is a result of research carried out by GSCA, commonly based on industry seismic data and rock samples from wells drilled by oil companies.

Using the data generated, GSCA staff members have published numerous papers providing details of the geology of the offshore basins and, in parallel, some impressive databases. Results have included erection of lithostratigraphic units (e.g., formations, which are distinctive packages of strata, and members, which are subunits of formations, generally of more limited areal extent), biostratigraphic zonation, and event schemes; such information contributes fundamentally to our understanding of the geological and paleoenvironmental history of a basin as well as of the potential oil and natural gas resources (petroleum systems). Considerable research has gone into determining the potential oil and natural gas resources in the offshore sedimentary basins. Resource evaluations, or resource appraisals, have been joint efforts with the Geological Survey of Canada offices in Calgary (Alberta) and Quebec City (Quebec). The results have revealed the impressive potential of some of the basins, an encouraging sign that oil and natural gas exploration will continue offshore for several decades to come.

Figure 1. Map of eastern Canada showing the locations, names (or numbers), and maximum thicknesses (kilometres) of the offshore Mesozoic-Cenozoic sedimentary basins (yellow hues); locations and names of places, features, and wells mentioned in the text are also given. Numerals refer to: 1 = Montagnais structure, 2 = Sable Island, 3 = Orpheus Graben, 4 = South Whale Basin, 5 = Whale Basin, 6 = Horseshoe Basin, 7 = Carson Basin, 8 = Flemish Pass Basin, 9 = St. Anthony Basin, and 10 = Cumberland Sound. Wells are identified by: A = Sable Island C-67, B = Tors Cove D-52, C = Grand Falls H-09, D = Terra Nova I-97, E = Texaco-Shell Blue H-28, and F = Leif E-38 (from Fensome et al. in press).

Within GSCA, some researchers have restricted their investigations to rocks formed over the past 220 million years, just before and during the opening of the North Atlantic Ocean, while others focussed on interpreting rocks older than 220 million years. This paper focusses on the former investigations.

HISTORY OF STUDY

Geoscientific studies of offshore eastern Canada have been ongoing for more than sixty years, beginning in 1950 with the first seismic refraction survey by the Lamont Geological Observatory of Columbia University (New York, NY). All initial studies were geophysical, including gravity, airborne and seaborne magnetics, and reflection and refraction seismic surveys; these remote sensing techniques reveal subsurface features such as sedimentary layering and igneous intrusions. Seismic, gravity, and magnetic studies can all be carried out from ships, and the last two are adaptable for use from aeroplanes. A major advantage of such remote sensing techniques is that we can learn much about the rocks without having to drill into them, an expensive operation beyond the capability of most oceanographic institutes and surveys.

The initial surveys revealed the probable existence of several deep sedimentary basins in offshore eastern Canada, prompting oil companies to acquire their own seismic data and to take out leases. When carrying out regional or detailed surveys of a sedimentary basin, oil companies rely largely on reflection seismic surveys. Originally, such surveys provided a two-dimension (2D) cross-section of subsurface rocks, somewhat like a slice through a layered ice-cream cake. In recent years, there has been a marked increase in three-dimensional (3D) surveys that give a three-dimensional view of the rocks and are much more informative (Fig. 2). Most of GSCA's studies have been based on 2D seismic, much of it as paper copies, but most have been digitized so that data can be manipulated on a computer. Digitizing the data is a time-consuming task necessitating help from numerous summer students and contractors.

Although the different surveys gave clues to the structures and types of rocks present in the basins and intervening basement highs, they provided few clues about rock types, their ages, or their potential as source and reservoir rocks for petroleum (oil and gas). To obtain what we call 'ground-truthing' (rock samples) from below the sea floor, we needed to drill wells or boreholes. The first samples from the subsurface of the east coast offshore prior to the drilling of petroleum exploration wells were obtained on the Grand Banks of Newfoundland in 1965 during a shallow-core-hole program by Pan American Petroleum Corporation and Imperial Oil. The results of the palynological analyses (a study of spores, pollen and dinoflagellates) and dating assemblages were presented by Williams and Brideaux (1975). Other biostratigraphic studies focussed on foraminifera. It was concluded that the cores ranged in age from about 100 to 2.6 million years old, although a few were older. This provided the first reliable age control and the first inkling of the ages of the rocks.

Anticipating the advent of drilling, the federal government set up a policy of obtaining and curating data from all offshore wells, including samples and logs, as well as geophysical data. The samples and logs provided the basis for 'ground-truthing' needed for detailed studies by GSCA staff.

Pan American Petroleum Corporation and Imperial Oil drilled the first east-coast offshore wells, both on the Grand Banks of Newfoundland, in 1966. These wells were the Tors Cove D-52 in the Scotian Basin and the Grand Falls H-09 in the Whale Basin. Tors Cove D-52, which was located on a salt dome, had a small natural gas show. Mobil Oil was the first oil company to find several natural gas shows and a small amount of light oil when it drilled Sable Island C-67 in the Scotian Basin in 1967. This enticement led to a flurry of drilling in the Scotian Basin. Farther north, drilling on the Labrador Margin started in 1971 when Tenneco Oil Company and partners drilled the Leif E-38 well in the Hopedale Basin.

Those were exciting times, with drilling increasing as new natural gas and oil discoveries were made. These finds included natural gas in the Hopedale and Saglek basins on the Labrador margin, natural gas, condensate (gases at higher temperature and depth and oil when at the surface), and oil in the Scotian Basin, and oil in the Jeanne d'Arc Basin. The first major regional compilation of the offshore geology of eastern Canada by the GSC was published in 1975 (van der Linden and Wade 1975). Highlights included the first paleogeographic maps for

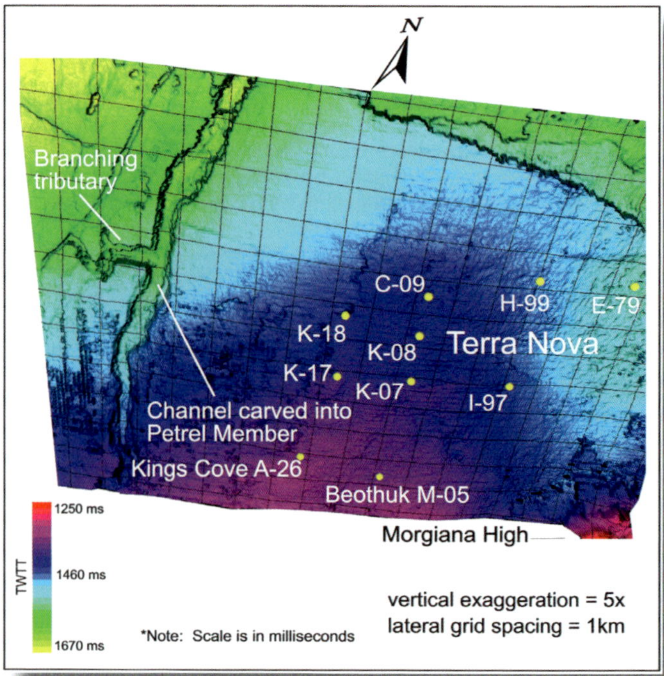

Figure 2. Time structure map of a Cretaceous horizon revealed in a 3D seismic survey of the Terra Nova oil field, Jeanne d'Arc Basin, Grand Banks, Newfoundland. Visible are morphological details (e.g., a channel and its tributary) that can be imaged with a grid survey at 1 km line spacing. TTWT = Two-way travel times of reflected seismic waves. For location, see the Terra Nova I-97 well site on Figure 1: D (from Deptuk et al. 2003).

the North Atlantic based on plate-tectonic reconstructions and the first conjugate geological comparison of the Scotian Basin with a northwest Moroccan counterpart, the Essaouira Basin. Subsequent syntheses of the subsurface geology of offshore eastern Canada were published in four major compilations: Labrador Sea (Bell et al. 1989), Scotian Shelf (Ross and Lewis 1991), Grand Banks of Newfoundland (Fensome et al. 1997), and the continental margin of eastern Canada (Keen and Williams 1990). Subsequent publications have focussed on upgrading our knowledge further.

Today, offshore eastern Canada remains an area of interest to the oil industry. Natural gas and condensate are being produced from the Scotian Basin and oil from the Jeanne d'Arc Basin. Further exploration is focussing on drilling in deeper water. This means further challenges for the biostratigraphers calling for integration of data from foraminiferal, palynological, and nannofossil studies. But the results are dramatic as shown by the Nova Scotia Offshore Energy Technical Research Association's Play Fairway Project (Offshore Energy Technical Research Association 2011, Weston et al. 2012). In this project, GSCA played a key role by supplying and assisting with crustal modelling and biostratigraphic data invaluable in development of the Play Fairway model that is stimulating renewed exploration on the Scotian Margin.

Exploration activity in offshore eastern Canada has been comparatively small. By the end of 2010, about 520 wells had been drilled in the region in contrast to more than 50,000 in the Gulf of Mexico. Thus, even if we studied all the wells in detail, coverage would be relatively sparse for such a large area.

TECHNICAL CAPABILITIES

Unravelling the complex subsurface geology of offshore eastern Canada demands expertise in regional geology, geophysics, lithostratigraphy, and biostratigraphy. All these skills exist within the GSCA at BIO, but they would be ineffective without the 'raw material' for the research: i.e., remote field, seismic, and well data including samples of the rocks. Much of the remote sensing data has been obtained on BIO multiparameter cruises. During cruises on CSS *Baffin* and CSS *Hudson*, gravity and magnetic data were obtained simultaneously with bathymetry surveys being undertaken by the Canadian Hydrographic Service (CHS). Refraction seismic data were also collected on some of the cruises. However, most of the refraction seismic data have been generated by industry. Biostratigraphic studies of offshore wells have been based on microscopic fossils that vary in size from less than 0.1 mm to about 2 mm. Such microfossils include palynomorphs (dinoflagellate cysts, pollen and spores - Fig. 3), foraminifera, and ostracods. We have utilized two major groups of foraminifera, planktonic and benthic. Dinoflagellates are especially useful for providing information on the age of rocks. In biostratigraphic studies of wells, we have to rely largely on the youngest (last or topmost) occurrence of a species (i.e., its extinction) as cuttings commonly tumble or cave down the well, sometimes for several tens or hundreds of meters from where they originated, thus contaminating lower samples. This explains why a series of plots have been developed to show 'events' or extinctions for index fossils from different ages and basins (e.g., Fig. 4); the events generally occur at a consistent age in different basins.

Paleoenvironmental determinations are based on benthic foraminifera, ostracods, and palynomorphs. Presence or absence of dinoflagellates tells us if paleoenvironments were marine or non-marine. We can ascertain whether sediments were deposited far from shore from the ratio of spores and pollen to dinoflagellates and what the approximate water depths were from the composition of the dinoflagellate assemblages.

Other vital contributions to our knowledge base are maturation studies which involve examination of organic matter to determine if a body of rock has been heated to the right temperatures (and not beyond) to produce oil or natural gas. Most such studies on Canadian offshore east-coast basins have been based on organic geochemistry carried out at GSC-Calgary, but at GSCA, microscopic studies of kerogen type, degree of maturation, and visual kerogen analysis have been undertaken (Bujak et al. 1977a, 1977b). Another important source of data is vitrinite reflectance studies, originally part of GSCA research on coals of the Maritime Provinces, but now carried out exclusively on offshore well samples. These studies reveal the well depths at which oil and natural gas can be sourced.

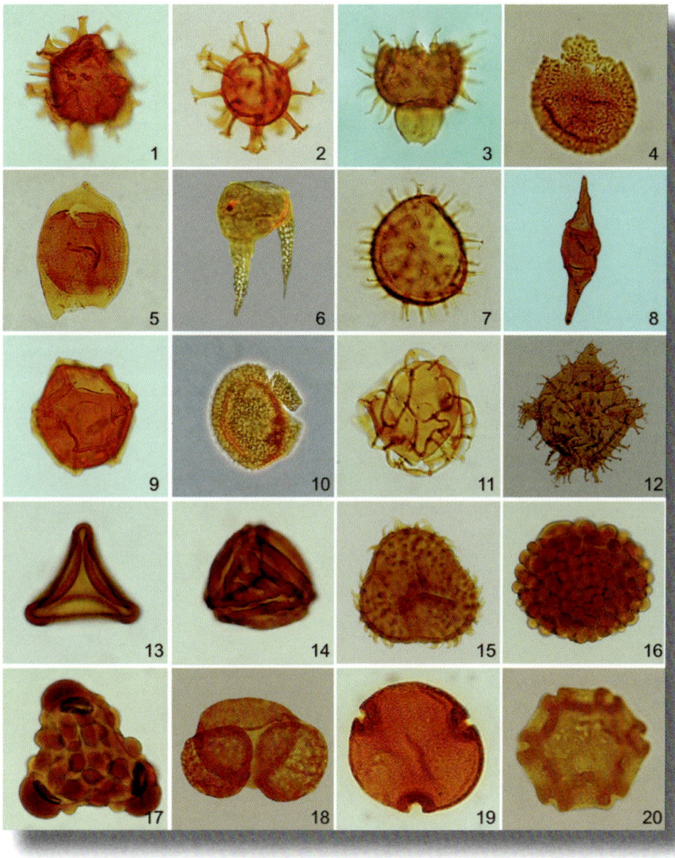

Figure 3. Photomicrographs of selected palynomorph (organic-walled microfossils) used to determine age and paleoenvironmental information on Cretaceous and Cenozoic rocks (specimens have been artificially stained and magnified for easier viewing). Dinoflagellate cysts (dinocysts) from the Scotian Margin (1-12): 1 = *Achilleodinium biformoides,* 2 = *Cordosphaeridium delimurum,* 3 = *Diphyes ficusoides,* 4 = *Elytrocysta druggii,* 5 = *Isabelidinium cooksoniae,* 6 = *Odontochitina porifera,* 7 = *Operculodinium centrocarpum,* 8 = *Palaeocystodinium sp.,* 9 = *Pentadinium laticinctum,* 10 = *Cerebrocysta waipawaense,* 11 = *Unipontidinium aquaductum,* and 12 = *Wetzeliella articulata.* Fern spores from small Early Cretaceous basins, onshore Nova Scotia (13-17): 13 = *Concavisporites toralis,* 14 = *Cicatricosisporites sp.,* 15 = *Pilosisporites trichopapillosus,* 16 = *Rotverrusporites varians,* and 17 = *Trilobosporites canadensis.* Bisaccate conifer pollen from offshore Nova Scotia (18). Angiosperm pollen from offshore Nova Scotia (19-20): 19 = *Tilliaepollenites sp.,* and 20 = *Alnuspollenites sp.* The maximum dimensions of all specimens range in size from about 20 to 100 microns; in fine-grained sedimentary rocks they may occur in thousands per teaspoon-sized sample.

SCIENTIFIC DISCOVERIES

Research by GSCA scientists at BIO has provided an abundance of new knowledge about the subsurface geology of offshore eastern Canada, findings that have been of fundamental importance to offshore exploration. As indicated earlier, several basins of offshore eastern Canada originated during the opening of the North Atlantic Ocean and Labrador Sea. The results and significance of GSCA's research in these basins are presented below, from south to north.

Fundy Basin

The breakup of the supercontinent Pangea began during the Triassic, about 220 million years ago, with doming and then rifting along lines of weakness within the Appalachian Orogen, resulting in a series of rift basins similar to the African Rift Valley of today. The Fundy Basin, the most southwesterly of the basins that we discuss (Fig. 1), started life as such a rift and did not evolve beyond that stage. It was filled mainly with clastic sediments (fragments eroded from existing rocks and composed mainly of clay, silt, sand or gravel) and basalt. Also present among the mostly red clastics were gypsum deposits which are indicative of a warm, dry climate. GSCA scientists determined the sedimentary sequences in the two wells drilled in the Bay of Fundy and related these to the onshore rocks. They also recorded the ages of rocks in the Fundy Basin as Late Triassic-Early Jurassic.

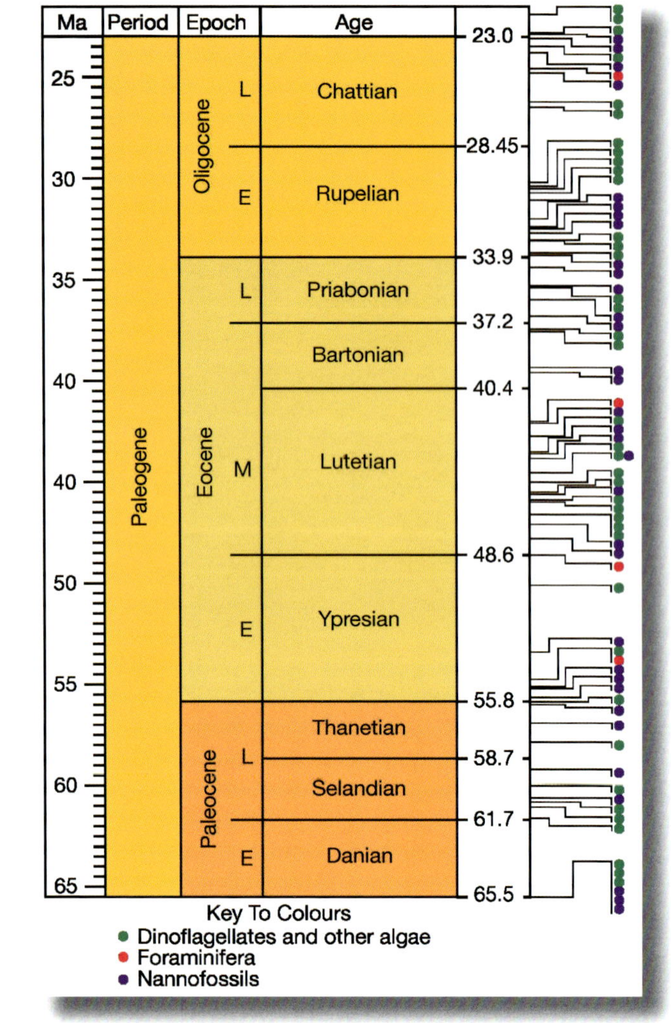

Figure 4. An example events plot showing the ages of numerous 'Last Appearance Datums' (LADs; or extinctions) of selected types of planktonic foraminiferal, coccolith, dinocyst, and spore and pollen species in the Paleogene on the Scotian Margin. Each line represents a species, collectively showing the rich array of index fossils that can be used to determine ages. Ma = age in millions of years; 'Age' column shows the standard units of the international time scale (from Fensome et al. 2008).

Scotian Basin and Adjacent Areas

The Scotian Basin, which became a focus of deposition as the Atlantic Ocean began to develop, lies to the southeast of the Fundy Basin and present-day Nova Scotia (Fig. 1). As in the Fundy Basin, the rock sequences at first were predominantly red clastics and evaporates (Fig. 5), indicative of hot and periodically dry climatic conditions. We know from the age of the rocks, as dated by GSCA's biostratigraphers and comparison with those now found in the Bay of Fundy, that the smaller rift basins that now underlie the Scotian Basin started to form more than 200 million years ago within the Late Triassic. Jansa and Wade (1975) placed the change from rifting to drifting, the earliest formation of oceanic crust in the Basin, at about 175 million years ago. Wade and MacLean (1990) placed the breakup unconformity, the time when drifting started, at about 189 million years ago.

Today, based on magnetic-reversal data derived from the basaltic oceanic crust in the North Atlantic, we consider the age of the onset of drifting to be about 180 million years ago. Magnetic reversals are shown by the direction and orientation of magnetic minerals in basaltic and other igneous rocks when they cool. The different aspects of these two parameters reflect the position of the North and South poles when the basalts were forming. Surprisingly, the two poles reverse periodically, the North Pole becoming the South Pole and vice versa. A single reversal episode is recorded in the basalt as a broad magnetic stripe of the same polarity whose age has been independently determined from radiometric data. Thus, pole reversals provide a series of magnetic stripes, somewhat like a bar code used in stores to determine the price of a product, which collectively provide a time scale for measuring ages in oceanic crust. Magnetic striping patterns in the North Atlantic show us that the ocean continued to widen, but in a somewhat unusual fashion, very like a zipper running from south to north. This has been an important aspect of the evolution of the basins of offshore eastern Canada.

What have the seismic data shown us? A startling early discovery was the presence of large salt diapirs (i.e., domes of salt squeezed upward) forming what Jansa and Wade (1975) termed the "Sedimentary Ridge Province" which runs along the outer margin of the Scotian Basin beneath

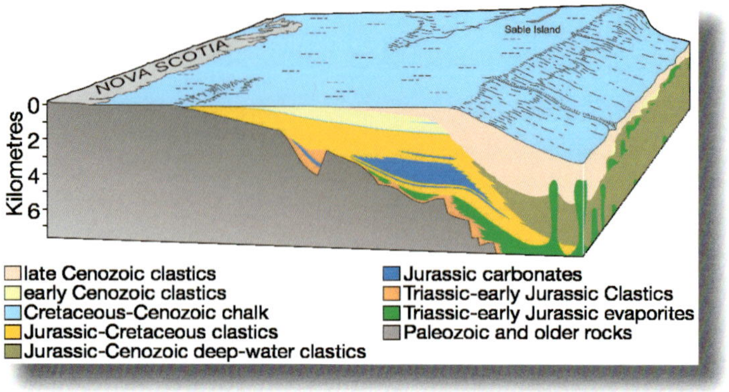

Figure 5. Cross section of the Scotian Basin off Nova Scotia. In contrast to the onshore geology where Paleozoic rocks underlie most of the Maritime Provinces, there is a sequence of Mesozoic-Cenozoic rocks up to 20 km thick in the Scotian Basin, which reflect the evolution of a passive margin as the Atlantic Ocean developed from a series of middle Triassic to early Jurassic rift basins (adapted from a figure by J. Wade).

the continental slope and rise. Wade and MacLean (1990) renamed this area the "Diapiric Slope Province". Jansa and Wade (1975) believed it was a series of elongated or ridge-like structures. Recently, J. Shimeld and J. Wade (pers. comm.) have re-interpreted many of the structures to involve complex intrusions of salt of various shapes, such as canopies and pinched off 'pillows' rather than just simple domes. This has some significance for exploration in salt-rich areas, as it would introduce the probability of new petroleum plays.

Perhaps the most dramatic find from our combined seismic and well studies of the subsurface geology of offshore eastern Canada is the roughly circular Montagnais structure located in the southwestern part of the Scotian Basin (Fig. 1). Jansa and Pe-Piper (1987) interpreted the structure as an impact crater, formed from a meteorite collision with the earth about 50 million years ago, during the Early Tertiary. This was the first time that an impact crater had been identified in the world's oceans. Although not on the scale of the impact crater that caused the extinction of the dinosaurs about 65 million years ago, it would certainly have led to massive destruction in the vicinity of its landing, as we are now beginning to glimpse with the most recent Offshore Energy Technical Research Association's Play Fairway Project (Offshore Energy Technical Research Association 2011, Deptuck and Campbell 2012, Weston et al. 2012).

The first lithostratigraphic framework for Mesozoic-Cenozoic rocks of the Scotian Basin was published by McIver (1972). Since then, geoscientists at GSCA have played a dominant role in revising this scheme, starting with Jansa and Wade (1975) who refined the Basin's lithostratigraphy (Fig. 6). Hardy (1975) tried to subdivide the Banquereau Formation, a term that McIver introduced for rocks in the Scotian Basin between about 70 and 2 million years old and which has also been used for similarly aged rocks on the Grand Banks of Newfoundland. Only one subsequent revision has been published that subdivides this gargantuan formation and that is based on data from the oldest sequences of the formation in the Jeanne d'Arc Basin on the Grand Banks of Newfoundland (Deptuck et al. 2003).

Biostratigraphic studies have played a key role in determining the age of the rocks, the environments of deposition, and the evolution of the Scotian Basin. GSCA published the first zonations and plots of species events for this basin with a series of papers on the foraminifera, ostracods, and palynomorphs (Gradstein et al. 1975, Williams 1975, Ascoli 1976). Williams (1975) showed that the age of the salt in the Scotian Basin is about the same as that of the Essaouira Basin off Morocco. This tied in with Jansa and Wade's (1975) reconstruction showing that the two basins were contemporaneous.

As summarized in Williams et al. (1990), GSCA paleontologists published several papers on the paleoenvironments of the Scotian Basin. The findings were based on data derived from foraminifera, ostracods, and palynomorphs which were related to the rock types or lithostratigraphy. Our results showed that non-marine to marginal marine paleoenvironments existed from about 230 to 200 million years ago, during the Triassic. The salt deposits indicated an evaporating water body and a hot, dry climate. From about 200 to 150 million years ago in the Jurassic, most of the sediments in the Scotian Basin were deposited in shallow marine waters, probably predominantly inner shelf. Until about 145 million years ago, warm tropical waters must have covered the Basin, as confirmed by the carbonate build-up (mainly the Abenaki Formation in Fig. 6) along the southeastern margin. Sea level fell substantially after this time and the dominance of spores and pollen in some of the samples, especially from the adjacent Orpheus Graben (a fault-bounded extension of the Scotian Basin in Fig. 1), indicated that at times the sediments were deposited in non-marine paleoenvironments such as rivers and lakes. These non-marine paleoenvironments persisted until about 140 million years, followed after about 20 million years by marginal to shallow marine conditions in many parts of the Basin. This was the time when a series of deltas developed, a principal one being the Sable Delta (mainly the Missisauga Formation in Fig. 6). The sediments the deltas and rivers deposited contain the natural gas that is now being produced around Sable Island (Fig. 1).

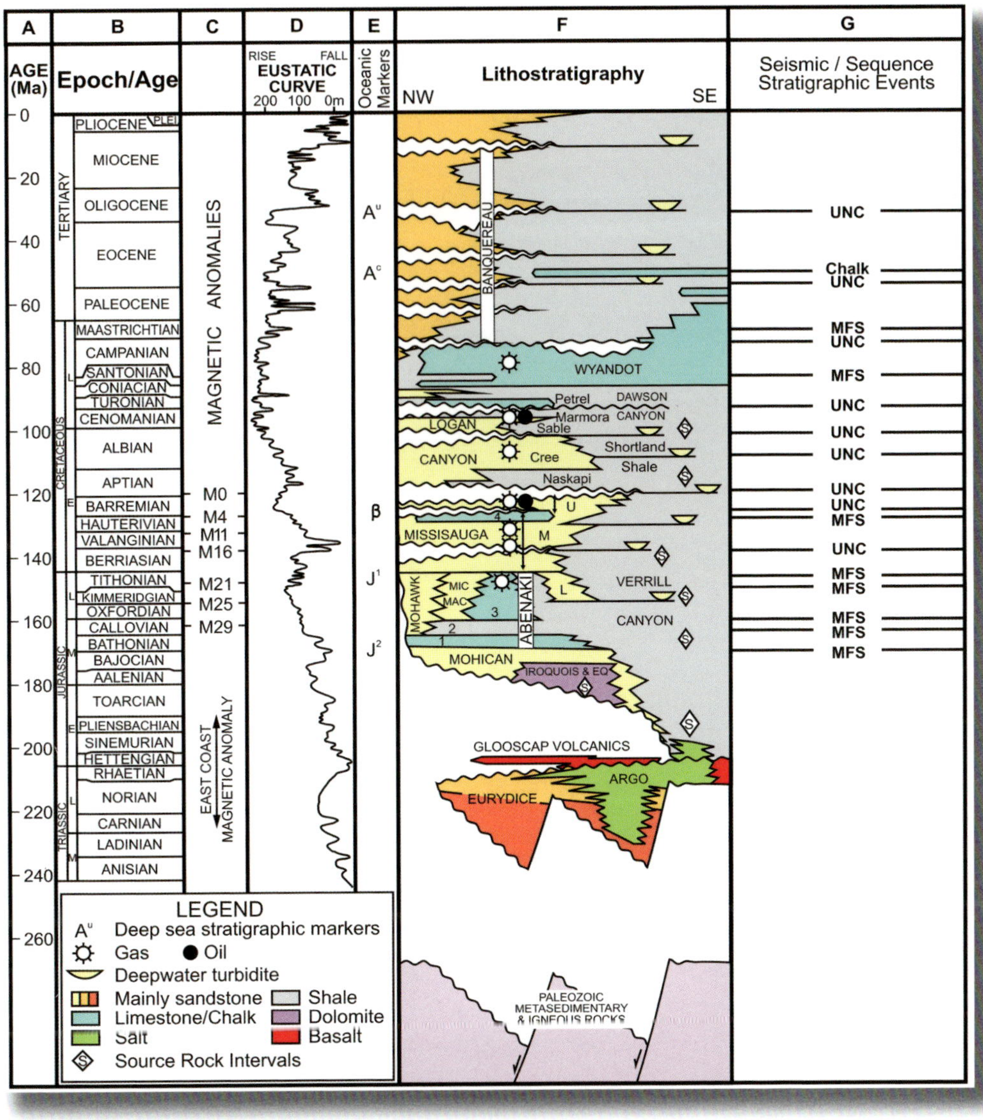

Figure 6. Synthesis of the stratigraphy of the Scotian Basin showing lithostratigraphy (column F) in relation to the geological timescale (column B) and age in millions of years (Ma) (column A) (both based on Gradstein et al. 2005), magnetic anomalies (column C), the eustatic sea-level curve after Haq et al. (1987) (column D), oceanic marker horizons (column E) and seismic /sequence stratigraphic events (column G). Column F also shows oil and gas, and petroleum source-rock occurrences. In column F, wiggly lines are unconformities (intervals not represented by sediment), and white areas indicate missing rock, either eroded or never deposited. L = lower, M = middle, Ma = millions of years, MFS = maximum flooding surface, U = upper, and Unc = unconformity. Numbers represent: 1. Scatarie Member, 2. Misaine Member, 3. Baccaro Member, all three of the Abenaki Formation, 4 = O Marker. (Overall compilation and columns F and G from Weston et al. 2012, building on earlier work by Wade and MacLean 1990, Wade et al. 1995 and CNSOPB 2008: at http//www.cnsopb.ns.ca/call.for.bids_08.2/cnsopb/subregional_geology.html).

From about 120 million years ago, marine paleoenvironments persisted in the Scotian Basin. Seas must have been subtropical around 85 to 65 million years ago, when chalks were deposited intermittently (the Wyandot Formation in Fig. 6). Marine conditions persisted until at least 2.6 million years ago, but there were differences in water depths. Settings varied from outer shelf to bathyal (deep water) between about 100 and 65 million years ago. Then during the Tertiary, from 65 to 2.6 million years ago, the waters became gradually shallower, with subsequently large parts of the Basin being exposed intermittently during sea-level lowerings of the Ice Age (from 2.6 million years ago to present).

One significant find was that of the overpressure zone in the Scotian Basin (Nantais 1985). Overpressuring occurs when gas or fluid pressures encountered in drilling are higher than hydrostatic pressure (the expected pressure due to the weight of pore water at a given depth); this excess pressure often causes a disastrous release of fluid known as a 'blowout'. Originally, when overpressured horizons were encountered in drilling a well, it was thought that there would be no reservoir rocks below this horizon, but, as one of the oil companies discovered in the Scotian Basin, this is not true. Thanks to GSCA research, we were able to correlate the relationship of overpressuring and maturation showing that with adequate seals some gas could remain trapped adjacent to the source rocks, with continuing gas generation causing overpressuring.

Important GSCA compilations relating to the Scotian Basin have included Jansa and Wade (1975), Wade and MacLean (1990), and Wade and MacLean (1993), which correlated the seismic reflection data with the logs, biostratigraphy, and lithostratigraphy of all wells drilled in the Scotian Basin to that time.

Grand Banks Basins and Adjacent Areas

Based on seismic and well data, Amoco and Imperial (1973) identified five basins on the Grand Banks of Newfoundland: South Whale, Whale, Horseshoe, Jeanne d'Arc, and Carson (Fig. 1). Jansa and Wade (1975) retained these names but considered the South Whale to be a sub-basin of the Scotian Basin. All these basins retain the southwest-northeast alignment reflecting the alignment of the underlying basement rocks. As with the Scotian Basin, the basins on the Grand Banks formed during the opening of the North Atlantic but tell a different story. Rather than drifting during the Jurassic Period from their conjugate margins now east of the North Atlantic, the Grand Banks basins reflect a temporary delay in the opening of the Atlantic Ocean at more northerly latitudes.

McAlpine (1990) and Grant and McAlpine (1990) recognized six stages in the evolution of the Grand Banks sedimentary basins. These were, from oldest to youngest: aborted rift, epeiric basin, late rift, transition to drift phase I, transition to drift phase II, and passive margin. It was not until about 140 million years ago that late rifting, marked by the Avalon Unconformity, started to separate the Grand Banks from Iberia. Jansa and Wade (1975) had previously postulated that the Avalon Unconformity, which they recognized in the Whale, Horseshoe, Carson, and Jeanne d'Arc basins, marked further opening of the North Atlantic. They considered the related uplift to be about 145 to 100 million years old. McAlpine (1990) narrowed this interval to between about 130 and 100 million years ago. We are now placing the onset at about 140 million years ago. From 100 to 60 million years ago, the Grand Banks of Newfoundland completely separated from western Europe and, as it continues to do today, drifted westward.

Seismic surveys of the Grand Banks basins have been intensive, especially since the discovery of oil and natural gas. Although obtained mostly by industry, many of the surveys have been made available to GSCA scientists. However, some of the data were obtained through a survey conducted by the United Kingdom's Institute of Oceanographic Sciences. Grant and McAlpine (1990) provided several cross-sections, including two showing the structure of the Jeanne d'Arc Basin. Of immediate interest are the folding, the listric faulting (fault surfaces that flatten with depth), the salt structures, the unconformities, the onlapping sequences, and the trans-basin fault zone. Deptuck et al. (2003) used 3D seismic data to identify and map erosional and depositional features and regional unconformities in the same basin (Fig. 2).

With the exception of some of the units first used for Scotian Basin rocks, the accepted terminology for the lithostratigraphic units in the Jeanne d'Arc Basin is essentially that proposed by McAlpine (1990) and modified by Deptuck et al. (2003). McAlpine recognized 17 formations, of which 14 were new, three were members of which two were new, and two new markers (thin intervals of distinct rock composition). Also, Jansa et al. (1980) previously recognized a salt unit, dated as 228 million years old, that they termed the Osprey Evaporites. This is the same age as the salts in the Lusitanian Basin, the conjugate basin off Spain (Jansa et al. 1980). The salts in the two basins are also of similar composition, thereby supporting the juxtaposition of the Grand Banks of Newfoundland and Iberia at that time.

McAlpine (1990) identified the Eurydice, Osprey, Argo and Iroquois formations, but all the succeeding ones except for the Dawson, Wyandot, and Banquereau formations were new (Fig. 7, right side). The terminology has been generally adopted by later workers, although there have been a few proposed changes. Deptuck et al. (2003), for example, formalized two informal members and introduced two new members for an Upper Cretaceous formation and three new members in the lower part of the Banquereau Formation (Fig. 7, right side).

Most of the ages for the formations, members, and markers identified by McAlpine (1990) were provided by GSCA staff. The fossil groups used were primarily foraminifera (Gradstein 1976) and palynomorphs (Barss et al. 1979). One significant find was that the Egret Member, the source rock for oil and natural gas, was of early Kimmeridgian age. As noted earlier, visual kerogen studies to evaluate source rock potential have been carried out on offshore east-coast wells, including several drilled on the Grand Banks. In one of the most intriguing studies, we identified the Jeanne d'Arc Basin as having considerable potential for the generation of oil (Bujak et al. 1977b), a prediction borne out by later discoveries such as the Hibernia Oil Field.

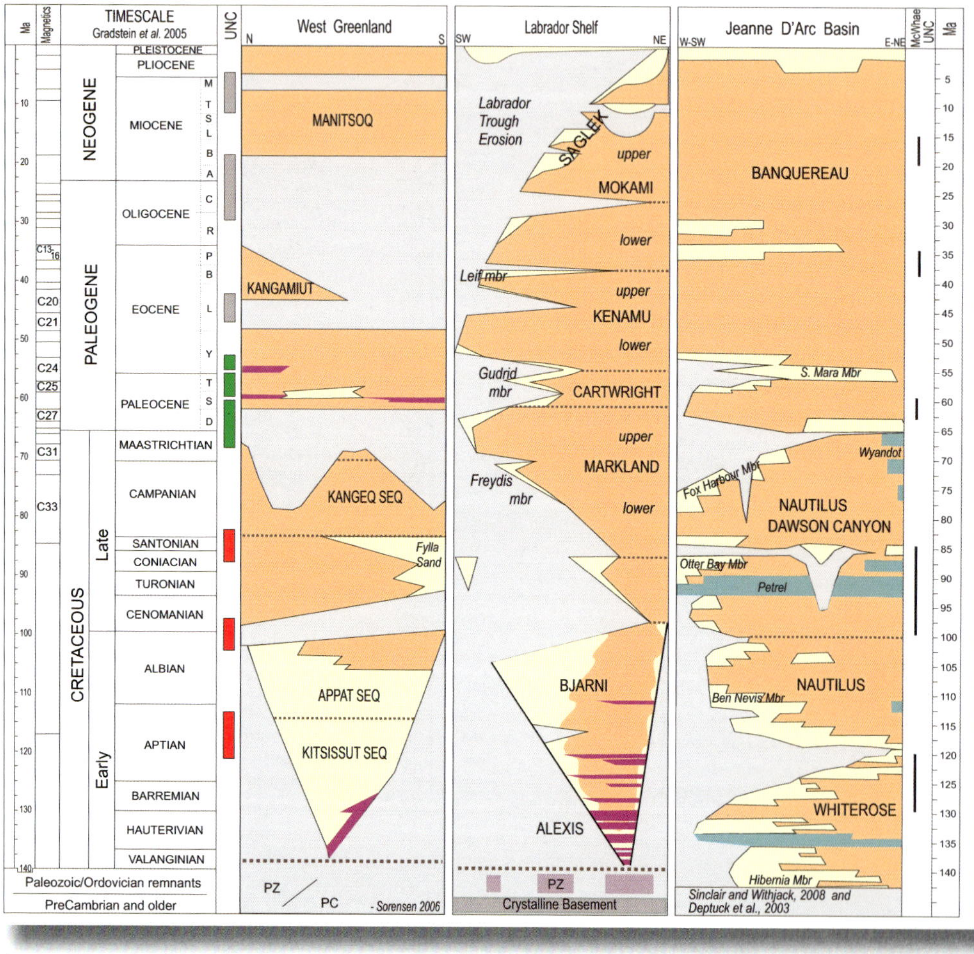

Figure 7. Lithostratigraphy of onshore west Greenland, the two Labrador Basins (Hopedale and Saglek) and the Jeanne d'Arc Basin offshore southeastern Newfoundland (after Dickie et al. 2011). Coloured intervals represent different lithologies (beige = clastic sediments other than sandstone, yellow = sandstone, purple = volcanics, blue = carbonates, and grey indicates the absence of rock). Ma = millions of years, UNC = unconformity.

Our results show that non-marine to marginal-marine paleoenvironments existed in the Carson and Horseshoe basins from about 230 to 200 million years ago, during the Triassic. The salt deposits indicated an evaporating water body and a hot, dry climate. Replenishment of the sea water after evaporation was from the forerunner of the Mediterranean Sea, the Tethys Ocean. From about 200 to 150 million years ago, during the Jurassic Period, most of the sediments in the basins were deposited from shallow marine waters, probably predominantly inner shelf. But there were non-marine episodes until about 130 million years ago in the Jeanne d'Arc Basin. Based on the presence of some chalks, widespread fully marine paleoenvironments returned about 130 million years ago with climates becoming subtropical. In the past 65 million years there has been a gradual shallowing of the region from slope and outer shelf depths to inner shelf settings with the Banks being often above sea level during the past two million years or so in the Ice Age when climates definitely became much cooler.

Important GSCA compilations relating to the Grand Banks basins have included McAlpine (1990), Grant and McAlpine (1990), and Fensome et al. (1997). An understanding of the geology of the Orphan Basin, offshore northeast Newfoundland, is still in its infancy because its situation in deep water means few wells have been drilled. But the oil companies are becoming more interested and are actively exploring this basin and the adjacent Flemish Pass Basin. To be prepared for the demand for more information, GSCA is presently completing a detailed study of this basin (Fig. 8).

Labrador-Baffin Seaway Basins

The Labrador-Baffin Seaway is the arm of the North Atlantic that extends up the Labrador Sea, through Davis Strait and into Baffin Bay (Fig.1). Much of it is underlain by oceanic crust. Geophysical studies by GSCA staff have shown that the Seaway evolved during the Cretaceous and early Cenozoic, but is no longer actively opening. There was an initial marine transgression about 130 million years ago that marked the onset of rifting. By analyzing the results of magnetic data, Srivastava (1978) and Roots and Srivastava (1984) postulated that rifting changed to drifting about 86 million years ago and ended at about 34 million years ago. Subsequent studies indicate that the onset of drifting was at about 62 million years ago. The cause of the cessation of drifting was probably the collision of the northern end of the Greenland Plate with Arctic Canada, the latter as part of the North American Plate. As a result, the Greenland Plate could no longer pivot away from the North American Plate and so became part of it, with drifting shifting to the Norwegian Sea between Greenland and Scandinavia.

For the past thirty years, the Labrador Margin has been of little interest to the oil industry, but GSCA has continued to study its subsurface rocks and correlate them with offshore western Greenland. The Labrador Margin lithostratigraphic framework was erected by Umpleby (1979). Most of the terms are still in use, although McWhae et al. (1980) proposed some new formations for rocks laid down in the last 100 million years or so. Since then the terminology has remained remarkably stable. Dickie et al. (2011) correlated six regional unconformities recognized in seismic sections, with the biostratigraphy, lithostratigraphy, and paleoenvironments determined from well samples. These unconformities can be matched with unconformities in offshore West Greenland and the Jeanne d'Arc Basin (Fig. 7). Most of the ages for the formations, members, and markers identified on the Canadian margin of the Labrador Sea were provided by GSCA staff. The fossil groups used were primarily foraminifera and palynomorphs.

Our biostratigraphic studies have shown that the oldest, albeit marginal, marine sediments in the Labrador Sea are Barremian in age (130–125 million years ago). But it was not until about 85 million years ago that fully marine conditions were established over the whole region. In the Baffin Bay area, the oldest known marine sediments are about 100 million years old. These were obtained from shallow core holes obtained by the BIO rock core drill in Cumberland Sound (MacLean et al. 1986). The BIO rock core drill was also successful in coring farther north in Baffin Bay where rock samples about 85 million years old were retrieved (MacLean et al. 2014).

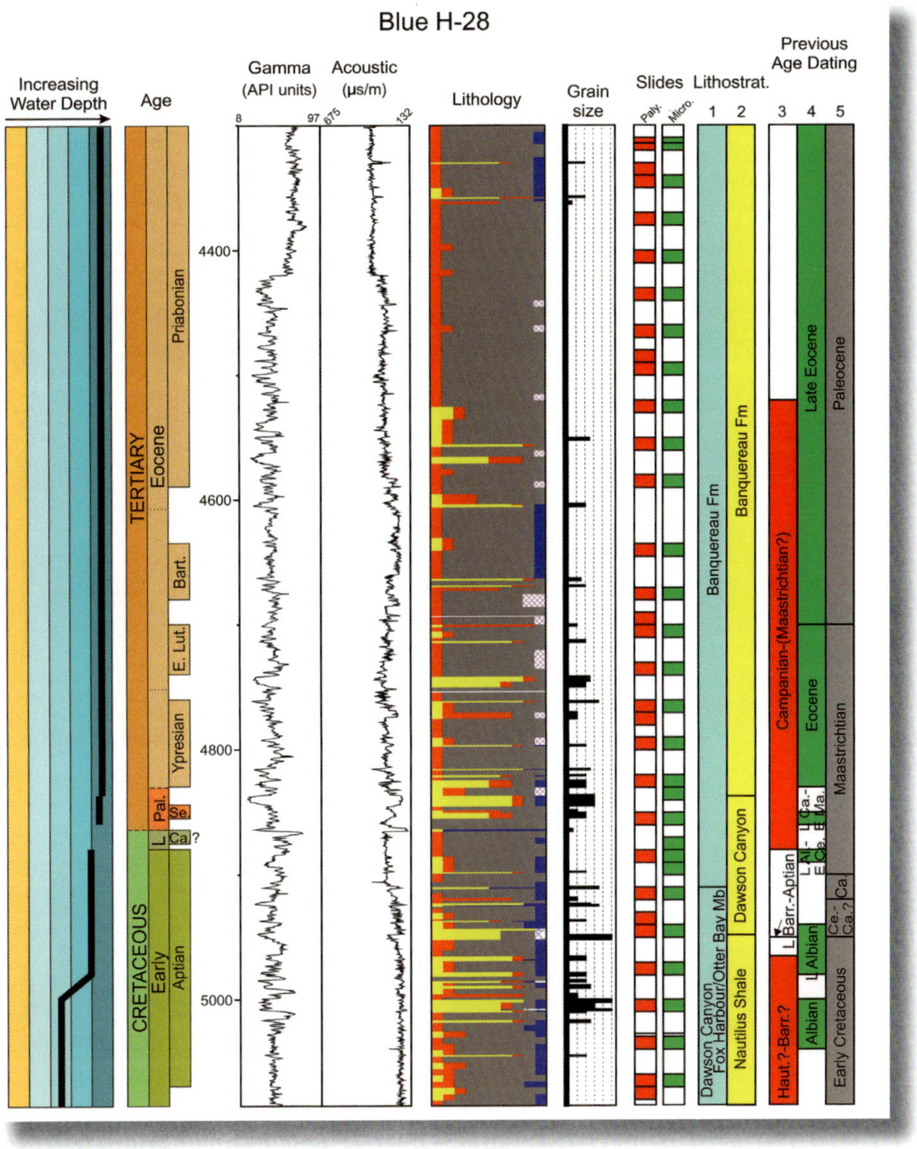

Figure 8. An example of a plot generated from multidisciplinary data in the BASIN database, from left to right, paleoenvironment, age, physical rock properties (gamma ray response to grain size), sampling interval for fossils (Paly. = palynomorphs, Micro. = microfossils), rock units (Lithostrat.), and previous age information from all well data sources in the BASIN data base by GSCA at BIO for public use. The example is for the 4,300-5,090 ft (1,310-1,551 m) interval of the Texaco-Shell Blue H-28 well in the Orphan Basin, located on Figure 1 at E. 1 = CNLOPB 2007 at (http://www.cnlopb.nl.ca/pdfs/wells/well58.pdf), 2 = McAlpine (pers. comm.), 3 = Ioannides (1998), 4 = Gradstein and Thomas (1983), 5 = Dolby et al. (1979) (plot courtesy of L. Dafoe).

Paleoenvironments in the Labrador Sea varied from non-marine to marginal marine until about 130 million years ago. Since then, marine conditions prevailed with episodes of outer shelf to upper slope conditions. From about 30 million years ago until about 2.6 million years ago, there was widespread shallowing before the onset of the Ice Age. Surprisingly, water temperatures in the Late Cretaceous and Tertiary were extremely warm at times. About 56 million years ago one could have gone swimming in the Labrador Sea in waters as warm as those today in the Caribbean.

The natural gas potential of the Labrador Sea region was demonstrated by the drilling of several discovery wells in the 1970s. Drilling results substantiated the kerogen data which indicated that the region was natural gas prone, but also had the potential for oil. The latter is supported by the presence of the freshwater fern *Azolla*, a potentially rich source of oil, in some samples about 49 million years old. More exploration wells are needed to substantiate these encouraging results.

Milestone GSCA publications on Labrador Sea geology include Umpleby (1979), Bell et al. (1989), Balkwill and McMillan (1990), and Dickie et al. (2011). Papers reviewing Baffin Bay include Srivastava (1978), Jackson et al. (1979), MacLean et al. (1990), and MacLean and Williams (2011).

DATABASES

As mentioned earlier, GSCA geoscientists rely almost exclusively on reflection seismic data, rock samples, and geophysical logs from wells when evaluating sedimentary basins. To curate all the data generated on the wells, GSCA developed BASIN, a comprehensive database. BASIN originated from WELLSYS, initiated in 1980. Originally, the well information was loaded by summer students, but is now kept up to date by a full-time employee who is responsible for loading, updating, and verifying data. BASIN, which is in great demand by government, academic, and industry personnel, is now available to the general public. Besides providing basic information, BASIN is the source of plots showing all the stratigraphic parameters, including well logs and location maps. One extremely useful feature is the capability to generate diagrams showing relative percentages of lithologies by sample and to superimpose these data on the stratigraphic column (Fig. 8). Now part of BASIN, but originally developed as a record of fossils in the offshore wells is BIOSTRAT with records going back to 1971. It records occurrences of the spores, pollen, and dinoflagellates found in the offshore wells together with their depth and processing number.

Another database, which originated with oil companies but in which GSCA played a prominent role, is PALYNODATA. This database catalogues all geographic and stratigraphic records of palynomorphs that have been published in scientific papers up to the last few years. The database, which covers more than 20,000 papers, is a useful resource for checking those species found in the offshore (Palynodata and White 2008). The major source for confirming nomenclature of dinoflagellate cysts is Fensome et al. (2009). For stratigraphic data on dinoflagellate cysts, we have relied primarily on the papers by Stover et al. (1996) and Williams et al. (2004).

GSCA's biostratigraphic group also developed the quantitative analytical techniques RAnking and SCaling in time (RASC) and Correlation And SCaling in time (CASC) (for details, see Gradstein and Agterberg 1982, 1985). Ranking and scaling techniques provide an average ordering of biostratigraphic events such as the oldest and/or youngest occurrences of fossil species in several wells. Doeven (1983) and Doeven et al. (1982) used this approach in a study of Late Cretaceous nannofossils from the Scotian Margin. The correlation and scaling technique provides a means of correlating stratigraphic sequences based on the results of a RASC analysis. By applying the methodology, Williamson (1987) determined the ages of eleven fossil zones identified in thirteen wells of the Jeanne d'Arc Basin.

IMPACTS OF RESEARCH

GSCA studies at BIO have provided a detailed framework of the structure, lithostratigraphy, and biostratigraphy of the east coast offshore basins. This information is accessible to everyone, whether industrial, government or academic scientists or the general public, through the numerous publications and the BASIN database. It supplies independent information about the geology of an area vital to Canada. Our detailed acquired knowledge of the subsurface geology provides us with a better understanding of the evolution of not only the basins, but also the North Atlantic Ocean and the Labrador-Baffin Seaway. Through visual kerogen studies and geochemical modelling of the wells, we have gleaned new evidence of potential source rocks for oil and natural gas. By identifying structures where the oil and natural gas may be trapped after migrating from the source rock (i.e., where the oil and natural gas originated), the GSCA basic research helps greatly in the search for these valuable resources.

One of the major material benefits of GSCA research is resource appraisal which provides estimates of how much oil and natural gas there may be in the different offshore basins. These estimates are available to federal and provincial governments, the general public, and oil companies considering investment in the offshore. Often a decision to invest will be based on the findings of GSCA. Our estimates of the potential reserves and resources are part of the federal government's ongoing resource appraisal of all the sedimentary basins of Canada. Other subdivisions of the GSC, notably GSC-Calgary, undertake similar appraisals. The impartial summaries give governments the information necessary for making informed decisions on policy development.

ACKNOWLEDGEMENTS

We would like to acknowledge the following people who, at various times, have been colleagues of the authors and members of the Marine Resources Geoscience Subdivision and/or its predecessors and thus have contributed to our present understanding of the subsurface geology of offshore eastern Canada: Piero Ascoli, Mike Avery, Sedley Barss, Jennifer Bates, Darrell Beaver, Sebastian Bell, Mel Best, Jon Bujak, Doug Cant, Janet Charest, Dave Clark, Donnie Clattenburg, Sheila Clyburne, Kevin Coflin, Gary Cook, Bernie Crilley, Lynn Dafoe, Ed Davies, Bhan Deonarine, Kate Dickie, Pete Doeven, Tony Edwards, Aubrey Fricker, Peter Giles, Paul Girouard, Felix Gradstein, Al Grant, Gary Grant, Peter Hacquebard, Ken Hale, Darrel Hardy, Iris Hardy, Ian Harris, Bob Howie, Art Jackson, Luba Jansa, Chris Jauer, Tony Jenkins, Charlotte Keen, Nelly Koziel, Paul Lake, Quingmou Li, Bernie MacLean, Bill MacMillan, Andrew MacRae, Ann Mazerall, Susan Merchant, Carol Mitchell, Phil Moir, Gordon Oakey, Lisa O'Neill, Ken Peters, Pat Purcell, Matt Salisbury, Bruce Sanford, John Shimeld, Rhonda Sutherland, Frank Thomas, Maisie Trapnell, David Umpleby, David Vaughan, John Wade, Hans Wielens, and Mark Williamson.

REFERENCES

Amoco Canada Petroleum Company Ltd. and Imperial Oil Ltd. 1973. Regional geology of the Grand Banks. Bulletin of Canadian Petroleum Geology 21: 479-503.

Ascoli, P. 1976. Foraminiferal and ostracod biostratigraphy of the Mesozoic-Cenozoic, Scotian Shelf, Atlantic Canada. Pages 653-771 *in* First International Symposium on Benthonic Foraminifera of Continental Margins, Part B: Paleoecology and Biostratigraphy (C.T. Schafer and B.R. Pelletier, Eds.). Maritime Sediments Special Publication No. 1, Dartmouth, NS.

Balkwill, H.R. and N.J. McMillan. 1990. Part 1: Mesozoic-Cenozoic geology of the Labrador Shelf. Pages 293-324 *in* Geology of the Continental Margin of Eastern Canada (M.J. Keen and G.L. Williams, Eds.). Geology of Canada No. 2, Geological Survey of Canada, Ottawa, ON.

Barss, M.S., J.P.Bujak, and G.L.Williams. 1979. Palynological zonation and correlation of sixty-seven wells, eastern Canada. Geological Survey of Canada Paper 78-24, Ottawa, ON.

Bell, J.S., R.D. Howie, N.J. McMillan, C.M. Hawkins, and J.L. Bates (Eds.). 1989. Labrador Sea Basin. Geological Survey of Canada, East Coast Atlas Series, Ottawa, ON. doi:10.4095/127152.

Bujak, J.P., M.S. Barss, and G.L. Williams. 1977a. Offshore eastern Canada – Part I, Organic type and colour and hydrocarbon potential. Oil and Gas Journal 75 (4 April 1977): 198-202.

Bujak, J.P., M.S. Barss, and G.L. Williams. 1977b. Offshore eastern Canada – Part II, Organic type and colour and hydrocarbon potential. Oil and Gas Journal 75 (11 April 1977): 96-100.

Deptuck, M.E. and C. Campbell. 2012. Widespread erosion and mass failure from the ~51 Ma Montagnais marine bolide impact off southwestern Nova Scotia, Canada. Canadian Journal of Earth Sciences 49: 1,567-1,594.

Deptuck, M.E., R.A. MacRae, J.W. Shimeld, G.L. Williams, and R.A. Fensome. 2003. Revised upper Cretaceous and lower Paleogene lithostratigraphy and depositional history of the Jeanne d'Arc Basin, offshore Newfoundland, Canada. American Association of Petroleum Geologists Bulletin 87: 1,459-1,483.

Dickie, K., C.E. Keen, G.L. Williams, and S.A. Dehler. 2011. Tectonostratigraphic evolution of the Labrador margin, Atlantic Canada. Marine and Petroleum Geology 28: 1,663-1,675.

Doeven P.H. 1983. Cretaceous nannofossil stratigraphy and paleoecology of the Canadian Arctic margin. Geological Survey of Canada Bulletin 356, Ottawa, ON.

Doeven, P.H., F.M. Gradstein, A. Jackson, F.P. Agterberg, and L.D. Nel. 1982: A quantitative nannofossil range chart. Micropaleontology 28: 85-92.

Dolby, G., E.M. Oliver, and B.V.A. Thorne. 1979. The micropaleontology, palynology and stratigraphy of the Texaco et al. Blue H-28 well. Robertson Research Centre Canada Limited Exploration Report No. 205, Calgary, AB.

Fensome, R A., G.L. Williams, P. Ascoli, M.S. Barss, J.P. Bujak, E.H. Davies, P. H. Doeven, F.M. Gradstein, and B. Stam. 1997. East Coast Basin Atlas Series, Grand Banks of Newfoundland, biostratigraphy and maturation data. Geological Survey of Canada, Open File 3458, Ottawa, ON. doi:10.4095/209222.

Fensome, R.A., J.A. Crux, I.G. Gard, R.A. MacRae, G.L.Williams, F.C. Thomas, F. Fiorini, and G. Wach. 2008. The last 100 million years on the Scotian Margin, offshore eastern Canada: an event-stratigraphic scheme emphasizing biostratigraphic data. Atlantic Geology 44: 93-126.

Fensome, R.A., G.L. Williams, and A. MacRae. 2009. Late Cretaceous and Cenozoic fossil dinoflagellates and other palynomorphs from the Scotian Margin, offshore eastern Canada. Journal of Systematic Palaeontology 7: 1-79.

Fensome, R.A., G.L. Williams, A. Achab, J.J. Clague, D. Corrigan, J.W.H. Monger, and G.S. Nowlan. In press. Four Billion Years and Counting: Canada's Geological Heritage. Canadian Federation of Earth Sciences, Calgary, AB, and Nimbus Publishing, Halifax, NS.

Gradstein, F.M. 1976. Biostratigraphy and biogeography of Jurassic Grand Banks Foraminifera. Pages 557-583 *in* First International Symposium on Benthonic Foraminifera of Continental Margins, Part B: Paleoecology and Biostratigraphy (C.T. Schafer and B.R. Pelletier, Eds.). Maritime Sediments, Special Publication No. 1, Dartmouth, NS.

Gradstein, F.M. and F.P. Agterberg. 1982. Models of Cenozoic foraminiferal stratigraphy northwestern Atlantic Margin. Pages 119-173 *in* Quantitative Stratigraphic Correlation (J.M. Cubitt and R.A. Reyment, Eds.). J. Wiley, Chichester, England.

Gradstein, F.M. and F.C. Thomas. 1983. Stratigraphy and depositional environment of Texas Blue H-28. Geological Survey of Canada Report No. EPGS-PAL 1-83FMG/FCT.

Gradstein, F.M. and F.P. Agterberg. 1985. Quantitative correlation in exploration micropaleontology. Pages 309-357 *in* Quantitative Stratigraphy (F.M. Gradstein, F.P. Agterberg, J.C. Brower, and W.S. Schwarzacher, Eds.). D. Riedel Publishing, Dordrecht, The Netherlands.

Gradstein, F.M., J. Ogg, and S.G. Smith. 2005. A geological time scale 2004. Cambridge University Press, Cambridge, MA.

Gradstein, F.M., G.L. Williams, W.A.M. Jenkins, and P. Ascoli. 1975. Mesozoic and Cenozoic stratigraphy of the Atlantic continental margin, eastern Canada. Pages 103-131 *in* Canada's Continental Margins and Offshore Petroleum Exploration (C.J. Yorath, E.R. Parker, and D.J. Glass, Eds.). Canadian Society of Petroleum Geologists Memoir 4, Calgary, AB.

Grant, A.C. and K.D. McAlpine. 1990. The continental margin around Newfoundland. Pages 239-292 *in* Geology of the Continental Margin of Eastern Canada (M.J. Keen, and G.L. Williams, Eds.). Geology of Canada No. 2, Geological Survey of Canada, Ottawa, ON.

Haq, B.U., J. Hardenbol, and P.R. Vail. 1987. Chronology of fluctuating sea levels since the Triassic. Science 235: 1,156-1,167.

Hardy, I.A. 1975. Lithostratigraphy of the Banquereau Formation of the Scotian Shelf. Pages 163-174 *in* Offshore Geology of Eastern Canada - Regional Geology (W.J.M. van der Linden and J.A. Wade, Eds.). Geological Survey of Canada Paper 74-30, Vol. 2, Ottawa, ON.

Ioannides, N.S. 1998. Palynology report on the Texaco, Shell et al. Blue H-28 well, Orphan Basin, Canada. Exxon Exploration Company (Technology Department, Global Studies-Geological Services Division, Biostratigraphy Section) C-NLOPB File No. 8932-J001-003E.

Jackson, H.R., C.E. Keen, R.K.H. Falconer, and K.P. Appleton. 1979. New geophysical evidence for sea-floor spreading in central Baffin Bay. Canadian Journal of Earth Sciences 16: 2,122-2,135.

Jansa, L.F. and J.A. Wade. 1975. Geology of the continental margin off Nova Scotia and Newfoundland. Pages 51-105 *in* Offshore Geology of Eastern Canada - Regional Geology (W.J.M. van der Linden and J.A. Wade, Eds.). Geological Survey of Canada Paper 74-30, Vol. 2, Ottawa, ON.

Jansa, L.F., J.P. Bujak, and G.L. Williams. 1980. Upper Triassic salt deposits of the western North Atlantic. Canadian Journal of Earth Sciences 17: 547-559.

Jansa, L.F. and G. Pe-Piper. 1987. Identification of an underwater extraterrestrial impact crater. Nature 327: 612-614.

Keen, M.J., and G.L. Williams (Eds.). 1990. Geology of the Continental Margin of Eastern Canada, Geology of Canada No. 2, Geological Survey of Canada, Ottawa, ON.

MacLean, B., G.L. Williams, A. Jennings, and C. Blakeney. 1986. Bedrock and surficial geology of Cumberland Sound, N.W.T. Geological Survey of Canada Paper 86-1B: 605-615.

MacLean, B., G.L. Williams, and S.P. Srivastava. 1990. Part 2: Geology of Baffin Bay and Davis Strait. Pages 325-348 *in* Geology of the Continental Margin of Eastern Canada (M.J. Keen and G.L. Williams, Eds.). Geology of Canada No. 2, Geological Survey of Canada, Ottawa, ON.

MacLean, B. and G.L. Williams. 2011. Cretaceous strata on the Baffin Island Shelf. American Association of Petroleum Geologists, IIIP Conference, Halifax, NS. Program with Abstracts, American Association of Petroleum Geologists, Tulsa, OK.

MacLean, B., G.L. Williams, and G.A. Fowler. 2014. Bedrock studies of the Baffin Island Shelf and Hudson Strait: a technological and scientific adventure. Pages 331-336 *in* Voyage of Discovery: Fifty Years of Marine Research at Canada's Bedford Institute of Oceanography (D.N. Nettleship, D.C. Gordon, C.F.M. Lewis, and M.P. Latremouille, Eds.). Bedford Institute of Oceanography-Oceans Association, Dartmouth, NS.

McAlpine, K.D. 1990. Mesozoic stratigraphy, sedimentary evolution, and petroleum potential of the Jeanne d'Arc Basin, Grand Banks of Newfoundland. Geological Survey of Canada Paper 89-17, Ottawa, ON.

McIver, N.L. 1972. Mesozoic and Cenozoic stratigraphy of the Nova Scotia Shelf. Canadian Journal of Earth Sciences 9: 54-70.

McWhae, J.R.H., R. Elie, D.C. Laughton, and P.R. Gunther. 1980. Stratigraphy and petroleum prospects of the Labrador Shelf. Bulletin of Canadian Petroleum Geology 28: 460-488.

Nantais, P.T. 1985. A reappraisal of the regional hydrocarbon potential of the Scotian Shelf. Geological Survey of Canada Open File 1175, Ottawa, ON.

Offshore Energy Technical Research Association. 2011. Play Fairway Analysis Atlas - offshore Nova Scotia. Nova Scotia Department of Energy Report 88-11-0004-01. http://www.novascotiaoffshore.com/analysis.

Palynodata Inc. and J.M. White. 2008. Palynodata datafile: 2006 version, with introduction by J.M. White. Geological Survey of Canada Open File 5793, Ottawa, ON. 1 CD-ROM, doi:10.4095/225704.

Roots, W.D. and S.P. Srivastava. 1984. Origin of the marine magnetic quiet zones in the Labrador and Greenland seas. Marine Geophysical Researches 6: 395-408.

Ross, D.I. and C.F.M. Lewis. 1991. Scotian Shelf. Pages 1-152 *in* East Coast Atlas Series, Frontier Geoscience Program (J.L. Bates, Ed.). Geological Survey of Canada, Ottawa, ON.

Sorensen, A.B. 2006. Stratigraphy, structure and petroleum potential of the Lady Franklin and Maniitsoq Basins, offshore southern West Greenland. Petroleum Geoscience 12: 221-234.

Sinclair, I.K. and M.O. Withjack. 2008. Mid to Late Cretaceous structural and sedimentary architecture at the Terra Nova Oilfield, offshore Newfoundland – Implications for the tectonic history of the North Atlantic. Pages 125-141 *in* Central Atlantic Conjugate Margins (D.E. Broen, Ed.). Dalhousie University, Halifax, NS.

Srivastava, S.P. 1978. Evolution of the Labrador Sea and its bearing on the early evolution of the North Atlantic. Geophysical Journal of the Royal Astronomical Society 52: 313-357.

Stover, L.E., H. Brinkhuis, S.P. Damassa, L. de Verteuil, R.J. Helby, E. Monteil, A.D. Partridge, A.J. Powell, J.B. Riding, M. Smelror, and G.L. Williams. 1996. Mesozoic-Tertiary dinoflagellates, acritarchs and prasinophytes. Pages 641-750 *in* Palynology: Principles and Applications, Vol. 2 (J. Jansonius and D.C. McGregor, Eds.). American Association of Stratigraphic Palynologists Foundation, Dallas, TX.

Umpleby, D.C. 1979. Geology of the Labrador Shelf. Geological Survey of Canada Paper 79-13, Ottawa, ON.

van der Linden, W.J.M. and J.A. Wade (Eds.). 1975. Offshore Geology of Eastern Canada, Vol. 2, Regional Geology. Geological Survey of Canada, Paper 74-30, Ottawa, ON.

Wade, J.A. and B.C. MacLean. 1990. The geology of the southeastern margin of Canada. Pages 167-238 *in* Geology of the Continental Margin of Eastern Canada (M.J. Keen and G.L. Williams, Eds.). Geology of Canada No. 2, Geological Survey of Canada, Ottawa, ON.

Wade, J.A. and B.C. MacLean. 1993. Seismic markers and stratigraphic picks in Scotian Basin wells. Pages 1-276 *in* East Coast Basin Atlas Series (J.L. Bates, Ed.). Geological Survey of Canada, Ottawa, ON.

Wade, J.A., B.C. MacLean, and G.L. Williams. 1995. Mesozoic and Cenozoic stratigraphy, eastern Scotian Shelf: new interpretation. Canadian Journal of Earth Sciences 32: 1,462-1,473.

Weston, J.F., M.K.E. Cooper, R.A. MacRae, P. Ascoli, R.A. Fensome, G.L. Williams, and D. Shaw. 2012. A revised biostratigraphic and well-log sequence-stratigraphic framework for the Scotian Basin, offshore eastern Canada. Canadian Journal of Earth Sciences 49: 1,417-1,462.

Williams, G.L. 1975. Dinoflagellate and spore stratigraphy of the Mesozoic-Cenozoic, offshore eastern Canada. Pages 107-161 *in* Offshore Geology of Eastern Canada - Regional Geology (W.J.M. van der Linden and J.A. Wade, Eds.). Geological Survey of Canada Paper 74-30, Vol. 2, Ottawa, ON.

Williams, G.L. and W.W. Brideaux. 1975. Palynologic analyses of Upper Mesozoic and Cenozoic rocks of the Grand Banks, Atlantic continental margin. Geological Survey of Canada Bulletin 236, Ottawa, ON.

Williams, G.L., P. Ascoli, M.S. Barss, J.P. Bujak, E.H. Davies, R.A. Fensome, and M.A. Williamson. 1990. Biostratigraphy and related studies. Pages 87-138 *in* Geology of the Continental Margin of Eastern Canada (M.J. Keen and G.L. Williams, Eds.). Geology of Canada No. 2, Geological Survey of Canada, Ottawa, ON.

Williams, G.L., H. Brinkhuis, M.A. Pearce, R.A. Fensome, and J.W. Weegink. 2004. Southern Ocean and global dinoflagellate cyst events compared: index events for the Late Cretaceous-Neogene. Pages 1-98 *in* The Tasmanian Gateway: Cenozoic Climatic and Oceanographic Development: Sites 1168-1172, Proceedings of the Ocean Drilling Program Scientific Results 189 (N.F. Exon, J.P. Kennett, and M.J. Malone, Eds.). Texas A&M University, College Station, TX. doi:10.2973/odp.proc.sr.189.2004

Williamson, M.A. 1987. A quantitative foraminiferal biozonation of the Late Jurassic and Early Cretaceous of the East Newfoundland Basin. Micropaleontology 33: 37-65.

26. MARINE GEOSCIENCE AND LAKES

C.F. Michael Lewis*, Brian J. Todd, Steve M. Blasco, Donald L. Forbes, Gordon D.M. Cameron, and Edward L. King

SUMMARY

Studies of the Great Lakes and Lake Winnipeg were undertaken during the 1990 and 2000 decades using the methods of marine and coastal geoscience. Expeditions were commonly conducted with collaborators to address societal concerns. Lake Ontario sediments and bedrock were surveyed for evidence of recent deformation and earthquake shaking, natural processes that pose concern for safety of nuclear power stations. Popups of surface bedrock were clearly buckled by compressive stress, but were found to relate more to glacial rebound and far-field tectonic stresses than earthquake stress. Glacial lake sediments under postglacial silty clay mud were imaged in most lakes, in places overlying drumlins, tunnel valleys, and moraines. Large shifts in the isotopic composition of fossils in lake sediments revealed new insights into the paleo-hydrology of the deglaciation. Studies in Lake Winnipeg implied that long term progressive lake-level rise resulting from differential glacial rebound of the lake's northern outlet enhanced shore erosion, a result that countered previous concerns that lake-level regulation for power generation was a cause of shore property losses. Submerged tree stumps and evidence of erosion beneath postglacial lake sediments indicated former low-lake levels in the Laurentian Great Lakes. Although the low water levels were initially thought to have resulted solely from tilting of lake basins by differential glacial rebound, it was discovered that the lakes had also descended metres to tens of metres as a result of intensive early to middle Holocene evaporation, a finding that underlined the susceptibility of large lakes to climate change.

Key words: Laurentian Great Lakes, Lake Winnipeg, deglaciation, glacial rebound, paleo-hydrology, seismic risk, closed-basin conditions, climate change.

***E-mail:** Michael.Lewis@NRCan-RNCan.gc.ca

The sedimentary records of the lakes of Canada are repositories of past hydrologic, climatic, tectonic, and glacio-isostatic conditions. Geoscientists and colleagues based at the Bedford Institute of Oceanography (BIO) have advanced the understanding of many eastern North American lakes using the principles and techniques of marine geoscience in basins of the Great Lakes (headwaters of the St. Lawrence River, hence Laurentian Great Lakes) and Lake Winnipeg in Manitoba, as well as lakes in Nova Scotia (Fig. 1). Advances were commonly founded on surveys of lakebed morphology and sediment stratigraphy using multibeam bathymetry and acoustic or seismic reflection surveys, followed by lakebed coring and analysis of sediment sequences to reveal sedimentary history with implications for basin stability, hydrological status, and other aspects of societal interest. In some cases, advances in understanding flowed from visual inspection and sampling of the lakebed using a manned submersible, and aerial reconnaissance, remote sensing, and shore-zone profiling for study of shoreline evolution and ice dynamics. Lake studies originating from Geological Survey of Canada (GSC) Atlantic were a new initiative conducted during the 1990 and 2000 decades with stakeholder interest and support, and in collaboration with researchers from other GSC divisions, universities, and provincial geological surveys.

SUBMERGED LAKESHORES IN NOVA SCOTIA

Shoreline features of former lakes in Atlantic coastal embayments have been revealed in multibeam sonar images from ~22 m water depth in Bedford Basin (Halifax Harbour), and ~25 m water depth in Bras d'Or Lake in Cape Breton (Fader and Miller 2008, Shaw et al. 2009). These lakes existed for thousands of years after the last deglaciation until they were submerged by rising sea level in the middle Holocene (Holocene = last 10,000 years of Earth history). Earlier study of sediment cores had shown that water in Bedford Basin was fresh (Lake Bedford) until ca. 6,000 years ago, and would have overflowed via the Narrows into a lower sea level in Halifax Harbour (Miller et al. 1982). Near the harbour, small lakes in Dartmouth were later investigated using miniaturized versions of marine geoscientific survey equipment (Fig. 2) and examination of short cores: similar submerged shorelines were found, but related, in these cases to a reduced water budget in a dry previous climate (Huppertz et al. 2008, Peters 2009). Preserved shoreline features of a presumed freshwater lake beneath the present brackish and saline Bras d'Or Lake are numerous and include shore platforms, barrier beaches and spits, and fluvial systems, possible sites of early human occupation (Shaw et al. 2009).

Figure 1. Map showing the lakes and features referred to in the text (Lakes Superior, Michigan, Huron, Erie, and Ontario = Laurentian Great Lakes, BP = Bruce Peninsula), and inset map showing Halifax Harbour and sites of 'Lake Bedford' (in Bedford Basin), and Lake Banook, NS.

Figure 2. An acoustic profiling survey being conducted by E. King from canoe in Lake Banook, NS.

LAKE ONTARIO

Although Lake Ontario is about 75 m above and 500 km upstream from tidal water today, during deglaciation ca. 12,900 years ago it was at the then current sea level (Fig. 3A). Only a strong outflow of freshwater prevented the Lake Ontario basin from becoming a marine environment (Anderson and Lewis 2012), as happened at Bedford Basin and Bras d'Or Lake basins of Nova Scotia.

In the eastern Great Lakes region today, where intra-plate earthquakes are common, pristine lakebeds and sedimentary sequences are recognized as places to look for records of potential neotectonic and paleo-seismic evidence. Such evidence can be used to refine the assessment of earthquake hazard, essential, for example, for gaining confidence in the long term safety of nuclear power stations, a particular concern of the

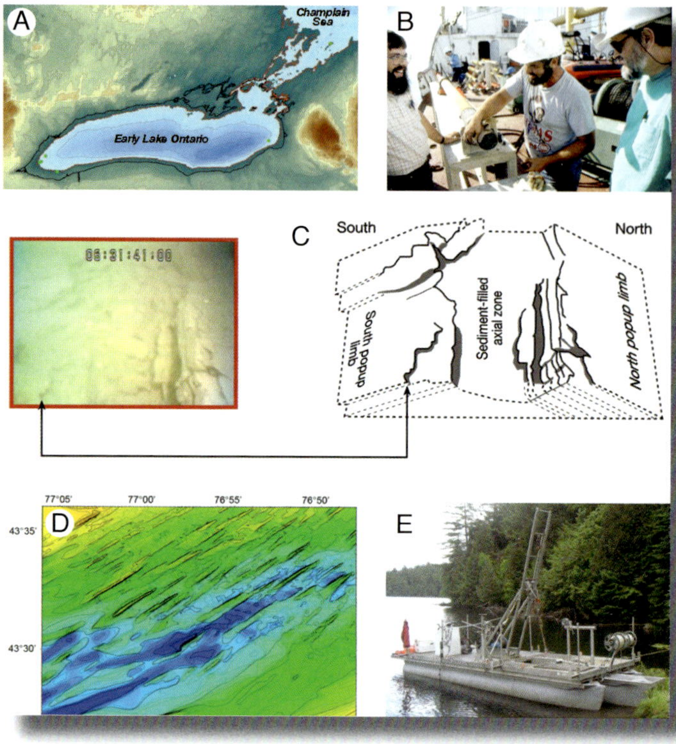

Figure 3. Lake Ontario early phase, coring activity, and geological features, and Lake Simcoe coring raft: (A) Early Lake Ontario at sea level about 12,500 years ago; black line shows the present shore of Lake Ontario (from Anderson and Lewis 2012); (B) Discussion about a piston core among (left to right) A. Sherin, F. Jodrey, and M. Lewis aboard CCGS *Griffon*; (C) Photo from a submersible with interpretative drawing showing a bedrock popup south of Toronto beneath the lake – the separation of the popup's two limbs across the axial zone is about 20 cm (from Jacobi et al. 2007); (D) Shaded-relief multibeam bathymetric map of eastern Lake Ontario ranging in water depth from about 170 m (yellow) to 244 m (blue) showing parallel ridges formed by underlying drumlins (elongated glacially-sculpted hills) (from NOAA map that incorporated GSC-Atlantic multibeam survey data: www.ngdc.noaa.gov/mgg/image/images/rochester.jpg), and (E) Pontoon raft used in smaller Lake Simcoe (for location of Lake Simcoe, see Fig. 1).

Canadian Nuclear Safety Commission (previously Atomic Energy Control Board or AECB). The continuity of sediment sequences and structure of the bedrock surface were profiled for earthquake evidence with boomer and air gun seismic reflection systems, and were sampled with piston cores (Fig. 3B) during surveys of Lake Ontario in 1992-93 aboard CCGS *Griffon* with support from the AECB (Lewis et al. 1995).

One of the most promising indicators of recent (neotectonic) bedrock faulting was a field of popups (i.e., upward buckles of compressed surface layers of sedimentary bedrock) on the lake floor south of Toronto, ON, discovered in 1987 (Thomas et al. 1993), near known deep underlying geophysical lineaments interpreted as Precambrian bedrock discontinuities. Popups were observed in many places in eastern North America and were thought by some to be evidence of earthquake stress release, and thus direct indicators of former earthquakes (Wallach et al. 1993). The BIO geoscientific investigations of exposed sedimentary bedrock beneath Lake Ontario south of Toronto, employing sidescan sonar, seismic reflection, multibeam and mini-sub tools, revealed numerous stress-release features in the form of sub-lakefloor buckles and lakebed bedrock popups (Fig. 3C). These features were found to be unaligned with the known major geophysical lineaments, but to be collinear with isobases of glacial rebound (contours of equal uplift). An observed rotation of older to younger popups from WNW to NNW paralleled the rotation of glacial lake isobases to those of recent basin tilting. These observations suggest that popups have been largely a response to glacial rebound stress, and as rebound declines with time, younger popups are responding increasingly to plate tectonic stresses, for example from Atlantic seafloor spreading (Jacobi et al. 2007).

The first multibeam sonar surveys in the lake revealed another feature of possible neotectonic origin. A hilly lakefloor of parallel ridges in the deep eastern basin had been tentatively interpreted as a result of normal faulting (Thomas et al. 1993). However, the multibeam data and seismic reflection profiles showed that the parallel ridges mimicked relief of underlying drumlins (glacial landforms), not faulted bedrock (Fig. 3D; Lewis et al. 1997).

In addition, linear acoustic backscatter zones across the western end of the lake were initially postulated to reflect surface expression of Precambrian geophysical lineaments beneath the lake; the backscatter zones were later shown to be reflections from accumulations of ash dumped during the steamship era on multiple voyages out of Toronto Harbour to ports on the opposite side of the lake (Lewis et al. 2000).

Overall, the Lake Ontario investigations showed that geological structures, initially thought to be geohazards, were benign features with respect to the stability of societal infrastructure.

LAKE SIMCOE

Groundwater is an important source of water supply, and could be a significant input to lakes, though little is known about this aspect of groundwater science. As environmental pressures increase in populated lake basins, knowledge of pathways and transport of water through sediment and bedrock units within basins and into lakes becomes increasingly important. Seismic surveys and sediment sampling in Lake Simcoe, north of Toronto, revealed records of postglacial and glacial lake sediments over till and sub-till sediments, with the ice-formed till surface shaped into drumlins and tunnel channels, the last features having sand and gravel infills (Todd et al. 2008). Such information about offshore sediment stratigraphy, similar to onshore watershed stratigraphy, contributes to constraint analysis for groundwater pathways and flow (Lewis et al. 2007a). Later, targeted surveys and coring (Fig. 3E) with the University of Rhode Island, combined with porewater isotopic analysis by the University of Western Ontario, revealed conduits of groundwater flow through lakebed sediment sequences (Longstaffe et al. 2008), indicating that modelling of groundwater inventory and movement should incorporate the lake and sub-lake sedimentary strata.

GEORGIAN BAY

Work with the Severn Sound Remedial Action Plan in southern Georgian Bay (Severn Sound) northwest of Toronto and Lake Simcoe revealed sedimentary barren zones devoid of pollen indicating episodes of subaerial (above water) exposure and hinting at former climate-driven lake lowstands, later shown to have resulted from excess evaporation (McCarthy et al. 2007, 2012).

Surveys to provide geological knowledge to support Fathom Five National Marine Park north of Bruce Peninsula (for location, see Fig. 1) revealed a remarkable occurrence of more than 6 tree stumps in growth position (Fig. 4A) with ages spanning 7,230 to 9,320 carbon-14-dated years before present in water depths down to 43 m (Blasco 2001). These finds of tree remains and evidence of former intermittent stream flow (Fig. 4B) on the lakebed between Lake Huron and Georgian Bay presented opportunities for discovery of the presence of prehistoric man (Blasco et al. 1997). The low lake-level implications of these observations resonated with local First Nations (Chippewa) people whose oral history contains stories of ancestors walking this same lakebed between Bruce Peninsula and Manitoulin Island (Fig. 1).

Other discoveries include facets of glacial and lake history, such as glacial bedrock grooves modified by high-velocity movement of meltwater, and a submerged river channel that re-occupied a sub-glacial discharge channel (Fig. 4B) during former periods of low lake levels and catastrophic inflows from northern sources. These discoveries are being incorporated into National Park displays and outreach programs to inform the public and to enhance conservation of marine and geological heritage of the Great Lakes.

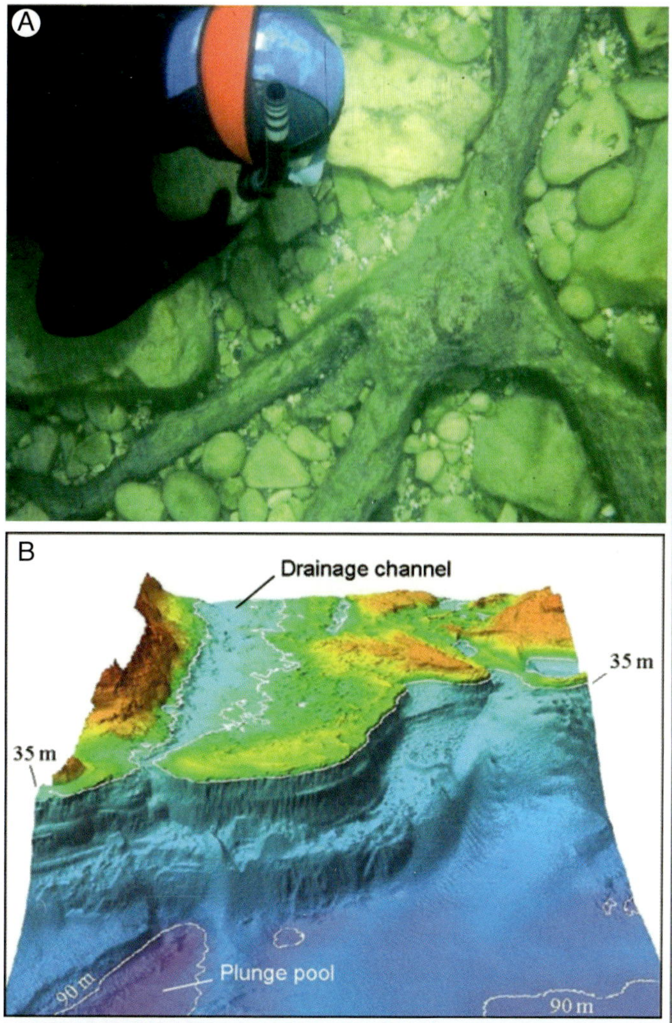

Figure 4. Features of the submerged escarpment between Georgian Bay and Lake Huron, north of Bruce Peninsula (for location, see Fig. 1): (A) Submerged tree stump (^{14}C age = 7,490±80 BP) in growth position on the lakebed; (B) Multibeam sonar bathymetry perspective image looking west at the submerged escarpment showing a cross-scarp drainage channel and plunge pool of a former waterfall below the escarpment.

LAKES MICHIGAN, HURON, AND SUPERIOR

In parallel with the foregoing discoveries in Georgian Bay, joint surveys with the University of Michigan, using the university research vessel MV *Laurentian*, delineated sediment sequences in northern parts of the Michigan, Huron, and Georgian Bay basins (Moore et al. 1994). Sediment cores yielded the first records of a surprising range of early Holocene $\delta^{18}O$ values in carbonate fossils which revealed a paleo-hydrology involving distinct alternation of non-glacial and glacial meltwater inflow (Rea et al. 1994a, b). Early to middle Holocene lake-level changes in the order of tens of metres resulting from alternating periods of meltwater overflow from northern glacial lakes and dry climate lowstands were later resolved from studies of bog and other sediment stratigraphy (Lewis and Anderson 2012). These data also provided evidence of teleconnection with the Pacific El Niño-La Niña oscillations in glacial lake records, and basin-specific anoxia (black FeS) occurrences in postglacial lake sediments suggesting that a warmer middle Holocene may be an analog for the Great Lakes during future climatic warming.

Seismic surveys with University of Minnesota-Duluth delineated sediment units off the northern shore of Lake Superior where fan deposits were found related to overflow from a late phase of glacial Lake Agassiz, but not earlier phases (Gary et al. 2012, Voytek et al. 2012). This find provided an example of massive freshwater outflows, some of which are known from changes in the sediment stratigraphy of downstream lakes (Lewis and Anderson 2012).

LAKE WINNIPEG

Farther west, a major multidisciplinary study of Lake Winnipeg using ship (CCGS *Namao*), launch, and aircraft operations was led by scientists from BIO, in partnership with the Manitoba Geological Survey, and others in the GSC, Freshwater Institute of Fisheries and Oceans Canada, and University of Manitoba, with support from Manitoba Hydro. Fundamental geological boundaries and features were mapped beneath this large lake, the eleventh largest in the world by area, including a part of the southwestern edge of Precambrian bedrock forming the Canadian Shield, and moraines (buried beneath lake sediments) which delineated ice margin positions during retreat of the last ice sheet (Todd et al. 1998). Records of outstanding clarity were obtained of deposits of the ensuing glacial Lake Agassiz (Fig. 5A), the largest lake yet known whose catastrophic discharges triggered the well-known abrupt climate change events in the North Atlantic basin– the Younger Dryas and 8.2 ka cold

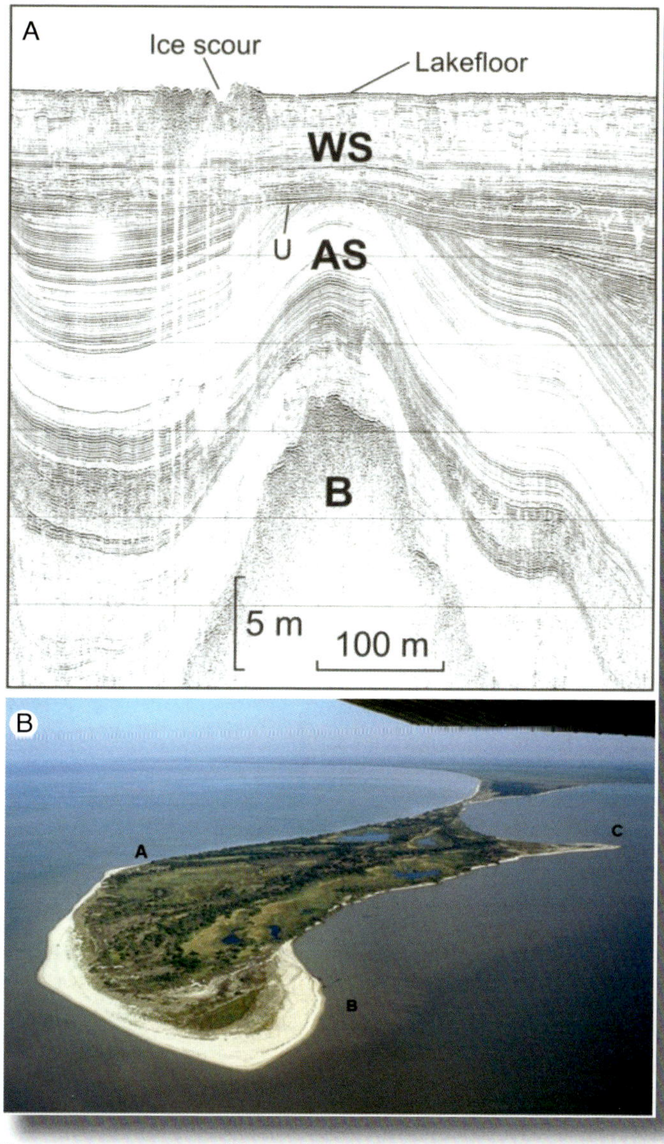

Figure 5. Subsurface and coastal features of Lake Winnipeg:
(A) High-resolution seismic profile showing the ice-scoured lakefloor of northern Lake Winnipeg in 16 m water depth resulting from sediment ploughing by a moving keel of a thick ridge of pressured and rafted lake ice, and the transition from acoustically stratified Lake Agassiz sediments (AS) to overlying postglacial Lake Winnipeg sediments (WS) which is gradational in places (right and left sides) and abrupt (eroded) above a till-covered bedrock peak B (centre, marked U); and
(B) Looking north across the complex structure of Disbrowe Point, a major Lake Winnipeg spit on the southeast shore of the lake's northern basin, in which sediment is presently transported southward (toward the viewer) along the outer shore of the spit and deposited at the outer end between A and B, and truncated beach ridges at A and anomalous ridge orientation at C, reflecting a complex history thought to have involved an earlier barrier or spit farther lakeward that broke up and retreated landward with lake-level rise which drowned marsh peat off the outer beach within the past 2,500 years.

events (Teller et al. 2002). An unexpected recovery of peaty deposits, remnants of former swamps and marshes now buried beneath southern Lake Winnipeg sediments, was initially thought to be the result of basin drainage via a glacio-isostatically down-tilted northern outlet. Later analysis led to the conclusion that excessive evaporation in an early to middle Holocene dry climate had reduced early Lake Winnipeg to a hydrologically-closed condition below its outlet (Lewis et al. 2001).

A wide diversity of coastal geomorphic features throughout the Lake Winnipeg shore zone was revealed by aerial and ground reconnaissance augmented by summer boat and winter ice surveys of nearshore sites (Forbes and Frobel 1996). Observations of the geomorphology of spit and barrier sediment complexes (Fig. 5B) combined with nearshore evidence of erosion and lake-level rise, including submerged remnants of tree stumps, provided a record of shore processes over the last few centuries to a millennium (Forbes 2000). In addition to long term water-level rise driven by isostatic tilting and outlet uplift, shorter term fluctuations of lake level were recognized, possibly related to climate change, for example, higher levels during the Little Ice Age (Nielsen 1998). Despite widespread suggestions that lake-level regulation (by a hydro-electric power dam) had caused an increase in shore erosion, it was shown that the dam had little effect on erosion rates because lake-level rise, which can accelerate shore erosion, had been ongoing since before the lake was regulated. In addition, clay-rich shorefaces, with little resistance to erosion, are common around Lake Winnipeg, and these erosion-susceptible shores, developed in fine-grained glacial Lake Agassiz deposits, had been present before the dam was constructed (Forbes 2000, Thorleifson et al. 2000).

Following the 1997 Red River flood, additional study of the surface sediments of southern Lake Winnipeg yielded a millennium-long record of flood events as a contribution to improved understanding of flood risk and influx of nutrients and contaminants to the lake (Simpson et al. 1999).

EARLY HOLOCENE CLIMATIC IMPACTS ON THE GREAT LAKES

The surprising discovery of closed-basin conditions in Lake Winnipeg precipitated a re-examination of lowstand evidence in the Laurentian Great Lakes (Lewis et al. 2008b, Lewis and King 2012), such as the Flowerpot Beach at 53 m water depth in Georgian Bay (Blasco 2001), the Stanley Unconformity at 70 m depth in northwestern Lake Huron (Lewis et al. 2007b), a mud-buried paleo-shoreface and wave-cut terrace 21 m to 28 m beneath Lake Erie (Lewis et al. 2012b), and paleo-nearshore sandy beds under mud up to 90 m below Lake Ontario (Anderson and Lewis 2012), all indicating lake lowstands within the early or middle Holocene (Fig. 6). This initiative to explore the sensitivity of these large lakes to climate change was of interest to many as the lake levels are closely integrated into coastal societal infrastructure and natural environments. In particular, interest was expressed by the Canada-United States International Joint Commission, an organization responsible for regulating lake levels, and by Parks Canada with regard to coastal wetland management.

The Lake Winnipeg experience showed that a new approach was required for reconstructing former water levels in large lake basins to separate the effects of basin tilting by differential glacial isostatic adjustment and water-level response to climatic change. Once a synthesis of tilted glacial lake shorelines and other evidence of differential rebound was completed, the original elevations of geological indicators of former lake levels and of basin overflow sills throughout the Great Lakes region were independently computed and compared (Lewis et al. 2005). With application of this approach it is now known that lakes in the southern basins of the Great Lakes system were depressed below their outlets by 10-40 m for 4-6 millennia in the dry early and middle Holocene climate (Edwards et al. 1996, Anderson and Lewis 2012, Lewis et al. 2012b). Lakes in the northern basins were also drawn down below their outlets by several tens of metres, but the lowstands were interrupted by northern inflows of glacial meltwater from lakes Agassiz and Ojibway (Lewis et al. 2007b, 2008a). While late meltwater presence in the upper Great Lakes basins in the midst of their lowstands needs to be better understood, the climatic reduction of these former Great Lakes shows that the extent of dry early Holocene climate was greater than previously thought. The lakes also serve as natural examples of the sensitivity and susceptibility of larger lakes to climate change (Lewis et al. 2008b), even the apparently stable Great Lakes whose mean annual levels have varied less than 2 m in the past 150 years.

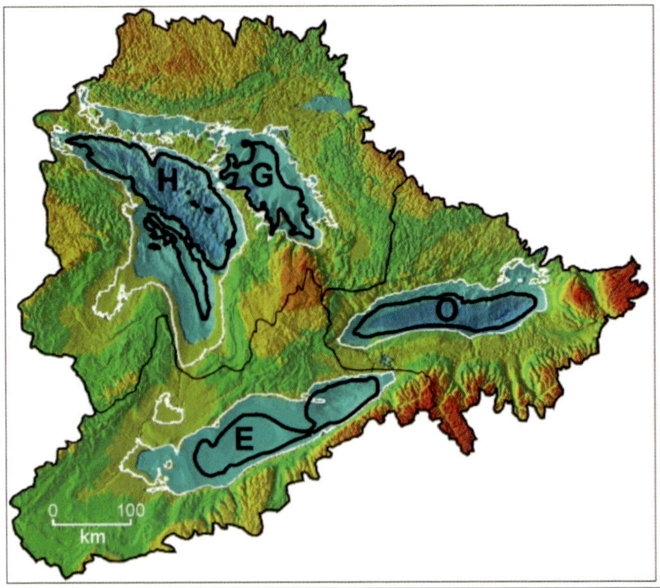

Figure 6. Lowstand shorelines (black) about 8,800 years ago in part of the Great Lakes watershed (coloured); thin black lines indicate internal watershed boundaries. Present Great Lake shorelines are shown in white: H= Lake Huron, G = Georgian Bay, E = Lake Erie, and O = Lake Ontario (from Lewis et al. 2008b).

SIGNIFICANCE

The application of BIO research methods in marine and coastal geoscience to some of the large lakes in North America has yielded several successful outcomes for understanding and formulating advice for societal concerns associated with geological aspects of these resources.

In Lake Ontario, studies focussed on features possibly affecting the geological stability of nuclear power stations, including: (1) lakebed ridges, (2) anomalous linear patterns of lakefloor acoustic reflectivity, and (3) buckles or popups in exposed sedimentary bedrock, all considered to be possible indicators of instability related to earthquakes. The formation of these features was found to be more likely related to past processes: (1) the sculpturing effects of former glaciation, (2) ash dumping during the era of steamship traffic, and (3) the long term combined effects of crustal unloading during deglaciation and Atlantic seafloor spreading, thereby raising confidence in the stability of nuclear power station sites around the lake.

In the Great Lakes region, studies of medium-sized Lake Simcoe showed that sediment stratigraphy beneath the lake basin was consistent with onshore sediment layering, and was part of the larger system of groundwater movement. This suggests that marine geoscience research methods can show whether large lake basins, such as the Great Lakes, are connected with and play a role in the groundwater dynamics of their surrounding watersheds, a connection for consideration in the future modelling and management of groundwater resources.

Using the data of differential postglacial rebound, independently reconstructed elevation histories of Great Lake basin outlets, and the offshore evidence of previous low water levels, showed that the low levels could not be explained by previously depressed outlets, but only as lowstands evaporated downward by the early to middle Holocene dry climate. The past occurrences of lowstands below outlets demonstrate the sensitivity of the Great Lakes to future climatically-driven changes in water supply. Overall, the past history of these lakes with their responses to previous climates, different than present, could provide some insight into future lake conditions in these and other large lakes in Canada if climates were to become similar to those in the past (Lewis et al. 2010).

In Lake Winnipeg, a possible relationship between unwanted shore erosion and lake-level regulation associated with operation of a lake outlet dam for electrical power generation was the concern. Here, the BIO coastal and offshore studies of postglacial earth history revealed substantial changes in the lake's boundaries related to past variations in basin water supply, backflooding of southern shores due to ongoing differential glacial rebound, and a lake basin setting on the floor of glacial Lake Agassiz giving rise to modern lake shores in erosion-susceptible, fine-grained glacial lake sediment. All of these factors predisposed the Lake Winnipeg shores to long-term and ongoing erosion independently of lake-level regulation, thereby diminishing the concern for regulation as a cause of enhanced shore erosion.

These 'voyages of discovery' in a subset of Canada's large lakes have revealed remarkable records of the mid-continent's postglacial history and a wide range of scientific insights with direct application to societal concerns and public policy.

ACKNOWLEDGEMENTS

We acknowledge improvements in this article resulting from reviews by R.B. Taylor and J. Shaw and the book editorial board. We thank K. Manchester, K. Moran, R. Parrott, R. Pickrill, D. Prior, and A. Sherin, colleagues at BIO, who supported our investigations, and many others at BIO who undertook the acquisition and analysis of lake data: K. Asprey, A. Atkinson, A. Boyce, B. Chapman, D. Frobel, P. Girouard, M. Gorveatt, L. Hopkinson, C. Jarrett, F. Jodrey, R. Murphy, P. Pledge, S. Solomon, D. Whalen, and B. Wile. We appreciate the contributions of colleagues from collaborating organizations: T.W. Anderson, R. Burns, M. Douma, R. Good, J. Hunter, S. Pullan, and L.H. Thorleifson (GSC Ottawa), W.M. Buhay (University of Winnipeg), J. Doering, W.M. Last, and J.T. Teller (University of Manitoba), J. Easton and M. Emms (Dixon Hydrogeology Limited), J.W. King and students (University of Rhode Island), F.J. Longstaffe and students (University of Western Ontario), L.A. Mayer and J. Hughes Clarke (University of New Brunswick), J.M. McAndrews, G.R. Brown, A.A. Mohajer, R.G. Pippert (University of Toronto), F.M.G. McCarthy (Brock University), S. McClelland and S. Parker (Parks Canada), T.C. Moore Jr., D.K. Rea and students (University of Michigan), E. Nielsen and G. Matile (Manitoba Geological Survey), P. Travaglini (Canadian Hydrographic Service - CHS, Burlington, ON), R.L. Thomas and J.P. Coakley (National Water Research Institute, Burlington, ON) and J.L. Wallach (Atomic Energy Control Board). The scientific work on the lakes was authorized and supported by components of Natural Resources Canada (NRCan), including the Marine Environmental Geology subdivision, GSC Atlantic, and the Climate Change Geoscience Program, NRCan Earth Sciences Sector. Additional support was provided by GSC Ottawa (Terrain Sciences Division where predecessor lake research was done), Manitoba Hydro, Manitoba Sustainable Development Innovations Fund, Atomic Energy Control Board, Ontario Hydro, Parks Canada, and Lake Simcoe Region Conservation Authority. Support-in-kind was provided by the Canadian Coast Guard (CCGS *Griffon*, *Frederick G. Creed*, *Samuel Risley*, *Limnos*, and *Namao*), Parks Canada (MV *Collins H*), Canadian Navy and Florida Atlantic University (submersible dives), CHS (multibeam surveys), Manitoba Geological Survey, Manitoba Natural Resources, and Severn Sound Remedial Action Plan. Moral support was provided by the International Joint Commission. This is contribution 2013058 of the Earth Sciences Sector of Natural Resources Canada.

REFERENCES

Anderson, T.W. and C.F.M. Lewis. 2012. A new water-level history for Lake Ontario basin: evidence for a climate-driven early Holocene lowstand. Journal of Paleolimnology 47: 513-530. doi 10.1007/s10933-011-9551-8.

Blasco, S.M. 2001. Geological history of Fathom Five National Marine Park over the past 15,000 years. Pages 45-62 *in* Ecology, Culture, and Conservation of a Protected Area: Fathom Five National Marine Park, Canada (S. Parker, and M. Munawar, Eds.). Ecovision World Monograph Series, Backhuys Publishers, Leiden, The Netherlands.

Blasco, S.M., S.E. Janusas, S. McClellan, and A. Amos. 1997. Prehistoric drainage across the submerged Niagara Escarpment north of Tobermory. Pages 218-228 *in* Leading Edge '97 Conference Proceedings. (S. Carty, R. Murzin, S. Powell, and D Ramsay, Eds.). Niagara Escarpment Commission, Georgetown, ON.

Edwards, T.W.D., B.B. Wolfe, and G.M. MacDonald. 1996. Influence of changing atmospheric circulation on precipitation $\delta^{18}O$ – temperature relations in Canada during the Holocene. Quaternary Research 46: 211-218.

Fader, G.B.J., and R.O. Miller. 2008. Surficial geology, Halifax Harbour, Nova Scotia. Geological Survey of Canada Bulletin 590, Ottawa, ON.

Forbes, D.L. 2000. Lake Winnipeg shoreline evolution: barrier growth and shore profile recession. Pages 361-401 *in* 1996 Lake Winnipeg Project: Cruise Report and Scientific Results (B.J. Todd, C.F.M. Lewis, D.L. Forbes, and L.H. Thorleifson, Eds.). Geological Survey of Canada, Open File 3470, Ottawa, ON.

Forbes, D.L. and D. Frobel. 1996. Shore-zone morphology and processes of Lake Winnipeg. Pages 355-391 *in* Lake Winnipeg Project: Cruise Report and Scientific Results (B.J. Todd, C.F.M. Lewis, and L.H. Thorleifson, Eds.). Geological Survey of Canada, Open File 3113, Ottawa, ON.

Gary, J.L., S.M. Colman, N.J. Wattrus, and C.F.M. Lewis. 2012. Post-Marquette discharge from Glacial Lake Agassiz into the Superior basin. Journal of Paleolimnology 47: 299-311. doi: 10.1007/s10933-011-95.3-3.

Huppertz, T.J., E.L. King, N.M. Peters, and G.D.M. Cameron. 2008. Geological setting of Lake Banook – sedimentation and habitat in an urban lake. Geological Survey of Canada, Open File 5877, 1 sheet, Ottawa, ON. doi:10.4095/226072.

Jacobi, R.D., C.F.M. Lewis, D.K. Armstrong, and S.M. Blasco. 2007. Popup field in Lake Ontario south of Toronto, Canada: indicators of late glacial and post-glacial strain. Pages 129-147 *in* Continental Intraplate Earthquakes: Science, Hazard, and Policy Issues (S. Stein and S. Mazotti, Eds.). Geological Society of America Special Paper 425, Boulder, CO. doi:10.1130/2007.2425(10).

Lewis, C.F.M. and T.W. Anderson. 2012. The sedimentary and palynological records of Serpent River Bog, and revised early Holocene lake-level changes in the Lake Huron and Georgian Bay region. Journal of Paleolimnology 47: 391-410. doi 10.1007/s10933-012-9595-4.

Lewis, C.F.M. and J.W. King. 2012. Introduction to "Holocene water levels and paleo-hydrology of the Laurentian Great Lakes". Journal of Paleolimnology 47: 293-297. doi 10.1007/s10933-012-9595-2.

Lewis, C.F.M., G.D.M. Cameron, E.L. King, B.J. Todd, and S.M. Blasco. 1995. Structural contour, isopach and feature maps of Quaternary sediments in western Lake Ontario. Atomic Energy Control Board Project No. 2.243.1 Report, Ottawa, ON.

Lewis, C.F.M., L.A. Mayer, G.D.C. Cameron, and B.J. Todd. 1997. Drumlins in Lake Ontario. Pages 48-49 *in* Glaciated Continental Margins: An Atlas of Acoustic Images (T.A. Davies, T. Bell, A.K. Cooper, H. Josenhans, L. Polyak, A. Solheim, M.S. Stoker, and J.A. Stravers, Eds.). Chapman & Hall, London, England.

Lewis, C.F.M., L.A. Mayer, P.K. Mukhopadhyay, M.A. Kruge, J.P. Coakley, and M.D. Smith. 2000. Multibeam sonar backscatter lineaments and anthropogenic organic components in lacustrine silty clay, evidence of shipping in western Lake Ontario. International Journal of Coal Geology 43: 307-324.

Lewis, C.F.M. and 23 others. 2001. Uplift-driven expansion delayed by middle Holocene desiccation in Lake Winnipeg, Manitoba, Canada. Geology 29: 743-746.

Lewis, C.F.M., S.M. Blasco, and P.L. Gareau. 2005. Glacial isostatic adjustment of the Laurentian Great Lakes basin: using the empirical record of strandline deformation for reconstruction of early Holocene paleo-lakes and discovery of a hydrologically closed phase. Géographie physique et Quaternaire 59: 187-210.

Lewis, C.F.M., B.J. Todd, J.W. King, D.R. Goodyear, and S.R. Slattery. 2007a. Hydrogeology of the Lake Simcoe basin: a geophysical view of stratigraphy beneath the lake. Pages 523-530 *in* Proceedings of OttawaGeo2007, 60th Canadian Geotechnical Conference and 8th Joint CGS/IAH-CNC Specialty Groundwater Conference. BiTech Publishers Ltd., Richmond, BC. (CD-ROM)

Lewis, C.F.M., C.W. Heil, Jr., J.B. Hubeny, J.W. King, T.C. Moore, Jr., and D.K. Rea. 2007b. The Stanley unconformity in Lake Huron basin: evidence for a climate-driven closed lowstand about 7900 ^{14}C BP, with similar implications for the Chippewa lowstand in Lake Michigan basin. Journal of Paleolimnology 37: 435-452. doi 10.1007/s10933-006-9049-y.

Lewis, C.F.M., P.F. Karrow, S.M. Blasco, F.M.G. McCarthy, J.W. King, T.C. Moore, Jr., and D.K. Rea. 2008a. Evolution of lakes in the Huron basin: deglaciation to present. Aquatic Ecosystem Health & Management 11: 127-136.

Lewis, C.F.M., and 16 others. 2008b. Dry climate disconnected the Laurentian Great Lakes. Pages 541-542 *in* EOS, Transactions American Geophysical Union 89 (52), 23 December 2008. American Geophysical Union, Washington,DC.

Lewis, C.F.M., D.K. Rea, J.B. Hubeny, T.A. Thompson, S.M. Blasco, J.W. King, M. Reddin, and T.C. Moore, Jr. 2010. Using geological history of the Laurentian Great Lakes to better understand their future. Aquatic Ecosystem Health & Management 13: 118-126.

Lewis, C.F.M., A.A.L. Miller, E. Levac, D.J.W. Piper, and G.V. Sonnichsen. 2012a. Lake Agassiz outburst age and routing by Labrador Current and the 8.2 cal ka cold event. Quaternary International 260: 83-97. doi 10.1016/j.quaint.2011.08.023.

Lewis, C.F.M., G.D.M. Cameron, T.W. Anderson, C.W. Heil Jr., and P.L. Gareau. 2012b. Lake levels in the Erie Basin of the Laurentian Great Lakes. Journal of Paleolimnology 43: 493-511. doi 10.1007/s10933-012-9578-5.

Longstaffe, F.J., C.F.M. Lewis, J.W. King, C.W. Heil, Jr., J.B. Hubeny, D.R. Goodyear, S.R. Slattery, and R.A. Macdonald. 2008. Stable isotope evidence for groundwater seepage into Kempenfelt Bay, Lake Simcoe. Page 91 *in* Book of Abstracts, International Association for Great Lakes Research, 51st Annual Conference on Great Lakes Research. International Association for Great Lakes Research, Ann Arbor, MI.

McCarthy, F.M.G., J.H. McAndrews, S.M. Blasco, and S.H. Tiffin. 2007. Spatially discontinuous modern sedimentation in Georgian Bay, Huron Basin, Great Lakes. Journal of Paleolimnology 37: 453–470.

McCarthy, F., S. Tiffin, A. Sarvis, J. McAndrews, and S. Blasco. 2012. Early Holocene brackish closed basin conditions in Georgian Bay, Ontario, Canada: microfossil (thecamoebian and pollen) evidence. Journal of Paleolimnology 43: 429-445. doi:10.1007/s10933-010-9415-7.

Miller, A.A.L., P.J. Mudie, and D.B. Scott. 1982. Holocene history of Bedford Basin, Nova Scotia: Foraminifera, dinoflagellate, and pollen records. Canadian Journal of Earth Sciences 19: 2,342-2,367.

Moore, T.C., Jr., D.K. Rea, L.A. Mayer, C.F.M. Lewis, and D.M. Dobson. 1994. Seismic stratigraphy of Lake Huron and Georgian Bay and postglacial lake level history. Canadian Journal of Earth Sciences 31: 1,606-1,617.

Nielsen, E. 1998. Lake Winnipeg coastal submergence over the last three

centuries. Journal of Paleolimnology 19: 335-342.
Peters, N. 2009. Glacial and climatic history of Lake Banook, Dartmouth, Nova Scotia. Unpubl. B.Sc. thesis, Dalhousie University, Halifax, NS.
Rea, D.K., T.C. Moore, Jr., T.W. Anderson, C.F.M. Lewis, D.M. Dobson, D.L. Dettman, A.J. Smith, and L.A. Mayer. 1994a. Great Lakes paleohydrology: complex interplay of glacial meltwater, lake levels, and sill depths. Geology 22: 1,059-1,062.
Rea, D.K., T.C. Moore, Jr., C.F.M. Lewis, L.A. Mayer, D.L. Dettman, A.J. Smith, and D.M. Dobson. 1994b. Stratigraphy and paleolimnologic record of lower Holocene sediments in northern Lake Huron and Georgian Bay. Canadian Journal of Earth Sciences 31: 1,586-1,605.
Shaw, J., G.B. Fader, and R.B. Taylor. 2009. Submerged early Holocene coastal and terrestrial landforms on the inner shelves of Atlantic Canada. Quaternary International 206: 24-34.
Simpson, S.L., L.H. Thorleifson, C.F.M. Lewis, and J.W. King. 1999. Executive summary. Pages 3-9 *in* 1999 Lake Winnipeg Project: Cruise Report and Scientific Results (S.L. Simpson, L.H. Thorleifson, C.F.M. Lewis, and J.W.King, Eds.). Geological Survey of Canada, Open File 4196, Ottawa, ON.
Teller, J.T., D.W. Leverington, and J.D. Mann. 2002. Freshwater outbursts to the oceans from glacial Lake Agassiz and their role in climate change during the last deglaciation. Quaternary Science Reviews 21: 879-887.
Thomas, R.L., J.L. Wallach, R.K. McMillan, J.R. Bowlby, S. Frape, D. Keyes, and A.A. Mohajer. 1993. Recent deformation in the bottom sediments of western and southeastern Lake Ontario and its association with major structures and seismicity. Géographie physique et Quaternaire 47: 325-335.
Thorleifson, L.H., D.L. Forbes, C.F.M. Lewis, E. Nielsen, and B.J. Todd. 2000. Overview of the Lake Winnipeg Project. Pages 5-30 *in* 1996 Lake Winnipeg Project: Cruise Report and Scientific Results (B.J. Todd, C.F.M. Lewis, D.L. Forbes, and L.H. Thorleifson, Eds.). Geological Survey of Canada, Open File 3470, Ottawa, ON.
Todd, B.J., C.F.M. Lewis, E. Nielsen, L.H. Thorleifson, R.K. Bezys, and W. Weber. 1998. Lake Winnipeg: geological setting and sediment seismostratigraphy. Journal of Paleolimnology 19: 215-244.
Todd, B.J., C.F.M. Lewis, and T.W. Anderson. 2008. Quaternary features beneath Lake Simcoe, Ontario, Canada: drumlins, tunnel channels, and records of proglacial to postglacial closed and overflowing lakes. Journal of Paleolimnology 39: 361-380. doi:10.1007/s10933-007-9111-4.
Voytek, E.B., S.M. Colman, N.J. Wattrus, J.L. Gary, and C.F.M. Lewis. 2012. Thunder Bay, Ontario, was not a pathway for catastrophic floods from Glacial Lake Agassiz. Quaternary International 260: 98-105. doi 10.1016/j.quaint.2011.10.040.
Wallach, J.L., A.A. Mohajer, G.H. McFall, J.R. Bowlby, M. Pearce, and D.A. McKay. 1993. Popups as geological indicators of earthquake-prone areas in intraplate eastern North America. Pages 67-83 *in* Neotectonics: Recent Advances (L.A. Owen, I. Stewart, and G. Vita-Finzi, Eds.). Quaternary Proceedings 3. Quaternary Research Association, Cambridge, England.

27. DISCOVERING THE SEAFLOOR OF THE BAY OF FUNDY

Brian J. Todd* and John Shaw

SUMMARY

Mapping of the Bay of Fundy by Europeans commenced in the 1600s and systematic geological mapping began in the 1960s, culminating with a published map in 1977. In partnership with the Canadian Hydrographic Service and the University of New Brunswick, the Geological Survey of Canada began a new round of systematic mapping of the Bay of Fundy with multibeam sonar in 2002. We discuss the survey strategies in this macrotidal environment and highlight a few of the scientific and engineering insights gained from this new mapping program.

Key words: Bay of Fundy, multibeam sonar, surficial geology, backscatter strength.
***E-mail:** Brian.Todd@NRCan-RNCan.gc.ca

The Bay of Fundy, located on the east coast of Canada between the provinces of Nova Scotia and New Brunswick (Fig. 1) is a macrotidal estuarine embayment (Amos et al. 1980) with tides approaching 17 m, the highest in the world (O'Reilly et al. 2005, Bishop 2008). The Bay is a southwest–northeast trending funnel-shaped body of water 155 km long that tapers to 48 km wide at its northeastern end where it bifurcates into Chignecto Bay and Minas Basin (Fig. 1). The floor of the Bay, although hummocky in detail, presents a gently dipping profile along its axis from northeast to southwest. Grand Manan Island and its adjacent southeastern shoals occupy nearly half the entrance to the Bay, and divide it into two channels. Between Brier Island and Grand Manan Island lies an elongated depression forming Grand Manan Basin which has a maximum water depth of 233 m. Grand Manan Channel, with water depths of about 80 m, separates the island from the coast of Maine.

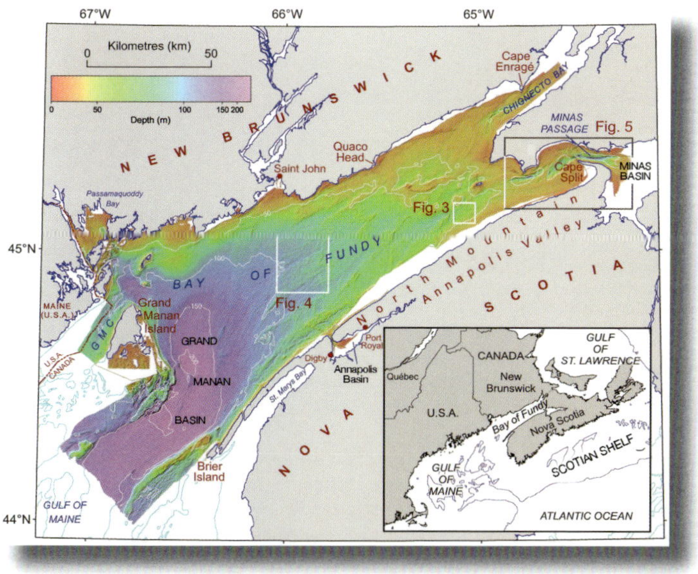

Figure 1. Seafloor relief in the Bay of Fundy based on multibeam sonar. Locations of Figures 3 and 4 are shown by white labelled boxes and Figure 5 by black and white margins. GMC denotes Grand Manan Channel between Maine and Grand Manan Island. Isobaths are in metres with 50 m interval. Isobaths on inset map denote 200 m water depth.

Archaeological evidence in the form of stone tools and artifacts indicates that the Bay of Fundy has been a region of human exploration and occupation since deglacial time about 10,000 years ago (Bonnichsen et al. 1991). The era of nautical charting in this region began four centuries ago with the arrival of Samuel de Champlain and establishment of Port Royal in 1605 on the shore of the Annapolis Basin (Champlain 1613).

GEOLOGICAL HISTORY OF THE BAY OF FUNDY

The Bay of Fundy is situated within the Carboniferous–Triassic lowland (Williams et al. 1972) and is underlain by Triassic and Early Jurassic sandstones, shales, and basalts (Wade et al. 1996). During the late Wisconsinan glacial maximum, culminating ca. 20,000 years before the present (years BP), the Bay of Fundy was covered by an ice sheet that terminated far to the south on the Scotian Slope (Schnitker et al. 2001, Hundert and Piper 2008). Ice-front retreat and glaciomarine deposition began as early as 18,000 years BP. Grounded ice was absent from the Gulf of Maine and Bay of Fundy by ca. 14,000 years BP (King and Fader 1986, Schnitker et al. 2001, Shaw et al. 2006). The Bay exhibits many geomorphological features formed during glaciation, including moraines, eskers, drumlins, megaflutes, and iceberg furrows.

After deglaciation, relative sea level fell rapidly to a -25 m lowstand at ca. 7,000 years BP (Amos and Zaitlin 1985) and then rose (Grant 1970). Tidal amplitude increased throughout the Holocene, and continues to expand today (Godin 1992, Shaw et al. 2010). Strong tidal currents have winnowed the seafloor, leaving veneers of coarse sediment which largely preserve glacial landforms beneath. As tidal energy increased in the Bay during the Holocene epoch, erosion of glacial sediments has created a unique suite of sandy bedforms and a number of large erosional troughs.

EARLY GEOLOGICAL MAPPING OF THE BAY OF FUNDY SEAFLOOR

Systematic regional surficial geology mapping of the Scotian Shelf seabed was initiated by the Geological Survey of Canada (GSC) in the 1960s and continued for two decades. This mapping was based on interpretation of closely-spaced (0.1 to 5 km) echogram profiles of the seabed (using a Kelvin-Hughes 26B echo sounder [model MS26B] with a frequency of 14.25 kHz) and a broad regional grid of seismic reflection profiles, interpreted in conjunction with thousands of textural and sedimentological analyses of seabed sediment grab samples, sediment cores, and seabed photographs (Fader et al. 1977, 2014, and references therein).

Five surficial sediment units were recognized overlying bedrock: (1) Scotian Shelf Drift, a glacial diamict (poorly sorted sediment containing a wide range of particle sizes) formed by contact with glacier ice; (2) Emerald Silt, a glaciomarine mud deposited from meltwater plumes; (3) Sambro Sand, deposited below the level of the postglacial sea-level lowering; (4) LaHave Clay, mud created by reworking of the glacial sediments; and (5) Sable Island Sand and Gravel, formed during the postglacial sea-level transgression by reworking of glacial sediments (Fader et al. 1977).

MODERN MAPPING USING MULTIBEAM SONAR

The importance of multibeam sonar as an essential marine geological mapping tool was recognized very early at the Bedford Institute of Oceanography (BIO) (Loncarevic et al. 1994). Although some early multibeam sonar mapping was undertaken in the Bay of Fundy from 1992 to 1999 for specific local scientific purposes, systematic mapping accelerated when the Bay was identified as a priority area for study under the auspices of Canada's Oceans Act (Parliament of Canada 1996). By the early 2000s, the mapping of benthic habitats had been successfully demonstrated offshore on the Scotian Shelf (Pickrill et al. 2014) and the Bay of Fundy presented an 'inshore' region of economic importance to extend the habitat mapping approach. As well, interest was growing within provincial and federal governments, and in the private sector, to develop tidal energy in the Bay of Fundy (EPRI 2005).

Multibeam sonar bathymetric data were collected systematically by the Canadian Hydrographic Service (CHS), GSC, and the University of New Brunswick (UNB) from 2002 to 2009. The broad intertidal zone was surveyed at high tide using shallow-draft survey vessels, thus overcoming operational challenges associated with deeper draft survey vessels. The survey employed a variety of survey vessels including:

- the Canadian Coast Guard Ship (CCGS) *Frederick G. Creed*, a SWATH (Small Waterplane Area Twin Hull) vessel equipped with Kongsberg EM1000 (prior to 2003) and Kongsberg EM1002 (post 2003) multibeam sonars;
- the CCGS *Matthew* equipped with a Kongsberg EM710 multibeam sonar; and
- hydrographic survey launches *Plover, Pipit*, and *Heron* equipped with Kongsberg EM3000 (prior to 2005) and Kongsberg EM3002 (post 2005) multibeam sonar systems.

The Differential Global Positioning System (GPS) was used for navigation and provided a positional accuracy of ±3 m. The sound velocity in the ocean was measured during multibeam sonar data collection and used to correct the effect of sonar beam refraction. The data were adjusted for tidal variation using tidal measurements and predictions from CHS. During the 2008 surveys, vessel elevations were also acquired using a combination of real-time kinematic GPS systems (Church et al. 2008) and hydrodynamic tidal models developed by CHS and the Fisheries and Oceans Canada Coastal Oceanography Group (Dupont et al. 2005).

Multibeam sonar mapping in the Bay of Fundy presented a number of practical challenges. Mapping the middle and upper Bay was logistically difficult because of the dearth of port facilities concomitant with the size of the survey vessels. Strong tidal currents, especially those in Minas Passage and those occurring on both sides of headlands, had to be taken into survey design account depending on the timing of the survey within the local tidal cycle. Large intertidal areas, especially adjacent to the shoreline of North Mountain in Nova Scotia (Fig. 1), limited the safe survey time in those areas. The high tidal range varies greatly over short distances within the Bay of Fundy, and as a result, the normal practice of installing local tide gauges could not be used; thus levelling errors plagued the raw, unprocessed data. Data collection using a suite of survey vessels produced sets of uncalibrated backscatter strength. To produce a backscatter strength map encompassing all the collected data, an empirical approach through inter-sonar comparisons was undertaken (see below).

The multibeam bathymetric image of the Bay of Fundy seafloor (Fig. 1) has a horizontal resolution 10 m/pixel. The shaded relief image was created by artificially illuminating the seafloor relief from the northwest and the superimposed colours indicate water depth. In order to apply the widest colour range to the most frequently occurring water depths, hypsometric analysis was applied to calculate the cumulative frequency of water depth. The resulting colour ramp highlights subtle variations in water depth that would otherwise be obscured.

MAPPING LANDFORMS BENEATH THE SEA

Regional and local landforms are revealed by the multibeam bathymetric image of the Bay of Fundy seafloor (Fig. 1). Landform studies traditionally have been subaerially based, with a critical component of the mapping conducted through the interpretation of aerial photographs, satellite imagery, or digital elevation models (Boulton and Clark 1990). The horizontal resolution of such imagery is on the order of metres, thus enabling identification and interpretation of large-scale (i.e., local) landforms over a small-scale (i.e., regional) map area. Until the advent of multibeam sonar technology, similar regional mapping using remote sensing was not possible in the marine environment because imagery at an equivalent resolution was not available. The use of multibeam sonar, in concert with traditional marine geoscience survey techniques, offers the capability to discriminate and locate objects on the seafloor as small as 0.5-1.0 m in size (Mayer 2006). Thus, multibeam technology now provides a subaqueous equivalent of a subaerial digital elevation model. The Bay of Fundy survey capitalizes on this new methodology to accomplish mapping of regional glacial landforms and local bedforms resulting from modern current flow (see below in 'Examples of Bay of Fundy Geomorphology').

BACKSCATTER STRENGTH: A PROXY FOR SEAFLOOR TEXTURE

In addition to bathymetric data, multibeam sonar technology records the intensity of echoes returned from the seabed. This backscatter intensity data is a measure of the reflectivity of the sea floor. High values represent relatively hard and/or rough seabed such as rock outcrop and gravel, whereas low values represent relatively soft and/or smooth seabed such as muddy sand and mud. Backscatter intensity images provide a rudimentary map of the distribution of bottom sediment type (Fig. 2).

Backscatter strength is of great value to marine geoscientists be-

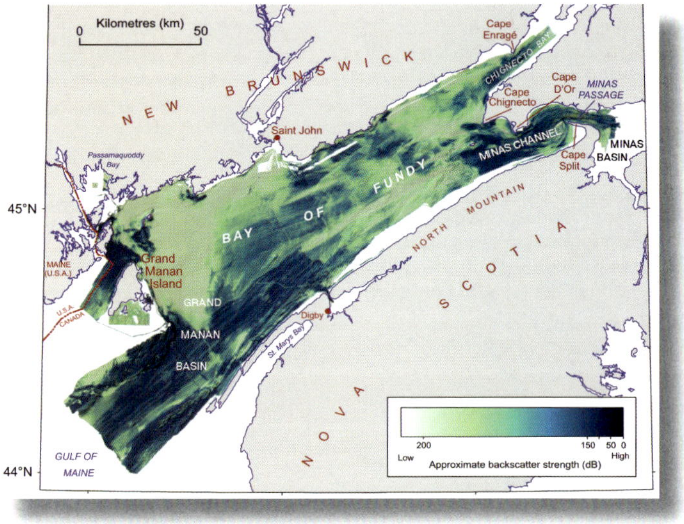

Figure 2. Backscatter strength in the Bay of Fundy based on multibeam sonar provides a rudimentary map of bottom sediment type. High values (blue) represent hard and/or rough seabed surfaces like bedrock and till; low values (light green) represent soft and/or smooth seabed like sand and mud.

cause it can be used as a proxy for roughness of the sea floor, and hence seafloor type and sediment texture. The backscatter strength data (Fig. 2) have been integrated into a single regional coverage from multi-year, multi-source, acoustic backscatter data using a range of theoretical and empirical corrections (Hughes Clarke et al. 2008). The confidence in the mean backscatter strength is ±2 dB. Therefore, subtle shifts in backscatter strength observed at the boundaries of the component survey areas are artifacts of the data processing and do not necessarily reflect differences in seabed physical properties. Keeping these limitations in mind, subjective interpretation of the backscatter strength data can be undertaken guided by the existing knowledge of the sedimentary facies in the Bay of Fundy (e.g., Swift et al. 1969, 1971; Pelletier and McMullen 1972; Fader et al. 1977; Todd et al. 2010).

The distribution of backscatter strength in the Bay of Fundy provides insight into ocean circulation and related modern seafloor sediment transport processes not apparent in the seafloor relief map (Fig. 1). Ocean circulation in the Bay of Fundy is subject to strong tides (Garrett 1972, Greenberg 1983). The general current direction is northeast along the Nova Scotia coast and southwest along the New Brunswick coast with a counter clockwise gyre in the lower Bay (Greenberg 1984). The winnowing and transport of fine-grained sediment under the influence of currents results in residual coarse-grained deposits. The seabed of central and outer Bay of Fundy and Grand Manan Channel is dominated by till deposited directly onto bedrock beneath the Laurentide Ice Sheet. The till is poorly sorted sediment containing angular fragments of pebble- to boulder-sized material, and sand, silt- and clay-sized sediments in varying proportions. Backscatter strength of the till is high and appears dark blue on the backscatter strength map (Fig. 2).

Mud (silt and clay) has accumulated in southwestern Bay of Fundy between Grand Manan Island and the coast of New Brunswick up the Bay as far as Saint John. This depocentre is likely the result of regional current circulation. Backscatter strength of the mud is low and appears light green on the backscatter strength map (Fig. 2). Sand occurs in broad sheets and as individual bedforms (metres to kilometres in plan view) throughout much of northeastern Bay of Fundy. This well-sorted sediment is mobilized through the action of strong tidal currents. Backscatter strength of the sand is low and appears light green on the backscatter strength map. Bedrock is exposed at the seabed only rarely in the Bay of Fundy (Todd and Shaw 2009). Where bedrock outcrops in Minas Passage, its backscatter strength is high.

EXAMPLES OF BAY OF FUNDY GEOMORPHOLOGY

Sandwaves

Sandwaves mapped in the Bay of Fundy using multibeam sonar present a continuum of amplitudes, wavelengths, and bedform widths (Fig. 3). The major axes of these flow-transverse sandwaves are oriented northwest–southeast, normal to the dominant direction of tidal current. Many of the large, solitary sandwaves reach heights between 10 and 20 m and major axis lengths of 600 m to over a kilometre. Their minor axis cross-sections are symmetrical, suggesting that these sediment bedforms do not have a preferred direction of migration. In fact, the terminations of the sand wave long axes generally appear embedded in 'moats', excavated often 5 or more metres below the level of the surrounding regional seafloor (Fig. 3: insets 'A' and 'B'). This geomorphology further suggests that these large sand bedforms are likely immobile. In contrast, sandwave fields are composed of bedforms with amplitudes of 5 m or less and wavelengths of about 100 m or less. Recent deployment of seabed instruments to measure sediment transport indicates that sediment within these sandwave fields is mobile.

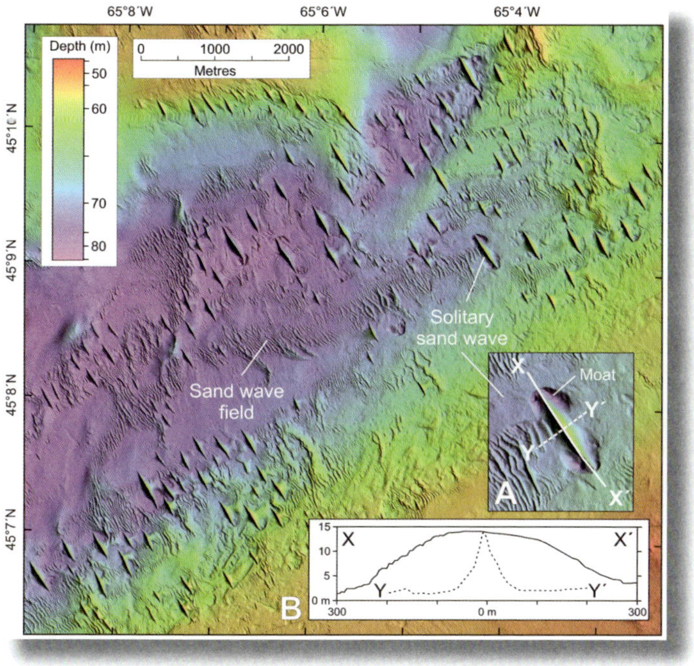

Figure 3. Shaded seafloor relief map of the Margaretsville Dune Field in northeastern Bay of Fundy. The labelled solitary sand wave is shown at larger scale in inset 'A' at right highlighting the moat formed at the ends of the sand wave. Elevation profiles of the major (solid line XX′) and minor (dashed line YY′) axes of the solitary sand wave are plotted at lower right in inset 'B'. See Figure 1 for location of map.

Recessional Moraines

Much of central Bay of Fundy, mapped in the 1970s as glacial till, harbours a wealth of information about the pattern and timing of the retreat of the Laurentide Ice Sheet from this region of Canada. Nested recessional moraines are ubiquitous geomorphological features in this part of the Bay (Fig. 4). Each moraine marks a still-stand period of an ice front, where material falling from the melting ice front accumulated. The moraines are curvilinear in plan view and convex to the southwest, indicating that overall retreat direction of the ice front was stepwise to the northeast. The pattern also makes clear that the ice front was convoluted, composed of 'fingers' of faster-flowing ice embedded in the slower moving ice mass. The discovery of the recessional moraine pattern is helping to build a clearer picture of the distribution of ice in and around the Bay of Fundy in the waning days of the Laurentide Ice Sheet.

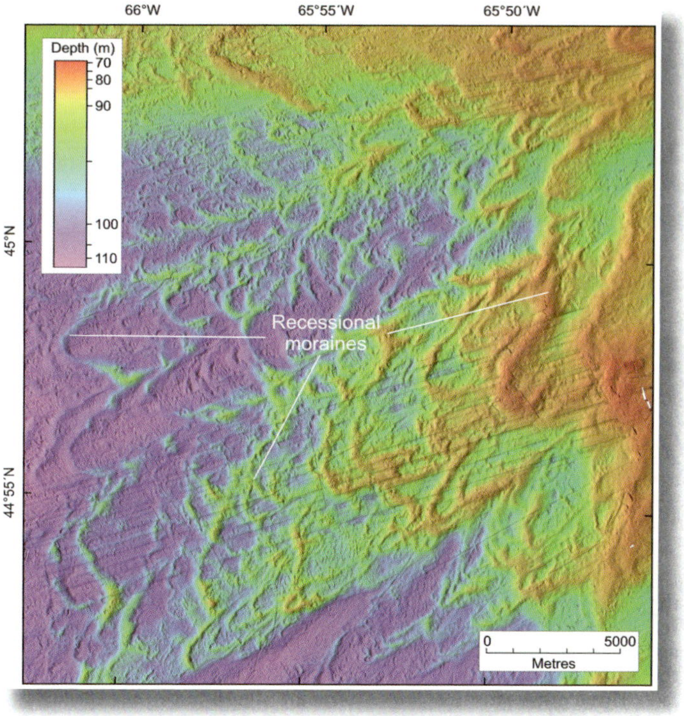

Figure 4. Shaded seafloor relief map of recessional moraines marking the still stands of former glacial ice front positions in central Bay of Fundy. See Figure 1 for location of map.

Tidal Energy Extraction and the Seabed

The large tides in the Bay of Fundy generate strong currents and the harnessing of these currents to generate power has been the focus of engineering schemes dating to 1910 (Baker 1982), and periodically has garnered attention through the twentieth century (Daborn and Dadswell 1988, Desplanque and Mossman 2004, Gordon et al. 2014). With revived interest in renewable energy, advances in engineering of marine structures, and the success of 'in-stream' electrical power generating installations elsewhere in the world, Minas Passage at the head of the Bay of Fundy (Figs. 1 and 5A) is now the subject of engineering studies as a site for electricity generation.

Multibeam sonar mapping of Minas Passage reveals a complex seafloor geomorphology much affected by tidal currents. During glacial and deglacial time, it is likely that sediment was deposited throughout Minas Channel and Minas Passage. During the post-glacial sea level transgression (Shaw et al. 2002), the extreme tidal range of the Bay of Fundy began to develop about 7,000 years BP (Scott and Greenberg 1983, Gehrels et al. 1995). Powerful currents sweeping through Minas Passage partially eroded the Quaternary sediments and created a scour trough that reaches a depth of 170 m and splays to the west and east in a series of separate, finger-like troughs. The seabed flanking the trough is less than 50 m deep. The volume of Quaternary sediment removed from the trough is conservatively estimated at 4 cubic kilometres. Outcropping bedrock lies at the present base of the scour trough.

The most important criterion in the selection of an installation site for in-stream tidal energy conversion infrastructure is tidal current speed;

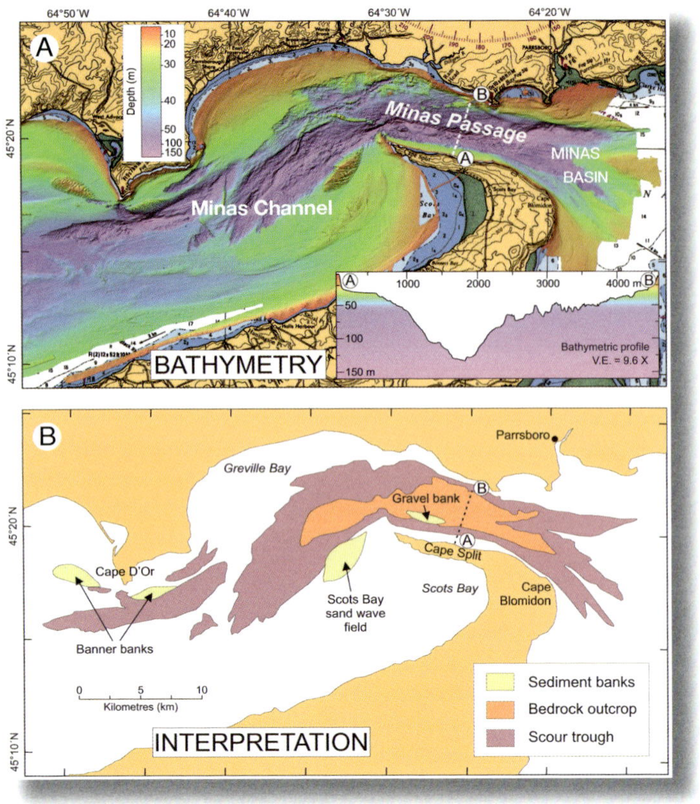

Figure 5. Minas Channel and Passage in the Bay of Fundy: (A) shaded relief bathymetric map; and (B) geomorphological interpretation of the Channel and Passage, the site of in-stream tidal power installations. Location and orientation of inset bathymetric cross section in (A) is indicated by the dashed white line AB across Minas Passage; for clarity this line is repeated in (B) as a dashed black line AB. See Figure 1 for location of map.

this is directly related to the amount of energy that can be extracted. Currents of 7-8 knots (13-15 km/h) occur on the south side of Minas Passage adjacent to Cape Split (Fig. 5B) with currents of 5-6 knots (9-11 km/h) on the north side (Canadian Hydrographic Service 2003).

Three other site selection criteria are significant in the case of Minas Passage: bathymetry, seafloor geology, and submarine cable routes. Firstly, once the tidal current energy resource has been established, bathymetry must be considered. For example, tidal rotors and turbines are large devices (reaching 25 m in diameter) that can require up to 35 m water depth for installation. In passages used by commercial shipping, the minimum water depth required for safe operation can reach almost 50 m (EPRI 2005). Water depths in central Minas Passage are well in excess of this minimum (Fig. 5A). Secondly, the geology of the sea floor must be suitable for the in-stream device foundation; regardless of the engineering design, the devices are situated on bedrock (EPRI 2005). Approximately 44 km^2 of bedrock is exposed in Minas Passage, almost all of which is below 50 m water depth (Fig. 5B). Thirdly, the submarine cable route to shore must be considered in terms of substrate composition, potential for sediment mobility, and changes to the seafloor over time. Although exposed bedrock predominates in Minas Passage and Minas Channel, there are notable current-formed sedimentary features, specifically the twinned sets of bedforms that are situated on either side of prominent headlands. A pair of these 'banner banks' (Dyer and Huntley 1999) occurs on either side of Cape D'Or and Cape Split, the Scots Bay sand wave field being associated with the latter (Fig. 5B). The orientation of the bedforms in the Scots Bay sand wave field indicates that bedform migration is counter clockwise, being to the south on the west side of the field and to the north on the east side of the field. This extensive sand deposit is surrounded by an immobile gravel sea floor (Fader and Miller 1991, Fader et al. 2014: Fig. 4B), which suggests that the sand wave field is a self-contained system, likely trapped within a large tidal eddy. The banner bank twin of the Scots Bay sand wave field is a 3-km long, 20-m thick body of gravel waves trapped in the deep bedrock trough north of Cape Split. To improve understanding of sediment transport on the seafloor in Minas Passage, *in situ* current measurements are required in this challenging environment.

CONCLUSION

The application of multibeam sonar in the Bay of Fundy has revealed the geomorphology of the seabed in unprecedented detail. This new knowledge, in conjunction with traditional marine geoscience techniques, is being used to improve our understanding of Quaternary history and sea-level change and to provide the basis for present and future in-stream tidal power development. Because the Bay of Fundy seabed relief and backscatter strength maps are available online (Todd et al. 2011a,b), we are confident that, like topographic maps on land, this new knowledge of the seafloor will be applied to a variety of future activities in the Bay of Fundy such as fisheries research (both benthic and pelagic) and commercial fishing, pollution studies, seabed engineering, and the possible establishment of marine parks and protected areas (for additional information, see Gordon et al. 2014).

ACKNOWLEDGEMENTS

B. MacGowan, M. Lamplugh, and J. Griffin of the Canadian Hydrographic Service (CHS) organized the multibeam-sonar surveys of the Bay of Fundy and oversaw data processing. CHS provided the data to the Geological Survey of Canada (GSC) for further processing and interpretation. J.E. Hughes Clarke of the Ocean Mapping Group (OMG), Department of Geodesy and Geomatics Engineering, University of New Brunswick (UNB, Fredericton, NB) supervised the earliest collection of multibeam-sonar data in the 1990s, followed by systematic mapping of the coastal areas of New Brunswick. Multibeam sonar data in Saint John Harbour, New Brunswick, were collected by D. Beaver (GSC), UNB and the Saint John Port Authority. D. Cartwright (OMG) processed the backscatter strength under contract to the GSC. The authors thank the officers and crews of the survey vessels for their efforts at sea. Geographical Information Systems and cartographic support were provided by S.E. Hayward, E. Patton, P. O'Regan, and P. Melbourne. We acknowledge improvements in this article resulting from reviews by R.B. Taylor (GSC-Atlantic) and the book editors, especially C.F.M. Lewis. This paper is ESS Contribution Number 20110264.

REFERENCES

Amos, C.L. and B.A. Zaitlin. 1985. The effect of changes in tidal range on a sublittoral macrotidal sequence, Bay of Fundy, Canada. Geo-Marine Letters 4: 161-169.

Amos, C.L., D.E. Buckley, G.R. Daborn, R.W. Dalrymple, S.B. McCann, and M.J. Risk. 1980. Geological Association of Canada Field Trip Guidebook Trip 23: Geomorphology and sedimentology of the Bay of Fundy. Geological Association of Canada, Waterloo, ON.

Baker, G.C. 1982. Some historical aspects of tidal power. Pages 1-9 *in* Proceedings of a Conference on New Approaches to Tidal Power. Bedford Institute of Oceanography, Dartmouth, NS.

Bishop, R. 2008. Tides and the Earth-Moon system. Pages 183-187 *in* Observer's Handbook 2009 (P. Kelly, Ed.). Royal Astronomical Society of Canada, Toronto, ON.

Bonnichsen, R., D. Keenlyside, and K. Turnmire. 1991. Paleoindian patterns in Maine and the Maritimes. Pages 1-36 *in* Prehistoric Archaeology in the Maritime Provinces: Past and Present Research (M. Deal and S. Blair, Eds.). Reports in Archaeology No. 8, New Brunswick Archaeological Services, Fredericton, NB.

Boulton, G.S. and C.D. Clark. 1990. A highly mobile Laurentide ice sheet revealed by satellite images of glacial lineations. Nature 346: 813-817.

Canadian Hydrographic Service. 2003. Bay of Fundy, Inner Portion. CHS Chart 4010, Scale 1:200,000. Canadian Hydrographic Service, Ottawa, ON.

Champlain, S. de. 1613. Les voyages du Sieur de Champlain, Xaintongeois, Capitaine ordinaire pour le Roy, en la marine, 2 volumes. J. Berjon, Paris, France.

Church, I., J.E. Hughes Clarke, S. Haigh, M. Santos, M. Lamplugh, J. Griffin, and D.R. Parrott. 2008. Using globally-corrected GPS solutions to assess the viability of hydrodynamic modelling in the Bay of Fundy. Paper 4-2 *in* Proceedings of the Canadian Hydrographic Conference and National Surveyors Conference. Canadian Hydrographic Association and Association of Canada Lands Surveyors. Victoria, BC. (CD-ROM)

Daborn, G.R. and M.J. Dadswell. 1988. Natural and anthropogenic changes in the Bay of Fundy-Gulf of Maine-Georges Bank system. Pages 547-560 *in* Natural and Man-Made Hazards (M.I. El-Sabh and T.S. Murty, Eds.). D. Reidel, Dordrecht, Netherlands.

Desplanque, C. and D.J. Mossman. 2004. Tides and their seminal impact on the geology, geography, history, and socio-economics of the Bay of Fundy, eastern Canada. Atlantic Geology 40: 1-130.

Dupont, F., C.G. Hannah, and D. Greenberg. 2005. Modelling the sea level of the upper Bay of Fundy. Atmosphere-Ocean 43: 33-47.

Dyer, K.R. and D.A. Huntley. 1999. The origin, classification and modelling of sand banks and ridges. Continental Shelf Research 19: 1,285-1,330.

EPRI (Electric Power Research Institute). 2005. Nova Scotia tidal in-stream energy conversion (TISEC): survey and characterization of potential project sites. Electric Power Research Institute, Palo Alto, CA.

Fader, G.B.J. and R.O. Miller. 1991. The Scots Bay sand wave field, Bay of Fundy: an example of potential environmental enhancement by extraction (abstract only). Page A35 *in* Program Geological Association of Canada-Mineralogical Association of Canada, Joint Annual Meeting, v. 16. Geological Association of Canada, Waterloo, ON.

Fader, G.B., L.H. King, and B. MacLean. 1977. Surficial geology of the eastern Gulf of Maine and the Bay of Fundy. Marine Sciences Paper 19, Geological Survey of Canada Paper 76-17 (1 map, Scale 1:300,000). Fisheries and Environment Canada, Energy, Mines and Resources Canada, Ottawa ON.

Fader, G.B.J., B. MacLean, H.W. Josenhans, and S.M. Blasco. 2014. Seabed sediment mapping at the Bedford Institute of Oceanography: from single beam to multibeam. Pages 191-199 *in* Voyage of Discovery: Fifty Years of Marine Research at Canada's Bedford Institute of Oceanography (D.N. Nettleship, D.C. Gordon, C.F.M. Lewis, and M.P. Latremouille, Eds.). Bedford Institute of Oceanography-Oceans Association, Dartmouth, NS.

Garrett, C.J.R. 1972. Tidal resonance in the Bay of Fundy and Gulf of Maine. Nature 238: 441-443.

Gehrels, W.R., D.F. Belknap, B.R. Pearce, and B. Gong. 1995. Modeling the contribution of M2 tidal amplification to the Holocene rise of mean water level in the Gulf of Maine and the Bay of Fundy. Marine Geology 124: 71-85.

Godin, G. 1992. Possibility of rapid changes in the tide of the Bay of Fundy, based on a scrutiny of the records from Saint John. Continental Shelf Research 12: 327-338.

Gordon, D.C., C.L. Amos, D.A. Greenberg, P.C. Smith, and G.B.J. Fader. 2014. Understanding the macrotidal environment of the Bay of Fundy and the impacts of tidal power development. Pages 373-382 *in* Voyage of Discovery: Fifty Years of Marine Research at Canada's Bedford Institute of Oceanography (D.N. Nettleship, D.C. Gordon, C.F.M. Lewis, and M.P. Latremouille, Eds.). Bedford Institute of Oceanography-Oceans Association, Dartmouth, NS.

Grant, D.R. 1970. Recent coastal submergence of the Maritime Provinces, Canada. Canadian Journal of Earth Sciences 7: 676-689.

Greenberg, D.A. 1983. Modeling the mean barotropic circulation in the Bay of Fundy and Gulf of Maine. Journal of Physical Oceanography 13: 886-904.

Greenberg, D.A. 1984. A review of the physical oceanography of the Bay of Fundy. Pages 9-30 *in* Update of the Marine Environmental Consequences of Tidal Power Development in the Upper Reaches of the Bay of Fundy (D.C. Gordon and M.J. Dadswell, Eds.). Canadian Technical Report of Fisheries and Aquatic Sciences No. 1256, Bedford Institute of Oceanography, Dartmouth, NS.

Hughes Clarke, J.E., K.K. Iwanowska, D.R. Parrott, G. Duffy, M. Lamplugh, and J. Griffin. 2008. Inter-calibrating multi-source, multi-platform backscatter data sets to assist in compiling regional sediment type maps: Bay of Fundy. Paper 8-2 *in* Proceedings of the Canadian Hydrographic Conference and National Surveyors Conference. Canadian Hydrographic Association and Association of Canada Lands Surveyors. Victoria, BC. (CD-ROM)

Hundert, T. and D.J.W. Piper. 2008. Late Quaternary sedimentation on the south-western Scotian Slope, eastern Canada: relationship to glaciation. Canadian Journal of Earth Sciences 45: 267-285.

King, L.H. and G.B.J. Fader. 1986. Wisconsinan glaciation of the Atlantic continental shelf of southeast Canada. Geological Survey of Canada Bulletin 363, Ottawa, ON.

Loncarevic, B.D., R.C. Courtney, G.B.J. Fader, P.S. Giles, D.J.W. Piper, G. Costello, J.E. Hughes Clarke, and R.R. Stea. 1994. Sonography of a glaciated continental shelf. Geology 32: 747-750.

Mayer, L.A. 2006. Frontiers in seafloor mapping and visualization. Marine Geophysical Researches 27: 7-17.

O'Reilly, C.T., R. Solvason, and C. Solomon. 2005. Where are the world's largest tides? Pages 44-46 *in* Bedford Institute of Oceanography: 2004 in Review (J. Ryan, Ed.). Bedford Institute of Oceanography, Dartmouth, NS.

Parliament of Canada. 1996. An act respecting the oceans of Canada. Acts of the Parliament of Canada passed in the year 1996, Chapter 31. House of Commons, Parliament of Canada, Queens Printer for Canada, Ottawa, ON. 51 p. (http://laws.justice.gc.ca/eng/acts/O2.4/page-1.html).

Pelletier, B.R. and R.M. McMullen. 1972. Sedimentation patterns in the Bay of Fundy and Minas Basin. Pages 153-187 *in* Tidal Power (T.J. Gray and O.K. Gashus, Eds.). Plenum Press, New York, NY.

Pickrill, R.A., B.J. Todd, S.J. Smith, J.V. Barrie, and K.W. Conway. 2014. Marine habitat mapping in Canada's oceans. Pages 185-190 *in* Voyage of Discovery: Fifty Years of Marine Research at Canada's Bedford Institute of Oceanography (D.N. Nettleship, D.C. Gordon, C.F.M. Lewis, and M.P. Latremouille, Eds.). Bedford Institute of Oceanography-Oceans Association, Dartmouth, NS.

Schnitker, D., D.F. Belknap, T.S. Bacchus, J.K. Friez, B.A. Lusardi, and D.M. Popek. 2001. Deglaciation of the Gulf of Maine. Pages 9-34 *in* Deglacial history and relative sea-level changes, northern New England and adjacent Canada (T.K. Weddle and M.J. Retelle, Eds.). Geological Society of America Special Paper 351. Geological Society of America, Boulder, CO.

Scott, D.B. and D.A. Greenberg. 1983. Relative sea-level rise and tidal development in the Fundy tidal system: Canadian Journal of Earth Sciences 20: 1,554-1,564.

Shaw, J., P. Gareau, and R.C. Courtney. 2002. Paleogeography of Atlantic Canada 13-0 kyr. Quaternary Science Reviews 21: 1,861-1,878.

Shaw, J., D.J.W. Piper, G.B. Fader, E.L. King, B.J. Todd, T. Bell, M.J. Batterson, and D.J.E. Liverman. 2006. A conceptual model of the deglaciation of Atlantic Canada. Quaternary Science Reviews 25: 2,059-2,081.

Shaw, J., C.L. Amos, D.A. Greenberg, C.T. O'Reilly, D.R. Parrott, and E. Patton. 2010. Catastrophic tidal expansion in the Bay of Fundy. Canadian Journal of Earth Sciences 47: 1,079-1,091.

Swift, D.J.P., B.R. Pelletier, A.K. Lyall, and J.A. Miller. 1969. Sediments of the Bay of Fundy – a preliminary report. Maritime Sediments 5: 95-100.

Swift, D.J.P., B.R. Pelletier, A.K. Lyall, and J.A. Miller. 1973. Quaternary sedimentation in the Bay of Fundy. Pages 113-151 *in* Earth Science Sympsium on Offshore Eastern Canada (P.J. Hood, Ed.). Geological Survey of Canada Paper 71-23, Ottawa, ON.

Todd, B.J. and J. Shaw. 2009. International Year of Planet Earth 5: Applications of seafloor mapping on the Canadian Atlantic continental shelf. Geoscience Canada 36: 81-94.

Todd, B.J., and others. 2010. Expedition report CCGS *Hudson* 2009-039: Bay of Fundy. Geological Survey of Canada Open File 6684, Ottawa, ON.

Todd, B.J., J. Shaw, and D.R. Parrott. 2011a. Shaded seafloor relief, Bay of Fundy, Sheet 1, offshore Nova Scotia-New Brunswick. Geological Survey of Canada Map 2174A, Scale 1:50,000, Ottawa, ON. (doi:10.4095/289508)

Todd, B.J., J. Shaw, D.R. Parrott, J.E. Hughes Clarke, D. Cartwright, and S.E. Hayward. 2011b. Backscatter strength and shaded seafloor relief, Bay of Fundy, Sheet 1, offshore Nova Scotia-New Brunswick. Geological Survey of Canada Open File 7024, Scale 1:50,000, Ottawa, ON. (doi: 10.4095/289508)

Wade, J.A., D.E. Brown, A. Traverse, and R.A. Fensome. 1996. The Triassic-Jurassic Fundy Basin, eastern Canada: regional setting, stratigraphy and hydrocarbon potential. Atlantic Geology 32: 189-231.

Williams, H.M.J., M.J. Kennedy, and E.R.W. Neale. 1972. The Appalachian structural province. Pages 182-261 *in* Variations in Tectonic Styles in Canada (R.A. Price and R.J.W. Douglas, Eds.). Geological Association of Canada Special Paper 11, Waterloo, ON.

28. LIVING AND POSTGLACIAL FORAMINIFERA AND THEIR ENVIRONMENTAL APPLICATIONS

Charles T. Schafer

SUMMARY
This article chronicles the evolution of modern Foraminifera research at the Bedford Institute of Oceanography (BIO) since its founding and the suite of environmental, paleoceanographic, and paleoclimate applications that were either developed or verified by scientific staff and associates. It tracks the projects of BIO foraminiferalogists within the Paleoecology Section of the Geological Survey of Canada and shows the transition from an early stage of 'curiosity-driven' basic research to a period of increasing emphasis on applied investigations, cross-discipline collaborations, and international networking that developed as the research matured. Collectively, the almost half century of research highlights the plethora of small steps that most marine scientists must take in their search for new understanding of Canada's ocean systems and resident species.

Key words: Foraminifera, pollution, environment, paleoecology, paleoceanography, ecology, mapping.
E-mail: CharlesTSchafer@gmail.com

Benthic and planktic Foraminifera belong to the Protoctista Kingdom and are classified under an exceptionally diverse Order (Foraminiferida) that includes hundreds of extant genera and thousands of species. Their external shell or exoskeleton is typically about the size of a small grain of sand (Fig. 1). Modern Foraminifera have been an important focus of micropaleontologists since the early part of the 19th century beginning in France with the investigations of Alcide d'Orbigny. Near the end of that century, a large volume of new information about contemporary deep sea Foraminifera species was published based on samples collected during the famous British HMS *Challenger* expedition (Brady 1884). After World War II, a few marine micropaleontologists turned their attention to the biological and environmental aspects of living planktic and benthic Foraminifera species to better understand the significance of their fossil remains in older marine sediments, and with a view to developing data for descriptive models for marine environmental mapping and monitoring applications. These researchers came to be known as foraminiferalogists. Fred Phleger was one of the best-known ecologically-focussed foraminiferalogists working in the United States in the mid-20th century. He studied benthic Foraminifera at the Scripps Institution of Oceanography (San Diego, CA) from 1949 to 1986 and is best remembered for his book on the ecology and distribution of modern Foraminifera (Phleger 1960). The book consolidated environmental and methodological baseline information from which subsequent basic and applied benthic Foraminifera research has developed. Textbooks that summarize a good measure of the current knowledge on the biology, environmental applications and investigative trends in modern Foraminifera research include those by Sen Gupta (1999) and Scott et al. (2001). This article describes the research on living and postglacial Foraminifera that was carried out at the Bedford Institute of Oceanography (BIO) during its first fifty years.

THE CURIOSITY-DRIVEN RESEARCH DECADE (1965-75)

B. Pelletier, head of the Marine Geology Section of the Geological Survey of Canada (GSC), nurtured government-based modern Foraminifera research soon after BIO was established. Much of the research undertaken by BIO foraminiferalogists between 1965 and 1975 was focussed on Canadian shallow-water benthic Foraminifera populations in both natural and contaminated (polluted) environments. It was complemented by studies aimed at improving sampling techniques and interlaced with laboratory studies. This diversity of field and laboratory activities quickly placed BIO in the mainstream of modern foraminiferal research.

Studies 1965-69

The first comprehensive investigations of modern Foraminifera populations inhabiting eastern Canadian inner continental shelf environments were conducted by G. Bartlett. His early investigations produced

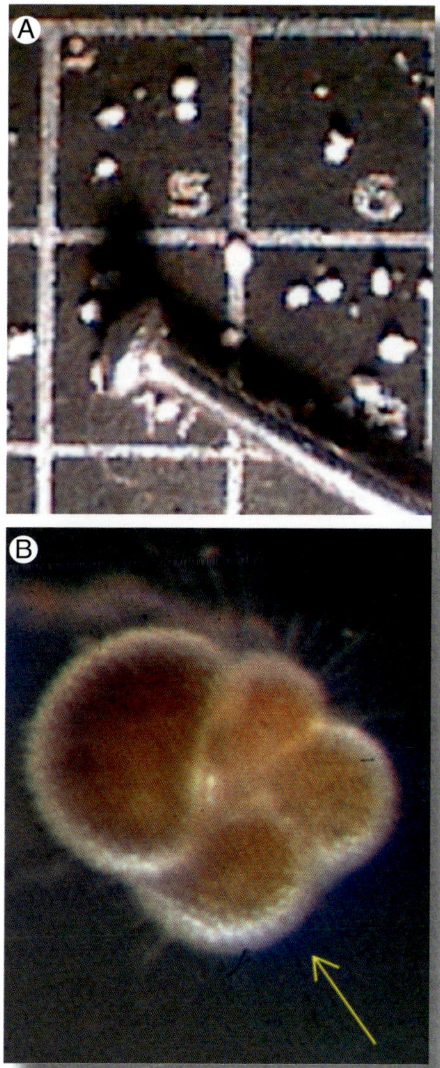

Figure 1. Benthic and planktic Foraminifera species collected from contemporary marine environments: (A) micropaleontology slide showing some Gulf of St. Lawrence benthic specimens (note their size in relation to the head of a small sewing pin); and (B) wet sample of a planktic specimen (*Neogloboquadrina pachyderma*), collected during the arctic leg of the *Hudson-70* expedition (photo: R. Smith).

new data on the interannual variation of Foraminifera population densities and on shoreward to seaward changes in specimen abundances and species diversity (Bartlett 1964a,b). Four major foraminiferal biofacies were mapped in St. Margarets Bay and Mahone Bay, Nova Scotia (Fig. 2), each marked by their characteristic indicator species. In the same year, G. Vilks investigated benthic Foraminifera distributions in East Bay, Mackenzie King Island (Fig. 2) in the Canadian Arctic (Vilks 1964). Soon after, Leslie (1965) investigated the ecology and paleoecology of Hudson Bay Foraminifera, and the distribution data for the only planktic species observed in the Bay *(Neogloboquadrina pachyderma)* indicated that the central of three channels that connected the Bay with Hudson Strait was the main conduit for marine water entering the Bay (Fig. 2). The same year also saw the release of a report on recent species of the common genus *Elphidium* in shallow waters of the Atlantic Provinces that addressed a number of important taxonomic and environmental issues (Bartlett 1965a).

By 1967, G. Bartlett and G. Vilks had been transferred permanently to BIO from the Ottawa office of the Geological Survey of Canada (GSC) along with mollusk expert F. Wagner, who had been studying arctic mollusks while working in Ottawa, Ontario, with the Polar Continental Shelf Project. These three researchers were joined that year by C. Schafer, D. Walker, and micropaleontology technicians F. Frape (Cole) and B. Baker. Critical mass had now been achieved, a Paleoecology Section was created, and the coming years witnessed a substantial increase in BIO foraminiferal research and surveys. As part of a later reorganization, B. Baker was replaced by B. Deonarine.

A study of benthic Foraminifera distributions in Tracadie Bay, Prince Edward Island (Fig. 2), described the relatively low diversity and eurybathic distribution of the Bay's Foraminifera population, a pattern that was often observed in later studies of semi-isolated shallow-water Canadian marine environments (Bartlett 1965b). Another study examined the modern Foraminifera populations of the Miramichi Estuary (Fig. 2) and showed how species distributions responded to the translocation of bay-mouth barriers and set the stage for later sediment core-based investigations (Bartlett 1966). A study of Bras D'Or Lakes (Fig. 2) Foraminifera described their patchy distribution patterns and the key physical and geographical factors (water depth, sediment texture, and proximity to open Atlantic water) controlling species occurrence (Vilks 1967). A study of Foraminifera in Northumberland Strait (Fig. 2), using SCUBA diving techniques to collect replicate sediment samples, revealed large numbers of a typically marsh-related taxon (*Miliammina fusca*; Schafer 1967) while concurrent coastal zone Foraminifera investigations highlighted patchy species distribution patterns that were linked to local passive transport processes. A study in Bedford Basin (in front of BIO, Fig. 2) involved the first use of a BIO custom-designed sediment trap to evaluate the passive transport of Foraminifera shells (Schafer and Prakash 1968). Over the winter of 1967-68, a survey of benthic Foraminifera was carried out in Castries Harbour (Fig. 2), St. Lucia, West Indies (Schafer and Sen Gupta 1968). Local benthic Foraminifera distribution patterns were observed to be clumped but warm water species assemblages were found, as expected, to be much more diverse compared to their northern temperate counterparts. The detailed differences between assemblages observed in reef patch environments and low energy (semi-isolated) open bay settings were later investigated (Sen Gupta and Schafer 1973).

The Foraminifera populations inhabiting intertidal zones of some polluted Maine and New Brunswick estuaries were also documented and it was noted that specimens were either rare or absent at some stations near pulp and paper mill waste outfalls in Saint John Harbour (Fig. 2; Schafer and Sen Gupta 1969). Other Foraminifera surveys were conducted on the Magdalen Shallows, Gulf of St. Lawrence (Fig. 2; Vilks 1968). The occurrence of sparse, low diversity populations of mostly arenaceous Foraminifera species (species whose skeletons incorporate various types of sediment particles) was among the key observations and, like many others that were to follow, would serve as a baseline reference of modern seafloor environments for future sediment core investigations designed to detect historical changes on time scales of decades to millennia.

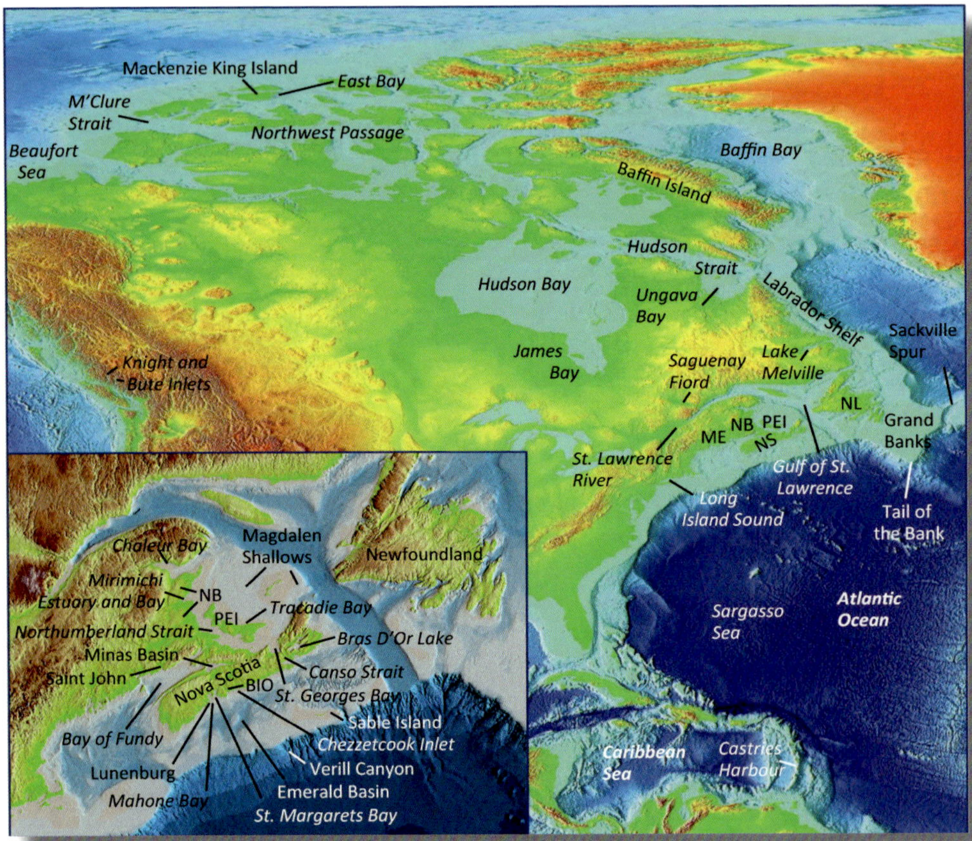

Figure 2. Locations of places or study sites mentioned in the text: ME=Maine, NB=New Brunswick, NL=Newfoundland, NS=Nova Scotia, and PEI=Prince Edward Island. [Notes: base maps from J. Shaw, GSC-Atlantic; oblique map of North America from United States-NOAA 5 arc-minute relief model (ETOPO5), and inset digital elevation map image of southeastern Canada from Shaw (2006).]

In 1969, BIO obtained its first scanning electron microscope (SEM) which was a wonderful new tool for foraminiferalogists. New techniques and applications of scanning electron microscopy in the marine sciences were subsequently developed (Walker and Buckley 1969). It was discovered in laboratory observations that a specimen of *Discorbis* sp. could repair a damaged skeleton in just one week (Walker 1969).

Investigations of recent Foraminifera in ice-covered seas of the Canadian Arctic revealed a boundary between shallow-water arenaceous species and deeper-living calcareous species at a water depth of about 200 m (Vilks 1969). In the same year, a joint study of Grand Banks (Fig. 2) Foraminifera and sediment facies was carried out (Sen Gupta and McMullen 1969; Sen Gupta 1971, 1972).

Studies 1970-75

In 1970, two summer students, B. St. John and R. Baker, provided field assistance for a survey of Foraminifera in estuaries along the west coasts of James and Hudson Bays (Fig. 2). Observations showed that modern estuarine populations were mixed with fossil extant species that had been eroded and re-deposited by spring floods from older postglacial raised marine deposits exposed along riverbanks (Schafer 1970a). The use of planktic Foraminifera as proxies of the circulation of surface waters was investigated in parts of the Canadian Arctic Archipelago (Vilks 1970). His sediment core sample results indicated a slow net eastward movement of water from the Arctic Ocean through M'Clure Strait (Fig.

2) for at least the past 2,500 years. A statistical analysis on samples collected in East Bay, Mackenzie King Island (Fig. 2), Canadian Arctic Archipelago , showed that the identified groupings of Foraminifera species were aligned with differences in faunal richness (Vilks et al. 1970).

Schafer (1970b) examined the links between a regional pollution gradient and trends of benthic Foraminifera species diversity in western Long Island Sound, New York (Fig. 2). That same year, he reported initial findings from the first field season of a multi-year systematic survey of benthic Foraminifera in Chaleur Bay (Fig. 2) and the Restigouche Estuary at the head of Chaleur Bay. The western estuarine part of the Bay offered a unique opportunity to study industrially-polluted marine environments. Forty-six benthic and one planktic species of Foraminifera were identified and grouped as either cosmopolitan (i.e., present mostly in the bay and estuary) or as outer estuary-restricted forms. Species occurrences offshore from several industrial installations (e.g., lead/zinc smelter, fertilizer plant, power plant, and chemical plant) were also documented to help establish a suite of indicator species and assemblages for assessing the condition of shallow near shore contaminated seafloor environments (Schafer 1970c).

In collaboration with the Lamont-Doherty Geological Observatory of Columbia University, G. Vilks examined the winter distribution of planktic Foraminifera between the Grand Banks and the Caribbean Sea (Fig. 2; Be et al. 1971). They defined a boundary at about 30°N that separated northern and southern Sargasso Sea (Fig. 2) species that could serve as a model for future climate change impact investigations. Another open ocean study investigated mid-Pacific planktic Foraminifera populations using samples collected with the BIO-designed Multiple Depth Plankton Sampler (redesigned by R. Vine) during the Tahiti to Vancouver leg of the *Hudson*-70 expedition (Wadhams 2014). Species distributions were correlated to several well-defined Pacific Ocean water masses that occurred between 10°S and 55°N along the 150°W meridian (Banerji et al. 1971).

Using replicate samples collected with diver-operated push cores from the lockout chamber of the Perry Shelf Diver submersible, the patchiness of benthic Foraminifera populations was studied in shallow sediments in the Gulf of St. Lawrence (Fig. 2; Schafer 1971). Using SEM observations, the etching of Foraminifera skeletons as a consequence of ingestion by a gastropod species was examined and the removal of the skeleton's surface veneer and the partial dissolution of the underlying layer of calcite was described for several benthic Foraminifera species (Walker 1971, Mageau and Walker 1976).

A study that mapped several near-abiotic environments close to effluent outfalls in Chaleur Bay identified some anomalously high species diversity zones where it was theorized that certain digestible components of effluents had generated an exceptionally favorable habitat for local benthic Foraminifera populations (Schafer 1973). A SEM study of the spinal ultrastructure of two modern planktic Foraminifera species provided proof that the genus *Globigerinella* is a valid genus and not a junior synonym of *Hastigerina* (Walker and Vilks 1973). Using a Q-mode cluster analysis statistical grouping technique, four major foraminiferal biotopes were delineated in Chaleur Bay (Schafer and Cole 1974a,b). Biotope boundaries marked seafloor environment changes from estuarine to open bay conditions and the aerial extent of upper estuarine conditions west of Dalhousie, New Brunswick (Chaleur Bay). The linkage of different phenotypes (skeleton shapes) of *Globorotalia pachyderma* to various oceanographic parameters were examined in the Northwest Passage and northern Baffin Bay (Fig. 2) and demonstrated their utility for interpreting arctic paleoceanography from the microfossil record (Vilks 1974). Vilks and Walker (1974) showed how the ultrastructure of tri-radiate spines of the planktic species *Orbulina universa* differed from those found in other spinose planktic taxa (Fig. 3). The excellent preservation of benthic Foraminifera skeletons in methane-saturated sediment confirmed previous studies regarding the positive effect of anaerobic conditions on the preservation of some exceptionally fragile Foraminifera skeletons (Vilks et al. 1974).

Figure 3. An SEM photograph of the spines of an *Orbulina universa* planktic specimen showing the tiny barb structures (SB) developed along the spine's edges (after Vilks and Walker 1974).

The distribution of benthic Foraminifera populations in the vicinity of a submerged pulp mill waste outfall on the north shore of Chaleur Bay was investigated (Schafer and Cole 1974b). The occurrence of several arenaceous Foraminifera species (e.g., *Eggerella advena*) close to the mouth of the outfall and an inverse relationship between coarse-textured organic matter and Foraminifera population density were noted. Back in the laboratory, a new staining technique for distinguishing living Foraminifera in samples of mixed living and dead specimens was developed which ultimately replaced the standard rose Bengal method in many laboratories around the world (Walker et al. 1974).

In 1975, Halifax was selected as the venue for the First International Symposium on Benthic Foraminifera, a triennial gathering that continues to this day. This event reflected the early development of a still-active collaboration between BIO foraminiferalogists and Dalhousie University (Halifax, NS) micropaleontologists, and established Canadian government and university micropaleontologists as important players in the field.

As part of the multidisciplinary Canso Strait (Fig. 2) Project, Schafer et al. (1975) described a zone populated by pollution-tolerant and opportunistic Foraminifera species such as *Eggerella advena* (Fig. 4A) just offshore from a nearshore Foraminifera-barren zone near Point Tupper (Fig. 4B). It was also shown that mollusks tended to favour less polluted substrates on the western (mainland) side of the Strait. As part of this project, G. Vilks compared Foraminifera observed in sediment cores from the Gulf and Atlantic sides of the Canso Causeway across Canso Strait, and assemblage differences were shown to be reflective of the distinctive water temperature and salinity regimes found on either side (Vilks et al. 1975). This project also showed how sediment and fossil Foraminifera assemblages changed from pre- to post-Causeway construction times. Using samples collected for the Canso Strait Project study, the first illustrated catalogue of Foraminifera and Ostracoda was prepared which served as a convenient reference for many typical north temperate shallow water species (Cole and Ferguson 1975).

The occurrence of *Globorotalia pachyderma* in the water column and sediments of the Beaufort Sea and the Northwest Passage (Fig. 2), and from different skeleton size distributions, suggested selective preservation of larger and older specimens (Vilks 1975). This observation led to refinements in Foraminifera-based paleoceanographic models used for interpreting the significance of fossil assemblages observed in core samples. In a collaborative effort with marine chemists M. Rashid and J. Leonard, the fossil Foraminifera assemblages were studied in a methane-rich basin in Chaleur Bay, and their excellent state of preservation provided insight into the benefits of sampling these kinds of oxygen-depleted sediments in future paleoceanographic investigations (Rashid et al. 1975).

YEARS OF APPLICATIONS AND COLLABORATIONS (1976-95)

Applications 1976-79

Beginning in 1976, the Paleoecology Section, led by C. Schafer and G. Vilks, placed increasing emphasis on applied studies of Foraminifera. These projects often involved collaboration with their technical support team and non-BIO researchers. Subjects still included fundamental

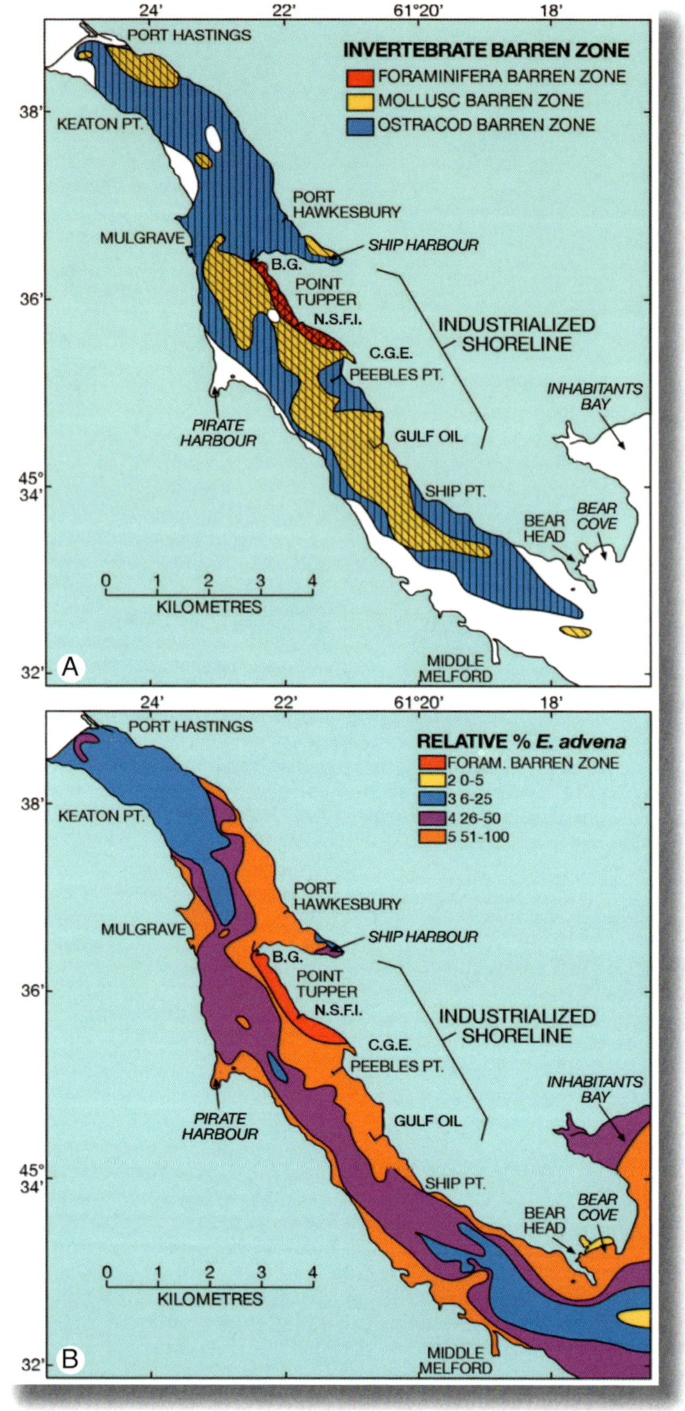

Figure 4. Sedimentary biological barren zones and distribution of pollution-tolerant Foraminifera in Canso Strait, Nova Scotia, observed in 1974 (after Schafer et al. 1975): (A) Foraminifera, mollusk, and ostracod barren zones in which the zone sizes indicate relative sensitivity of each type of organism to seafloor contamination from local industries; and (B) relative abundance (by percentage) distribution map of the pollution-tolerant benthic Foraminifera indicator species *Eggerella advena*. [Notes: Relative abundance of this species increases rapidly beyond the Foraminifera barren zone, and its distribution overlaps the mollusk and ostracod barren zones; parallel and cross-parallel line patterns show the spatial overlap between various barren zones. Abbreviations: B.G. = Bestwall Gypsum loading terminal, N.S.F.I = Nova Scotia Forest Industries wharf, C.G.E. = Canadian General Electric heavy water plant, GULF OIL = Gulf Oil refinery and ocean terminal.]

Foraminifera biology and ecology research topics (Schafer 1976, Walker 1976), but they were being increasingly complemented by a variety of applied studies in paleoceanography, paleoclimatology, and environmental monitoring and mapping using modern Foraminifera models. By this time, G. Bartlett had moved to Queens University in Kingston, Ontario, and D. Walker had transferred to the Mineral Resources Division of the GSC in Ottawa.

Earlier examples of applied investigations included several done by G. Bartlett at BIO in collaboration with R. Greggs of Queens University. They used data on warm temperate planktic Foraminifera species observed in carbonate rock cores raised from several Mid-Atlantic Ridge mountain tops to explain the environmental conditions responsible for the occurrence of both lithified and unlithified calcium carbonate-rich deposits (Bartlett and Greggs 1969, Bartlett 1970).

G. Vilks and M. Rashid conducted a study of paleoceanography of Emerald Basin (Fig. 2) on the Scotian Shelf in which benthic Foraminifera and geochemical data facilitated the formulation of a paleoceanographic model to define paleosea levels during post-glacial time and their impact on circulation patterns of local ocean currents (Vilks and Rashid 1976). Subsequent work emphasized late glacial and Holocene paleoceanography issues interspersed with Foraminifera-specific basic research. For example, fossil foraminiferal evidence for the early deglaciation of the Labrador Shelf (Fig. 2) was reported by Deonarine and Vilks (1977) and Vilks and Mudie (1978). At about this time, research on the modern Foraminifera of two Nova Scotia marshes confirmed the utility of two marsh indicator species (*Trochammina macresens* and *Miliammina fusca*) for establishing the boundary between upper and lower north temperate marsh environments (Deonarine 1979). Another study detailed the occurrence of Foraminifera and mollusks of the southeastern Labrador Shelf and Lake Melville (Fig. 2; Vilks et al. 1982) while a collaborative study with D. Krauel established a linkage between the circulation pattern of the Miramichi Estuary and its modern benthic Foraminifera distribution patterns (Vilks and Krauel 1981). Another study documented the evidence for postglacial paleoceanographic and paleoclimatic changes recorded in Lake Melville core samples (Vilks and Mudie 1983).

In collaboration with D. Scott and D. Younger of Dalhousie University, a study was conducted of several distinct Late Pleistocene and Holocene-age paleoceanographic events in three eastern Canadian margin basins which showed how associated proxy paleosignals degraded in deeper offshore environments. Basin study results also revealed a paleoceanographic shift along a north to south gradient during the same time (Scott et al. 1984). Another project reported on the quantitative paleoecology of benthic Foraminifera in Late Quaternary age sediments from Beaufort Sea and northeastern Canadian continental shelf environments using multivariate analysis (Mudie et al. 1984). Their results emphasized quantitative relationships between recent assemblage distributions, water depth, and bottom water salinity/temperature. A study of the oxygen 18 ($\delta^{18}O$) isotopic composition of planktic Foraminifera skeletons, conducted in collaboration with L. Keigwin of the Woods Hole Oceanographic Institution, enabled the identification of Wisconsinan coarse deep-sea sediments off Nova Scotia, likely derived from the adjacent Scotian Shelf. (Vilks et al. 1985). A study of 38 grab samples from the Labrador Shelf demonstrated an exceptionally high correlation between the oxygen isotopic composition of skeletons of the benthic Foraminifera species *Cibicides lobatulus* and bottom water salinity of the Labrador Current which facilitated the establishment of a proxy paleosalinity record for subarctic continental shelf environments (Vilks and Deonarine 1988). Another applied study at this time, conducted in collaboration with A. Aksu of Memorial University (St. John's, NL), described the evidence for a late Wisconsinan glacier re-advance on the outer Scotian shelf between about 26,000 and 21,000 years BP (Mosher et al. 1989).

While G. Vilks and his collaborators were busy investigating Canada's northern marine environments, C. Schafer and associates were active in several southeastern Canadian marine areas. In the Miramichi Estuary, Foraminifera and mollusk distribution patterns were compared to ambient sediment transport and water circulation processes based on samples collected using SCUBA diver-supported grid sampling and sediment trap methods deployed through the ice during the winter months. Foraminifera and mollusk biotope boundaries showed good overall agreement with the estuary's tidal circulation pattern and river water input (Schafer et al. 1977). Year-to-year changes in Miramichi Foraminifera distribution patterns were examined in a collaborative effort with D. Scott and F. Medioli of Dalhousie University and the results indicated only a few minor boundary changes, but noted the development of an estuarine transitional zone that consisted mostly of arenaceous species (Scott et al. 1977). The mobility of St. Georges Bay (Fig. 2) benthic Foraminifera was evaluated in several fish tank and *in situ* experiments. Tank results suggested that the more passive transport-susceptible species were also the most active crawlers within the living population. The *in situ* experiment focussed on Foraminifera colonization and passive transport processes at a 20-m deep location in the Bay and was monitored using a prototype underwater time-lapse television system built by C. Godden. Results showed that living specimens had started to recolonize sterile sand pads after just a few days. Nearshore species were passively transported to deeper and relatively quiescent environments during storm events as shown by chance during a passing hurricane (Schafer and Young 1977). Three decades later, these results were used in planning an investigation aimed at resolving ancient storm events in the foraminiferal fossil record (Schafer and Medioli 2009).

Various studies of benthic Foraminifera and mollusks were carried out in Chaleur Bay. A number of benthic Foraminifera/mollusk species associations were identified and used to document the impact of a cold (<10°C) westward flowing current on the species composition of assemblages between 40 and 80 m in the northern part of the Bay (Schafer and Wagner 1978). Detailed maps of key Foraminifera population parameters were prepared based on four years of survey data that reflected control by both bathymetric and tidal/river current circulation patterns, and relatively dense living populations were found to be closely associated with high primary production environments (Schafer and Cole 1978). In a shift to studies in deeper offshore environments, in collaboration with L. Carter from the New Zealand Oceanographic Institute, sediment types and living Foraminifera populations were mapped at depths of 500-3,000 m on the continental slope near 49°N off Newfoundland (Fig. 2). The linkages between benthic Foraminifera species diversity and living population density were described on a part of the lower continental slope that is in constant contact with the southward flowing Western Boundary Undercurrent (WBU; Carter et al. 1979). Evidence was obtained that the WBU sorted sediment and reworked Foraminifera skeletons (Carter and Schafer 1983).

Applications 1980-89

Using core samples collected from the Newfoundland continental shelf, Schafer et al. (1980) identified a probable mid-hypsithermal (5,000-7,000 years BP) climate event that was marked by the unusual occurrence of the warm water (Gulf Stream) planktic species *Globigerinoides ruber* along with several other apparent upper Holocene paleoceanographic changes. At the shallow end of the water column, Scott et al. (1980) developed an eastern Canadian estuarine framework model that was shown to have utility for resolving past changes in estuarine circulation patterns based on benthic Foraminifera and Thecamoebian species occurrences in sediment cores. This model was applied to samples collected by vibrocore in Inner Miramichi Bay to show the environmental effects of historical changes in openings and closings of the channels that divided the barriers along the mouth of the Bay (Wagner and Schafer 1980). In another study, Foraminifera and pollen were compared in two adjacent (1 m separation) diver-collected cores from 20 m water depth in southern St. Georges Bay, and the results indicated relatively greater spatial and temporal variation for benthic Foraminifera assemblages and highlighted caution in correlating quantitative benthic Foraminifera species data over distances of kilometres or greater in shallow marine environments (Schafer and Mudie 1980). Observations at ocean dumpsites in western Chaleur Bay, made in collaboration with S. MacKnight (private consultant) showed that two estuarine arenaceous benthic Foraminifera species (*Eggerella advena* and *Ammotium cassis*) had recolonized dumpsite deposits after only one month (MacKnight and Schafer 1980, Schafer 1982). In some deep offshore studies, the distributions and relative abundances of arenaceous versus calcareous benthic Foraminifera genera were compared to their Gulf of Mexico counterparts (Schafer et al. 1981). In addition, a report on taxonomic notes and illustrations of northeastern Newfoundland slope benthic Foraminifera species was prepared (Cole 1981).

Studies of benthic Foraminifera were also conducted in the Minas Basin (Fig. 2) and the distribution patterns of relatively common species and the effects of intensive passive transport of Foraminifera skeletons by tidal currents were determined (Thomas and Schafer 1982). In another continental slope study, Schafer and Cole (1982) detailed Foraminifera species distributions on the upslope side and in the core area of the Western Boundary Undercurrent (WBU) off Newfoundland that offered a species-based model for tracking spatial (upslope versus downslope) changes in the position of the WBU's axis. Using the Scott/Medioli/Schafer framework model (Scott et al. 1980), temporal variations of the Miramichi estuary's transitional zone species were traced between 1920 and 1975 based on Foraminifera assemblages observed in a Pb^{210} dated core. Transitional zone changes were ascribed to river discharge and tidal circulation variations over the 55-year interval recorded in the core (Schafer and Smith 1983).

Further applied studies documented the WBU foraminiferal facies. One of them detailed a high proportion of broken Foraminifera tests below the core of the WBU on the northeastern Newfoundland continental slope and rise (Schafer et al. 1983). With guidance from G. Vilks and C. Schafer, M. Williamson completed a PhD thesis at Dalhousie University which provided an overview of trends in benthic Foraminifera species diversity on the continental shelf and upper slope off Nova Scotia (Williamson 1983, 1985). Species distributions were shown to be strongly influenced by the continental shelf's physiography in concert with bottom water temperature, and salinity. Smith and Schafer (1984) showed that the enhanced bioturbation of middle slope sediment deposits, using a Pb^{210} tracer, was characterized by a reduction in the down-core temporal variation of some relatively abundant fossil species of benthic Foraminifera compared with their upper continental rise counterparts, thus limiting their usefulness for studying short-duration paleoceanographic events in WBU depths. Scott et al. (1984) used Foraminifera, dinoflagellate and pollen evidence to distinguish longer-term Late Pleistocene and Holocene paleoceanographic events in several Scotian Shelf basins while Schafer et al. (1985) applied knowledge on displaced shelf and upper slope benthic Foraminifera species observed in sediment cores to identify postglacial turbidity current deposition events.

In 1986, a reconnaissance survey of benthic Foraminifera was conducted in ten fiords on the east coast of Baffin Island (Fig. 2). The dominance of arenaceous species indicative of cold (<0.00°C) Arctic water and the occurrence of calcareous species in the deeper parts of some fiord basins that are flooded by relatively warmer and more saline Atlantic water were described (Schafer and Cole 1986). Off Nova Scotia, Medioli et al. (1986) surveyed benthic Foraminifera in waters surrounding Sable Island (Fig. 2) where several regional assemblage zones overlap. Foraminifera-barren areas were observed to be associated with shallow environments characterized by high wave turbulence conditions that they speculated had winnowed and transported indigenous species to deeper and relatively quiescent seafloor settings. Schafer and Smith (1987) applied data on the occurrences of re-deposited calcareous Foraminifera species characteristic of older late glacial-age deposits found on some Saguenay Fiord (Fig. 2) hillsides to document the source of sediments from a 1663 earthquake-triggered landslide which had carried an estimated 210 million m^3 of fossil-rich clay-textured sediment into the upper end of the Fiord. In collaboration with F. Tan, the paleoenvironments of Holocene sediments of Lake Melville in southeastern Labrador were examined using stable organic carbon isotopes (Tan and Vilks 1987). Studies were also conducted in Knight and Bute inlets (Fig. 2) in British Columbia where Foraminifera proxy indicator species were employed to trace fresh water discharge, bottom water renewal and sediment gravity flow processes (Schafer et al. 1989).

Further studies examined evidence for Wisconsinan glaciations (relatively short-term advances and retreats) in the sedimentary record of the Verrill Canyon (Fig. 2) area of the Scotian slope (Mosher et al. 1989) and the ecology of arctic continental shelf Foraminifera (Vilks 1989). In addition, foraminiferal research formed an important component of studies of the seafloor geology and paleoceanographic record in some channels of the Canadian Arctic Archipelago using CSS *Hudson* and through-the-ice-sampling techniques that were supported by the GSC Northern Oil and Gas Action Program (NOGAP; MacLean and Vilks 1986, MacLean et al. 1989). In collaboration with L. Kennard of ESSO Resources Canada, benthic Foraminifera evidence was employed to identify sediment slumping and turbidity current activity on the north flank of the Sackville Spur (Fig. 2) on the Newfoundland continental slope during postglacial time (Kennard et al. 1990).

Applications 1990-95

In the early 1990s, additional fundamental and applied foraminiferal studies were motivated by new government programs aimed at gaining a more comprehensive view of the potential impact of climate change on Canadian marine environments. Vilks and Buckley (1990) described an investigation of dissolution and sorting of planktic Foraminifera in Pleistocene sediments recorded in Ocean Drilling Program (ODP) core 708A (Indian Ocean). Vilks et al. (1990) examined foraminiferal stratigraphy in Gulf of St. Lawrence, and Vilks (1991) reported on Foraminifera that occupied deep-sea, ice-covered Canadian ocean environments, still one of the most poorly understood marine environments at that time. Schafer et al. (1991) conducted a repeat survey of an area near the head of Saguenay Fiord, and described how some formerly oxygen-depleted barren fiord bottom areas had been recolonized by a number of arenaceous taxa between 1976 and 1988. In collaboration with K. You and X. Zhu of Nanjing University (China), the disturbance of benthic and planktic Foraminifera distribution patterns by tidal flushing and dredging in Sanya Harbour (Hainan Island), China, was mapped (Schafer et al. 1992). On the Canadian scene, studies on the depositional environments and the Late Quaternary sedimentary record of Hudson Strait and Ungava Bay (Fig. 2) were conducted in conjunction with colleagues from other institutions, notably A. Jennings, A. Silis and J. Ceman (Vilks et al. 1989, MacLean et al. 1992, Jennings et al. 2001, and MacLean et al. 2001). These investigations were important in establishing a chronological record for sediment deposits since age dates were derived primarily using foraminiferal assemblages. In collaboration with C. Rodriques of University of Windsor, a discussion of the significance of freshwater flux from eastern Canada to the North Atlantic Ocean for inducing past climate changes between 11,600 and 8,000 years BP was based on the fossil Foraminifera record in the sediments of former postglacial-age Champlain and Goldthwait seas (upper St. Lawrence River valley [Fig. 2] and Gulf of St. Lawrence areas; Rodriques and Vilks 1994). In the late 1980s and early 1990s, G. Vilk's growing international reputation was exemplified by a series of invited lecture presentations made in Denmark and China.

As the program evolved further during this period, projects on the impacts of shellfish and finfish aquaculture were conducted. One study, conducted in collaboration with several Dalhousie University colleagues and P. Pocklington (private consultant), focussed on changing seafloor environments and species distributions at some suspended mussel culture operations near Lunenburg, Nova Scotia (Fig. 2). It detailed the replacement of the indigenous calcareous Foraminifera species *Heynesina orbiculare* by several organic matter-tolerant arenaceous species. Degraded seafloor habitats marked by reduced foraminiferal species richness and abundance were found where higher concentrations of organic matter had accumulated on the seafloor in active aquaculture areas (Grant et al. 1995, Scott et al. 1995). In another study, conducted in collaboration with C. Honig of St. Mary's University (Halifax, NS) and P. Pocklington at finfish farms in southwest Bay of Fundy (Fig. 2), it was observed that about 30% of the sediment samples contained no living Foraminifera and that there was a general inverse relationship between the number of species per sample and organic matter concentration which was more pronounced during the summer months (Schafer et al. 1995). These results highlighted the importance of both seasonal and anthropogenic factors in developing benthic community assemblage models for environmental monitoring applications. In another study, Schafer and Cole (1995) documented marine habitat recovery from industrial waste contamination in the North Arm of the Saguenay Fiord. Also, foraminiferal study results were compiled for southeastern Labrador Shelf and Lake Melville (Vilks and Deonarine 1995).

The year 1995 was pivotal for modern Foraminifera research at BIO. As a consequence of the government's effort to address Canada's growing budget deficit, there was a 20% downsizing of many parts of the federal civil service. In response, the GSC chose to disband some of its marine environmental-focussed programs and decades of marine ecology and chemistry research experience were lost. One of the unfortunate outcomes was the demise of the Paleoecology Section at BIO. However, a mitigating outcome of the cuts in many of the down-sized federal departments was rekindled support for government research scientist emeritus programs. These allowed qualified pensioned research scientists to complete, as volunteers, studies already in progress, thereby extracting full value from the original funding of those projects.

THE POST-PALEOECOLOGY SECTION YEARS (1996 - 2011)

The post-1995 period witnessed an ongoing but reduced stream of basic and applied Foraminifera studies conducted by some members of the former Paleoecology Section. The program was also reduced further by the untimely death of G. Vilks in 1997.

In collaboration with M. Buzas of the Smithsonian Institution (Washington, DC), a novel *in situ* field experiment was carried out at 7 m depth in Bedford Basin adjacent to BIO (Schafer et al. 1996). The Benthonic Foraminifera Temperature Experiment (BFTREX) was designed to explore the effect on benthic Foraminifera populations of a permanent increase in bottom water temperature throughout the year from a persistent warming trend. BFTREX involved the deployment of a cluster of heated and unheated trays of sterile sand implanted with partially sand-filled vials that were subsampled by SCUBA divers at regular intervals between July 1990 and October 1991 (462 days) (Fig. 5A,B). Observations indicated that certain species of benthic Foraminifera preferred the heated pans during the colder seasons suggesting that they might react quickly to long-term water temperature changes.

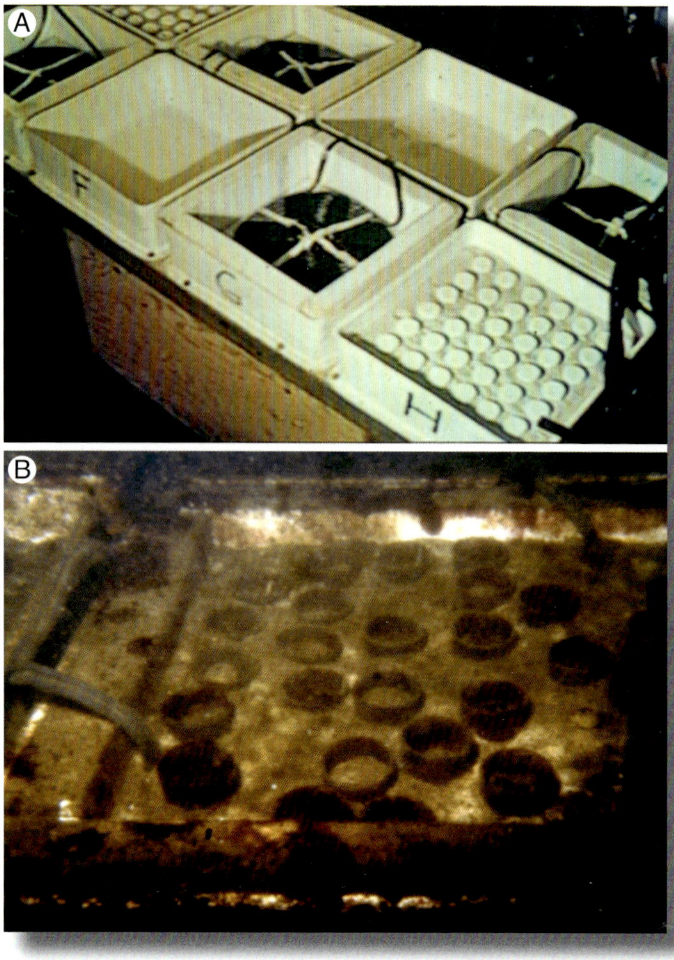

Figure 5. Benthonic Foraminifera Temperature Experiment (BFTREX) to assess the effects of a warming trend: (A) photograph of BFTREX experimental equipment being prepared for its deployment in the Bedford Basin (Halifax Harbour, Nova Scotia) just north of the BIO finger pier; half of the sterile sand-filled trays were heated by coils of heating tape - black circular structures visible in four segments with trays removed. (B) underwater photograph of the experiment after 131 days showing algal colonization of partially sand-filled sample vials that were set in trays of heated and unheated sand. [Note: Temperature of heated trays was controlled at 4°C above ambient bottom water temperature by a data link through a multiconductor submarine cable connection to a dockside control/video recorder system.]

Along with Dalhousie University colleagues D. Scott and F. Medioli, C. Schafer prepared a textbook on modern Foraminifera and Thecamoebian monitoring and mapping applications that had been developed by the world's cadre of foraminiferalogists during the last four decades of the 20th century (Scott et al. 2001). In addition, Schafer (2000) compiled a review of the protocols and pitfalls of using benthic Foraminifera in applied studies as environmental sentinels and indicators in shallow nearshore environments that included temporal and spatial species distribution variability in various marine environments, sample processing, and taphonomic (post-mortem and post-burial) factors in relation to specimen preservation, and some other methodological issues.

In 2004, a paleohydrologic and environmental mapping study was carried out in the St. Lawrence Estuary (Schafer and Smith 2004). It relied on data from both box and Lehigh gravity cores to evaluate historical changes in the discharge of the St. Lawrence River. Textural, magnetic susceptibility, and Foraminifera species proxy indicators were defined to delineate five ecotones along the estuary's axis ranging from a sandy, fluvially-dominated upstream environment to a finer-grained, deeper downstream setting in the western part of the Gulf. Three Foraminifera species *(Spiroplectammina biformis, Cassidulina reniforme,* and *Bulimina exilis)* showed well-defined water depth and bottom water temperature/salinity-related distributions that helped in establishing ecotone boundaries and tracing historical changes in the dynamics and mixing patterns of indigenous water masses.

As a belated contribution to Natural Resources Canada's Global Change Initiative Program, that had been active in the early 1990s, a study was conducted on fossil Foraminifera evidence for onshore-directed Nova Scotia storms over the past several hundred years in two vibrocores collected in Chezzetcook Inlet (Fig. 2; Schafer and Medioli 2009). The design of this applied study incorporated ideas learned from basic experimental work and field studies on Foraminifera transport processes in the late 1960s and 1970s (Schafer and Young 1977). Microfossil evidence of onshore-directed storms in the cores was marked by the passive transport and redeposition of offshore, inner shelf Foraminifera species that do not usually inhabit estuarine environments. The offshore species were similar to those presently found on the shoreward side of the Inlet's bay mouth barrier. The impact of storms on the position and size of bay-mouth barrier channels was revealed by fossil Foraminifera indicators of salinity changes which showed that, in one instance, the barrier channels appeared to have persisted for several decades after an apparent early 18th century relatively stormy interval (Schafer and Medioli 2009).

THE FUTURE OF FORAMINIFERA RESEARCH

Modern Foraminifera research has now been on the 'back burner' of the GSC at BIO for more than a decade. However, the new generation of foraminiferalogists working at other marine research institutions around the world confirms that this field is still very much alive and prospering. Monitoring modern Foraminifera research trends through monthly Internet scans of appropriate scientific journals revealed that more than 300 modern Foraminifera papers were published in the peer-reviewed literature between 2000 and 2010. Many fell into the classic categories of species distributions and their habitats, experimental biology, pollution mapping, environmental monitoring, field experiments, the use of Foraminifera as tracers of fluvial transport processes in space and time, and taxonomic investigations. However, a year-by-year analysis also suggests an increasing post-2006 emphasis on applications involving the use of isotopic, physical, and biochemical techniques to extract new information about paleoceanographic and paleoclimatic events recorded in the mineral composition of Foraminifera skeletons. Collectively, the papers reaffirm an ongoing scientific interest in modern Foraminifera that appears to span the full spectrum of ocean depths and physical settings. While no further programs are underway at BIO, modern Foraminifera investigators currently employed at a number of Canadian universities are maintaining Canada's link to this field of marine research.

Over the span of BIO's first fifty years, studies of the Foraminifera have revealed their ubiquitous presence and the varying characteristics of their populations in a wide range of settings from sub-tropical to arctic, and from coastal to offshore (Fig. 2). The research at BIO has also shown the sensitivity of these organisms to oceanographic changes, and to various forms of marine pollution arising from pulp and paper, and aquaculture operations, for example. Such knowledge is an impressive legacy in its own right, but it also provides a resource for future management of the marine environment. For example, future studies of Foraminifera will likely continue to be useful components of paleoceanographic research, the results of which will allow a better understanding of oceanic climate-change processes and effects, needed for specifying effective adaptation measures. In addition, such studies are expected to be useful components of the assessment and monitoring of marine environmental quality in the presence of coastal and offshore economic development.

ACKNOWLEDGEMENTS

I would like to thank Brian MacLean, Michel Latremouille and Michael Lewis for their review and suggestions for improving an earlier draft of this paper, and the editors for the final product. I would also like to extend my appreciation to Bhan Deonarine for providing some references to work that he completed with Gus Vilks and to Francis Kelly for his assistance in enhancing the colour of the Canso Strait species distribution and barren zones maps.

REFERENCES

Banerji, R.K., C.T. Schafer, and R. Vine. 1971. Environmental relationships and distribution of planktonic Foraminifera in the equatorial and northern Pacific waters. BIO Atlantic Oceanographic Laboratory Report 1971-7, Dartmouth, NS.

Bartlett, G.A. 1964a. A preliminary study of foraminiferal distribution on the Atlantic continental shelf, southeastern Nova Scotia. Geological Survey of Canada Paper 64-5, Ottawa, ON.

Bartlett, G.A. 1964b. Benthic foraminiferal ecology in St. Margaret's Bay and Mahone Bay, southeast Nova Scotia. BIO Report 64-8, Dartmouth, NS.

Bartlett, G.A. 1965a. Preliminary notes on recent species of Elphidiidae in shallow waters of the Atlantic provinces of Canada. BIO Report 65-13, Dartmouth, NS.

Bartlett, G.A. 1965b. Preliminary investigation of benthic foraminiferal ecology in Tracadie Bay, Prince Edward Island. BIO Report 65-3, Dartmouth, NS.

Bartlett, G.A. 1966. Distribution and abundance of Foraminifera and Thecamoebians in Miramichi River and Bay. BIO Report 66-2, Dartmouth, NS.

Bartlett, G.A. 1970. The Mid-Atlantic Ridge near 45°N. VIII. Carbonate lithification on oceanic ridges and seamounts. Canadian Journal of Earth Sciences 7: 257-267.

Bartlett, G.A. and R.G. Greggs. 1969. Carbonate sediments: Oriented lithified samples from the North Atlantic. Science 166: 740-741.

Be, A.W.H., G. Vilks, and L. Lott. 1971. Winter distribution of planktonic Foraminifera between the Grand Banks and the Caribbean Sea. Micropaleontology 17: 31-42.

Brady, H. 1884. Report on the Foraminifera dredged by HMS *Challenger* during the years 1873 to 1876. Pages 1-814 *in* Volume 9 of the Report on the Scientific Research of the Voyage of the HMS *Challenger* during the years 1873-1876: Zoology (J. Murray, Ed.). Neil and Company, Edinburgh, Scotland.

Carter, L. and C.T. Schafer 1983. Interaction of the Western Boundary Undercurrent with the continental margin off Newfoundland. Sedimentology 30: 751-768.

Carter, L., C.T. Schafer, and M.A. Rashid. 1979. Observations on depositional environments and benthos of the continental slope and rise, east of Newfoundland. Canadian Journal of Earth Sciences 16: 831-846.

Cole, F.E. 1981. Taxonomic notes on the bathyal zone benthic foraminiferal species off northeast Newfoundland. BIO Report BI-R-81-7, Dartmouth, NS.

Cole F.E. and C. Ferguson. 1975. An illustrated catalog of Foraminifera and Ostracoda from Canso Strait and Chedabucto Bay. BIO Report BI-R-75-5, Dartmouth, NS.

Deonarine, B. 1979. Foraminifera distribution in two Nova Scotia marshes. Maritime Sediments 15: 35-46.

Deonarine, B. and G. Vilks. 1977. Foraminifera in sediment cores from the Labrador Shelf. Geological Survey of Canada Open File Report No. 485, Ottawa, ON.

Grant, J., A. Hatcher, D. Scott, P. Pocklington, C.T. Schafer, and G.V. Winters. 1995. A multidisciplinary approach to evaluating impacts of shellfish aquaculture on benthic communities. Estuaries 18: 124-144.

Jennings, A., G. Vilks, B. Deonarine, A. Silis, and N. Weiner. 2001. Foraminiferal biostratigraphy and paleoceanography of Hudson Strait. Pages 127-146 *in* Geological Survey of Canada Bulletin 566 (B. MacLean, Ed.), Ottawa, ON.

Kennard, L., C.T. Schafer, and L. Carter. 1990. Late Cenozoic evolution of Sackville Spur: a sediment drift on the Newfoundland continental slope. Canadian Journal of Earth Sciences 27: 863-878.

Leslie, R.J. 1965. Ecology and paleoecology of Hudson Bay Foraminifera. BIO Report 65-6, Dartmouth, NS.

MacKnight, S. and C.T. Schafer. 1980. Geochemistry and benthic ecology at the Dalhousie, New Brunswick, Ocean Dump Site. Pages 761-781 *in* Proceedings of the 9th World Dredging Conference (WODCON IX), Vancouver, BC (J. Powers, Ed.). Symcon Publishing Company, Long Beach, CA.

MacLean, B., and G. Vilks. 1986. Marine geological program in the Byam Martin Channel-Lougheed Island region, District of Franklin. Pages 769-774 *in* Current Research, Part A, Geological Survey of Canada Paper 86-1A, Ottawa, ON.

MacLean, B., G.V. Sonnichsen, G. Vilks, C. Powell, K. Moran, A. Jennings, D. Hodgson, and B. Deonarine. 1989. Marine geological and geotechnical investigations in Wellington, Byam Martin, Austin, and adjacent channels, Canadian Arctic Archipelago. Geological Survey of Canada Paper 89-11, Ottawa, ON.

MacLean, B., G. Vilks, and B. Deonarine. 1992. Depositional environments and history of Late Quaternary sediments in Hudson Strait and Ungava Bay: further evidence from seismic and biostratigraphic data. Géographie physique et Quaternaire 46: 311-329.

MacLean, B., G. Vilks, I.A. Hardy, B. Deonarine, A. Jennings, and W. Manley. 2001. Quaternary sediments in Hudson Strait and Ungava Bay. Pages 71-125 *in* Geological Survey of Canada Bulletin 566, Ottawa, ON.

Mageau, N.C. and D.A. Walker. 1976. Effects of ingestion of Foraminifera by larger invertebrates. Pages 89-105 *in* Part A, First International Symposium on Benthonic Foraminifera of Continental Margins, Maritime Sediments Special Publication No. 1. (C.T. Schafer and B.R. Pelletier, Eds.). Dartmouth, NS.

Medioli, F. S, C.T. Schafer, and D.B. Scott. 1986. Distribution of recent Benthonic Foraminifera near Sable Island, Nova Scotia. Canadian Journal of Earth Sciences 23: 985-1,000.

Mosher, D.C., D.J.W. Piper, G. Vilks, A. Aksu, and G.B.J. Fader. 1989. Evidence for Wisconsinan glaciations in the Verrill Canyon area, Scotian slope. Quaternary Research 31: 27-40.

Mudie, P.J., C.E. Keen, I.A. Hardy, and G. Vilks. 1984. Multivariate analysis and quantitative paleoecology of benthic Foraminifera in surface and Late Quaternary shelf sediments, northern Canada. Marine Micropaleontology 8: 283-313.

Phleger, F.B. 1960. Ecology and Distribution of Recent Foraminifera. Johns Hopkins University Press, Baltimore, MD.

Rashid, M.A., G. Vilks, and J. D. Leonard 1975. Geological environment of a methane-rich recent sedimentary basin in the Gulf of St. Lawrence. Chemical Geology 15: 83-96.

Rodrigues, C.G. and G. Vilks. 1994. The impact of glacial lake runoff on the Goldthwait and Champlain seas: the relationship between glacial Lake Agassiz runoff and the Younger Dryas. Quaternary Science Reviews 13: 923-944.

Schafer, C.T. 1967. Preliminary survey of the distribution of living Benthonic Foraminifera populations in Northumberland Strait. Maritime Sediments 3: 105-108.

Schafer, C.T. 1970a. Distribution of Foraminifera along the west coasts of Hudson and James bays: A preliminary report. Maritime Sediments 5: 90-94.

Schafer, C.T. 1970b. Pollution and benthonic Foraminifera species diversity in Long Island Sound. Page 141 *in* United Nations Food and Agricultural Organization Technical Conference on Marine Pollution and its Effects on Living Resources and Fishing (M. Ruivo, Ed.). Food and Agriculture Organization of the United Nations, Rome, Italy.

Schafer, C.T. 1970c. Studies of Foraminifera in the Restigouche estuary: faunal distribution patterns near pollution sources. Maritime Sediments 6: 121-134.

Schafer, C.T. 1971. Sampling and spatial distribution of benthonic Foraminifera. Limnology and Oceanography 16: 944-951.

Schafer, C.T. 1973. Distribution of Foraminifera near pollution sources in Chaleur Bay. Water, Air and Soil Pollution 2: 219-233.

Schafer, C.T. 1976. *In situ* environmental responses of benthonic Foraminifera. Report of Activities, Paper 76-1C, Part C, Geological Survey of Canada, Ottawa, ON.

Schafer, C.T. 1982. Foraminiferal colonization of an offshore dumpsite in Chaleur Bay, New Brunswick, Canada. Journal of Foraminiferal Research 12: 317-326.

Schafer, C.T. 2000. Monitoring nearshore marine environments using benthic Foraminifera: Some protocols and pitfalls. Micropaleontology 46: 161-169.

Schafer, C.T. and A. Prakash. 1968. Current transport and deposition of foraminiferal tests, planktonic organisms and lithogenic particles in Bedford basin, Nova Scotia. Maritime Sediments 4: 100-103.

Schafer, C.T. and B.K. Sen Gupta. 1968. Benthonic foraminiferal ecology in Port Castries Bay, St. Lucia, BWI: a preliminary report. Maritime Sediments 4: 57-63.

Schafer, C.T. and B.K. Sen Gupta. 1969. Foraminiferal ecology in polluted estuaries of New Brunswick and Maine. Bedford Institute of Oceanography Report 69-1, Dartmouth, NS.

Schafer, C.T. and F.E. Cole. 1974a. Environmental geology of Chaleur Bay. Geological Survey of Canada Paper 74-1, Part B, Ottawa, ON.

Schafer, C.T. and F.E. Cole. 1974b. Distribution of Benthonic Foraminifera. Their use in delimiting local nearshore environments. Pages 103-108 *in* Offshore Geology of Eastern Canada, Volume 1, Concepts and Applications in Environmental Marine Geology (B.R. Pelletier, Ed.). Geological Survey of Canada Paper 74-30, Ottawa, ON.

Schafer, C.T. and J. Young. 1977. Experiments on mobility and transportability of some nearshore Benthonic Foraminifera species. Pages 27-31 *in* Geological Survey of Canada Paper 77-1C, Ottawa, ON.

Schafer, C.T. and F.E. Cole. 1978. Distribution of Foraminifera in Chaleur Bay, Gulf of St. Lawrence. Geological Survey of Canada Paper 77-30, Ottawa. ON.

Schafer, C.T. and F.J.E. Wagner. 1978. Foraminifera-mollusk associations in eastern Chaleur Bay. Canadian Journal of Earth Sciences 15: 889-901.

Schafer, C.T. and P.J. Mudie. 1980. Spatial variability of Foraminifera and pollen in nearshore sediment sites, St. Georges Bay, Nova Scotia. Canadian Journal of Earth Sciences 17: 313-324.

Schafer, C.T. and F.E. Cole. 1982. Living benthic Foraminifera distributions on the continental slope and rise off Newfoundland. Geological Society of America Bulletin 93: 207-217.

Schafer, C.T. and J.N. Smith. 1983. River discharge, sedimentation and benthic environmental variations in Miramichi Inner Bay, New Brunswick. Canadian Journal of Earth Sciences 20: 388-398.

Schafer, C.T. and F.E. Cole. 1986. Reconnaissance survey of Benthonic Foraminifera from Baffin Island fiord environments. Arctic 39: 232-239.

Schafer, C.T. and J.N. Smith. 1987. Hypothesis for a submarine landslide and cohesionless sediment flows resulting from a 17th century earthquake-triggered landslide in Quebec. Geo-Marine Letters 7: 31-37.

Schafer, C.T. and F.E. Cole. 1995. Marine habitat recovery in the Saguenay Fiord, Canada: the legacy of environmental contamination. Pages 925-940 *in* Challenges of Our Changing Global Environment, Proceedings of Oceans'95 Marine Technology Society/Institute of Electrical and Electronics Engineers Conference, San Diego, CA, Volume 2.The Marine Technology Society, Washington, DC.

Schafer, C.T. and J.N. Smith. 2004. Possible proxy, textural, magnetic susceptibility and microfossil indicators of historical changes in river discharge into the lower St. Lawrence estuary. Geological Survey of Canada Open File Report, Ottawa, ON.

Schafer, C.T. and F.S. Medioli. 2009. Pilot study of fossil evidence of onshore-directed storm events in estuarine sediments: Chezzetcook Inlet, Nova Scotia. Canadian Journal of Earth Sciences 46: 193-205.

Schafer, C.T., F.J.E. Wagner, and C. Ferguson. 1975. Occurrence of Foraminifera, Mollusks and Ostracods adjacent to the industrialized shoreline of Canso Strait, Nova Scotia. Water, Air and Soil Pollution 5: 79-96.

Schafer, C.T., F.E. Cole, and F.J.E. Wagner. 1977. Relationship of Foraminifera distribution patterns to sedimentary processes in the Miramichi estuary. Pages 1-7 *in* Geological Survey of Canada Report of Activities, Paper 77-1C, Ottawa, ON.

Schafer, C.T., J.N. Smith, and F.E. Cole. 1980. Record of paleoceanographic events in Holocene sediments, Newfoundland continental slope and rise. Pages 223-243 *in* Proceedings of Workshop on Research in the Labrador Coastal and Offshore Region, Goose Bay, NL. Memorial University of Newfoundland, St. John's, NL.

Schafer, C.T., F.E. Cole, and L. Carter. 1981. Bathyal zone benthic foraminiferal genera off northeast Newfoundland. Journal of Foraminiferal Research 11: 295-316.

Schafer, C.T., F.E. Cole, and L. Carter. 1983. Paraecology of bathyal zone arenaceous Foraminifera genera and species associations off northeast Newfoundland. Pages 133-143 *in* Proceedings of the First Workshop on Arenaceous Foraminifera, Free University, Amsterdam (J.G. Verdenius, J.E. van Hinte, and A.R. Foruin, Eds.). Publication 108, Continental Shelf Institute, Trondheim, Norway.

Schafer, C.T., F.C. Tan, D.F. Williams, and J.N. Smith. 1985. Late glacial to recent stratigraphy, paleontology and sedimentary processes: Newfoundland continental slope and rise. Canadian Journal of Earth Sciences 22: 266-282.

Schafer, C.T., F.E. Cole, and J.P.M. Syvitski. 1989. Bio- and lithofacies of modern sediments in Knight and Bute inlets, British Columbia. Palaios 4: 107-126.

Schafer, C.T., E. Collins, and J.N. Smith. 1991. Relationship of Foraminifera and Thecamoebian distributions to sediments contaminated by pulp mill effluent: Saguenay Fiord, Quebec. Marine Micropaleontology 17: 255-283.

Schafer, C.T., K. You, F.E. Cole, and X. Zhu. 1992. Foraminifera distribution patterns as markers of tidal circulation modes in Sanya Harbour, China. Pages 221-241 *in* Island Environment and Coast Development (Wang Ying and C.T. Schafer, Eds.). Nanjing University Press, Nanjing, China.

Schafer, C.T., G.V. Winters, D.B. Scott, P. Pocklington, F.E. Cole, and C. Honig. 1995. Survey of living Foraminifera and polycheate populations at some Canadian aquaculture sites: potential for impact mapping and monitoring. Journal of Foraminiferal Research 25: 236-259.

Schafer, C.T., F.E. Cole, D. Frobel, N. Rice, and M. Buzas. 1996. An *in situ* experiment on temperature sensitivity of nearshore temperate Benthonic Foraminifera. Journal of Foraminiferal Research 26: 53-63.

Scott, D.B., F.S. Medioli, and C.T. Schafer. 1977. Temporal changes in foraminiferal distribution in Miramichi River estuary, New Brunswick. Canadian Journal of Earth Sciences 14: 1,566-1,587.

Scott, D.B., C.T. Schafer, and F.S. Medioli. 1980. Eastern Canadian estuarine Foraminifera: A framework for comparison. Journal of Foraminiferal Research 10: 205-234.

Scott, D.B., P.J. Mudie, G. Vilks, and D.C. Younger. 1984. Latest Pleistocene-Holocene paleoceanographic trends on the continental margin of eastern Canada: Foraminiferal, dinoflagellate and pollen evidence. Marine Micropaleontology 9: 181-218.

Scott, D.B., C.T. Schafer, C. Honig, and D. Younger. 1995. Temporal variations of benthic foraminiferal assemblages under or near aquaculture operations: documentation and impact history. Journal of Foraminiferal Research 25: 224-235.

Scott, D.B., F.S. Medioli, and C.T. Schafer. 2001. Monitoring in Coastal Environments Using Foraminifera and Thecamoebian Indicators. Cambridge University Press, Cambridge, England.

Sen Gupta, B.K., 1971. The benthonic Foraminifera of the Tail of the Grand Banks. Micropaleontology 17: 69-98.

Sen Gupta, B.K. 1972. Distribution of Holocene benthonic Foraminifera on the Atlantic continental shelf of North America. Pages 125-134 *in* Section 8, Marine Geology and Geophysics (J.W. Murray, B.R. Pelletier, and J.R. Luternauer, Eds.), 24th International Geological Congress, Montreal, QC. 24th International Geological Congress, 601 Booth St., Ottawa, ON.

Sen Gupta, B.K. (Ed.). 1999. Modern Foraminifera. Kluwer Academic Publishers, Dordrecht, The Netherlands.

Sen Gupta, B.K. and R.M. McMullen. 1969. Foraminifera distribution and sedimentary facies on the Grand Banks of Newfoundland. Canadian Journal of Earth Sciences 6: 475-487.

Sen Gupta, B.K. and C.T. Schafer. 1973. Holocene benthonic Foraminifera in leeward bays of St. Lucia, West Indies. Micropaleontology 19: 341-365.

Shaw, J., D.J.W. Piper, G.B.J. Fader, E.L. King, B.J. Todd, T. Bell, M.J. Batterson, and D.G.E. Liverman. 2006. A conceptual model of the deglaciation of Atlantic Canada. Quaternary Science Reviews 25: 2,059-2,081.

Smith, J.N. and C.T. Schafer. 1984. Bioturbation processes in continental slope and rise sediments delineated by Pb^{210}, microfossil and textural indicators. Journal of Marine Research 42: 1,117-1,145.

Tan, F.C. and G. Vilks. 1987. Organic carbon isotope ratios and paleo-environmental implications for Holocene sediments in Lake Melville, southeastern Labrador. Canadian Journal of Earth Sciences 24: 1,994-2,003.

Thomas, F.C. and C.T. Schafer. 1982. Distribution and transport of some common foraminiferal species in the Minas Basin, eastern Canada. Journal of Foraminiferal Research 12: 24-38.

Vilks, G. 1964. Foraminiferal study of East Bay, MacKenzie King Island, District of Franklin (Polar Continental Shelf Project). Geological Survey of Canada Paper 64-53, Ottawa, ON.

Vilks, G. 1967. Quantitative analysis of Foraminifera in Bras d'Or Lakes. BIO Report 67-1, Dartmouth, NS.

Vilks, G. 1968. Foraminiferal study of the Magdalen Shallows, Gulf of St. Lawrence. Maritime Sediments 4: 14-21.

Vilks, G. 1969. Recent Foraminifera in the Canadian Arctic. Micropaleontology 15: 35-60.
Vilks, G. 1970. Circulation of surface waters in parts of the Canadian Arctic Archipelago based on foraminiferal evidence. Arctic 23: 100-111.
Vilks, G. 1974. The distribution of planktonic Foraminifera in the sediments and water of the NW Passage and northern Baffin Bay: a tool for paleoceanographic synthesis. Pages 109-121 *in* Offshore Geology of Eastern Canada, Volume 1, Concepts and Applications in Environmental Marine Geology (B.R. Pelletier, Ed.). Geological Survey of Canada Paper 74-30, Ottawa, ON.
Vilks, G. 1975. Comparison of *Globorotalia pachyderma* (Ehrenberg) in the water column and sediments of the Canadian Arctic. Journal of Foraminifera Research 5: 313-325.
Vilks, G. 1989. Ecology of recent Foraminifera on the Canadian continental shelf of the Arctic Ocean. Pages 497-569 *in* The Arctic Seas: Climatology, Oceanography, Geology and Biology (Y. Herman, Ed.). Van Nostrand Reinhold, New York, NY.
Vilks, G. 1991. Benthic Foraminifera in the surface sediments of the deep-sea Arctic Ocean. Journal of Foraminiferal Research 21: 20-38.
Vilks, G. and D.A. Walker. 1974. Morphology of *Orbulina universa* d' Orbigny in relation to other spinose planktonic Foraminifera. Journal of Foraminiferal Research 4: 1-8.
Vilks, G. and M.A. Rashid. 1976. Post-glacial paleo-oceanography of Emerald Basin, Scotian Shelf. Canadian Journal of Earth Sciences 13: 1,256-1,267.
Vilks, G. and P.J. Mudie. 1978. Early deglaciation of the Labrador Shelf. Science 202: 1,181-1,183.
Vilks, G. and D.P. Krauel. 1981. Environmental geology of the Miramichi estuary: Physical oceanography. Geological Survey of Canada Paper 81-24, Ottawa, ON.
Vilks, G. and P.J. Mudie. 1983. Evidence for postglacial paleoceanographic and paleoclimatic changes in Lake Melville, Labrador, Canada. Journal of Arctic and Alpine Research 15: 307-320.
Vilks, G. and B. Deonarine. 1988. Labrador shelf benthic Foraminifera and stable oxygen isotopes of *Cibicides lobatulus* related to the Labrador Current. Canadian Journal of Earth Sciences 25: 1,240-1,255.
Vilks, G. and D.E. Buckley. 1990. Evidence for dissolution and sorting of planktonic foraminifers in Pleistocene sediments at Hole 708A. Pages 621-625 *in* Proceedings of the Ocean Drilling Program, Scientific Results, Volume 115 (E.M. Barbu, Ed.). Ocean Drilling Program, Texas A&M University, College Station, TX.
Vilks, G. and B. Deonarine. 1995. Foraminifera in cores from the continental shelf of northern and eastern Canada. Geological Survey of Canada Open File Report 3051, Ottawa, ON.
Vilks, G., E.H. Anthony, and W.T. Williams. 1970. Application of association analysis to distribution studies of recent Foraminifera. Canadian Journal of Earth Sciences 7: 1,462-1,469.
Vilks, G., M.A. Rashid, and W.J. van der Linden. 1974. Methane in recent sediments of the Labrador Shelf. Canadian Journal of Earth Sciences 11: 1,427-1,434.
Vilks, G., C.T. Schafer, and D.A. Walker. 1975. The influence of a causeway on oceanography and Foraminifera in the Strait of Canso. Canadian Journal of Earth Sciences 12: 2,085-2,102.
Vilks, G., B. Deonarine, F.J.E. Wagner, and G.V. Winters. 1982. Foraminifera and Molluska in surface sediments of the southeastern Labrador shelf and Lake Melville, Canada. Geological Society of America Bulletin 93: 225-238.
Vilks, G., D.E. Buckley, and L.D. Keigwin. 1985. Late Quaternary sedimentation on the southern Sohm abyssal plain. Sedimentology 32: 69-82.
Vilks, G., B. MacLean, C.G. Currie, and K. Moran. 1989. Late Quaternary paleoceanography and sedimentary environments in Hudson Strait. Géographie physique et Quaternaire 43: 161-178.
Vilks, G., B. Maclean, and C.G. Rodrigues. 1990. Quaternary high-resolution seismic and foraminiferal stratigraphy in the Gulf of St. Lawrence. Current Research Part B, Geological Survey of Canada Paper 90-01B, Ottawa, ON.
Wadhams, P. 2014. The *Hudson-70* voyage of discovery: first circumnavigation of the Americas. Pages 21-28 *in* Voyage of Discovery: Fifty Years of Marine Research at Canada's Bedford Institute of Oceanography (D.N. Nettleship, D.C. Gordon, C.F.M. Lewis, and M.P. Latremouille, Eds.). Bedford Institute of Oceanography-Oceans Association, Dartmouth, NS.
Wagner, F.J.E. and C.T. Schafer. 1980. Upper Holocene paleoceanography of Inner Mirimichi Bay. Atlantic Geology 16: 5-10.
Walker, D.A. 1969. Observations of the regeneration of a new test by the foraminifer *Discorbis sp*. Canadian Journal of Zoology 47: 543-545.
Walker, D.A. 1971. Etching of the test surface of benthonic foraminifers due to ingestion by the gastropod *Littorina littorea* Linné. Canadian Journal of Earth Sciences 8: 1,487-1,491.
Walker, D.A. 1976. An *in situ* investigation of life cycles of benthonic mid-littoral Foraminifera. Pages 51-60 *in* First International Symposium on Benthonic Foraminifera of Continental Margins, Part A (C.T. Schafer and B.R. Pelletier, Eds.). Maritime Sediments Special Publication No. 1, Halifax, NS.
Walker, D.A. and D.E. Buckley. 1969. Some techniques and applications of scanning electron microscopy in the fields of marine science. Maritime Sediments 5: 113-118.
Walker, D.A. and G. Vilks. 1973. Spinal ultrastructure of the planktonic foraminifers *Hastigerina* Thomson and *Globigerinella* Cushman. Journal of Foraminiferal Research 3: 196-198.
Walker, D.A., A. Linton, and C.T. Schafer. 1974. Sudan Black B: a superior stain to Rose Bengal for distinguishing living from non-living Foraminifera. Journal of Foraminiferal Research 4: 205-215.
Williamson, M.A. 1983. Benthic foraminiferal assemblages in the continental margin off Nova Scotia: a multivariate approach. Ph.D. thesis, Dalhousie University, Halifax, NS.
Williamson, M.A. 1985. Recent foraminiferal diversity on the continental margin off Nova Scotia, Canada. Journal of Foraminiferal Research 15: 43-51.

29. DISCOVERIES IN ENVIRONMENTAL MARINE GEOLOGY

Dale E. Buckley

SUMMARY

Beginning with just one geologist in 1962, the Bedford Institute of Oceanography marine geoscience program steadily developed during the first decade adding expertise from a large number of disciplines. In 1972 the Environmental Marine Geology (EMG) group was formed with expertise in micropaleontology, coastal geomorphology, and geochemistry. The mechanisms of chemical transport in estuaries and bays with input from other disciplines in EMG were topics of initial projects, including studies of the LaHave Estuary and Strait of Canso in Nova Scotia, and Miramichi River and Estuary, New Brunswick. Later in the 1980s, deep-sea sediments were assessed as a medium for disposal of radioactive waste. Additional activities included scientific exchange visits in China, and recognition that corrosion of the RMS *Titanic* wreck was by biogeochemical processes stimulated by bacteria. The sedimentological and geochemical processes affecting surficial sediments in Scotian Shelf basins were examined, and finally the deposition of waste chemicals in Halifax Harbour was investigated in the 1990s. These studies help to ensure that Canadian marine environments are sustainably developed and managed.

Key words: environmental marine geology, marine geochemistry of estuaries and bays, LaHave Estuary, Miramichi Estuary, Halifax Harbour, deep-sea radioactive waste disposal, RMS *Titanic*.

E-mail: DBuckley@ns.sympatico.ca.

Among the first staff to be located at the new Bedford Institute of Oceanography (BIO) in 1962 was a single geologist, D. Buckley. He was almost immediately assigned to the first BIO field investigation, carried out at Ellerslie, Prince Edward Island, which was designed to determine why there were several major population shifts in oysters in the estuaries of the Island, such as Malpeque Bay (Fig. 1). The most significant factor was found to be changes in sedimentation in the creeks and estuaries due to deforestation and development of agriculture (Buckley 1969).

In 1963, several new staff were added from Ottawa, Ontario, and elsewhere, and consolidated as a Marine Geology Section led by B. Pelletier, a group that was already engaged in marine geology studies of the arctic Canadian polar shelf and adjacent inter-island channels. The new staff included laboratory technicians, field sampling and survey technicians, and specialists in various disciplines, including physical geology, coastal geomorphology, micropaleontology, and geochemistry. Investigations continued on the Arctic Ocean shelf and inter-island passages,

Figure 1. Map showing locations of studies in the Maritimes region (courtesy: J. Shaw, GSCA).

and studies of organic deposition were begun on the Scotian Shelf (Fig. 1). As a prerequisite for understanding organic matter in sediments, the Scotian Shelf activity focussed on the identification of sedimentary units from samples and acoustic reflection records which led to pioneering interpretations of offshore surficial geology. This research included interpretation of the uppermost sediment layers from the character of conventional hydrographic 14.25 kHz acoustic signals reflected back to survey ships and recorded on graphical echo sounder records. With time and experience, the marine geology group was able to identify sediments and rocks of various geological ages. This was the beginning of marine surficial geological mapping based on acoustic reflection data and was the only such activity underway anywhere in the world at the time (Fader et al. 2014).

During the mid-1960s a major effort was devoted to building up the capability of the laboratories at BIO. This included research microscopes for micropaleontology, the mineralogy laboratory based on the X-ray diffraction system, an organic chemical analytical laboratory to separate and characterize organic material, and an atomic absorption laboratory to quantitatively determine elemental content in water and sediments.

During the 1960s, thought was being given to developing integrated multidisciplinary teams of geoscientists. Such teams would be ideal for studying complex systems such as estuaries and bays. The first such project was undertaken in 1963 and was designed to evaluate the present processes controlling the Point Belledune area in northern New Brunswick (Fig. 1; Buckley and Grant 1964). In 1966 and 1967, research was carried out in an Alaskan fiord from the University of Alaska to determine the transition that water and sediment goes through during passage to the sea (Buckley and Cranston 1971).

ESTABLISHMENT OF ENVIRONMENTAL MARINE GEOLOGY

Following the transfer of the Atlantic Oceanographic Laboratory and the Marine Ecology Laboratory to the new Department of the Environment in 1971, the earth science units at BIO remained in Energy, Mines, and Resources Canada, and were reorganized as the Atlantic Geoscience Centre (AGC), later renamed Geological Survey of Canada Atlantic (GSCA) in 1996. Many components of the former Marine Geology Section were re-established in the Environmental Marine Geology (EMG) subdivision of AGC formed in late 1972 with D. Buckley as its Head. The program of EMG was organized in four scientific themes: Paleo-ecology, Coastal Geodynamics, Organic Geochemistry, and Inorganic Geochemistry (Fig. 2). The first two themes are described by Schafer (2014) and Taylor et al. (2014), respectively. Organic geochemistry was led by M.A. Rashid whose group participated in EMG multidisciplinary studies and contrib-

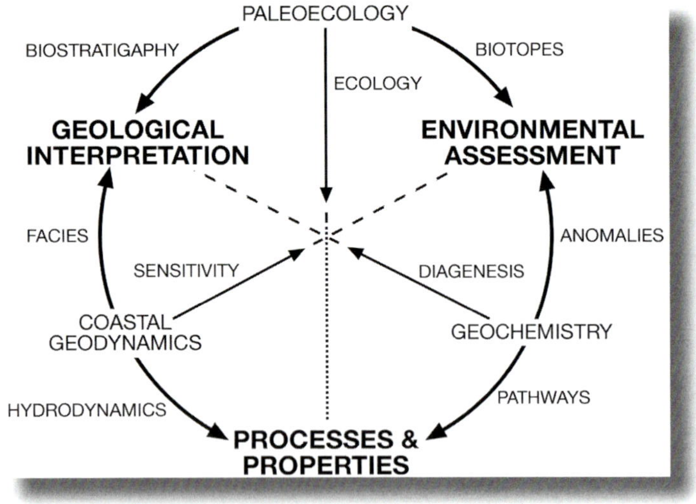

Figure 2. Relationships among the different components of the Environmental Marine Geology program.

uted analyses of organic carbon and gaseous hydrocarbons for evaluation of the oil and gas potential in the sedimentary basins of offshore eastern Canada (Williams et al. 2014). Other activities in EMG focussed on geotechnical and seabed hazard issues (Lewis et al. 2014). Here, some highlights of EMG and the inorganic geochemistry program during the 1970s to 1990s are presented.

INORGANIC GEOCHEMISTRY AND MULTIDISCIPLINARY STUDIES

Through the 1970s, the inorganic geochemical research program of EMG was directed at understanding the mechanisms of chemical transport and deposition in estuaries and bays. This knowledge would help in developing guidelines for environmental assessment and management.

LaHave Estuary

The first estuarine system studied was the LaHave Estuary (Fig. 1) on the southwest coast of Nova Scotia in 1972. This rather simple system was dominated by fresh water discharge that varied with the prevailing weather conditions and the season of the year. It was observed that dissolved mercury released in industrial wastes was dissipated through both dilution and absorption to suspended particulate matter (Cranston and Buckley 1973).

Strait of Canso

In 1974, the entire EMG subdivision staff and most of the laboratory equipment was transferred to a school in the Strait of Canso area so that continuous operations including survey and sampling of the water and sediment of the Strait could be carried out during the days and some nights. This extensive field program eventually led to one of the most comprehensive coastal research projects ever undertaken in Canada (Buckley et al. 1974). The Strait of Canso was a deep-water channel between the mainland of Nova Scotia and the Island of Cape Breton (Fig. 1). In 1956, a causeway was constructed across the Strait to provide a highway and rail link between the Nova Scotia mainland and Cape Breton. This created two artificial fiords, one opening to the southeast into Chedabucto Bay and the North Atlantic, and the other to the northwest into St. Georges Bay and the Gulf of St. Lawrence; details of the St. Georges Bay ecosystem are provided by Lambert et al. (2014). The causeway blocked any open seawater exchange between the northwest and the southeast and inadvertently created an excellent deep-water port on the southeast side of the causeway. In addition, the causeway blocked the flow of winter ice through the Strait, creating an ice-free port open to the North Atlantic. The serendipitous creation of an ice-free fiord provided an excellent area for new industries to establish along the shoreline of Cape Breton. New establishments included a pulp and paper mill, a heavy water plant, an oil refinery, a gypsum washing plant, and an electrical power generating station fueled by oil. The effluent from all of these industrial developments was discharged into Canso Strait.

Data from our environmental investigations showed anomalous concentrations of metals and suspended particulate matter in the water column along the industrially developed shoreline. Chemical analyses of the bottom sediments showed high concentrations of industrial metals such as copper, lead, and zinc (Fig. 3A). Of considerable concern was the high concentration of mercury in the bottom sediments. Sediments from the shoreline adjacent to the industrial sites and the town waterfront were highly contaminated with organic matter. Information on the impact of these sediments and water quality anomalies on biota was obtained by the paleontologists who demonstrated a gradient of increasing sensitivity and loss of biota towards the industrial sites based on a distributional sequence of the most sensitive benthic life forms — molluscs and ostracods — through the least sensitive microorganisms (Foraminifera), to barren zones closest to the sites (Fig. 3B; Schafer 2014).

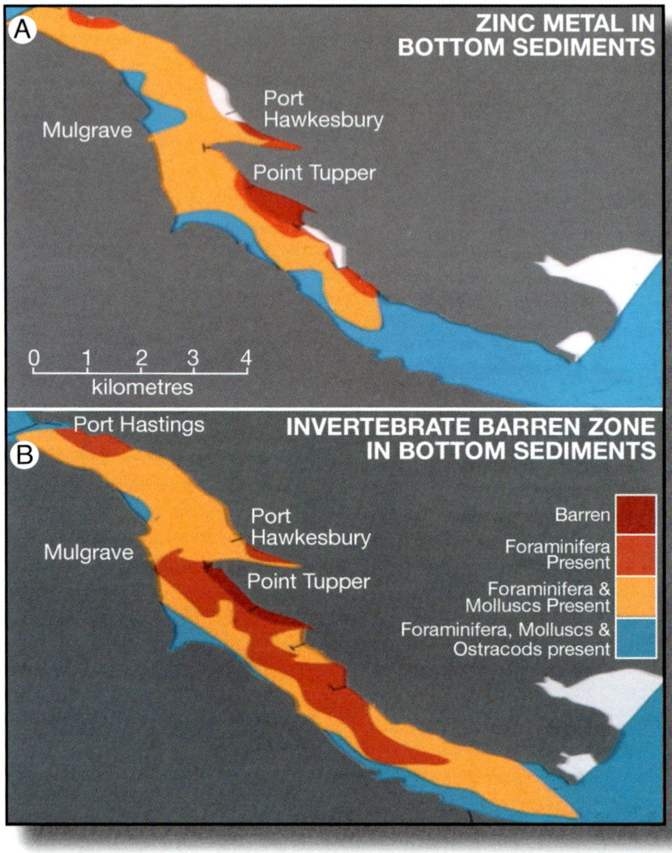

Figure 3. Sediment property distribution in the Strait of Canso: (A) zinc concentrations (dark red = highest, blue = lowest) and (B) benthic invertebrate organisms.

Part of the study program of the coastal geodynamics group was to re-examine the coastal areas in Chedabucto Bay that had been heavily oiled after the sinking of the tanker *Arrow* in 1970 (Fig. 4; Gordon et al. 2014a). The coastal studies, led by E. Owens, revealed that several types of shorelines had recovered well as oil residues were eroded or were buried under new sediments. However, some low energy coastlines were still heavily oiled in 1973 (Owens 1978). This study provided a basis for developing advice on clean-up strategies for oil-contaminated shorelines.

Miramichi Estuary

Beginning in 1975, a multiyear environmental assessment was begun on the Miramichi River and Estuary (Fig. 1). This system had been partially studied by several groups over the years starting in the 1920s. The main concern was the impact of the forest industry on the quality of the river and estuary. Great quantities of wood products had been harvested for a number of years in the upper reaches of the river, with wood waste products dumped in the river. In the previous 75 years, pulp and paper mills had been established in the head of the tidal estuary, with the usual consequence of waste discharge in the estuary. A side effect of the deforestation was an increase in soil erosion products that could be carried down the river to the tidal estuary. Because the estuary was an important port facility for shipping forest products and other industrial production,

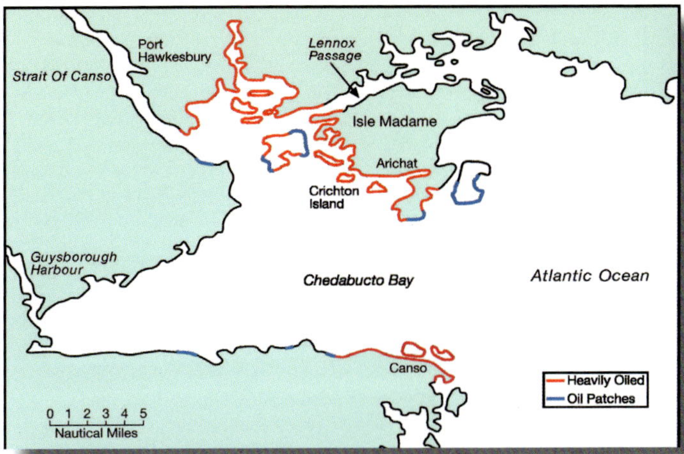

Figure 4. Shoreline of Chedabucto Bay, NS, showing areas contaminated by the 1970 *Arrow* oil spill.

there was a need to maintain the shipping channels through Miramichi Bay and lower parts of the river channels.

Previous studies had already established that the channels through the inner bay and the barrier islands were constantly changing with enormous quantities of sand being shifted from one deposition site to another. Periodic efforts to dredge through the barrier islands or the sand deposits in the inner bay were usually futile as the movement of sand by natural processes was so great.

During the winter and summer, contaminants discharged into the river were carried out into the inner bay and to various sites of deposition along the main channel (Buckley and Winters 1983). Over about 40 days in spring, the annual flood of the Miramichi River caused the flow of fresh water to increase up to 10 times the annual average daily discharge. This is typical of seasonal river-dominated estuaries which are poorly flushed over most of the year but experience very significant flushing of sediments and contaminants during the spring flood period.

Owing to the obvious seasonal variability in the freshwater discharge and in the nature of deposition patterns over the year, an effort was made to monitor these processes during different seasons to arrive at values of average annual geochemical transports (Fig. 5). This entailed setting up monitoring stations in the upper estuary, lower river estuary, and in the centre of the inner bay. Some of these monitoring stations were established in mid-winter when most of the surface of the estuary was frozen. In spite of difficult conditions, monitoring and sampling were carried out

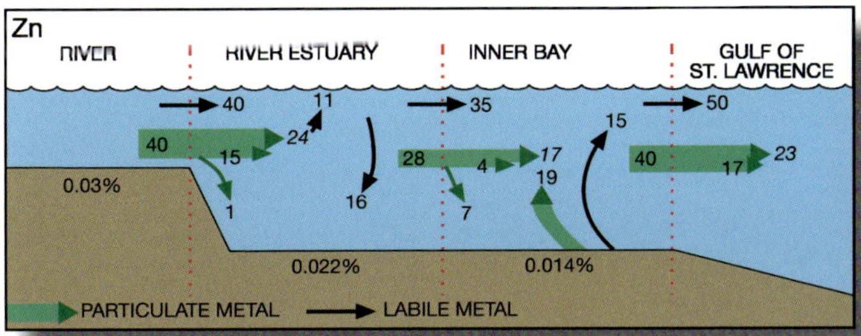

Figure 5. Schematic model of annual geochemical transport modes in the Miramichi Estuary. Code: numbers after the arrows represent tonnes of metal per year; numbers in italics represent the annual amount of reactive (chemically active) metal; and percentages shown are concentrations of metal in bottom muds (from Buckley and Winters 1983).

on a 24-hour basis. In winter a sampling hut was dragged to the main channel area in the inner bay over a hole cut through the ice.

Although the Miramichi project was undertaken as a multidisciplinary study intended to last at least three years, some EMG scientists with expertise in coastal geomorphology and sedimentation were committed to studies in other areas. These included renewed studies of the Bay of Fundy with a view of understanding the potential impacts of tidal power development (Gordon et al. 2014b) and determining the sensitivity of coastal areas to oil spills (Gordon et al. 2014a).

The Deep Sea and Radioactive Waste

In 1979, the subdivision began to plan a major international cooperative project to evaluate the feasibility of using the deep-sea sediments as a medium for disposal of radioactive waste. This concept had been discussed by a few countries a number of years earlier, but scientific technical and political aspects prevented the concept from being seriously considered. By 1978 sufficient progress had been made in oceanographic institutes to explore the deep sea in more detail. A number of countries including the United States, Great Britain, France, The Netherlands, and Japan were prepared to cooperate on surveys and sampling programs to learn more about the nature of deep-sea sediments. Canada was invited to participate in these studies because it was recognized that BIO had the scientific and technical expertise to be a significant contributor to the research program. A series of discussion and planning meetings were held in 1978 and 1979, and plans were made for several oceanographic cruises in 1980 and 1981. These cruises surveyed several areas in the North At-

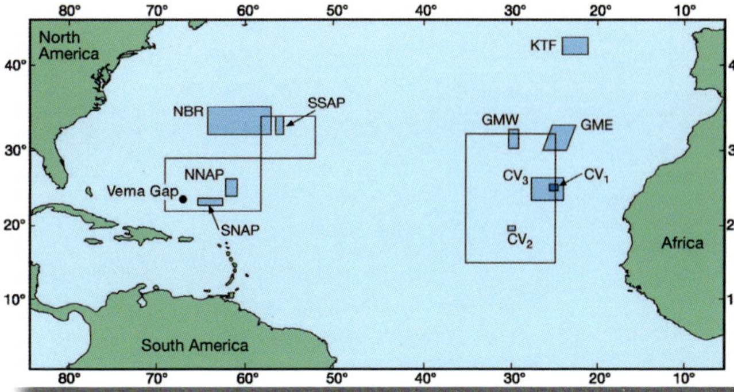

Figure 6. North Atlantic Ocean with study areas for radioactive waste disposal identified: NBR - Northern Bermuda Rise; SSAP - Southern Sohm Abyssal Plain; NNAP - Northern Nares Abyssal Plain; SNAP - Southern Nares Abyssal Plain; GMW - Great Meteor West; GME - Great Meteor East; KTF - Kings Trough Flank; and CV - Cape Verde.

lantic, mainly the abyssal plain areas in both the eastern and western North Atlantic Ocean (Fig. 6).

Potential disposal sites would be located in deep-sea areas with minimum water depths of 3,500 m and sediment thickness of at least 300 m. It was decided that ideal areas would have flat lying, fine-grained sediments, with no active volcanic or tectonic features. Such conditions were possible in the distal abyssal plains where sedimentation rates were slow, averaging less than 1 cm per 1,000 years. The first Canadian investigation was carried out on the Sohm Abyssal Plain, southeast of Bermuda, using CSS *Hudson* in 1980. Several conventional piston cores were taken in the soft mud at the surface of the abyssal plain in 1980 and 1982. The recovered mud showed several different colours and changes in sediment texture down core. Detailed geochemical and sedimentological analyses indicated that these sediments were part of the distal ends of turbidite deposition, deposits of turbidity currents that had travelled from the eastern margin of Canada down the deep abyssal plain off the eastern continental shelf of North America, and across the Northern Bermuda Rise to the Southern Sohm Abyssal Plain (SSAP). Because of the several changes in sediment texture these sediments were not considered to be ideal disposal sites for radioactive waste.

In order to find better conditions for the radioactive waste disposal option, attention was shifted to the Southern Nares Abyssal Plain (SNAP) in 1984. Again, CSS *Hudson* was used for the investigations that included conventional piston coring and some box coring. Coring sites were selected in the central part of the SNAP as far removed from any seamounts as possible. The sediments in this area appeared to be nearly flat lying and without any sign of disturbance from volcanic or tectonic activity. Cores of the mud showed that the sediments were very fine-grained with very little sand-sized material. They did show frequent changes in colour and silt content, which suggested that these sediments may have been deposited from turbidity currents that had travelled through the Vema Gap on its way south and east of the American Continental Shelf (Buckley and Cranston 1988).

One of the surprising discoveries in examining the acoustic profile records (Fig. 7) from the SNAP was the presence of features that appeared to be faults in the sediments with displacement along the plane of the fault. The importance of these features, if they did prove to be faults, is that they would provide a conduit for the advection of pore fluids (Fig. 8; Buckley and Grant 1985). These types of features were found in both the SNAP and the Great Meteor East Abyssal Plain (GMEAP, GME in Fig.

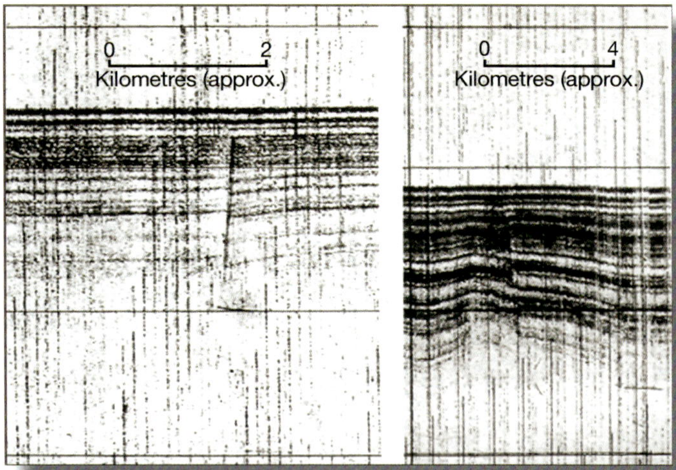

Figure 7. Parts of acoustic reflectance records from a 12 kHz acoustic profiler; both records show a fracture line with some apparent displacement of sediment layers, suggestive of a fault.

6). Because most conventional piston corers were limited in the length of sediment core they could retain, an effort was made to build a new corer with a fixed reference piston and long core barrel that would be capable of sampling to a sub-bottom depth of about 35 m. Such a device was fabricated by the French Petroleum Institute for deployment on the French Antarctic research ship *Marion Dufresne*. Subsequent investigations from this ship targeted the area where apparent faults were seen in the acoustic records, and piston cores up to 37 m long, from both GMEAP and SNAP, intersected what appeared to be part of a fracture system.

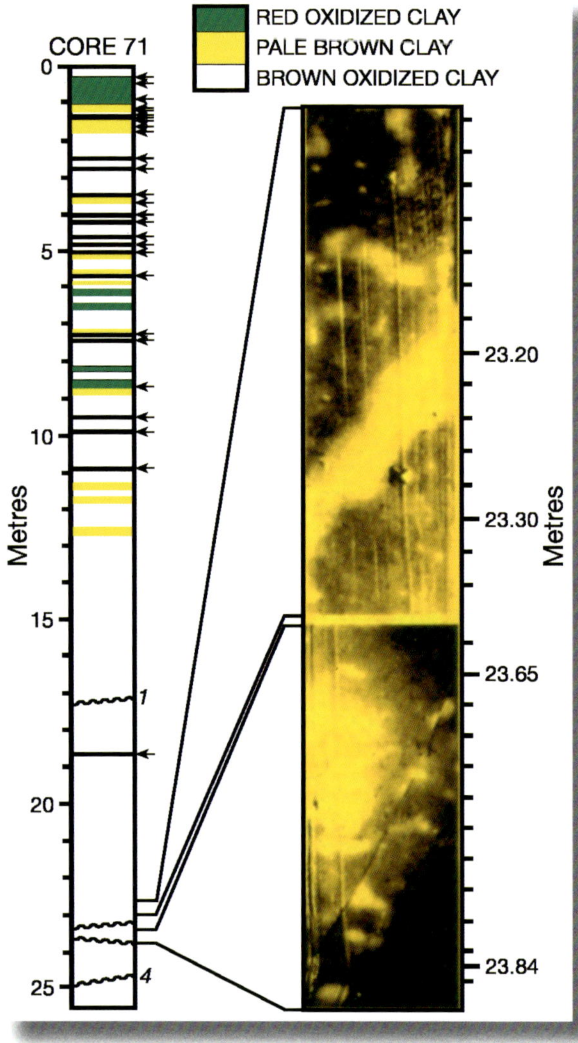

Figure 8. Log and x-radiograph of a core section containing fractures, the upper one at 23.2 m with an alteration halo from pore fluid migration along the fracture plane.

Samples acquired by the CSS *Hudson* expeditions were also studied at BIO for the role of biological processes in creating transport pathways of leached waste products into the abyssal food web (Gordon et al. 2014c). During the latter part of the 1980s, laboratory analyses were completed on thousands of samples obtained by the long coring device. These data, together with survey results, allowed a preliminary assessment to be made of the potential waste disposal sites in the SNAP and GMEAP. It was decided that neither site was entirely suitable for selection as a waste disposal site (Shephard et al. 1988). This was due to the presence of sand lenses in the sediments from the GMEAP, limited consistent sediment type in SNAP, and the presence of faults and fractures in both areas.

China Connection

By 1979, scientists from China were visiting BIO beginning with Y. Wang. In 1982 contact was made with oceanographic scientists at the institutes of oceanographic science in several Chinese cities. G. Vilks visited three institutes during 1981 and established contacts for future scientific exchange. In the following year, an exchange was arranged with D. Buckley representing Canada. Subsequently, a series of 33 lectures were given by D. Buckley at Beijing, Quingdao, Nanjing, Hang Zhou, Xiamen, and Quangshou during his visit. These lectures and some additional information were combined into a single volume that was translated into Chinese and published as a textbook for Chinese oceanographers (Buckley 1984). During his 1983 visit, D. Buckley participated in the planning for a multidisciplinary study of the Chang Jiang (Yangtze) River Estuary, southeast China.

RMS *Titanic* Corrosion

In the late 1980s, extensive searches were underway to find the wreck of RMS *Titanic* in deep water off the southeastern margin of the Grand Banks of Newfoundland. A Russian research vessel equipped with manned submersibles visited the wreck near the bottom of the slope of the Grand Banks (Fig. 9). This was of immediate interest to many people as the wreck had not been seen by anyone since it sank in 1912. Arrangements were made to have the Russian submarine obtain samples of the metal from the deck of the RMS *Titanic*. Some of these samples were returned to BIO for chemical and mineralogical analyses. It was found that the *Titanic* is corroding by biogeochemical processes stimulated by bacteria (Stoffyn-Egli and Buckley 1993).

Scotian Shelf Basins

A re-examination of some of the well-known features of the continental shelf was undertaken at this time. These included some examination of the geological processes dominating the basins and depressions on the Scotian Shelf. Although Emerald Basin and LaHave Basin (Fig. 1) had been surveyed before to compile the marine geological maps of these features within the Scotian Shelf, there had not been detailed studies of the

Figure 9. Forward deck of RMS *Titanic* with deck winches highly corroded by bacterial activity (image taken by the MIR-2 submersible operated by the Russian Academy of Sciences Akademik Kalydysh, courtesy of IMAX Corporation).

sedimentological and geochemical processes. Thus, the studies in the late 1980s attempted to fill some of the gaps by taking core samples within the basins. Research on the nature of marine sediments in Emerald Basin showed that there was a nearly continuous record of sedimentation for the past 14,000 years (Buckley 1991).

Halifax Harbour

Since its founding in 1749, domestic and industrial waste from Halifax, Nova Scotia, was not treated before discharge into the harbour (Fig.1). As a result, carbon-rich waste and chemical residues accumulated in bottom sediments, especially along the shipyards and off the domestic sewers (Fig. 10A). The water column also received waste chemicals that dispersed with the dominant currents and winds. The two main current systems in Halifax Harbour are the flood tide and the ebb tide. The ebb tidal currents are mainly the result of fresh water flow from the Sackville River that enters the northwest end of the harbour at Bedford Bay (Fig. 10A). This flow is heavily dependent on rainfall and season of the year. On average the fresh water flow is about one tenth of the tidal flow, so the flushing power of the fresh water flow is relatively weak and the system is dominated by the tidal currents. As a consequence of these characteristics, Halifax Harbour is not deemed to be a well-flushed system.

Several discrete zones of high concentrations of mercury were evident in the harbour sediments (Fig. 10B). These zones reflect poor harbour flushing. As an example, a point source of mercury contamination off the shipping terminal in the southern part of the western side of the harbour between McNabs Island and Halifax is distinct (Fig. 10B), and demonstrates that very little of the metal is flushed from this site out to sea. It appears that this condition has existed for over 100 years as shown by the profiles of enhanced contaminant metal since 1900 in sediment cores taken from the harbour (Fig. 11; Buckley and Winters 1992). These results played an important role in the development of recommendations for the design of a sewage treatment system by the Halifax Harbour Task Force (Fournier 1990).

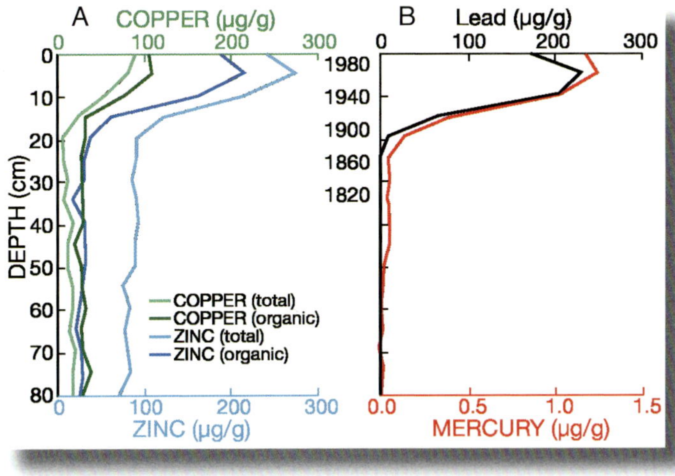

Figure 11. Profiles of metals in sediment cores taken from south central Halifax Harbour: (A) concentration versus depth, and (B) concentration versus calendar date.

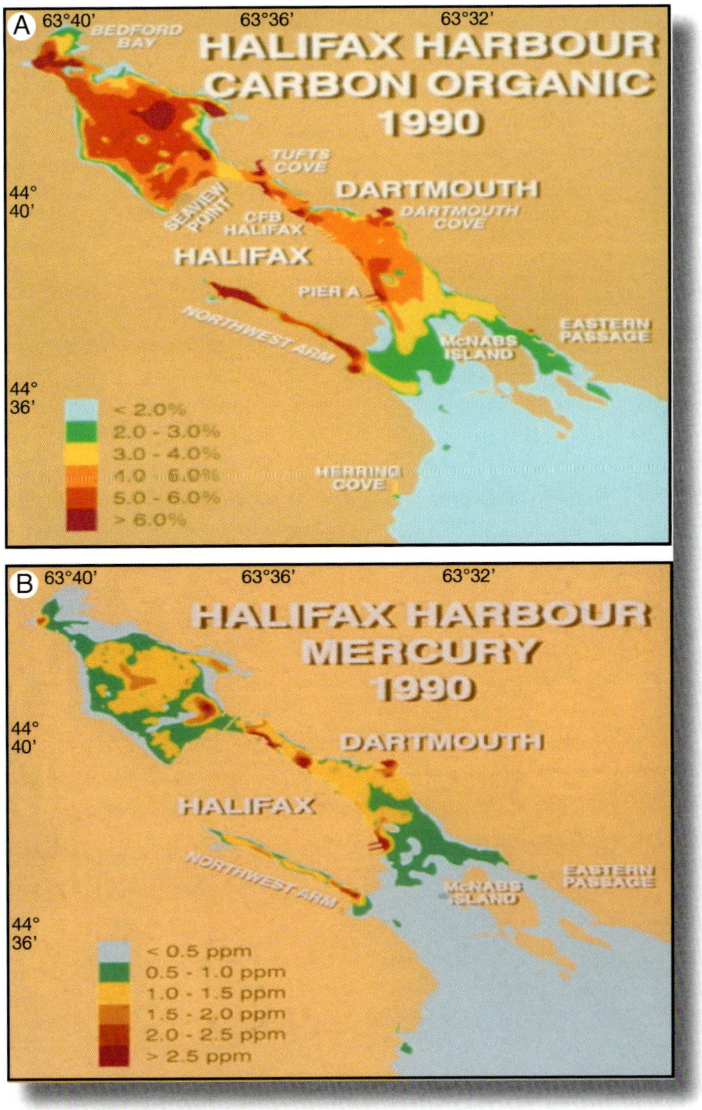

Figure 10. Organic carbon and mercury in surficial sediments of Halifax Harbour, 1990: (A) organic carbon, and (B) mercury.

THE FUTURE

Over the years, the research carried out by the Environmental Marine Geology group and associates has enhanced our understanding of marine processes and indicated ways in which the environmental quality of the deep-sea and nearshore areas may be managed. Over the last decade and continuing, M. Parsons has been extending this type of research to include assessment of unhealthy metals such as arsenic deposited in tailings from former gold mining sites in Nova Scotia. Some of the findings of environmental quality in nearshore and estuarine environments also indicate how long it has taken for some environmental problems to be recognized. As can be seen from our brief review of environmental studies at BIO, the sensitivity of our investigations has improved over the years and we are now able to project the feasibility of various waste management strategies. Clearly, indiscriminate waste dumping is no longer acceptable and that even well-considered waste disposal options must be critically examined. The experience gained and methods of study developed at BIO will be important in the future to ensure that Canadian marine environments are sustainably developed and managed.

ACKNOWLEDGEMENTS

I acknowledge the importance of BIO ships, facilities and scientific community for these studies, and I thank the many colleagues and collaborators in the Atlantic Geoscience Centre (later Geological Survey of Canada Atlantic), in other components of BIO, and from institutions elsewhere who have contributed to the program of geochemical and multidisciplinary projects in Environmental Marine Geology highlighted in this article. These include: C.L. Amos, K.W. Asprey, J.M. Bewers, L.C. Brown, D. Clattenburg, R.E. Cranston, J.A. Dalziel, R. Fanjoy, R.A. Fitzgerald, M. Gardner, J.N. Gearing, B.T. Hargrave, S. Hughes, D.P. Krauel, E. Larsen, D. Lawrence, C.F.T. Lay, W.K.G. LeBlanc, J. Leonard, T.C. Loder, B. Long, D.H. Loring, I.D. MacCauley, M. McIntosh, E.H. Owens, D.L. Peer, S. Penney, C.L. Perkins, B. D. Petrie, N.J. Prouse, R.T.T. Rantala, M.A. Rashid, K.R. Robertson, S. Salomon, C.T. Schafer, L.E. Shephard, A. Sherin, J.N. Smith, M. Stoffyn, P. Stoffyn-Egli, B. Sundby, G. Vilks, F.J.E. Wagner, T. Willar, J.D. Willey, G.V. Winters, and P.A. Yeats.

REFERENCES

Buckley, D.E. 1969. Sedimentological studies at Malpeque Bay, Prince Edward Island. Atlantic Oceanographic Laboratory Report 69-3. Dartmouth, NS.

Buckley, D.E. 1984. Multidisciplinary studies in the marine sciences. China Ocean Press, Beijing, China (translated by Second Institute of Oceanography, National Bureau of Oceanography).

Buckley, D. E. 1991. Deposition and diagenetic alteration of sediments in Emerald Basin, The Scotian Shelf. Continental Shelf Research 11: 1,099-1,122.

Buckley, D.E. and A. C. Grant. 1964. A preliminary statement on a sedimentological study of the beach and marine area at Belledune Point, Chaleur Bay, New Brunswick. Bedford Institute of Oceanography Report 64-12, Dartmouth, NS.

Buckley, D.E. and R.E. Cranston. 1971. Geochemical data for an Alaskan fjord. Atlantic Oceanographic Laboratory Report 1971-8-D, Dartmouth, NS.

Buckley, D.E. and G.V. Winters. 1983. Geochemical transport through Miramichi Estuary. Canadian Journal of Fisheries and Aquatic Sciences 40 (Supplement 2): 162-182.

Buckley, D.E. and A.C. Grant. 1985. Faultlike features in abyssal plain sediments: possible dewatering structures. Journal of Geophysical Research 90: 9,173-9,180.

Buckley, D.E. and R.E. Cranston. 1988. Early diagenesis in deep sea turbidites: the imprint of paleo-oxidation zones. Geochimica et Cosmochimica Acta 52: 2,925-2,939.

Buckley, D.E. and G.V. Winters. 1992. Geochemical characteristics of contaminated surficial sediments in Halifax Harbour: impact of waste discharge. Canadian Journal of Earth Sciences 29: 2,617-2,639.

Buckley, D.E., E.H. Owens, C.T. Schafer, G. Vilks, R.E. Cranston, M.A. Rashid, F.J.E. Wagner, and D.A. Walker. 1974. Canso Strait and Chedabucto Bay: a multidisciplinary study of the impact of man on the marine environment. Pages 133-160 *in* Offshore Geology of Eastern Canada, Volume 1: Concepts and Applications in Environmental Marine Geology (B.R. Pelletier, Ed.). Geological Survey of Canada Paper 74-30, Ottawa, ON.

Cranston R.E. and D.E. Buckley. 1973. Mercury pathways in a river and estuary. Environmental Science and Technology 6: 274-278.

Fader, G.B.J., B. MacLean, H.W. Josenhans, and S.M. Blasco. 2014. Seabed sediment mapping at the Bedford Institute of Oceanography: from single beam to multibeam. Pages 191-199 *in* Voyage of Discovery: Fifty Years of Marine Research at Canada's Bedford Institute of Oceanography (D.N. Nettleship, D.C. Gordon, C.F.M. Lewis, and M.P Latremouille, Eds.). Bedford Institute of Oceanography-Oceans Association, Dartmouth, NS.

Fournier, R.O. 1990. Halifax Harbour Task Force Final Report, Nova Scotia Department of Environment, Halifax, NS.

Gordon, D.C., K. Lee, P.G. Wells, and P.D. Keizer. 2014a. The impacts of oil and gas activities on the marine environment. Pages 361-371 *in* Voyage of Discovery: Fifty Years of Marine Research at Canada's Bedford Institute of Oceanography (D.N. Nettleship, D.C. Gordon, C.F.M. Lewis, and M.P. Latremouille, Eds.). Bedford Institute of Oceanography-Oceans Association, Dartmouth, NS.

Gordon, D.C., C.L. Amos, D.A. Greenberg, P.C. Smith, and G.B.J. Fader. 2014b. Understanding the macrotidal environment of the Bay of Fundy and the impacts of tidal power development. Pages 373-382 *in* Voyage of Discovery: Fifty Years of Marine Research at Canada's Bedford Institute of Oceanography (D.N. Nettleship, D.C. Gordon, C.F.M. Lewis, and M.P Latremouille, Eds.). Bedford Institute of Oceanography-Oceans Association, Dartmouth, NS.

Gordon, D.C., E.L.R. Kenchington, B.T. Hargrave, and D.L. Peer. 2014c. Life at the bottom of the sea: advances in understanding benthic ecosystems. Pages 87-97 *in* Voyage of Discovery: Fifty Years of Marine Research at Canada's Bedford Institute of Oceanography (D.N. Nettleship, D.C. Gordon, C.F.M. Lewis, and M.P Latremouille, Eds.). Bedford Institute of Oceanography-Oceans Association, Dartmouth, NS.

Lambert, T.C., G.C. Harding, K.F. Drinkwater, and B.T. Hargrave. 2014. St. Georges Bay ecosystem study: an exercise in interdisciplinary science. Pages 105-112 *in* Voyage of Discovery: Fifty Years of Marine Research at Canada's Bedford Institute of Oceanography (D.N. Nettleship, D.C. Gordon, C.F.M. Lewis, and M.P. Latremouille, Eds.). Bedford Institute of Oceanography-Oceans Association, Dartmouth, NS.

Lewis, C.F.M., S.M. Blasco, D.J.W. Piper, and G.V. Sonnichsen. 2014. Seabed geohazard knowledge for safe hydrocarbon development. Pages 383-394 *in* Voyage of Discovery: Fifty Years of Marine Research at Canada's Bedford Institute of Oceanography (D.N. Nettleship, D.C. Gordon, C.F.M. Lewis, and M.P. Latremouille, Eds.). Bedford Institute of Oceanography-Oceans Association, Dartmouth, NS.

Owens, E.H. 1978. Mechanical dispersion of oil stranded in the littoral zone. Journal of the Fisheries Research Board of Canada 35: 563-572.

Schafer, C.T. 2014. Living and postglacial foraminifera and their environmental applications. Pages 237-245 *in* Voyage of Discovery: Fifty Years of Marine Research at Canada's Bedford Institute of Oceanography (D.N. Nettleship, D.C. Gordon, C.F.M. Lewis, and M.P. Latremouille, Eds.). Bedford Institute of Oceanography-Oceans Association, Dartmouth, NS.

Shephard, L.E., G.A. Auffret, D.E. Buckley, R.T.E. Schuttenhelm, and R.C. Searle. 1988. Feasibility of disposal of high-level radioactive waste into the seabed: geoscience characterization studies. Sandia Report SAND87-1913, UC 70, Sandia National Laboratories, Albuquerque, NM.

Stoffyn-Egli, P. and D.E. Buckley. 1993. What is happening to the TITANIC? Pages 12-13 in Electron Microscopy Newsletter, Texas A & M University, College Station, TX.

Taylor, R.B., D.L. Forbes, D. Frobel, G.K. Manson, and J. Shaw. 2014. Coastal geoscience studies at the Bedford Institute of Oceanography, 1962-2012. Pages 203-210 *in* Voyage of Discovery: Fifty Years of Marine Research at Canada's Bedford Institute of Oceanography (D.N. Nettleship, D.C. Gordon, C.F.M. Lewis, and M.P. Latremouille, Eds.). Bedford Institute of Oceanography-Oceans Association, Dartmouth, NS.

Williams, G.L., R.A. Fensome, and S.A. Dehler. 2014. Rocks of the deep: the subsurface geology of offshore eastern Canada. Pages 215-223 *in* Voyage of Discovery: Fifty Years of Marine Research at Canada's Bedford Institute of Oceanography (D.N. Nettleship, D.C. Gordon, C.F.M. Lewis, and M.P. Latremouille, Eds.). Bedford Institute of Oceanography-Oceans Association, Dartmouth, NS.

Fisheries, Ecosystems & Aquaculture

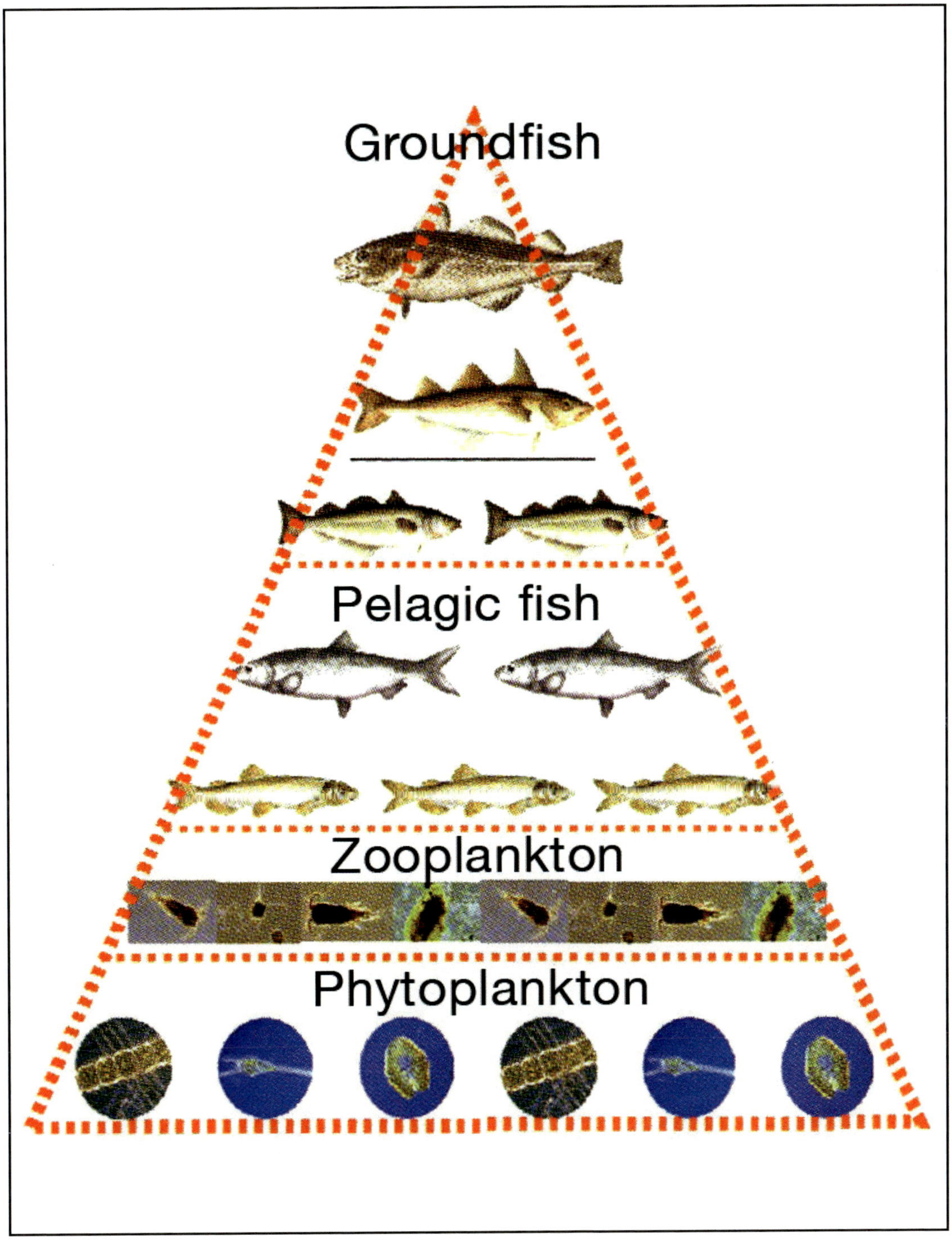

Simplified food chain on the Scotian Shelf, Nova Scotia

Fisheries, Ecosystems, and Aquaculture

30. ECOSYSTEM MANAGEMENT BRANCH AT THE BEDFORD INSTITUTE OF OCEANOGRAPHY: FRONT LINE FOR OCEAN POLICY DEVELOPMENT AND MANAGEMENT

Odette C. Murphy*, André J. Ducharme, Jason G. Naug, Paul A. Macnab, and Catherine B. Merriman

SUMMARY

The emergence of the Habitat Management, Oceans, and Species at Risk programs in Fisheries and Oceans Canada-Maritimes Region and their roles in relation to Bedford Institute of Oceanography-Science are described. The mandate of each program, in relation to its legislative and policy basis, is summarized with major achievements highlighted. Collectively, the three programs have contributed significantly to an improved management and sustainable use of marine and freshwater environments. The structure and organization of the programs developed over a 25-year period in relation to amendments and the introduction of new legislation and policies. The programs are poised for further change with legislative and policy reviews currently underway.

Key words: ecosystem management, habitat management, ocean and coastal management, species at risk management, operational programs, management of freshwater and marine environments, BIO Science, Fisheries Act, Oceans Act, Species at Risk Act, Canadian Environmental Assessment Act, fish habitat policy.
***E-mail:** Odette.Murphy@dfo-mpo.gc.ca

Ecosystem Management is about managing human activities that impact on habitats and resources they sustain. It denotes an operational sector of Fisheries and Oceans Canada (DFO) at the Bedford Institute of Oceanography (BIO) that relies on the results of marine research and ecosystem-based science to aid the decision-making process on how to manage human activity in relation to fisheries resources and fish habitats. Through three key programs – Habitat Management, Oceans, Species at Risk – and in close collaboration with BIO Science, Ecosystem Management helps DFO meet its obligations to ensure sustainable use of our ocean, coastal, and freshwater resources under the federal Fisheries Act, Canadian Environmental Assessment Act (CEAA), Oceans Act, and Species at Risk Act (SARA).

In contrast to most other papers in 'Voyage of Discovery' which focus largely on scientific achievements, this review article attempts to show the essence of Ecosystem Management's programs, the evolution of their linkages to BIO Science, major accomplishments, and key roles played in shaping improvements to the management of marine and freshwater habitat resources in the DFO Maritimes Region of eastern Canada. The paper also outlines the legislative and policy context, and provides overviews of the Branch's three major programs: Habitat Management, Oceans, and Species at Risk. At the end, a brief synopsis is given that includes an outlook on emerging issues and challenges.

LEGISLATIVE AND POLICY CONTEXT

Mandates for federal departments and agencies are derived from Acts of Parliament. They are further refined by policies and regulations pursuant to those Acts and carried out through the establishment and delivery of specific programs. The mandate of Ecosystem Management is derived from the Fish Habitat Provisions of the Fisheries Act, CEAA, Oceans Act, and SARA. The significance of these Acts to the three Ecosystem Management programs to 2012 is summarized in Appendix A with a list of supporting strategy and policy documents.

The protection of fish and their habitats against harmful human activity falls under the purview of the Fisheries Act of Canada. This powerful legal document dates back to Confederation (1867). It was amended in 1985 to introduce specific fish habitat protection provisions. In 1986, to put these enhanced protection measures into practice, DFO introduced a 'Policy for the Management of Fish Habitat' (DFO 1986). This important document, known as the Habitat Policy, became a key guidance document for departmental officials and other interested parties for the ensuing 25 years. It introduced a long term policy objective of overall 'Net Gain' and an ambitious guiding principle of 'No Net Loss' of the productive capacity of fish habitats. The Habitat Policy further sets forth goals of fish habitat conservation – supported by the 'No Net Loss' principle – as well as restoration and development, which together contribute to the achievement of 'Net Gain' of habitat for the nation's fisheries resources. In addition, implementation strategies were prescribed to allow for development to proceed where the loss of fish habitat was deemed acceptable and could be compensated to achieve 'No Net Loss'. Currently, the Habitat Management Program continues to be guided by the Fisheries Act and associated legislation and policy. However, changes in the legislative and policy basis for the Habitat Management Program is underway, and as a consequence, the review given below pertains to how the program was carried out between 1986 and 2012.

Following the Fisheries Act amendments in 1985 and the companion Habitat Policy (DFO 1986) that introduced powerful federal controls over pollution and marine habitat, DFO released an oceans policy discussion paper calling for a new act that would create the legislative basis for oceans management in Canada (DFO 1987). Pressures from growth industry sectors (e.g., aquaculture and hydrocarbon production, Atlantic Groundfish Moratorium) and global events (e.g., World Summit on Sustainable Development, Code of Conduct for Responsible Fisheries, and Convention on Biological Diversity) brought about the initiation of a framework for legislation of Canada's oceans (National Advisory Board on Science and Technology 1994). The resulting Oceans Act received Royal Assent in December 1996 and came into force on 31 January 1997, which made Canada the first nation in the world to have comprehensive oceans management legislation.

The three parts of the Oceans Act laid the foundations for modern oceans governance in Canada. Part I defines Canada's maritime territory, including the declaration of an Exclusive Economic Zone in accordance with the provisions of United Nations Convention on the Law of the Sea (UNCLOS; see Verhoef et al. 2014). Part II assigns a leadership role to the Minister of DFO for oceans stewardship and the management of all activities in or affecting estuarine, coastal and marine ecosystems in Canadian waters. Part III clarifies and consolidates federal oceans responsibilities. Overall, the Oceans Act enshrines the fundamental principles of sustainable development, the precautionary approach and integrated management, and calls for collaborative and cooperative management arrangements that respect assigned constitutional and legislative responsibilities including Aboriginal and treaty rights. A parallel effort was invested in policy development to interpret the intent of the Oceans Act and to help guide practitioners in the delivery of key program areas that developed from the legislation (for details, see Appendix A).

Similarly over a nine-year time frame, initiatives were underway to develop an Act to protect wildlife in Canada. The resulting Species at Risk Act received Royal Assent on 12 December 2002 and came into effect in two phases. Listing, stewardship, and recovery components were enacted in June 2003, while prohibitions and enforcement provisions came into force in June 2004. SARA is an important tool for conserving and protecting Canada's biodiversity, and is administered by Environment Canada with DFO and Parks Canada sharing responsibility for its implementation and management. DFO is responsible for aquatic species listed under SARA, which are defined as all life stages of fish, shellfish, crustaceans, marine animals and marine plants. SARA complements the Fisheries Act and Oceans Act which protect and conserve species not listed under SARA. SARA establishes a process for conducting scientific assessments of the conservation status of individual wildlife species (plant and animal) and provides a mechanism for listing species assessed as extirpated, endangered, threatened, or of special concern. SARA provides legal protection to listed wildlife species and their critical habitat, and requires the preparation of recovery documents for listed species within prescribed timeframes.

LINKAGES WITH SCIENCE

After 1985, the legislative and policy context contributed to fish habitat resource managers being faced with making decisions that impacted both habitat resources and project developers. The multidisciplinary aspect and complexity of many projects combined with potential impacts on fish habitat often caused habitat managers to seek advice from research scientists within BIO. To facilitate easy access to this scientific expertise, the Marine Assessment and Liaison Division (MALD) was established at BIO in 1987 (MacPhee et al. 1988). MALD coordinated requests necessitating input from more than one specialist group, and by doing so, allowed scientists and managers to work together to make scientifically-based decisions on proposed development projects. Ducharme (1992) provides details of the mechanism for interaction between BIO scientists and habitat managers. The types of research advice and the role of BIO in addressing fish habitat impact issues in the coastal zone in support of management decisions during the MALD years (1987-96) are well documented (e.g., Nicholls 1989, 1993; Boudreau 1994).

Although MALD was terminated in 1996, the cooperative relationship between BIO Science and the Habitat group in Ecosystems Management continues. At present, formal science advice is provided by BIO's Centre for Science Advice to all DFO groups including Habitat, Oceans, Species at Risk, as well as Fisheries Management (O'Boyle et al. 2014). The Centre for Science Advice provides a mechanism to coordinate expert advice and peer review of scientific response issues and management questions, including urgent and unforeseen requests, posed by DFO operational programs in the Maritimes Region. Through this process, biologists and managers within the Habitat Management Program are able to make informed decisions on a wide range of projects such as: Tidal In-Stream Energy Conversion pilot project in Minas Basin, deepening of Sydney Harbour Channel, and Sydport Container Terminal in Cape Breton.

An equally important area of cooperation that emerged between BIO Science and Ecosystem Management programs over the years is their co-participation on a number of internal working groups and external advisory committees. Numerous examples exist in all three Ecosystem Management programs, ranging from committees to advance Working Agreements under the Habitat Management Program, Species at Risk Recovery Teams to Stakeholder Advisory Committees established under the Oceans Program.

While the Habitat Management and Oceans programs are regular users of formal advice from BIO's Centre for Science Advice, the Species at Risk Program is the most heavily dependent on the formal science advisory process offered by the Centre. Science advice ensures that SARA listing recommendations, planning processes, and recovery actions are based on the best available scientific information. An essential element of the Species at Risk Program delivery is a core coordination role across operational sectors of DFO which have a degree of shared responsibility under the SARA legislation. This is a key role of the Species at Risk Management Division of Ecosystem Management, together with its lead responsibility for listing recommendations and recovery planning. To that end, the Species at Risk Management Division coordinates essential input from BIO Science to the assessment of species status, the identification of critical habitat for listed species, the implementation of recovery activities, and monitoring the success of recovery measures. The Species at Risk Management Division also solicits input from BIO Science about Habitat Stewardship Program funding proposals. Examples of such collaborations are well represented among the major accomplishments of the Species at Risk Program.

Though formal advice received from the Centre for Science Advice and via co-participation on external committees are indispensable to all three Ecosystem Management programs, decisions are achieved through a regional governance process and not through a direct function of co-location. However, it remains clear that many important stakeholder partnerships and collaborations undertaken by Ecosystem Management have been with the BIO scientific community. The decision to locate the Ecosystem Management sector at BIO, Canada's premier marine research centre, has provided invaluable benefits to the development of operational programs in the Maritimes Region. The multidisciplinary strengths and team building customs that characterize BIO have been instrumental for implementing science-based approaches to the management of oceans, habitat, and species at risk. Placing marine planners, habitat biologists, conservation practitioners, and ocean managers with scientific, engineering and technical specialists from diverse fields has engendered collective learning and joint problem solving. A distinct community of practice has been created in the process. Innovations, trail-blazing, and national/international leadership in ocean management and marine environmental protection are undoubtedly the result of co-location, the efficient exchange and transfer of information from genuine collegiality that exists at BIO.

The nature of the collaborative success experienced at BIO is evidenced by the many co-sponsored workshops, team authorship on technical documents and academic papers, shared priority setting, precautionary decision-making, cooperative cruise planning, leading-edge data handling partnerships and cross assignments. A fruitful and productive two-way exchange of knowledge has allowed scientists and managers to better understand, appreciate, and respond to the needs of each other and to ocean management *per se*. This has ultimately helped scientists provide the kinds of fundamental and applied science required for biophysical description, ecosystem-based management, conservation planning and risk assessment – all foundations for contemporary ocean management, recovery of species at risk, and habitat protection. Overall, Ecosystem Management staff at BIO learned first-hand about the conduct of offshore and coastal marine science by co-writing proposals, participating in field work and contributing to peer reviews. The resulting enhanced awareness of science processes has allowed staff within Ecosystem Management to better explain information needs to scientists in ways that satisfy both manifest and latent research interests. The combined BIO effort to study, monitor, and manage hydrocarbon exploration pressures vividly illustrates the nature and benefits of inter-branch multidisciplinary collaboration (see Text Box 1).

HABITAT MANAGEMENT PROGRAM

All living creatures have a preferred living space without which their numbers dwindle and eventually disappear. The valuable fishery resource of Canada's marine and freshwater regions is no exception to this universal rule.

History

From the late 1960s to the late 1980s fish habitat protection was delivered by a small group within the Freshwater and Anadromous Branch of DFO Science, called the Stream Alteration Unit. Initially its operation was confined primarily to inland areas (i.e., lakes and streams) and marine shorelines of the Maritimes Region.

In 1985, amendments to the Fisheries Act introduced section 35 (1) which stated that: "No person shall carry out any work or undertaking that results in harmful alteration, disruption or destruction of fish habitat." DFO's first response to this new responsibility was to develop the 1986 Policy for the Management of Fish Habitat (DFO 1986). Secondly, DFO established resource manager groups in all six DFO Regions of the country. The Habitat Management Program of the Maritimes Region

Text Box 1: Collaboration at BIO
Monitoring and Management of Hydrocarbon Exploration

Convergent mandates and program responsibilities often make intra- and inter-branch collaboration essential. When plans were announced to acquire seismic data near The Gully, Marine Protected Area (MPA), and its endangered population of acoustically sensitive Northern Bottlenose Whales (*Hyperoodon ampullatus*), a central issue for environmental assessment and related decision-making was the potential effect of intense underwater noise. Consultations with the proponent and regulator commenced immediately. With limited knowledge available to the newly-formed Ecosystem Management Branch on the stressor and appropriate mitigation measure, or the technical requirements for *in-situ* monitoring, the need for BIO engagement had never been greater. Could Ecosystem Management predict the vulnerabilities and allow hydrocarbon exploration to proceed without imposing unnecessary restrictions or costs on industry?

The multidisciplinary strengths and BIO team-building customs were leveraged to support the precautionary nature of the situation. The Science Advisory Committee for Offshore Petroleum Activities examined the proponent's environmental impact assessment and a team of scientists mobilized to assemble an acoustic effects monitoring program. Habitat Management allowed seismic activity to proceed once this program and other safeguards were in place. Researchers were on hand to observe Northern Bottlenose Whale behaviours while simultaneously recording exploration sounds with Geological Survey of Canada ocean-bottom seismometers. The partnership proved effective on many fronts: protection goals were implemented, innovative expertise was applied on short notice, knowledge gains were made, conservation policy was enhanced, and future decision-making was clarified for industry. Results were published (Lee et al. 2005) and the information has been used by Ecosystem Management to inform environmental assessment, MPA management, and the species-at-risk recovery team for planning to this day.

became officially operational in 1987. This group, made up partly from Stream Alteration Unit staff, became the focal point for all habitat-related matters in both marine and freshwater environments of the Maritimes Region. The Habitat Management Program group was first stationed near the Halifax waterfront in 1987, and then relocated to BIO in 1999.

An important element in the history of the Habitat Management Program is its close collaboration with the Maritime Provinces, an association that began in the late 1970s. Provincial 'low risk guidelines' (LRG) were formulated for certain types of work known to pose minimal risk to fish habitat. These LRG were updated in 1994 to help consolidate the 'One-Window' approach implemented jointly by DFO Maritimes and Gulf Regions with the Provinces of Nova Scotia, New Brunswick, and Prince Edward Island. The 'One-Window' approach simplifies the review procedure by allowing the proponent of a project to submit its application to a single government department that coordinates the exchange of information between the regulatory authorities. The approach increases the efficiency of the process greatly. The Habitat Management Program and the Provinces also collaborated on the development of certification processes for specific industry sectors (e.g., forestry) to institute best practices among its practitioners for minimizing the impact on fish habitat and the need for project reviews.

Mandate and Function

The increasing demand for oil and gas developments, aquaculture, tidal energy, and coastal development are just some of the areas that may impact fish and fish habitats. The Habitat Management Program plays a vital role in the conservation and protection of fish habitat in Canada by working to address impacts from these emerging land-uses on or near water, as well as those associated with traditional uses of road and bridge construction, commercial and residential developments, wharves, and breakwaters.

The Habitat Management Program relies on a range of approaches to address the potential impacts to fish and their habitats resulting from development in or near marine and freshwater environments. Each approach is based on the potential risk the proposed activity represents and whether the activity might result in the harmful alteration, disruption, or destruction (HADD) of fish habitat. Low risk projects are streamlined through the provincial 'One-Window' referral process. Where the risks are greater, a 'Letter of Advice' may be issued that includes the mitigation measures that should be used to avoid harmful impacts. For projects where DFO issues a HADD Authorization, the proponent must follow a number of conditions aimed at mitigating or compensating for the expected habitat damage at a prescribed ratio to ensure a 'No Net Loss' requirement is achieved.

In order to ensure that proponents follow the advice and guidance provided by the Habitat Management Program – i.e., Low Risk Guidelines, Letters of Advice, or HADD Authorization – a Habitat Compliance Monitoring Program is now in place. This monitoring program assesses compliance with the conditions set by Habitat Management both during and after construction. Collection of these monitoring data allows the Habitat Management Program to adapt its operations, engage relevant sectors, and ensure proponents remain in compliance with the objectives of the Habitat Policy. DFO Conservation and Protection officers assist with enforcement action in instances of non-compliance, as do their provincial counterparts.

The DFO Habitat Management Program also pursues a range of stewardship and partnering initiatives, including numerous formal Working Agreements with external partners who help promote not only compliance, but also pro-active planning with habitat provisions of the Fisheries Act in mind. Many of these collaborations are supported by DFO Science at BIO whose representatives either sit on Steering Committees established under formal Working Agreements or conduct research in support of specific projects. A project to assess the effectiveness of 'Artificial Reef Balls' as an appropriate means of habitat compensation illustrates this type of collaboration (see Text Box 2).

Major Accomplishments

Since its formation in 1987, the Habitat Management Program has worked hard to implement the fish habitat provisions of the Fisheries Act and help make the objectives contained in the national 'Policy for the Management of Fish Habitat' operational. A range of tools and techniques have been used by the Habitat Management Program over the years to accomplish these goals in addition to strategies generated from discussions with DFO Science at BIO.

In the late 1980s and early 1990s, Habitat Management Program managers focussed on communication and education activities such as habitat seminars, presentations to the Road Builders Association of Nova Scotia and to graduating classes of engineers. Performance tended to be measured in terms of successful court actions against extreme offenders of the Fisheries Act fish habitat provisions. For example, between 1987 and 1994, the Habitat Management group, in co-operation with DFO Conservation and Protection staff, engaged in 16 successful court actions. Initially, the fines levied by the courts were low, failing as deterrents against future offenses, and none of the fine proceeds could be used for environmental repairs or mitigation. Gradually, with the help of crown legal counsels, Habitat Management Program managers succeeded in having the courts alter penalties from fines to mitigation, restoration or compensation orders based on the habitat damage actually done. Notwithstanding the deterrent value of court actions *per se*, the consent of the court to order habitat repairs was considered a significant success.

Over the years, primarily through continued development and enhancement of partnering and stewardship initiatives with the provincial governments and key proponents, the focus shifted toward prevention and mitigation of damage, as well as the restoration of habitat. While the current 'performance indicators' used in DFO performance reports focus on the numbers of 'Letters of Advice' and 'Authorizations' issued annually by each DFO Region, more recent accomplishments show significant progress in terms of improved outcomes for fish habitat, proponents, partners, and stakeholders. Some highlights of these accomplishments follow:

- Strengthened by the provision of the Fisheries Act and supported by both the Habitat Policy and DFO Science, Habitat Management Program biologists entered into negotiations with the Departments of Highways and Agriculture of the three Maritime Provinces on works they were conducting in and around inland waters. These negotiations lead to the formation of a referral system that captured a wide range of work proposals in and around inland waters that previously went unmanaged.
- The LRG coupled with the 'One-Window' approach and provincially delivered certification processes in the forestry sector contributed to the reduction in project referrals that required DFO review, from close to 3,000 per year in 1996-97 and declining to 600-800 per year in each of the 2004-05 to 2011-12 fiscal years in the DFO Maritimes Region (W. Morrell unpubl., Habitat Program Services Branch, DFO, Ottawa, ON). The result is a more timely and efficient review and permit issuance process for proponents, an alignment of reviews with federal and provincial environmental regulations, and more time for Habitat Management Program biologists to concentrate on high risk undertakings. As a consequence, the provincial LRG developed in the Maritime Provinces has served as a model for the establishment of similar 'Operational Statements' by DFO Habitat Management Program nationally.
- The Habitat Management group received an Award of Environmental Excellence in 2002 by the International Erosion Control Association. Their submission documented the period from 1982 to 2001 during which the Habitat Management Program, together with the Centre for Water Resources Studies and various provincial and federal agencies, developed projects, studies and training materials that led to significant reductions or elimination of construction sediments in urban developments, pipeline projects, and highway construction on the water resources of Nova Scotia. The results also provided a useful example to other Canadian jurisdictions for consideration (B. Jollymore pers. comm.).
- Workshops, field assistance, technical support, and reviews of funding proposals were provided to Non-Government Organizations, communities, and individuals to build capacity and help optimize collaborative opportunities for fish habitat restoration activities in the region. Stewardship and community efforts to improve the state of fish habitat in the Maritime Provinces became more main-stream as a result and used restoration approaches endorsed by DFO.
- Formal working agreements were signed with Nova Scotia Power in 2008 and with New Brunswick Power in 2010 to incorporate fish habitat improvement strategies into the long-term capital planning of these large corporations. The agreements, which set out action plans and timelines for achieving them, promote compliance and accountability. They also provide an effective tool in advancing the DFO fish-passage requirements associated with hydro-electric facilities.
- In 2008, the Habitat Management Program was reorganized into three sections: Marine Habitat Protection, Freshwater Habitat Protection, and Operational Policy and Planning. The new structure allowed for better client-based service while strengthening the knowledge base in key areas such as marine habitat compensation, freshwater sediment and erosion control, and fish passage. In 2010, the Habitat Management Program expanded its ability to assess potential impacts of ongoing projects and proposals by acquiring a remotely-operated vehicle (ROV) that allowed habitat biologists to view vulnerable marine and freshwater habitats directly. The ROV is also used to monitor projects and assess compensation activities for compliance with the authorization issued.
- The Habitat Management Program has worked with DFO Small Craft Harbours, Nova Scotia Department of Transportation and Infrastructure Renewal, and New Brunswick Department of Transportation to create fish habitat banks throughout most of the Maritimes. Fish habitat banks are large habitat compensation projects created through the restoration, enhancement or creation

Text Box 2: Artificial Reef Balls

Given the increase in the use and development taking place in Canadian marine and coastal waters, the Habitat Management Program must ensure that appropriate habitat compensation takes place in affected areas. The challenge in doing so is choosing appropriate methods of compensation and ensuring their efficacy at replacing the habitat that is lost to any DFO-authorized development project. To this end, a good partnership took place between BIO Science and the Habitat Management Program in 2005 to assess the effectiveness of 'Artificial Reef Balls'. These are concrete beehive shaped structures designed to replace coral reefs damaged by storms or human impacts (Fig. 1A). In this case the reef balls were tested to see if they were a suitable replacement for benthic habitat lost to an 'infill' project in Halifax Harbour. A science program was developed that positioned 40 reef balls and monitored colonization by marine biota monthly over one year to assess their effectiveness as replacements for lost lobster habitat. The results indicated that the reef balls were colonized rapidly by 55 marine species present after 12 months (Fig. 1B). A canopy of kelp (*Laminaria* species) developed with several fish species (e.g., juvenile stages of fish, blennies, sculpins, snail fish, lumpfish and hake) inhabiting it for new food sources. The experiment also showed that reef balls were limited in their use as lobster replacement habitat, as each ball could only hold one lobster and were only occupied periodically through the year. In summary, the study showed that reef balls were not an optimal replacement for lobster habitat, but did serve to increase the overall complexity, productivity, and biodiversity of the site (Sharp et al. 2007). Based on this work, Habitat Management Program managers were able to make informed decisions about the use of this tool for compensation projects in marine environments.

Figure 1. Reef Balls: (A) placement of Reef Balls at Paddy's Head, St. Margaret's Bay, Nova Scotia, June 2005; and (B) stages in community development and habitat complexity of Reef Balls, June 2005 to May 2006 (from Sharp et al. 2007).

of fish habitat. The banks created to 2012 include Cheverie salt marsh, St. Frances Harbour, Sambro reef, and Aulac salt marsh, and are used to offset smaller, cumulative impacts to fish habitat as a result of multiple infrastructure projects over the years. This allows the 'No Net Loss' requirement under the 1986 Habitat Policy to be attained. In total, about 550,000 m^2 of salt marsh and estuarine habitat have been restored in Nova Scotia and New Brunswick through the establishment of these banks (M. McLean pers. comm.).

OCEANS PROGRAM

History

The Oceans Act Coordination Office, later renamed Oceans and Coastal Management Division (OCMD), was established at BIO in 1997, the same year the Oceans Act came into force to develop the Oceans Program as envisaged by the new legislation. This was the first regional structure created under the Oceans Act, predating the creation of a National Oceans Sector at DFO Headquarters in Ottawa. Cooperation and interaction with DFO scientists was at the core of the decision to locate the Office at BIO, as was the decision to draw on DFO Science personnel to complete the ranks of the original staff complement.

OCMD initiated several regional projects in the late 1990s to further develop Oceans Act program areas. By 1996, pressures associated with offshore hydrocarbon development made The Gully, a submarine canyon on the Scotian Shelf near Sable Island, a regional conservation priority owing to its ecological importance for a wide range of biota including deep sea coral, cetaceans, and seabirds (Macnab 2005). Two other MPA initiatives, both coastal sites with broad community and provincial support, were launched around the same time: the Musquash Estuary in southwest New Brunswick (Singh et al. 2000) and the Basin Head Lagoon in eastern Prince Edward Island (Boyd and Smith 2002, Sharp et al. 2003).

Canada's first Integrated Management project, the Eastern Scotian Shelf Integrated Management (ESSIM) initiative was launched in 1998 (Rutherford et al. 2005). ESSIM was intended to provide an umbrella for integrated sea-use planning and decision-making in offshore waters to the edge of the 200-mile Extended Economic Zone. Staff started to build the knowledge base and governance structures required of integrated oceans management while tackling emergent issues such as the conflict between fisheries and cables (Coffen-Smout and Herbert 2000). Meanwhile, the Bras d'Or Lakes in Cape Breton became a priority for coastal management. Compelled by the strong First Nations Mi'kmaq interest in maintaining and restoring the health of the Lakes, OCMD worked to build lasting relationships with all five First Nation Bands in Cape Breton under a Collaborative Environmental Planning Initiative (Parker et al. 2007).

These early projects anchored the Oceans Act and demonstrated its potential. OCMD initiatives provided for immediate application, testing, and further refinement of evolving program and policy frameworks, and related advice, including science-based approaches to achieving ecosystem-based ocean management (Curran et al. 2012, O'Boyle et al. 2014). OCMD capacity expanded between 1998 and 2002 to cover the wide range of knowledge, skills and expertise demanded of an office occupying the interface of marine science, oceans policy, and ocean-use decision making.

Mandate and Function

The Oceans Act laid the statutory foundation for modern oceans governance and management in Canada. Two major program areas evolved from the legislation: the integrated management of marine and coastal activities and MPAs. Both the Integrated Management and MPA programs are advanced using an ecosystem approach to management (i.e., places the ecosystem at the forefront of management considerations). Integrated Management provides for a consistent and coordinated approach to management of marine activities and ocean resources. The primary aim is to achieve a balance between sustainable economic activity and marine ecosystem conservation. This can be accomplished by developing and implementing Integrated Management plans though a transparent and collaborative governance process. MPAs are special areas of the sea protected by law to safeguard an important feature of the marine environment. Canada has committed to establishing a network of MPAs across the country to help meet a range of environmental and cultural conservation goals. OCMD works across DFO sectors with other federal and provincial departments and agencies to plan and implement this national network. OCMD also manages MPAs declared under the Oceans Act to protect important fish and mammal habitats, endangered species, unique features, and areas of high biodiversity and productivity.

Decision making in the marine domain typically requires the compilation of information obtained from the natural and social sciences along with economic, legal, cultural, and local knowledge sources. OCMD produces syntheses of existing information and reports of findings to assist planning processes and regulatory/operational decision making. Spatial decision support has developed as a core function of OCMD owing to the need for geographic data and visualization tools for ocean and coastal management. OCMD compiles maps of human uses including fisheries, shipping, and oil and gas activities (e.g., Breeze and Horsman 2005). Typical advisory and decision-making applications of this information include responding to environmental assessments, examining exploratory fisheries and habitat interactions, undertaking conflict analyses, designing MPA sites and networks, assessing risk in space and time, and selecting stations for research cruises. Geospatial tools are also employed for statutory purposes such as the delineation, surveillance, and control of MPAs, coral conservation areas, and SARA critical habitats.

Meaningful engagement and effective collaboration is central to the work of OCMD. Coordination and partnerships with the many levels and departments of government involved in regulating and managing marine activities are critical to attaining management goals. The involvement of interested and affected parties – the users, stewards, and would-be guardians of Canada's oceans – is also essential. OCMD has fostered close ties with Aboriginal groups, industry sectors, academics, coastal communities, and conservation organizations using a variety of methods to engage groups and individuals. Formal governance mechanisms include the ESSIM Stakeholder Advisory Council (Rutherford et al. 2005, Government of Canada 2007, Arbour 2009) and MPA Advisory Committees struck for The Gully and Musquash MPAs. OCMD plays an important role in activities of other groups such as the Gulf of Maine Council on the Marine Environment. Raising public awareness of the importance of Canada's oceans is another key role for OCMD. To that end, OCMD participates in outreach events and develops educational materials, including the 'Oceans 11' science curriculum developed with the Nova Scotia Department of Education.

Major Accomplishments

Many actions have been taken by OCMD pursuant to the Oceans Act mandate. A conservation milestone was reached in 2004 when regulations established The Gully MPA (see Text Box 3), the first Atlantic Canadian designation under the Oceans Act (Canada 2004). The MPA protects the largest submarine canyon in eastern North America, an offshore ecosystem recognized nationally and internationally for its features and inhabitants including endangered whales and the highest diversity of coral in Canada. Situated in a complex offshore setting subject to commercial fisheries, shipping, hydrocarbon development, and multinational scientific research, The Gully served as a regulatory prototype. The Gully MPA Management Plan supports the regulations by setting out specific actions for regulators and marine users (DFO 2008a). The site remains an influential test case for many aspects of MPA policy and ocean management in Canada (VanderZwaag and Macnab 2011).

Regulations creating the Musquash Estuary MPA were passed in 2006 (Canada 2006) and a management plan followed two years later (DFO 2008b). Located 20 km southwest of Saint John, New Brunswick, Musquash stands out among Bay of Fundy estuaries because of its size, expansive salt marshes, and relatively undisturbed condition. It is regarded as one of the last ecologically-intact estuaries in the Bay of Fundy (Harvey et al. 1998). The estuary's location, shape, and oceanographic characteristics support diverse habitat, abundant wildlife, high marine biological productivity and commercial fisheries. Other noteworthy protective measures with strong OCMD involvement include two coral conservation areas established on the Scotian Shelf in 2002 and 2004, respectively, to protect dense aggregations of corals in the Northeast Channel and reef-building *Lophelia pertusa* at the mouth of the Laurentian Channel (Breeze and Fenton 2007, Gordon et al. 2014). The Coral

Text Box 3: The Gully Marine Protected Area

BIO knowledge covering every facet of The Gully ecosystem was critical to its designation as an MPA (e.g., Harrison and Fenton 1998, Gordon and Fenton 2002). The site remains a locus for fundamental and applied research, with a cadre of researchers, technicians and OCMD staff sustaining multidisciplinary support from across the BIO science community. Management of the site benefits from traditional BIO strengths like oceanographic moorings, geological mapping, hydrographic charting, and biophysical sampling, as well as new millennium frontiers such as genetics, autonomous acoustic recorders, and real-time spatial decision support systems. BIO studies span canyon depths from the seabed to the sea surface and from microbes to top-trophic predators (e.g., Yeung et al. 2010, Kenchington et al. 2009, Cameron et al. 2008, Mortensen and Buhl-Mortensen 2005). BIO scientists also assess and monitor stressors including contaminants and underwater noise (e.g., Yeats et al. 2009, Lee et al. 2005). The provision of science advice continues, most recently for an ecosystem monitoring program to track how well the MPA is meeting its objectives (DFO 2010). These and many other lines of inquiry have built an impressive scientific foundation for MPA management, helping cement The Gully's reputation as an international model for offshore conservation. A variety of venues and techniques are used to disseminate knowledge of The Gully. Spectacular imagery, specimen collections, and multi-media products derived from BIO research (e.g., DFO 1999a) are employed to communicate with diverse audiences and promote the significance of this distant water MPA to Canadians (Fig. 2 A,B).

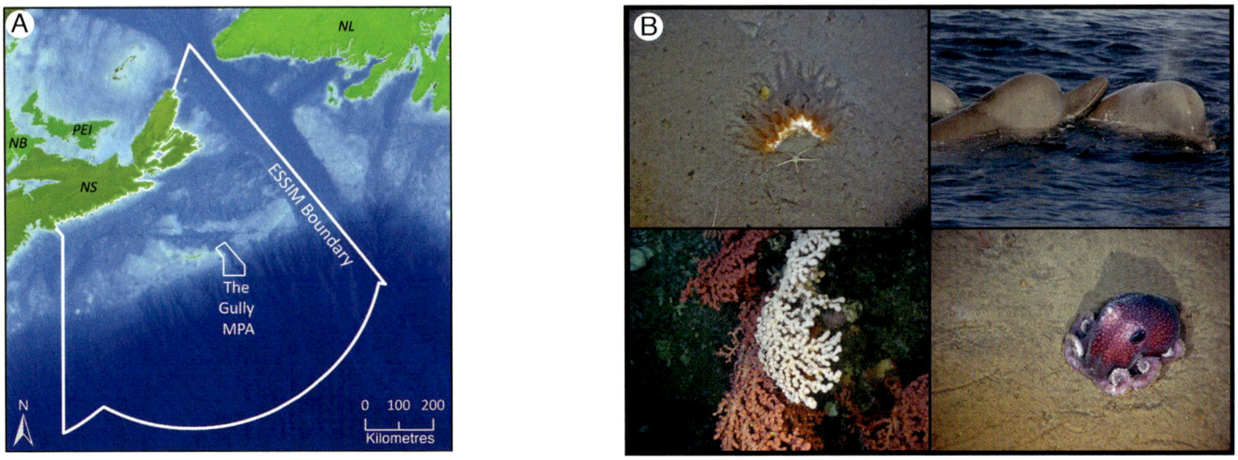

Figure 2. The Gully Marine Protected Area: (A) map showing the MPA within the Eastern Scotian Shelf Integrated Management (ESSIM) area; and (B) collage of sea life (photos: top right H. Moors-Murphy; others, T.J. Kenchington).

Conservation Plan (DFO 2006) spells out objectives and actions required to address the management and scientific needs of this emerging conservation requirement.

The ESSIM initiative matured into the most advanced of the ocean planning processes formally pursued by DFO. In contrast to traditional sector-based management, which addresses individual industries on a case-by-case basis, the ESSIM planning process considered the ecosystem and all of its users in a comprehensive manner. The initiative brought regulatory authorities from all levels of government together with a wide array of ocean stakeholders. Close to a decade of investments in ecosystem and human-use studies, collaborative governance, and strategic planning culminated in the release of the ESSIM Integrated Ocean Management Plan (Government of Canada 2007). The first of its kind in Canada, the ESSIM Plan provides long-term direction for integrated, ecosystem-based and adaptive management of marine activities. The plan uses an objectives-based approach to guide sustainable resource use, conservation, and coordinated management of the eastern Scotian Shelf.

OCMD has also worked on many other pressing oceans management issues to provide information and advice concerning resource development projects and conservation initiatives. A family of ecological reports has been especially valuable in these processes. For example, Breeze et al. (2002) collated and summarized a large volume of BIO-generated knowledge that has become a fundamental reference source, particularly for offshore environmental assessments. Additional reports identified distinct places and habitats where precautionary management is necessary owing to their biological significance and sensitivity (e.g., Breeze 2004, Schaefer et al. 2004, McCullough et al. 2005, Doherty and Horsman 2007, Buzeta and Singh 2008). More recently, OCMD has coordinated on-going state of the ocean reporting for the Scotian Shelf and the Gulf of Maine. An overview document was prepared for each region (Thompson 2010, Oceans and Coastal Management Division n.d.) and theme papers have been drafted for a variety of issues including ocean acidification (Curran and Azetsu-Scott 2012) and offshore habitats (Parker 2012).

SPECIES AT RISK PROGRAM

History

In 1992, Canada was the first of 130 nations to sign the Convention on Biological Diversity (CBD) at the Rio Earth Summit in Rio de Janeiro, Brazil. Canada subsequently developed the Canadian Biodiversity Strategy to support implementation of the CBD (Environment Canada 1995). Two of the three pillars of that strategy, notably the 'Species at Risk Act' and the 'Habitat Stewardship Program' are at the root of the DFO Species at Risk Program. DFO recognized that it would need to develop a strong capacity for internal and external coordination to meet its regional, national, and international obligations under the Canadian Biodiversity Strategy and SARA. In anticipation of the legislation to protect at-risk species, DFO Maritimes Region has operated a Species at Risk Program at BIO since 1999, centred in a coordination office which has changed departmental homes and names several times since its inception. Originally, it was placed within the DFO Science organizational structure at BIO, later moved to a corporate reporting structure, and currently restructured as the Species at Risk Management Division (SARMD) within the Ecosystem Management sector. Since SARA was proclaimed in June 2003, and came fully into force the following year, staff within a Species at Risk Program office have been coordinating and managing the activities involved in meeting departmental responsibilities under SARA.

The Habitat Stewardship Program is a funding program that was established in 2000 and managed cooperatively by Environment Canada, DFO, and Parks Canada. It is one of the most important ways for the DFO Species at Risk Program to collaborate with Non-Government Organizations, interest groups, and individuals in supporting projects that encourage the protection and recovery of at-risk species and their habitats. Together, SARA and the Habitat Stewardship Program remain the integral drivers of the DFO Species at Risk Program and SARMD activities today.

Mandate and Function

SARA mandates specific processes with timelines for the activities that comprise the SARA conservation cycle. The cycle begins with a listing process that is triggered when the Committee on the Status of Endangered Wildlife in Canada (COSEWIC) assigns an 'at-risk' category to an aquatic species within DFO jurisdiction. DFO then reviews COSEWIC's assessments to determine whether to list the species in question under SARA. Overall, DFO is responsible for, or has involvement in, the assessment, listing, protection, recovery, monitoring, and evaluation of aquatic species under its jurisdiction. To date, related activities have been directed toward a wide range of species including marine mammals, sea turtles, marine-diadromous-freshwater fish, and freshwater mussels. Activities undertaken by SARMD at BIO contribute directly to the DFO federal role for all relevant aquatic species within or overlapping with the DFO Maritimes Region geographic area.

While SARMD coordinates the cyclical process for each at-risk species, the effective implementation of the SARA mandate requires the involvement of other DFO sectors, as well as many external stakeholders at all stages of the process. Thus, since its inception, SARMD (or earlier equivalent offices) has worked with partners inside and outside of BIO and DFO to promote a better understanding of at-risk species and the conservation requirements and activities necessary for their recovery.

Major Accomplishments

DFO Maritimes convened the Region's first species recovery team in 1997 to prepare a recovery plan for the endangered North Atlantic Right Whale (*Eubalaena glacialis*). This was done in anticipation of new endangered species legislation. DFO recognized that this legislation would have significant implications for the protection of marine and freshwater species under its jurisdiction, and chose to be proactive in commencing work on a recovery plan.

The Right Whale Recovery Team included scientific experts, environmental groups, fishing and shipping industry representatives, federal and provincial governments, and other partners who identified the threats to the species, as well as measures that needed to be undertaken to contribute to the future welfare and recovery of the Right Whale. This recovery team not only laid the foundation for important achievements toward Right Whale recovery, but also for subsequent recovery teams working on other at-risk species (see Text Box 4).

When SARA came into force, it placed timelines on DFO to produce recovery strategies and action plans for listed aquatic species. At this time, DFO Maritimes had also proactively formed multi-partner recovery teams for the Leatherback Turtle (*Dermochelys coriacea*), Inner Bay of Fundy population of Atlantic Salmon (*Salmo salar*), and the Atlantic Whitefish (*Coregonus huntsman*), all assessed as endangered by COSEWIC prior to SARA's enactment. In 2012, there are 18 aquatic spe-

Text Box 4: North Atlantic Right Whale Recovery

In 2003, the North Atlantic Right Whale population in the North Atlantic was estimated to be 350 animals (Hamilton et al. 2007). The North Atlantic Right Whale Consortium estimated that by the end of 2011, the population was close to 500 animals (Pettis 2012)). Reasons for the increase are uncertain, but it does seem likely that recovery activities initiated in Canadian waters have helped to reverse the population's decline.

Collisions with ocean vessels was identified as one of the main threats to North Atlantic Right Whales in the first Recovery Plan completed in 2000 (Right Whale Recovery Team 2000). Two critical habitat areas for Right Whales have been identified in Atlantic Canadian waters. They are Grand Manan Basin in the Bay of Fundy, and Roseway Basin on the Scotian Shelf. Both areas coincide with high shipping traffic zones. To reduce the risk of collisions, several partners worked together to change the configuration and location of the international shipping lanes that pass through the Bay of Fundy. The revised routing plan came into effect in 2003. In 2008, a second initiative resulted in an international advisory for large vessel traffic to avoid the Right Whales' Roseway Basin habitat.

To maximize understanding of and compliance with these changes, the Habitat Stewardship Program has supported 'outreach' to the shipping industry in Roseway Basin. As a consequence, vessel traffic decreased dramatically in the Roseway Basin habitat of the Right Whales with the expected decline in risk of ship-whale conflicts (Vanderlaan and Taggert 2009) - see Figure 3A and B. While jurisdiction over shipping lanes rests with the Canadian government and the International Maritime Organization, the success of these projects relied on the collaboration of many partners including the Canadian Whale Institute (Dalhousie University, Halifax, NS) and the shipping and fishing industries.

Work remains to be done, and while the North Atlantic Right Whale population is still perilously low, results like these (i.e., reduced risk of collisions) are encouraging to all partners involved in recovery activities. Recovery efforts for Right Whales are enhanced by the participation of national and regional conservation groups, academic researchers, the governments of Nova Scotia and New Brunswick, and the United States National Oceanographic and Atmospheric Administration (NOAA).

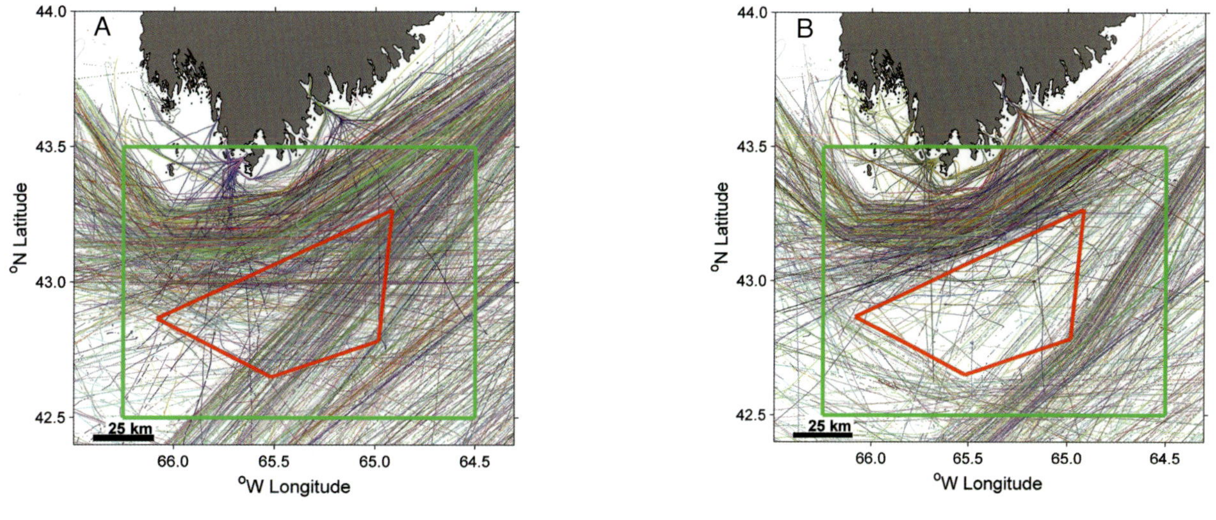

Figure 3. Bathymetric charts of Roseway Basin region on the southwest Scotian Shelf illustrating the 'Vessel Domain' (green rectangle), 'Area To Be Avoided' (ATBA - red polygon), and 'Navigation Tracks' (thin lines) for each vessel and trip through the region from: (A) 15 June to 31 October 2007, and (B) 1 June to 31 October 2008, prior to and following the implementation of the ATBA, respectively (from Vanderlaan and Taggart 2009).

Table 1. Summary of 18 aquatic species found in the DFO Maritimes Region listed under SARA as of 2012 and the status of recovery documents completed or in preparation with Maritimes lead or support.

DFO MARITIMES REGION LISTED SPECIES

	SARA Listing		
Species	**Listing Status**	**Date Listed**	**Recovery Documents: Maritimes Lead (L) or Support (S)**
MARINE species			
Atlantic Walrus, Northwest Atlantic population *(Odobenus rosmarus rosmarus)*	Extirpated	June 2003	Recovery Strategy 2008 (L)
Grey Whale, Atlantic population *(Eschrichtius robustus)*	Extirpated	June 2003	Recovery Strategy 2007 (L)
Blue Whale, Northwest Atlantic population *(Balaenoptera musculus)*	Endangered	January 2005	Recovery Strategy 2010 (S)
Leatherback Turtle *(Dermochelys coriaciae)*	Endangered	June 2003	Recovery Strategy 2007; Action Plan in preparation (L)
Northern Bottlenose Whale *(Hyperoodon ampullatus)*	Endangered (Scotian Shelf population)	April 2006	Recovery Strategy 2010; Action Plan in preparation (L)
North Atlantic Right Whale *(Eubalaena glacialis)*	Endangered	April 2004	Recovery Strategy 2009; Action Plan in preparation (L)
White Shark *(Carcharodon carcharias)*	Endangered	July 2011	Recovery strategy in preparation (L)
Northern Wolffish *(Anarhichas denticulatus)* and **Spotted Wolffish** *(Anarhichas minor)*	Threatened	June 2003	Joint Recovery Strategy 2007 Management plan for 3 wolffish species prepared; Action Plan in preparation (S)
Atlantic Wolffish *(Anarhichas lupus)*	Special concern		
Fin Whale, Atlantic population *(Balaenoptera physalus)*	Special concern	September 2006	Management Plan in preparation (S)
Sowerby's Beaked Whale *(Mesoplodon bidens)*	Special concern	July 2011	Management Plan due in 2016 (L)
FRESHWATER AND DIADROMOUS species			
Dwarf Wedgemussel *(Alasmidonta heterodon)*	Extirpated	June 2003	Recovery Strategy 2007 (L)
Atlantic Salmon, Inner Bay of Fundy population *(Salmo salar)*	Endangered	June 2006	Recovery Strategy 2010; Action Plan in preparation (L)
Atlantic Whitefish *(Coregonus huntsmani)*	Endangered	June 2003	Recovery Strategy 2007; Action Plan in preparation (L)
Lake Utopia Rainbow Smelt, small-bodied population (LURS-sbp; formerly LU'dwarf'S) *(Osmerus mordax)*	Threatened	November 2009	Recovery Strategy in preparation (L)
Yellow Lampmussel *(Lampsilis cariosa)*	Special Concern	July 2005	Management Plan 2010 (L)
Shortnose Sturgeon *(Acipenser brevirostrum)*	Special Concern	March 2009	Management Plan due in 2014 (L)

cies under DFO jurisdiction (8 fish, 6 whales, walrus, 1 turtle, 2 mussels) listed under SARA in Atlantic Canada. DFO Maritimes Region is leading the development and implementation of associated recovery processes for 13 of these species, and supports other DFO Atlantic Regions on the remaining four species (Table 1).

Since its inception, SARMD (and its preceding offices) has worked with partners inside and outside DFO to promote understanding of at-risk species and the activities necessary to support their recovery. In addition to the coordination required to ensure the smooth intersection of SARA-compliant activities with those that support the Fisheries Act, the Species at Risk Program has endeavoured to develop relationships with external partners whose knowledge and participation are critical for the successful attainment of species recovery goals. Examples of internal and external collaborations on species recovery projects include:

- support for scientific research and communications activities in support of North Atlantic Right Whale recovery;
- multi-year research program on the population biology and habitat requirements of the Atlantic Whitefish, an endangered species endemic to Nova Scotia;
- initiation of a recovery planning team for the Leatherback Turtle, and support for research on the species' distribution and critical habitat in Atlantic Canadian waters; and
- the facilitation of a recovery team for the Inner Bay of Fundy population of Atlantic Salmon, which involves all the important stakeholders who provide guidance on the development and implementation of a recovery strategy and action plan.

The Habitat Stewardship Program for Species at Risk is one of the most important ways that DFO collaborates with non-federal partners. The Habitat Stewardship Program supports projects that encourage and enable the protection of at-risk species' habitat by engaging all Canadians in conservation actions to benefit wildlife. In the case of aquatic species, such actions may be carried out by private citizens, resource users, and/or provincial governments. The Species at Risk office at BIO plays an important role in identifying and recommending Habitat Stewardship Program projects for funding, and in providing ongoing guidance to projects.

In marine ecosystems, stewards are most typically also resource users. That fact presents both significant challenges and opportunities in developing and implementing stewardship and recovery measures. Examples of successful projects in DFO Maritimes include the Canadian Sea Turtle Network which, with support from the Habitat Stewardship Program, has worked with commercial fisheries to permit a better understanding of the presence of endangered Leatherback Turtles in their fishing areas. This work helps reduce the risk of turtles drowning in fishing gear, and of fishermen damaging their gear through efforts to release turtles. This project has contributed to knowledge of this wide-ranging marine species and the formulation of solutions to protect the species in Canadian waters.

For anadromous aquatic species, a common threat to species recovery is the presence of barriers that prevent access to parts of their freshwater habitat. The Habitat Stewardship Program has supported work by community groups and First Nations to restore habitat for the once-abundant Inner Bay of Fundy population of Atlantic Salmon. This includes efforts to document changes in the Petitcodiac River before and after the opening of the causeway in Moncton, New Brunswick, which may restore access by Inner Bay of Fundy Atlantic Salmon to their former habitat.

SYNOPSIS AND FUTURE OUTLOOK

The name, mandate, and composition of the Ecosystem Management sector evolved over time, as did its dynamics in relation to BIO Science. It grew from a single Habitat Management Group in the mid-1980s to a multi-faceted sector that today delivers Habitat, Oceans and Species at Risk management programs across the DFO Maritimes Region. Though they emerged at different junctures in DFO's history in Atlantic Canada and stem from different legislative mandates, all three programs eventually coalesced within one sector that can be described as 'the meeting place of science, policy development, and management.' As such, programs within Ecosystem Management have become 'satellites' to the BIO Science group. This ensures that aquatic ecosystem conservation, protection, and planning activities, and decisions are based upon science and that all relevant agencies are working in the same direction to achieve sustainable ecosystem use.

Looking forward, Ecosystem Management and the specifics of its programs will be influenced primarily by changes or shifts in mandates stemming from legislative and policy reviews, regulatory amendments, or responses to program evaluations and audits that occur from time to time. Program adaptations to the amended Canadian Environmental Assessment Act (CEAA), passed on 6 July 2012, have already taken place, and pending legislative amendments to the Fish Habitat Provisions of the Fisheries Act will lead to a comprehensive review of the 1986 Habitat Policy. Though no date has been set by Environment Canada to lead a legislative review of the Species at Risk Act, there is an outstanding requirement to do so and the outcome can be expected to influence the direction and activities of the Species at Risk Program. Lastly, the Oceans' Integrated Management Program underwent a formal evaluation from April to June 2012, the results of which will be instrumental in making appropriate adjustments in the future. Reviews of this nature are cyclical and can lead to immediate program responses as well as to longer term adjustments in mandates and program-delivery elements. Ecosystem Management programs have been no stranger to change over the years and will continue to adapt to these driving forces.

More pertinent to the BIO context, however, are transformations emerging as a result of advances in ecosystem-level research, which underpins the 'paradigm shift in oceans management', explained by O'Boyle et al. (2014) in the context of an Ecosystem Approach to Management that extends beyond traditional fisheries management. The Ecosystem Approach to Management is placing the Oceans Program in an increasingly important role in establishing frameworks for integrated coastal and ocean planning at bio-regional scales. The Ecosystem Approach to Management form is likely to play an increasingly important role and expand from a regional pilot approach to a national standard. And finally, the Ecosystem Approach to Management presents an opportunity for the continued integration of fish habitat and species at risk considerations for a range of decision making across multiple sectors that we predict will withstand the test of time and shifts in the legislative and policy landscape.

ACKNOWLEDGEMENTS

Crafting a historical account and outcomes of operational programs spanning 25 years would not be possible without delving into the corporate memories of a few key players among the original staff. To that end, thanks are owed to: Faith Scattolon, current RDG and formerly Director of the Oceans Act Coordination Office, who provided the authors with her documented recollection of the early history of the Oceans Program at BIO; John Loch, retired Director Aquatic Species-at-Risk Office, for his particularly insightful comments on early drafts of the Species-at-Risk section; and Joe Arbour, former Regional Manager of the Oceans Program, for his review of the Oceans Program section of the manuscript. The authors also thank Jane Avery, Hillary Moors, Dan Shervill, Anita Hamilton, Roland Cormier, Mark McLean and Brian Jollymore for contributions of photos, illustrations, or selected content, and acknowledge Sandy Skinner for her assistance with manuscript formatting. Last but not least, the authors would like to express their sincere gratitude to Mike Sinclair for early discussions that helped shape the idea for this manuscript, to the editors of 'Voyage of Discovery' for their very helpful feedback on the manuscript, and to the BIO-Oceans Association for making the BIO 50th Anniversary commemorative book possible. It was a pleasure to work with them on this project.

REFERENCES

Arbour, J. 2009. The evolution of governance mechanisms for the Eastern Scotian Shelf Integrated Management Initiative. Pages 295-305 *in* Integrated Coastal Zone Management (E. Moksness, E. Dahl, and J. Støttrup, Eds.). Wiley-Blackwell, Oxford, England.

Boudreau, P.R. 1994. Habitat sensitivity mapping system: a method of linking science with managers. Pages 36-39 *in* Science Review 1992 & '93 of the Bedford Institute of Oceanagraphy, Halifax Fisheries Research Laboratory, St. Andrews Biological Station (A. Fiander, Ed.). Fisheries and Oceans Canada, (Scotia-Fundy Region), Dartmouth, NS.

Boyd, P. and B. Smith. 2002. Working together to conserve and protect a unique ecosystem: Basin Head, Prince Edward Island. Pages 1,367-1,377 *in* Managing Protected Areas in a Changing World (S. Bondrup-Nielsen, N.W.P. Munro, G. Nelson, J.H.M. Willison, T.B. Herman, and P. Eagles, Eds.). Science and Management of Protected Areas Association, Wolfville, NS.

Breeze, H. 2004. Review of Criteria for Selecting Ecologically Significant Areas of the Scotian Shelf and Slope: A Discussion Paper. Oceans and Coastal Management Report 2004-04, Fisheries and Oceans Canada, Dartmouth, NS.

Breeze, H., D.G. Fenton, R.J. Rutherford, and M.A. Silva. 2002. The Scotian Shelf: an ecological overview for ocean planning. Canadian Technical Report of Fisheries and Aquatic Sciences 2393, Fisheries and Oceans Canada, Dartmouth, NS.

Breeze, H. and D. Fenton. 2007. Designing management measures to protect cold-water corals off Nova Scotia, Canada. Bulletin of Marine Science 81: 123-133.

Breeze, H. and T. Horsman. 2005. The Scotian Shelf: An Atlas of Human Activities. Fisheries and Oceans Canada, Dartmouth, NS.

Buzeta, M.-I. and R. Singh. 2008. Identification of Ecologically and Biologically Significant Areas in the Bay of Fundy, Gulf of Maine, Volume 1: Areas identified for review, and assessment of the Quoddy Region. Canadian Technical Report of Fisheries and Aquatic Sciences 2788, Fisheries and Oceans Canada, Dartmouth, NS.

Cameron, G.D.M., E.L. King, and D.C. Campbell. 2008. Surficial geology and sun-illuminated seafloor topography, The Gully, Scotian Shelf, offshore Eastern Canada. Geological Survey of Canada "A" Series Map 2123A, Dartmouth, NS.

Canada. 2004. Gully Marine Protected Area Regulations. SOR/2004-112, Fisheries and Oceans Canada, Ottawa, ON.

Canada. 2006. Musquash Estuary Marine Protected Area Regulations. SOR/2006-354, Fisheries and Oceans Canada, Ottawa, ON.

Coffen-Smout, S. and G.J. Herbert. 2000. Submarine cables: a challenge for ocean management. Marine Policy 24: 441-448.

Curran, K. and K. Azetsu-Scott. 2012. Ocean Acidification. State of the Scotian Shelf Report, Atlantic Coastal Zone Information Steering Committee and Fisheries and Oceans Canada, Fisheries and Oceans Canada, Dartmouth, NS.

Curran, K.J., A. Bundy, M. Craig, T. Hall, P. Lawton, and S. Quigley. 2012. Recommendations for Science, Management, and an Ecosystem Approach in Fisheries and Oceans Canada, Maritimes Region. Canadian Science Advisory Secretariat Research Document 2012/061, Fisheries and Oceans Canada, Ottawa, ON.

DFO. 1986. Policy for the Management of Fish Habitat. Fisheries and Oceans Canada, Ottawa, ON.

DFO. 1987. Toward Canada's Oceans Strategy: Discussion Paper. Communications Directorate, Fisheries and Oceans Canada, Ottawa, ON.

DFO. 1999a. The Sable Gully: A Virtual Tour. Department of Fisheries and Oceans, Oceans Act Coordination Office, Dartmouth, NS.

DFO. 1999b. Marine Protected Areas Policy. Fisheries and Oceans Canada (March 1999), Ottawa, ON.

DFO. 1999c. National Framework for Establishing and Managing Marine Protected Areas – A Working Document. Fisheries and Oceans Canada (March 1999), Ottawa, ON.

DFO. 2006. Coral Conservation Plan Maritimes Region (2006-2010). Oceans and Coastal Management Report 2006-01, Fisheries and Oceans Canada, Dartmouth, NS.

DFO. 2008a. The Gully Marine Protected Area Management Plan. Fisheries and Oceans Canada, Dartmouth, NS.

DFO. 2008b. Musquash Estuary: A Management Plan for the Marine Protected Area and Administered Intertidal Area. Fisheries and Oceans Canada, Dartmouth, NS.

DFO. 2010. Gully Marine Protected Area monitoring indicators, protocols and strategies. Canadian Science Advisory Secretariat Science Advisory Report 2010/066, Fisheries and Oceans Canada, Dartmouth, NS.

Doherty, P. and T. Horsman. 2007. Ecologically and Biologically Significant Areas of the Scotian Shelf and environs: a compilation of scientific expert opinion. Canadian Technical Report of Fisheries and Aquatic Sciences 2774, Fisheries

and Oceans Canada, Dartmouth, NS.
Ducharme, A. 1992. Links Between Science and Habitat Management. Pages 141-157 *in* Proceedings of the Gulf of Maine Scientific Workshop. Urban Harbors Institute, University of Massachusetts, Boston, MA.
Environment Canada. 1995. Canadian Biodiversity Strategy: Canada's Response to the Convention on Biological Diversity 1995. Environment Canada, Hull, QC.
Gordon, D.C. and D.G. Fenton (Eds.). 2002. Advances in understanding the Gully Ecosystem: a summary of research projects conducted at the Bedford Institute of Oceanography (1999-2001). Canadian Technical Report of Fisheries and Aquatic Sciences 2377, Fisheries and Oceans Canada, Dartmouth, NS.
Gordon, D.C., E.L.R. Kenchington, B.T. Hargrave, and D.L. Peer. 2014. Life at the bottom of the sea: advances in understanding benthic ecosystems. Pages 87-97 *in* Voyage of Discovery: Fifty Years of Marine Research at Canada's Bedford Institute of Oceanography (D.N. Nettleship, D.C. Gordon, C.F.M. Lewis, and M.P. Latremouille, Eds.). Bedford Institute of Oceanography-Oceans Association, Dartmouth, NS.
Government of Canada. 2002. Canada's Oceans Strategy: Our Oceans, Our Future. Policy and Operational Framework for Integrated Management of Estuarine, Coastal and Marine Environments in Canada. Fisheries and Oceans Canada, Ottawa, ON.
Government of Canada. 2005. Canada's Federal Marine Protected Areas Strategy. Fisheries and Oceans Canada, Ottawa, ON.
Government of Canada. 2007. Eastern Scotian Shelf integrated ocean management plan. Fisheries and Oceans Canada, Dartmouth, NS.
Government of Canada. 2011. National Framework for Canada's Network of Marine Protected Areas. Fisheries and Oceans Canada, Ottawa, ON.
Hamilton, P.K., A.R. Knowlton, and M.K. Marx. 2007. Right Whales tell their own stories: the photo-identification catalog. Pages 75-104 *in* The Urban Whale: North Atlantic Right Whales at the Crossroads (S.D. Kraus and R.M. Rolland, Eds.). Harvard University Press, Cambridge, MA.
Harrison, W.G. and D.G. Fenton (Eds.). 1998. The Gully: A Scientific Review of its Environment and Ecosystem. Canadian Stock Assessment Secretariat Research Document 98/83, Fisheries and Oceans Canada, Dartmouth, NS.
Harvey, J., D. Coon, and J. Abouchar. 1998. Habitat lost: taking the pulse of estuaries in the Canadian Gulf of Maine. Conservation Council of New Brunswick, Frederiction, NB.
Kenchington, T.J., M. Best, C. Bourbonnais-Boyce, P. Clement, A. Cogswell, B. MacDonald, W.J. MacEachern, K. MacIsaac, P. MacNab, L. Paon, J. Reid, S. Roach, L. Shea, D. Themelis, and E.L.R. Kenchington. 2009. Methodology of the 2007 Survey of Meso- and Bathypelagic Micronekton of the Sable Gully: Cruise TEM768. Canadian Technical Report of Fisheries and Aquatic Sciences 2853, Fisheries and Oceans Canada, Dartmouth, NS.
Lee, K., H. Bain, and G. Hurley (Eds.). 2005. Acoustic Monitoring and Marine Mammal Surveys in The Gully and Outer Scotian Shelf Before and During Active Seismic Programs. Environmental Studies Research Funds Report 151, Fisheries and Oceans Canada, Dartmouth, NS.
Macnab, P. 2005. The Gully Marine Protected Area and Northern Bottlenose Whales on the Scotian Shelf. Pages 1-14 *in* Acoustic Monitoring and Marine Mammal Surveys in The Gully and Outer Scotian Shelf Before and During Active Seismic Programs (K. Lee, H. Bain, and G. Hurley, Eds.). Environmental Studies Research Funds Report 151, Fisheries and Oceans Canada, Dartmouth, NS.
MacPhee, S.B., J.A. Elliot, M.M. Sinclair, and T.B. Smith. 1988. The Science Program of Scotia-Fundy Region. Pages 4-9 *in* Science Review 1987 (B. Bennett, Ed.). Fisheries and Oceans Canada, Scotia-Fundy Region, Dartmouth, NS.
McCullough, D.M., P.A. Doherty, H.L. Schaefer, C. Deacoff, S.K. Johnston, D.R. Duggan, B.D. Petrie, and V.V. Soukhovtsev. 2005. Significant Habitats: Atlantic Coast Initiative (SHACI). Halifax Regional Municipality - Units 4-6. Canadian Manuscript Report of Fisheries and Aquatic Sciences 2724, Fisheries and Oceans Canada, Dartmouth, NS.
Mortensen, P.B. and L. Buhl-Mortensen. 2005. Deep-water corals and their habitats in The Gully, a submarine canyon off Atlantic Canada. Pages 247-277 *in* Cold-water Corals and Ecosystems (A. Freiwald and J.M. Roberts, Eds.). Springer, Berlin, Germany.
National Advisory Board on Science and Technology. 1994. Opportunities from our Oceans: Report of the Committee on Oceans and Coasts. National Advisory Board on Science and Technology, Ottawa, ON.
Nicholls, H.B. 1989. Research in support of fish habitat impact issues in the coastal zone. Pages 988-995 *in* Coastal Zone '89: Proceedings of the Sixth Symposium on Coastal and Ocean Management (O.T. Magoon, H. Converse, D. Miner, L.T. Tobin, and D. Clark, Eds.). American Society of Civil Engineers, New York, NY.
Nicholls, H.B. 1993. The role of the Bedford Institute of Oceanography in addressing marine coastal zone issues. Pages 213-221 *in* Coastlines of Canada (L.P. Hildebrand and O.T. Magoon, Eds.). American Society of Civil Engineers, New York, NY.
O'Boyle, R.N., M.M. Sinclair, and R.R. Claytor. 2014. Research in support of harvest fisheries and their ecological interactions: the Scotian Shelf. Pages 267-277 *in* Voyage of Discovery: Fifty Years of Marine Research at Canada's Bedford Institute of Oceanography (D.N. Nettleship, D.C. Gordon, C.F.M. Lewis, and M.P. Latremouille, Eds.). Bedford Institute of Oceanography-Oceans Association. Dartmouth, NS.
Oceans and Coastal Management Division. n.d. The Scotian Shelf in Context - State of the Scotian Shelf Report. Atlantic Coastal Zone Information Steering Committee and Fisheries and Oceans Canada, Fisheries and Oceans Canada, Dartmouth, NS.
Parker, M. 2012. Offshore Ecosystems and Habitats. State of the Gulf of Maine Report. Gulf of Maine Council on the Marine Environment, Annapolis Royal, NS.
Parker, M., M. Westhead, P. Doherty, and J. Naug. 2007. Ecosystem overview and assessment report for the Bras d'Or Lakes. Nova Scotia. Canadian Manuscript Report of Fisheries and Aquatic Science 2789, Fisheries and Oceans Canada, Dartmouth, NS.
Pettis, H. 2012. North Atlantic Right Whale Consortium 2012 Annual Report Card. Committee on the Status of Endangered Wildlife in Canada, Ottawa, ON. http://www.narwc.org/pdf/2012_Report_Card.pdf.
Right Whale Recovery Team. 2000. Canadian North Atlantic Right Whale Recovery Plan. Committee on the Status of Endangered Wildlife in Canada, Ottawa, ON.
Rutherford, R.J., G.J. Herbert, and S.S. Coffen-Smout. 2005. Integrated ocean management and the collaborative planning process: The Eastern Scotian Shelf Integrated Management (ESSIM) Initiative. Marine Policy 29: 75–83.
Schaefer, H.L., D.M. McCullough, S.K. Johnston, and D.R. Duggan. 2004. Significant Habitats: Atlantic Coast Initiative (SHACI). Sydney Bight - Unit 11. Canadian Manuscript Report of Fisheries and Aquatic Sciences 2650, Fisheries and Oceans Canada, Dartmouth, NS.
Sharp, G., R. Semple, K. Connolly, R. Blok, D. Audet, D. Cairns, and S. Courtenay. 2003. Ecological assessment of the Basin Head lagoon: a proposed marine protected area. Canadian Manuscript Report of Fisheries and Aquatic Sciences 2641, Fisheries and Oceans Canada, Dartmouth, NS.
Sharp, G., B. Semple, and M. Veinot. 2007. Artificial reefs: homes for benthic diversity. Pages 16-18 *in* Bedford Institute of Oceanography 2006 in Review (J. Ryan, Ed.). Natural Resources Canada and Fisheries and Oceans Canada, Dartmouth, NS.
Singh, R., M.I. Buzeta, M. Dowd, J.L. Martin, and M. LeGresley. 2000. Ecological overview of Musquash Estuary: a proposed marine protected area. Canadian Manuscript Report of Fisheries and Aquatic Sciences 2538, Fisheries and Oceans Canada, Dartmouth, NS.
Thompson, E. 2010. The Gulf of Maine in Context: State of the Gulf of Maine Report. Gulf of Maine Council on the Marine Environment, Annapolis Royal, NS.
Vanderlaan, A.S.M. and C.T. Taggart. 2009. Efficacy of a voluntary area to be avoided to reduce risk of lethal vessel strikes to endangered whales. Conservation Biology 23: 1,467-1,474.
VanderZwaag, D.L. and P. Macnab. 2011. Marine protected areas: legal framework for The Gully off the coast of Nova Scotia (Canada). Supplementary case study for Guidelines for Protected Areas Legislation (B. Lausche. Ed.). International Union for Conservation of Nature, Environmental Policy and Law Paper No. 81. Gland, Switzerland. http://cmsdata.iucn.org/downloads/the_gully.pdf
Verhoef, J., D.C. Mosher, and S.R. Forbes. 2014. Defining Canada's extended continental shelves. Pages 407-414 *in* Voyage of Discovery: Fifty Years of Marine Research at Canada's Bedford Institute of Oceanography (D.N. Nettleship, D.C. Gordon, C.F.M. Lewis, and M.P. Latremouille, Eds.). Bedford Institute of Oceanography-Oceans Association, Dartmouth, NS.
Yeats, P., J. Hellou, T. King, and B. Law. 2009. Measurements of Chemical Contaminants and Toxicological Effects in The Gully. Canadian Science Advisory Secretariat Research Document 2008/066, Fisheries and Oceans Canada, Dartmouth, NS.
Yeung, C.W., K. Lee, L.G. Whyte, and C.W. Greer. 2010. Microbial community characterization of the Gully: a marine protected area. Canadian Journal of Microbiology 56: 421-431.

APPENDIX A

Summary of legal and policy framework of DFO Ecosystem Management Programs

(a) Summary of Legislation and Weblinks:

Enabling Legislation	**Relevant Programs**	**Purpose/ Key Provisions**
Fisheries Act (R.S.C. 1985, c. F-14)	Habitat Management Program	One of the oldest Acts in Canada. Contains key provisions for habitat protection and pollution prevention that provide DFO with the authorities and powers for regulating associated impacts to fish and fish habitat including: • dealing with obstructions impeding the free passage of fish and the minimum flow of water for fish • prohibiting the killing of fish by any means other than fishing without authorization • prohibiting the harmful alteration, disruption or destruction (HADD) of fish habitat without an authorization; and • prohibiting the deposit of deleterious substances in fish-bearing waters without authorization Link: http://laws-lois.justice.gc.ca/eng/acts/F-14/ Updates to these provisions were underway at the time of writing.
Canadian Environmental Assessment Act [Repealed] (S.C. 1992, c. 37)	Habitat Management Program	Established responsibilities and procedures for assessing environmental effects of projects where a federal authority made decisions as a proponent, land administrator, source of funding, or regulator. Section 5 of CEAA [Repealed] required DFO to ensure that an Environmental Assessment was conducted in relation to works or undertakings prior to regulatory decisions being made by DFO, including issuance of authorizations of a HADD under the Fisheries Act. Link: http://laws-lois.justice.gc.ca/eng/acts/C-15.2/ Replaced by Canadian Environmental Assessment Act 2012 (S.C. 2012, C. 19, S. 52) on 6 July 2012.
Oceans Act (S.C. 1996, c. 31)	Oceans Program	Sets out a legal commitment for the federal government to conserve, protect and develop the oceans in a sustainable manner, and assigns DFO the lead role in its implementation, in collaboration with other federal departments and agencies, and respecting jurisdictional authorities. Link: http://laws-lois.justice.gc.ca/eng/acts/O-2.4/
Species at Risk Act (S.C. 2002, c. 29)	Species at Risk Program Habitat Management Program Oceans Program	Created to prevent wildlife species from becoming extinct; to provide for the recovery of threatened, endangered and extirpated species; and to manage species of special concern to prevent them from becoming endangered or threatened. SARA is administered by Environment Canada. DFO, Parks Canada, and Environment Canada share responsibility for the implementation of the Act, and jointly manage the Species at Risk Program. Under SARA, DFO is responsible for the recovery and protection of aquatic species in Canada (including all life stages of fish, shellfish, crustaceans, marine animals and marine plants, except those on federal lands under the responsibility of Parks Canada). The Act provides legal protection to listed wildlife species and their critical habitat, and requires the preparation of recovery documents for listed species. Link: http://laws-lois.justice.gc.ca/eng/acts/S-15.3/

(b) List of Strategic and Policy Documents:

Habitat Management Program

The Department of Fisheries and Oceans Policy for the Management of Fish Habitat (DFO 1986).

Oceans Program

Marine Protected Areas Policy (DFO 1999b).

National Framework for Establishing and Managing Marine Protected Areas – A Working Document (DFO 1999c).

Policy and Operational Framework for Integrated Management of Estuarine, Coastal and Marine Environments in Canada (Government of Canada 2002).

Federal Marine Protected Areas Strategy (Government of Canada 2005).

National Framework for Canada's Network of Marine Protected Areas (Government of Canada 2011).

Species at Risk Program

Canadian Biodiversity Strategy (Environment Canada 1995).

Habitat Stewardship Program for Species at Risk (Environment Canada – On-line).

Link: http://www.ec.gc.ca/hsp-pih/default. asp?lang=En&n=59BF488F-1

31. RESEARCH IN SUPPORT OF HARVEST FISHERIES AND THEIR ECOLOGICAL INTERACTIONS: THE SCOTIAN SHELF

Robert N. O'Boyle*, Michael M. Sinclair, and Ross R. Claytor

SUMMARY

Before extension of the Canadian Extended Economic Zone in 1977, research at the Bedford Institute of Oceanography (BIO) on fisheries resources was devoted to food chain and process studies on a wide range of species. This work significantly expanded in scope after 1977 to meet the demands of domestic fisheries management. In these early days, fishery monitoring systems were established, data processing and archiving methodologies designed, and algorithms developed to assess the status of fish stocks. As well, extending the work prior to 1997, a wide range of research in support of fisheries management was undertaken. The collapse of the groundfish resources on the Scotian Shelf in 1993 led to an expansion of assessment and associated research on newly exploited species, including new monitoring systems and analytical techniques for fisheries with little data. After 2000, in response to Canada's Oceans Act, another dimension was added to the research program to support an ecosystem approach to fisheries. Programs extended the earlier single species activities as well as placed renewed emphasis on the study of the ecosystem impacts of fishing. The profile of research on harvest fisheries fifty years after the founding of BIO is the result of a long evolution of a program which has adaptively responded to the requirements of management. The program developed a well-deserved reputation in the international fisheries science community for high quality and innovative research. This legacy is now passed on to the next generation of fishery scientists who will no doubt rise to future challenges in the same spirit as their predecessors.

Key words: fisheries science, stock assessment, ecosystem approach to fisheries, Scotian Shelf.
***E-mail:** BCubed@accesswave.ca

The Atlantic Ocean off Canada's east coast is inhabited by marine ecosystems rich in natural and renewable resources which have been long exploited by both Canadian and international fishing fleets. The wise management of these resources requires state-of-the-art science to inform decision-makers and attain conservation goals. Since its founding in 1962, the Bedford Institute of Oceanography (BIO) has conducted research on fisheries resource management that has been applied both locally and internationally. This article highlights these research efforts by focussing on major commercial groundfish species on the Scotian Shelf (Fig. 1).

EARLY YEARS AND THE MARINE ECOLOGY LABORATORY (1965-87)

The Marine Ecology Laboratory (MEL) was established in 1965, soon after the founding of BIO. Its primary mandate was to conduct research on ecosystem energetics and trophic dynamics. At the time, fisheries in the waters off Canada's east coast were under the stewardship of the International Commission of Northwest Atlantic Fisheries (ICNAF) which made decisions on appropriate harvesting by the domestic and foreign fishing fleets operating beyond Canada's twelve mile limit. Stock assessments and associated research and monitoring in support of ICNAF were con-

Figure 1. Major commercial groundfish species on the Scotian Shelf: (A) Haddock *Melanogrammus aeglefinus*, (B) Atlantic Cod *Gadus morhua*, (C) Atlantic Halibut *Hippoglossus hippoglossus*, and (D) Redfish *Sebastes marinus* (photos: H. Wiele).

ducted at the St. Andrews Biological Station (SABS) in New Brunswick. MEL was ahead of its time in undertaking research of global significance on the structure and function of marine ecosystems (Li 2014). Several of the contributions by MEL fishery scientists have been significant with respect to fisheries management and are addressed here.

In a landmark paper, Sheldon et al. (1972) showed that as particles in an ocean ecosystem increase in size from phytoplankton to whales, their abundance per size class decreases but the biomass in each size class remains relatively constant (Duplisea et al. 2014; Fig. 2). This concept led to further work on energy transfer along the food chain to learn about its relation to fish production (Sheldon et al. 1977) and the processes underlying ecosystem functioning (Dickie et al. 1987).

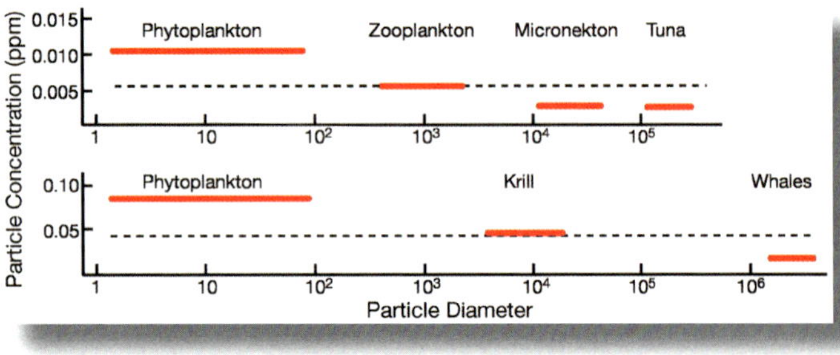

Figure 2. Theoretical relationship between body size and production for various animal groups in two regions (top panel - equatorial Pacific, bottom panel - Antarctic): vertical axis indicates biomass (ppm) and horizontal axis indicates particle size (µm): thick red lines are estimates of standing stock for various species groups while thin broken black line is an estimate of true or potential biomass (from Sheldon et al. 1972).

Another line of research involved the processes that influence recruitment to fish populations, a topic that remains critical to this day. Sutcliffe et al. (1977) found significant correlations between environmental factors, in particular freshwater runoff from the St. Lawrence River, and Atlantic Lobster (*Homarus americanus*) catch in the Gulf of Maine. While these correlations ultimately did not stand up to further observations, the study offered insight into some of the driving forces behind recruitment. In another landmark paper, Ware (1980) explored the bioenergetics between stock and recruitment. The classic work of Ricker (1954) on the Pacific Coast described recruitment as a function of spawning stock biomass and Ware (1980) provided an energetics basis for this relationship. Lambert (1987), who worked with D. Ware, showed that recruitment success of Atlantic Herring (*Clupea harengus*) stocks was highly influenced by the age structure of the adult population. A wide age span produced a larger number of recruitment ways, 'hedging bets' in a highly variable and hostile environment.

YEARS AFTER EXTENSION OF JURISDICTION (1977-93)

Until 1977, BIO had no group devoted to the provision of scientific advice in support of fisheries management. MEL conducted research on the role of fish populations within an ecosystem context, but it was not directly involved in management issues. The fisheries research group based at SABS had the mandate to conduct assessment and associated research to determine the distribution and abundance of fish in the fisheries resources of the Gulf of St. Lawrence, Scotian Shelf, and Gulf of Maine and interacted regularly with ICNAF. All this changed in 1977 with the extension of Canada's jurisdiction to 200 nautical miles (Extended Economic Zone, the EEZ). Management of domestic fisheries, previously overseen by ICNAF, was transferred to the federal Department of Fisheries and Environment. To facilitate the science needs of fisheries management within the Scotia-Fundy Region, a component of the SABS fisheries group led by R. Halliday, was moved to BIO and became the nucleus of the new Marine Fish Division (MFD). Its focus was to be on finfish and marine mammal stock assessment while SABS continued to work on pelagic and invertebrate species, as well as on sampling, aging, and survey activities.

To support the research, assessment and monitoring needs of domestic fisheries management, MFD established a number of new monitoring programs, many of which continue to this day. Since 1970, the SABS fisheries group has coordinated and conducted the annual summer bottom trawl survey (Fig. 3).

This survey conducts about 200 standardized bottom trawl sets covering the entire Scotian Shelf each July to August, which allows mapping of the distribution of finfish species (e.g., distribution of haddock determined by the 2009 survey - see Fig. 4). It also provides Maritimes stock assessments with the primary indices of finfish stock abundance as well as their age and size composition. For instance, long-term trends in haddock biomass (tonnage of fish) by area are shown in Figure 5. This dataset has been and continues to be extensively used by BIO scientists in their study of the natural processes that govern the distribution and abundance of finfish on the Scotian Shelf.

BIO scientists supplemented the summer survey with spring and fall surveys which were conducted during the 1980s and 1990s. As well, deepwater surveys were conducted during the 1990s to determine the distribution and abundance of species which inhabit the waters off the Scotian Shelf and on the continental slope (Zwanenburg 1985, Halliday et al. 2012). The International Observer Program (IOP) was established to obtain at-sea observations of fishing vessel activities. This program involved the deployment of observers on fishing vessels to record on-board activities at sea such as the species and size composition of the catch of each fishing set, logistics (time and area) of fishing operations, and the collection of special samples (e.g., diet samples) for BIO scientists. In addition, some shorter duration programs were initiated. An ambitious one was the Scotian Shelf Ichthyoplankton Program (SSIP). Conducted from 1978 through 1982, it mapped the seasonal distribution of the early life history stages of finfish and created an invaluable dataset which is

Figure 3. CCGS *Needler* conducting groundfish surveys on the Scotian Shelf using an otter trawl (photo: D. Roddick).

still being used to assist management efforts: e.g., the deliberations on spatial planning for the identification of Ecologically and Biologically Significant Areas (EBSAs). The SSIP observations (Fig. 6) generated knowledge on the spatial distribution and timing of spawning for a wide range of fish species as well as new concepts to explain the underlying reasons for the observed patterns. For instance, based on their egg and larval distributions, Atlantic cod were observed to spawn on the offshore banks first in November-December around Sable Island, then along the coast of western Nova Scotia and by April-May off Southwest Nova Scotia on Browns Bank (O'Boyle et al. 1984). This dataset showed for a wide range of species that spawning primarily took place on the offshore banks with the larvae retained by oceanographic gyres that no doubt improved survivorship.

Research groups were established to study the population dynamics of a range of species. For instance, the marine mammal group was set up to study the dynamics of Grey (*Halichoerus grypus*) and Harbour (*Phoca vitulina*) seals of the Maritimes (Bowen 2014). The assemblage structure of the Scotian Shelf groundfish communities (also known as demersal fish communities) was pursued, in part stimulated by the technical analyses undertaken during the Georges Bank Canada-United States boundary dispute (Mahon and Smith 1989). Stimulated by the availability of the SSIP dataset, a number of groups initiated research of the early life history dynamics of groundfish, including Atlantic Cod (*Gadus morhua*; Gagné and O'Boyle 1984). Many of these studies culminated in the Fisheries Ecology Program (FEP) discussed below.

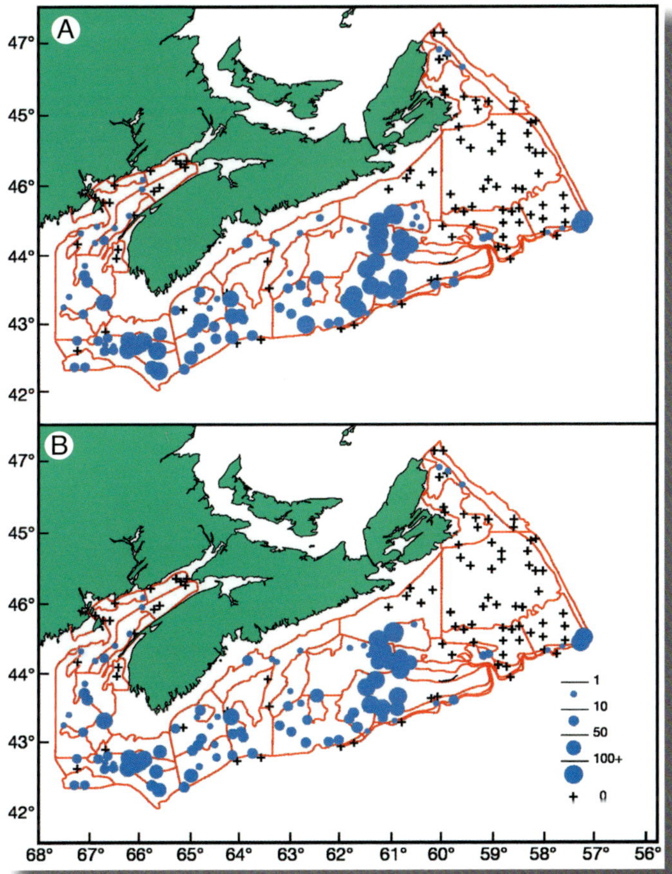

Figure 4. Distribution of Haddock (*Melanogrammus aeglefinus*) catches on the Scotian Shelf during the July-August 2009 summer bottom trawl survey. Relative size of dots indicates numbers (A) and biomass (B) of haddock per survey tow according to legend; areas demarcated in red are the survey areas used to distribute total number of tows taken on a survey (from Clark et al. 2010).

The early days of MFD were dominated by the setup of both fisheries monitoring activities, such as the international fisheries observer program noted above, and, equally important, the structure and quality assurance of the long-term datasets needed to support assessment. Although not a 'glorious' activity, the importance of data management was established during this period and set the foundations for long-term data processing and archiving. For instance, the IOP and SSIP programs were the first in the region to use relational databases to store the data and facilitate their analysis. Previously, flat ASCII files were the method of storage, but these new programs introduced extensive hierarchical data editing procedures, approaches that are still used today. The strong commitment to data management had spin-offs that became obvious very quickly. For example, between 1980 and 1984, Canada was involved in a dispute with the United States over the international boundary in the Gulf of Maine. The capacity of BIO to support the scientific arguments of Canada's lawyers through the mapping and analysis of large transboundary databases was a key element of the case's ruling for Canada by the International Court of Justice (Sinclair and O'Boyle 2014).

Stock assessments in support of the Canadian east coast fisheries were peer reviewed at that time by the Canadian Atlantic Fisheries Scientific Advisory Committee (CAFSAC), an organization set up in 1977 to replace the ICNAF review process and headquartered at BIO. When MFD was created, there was limited software available to conduct stock assessments. Within a short period of time, the new MFD assessment team developed a full suite of packages in the computer language APL which over the next decade became the 'lingua franca' of stock assessment on Canada's east coast (Rivard 1980). APL was very flexible for the manipulation of matrices, a feature of great importance for the assessment models. These early days of stock assessment were dominated by Cohort Analysis (Pope 1972) which had been first used in ICNAF into which Virtual Population Analysis (VPA) methods had been introduced by European scientists. Initially, optimization procedures for these models were basic (O'Boyle 1981), relying on visual inspection of model outputs versus survey trends. Optimization methods, however, were certainly well known at the time (Smith 1979) and the need to incorporate them into assessment models well recognized. Based on the efforts of MFD and SABS scientists, the ADAPT model was developed (Gavaris 1988) and became the international standard for VPAs, so named due to the ease of 'adapting' models in APL to address the problem at hand. In essence, ADAPT allowed optimization of the fit between the aggregate observations of both trends in abundance from the research surveys and the estimates of catch per unit of effort (CPUE) from the fishing fleets with the model VPA outputs.

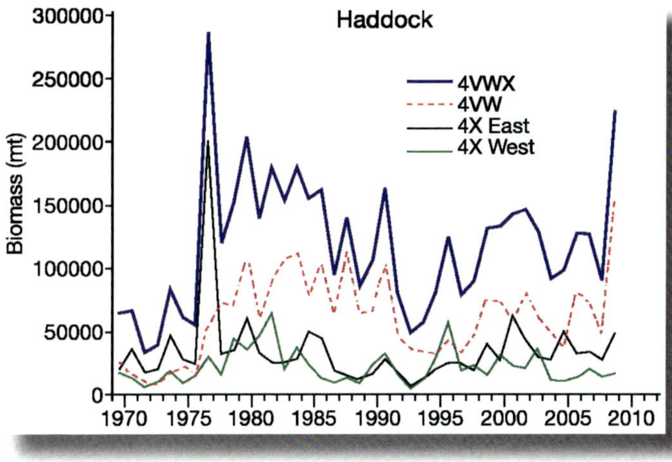

Figure 5. Trends in biomass (tonnage of fish caught) of Haddock (*Melanogrammus aeglefinus*) by NAFO Divisions from the summer bottom trawl survey between 1969 and 2009. See Figure 8 for locations of NAFO Divisions presented: 4VWX is NAFO divisions 4Vn, 4Vs, 4W, and 4X combined while 4X east and 4X west splits NAFO division roughly down the middle off Yarmouth (from Clark et al. 2010).

Stock assessments are recognized as being highly complex with many problems to be surmounted to provide fisheries managers with unbiased and accurate estimates of abundance (Quinn and Deriso 1999). Quite early, the issue of systematic overestimation/underestimation of abundance from the VPA models, and underestimation/overestimation of fishing mortality, was recognized by BIO scientists during Atlantic Herring assessments (Sinclair et al. 1985). This systematic bias in model outputs quickly became significant at the international level. Coined the 'retrospective' pattern, a systematic bias with abundance either under- or over-estimated was uncovered as more years of data were added to the assessment. A CAFSAC working group studied the issue based on work by BIO scientists. This discussion led to a national workshop to both characterize why it occurred and what could be done to resolve it (Sinclair et al. 1991). Mohn (1999) subsequently developed an indicator of the magnitude of the retrospective effect in a stock assessment which is now referred to as 'Mohn's rho' in the international stock assessment community.

The understanding of and correction for errors in stock assessments were, and continue to be, an active area of research. Numerous influential contributions were made by BIO scientists from 1977 to 1993. Mohn (1980) studied how errors impact the logistic modelling of fish populations, while Mohn (1983) studied the effects of error in sampling and abundance indices of cohort analysis. Efforts to 'calibrate' stock assessments, particularly with survey data, stimulated a great deal of innova-

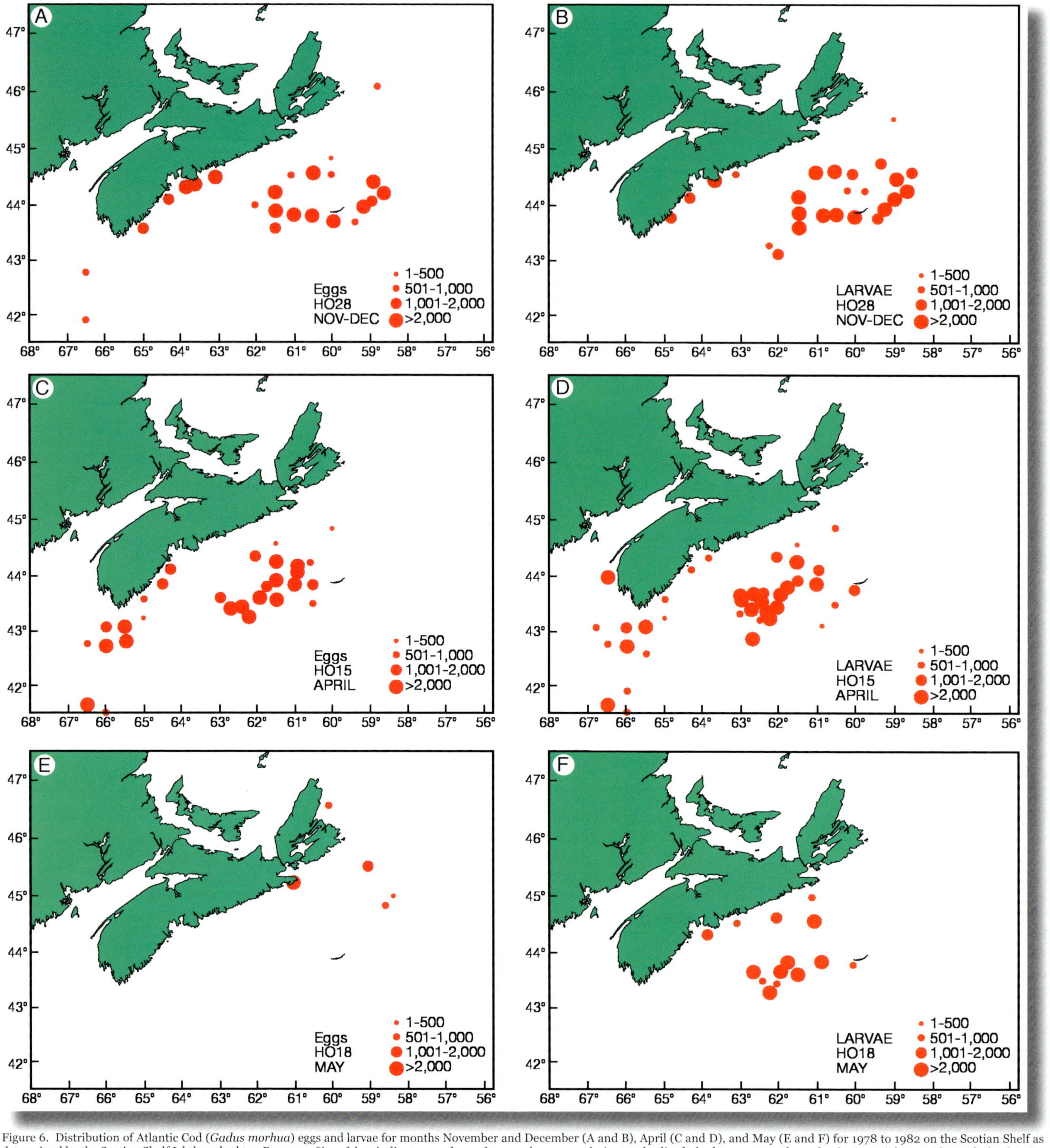

Figure 6. Distribution of Atlantic Cod (*Gadus morhua*) eggs and larvae for months November and December (A and B), April (C and D), and May (E and F) for 1978 to 1982 on the Scotian Shelf as determined by the Scotian Shelf Ichthyoplankton Program. Size of dots indicates numbers of eggs or larvae caught in standardized plankton net tow; legend at bottom right provides scale for dot size (from O'Boyle et al. 1984).

tive and influential research. A particular focus was on how to characterize the uncertainty of abundance indices and their relationships with oceanographic conditions. The goal was to provide more precise survey estimates of population size. Gavaris and Smith (1987) studied how best to allocate survey sampling effort (e.g., determine the number of survey sets to take in each sampling area of the survey) to achieve a specified level of accuracy. Smith (1990) studied the relationship between Atlantic Cod age and hydrographic conditions during survey catches in an effort to determine what oceanographic processes are important to the geographic distribution of that species, determining that a combination of water depth, salinity and temperature were influential in the distribution of the age groups of cod.

There were many important contributions to the biology of the fisheries resources during this period. Sinclair (1988) proposed a theory for the spatial organization of marine populations. Under his member/vagrant hypothesis, the number of populations within a species, as well as the location of their spawning, is determined by oceanographic processes, such as gyres, that enhance retention of the early life history stages of eggs and larvae. Another notable initiative was the Fisheries Ecology Program (FEP) which was undertaken as a comprehensive study of all life history stages of the Haddock (*Melanogrammus aeglefinus*) of the southwest coast of Nova Scotia. These fish are one of the keystone resources in the Maritimes fishery and were being heavily over-exploited at the time (Mohn et al. 2010). The FEP was a collaboration of BIO scientists from the fields of oceanography and fisheries assessment which culminated in a major publication (Dickie and Smith 1989). One of its main findings was that while Haddock spawned on Browns Bank off southwest Nova Scotia in the spring, a portion of the eggs and larvae were retained by an oceanographic gyre on the bank while another portion was carried by prevailing currents into the Bay of Fundy (Campana et al. 1989). The Browns Bank gyre was therefore considered to be 'leaky'. Typically, the early life stages of fish were expected to be entrained by oceanographic gyres around banks after spawning (Sinclair 1988). Observing a gyre that entrained part of the spawned eggs and larvae, but let part drift to another area represented a new phenomenon. This finding explained the strong size differences between adult Browns Bank and Bay of Fundy Haddock within one spawning population. The research was supported by a large array of studies on the physical oceanography of the area and the impact of the oceanographic findings on the distribution of Haddock eggs and larvae (Dickie and Smith 1989).

Research on fisheries oceanography during this period included early musings on the impacts of climate change on fisheries. Frank et al. (1988), in an insightful report, made predictions on how the distributions and productivity of fisheries would change in response to global warming, some of which, such as the distribution of warm water species farther north along the Atlantic coast, appear today to be coming true. This and other studies highlighted the need to better understand the structure and function of marine ecosystems and how these respond to both natural perturbations and human threats. The modelling work of Dickie et al. (1987) highlighted the importance of size-based processes, while a number of other studies focussed on the interaction between benthic organisms and the overlying water column (Gordon et al. 2014).

As a start towards an ecosystem approach to management, stimulated by the scientific community, a workshop was held at BIO to discuss what was known about the Scotian Shelf ecosystem and consider how best to incorporate this knowledge in fisheries management (Mahon 1985). While BIO scientists had provided much information to managers on the yield implications of various gear regulations (e.g., Waldron et al. 1985), little consideration had been given to the broader 'ecological footprint' of fisheries. This workshop occurred well before the recent efforts taken in response to Canada's 1997 Oceans Act and was one of the first of its kind to take this broader ecological perspective.

The enhanced focus on research in support of fisheries management during this period was a direct result of extended jurisdiction in 1977. There was a rapid expansion of the Canadian fishing fleets to fill the void left by the departing European fleets. By the early 1980s, it was evident that this increasing fleet capacity was not only creating socio-economic issues (e.g., conflict over quota sharing) in coastal communities, but was also severely stressing the fish populations and marine ecosystems through overfishing off Atlantic Canada. BIO scientists were heavily engaged during this period in informing fisheries managers of not only the risks of enhanced fleet capacity, but also of measures to address this hazard. There were numerous studies by BIO scientists on the efficacy of specific management measures. For example, Fanning et al. (1987) and Halliday (1988) studied the impact of closed areas on groundfish population fluctuations, showing that unless they are carefully designed both temporally and spatially, they can be of limited utility for the conservation of the species. Halliday and White (1989) considered the yield implications of fishing gear mesh-size changes, providing evidence for generally increased yield as mesh sizes are increased. The growth in fleet capacity also stimulated research on the dynamics of the fleets themselves. In an innovative paper, Allen and McGlade (1986) described how vessels share information on the fishing grounds to optimize catch rates and thus maximize revenue gains.

The groundfish fisheries of Atlantic Canada collapsed in 1992, so that by the end of 1993, most fisheries north of Halifax, Nova Scotia, including stocks in the Gulf of St. Lawrence and off Newfoundland, were closed to fishing. The details of the rapid declines in cod abundance varied among the several management units from the eastern Scotian Shelf to the shelf seas off Labrador. BIO scientists organized and led two workshops to evaluate the causes of the cod fluctuations on the Scotian Shelf within the eastern Scotian Shelf and the western Scotian Shelf management units (Angel et al. 1994), as well as what should be done to improve the management system (Burke et al 1996). Paradoxically, under the same management regime, the stock on the eastern Scotian Shelf had collapsed, whereas that on the western Scotian Shelf did not. It was concluded in retrospect that, although overfishing had occurred in both management units, natural mortality had increased significantly (starting in the 1980s) in the eastern Scotian Shelf. The difficulty in identifying this change in a timely manner had led to the assessments being too optimistic for the eastern Scotian Shelf management unit, and thus, the associated overfishing and ultimately the collapse (Sinclair et al. 1997). Precise causes for the differences in the trends in groundfish abundance on the Scotian Shelf, and the reasons for the differences in the trends in natural mortality of cod, have been hotly debated and are addressed in the next section. This event had huge consequences for the coastal communities of Atlantic Canada, the repercussions of which are still felt to this day. The fishery collapses also galvanized the research community at BIO to address the causes, as well as the lessons that could be learned to improve the advisory products and management systems.

POST-GROUNDFISH COLLAPSE (1993-2012)

The collapse of the east coast groundfish fisheries in the early 1990s put in motion a number of significant changes that rippled throughout the BIO research community. In the big picture, there was a realization that a focus on single-species management had taken attention away from the need to conserve ecosystems. In 1997, Canada enacted the Oceans Act, which required government, industry, and stakeholders to put fisheries management in the broader context of an 'ecosystem approach to management' (EAM). Within BIO, since 1993, there had been a growth in research on EAM. At the same time, there was a need to both rebuild the depleted fish populations and limit fishery impacts on other ecosystem components. In 2003, Canada enacted its Species at Risk Act (SARA) which legislated that governments are mandated to rebuild and protect depleted populations. The overall impact of SARA has been to shift BIO research resources from commercially fished finfish stocks to those requiring assessment and associated research under SARA. Furthermore, for the commercial fisheries under amendments to the Fisheries Act, a new precautionary approach had been mandated. This outlined another list of 'must dos' for regional managers which in turn placed new demands on the BIO scientific community. Key among these is the need to define harvest control rules for each stock consisting of both biomass and fishing mortality limits and target reference points. These require knowledge of the production dynamics of each stock which has required new innovative population modelling efforts, in some situations with poor data.

Some of the void created by these shifts in research priorities, driven by the new legislation, has been filled by the fishing industry. Since the early 1990s, when quasi-property rights were introduced into Maritimes fisheries, there has been a trend of increasing involvement of fishing fleets in population monitoring and associated research. For instance, a number of industry-DFO science surveys were initiated which now provide the key abundance indicators for stock assessments of groundfish (O'Boyle et al. 1995), shrimp (*Pandalus borealis*; Koeller et al. 2011), and snow crab (*Chionoecetes opilio*; Choi and Zizzerson 2011).

As well, the Fishermen and Scientists Research Society (FSRS) was created to facilitate collaboration on science projects and surveys of joint interest with the inshore groundfish industry. Since its start in 1994, the FSRS has conducted an annual survey every fall on the eastern Scotian Shelf employing longliner fishing vessels. Collaborative projects have now expanded to Atlantic Lobster (*Homarus americanus;* Tremblay et al. 2014). The FSRS continues to be an important member of the fisheries community, being active in an ever increasing number of fishermen-scientist collaborations (for details, go to: www.fsrs.ns.ca).

While the direction of fisheries research was changing, so too were the scientific institutions. CAFSAC, which had been the peer review forum for fisheries stock assessments, was replaced by the Regional Advisory Process (RAP) which fostered broader participation by stakeholders in scientific peer review of fishery management advice. In 1999, the invertebrate fisheries science group moved from the Halifax Fisheries Research Laboratory to BIO, while the diadromous fisheries research group was consolidated at BIO in 2000 after years of being spread across a number of locations. These changes led to the greatest concentration of fisheries science expertise at BIO since its founding in 1962.

The 1997 Canada Oceans Act required that all oceans activities, including fisheries, take an EAM. To facilitate the implementation of the Act, the Oceans Act Coordination Office (OACO) was established at BIO (Murphy et al. 2014). One of the first tasks was to define the conservation objectives which would be used to guide EAM. These were articulated at a national Fisheries and Oceans Canada (DFO) workshop in 2000 in which a number of BIO scientists played a major role (Jamieson et al. 2001, O'Boyle and Jamieson 2006). Objectives were defined to conserve ecosystem biodiversity at the community, population, and species levels, productivity by trophic level and population, and the habitats of the seafloor and water column. Ultimately, these objectives influenced the direction of ecosystem research at BIO and elsewhere in DFO. However, initial efforts focussed on policy defining EAM, and pilot projects were established in each DFO region to explore implementation options. In the Maritimes Region, a pilot project was established on the eastern Scotian Shelf, entitled the Eastern Scotian Shelf Integrated Management (ESSIM) initiative. BIO scientists worked with the OACO in outlining best practices for ESSIM. Early on it was recognized that much could be learned from EAM initiatives in Australia and thus, a long-term collaboration was initiated between BIO and Australian scientists at the Commonwealth Scientific and Industrial Research Organization (CSIRO). One of the indirect products of this collaboration was the production of an implementation template, elements of which have guided ESSIM efforts (O'Boyle et al. 2005).

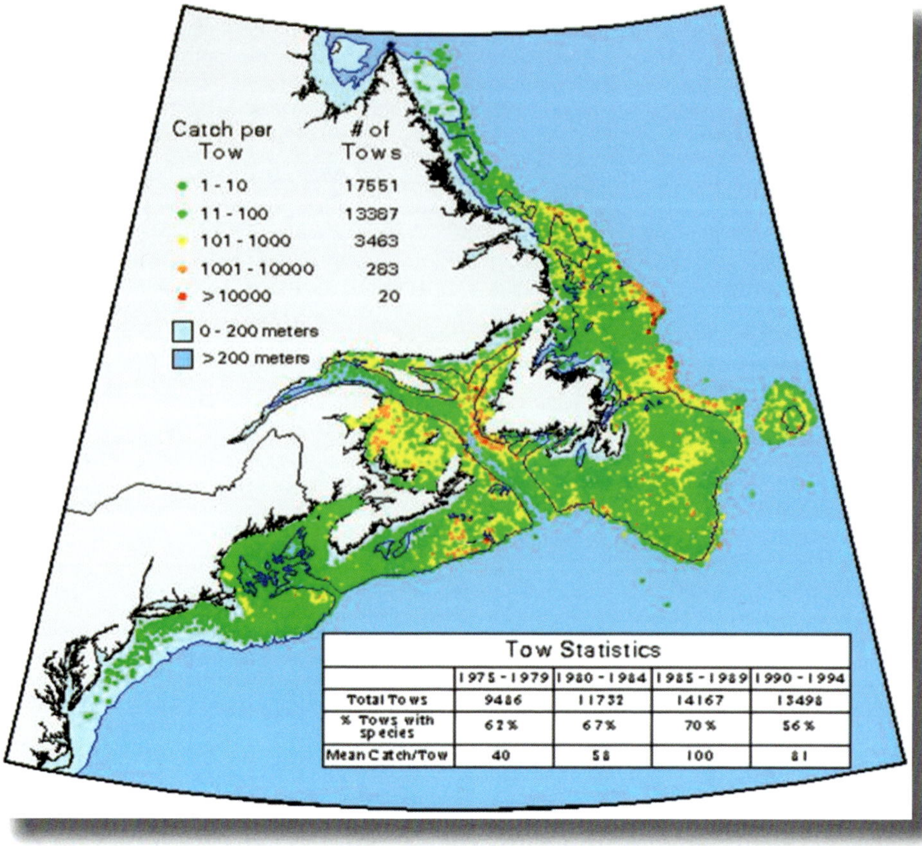

Figure 7. East coast distribution of Atlantic Cod (*Gadus morhua*) determined by the DFO/NOAA East Coast of North America Strategic Assessment project (ECNASAP); colours indicate relative abundance of cod based upon catch per tow as indicated in the legend (from online atlas located at: http://coinatlantic.ca/documents/aczisc_miscellaneous%20_documents/96ecnasap_groundfish.pdf).

Biodiversity figures prominently in EAM, and BIO scientists have undertaken innovative research on the structure and changes of the Scotian Shelf ecosystem. One of the first of these was collaboration with scientists of the United States National Oceanographic and Atmospheric Administration (NOAA) to study the changes in groundfish communities on the east coast of North America since the early 1970s. This East Coast of North America Strategic Assessment Project (ECNASAP) identified biogeographic patterns of fish communities and how they have changed over time (Mahon et al. 1998; Fig. 7).

There was a growing realization from this work that the ecosystems of the Scotian Shelf, particularly on the eastern half, had dramatically changed in the 1980s. The review by Zwanenburg et al. (2002) focussed on the marked differences in species trends on the eastern and western portions of the shelf, concluding that overfishing was a major driver of change, but also that environmental variability was also involved. Where once the groundfish stocks had dominated the ecosystem, pelagic species such as Atlantic Herring now represented the most abundant fish species.

It was considered important to document these long-term changes in the eastern Scotian Shelf ecosystem for the ESSIM managers. Therefore, in the early 2000s, a working group led by K. Frank was tasked with undertaking an 'integrated assessment' to produce the first Ecosystem Status Report (Department of Fisheries and Oceans 2003) in Atlantic Canada. This work was part of the broader research efforts by the team of J. Choi, J. Fisher, K. Frank, B. Leggett, B. Petrie, and N. Shackell on the dynamics of the Scotian Shelf ecosystem which has produced a series of internationally recognized papers on the structure and function of marine ecosystems. For example, Choi et al. (2005), examining trends in survey and fisheries datasets, observed community-level reductions in body size, biomass, and physiological condition in groundfish species. They concluded that there had been a decoupling of benthic and pelagic systems which reduced the energy flow to the benthic system. This decoupling was interpreted as being due to a complex set of factors that were triggered by the cumulative removal of biomass of groundfish species and exacerbated by decadal scale variability in bottom temperature and water column stratification. Frank et al. (2005) interpreted the trophic level changes on the eastern Scotian Shelf owing to the cascading impacts of the removal of large fish, in particular the larger cod. They hypothesized that the release of predation on mid-trophic level fish caused by overfishing of larger fish led to increases in the relative abundance of small pelagic species such as Herring and benthic invertebrates such as Atlantic Snow Crab. This in turn was interpreted to have caused decreases in zooplankton abundance and lower predation on phytoplankton resulting in higher biomass at the base of the food-chain.

Later, Shackell et al. (2010) interpreted the different features of the western Scotian shelf temporal dynamics also as evidence of trophic cascades in response to the reduction in abundance of larger fish. Trophic cascades can occur when the reduction of a predator of a prey results in the increase in abundance of that prey which in return leads to a reduction in the abundance of the prey of that species. In this case, the biomass of the top predators had not declined during the past several decades, but their average size had. They inferred that the change in the size composition of the predators had led to an increase in the biomass of prey with subsequent effects, such as reduced abundance of species at lower trophic levels. Frank et al. (2006, 2007), taking a meta-analysis approach to the North Atlantic observations on trophic level fluctuations, concluded that top-down impacts due to overfishing of large fish are prevalent and lead to lower species diversity at lower temperatures. More recently, Frank et al. (2011) updated their earlier integrated assessment of the eastern Scotian Shelf and suggested that, overall, the state of the ecosystem may be returning to that observed during the 1980s with fewer pelagic fish and somewhat higher abundance of groundfish. More years of observations are required to confirm whether or not this process is underway.

Fisher et al. (2008) provided a summary of the temporal shifts in the distribution of fish species off Atlantic Canada with an emphasis on species diversity in relation to the North Atlantic Oscillation (NAO). Although the expected bottom temperature response to the oscillations was estimated to be minimal at the latitudes of the Scotian Shelf, there has been about a 5 to 10% difference in diversity during the three decades in response to NAO fluctuations. This work was followed up in a global study of how fish body size and biodiversity relate to ecosystem functioning (Fisher et al. 2010). There was a negative correlation between mean fish species length per 'large marine ecosystem' (LME) and the annual percent change in predator landings per year among 30 LMEs during periods when the trophic level of the catch declined in each LME. In contrast, there was a positive correlation between species richness per LME and the annual percent change in predator landings per year among 30 LMEs during periods when the trophic level of the catch declined in each LME.

Starting about 2003, ecosystem modelling of the Scotian Shelf was also undertaken as part of a DFO project entitled 'Comparative Dynamics of Exploited Ecosystems in the Northwest Atlantic' (CDEENA). The overall goal of this project was to gain a better understanding of the structure and function of eastern Canadian marine ecosystems. Bundy (2004, 2005) and Bundy and Fanning (2005) used a trophic dynamic modelling approach called ECOPATH to tease out the relative importance of processes that have prevented the recovery of Atlantic Cod on the eastern Scotian Shelf. They concluded that the systematic removal of larger fish, a practice also known as fishing down the food chain, has resulted, through trophic cascade dynamics, in an increase of abundance of species situated at the middle of the food chain. These species, through enhanced predation on young cod, are interpreted to have generated a higher level of natural mortality for small cod, as well as a reduction in condition (fish 'plumpness') due to competition. However, the estimated high level of mortality of larger cod since the early 1990s is not easily interpreted in this modelling approach. In a broader sense, it was interpreted that the ecosystem has changed fundamentally from a 'demersal-feeder-dominated' system to a 'pelagic-feeder-dominated' system. The authors concluded that the changes in ecological processes are consistent with the 'cultivation-depensation' hypothesis of Walters and Kitchell (2001) and that cod are trapped in this alternate state of low productivity. When groundfish like cod are abundant, they control the forage fish through predation and so limit the predation on their eggs, as well as the competition between forage fish and their juveniles. When cod decline, the forage fish can become so abundant that they consume eggs, compete with the juveniles, and suppress recovery. In such conditions, there would be a time-lagged recovery of the stock.

Bundy et al. (2010) used a similar modelling approach to compare four geographic areas off Atlantic Canada, including the eastern Scotian Shelf. The conclusions were similar to the earlier studies, but a variant of their 'cultivation-depensation' hypothesis was suggested. As well as interpreting that forage species out-compete small cod for small zooplankton, they suggested that these competitors also prey on larval cod, thus reducing recruitment success.

Halliday and Pinhorn (2009) provided a different perspective on the relative importance of fishing and environmental change on groundfish populations for the northwest Atlantic. The assessment of the 4VsW (Fig. 8) cod stock determined that, subsequent to the closure of the fishery in 1992, total mortality was still high, implying that natural mortality had remained high. Elevated high natural mortality has also been seen in the Gulf of St. Lawrence and western Scotian Shelf cod stocks. They concluded that increases in natural mortality of cod began in the late 1980s, contiguous with the collapses of the several cod stocks off Atlantic Canada, and that this phenomenon was widespread. They also suggested that environmental conditions, at the scale of the Northwest Atlantic, influenced the productivity of groundfish species on decadal time scales. In summary, their analysis concluded that a combination of overfishing and climate variability has been responsible for the observed fluctuations in groundfish populations. They do not, however, specify the ecological processes involved in the changes in productivity.

The above studies addressed the overall ecosystem components. In addition, there are a number of papers by BIO scientists that considered more narrowly the interactions between Grey Seals and Atlantic Cod. These studies have greatly benefited from the research program conducted on Grey Seals since the establishment of MFD (Bowen 2014). Mohn and Bowen (1996), based on a 'minimum realistic' predator/prey model for the eastern Scotian Shelf for the 1970-94 period, concluded that Grey Seals were not a major factor in the collapse of the cod stock. In contrast, Sinclair et al. (1997), based on a comparative analysis of fisheries management practices on the eastern (4VsW) and western (4X) Scotian Shelf, concluded that a combination of poor environmental conditions and increases in natural mortality due in part to seal predation had contributed to the decline in stock production and recruitment of cod. Fu et al. (2001) evaluated the causes of the lack of recovery of cod on the eastern Scotian Shelf following the 1993 fishery closure and concluded that seal predation was not a significant factor. Trzcinski et al. (2006) also focussed on the lack of recovery of cod since 1993 and concluded that Grey Seals had made some contribution to increases in cod natural mortality in the post-fishery closure period, but that unknown sources of mortality were also contributing to the failure of cod to recover. Trzcinski et al. (2009) updated their model and included an analysis of the western Scotian Shelf management area. For both management areas, they concluded that seal predation on cod is a minor contribution to natural mortality, but that other unknown sources have caused the stocks to decline and not recover. Recently, O'Boyle and Sinclair (2012) examined the assumptions and data used in the previous models and concluded that not only were the estimates of the percent cod in a seal's diet too low, but also that seals may be eating a wide range of cod sizes and not just small individuals as had been previously stated (Trzcinski et al. 2006). The conclusion drawn from these findings was that seals may explain the high recent mortality of cod (O'Boyle and Sinclair 2012). Further study is required to help resolve these contrasting perspectives.

While the above studies focussed on predator-prey interactions, the work of assessing the status of stocks continued. With the collapse of populations of Atlantic Cod, Haddock, and Pollock (*Pollachius virens*), exploratory fisheries on a wide range of other species such as skates (*Raja* spp.), Monkfish (*Lophius americanus*), Atlantic Hagfish (*Myxine glutinosa*), and blood worms (*Glycera* spp.) were initiated to give fishermen displaced from the collapsed fisheries new employment opportunities.

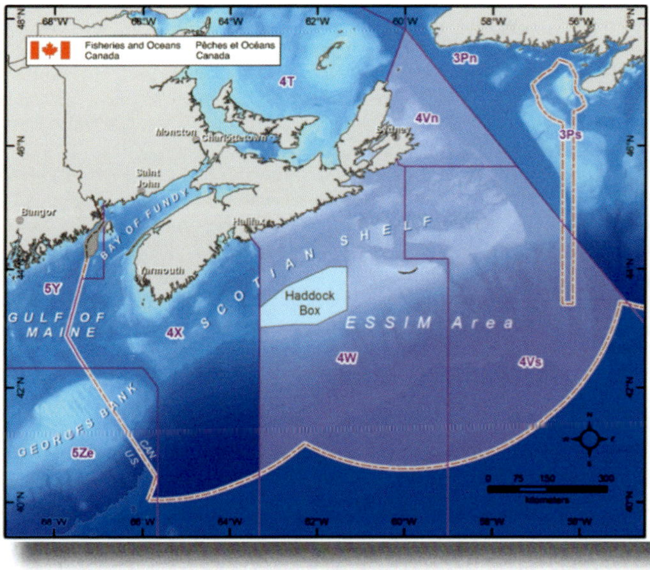

Figure 8. Map of the NAFO Divisions of the Scotian Shelf which are used to designate finfish stock areas.

This put additional demands on BIO fishery scientists to initiate new data collection programs for these fisheries and design new assessment procedures for these little known and data-poor stocks. Caddy (2002) had designed an assessment method for data-poor situations encountered in many parts of the world. Termed the 'Traffic Light Approach' (TLA), it consisted of tabulating indices of stock recruitment, growth, mortality, and ecosystem trends using a wide range of data sources and without explicitly using a mathematical model to describe relationships among the data. A number of BIO fishery scientists felt that one cause of the groundfish collapse was excessive dependence on assessment models that could only consider a narrow range of the data potentially available. The TLA was seen as a way of not only addressing data-poor stock situations, but also broadening the scope of assessments (Halliday et al. 2001). Through the efforts of the Fisheries Management Studies working group (for more details on this group, see below), the design of a TLA assessment to meet the needs of Maritimes fisheries was articulated and implemented in a number of groundfish and invertebrate assessments. However, efforts to integrate the TLA with modelling approaches proved difficult and, by 2005, the method had fallen out of use in groundfish stock assessments.

Nevertheless, it has continued to be used for the eastern Scotian Shelf shrimp stock (Koeller et al. 2011).

Assessment modelling, on the other hand, has made a transition from the Virtual Population Analysis (VPA) methods common in the 1980s and 1990s to Statistical Catch at Age (SCAA) methods which has grown in prominence in other parts of the world (Quinn and Deriso 1999). The key difference between the two approaches is that VPA assumes no error in the catch at age while SCAA makes no such assumption. SCAA models are generally more complex than VPA models as exemplified by the ADAPT framework, but has allowed a greater range of data and issues to be included in assessment models. The model developed by Trzcinski et al. (2011) for Atlantic Halibut (*Hippoglossus hippoglossus*) is an example of the SCAA approach as currently implemented by BIO assessment scientists. Bayesian modelling approaches in which variation of input parameters are updated as new observations become available also have come into use, especially for the scallop fishery (Smith and Lundy 2002). Overall, since the collapse of the groundfish stocks in the early 1990s, there has been a dramatic change in the models used to assess fish stocks.

These changes in assessment models were timely from another perspective. For the depleted stocks, such as eastern Scotian Shelf Atlantic Cod, DFO has introduced a new framework termed the Recovery Potential Assessment (RPA) which requires that not only must the status and threats of a depleted stock be assessed but also its recovery potential under a range of future yields. For commercially fished stocks, DFO has introduced a precautionary fisheries framework consisting of a target biomass ('Upper Stock Threshold') and limit biomass ('Lower Reference Point') below which fishing is not permitted. BIO scientists have been influential in the determination of stock reference points. This is exemplified by Smith et al. (1993), a benchmark publication on biological reference points. Reference points have required explicit modelling of the production dynamics of a stock and their uncertainty for which SCAA methods are well suited. Good examples of SCAA uses for RPAs implemented for depleted species include that for Porbeagle Shark (*Lamna nasus*; Gibson and Campana 2005) and Atlantic Salmon (*Salmo salar*; Gibson et al. 2009).

However, assessment models ultimately depend upon new data on the biology and dynamics of the species under consideration. For a wide range of depleted species, new research programs have been initiated since 1993 to fill gaps in knowledge of these species. A good example of this is that for Porbeagle Shark. Since the initiation of the shark research program in 1998, a number of significant findings have been made including the species' growth dynamics, maturation at age, diet, and population dynamics. Most recently, through the use of satellite tagging, Campana et al. (2010) discovered that adult Porbeagle females annually migrate to the Sargasso Sea to mate, travelling almost 1 km below the surface to avoid the warm water of the Gulf Stream (Fig. 9). Indeed, migration studies have figured prominently throughout the history of fisheries studies at BIO. Campana et al. (1999) used acoustic tags to determine the stock origins of Atlantic Cod mixing off Cape Breton each fall and winter while Stobo and Fowler (2006) have summarized tagging studies conducted between 1953 and 1985.

Another aspect of biological studies of Scotian Shelf species includes their use and dependence of the benthic habitat. It has been recognized for some time that fishing gear such as trawls and dredges can have significant impacts on the seabed and this has prompted a large number of studies at BIO focussed on the response of benthic habitat and organisms to fishing disturbance (Gordon and Kenchington 2014). This work benefited from the development of a wide array of bottom sampling and imaging equipment developed by BIO engineers (Gordon et al. 2014). Studies have also been conducted by BIO on deep-water corals (Mortensen and Buhl-Mortensen 2005, Mortensen et al. 2005) and the results have been instrumental in the delineation of areas closed to fishing to protect these highly sensitive species (Gordon et al. 2014). Robert (2002) reported on an interesting study done in collaboration with the scallop fishing industry which identified both the preferred habitat of this species and the target fishing area which in turn limited the habitat impacts of the fishery. Finally, a theoretical framework has been developed by Kostylev and Hannah (2007) that describes the sensitivity of benthic habitat as a function of both the level of natural disturbance it experiences and its scope for growth based on production characteristics. This work has been used by the Oceans, Habitat and Species at Risk Branch at BIO to define Marine Protected Areas (MPAs) in order to protect sensitive habitat.

The research described on harvest fisheries and ecological interactions in this paper has necessarily called upon the work of a number of different scientists each working towards a diverse set of initial objectives, each with a differing data collection and management philosophy, and from a variety of sites. Ecological analysis requires data that is centrally available, with well documented formats (meta-data), and where possible, well defined computer programs for data extraction and analysis. Project leaders working with data scientists at BIO devised a unique web application to overcome the most important of these challenges by developing a web-based common computer working environment called the Virtual Data Centre (VDC). The VDC has become the central standard location for a variety of survey data, each with a well-documented set of metadata allowing scientists within and outside DFO to access the survey and fishery data needed for ecological analyses. It has also become a location where standardized data extraction and analysis programs are maintained and improved. This centralization of data and software has helped to ensure that researchers comparing across spatial zones and across time are drawing conclusions that are related directly to the ecological phenomena being investigated and are not biased by unknown aspects of the data. The VDC has been a valuable component

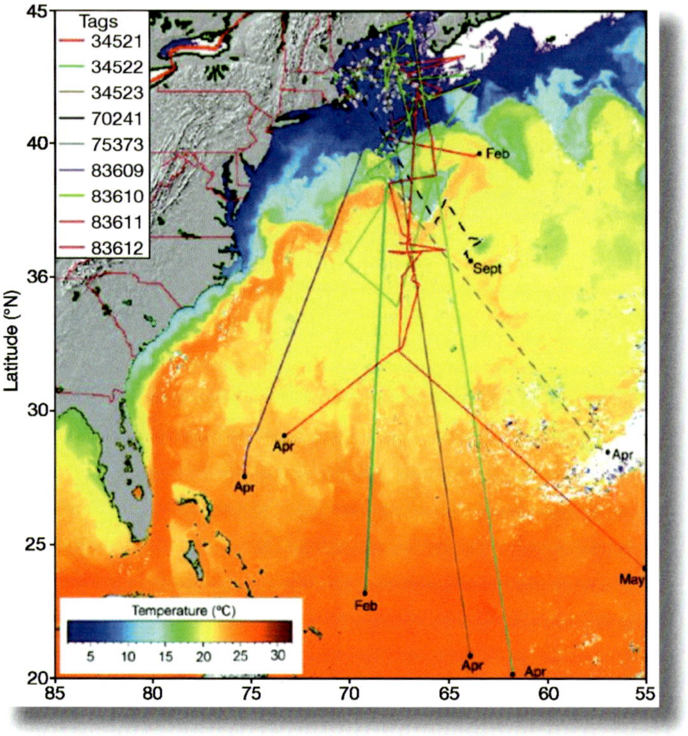

Figure 9. Migratory pathways of mature female Porbeagle Sharks (*Lamna nasus*) to the Sargasso Sea (white area at lower centre-right) and under the Gulf Stream (stronger yellow and orange areas immediately offshore of the cooler water [blue colours] adjacent to United States east coast) determined from 'pop-up' archival transmission tags. Spatial tracks of nine 'pop-up' archival tags are presented with month of last transmission given at end of each track (from Campana et al. 2010).

for the ecological work described in this paper and has enabled objectives beyond those originally intended for by the original data collections to be investigated.

It is evident that BIO fishery scientists have been supporting fisheries and oceans managers with science information to allow informed regulatory decisions. Fisheries management studies undertaken at BIO have addressed a wide spectrum of issues. These have included the delineation and impact of spatial and temporal closures to address specific issues. Some of these were undertaken under the auspices of the regional Fisheries Management Studies Working Group, which was a DFO Fisheries Management/Science body created to facilitate dialogue between managers and scientists on the research needs of fisheries management. For example, Halliday (1988) evaluated the use of seasonal spawning closures off southwest Nova Scotia while Fanning et al. (1987) and Frank et al. (2000) considered the design and impact of a closure on Emerald and Western banks to protect juvenile Haddock. Other studies range from

Halliday and White (1989) and Halliday (2002) on fish selectivity characteristics of trawl mesh and longline hook sizes to Halliday and Pinhorn's (1996) examination of North Atlantic fisheries management systems in general. These examples represent only a small sample of the studies that BIO scientists have conducted in support of fisheries management.

On a last note, the market place is being more proactive in encouraging sustainable fishing. The international Marine Stewardship Council (MSC), based in London, England, was created in 1997 to provide a set of criteria against which the sustainability of a fishery can be measured. Increasingly, markets are only accepting fish product from processors that carry the MSC eco-label. A number of Nova Scotia fisheries have undergone MSC certification, aided by scientists at BIO.

THE FUTURE

It is always fun, but perhaps perilous, to 'crystal ball' about what the future will bring for fisheries research at BIO. O'Boyle (2009) attempted to do this based upon considerations of current research and ocean management trends, and his conclusions are still considered valid several years later. As noted, since early 2000, a paradigm shift in oceans management has been underway which will continue to influence the future of research at BIO and elsewhere. On one hand, fisheries are increasingly being seen as one ocean sector among many with numerous new objectives being sought under an Ecosystem Approach to Management (EAM). On the other hand, there is growing acceptance that stock assessment needs to be considered as only one element of a more comprehensive management strategy evaluation (MSE). MSE consists of a linked suite of processes that include monitoring, assessment, harvest control rules, and implementation. Both these trends have implications for science support of future MSEs and the process whereby this science is managed and delivered. There will be a move towards ecosystem models that propose plausible hypotheses of ecosystem functioning. To support these, there will need to be theoretical developments on ecosystem control, spatial dynamics, and the habitat-productivity linkage. Growth in monitoring technology will provide unprecedented opportunities to enhance our knowledge and will fundamentally impact EAM and MSE. Indeed, the strong legacy of monitoring programs places BIO in an excellent position to take advantage of these advancements. Stock assessment will initially be similar to current approaches, but will increasingly be required to report on ecosystem-related impacts. Decision-making will require the evaluation of the merits of competing management strategies in relation to achievement of EAM objectives in the face of uncertainty. It will be revealing to see whether or not these predictions come to pass at the 100th anniversary of the founding of the Bedford Institute of Oceanography.

ACKNOWLEDGEMENTS

The authors have worked over 30 years with virtually all the scientists whose work is referenced in this chapter. Support staff, including scientific technicians, computer scientists, ships personnel, international colleagues, industry collaborators, fishermen, and fishing associations have made these programs possible. Although their names do not appear on papers or in publications, they have been integral to the scientific advances that these programs have produced. We wish to acknowledge their collective contributions to marine science. The manuscript benefited greatly from the comments of Don Gordon, Mike Lewis, and David Nettleship for which the authors are most grateful.

REFERENCES

Allen, P.M. and J.M. McGlade. 1986. Dynamics of discovery and exploitation: the case of the Scotian Shelf groundfish fisheries. Canadian Journal of Fisheries and Aquatic Sciences 43: 1,187-1,200.

Angel, J.R., D.L. Burke, R.N. O'Boyle, F.G. Peacock, M. Sinclair, and K.C.T. Zwanenburg. 1994. Report of the Workshop on Scotia-Fundy Groundfish Management from 1977 to 1993. Canadian Technical Report of Fisheries and Aquatic Sciences 1979, Dartmouth, NS.

Bowen, W.D. 2014. Whale and seal research at the Bedford Institute of Oceanography through five decades. Pages 113-122 *in* Voyage of Discovery: Fifty Years of Marine Research at Canada's Bedford Institute of Oceanography (D.N. Nettleship, D.C. Gordon, C.F.M. Lewis, and M.P. Latremouille, Eds.). Bedford Institute of Oceanography-Oceans Association, Dartmouth, NS.

Bundy, A. 2004. Mass balance models of the eastern Scotian Shelf before and after the cod collapse and other ecosystem changes. Canadian Technical Report of Fisheries and Aquatic Sciences 2520, Dartmouth, NS.

Bundy, A. 2005. Structure and functioning of the eastern Scotian Shelf ecosystem before and after the collapse of groundfish stocks in the early 1990s. Canadian Journal of Fisheries and Aquatic Sciences 62: 1,453-1,473.

Bundy, A. and L.P. Fanning. 2005. Can Atlantic cod (*Gadus morhua*) recover? Exploring trophic explanations for the non-recovery of the cod stock on the eastern Scotian Shelf, Canada. Canadian Journal of Fisheries and Aquatic Sciences 62: 1,474-1,489.

Bundy, A., J.J. Heymans, L. Morissette, and C. Savenkoff. 2010. Seals, cod and forage fish: a comparative exploration of variations in the theme of stock collapse and ecosystem change in four Northwest Atlantic ecosystems. Progress in Oceanography 81: 188-206.

Burke, D.L., R.N. O'Boyle, P. Partington, and M. Sinclair. 1996. Report of the Second Workshop on Scotia-Fundy Groundfish management. Canadian Technical Report of Fisheries and Aquatic Sciences 2100, Dartmouth, NS.

Caddy, J. 2002. Limit reference points, traffic lights, and holistic approaches to fisheries management with minimal stock assessment input. Fisheries Research 56: 133-137.

Campana, S.E., S.J. Smith, and P.C.F. Hurley. 1989. A drift-retention dichotomy for larval haddock (*Melanogrammus aeglefinus*) spawned on Browns Bank. Canadian Journal of Fisheries and Aquatic Sciences 46 (Supplement 1): 93-102.

Campana, S.E., G.A. Chouinard, J.M. Hanson, and A. Frechet. 1999. Mixing and migration of overwintering Atlantic cod (*Gadus morhua*) stocks near the mouth of the Gulf of St. Lawrence. Canadian Journal of Fisheries and Aquatic Sciences 56: 1,873-1,881.

Campana, S.E., W. Joyce, and M. Fowler. 2010. Subtropical pupping ground for a cold-water shark. Canadian Journal of Fisheries and Aquatic Sciences 67: 769-773.

Choi, J.S., K.T. Frank, and W.C. Leggett. 2005. Integrated assessment of a large marine ecosystem: a case study of the devolution of the eastern Scotian Shelf, Canada. Oceanography and Marine Biology Annual Review 43: 47-67.

Choi, J.S. and B.M. Zisserson. 2011. Assessment of Scotian Shelf Snow Crab in 2010. Canadian Science Advisory Secretariat Research Document 2011/110, Fisheries and Oceans Canada, Dartmouth, NS.

Clark, D., J. Emberley, C. Clark, and B. Peppard. 2010. Update of the 2009 Summer Scotian Shelf and Bay of Fundy Research Vessel Survey. Canadian Science Advisory Secretariat Research Document 2010/008, Fisheries and Oceans Canada, Dartmouth, NS.

Department of Fisheries and Oceans. 2003. State of the eastern Scotian Shelf ecosystem. Canadian Science Advisory Secretariat Ecosystem Status Report 2003/004, Dartmouth, NS.

Dickie, L.M., S.R. Kerr, and P.R. Boudreau. 1987. Size-dependent processes underlying regularities in ecosystem structure. Ecological Monographs 57: 233-250.

Dickie, L.M. and P.C. Smith. 1989. Fisheries Ecology Program (FEP): general introduction. Canadian Journal of Fisheries and Aquatic Sciences 46: 538.

Duplisea, D.E., P.R. Boudreau, and L.M. Dickie. 2014. The size-structured view of marine ecosystems. Pages 99-103 *in* Voyage of Discovery: Fifty Years of Marine Research at Canada's Bedford Institute of Oceanography (D.N. Nettleship, D.C. Gordon, C.F.M. Lewis, and M.P. Latremouille, Eds.). Bedford Institute of Oceanography-Oceans Association, Dartmouth, NS.

Fanning, F.P., K. Zwanenburg, and M. Showell. 1987. Haddock nursery closed areas: delineation and impact. Canadian Atlantic Fisheries Scientific Advisory Committee Research Document 87/59, Dartmouth, NS.

Fisher, J.A.D, K.T. Frank, B. Petrie, W.C. Leggett, and N.L. Shackell. 2008. Temporal dynamics within a contemporary latitudinal diversity gradient. Ecological Letters 11: 883-897.

Fisher, J.A.D., K.T. Frank, and W.C. Leggett. 2010. Global variation in marine fish body size and its role in biodiversity-ecosystem functioning. Marine Ecology Progress Series 405: 1-13.

Frank, K.T., R.I. Perry, K.F. Drinkwater, and W.H. Lear. 1988. Changes in the fisheries of Atlantic Canada associated with global increases in atmospheric carbon dioxide: a preliminary report. Canadian Technical Report of Fisheries and Aquatic Sciences Number 1652, Fisheries and Oceans Canada, Dartmouth, NS.

Frank, K.T., N.L. Shackell, and J.E. Simon. 2000. An evaluation of the Emerald/Western Bank juvenile haddock closed area. ICES Journal of Marine Science 57: 1,023-1,034.

Frank, K. T., B. Petrie, J.S. Choi, and W.C. Leggett. 2005. Trophic cascades in a formerly cod-dominated ecosystem. Science 308: 1,621-1,623.

Frank, K.T., B. Petrie, N.L. Shackell, and J.C. Choi. 2006. Reconciling differences in trophic control in mid-latitude marine ecosystems. Ecology Letters 9: 1,096-1,105.

Frank, K.T., B. Petrie, and N.L. Shackell. 2007. The ups and downs of trophic control in continental shelf ecosystems. Trends in Ecology and Evolution 22: 236-242.

Frank, K.T., B. Petrie, J.A.D. Fisher, and W.C. Leggett. 2011. Transient dynamics of an altered large marine ecosystem. Nature 477: 86-91.

Fu, C., R. Mohn, and L.P. Fanning. 2001. Why the Atlantic Cod (*Gadus morhua*) stock off eastern Nova Scotia has not recovered. Canadian Journal of Fisheries and Aquatic Sciences 58: 1,613-1,623.

Gagné, J.A. and R.N. O'Boyle. 1984. The timing of cod spawning on the Scotian Shelf. Flodevigen Rapportser 1: 501-517.

Gavaris, S. 1988. An adaptive framework for the estimation of population size. Canadian Atlantic Fisheries Scientific Advisory Committee Research

Document 88/29, Dartmouth, NS.

Gavaris, S. and. S.J. Smith. 1987. Effect of allocation and stratification strategies on precision of survey abundance estimates for Atlantic cod (*Gadus morhua*) on the eastern Scotian Shelf. Journal of Northwest Atlantic Fishery Science 7: 137-144.

Gibson, A.J.F. and S.E. Campana. 2005. Status and recovery potential of Porbeagle Shark in the Northwest Atlantic. Canadian Science Advisory Secretariat Research Document 2005/053, Fisheries and Oceans Canada, Dartmouth, NS.

Gibson, A.J.F., R.A. Jones, and P.G. Amiro. 2009. Equilibrium analyses of the recovery feasibility of four Atlantic salmon (*Salmo salar*) stocks in Nova Scotia and Southwest New Brunswick. Canadian Science Advisory Secretariat Research Document 2008/010, Fisheries and Oceans Canada, Dartmouth, NS.

Gordon, D.C. and E.L.R. Kenchington. 2014. The impact of fishing gear on benthic habitat and communities. Pages 295-300 *in* Voyage of Discovery: Fifty Years of Marine Research at Canada's Bedford Institute of Oceanography (D.N. Nettleship, D.C. Gordon, C.F.M. Lewis, and M.P. Latremouille, Eds.). Bedford Institute of Oceanography-Oceans Association, Dartmouth, NS.

Gordon, D.C., E.L.R. Kenchington, B.T. Hargrave, and D.L.Peer. 2014. Life at the bottom of the sea: advances in understanding benthic ecosystems. Pages 87-97 *in* Voyage of Discovery: Fifty Years of Marine Research at Canada's Bedford Institute of Oceanography (D.N. Nettleship, D.C. Gordon, C.F.M. Lewis, and M.P. Latremouille, Eds.). Bedford Institute of Oceanography-Oceans Association, Dartmouth, NS.

Halliday, R.G. 1988. Use of seasonal spawning area closures in the management of haddock fisheries in the northwest Atlantic. NAFO Scientific Council Studies 12: 27-36.

Halliday, R.G. 2002. A comparison of size selection of Atlantic cod (*Gadus morhua*) and haddock (*Melanogrammus aeglefinus*) by bottom longlines and otter trawls. Fisheries Research 57: 63-73.

Halliday, R.G. and G.N. White. 1989. The biological/technical implications of an increase in minimum trawl mesh size for groundfish fisheries in the Scotia-Fundy region. Canadian Technical Report of Fisheries and Aquatic Sciences Number 1691, Fisheries and Oceans Canada, Dartmouth, NS.

Halliday, R.G. and A.T. Pinhorn. 1996. North Atlantic fishery management systems: A comparison of management methods and resource trends. Journal of Northwest Atlantic Fishery Science 20: 1-143.

Halliday, R.G., L.P. Fanning, and R.K. Mohn. 2001. Use of the traffic light method in fishery management planning. Canadian Science Advisory Secretariat Research Document 2001/108, Fisheries and Oceans Canada, Dartmouth, NS.

Halliday, R.G. and A.T. Pinhorn. 2009. The roles of fishing and environmental change in the decline of northwest Atlantic groundfish populations in the early 1990s. Fisheries Research 97: 163-182.

Halliday, R.G., L. Van Guelphen, and D.E. Themelis. 2012. Demersal fish fauna of the continental slope off Nova Scotia, Canada, based on exploratory bottom trawl surveys in 1994–95. Journal Northwest Atlantic Fisheries Science 44: 41-60.

Jamieson, G., R. O'Boyle, J. Arbour, D. Cobb, S. Courtenay, R. Gregory, C. Levings, J. Munro, I. Perry, and H. Vandermeulen (Eds.). 2001. Proceedings of the National Workshop on Objectives and Indicators For Ecosystem-based Management. Canadian Science Advisory Secretariat Proceedings Series 2001/09, Fisheries and Oceans Canada, Dartmouth, NS.

Koeller, P., C. Fuentes-Yaco, M. Covey, M. King, and B. Zisserson. 2011. The last traffic light on the Scotian Shelf: Shrimp 2009-2010. Canadian Science Advisory Secretariat Research Document 2011/061, Fisheries and Oceans Canada, Dartmouth, NS.

Kostylev, V.E. and C.G. Hannah. 2007. Process-driven characterization and mapping of sea-bed habitats. Pages 177-184 *in* Mapping the Seafloor for Habitat Characterization (B.J. Todd and H.G. Greene, Eds). Geological Association of Canada Special Paper Number 47, St. John's, NL.

Lambert, T.C. 1987. Duration and intensity of spawning in herring (*Clupea harengus*) as related to the age structure of the mature population. Marine Ecology Progress Series 39: 209-220.

Li, W.K.W. 2014. Plankton ecology at the Bedford Institute of Oceanography, 1962-2012. Pages 77-86 *in* Voyage of Discovery: Fifty Years of Marine Research at Canada's Bedford Institute of Oceanography (D.N. Nettleship, D.C. Gordon, C.F.M. Lewis, and M.P. Latremouille, Eds.). Bedford Institute of Oceanography-Oceans Association, Dartmouth, NS.

Mahon, R. 1985. Towards the inclusion of fishery interactions in management advice. Canadian Technical Report of Fisheries and Aquatic Sciences Number 1347, Fisheries and Oceans Canada, Dartmouth, NS.

Mahon, R. and R.W. Smith. 1989. Demersal fish assemblages on the Scotian Shelf, Northwest Atlantic: spatial distribution and persistence. Canadian Journal of Fisheries and Aquatic Sciences 46 (Supplement 1): 134-152.

Mahon, R., S.K. Brown, K.C.T. Zwanenburg, D.B. Atkinson, K.R. Buja, L. Calflin, G.D. Howell, M.E. Monaco, R.N. O'Boyle, and M. Sinclair. 1998. Assemblages and biogeography of demersal fishes of the east coast of North America. Canadian Journal of Fisheries and Aquatic Sciences 55: 1,704-1,738.

Mohn, R.K. 1980. Bias and error propagation in logistic production models. Canadian Journal of Fisheries and Aquatic Sciences 37: 1,276-1,283.

Mohn, R.K. 1983. Effects of error in catch and effort data on tuning cohort analysis, with a postscript on logistic production models. Canadian Special Publication of Fisheries and Aquatic Sciences 66: 141-150.

Mohn, R.K. 1999. The restrospective problem in sequential population analysis: an investigation using cod fishery and simulated data. ICES Journal of Marine Science 56: 473-488.

Mohn, R. and W.D. Bowen. 1996. Grey seal predation on the eastern Scotian Shelf: modelling the impact on Atlantic cod. Canadian Journal of Fisheries and Aquatic Sciences 53: 2,722-2,738.

Mohn, R.K., M.K. Trzcinski, G.A.P. Black, S. Armsworthy, G.A. Young, P.A. Comeau, and C.E. den Heyer. 2010. Assessment of the Status of Division 4X5Y Haddock in 2009. Canadian Science Advisory Secretariat Research Document 2010/085, Fisheries and Oceans Canada, Dartmouth, NS.

Mortensen, P.B. and L. Buhl-Mortensen. 2005. Deep-water corals and their habitats in The Gully, a submarine canyon off Atlantic Canada. Pages 247-277 *in* Cold-water Corals and Ecosystems (A. Freiwald and J.M. Roberts, Eds.). Springer, Berlin, Germany.

Mortensen, P.B., L. Buhl-Mortensen, D.C. Gordon, Jr., G.B.J. Fader, D.L. McKeown, and D.G. Fenton. 2005. Effects of fisheries on deepwater gorgonian corals in the Northeast Channel, Nova Scotia. American Fisheries Society Symposium 41: 369-382.

Murphy, O.C., A.J. Ducharme, J.G. Naug, P.A. Macnab, and C.B. Merriman. 2014. Ecosystem Management Branch at the Bedford Institute of Oceanography: front line for ocean policy development and management. Pages 255-265 *in* Voyage of Discovery: Fifty years of Marine Research at Canada's Bedford Institute of Oceanography (D.N. Nettleship, D.C. Gordon, C.F.M. Lewis, and M.P. Latremouille, Eds.). Bedford Institute of Oceanography-Oceans Association, Dartmouth, NS.

O'Boyle, R.N. 1981. The generation of input parameters for sequential population analysis. Canadian Atlantic Fisheries Scientific Advisory Committee Research Document 81/78, Fisheries and Oceans Canada, Dartmouth, NS.

O'Boyle, R. 2009. The implications of a paradigm shift in ocean resource management for fisheries stock assessment. Pages 49-76 *in* The Future of Fisheries Science in North America (R.J. Beamish and B.J. Rothschild, Eds.). Springer, Berlin, Germany.

O'Boyle, R. and G.T. Jamieson. 2006. Observations on the implementation of ecosystem-based management: Experiences on Canada's east and west coasts. Fisheries Research 79: 1-12.

O'Boyle, R. and M. Sinclair. 2012. Seal-cod interactions on the eastern Scotian Shelf: reconsideration of modelling assumptions. Fisheries Research 115-116: 1-13.

O'Boyle, R.N., M. Sinclair, R.J. Conover, K.H. Mann, and A.C. Kohler. 1984. Temporal and spatial distribution of ichthyoplankton communities of the Scotian Shelf in relation to biological hydrological and physiographic features. Rapports et Proces-verbaux des Réunions, Conseil International pour l'Éxploration de la Mer 183: 27-40.

O'Boyle, R., D. Beanlands, P. Fanning, J. Hunt, P. Hurley, T. Lambert, J. Simon, and K. Zwanenburg. 1995. An overview of joint science/industry surveys on the Scotian Shelf, Bay of Fundy, and Georges Bank. Canadian Science Advisory Secretariat Research Document 95/133, Fisheries and Oceans Canada, Dartmouth, NS.

O'Boyle, R., M. Sinclair, P. Keizer, K. Lee, D. Ricard, and P. Yeats. 2005. Indicators for ecosystem-based management on the Scotian Shelf: bridging the gap between theory and practice. ICES Journal of Marine Science 62: 598-605.

Pope, J.G. 1972. An investigation of the accuracy of virtual population analysis using cohort analysis. ICNAF Research Bulletin 9: 65-74.

Quinn, T.J. and R.B. Deriso. 1999. Quantitative Fish Dynamics. Oxford University Press. New York, NY.

Ricker, W.E. 1954. Stock and recruitment. Journal of the Fisheries Research Board of Canada 11: 559-623.

Rivard, D. 1980. APL programs for stock assessment. Canadian Technical Report of Fisheries and Aquatic Sciences Number 1091, Fisheries and Oceans Canada, Dartmouth, NS.

Robert, G. 2002. Impact of multibeam surveys on scallop fishing efficiency and stock assessment. Pages 40-42 *in* Bedford Institute of Oceanography 2001 in Review (D. Geddes, Ed.). Bedford Institute of Oceanography, Dartmouth, NS.

Shackell, N.L., K.T. Frank, J.A.D. Fisher, B. Petrie, and W.C. Leggett. 2010. Decline in top predator body size and changing climate alter trophic structure in an oceanic ecosystem. Proceedings of the Royal Society of London B Biological Sciences 277: 1,353-1,360.

Sheldon, R.W., A. Prakash, and W.H. Sutcliffe. 1972. The size distribution of particles in the ocean. Limnology and Oceanography 17: 327-340.

Sheldon, R.W., W.H. Sutcliffe, and M.A. Paranjape. 1977. Structure of pelagic food chain and relationship between plankton and fish production. Journal of the Fisheries Research Board of Canada 34: 2,344-2,353.

Sinclair, M. 1988. Marine Populations. Washington Sea Grant Program, University of Washington Press, Seattle, WA.

Sinclair, M., V.C. Anthony, T.D. Iles, and R.N. O'Boyle. 1985. Stock assessment problems in Atlantic Herring (*Clupea harangus*) in the Northwest Atlantic. Canadian Journal of Fisheries and Aquatic Sciences 42: 888-898.

Sinclair, A., D. Gascon, R. O'Boyle, D. Rivard, and S. Gavaris. 1991. Consistency of some Northwest Atlantic groundfish assessments. NAFO Scientific Council Studies. 16: 59-77.

Sinclair, M., R. O'Boyle, D.L. Burke, and G. Peacock. 1997. Why do some fisheries survive and others collapse? Pages 23-35 *in* Developing and Sustaining World Fisheries Resources. The State of Science and Management, 2nd World Fisheries Congress (D.A. Hancock, D.C. Smith, A. Grant, and J.P. Beumer, Eds.). CSIRO Publishing, Collingwood, Australia.

Sinclair, M.M. and R.N. O'Boyle. 2014. The Gulf of Maine boundary dispute: the role of the Bedford Institute of Oceanography. Pages 397-405 *in* Voyage of Discovery: Fifty years of Marine Research at Canada's Bedford Institute of Oceanography (D.N. Nettleship, D.C. Gordon, C.F.M. Lewis, and M.P.

Latremouille, Eds.). Bedford Institute of Oceanography-Oceans Association, Dartmouth, NS.
Smith, S.J. 1990. Use of statistical models for the estimation of abundance from groundfish trawl survey data. Canadian Journal of Fisheries and Aquatic Sciences 47: 894-903.
Smith, S.J., J.J. Hunt, and D. Rivard. 1993. Risk evaluation and biological reference points for fisheries management. Canadian Special Publication of Fisheries and Aquatic Science 120, Fisheries and Oceans Canada, Ottawa, ON.
Smith, S.J. and M.J. Lundy. 2002. Scallop production Area 4 in the Bay of Fundy: stock status and forecast. Canadian Science Advisory Secretariat Research Document 2002/018, Fisheries and Oceans Canada, Dartmouth, NS.
Smith, W.R. 1979. Parameter estimation in non-linear models of biological systems. Fisheries Marine Service Technical Report 889, Fisheries and Oceans Canada, Dartmouth, NS.
Stobo, W.T. and G.M. Fowler. 2006. Canadian tagging of commercial groundfish and small pelagic fish in the vicinity of the Scotian Shelf and Gulf of St. Lawrence, 1953-1985. Canadian Technical Report of Fisheries and Aquatic Sciences 2669, Fisheries and Oceans Canada, Dartmouth, NS.
Sutcliffe, W.H., K.F. Drinkwater, and B.S. Muir. 1977. Correlations of fish catch and environmental factors in the Gulf of Maine. Journal of the Fisheries Research Board of Canada 34: 19-30.
Tremblay, M.J., J.S. Choi, P.A. Koeller, R.J. Miller, D.L. Roddick, and S.J. Smith. 2014. Science in support of the management of invertebrate fisheries. Pages 279-288 *in* Voyage of Discovery: Fifty Years of Marine Research at Canada's Bedford Institute of Oceanography (D.N. Nettleship, D.C. Gordon, C.F.M. Lewis, and M.P. Latremouille, Eds.). Bedford Institute of Oceanography-Oceans Association, Dartmouth, NS.
Trzcinski, M.K., R. Mohn, and W. D. Bowen. 2006. Continued decline of an Atlantic cod population: how important is grey seal predation? Ecological Applications 16: 2,276-2,292.
Trzcinski, M.K., R. Mohn, and W.D. Bowen. 2009. Estimating the impact of Grey Seals on the Eastern Scotian Shelf and Western Scotian Shelf cod populations. Canadian Science Advisory Secretariat Research Document 2009/052, Fisheries and Oceans Canada, Dartmouth, NS.
Trzcinski, M.K., S.L. Armsworthy, S. Wilson, R.K. Mohn, and S.E. Campana. 2011. A framework for the assessment of Scotian Shelf and Southern Grand Banks Atlantic Halibut Stock. Canadian Science Advisory Secretariat Research Document 2011/002, Fisheries and Oceans Canada, Dartmouth, NS.
Waldron, D.E., T.E. Iles, and G.V. Hurley. 1985. Estimating the effects of introducing a minimum 130 mm mesh regulation on the 4X groundfish fishery. Canadian Technical Report of Fisheries and Aquatic Sciences 1400, Fisheries and Oceans Canada, Dartmouth, NS.
Walters, C. and J.F. Kitchell. 2001. Cultivation/depensation effects on juvenile survival and recruitment: implications for the theory of fishing. Canadian Journal of Fisheries and Aquatic Sciences 58: 39-50.
Ware, D. 1980. Bioenergetics of stock and recruitment. Canadian Journal of Fisheries and Aquatic Sciences 37: 1,012-1,024.
Zwanenburg, K.C.T. 1985. Redfish in management unit 4VWX: A history of stock definition and assessment of present status. Canadian Science Advisory Secretariat Research Document 1985/061, Fisheries and Oceans Canada, Dartmouth, NS.
Zwanenburg, K.C.T., D. Bowen, A. Bundy, K. Drinkwater, K. Frank, R. O'Boyle, D. Sameoto, and M. Sinclair. 2002. Decadal changes in the Scotian Shelf large marine ecosystem. Pages 105-150 *in* Large Marine Ecosystems of the North Atlantic: Changing States and Sustainability (K. Sherman and H.R. Skoldal, Eds.). Elsevier Press, Amsterdam, The Netherlands.

FISHERIES, ECOSYSTEMS, AND AQUACULTURE

32. SCIENCE IN SUPPORT OF THE MANAGEMENT OF INVERTEBRATE FISHERIES

M. John Tremblay*, Jae S. Choi, Peter A. Koeller, Robert J. Miller, Dale L. Roddick, and Stephen J. Smith

SUMMARY

Scientists providing support for the management of invertebrate fisheries off the coast of Nova Scotia began to work out of the Bedford Institute of Oceanography (BIO) in 1998. Invertebrate fisheries are significant in terms of both landed value and weight. The landed value of invertebrate fisheries in Atlantic Canada has represented 75-85% of all landings since 1998. Major species are lobster, scallops, snow crab, shrimp, and offshore clams. This paper reviews the science done at BIO on these species, as well as some other invertebrates of lesser commercial value. Four themes are evident: (1) increased collaboration with industry to increase the available data and buy-in from industry; (2) studies of life history, distribution, growth, reproduction, and mortality that underpin all of the advice that is given to fisheries and ocean managers; (3) new assessment methods and surveys that have informed management and industry on the consequences of different fishing and management strategies; and (4) the emergence of an ecosystem approach to assessing exploited populations and the fisheries directed at them, as evidenced by studies of the bottom impact of dredges, application of habitat information to survey design, assessment of bycatch, and incorporation of physical and biological information into assessments. The location at BIO of the groups working on invertebrate fisheries has increased collaboration with physical oceanographers, geologists, and benthic ecologists.

Key words: invertebrates, population ecology, assessment, surveys, fisheries science.
***E-mail:** John.Tremblay@dfo-mpo.gc.ca

Lobsters, scallops, crabs, shrimp, and clams: the favourite of many epicures. How do biologists think of these creatures? Lobsters, crabs, and shrimp are crustaceans (from the Latin 'crust' for shell); scallops and clams are molluscs (from the Latin 'moll' for soft). Commercially fished groups of crustacea and molluscs are often termed shellfish. Shellfish lack spinal columns and thus fall into the more general group of animals known as invertebrates. In Atlantic Canada, most of the commercially fished invertebrates are shellfish.

Science supporting the management of invertebrate fisheries has been conducted in federal labs for many years, but only since 1998 at the Bedford Institute of Oceanography (BIO). That year marked the move of Invertebrate Fisheries Division (IFD) from the Halifax Fisheries Research Lab, a facility on the Halifax waterfront dating from 1925 (Stewart and Safer 2005). In 2005, IFD joined two other divisions to form the Population Ecology Division. This review describes the science conducted at BIO in support of the management of commercial invertebrate fisheries. Where appropriate, reference is made to earlier work, but the emphasis here is on 1998 to 2012. While most of the attention is directed at shellfish, we also highlight some research on other invertebrates.

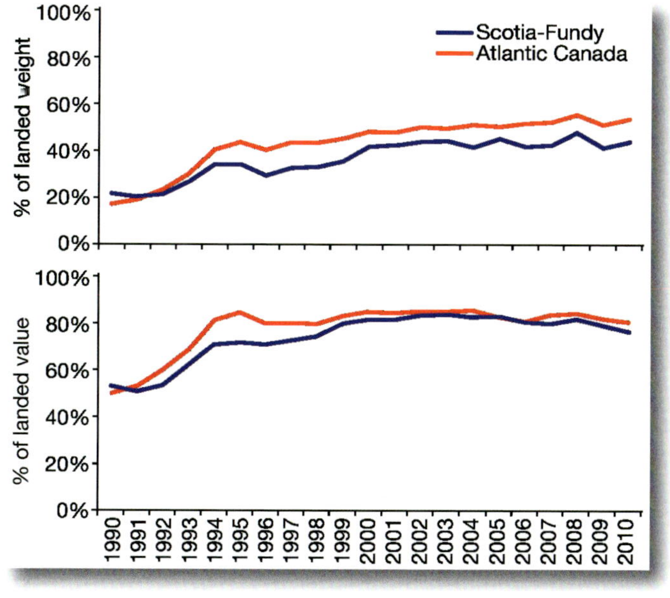

Figure 1. The relative importance of invertebrates in commercial fisheries from 1990 to 2010. Shown is the percentage of total landed weight (upper panel) and the percentage of total landed value (lower panel) represented by invertebrates for the waters off the Atlantic coast of Nova Scotia and the Bay of Fundy (Scotia-Fundy) and for all of Atlantic Canada (NS, NB, PEI, QC, and NL). Data obtained from DFO Internet site (http://www.dfo-mpo.gc.ca/stats/commercial/land-debarq-eng.htm) in April 2012.

IMPORTANCE OF COMMERCIALLY FISHED INVERTEBRATES

Invertebrates as a group have traditionally commanded higher prices than finfish, and the landed value of commercial fisheries for invertebrates in Atlantic Canada has represented 60-85% of the value of all landings since 1992 and 75-85% since 1998 (Fig. 1). Since 2002, even the landed weight of invertebrates has surpassed that of other fisheries in Atlantic Canada (Fig. 1). The increased importance of invertebrate fisheries over the last twenty years follows a global trend and has raised concern about ecosystem effects (Anderson et al. 2011), but two of the key invertebrate species discussed here (lobsters and scallops) have a long history of exploitation in Atlantic Canada.

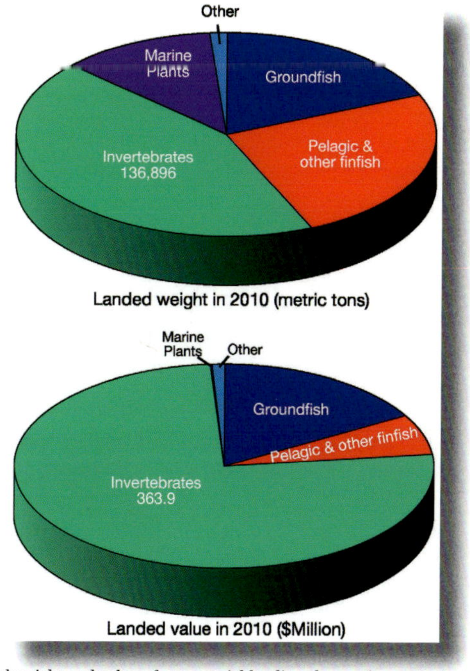

Figure 2. Landed weight and value of commercial landings by species group in 2010 from the waters off the Atlantic coast of Nova Scotia and Bay of Fundy ('Scotia-Fundy').

Scientists at BIO have been concerned primarily with those fisheries on the Atlantic coast of Nova Scotia and in the Bay of Fundy, sometimes termed the Scotia-Fundy region. In 2010, the landed quantity of invertebrates in Scotia-Fundy was 137,000 metric tons with a landed value of \$364M (Fig. 2). This represents 76% of the total of all fisheries. Lobster continues to be the single most valuable species fished in the Maritimes and in Canada as a whole with a 2010 landed value in Scotia-Fundy of \$187M. Scallops had the next highest landed value in Scotia-Fundy at \$78M, followed by snow crab at \$55M, and shrimp at \$38M. Below, we review some of the science done at BIO in support of the fisheries for lobster, scallops, snow crab, shrimp, offshore clams, and some other species that have been the target of smaller fisheries.

Lobster *(Homarus americanus)*

The context for lobster science at BIO in 1998 was a 1995 report entitled "A Conservation Framework for Atlantic Lobster" by the Fisheries Resource Conservation Council (FRCC 1995). The report originated from a concern about a recent decline in lobster landings. Lobster landings in Canada had trended upwards from the early 1980s to a peak in 1991, a pattern evident in the landings for the Lobster Fishing Areas (LFAs) off Atlantic Nova Scotia and in the Bay of Fundy (Fig. 3). In 1992 and 1993, there was a decline in Canadian landings of 15%. In hindsight, we can see how temporary this decline in landings was. Landings increased from the mid-1990s until the present, and biologists concur that the increased landings resulted mainly from increased abundance rather than increased fishing effort.

Key recommendations from FRCC (1995) were to reduce fishing effort and to take steps to allow the average lobster to produce more eggs. The Department of Fisheries and Oceans (DFO) minister of the day, David Anderson, responded to the report in late 1997 by asking lobster fishermen "to prepare conservation harvesting plans to include multi-year conservation measures that will lead to doubling of lobster egg production in the next two to three years". Failure to adopt the necessary conservation measures would lead to the imposition of mandatory measures. This set the stage for many sometimes boisterous industry meetings involving government scientists advising on conservation measures. The 1995 FRCC report also recommended science priorities: (1) definition and assessment of conservation measures; (2) monitoring current stock status; and (3) understanding long-term trends. The lobster science at BIO since 1998 fits primarily under the first two categories. Some of this work was funded by an Atlantic-wide program funded by DFO called the Canadian Lobster Atlantic Wide Studies (CLAWS; Tremblay and Saint-Marie 2001).

Monitoring stock status – Since 1998 there have been significant increases in the data available for assessing the health of lobster stocks. Much of the new data has come from industry. Beginning in 1998, lobster fishermen in LFA 34 were required to provide data on their daily catch, effort, and fishing location. These data were used in assessments to estimate catch rates as a proxy for lobster abundance. Some voluntary log data were available prior to 1998, but from only a small percentage of fishermen. Mandatory catch and effort logs expanded to include all LFAs in Figure 3 by 2007.

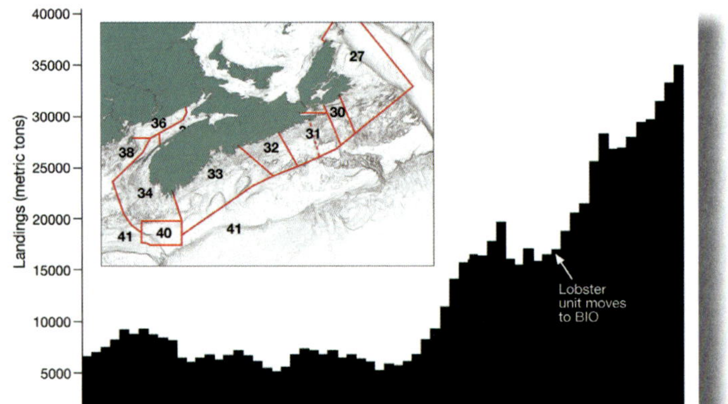

Figure 3. Lobster landings in weight from 1947-2010 for lobster fisheries off the Atlantic coast of Nova Scotia and in the Bay of Fundy. The inset map shows associated Lobster Fishing Areas (LFAs).

Data on the abundance of smaller lobsters ('pre-recruits', below commercial size) not captured well by commercial traps were provided by an industry-science group known as the Fishermen and Scientists Research Society (FSRS). Established in 1994 and located at BIO, the FSRS initiated a lobster recruitment trap study in 1999 whereby individual fishermen tracked their daily catch during the fishing season using traps designed to retain smaller lobsters. In 2011, data were collected by over 160 fishermen distributed along the Atlantic coast of Nova Scotia and the Bay of Fundy. This represents 5% of the approximately 3,133 lobster licenses in this region. The FSRS data are not totally independent of the fishery because they are obtained during the fishing season. However, since the traps are standardized, fished in fixed locations, and modified to retain lobsters below the minimum legal size, the derived catch rates are better indicators of pre-recruit lobster abundance than those derived from commercial traps. The FSRS data have been used to estimate exploitation rate (Claytor and Allard 2003, Tremblay et al. 2011) for indicators of abundance (Tremblay and Lanteigne 2005) and to depict spatial patterns (Tremblay et al. 2009a; Fig. 4).

Fishery independent measures of lobster abundance would greatly improve evaluations of stock health and the response to management measures. While there are no directed surveys in place in the region, progress has been made at BIO in obtaining data on lobsters from other surveys, and in approaches to measure lobster abundance. Since 1999, lobster size and length have been recorded on DFO's annual trawl surveys (Tremblay et al. 2007), and in the 2000s, lobsters began to be systematically recorded in some surveys that are targeted at other species (e.g., scallops, groundfish). Although the gear is not designed for lobster, lobsters are captured as a bycatch, occasionally in high numbers. Fishery independent trap surveys hold promise, but variable catchability would need to be accounted for (Smith and Tremblay 2003). Underwater video could be used to survey lobsters and estimate abundance in some areas

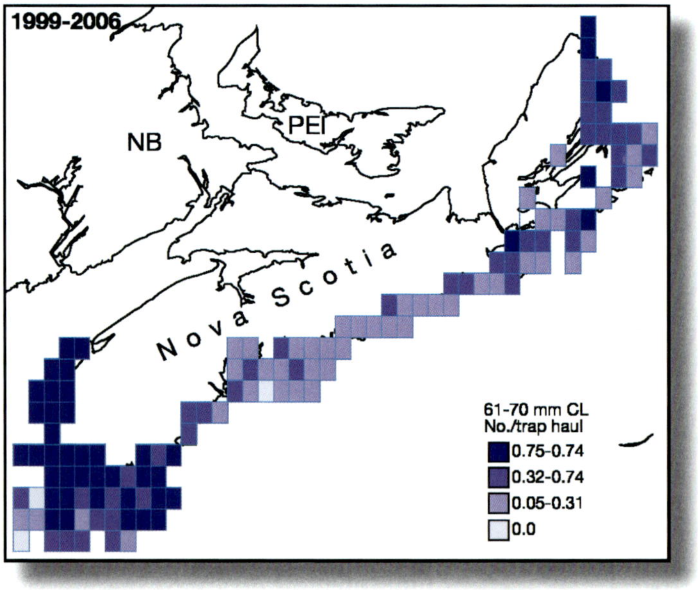

Figure 4. Composite spatial patterns in relative abundance (catch-per-unit-effort, CPUE) for sublegal lobsters of 61-70 mm carapace length (CL), 1999-2006, from data collected from traps deployed by the Fishermen and Scientists Research Society (FSRS). Data are for the month of May only, all years combined (from Tremblay et al. 2009a).

(Tremblay et al. 2009b). A new tool to measure the abundance of very young lobsters has been developed since 2007. Settlement collectors mimic the habitat of newly settled lobsters and provide density estimates similar to those obtained by underwater diving (Wahle et al. 2013). Data from the collectors yield a fishery-independent abundance index for young-of-the-year lobsters.

Definition and assessment of conservation measures – In 1998, potential conservation measures were assessed in terms of the lifetime egg production ('eggs per recruit') by the average female. Eggs per recruit models were used to assess different conservation measures (Tremblay and Eagles 1998, Lawton et al. 1999, Idoine et al. 2001) and management changes were adopted to varying degrees within different Lobster Fishing Areas from 1998 to 2002. Within LFAs 27-38, the most significant change occurred in LFA 27. This area had historically retained smaller lobsters ('canners') and an assessment document published 11 years earlier (Miller et al. 1987) indicated that a large benefit in yield and dollar value would result from an increased minimum legal size (MLS). Mark-recapture studies were used to verify growth and movement rates for the area, and they demonstrated that, in one moult, lobsters would grow by 12-16% in length (36-50% in weight) and that most would move less than 5 km from one year to the next (Tremblay and Eagles 1997, Tremblay et al. 1998). Between 1998 and 2003, the minimum legal size was increased from 70 to 76 mm carapace length followed by an additional increase of 5 mm from 2007 to 2009. The conservation value of these measures was demonstrated through analysis of catch rates of females with eggs – the abundance of mature, reproducing females has increased because more are able to reach sexual maturity prior to harvest (Tremblay et al. 2012).

Lobster 'catchability' is a measure of the probability that lobsters in the vicinity of a trap will enter it. This is important to understand because lobsters are fished exclusively by traps and catch rate is often used as an abundance indicator. Building upon the work of R.J. Miller (1990, 1995), studies confirmed the effects of size and sex, and demonstrated effects of season and habitat (Tremblay and Smith 2001). Studies in an area unique for its aggregations of large lobsters (off Grand Manan, NB) found that catchability was unaffected by size between 80 and 160 mm carapace length, that it could vary interannually, and that high densities and large sizes may reduce the tendency of lobsters to enter traps (Tremblay et al. 2006).

Knowledge of the sizes at which lobsters reproduce are needed for biological models such as eggs per recruit, and to ensure that a good proportion of females can reproduce prior to capture by the fishery. Detailed studies of the size at onset of maturity have demonstrated spatial and temporal differences at several scales (Miller and Watson 1991, Reeves et al. 2011, Silva et al. 2012).

Although conservation measures for lobster are often measured in terms of their effect on egg production, analyses done at BIO indicate the relationship between egg production and successful recruitment to the fishery is complex. At some low level of egg production, there must be a relationship with weight of lobsters available to the fishery, but egg production in itself does not explain differences in lobster yield from area to area. Egg production was negatively correlated with lobster landings among six areas along the South Shore of Nova Scotia (Miller 1997) and unrelated among eight areas around Prince Edward Island (Miller et al. 2006). On the other hand, the density of post-larvae, the stage that leaves the water column and swims to the bottom, was correlated with landings around Prince Edward Island and along Nova Scotia's South Shore. This doesn't mean that eggs are unimportant, but that larval survival is spatially variable and that some areas require more eggs than others to produce a lobster that survives to enter the fishery. A management target could be established in terms of eggs per fishing ground. The potential for such a scheme was demonstrated by a project on the Eastern Shore of Nova Scotia whereby fishermen conducted inexpensive mark-recapture studies to measure abundance of ovigerous females, i.e., with exterior eggs (Miller 2010). When combined with female size, annual egg production on a fishing ground can be estimated.

Whatever conservation measures are used, there must be a decision as to the spatial scale of application. The optimum size of a lobster fishery management area is unresolved and is almost certainly not uniform. A study that modelled larval drift and survival between hatching and settlement locations around Prince Edward Island identified five cells that were somewhat self-contained (Chasse and Miller 2010).

How effective has management of lobster fisheries been? There are several approaches that might be taken to evaluate this, and one is by comparative study. A recent comparison of Nova Scotia and New Zealand lobster fisheries concluded that, based on performance, management of both lobster fisheries can be considered successful, but management could be improved by clearer statements of objectives, more efficient mechanics of governance, and quicker response to changes in stocks or fisheries (Miller and Breen 2010).

Scallops (Placopecten magellanicus)

The move of the scallop group to BIO in 1998 was preceded by a change in the approach to managing inshore fisheries – the introduction of quotas

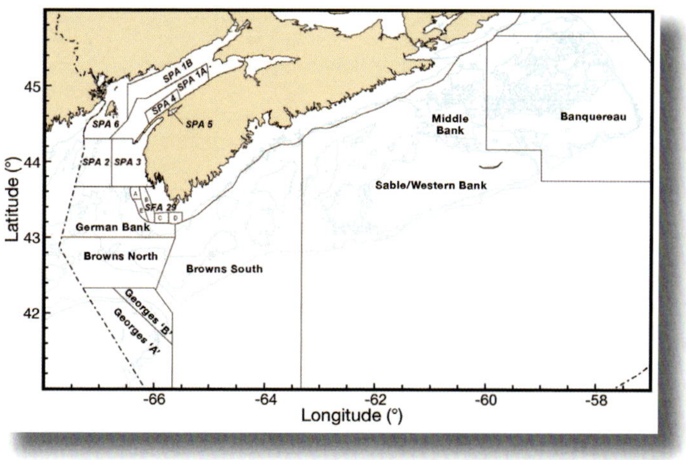

Figure 5. Scallop fishing management areas of Fisheries and Oceans Canada in the Maritimes Region. SPA (Scallop Production Area) 1-6 and SFA (Scallop Fishing Area) 29 are inshore management areas: all others are offshore fishing areas.

for the inshore fisheries. The fisheries for sea scallops in the Maritimes region are managed geographically as offshore fisheries (Fig. 5: Georges, Browns, German, Sable, Western and Middle banks) and inshore fisheries (Fig. 5: SPA - Scallop Production Area, 1 to 6; SFA - Scallop Fishing Area, 29 A to E). The offshore fisheries had been operating under quota since 1986. The introduction of quotas to the inshore fisheries in 1997 required the development of methods to provide scientific advice on potential catch levels for setting the annual quotas. During its tenure at BIO, the scallop group has made significant advancements in assessment methods and surveys including the role of spatial variation in growth and links between scallops and habitat. In addition, progress has been made in understanding the benthic impacts of scallop fishing.

Improved assessment methods and surveys – In all areas, the fishery and the scallop population are regularly monitored by annual scientific surveys and commercial log books. Port sampling is also used to monitor the offshore fishery. A size-based population model was introduced to estimate population biomass, recruitment to the fishery, and exploitation rate and to provide advice on future catch levels (Smith and Lundy 2002). This model used a Bayesian state-space structure and provided advice on potential catches in terms of probabilities of exceeding a target exploitation rate. Currently, this model is used for both inshore and offshore scallop stock assessments (Jonsen et al. 2009, Hubley et al. 2011, Smith et al. 2012).

One of the important features of this stock assessment model was the incorporation of the spatial distribution of growth patterns exhibited by the scallops. Scallops are sedentary bivalves that have limited range of movement as adults. Their growth characteristics reflect the suitability of conditions they live in. Scallops with the same size shell may have very different weights of scallop meat depending upon water depth, current speeds, temperature, and other conditions (Smith et al. 2001). The productivity of a scallop stock will for the most part be determined by the spatial distribution of growth and recruitment (Smith and Rago 2004).

Estimates of the abundance and biomass of the scallops from annual surveys of the scallop beds are the main monitoring tool used to understand the impact of the fishery on the scallop populations. These surveys are conducted on commercial fishing vessels through various arrangements with the fishing industry. Given the patchy spatial distribution of scallops, research has focussed on efficient survey designs appropriate to these distributions. In some areas, adaptive designs have been developed to respond to density patterns observed during the survey (Smith and Lundy 2006), and on Georges Bank, historical distribution patterns observed over many years of surveys were used to update the survey design (Hubley et al. 2009).

The most fruitful line of research has been directed towards the degree to which bottom type determines the spatial distribution of scallops. Earlier work had promoted this approach (e.g., Thouzeau et al. 1991, Smith and Robert 1998) in anticipation of bottom mapping (see Pickrill et al. 2014). In general, scallops are found more often on gravel lag or till bottom types (Kostylev et al. 2003, Todd et al. 2012). The scallop surveys of Browns Bank and SFA 29 are now designed using sediment type to define the different sampling areas or strata (Hubley et al. 2011, Smith et al. 2009). Recent research has focussed on refining the relationship between bottom type and scallop habitat suitability (Brown et al. 2012).

Impact of scallop fishing — The impact of scallop fishing on benthic communities has received some attention. Kenchington et al. (2007) compared epifaunal species in the Bay of Fundy captured in surveys in 1966–67 and in 1997. The same species were found in both surveys, but the number of species found in any one area was reduced in 1997, and motile scavengers and filter-feeders, along with robust burrowing filter-feeders, were more common relative to more fragile attached epifaunal filter-feeders. Kenchington et al. (2007) suggested that the primary cause for this change was physical impacts of fishing gear, even though trawling and scallop dragging in the area was neither intense nor had necessarily increased over time. An effect of fishing was also suggested by comparison of hydroid assemblages on cobble substrates with those on scallop shells in the Bay of Fundy (Henry and Kenchington 2004). The scallop shells were considered 'island habitats' while the cobbles were 'disturbed habitats'. The number of taxa was significantly lower on cobbles, and it was suggested that the differences could be related to fishing. Comparison of closed and open fishing areas found larger numbers of small scallops (<60 mm shell height) in the closed areas (Brocken and Kenchington 1999). Recently, the ecosystem impacts of scallop fishing have been evaluated from bycatches of groundfish, lobsters, and skates reported by onboard observers (Gavaris et al. 2010, Sameoto and Glass 2012).

Atlantic Snow Crab (*Chionoecetes opilio*)

When the Invertebrate Fisheries Division moved to BIO in 1998, the mandate for snow crab science had been with the DFO Gulf Fisheries Centre in Moncton for two years. It was not until six years later that science supporting snow crab in the Scotian Shelf Ecosystem (SSE) was conducted at BIO. The relative abundance of snow crab in the SSE prior to 1998 was poorly established. The earliest records indicate most activity in the nearshore areas of eastern Nova Scotia where a fishery existed since the early 1970s. Fishery landings peaked in 1979 and then declined substantially; the snow crab fishery was considered collapsed in the mid-1980s (Tremblay and Eagles 1995). Since that time, landings and its economic importance have increased considerably.

With the move of the snow crab science mandate to the Gulf Fisheries Centre in 1996, an Industry-DFO Joint Project Agreement was established to assess the abundance and population structure of snow crab using a fisheries-independent trawl survey funded completely by the fishing industry (Biron et al. 1997). The Gulf Fisheries Centre snow crab group used their experience with trawl surveys in the southern Gulf of St. Lawrence to develop the trawl survey on the Scotian Shelf. It was officially accepted as an abundance assessment tool in 1999. Studies of the groundfish research vessel surveys (Tremblay 1997) and the early snow crab surveys demonstrated the presence of unexploited crab in offshore areas of the SSE. This led to large increases in fishing effort, landings, and catch rates and the addition of many new participants. Trawl surveys were formally extended to the western portion of the SSE in 2004. This Joint Project Agreement continues to the present and represents an excellent example of co-operation and co-management between industry and DFO Science.

The transfer of the SSE snow crab mandate to BIO in 2004 resulted in the formation of a new snow crab group, and the first BIO-based assessment was conducted in 2005 (Choi et al. 2005a). Prior to 2004, scientific efforts focussed upon understanding basic life history cycles and reproductive behaviour of snow crab with the majority of these efforts directed at snow crab outside of the SSE. After 2004, more research specific to the SSE was initiated and continues to this date. The focus of the research since 2004 has been in the areas of life history cycles, egg production (Kuhn and Choi 2011, Kuhn et al. 2011), moult cycles, growth studies, movement studies, habitat requirement studies (Choi 2010), improved survey design, and methods of abundance estimation. This information has been integrated into coherent population models and ecosystem indicator-based assessments of SSE snow crab (Choi et al. 2005b, Choi and Zisserson 2011; Fig. 6).

At present, an important and timely challenge is how best to incorporate the Precautionary Approach (PA) into the management of this fishery. The following are important characteristics of the SSE snow crab fishery in the PA context: (1) it exploits post-spawned males larger than 95 mm carapace width; (2) the spawning stock biomass is completely protected as almost all reproductive females are less than 80 mm carapace width and it is illegal to fish females; (3) sub-legal sized males and immature males are able to reproduce; (4) generally conservative exploitation strategies are followed; and (5) transparent reporting mechanisms and communication are used between all stakeholders.

These factors reduce the risks associated with disturbing the long-term sustainability of the resource, and so, by definition, are compliant with the PA (WSSD 2002). However, it is also important to maintain the sustainability and viability of the fishery itself and the socio-economic base that it supports. Fortunately, long-term sustainability of the resource will necessarily ensure the long-term sustainability of the fishery.

Another major and persistent challenge in the SSE has been the very dynamic nature of the area in terms of the ocean currents and associated changes in temperatures, as well the major alterations in food web structure implied by the collapse of groundfish in the 1990s (Choi et al. 2004, Choi et al. 2005b). To deal with this environmental and ecological variability in space and time, new methods of assessment have been developed that directly incorporate habitat information, currently popularized as Species Distribution Models (Choi 2010; Fig. 7). The research emphasis will be to continue to refine our knowledge of the habitat preferences of snow crab of various life stages and to integrate this knowledge via traditional and agent-based simulation modelling approaches. These efforts will improve abundance estimates, short-term projections, identification of the potential effects of climate change, and perhaps improve our understanding of the snow crab's ecological role in the very complex Scotian Shelf Ecosystem.

Northern Shrimp (*Pandalus borealis*)

From 1998 to the present, the shrimp group at BIO has conducted research and monitored the shrimp stock on the Scotian Shelf. It also contributed to management of the entire North Atlantic cold-water shrimp industry, one of the largest in the world (valued at ~$500M annually), through participation in the stock assessment committees of the Northwest Atlantic Fisheries Organization (NAFO) and International Council for the Exploration of the Sea (ICES), and through the execution of international research projects. The shrimp group also collaborated with biological oceanographers at BIO and shrimp biologists in other countries to better understand shrimp ecology. Below, we discuss the development of the shrimp fishery, the assessment process, and application of the 'Traffic Light' approach, and research topics.

Development and expansion of the shrimp fishery — Compared to the 'big three' invertebrate fisheries (lobster, snow crab, and scallops), landings and landed value of shrimp caught on the Scotian Shelf have always been modest (<6,000 metric tons and $10M). Commercial quantities of shrimp were known to exist on the Scotian Shelf by the 1960s, but the modern shrimp fishery was not enabled until the 1990s, when the groundfish fishery collapsed and there was significant innovation in fishing gear technology. Prior to the 1990s, fishermen targeted groundfish and shrimp trawling had a problem with excessive bycatch of other species. Shrimp offered an alternative species for groundfish fishermen after the collapse. The innovation was the Nørdmore grate, a device in the trawl's cod end which reduces fish bycatch to near zero while retaining shrimp. Invented by a Norwegian fisherman, it was introduced to Canadian shrimpers in the early 1990s by DFO's Industrial Development Branch. The 1990s also saw increased interest in shrimp trapping as a way to help revitalize the inshore fishery.

The first important finding from the Scotian Shelf shrimp survey program was the discovery of large concentrations of shrimp along the Cape Breton shore, from Fourchu into Chedebucto Bay. This area, named 'The Noodles' (Fig. 8) because of the shape of the bottom contours, appeared to be an extension of the well-known offshore stock (Koeller 1996). This allowed an expansion of the fishery, including additional quota for trawlers, and development of the inshore trap fishery in Chedabucto Bay. The latter was aided by submersible observations of the trapping process by DFO scientists and fishermen on the last dives by manned Canadian submersibles in 1995 and 1996. These observations helped in the development of a snow crab exclusion device by M. Newell, the Canso fisherman credited with initiating the trap fishery. The success of this fishery, made permanent in 1996, led to a number of cooperative experimental trapping programs from Grand Manan to northern Cape Breton and the discovery of additional inshore trapping grounds in Mahone and St. Margaret's bays, Nova Scotia (Koeller et al. 1995, 2007a).

Figure 6. Ecosystem indicators used to summarize temporal change in ecosystem structure in the SSE. The indices are in standard deviation (SD) units with red representing low values (-2.5 SD) and green representing high values (+2.5 SD); white blocks indicate no data. Note the systemic change in large groups of indicators especially in the period of the groundfish collapse (late 1980s to early 1990s). This type of information is utilized in snow crab population assessments to monitor ecosystem change and so provide contextual information for the assessment. See Choi and Zisserson (2011) for more information on data sources and methods. Numbers in brackets {} are the first two ordination scores associated with a Principle Components Analysis of the indicators.

The assessment process — The assessment process for shrimp from the mid-1990s to 2012 can be characterized as a cooperative, government-industry venture, one of the first of its kind. Essentially, DFO provided the research expertise and management framework, and industry provided the funds and ships to conduct surveys, the commercial sampling/ monitoring program, and some research projects. Data collected by the shrimp group at BIO indicated that the Scotian Shelf stock is probably more vulnerable to overfishing than the more northern stocks. Consequently, the Integrated Management Plan for the stock, the first in the region, took a conservative approach to harvesting. In addition, a new stock assessment methodology using multiple indicators of stock health and environmental conditions – the 'Traffic Light' approach – was developed and implemented (Caddy 1998; Koeller et al. 2000a, 2011; Koeller 2003, 2008), taking its cue from the new emphasis on an ecosystem approach to fisheries management. It was the first to do so in the region, and the resultant advice and subsequent management actions led to conservation measures that contributed to long-term sustainability.

Research — Analysis of data from various commercial and survey sources, including the new shrimp surveys, provided the biological basis for the management of the Scotian Shelf shrimp stock including its distribution, migrations, size, life cycle, growth rates, recruitment mechanisms, and the importance of environmental and ecological influences on its production cycles (Koeller 2000, 2006; Koeller et al. 2000b, 2003, 2007b; Ramseir et al. 2000). Much of this research was presented during an international symposium in 1999, prompted by the expansion of shrimp fisheries throughout the North Atlantic in the 1990s. The symposium was initiated and organised by BIO scientists, and jointly sponsored by the ICES, the North Pacific Marine Science Organization, and NAFO, with the proceedings published in the Journal of Northwest Atlantic Fisheries Science (Koeller et al. 2000c).

From 2006 to 2009, the shrimp group collaborated with other BIO scientists to lead an international research project to test one of the most famous concepts in marine science – David Cushing's 'match-mismatch hypothesis' (Cushing 1974). This work culminated in a contribution to the journal Science (Koeller et al. 2009). According to the match-mis-

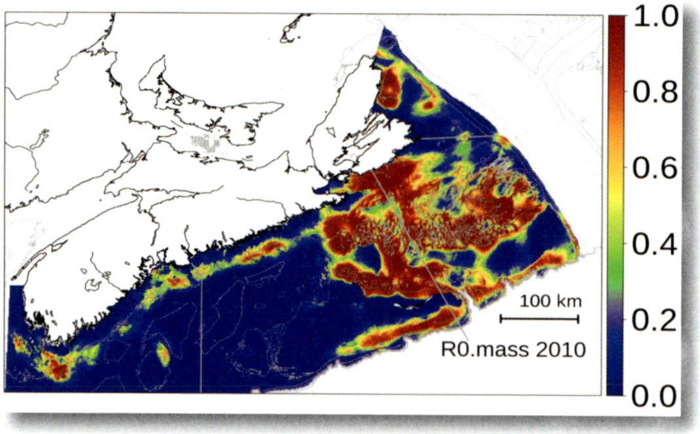

Figure 7. Probability of observing Atlantic Snow Crab in 2010. Red areas indicate where there is a high probability (1 or 100%) of observing snow crab and blue areas where there is little to no chance of observing snow crab. This non-random spatial pattern is determined by numerous factors, including depth, temperature, sediment grain size, and species composition. This type of information is utilized for species abundance estimation in population assessments and also for monitoring environmental and ecosystem change which ultimately provides the contextual information necessary for species and ecosystem assessments (for details, see Choi and Zisserson 2011).

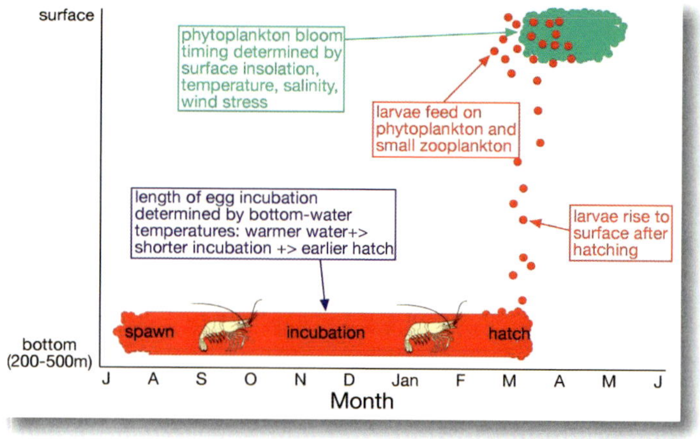

Figure 9. Shrimp life cycle in relation to key environmental factors. Shrimp larvae are both herbivorous and carnivorous, feeding near the surface on diatoms, and small zooplankton directly dependant on the spring phytoplankton bloom. Short-term variability in oceanographic conditions can lead to annual differences in the time when shrimp eggs hatch, and in the onset of the spring bloom. Only some years will have a 'perfect match' between larval release and food production, resulting in the relatively rare, large year-classes on which the shrimp fisheries depend (see Koeller et al. 2009).

match hypothesis, the survival of fish or invertebrate larvae and the success of year classes (and fisheries) is related to how closely the hatching times of larvae match the arrival of their food in the form of the annual spring phytoplankton bloom (Fig. 9). Using satellite imagery of spring bloom development and shrimp egg hatching times, the team was able to show that, on average, shrimp egg hatch and phytoplankton bloom times match closely throughout the north Atlantic from Cape Cod to the Arctic Circle, despite the fact that egg development and bloom times vary greatly throughout this wide range. Shrimp have adapted their life cycle to these local differences so that hatch and bloom indeed match. The results have implications for climate change on shrimp populations because egg development, hatching, and bloom times are all strongly influenced by temperature. Climate change could alter the delicate match between shrimp and its food which has been developed over evolutionary time periods. Because northern shrimp are a keystone species in the food web, this could have important consequences for some marine ecosystems as well as the fisheries.

Offshore Clams

The offshore clam fishery off eastern Canada had been active for just 12 years when the science group supporting the clam fishery moved to BIO in 1998. Since 1998, work has focussed on surveys and assessment, life history research, and the effects of the dredge gear on the bottom (Roddick 2005).

Surveys and assessment — Surveys from 1980 to 1983 found commer-

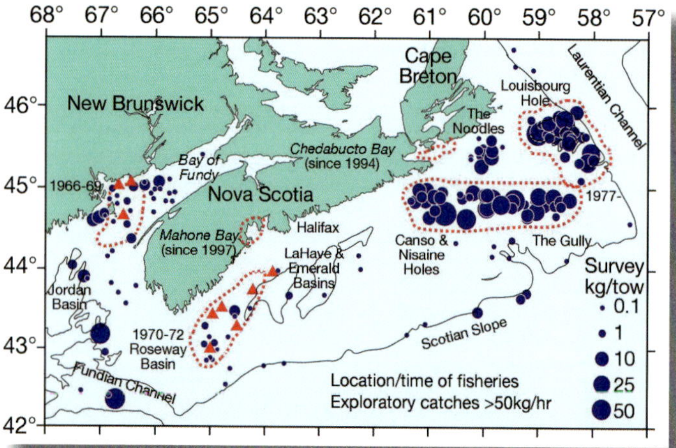

Figure 8. A composite map of the areas of current and historical fishing for northern shrimp on the Scotian Shelf. Dashed lines outline fishery locations and associated text gives the period of fishery. Expanding symbols provide a measure of abundance from directed surveys (kg/tow); triangles show locations with exploratory fishing catches of >50 kg/h.

cial quantities of Ocean Quahogs *(Arctica islandica)* and Arctic Surfclams *(Mactromeris polynyma)*, on Banquereau Bank. Arctic Surfclams caught the interest of processors because of the purple colour on the outer section of the foot, siphon, and mantle. This turns red when blanched, similar to lobster and shrimp. Although the colour made it unsuitable for the initial target market of United States clam strips and chowder, the red and white colouration was very attractive to the Japanese sushi and sushimi market, where it commanded a high price. Currently Japan and China are the largest consumers.

There was little information on Arctic Surfclam populations in the 1980s to guide management of the fishery. Commercial data on catch, effort, and area fished were initially used to monitor the fishery, but as the fishing vessels moved around to get the best catch rates and the Arctic Surfclams are sedentary, there were concerns that the catch rate data would not detect stock depletion. By the late 1990s, industry was facing large investments in vessel replacement, and wanted to be certain of the future of the fishery. A fishery-independent survey was needed, but DFO lacked the resources to conduct such a survey. As a result, a series of Joint Project Agreements were initiated between DFO and industry to conduct surveys and research in support of the surfclam fishery. Industry provided a vessel, gear, and funding, while DFO conducted the surveys, analyzed the results, and directed the research program. There have been three such industry-DFO surveys of Banquereau Bank (Roddick et al. 2007a), one of Sable Bank (Roddick et al 2007b), and two of Grand Banks (Roddick et al 2011).

Life history research and management implications — In addition to abundance estimates, research has focussed on growth and mortality rates, size and age at maturity, gear selectivity, recruitment, and bycatch. Research has examined how to best use the survey estimates for absolute biomass rather than an index. Dredge selectivity and efficiency were studied on the fishing grounds using dredge sensors to monitor tow distance (Roddick et al 2011).

Research also addressed the distribution, abundance, growth rate, and size and age of maturity of other large clams (Figs. 10 and 11) of commercial interest (Kilada et al. 2007a, 2007b, 2009). The longest lived of the offshore clams is the Ocean Quahog. The oldest quahog aged to date from Sable Bank was 210 years old, and a quahog from elsewhere in the North Atlantic was estimated to be 507 years old (Wanamaker et al. 2012).

Although faster growing than Ocean Quahogs, most of the clam species of commercial interest, including the Arctic Surfclam, are slow growing and have long life spans. This has important implications for management of these fisheries as the low productivity will permit only a small percentage of the biomass to be harvested annually. Low harvest rates and long life spans mean that there will be little detectable change in biomass from fishing or natural processes, on time scales of years to decades. As a result, it is difficult to fit parameters for model based approaches to stock assessment, at least in the short term.

Gear impacts on bottom — Clam dredges have a large immediate impact on the substrate and there are concerns about the impacts on habitat. Clam dredges have a cutting blade in front of the dredge that digs into the sediment. High-pressure water is pumped from the ship down a hose to liquefy sediments, which enhances the performance of the blade and excavation of the clams. Dredge tracks can be as deep as 20 cm. To examine the long term impacts on habitat, a large multi-year study was initiated in 1998 in collaboration with benthic ecologists and geologists at BIO and DFO Newfoundland Region. This project followed an experimental site with dredged and control plots at 70-m depth on Banquereau for 10 years. Sampling took place prior to dredging, immediately following dredging, and at intervals of 2 weeks, and 1, 3, 5, and 10 years post-dredging. Sampling included grab samples, still and video photography, sidescan sonar and other acoustic and direct sampling methods.

Figure 10. Large offshore clams of commercial interest in eastern Canada.

One year after dredging, still and video photography could not discern dredge tracks. Sidescan imaging, on the other hand, could still detect some of the dredge tracks even after 10 years, indicating that the substrate had still not fully recovered to its pre-dredging state. After three years, species composition in both the dredged and reference boxes was dominated by colonizing species of polychaetes and amphipods, which showed large fluctuations in abundance. The polychaete *Spiophanes bombyx* was numerically the most abundant organism (Gilkinson et al. 2003, 2005a,b). Due to their long life and slow growth, the biomass of the large clams removed by dredging is not expected to recover for more than ten years. Hydraulic clam dredge fisheries occur on fairly mobile, well-sorted sand, and with few vessels the footprint of the fishery is small. These factors help to mitigate the overall impact on some elements of the benthic community.

As of 2011, the Arctic Surfclam fishery employed approximately 350 people and had annual sales exceeding $50M. The research program has informed management of the fishery as it has developed. The Arctic Surfclam fishery has applied for certification by the Marine Stewardship Council as a sustainable fishery and the research conducted from BIO has been very important to their application.

Other Invertebrates

Fisheries for invertebrates, other than the major species, lack long management histories, and usually involve fewer fishermen. They provide good opportunities to involve fishermen in data collection and fishery management. Such involvement can make fishermen more supportive of the management regime and reduce costs. The fisheries for Jonah Crab (*Cancer borealis*), blood worms, and sea urchins all had significant fishermen involvement.

In the late 1990s, Jonah Crab fishermen on Nova Scotia's South Shore formed an association and worked closely with DFO in conducting experiments (Adams et al. 2000). A minimum legal size and detailed reporting of catch statistics were agreed upon. Results of experiments on the location and size of trap entrance and escape openings increased the catch of legal-sized crabs, decreased the size of undersized crabs, and reduced the bycatch of other species to almost nil. A new regulation prohibited retention of Jonah Crabs by other nearshore fisheries. Crab mortality before processing was reduced by eliminating the transfer of crabs between containers. The weight of crabs placed in a container had no effect on mortality. In bait comparisons, shark was best, and catch rate was unrelated to bottom temperature. Each fisherman accepted assigned fishing areas outside his normal fishing area to map the extent of the resource.

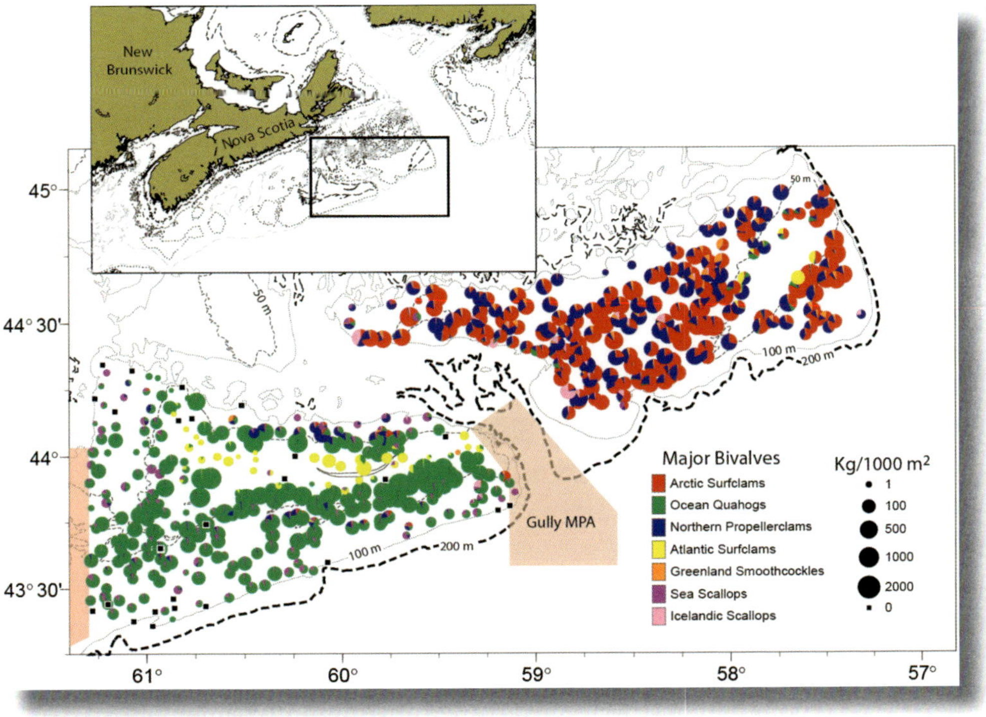

Figure 11. Distribution of large bivalve species of commercial interest caught during the Sable Bank (2003) and Banquereau (2004) offshore clam surveys. There are currently commercial fisheries for the Arctic Surfclam (*Mactromeris polynyma*) and Sea Scallops, while Ocean Quahogs (*Arctica islandica*), Greenland Smoothcockles (*Serripes groenlandicus*), and Northern Propellerclams (*Cyrtodaria siliqua*) are caught as a bycatch in the Arctic Surfclam fishery.

Blood worms are dug on intertidal mud flats and sold at high prices in the United States and western Europe as sport fishing bait. Worm harvesters from southwest Nova Scotia and the Minas Basin resisted new regulations on an old, unregulated fishery in decline. However, after participating in the development of a management regime most gradually became supportive. The ability of flats to sustain harvests changes on a spatial scale of kilometres (Miller and Smith 2011) and so, stocks need to be regulated flat-by-flat. In order that harvesters could accept some of the responsibility for surveying worm size and density, DFO and the harvesters jointly developed a simple but statistically robust survey method.

Sea urchins are harvested for their gonads by underwater scuba divers in autumn and winter, and exported to Japan as a luxury product. Depending on food supply, sea urchin quality can vary over a distance of a few metres from valuable to worthless. Also, sea urchins can be ready for harvest as early as mid-August or as late as November. The same bed can be productive enough to yield three harvests in a season or only one (Miller and Nolan 2008). A management agency could never regulate fishing on this fine spatial and temporal scale. Therefore, harvesters were allotted individual (i.e., exclusive) fishing areas and held accountable for managing the stock within their areas.

Management strategies included altering the distribution of sea urchins and their food to increase yields over natural levels, and adapting harvest times to market demand. Seaweeds are the principal food of sea urchins, but the abundance of predator and prey can easily get out of balance. Because harvesters did not share fishing areas, they alone benefited from resource enhancement. Their modest compliance requirements included reporting catch by harvest bed, mapping the resource in their area, and after 4-years paying for an area audit that measured success of their resource management.

Some Common Themes

Some common themes are evident within the science conducted at BIO in support of invertebrate fisheries. The first is the collaboration with industry to collect scientific data. This collaboration has been via formal agreements such as those involving snow crab and offshore clams, through societies such as the FSRS, and through smaller less formal associations built around problem solving (e.g., shrimp, Jonah Crab, and worms). In many cases industry has contributed to the costs of surveys. Industry has also participated in science peer review processes, leading to better understanding in the industry of how science-based decisions are made, and providing on-the-water observations of stock status for the benefit of the scientists. In future, there is the possibility of further increasing industry involvement in data collection and observations given the widespread use of social media. A second theme is what might be called the 'meat and potatoes' of fisheries science — studies of life history, distribution, growth, reproduction, and mortality. These studies are essential as they underpin all of the advice given to fisheries and ocean managers. With climate change, population parameters may well change and these studies will need to be continued. A third theme is the development of new assessment methods and surveys for invertebrates. Scallop, snow crab, and shrimp assessments have all introduced new methods and approaches for both the analysis and synthesis of data. In particular, the importance of the spatial component of populations has been recognized. The improvements to surveys and assessment methods have informed management and industry on the consequences of different fishing and management strategies. Finally, the last 15 years has seen an emergence of an ecosystem approach to assessing exploited populations and the fisheries directed at them. This is evidenced by studies of the bottom impact of scallop and clam dredges, application of habitat information to scallop survey design, assessment of bycatch in all fisheries, and incorporation of physical and biological information into assessments for shrimp and snow crab. The location at BIO of the groups working on invertebrate fisheries has increased collaboration with physical oceanographers, geologists, and benthic ecologists. This collaboration should be nurtured and encouraged as Canada adopts a more comprehensive ecosystem-based approach to managing fisheries.

In conclusion, the science done at BIO since 1998 in support of invertebrate fisheries has been innovative and has contributed to increased value and sustainability of some of the most important fisheries in Canada. As science-based decisions are required more and more, solid investments are needed in ships, infrastructure, and operations that support scientific research. Given these investments, we can expect that future science done at BIO will contribute substantially to meeting Canada's goals in the management of its living marine resources.

ACKNOWLEDGEMENTS

We are grateful to the many fisheries technicians, biologists, and research scientists who contributed to the studies and assessments conducted at BIO since 1998. In particular, we acknowledge Stephen Nolan who passed away suddenly in 2009 – his skills and dedication as an 'on-the-water' field technician are missed. We also thank the managers of the several divisions within which the invertebrate group resided at BIO (Michael Chadwick: 1998-99; Bob Miller: 1999; Stephen Smith: 1999-2000; René Lavoie: 2000-05; and Ross Claytor: 2005-present).

REFERENCES

Adams, B., A. Reeves, and R.J. Miller. 2000. Exploratory Jonah crab, *Cancer borealis*, fishery in lobster fishing area 33 (1997-1999). Canadian Science Advisory Secretariat Research Document 2000/27, Dartmouth, NS.

Anderson, S.C., J.M. Flemming, R. Watson, and H.K. Lotze. 2011. Rapid global expansion of invertebrate fisheries: trends, drivers, and ecosystem effects. PLoSONE 6(3): e14735. doi:10.1371/journal.pone.0014735.

Biron, M., M. Moriyasu, E. Wade, P. DeGrace, R. Campbell, and M. Hebert 1997. Assessment of the 1996 snow crab (*Chionoecetes opilio*) fishery off eastern Cape Breton, Nova Scotia (CFAs 20 to 24, and 4X). Canadian Stock Assessment Secretariat Research Document 97/102, Moncton, NB.

Brocken, F. and E.L.R. Kenchington. 1999. A comparison of scallop (*Placopecten magellanicus*) population and community characteristics between fished and unfished areas in Lunenburg County, N.S., Canada. Canadian Technical Report of Fisheries and Aquatic Sciences 2258, Dartmouth, NS.

Brown, C.J., J.A. Sameoto, and S.J. Smith. 2012. Multiple methods, maps, and management applications: purpose made seafloor maps in support of Ocean Management. Journal of Sea Research 72: 1-13.

Caddy, J.F. 1998. A short review of precautionary reference points and some proposals for their use in data-poor situations. FAO Fisheries Technical Paper 379, Rome, Italy.

Chasse, J. and R.J. Miller. 2010. Lobster larval transport in the southern Gulf of St. Lawrence. Fisheries Oceanography 19: 319-338.

Choi, J.S. 2010. Habitat preferences of the snow crab, *Chionoecetes opilio*: where stock assessment and ecology intersect. Pages 361-376 *in* Biology and Management of Exploited Crab Populations under Climate Change (G.H. Kruse , G.L. Eckert, R.J. Foy, R.N. Lipcius, B. Sainte-Marie, D.L. Stram, and D. Woodby, Eds.). Alaska Sea Grant, University of Alaska, Fairbanks, AK. AK-SG-10-01: doi 10.4027/bmecpcc.2010.02.

Choi, J.S. and B.M. Zisserson. 2011. Assessment of Scotian Shelf snow crab in 2010. Canadian Science Advisory Secretariat Research Document 2011/110, Dartmouth, NS.

Choi, J.S., K.T. Frank, W.C. Leggett, and K. Drinkwater. 2004. Transition to an alternate state in a continental shelf ecosystem. Canadian Journal of Fisheries and Aquatic Sciences 61: 505-510.

Choi, J., B. Zisserson, and A. Reeves. 2005a. An assessment of the 2004 snow crab populations resident on the Scotian Shelf (CFAs 20 to 24). Canadian Science Advisory Secretariat Research Document 2005/028, Dartmouth, NS.

Choi, J.S., K.T. Frank, B. Petrie, and W.C. Leggett. 2005b. Integrated assessment of a large marine ecosystem: a case study of the devolution of the eastern Scotian Shelf, Canada. Oceanography and Marine Biology: An Annual Review 43: 47-67.

Claytor, R. and J. Allard. 2003. Change-in-ratio estimates of lobster exploitation rate using sampling concurrent with fishing. Canadian Journal of Fisheries and Aquatic Sciences 60: 1,190-1,203.

Cushing, D.H. 1974. The natural regulation of fish populations. Pages 399-412 *in* Sea Fisheries Research (F.R. Harden Jones, Ed.). Elek Science, London, England.

FRCC. 1995. A Conservation Framework for Atlantic Lobster. A report to the Minister of Fisheries and Oceans by the Fisheries Resource Conservation Council (FRCC). FRCC95.R.1, Nov. 1995. Minister of Supply and Services Canada, Cat. No. FS23-278/1995E, Ottawa, ON.

Gavaris, S., K.J. Clark, A.R. Hanke, C.F. Purchase, and J. Gale. 2010. Overview of discards from Canadian commercial fisheries in NAFO Divisions 4V, 4W, 4X, 5Y and 5Z for 2002-2006. Canadian Technical Report of Fisheries and Aquatic Sciences 2873, St. Andrews, NB.

Gilkinson, K.D., G.B.J. Fader, D.C. Gordon, Jr., R. Charron, D. McKeown, D. Roddick, E.L.R. Kenchington, K. MacIsaac, C. Bourbonnais, W.P. Vass, and Q. Liu. 2003. Immediate and longer-term impacts of hydraulic clam dredging on an offshore sandy seabed: effects on physical habitat and processes of recovery. Continental Shelf Research 23: 1,315-1,336.

Gilkinson, K.D., D.C. Gordon, Jr., K. MacIsaac, D.L. McKeown, E.L.R. Kenchington, C. Bourbonnais, and W.P. Vass. 2005a. Immediate impacts and recovery trajectories of macrofaunal communities following hydraulic clam dredging on Banquereau, eastern Canada. ICES Journal of Marine Science 62: 925-947.

Gilkinson, K.D., D.C. Gordon, Jr., D. McKeown, D. Roddick, E.L.R. Kenchington, K.G. MacIsaac, C., Bourbonnais, and W. P. Vass. 2005b. Susceptibility of soft corals *Gersemia rubiformis*, to capture by hydraulic clam dredges off eastern Canada: the significance of soft coral-shell associations. Pages 383-390 *in* American Fisheries Society Symposium 41 (P.W. Barnes and J.P Thomas, Eds.). American Fisheries Society, Bethesda, MD.

Henry L.-A. and E.L.R. Kenchington. 2004. Differences between epilithic and epizoic hydroid assemblages on commercial scallop grounds in the Bay of Fundy, northwest Atlantic. Marine Ecology Progress Series 266: 123-134.

Hubley, B., S.J. Smith, I.D. Jonsen, and J. Sameoto. 2009. Georges Bank 'a' scallop annual stock assessment: survey design. Canadian Science Advisory Secretariat Research Document 2009/033, Dartmouth, NS.

Hubley, P.B., A. Glass, A. Reeves, J. Sameoto, and S.J. Smith. 2011. Browns Bank "north" scallop (*Placopecten magellanicus*) stock assessment. Canadian Science Advisory Secretariat Research Document 2011/042, Dartmouth, NS.

Idoine, J.S., D.S. Pezzack, P.J. Rago, C.M. Frail, and I.M. Gutt. 2001. A comparison of different fishing strategies on yield and egg production of American lobsters in nearshore Gulf of Maine. Canadian Technical Report of Fisheries and Aquatic Sciences 2328: 64-68, Dartmouth, NS.

Jonsen, I.D., A. Glass, B. Hubley, and J. Sameoto. 2009. Georges Bank 'a' scallop (*Placopecten magellanicus*) framework assessment: data inputs and population models. Canadian Science Advisory Secretariat Research Document 2009/034, Dartmouth, NS.

Kenchington E.L.R., T.J. Kenchington, L.-A. Henry, S.D. Fuller, and P.Gonzalez. 2007. Multi-decadal changes in the megabenthos of the Bay of Fundy: the effects of fishing. Journal of Sea Research 58: 220-240.

Kilada, R.W., S.E. Campana, and D. Roddick. 2007a. Validated age, growth, and mortality estimates of the ocean quahog (*Arctica islandica*) in the western Atlantic. ICES Journal of Marine Science 64: 31-38.

Kilada, R.W., D. Roddick, and K. Mombourquette. 2007b. Age determination, validation, growth and minimum size of sexual maturity of the Greenland smoothcockle (*Serripes groenlandicus*, Bruguiere, 1789) in eastern Canada. Journal of Shellfish Research 26: 443-450.

Kilada, R.W., S.E. Campana, and D. Roddick. 2009. Growth and sexual maturity of the northern propellerclam (*Cyrtodaria siliqua*) in Eastern Canada, with bomb radiocarbon age validation. Marine Biology 156: 1,029-1,037.

Koeller, P.A. 1996. The Scotian Shelf shrimp (*Pandalus borealis*) fishery in 1996. Atlantic Fisheries Research Document 1996/8, Halifax, NS.

Koeller. P.A. 2000. Relative importance of environmental and ecological factors to the management of the northern shrimp (*Pandalus borealis*) fishery on the Scotian Shelf. Journal of Northwest Atlantic Fisheries Science 27: 21-33.

Koeller, P. 2003. The lighter side of reference points. Fisheries Research 62: 1-6.

Koeller, P. 2006. Inferring shrimp (*Pandalus borealis*) growth characteristics from life history stage structure analysis. Journal of Shellfish Research 25: 595-608.

Koeller, P. 2008. Ecosystem-based psychology, or, how I learned to stop worrying and love the data. Fisheries Research 90: 1-5.

Koeller, P., M. King, M. Newell, A. Newell, and D. Roddick. 1995. An inshore shrimp trap fishery for eastern Nova Scotia? Canadian Technical Report of Fisheries and Aquatic Sciences 2064, Halifax, NS.

Koeller, P.A., L. Savard, D. Parsons, and C. Fu. 2000a. A precautionary approach to assessment and management of shrimp stocks in the Northwest Atlantic. Journal of Northwest Atlantic Fisheries Science 27: 235-246.

Koeller, P., R. Mohn, and M. Etter. 2000b. Density dependent sex-reversal in pink shrimp, *Pandalus borealis*, on the Scotian Shelf. Journal of Northwest Atlantic Fisheries Science 27: 107-118.

Koeller, P., J. Boutillier, and S. Tveite (Eds.). 2000c. Pandalid Shrimp Fisheries - Science and Management at the Millennium. Journal of Northwest Atlantic Fisheries Science 27: 1-289.

Koeller, P., M. Covey, and M. King. 2003. Is size at transition a measure of growth or abundance in Pandalid shrimp? Fisheries Research 65: 217-230.

Koeller, P., M. Covey, and M. King. 2007a. Biological and environmental requisites for a successful trap fishery of the northern shrimp *Pandalus borealis*. Proceedings of the Nova Scotian Institute of Science 44: 51-71.

Koeller, P., C. Fuentes-Yaco, and T. Platt. 2007b. Decreasing shrimp (*Pandalus borealis*) sizes off Newfoundland and Labrador - environment or fishing? Fisheries Oceanography 16: 105-115.

Koeller, P., C. Fuentes-Yaco, T. Platt, S. Sathyendranath, A. Richards, P. Ouellet, D. Orr, U. Skúladóttir, K. Wieland, L. Savard, and M. Aschan. 2009. Basin-scale coherence in phenology of shrimps and phytoplankton in the North Atlantic Ocean. Science 324: 791-793.

Koeller, P., C. Fuentes-Yaco, M. Covey, M. King, and B.M. Zisserson. 2011. The last traffic light on the Scotian Shelf: shrimp 2009-2010. Canadian Science Advisory Secretariat Research Document 2011/061, Ottawa, ON.

Kostylev, V.E., R.C. Courtney, G. Robert, and B.J. Todd. 2003. Stock evaluation of giant scallop (*Placopecten magellanicus*) using high-resolution acoustics for seabed mapping. Fisheries Research 60: 479-492.

Kuhn, P.S. and J.S. Choi. 2011. Influence of temperature on embryo developmental cycles and mortality of female *Chionoecetes opilio* (snow crab) on the Scotian Shelf, Canada. Fisheries Research 107: 245-252.

Kuhn, P.S., S. Graham, and J.S. Choi. 2011. Influence of senescent algae, temperature, tides, currents, and embryo detachment on *Chionoecetes opilio* (snow crab) larval release. Journal of Crustacean Biology 31: 100-105.

Lawton, P., D.S. Pezzack, D.R. Duggan, D.A. Robichaud, M.B. Strong, and I.M. Gutt. 1999. The American lobster, *Homarus americanus*, fishery in the Bay of Fundy (Lobster Fishing Areas 35, 36, and 38). Canadian Science Advisory Secretariat Research Document 1999/31, St. Andrews, NB.

Miller, R.J. 1990. Effectiveness of crab and lobster traps. Canadian Journal of Fisheries and Aquatic Sciences 47: 1,228-1,251.

Miller, R.J. 1995. Catchability coefficients for American lobster (*Homarus americanus*). ICES Marine Science Symposium 199: 349-356.

Miller, R.J. 1997. Spatial differences in the productivity of American lobster in Nova Scotia. Canadian Journal of Fisheries and Aquatic Sciences 54: 1,613-1,618.

Miller, R.J. 2010. Tagging by lobster fishermen to estimate abundance of the discarded portions of their catch. Fisheries 35: 595-600.

Miller R.J. and F.L. Watson. 1991. Change in lobster size at maturity among years and locations. Journal of Shellfish Research 10: 286-287.

Miller, R.J. and S.C. Nolan. 2008. Management methods for a sea urchin dive fishery with individual fishing zones. Journal of Shellfish Research 37: 929-938.

Miller, R.J. and P.A. Breen. 2010. Are lobster fisheries being managed effectively? Examples from New Zealand and Nova Scotia. Fisheries Management and Ecology 17: 394-403.

Miller, R.J. and S.J. Smith. 2011. Nova Scotia's bloodworm harvest: assessment, regulation, and governance. Fisheries Research 113: 84-93.

Miller, R.J., D.S. Moore, and J.D. Pringle. 1987. Overview of the inshore lobster resources in the Scotia-Fundy region. Canadian Atlantic Fisheries Scientific Advisory Committee Research Document 1987/085, Halifax, NS.

Miller, R.J., M. Mallet, M. Lanteigne, and R. MacMillan. 2006. Bottlenecks to fishery yield for American lobster in a portion of the Gulf of St. Lawrence. North American Journal of Fisheries Management 26: 765-776.

Pickrill, R.A., B.J. Todd, S.J. Smith, J.V. Barrie, and K.W. Conway. 2014. Marine habitat mapping in Canada's oceans. Pages 185-190 *in* Voyage of Discovery: Fifty Years of Marine Research at Canada's Bedford Institute of Oceanography (D.N. Nettleship, D.C. Gordon, C.F.M. Lewis, and M.P. Latremouille, Eds.). Bedford Institute of Oceanography-Oceans Association, Dartmouth, NS.

Ramseier, R.O., C. Garrity, D.G. Parsons, and P. Koeller. 2000. Influence of particulate organic carbon sedimentation within the seasonal sea-ice regime on the catch distribution of Northern Shrimp (*Pandalus borealis*). Journal of Northwest Atlantic Fisheries Science 27: 35-44.

Reeves, A.R., J.S. Choi, and J. Tremblay. 2011. Lobster size at maturity estimates in eastern Cape Breton, Nova Scotia. Canadian Science Advisory Secretariat Research Document 2011/079, Dartmouth, NS.

Roddick, D.L. 2005. The Scotian Shelf experience with emerging bivalve fisheries. Pages 305-321 *in* Fisheries assessment and management in data-limited situations (G.H. Kruse, V.F. Gallucci, D.E. Hay, R.I. Perry, R.M. Peterman, T.C. Shirley, P.D. Spencer, B. Wilson, and D. Woodby, Eds.). Alaska Sea Grant, University of Alaska, Fairbanks, AK. AK-SG-05-02: doi 10.4027/famdls.2005.

Roddick, D., R. Kilada, and K. Mombourquette. 2007a. Survey for Arctic surfclams (*Mactromeris polynyma*) on Banquereau, 2004. Canadian Science Advisory Secretariat Research Document 2007/035, Dartmouth, NS.

Roddick, D., R. Kilada, and K. Mombourquette. 2007b. Ocean quahog (*Arctica islandica*) survey and yield estimates for Sable Bank. Canadian Science Advisory Secretariat Research Document 2007/036, Dartmouth, NS.

Roddick, D., J. Brading, L. Carrigan, T. Davignon-Burton, S. Graham, and C. McEwen. 2011. Assessment of the Arctic surfclam (*Mactromeris polynyma*) stock on Grand Bank. Canadian Science Advisory Secretariat Research Document 2011/52, Dartmouth, NS.

Sameoto, J.A. and A. Glass. 2012. An overview of discards from the Canadian inshore scallop fishery in SFA 28 and SFA 29 West for 2002 to 2009. Canadian Technical Report of Fisheries and Aquatic Sciences 2979, Dartmouth, NS.

Silva, M.A., M.J. Tremblay, and D.S. Pezzack. 2012. *Homarus americanus* size at onset of sexual maturity in Nova Scotia 2008-2011: Canso, Tangier, Port Mouton and Lobster Bay - A progress report. Canadian Science Advisory Secretariat Research Document 2012/59, Dartmouth, NS.

Smith, S.J. and G. Robert. 1998. Getting more out of your survey information: an application to Georges Bank scallops (*Placopecten magellanicus*). Pages 3-13 *in* North Pacific Symposium on Invertebrate Stock Assessment and Management (G. Jamieson and A. Campbell, Eds.). Canadian Special Publication of Fisheries and Aquatic Science 25, Ottawa, ON.

Smith, S.J. and M.J. Lundy. 2002. Scallop Production Area 4 in the Bay of Fundy: Stock status and forecast. Canadian Science Advisory Secretariat Research Document 2002/18, Dartmouth, NS.

Smith, S.J. and M.J. Tremblay. 2003. Fishery-independent trap surveys of lobsters (*Homarus americanus*): design considerations. Fisheries Research (Amsterdam) 62: 65-75.

Smith, S.J. and P. Rago. 2004. Biological reference points for sea scallops (*Placopecten magellanicus*): The benefits and costs of being nearly sessile. Canadian Journal of Fisheries and Aquatic Sciences 61: 1,338-1,354.

Smith, S.J. and M.J. Lundy. 2006. Improving the precision of design-based scallop drag surveys using adaptive allocation methods. Canadian Journal of Fisheries and Aquatic Sciences 63: 1,639-1,646.

Smith, S.J., E.L.R. Kenchington, M.J. Lundy, G. Robert, and D. Roddick. 2001. Spatially specific growth rates for sea scallops (*Placopecten magellanicus*). Pages 211-231 *in* Spatial Processes and Management of Marine Populations (G.H. Kruse, N. Bez, A. Booth, M. Dorn, S. Hills, R.N. Lipcius, D. Pelletier, C. Roy, S.J. Smith, and D. Witherell, Eds.). Alaska Sea Grant, University of Alaska Fairbanks, AK. AK-SG-01-02.

Smith, S.J., J. Black, B.J. Todd, V.E. Kostylev, and M.J. Lundy. 2009. The impact of commercial fishing on the determination of habitat associations for sea scallops (*Placopecten magellanicus*, Gmelin). ICES Journal of Marine Science 66: 2,043-2,051.

Smith, S.J., B. Hubley, L. Nasmith, J. Sameoto, H. Bourdages, and A. Glass. 2012. Scallop production areas in the Bay of Fundy: stock status for 2011 and forecast for 2012. Canadian Science Advisory Secretariat Research Document 2012/009, Dartmouth, NS.

Stewart, J.E. and A. Safer. 2005. A retrospective: three quarters of a century at the Halifax Fisheries Research Laboratory. Proceedings of the Nova Scotian Institute of Science 43: 19-44.

Thouzeau, G., G. Robert, and S.J. Smith. 1991. Spatial variability in distribution and growth of juvenile sea scallops, *Placopecten magellanicus* (Gmelin), on eastern Georges Bank (Northwest Atlantic). Marine Ecology Progress Series 74: 205-218.

Todd, B. J., V.E. Kostylev, and S.J. Smith. 2012. Seabed habitat of a glaciated shelf, German Bank, Atlantic Canada. Pages 555-568 *in* Seafloor Geomorphology as Benthic Habitat: GeoHab Atlas of Seafloor Geomorphic Features and Benthic Habitats (P.T. Harris and E.K. Baker, Eds.). Elsevier,

Amsterdam, The Netherlands.
Tremblay, M.J. 1997. Snow crab (*Chionoecetes opilio*) distribution limits and abundance trends on the Scotian Shelf. Journal of Northwest Atlantic Fisheries Science 21: 7-22.
Tremblay, M.J. and M.D. Eagles. 1995. Assessment of the 1994 snow crab fishery off eastern Cape Breton (Areas 20-24). DFO Atlantic Fisheries Research Document 1995/1, Halifax, NS.
Tremblay, M.J. and M.D. Eagles. 1997. Molt timing and growth of the lobster, *Homarus americanus*, off northeastern Cape Breton Island, Nova Scotia. Journal of Shellfish Research 16: 383-394.
Tremblay M.J. and M.D. Eagles. 1998. Eastern Cape Breton Lobster (LFA 27-30): stock status and eggs per recruit estimates. Canadian Science Advisory Secretariat Research Document 1998/124, Dartmouth, NS.
Tremblay, M.J. and B. Sainte-Marie (Eds.). 2001. Canadian Lobster Atlantic Wide Studies (CLAWS) symposium: Abstracts and Proceedings Summary. Canadian Technical Report of Fisheries and Aquatic Sciences 2328, Dartmouth, NS.
Tremblay, M.J. and S.J. Smith. 2001. Lobster (*Homarus americanus*) catchability in different habitats in late spring and early fall. Marine and Freshwater Research 52: 1,321-1,331.
Tremblay, M.J. and M. Lanteigne. 2005. Trap-based indicators of egg production following increases in minimum legal size in *Homarus americanus* fisheries. New Zealand Journal of Marine and Freshwater Research 39: 775-783.
Tremblay, M.J., M.D. Eagles, and G.A.P. Black. 1998. Movements of the lobster, *Homarus americanus*, off northeastern Cape Breton Island, with notes on lobster catchability. Canadian Technical Report of Fisheries and Aquatic Sciences 2220, Dartmouth, NS.
Tremblay, M.J., S.J. Smith, D.A. Robichaud, and P. Lawton. 2006. The catchability of large American lobsters (*Homarus americanus*) from diving and trapping studies off Grand Manan Island, Canadian Maritimes. Canadian Journal of Fisheries and Aquatic Sciences 63: 1,925-1,933.
Tremblay, M.J., G.A.P. Black, and R.M. Branton. 2007. The distribution of common decapod crustaceans and other invertebrates recorded in annual ecosystem surveys of the Scotian Shelf 1999-2006. Canadian Technical Report of Fisheries and Aquatic Sciences 2762, Dartmouth, NS.
Tremblay, M.J., C. MacDonald, and R.R. Claytor. 2009a. Indicators of abundance and spatial distribution of lobsters (*Homarus americanus*) from standard traps. New Zealand Journal of Marine and Freshwater Research 43: 387-399.
Tremblay, M.J., S.J. Smith, B.J. Todd, P.M. Clement, and D.L. McKeown. 2009b. Associations of lobsters (*Homarus americanus*) off southwestern Nova Scotia with bottom type from images and geophysical maps. ICES Journal of Marine Science 66: 2,060-2,067.
Tremblay, M.J., D.S. Pezzack, C. Denton, A.R. Reeves, S. Smith, A. Silva, and J. Allard. 2011. Framework for assessing lobster off the coast of eastern Cape Breton and the eastern and south shores of Nova Scotia (LFAs 27-33). Canadian Science Advisory Secretariat Research Document 2011/58, Dartmouth, NS.
Tremblay M.J., D.S. Pezzack, C. Denton, M. Cassista-Da Ros, S. Smith, A. Reeves, A. Silva, and S. Armsworthy. 2012. Assessment of lobster off the coast of eastern Cape Breton and the eastern and south shores of Nova Scotia (LFAs 27-33). Canadian Science Advisory Secretariat Research Document 2012/22, Dartmouth, NS.
Wahle, R.A., C. Bergeron, J. Tremblay, C. Wilson, V. Burdett-Coutts, M. Comeau, R. Rochette, P. Lawton, R. Glenn, and M. Gibson. 2013. The geography and bathymetry of American lobster benthic recruitment as measured by diver-based suction sampling and passive collectors. Marine Biology Research 9: 42-58.
Wanamaker, A.D., P.G. Butler, Jr., J.D. Scourse, J. Heinemeir, J. Eiriksson, K.L. Knudsen, and C.A. Richardson. 2012. Surface changes in the North Atlantic meridional overturning circulation during the last millennium. Nature Communications 3: 899. doi: 10.1038/ncomms1901.
WSSD (World Summit on Sustainable Development). 2002. Report of the World Summit on Sustainable Development, Johannesburg, South Africa. United Nations, New York, NY.

FISHERIES, ECOSYSTEMS, AND AQUACULTURE

33. ENVIRONMENTAL EFFECTS OF SALMON AND MUSSEL AQUACULTURE

Barry T. Hargrave*, David J. Wildish, and Peter J. Cranford

SUMMARY

Culture of Atlantic Salmon in floating net-pens in the Western Isles region of the Bay of Fundy and of Blue Mussels on suspended long-lines in Prince Edward Island expanded between 1980 and 1990. Both types of aquaculture can potentially cause adverse environmental changes in water and sediments where depth is shallow and tidal exchange with offshore waters is restricted. High fish biomass, metabolism, and feed pellet deposition may cause nutrient enrichment during salmon cage culture if the capacity of an inlet to assimilate additional organic matter is exceeded. Mussels filter natural suspended matter, but the release of faecal matter increases sedimentation and the potential for benthic enrichment. Starting in the 1990s, research staff from the Bedford Institute of Oceanography, St. Andrews Biological Station, provincial governments, and university laboratories collaborated to examine farm- to ecosystem-scale environmental effects associated with intensive salmon and mussel culture. Physical and bioenergetic models were developed to describe local and inlet-wide effects such as dissolved oxygen and suspended-matter depletion, increased sedimentation, and changes in benthic communities and habitats in areas where salmon and mussel farms were concentrated. The research provided environmental managers and provincial licensing authorities with information to identify local and far-field environmental problems potentially due to aquaculture and suggested approaches to mitigate effects once changes occur. The aim was to allow salmon and shellfish aquaculture industries to expand while operating in an environmentally sustainable manner.

Key words: mariculture, production, ecological carrying capacity, ecosystem impacts.
***E-mail:** HargraveB@rogers.com

Research on factors controlling growth in bivalves such as the Blue Mussel (*Mytilus edulis*) and Common Oysters (*Crassostrea virginica)* was carried out in the 1950s and 1960s in southwestern New Brunswick (SWNB) and at the Fisheries and Oceans Canada (DFO) field station at Ellerslie, Prince Edward Island (Fig. 1). The research was focussed on establishing optimal conditions for oyster and mussel culture and in addition considered habitat, morphological variations, and genetic diversity effects on growth and diseases in natural populations. Research on Atlantic Salmon (*Salmo salar*) in the 1970s was focussed primarily on nutritional requirements and husbandry practices to optimize growth and disease protection (Anderson 2007). Lack of knowledge about the control and treatment of aquatic diseases was a limiting factor impeding the growth of salmon and oyster aquaculture industries at the time.

As knowledge about the control and treatment of aquatic diseases and the development of optimal conditions for salmon nutrition increased, the marine environment was considered but only in terms of how physical conditions affected growth and tissue quality of wild and cultured species. Few studies considered the converse: i.e., how the growth of cultured animals affects the environment. An associated question was: are there ways to determine the optimum holding capacity (for salmon) or production carrying capacity (for molluscs) in an inlet or bay that allows production to be optimized while preventing adverse environmental changes? Research programs initiated in the 1980s within the DFO Science Branch at Bedford Institute of Oceanography (BIO) in collaboration with staff at St. Andrews Biological Station (SABS), St. Andrews, New Brunswick, were designed to address these questions. The research assisted habitat managers and provincial fisheries and aquaculture authorities with licensing and regulatory responsibilities for these new and expanding industries.

With the exception of Prince Edward Island, where DFO has regulatory authority for site approval, licensing of aquaculture leases in Canada is controlled by the fisheries and aquaculture departments in provincial governments. The mandate during the 1980s was to expand aquaculture industries as fast as possible to provide employment and economic development, particularly in rural areas where incomes from traditional harvest fisheries were in decline. The hope was that aquaculture production could replace some of the losses in traditional harvest fisheries which had markedly declined in eastern Canada between mid-1960 and 1980.

Cultivation methods for various invertebrate and finfish species were being investigated around the world in the 1970s based on advances in developing broodstock and rearing of juveniles for stocking purposes. Environmental conditions in some coastal areas of eastern Canada such as SWNB were especially favourable for salmon aquaculture. Farms were established where physical conditions such as temperature, salinity, and protection from excessive wave action and high currents allowed salmon culture. In the case of Blue Mussels, natural suspended particulate matter (seston) in the water is the food supply, so culture conditions are most favourable in inlets where water exchange provides a continuous supply of particles suitable for ingestion.

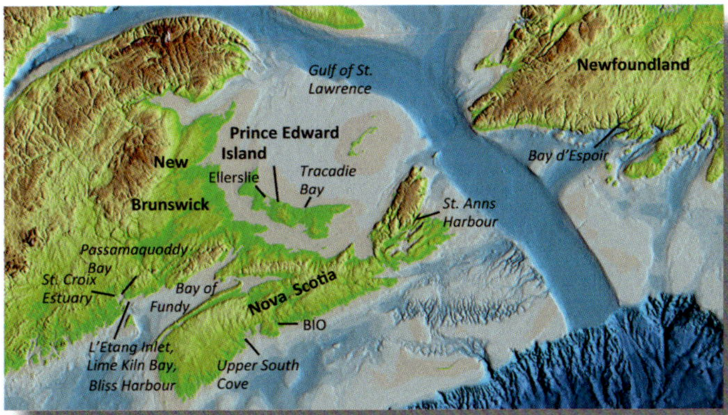

Figure 1. Map showing locations of sites in the Atlantic Provinces mentioned in the text (base map from Shaw et al. 2006).

Finfish and shellfish aquaculture can have both positive and negative environmental consequences (Fig. 2). The major difference is that growth of salmon in floating net-pens requires addition of food pellets which if uneaten along with fecal matter settle to the bottom. Potential adverse effects of salmon aquaculture were reviewed by Fisheries and Oceans Canada (2003, 2004, 2006). High fish biomass creates opportunities for viral and bacterial diseases such as Bacterial Kidney Disease, Furunculosis, and Infectious Salmon Anaemia or parasitic infections to develop which are often controlled by application of therapeutants and vaccines. Antibiotics and other drugs used for disease treatment can have potentially negative effects on non-target species. In addition, naturally occurring bacterial populations can develop resistance to antibiotics added to fish feed. Escapement of salmon and resulting negative interactions with wild stocks is another important issue occurring whenever net pens are located close to migratory routes of natural stocks.

Mussels feed on naturally available suspended particulate matter (seston) so no organic matter (OM) or nutrients are added. The potential

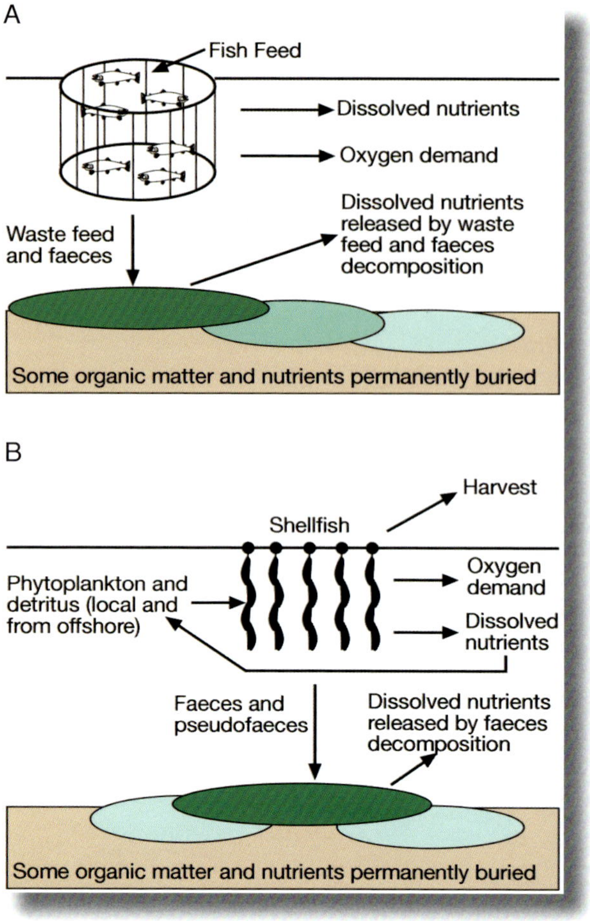

Figure 2. Principal pathways of dissolved and particulate waste products from: (A) finfish, and (B) shellfish aquaculture (after Cranford et al. 2006: Figs. 3.2 and 3.3). Green areas indicate deposition of settled particulate material on the bottom generally concentrated directly under fish pens and mussel long-lines. Distances and horizontal directions of sediment accumulation are affected by the size, number, and configuration of cage and culture line arrays and local variations in currents and bottom topography.

environmental effects of mussel culture are related in large part to how the cultured population interacts with the ecosystem by means of removing particles during suspension feeding. Food depletion by extensive mussel stocking ultimately limits the maximum aquaculture yield (i.e., production carrying capacity) in the water body. Other changes in ecological processes, species, populations, or communities will accompany seston depletion by mussels and knowledge of these effects is required to assess the 'ecological' carrying capacity of a region. Changes in ecosystem processes and structure from the byproducts of suspension feeding, including ammonia excretion and faeces production were reviewed in Fisheries and Oceans Canada (2003) and Cranford et al. (2006). The latter increases nutrients and OM in sediments leading to enhanced benthic organic enrichment. When the stock is harvested, OM and nutrients are removed in mussel tissue which could potentially decrease eutrophication caused by nutrient enrichment from other sources (e.g., agricultural runoff, discharges from fish processing plants, etc.).

Mussels on suspended long-lines provide a large area of solid surfaces in the water column which may be colonized by attached invertebrates such as tunicates. These filter feeders consume a similar size range of suspended material as food, as do mussels, and their feeding activity can reduce mussel growth and increase rates of particle removal from the water column. Evidence from observations in Prince Edward Island inlets shows that far-field (inlet-wide) changes in the trophic balance between autotrophs (phytoplankton) and heterotrophs (bacteria) may occur as a result of the selective filtration of particles by mussels (Harrison et al. 2005, Kepkay et al. 2005). Similarly, the limited capacity of mussels to filter small particles can result in a shift towards smaller phytoplankton species dominating the base of the food chain (Cranford et al. 2006).

The major physical, chemical, and biological factors affecting marine finfish and mussel culture have been well known since the 1990s. Adequate depth and water movement within farms are required to supply dissolved oxygen (DO) and disperse/dilute excretory products and, in the case of mussels, sufficient concentrations of phytoplankton and suspended particles. However, the physical structure of salmon cages and mussel long-lines can interfere with water circulation. Oxygen availability may be reduced within salmon pens due to fish respiration that exceeds DO supply during periods of slack water (Page et al. 2005). The addition of salmon feed can also increase sedimentation under cages and the oxygen demands of deposited OM in feed pellets and faeces which may result in hypoxic (low oxygen) or anoxic (no oxygen) surface sediments (Hargrave et al. 1993, 1997). The changes in sediments due to oxygen depletion may limit growth or pose health risks to the cultured stock as well as create deleterious effects on wild populations of fish, shellfish, and other invertebrates.

In addition to local effects under salmon pens or around long-lines, far-field changes distant from farms or on an inlet-wide scale may arise from nutrient enrichment (i.e., eutrophication). Release of excretory products, increased sedimentation, OM enrichment, and accumulation of fine particles in sediments and changes in planktonic and benthic food webs can significantly alter species composition in the water column and benthic communities. Many of these factors were discussed in the Fisheries and Oceans Canada (2003, 2004, 2006) science reviews where potential negative local and far-field environmental effects due to culture operations were summarized. An International Council for the Exploration of the Seas (ICES) workshop held at BIO in September 1995 (Silvert and Hargrave 1995) concluded that sustainable development of aquaculture in the coastal zone required integration of models of environmental impacts with application of tools such as expert systems to assist with management decisions.

RESEARCH PROGRAMS AND FUNDING SOURCES

As salmon and mussel aquaculture industries expanded in New Brunswick, British Columbia, and to some degree Quebec and Newfoundland after 1980, DFO funding was available for research on aquaculture-environment interactions. Projects by Wildish et al. (1988, 1990) compared water column and sediment properties proximate to and distant from salmon farms to determine if environmental changes could be detected. Salmon farms were highly concentrated in specific areas (L'Etang Inlet, Lime Kiln Bay, and Bliss Harbour) and research was focussed in these locations (Fig. 3). The Coastal Oceanography for Sustainable Aquaculture (COSAD) program was also formed within the Ocean and Ecosystem Science Branch of DFO at the same time with the aim of supporting physical and biological observations in coastal areas where salmon and mussel culture facilities were expanding (Page et al. 1999).

In 2000, the Environmental Sciences Strategic Research Fund (ESSRF) supported scientists from BIO, SABS and local universities to collaborate in expanding aquaculture-environment interactions research. Environmental Studies for Sustainable Aquaculture (ESSA) was a three-year (2000-03) ESSRF-supported project to identify measures and model far-field effects of salmon aquaculture with study sites in SWNB, Newfoundland and British Columbia. Although SWNB had been a focus for the initial research on environmental effects of salmon aquaculture on water and sediments, projects in Bay d'Espoir, Newfoundland, and the Broughton Archipelago, British Columbia, co-ordinated by R. Anderson and T. Sutherland, respectively, contributed significantly to the national scope of the project (Anderson et al. 2005, Stucchi et al. 2005). Prior studies had focussed on local impacts on, under and in close proximity to net-pens, but physical circulation models describing the distribution of DO, nutrients, and suspended particulate matter developed during the ESSA project provided a framework for estimating the dispersion of dissolved and particulate waste from farms (Hargrave 2004).

The Aquaculture Collaborative Research and Development Program (ACRDP) was also initiated within DFO in 2000. ACRDP projects required industry partnerships that provided up to 30% of the funding with the aim of supporting studies to increase the competitiveness of the Canadian aquaculture industry. Projects had to show benefits to the industry, and it proved difficult to establish partnerships and

Figure 3. Photograph looking east-northeast across Lime Kiln Bay, New Brunswick, prior to 1997 showing locations of salmon net pens; L'Etang Inlet is visible in the distance (photo: K. Haya/J. Martin, DFO-SABS, NB).

Figure 4. Harvesting mussels in Tracadie Bay, Prince Edward Island, July 2002.

obtain funding for environmental research that might show negative effects which could ultimately limit expansion of culture activities. The COSAD program supported studies of mussel-environment interactions to develop physical models describing water exchange in Prince Edward Island inlets where intensive mussel aquaculture was established. The first field studies occurred in Tracadie Bay, an inlet intensively studied over the next decade to measure environmental effects of intensive mussel culture (Page et al. 1999).

Research on factors affecting bivalve growth and environmental interactions was also enabled by the establishment of research networks within the Natural Sciences and Engineering Research Council (NSERC) in 1990. NSERC supports university-based research, but collaboration with government and industry laboratories is encouraged. DFO staff from BIO participated in the Ocean Production Enhancement Network (OPEN) from 1990 to 1994, one of NSERC's first research networks. The multidisciplinary study identified factors controlling fish and shellfish growth and reproduction. It provided opportunities for graduate students, and university and government researchers to investigate growth and physiological responses of bivalves (mussels and scallops) to environmental changes and indirectly to environmental effects caused by culture activities. While OPEN focussed on Atlantic Cod (*Gadus morhua*) and scallops, factors important for bivalve growth in coastal waters in general were investigated by assessing water column and benthic effects of mussel and scallop culture in Upper South Cove near Lunenburg, Nova Scotia (O'Dor and Thompson 1996).

DFO-based studies initiated during OPEN continued after 2000 supported by an ESSRF project (Integrated Ecosystem Studies for Modelling Mussel Aquaculture-Environment Interactions) with collaboration between research scientists and biologists from DFO (Maritimes, Gulf, and Quebec regions), Dalhousie University (Halifax, NS), and IFREMER (Institut français de recherche pour l'exploitation de la mer, France). Results from investigations of the consequences of mussel culture to ecosystem structure and function were incorporated into numerical models to benefit from their predictive power. The project was notable at the time for taking a multidisciplinary ecosystem approach that utilized the broad oceanographic capabilities of BIO scientists. Modelling activities combining research in physical, chemical, and biological oceanography addressed broad-scale questions regarding system productive capacity, food depletion, nutrient cycling, and aquaculture/land-use interactions. Research was primarily located in Tracadie Bay, the most extensively leased mussel aquaculture embayment in Canada (Fig. 4), but mussel culture effects on ecosystem processes were also assessed in other Prince Edward Island inlets (Cranford et al. 2006, 2007, 2009; Grant et al. 2008; Hargrave et al. 2008).

The Program for Aquaculture Regulatory Research (PARR) was established in 2008 to fund DFO projects seeking new knowledge to support and advise ecosystem-based environmental regulations and decision making related to aquaculture. PARR funded an assessment of the spatial and temporal scales of environmental effects of mussel aquaculture in St. Anns Harbour, Nova Scotia, the location of the largest mussel lease application approved (2003) in the Maritimes. Scientists from BIO and Dalhousie University collaborated with Nova Scotia Fisheries and Aquaculture to test the effectiveness of environmental impact assessment predictions and assess the environmental monitoring program (EMP). In 2008 an intensive synoptic survey was conducted to test the effectiveness of the EMP for detecting benthic changes due to mussel culture operations. The project documented temporal and spatial changes in benthic and pelagic performance indicators, provided an assessment of the effectiveness of the current EMP, and made recommendations for improving monitoring methods (Cranford et al. 2010).

MAJOR RESEARCH RESULTS

Local Versus Far-field Effects Studies

DFO research on aquaculture-environment interactions in the Maritimes described above focussed on studies of local effects within salmon and mussel farm boundaries. Increased OM sedimentation, sediment-water exchange of DO and ammonia, and altered biomass and species composition of benthic invertebrates (macrofauna) were observed in some locations under and adjacent to salmon net-pens and mussel lines but effects decreased with distance (Fisheries and Oceans Canada 2003). Depending on water depth and current speed, measureable differences from reference (non-farm) sites were restricted to within 50 m of culture facilities. Changes in DO and ammonia in the water column within a salmon farm leased area were more difficult to detect. DO varied with tidal currents, but more importantly, with the reduced tidal volumes associated with low water during a tidal cycle. If changes in concentrations were detected, they only occurred briefly when water currents were low (Wildish at al. 1993). The observations were consistent with model calculations for oxygen budgets in SWNB (Trites and Petrie 1995, Strain et al. 1995, Page et al. 2005) where fish respiration and water circulation were concluded to be major factors controlling DO within salmon cages.

Local effects of salmon net-pen culture on sediments measured in SWNB in the mid to late 1990s (Hargrave et al. 1997) suggested that it might be possible to monitor environmental effects of farms using observations at individual sites. Comparisons of benthic biological and geochemical variables at different salmon leases in SWNB showed that total dissolved free sulfides (S) and oxidation-reduction potentials (Eh) in the surface (upper 2 cm) sediment were sensitive to excessive OM sedimentation. These variables were recommended as the basis for monitoring programs in an EMP (Wildish et al. 1999). There was widespread interest in this approach by regulatory agencies since it would make lease owners responsible for monitoring their farm site. Licensing could require that an EMP be applied by an operator within their leased area with results reported annually to provincial regulatory agencies.

The review that examined potentially negative environmental effects of salmon net-pen and mussel long-line culture over areas larger than individual farms or lease areas (Fisheries and Oceans Canada 2003) emphasized the lack of far-field environmental effects studies. Observations at the scale of a single farm or within a lease that described local environmental conditions could not be used to determine the capacity of an inlet or bay to assimilate additional dissolved and particulate nutrients released from culture operations. The examples below show how field observations and model calculations were combined in attempts to consider inlet-wide impacts of multiple salmon or mussel farm leases.

Evidence for Far-field Effects Due to Salmon Culture in the Bay of Fundy

The first evidence for far-field effects of salmon culture in SWNB was provided by Pohle et al. (2001) in a study of benthic macrofauna communities and other sediment variables. The temporal study (1994-99) with annual sampling was located in areas of SWNB where intensive salmon culture had developed with sites at least 200 m away from operational farms. Significant changes in benthic community structure were noted in the first year (1994-95), coincident with an increase in salmon culture production, which persisted for the remainder of the study. A second study (Wildish and Pohle 2005) compared macrofauna data collected from the same area before salmon culture had begun (1974-75) with similar data collected in 1997 and 2000 after the industry was well developed. Macrofauna community structure at a reference station in the St. Croix Estuary in SWNB covering 10 km had not changed during this period showing that no general, long-term changes in biomass or taxonomic composition had occurred during the study period.

A characteristic feature of benthic macrofauna communities in the lower L'Etang in SWNB in 1975 was the presence of extensive beds of burrowing, filter-feeding amphipods. Increased sedimentation of flocculated fine-grained sediment throughout the inlet during the 1990s is thought to have caused the disappearance of these communities (Milligan and Law 2005). By 1997 to 2000, amphipod beds, historically an important food resource for young groundfish such as haddock and cod, had completely disappeared from Lime Kiln Bay. An independent study by Robinson et al. (2005) demonstrated that macroalgal eutrophication had occurred on local beaches in SWNB due to nutrients released from salmon farms. Intertidal areas near salmon farms had high standing crops of the green alga *Ulva* spp. that was found to reduce recruitment, growth, and survival, and cause behavioural changes in commercially important Soft-shelled Clam (*Mya arenaria*) populations. Circumstantial evidence, in the form of increased levels of zinc in sediments (derived from high levels in salmon feed), suggested that increased *Ulva* biomass was due to nutrients released from the nearby salmon farm. Yeats et al. (2005) showed that depending on mineralogy and grain size, elevated Zn and Cu, normalized for lithium, could be detected above concentrations normally present in sediments at some distance from salmon cage sites in depositional areas of SWNB.

Numerical and Finite Element Circulation Modelling

The linkage between water circulation and holding capacity for salmon management in the L'Etang Inlet in SWNB was first investigated by Loucks (1988, 1991) and Trites (1991) using a numerical model (de Margerie et al. 1990) described in Wildish et al. (1990). Measurements over two months (May to December in 1989) showed complex horizontal currents with a net inward flow. Greenberg et al. (2005) described the tidally-driven circulation in Passamaquoddy Bay and inlets within SWNB in more detail using a finite element model. Trajectories of soluble material or neutrally buoyant particles added at different locations could be followed hourly over 2.5 tidal cycles. The model output clearly showed large horizontal exchanges in the L'Etang area. Tidally-driven water movement, as in many locations favourable for salmon culture, can transport dissolved substances and suspended particles over long distances between adjacent inlets over a few tidal cycles. The particle-tracking feature of the model could be used to examine the spread of disease, to determine minimum currents required to replenish oxygen consumed by fish within cage arrays, and to predict sedimentation patterns around farms. The modelled trajectories of water and suspended particles show that management practices in one bay should take into account culture operations in adjacent inlets.

Mass Balance Models

Several studies have used a mass balance approach to compare physical and biological processes of DO supply and loss on an inlet-wide basis to assess the relative importance of fish metabolism to other processes in SWNB. Page et al. (2005) summarized DO dynamics to show that fish respiration could be an important process causing oxygen depletion within salmon net-pens. Wildish et al. (1990), Trites and Petrie (1995), and Strain and Hargrave (2005) made similar calculations showing that if salmon biomass was sufficiently high, localized DO reductions could occur in areas where currents are weak or water residence times are long. Anecdotal information from some farms in such areas confirmed model predictions that localized oxygen depletion had occurred within fish pens at some locations (Page et al. 2005).

The fate of nitrogen in dissolved and particulate wastes released from all salmon farm sites in SWNB in 2002 was also described using mass balance calculations (Strain and Hargrave 2005). A fish-growth model to estimate particulate and dissolved nitrogen loss from feed application and salmon metabolism during a 2-year grow-out cycle showed that most nitrogen release occurs as dissolved ammonia. Faeces production represents a much smaller loss (~10%), but as the particulate matter is almost neutrally buoyant it is potentially available for transport over relatively long distances. While heavier waste feed pellets are buried locally, more buoyant faecal matter can be transported over relatively long distances to be either decomposed in the water column or buried. The mass balance calculations compared nitrogen fluxes through salmon farms with those due to natural processes to show that, where farms were most concentrated, fluxes due to salmon could be increased by more than 300%.

Nitrogen Fluxes in Tracadie Bay

Similarly to finfish culture, mussel aquaculture influences some fundamental ecosystem processes with a complexity of interactions. Particle depletion by filter feeding and increased biodeposition are key processes with potentially negative ecological effects at inlet-wide scales (Cranford et al. 2006, 2007, 2009; Grant et al. 2008) and models are essential for predicting these effects.

A nitrogen budget and dynamic water exchange model developed for Tracadie Bay, Prince Edward Island, showed that most nitrogen flux for the entire inlet occurs as a result of tidal exchange (Cranford et al. 2007). More nitrogen leaves via offshore tidal exchange than enters as river input. The mussel harvest also removes nitrogen from the system, but the amount is small compared to input from river and agricultural sources. The mussels can contribute significantly to the retention of nutrients in the coastal zone, the amounts excreted, sedimented, and buried in sediments. Mussel biodeposition can significantly increase nitrogen flux and concentrations of OM in sediments in shallow inlets with limited water exchange such as Tracadie Bay. Particulate nitrogen fluxes within the bay are dominated by mussel ingestion of suspended material and faecal matter production. Calculations show that benthic enrichment can be expected when biodeposits are buried.

Mapping Inlet-wide Effects of Mussel Culture

Seston depletion and sediment OM enrichment as a result of increased mussel biodeposition can extend over areas much larger than lease boundaries. Eutrophication effects were appearing in sediments in Prince Edward Island inlets as intensive mussel culture expanded (Cranford et al. 2009), and Tracadie Bay served as a suitable case study to evaluate inlet-wide effects. Key sediment variables (water content, grain size, OM, Eh, and dissolved sulfides) measured throughout the inlet showed spatial variations within and outside of lease areas (Cranford et al. 2007, Hargrave et al. 2008). The geochemical variables were used to group stations into benthic enrichment categories that separated mussel lease and non-lease areas. The enrichment gradient was similar to changes occurring as a result of high OM sedimentation near salmon pens described by Hargrave et al. (1993). Shallow water depths, low currents, and a large biomass of cultured mussels in an inlet are required for sedimentation and accumulation of biodeposits to reach the high levels of benthic enrichment observed near salmon pens.

Detection of the magnitude and zone of food depletion in and around mussel aquaculture sites is complicated by the large degree of natural variation in phytoplankton and seston concentrations in coastal waters. Two new approaches were developed at BIO to document the scale of phytoplankton depletion. The first was based on conducting rapid high-resolution three-dimensional surveys of phytoplankton and suspended particles with a towed undulating sensor vehicle (Cranford et al. 2006,

Grant et al. 2008). This approach has permitted the routine mapping of depletion zones in many mussel aquaculture regions in Canada and Europe. The second approach specifically targets ecosystem-scale effects of phytoplankton depletion by measuring changes in phytoplankton size-structure resulting from the size-selective feeding behaviour of mussels. Size-fractioned chlorophyll *a* analysis was shown to be an ecologically relevant and inexpensive indicator of bay-scale changes at the base of the pelagic food web. Picophytoplankton (0.2 to 2.0 µm size range) were shown to dominate in Prince Edward Island embayments where feeding by cultured mussels removes food particles faster than they can be replaced by tidal exchange (Harrison et al. 2005).

PROVISION OF ADVICE TO HABITAT MANAGEMENT

DFO research on aquaculture-environmental interactions has been and continues to be focussed on providing advice for habitat managers to support development of sustainable salmon and mussel culture industries. Research results have been used to recommend management approaches to avoid a Harmful Alteration, Disruption, or Destruction (HADD) of marine fish habitat as required under the federal *Fisheries Act*.

Methodologies for habitat impact assessment resulting from the research over the past two decades have become part of a standardized EMP for determining benthic enrichment effects associated with salmon and mussel aquaculture (Wildish et al. 1990, 1999; Cranford et al. 2006). A Canadian Science Advisory Secretariat (CSAS) research document prepared for DFO Habitat Management (Wildish et al. 2005) recommended monitoring methods and identified thresholds for variables shown to be sensitive indicators of benthic organic enrichment (free sulfides and redox potentials) in surface sediments (Hargrave et al. 1997) to assess environmental effects of salmon aquaculture. The methods and assessment approaches are currently applied in an annual EMP at all licensed aquaculture sites in Newfoundland, Nova Scotia, New Brunswick, and British Columbia.

Decision support tools were also developed to assist managers with regulatory responsibility (Silvert 1994). A decision support system (DSS) described by Hargrave (2002) consisted of questions about far- and near-field variables potentially affected by salmon aquaculture. Input data for farm variables (the number and sizes of pens and fish stocking density) were combined with physical (mean water depth, presence or absence of sills, tidal amplitude and variations in current speed) and sediment variables (grain size, organic content, S and redox potentials). Scoring based on input data was used to provide a score that reflected the degree that environmental conditions might be adversely affected by the increased organic input due to the presence of the farm. This DSS has been used by DFO Habitat Management staff in the Maritimes Region since 2003 to screen new applications to determine if a potential exists for a proposed farm site to create conditions for a HADD.

The CSAS research document of Cranford et al. (2006) recommended a tiered approach for assessing environmental risks of mussel aquaculture where, depending on previous observations and the type of environment and operational nature of the shellfish lease, different levels of monitoring would be applied. In addition, shellfish aquaculture management approaches, developed in part from DFO research, have been recommended to address the needs of worldwide legislations requiring an ecosystem-based management framework (Cranford et al. 2012). Benthic performance indicators and classifications have been implemented as part of global sustainability standards for the certification of cultured shellfish (World Wildlife Fund 2010). Research to improve monitoring methods and develop new approaches continues as both salmon and mussel aquaculture industries wish to expand existing leases and locate new farm sites.

SYNTHESIS AND FUTURE RESEARCH

Our understanding of near-field environmental effects of salmon and mussel culture based on studies in SWNB and Prince Edward Island increased rapidly during the 1990s through collaborative research projects at BIO and SABS. Geochemical variables in surface sediments (S and Eh potentials) and, for salmon farms, trace metals were found to be sensitive indicators of benthic enrichment. Increased sedimentation of fecal matter and waste feed was associated with decreased benthic macrofauna biomass and changes in community structure and the formation of hypoxic or anoxic sediments under and close to net pen and long line arrays. In the past decade these geochemical variables have been applied in provincial EMP programs in Newfoundland, Nova Scotia, New Brunswick, and British Columbia to assess benthic enrichment effects at farm sites due to salmon and mussel aquaculture.

While these studies provided information on local benthic enrichment at individual farm sites, they did not allow conclusions about far-field or inlet-wide effects. Numerous field programs (COSAD, OPEN, ESSA, and more recently PARR-funded projects) combined physical, chemical, and biological oceanographic observations and the application of circulation models to determine if effects of salmon and mussel culture could be detected at scales larger than a farm lease. The exchange of water between adjacent inlets in areas of intensive salmon aquaculture in SWNB was demonstrated by a finite element physical mixing model driven by tidal circulation. Model results support a bay management, rather than a farm-by-farm approach for setting stocking densities in areas where many leases are located in close proximity. Mass balance models comparing sources and sinks for DO, particulate carbon and dissolved nitrogen in SWNB where salmon farms are concentrated also showed that chemical fluxes due to cultured salmon could exceed natural fluxes by several times. These observations led to the recommendation that stocking density should be limited in some areas to avoid long-term environmental degradation.

A major strength of both near- and far-field aquaculture environment effects studies has been the multidisciplinary nature of the research. The collaboration of physical, chemical, and biological oceanographers was made much easier because research staff in different disciplines were co-located. In a similar manner, having DFO Habitat Management staff located at BIO allowed research projects to be designed to answer specific, practical questions with results more likely to be used by managers. The development of DSS tools for assessing site suitability for new salmon farms and the tiered approach for EMPs monitoring of mussel farm sites have assisted federal government habitat managers, provincial aquaculture regulators, and salmon and mussel farm operators who apply the site monitoring methods. In addition, DFO research staff have been involved in some EMP monitoring studies which assisted both farm operators and provincial regulators in interpreting the results.

Future studies concerning aquaculture-environment interactions must focus on large-scale and long-term effects, impacts on hard bottom areas, and, in the case of finfish aquaculture, the location of farms in deeper water at offshore sites. The geochemical methods currently used in EMPs for assessing aquaculture benthic impacts are only suitable for mud and sand bottom areas where samples can be collected by cores or grabs. Wildish et al. (1999) emphasized that research on monitoring methods should be continued and updated annually. Quantitative methods to assess enrichment effects on rock and cobble substrates and in deeper water must also be developed. Short-term (e.g., annual) and local measures of effects within or close to leases will continue to be carried out by individual aquaculture site operators and companies holding leases as part of ongoing EMP requirements. It is unclear, however, who has the responsibility to consider larger-scale effects beyond lease boundaries that could have broad-scale habitat impacts or effects on non-commercial populations of invertebrates and fish. In the past, aquaculture industries for salmon and mussel culture have not been willing to collect data outside of their lease boundaries. However, DFO does not have the mandate and has limited resources to conduct far-field monitoring studies. Despite the current reduction in research budgets and staffing limitations, research to find practical methods to observe far-field effects must continue. In addition, collaborative management approaches must be developed that consider both local and far-field environmental effects of the growing aquaculture industries.

ACKNOWLEDGEMENTS

We are grateful to H. Akagi, S. Armsworthy, J. Bugden, R. Losier, G. Phillips, and A. Wilson for valuable technical assistance during various research projects on aquaculture-environment interactions conducted at the Bedford Institute of Oceanography and St. Andrews Biological Station over two decades. We thank S. Armstrong, G. Bugden, M. Dowd, J. Grant, D. Greenberg, G. Harrison, K. Haya, E. Horne, P. Kepkay, W. Li, F. Page, J. Martin, T. Milligan, S. Robinson, W. Silvert, J. Smith, P.

Strain, and P. Yeats for their collaboration and participation in field work, data analysis, and modelling. Honours and graduate students L. Auffrey, F. Bouvet, L. Doucette, D. Duplisea, F. Friars, N. Hamilton, and E. Pfeiffer contributed significantly to the projects through their dissertation research. Ron Loucks, Ruth Smith, and Robin Anderson kindly commented on the manuscript.

REFERENCES

Anderson, J.M. 2007. The Salmon Connection. Glen Margaret Publishing, Tantallon, NS.

Anderson, M.R., M.F. Tlusty, and V.A. Pepper. 2005. Organic enrichment at cold water aquaculture sites - the case of coastal Newfoundland. Handbook of Environmental Chemistry 5, Part M: 99-114.

Cranford, P.J. and others. 2006. Indicators and thresholds for use in assessing shellfish aquaculture impacts on fish habitat. Canadian Science Advisory Secretariat Research Document 2006/034, Fisheries and Oceans Canada, Ottawa, ON.

Cranford, P.J., P.M. Strain, M. Dowd, J. Grant, B.T. Hargrave, and M.-C. Archambault. 2007. Influence of mussel aquaculture on nitrogen dynamics in a nutrient enriched coastal embayment. Marine Ecology Progress Series 347: 61-78.

Cranford, P.J., B.T. Hargrave, and L.I. Doucette. 2009. Benthic organic enrichment from suspended mussel (*Mytilus edulis*) culture in Prince Edward Island, Canada. Aquaculture 292: 189-196.

Cranford, P.J., T. Balch, C. Buchan, J. Crocker, R. Filgueira, J. Grant, B.T. Hargrave, B. Law, W. Li, L. Lu, D. Sephton, S. Roach, and R. Stuart. 2010. Mussel aquaculture regulatory effectiveness monitoring: validation of the St. Ann's Harbour Environmental Assessment and Monitoring Program. Canadian Technical Report of Fisheries Aquatic Sciences 2905, Fisheries and Oceans Canada, Dartmouth, NS.

Cranford, P.J., P. Kamermans, G. Krause, A. Bodoy J. Mazurié, B. Buck, P. Dolmer, D. Fraser, K. Van Nieuwenhove, F.X. O'Beirn, A. Sanchez-Mata Fisheries and Oceans Canada. 2006. A scientific review of the potential environmental effects of aquaculture in aquatic ecosystems. Canadian Technical Report of Fisheries and Aquatic Sciences 2450, Volume IV, Fisheries and Oceans Canada, Ottawa, ON.

Grant, J., C. Bacher, P.J. Cranford, T. Guyondet, and M. Carreau. 2008. A spatially explicit ecosystem model of seston depletion in dense mussel culture. Journal of Marine Systems 73: 155-168.

Greenberg, D.A., J.A. Shore, F.H. Page, and M. Dowd. 2005. A finite element circulation model for embayments with drying intertidal areas with application to the Quoddy region of the Bay of Fundy. Ocean Modelling 10: 211-231.

Hargrave, B.T. 2002. A traffic light decision system for marine finfish aquaculture siting. Ocean and Coastal Management 45: 215-235.

Hargrave, B.T. 2004. Environmental Studies for Sustainable Aquaculture (ESSA): 2004 Symposium Report. Canadian Technical Report of Fisheries Aquatic Sciences 2542, Fisheries and Oceans Canada, Dartmouth, NS.

Hargrave, B.T., D.E. Duplisea, E. Pfeiffer, and D.J. Wildish. 1993. Seasonal changes in benthic fluxes of dissolved oxygen and ammonium associated with marine cultured Atlantic salmon. Marine Ecology Progress Series 96: 249-257.

Hargrave, B.T., G.A. Phillips, L.I. Doucette, M.J. White, T.G. Milligan, D.J. Wildish, and R.E. Cranston. 1997. Assessing benthic impacts of organic enrichment from marine aquaculture. Water, Air, Soil Pollution 99: 641-650.

Hargrave, B.T., L.I. Doucette, P.J. Cranford, B.A. Law, and T.G. Milligan. 2008. Influence of mussel aquaculture on benthic organic enrichment in a nutrient-rich coastal embayment. Marine Ecology Progress Series 365: 137-149.

Harrison, W.G., T. Perry, and W.K.W. Li. 2005. Ecosystem indicators of water quality. Part I. Plankton biomass, primary production and nutrient demand. Handbook of Environmental Chemistry 5, Part M: 59-82.

Kepkay, P.E., W.G. Harrison, and J.B.C. Bugden. 2005. Ecosystem indicators of water quality. Part II. Oxygen production and oxygen demand. Handbook of Environmental Chemistry 5, Part M: 83-97.

Loucks, R.H. 1988. Preliminary oceanographic information for salmonid aquaculture in L'Etang Inlet, New Brunswick. Contractor's Report to DFO, St. Andrews Biological Station, St. Andrews, NB.

Loucks, R.H. 1991. Measurement of dispersion in L'Etang Inlet and approaches using drifters. Contractor's report prepared for New Brunswick Department of Fisheries and Aquaculture, Fredericton, New Brunswick.

Milligan, T.G. and B.A. Law. 2005. The effect of marine aquaculture on fine sediment dynamics in coastal inlets. Handbook of Environmental Chemistry 5, Part M: 239-251.

O'Dor, R.K and R. Thompson. 1996. Ocean production enhancement network (OPEN): fourth annual scientific meeting contribution. Marine Biology 124: 591-592.

Page, F., D. Greenberg, G. Bugden, R. Losier, J. Shore, E. Horne, S. Robinson, B. Chang, and T. Sephton. 1999. Oceanographic component of the Canadian Department of Fisheries and Oceans Science Strategic Research Program on Coastal Oceanography for sustainable aquaculture development (COSAD). Bulletin of the Aquaculture Association of Canada 99-2: 14-16.

Page, F.H., R. Losier, P. McCurdy, D. Greenberg, J. Chaffey, and B. Chang. 2005. Dissolved oxygen and salmon cage culture in the Southwestern New Brunswick Portion of the Bay of Fundy. Handbook of Environmental Chemistry 5, Part M: 1-28.

Pohle, G., B. Frost, and R. Findlay. 2001. Assessment of regional benthic impact of salmon mariculture within L'Etang Inlet, Bay of Fundy. ICES Journal of Marine Science 58: 417-426.

Robinson, S.M.C., L.M. Auffrey, and M.A. Barbeau. 2005. Far-field impacts of eutrophication on the intertidal zone in the Bay of Fundy, Canada with emphasis on the soft shell clam, *Mya arenaria*. Handbook of Environmental Chemistry 5, Part M: 253-274.

Shaw, J., D.J.W. Piper, G.B.J. Fader, E.L. King, B.J. Todd, T. Bell, M.J. Batterson, and D.G.E. Liverman. 2006. A conceptual model of the deglaciation of Atlantic Canada. Quaternary Science Reviews 25: 2,059-2,081.

Silvert, W. 1994. Decision support systems for aquaculture licensing. Journal of Applied Ichthyology 10: 307-311.

Silvert, W. and B. Hargrave. 1995. Report on International Workshop on Modelling Environmental Interactions of Mariculture. Proceedings of an ICES Annual Science Conference, C. 1995/F: 6 (Session F), Copenhagen, Denmark.

Strain, P.M. and B.T. Hargrave. 2005. Salmon aquaculture, nutrient fluxes and ecosystem processes in southwestern New Brunswick. Handbook of Environmental Chemistry, 5, Part M: 29-57.

Strain, P.M., D.J. Wildish, and P.A. Yeats. 1995. The application of simple models of nutrient loading and oxygen demand to the management of a marine tidal inlet. Marine Pollution Bulletin 30: 253-261.

Stucchi, D., T.F. Sutherland, C. Levings, and D. Higgs. 2005. Near-field depositional model for salmon aquaculture waste. Handbook of Environmental Chemistry 5, Part M: 157-180.

Trites, R.W. 1991. Measurement of dispersion in L'Etang Inlet and approaches using drifters. R.H. Loucks Oceanology Limited, Dartmouth, NS.

Trites, R.W. and L. Petrie. 1995. Physical oceanographic features of L'Etang Inlet including evaluation and results from a numerical model. Canadian Technical Report of Hydrography and Ocean Sciences 163, Fisheries and Oceans Canada, Dartmouth, NS.

Wildish, D.J. and G.W. Pohle. 2005. Benthic macrofaunal changes resulting from finfish mariculture. Handbook of Environmental Chemistry 5, Part M: 275-304.

Wildish, D.J., J.L. Martin, A.J. Wilson, and A.M. DeCoste. 1988. Environmental monitoring of the Bay of Fundy salmonid mariculture industry during 1986 and 1987. Canadian Technical Report of Fisheries and Aquatic Sciences 1648, Fisheries and Oceans Canada, St. Andrews, NB.

Wildish, D.J., J.L. Martin, R.W. Trites, and A.M. Saulnier. 1990. A proposal for environmental research and monitoring of organic pollution caused by salmonid mariculture in the Bay of Fundy. Canadian Technical Report of Fisheries and Aquatic Sciences 1724, Fisheries and Oceans Canada, St. Andrews, NB.

Wildish, D.J., P.D. Keizer, A.J. Wilson, and J.L. Martin. 1993. Seasonal changes of dissolved oxygen and plant nutrients in seawater near salmonid net pens in the macrotidal Bay of Fundy. Canadian Journal of Fisheries and Aquatic Sciences 50: 303-311.

Wildish, D.J., H.M. Akagi, N. Hamilton, and B.T. Hargrave. 1999. A recommended method for monitoring sediments to detect organic enrichment from mariculture in the Bay of Fundy. Canadian Technical Report of Fisheries and Aquatic Sciences 2286, Fisheries and Oceans Canada, St. Andrews, NB.

Wildish, D.J., G.W. Pohle, B.T. Hargrave, T.F. Sutherland, and M.R. Anderson. 2005. Benthic monitoring methods for habitat management of finfish mariculture in Canada. Canadian Science Advisory Secretariat Research Document 005/039, Fisheries and Oceans Canada, Ottawa, ON.

World Wildlife Fund. 2010. Bivalve Aquaculture Sustainability Standards. World Wildlife Fund, Toronto, ON. www.worldwildlife.org/what/globalmarkets/aquaculture/ WWFBinaryitem17872.pdf: 50 p.

Yeats, P.A., T.G. Milligan, T.F. Sutherland, S.M.C. Robinson, J.A. Smith, P. Lawton, and C.D. Levings. 2005. Lithium-normalized zinc and copper concentrations in sediments as measures of trace metal enrichment due to salmon aquaculture. Handbook of Environmental Chemistry 5, Part M: 207-220.

34. THE IMPACT OF FISHING GEAR ON BENTHIC HABITAT AND COMMUNITIES

Donald C. Gordon* and Ellen L.R. Kenchington

SUMMARY

A multidisciplinary team of scientists at the Bedford Institute of Oceanography (BIO), in collaboration with the Northwest Atlantic Fisheries Centre, conducted an extensive field program studying the effects of bottom-contacting mobile fishing gear on benthic habitat and communities. Experiments were conducted using otter trawls, scallop dredges, and hydraulic clam dredges on sand and gravel habitats off Atlantic Canada. The success of the program was heavily dependent on recent advances in navigational technology and new seabed sampling and imaging gear developed at BIO. The results provided information on the impacts of fishing disturbance, as well as recovery periods. Impacts were found to be variable and dependent upon the kind of gear, how it is used, the return period of the disturbance, the substrate, and the species composition and life history characteristics of the benthic community. Sandy habitats were the easiest to disturb, but recovered faster than gravel habitats; hydraulic clam dredges caused the greatest damage. The most sensitive species were large epibenthic animals, especially sessile species with low growth rates, such as deep-water corals. The impacts of bottom-contacting mobile fishing gear is an important issue that needs to be considered as Canada moves to adopt an ecosystem approach to fisheries management.

Key words: benthic habitat and communities, otter trawls, scallop dredges, hydraulic clam dredges.
***E-mail:** Donald.Gordon@ns.sympatico.ca

Bottom-contacting fishing gear such as trawls, rakes, and dredges has been widely used by the fishing industry for many years in Atlantic Canada. Damage to benthic habitat and communities was suspected but received little attention, except for some early studies conducted at the St. Andrews Biological Station, New Brunswick, and the Halifax Fisheries Research Laboratory, Nova Scotia. However, this changed in the late 1980s when groundfish resources started to decline and many began to wonder whether seabed disturbance by fishing gear was an important contributing factor. The issue became controversial and international in scope with the fishing industry and environmental organizations having different viewpoints. There was a need for objective research and quantitative data to help resolve this issue and provide guidance to fisheries managers. Also, in 1986, the Department of Fisheries and Oceans Canada (DFO) released its new policy on fish habitat (Fisheries and Oceans Canada 1986) that called for new research to address high priority habitat issues, such as fishing gear impacts.

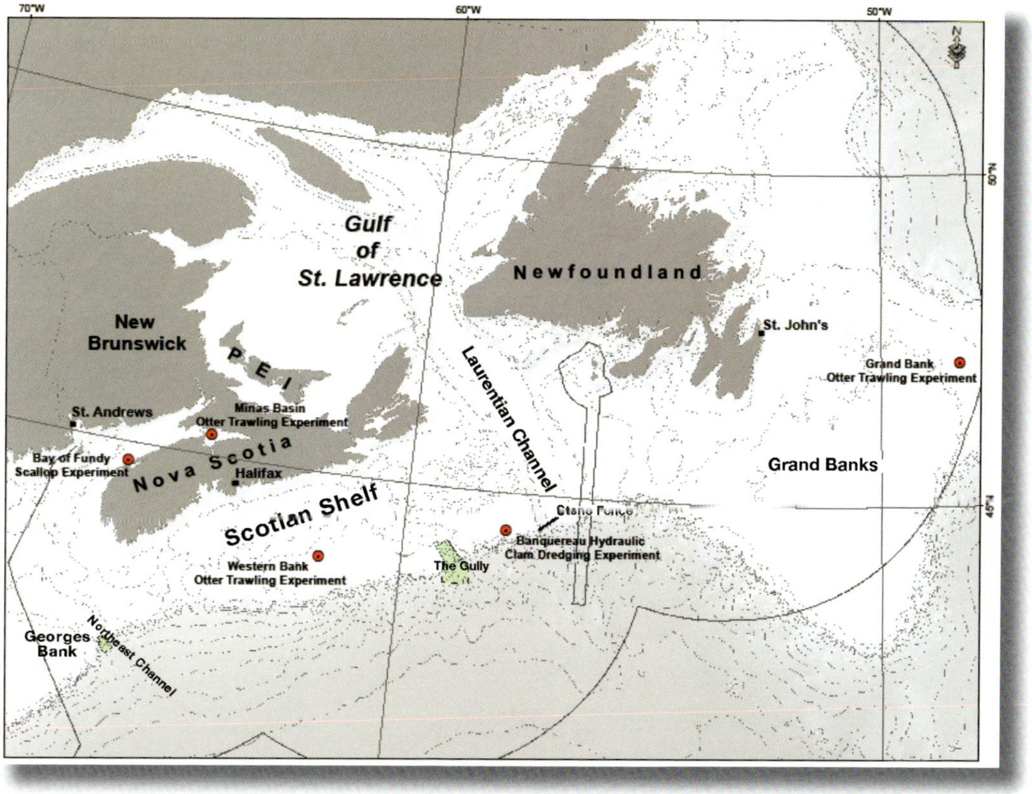

Figure 1. Map showing the location of study sites (red circles) and other geographic locations and features in Atlantic Canada.

A long-term program on the impacts of fishing gear on benthic habitats and communities was established at the Bedford Institute of Oceanography (BIO) in 1990. This program was led by the newly created Habitat Ecology Division with strong collaboration from the Northwest Atlantic Fisheries Centre (NAFC) in St. John's, Newfoundland, Geological Survey of Canada Atlantic (GSCA), numerous contractors, universities, and the fishing industry. The BIO component was coordinated by D. Gordon while the NAFC participation was initially led by P. Schwinghamer, and later K. Gilkinson. BIO staff involved at the outset of the program included D. Peer, T. Rowell, P. Woo, D. McKeown, P. Vass, D. Reimer, and J. Prena (a visiting scientist from Germany), with others joining the team later including E. Kenchington, C. Bourbonnais, K. MacIsaac, L.-A. Henry, and G. Fader. A large number of technical staff also contributed. The intent of this applied science program was to conduct multiyear experiments examining the impacts of different gear types on various habitats in Atlantic Canada (Fig. 1), as well as to study recovery from disturbance. It was also recognized that this program would provide new and valuable knowledge of benthic ecosystems off eastern Canada.

Program planning included input from fisheries biologists and habitat managers, the fishing industry, and European scientists with experience in studying fishing gear impacts. Funding sources included the DFO A-Base, Northern Cod Science Program, Atlantic Fisheries Adjustment Program (AFAP), Green Plan Sustainable Fisheries Program, Environmental Science Strategic Research Fund (ESSRF), and the fishing industry. One of the first steps in the program was a literature review of the effects of trawling, dredging and ocean dumping in Atlantic Canada (Messieh et al. 1991). Analysis of historical sidescan sonar records by GSCA provided information on the degree and distribution of mobile gear disturbance on the continental shelf off Newfoundland and Nova Scotia (Harrison et al. 1991, Jenner et al. 1991). Considerable attention was given to selecting suitable study sites (Prena et al. 1996). Important factors included ensuring that sites had not been disturbed in recent years and were protected from fishing disturbance for the duration of the experiments.

In order to meet the objectives of this program, it was essential to assemble a suite of equipment that could sample different seabed types, collect a range of benthic organisms, and provide imagery. Sidescan sonar support was available from GSCA. Improvements were made by BIO engineers to BRUTIV (a towed bottom-referencing video platform) and an epibenthic sled (Rowell et al. 1997). In addition, BIO engineers developed three new seabed sampling tools, Videograb, Campod and Towcam, which are described in Gordon et al. (2014) and played a major role in this program. Concurrent with the development of these new tools were significant improvements to navigation (McKeown and Gordon 1997), including the development of the Atlantic Geoscience Centre navigation system (AGCNAV), the installation of dGPS on BIO ships, and the availability of a Trackpoint II system through GSCA that allowed tracking the

Figure 2. Recently trawled mud flat in the Minas Basin at low tide showing the disturbance from doors and footgear.

position of gear in relation to the ship. These improvements meant that the location of all equipment on the seabed could be determined with an accuracy of just a few metres. The assembled technology was unique and the envy of other laboratories around the world. These critical technological developments would not have been possible without the dedicated support of BIO engineers, both DFO and GSCA.

MINAS BASIN OTTER TRAWLING EXPERIMENT (1990-91)

This first experiment was run in collaboration with Acadia University (Brylinsky et al. 1994) while equipment and plans were being developed for offshore experiments. The Minas Basin (Fig. 1) is a high energy, macrotidal area fished by small draggers for winter flounder. Dominant benthic organisms at the study site were diatoms, nematodes, and polychaetes. Except for a few mud snails, there were no epibenthic organisms. Single otter-trawl sets were made at high tide using a commercial dragger, when flats were flooded with 6-8 m of water, and observations were made at low water when flats were exposed (Fig. 2). Sampling was done in the furrows made by the doors, the roller marks between the door furrows, and control sites outside of the trawl path, over several months, after trawling. The overall impacts were judged to be minor and short-lived compared to the natural stress imposed by tidal inundation, storms, and winter ice, but results could not be applied to offshore fishing banks with much different environmental settings.

GRAND BANKS OTTER TRAWLING EXPERIMENT (1993-95)

A 20 x 20 km experimental site (average depth 137 m) selected on the Grand Banks was relatively flat and composed primarily of sand (Fig. 1). Analysis of commercial fishing effort data indicated that the site had not been trawled since 1980 and sidescan sonar surveys showed no seabed disturbance. DFO closed the site to all fishing activity for the duration of the experiment, with an additional degree of protection provided from the groundfish moratorium established in 1992. Some iceberg scours were present but not abundant enough to interfere with the experiment.

Three, 13-km long experimental lines were established, each with a different heading and parallel control line. These were trawled 12 times in 1993, 1994, and 1995 by the CCS *Templeman* using an Engel 145 otter trawl (Fig. 3A). The distance between the doors averaged 60 m and the width of the rockhopper foot-gear was about 20 m. This intensity of trawling disturbance was considered to be higher than typical commercial fishing conditions. The trawl catch, both fish and invertebrates, was processed. Benthic sampling was done before and after trawling each year along both experimental and control lines by CCS *Parizeau* (Fig. 3B) using sidescan sonar, BRUTIV, the epibenthic sled (Fig. 3C), and Videograb (Fig. 3D). Equal numbers of samples were randomly collected along both the experimental and control lines to assess the impacts of trawling treatment over time. High-precision navigation ensured that samples collected along the experimental lines after trawling were in fact collected within the disturbed areas.

A diverse benthic community was present at the experimental site: in total, there were 246 invertebrate taxa with the dominant taxonomic groups being echinoderms, polychaetes, molluscs, and crustaceans. In this sandy habitat, most species were free-living or burrowing, with an abundant epibenthic community dominated by Sand Dollars (*Echinarachnius parma*), Brittlestars (*Ophiura sarsi*), Sea Urchins (*Strongylocentrotus pallidas*), Snow Crabs (*Chionoecetes opilio*), Soft Corals (*Gersemia sp.*), and molluscs (Fig. 4). Fish catch in the otter trawl was low and dominated by American Plaice (*Hippoglossoides platessoides*) and Thorny Skate (*Raja radiata*), with a small invertebrate bycatch dominated by Snow Crabs, Basket Stars (*Gorgonocephalus arcticus*), and Sea Urchins.

The immediate physical impacts of trawling on the seabed were readily visible and tended to decrease habitat complexity. Significant immediate effects of trawling were detected on some species of large epibenthic organisms including Snow Crabs, Sand Dollars, Brittlestars, Sea Urchins, and Soft Corals (Prena et al. 1999). However, indirect evidence suggested recovery of these species within a year, likely through migration from undisturbed areas adjacent to the trawled lines (Schwinghamer et al. 1998). The immediate effects of experimental otter trawling on the abundant and diverse macrobenthic organisms were relatively minor, restricted primarily to some species of polychaetes (Kenchington et al. 2001), with recovery within a year. Overall, there was no evidence of longer-term biological impacts due to annual trawling disturbance at this site on the Grand Banks (Gordon et al. 2005). The major signal observed in the data was a natural trend in the structure of the benthic community over the three-year experiment.

WESTERN BANK OTTER TRAWLING EXPERIMENT (1997-99)

This experiment was designed to investigate the impacts of otter trawling on a gravel seabed, a different habitat and biological community than present at the sandy Grand Banks site. A 2 x 2 km experimental site (average depth 70 m) was selected on Western Bank (Fig. 1) inside a haddock nursery area, closed to trawling since 1987. The seabed was relatively flat and composed of a mostly pebble and cobble gravel lag. (Fig. 5).

One experimental and three parallel control lines, each 2 km long, were established. The experimental line was trawled 12-14 times in 1997, 1998, and 1999, using the same Engel 145 otter trawl as used in the Grand Banks experiment, by either the CCGS *Needler* or CCGS *Teleost*. The trawl catch was processed, including the stomach contents of fish. Habitat and benthic communities were sampled before and after trawling by either the CCGS *Parizeau* or CCGS *Hudson* using sidescan sonar, BRUTIV or

Figure 3. Grand Banks otter trawling experiment. (A) The Engel otter trawl about to be deployed from the CSS *Templeman*; the black disks are the rock hopper footgear and the trawl doors are hanging in the gallows over the stern. (B) Research staff on CSS *Parzeau* (left to right): D. Gordon, P. Vass, D. Reimer, T. Milligan, M. Hawryluk, K. Muschenheim, D. McKeown, T. Rowell, K. Saunders, K. MacIsaac, and A. Ducharme. (C) Unloading the catch of the epibenthic sled. (D) Dumping a sediment sample collected by Videograb.

Figure 4. Epibenthic organisms common at the Grand Banks experimental site including Basket Stars (*Gorgonocephalus arcticus*), Snow Crabs (*Chionoecetes opilio*), Sand Dollars (*Echinarachnius parma*), Brittlestars (*Ophiura sarsi*), and Sea Urchins (*Strongylocentrotus pallidas*).

Towcam, Campod, and Videograb. Equal numbers of samples were randomly collected along both the experimental and control lines to assess the impacts of trawling over time. High-precision navigation ensured samples collected along the experimental line after trawling were collected within the disturbed area. A multibeam survey of the experimental site was conducted by the Canadian Hydrographic Service soon after the experiment began.

A total of 341 benthic taxa were identified, the majority of species being epifaunal, dominated by polychaetes, amphipods, and molluscs. Biomass was dominated by Horse Mussels (*Modiolus modiolus*) while a tube-building amphipod was the most abundant species. Twenty-two species of fish and five invertebrate species were captured in the trawl. Atlantic Cod (*Gadus morhua*), Haddock (*Melanogrammus aeglefinus*), and Winter Flounder (*Pseudopleuronectes americanus*), all visual predators, increased in abundance in successive trawl sets which suggests scavenging behaviour (Kenchington et al. 2005). Analysis of the stomach contents of Atlantic Cod, Haddock, American Plaice (*Hippoglossoides platessoides*), Yellowtail Flounder (*Limanda ferruginea*), and Winter Flounder showed significant quantitative and qualitative changes in diet attributed to the availability of benthic organisms damaged by the trawling disturbance.

Only minor impacts were observed on the gravel lag habitat, which is difficult to disturb because of its armoured nature, but recovery appeared to be slow (Gordon et al. 2008). Immediate impacts on organisms were relatively minor. The overall proportion of epifaunal biomass declined significantly over the three-year experiment, and the most affected species were large and attached epibenthic forms (Henry et al. 2005, Kenchington et al. 2006). Some affected organisms are long lived, such as Horse Mussels, and are expected to take a long time to recover. As in the Grand Banks experiment, significant natural changes with time were also observed in the benthic communities.

Figure 5. Gravel lag seabed habitat at the Western Bank experimental site.

BANQUEREAU HYDRAULIC CLAM DREDGING EXPERIMENT (1998-2000)

This experiment was designed to examine the impacts of hydraulic clam dredges used to harvest offshore clams in Atlantic Canada. It was conducted under a Joint Project Agreement with Clearwater Fine Foods, Halifax, Nova Scotia. A 1.5 km by 2 km experimental site (average depth 75 m) was established on Banquereau, an expansive sandy bank on the eastern Scotian Shelf (Fig. 1). The seabed was relatively flat and consisted of well-sorted fine-grained sand (Fig. 6). No evidence of previous fishing disturbance was detectable.

Three experimental treatment boxes, each 100 by 500 m, were established. Two of these were dredged. In one, the bycatch was released immediately within the box, following standard commercial procedures. In the other, the bycatch was held and later dumped in the third treatment box. Two control boxes were situated nearby. Experimental dredging was conducted on just one occasion (1998) by MV *Atlantic Pursuit* (Fig. 7A) operated by Clearwater, following standard commercial practices. The paired dredges were 4 m wide and the cutting blade was set at a depth of 20 cm (Fig. 7B). A total of 12 successive tows were made in alternating directions within each dredged box and, after each tow, the dredges were retrieved and the contents dumped for processing before being re-deployed. Benthic sampling was conducted by the CCGS *Hudson* before experimental dredging, immediately after dredging, two weeks after dredging, and one and two years after dredging. Sampling tools included sidescan, BRUTIV or Towcam, Campod, and Videograb. Equal numbers of samples were randomly collected in the treatment boxes to assess the impacts of dredging over time. High-precision navigation again ensured that samples collected in experimental boxes after dredging were within the disturbed areas. A multibeam survey of the experimental site was conducted by the Canadian Hydrographic Service soon after the experiment began.

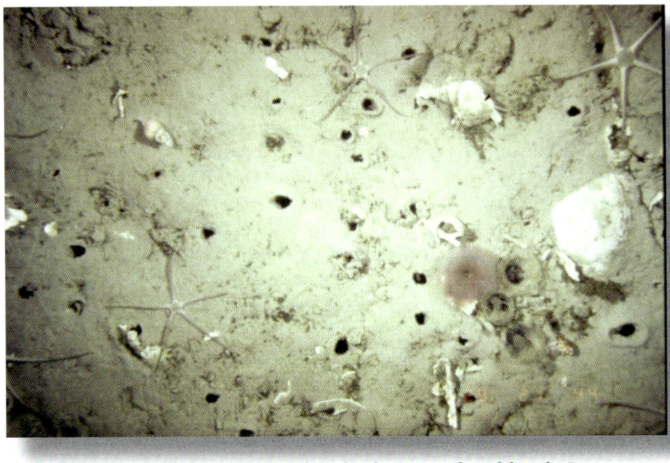

Figure 6. Sandy seabed habitat with abundant clam burrows and starfish at the Banquereau experimental site.

A total of 270 benthic taxa were observed, dominated by amphipods, polychaetes, and molluscs. Biomass was dominated by the Northern Propellerclam (*Cyrtodaria siliqua*). The most common epibenthic species included Sand Dollars, Sea Cucumbers (*Cucumaria frondosa*), Brittlestars, Sea Urchins, and Soft Corals. A total of 35 taxa were collected by the dredges with Propellerclams, Sea Cucumbers, and Sand Dollars comprising more than 80% of the biomass. Arctic Surfclams (*Mactromeris polynyma*), Greenland Cockles (*Serripes groenlandicus*), and Ocean Quahogs (*Arctica islandica*), the target species, were also caught.

Dredging effects were readily detectable against a background of natural temporal and large-scale spatial variability. The most obvious effect on habitat was a dramatic change in seabed topography due to the numerous overlapping curvilinear furrows made by the dredges, which covered 53-68% of the area of dredged boxes (Gilkinson et al. 2003). The loss of burrows, tubes, and shells created a smooth surface within the furrows. Furrows gradually degraded with time through the combined actions of slumping, sediment transport, and bioturbation. While not visible in video after one year, the sidescan data indicated that they lasted at least three years and acted as traps accumulating empty shells. Differences in patterns of acoustic reflectance between dredge furrows and the surrounding seabed indicated long-lasting effects on sediment structure. Densities of clam burrows within the furrows were reduced by up to 90% with no signs of recovery after three years due to the high mortalities of their architects and lack of recolonization.

Figure 7. Clam dredging. (A) The MV *Atlantic Pursuit* conducting the experimental clam dredging. (B) The commercial hydraulic clam dredge used in the Banquereau experiment.

Immediately after dredging, most macrofaunal species decreased in abundance with the greatest declines found inside dredge furrows (Gilkinson et al. 2005). The Brittlestar showed scavenging behaviour with a significantly greater proportion of the animals feeding immediately after dredging (Harris et al. 2009). Large numbers of Propellerclams were excavated to the seabed surface. Following initial declines in abundance and biomass of most taxa, there were marked increases in abundance of polychaetes and amphipods one year later. Two years after dredging, abundance of opportunistic species was generally elevated by more than 100% relative to pre-dredging levels. As expected, the dredging resulted in pronounced reductions in the biomass of target bivalves and there was no sign of recovery after two years. Longer-term site recovery was investigated in 2008, ten years after the disturbance. Sediment structure and/or compaction had largely returned to pre-dredging levels while commercial bivalves showed little recruitment (K.D. Gilkinson pers. comm.).

IMPACTS OF SCALLOPING IN THE BAY OF FUNDY (1997-2000)

This study was non-manipulative, a comparison of two data sets collected 30 years apart in an area of chronic fishing disturbance. It was carried out in the Bay of Fundy off Digby, Nova Scotia, where scallop dredging has occurred since 1921 (Fig. 1). The seabed in the area (average depth 70 m) is a gravel lag with sand patches and strong tidal currents.

The two surveys were conducted in 1966-67 (Caddy 1970) and 1997

(Fuller et al. 1998) using similar sampling and processing methods. Sampling was done using Digby scallop drags (Fig. 8) and the presence and absence of bycatch taxa were tabulated. The combined data set contained 35 megafauna taxa, most identified to the level of species or genus. A rich megafauna community was present at the time of both surveys; the dominant groups were sponges, cnidarians, brachiopods, molluscs, polychaetes, crustaceans, echinoderms, and tunicates.

Significant changes in the composition of the megafaunal community were observed over the 30-year period (Kenchington et al. 2007). The mean number of taxa per station increased and the community became more homogeneous. The frequencies of occurrence of dominant taxa changed markedly, with polychaetes, tunicates, sponges, and Horse Mussels decreasing in frequency, and whelks, sunstars, starfish, burrowing clams, hermit crabs, and brittlestars increasing. There was no evidence that any species was lost from the area. Biological traits analysis indicated that mobility, degree of attachment, habitat, feeding mode, body flexibility, and regenerative powers could explain some of the changes observed. There was a relative decline in fragile, attached, and colonial taxa but an increase in robust, mobile, and scavenging taxa. Taxa with a low ability to regenerate declined and there appeared to be a shift towards smaller taxa.

Owing to the nature of the data set, it is not possible to draw firm conclusions on the reasons for the observed changes in megafauna community structure. However, the changes are the kind that would be expected to result from the repeated physical impact of scallop drags and otter trawls. A related study indicated that chronic scallop dredging can change the taxonomic structure of hydroid assemblages on gravel seabeds (Henry and Kenchington 2004a), as well as their reproductive strategy of cloning versus sexual reproduction (Henry and Kenchington 2004b).

OBSERVATIONS ON DEEPWATER CORALS (2000-03)

Numerous observations of damage from fishing gear were made during the BIO deep-water coral program (Gordon et al. 2014). Video of coral communities was collected using Campod deployed from CCGS *Hudson* at several prime coral habitat sites off Nova Scotia including the Northeast Channel, Scotian Slope, Gully, and Stone Fence at the mouth of the Laurentian Channel (Fig. 1). Water depths ranged from 200 to 500 m. Bottom type was variable, but all sites had some stable substrate to support corals (i.e., cobble, boulder, bedrock). All sites had been exposed to fishing activity.

In the Northeast Channel, a heavily fished area with an abundance of large gorgonian corals, visible signs of fishing impact included scattered skeletons and tilted and broken live corals, with 4% of observed colonies damaged (Mortensen et al. 2005). Damage may make corals more susceptible to parasites since a parasitic anemone was more common on damaged colonies. Tracks on the seabed, either from longline anchors or parts of otter trawl gear, and lost gillnets were observed. Lines were observed on the seabed or entangled in corals. On the Scotian Slope, no signs of damage to corals were observed, possibly because the dominant species, small free-living cup corals, are less prone to damage from fishing gear. Little sign of fisheries damage to corals was observed in The Gully, only a few trawl tracks and one corroded lost trawl wire. The *Lophelia* reef complex at the Stone Fence was clearly impacted by fishing gear (Mortensen et al. 2006). All live colonies were either small (Fig. 9A) or broken in an unnatural way. Furrows caused by trawl doors were visible and an extensive rubble zone surrounded the reef (Fig. 9B). Many cobbles and boulders showed signs of being overturned and a fragment of a net was observed.

Figure 8. Typical scallop dredge used in the commercial offshore fishery.

Figure 9. The stony coral *Lophelia pertusa* at the Stone Fence. (A) A small healthy colony with a red fish (*Sebastes spp.*) taking shelter. (B) Rubble from fishing damage.

These direct observations demonstrated that large deep-water corals can be significantly impacted by all types of bottom-tending fishing gear. Due to very slow growth rates, expected recovery from such disturbance is on the order of decades to centuries. A related study showed that not all corals are as vulnerable to disturbance. Experiments with the Soft Coral *Gersemia rubiformis* showed it to be able to withstand a certain degree of disturbance; however chronic disturbance eventually resulted in weakened stalks and possibly pre-mature release of larvae (Henry et al. 2003).

SYNTHESIS AND THE FUTURE

This research program examined the impacts of the three most widely used types of bottom-contacting mobile fishing gear on benthic habitat and communities in Atlantic Canada. Long-term experiments were conducted on sand and gravel habitats using a wide variety of survey tools to collect information on the benthic ecosystem over a broad range of spatial scales. The three-year otter trawling experiments on the Grand Banks and Western Bank, and the three-year hydraulic clam dredging experiment on Banquereau Bank, are some of the most detailed gear-impact experiments ever conducted around the world and answer many important questions. These experiments, the first of their kind conducted in Canada, could only have been done at an institution such as BIO, which at the time had the scientific and engineering expertise, equipment, and research vessels required to carry out the research. The work was heavily dependent on technology developed at BIO. The program also made significant contributions to the understanding of benthic communities on the continental shelf and slope off Atlantic Canada.

This research clearly demonstrated that the impacts of bottom-contacting mobile fishing gear are variable and depend upon the kind of gear, how it is used, the return period of the disturbance, the kind of seabed habitat, and the characteristics of the benthic community (Gordon et al. 2006). These impacts are an important issue that needs to be considered as Canada moves to adopt an ecosystem approach to fisheries management. Because of this research program, and other related studies conducted around the world, an extensive knowledge base now exists that can be used to move forward. Effective management measures for sustainable fisheries include effort control, gear modification and substitution, and establishment of closed areas. One area of particular importance in future research is continued spatial mapping of seabed habitat and communities and the distribution of fishing disturbance.

Considerable effort was given to communicating the results of this program to all clients in an open manner. The results have been published in the scientific literature, presented at numerous national and international conferences and workshops, and cited in major international reviews. BIO scientists have participated in numerous working groups under the International Council for the Exploration of the Sea (ICES). On the local level, numerous briefings were given to the fishing industry, fisheries managers, and environmental organizations as the program evolved and objective advice was offered as requested. Results have been used by the Marine Stewardship Council in their assessment of the sustainability of specific fisheries under review for marketplace certification. The results also contributed to a national review of fishing gear impacts on benthic habitats and the living things that occupy them (Fisheries and Oceans Canada 2006).

ACKNOWLEDGEMENTS

We thank our many colleagues, many of whom are identified as authors in the references listed below, for their enthusiastic participation in this program, including spending lots of time at sea, looking through a microscope, and analyzing imagery. The success of this program was also critically dependent upon the dedication of many other BIO and NAFC staff who contributed behind the scenes by developing equipment, collecting and processing samples, analyzing data, and providing administrative and field support. We thank Kevin MacIsaac and Kent Gilkinson for their review of this manuscript; Mike Latremouille, David Nettleship and Mike Lewis for their editorial assistance; and Cam Lirette for preparing Figure 1. And finally, we thank BIO and NAFC managers and the funding agencies, including Clearwater Fine Foods, for their support in carrying out this research.

REFERENCES

Brylinsky, M., J. Gibson, and D.C. Gordon, Jr. 1994. Impacts of flounder trawls on the intertidal habitat and community of the Minas Basin, Bay of Fundy. Canadian Journal of Fisheries and Aquatic Sciences 51: 650-661.

Caddy, J.F. 1970. Records of associated fauna in scallop dredge hauls from the Bay of Fundy. Fisheries Research Board of Canada Technical Report 225, Fisheries and Oceans Canada, St. Andrews, NB.

Fisheries and Oceans Canada. 1986. The Department of Fisheries and Oceans policy for the management of fish habitat. Fisheries and Oceans Canada, Ottawa, ON.

Fisheries and Oceans Canada. 2006. Impacts of trawl gears and scallop dredges on benthic habitats, populations and communities. Canadian Science Advisory Secretariat Science Advisory Report 2006/025, Ottawa, ON.

Fuller, S., E. Kenchington, D. Davis, and M. Butler. 1998. Associated fauna of commercial scallop grounds in the lower Bay of Fundy. Marine Issues Committee Special Publication 2, Ecology Action Centre, Halifax, NS.

Gilkinson, K.D., G.B.J. Fader, D.C. Gordon, Jr., R. Charron, D.L. McKeown, D. Roddick, E.L.R. Kenchington, K. MacIsaac, C. Bourbonnais, W.P. Vass, and Q. Liu. 2003. Immediate and longer-term impacts of hydraulic clam dredging on an offshore sandy seabed: effects on physical habitat and processes of recovery. Continental Shelf Research 23: 1,315-1,336.

Gilkinson, K.D., D.C. Gordon, Jr., K.G. MacIsaac, D.L. McKeown, E.L.R. Kenchington, C. Bourbonnais, and W.P. Vass. 2005. Immediate impacts and recovery trajectories of macrofaunal communities following hydraulic clam dredging on Banquereau, eastern Canada. ICES Journal of Marine Science 62: 925-947.

Gordon, D.C., Jr., K.D. Gilkinson, E.L.R. Kenchington, C. Bourbonnais, K.G. MacIsaac, D.L. McKeown, and W.P. Vass. 2005. Summary of the Grand Banks otter trawling experiment (1993-1995): effects on benthic habitat and macrobenthic communities. American Fisheries Society Symposium 41: 411-424.

Gordon, D.C., Jr., E.L.R. Kenchington, and K.D. Gilkinson. 2006. A review of Maritimes Region research on the effects of mobile fishing gear on benthic habitat and communities. Canadian Science Advisory Secretariat Research Document 2006/056, Dartmouth, NS.

Gordon, D.C., Jr., E.L.R. Kenchington, K.D. Gilkinson, G.B.J. Fader, C. Bourbonnais-Boyce, K.G. MacIsaac, D.L. McKeown, L.-A. Henry, and W.P. Vass. 2008. Summary of the Western Bank otter trawling experiment (1997-1999): effects on benthic habitat and communities. Canadian Technical Report of Fisheries and Aquatic Sciences 2822, Fisheries and Oceans Canada, Dartmouth, NS.

Gordon, D.C., E.L.R. Kenchington, B.T. Hargrave, and D.L. Peer. 2014. Life at the bottom of the sea: advances in understanding benthic ecosystems. Pages 87-97 *in* Voyage of Discovery: Fifty Years of Marine Research at Canada's Bedford Institute of Oceanography (D.N. Nettleship, D.C. Gordon, C.F.M. Lewis, and M.P. Latremouille, Eds.). Bedford Institute of Oceanography-Oceans Association, Dartmouth, NS.

Harris, J., K. MacIsaac, K. Gilkinson, and E. Kenchington. 2009. Feeding biology of *Ophiura sarsi* Lütken, 1855 and the effects of fishing. Marine Biology 156: 1,891-1,902.

Harrison, P.H., K.W. Strong, and K.A. Jenner. 1991. A review of fishing-related seabed disturbance on the Grand Banks of Newfoundland. Final contractors report to Fisheries and Oceans Canada from Maritime Testing Limited, Dartmouth, NS.

Henry, L.-A., E.L.R. Kenchington, and A. Silvaggio. 2003. Effects of experimental disturbance on aspects of colony behaviour, reproduction and regeneration in the cold water octocoral *Gersemia rubiformis* (Ehrenberg, 1834). Canadian Journal of Zoology 81: 1,691-1,701.

Henry, L.-A. and E. Kenchington. 2004a. Differences between epilithic and epizoic hydroid assemblages from commercial scallop grounds in the Bay of Fundy, northwest Atlantic. Marine Ecology Progress Series 266: 123-134.

Henry, L.-A. and E. Kenchington. 2004b. Ecological and genetic evidence for impaired sexual reproduction and induced clonality in the hydroid *Sertularia cupressina* (Cnidaria: Hydrozoa) on commercial scallop grounds in Atlantic Canada. Marine Biology 145: 1,107-1,118.

Henry, L.-A., E.L.R. Kenchington, T.J. Kenchington, K.G. MacIsaac, C. Bourbonnais, and D.C. Gordon, Jr. 2005. Impacts of trawling on colonial epifaunal assemblages on a cobble bottom ecosystem on Western Bank (northeast Atlantic). Marine Ecology Progress Series 306: 63-78.

Jenner, K., K.W. Strong, and P. Pocklington. 1991. A review of fishing-related seabed disturbance in the Scotia-Fundy Region. Industry Services and Native Fisheries Branch, Fisheries and Oceans Canada Project Report 166, Halifax, NS.

Kenchington, E.L.R., J. Prena, K.D. Gilkinson, D.C. Gordon, Jr., K.MacIsaac, C. Bourbonnais, P.J. Schwinghamer, T.W. Rowell, D.L. McKeown, and W.P. Vass. 2001. The effects of experimental otter trawling on the macrofauna of a sandy bottom ecosystem on the Grand Banks of Newfoundland. Canadian Journal of Fisheries and Aquatic Sciences 58: 1,043-1,057.

Kenchington, E.L.R., D.C. Gordon, Jr., C. Bourbonnais, K.G. MacIsaac, K.D. Gilkinson, D.L. McKeown, and W.P. Vass. 2005. Effects of experimental otter trawling on the feeding of demersal fish on Western Bank, Nova Scotia. American Fisheries Society Symposium 41: 391-409.

Kenchington, E.L.R., K.D. Gilkinson, K.G. MacIsaac, C. Bourbonnais-Boyce, T.J. Kenchington, S.J. Smith, and D.C. Gordon, Jr. 2006. Effects of experimental otter trawling on benthic assemblages on Western Bank, northwest Atlantic Ocean. Journal of Sea Research 56: 249-270.

Kenchington, E.L.R. T. J. Kenchington, L.-A. Henry, S. Fuller, and P. Gonzalez. 2007. Multi-decadal changes in the megabenthos of the Bay of Fundy: the effects of fishing. Journal of Sea Research 58: 220-240.

McKeown, D.L. and D.C. Gordon, Jr. 1997. Grand Banks otter trawling impact experiment: II. Navigation procedures and results. Canadian Technical Report of Fisheries and Aquatic Sciences 2159, Fisheries and Oceans Canada, Dartmouth, NS.

Messieh, S.N., T.W. Rowell, D.L. Peer, and P.J. Cranford. 1991. The effects of trawling, dredging and ocean dumping on the eastern Canadian continental shelf seabed. Continental Shelf Research 11: 1,237-1,263.

Mortensen, P.B., L. Buhl-Mortensen, D.C. Gordon, Jr., G.B.J. Fader, D.L. McKeown, and D.G. Fenton. 2005. Effects of fisheries on deepwater gorgonian corals in the Northeast Channel, Nova Scotia. American Fisheries Society Symposium 41: 369-382.

Mortensen, P.B., L. Buhl-Mortensen, S.E. Gass, D.C. Gordon, Jr., E.L.R. Kenchington, C. Bourbonnais, and K.G. MacIsaac. 2006. Deep-water corals in Atlantic Canada: A summary of ESRF-funded research (2001-2003). Environmental Studies Research Funds Report 143, Calgary, AB.

Prena, J., T.W. Rowell, P. Schwinghamer, K. Gilkinson, and D.C. Gordon, Jr. 1996. Grand Banks otter trawling experiment: I. Site selection process, with a description of macrofaunal communities. Canadian Technical Report of Fisheries and Aquatic Sciences 2094, Fisheries and Oceans Canada, Dartmouth, NS.

Prena J., P. Schwinghamer, T.W. Rowell, D.C. Gordon, Jr., K.D. Gilkinson, W.P. Vass, and D.L. McKeown. 1999. Experimental otter trawling on a sandy bottom ecosystem of the Grand Banks of Newfoundland: analysis of trawl bycatch and effects on epifauna. Marine Ecology Progress Series 181: 107-124.

Rowell, T.W., P. Schwinghamer, K.D. Gilkinson, D.C. Gordon, Jr., E. Hartgers, M. Hawryluk, D.L. McKeown, J. Prena, W.P. Vass, and P. Woo. 1997. Grand Banks otter trawling impact experiment: III. Experimental design and sampling equipment. Canadian Technical Report of Fisheries and Aquatic Sciences 2190, Fisheries and Oceans Canada, Dartmouth, NS.

Schwinghamer, P., D.C. Gordon, Jr., T.W. Rowell, J. Prena, D.L. McKeown, G. Sonnichsen, and J.Y. Guigné. 1998. Effects of experimental otter trawling on surficial sediment properties of a sandy bottom ecosystem on the Grand Banks of Newfoundland. Conservation Biology 12: 1,215-1,222.

35. A BRIEF FORAY INTO STUDIES ON TOXIGENIC MARINE ALGAE

James E. Stewart

SUMMARY

In 1987, food poisoning in Prince Edward Island was associated with the consumption of Blue Mussels (*Mylilus edulis*) which had been feeding upon the pennate diatom, *Pseudo-nitzschia multiseries*. This poisoning caused three and possibly five deaths and left 106 people affected, about 12 disabled permanently. As a result, the molluscan fisheries in eastern Canada were closed and the event was investigated through intensive collaborative efforts by government agencies and academic institutions which identified the cause as a toxin, domoic acid (DA), produced by diatoms. Studies were undertaken to identify: (1) shellfish toxins likely to occur locally, (2) their sources, (3) methods and bases for detection and prediction of their occurrence, and (4) management of the problems. The research efforts, in which the Bedford Institute of Oceanography played a significant role, produced an understanding of the impact of the toxin upon affected consumers, the setting of 20 µg DA/g as the maximum value of toxin permitted in the shellfish portion consumed, implementation of suitable survey and testing regimes and findings that production of DA by the diatoms was induced and enhanced by nutritional deficiencies in phosphorus or silicon. The evidence assembled showed that DA, although poisonous to susceptible people, also actually illustrates the fundamental capacity of biological systems to evolve mechanisms to acquire scarce, but essential nutrients to ensure their own survival and growth under otherwise hostile and adverse conditions. It also demonstrated that our understanding of the physiology and interactions of phytoplankton, representing some 95% of the living carbon in the sea and the foundation of all marine life, is far from adequate and that research on these topics to date has been reactive rather than strategic.

Key words: domoic acid, amnesic shellfish poison, Blue Mussels, diatoms, gluconolactone, *Pseudo-nitzschia*.
E-mail: JStewart@ns.sympatico.ca

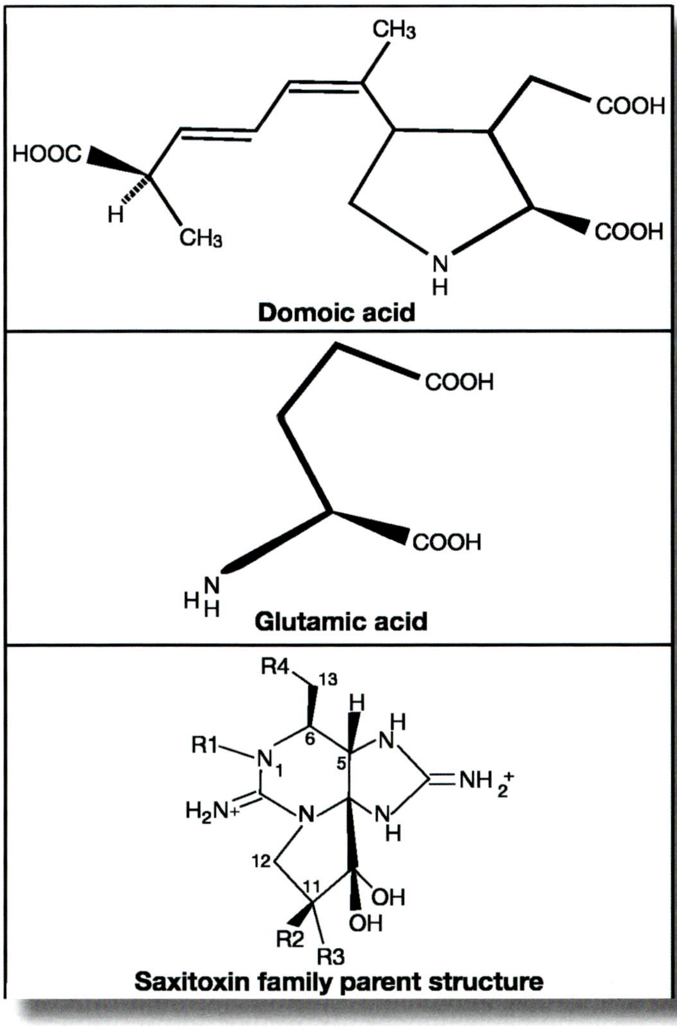

Figure 1. Domoic acid, glutamic acid, and the saxitoxin family parent structure.

In late fall 1987, consumers of cultured Blue Mussels (*Mytilus edulis*) from sites in Prince Edward Island (PEI) suffered apparent food poisoning. The epidemiological symptoms and the effects on mice injected with extracts from the mussels indicated that this was neither the familiar Paralytic Shellfish Poisoning (PSP) caused by members of the saxitoxin chemical group, nor Diarrhetic Shellfish Poisoning (DSP). The symptoms were sufficiently different to confirm the existence of a new toxin, which turned out to be domoic acid (DA) contained in the mussels (Wright et al. 1989; Fig. 1) in concentrations as high as 900 µg/g of soft mussel tissue (Quilliam et al. 1989).

DA is a small (molecular weight 311.3), water soluble, heat stable, excitatory glutamic acid analogue originally isolated in Japan from the Red Alga (*Chondria armata*) and described by Daigo (1958) and Ohfune and Tomita (1982). In Japan, it had also been shown to be an antihelminthic agent and a natural insecticide (Maeda et al. 1984, 1987). Its neurotoxic properties leading to human deaths, however, were revealed for the first time by its identification as the cause of the PEI acute human poisoning episode (Bird et al. 1988, Subba Rao et al. 1988, Bates et al. 1989, Wright et al. 1989, Perl et al. 1990, Todd 1993). The source of the DA was shown to be the diatom (Subba Rao et al. 1988, Bates et al. 1989) *Pseudo-nitzschia multiseries* (Hasle 1995; Fig. 2) upon which the mussels had been feeding. This finding also marked the first time that a diatom was shown to produce a toxin. At least three people and possibly five died as a result and 106 others were hospitalized; around 12 people were seriously and apparently permanently disabled. As one of the lasting effects of the severe poisoning was the loss of short-term memory, the DA poisoning was dubbed Amnesic Shellfish Poisoning (ASP) (Todd 1993).

Since 1987, DA has been detected periodically in shellfish and diatoms worldwide; a partial list of affected shellfish includes Deep-Sea Scallops (*Placopecten magellanicus*) from the Bay of Fundy and Maine, King Scallops (*Pecten maximus*) in Ireland and Scotland, Bay Scallops (*Argopecten irradians*) from Nantucket Shoals and Georges Bank, and Blue Mussels and Soft-shelled Clams (*Mya arenaria*) from the Bay of Fundy. DA has also been reported from various parts of Asia and Europe as well as from Australia, New Zealand, the Gulf of Mexico, and the west coast of North America where amounts exceeding the legal standards were recorded for razor clams and Dungeness Crabs (*Metacarcinus magister* formerly *Cancer magister*) along the coasts of Washington, Oregon, and California (reviewed by Villac et al. 1993, Todd 1993, Rhodes et al. 1998, Bates 2000, Lelong et al. 2012).

Elevated DA levels also caused the death of pelicans and cormorants in Monterey Bay, California, where the birds had been feeding on ancho-

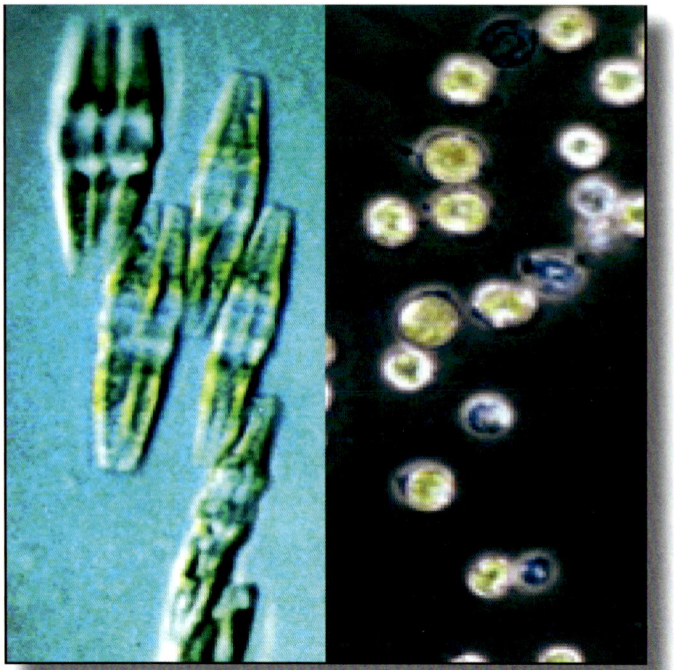

Figure 2. Left: *Pseudo-nitzschia multiseries* x400; right: *Alexandrium excavatum* (now known as *A. tamarense*) x200.

vies that contained high levels of the toxin (Work et al. 1993). Interestingly, the death of the birds in California gave rise to speculation as to whether a similar event affecting the behaviour of birds locally was influential in Alfred Hitchcock's production of the 1963 classic thriller *'The Birds'*, the adaptation of Daphne du Maurier's short story of the same name.

Although the DA episode was devastating, it was not the first threat to the consumption of shellfish in the Maritimes area. Shellfish toxicity in the Bay of Fundy has been a hazard for years: for example, between 1880 and 1970 known PSP deaths for the combined St. Lawrence and Fundy regions totalled 24 (Medcof 1985). Intermittent testing using the acid PSP extraction/mouse bioassay method developed by Sommer and Meyer (1937) in California and its various improvements have provided a more general picture of the scale of the PSP occurrences in eastern Canada. World War II brought a growing demand to exploit shellfish which led to the organization then called Canada Department of Fisheries implementing year-round PSP assays of both clams and mussels. Monitoring the toxicity of shellfish in the Bay of Fundy began in 1943 (Medcof 1985); this activity continues today and constitutes the longest continuous data set of its kind anywhere.

In Canada, the immediate regulatory response to the 1987 food poisoning traced to the mussels was the implementation of a moratorium on the sale of all molluscan shellfish harvested from Canadian east coast waters. This ban remained in effect until the toxin was identified and sufficient information was generated to relax it for particular species. This, of course, constituted a heavy, but unavoidable, economic blow to the invertebrate fisheries, which by the 1980s were the most valuable fisheries in the five east coast provinces and in particular to the highly profitable scallop fisheries and the burgeoning mussel culture industry.

In 1987, as a direct result of the DA incident, elements of the Bedford Institute of Oceanography (BIO) and other regional laboratories of the Fisheries and Oceans Canada (DFO) Biological Sciences Branch (Halifax, NS; St. Andrews and Moncton, NB) and the DFO Fish Inspection Services in the several Atlantic regions, the Halifax Laboratory of the National Research Council (NRC), Dalhousie University (Halifax, NS), the University of Prince Edward Island (UPEI, Charlottetown, PEI), and National Health and Welfare Canada (NHW, Ottawa, ON) immediately responded by joining forces to identify the various factors involved to acquire an adequate and fundamental understanding sufficient to provide for safe practices and to ensure the safety of consumers of shellfish products. Additional funds were allocated by DFO headquarters to their regional laboratories to ensure that the required work could proceed expeditiously.

Fortuitously, something of a head start on dealing with algal toxins had been arranged between the DFO Scotia-Fundy Region's Biological Sciences Branch and the Halifax NRC Laboratory. The relatively new NRC Laboratory director (R. Foxall) had become aware of the PSP problem affecting the scallop (*P. magellanicus*) and to a lesser degree, mussel culture. At the time, scallop harvesters and mussel growers had no capabilities for detecting the presence or level of PSP toxins themselves and had to rely entirely on testing by government laboratories using the relatively laborious and slow mouse bioassay. Unlike mussels that depurate DA and/or PSP toxins readily over periods of days to a few weeks, the scallop, following consumption of the microalgae producing DA or PSP toxins, retains these toxins more or less permanently in all parts of its tissues, except the adductor muscles (the muscles responsible for opening and closing the valves). Thus the scallop adductor muscle is the only portion of the scallop soft tissue generally available for sale from the Maritime Provinces. As inclusion of the remainder of the scallop soft tissues would add greatly to the value of the scallop fisheries, the research premise sketched was to develop a rapid, accurate, and reliable spot test for measuring PSP toxins in scallop tissues, thus making it possible to determine aboard the scallop draggers, or shortly after landing, whether the scallop tissues were free of PSP toxins. Such a test could also be applied in the rapidly expanding mussel culture industry to determine whether mussels, otherwise ready for harvest, contained levels of PSP toxins preventing sales and also to monitor the elimination of the PSP toxins from the mussels and aid the mussel growers in scheduling their harvesting more efficiently. It is gratifying to be able to note that the studies begun originally to provide a spot test for PSP toxins were continued by NRC and ultimately led to a complete suite of PSP toxins produced by NRC and certified as chemical standards for sale internationally (web: http://www.nrc-cnrc.gc.ca/eng/programs/imb/crmp.htm).

The work involved in developing such a test for PSP toxins had been underway for several months when the mussel toxicity crisis struck. As the project had involved the growth and acquisition of sufficient amounts of cells of a dinoflagellate, *Alexandrium excavatum* (now designated *A. tamarense*; Fig. 2), producing the PSP toxins, chemical preparation of the toxins and analytical methods to measure them, mental attitudes were in tune, and many of the skills and much of the equipment were available when the unexpected DA crisis was thrust on the Atlantic region. Thus, NRC, when contacted at the outset, was prepared and in a position to provide the early analytical studies and methodology that led to the rapid and early identification of the problem agent as DA (Bird et al. 1988, Subba Rao et al. 1988, Wright et al. 1989). The analytical technique applied successfully was based on high performance liquid chromatography (HPLC).

It was agreed early during regional and interregional meetings that the problems created by the occurrence of phycotoxins in the Canadian Atlantic molluscan shellfish industries (wild and cultured stocks) constituted a zonal rather than a regional dilemma. These problems were defined and grouped under four main headings:

(1) Identity of phycotoxins known to occur locally or likely to occur within the Atlantic zone.
(2) Sources of these toxins.
(3) Detection and prediction of the occurrence of the phycotoxins.
(4) Management of the problems.

It was generally agreed that the 18 or so PSP toxins and DA should be the toxins of prime concern, with the possibility of those causing DSP a likely third candidate. Atlantic area-wide direction for the immediate regulatory actions and accompanying surveys for DA in the commercial shellfish fisheries were overseen and directed by a task force located in the DFO Gulf Region headed by R. Bourque, Chief of Fisheries Inspection Service for that Region.

As described earlier, the troublesome toxin, DA, had been identified relatively quickly by NRC analysts and was shown subsequently to be present in the diatom *Pseudo-nitzschia multiseries* from samples drawn from waters around Cardigan Bay, PEI. This diatom was isolated and brought into culture by a team from BIO composed of P. Vass, P. Dickie, and D.V. Subba Rao with inputs from DFO PEI Fisheries Inspection staff and L. Hanic of UPEI. It was agreed early, as a result of the field and laboratory studies, that *P. multiseries* appeared to be the major and apparently the only producer of DA locally and as oysters and clams were not feeding on this diatom they could be released from the general ban imposed upon molluscan shellfish. This left the two largest species by volume and value, mussels and scallops, as the species of prime concern, although all commercially handled shellfish continued to be monitored carefully throughout by the DFO Fisheries Inspection Service in all regions.

Concurrently, under the aegis of the NHW Laboratories in Ottawa, clinical studies on the physiological effects of DA were undertaken to provide the basis for setting safe limits for DA in shellfish tissues offered for sale. As DA is a small, water soluble, foreign molecule, it was expected that it should be filtered readily from the blood stream by the kidneys or modified by the liver and excreted promptly. Further, it was also considered possible that as DA is an analogue of the naturally occurring neurotransmitter, glutamic acid (Fig. 1), any DA retained might function similarly to it (i.e., bind temporarily to receptors on a 'rapid make and break' system to transmit nervous signals). Unfortunately, in some individuals the DA crossed the blood/brain barrier in quantity, and as the binding of DA to neuronal receptors apparently was more permanent than is the case for glutamic acid, it generated a short period of hyperactivity causing the receptors to continuously transmit impulses until they 'burned out', causing memory loss or death when the damage was great enough. As DA had been shown to be eliminated readily from healthy individuals without causing harm, it was apparent that the victims most affected were those whose liver and kidney processes were impaired.

By 1988, the identification of this new toxin as DA, the development of suitable analytical methods to measure it, its production by the diatom *P. multiseries*, and an understanding of its mode of action led to the setting of a DA legal limit of 20 μg/g of soft tissue. The implementation of a suitable survey and testing regime permitted the authorities to lift the remaining ban on the marketing of shellfish in the spring of 1988, only 3 months after the DA toxin incident was first manifested.

The accomplishment of these major landmarks plus the isolation of the diatom and the culture of it now changed the focus of the studies. Thus, while studies by scientists at the NRC Laboratories and the BIO group led by R. Pocklington continued on various of the initial lines (i.e., improvements to analytical methods and toxicity studies at a number of laboratories in the Maritimes and Ottawa, and provision of chemical analyses for work at BIO), new studies on the depuration of the toxin from shellfish were initiated at UPEI and the DFO Biological Sciences Halifax Laboratory, while studies on the growth of diatoms, the bio-production of DA, and determination of the role of bacteria in both production and elimination of the toxin were undertaken at BIO, the DFO Gulf Region Laboratory (Moncton) and NRC Halifax. As well, contracts were arranged for collections by field teams to acquire a more complete picture of the various genera and species of microalgae and their successions in relation to the different oceanographic profiles occurring at different seasons in Nova Scotian coastal waters.

The experimental growth studies showed that the various strains of *P. multiseries* yielded varying amounts of toxin. All strains producing DA, however, exhibited a common trait; they produced DA mainly after growth had entered the stationary phase (Subba Rao et al. 1990, Bates et al. 1991). This is the phase reached by growing cultures after one or another of the nutrients sustaining growth is depleted and/or the culture conditions have deteriorated. Furthermore, as shown by both of these investigations, the DA was not retained by the diatom cells, but instead most was released to the surrounding medium as it was produced. Subsequently, work by these authors and Pan et al. (1996a, b, c) showed this same production mode was repeated when limitations on key nutrients (i.e., silicate or phosphate) were imposed (Fig. 3). In addition, Bates et al. (1993) showed that supplying nitrogen in the form of ammonium ions in excess of 110 μM slowed the rate of cell division and concomitantly increased DA production. Importantly, it was also shown (Douglas and Bates 1992, Bates et al. 1995) that the low production of DA by axenic (bacteria-free) cultures of *P. multiseries* could be enhanced by inclusion of particular, but unidentified bacteria in these cultures. As DA has the structure of a chelating or chemical scavenging agent and its production was induced by the reduction of essential nutrients, it suggested that the probable benefit of the release of DA to the surrounding milieu could be to secure and lock up nutrients exclusively for the sustenance of the diatom.

Interestingly, at about this time another set of investigators working at NRC Ottawa had been attempting to detect DA using a modification of a device originally designed to detect traces of explosives emanating from luggage or parcels that might be smuggled aboard to destroy an aircraft. They detected in mussels a very strong signal which occurred only in those mussels that had been shown by HPLC to contain DA. It turned out, however, that the signal was not attributable to the DA, but was generated by another compound, gluconolactone (McLachlan et al. 1993, D.G. McLachlan pers. comm.). Subsequent studies at BIO showed that certain bacteria (*Alteromonas* spp.) associated with every DA-producing *P. multiseries* strain examined produced gluconolactone (or more properly a mixture of gluconic acid and its lactone in equilibrium referred to as GLAC) (Fig. 4) from glucose in considerable quantities (Stewart et al. 1997).

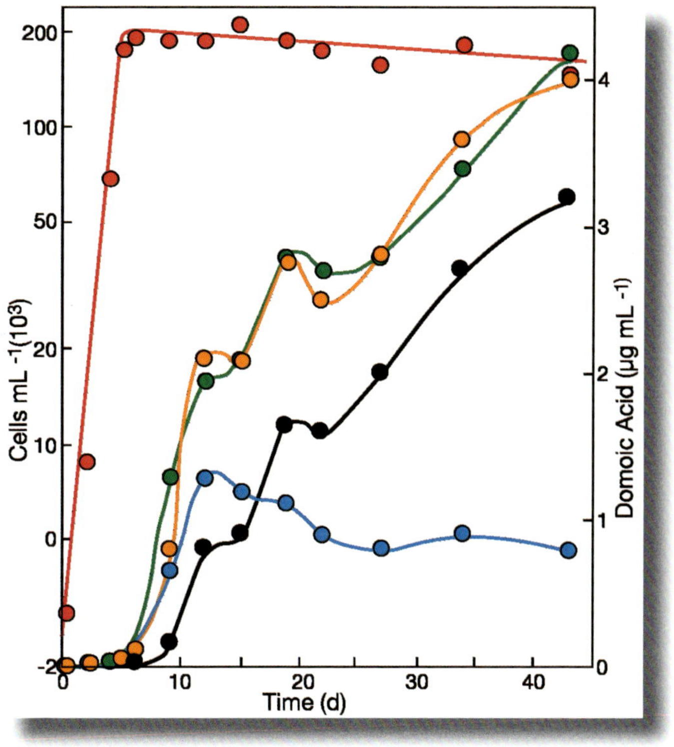

Figure 3. Growth and domoic acid (DA) production by *P. multiseries* in batch culture (redrawn from Bates 1998). Diatom cell numbers (red); DA in 'whole culture' cells sonicated with growth medium (green); DA in cells plus DA in filtrate (orange); DA in filtrate only (black); and DA in cells only (blue).

This investigation at BIO was extended by a visiting scientist from Japan, M. Osada, who showed that when low concentrations of GLAC were added to axenic cultures of DA-producing *P. multiseries*, the DA production increased materially (Osada and Stewart 1997). Of considerable interest is the fact that both DA and the gluconate radical are powerful chelating (chemical scavenging) agents.

Further studies showed that GLAC-producing bacteria and other bacteria live in close association with the different strains of *P. multiseries* and enjoy a symbiotic relationship with the diatoms, which at dif-

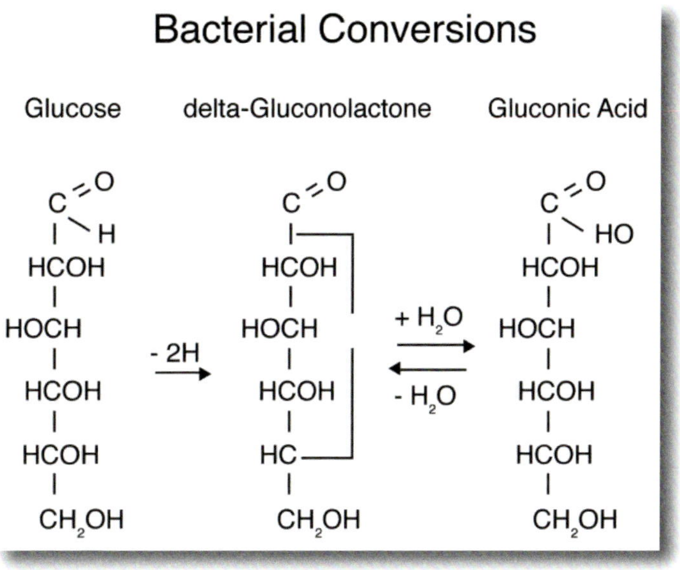

Figure 4. Bacterial conversion of glucose to gluconolactone and gluconic acid.

ferent salinities have substantial amounts of glucose free in their cells; the release of this glucose provides a suitable substrate for these bacteria to form GLAC. It was concluded that ingestion by mussels of masses of *P. multiseries* containing varying levels of DA and having the capacity to generate more, prior to their digestion by the mussels, would bring together the ingredients required to produce the results detected by McLachlan et al. (1993, D.G. McLachlan pers. comm.).

Studies on the depuration of DA from the shellfish at UPEI and the DFO Halifax Laboratory showed that following the decline of the diatom bloom and thus its disappearance as food for the shellfish, the DA content of the mussels declined gradually over a two to three week period to levels below the legal limit. This depuration of the mussels appears to result from a combination of the elimination of the diatom by digestion and excretion by the mussel and by the degradation of the DA by certain bacteria associated with the diatom and those resident in the digestive tract of the mussel (Stewart et al. 1998).

When all of these data were assembled, it was apparent that a dynamic and competitive set of interactions was occurring; DA is produced either not at all or only in small quantities through the diatom's logarithmic growth phase. As its growth slows through depleting one or another nutrient, the diatom experiences nutrient stress exacerbated by bacterial products (GLAC) and DA production is greatly enhanced. At this point, the growth of other bacteria also associated with the diatom, but capable of utilizing moderate concentrations of DA, would be enhanced and begin metabolizing the DA. Thus the DA measured in culture or within the shellfish would be a balance between the DA production rates enhanced by bacterial stimulation and bacterial destruction of DA (Stewart 2008). The interplay of the two chelating agents would be expected to heighten the production of DA in the digestive system of the mussel and offers reasonable explanations for the extremely high levels of DA in mussels in certain instances and the apparently slower than expected rates of depuration discussed by Silvert and Subba Rao (1992). As mentioned earlier, depuration of DA from mussels is in marked contrast to the situation with the scallop where DA and/or PSP toxins appear to be laid down and retained more or less permanently in all tissues except the adductor muscle.

Recent studies by Maldonado et al. (2002) and Wells et al. (2005) in California have added materially to our understanding of possible functions of DA and underscore the adaptability of phytoplankton in coping with limited and restrictive growth situations. According to Maldonado et al. (2002), the growth of the diatom is reduced by iron limitation or by copper toxicity. Both of these conditions enhance DA production, which can then be utilized to reduce copper toxicity and enhance iron uptake, thereby allowing DA-producing diatoms to flourish under otherwise adverse conditions. Wells et al. (2005) added to this picture by showing that less than toxic concentrations of copper are essential for the diatom's acquisition of essential iron levels and hypothesize that DA is used to acquire copper in a manner similar to that functioning in the high-affinity complex enzyme system possessed by the yeast *Saccharomyceus cerevisiae* to acquire the requisite levels of iron as described by Dancis et al. (1994) and Crichton and Pierre (2001). These conclusions suggest that the ubiquity of the diatoms in otherwise hostile, coastal growth conditions is to a large extent dependent upon the diatom's graded production of the highly flexible and versatile chelating agent, DA. These data also indicate and probably illustrate the kinds of mechanisms developed generally by phytoplankton to acquire and concentrate scarce nutrients; an area of phytoplankton physiology insufficiently explored to date.

The major question as to why this diatom and others closely related to it, occurring widely in most of the coastal waters of the world, suddenly gave rise to this problem has not been answered completely. *Pseudo-nitzschia multiseries* and closely related species usually proliferate at a time of year when conditions are unfavourable for other algal species, i.e., light is low and most species of algae are unable to grow optimally (Bates 1998, Hagström et al. 2007). Blooms occur usually in the spring and late fall when phosphorous and silicate concentrations are depleted in surface waters, thus imposing specific nutrient limitations shown to induce DA production. As nitrogen should be relatively high, however, as a result of rain and melting snow increasing its transport from land to sea there are expectations for growth of the diatom at those times of the year. DA production by diatoms is a direct response to generally diminished nutrient supplies or to nitrogen supplied at high levels, but in the form of the ammonium ion, that can occur in high concentrations in the vicinity of fish or shellfish culture operations. The occurrence of DA in the mussels, at troublesome levels, would likely become apparent only after intensive mussel culture became widespread in the Canadian Maritime Provinces where the harvesting of mussels occurs in the spring and late fall. Thus, the commercial production of mussels would not only greatly increase the supply of mussels, but also the numbers of consumers including those susceptible because of impaired liver and/or kidney functions.

Earlier it was mentioned that field studies had been contracted to acquire a realistic accounting of the various microalgae and their successions in relation to oceanographic profiles occurring at different seasons. Beginning in November 1988, surveys were mounted from BIO at five Nova Scotian coastal sites covering a period of three years. Approximately 26 times each year samples were collected from three depths at each site: Whitehaven Harbour, Ship Harbour, St. Margarets Bay, Woods Harbour, and Annapolis Basin. The oceanographic, chemical and phytoplankton measurements obtained have been compiled and are available (Keizer et al. 1996a) along with the results from a subsequent monitoring program on material collected from Indian Point and Sambro, incorporating the same measurements, for July 1992 to December 1994 (Keizer et al. 1996b). These reports provide the kind of database sorely lacking in 1987 when the DA crisis raised questions as to whether this episode resulted from unusual conditions and organisms.

Space permits only a brief mention of studies at BIO involving the PSP toxins. As international pressure had been developing to find an alternative method to the live mouse bioassay, a comprehensive and intensive study was conducted to standardize and provide an automated end point determination for the tissue culture method of Kogure et al. (1988) for determining the toxicity of extracts of shellfish. This study by Jellett et al. (1992) was very successful. Unfortunately, although completely valid, the tissue culture assay was not rapid enough nor was it possible to determine with it which specific PSP toxins were present or their individual concentrations. Chemical methods such as HPLC have proven to be more rapid and are suitable for measuring the concentrations of the individual toxins. Other studies on *Alexandrium* species producing PSP toxins included examining the important survival step of their encystment shown to be fostered by increased concentrations of nitrogen in the form of the ammonium ion (Subba Rao and Stewart 2011) and the involvement of at least one of the PSP toxins (B1) in the reduction or binding of iron available to the PSP-producing dinoflagellate (Stewart 2011).

The responses arising from this major threat to human health from a major food poisoning event have shown clearly what can be achieved rapidly by the effective mobilization and minor supplementation of existing resources. Despite the brief span of time, concentrated, collaborative, practical, and fundamental studies rapidly identified the cause, the underlying combination of circumstances that made such an event a continuing hazard and produced reasonable approaches for effective detection and control. Although the crisis and subsequent events undoubtedly caused strains in some relationships, they also resulted in identifying new opportunities for successful cooperative ventures. Unfortunately, with the reduction of resources including qualified personnel at most of the participating entities, it would now be very difficult, if not impossible, to mount an equivalent effort again.

Two key groups of questions are derived from these and other studies on toxic products from other toxigenic algae. First, are the algal products, highly toxic primarily to life forms several trophic levels removed from the producing microalgae, generated for defensive purposes or are they actually elements of microalgal nutrient acquisition systems and their normal metabolic and nutrient storage systems whose toxicity is largely or wholly coincidental? And second, based on conclusions reached by a panel of leading scientists studying a wide variety of toxigenic algae that the global increase in harmful algae and the associated problems are largely a result of increasing supplies of suitable nutrients released to inshore environments in which the composition, not just the total quantity of the nutrient pool, is critical (Heisler et al. 2008), the question becomes what measures will be necessary to define and cope with the particular problems?

Clearly, in addition to reducing the release of nutrients, detailed and fundamental studies of the physiology and interactions of the phytoplankton with each other and with other microbial forms in the sea (Eubacteria, Archaebacteria, Viruses, and with the other microbial eukaryotes) will be essential to gain an adequate understanding of the factors involved. Effectively the studies required will encompass what is now largely included under the sobriquet 'Primary Productivity'. As increased attention to the other microorganisms in the sea is required, the essential more comprehensive integrated approach would be better described as 'Microbial Oceanography' as discussed by Harrison (2006).

Closure for the studies on toxigenic algae came rather abruptly in 1995 with the resolution of the most pressing of the DA problems. Other research demands, coupled with reductions in budgets and staff, resulted in the termination of organized studies on toxic algae at BIO and to a large extent throughout the several DFO regions in eastern Canada. Some elements of the program at BIO, however, were continued for a time at lower levels of activity through the Emeritus Scientist program.

ACKNOWLEDGEMENTS

I thank Dr. S.S. Bates for the kind contribution of Figure 3 and Dr. Bates, Dr. W.G. Harrison, and Dr. D.C. Gordon for reading the manuscript and offering suggestions for improvement.

REFERENCES

Bates, S.S. 1998. Ecophysiology and metabolism of ASP toxin production. Pages 405-426 *in* Physiological Ecology of Harmful Algal Blooms, NATO ASI Series, Series G, Ecological Sciences vol. 41 (D.M. Anderson, A.D. Cembella, and G.M. Hallegraeff, Eds.). Springer-Verlag, Berlin, Germany.

Bates, S.S. 2000. Domoic acid-producing diatoms: another genus added! Journal of Phycology 36: 978-983.

Bates, S.S. and 16 others. 1989. Pennate diatom *Nitzschia pungens* as the primary source of domoic acid, a toxin in shellfish from eastern Prince Edward Island, Canada. Canadian Journal of Fisheries and Aquatic Sciences 46: 1,203-1,215.

Bates, S.S., A.S.W. de Freitas, J.E. Milley, R. Pocklington, M.A. Quilliam, J.C. Smith, and J. Worms. 1991. Controls on domoic acid production by the diatom *Nitzschia pungens f. multiseries* in culture: nutrients and irradiance. Canadian Journal of Fisheries and Aquatic Sciences 48: 1,136-1,144.

Bates S.S., J. Worms, and J.C. Smith. 1993. Effects of ammonium and nitrate on growth and domoic acid production by *Nitzschia pungens* in batch culture. Canadian Journal of Fisheries and Aquatic Sciences 50: 1,248-1,254.

Bates, S.S., D.J. Douglas, G.J. Doucette, and C. Leger. 1995. Enhancement of domoic acid production by re-introducing bacteria to axenic cultures of the diatom *Pseudo-nitzschia multiseries*. Natural Toxins 3: 428-435.

Bird, C.J. and 37 others. 1988. Identification of domoic acid as the toxic agent responsible for the P.E.I. contaminated mussel incident. Atlantic Research Laboratory Technical Report 56: 1-86.

Crichton R.R. and J.-L. Pierre. 2001. Old iron, young copper: from Mars to Venus. Biometals 14: 99-112.

Dancis, A., D.S. Yuan, D. Halle, C. Askwith, D. Eide, C. Moehle, J. Kaplan, and R.D. Klausner. 1994. Molecular characterization of a copper transport protein in *S. cereviae*: An unexpected role for copper in iron transport. Cell 76: 393-402.

Daigo, K. 1958. Studies on the constituents of *Chondria armata* II. Isolation of an antihelmintical constituent. Yakugaku Zasshi 79: 353-356.

Douglas, D.J. and S.S. Bates. 1992. Production of domoic acid, a neurotoxic amino acid by an axenic culture of the marine diatom *Nitzschia pungens f. multiseries* Hasle. Canadian Journal of Fisheries and Aquatic Sciences 49: 85-90.

Hagström, J.A., E. Granéli, I. Maneiro, A. Barreiro, A. Petermann, and C. Svensen. 2007. Release and degradation of amnesic shellfish poison from decaying *Pseudo-nitzschia multiseries* in presence of bacteria and organic matter. Harmful Algae 6: 175-188.

Harrison, W.G. 2006. Biological Oceanography in Canada (with special reference to federal government science). Proceedings of the Nova Scotian Institute of Science 43: 129-158.

Hasle, G.R. 1995. *Pseudo-nitzschia pungens* and *P. multiseries* (Bacillariophyceae) nomenclatural history, morphology, and distribution. Journal of Phycology 31: 428-435.

Heisler, J. and 16 others. 2008. Eutrophication and harmful algal blooms: a scientific consensus. Harmful Algae 8: 3-13.

Jellett J.F., L.J. Marks, J.E. Stewart, M.L. Dorey, W. Watson-Wright, and J.F. Lawrence. 1992. Paralytic shellfish poison (Saxitoxin family) bioassays: automated endpoint determination and standardization of the *in vitro* tissue culture bioassay, and comparison with the standard mouse bioassay. Toxicon 30: 1,143-1,156.

Keizer, P.D., T.G. Milligan, D.V. Subba Rao, P.M. Strain, and G. Bugden. 1996a. Phytoplankton monitoring program: Nova Scotia component - 1989 to 1994. Canadian Technical Report of Fisheries and Aquatic Sciences 2136, Dartmouth, NS.

Keizer, P.D., G. Bugden, D.V. Subba Rao, and P.M. Strain. 1996b. Long-term monitoring program: Indian Point and Sambro, for the period July 1992 to December 1994. Canadian Data Report of Fisheries and Aquatic Sciences 980, Dartmouth, NS.

Kogure, K., M.L. Tamplin, U. Simidu, and R.R. Colwell. 1988. A tissue culture assay method for PSP and related toxins. Toxicon 26: 191-197.

Lelong, A., H. Hégaret, P. Soudant, and S.S. Bates. 2012. *Pseudo-nitzschia* (Bacillariophyceae) species, domoic acid and amnesic shellfish poisoning: revisiting previous paradigms. Phycologia 51: 168-216.

Maeda, M., T. Kodama, T. Tanaka, Y. Ohfune, K. Nomoto, K. Ishimura, and T. Fujita. 1984. Insecticidal and neuromuscular activities of domoic acid and its related compounds. Journal of Pesticide Science 2: 27-32.

Maeda, M., T. Kodama, M. Saito, T. Tanaka, H. Yoshizumi, K. Nomoto, and T. Fujita. 1987. Neuromuscular action of insecticidal domoic acid in the American cockroach. Pesticide Biochemistry and Physiology 28: 85-92.

Maldonado, M.T., M.P. Hughes, and E.L. Rue. 2002. The effect of Fe and Cu on growth and domoic acid production by *Pseudo-nitzschia multiseries* and *Pseudo-nitzschia australis*. Limnology and Oceanography 47: 515-526.

McLachlan, D.G., A.H. Lawrence, and L. Elias. 1993. Rapid IMS analysis for the shell fish biotoxin, domoic acid. Abstract, 39th Canadian Spectroscopy Conference, Spectroscopy Society of Canada, Ottawa, ON.

Medcof, J.C. 1985. Life and death with *Gonyaulax*: an historical perspective. Pages 1-8 *in* Toxic Dinoflagellates (D.M. Anderson, A.W. White, and D.G. Baden, Eds.). Elsevier, New York, NY.

Ohfune, Y. and M. Tomita. 1982. Total synthesis of domoic acid: a revision of the original structure. Journal of the American Chemical Society 104: 3,511-3,513.

Osada M. and J.E. Stewart. 1997. Gluconic acid/gluconolactone: physiological influences on domoic acid production by bacteria associated with *Pseudo-nitzschia multiseries*. Aquatic Microbial Ecology 12: 203-209.

Pan, Y., D.V. Subba Rao, and K.H. Mann. 1996a. Changes in domoic acid production and cellular chemical composition of the toxigenic diatom *Pseudo-nitzschia multiseries* under phosphate limitation. Journal of Phycology 32: 371-381.

Pan, Y., D.V. Subba Rao, K.H. Mann, R.G. Brown, and R. Pocklington. 1996b. Effects of silicate limitation on production of domoic acid, a neurotoxin, by the diatom *Pseudo-nitzschia multiseries*. I. Batch culture studies. Marine Ecology Progress Series 131: 225-233.

Pan, Y., D.V. Subba Rao, K.H. Mann, W.K.W. Li, and W.G. Harrison. 1996c. Effects of silicate limitation on production of domoic acid, a neurotoxin, by the diatom *Pseudo-nitzschia multiseries*. II. Continuous culture studies. Marine Ecology Progress Series 131: 235-243.

Perl, T.M., L. Bedard, T. Kosatsky, J.C. Hockin, E.C.D. Todd, L.A. McNutt, and R.S. Remus. 1990. An outbreak of toxic encephalopathy caused by eating mussels contaminated with domoic acid. New England Journal of Medicine 322: 1,775-1,780.

Quilliam, M.A., P.G. Sim, A.W. McCulloch, and A.G. McInnes. 1989. High performance liquid chromatography of domoic acid, a marine neurotoxin, with application to shellfish and plankton. International Journal of Environmental Analytical Chemistry 36: 139-154.

Rhodes, L., C. Scholin, and I. Garthwaite. 1998. *Pseudo-nitzschia* in New Zealand and the role of DNA probes and immunoassays in refining marine biotoxin programmes. Natural Toxins 6: 105-111.

Silvert, W. and D.V. Subba Rao. 1992. Dynamic model of the flux of domoic acid, a neurotoxin, through a *Mytilus edulis* population. Canadian Journal of Fisheries and Aquatic Sciences 49: 400-405.

Sommer, H. and K.F. Meyer. 1937. Paralytic shellfish poisoning. Archives of Pathology 24:560-598.

Stewart, J.E. 2008. Bacterial involvement in determining domoic acid levels in *Pseudo-nitzschia multiseries* cultures. Aquatic Microbial Ecology 50: 135-144.

Stewart, J.E. 2011. Enhancement by gonyautoxin V of the iron (III) reducing or binding activity produced by the dinoflagellate, *Alexandrium excavatum*. Harmful Algae 10: 706-712.

Stewart J.E., L.J. Marks, C.R. Woods, S.M. Risser, and S. Gray. 1997. Symbiotic relations between bacteria and the domoic acid producing diatom, *Pseudo-nitzschia multiseries* and the capacity of these bacteria for gluconic acid/gluconolactone formation. Aquatic Microbial Ecology 12: 211-221.

Stewart J.E., L.J. Marks, M.W. Gilgan, E. Pfeiffer, and B.M. Zwicker. 1998. Microbial utilization of the neurotoxin domoic acid: blue mussels (*Mytilus edulis*) and soft shell clams (*Mya arenaria*) as sources of the microorganisms. Canadian Journal of Microbiology 44: 456-464.

Subba Rao, D.V., M.A. Quilliam, and R. Pocklington. 1988. Domoic acid – a neurotoxic amino acid produced by the marine diatom *Nitzschia pungens* in culture. Canadian Journal of Fisheries and Aquatic Sciences 45: 2,076-2,079.

Subba Rao, D.V., A.S.W. de Freitas, M.A. Quilliam, R. Pocklington, and S.S. Bates. 1990. Rates of production of domoic acid, a neurotoxic amino acid in the pennate diatom *Nitzschia pungens*. Pages 504-508 *in* Toxic Marine Phytoplankton (E. Granéli, B. Sundström, L. Edler, and D.M. Anderson, Eds.). Elsevier, New York, NY.

Subba Rao, D.V. and J.E. Stewart. 2011. A preliminary study of the formation of a third category of cysts by a toxigenic dinoflagellate, *Alexandrium fundyense* in response to elevated concentrations of ammonium chloride. Harmful Algae 10: 512-520.

Todd, E.C.D. 1993. Domoic acid and amnesic shellfish poisoning – a review. Journal of Food Protection 56: 69-83.

Villac, M.C., D.L. Roelke, T.A. Villareal, and G.A. Fryxell. 1993. Comparison of two domoic acid producing diatoms: a review. Pages 213-224 *in* 12th International Diatom Symposium (H. van Dam, Ed.). Hydrobiologia 269/270.

Wells, M., C.G. Trick, W.P. Cochlan, M.P. Hughes, and V.L. Trainer. 2005. Domoic acid: the synergy of iron, copper and the toxicity of diatoms. Limnology and Oceanography 50: 1,908-1,917.

Work, T.M., B. Barr, A.M. Beale, L. Fritz, M.A. Quilliam, and J.L.C. Wright. 1993. Epidemiology of domoic acid poisoning in Brown Pelicans (*Pelecanus occidentalis*) and Brandt's Cormorants (*Phalacrocorax penicillatus*) in California. Journal of Zoo and Wildlife Medicine 24: 54-62.

Wright, J.L.C. and 18 others. 1989. Identification of domoic acid in toxic mussels from eastern Prince Edward Island. Canadian Journal of Chemistry 67: 481-490.

Marine Contamination

Grounded tanker spilling oil

Marine Contamination

36. ORGANOCHLORINE POLLUTANTS IN MARINE ECOSYSTEMS

Richard F. Addison*, Barry T. Hargrave, and Gareth C. Harding

SUMMARY

Studies on the distribution, pathways, and effects of organochlorine (OC) pollutants have been carried out at the Bedford Institute of Oceanography since the early 1970s. Initially, these focussed on the DDT group of insecticides (which had been used extensively in eastern Canada for spruce budworm control) and on polychlorinated biphenyls (PCBs) that had been used in most developed countries in a variety of industrial applications. In this review, we describe studies of transfer pathways and bioaccumulation of OCs in marine food webs at the population and community levels. Results are presented using case studies of OC distribution and temporal trends in Arctic and Sable Island seal populations, and complex ecosystems such as those of St. Georges Bay, Nova Scotia, and the Arctic Ocean. These studies have led to significant contributions to our general understanding of OC dynamics in marine systems; more specifically, they have shown clear declines in OC concentrations in both western Arctic and eastern Canadian marine ecosystems at various trophic levels thus confirming the importance of controlling the sources and inputs of known or potential contaminants.

Key words: organochlorines, dynamics and pathways, boreal and arctic food webs, DDT, PCB, seals, zooplankton, bioaccumulation.
***E-mail:** RFAddison@shaw.ca

The spill of elemental phosphorus in Newfoundland in 1969 (Jangaard 1972) and the MV *Arrow* oil spill in February 1970 in Chedabucto Bay, Nova Scotia (Vandermeulen and Gordon 1976, Vandermeulen 1977), led to an increased awareness of marine pollution in the region. This led to the development of a Marine Environmental Quality (MEQ) program, based in the Marine Ecology Laboratory (MEL) at Bedford Institute of Oceanography (BIO), in 1970. The general objective of MEL's contaminant studies was to understand the processes and factors which controlled the distribution and transport of pollutants within marine food webs. One aspect of the MEQ program dealt with organochlorine (OC) contaminants which included the insecticide DDT and its metabolites, and the polychlorinated biphenyls (PCBs) which were widely used in industrial applications; both groups of compounds were becoming recognised as environmental pollutants at that time. Studies included measurements of biochemical effects on individual organisms, food web biomagnification, and environmental pathways of the DDT-group and PCBs (and later, other OCs) in marine ecosystems.

DDT was first introduced as an insecticide in the mid-1940s and became widely used in eastern Canada to control the spruce budworm. In 1957, the year of maximum use in the New Brunswick forest spraying program, the amount of DDT sprayed represented more than 5% of total DDT exports from the United States in 1955-56 (Addison and Stobo 2001). Insecticidal DDT is a mixture of compounds consisting of about 80% *p,p'*-DDT and about 20% *o,p'*-DDT, and is almost always reported nowadays as the 'parent' compound, *p,p'*-DDT, with its two main degradation products p,p'-DDE (probably a metabolic dead-end) and *p,p'*-DDD, which may be an intermediate in the eventual degradation of *p,p'*-DDT. PCBs were widely used since the 1930s in industrial applications where stable chemicals with a wide range of physical properties (from liquid to waxy solids) were required; applications included use in hydraulic fluids, electrical transformers, and capacitor insulators, etc. (Addison 1983). As the MEQ program evolved, studies included compounds such as the hexachlorocyclohexane (HCH) insecticides, dieldrin, nonachlor, and toxaphene.

All of these OCs have the general features (which vary in degree) of chemical stability, which leads to environmental persistence; fat solubility, which leads to accumulation in adipose tissue, which usually turns over relatively slowly and so exacerbates persistence; and volatility, which leads to wide dispersal via atmospheric transport. Concerns about the persistence and possible toxic effects of these and related OCs led to many of them being banned in most western countries in the early 1970s (Dunlap 1981).

In this review, we describe some of the studies undertaken within the MEL program spanning a wide geographic area in Arctic and Eastern Canada (Fig. 1). We do not intend this as a comprehensive survey of all the work that was done; instead we have selected four topics which illustrate the theme of understanding the processes that control contaminant distribution.

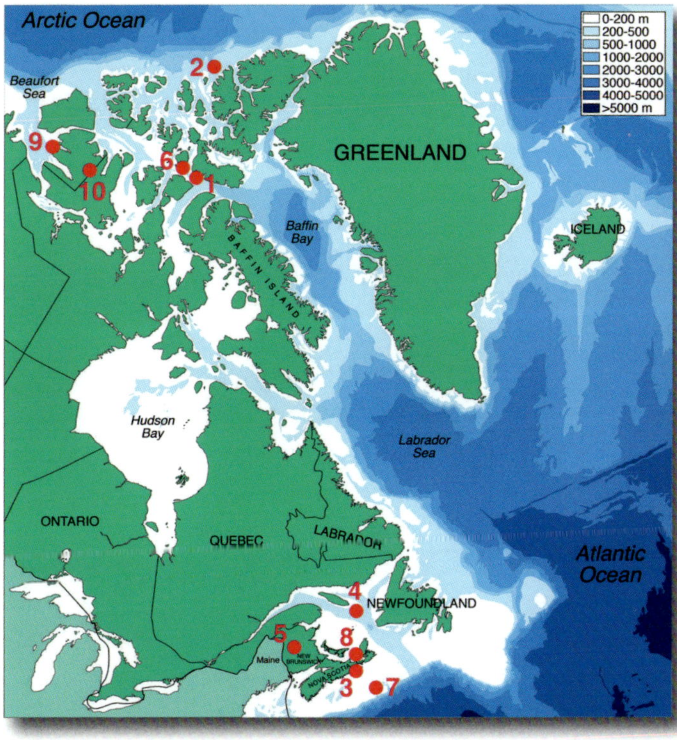

Figure 1. Map showing principal geographic features and study locations in Arctic and Eastern Canada referred to in the text and figures: Barrow Strait (1); Canadian Ice Island (2); Chedabucto Bay (3); Gulf of St. Lawrence (4); New Brunswick (5); Resolute Bay, Cornwallis Island (6); Sable Island (7), St. Georges Bay (8); Ulukhaktok/Holman (9); and Victoria Island (10).

ORGANOCHLORINES IN SEALS

Seals occupy high trophic levels in marine food webs (i.e., they are usually high or top level predators) and through a process of biomagnification accumulate high levels of pollutants like the DDT-group and PCBs (Muir et al. 1999). During the 1960s, DDT-group concentrations were reported in seals from various locations in Canada, but data were sporadic and variable, and so were difficult to interpret. In 1972, we examined (collaboratively with the Arctic Biological Station, Ste. Anne de Bellevue, QC) DDT-group and PCB concentrations in blubber of Ringed Seals (*Phoca hispida*) from a western arctic population at Ulukhaktok, Northwest Territories (formerly Holman, NWT; Fig. 1) in which detailed biological data (age, sex, and condition) were recorded for each animal analyzed.

The results showed clearly that the accumulation of these compounds differed between the sexes, males accumulating higher concentrations than females. In males, concentrations increased with age, but did not in females, and concentrations varied inversely with the animal's condition, i.e., higher in thin and lower in fat animals (Addison and Smith 1974). The simplest explanation of the first two of these results is that female Ringed Seals, which usually breed every year after they reach maturity, lose their burden of DDT-group and PCBs by some route that is closed to the males. The most probable process is that of lactation: most seals nurse their pups for a short time after birth with milk which is very rich in fat, and it seemed likely that the DDT-group and the PCBs present in blubber fat would be mobilized along with the fat to produce this milk. Subsequent studies of Grey Seals (*Halichoerus grypus*) from Sable Island, Nova Scotia (Fig. 1), showed that this was indeed the case, and that a nursing Grey Seal could lose about one-third of her total body burden of DDT-group, approximately the amount accumulated in the previous year's feeding (Addison and Brodie 1977, 1987).

As well as identifying the causes of much of the variability in previous data, the results of this 1972 arctic sampling were valuable for two reasons. First, female seals were shown to be good candidates for long-term monitoring of trends in DDT-group and PCBs (and presumably other organochlorines with similar physico-chemical properties) since they essentially 'sample' their environment each year and then discard a significant fraction of the sample during lactation. As an example of trend monitoring, Figure 2A shows the decline in total DDT-group concentrations in maternal Grey Seals from Sable Island between 1974 and 1994; the exponential half-life of the DDT-group in these animals was estimated to be about 4.5 years. The steady (linear) increase in the proportion of the DDT-group represented by *p,p'*-DDE (Fig. 2B) shows that no 'new' *p,p'*-DDT entered the system since the mid-1970s (i.e., the DDT-group residues in these female Grey Seals came from insecticidal DDT used before 1974) and implies that essentially all the DDT-group will be in the form of *p,p'*-DDE by now.

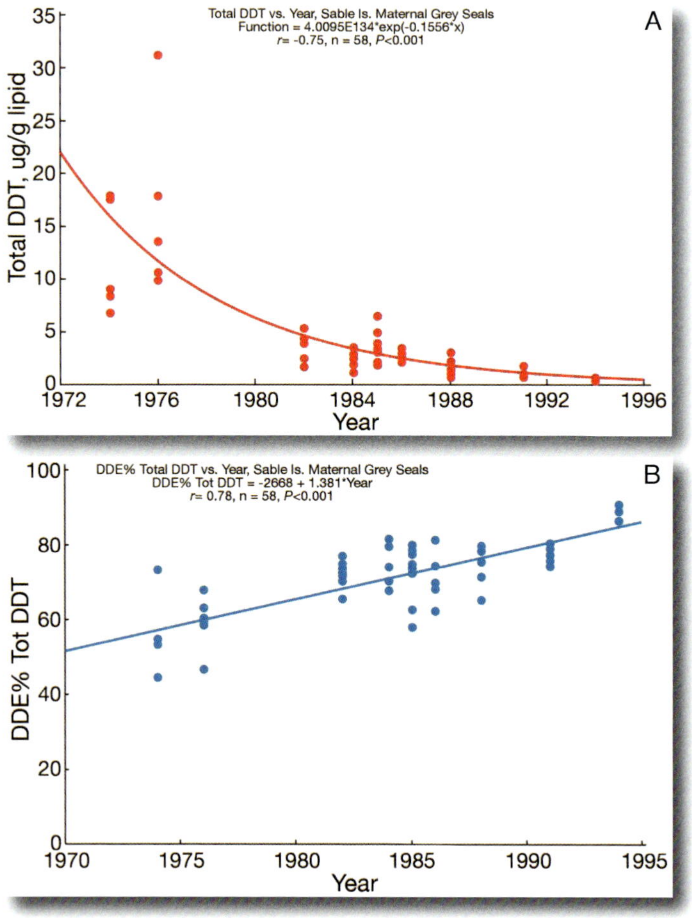

Figure 2. Organochlorines monitored in seals: (A) Total DDT-group residues, and (B) *p,p'*-DDE as a percentage of total DDT-group in maternal Grey Seals (*Halichoerus grypus*) from Sable Island, Nova Scotia, sampled at intervals between 1974 and 1994.

The second useful outcome was that these 1972 analyses represented a 'baseline' with which later OC analyses could be compared; the Ulukhaktok Ringed Seals now comprise one of the longest time series of OC measurements in marine mammals. Figure 3 shows the declines in total DDT-group concentrations in both male and female Ringed Seals from Ulukhaktok between 1972 and 2010 (Addison et al. 1986, Addison and Smith 1998, Addison et al. 2014). Exponential half-lives in the Ringed Seals were calculated to be 15-20 years, much longer than at Sable Island. Since seals are homeotherms, both Grey and Ringed Seals might be expected to degrade the DDT-group at roughly similar rates, but that was not the case. A possible explanation for the difference between Arctic and NW Atlantic seals is that much of the DDT-group degradation actually occurs in the food web within which the seals feed. This process would be expected to be faster in the NW Atlantic because environmental temperatures are higher throughout the year. Some support for this view is that another OC, trans-nonachlor, has declined faster in Sable Island Grey Seals than in Ringed Seals over the 15-year time interval (1980–95). Although 'starting' concentrations of trans-nonachlor were much higher in the Sable Island Grey Seals than in the arctic Ringed Seals, the rate of decline was also much faster. The exponential half-life was ca. 18 years in the northern Ringed Seals, but only ca. 5 years in Sable Island Grey Seals (Addison and Stobo 2001, R.F. Addison unpubl. data).

The BIO studies of seal-organochlorine interactions have contributed to a general understanding of some of the factors that control how chemicals like DDT and PCBs accumulate in marine mammals in general.

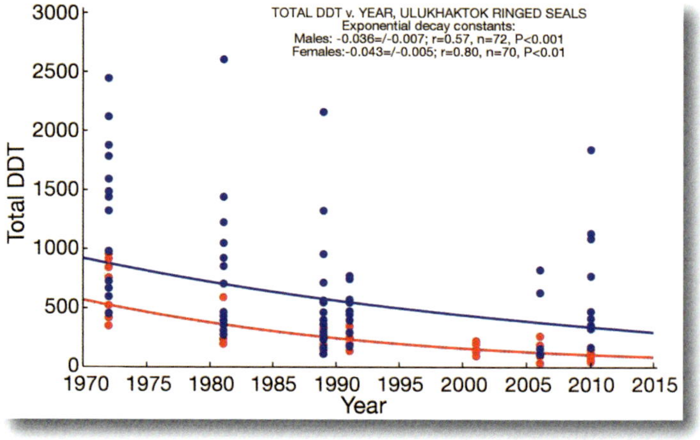

Figure 3. Declines in total DDT-group concentrations in Ringed Seals (*Phoca hispida*) from Ulukhaktok, Northwest Territories (formerly Holman, NWT) between 1972 and 2010. Data for males are in blue and for females in red.

This in turn has led to the development of reliable and informative monitoring programs which have demonstrated the effectiveness of source control by environmental regulations (e.g., the Arctic Monitoring and Assessment Program - AMAP).

ORGANOCHLORINE DYNAMICS IN ZOOPLANKTON

In the 1970s, little was known about the dynamics of OCs in marine organisms, particularly in zooplankton which occupy a key position in marine food webs. OC concentrations in an east coast estuary were found to be three orders of magnitude greater in zooplankton than in seawater, and another three orders of magnitude higher in Double-crested Cormorants (*Phalacrocorax auritus*) and *Larus* gulls than in zooplankton (Woodwell et al. 1967), but the pathways and dynamics of processes leading to the bioaccumulation had not been identified (Harding 1986, Harding and Addison 1987). At the time, there was considerable controversy about whether OCs were accumulated by low-trophic level biota through a 'passive' process of adsorption to external surfaces (bioconcentration), or actively through feeding (i.e., biomagnification).

In an MEL project designed to clarify these processes, DDT was chosen as a representative persistent OC, not only because it was readily available in radioactive form for tracer studies, but because it had been sprayed intensely on the nearby forests of New Brunswick and Maine to control the spread of spruce budworm between the 1950s and 1970s

(Dimond and Owen 1996). Rates of uptake and clearance, directly from or to seawater, were first determined for the most abundant boreal copepod, *Calanus finmarchicus* (Harding and Vass 1977). It had previously been shown that *p,p'*-DDT degradation in *Calanus* was insignificant over a two-month period, which can be a generation length for this species during summer (Darrow and Harding 1975). A technique was then developed to measure the surface area of the common krill in Atlantic waters, *Thysanoessa raschii*, as a possible predictor of contaminant uptake (Harding 1977). Uptake and clearance rate constants for *p,p'*-DDT in this species were found to be essentially the same as those in *C. finmarchicus*, in spite of a three-fold difference in body volume (Harding and Vass 1979). Surface area alone, therefore, could not explain *p,p'*-DDT uptake in pelagic crustaceans. However, if the surface area of an organism exposed was expressed as a function of time, the anticipated positive relationship between surface area exposed per unit time and contaminant uptake was satisfied (Harding and Vass 1979). Feeding studies were then performed with *C. finmarchicus* to evaluate this avenue of *p,p'*-DDT uptake, which was found to be much more important than direct uptake from seawater (Harding et al. 1981). Thus, biomagnification through contaminant retention from feeding is more significant in these organisms than is bioconcentration from seawater.

ORGANOCHLORINE BIOMAGNIFICATION IN A BOREAL SEA: SOUTHERN GULF OF ST. LAWRENCE

Incorporation of contaminant measurements into an ecological study of an inshore ecosystem provided an opportunity to interpret contaminant data in the context of ecological, physical and chemical oceanographic information. The ecosystem studied – St. Georges Bay (Fig. 1), Nova Scotia – was a nursery ground for pelagic fisheries, specifically Atlantic Mackerel (*Scomber scombrus*) and Atlantic Herring (*Clupea harengus*) (see also Lambert et al. 2014). PCBs, measured as five dominant chromatographic peaks of Aroclor 1254, were chosen as the contaminants for study. An ambitious food web study was pursued, involving measurement of PCBs in plankton separated using a $\log_2$ series of screen mesh sieves, starting with microplankton (those retained on a 25 µm mesh) and in organisms up to fish as large as Bluefin Tuna (*Thunnus thynnus*). PCB values determined for marine mammals from other studies in the Gulf of St. Lawrence in the 1970s were included in our synthesis. Dramatic biomagnification of PCBs was seen in the upper trophic levels as defined either by food type or size-spectrum, consistent with the theory that, in general, an organism feeds or preys on organisms 2 to 3 orders of magnitude smaller than itself (Sheldon et al. 1972, Kerr and Dickie 2001). PCB distribution in all categories of biota met this expectation well: e.g., active mammalian predators, such as porpoises, dolphins, and seals, had PCB concentrations consistent with those in the larger predatory fish such as Swordfish (*Xiphias gladius*) and Bluefin Tuna. Exceptions to the rule were a few organisms known to feed well down the food chain, such as ambush predatory jellyfish and the water-straining baleen whales (Harding et al. 1997). However, bioaccumulation within the planktonic-size spectrum from microplankton (>25 µm) to macroplankton (>2 mm) appeared to be similar because PCB concentrations were constant between size groups, rather than being biomagnified. This unexpected finding meant that either the cumulative contaminant uptake from feeding was lost to the zooplankton due to rapid excretion, or more probably due to the rapid turnover time of the larger zooplankton populations resulting from predation. PCB concentrations increased exponentially once the trophic levels of free-swimming categories (nekton, larval fish, shrimp, and krill) were reached (Harding et al. 1997).

Approximately twenty years after the original St. Georges Bay project was undertaken, OC concentrations in biota from selected trophic levels were measured (Harding et al. 1996). The PCB levels in the plankton categories may have declined slightly between 1976 and 1994 (Harding et al. 1996), but the concentrations in clupeids (Atlantic Herring, Gasperau *Alosa pseudoharengus*, and Blueback Herring *A. aestivalis*) declined significantly over the same time period (Fig. 4). These, and the preceding (mid-1970s) results, contributed to the assessment process held before the raising in 1996 of the *Irving Whale* barge, which had sunk in 1970 with its load of bunker oil and accompanying PCB-based hydraulic fluids in the southern Gulf of St. Lawrence (Gilbert and Walsh 1996).

Sufficient time has now elapsed such that a further sampling in St. Georges Bay is warranted to confirm the declining trend in OC concentrations in clupeids, and to establish the current degree of contamination.

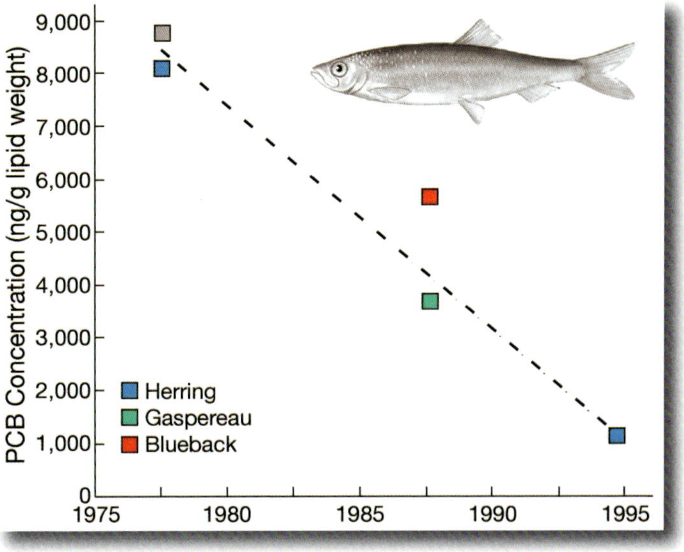

Figure 4. Mean PCB content of clupeid fish in southern Gulf of St. Lawrence between 1977 and 1994.

ORGANOCHLORINE TRANSFERS IN THE ARCTIC OCEAN AND BIOCONCENTRATION IN LOWER TROPHIC LEVEL BIOTA

Research in the early 1980s showed that OCs were widely distributed in fish and mammals collected from circumpolar regions including the Canadian Arctic (Barrie et al. 1992). The contaminants were also measured in milk from nursing mothers in northern Inuk populations in concentrations that in some cases exceeded Health Canada guidelines (DeWailly et al. 1989). With the exception of abandoned Distant Early Warning sites, there were no regional sources of OCs that could explain the source of contamination. The Department of Indian Affairs and Northern Development (DIAND) had a mandate to protect northern human populations, and DIAND-funded research within Fisheries and Oceans Canada and other agencies (e.g., Environment Canada) to determine sources and pathways of the pollutants (Barrie et al. 1992, Muir et al. 1992).

Atmospheric transport associated with aerosols from southern latitudes and vapour/aerosol transport to high latitudes were considered to be the most likely sources of OCs entering polar regions (Hargrave et al. 1988, Bidleman et al. 1989, Patton et al. 1989). Evidence to support the idea of global distillation was based largely on modelling the relative concentrations in seawater and overlying air and estimating air-sea gas exchange (with partitioning into water favoured for many OCs at the colder temperatures in polar regions). However, no studies had been completed at the time to provide data from the Canadian Arctic to verify model calculations. In 1985, the Polar Continental Shelf Project (PCSP) of the Department of Energy, Mines and Resources (DEMR, now Natural Resources Canada - NRCan) established a research camp on a tabular iceberg named the Canadian Ice Island (Fig. 1; for details, see Mudie and Jackson 2014). The 6 x 9 km long and 43-45 m thick iceberg had calved from the Ward Hunt ice shelf off Ellesmere Island and was slowly drifting with the seasonal arctic ice pack (Vincent et al. 2001). It provided a stable platform and the only practical means of obtaining samples of OCs in a permanently ice-covered region of the Arctic Ocean in Canada. Funding was obtained from DIAND and Supply and Services Canada for MEL researchers to use the Canadian Ice Island (CII) to measure OCs in various environmental compartments such as air, seawater, ice, snow, sediment, and lower trophic level organisms including epontic ice algae, phytoplankton, planktonic and benthic zooplankton, and invertebrates such as amphipods.

Battery-operated pumps with pre-filters and XAD ion exchange resin columns that adsorbed OCs were suspended under first-year ice adjacent to CII during summer and fall months from 1986 to 1990. Known amounts of seawater were pumped through the resin columns and OCs were later extracted using organic solvents prior to analysis by gas chromatography and mass spectrometry. Filter and resin samples obtained from pumps suspended at various depths were analyzed separately to provide measurements of particulate and dissolved OC phases. Air samplers with prefilters and polyurethane foam plugs were used in a similar manner to measure OCs in vapour and particulate phases. Plankton nets and under-ice and on-bottom baited traps provided samples of planktonic and benthic invertebrates. Multi-cup sediment traps were suspended at 100 m below the CII over two annual periods (1988 to 1990) to collect settling particles at monthly to bi-monthly intervals.

OCs such as hexachlorobenzene, hexachlorocyclohexanes (HCH), chlordane, DDT and its metabolites, toxaphene, and PCBs, were detectable and quantified in most air, snow, ice, and seawater samples collected from the CII. The most abundant compounds were α- and γ- HCH. Seawater concentrations were highest in surface water layers, but were among the lowest reported for any world ocean (Hargrave et al. 1992). PCBs, *p,p'*-DDT, *p,p'*-DDE and some cyclodiene pesticides (chlordane, dieldrin, α-endosulphan and heptachlor) were present at trace levels in air and water but relatively concentrated in melted snow, indicating scavenging from air. Some OCs (*cis*-chlordane, *p,p'*-DDE and PCBs) were detected in surface sediments showing that transfers to the bottom occurred with sedimenting particles (Muir et al. 1992, Hargrave et al. 1994).

The ubiquitous presence of OCs in the Arctic Ocean distant from sources emphasized the global nature of atmospheric transport. Due to increasingly restricted use, atmospheric concentrations of many OCs in the Arctic had decreased after 1980 (Barrie et al. 1997). However, the decrease in the atmosphere was accompanied by an increase of the most soluble OCs in the Arctic Ocean surface layer, which had become supersaturated (Hargrave et al. 1988, Hargrave et al. 1997). The upper 50 m in the Arctic Ocean comprises Atlantic Ocean sub-surface water (AMAP 1998, Wassmann et al. 2003, Jones 2014). The lack of concentration gradients in OCs in this layer indicated that advection of water from the Atlantic Ocean was an important source of these compounds to the Arctic Ocean in Canada. The observations showed that OCs entered the Arctic Ocean through vapour exchange during ice-free periods and through advection of North Atlantic Ocean waters throughout the year (Hargrave et al. 1988, 1989, 1992; Bidleman et al. 1989, 1990; Patton et al. 1989; Barrie et al. 1992, 1997; Hargrave et al. 1997).

While the dynamics of OCs with higher solubility in seawater appear to be controlled by air-sea vapour exchanges, pathways for less water-soluble compounds (such as DDT and heavier PCB congeners) are related to transfers of particles (Hargrave et al. 2000). Soluble OCs are absorbed and incorporated into lipids in phytoplankton and epontic under-ice algae which either settle to become incorporated in bottom sediments or are consumed by grazing animals such as zooplankton and under-ice grazing amphipods. Fecal and other non-living particulate matter from organisms in the pelagic food web produces sedimenting material which can provide a mechanism to rapidly transfer material from the water column to sediments (Hargrave et al. 1994).

Sediment traps deployed from the CII to collect settling material over monthly to bi-monthly intervals provided the first measurements of vertical particle flux under ice in the Arctic Ocean (Hargrave et al. 1989, Hargrave et al. 1994, Wassmann et al. 2003). Highest rates of sedimentation occurred during August and September when ice cover is at a seasonal minimum and phytoplankton production is maximum. This was the time of year when OC concentrations in seawater and tissues of lower trophic levels biota were reduced, which implies that the inventory of particle-reactive OCs in the water column available for uptake by planktonic organisms was being reduced by adsorption onto settling particles. Small mineral particles were aggregated in settled material showing an atmospheric supply in addition to particles derived from planktonic production since particles with a similar mineralogy also occurred in ice cores from the CII (Hargrave et al. 1994).

The Northern Contaminants Program (NCP) was established in 1991 with combined funding from several Canadian federal government departments with a mandate to address concerns about elevated levels of persistent contaminants in the traditional diets of northern Aboriginal peoples. NCP funding was provided between 1993 and 1995 to measure OCs in seawater and ice algae, phytoplankton, zooplankton and pelagic and benthic amphipods during a one-year seasonal study (POLARPRO) in Barrow Strait (Fig.1). Sampling was conducted from the ice or by small boat during the July-September period of open water using DFO's South Camp facilities at Resolute Bay, Cornwallis Island.

Comparisons of OCs in lower trophic level biota measured in Barrow Strait during 1993 combined with observations of OCs in other organisms from different Canadian arctic locations demonstrate the degree of biomagnification of OCs occurring between potential predator-prey links in the arctic marine food web (Fig. 5). Toxaphene transfer in the food web is expressed as ng/g lipid since OCs are preferentially accumulated in fat-rich tissues. Under-ice amphipods such as *Gammarus* and *Parathemisto* feed on epontic ice algae and suspended phytoplankton. These amphipods are common prey for Arctic Cod (*Boreogadus saida*). The biomagnification factors were ~10 between these trophic levels. Ringed Seals and Polar Bears (*Ursus maritimus*) bioaccumulate toxaphene to a lesser degree and much less than Narwhal (*Monodon monoceros*) and Beluga (*Delphinapterus leucas*; Zhu and Norstrom 1993). Scavenging benthic amphipods that feed on carcasses of fish and mammals reaching the seabed have very high levels of toxaphene and other OCs (Hargrave et al. 1993).

As with measurements from the CII, HCHs, chlordane, dieldrin, toxaphene, PCBs, and DDT were the most abundant compounds in seawater and lower trophic level biota in Barrow Strait. Highest concentrations occurred in microalgae and zooplankton during the winter-spring period of maximum ice-cover when phytoplankton production was minimum (Hargrave et al. 2000). Concentrations of most compounds decreased during the open water period when suspended particulate matter (SPM) and lipid concentrations in biota increased. Lower concentrations of OCs in seawater during the summer coincided with higher SPM concentrations and seasonal minima in bioconcentration factors. The deviations from the physical-chemical equilibrium were greatest during the open water period probably due to more continuous input, zooplankton growth, lipid storage and metabolism, and higher SPM concentrations (Hargrave et al. 1989).

The Arctic Monitoring and Assessment Programme (AMAP) was formed by the Arctic Council in 1991 to report on transport pathways and rates of transfer of OCs and other persistent anthropogenic pollutants (metals and radionuclides) in arctic environments and human health effects on northern populations. Canada joined the program and continues to be an active member of AMAP. OC measurements in the Arctic Ocean from the CII and in Barrow Strait from Resolute Bay have been summarized in AMAP publications (Muir et al. 1992, 1997, 1999; AMAP 1998). The observations can be used as a baseline to evaluate future trends in OC concentrations in lower trophic level biota from different locations in the Arctic Ocean.

ENVOI

In this review, we have tried to illustrate the point that by understanding the factors and processes that control OC distribution in marine ecosystems, we can anticipate the kind of chemicals that are likely to become environmental 'problems' in terms of distribution, persistence, and po-

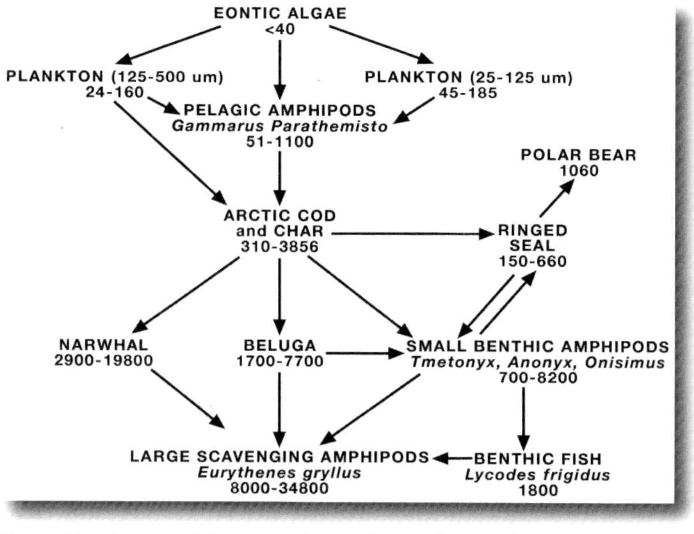

Figure 5. Toxaphene transfer between predators and potential prey in a hypothetical food web for the Arctic Ocean. Concentrations for various types of organisms are shown as ranges of measured values as ng/g lipid (after Hargrave et al. 1993 with additional data from Zhu and Norstrom 1993, Muir et al. 1999, Hargrave et al. 2000).

tential toxicity. We can devise approaches to mitigate their impact (usually source control) and we can devise monitoring programs to evaluate the success of mitigative measures. The case studies of both the St. Georges Bay and the Arctic marine systems emphasize the value of this approach.

Restrictions on the use of both DDT and PCBs introduced in the early 1970s ('source control') have led to generally declining concentrations in many environmental compartments. However, residues of these (and other OCs) remain and are probably being recycled to some extent through the environment (while at the same time being slowly degraded). Even in the NW Atlantic, which has been studied relatively intensively by scientists from agencies in both Canada and the United States, questions remain about the rates and routes of these recycling pathways, and about the ultimate fate of the residues. The work described here has provided both a baseline against which to assess future analytical data, and also some guidance about the direction of future research and monitoring activities. However, these questions can be answered only by continued field and laboratory research, and by appropriate monitoring programs.

A similar situation exists in the Canadian Arctic. The observations of OCs in the arctic atmosphere, seawater, and biota provide a baseline to evaluate future trends in the Arctic Ocean. Although many pathways deliver and redistribute contaminants to high latitudes, the research has shown that differences in water and lipid solubility among different groups of OCs affect transfer rates between major environmental compartments and organisms in the arctic marine food web (AMAP 1998). Decreases in levels of some OCs in the atmosphere in recent decades have been accompanied by an increase in concentrations in the ocean surface layer. On the other hand, OCs with a low water solubility and affinity for fat are accumulated in the marine food web and stored in lipids (Hargrave et al. 1992, 1993, 2000). Continued research is needed to provide temporal data for lower marine food web organisms and to understand processes controlling the transfer and bioaccumulation of these contaminants by higher trophic level organisms such as Arctic Cod, seals, and Polar Bears. Studies to document changes in water soluble contaminants which appear to move into the Arctic through transfer of ocean water and vapour exchange between the ocean and air must also continue to verify that atmospheric concentrations are continuing their downward trend.

ACKNOWLEDGEMENTS

We thank Maurice Zinck, Doug Willis, Jackie Dale, and Reynald LeBlanc for providing laboratory support throughout these programs. Georgina Phillips, Peter Vass, and Harold Welch provided technical and scientific assistance for studies of OCs from the Canadian Ice Island (1986-88) and in Barrow Strait (1993). Their participation in field and laboratory work and technical expertise were critical for the completion of the studies summarized here. We also thank Harold Welch for comments on the manuscript.

REFERENCES

Addison R.F. 1983. PCB replacements in dielectric fluids. Environmental Science and Technology 17: 486A-494A.
Addison R.F. and T.G. Smith. 1974. Organochlorine residue levels in arctic ringed seals: variation with age and sex. Oikos 25: 335-337.
Addison R.F. and P.F. Brodie. 1977. Organochlorine residues in maternal blubber, milk and pup blubber from grey seals (*Halichoerus grypus*) from Sable Island, Nova Scotia. Journal of the Fisheries Research Board of Canada 34: 937-941.
Addison R.F. and P.F. Brodie. 1987. Transfer of organochlorine residues from blubber through the circulatory system to milk in the lactating grey seal *Halichoerus grypus*. Canadian Journal of Fisheries and Aquatic Sciences 44: 782-786.
Addison R.F. and T.G. Smith. 1998. Trends in organochlorine residue concentrations in ringed seal (*Phoca hispida*) from Holman, NWT, 1972-1991. Arctic 51: 253-261.
Addison, R.F. and W.T. Stobo. 2001. Trends in organochlorine residue concentrations and burdens in grey seals (*Halichoerus grypus*) from Sable Is., NS, Canada, between 1974 and 1994. Environmental Pollution 112: 505-513.
Addison R.F., M.E. Zinck, and T.G. Smith. 1986. PCBs have declined more than DDT group residues in Arctic ringed seals (*Phoca hispida*) between 1972 and 1981. Environmental Science and Technology 20: 253-256.
Addison, R.F., D.C. Muir, M.G. Ikonomou, L. Harwood, T.G. Smith, and J. Alikamik. 2014. Temporal trends in 'legacy' organochlorine contaminants in blubber of Ringed Seals (*Phoca hispida*) from Ulukhaktok, NT, Canada between 1972 and 2010. Science of the Total Environment 466-467:564-576 .
AMAP. 1998. AMAP Assessment Report: Arctic Pollution Issues. Arctic Monitoring and Assessment Programme (AMAP), Oslo, Norway.
Barrie, L.A., D. Gregor, B. Hargrave, P. Lake, D. Muir, R. Shearer, B. Tracey, and T. Bidleman. 1992. Arctic contaminants: sources, occurrence and pathways. Science of the Total Environment 122: 1-74.
Barrie, L.A. and 23 others. 1997. Arctic contaminants: five years of progress in understanding sources, occurrence and pathways. Chapter 2: Sources, Occurrence and Pathways. Pages 25-182 *in* Canadian Arctic Contaminants Assessment Report (J. Jensen, K. Adare, and R. Shearer, Eds.). Department of Indian and Northern Affairs Canada, Ottawa, ON.
Bidleman, T.F., G.W. Patton, M.D. Walla, B.T. Hargrave, W.P. Vass, P. Erickson, B. Fowler, V. Scott, and D.J. Gregor. 1989. Toxaphenes and other organochlorines in Arctic Ocean fauna: evidence for atmospheric delivery. Arctic 42: 307-313.
Bidleman, T.F., G.W. Patton, D.A. Hinckley, M.D. Walla, W.E. Cotham, and B.T. Hargrave. 1990. Chlorinated pesticides and polychlorinated biphenyls in the atmosphere of the Canadian Arctic. Pages 347-372 *in* Long Range Transport of Pesticides (D. Kurtz, Ed.). American Chemical Society Advances in Chemistry Series. Lewis Publishing, Chelsea, MI.
Darrow, D.C. and G.C. Harding. 1975. Accumulation and apparent absence of DDT metabolism by marine copepods, *Calanus spp.*, in culture. Journal of the Fisheries Research Board of Canada 32: 1,845-1,849.
Dewailly E., A. Nantel, J.P. Weber, and F. Meyer. 1989. High levels of PCBs in breast milk of Inuit women from Arctic Quebec. Bulletin of Environmental Contamination and Toxicology 43: 641-646.
Dimond J.B. and R.B. Owen. 1996. Long-term residue of DDT compounds in forest soils in Maine. Environmental Pollution 92: 227-230.
Dunlap, T.R. 1981. DDT: Scientists, Citizens and Public Policy. Princeton University Press, Princeton, NJ.
Gilbert, M. and G. Walsh. 1996. Potential consequences of a PCB spill from the barge *Irving Whale* on the marine environment of the Gulf of St. Lawrence. Canadian Technical Report of Fisheries and Aquatic Sciences 2113: 1-59.
Harding, G.C.H. 1977. Surface area of the euphausiid *Thysanoessa raschii* and its relation to body length, weight, and respiration. Journal of the Fisheries Research Board of Canada 34: 225-231.
Harding, G.C. 1986. Organochlorine dynamics between zooplankton and their environment, a reassessment. Marine Ecology Progress Series 33: 167-191.
Harding, G.C.H. and W.P. Vass. 1977. Uptake from sea water and clearance of ^{14}C- *p, p´*-DDT by the marine copepod *Calanus finmarchicus*. Journal of the Fisheries Research Board of Canada 34: 177-182.
Harding, G.C.H. and W.P. Vass. 1979. Uptake from sea water and clearance of *p,p'*-DDT by marine planktonic crustacea. Journal of the Fisheries Research Board of Canada 36: 247-254.
Harding, G.C. and R.F. Addison. 1987. Accumulation and effects of PCBs in marine invertebrates and vertebrates. Pages 9-30 *in* PCBs in the Environment, Volume II (J.S Waid, Ed.). CRC Press, Boca Raton, FL.
Harding, G.C., W.P. Vass, and K.F. Drinkwater. 1981. Importance of feeding, direct uptake from sea water, and transfer from generation to generation in the accumulation of an organochlorine (*p, p´*¹-DDT) by the marine planktonic copepod *Calanus finmarchicus*. Canadian Journal of Fisheries and Aquatic Sciences 38: 101-119.
Harding, G., P. Vass, and B. Hargrave. 1996. Organochlorine levels in the marine food web of the southern Gulf of St. Lawrence. Pages 41-44 *in* Science Review 1994 & '95 (A. Fiander, Ed.). Fisheries and Oceans (Maritimes Region), Bedford Institute of Oceanography, Dartmouth, NS.
Harding, G.C., R.J. LeBlanc, W.P. Vass, R.F. Addison, B.T. Hargrave, S. Pearre, Jr., A. Dupuis, and P.F. Brodie. 1997. Bioaccumulation of polychlorinated biphenyls (PCBs) in the marine pelagic food web, based on a seasonal study in the southern Gulf of St. Lawrence, 1976-1977. Marine Chemistry 56: 145-179.
Hargrave, B.T., W.P. Vass, P.E. Erickson, and B.R. Fowler. 1988. Atmospheric transport of organochlorines to the Arctic Ocean. Tellus 40B: 480-493.
Hargrave, B.T., B. von Bodungen, R.J. Conover, A.J. Fraser, G. Phillips, and W.P. Vass. 1989. Seasonal changes in sedimentation of particulate matter and lipid content of zooplankton collected by sediment trap in the Arctic Ocean off Axel Heiberg Island. Polar Biology 9: 467-475.
Hargrave, B.T., G.C. Harding, W.P. Vass, P.E. Erickson, B.R. Fowler, and V. Scott. 1992. Organochlorine pesticides and polychlorinated biphenyls in the Arctic Ocean food web. Archives of Environmental Contamination and Toxicology 22: 41-54.
Hargrave, B.T., D.C.G. Muir, and T.F. Bidleman. 1993. Toxaphene in amphipods and zooplankton from the Arctic Ocean. Chemosphere 27: 1,949-1,963.
Hargrave, B.T., B. von Bodungen, P. Stoffyn-Egli, and P.J. Mudie. 1994. Seasonal variability in particle sedimentation under permanent ice cover in the Arctic Ocean. Continental Shelf Research 14: 279-293.
Hargrave, B.T., L.A. Barrie, T.F. Bidleman, and H.E. Welch. 1997. Seasonality in exchange of organochlorines between arctic air and seawater. Environmental Science and Technology 31: 3,258-3,266.
Hargrave, B.T., G.A. Phillips, W.P. Vass, P. Bruecker, H.E. Welch, and T.D. Siferd. 2000. Seasonality in bioaccumulation of organochlorines in lower trophic level arctic marine biota. Environmental Science and Technology 34: 980-987.
Jangaard P.M. (Ed.) 1972. Effects of elemental phosphorus on marine life. Circular Number 2, Atlantic Regional Office, Research and Development, Fisheries Research Board of Canada, Halifax, NS.
Jones, E.P. 2014. The Arctic Ocean: its waters and global significance. Pages 31-35 *in* Voyage of Discovery: Fifty Years of Marine Research at Canada's Bedford Institute of Oceanography (D.N. Nettleship , D.C. Gordon, C.F.M. Lewis, and M.P. Latremouille, Eds.). Bedford Institute of Oceanography-Oceans Association, Dartmouth, NS.

Kerr, S.R. and L.M. Dickie. 2001. The biomass spectrum: a predator-prey theory of aquatic production. Columbia University Press, New York, NY.
Lambert, T.C., G.C. Harding, K.F. Drinkwater, and B.T. Hargrave. 2014. St. Georges Bay ecosystem study: an exercise in interdisciplinary science. Pages 105-112 *in* Voyage of Discovery: Fifty Years of Marine Research at Canada's Bedford Institute of Oceanography (D.N. Nettleship, D.C. Gordon, C.F.M. Lewis, and M.P. Latremouille, Eds.). Bedford Institute of Oceanography-Oceans Association, Dartmouth, NS.
Mudie, P.J. and H.R. Jackson. 2014. The Canadian Ice Island Program: discoveries from a ship of ice. Pages 59-67 *in* Voyage of Discovery: Fifty Years of Marine Research at Canada's Bedford Institute of Oceanography (D.N. Nettleship, D.C. Gordon, C.F.M. Lewis, and M.P. Latremouille, Eds.). Bedford Institute of Oceanography-Oceans Association, Dartmouth, NS.
Muir, D.C.G, R. Wagemann, B.T. Hargrave, D.J. Thomas, D.B. Peakall, and R.J. Norstrom. 1992. Arctic marine ecosystem contamination. Science of the Total Environment 122: 74-134.
Muir, D. and 23 others. 1997. Chapter 3: Ecosystem Uptake and Effects. Pages 191-294 *in* Canadian Arctic Contaminants Assessment Report (J. Jensen, K. Adare, and R. Shearer, Eds.). Department of Indian and Northern Affairs Canada, Ottawa, ON.
Muir, D., B. Braune, B. DeMarch, R. Norstrom, R. Wagemann, L. Lockhart, B. Hargrave, D. Bright, R. Addison, J. Payne, and K. Reimer. 1999. Spatial and temporal trends and effects of contaminants in the Canadian Arctic marine ecosystem: a review. Science of the Total Environment 230: 83-144.
Patton, G.W., D.A. Hinckley, M.D. Walla, T.F. Bidleman, and B.T. Hargrave. 1989. Airborne organochlorines in the Canadian high Arctic. Tellus 41B: 243-255.
Sheldon, R.W., A. Prakash, and W.H.Sutcliffe, Jr. 1972. The size distribution of particles in the ocean. Limnology and Oceanography 17: 327-340.
Vandermeulen, J.H. 1977. The Chedabucto Bay oil spill - *Arrow*, 1970. Oceanus 20: 31-39.
Vandermeulen, J.H. and D.C. Gordon, Jr. 1976. Re-entry of five-year-old standard Bunker C fuel oil from a low-energy beach into the water, sediments, and biota of Chedabucto Bay, Nova Scotia. Journal of the Fisheries Research Board of Canada 33: 2,002-2,010.
Vincent, W.F., J.A.E. Gibson, and M.O. Jeffries. 2001. Ice-shelf collapse, climate change, and habitat loss in the Canadian high Arctic. Polar Record 37: 133-142.
Wassmann, P., E. Bauernfeind, M. Fortier, M. Fukuchi, B. Hargrave, B. Moran, T. Noji, E.-M. Nöthig, R. Peinert, H. Sasaki, and V. Shevchenko. 2003. Particulate organic carbon flux to the Arctic Ocean sea floor. Pages 101-138 *in* The Organic Carbon Cycle in the Arctic Ocean (R. Stein and R.W. Macdonald, Eds). Springer, Berlin, Germany.
Woodwell, G.M., C.F. Wurster, Jr., and P.A. Isaacson. 1967. DDT residues in an east coast estuary: a case of biological concentration of a persistent insecticide. Science 156: 821-823.
Zhu, J. and R.J. Norstrom. 1993. Identification of polychlorocamphenes (PCCs) in the Polar Bear (*Ursus maritimus*) food chain. Chemosphere 27: 1,923-1,936.

37. APPLIED AQUATIC TOXICOLOGY: PROTECTING THE WATERS OF ATLANTIC CANADA

Peter G. Wells* and Kenneth G. Doe

SUMMARY

Aquatic toxicology studies, basic and applied, were conducted from 1971 to 1997 by the Toxicity Evaluation Section (TES), Environmental Quality Laboratory, Environment Canada, at the Bedford Institute of Oceanography (BIO). This was largely applied research for the environmental protection of fresh and coastal waters of the four provinces of Atlantic Canada. The absence of toxicity (harmful biological effects) in industrial discharges and widely used chemicals such as pesticides was a criterion that had to be met under new provisions of the Canadian Fisheries Act and other environmental legislation introduced in the 1970s and 1980s. Acute toxicity tests were developed with numerous species, especially fish and crustaceans. Toxicity tests and related experiments were conducted with industrial wastewater effluents, chemical constituents of effluents, contaminated ocean sediments, oil spill dispersants, and pesticide formulations and their components. Owing to the interdisciplinary nature of water pollution research, and the many oceanographic disciplines represented at BIO, there were many beneficial interactions and collaborations with other units within the Institute. The TES's staff conducted research and provided advice for many national and international initiatives to protect aquatic ecosystems, freshwater, coastal and marine. The TES was relocated to Moncton, New Brunswick, in 1997.

Key words: aquatic toxicology, Atlantic provinces, coastal pollution, environmental effects monitoring (EEM), Fisheries Act, pollution control, toxicity-test development.
***E-mail:** Oceans2@ns.sympatico.ca

Aquatic toxicology studies, basic and applied, were conducted by staff of the Environmental Protection Service, Environment Canada, in the aquatic toxicology laboratories at the Bedford Institute of Oceanography (BIO) from 1971 to 1997. The studies represented applied research for the environmental protection of fresh and coastal waters of the four provinces of Atlantic Canada (Fig. 1). There was considerable interaction with other research units at BIO in marine pollution, ecotoxicology, and biological and chemical oceanography over this 26-year period.

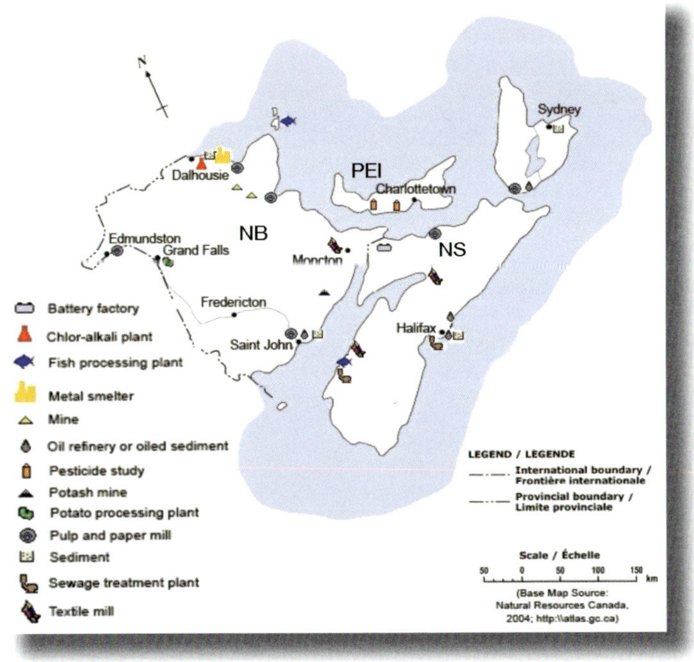

Figure 1. The distribution of study areas and monitoring sites in Atlantic Canada investigated by the Environmental Quality Laboratory, Environment Canada, at the Bedford Institute of Oceanography.

A new federal Department of Environment (DOE) was established in 1971 from the Departments of Fisheries and Forestry, and Energy Mines and Resources. One of the new agencies created with this reorganization was the Environmental Protection Service (EPS). The original primary mandate of EPS was laid out under the Canadian Fisheries Act and the new Ocean Dumping Control Act (ODCA). The legislative mandate was expanded in the mid-1980s to include the Canadian Environmental Protection Act (CEPA), that absorbed the ODCA and the Pest Control Products Act (PCPA), both of which were regulatory legislation that invoked biological testing criteria (Blaise et al. 1988, Day et al. 1988, Taylor et al. 2013). The Fisheries Act was revised in 1972 with Section 33 (now 36) covering pollution control requirements. Canadian industrial effluent control regulations and guidelines were to be developed on an industrial sector basis, with provisions for comprehensive effluent quality and the requirement that the effluents at source would be non-toxic (i.e., non-lethal to fish exposed for short time periods, generally four days). EPS Atlantic Region took the lead in developing the technical requirements for effluent regulations and guidelines under the Fisheries Act, which included choosing a suitable fish bioassay or toxicity test. Protected under the revised Fisheries Act, 'fish' were considered to be all aquatic organisms in all of their life stages, but as part of the first step in pollution control, the Rainbow Trout (*Salmo gairdneri*, now *Oncorhynchus mykiss*; Fig. 2) was recommended as the species of choice for the regulatory toxicity tests (Pessah and Cornwall 1980).

Figure 2. Rainbow Trout (*Oncorhynchus mykiss*) - the primary test species used in Canadian regulatory toxicity testing.

The Pollution Division of EPS established the Environmental Quality Laboratory (EQL) at BIO in 1971. This unique laboratory consisted of analytical chemistry, microbiology and aquatic toxicity testing facilities (labs and offices) and staff, and a group for biological monitoring and surveillance. The laboratory first utilized the Fish Laboratory and a set of offices and dry laboratories housed in trailers, but later moved to the Strickland Building in 1979. The primary mandate of the Toxicity Evaluation Section (TES), later renamed the Aquatic Toxicity Section (ATS) in 1985, was industrial effluent toxicity testing and assessment. As TES and its Division grew (reaching 30-35 staff in 1978), other study programs were developed including: development of tests for toxicity protocols, contaminated marine sediments, oil spill dispersants (for effectiveness and toxicity), pesticide formulations (for regional spruce budworm control), water quality monitoring and surveillance programs, and contributions to international use of aquatic toxicology methods in the management of industrial effluents and toxic chemicals (Pessah and Cornwall 1980, Wells et al. 1998).

Aquatic toxicology is highly interdisciplinary, requiring an interplay of basic toxicology with several biological and chemical fields, and methods essential for investigating marine pollution evolved greatly during this period. The water pollution studies benefited from, and contributed to, the marine ecology and oceanography mission of BIO. Interaction with specialists in other disciplines, and access to the facilities of an established institute (for vessels, specialized equipment, machine shops, library, etc.) were essential to the studies undertaken on water pollution. Short descriptions of the activities and scientific output of the TES programs during these highly productive years at BIO are given below.

Figure 3. BIO Toxicology Laboratory staff in 1988 (left to right): S. Wade, D. Vaughan, K. Doe, and M. MacLean.

REGULATORY TOXICITY TESTING OF INDUSTRIAL EFFLUENTS

The Canadian Fisheries Act (revised 1972, herein called the Fisheries Act) was now in place, with pollution control provisions that included the need for toxicological information on wastewater effluents at source. Various effluents were tested for acute toxicity over the years, from petroleum refineries, pulp mills, mining operations, and chlor-alkali plants, to fish and food processing plants (meat, poultry, potato), landfill leachates, and sewage treatment plants. The TES laboratory was set up to conduct static, static with replacement, and flow-through acute toxicity tests using hatchery-reared, fingerling Rainbow Trout as the primary test organism (Pessah and Cornwall 1980). For many years, the TES laboratory at BIO was the main EPS toxicity lab for effluent testing and toxicity test methods development (Fig. 3).

One of the first studies was on the toxicity of petroleum refinery effluents, the objective being to contribute to the proposed provisions of the refinery regulations and guidelines being drafted under the Fisheries Act. Information was needed on the detailed physico-chemical and toxicity characteristics of these effluents. A study was conducted in 1972 on the final effluents from the Saint John, New Brunswick, Irving Refinery to Rainbow Trout and American Lobster (*Homarus americanus*) larvae (Parker and Cote 1973, Wells 1973). Short-term lethality tests showed that the untreated final effluents were extremely toxic to both organisms. Further studies were then conducted on effluents from various sources, due to concerns about both the toxicity and bioaccumulation potential of their persistent oil constituents and metals. At the time, there were five oil refineries in Atlantic Canada: Irving (Saint John, NB), Texaco and Imperial/Esso (Halifax, NS), Gulf Oil (Port Hawkesbury, NS), and Eagle (Placentia Bay, NL). Trout bioassays demonstrated the high toxicity of the final untreated effluents being discharged into coastal waters (Parker and Cote 1973) and identified the source of acute toxicity (metals, polycyclic aromatic hydrocarbons, sulphides). The toxicity data were used to recommend safe limits for these substances in the final treated effluents, under the new regulations and guidelines.

Following attention to refineries, water pollution control in the Atlantic Provinces focussed largely on pulp mills, mining, smelters, chlor-alkali plants, a battery plant, and fish plant effluents. For many years, pulp-mill effluents in the region and across Canada were investigated, in the laboratory and field, for the toxicity of the various internal waste streams and final effluents, and for biological effects in receiving waters (Dafoe et al. 1987). Pulp mills use huge quantities of water for processing wood fibre and emit similar volumes of effluent into waterways. Many regional mills in the Atlantic region were monitored for acute toxicity to fish, with large volumes of effluents being trucked to BIO for testing in 4-day, flow-through tests, as well as toxicity being measured on-site using mobile, fully-equipped bioassay trailers. The data were used for developing the toxicity criteria in the regulations and guidelines for this industrial sector. As well, joint industry-government, Canada-wide task groups for each industrial sector were established, cooperating in this task of pollution control; sources of toxicity in the effluents were identified and environmental effects monitoring (EEM) programs were established to ensure protection of receiving waters. Significant investments by industry (several billion dollars) contributed to eventual acute toxicity removal from most pulp-mill effluents (Colodey and Wells 1992). Work then began in earnest on sub-lethal toxic effects detection, both in the laboratory and field under a detailed EEM program, as there were low concentrations of many persistent, plant-derived organic compounds that could be harmful to growth, development, and reproduction of aquatic organisms. The TES laboratory at BIO worked with teams across the country on this industrial sector into the 1990s (Dafoe et al. 1987, Parker et al. 1991, Colodey and Wells 1992). This work eventually led to the substantial studies contributing to the Phase II EEM of pulp mills, led by EPS-Conservation and Protection Ottawa in the 1990s (R. Scroggins pers. comm.).

The effluents of base metal mines in New Brunswick also were studied in the 1970s, especially those from Heath Steele Mines on the Miramichi River watershed (Wells et al. 1974). Concerns focussed on the effects of low levels of dissolved metals such as copper, especially on fish avoidance behaviour identified in earlier studies. Raw mining effluents could be quite toxic, at source and in the acid-stressed river waters (Wells et al. 1974), as well as in the Miramichi Estuary. Data from the Heath Steele Mines study and similar ones across Canada (Dafoe et al. 1987) contributed to the development of the Canadian Metal Mining Liquid Effluent Regulations (pursuant to the Fisheries Act) implemented in 1977. Fish plant wastes were also studied in advance of regulations and effluent control; extensive toxicity studies of fish plants in Nova Scotia were undertaken (Wells and Schneider 1975), which showed toxicity to fish to be caused by suspended solids, fish oils, low oxygen and ammonia in the fish-plant wastes. Other types of effluents studied for pollution control purposes included those from base metal smelters, chlor-alkali plants, battery plants, textile mills (Rutherford et al. 1992), wood treatment plants, tire manufacturing plants, municipal wastewater treatment plants (Rutherford et al. 1994), landfill leachates (Ernst et al. 1994, Rutherford et al. 2000), and aluminum smelters (for details, see Eaton et al. 1994). Considerable work was done with the industries to reduce the toxicity of their discharges. A study was also completed on the effects of a local municipal effluent and an elastics plant effluent on the reproduction of Striped Bass (*Morone saxatilis*) in the Annapolis River, Nova Scotia, and its estuary (Parker and Doe 1981).

Ancillary studies associated with effluents included investigations of reference toxicants (Pessah et al. 1976), effects of variation in water quality (Wells and Horne 1977), the influence of salinity on test species responses (Himmelman et al. 1984), effects of fish size, effects of nutrition, and measurements of organism behaviour under chemical stress (Olla et al. 1980). Many of these studies were conducted concurrent with the development of the standardized Rainbow Trout test.

DEVELOPING STANDARD AQUATIC TOXICITY TESTING PROCEDURES

The TES laboratory at BIO was designated a primary laboratory for the development of the Rainbow Trout regulatory toxicity test, as well as for developing other toxicity tests (lethal and sub-lethal) for future applications, either on pollutants at source or in ambient (natural) environments. Considerable cooperative work was conducted with other federal and provincial laboratories across Canada. Many contributions were made to the Intergovernmental Aquatic Toxicity Technical Group (IGATG), now called the Intergovernmental Ecotoxicity Testing Group (IGETG). IGATG was established in 1976 as the technical group supporting regulation development under the Fisheries Act and is responsible for developing biological assessment methods (i.e., toxicity tests), using a variety of test species; the group is still very active (Blaise et al. 1988, 1998; Wells 1989; Taylor et al. 2013).

Work first progressed to standardize the Rainbow Trout fingerling test protocol, completed in 1980 (Environment Canada 1980), and later further developed and updated (Environment Canada 1990a). Research was also initiated at BIO in 1976 to develop salt-water assays, with an emphasis on zooplankton (Wells 1984a, Persoone and Wells 1987), sea urchins (Wells 1982, Jonczyk et al. 1991), polychaete worms (Pocklington and Wells 1992), and estuarine fish (Mummichogs *Fundulus heteroclitis*, and Three-spine Sticklebacks *Gasterosteus aculeatus*). Work also progressed on a freshwater zooplankton assay utilizing water fleas (*Daphnia magna* and *D. pulex*), which has become an important regulatory method complementing the Rainbow Trout test. Toxicity test development in the 1980s involved collaboration and inter-laboratory studies among regional EPS laboratories, and produced the standardized '*Daphnia magna*' toxicity test method used throughout Canada by federal, provincial, and private laboratories (Environment Canada 1990b).

While TES was based at BIO, many contributions were made to the development and standardization of a variety of regulatory toxicity tests now in use across Canada. This involved cooperative work with other Canadian laboratories on the culture and feeding of test organisms, 'round-robin' or inter-laboratory testing, improved quality assurance and quality control (MacGregor and Doe 1987), and final preparation of protocols (Schlekat et al. 1995, Pocklington and Doe 1998, Tay et al. 1998, Ross et al. 1999, Taylor et al. 2013). In addition, guidelines on the general conduct of aquatic toxicity tests and statistical considerations were prepared through IGETG (for details, see: www.ec.gc.ca/faunecanada-wildlifescience).

Over the years, the TES laboratory contributed substantially to the background science, methods, and applications of small-scale or microscale aquatic toxicity tests used in Canada and around the world (Persoone and Wells 1987, Wells 1994, Lee et al. 1998, Wells et al. 1998, Taylor et al. 2013). Such small-scale toxicity tests utilize marine bacteria (Fig. 4), small macro-invertebrates such as copepods from the plankton, and young life stages (gametes, embryos, larvae, post-larvae) of organisms such as crustaceans and echinoderms that are sensitive to low-level chemical exposures; the tests are inexpensive, rapid, and increasingly automated (Wells et al. 1998). TES was particularly involved with developing the sea urchin sperm inhibition test (Fig. 5), as well as the *Daphnia* assay. After more than 40 years, numerous standardized toxicity tests now have world-wide application in water pollution studies, pollution regulations, and environmental monitoring.

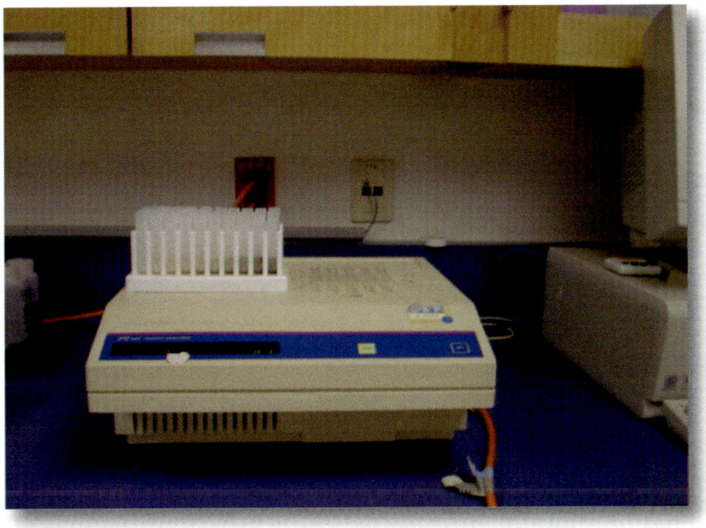

Figure 4. The Microtox 500 analyser used to test sediment and water samples for toxicity to bacteria.

SEDIMENT TOXICITY TESTING AND MONITORING TECHNIQUES

The Ocean Dumping Control Act became federal law in 1975 and became part of the Canadian Environmental Protection Act in 1988. The Act required toxicity testing of harbour dredging spoils that were designated for offshore disposal, as well as monitoring for possible environmental effects at designated offshore dumping sites. Suitable regulatory sediment toxicity tests were developed over many years at the BIO TES-laboratory in collaboration with the Pacific and Yukon laboratory in Vancouver, BC, with an emphasis on polychaete worm tests (Pocklington and Doe 1998), marine amphipod (beach flea) sediment tests (Fig. 6; Schlekat et al. 1995), and marine bacteria solid-phase tests (Tay et al. 1998, Ross et al. 1999, Doe et al. 2005). The procedures were further evaluated using metal contaminated sediments from New Brunswick, and interpretative guidance was developed (Porebski et al. 1998, 1999). Regulatory sediment toxicity tests are now in place for each of these species (for details, see: www. ec.gc.ca/faunecanada-wildlifescience).

Figure 5. Wet spawning of male and female sea urchins (*Strongylocentrotus droebachiensis*) with collected gametes used to study the effects of toxicants on the species' fertilization and early development.

Figure 6. Adding the marine amphipod *Corophium volutator* to test jars in a toxicity study to evaluate the health of the test organism after 10 days exposure to the test sediment.

The above sediment toxicity tests were also utilized by marine researchers, in combination with chemical analyses and other biological monitoring techniques, to assess the quality of harbour sediments in Halifax (Tay et al. 1992) and Sydney (Zajdlik et al. 2000), Nova Scotia, and at ocean dumpsites across Atlantic Canada (Tay et al. 1997). The methods have been used for monitoring toxicity trends during an oil spill bioremediation experiment (Mearns et al. 1995), for assessing recovery of oiled sediments from the 1970 *Arrow* Bunker C oil spill in Chedabucto Bay, Nova Scotia (Lee et al. 2002), for measuring the effectiveness of remediation techniques for oiled marine sediments (Doe et al. 2002), and in monitoring habitat recovery in a crude-oil contaminated salt marsh following bio-restoration techniques (Lee et al. 2002).

THE TOXICITY OF COMPLEX MIXTURES

Many aquatic pollutants are not single compounds or elements, but rather highly complex mixtures, demanding considerable innovative research to identify the compounds primarily responsible for toxicity to exposed organisms and to understand the types of toxic interactions created by the mixtures. Besides studying industrial effluents in this context, research at BIO focussed on oil spill dispersants, drilling muds, and pesticides.

Oil Spill Dispersant Toxicity Program Studies, 1973-85

After the *Arrow* oil spill in 1970, a decision was made by oil spill emergency personnel in Environment Canada to consider chemical dispersants as a countermeasure option at oil spills in Canadian waters (Gordon et al. 2014). The plan was to identify and use products that were effective at oil dispersal and of low acute lethal toxicity to fish. A major research program was established by TES in 1973 to test the effectiveness and toxicity of commercially available, oil spill dispersant formulations available for use in North America and to identify products acceptable for use in Canadian waters. Studies were conducted in the BIO Fish Laboratory from 1973-80, leading to the development of dispersant use guidelines for Canada (Environment Canada 1984). The studies provided an overall understanding of the acute toxicity of oil spill dispersants and a first list of 'acceptable' dispersant products for use in marine waters in Canada (Wells and Doe 1976, Doe and Wells 1978, Environment Canada 1984, Wells 1984b, Gordon et al. 2014). Key findings were reported in Wells (1984b) and summarized at numerous oil spill meetings and conferences including the Gordon Research Conference (1978) in New Hampshire. Importantly, the research gave guidance to Canadian oil spill responders and emergency preparedness authorities charged with stock-piling dispersants for use at coastal and near-shore oil spills.

Additional research studies on the fate and effects of chemically-dispersed oils were conducted at BIO, working closely with environmental scientists in the Fisheries and Oceans Canada (DFO) Marine Ecology Laboratory (MEL) (Wells and Keizer 1975, Harris and Wells 1979, Wells and Harris 1979). There were also collaborative studies on oil and dispersants with K. Lee (Gordon et al. 2014). An open-tank experiment conducted with MEL provided some of the first data on the levels of hydrocarbons to be expected under chemically-dispersed oil slicks (Wells and Keizer 1975).

Moreover, further information and advice important for dispersant use and spill countermeasure policies were provided to the federal government (Sprague et al. 1981, Harris et al. 1986) and by invitation to the United States Government (National Research Council 1985, 1989), the United Kingdom's oil dispersant testing program at Burnham-Upon-Crouch, and the oil pollution program of the State Environmental Protection Agency (Companhia de Tecnologia de Saneamento Ambiental), State of Sao Paulo, Brazil (Arajou et al. 1987). Furthermore, P. Wells joined five other BIO staff on the Canadian sponsored scientific field trip to the site of the massive *Amoco Cadiz* crude oil spill off the coast of Brittany, France, in April 1978. Many observations were made on crude oil movement and deposition in coastal salt marshes and on rocky and sandy shorelines, and the lessons learned by Canadians from the *Arrow* spill about oil fate and effects in temperate marine waters were transferred to French investigators (Vandermeulen 1982, Gordon et al. 2014).

Offshore Oil Studies

A collaborative laboratory study with the MEL on oiled mud cuttings took place in the early 1980s. These complex mixtures are deposited on the offshore ocean floor by exploration and production oil rigs, after they are ejected at the well head. Little was known at the time about possible effects of such mud cuttings on pelagic (offshore) or benthic (bottom-dwelling) organisms. A laboratory study with Winter Flounder (*Pleuronectes americanus*) showed no measureable effects related to exposure to such mud cuttings (Addison et al. 1984).

Pesticide Toxicity Studies, 1976-90

The research and routine testing of newly introduced pesticides (organophosphates, carbamates) and their formulations were stimulated by concerns about inland water quality due to their use over large swaths of New Brunswick forests in the decades-long battle against the spruce budworm. During the post-chlorinated hydrocarbon (DDT) days of the 1970s and 1980s, the federal government took the lead in this research with studies conducted by DOE, and later by both DOE and DFO. Investigations focussed on the acute toxicity to wild Atlantic Salmon (*Salmo salar*) and other salmonids of the different registered pesticide products, and the toxicity of their various formulations; the parent pesticide or active ingredient was always applied in a solvent which was often unknown (to non-industry investigators) and of variable composition. There were many concerns about the possible effects of the pesticides on both human and ecosystem health, as they were often sprayed on forests adjacent to residential areas and water bodies. Reports on the research (e.g., Lord et al. 1978; Wells et al. 1978, 1979; Ernst et al. 1980) provided advice to senior managers and policy makers about the ecological risks associated with pesticide spraying.

To further understand the aquatic impacts of pesticides, effects of environmental variables such as pH on the acute and sub-lethal toxicity of three commonly used products were studied (Doe et al. 1988). Ernst and Doe (1989) compared the aquatic toxicity and bioaccumulation of two formulations of the heavily-used fenitrothion to a variety of organisms. Eventually, guidelines for appropriate pesticide use were developed. One important and serendipitous discovery during the research at BIO was that the solvent in the fenitrothion pesticide formulation was the main toxic agent in the mixture (Wells et al. 1978, 1979), a finding verified simultaneously by chemical analysis and identified as being nonyl-phenols at the St. Andrews Biological Station, New Brunswick (V. Zitko pers. comm.). Nonyl-phenols are extremely toxic to fish and hazardous to humans, being implicated in Reye's Syndrome, a serious but rare brain and liver disease in children. Largely due to these health concerns, nonyl-phenols were quickly banned from use in the pesticide formulation (Bagnall et al. 1978).

Fish kill episodes in Prince Edward Island and concerns about contamination of surface water from off-target drift and runoff of pesticides used in agriculture led to further research. Studies were conducted on toxicity to aquatic organisms of off-target deposition of endosulfan applied by aircraft (Ernst et al. 1991a), and on the toxicity of chorothalonil to aquatic fauna and the impact of its operational use on pond ecosystems (Ernst et al. 1991b).

NATIONAL AND INTERNATIONAL CONTRIBUTIONS TO AQUATIC TOXICOLOGY

Various contributions were made over the years to the field of aquatic toxicology by staff and affiliates of the TES at BIO. TES staff were founding members of the Canadian Annual Aquatic Toxicity Workshops, an internationally-recognized meeting for environmental scientists and a fore-runner to the Society of Environmental Toxicology and Chemistry. Members also served on Committee E47 of the American Society for Testing and Materials (ASTM), working on the development of standard techniques for environmental toxicity testing and monitoring. Contributions were made to North American-wide approaches to the use of toxicity testing at source to control pollution discharges (Dafoe et al. 1987). Advice was offered to the Organization for Economic Cooperation and Development (OECD) working group on toxicity testing methods and effluent toxicity testing. Contributions were also made to the United Nations Joint Group of Experts on the Scientific Aspects of Marine Pollution (GESAMP) and the International Maritime Organization (IMO) on biological monitoring and chemical hazard evaluation (Howells et al. 1990, Persoone et al. 1990, GESAMP 2002).

CONCLUSIONS

The Environmental Quality Laboratory (EQL) of DOE operated at the BIO from 1971 to 1997. Its Toxicity Evaluation Section (TES) was at the forefront of Canadian water pollution studies for over 25 years, contributing to the nascent field of aquatic toxicology and the broader field of marine ecotoxicology, helping to quell industrial, pesticide, and coastal pollution in waters of Atlantic Canada. Many benefits came from being located at BIO, as its facilities and vessels, equipment, and scientists facilitated an exceptionally stimulating and productive work place. Sadly, due to continued federal cutbacks to the Public Service in the 1990s, the EQL laboratory was vastly reduced in size by 1997 and remaining personnel were moved to the DOE Environmental Sciences Centre on the campus of the University of Moncton, New Brunswick. TES continues to operate in its new location today, but as a consequence of the move, an exciting and productive chapter of aquatic toxicology and marine environmental science at BIO, so important for protecting the health of aquatic ecosystems, came to a close.

Coincident with the closure of the EQL and TES laboratories at BIO, and somewhat ironically, was the passing into legislation of Canada's Oceans Act in 1996, proclaiming Canada's leadership in integrated coastal and ocean management, the establishment of marine protected areas, and marine environmental quality (i.e., health of the oceans). DFO was identified as the lead federal agency for the Oceans Act that was established to advance Canada's collective ability to conserve and protect its ocean spaces and species. Such responsibility requires that the responsible federal government departments have and maintain scientific expertise in areas such as aquatic toxicology (now part of the broader field of ecotoxicology), environmental monitoring, and environmental assessment. Given the many known chemical stresses impinging on the waters and species of the northwest Atlantic, especially due to climate change (e.g., ocean acidification) and persistent toxic substances, the need for this science is more urgent now than ever before. It is hoped that over the next few years, the various government agencies and private sector partners at BIO will re-invest in such science, basic and applied. The science is needed to protect Canadian fishery resources, marine habitats and ecosystems, and ocean wildlife, and to maintain Canada's reputation as a leader in marine environmental protection and conservation.

ACKNOWLEDGEMENTS

Many people, staff, and summer students contributed to the leadership and work of the Toxicity Evaluation Section. They are thanked for their efforts and dedication in the early days of aquatic toxicology for water pollution control in Canada. We especially recognize Ray Coté, Bill Ernst, Gary Harris, Amanda Huybers, Paula Jackman, Desmond Lord, Roy Parker, Ed Pessah, John Schneider, K.-L. Tay, David Vaughan, Suzanne Wade, Gary Westlake, and Gary Wohlgeschaffen. We apologize to others whose names do not appear, especially the dedicated support staff and the many hard-working summer students that have contributed over the years.

REFERENCES

Addison, R.F., K. Doe, and A. Edwards. 1984. Effects of oil based drilling mud cuttings on winter flounder (*Pseudopleuronectes americanus*): absence of acute toxicity or mixed function oxidase induction. Canadian Technical Report of Fisheries and Aquatic Sciences 1307, Ottawa, ON.

Araujo, A.R.P., K. Momo, E. Gherardi Goldstein, M.G. Nipper, and P.G. Wells. 1987. Marine dispersant program for licensing and research in Sao Paulo State, Brazil. Pages 289-292 *in* Proceedings 1987 Oil Spill Conference (Prevention, Behavior, Control, Cleanup), Tenth Biennial, April 6-9, 1987, Baltimore, Maryland. American Petroleum Institute Publication No. 4452, Washington, DC.

Bagnall, P.C., J.F.S. Crocker, and R.L. Ozere. 1978. Reye's syndrome in Canadian Maritime Provinces. Chemosphere 7: 565-571.

Blaise, C., G. Sergy, P.G. Wells, N. Bermingham, and R. Van Coillie. 1988. Biological testing development, application and trends in Canadian environmental protection laboratories. Toxicity Assessment 3: 385-406.

Blaise, C., P.G. Wells, and K. Lee. 1998. Microscale testing in aquatic toxicology: introduction, historical perspective, and context. Pages 1-9 *in* Microscale Testing in Aquatic Toxicology - Advances, Techniques and Practice (P.G. Wells, K. Lee, and C. Blaise, Eds.). CRC Press, Boca Raton, FL.

Colodey, A.G. and P.G. Wells. 1992. Effects of pulp and paper mill effluents on estuarine and marine ecosystems in Canada: a review. Journal of Aquatic Ecosystem Health 1: 201-226.

Dafoe, T., J.H. Carey, S.H. McCrindle, P.G. Wells, and R.C.H. Wilson. 1987. Relationship between the biological testing of industrial effluents and the quality of receiving waters - some Canadian case studies. Water Pollution Research Journal of Canada 22: 251-269.

Day, K.E., E.D. Ongley, R.P. Scroggins, and H.R. Eisenhauer. 1988. Biology in the new regulatory framework for aquatic protection. Proceedings of the Alliston Workshop, April 26-28th, 1988 (K.E.Day, E.D. Ongley, R.P. Scroggins, and H.R. Eisenhauer, Eds.). National Water Research Institute, Burlington, ON.

Doe, K.G. and P.G. Wells. 1978. Acute aquatic toxicity and dispersing effectiveness of oil spill dispersants: results of a Canadian Oil Dispersant Testing Program (1973-1977). Pages 50-65 *in* Chemical Dispersants for the Control of Oil Spills, ASTM STP 659 (L.T. McCarthy, Jr., G.P. Lindblom, and H.F. Walters, Eds.). American Society for Testing and Materials, Philadelphia, PA.

Doe, K.G., W.R. Ernst, W.R. Parker, G.R.J. Julien, and P.A. Hennigar. 1988. Influence of pH on the acute lethality of fenitrothion, 2,4-D and aminocarb, and some pH altered sublethal effects of aminocarb on rainbow trout (*Salmo gairdneri*). Canadian Journal of Fisheries and Aquatic Sciences 45: 287-293.

Doe, K.G., P.M. Jackman, and K. Lee. 2002. Measuring the effectiveness of remediation techniques using sediment toxicity tests with the amphipod *Eohaustorius estuarius*. Pages 369-378 *in* Proceedings of the Twenty-Fifth Arctic and Marine Oilspill Program (AMOP) Technical Seminar, June 11-13, 2002, Calgary, Canada (M. Fingas, Ed.). Environment Canada, Ottawa, ON.

Doe, K., P. Jackman, R. Scroggins, D. McLeay, and G. Wohlgeschaffen. 2005. Solid-phase test for sediment toxicity using the luminescent bacterium, *Vibrio fischeri*. Pages 107-136 *in* Small-scale Freshwater Toxicity Investigations: Volume 1 - Toxicity Test Methods (C. Blaise and J.-F. Férard, Eds.). Springer, Dordrecht, The Netherlands.

Eaton, P.B., A.G. Gray, P.W. Johnson, and E. Hundert. 1994. State of the Environment for the Atlantic Region. Technical Report, Environment Canada - Atlantic Region, Dartmouth, NS.

Environment Canada. 1980. Standard procedure for testing the acute lethality of liquid effluents. Environmental Protection Service Report EPS 1 WP 80 1, Environment Canada, Ottawa, ON.

Environment Canada. 1984. Guidelines on the use and acceptability of oil spill dispersants, 2nd Edition. Environmental Protection Service Report EPS 1 EP 84 1, Environment Canada, Ottawa, ON.

Environment Canada. 1990a. Biological test method: acute lethality test using rainbow trout. Environmental Protection Service Report EPS 1/RM/9, Environment Canada, Ottawa, ON.

Environment Canada. 1990b. Biological test method: Acute lethality test using *Daphnia* spp. Environmental Protection Service Report EPS 1/RM/11, Environment Canada, Ottawa, ON.

Ernst, B., G. Julien, K. Doe, and R. Parker. 1980. Environmental investigations of the 1980 spruce bud-worm program in New Brunswick. Environmental Protection Service Report EPS-5-AR-81-3, Environment Canada, Halifax, NS.

Ernst, W.R. and K.G. Doe. 1989. A comparison of the aquatic toxicity of fenitrothion flowable and fenitrothion liquid technical formulations. Water Pollution Research Journal of Canada 24: 553-568.

Ernst, W.R., P. Jonah, K. Doe, G. Julien, and P. Hennigar. 1991a. Toxicity to aquatic organisms of off-target deposition of endosulfan applied by aircraft. Environmental Toxicology and Chemistry 10: 103-114.

Ernst, W.R., K. Doe, P. Jonah, J. Young, G. Julien, and P. Hennigar. 1991b. The toxicity of chorothalonil to aquatic fauna and the impact of its operational use on a pond ecosystem. Archives of Environmental Contamination and Toxicology 21: 1-9.

Ernst, W.R., P. Hennigar, K. Doe, S. Wade, and G. Julien. 1994. Characterization of the chemical constituents and toxicity to aquatic organisms of a municipal landfill leachate. Water Pollution Research Journal of Canada 29: 89-101.

GESAMP (Joint Group of Experts on Scientific Aspects of Marine Environmental Protection). 2002. The revised Group of Experts on the Scientific Aspects of Marine Pollution hazard evaluation procedure for chemical substances carried by ships. Group of Experts on the Scientific Aspects of Marine Enviromental Protection Report and Studies No. 64, International Maritime Organization, London, England.

Gordon, D.C., K. Lee, P.G. Wells, and P.D. Keizer. 2014. The impacts of oil and gas activities on the marine environment. Pages 361-371 *in* Voyage of Discovery: Fifty Years of Marine Research at Canada's Bedford Institute of Oceanography (D.N. Nettleship, D.C. Gordon, C.F.M. Lewis, and M.P. Latremouille, Eds.). Bedford Institute of Oceanography-Oceans Association, Dartmouth, NS.

Harris, G.W. and P.G. Wells. 1979. A laboratory study of the adhesion of crude oil to beach sand in the presence of a dispersant. Spill Technology Newsletter 4: 293-298.

Harris, G.W., P.G. Wells, A. Bobra, and F. Abbott. 1986. The comparative toxicology of oil spill dispersants to fish-implications for Canada's dispersant toxicity guidelines and the protection of marine environmental quality. Pages 485-495 *in* Proceedings of the Ninth Arctic Marine Oilspill Program Technical Seminar, Edmonton, AB, June 1986 (M. Fingas, Ed.). Environment Canada, Ottawa, ON.

Himmelman, J.H., H. Guderley, G. Vignault, G. Drouin, and P.G. Wells. 1984. Response of the sea urchin, *Strongylocentrotus droebachiensis*, to reduced salinities: importance of size, acclimation, and inter-population differences. Canadian Journal of Zoology 62: 1,015-1,021.

Howells, G., D. Calamari, J.S. Gray, and P.G.Wells. 1990. An analytical approach to assessment of long term effects of low levels of contaminants in the marine environment. Marine Pollution Bulletin 21: 371-375.

Jonczyk, E., K.G. Doe, P.G. Wells, and S.G. Yee. 1991. Technical evaluation of the sea urchin fertilization test: proceedings of a workshop in Dartmouth, Nova Scotia. Pages 323-330 *in* Proceedings of the 17th Annual Toxicity Workshop, November, 1990, Vancouver, B.C. (P. Chapman, F. Bishay, E. Power, K. Hall, L. Harding, D. McLeay, M. Nassichuk, and W. Knapp, Eds.). Canadian Technical Report of Fisheries and Aquatic Sciences, No. 1774, Vol. 1, Ottawa, ON.

Lee, K., P.G. Wells, and C. Blaise. 1998. Chapter 44. Microscale testing in aquatic toxicology: conclusions and future directions. Pages 647-649 *in* Microscale Testing in Aquatic Toxicology - Advances, Techniques and Practice (P.G.Wells, K. Lee, and C. Blaise, Eds.). CRC Press, Boca Raton, FL.

Lee, K., S. Cobanli, G. Wohlgeschaffen, A.D. Venosa, M.T. Suidan, J. Gauthier, G.H. Tremblay, C.W. Greer, and K.G. Doe. 2002. Habitat recovery in a crude-oil contaminated saltmarsh following bio-restoration techniques. Pages 329-339 *in* Proceedings of the Twenty-Fifth Arctic and Marine Oilspill Program (AMOP) Technical Seminar, June 11-13, 2002, Calgary, AB (M. Fingas, Ed.). Environment Canada, Ottawa, ON.

Lord, D.A., R.A.F. Matheson, L. Stuart, J.J. Swiss, and P.G. Wells. 1978. Environmental monitoring of the 1976 spruce budworm spray program in New Brunswick, Canada. Environmental Protection Service Surveillance Report EPS 5 AR 78 3, Fisheries and Environment Canada, Ottawa, ON.

MacGregor, D. and K. Doe. 1987. Basic elements of quality assurance in ecotoxicological testing. Pages 75-88 *in* Recommendations on Aquatic Biological Tests and Procedures for Environmental Protection (G. Sergy, Ed.). Conservation and Protection, Environment Canada, Ottawa, ON.

Mearns, A., K. Doe, W. Fisher, R. Hoff, K. Lee, R. Siron, C. Mueller, and A. Venosa. 1995. Toxicity trends during an oil spill bioremediation experiment on a sandy shoreline in Delaware, USA. Pages 1,133-1,145 *in* Proceedings of the Eighteenth Arctic and Marine Oilspill Program (AMOP) Technical Seminar, June 14 to 16, 1995, Edmonton, AB (M. Fingas, Ed.). Environmental Technology Centre, Environment Canada, Ottawa, ON.

National Research Council. 1985. Oil in the Sea: Inputs, Fates and Effects. Marine Board, National Research Council, National Academy of Sciences. National Academy Press, Washington, DC.

National Research Council. 1989. Using Oil Spill Dispersants on the Sea. Marine Board, National Research Council, National Academy of Sciences. National Academy Press, Washington, DC.

Olla, B.L., J. Atema, R. Forward, J. Kittredge, R.J. Livingston, D.W. McLeese, D.C. Miller, W.B. Vernberg, P.G. Wells, and K. Wilson. 1980. The role of behavior in marine pollution monitoring. Behavior Panel Report. International Council for the Exploration of the Sea 179: 174-181.

Parker, W.R. and R.P Cote. 1973. A toxicity study of an oil refinery effluent in Saint John, New Brunswick. Environmental Protection Surveillance Report EPS 5 WP 73 1, Environment Canada, Ottawa, ON.

Parker, W.R. and K.G. Doe. 1981. Studies on the reproduction of striped bass *Morone saxatilis* (Walbaum) from the Annapolis River, Nova Scotia. Environmental Protection Service Surveillance Report EPS-5-AR-81-6, Environment Canada, Halifax, NS.

Parker, W.R., K.G. Doe, and P.G. Wells. 1991. Application of marine biological tests in assessing and controlling the acute and chronic toxicities of effluents. Pages 135-151 *in* Proceedings of the 17th Annual Aquatic Toxicity Workshop, November 1990, Vancouver, B.C. (P. Chapman, F. Bishay, E. Power, K. Hall, L. Harding, D. McLeay, M. Nassichuk, and W. Knapp, Eds.). Canadian Technical Report of Fisheries and Aquatic Sciences 1774, Vol. 1, Ottawa, ON.

Persoone, G. and P.G. Wells. 1987. *Artemia* in aquatic toxicology: a review. Pages 259-275 *in Artemia* Research and its Applications, Vol. I. Morphology, Genetics, Strain Characteristics, Toxicology (P. Sorgeloos, D.A. Bengtson, W. Declair and E. Jaspers, Eds.). Universa Press, Wetteren, Belgium.

Persoone, G., D. Calamari, and P.G. Wells. 1990. Chapter 18. Possibilities and limitations of predictions from short term tests in the aquatic environment. Pages 301-312 *in* Short Term Toxicity Tests for Non Genotoxic Effects (P. Bourdeau, E. Somers, G.M. Richardson, and J.R. Hickman, Eds.). John Wiley, New York, NY.

Pessah, E., P.G. Wells, and J.R. Schneider. 1976. Dodecyl sodium sulphate (DSS) as an intra-laboratory reference toxicant in fish bioassays. Pages 93-121 *in* Proceedings 2nd Annual Aquatic Toxicity Workshop, 1975 (G.R. Craig, Ed.). Ontario Ministry of the Environment, Toronto, ON.

Pessah, E. and G.M. Cornwall. 1980. Use of toxicity tests in regulating the quality of industrial wastes in Canada. Pages 130-141 *in* Aquatic Toxicology, ASTM STP 707 (J.G. Eaton, P.R. Parrish, and A.C. Hendricks, Eds.). American Society for Testing and Materials, Philadelphia, PA.

Pocklington, P. and K.G. Doe. 1998. Development of a Canadian marine toxicity test for whole sediments using cultured spionid worms. Pages 395-407 *in* Microscale Testing in Aquatic Toxicology: Advances, Techniques, Practice (P.G. Wells, K. Lee, and C. Blaise, Eds.). CRC Press, Boca Raton, FL.

Pocklington, P. and P.G. Wells. 1992. Polychaetes: key taxa for marine environmental quality monitoring. Marine Pollution Bulletin 24: 593-598.

Porebski, L., K. Doe, B. Zajdlik, D. Lee, P. Pocklington, G. Atkinson, and J. Osborne. 1998. Interpretive guidance for bioassays using pollution gradient studies - Belledune, NB. Marine Environment Division Report WM-20, Environment Canada, Ottawa, ON.

Porebski, L.M., K.G. Doe, B.A. Zajdlik, D. Lee, P. Pocklington, and J. Osborne. 1999. Evaluating the techniques for a tiered testing approach to dredged sediment assessment - a study over a metal concentration gradient. Environmental Toxicology and Chemistry 18: 2,600-2,610.

Ross, P. and others. 1999. Inter-laboratory precision study of a whole sediment toxicity test with the bioluminescent bacterium *Vibrio fischeri*. Environmental Toxicology 14: 339-345.

Rutherford, C.A., P.A. Hennigar, K.G. Doe, M.L. Nicol, M.M.E. Holmes, B.C. MacDonald, and W.H. Horne. 1992. Chemical characterization, aquatic toxicity and environmental impact of untreated effluent discharges from three textile mills in the Atlantic Region. Environmental Protection Service Report EPS-5-AR-93-1, Environment Canada, Ottawa, ON.

Rutherford, L.A., K.G. Doe, S.J. Wade, and P.A. Hennigar. 1994. Aquatic toxicity and environmental impact of chlorinated wastewater effluent discharges from four sewage treatment facilities in the Atlantic Region. Pages 179-195 *in* Proceedings of the Twentieth Annual Aquatic Toxicity Workshop, October 17-21, 1993, Quebec City, QC (R. VanCoillie, Y. Bois, P.G.C. Campbell, P. Lundahl, L. Martel, M. Michaud, P. Riebel, and C. Thellen, Eds.). Canadian Technical Report of Fisheries and Aquatic Sciences 1989, Ottawa, ON.

Rutherford, L.A., S.L. Matthews, K.G. Doe, and G.R.J. Julien. 2000. Aquatic toxicology and environmental impact of leachate discharges from a municipal landfill. Water Quality Research Journal of Canada 35: 39-57.

Schlekat, C.E., K.J. Scott, R.C. Swartz, B. Albrecht, L. Antrim, K. Doe, S. Douglas, J.A. Ferrati, D.J. Hansen, D.W. Moore, C. Mueller, and A. Tang. 1995. Inter-laboratory comparison of a 10-day sediment toxicity test method using *Ampelisca abdita*, *Eohaustaurius estuarius*, and *Leptocheirus plumulosus*. Environmental Toxicology and Chemistry 14: 2,163-2,174.

Sprague, J.B., J.H. Vandermeulen, and P.G. Wells. 1981. Oil and dispersants in Canadian seas: recommendations from a research appraisal. Marine Pollution Bulletin 12: 45-46.

Tay, K.-L., K.G. Doe, and A.J. MacDonald. 1997. Monitoring of the Black Point ocean disposal site, Saint John Harbour, New Brunswick, 1992-1994. Ocean Disposal Report 9. Environment Canada - Atlantic Region, Dartmouth, NS.

Tay, K.-L., K.G. Doe, A.J. MacDonald, and K. Lee. 1998. The influence of particle size, ammonia, and sulfide on toxicity of dredged materials for ocean disposal. Pages 559-574 *in* Microscale Testing in Aquatic Toxicology: Advances, Techniques, Practice (P.G. Wells, K. Lee, and C. Blaise, Eds.). CRC Press, Boca Raton, FL.

Tay, K.-L., K.G. Doe, S.J. Wade, J.D.A. Vaughan, R.E. Berrigan, and M.J. Moore. 1992. Sediment bioassessment in Halifax Harbour. Environmental Toxicology and Chemistry 11: 1,567-1,581.

Taylor, L.N., K.G. Doe, R.P. Scroggins, and P.G. Wells. 2013. A history of the inter-governmental ecotoxicological testing group and the evolution of ecotoxicological testing in Canada for regulatory applications. Water Quality Research Journal of Canada 48: 14-29.

Vandermeulen, J.H. 1982. Some conclusions regarding long-term biological effects of some major oil spills [and Discussion]. Philosophical Transactions of the Royal Society of London B 297: 335-351.

Wells, P.G. 1973. Acute toxicity bioassay with an oil effluent and larvae of *Homarus americanus*. Pages 14-19 *in* A Toxicity Study of an Oil Refinery Effluent in Saint John, New Brunswick, Environmental Protection Surveillance Report, EPS 5 WP 73 1 (W.R. Parker and R.P. Côté, Eds.). Environmental Protection Service, Environment Canada, Dartmouth, NS.

Wells, P.G. 1982. Green sea urchins (*Strongylocentrotus droebachiensis*) as toxicity test organisms and monitors of pollutants in Canadian marine coastal waters. DOE Spill Technology Newsletter 7: 114-120.

Wells, P.G. 1984a. Marine ecotoxicological tests with zooplankton. Pages 215-256 *in* Ecotoxicological Testing for the Marine Environment, Vol. 1 (G. Persoone, E. Jaspers, and C. Claus, Eds.). State University of Ghent, Ghent and Institute of Marine Scientific Research, Bredene, Belgium.

Wells, P.G. 1984b. The toxicity of oil spill dispersants to marine organisms - a current perspective. Pages 177-202 *in* Oil Spill Chemical Dispersants: Research, Experience and Recommendations, STP 840 (T.E. Allen, Ed.). American Society for Testing and Materials, Philadelphia, PA.

Wells, P.G. 1989. History and practice of biological effects assessment for aquatic protection in Canada: a synopsis. Pages 25-29 *in* Biology in the New Regulatory Framework for Aquatic Protection, Proceedings of the Alliston Workshop, April 1988, Technical Report (K.E. Day, E.D. Ongley, R.P. Scroggins, and H.R. Eisenhauer, Eds.). National Water Research Institute, Environment Canada, Burlington, ON.

Wells, P.G. 1994. Bioassays. Pages 15-17 *in* Biological Indicators of the Health of Marine Ecosystems, GESAMP Report and Studies No. 55. UNESCO-IOC, Geneva, Switzerland.

Wells, P.G., E. Pessah, and W.R. Parker. 1974. The toxicity of raw and treated drainage from Heath Steele Mines, N.B., during period of September-October, 1974. Environmental Protection Service Surveillance Report EPS 5 AR 74 14, Environment Canada, Dartmouth, NS.

Wells, P.G. and P.D. Keizer. 1975. Effectiveness and toxicity of an oil dispersant in large outdoor salt water tanks. Marine Pollution Bulletin 6: 153-157.

Wells, P.G. and J.R. Schneider. 1975. Characteristics of fish plant wastes in Nova Scotia and their effects on coastal bays. III. Toxicity Studies. Environmental Protection Service Impact and Assessment Report EPS 8 AR 75 4, Environment Canada, Dartmouth, NS.

Wells, P.G. and K.G. Doe. 1976. Results of the EPS oil dispersant testing program: concentrates, effectiveness testing and toxicity to marine organisms. DOE Spill Technology Newsletter 1: 9-16.

Wells, P.G. and W. Horne. 1977. Some characteristics of a diluent fresh water used for aquatic bioassays January 1975 to December 1976. Environmental Protection Service Surveillance Report EPS 5 AR 77 16, Environment Canada, Dartmouth, NS.

Wells, P.G., W.R. Parker, and D. Vaughan. 1978. The acute toxicity of four insecticides and their formulations to fingerling rainbow trout, *Salmo gairdneri*. Pages 84-110 *in* Environmental Monitoring of the 1976 Spruce Budworm Spray Program in New Brunswick, Canada. Environmental Protection Service , Environment Canada, Dartmouth, NS.

Wells, P.G. and G.W. Harris. 1979. Dispersing effectiveness of some oil spill dispersants: tests with the Mackay Apparatus and Venezuelan Lago Medio crude oil. DOE Spill Technology Newsletter 4: 232-241.

Wells, P.G., R.A. Matheson, D.A. Lord, and K.G. Doe. 1979. Environmental monitoring of the 1978 spruce budworm spray program in New Brunswick, Canada - field sampling and aquatic toxicity studies with fish. Environmental Protection Service Surveillance Report EPS 5 AR 79 1, Environment Canada, Ottawa, ON.

Wells, P.G., K. Lee, and C. Blaise (Eds.). 1998. Microscale testing in aquatic toxicology: advances, techniques and practice. CRC Press, Boca Raton, FL.

Zajdlik, B.A., K.G. Doe, and L.M. Porebski. 2000. Report on biological toxicity tests using pollution gradient studies - Sydney Harbour. Marine Environment Division, Environmental Protection Service Report EPS 3/AT/2, Environment Canada, Ottawa, ON.

Technology & Instrument Development

BIO Videograb for seabed sampling

Technology and Instrument Development

38. DEGLACIATION AND POSTGLACIAL SEA-LEVEL CHANGES IN ATLANTIC CANADA: SCIENCE DRIVEN BY TECHNOLOGY

John Shaw

SUMMARY

The study of offshore glacial history and relative sea-level changes has benefited from technologic advances in the past few decades, including improved radiocarbon dating, advent of the Huntec Deep Tow Seismic Reflection system, use of computers for data manipulation and visualization, and the application of multibeam sonar to geological mapping. It is generally accepted that the Laurentide Ice Sheet extended to the edges of the continental shelves at the last glacial maximum about 20,000 years before present. Multibeam sonar imagery reveals the landforms that were created by the movement and retreat of the ice, and Olex bathymetric data reveal evidence of large-scale glaciotectonism. While complex relative sea-level changes in the postglacial period have left an imprint on the seafloor, submerged coastal and terrestrial landforms are preserved only in special circumstances.

Key words: radiocarbon dating, Huntec, multibeam sonar, glaciation, sea-level change.
E-mail: John.Shaw@nrcan.gc.ca

Over the last 50 years, technologic advances have changed the conduct of geological research on the continental shelves of Atlantic Canada (Fig. 1). For example, radiocarbon dating of marine sediments was revolutionized in the late 1980s by the introduction of the Atomic Mass Spectrometry (AMS) technique to date minute samples (Currie 2004). The advent of the Huntec Deep Tow Seismic Reflection system (DTS) (Hutchins et al. 1976, McKeown et al. 2014) permitted observation of the acoustic structure of sedimentary layers in high resolution even from a wave- and swell-prone sea surface. Also, the use of increasingly powerful computers allowed storage of vast quantities of data, and its manipulation and visualization in Geographic Information Systems (GIS). Notably, in the mid-1990s, Geological Survey of Canada (GSC) researchers began applying multibeam sonar to geological mapping (e.g., Loncarevic et al. 1994) in partnership with the Canadian Hydrographic Service (CHS). To maximize the value of multibeam data, GSC scientists developed a methodology to extract backscatter – a proxy for seafloor texture. Finally, the advent of the Olex AS system permitted users to pool digital bathymetric data and create bathymetric maps of large areas of the sea floor that would never be mapped otherwise. This short paper focusses on the history of the deglaciation and postglacial sea-level change in Atlantic Canada. Scientists based at the Bedford Institute of Oceanography (BIO) played a leading role in this research, but also collaborated with researchers based at other government laboratories and at universities around the globe.

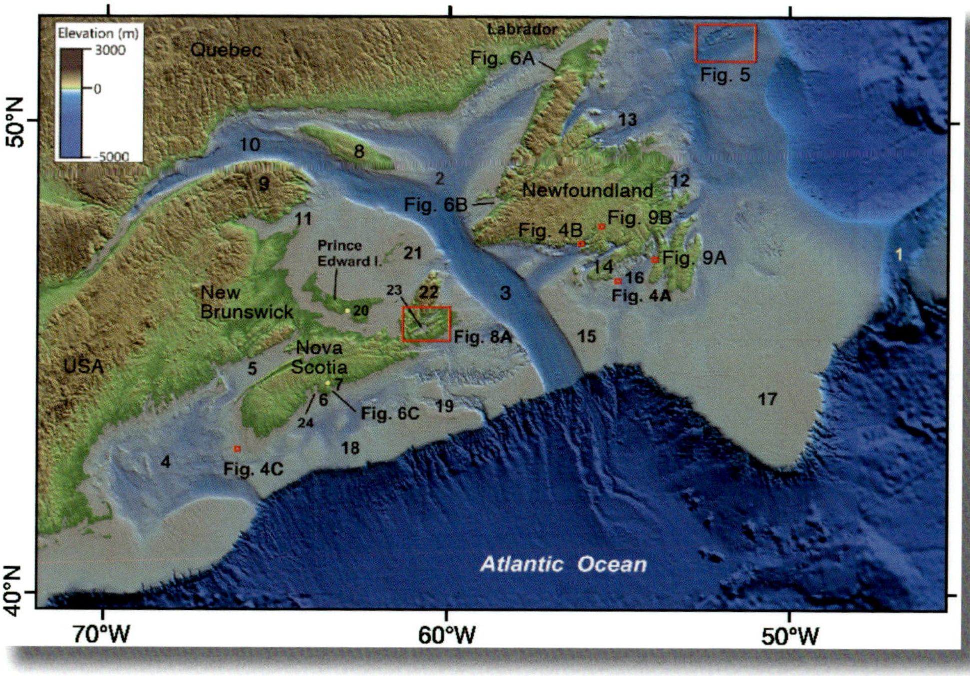

Figure 1. The coast of Atlantic Canada today. A series of glacially-overdeepened troughs cross the offshore banks and reach the edge of the continental shelves. Locations: (1) Flemish pass; (2) Gulf of St. Lawrence; (3) Laurentian Channel; (4) Gulf of Maine; (5) Bay of Fundy; (6) Peggy's Cove; (7) Halifax; (8) Anticosti Island; (9) Gaspé Peninsula; (10) St. Lawrence Estuary; (11) Chaleur Bay; (12) Bonavista Bay; (13) Notre Dame Bay; (14) Burin Peninsula; (15) St. Pierre Bank; (16) Placentia Bay; (17) Grand Bank; (18) Scotian Shelf; (19) Sable Island; (20) Charlottetown; (21) Magdalen Islands; (22) Cape Breton Island; (23) Bras d'Or Lakes; and (24) St. Margaret's Bay. Location of other figures indicated.

GLACIAL HISTORY

Identification of Glacial Deposits Offshore

Researchers mapping the surficial geology of offshore Atlantic Canada using data from single-beam echo sounders (King 1970, MacLean and King 1971, Drapeau and King 1972, Fader et al. 1977, MacLean et al. 1977) identified two principal glacial formations: (1) Scotian Shelf Drift (Grand Banks Drift in Newfoundland), acoustically incoherent till deposited under glacial ice; and (2) Emerald Silt (Downing Silt), acoustically stratified sediment deposited by meltwater plumes. These formations were mapped across vast areas, testifying to the former extent of glacier ice (Fader et al. 2014). The Scotian Shelf Drift, for example, constituted the vast Scotian Shelf Submarine Moraine (King 1969) that stretched hundreds of kilometres. High-resolution Huntec DTS data revealed the complex relationship between these glacial formations in certain settings. Till tongues were wedge-shaped deposits of Scotian Shelf Drift interbedded with Emerald Silt, commonly rooted in large constructional moraines and formed at the margins of grounded ice sheets (King and Fader 1986, King 1996, Gipp and Piper 1989).

Chronology

It was originally thought that the ice margin at the last glacial maximum (LGM), about 20,000 years before present (BP), lay close to the modern coast (Dyke and Prest 1987). While glacial sediments had been mapped far offshore, they were attributed to an earlier glaciation on the basis of radiocarbon evidence (King and Fader 1986). Prior to the late 1980s, radiocarbon dating of marine sediments required bulk samples that yielded anomalously old dates due to incorporation of old, recycled carbon. Thus, published dates from the Emerald Silt ranged up to 40,000 years BP (King and Fader 1986). AMS dating, pioneered in 1977 (Currie 2004) permitted dating of organic samples weighing as little as 30 mg, with dramatic results. The Emerald Silt Formation was dated to 14,900 to 18,300 years BP (King and Fader 1988), setting the stage for a revised chronology of glaciation (Dyke et al. 2002, Shaw et al. 2006). In this paper, cited ages are radiocarbon ages. When corrections for variations in the rate of production of the radiocarbon isotope in the atmosphere over time, which can amount to approximately 20%, are applied to laboratory determinations or radiocarbon ages, the resulting ages are said to be calibrated (Stuiver and Reimer 1993).

Determining Ice Limits at the Last Glacial Maximum

The map of the glacial maximum in Atlantic Canada (Fig. 2) is based on the revised chronology. Information from continental shelf margins has proven critical in constraining this ice limit. Till tongues pinching out at present water depths of 450-500 m are recognized along much of the margin (Bonifay and Piper 1988, Mosher et al. 1989). A small number of AMS radiocarbon dates associate these ice margins with the Last Glacial Maximum (LGM). For example, Mosher et al. (1989) published an AMS date of 18,320 ± 440 years BP on shell in glaciomarine sediments at ~650 m depth on the Scotian Slope. This unit extends upslope into a till tongue dated at 20,800 years BP (King 1996). Many mass-transport deposits on continental slopes are related to the presence of glacier ice on adjacent shelves. Huppertz and Piper (2009) noted the absence of such deposits at Oxygen Isotope Stage 2 (i.e., LGM) on Flemish Pass, which suggests that LGM ice did not reach the shelf edge there.

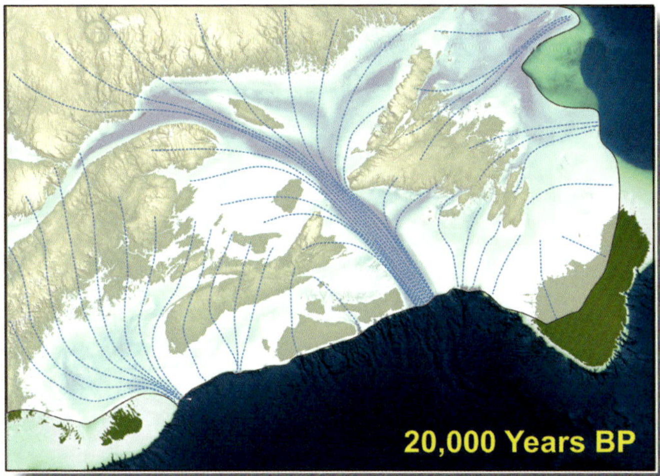

Figure 2. A generalized depiction of the extent of the Laurentide Ice Sheet at the Last Glacial Maximum (LGM) about 20,000 years BP. The dashed lines are approximate flow lines. The Laurentian Channel was occupied by a major ice stream and the exposed land is shown in green.

The Ice Sheet at LGM

The LGM reconstruction of the Laurentide Ice Sheet depicted in Figure 2 draws heavily on the literature of ice streams. On modern ice sheets these are narrow, fast-flowing, longitudinal zones separated by low-velocity zones, reaching far into the interior (Bamber et al. 2000, Boulton et al. 2001). Hughes (1998) depicted hypothetical ice streams on the southeast margin of the Laurentide Ice Sheet, and a similar pattern is described in Figure 2. Ice flowed from catchments towards the periphery of the ice sheet, converging and feeding fast-flow features. Ice streams occupied and over-deepened troughs on the shelves. The major ice stream in the Laurentian Channel drained western and southwestern Newfoundland in addition to other areas of the mainland around the Gulf of St. Lawrence.

Deglaciation

Deglaciation was initially accomplished by ice calving along deep channels. Figure 3 is a 'snapshot' of conditions 14,000 years BP when ice margins lay close to modern coasts. The ice sheet had become a series of isolated ice caps, similar in configuration to the ice caps which Stea (2004) argued had been the nuclei for the more extensive ice at the LGM. In the Gulf of Maine and Bay of Fundy (Schnikter et al. 2001) a tidewater margin developed

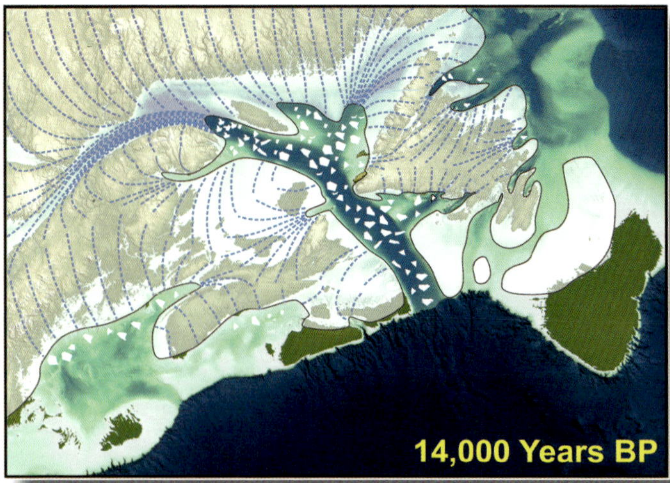

Figure 3. Glacial ice extent about 14,000 years BP. The Laurentian Channel was in the throes of massive calving of ice and ice margins were retreating to the modern coasts in most areas. The exposed land is shown in green.

near modern coasts. Peggy's Cove, near Halifax, Nova Scotia, was ice-free by about 14,000 years BP (MacDonald et al. 2003). Farther east, landward retreat of ice grounded in shallow water was punctuated by still stands or slight readvances, forming moraines just offshore (Stea et al. 1992, 1996). Ice remained at the mouth of the Laurentian Channel until 14,200 years BP (Piper and Macdonald 2001). A retreating calving embayment halted briefly in the Laurentian Channel (Josenhans and Lehman 1999) and rapidly moved northwest into the Gulf of St. Lawrence where Rodriques et al. (1993) reported open water between Anticosti Island and the Gaspé Peninsula by 14,040 ± 240 years BP. The embayment reached the St. Lawrence Estuary by 13,500 years BP (Locat 1977) and the head of Chaleur Bay by 13,900 years BP (Rodrigues et al. 1993).

By 14,000 years BP, calving ice margins had reached the south and southwest coasts of Newfoundland (Shaw et al. 2000, Shaw 2003), including St. George's Bay (Forbes et al. 1993; Liverman and Bell 1996; Bell et al. 2001, 2003). The ice had gone from Bonavista Bay by 13,500 years BP (Cumming et al. 1992). In Notre Dame Bay the calving margin was grounded on the flanks of the Notre Dame Channel (Shaw 2003). The ice cap shown extending down the Burin Peninsula and onto St. Pierre Bank provides a mechanism for the formation of the Burin Moraine (Fader et al. 1982). Tucker and McCann (1980) argued that the last ice on the Burin Peninsula approached from offshore, and this has been confirmed by multibeam mapping (Shaw et al. 2008). After 14,000 years BP, ice was on land, and retreating as it melted. It lingered a long time in the region and persuasive arguments have been made for extensive glacier ice in Nova Scotia and parts of the adjacent continental shelves as late as the Younger Dryas cold period of 11,000 to 10,000 years BP (King 1993, Stea and Mott 1998).

EVIDENCE OF GLACIAL PROCESSES ON SHELVES

Landforms oriented parallel to former ice flow indicate directions and velocities of motion. For example, in Placentia Bay, Newfoundland, fields of drumlins (Fig. 4A) indicate flow to the southeast. Towards the south, in deeper water, they converge, become more elongated, and are denoted as 'megaflutes' (Evans 2003), demonstrating an accelerated flow of ice down Placentia Bay (Brushett et al. 2007). Flow-transverse landforms indicate positions of former ice margins during retreat. In southern Newfoundland, large, arcuate, lobate submarine moraines (Fig. 4B) formed when retreating glaciers halted at fiord mouths about 14,000 years BP (Shaw et al. 2000, Shaw 2003, Shaw et al. 2008). A large variety of moraines has been observed, including de Geer moraines (Fig. 4C), formed by the incremental retreat of grounded ice.

Olex AS of Norway initiated a remarkable experiment in data collection. Users of Olex sounders store data and send it to Olex who compile it. Bathymetric data sets are created, intermediate in resolution between compilations based on single-beam sounder data and those based on multibeam sonar data. Using Olex data, we recognized a large

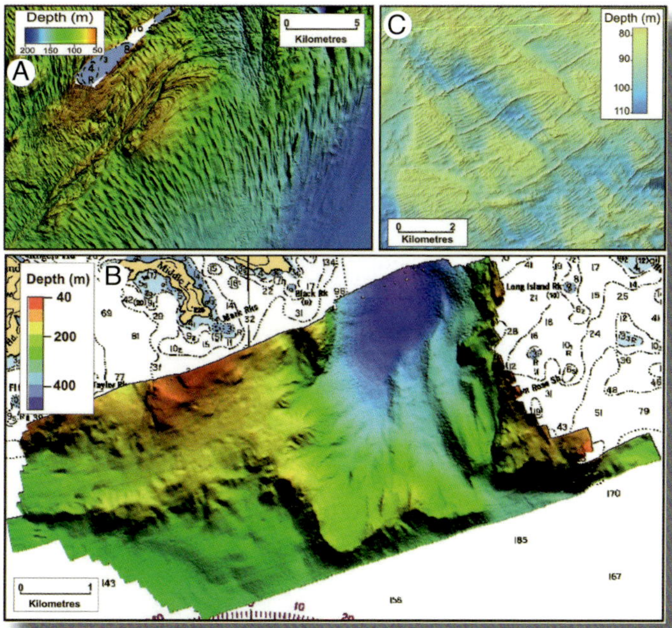

Figure 4. Evidence of glaciation from multibeam surveys: (A) a field of drumlins in Placentia Bay, Newfoundland; (B) a fiord-mouth moraine at the entrance to Bay d'Espoir, Newfoundland; and (C) de Geer moraines on German Bank, Nova Scotia.

area of anomalous bathymetry on the northeast Newfoundland Shelf (Shaw et al. 2012) that had attracted interest many years earlier (Warren 1976). Large blocks of stacked till (Fig. 5) have been transported and deformed. Given the very low gradients involved, glaciotectonism is the most likely process that can account for this process.

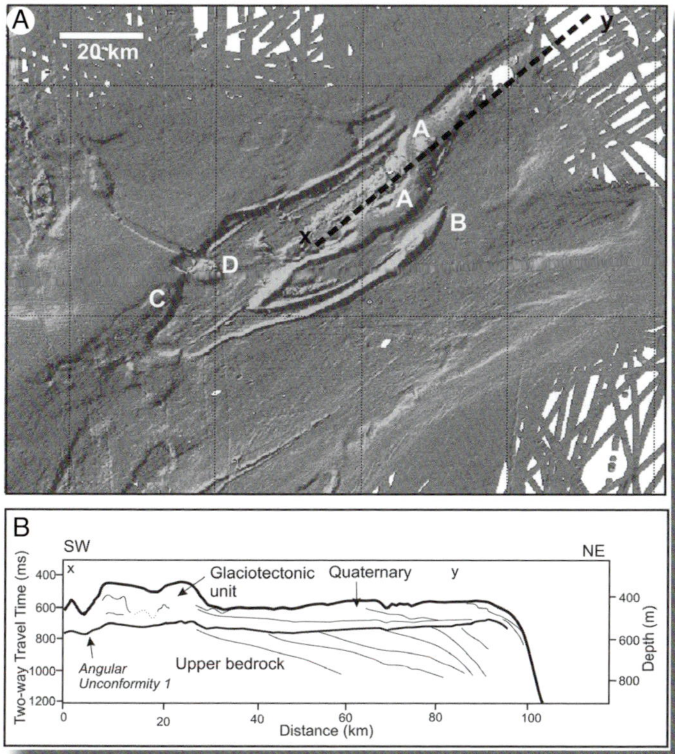

Figure 5. Evidence of glaciotectonism on the northeast Newfoundland Shelf as observed using Olex bathymetric data: (A) block A has been deformed, transported, and thrust over Quaternary sediments, and block B has left in its wake a 100 m-deep trench flanked by 90 m-high berms; these movements created a 150 m-high escarpment (C) extending 110 km along the flank of the Notre Dame glacial trough, and block D moved by gravity alone (not by ice). (B) Air-gun seismic cross-section showing subsurface features and the glaciotectonically-deformed Quaternary sediments on the left; the location of the cross-section, which extends beyond the image to the continental slope, is indicated by the dashed black line in (A).

SEA-LEVEL CHANGES

Sea-level Curves

From the 1850s onwards, researchers investigating the history of late and post glacial relative sea-level change in Atlantic Canada observed that tilted raised shorelines indicated regional variations in sea-level history from which the locations of greatest ice-loading might be inferred (Grant 1977). With the advent of radiocarbon dating, the ages of raised beaches could be ascertained. By dating collections of shells from terrestrial sites researchers were able to plot elevation against age, and create sea-level curves that showed the fall of relative sea level at particular locations (e.g., Grant 1989; Fig. 6). These falls were attributed to crustal rebound following deglaciation. As Grant (1989) and others demonstrated, a line could be drawn across Atlantic Canada, south of which raised beaches did not exist. Offshore, however, researchers identified a widespread postglacial lowstand of 110-120 m on the continental shelves (cf., Fader

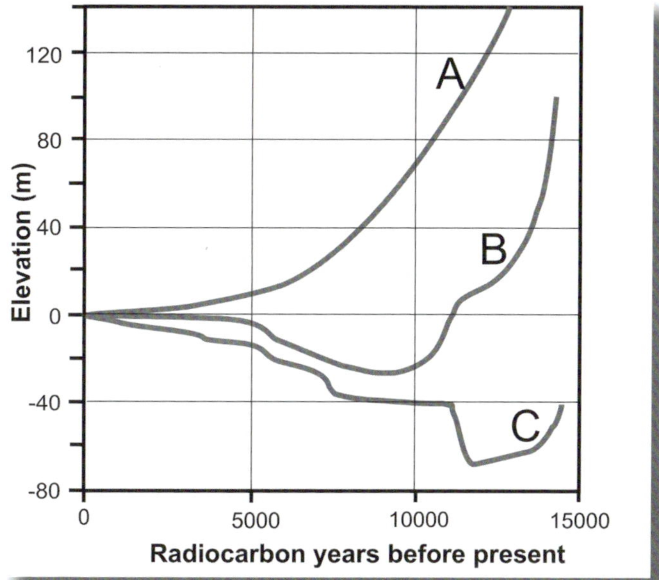

Figure 6. Three sea-level records illustrating the diversity of relative sea-level changes in Atlantic Canada: (A) northern Newfoundland (Grant 1989), dominated by crustal rebound; (B) St. George's Bay, Newfoundland (Bell et al. 2003), a type of curve common in Atlantic Canada, showing a postglacial sea level lowstand; and (C) the Halifax area showing near-continuous relative sea-level rise following an early fall (Stea et al. 1994).

1989). These apparent disparities were resolved by Quinlan and Beaumont (1981, 1982) who used crustal modelling to define four classes of relative sea-level history: (1) falling continuously; (2) dropping below the modern level before rising once more; (3) always below the modern level, but dropping for a time to a lowstand, then rising; and (4) always rising. The theory of glacio-isostasy explained these variations (cf., Peltier 1998). Collecting empirical data to ascertain sea-level histories below modern sea levels demanded new approaches. Cores from salt marshes could be used to track the rise of sea level, a task that was given rigour by the technique of using Foraminifera to determine former high water levels (cf., Scott and Medioli 1980). Submerged salt marsh and estuarine deposits identified offshore by geophysical surveys were dated, leading to a sea-level curve for the Halifax area (Forbes et al. 1991) that evolved with the addition of new data (Shaw et al. 1993, Stea et al. 1994, Edgecombe et al. 1999; Fig. 6).

Determining maximum sea-level lowering has been one of the more difficult tasks in sea-level reconstruction (Fader 1989). In St. George's Bay, Newfoundland, deltas formed 25 m below modern sea level during the postglacial sea-level lowstand (Shaw and Forbes 1990, 1992; Forbes et al. 1993). AMS radiocarbon dating showed that they formed ca. 9,000 years BP (Bell et al. 2003; Fig. 6) when sea level was lowest in the Gulf of St. Lawrence (Fig. 7; Shaw et al. 2002). Shaw and Forbes (1995) recognized similar submerged deltas across southern Newfoundland. Parkes et al. (2002) did not have evidence of submerged deltas, but had sufficient evidence to delineate a -43 m postglacial sea-level minimum at Charlottetown, Prince Edward Island. For comparison, Josenhans et al.

Figure 7. Palaeogeography 9,000 years BP. Large islands on the continental shelves are shrinking in extent as sea level rises. Concurrently, falling sea levels (due to land uplift outpacing sea-level rise) have connected Prince Edward Island with the mainland. In the north where land uplift dominates, sea levels remain high at this time so that the northern tip of Newfoundland is submerged.

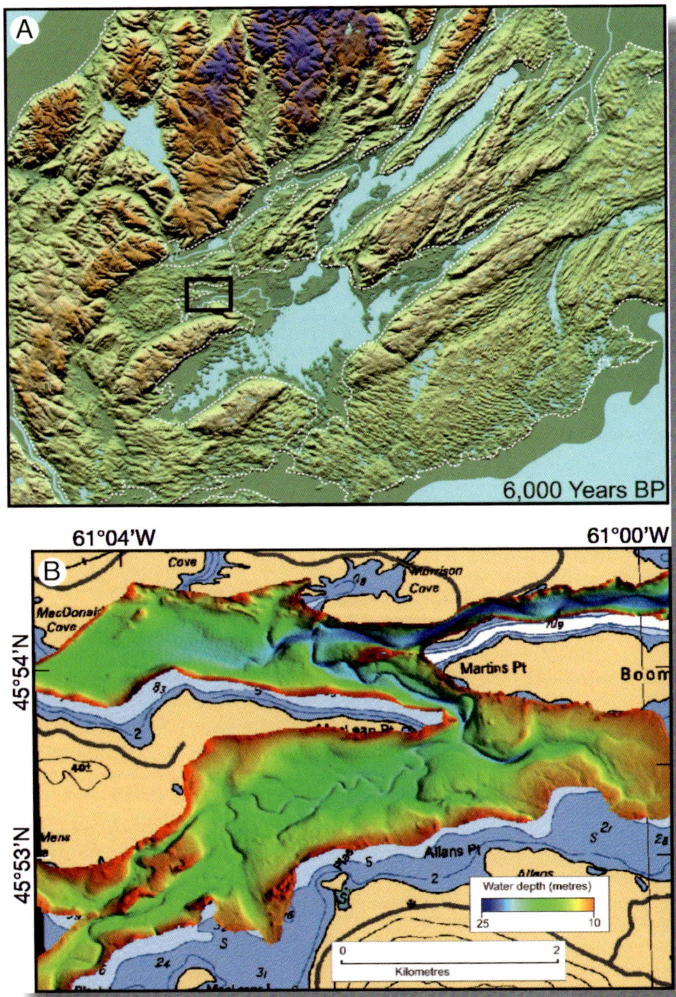

Figure 8. Sea-level change in the Bras d'Or Lakes, Nova Scotia: (A) 6,000 years BP with present shoreline shown in dashed white line, and rectangle showing area of (B); (B) multibeam bathymetry showing submerged river channels in Denys Basin.

(1997) showed that the postglacial sea-level lowstand on the continental shelf of British Columbia reached the extreme depth of 153 m below modern sea level.

Great steps have been taken in recent years to advance geodynamic modelling, a technique that allows sea-level histories to be reconstructed

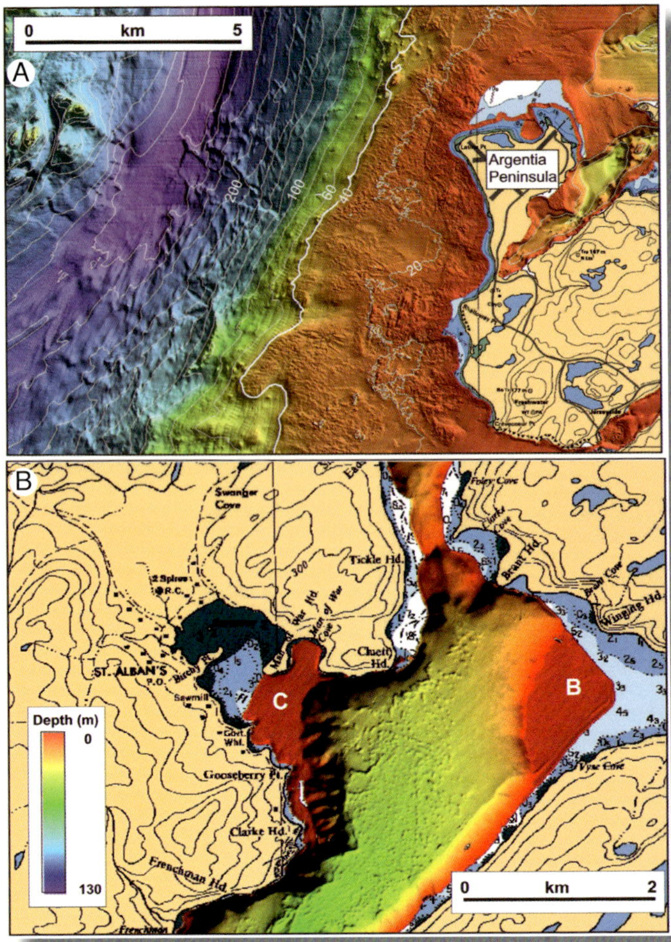

Figure 9. Multibeam imagery from Placentia Bay and Bay d'Espoir, Newfoundland: (A) Multibeam imagery from the Argentia area, Placentia Bay, showing an extensive wave-cut platform eroded into glacial sediments (notes: sea floor below a depth of ca. 35 m retains its original morphology, the lowstand was slightly shallower, as erosion occurred a distance below the low water mark; isobaths given in metres); and (B) Multibeam bathymetry from the head of Bay d'Espoir, a submerged delta at B and a wave-cut submerged platform incised into glaciomarine sediments at C.

at any location (cf., Peltier 2004). Efforts to understand sea-level change in high resolution (Shaw and Ceman 1999) yielded evidence of fluctuating rates of sea-level rise over the past 3,000 years.

Palaeogeography

Early reconstructions of the postglacial geography of Atlantic Canada showed large islands on the shelves (e.g., Dyke and Prest 1987). With the benefit of computers and GIS systems, new sea-level curves, and access to computer models of glacio-isostasy (Peltier 1998), it became possible in the late 1990s to make improved reconstructions (e.g., Shaw et al. 2002). Figure 7 shows Atlantic Canada at ca. 9,000 years BP. Grand Bank southeast of Newfoundland and Sable Island remain emergent, much shrunken from their size in previous millennia. By contrast, emergent areas around Prince Edward Island, the Magdalen Islands, and Cape Breton Island have reached their greatest extent. Some large embayments were disconnected from the ocean when sea level was lower, including Bedford Basin in Halifax Harbour (Miller et al. 1982, Shaw et al. 2009). A reconstruction of the Bras d'Or Lakes ca. 6,000 years BP is shown in Figure 8A.

Evidence of Submerged Landscapes in Multibeam Sonar Data

The rapidity of sea-level change, high wave and current levels in exposed areas, and the brevity of lowstands tended to reduce the probability that coastal landforms would be formed and preserved during the postglacial transgression (Shaw 2005). In some situations an erosional terrace may indicate the extent of postglacial sea-level lowering, and along the south coasts of Newfoundland submerged early Holocene deltas exist in fiords at depths of 10 to 30 m (Fig. 9; Shaw and Forbes 1990). The optimum situation within which to find well-preserved shorelines is where large coastal lakes existed for many thousands of years before being connected to the ocean by rising sea levels. Good examples are Bedford Basin in Halifax Harbour and the Bras d'Or Lakes (Fig. 8B) in Nova Scotia (Shaw et al. 2009).

THE BIO CONTRIBUTION AND FUTURE DIRECTIONS

BIO scientists have greatly contributed to the understanding of glacial processes and sea-level history, primarily because of access to the vessels and equipment necessary for the conduct of research on Canada's inhospitable continental shelves. The research outlined in this paper was rarely curiosity-driven, but was determined by a range of issues that changed over time and included, for example, understanding the impacts of rising sea levels, evaluating hazards to offshore petroleum developments, assessing mineral potential, and even responding to national disasters, notably the crash of Swissair Flight 111 off St. Margaret's Bay, Nova Scotia, in 1998. One of the unforeseen impacts of the sea-level research was the application of the data to biological questions, such as, for example, the colonization of Atlantic Canada by freshwater fishes (Curry 2007).

This paper is too brief to provide a comprehensive account of the BIO contribution. Perhaps the greatest debt is owed to those pioneers of the 1960s and 1970s who laid the groundwork for later researchers. While advances continue to be made – notably on the upper continental slopes where researchers are learning more about the LGM and preceding glacial and interglacial periods – research is nevertheless being increasingly focussed on applied topics. Large numbers of senior researchers are leaving BIO and not being replaced. It is clear that the pace of advance made over the past 50 years is not being maintained. SEAMAP, a project to systematically map Canada's offshore lands (Pickrill 2014), might have made a difference, but this interdepartmental plan was not embraced in Canada, although adopted enthusiastically elsewhere, notably in Ireland (Dorschel et al. 2010). However, researchers supportive of the SEAMAP concept were nevertheless able to map large areas such as the Bay of Fundy (Todd and Shaw 2014) and Placentia Bay with funding from Canada's Ocean Action Plan.

Arguably the greatest advances to be made in the next few decades might come from a renewed effort to systematically map the Canadian continental shelves, an effort that would require a renewal of the fruitful partnership between the GSC and the Department of Fisheries and Oceans Canada. With specific regard to sea-level studies, at a time of concern about climate change impacts it is increasingly important to determine ongoing trends in coastal areas, and in particular, to disentangle the signals of crustal motion from those of a eustatic nature. The tide gauge program operated by the CHS remains valuable in this respect.

ACKNOWLEDGEMENTS

My grateful thanks to my colleagues in the Geological Survey of Canada who collaborated on research, participated in discussions, and reviewed my work over the years. Special gratitude is due to C.L. Amos, R.C. Courtney, G.B. Fader, D.L. Forbes, H.W. Josenhans, C.F.M. Lewis, M.Z. Li, D.R. Parrott, D.J.W. Piper, D.P. Potter, J.P.M Syvitski, R.B. Taylor, and B.J. Todd. Thanks are also due to the skilled technical support staff who made marine surveys possible, notably K.A. Asprey, A.S. Atkinson, D.E. Beaver, B. Chapman, D. Frobel, P. Girouard, F. Jodrey, L. Johnston, D. Locke, R. Murphy, A. Robertson, and B. Wile. The expertise of masters and crews of research vessels CSS *Baffin*, CSS *Dawson*, CSS *F.G. Creed*, CSS *Hart*, CSS *Hudson*, CSS *Navicula*, CSS *Matthew*, CSS *Shamook*, and CSS *Parizeau* are acknowledged. The research described here was facilitated by the support and encouragement of managers, particularly R. Pickrill. Hydrographers of the Canadian Hydrographic Service collaborated with the GSC, with M. Lamplugh and G. Costello being worthy of mention. This paper was reviewed by D.L. Forbes and G.D.M. Cameron, and edited with care by C.F.M. Lewis and D.N. Nettleship.

REFERENCES

Bamber, J.L., D.J. Vaughan, and I. Joughin. 2000. Widespread complex flow in the interior of the Antarctic Ice Sheet. Science 287: 1,248-1,250.

Bell, T., D.G.E. Liverman, M. Batterson, and K. Sheppard. 2001. Late Wisconsinan stratigraphy and chronology of southern St. George's Bay, Newfoundland: a re-appraisal. Canadian Journal of Earth Sciences 38: 851-869.

Bell, T., M.J. Batterson, D.G.E. Liverman, and J. Shaw. 2003. A new late-glacial sea-level record for St. George's Bay, Newfoundland. Canadian Journal of Earth Sciences 40: 1,953-1,970.

Bonifay, D. and D.J.W. Piper. 1988. Probable late Wisconsinan ice margin on the upper continental slope off St. Pierre Bank, eastern Canada. Canadian Journal of Earth Sciences 25: 853-865.

Boulton, G.S., P. Dongelmans, M. Punkari, and M. Broadgate. 2001. Palaeoglaciology of an ice sheet through a glacial cycle: the European ice sheet through the Weichselian. Quaternary Science Reviews 20: 591-625.

Brushett, D., T. Bell, M.J. Batterson, and J. Shaw. 2007. Ice-flow history of Placentia Bay, Newfoundland: multibeam seabed mapping. Pages 215-228 *in* Current Research, Newfoundland and Labrador Department of Natural Resources, Geological Survey of Canada, Report 07-1, Ottawa, ON.

Cumming, E.H., A.E. Aksu, and P.J. Mudie. 1992. Late Quaternary glacial and sedimentary history of Bonavista Bay, northeast Newfoundland. Canadian Journal of Earth Sciences 29: 222-235.

Currie, L.A. 2004. The remarkable metrological history of radiocarbon dating [II]. Journal of Research of the National Institute of Standards and Technology 109: 185-217.

Curry, R.A. 2007. Late glacial impacts on dispersal and colonization of Atlantic Canada and Maine by freshwater fishes. Quaternary Research 67: 225-233.

Dorschel, B., A.J. Wheeler, X. Monteys, and K. Kerbruggen. 2010. Atlas of the deepwater seabed: Ireland. Springer, Dordrecht, The Netherlands.

Drapeau, G. and L.H. King. 1972. Surficial geology of the Yarmouth-Browns Bank map area. Marine Sciences Paper 2, Geological Survey of Canada Paper 72-24, Ottawa, ON.

Dyke, A.S. and V.K. Prest. 1987. Late Wisconsinan and Holocene history of the Laurentide Ice Sheet. Géographie physique et Quaternaire 41: 237-263.

Dyke, A.S., J.T. Andrews, P.U. Clark, J.H. England, G.H. Miller, J. Shaw, and J.J. Veillette. 2002. The Laurentide and Innuitian ice sheets during the last glacial maximum. Quaternary Science Reviews 21: 9-31.

Edgecombe, R.B., D.B. Scott, and G.B. Fader. 1999. New data from Halifax Harbour: palaeoenvironment and a new Holocene sea-level curve for the inner Scotian Shelf. Canadian Journal of Earth Sciences 36: 805-817.

Evans, D.J.A. 2003. Glacial Landsystems. Arnold, London, England.

Fader, G.B.J. 1989. A late Pleistocene low sea-level stand of the southeast Canadian offshore. Pages 71-103 *in* Late Quaternary Sea-Level Correlation and Applications (D.B. Scott, P.A. Pirazolli, and C.A. Honig, Eds.). Kluwer Academic Publishers, Dordrecht, The Netherlands.

Fader, G.B.J., L.H. King, and B. MacLean. 1977. Surficial geology of the eastern Gulf of Maine and Bay of Fundy. Marine Sciences Paper 19, Geological Survey of Canada Paper 76-17, Ottawa, ON.

Fader, G.B., L.H. King, and H.W. Josenhans. 1982. Surficial geology of the Laurentian Channel and the western Grand Banks of Newfoundland. Marine Sciences Paper 21, Geological Survey of Canada Paper 81-22, Ottawa, ON.

Fader, G.B.J., B. MacLean, H.W. Josenhans, and S.M. Blasco. 2014. Seabed sediment mapping at the Bedford Institute of Oceanography: from single beam to multibeam. Pages 191-199 *in* Voyage of Discovery: Fifty Years of Marine Research at Canada's Bedford Institute of Oceanography (D.N. Nettleship, D.C. Gordon, C.F.M. Lewis, and M.P. Latremouille, Eds.). Bedford Institute of Oceanography-Oceans Association, Dartmouth, NS.

Forbes, D.L., R. Boyd, and J. Shaw. 1991. Late Quaternary sedimentation and sea level changes on the inner Scotian Shelf. Continental Shelf Research 11: 1,155-1,179.

Forbes, D.L., J. Shaw, and B.G. Eddy. 1993. Late-Quaternary sedimentation and the postglacial sea-level minimum in Port-au-Port Bay and vicinity, west Newfoundland. Atlantic Geology 29: 1-26.

Gipp, M.R. and D.J.W. Piper. 1989. Chronology of Late Wisconsinan glaciation, Emerald Basin, Scotian Shelf. Canadian Journal of Earth Sciences 26: 333-335.

Grant, D.R. 1977. Glacial style and ice limits, the Quaternary stratigraphic record, and changes of land and ocean level in the Atlantic Provinces, Canada. Géographie physique et Quaternaire 31: 247-260.

Grant, D.R. 1989. Quaternary geology of the Atlantic Appalachian region of Canada. Pages 393-440 *in* Quaternary Geology of Canada and Greenland (R.J. Fulton, Ed.). Geology of Canada, No. 1, Geological Survey of Canada, Ottawa, ON.

Hughes, T.J. 1998. Ice Sheets. Oxford University Press, Oxford, England.

Huppertz, T.J. and D.J.W. Piper. 2009. The influence of shelf-crossing glaciation on continental slope sedimentation, Flemish Pass, eastern Canadian continental margin. Marine Geology 265: 67-85.

Hutchins, R.W., D.L. McKeown, and L.H. King. 1976. A deep tow high-resolution seismic system for continental shelf mapping. Geoscience Canada 3: 95-100.

Josenhans, H.W. and S. Lehman. 1999. Quaternary stratigraphy and glacial history of the Gulf of St. Lawrence, Canada. Canadian Journal of Earth Sciences 36: 1,327-1,345.

Josenhans, H.W., D. Fedje, R. Pienitz, and J. Southon. 1997. Early humans and rapidly changing Holocene sea levels in the Queen Charlotte Islands-Hecate Strait, British Columbia, Canada. Science 227: 71-74.

King, L.H. 1969. Submarine end moraines and associated deposits of the Scotian Shelf. Geological Society of America Bulletin 80: 83-96.

King, L.H. 1970. Surficial geology of the Halifax-Sable Island area. Marine Sciences Branch Paper 1, Department of Energy, Mines and Resources, Ottawa, ON.

King, L.H. 1993. Proposed Younger Dryas glaciation of the eastern Scotian Shelf. Canadian Journal of Earth Sciences 31: 401-417.

King, L.H. 1996. Late Wisconsinan ice retreat from the Scotian Shelf. Geological Society of America Bulletin 108: 1,056-1,067.

King, L.H. and G.B.J. Fader. 1986. Wisconsinan glaciation of the Atlantic continental shelf of southeast Canada. Geological Survey of Canada Bulletin 363, Ottawa, ON.

King, L.H. and G.B.J. Fader. 1988. Late Wisconsinan ice on the Scotian Shelf. Geological Survey of Canada, Open File 1972, Ottawa, ON.

Liverman, D. and T. Bell. 1996. Late Quaternary glacial and glaciomarine sediments in Southern St. George's Bay. Pages 29-40 *in* Current Research, Newfoundland and Labrador Department of Natural Resources, Geological Survey, Report 96-1, St. John's, NL.

Locat, J. 1977. L'émersion des terres dans la région de Baie-des-Sables/Trois-Pistoles, Québec. Géographie physique et Quaternaire 31: 297-306.

Loncarevic, B.D., R.C. Courtney, G.B.J. Fader, P.S Giles, D.J.W Piper, G. Costello, J.E. Hughes Clark, and R.R. Stea. 1994. Sonography of a glaciated continental shelf. Geology 22: 747-750.

MacDonald, F.H., J.C. Gosse, and G. Yank. 2003. Glacial geology and chronology of the Peggy's Cove region. Pages A70-A71 *in* Program and Abstracts, Canadian Quaternary Association (CANQUA)/Canadian Geomorphological Research Group Meeting, Halifax, NS.
MacLean, B. and L.H. King. 1971. Surficial geology of the Banquereau and Misaine Bank map area. Marine Sciences Paper 3, Geological Survey of Canada Paper 71-52, Ottawa, ON.
MacLean, B., G.B.J. Fader, and L.H. King. 1977. Surficial geology of Canso bank and adjacent areas. Marine Sciences Paper 20, Geological Survey of Canada Paper 76-15, Ottawa, ON.
McKeown, D.L., P.G. Simpkin, G.B.J. Fader, D.R. Parrott, and D.C. Mosher. 2014. The Huntec Deep Tow Seismic System: a revolution in high resolution profiling. Pages 337-341 *in* Voyage of Discovery: Fifty Years of Marine Research at Canada's Bedford Institute of Oceanography (D.N. Nettleship, D.C. Gordon, C.F.M. Lewis, and M.P. Latremouille, Eds.). Bedford Institute of Oceanography-Oceans Association, Dartmouth, NS.
Miller, A.A.L., P.J. Mudie, and D.B. Scott. 1982. Holocene History of Bedford Basin, Nova Scotia: foraminifera, dinoflagellate and pollen records. Canadian Journal of Earth Sciences 19: 2,342-2,367.
Mosher, D.C., D.J.W. Piper, G. Vilks, A.E. Aksu, and G.B.J Fader. 1989. Evidence for Wisconsinan glaciations in the Verrill Canyon area, Scotian Slope. Quaternary Research 31: 27-40.
Parkes, G.S., D.L. Forbes, and L. Ketch. 2002. Sea-level rise. Supporting Document 1 *in* McCulloch, M.M., D.L. Forbes, R.W. Shaw, and CCAF Team. Coastal impacts of climate change and sea-level rise on Prince Edward Island (D.L. Forbes and R.W. Shaw, Eds.). Geological Survey of Canada, Open File 4261, Ottawa, ON.
Peltier, W.R. 1998. Postglacial variations in the level of the sea: implications for climate dynamics and solid earth geophysics. Reviews of Geophysics 36: 603-690.
Peltier, W.R. 2004. Global glacial isostasy and the surface of the ice-age Earth: the ICE-5G (VM2) model and GRACE. Annual Review of Earth and Planetary Science 32: 111-149.
Pickrill, R.A., B.J. Todd, S.J. Smith, J.V. Barrie, and K.W. Conway. 2014. Marine habitat mapping in Canada's oceans. Pages 185-190 *in* Voyage of Discovery: Fifty Years of Marine Research at Canada's Bedford Institute of Oceanography (D.N. Nettleship, D.C. Gordon, C.F.M. Lewis, and M.P. Latremouille, Eds.). Bedford Institute of Oceanography-Oceans Association, Dartmouth, NS.
Piper, D.J.W. and A. Macdonald. 2001. Timing, position of late Wisconsinan ice margins on the upper slope seaward of Laurentian Channel. Géographie physique et Quaternaire 55: 131-140.
Quinlan, G. and C. Beaumont. 1981. A comparison of observed and theoretical postglacial relative sea level in Atlantic Canada. Canadian Journal of Earth Sciences 18: 1,146-1,163.
Quinlan, G. and C. Beaumont. 1982. The deglaciation of Atlantic Canada as reconstructed from the postglacial sea-level record. Canadian Journal of Earth Sciences 19: 2,232-2,246.
Rodrigues, C.G., J.A. Ceman, and G. Vilks. 1993. Late Quaternary paleoceanography of the deep and intermediate water masses off Gaspé Peninsula, Gulf of St. Lawrence: foraminiferal evidence. Canadian Journal of Earth Sciences 30: 1,390-1,403.
Schnikter, D., D.F. Belknap, T.S. Bacchus, J.K. Friez, B.A. Lusardi, and D.M. Popek. 2001. Deglaciation of the Gulf of Maine. Geological Society of America Special Paper 351: 9-34.
Scott, D.B. and F.S. Medioli. 1980. Quantitative studies of marsh foraminiferal distributions in Nova Scotia: implications for sea level studies. Cushman Foundation for Foraminiferal Research, Special Publication 17: 1-59.
Shaw, J. 2003. Submarine moraines in Newfoundland coastal waters: implications for the deglaciation of Newfoundland and adjacent areas. Quaternary International 99-100: 115-134.
Shaw, J. 2005. Geomorphic evidence of postglacial terrestrial environments on Atlantic Canadian continental shelves. Géographie physique et Quaternaire 59: 141-154.
Shaw, J. and D.L. Forbes. 1990. Late-Quaternary sedimentation in St. George's Bay, southwest Newfoundland: acoustic stratigraphy and surficial deposits. Canadian Journal of Earth Sciences 27: 964-983.
Shaw, J. and D.L. Forbes. 1992. Barriers, barrier platforms, and spillover deposits in St. George's Bay, Newfoundland: paraglacial sedimentation on the flanks of a deep coastal basin. Marine Geology 105: 119-140.
Shaw, J. and D.L. Forbes. 1995. The post-glacial relative sea-level lowstand in Newfoundland. Canadian Journal of Earth Sciences 32: 1,308-1,330.
Shaw, J. and J. Ceman. 1999. Salt-marsh aggradation in response to late Holocene sea-level rise at Amherst Point, Nova Scotia. The Holocene 9: 439-451.
Shaw, J., R.B. Taylor, and D.L Forbes. 1993. Impact of the Holocene transgression on the Atlantic coastline of Nova Scotia. Géographie physique et Quaternaire 47: 221-238.
Shaw, J., D.R. Grant, J.-P. Guilbault, T.W. Anderson, and D.R. Parrott. 2000. Submarine and onshore end moraines in southern Newfoundland: implications for the history of late Wisconsinan ice retreat. Boreas 29: 295-314.
Shaw, J., P. Gareau, and R.C. Courtney. 2002. Paleogeography of Atlantic Canada 13-0 kyr. Quaternary Science Reviews 21: 1,861-1,878.
Shaw, J., D.J.W. Piper, G.B.J. Fader, E.L. King, B.J. Todd, T. Bell, M.J. Batterson, and D.J.E. Liverman. 2006. A conceptual model of the deglaciation of Atlantic Canada. Quaternary Science Reviews 25: 2,059-2,081.
Shaw, J., B.J. Todd, D. Brushett, D.R. Parrott, and T. Bell. 2008. Late Wisconsinan glacial landsystems on Atlantic Canadian shelves: new evidence from multibeam and single-beam sonar data. Boreas 38: 146-159.
Shaw, J., G.B.J. Fader, and R.B Taylor. 2009. Submerged early Holocene coastal and terrestrial landforms on the inner shelves of Atlantic Canada. Quaternary International 206: 24-34.
Shaw, J., D.J.W. Piper, T. Skulski, M. Lamplugh, A. Craft, A. Roy, and R.C. Courtney. 2012. New evidence for widespread mass transport on the Northeast Newfoundland Shelf revealed by Olex single-beam echo sounding. Geo-Marine Letters 32: 5-15. doi 10.1007/s00367-011-0233-3.
Stea, R.R. 2004. The Appalachian glacier complex in Maritime Canada. Pages 213–232 *in* Quaternary Glaciations - Extent and Chronology, Part II. (J. Ehlers, and P.J. Gibbard, Eds.). Developments in Quaternary Science 2b. Elsevier, Amsterdam, The Netherlands.
Stea, R.R. and R.J. Mott. 1998. Deglaciation of Nova Scotia: stratigraphy and chronology of lake sediment cores and buried organic sections. Géographie physique et Quaternaire 52: 3-21.
Stea, R.R., G.B.J. Fader, and R. Boyd. 1992. Quaternary seismic stratigraphy of the inner shelf region, Eastern Shore, Nova Scotia. Pages 179-188 *in* Current Research, Part D. Geological Survey of Canada, Paper 92-1D, Ottawa, ON.
Stea, R.R., R. Boyd, G.B.J. Fader, R.C. Courtney, D.B. Scott, and S.S. Pecore. 1994. Morphology and seismic stratigraphy of the inner continental shelf off Nova Scotia, Canada: evidence for a -65 m lowstand between 11,650 and 11,250 C^{14} yr B.P. Marine Geology 117: 135-154.
Stea, R.R., R. Boyd, O. Costello, G.B.J. Fader, and D.B. Scott. 1996. Deglaciation of the inner Scotian Shelf, Nova Scotia: correlation of terrestrial and marine glacial events. Pages 77-101 *in* Late Quaternary Palaeoceanography of the North Atlantic margin (J.T. Andrews, W.E.N. Austin, H. Bergsten and A.E. Jennings, Eds.). Geological Society Special Publication No. 111, The Geological Society, London, England.
Stuiver, M. and P.J. Reimer. 1993. Extended ^{14}C database and revised CALIB radiocarbon calibration program. Radiocarbon 35: 315-330.
Todd, B.J. and J. Shaw. 2014. Discovering the seafloor of the Bay of Fundy. Pages 231-235 *in* Voyage of Discovery: Fifty Years of Marine Research at Canada's Bedford Institute of Oceanography (D.N. Nettleship, D.C. Gordon, C.F.M. Lewis, and M.P. Latremouille, Eds.). Bedford Institute of Oceanography-Oceans Association, Dartmouth, NS.
Tucker, C.M. and S.B. McCann. 1980. Quaternary events on the Burin Peninsula, Newfoundland, and the islands of St. Pierre and Miquelon, France. Canadian Journal of Earth Sciences 17: 1,462-1,479.
Warren, J.S. 1976. The morphology of two transverse channels on the Northeast Newfoundland Shelf. Maritime Sediments 12: 19-32.

39. BEDROCK STUDIES OF THE BAFFIN ISLAND SHELF AND HUDSON STRAIT: A TECHNOLOGICAL AND SCIENTIFIC ADVENTURE

Brian MacLean*, Graham L. Williams, and George A. Fowler

SUMMARY

During the 1970s and 1980s, engineers at the Bedford Institute of Oceanography (BIO) developed a series of underwater rock core drills that have been used to investigate the bedrock geology of Hudson Strait and the continental shelf east of Baffin Island. The capability of recovering rock cores in water depths as great as 900 m opened new vistas to the mysteries of the type, ages, and petroleum potential of rocks below the sea floor. It is now known that Paleozoic (472 to 444 million years old) rocks underlie most of Hudson Strait and predominantly late Cretaceous (100 to 66 million years old) rocks, with potential as a source of hydrocarbons, underlie the northeastern Baffin Shelf. The samples recovered during the drilling programs continue to provide an invaluable resource for research and reveal geological surprises. The benefits of this work suggest that a renewed drilling program would be a worthy successor to the pioneer efforts of BIO more than four decades ago, especially in an era of increased interest in offshore exploration for hydrocarbons.

Key words: rock core drills, bedrock cores, Baffin Shelf, Hudson Strait, dinoflagellate cysts, Cretaceous, Paleozoic.
***E-mail:** Brian.MacLean@NRCan-RNCan.gc.ca

When the Bedford Institute of Oceanography (BIO) opened in 1962, very little was known about the rocks underlying the Baffin Island continental shelf and Hudson Strait. It was thought that rocks younger than the Precambrian metamorphic and igneous rocks that compose most of Baffin Island would be present on the Baffin Shelf, but there were no samples. However, thanks to the development of a series of rock core drills at BIO, bedrock cores were later collected that provided insight into the geology of this region.

Early geological studies in the region were carried out by Robert Bell who, in 1884-85, examined the shoreline geology while on a voyage through Hudson Strait into Hudson Bay. Albert Low undertook geological studies in Labrador in 1894-95, and in 1903-04 the crew of the *Neptune* investigated the geology of the Hudson Bay-Southampton Island region (Vodden 1992). Systematic scientific studies of the offshore began with hydrographic surveys which included charting of Hudson Bay by CSS *Acadia* in 1913. Geological studies of marine areas using modern geological and geophysical techniques started in the mid-1960s with echo sounding, seismic, magnetic, and gravity surveys conducted from CSS *Hudson,* CCGS *d'Iberville* and CCGS *Labrador*. These latter investigations included geophysical studies in eastern Hudson Strait (Grant and Manchester 1970) and on the southeastern Baffin Shelf (Grant 1975).

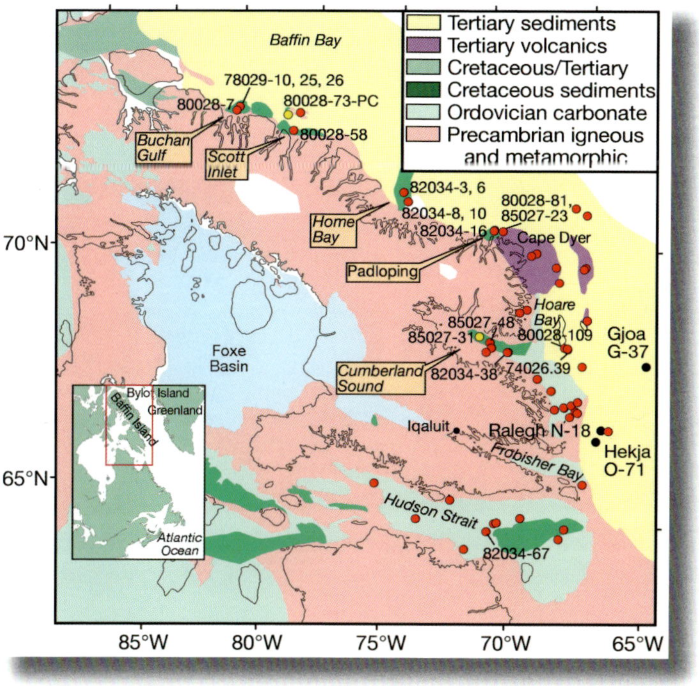

Figure 1. Map showing the main bedrock units in Hudson Strait and on the Baffin Shelf. Red dots identify successful rock core drill localities, black dots mark petroleum industry exploratory well locations and yellow dots indicate where semi-consolidated bedrock samples were recovered in piston cores. Rock core drill locations cited in Figures 5 and 7 are denoted by cruise and station number. Inset map of eastern Canada shows main map area.

Data from these cruises and additional conventional seismic reflection data and profiles from the newly-developed Huntec deep-towed high-resolution seismic system (Hutchins et al. 1976, McKeown et al. 2014) were utilized in determining sites for the first core holes drilled in 1974 into bedrock on the Baffin Island Shelf (Srivastava 1974, MacLean et al. 1977) with the newly developed BIO underwater electric rock core drill (Fowler and Kingston 1975). These successes led to a further six drilling cruises aboard CSS *Hudson* in the region over the next 11 years. The investigations focussed on sampling and identification of the main bedrock units in Hudson Strait and on the Baffin Island Shelf (Fig. 1). Deep water, strong currents, thick overburden comprising mostly glacial sediments with rock fragments (i.e., till), poor weather, and less precise navigation systems than those now available presented major challenges, but the cores obtained during this time have yielded valuable data and continue to do so.

TECHNOLOGY DEVELOPMENTS AND APPLICATIONS IN THE FIELD

Rock core drills used for bedrock sampling were designed and built by BIO's Metrology Division over two decades. The development of the design of these drills was influenced by the particular geophysical/geological application for which each was intended, innovation, and advances in technology.

Hydrostatic Rock Core Drill

The first drills, developed in the early 1960s, were designed for use on the Mid-Atlantic Ridge to complement geophysical surveys being conducted to confirm and quantify the influence of seafloor spreading in the new theory of plate tectonics. Two operational requirements defined the design of the drills. Firstly, because the ridges were relatively deep (minimum water depth 800 m) for the technological capability of the time, powering the drill was a major challenge which forced the development of a device with an independent power source. Secondly, but on a more positive note, it was anticipated that since the ridges were relatively new in geological terms and the areas had never been glaciated, basaltic bedrock would be exposed. This permitted the design of a relatively small diamond drill coring system with limited bottom penetration that could be deployed from an oceanographic vessel (Brooke and Gilbert 1968).

To overcome the power problem, advantage was taken of the hydrostatic pressure that exists at depth. By allowing high-pressure seawater to flow into an empty reservoir, which had been lowered to the bottom, power could be derived to recover a small 2.5-cm diameter core. The drill eventually became known as the hydrostatic rock core drill. However, the task of creating a fully operational system was extremely difficult and time consuming.

Major obstacles that had to be overcome included the handling of long lengths of neutrally buoyant synthetic rope to ensure that the ship's motion did not contribute to drill rig instability. As the drill was powered by seawater, many of the required hydraulic components had to be adapted to unusual conditions. Using a system that injected soluble oil into the seawater flow alleviated many of the difficulties and provided the necessary power from a standard, positive displacement hydraulic motor.

The elegant innovation that really made the drill work, however, was the creation of a load-sensing automatic download mechanism. Using the pressure at different points in the hydraulic circuit in conjunction with a hydraulic cylinder, the power being consumed by the hydraulic motor was sensed and used to apply the appropriate download to the drill bit for optimum performance. The ability to create down-loading without mass at the top of the drill structure was a great advantage since drill stability on the sea bottom was a continuing concern. While the power to run the system was essentially 'free' because the drill took advantage of ambient water pressure, the reservoirs represented buoyancy and caused rig instability. At the beginning of the project, empty compressed air cylinders were used as reservoirs giving about 7 minutes of running time (Fig. 2A). These were later replaced by large spheres that increased running time to 22 min but negatively affected the drill's centre of gravity.

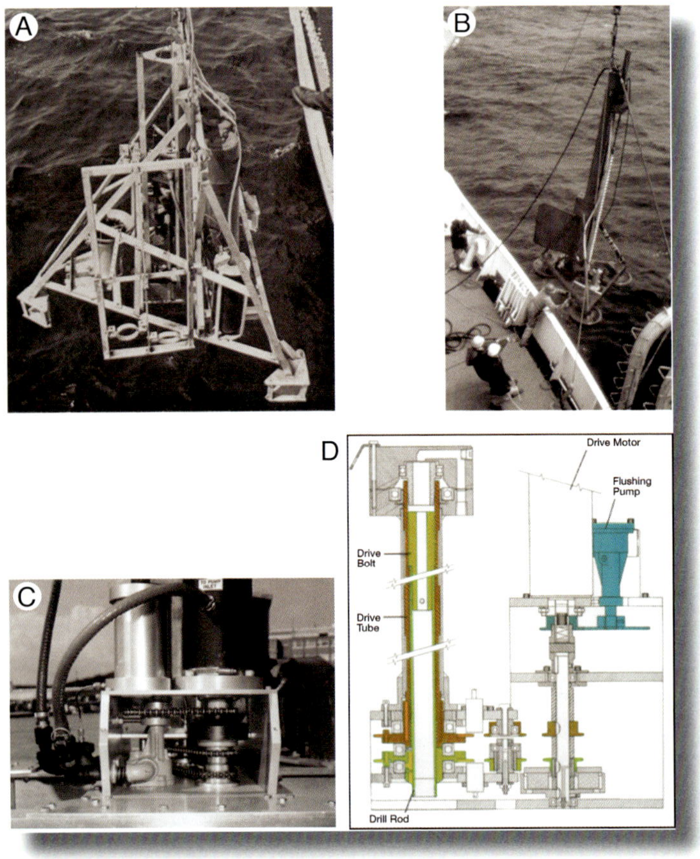

Figure 2. Early rock core drills: (A) an early version of the hydrostatic rock core drill (ca. 1967) - note compressed gas cylinders used as low pressure reservoirs on right of the 2.5-m high frame; (B) Godden electric rock core drill being readied for deployment (ca. 1970); (C) original electric rock core drill drive mechanism layout with (D) cross-sectional view of the internally-threaded 'drive tube' mechanism (ca. 1977).

Throughout the life of the project, the difficulty in controlling and monitoring drill operation on the sea floor was a major limitation. Eventually, some drilling parameters like bit penetration and motor pressure drop were recovered using acoustic telemetry, but the level of received information was limited. Problems aside, various versions of the hydrostatic rock core drill were successfully used during several programs from 1974 to 1985 to obtain valuable bedrock samples that would not have been possible without using much more expensive equipment such as a specialized drill ship.

Electric Rock Core Drill

Success with the hydrostatic rock core drill in deep water spurred an interest in having the same capability for drilling on the continental shelf where operational requirements were quite different. Surficial geology surveys had shown that significant overburden covered the bedrock and some of the rocks were expected to be hard to drill. Thus, the drill would have to possess significant bottom penetration capability and greater power.

Early attempts to develop a usable drill to sample bedrock on the continental shelf included one designed and assembled by C. Godden of the Atlantic Geoscience Centre (Fig. 2B). The Godden drill used a double-walled core barrel and saw limited operation on both the Flemish Cap (Pelletier 1971) and in the high arctic during the *Hudson*-70 voyage. This system was superseded by the BIO underwater electric rock core drill.

Laboratory testing showed that it would be possible to power a diamond drill from the surface through an umbilical cable operating at 440 volts in water depths of 200 m. A mechanism was developed that could operate underwater using the limited control capability of that time. The mechanism was driven by an 'off-the-shelf', 5 HP, 3-phase, deep-well pump motor which also drove a small fixed displacement water pump for bit flushing. Other features were the ability to rotate and extend or retract a threaded and keyed drill barrel, operating much like a nut and bolt, at the base of the drill frame. This enhanced rig stability permitting the use of 6 m long drill barrels (for details of the mechanism, see Fig. 2C).

Unlike the hydrostatic drill, uninterrupted electrical connection was maintained so that the drill's operation could be observed, powered, and controlled from the surface (Fig. 3A), a significant improvement over earlier systems (Fowler and Kingston 1975). Servicing was straightforward, although chilly at times (Figs. 3B and C).

Figure 3. Operating and servicing the electric rock core drill: (A) R. Cassivi remotely controlling the electric rock core drill from the drill console aboard CSS *Hudson*; (B) W. MacKinnon and G. Williams servicing the electric rock core drill; and (C) W. Whiteway and F.Ewing retrieving a drill core from the core barrel of the electric rock core drill.

Initial sea trials were reasonably successful, but the exposed threaded drill barrel proved to be a serious weakness when drilling in tills. This problem was resolved by creating a threaded drive tube enclosed within the drive mechanism so that only the keyway on the barrel was exposed to potential damage (Fig. 2D). This type of drill and later variants, which included an extension of seafloor penetration capability from the original 6 m to 9 m, was employed on several hundred drill stations along Canada's eastern continental shelves from the Bay of Fundy to the high arctic. Core recovery was highly variable, being largely governed by overburden thickness and bedrock type.

Throughout the life of the drilling project, we wanted to drill bedrock in ever deeper water. But reaching these depths was hampered by difficulties associated with handling the long cables, supplying power, and failure of electrical components. However, all of these problems were eventually overcome. The electric drills were deployed using a neutrally buoyant lowering line along with an electrical or umbilical cable which delivered power to the bottom and returned drill operational data. The umbilical cable was rendered buoyant with the addition of mid-water trawl floats (Fig. 4A). Over time, system power was increased to 600 volts with larger diameter conductors to triple operational sampling depths. However, in deeper water or in strong water currents, umbilical handling was still difficult and time consuming, sometimes making the drill rig unstable.

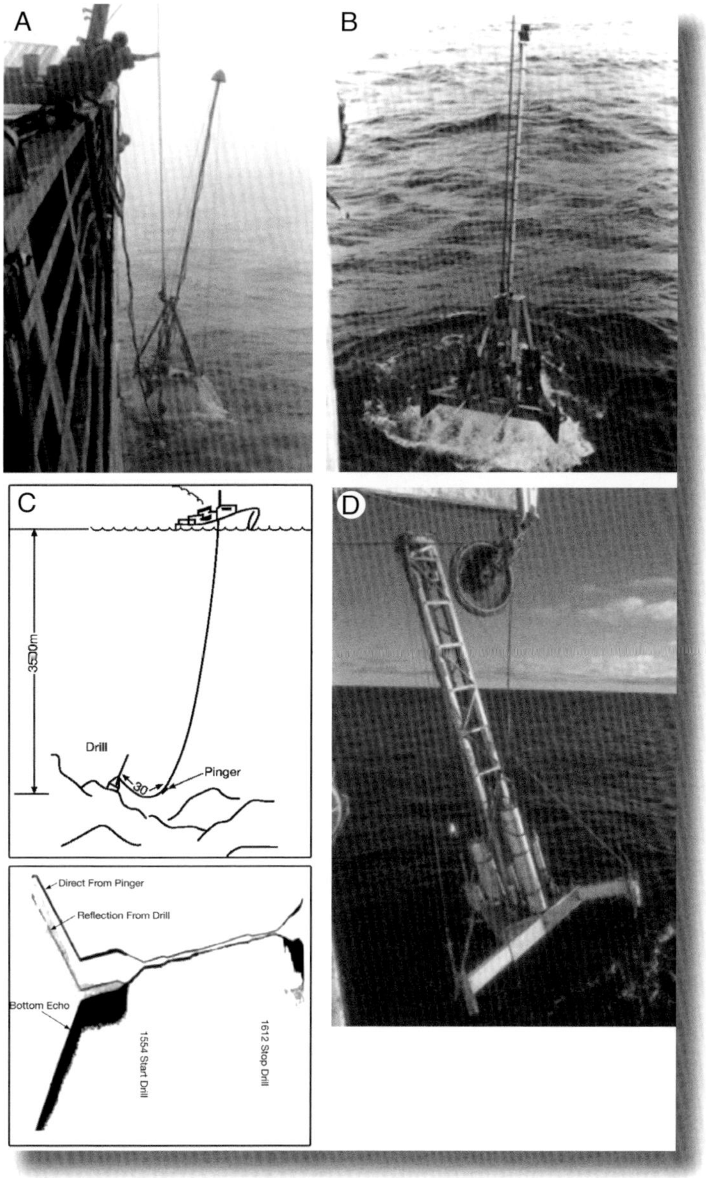

Figure 4. Drilling in deeper water: (A) early version of electric rock core drill – note the slack umbilical cable with attached trawl floats to render it neutrally buoyant (ca. 1972); (B) deep-water version of the electric rock core drill (ca. 1981) - note the single handling cable; (C, upper) sketch of CSS *Hudson* operating the deep-water electric rock core drill; (C, lower) direct and bottom-reflected sound waves from a pinger on the drill cable are recorded on a precision graphic recorder and reveal the position of the cable relative to seafloor; and (D) 6-m Nordco electric rock core drill (ca. 1985).

Realizing that the BIO electric rock core drill had the potential to operate in depths approaching that of the mid-ocean ridges, P. Ryall and J. Ade-Hall of Dalhousie University (Halifax, NS) procured funding from Natural Sciences and Engineering Research Council (NSERC) and provided leadership in redeveloping the drill in concert with BIO. Following pioneering work at the Scripps Institution of Oceanography where the high voltage capacity of co-axial cables was employed to power instrumentation at greater depths, a similar technique was tried for the electric rock core drill. Through a series of increasingly sophisticated prototypes, the drill system was made to operate with a single cable. The drill frame was redesigned with a larger 'footprint' to improve its stability on the anticipated rough terrain (Fig. 4B).

Mechanically, the drill mechanism remained unchanged except for modifications to the primary drive which included transforming ship's power to 2300 volts and driving a high voltage oil-filled submersible motor on the mechanism through a 5,000-m long, double-armoured tri-axial cable. This cable presented three challenges. Firstly, data, such as bit extension, tilt, and flushing pressure, had to be acquired using a specially-designed inductively coupled multiplexing system. Secondly, the axial configuration of the three conductors and interstitial insulation, combined with the very long length of the cable, produced a capacitive imbalance among the three phases. This imbalance upset the system's voltage/current relationship to such an extent that virtually no useful power was transmitted to the drill motor. Shipboard inductive/capacitive circuitry overcame this problem successfully. Thirdly, the weight of the cable suspended from the ship seriously impaired ship station-keeping ability. The visible angle of previously-used slightly buoyant handling lines gave a rough indication of the ship's position relative to the drill. With a wire cable, however, this indication was lost as the heavy cable always headed straight down. To eliminate, or at least control, ship/drill interaction, a pinger was mounted on the wire about 30 m above the drill. Monitoring pinger/bottom separation, as shown by a precision graphic recorder (Fig. 4C), provided an indication as to when to pay out cable to avoid any dragging. This simple solution proved to be surprisingly effective (Ryall 1990). The successful introduction of the single cable handling system dramatically improved the effectiveness of the whole drilling program.

While good sample recovery was achieved in many rock types, the drill's effectiveness in glassy-surfaced and highly stressed basalts was disappointing because cores fractured readily and caused frequent jamming in the core tube. In addition, pebbles in tills overlying the bedrock jammed in the drill tube's core catcher, thus limiting further penetration. Several modifications to resolve this difficulty were tried, but none proved to be successful.

To overcome the jamming problem and to core bedrock under tills, the Newfoundland Offshore Research and Development Corporation (Nordco) in St. John's, Newfoundland, building upon the BIO experience, designed and built an entirely new electric rock core drill (Fig.4D). The Nordco drill contained a 6-m long auger to remove the overburden down to the bedrock surface, at which point a 6-m long diamond drill was extended through the centre of the auger. Owing to the heavy auger and additional drive systems, the Nordco drill was a significantly larger unit to deploy and service, but it was successful in recovering bedrock cores (Ryall 1987).

Throughout the life of the BIO drilling program, the major factor in core recovery was the nature of the site. If the drill landed on an outcrop of suitable rock, good core recovery might be expected, but such sites were rare. Even so, drilling on the continental shelves proved successful and yielded an acceptable return of cores for the effort expended.

SEISMIC AND NAVIGATIONAL SYSTEMS AND OPERATIONAL CONSTRAINTS

Regional geophysical surveys provided background information on the rock units underlying the Baffin Shelf. These surveys were used to identify potential drill sites that were further evaluated using high-resolution seismic systems. Improvements to these systems during the course of this program helped us find locations where bedrock was within reach of the drill's bottom penetration capability. In the early years, the seismic reflection systems in use produced a ringing or bubble pulse that seriously impaired resolution in the first 9 to 12 metres below the seafloor. The availability, part way through the program, of a small, 6 m-long hydrophone array developed by the Nova Scotia Research Foundation

(NSRF), in which bubble pulse masking was only 6 m, improved site selection immensely. But the tool most valuable in finding accessible drill sites was the Huntec deep-towed, high-resolution seismic reflection system. Huntec development relied heavily on BIO support (McKeown et al. 2014).

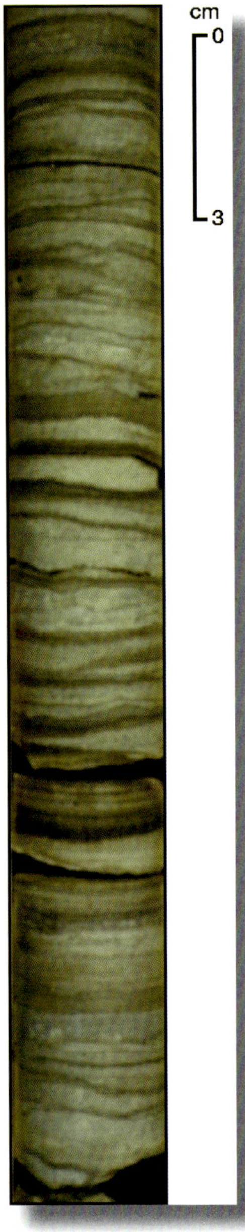

Figure 5. An example drill core of Ordovician brown- and grey-banded limestone from site 82034-67 in Hudson Strait (Fig. 1) that correlates with known rock formations in the Hudson Bay area. Approximately 2 m of core (2.54 cm diameter) were recovered from this site.

Ship navigation at the time of the field program relied on BIONAV, which incorporated a combination of satellite navigation and Loran-C, together with radar when coastal features were in range (Grant and Wells 2014). With this system, positional errors ranged up to 1,500 m. On drill sites, the core barrel, with an extension rate of 15 cm/min, often was in the seabed for more than an hour. During this time the ship had to avoid pulling on the drill, presenting severe challenges for the captain and officers to maintain the ship's position. Early in the program, buoys were deployed prior to drilling to provide the ship with a reference marker, but they were sometimes pulled under by strong currents. Later introduction of a short baseline positioning system, developed by D. McKeown, assisted in staying on location.

As indicated earlier, many drill holes were terminated prematurely because pebbles in the glacial overburden jammed in the core barrel. However, the practice of drilling at least three holes after poor or no core recovery on the first try proved worthwhile as subsequent attempts were often successful, even though there was no rational explanation for the improved outcome. Also, recovery of multiple cores of similar rocks at a site confirmed that the samples were from the bedrock and not just a glacially-transported boulder. In later operations when the drill had a single electro-mechanical cable, drill station recovery/re-deployment time was greatly reduced due to improved cable handling.

BEDROCK IN HUDSON STRAIT AND ON THE BAFFIN ISLAND SHELF

Bedrock cores (Fig. 5) were recovered at more than 40 localities from Hudson Strait to the northern end of the Baffin Island Shelf (Fig. 1). On the northeastern Baffin Shelf, we recovered core samples from four main areas (Fig.1). These cores were dated using dinoflagellates and spores (organic-walled microfossils called palynomorphs; see Fig. 6).

Two of these cores, near Padloping Island (northern Cumberland Peninsula), contained Cretaceous spore assemblages but no dinoflagellates, which indicated that the sediments were laid down in a non-marine environment. Cores from Buchan Gulf, Scott Inlet, and Home Bay were late Cretaceous in age (from about 88 to 81 million years old). Cores from Home Bay consisted of organic rich mudstone of Santonian to early Campanian age (about 86 to 81 million years old; Fig. 7). One of these emitted a strong petroliferous odour which was an exciting discovery. Farther north at Scott Inlet, in the vicinity of a submarine oil seep, recovered shale was late Coniacian to early Santonianin age (about 88 to 84.5 million years old), providing an indication of the age of the rock from which the seep originates. Cores of organic-rich mudstones were collected from five holes at two localities at Buchan Gulf and these were dated as Coniacian to Santonian in age (about 88 to 83.5 million years old; Fig. 7).

Figure 6. Photomicrograph images exemplifying index fossils in rock cores from offshore eastern Baffin Island (scale bar has the following values: for x40 = 25 µm, for x50 = 20 µm, for x63 = 15µm; where no scale bar is indicated, size is given in the caption):
1. *Alisogymnium* sp. Dinocyst (sample 78029-10-M01; P5110-9C. x63); 2. *Areoligera gippingensis*. Dinocyst (sample 80028-109-M01; slide P5110-3C. x50); 3. *Elytrocysta druggii*. Dinocyst (sample 82034-8-M01; slide P5110-10E. x63); 4. *Endoscrinium obscurum*. Dinocyst (sample 82034-3-M01; slide P5111-1C. x40); 5. *Gonyaulacysta*. sp. Dinocyst (sample 80028-7-M01; slide P5110-10D. x63); 6. *Heterosphaeridium difficile*. Dinocyst (sample 80028-7-M02; slide P5110-5C. x50); 7. *Kleithriasphaeridium cooksoniae*. Dinocyst (sample 80028-7-M01; slide P5110-4C. x50); 8. *Odontochitina costata*. Dinocyst (sample 82034-8-M01; slide P5110-10C. x40); 9. *Raphidodinium fucatum*. Dinocyst (sample 80028-7-M01; slide P5110-4D. x63); 10. *Stiphrosphaeridium anthophorum*. Dinocyst (sample 80028-7-M01; slide P5110-4C. x63); 11. *Trithyrodinium suspectum*. Dinocyst (sample 80028-7-M01; slide P5110-4C. x50); 12. *Fromea fragilis*. Acritarch (sample 78029-25-M01; slide P5110-8D. x50); 13. *Appendicisporites* cf. *bilateralis* (lower view). Spore (sample 80028-08; slide P5274-1C. x50); 14. *Cicatricosisporites augustus*. Spore (sample 85027-0048-R02; slide P5274-4D. x50); 15. *Appendicisporites problematicus*. Spore (sample 85027-0031. P5274-5B . Width = x50); 16. *Cicatricososporites sp*. Spore (sample 82034-3-M01; slide P5110-11D. x50); 17. *Costatoperforosporites fistulosus*. Spore (sample 80028-081; slide P5274-1B. x50); 18. *Trilobosporites apiverrucatus* . Spore (sample 85027-003; P5274-5D. Width = x50); 19. *Parvisaccites radiatus*. Pollen (sample 85027-0031; P5274-9C. Length = x40); 20. *Extratriporopollenites* sp. Pollen (sample 80028-109-M01; slide 5110-3D. x50).

It has since been discovered that strata of similar age and dinoflagellate assemblages occur in tectonically elevated sections on Bylot Island (Haggart et al. 2011), which lies at the northern end of Baffin Island, and these assemblages can be correlated with those found onshore West Greenland as described by Nøhr-Hansen (1996). Our findings regarding the age of the strata and depositional environments provide a better understanding of the geological evolution of Baffin Bay during the critical phases of the late Cretaceous (Williams et al. 2014).

To the north of Cumberland Sound, early Tertiary volcanic rocks occur onshore along the coast from near Cape Dyer northward to Padloping Island (Clarke and Upton 1972) and extensively offshore from Cape Dyer to mid-Davis Strait (Fig. 1). Short drill core samples were obtained from several localities in this area (MacLean et al. 1978, 1990). Success in coring the volcanic rocks was limited because of their tendency to break into fragments and jam in the core barrel.

Cores from the northeastern half of Cumberland Sound consisted of semi-consolidated organic rich mudstones and studies of dinoflagellates and spores indicated that the samples were early Cretaceous in age (about 126 or older to 99 million years old; Fig. 7).

The dinoflagellate and spore assemblages indicated that sedimentary rocks of Cretaceous–Tertiary age occur in cores from the shelf seaward of Cumberland Sound (Fig. 7). Volcanic rocks associated with the Tertiary sedimentary rocks are also considered to be of Tertiary age. These volcanic rocks were emplaced during seafloor spreading when the Labrador Sea, Davis Strait, and Baffin Bay were forming. The presence of diapiric (upward-directed) structures may indicate the presence of oil or gas traps in the flanking strata, an interpretation supported by the observation of gas in one of the cores.

The carbonate rock cores from Hudson Strait (Fig. 5) contained organic-walled microfossils called chitinozoa which were middle to late Ordovician (472 to 444 million years old; Miller and Williams 1988). Cores obtained from the inner part of the southeastern Baffin Shelf and in the inner part and southwestern half of Cumberland Sound were hard, competent Precambrian metamorphic and igneous rocks (more than 542 million years old). Since these sites had minimal sediment cover, bedrock was within range of the drill's penetration capability and pebbles did not present a problem. As a consequence, we recovered good cores on the first attempt. Limestones were found on the southeastern Baffin Shelf between Frobisher Bay and Cumberland Sound and these were of the same age and type as the limestones found in Hudson Strait and onshore near the head of Frobisher Bay.

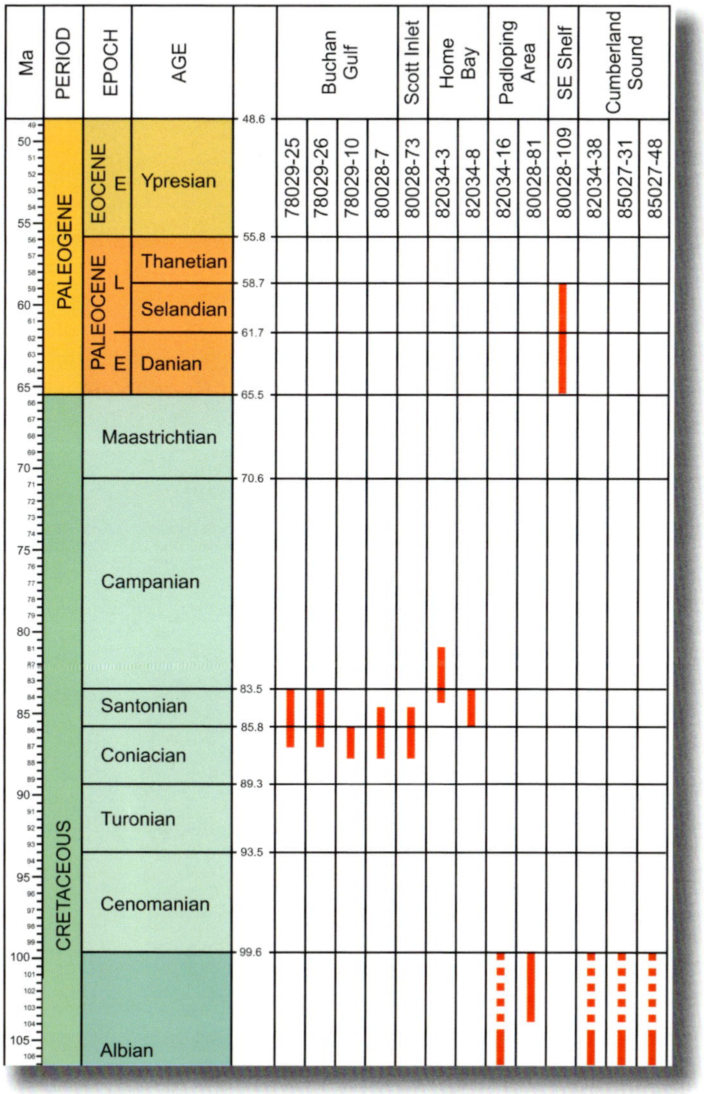

Figure 7. Geological ages of cores from the Baffin Island Shelf as determined by analysis of microfossils (palynomorphs). Codes: Ma is millions of years ago; 'Age' is geological age; 'Paleogene' is early part of Tertiary Period; E = Early, L = Late. Hyphenated number at top of each column is the cruise and station number for the core whose age is indicated by a red bar in the same column.

Information on the age, composition, and physical properties of cores obtained through drilling operations has been used to create regional geological maps and reports. These data represent the sole source of bedrock geological information for most of the length of the Baffin Island Shelf and Hudson Strait.

POTENTIAL RESOURCE SIGNIFICANCE

The potential for the formation of petroleum source rocks is closely related to plate tectonics, type of sediments, climate, productivity of organisms, and seawater circulation. But perhaps a more important control is the preservation of organic material in anoxic environments. Such anoxic events have occurred at periodic intervals in the evolution of the oceans when oxygen is found only near the surface. This means that when marine organisms die and fall to the sea floor, they are preserved and over a long period of time can become a major source of oil and gas. The Cretaceous rocks found in Baffin Bay are of an age that spanned two anoxic events, one in the Cenomanian–Turonian Age and one in the Coniacian–Santonian Age (Fig. 7). These occurrences could explain the origin of the submarine oil seep at Scott Inlet, an interpretation now supported by new analyses of the oil which indicate it is of late Cretaceous marine origin (Moir et al. 2011). To add further confirmation, studies of the organic carbon content of the drill samples from these strata are being undertaken to determine the conditions relevant to the oil formation processes in Baffin Bay. Discovery of wet gas in the Hekja O-71 exploratory well (Fig. 1) in 1979 is a further example of hydrocarbon potential of the region.

One overriding conclusion of this project is that recovering bedrock cores using bottom-operating equipment is a difficult but not an impossible task. Such drilling merits further pursuit if more is to be learned about the bedrock and bedrock resources of offshore eastern Canada. This coming decade could be an exciting time for geological studies of Baffin Bay, but new breakthroughs in knowledge will be dependent on future access to bedrock samples. The only way to get these economically is by using an underwater electric rock core drill and perhaps now is the time to start designing a new one that can be operated from a new 'state-of-the-art' multi-functional oceanographic vessel.

ACKNOWLEDGEMENTS

The successes achieved during this program would not have been possible without the skill and dedication of the drill teams, all members of the scientific staff, and the hard work by the crew and the outstanding station keeping provided by the captains and bridge officers of the CSS *Hudson*. We extend our sincere gratitude to each of these individuals who truly were co-adventurers in this work: Captains David Deer, Fred Mauger, Lorne Strum and crews of CSS *Hudson*. We also thank Tony Atkinson, Darrell Beaver, Ted Bendell, Austin Boyce, John Brooke, Roger Cassivi, Borden Chapman, Vern Coady, Bill Cooke, Gerry Connolly, Tom Courtney, Claudia Currie, Fred Ewing, Robin Falconer, Reg Gilbert, Paul Girouard, Mike Gorveatt, Iris Hardy, Bob Harmes, Mike Hughes, Barry Inkpen, Kate Jarrett, Anne Jennings, Fred Jodrey, Larry Johnston, Paul Jollymore, Peter Kingston, Bill LeBlanc, David Livingstone, Don Locke, Bill MacKinnon, Keith Manchester, David McKeown, Susan Merchant, Bob Murphy, Jess Neilsen, Patrick Potter, Kevin Robertson, Bruce Sanford, Andy Sherin, Roy Sparkes, Shiri Srivastava, Dick Vine, Bill Whiteway of BIO, Charlie Walls of Dalhousie University, Fred Learning and David Wilson of Geomarine Associates, George Bica, Graham Standen, and Martin Uyesugi of Geoforce, Joe Coombs, A. Fagan, B. Henderson and D. Millan of Nordco, John Osborne of the Nova Scotia Research Foundation, and Dick Sircum of Surfline Engineering. We acknowledge the special contributions made by Pat Ryall and Jim Ade-Hall of Dalhousie University in the final stages of drill development. Without their support, insight, and direction, many of the achievements noted here might never have occurred. Similarly, we gratefully acknowledge the ongoing support provided to this program by Bosko Loncarevic, David Ross, and Mike Keen, Directors of the Atlantic Geoscience Centre. Special thanks are also extended to Bosko Loncarevic for his review of this paper and helpful comments.

REFERENCES

Brooke, J. and R.L.G. Gilbert. 1968. The development of the Bedford Institute deep sea drill. Deep-Sea Research 15: 483-490.

Clarke, D.B. and B.G.J. Upton. 1972. Tertiary basalts of Baffin Island: field relations and tectonic setting. Canadian Journal of Earth Sciences 8: 248-258.

Fowler, G.A. and P.F. Kingston. 1975. An underwater drill for continental shelf exploration. Society for Underwater Technology 1: 18-22.

Grant, A.C. 1975. Geophysical results from the continental margin off southern Baffin Island. Pages 411-431 *in* Canada's Continental Margins and Offshore Petroleum Exploration (C.J. Yorath, E.R. Parker, and D.J. Glass, Eds.). Canadian Society of Petroleum Geologists Memoir 4, Calgary, AB.

Grant, A.C. and K.S. Manchester. 1970. Geophysical investigation in the Ungava Bay-Hudson Strait region of Northern Canada. Canadian Journal of Earth Sciences 7: 1,062-1,076.

Grant, S.T. and D.E. Wells. 2014. The Bedford Institute of Oceanography integrated navigation system (BIONAV). Pages 353-357 *in* Voyage of Discovery: Fifty Years of Marine Research at Canada's Bedford Institute of Oceanography (D.N. Nettleship, D.C. Gordon, C.F.M. Lewis, and M.P. Latremouille, Eds.). Bedford Institute of Oceanography-Oceans Association, Dartmouth, NS.

Haggart, J.W., H.R. Sweet, G.L. Williams, L. Currie, V. McNicoll, E.T. Burden, P.H. Benham, and J. Galloway. 2011. Paleoenvironments and correlations of Cretaceous-Paleogene strata, Bylot Island, Nunavut. Abstracts, Search and Discovery Article #90130, 3P Polar Petroleum Potential Conference, Halifax, Nova Scotia. American Association of Petroleum Geologists, Tulsa, OK.

Hutchins, R.W., D.L. McKeown, and L.H. King. 1976. A deep tow high resolution seismic system for continental shelf mapping. Geoscience Canada 3: 95-100.

MacLean, B., L.F. Jansa, R.K.H. Falconer, and S.P. Srivastava. 1977. Ordovician strata on the Southeastern Baffin Island shelf revealed by shallow drilling. Canadian Journal of Earth Sciences 14: 1,925-1,939.

MacLean, B., R.K.H. Falconer, and D.B. Clarke. 1978. Tertiary basalts of western Davis Strait: bedrock core samples and geophysical data. Canadian Journal of Earth Sciences 15: 773-780.

MacLean, B., G.L. Williams, and S.P. Srivistava. 1990. Geology of Baffin Bay and Davis Strait. Pages 293-348 *in* Geology of Canada No. 2: Geology of the Continental Margin of Eastern Canada (M.J. Keen, and G.L. Williams, Eds.). Geological Survey of Canada, Ottawa, ON.

McKeown, D.L., P.G. Simpkin, G.B.J. Fader, D.R. Parrott, and D.C. Mosher. 2014. The Huntec Deep Tow Seismic system: a revolution in high resolution profiling. Pages 337-341 *in* Voyage of Discovery: Fifty Years of Marine Research at Canada's Bedford Institute of Oceanography (D.N. Nettleship, D.C. Gordon, C.F.M. Lewis, and M.P. Latremouille, Eds.). Bedford Institute of Oceanography-Oceans Association, Dartmouth, NS.

Miller, A.M. and G.L. Williams. 1988. The essential role of palynology for bedrock mapping in Hudson Strait. Palynology 12: 224.

Moir, P.N., G.N. Oakey, R. Bennett, K. Dickie, P. Budkewitsch, M. Obermajer, and M. Fowler. 2011. A synthesis of the Scott Inlet oil seep, Baffin Bay, Canada. Abstracts, Search and Discovery Article #90130, 3P Polar Petroleum Potential Conference, Halifax, Nova Scotia. American Association of Petroleum Geologists, Tulsa, OK.

Nøhr-Hansen, H. 1996. Upper Cretaceous dinoflagellate cyst stratigraphy, onshore West Greenland. Grønlands Geologiske Undersøgelse (Geological Survey of Denmark and Greenland) Bulletin 170, Copenhagen, Denmark.

Pelletier, B.R. 1971. A granodioritic drill core from the Flemish Cap, eastern Canadian continental margin. Canadian Journal of Earth Sciences 8: 1,499-1,503.

Ryall, P. 1987. Remote drilling technology. Marine Mining 6: 149-187.

Ryall, P. 1990. An electric drill for deep-sea coring. Pages 201-210 *in* Gorda Ridge (G.R. Murray, Ed.). Springer-Verlag, New York, NY.

Srivastava, S.P. 1974. Cruise Report No. 74-026, CSS *Hudson*. Bedford Institute of Oceanography Internal Report, Dartmouth, NS.

Vodden, C. 1992. No stone unturned: the first 150 years of the Geological Survey of Canada. Geological Survey of Canada Miscellaneous Paper G12, Energy, Mines and Resources Canada, Ottawa, ON.

Williams, G.L., R.A. Fensome, and S.A. Dehler. 2014. Rocks of the deep: the subsurface geology of offshore eastern Canada. Pages 215-223 *in* Voyage of Discovery: Fifty Years of Marine Research at Canada's Bedford Institute of Oceanography (D.N. Nettleship, D.C. Gordon, C.F.M. Lewis, and M.P. Latremouille, Eds.). Bedford Institute of Oceanography-Oceans Association, Dartmouth, NS.

40. THE HUNTEC DEEP TOW SEISMIC SYSTEM: A REVOLUTION IN HIGH RESOLUTION PROFILING

David L. McKeown*, Peter G. Simpkin, Gordon B.J. Fader, D. Russell Parrott, and David C. Mosher

SUMMARY
During the late 1960s and early 1970s, the Marine Geology Section at the Bedford Institute of Oceanography (BIO) engaged in systematic mapping of surficial sediments on the Scotian Shelf and adjacent areas. To support and extend this initiative, Huntec '70 Limited, a geophysical operations company based in Toronto, and BIO staff developed a new towed high resolution seismic reflection profiler to operate in water depths up to 300 m. The Huntec Deep Tow Seismic system utilized a pressure-equalized, electro-dynamic boomer plate for the seismic source, providing a highly repeatable impulsive signature having a frequency spectrum from 800 Hz to 10 kHz. The sound energy generated over this range of frequencies permitted imaging the subsurface geology down to 300 m below the seafloor. Towing the system close to the seabed reduced the acoustic footprint size and also reduced the effect of sea-state noise; pressure equalization stabilized the source signature. The outstanding success of initial trials undertaken in 1974 led to the creation of the first 'Seabed Project', a five-year research and development program to further develop the Deep Tow Seismic system and to support the government's offshore geological/geophysical mapping initiative. This program included the incorporation of automatic heave compensation and the first real-time acoustic seafloor reflectivity measurements. These technological advances combined to advance the collection, analysis, presentation, and interpretation of high resolution seismic profiles collected from continental shelf depth, open ocean areas. Subsequently, the Seabed II Project was initiated with the goal of extending this survey technology to depths greater than 2,000 m. The original Deep Tow Seismic system is still the preferred high resolution profiling equipment used by BIO researchers today, and more than 250,000 line-km of data have been acquired in Canadian waters since the inception of the Seabed Project.

Key words: Huntec, high-resolution seismic reflection system, deep-tow profiler.
***E-mail:** DavidMckeown@hfx.eastlink.ca

During the late 1960s and early 1970s, the Marine Geology Section at the Bedford Institute of Oceanography (BIO) undertook a major program to systematically map surficial sediments and shallow sub-surface stratigraphy on the Scotian Shelf and adjacent areas. Lead researcher L. King realized that echograms collected by the Canadian Hydrographic Service (CHS), particularly those produced by the Kelvin-Hughes MS26B echo sounder, produced distinctive characteristics for a variety of bottom sediment types. When correlated with data from detailed analyses of seabed samples, a powerful method was developed that could be used to categorize and map large areas of the seabed. The echograms from the MS26B sounder showed up to 20 m of penetration into softer glacial and Holocene muddy sediments, while other seabed types, such as bedrock and till, displayed distinctive echo characteristics, but no penetration. The first map, based on these data, in what became a new series of BIO publications was the Halifax to Sable Island Surficial Geology Map and accompanying report (King 1970). At the same time, other BIO geologists were analyzing CHS echograms and mapping additional regions — Gulf of Maine/Bay of Fundy, Yarmouth to Browns Bank, Banquereau/ Misaine — using BIO ships to collect the 5,000 seafloor samples required to 'ground-truth' geophysical interpretations of the echograms for the Scotian Shelf (Fader et al. 2004).

Seismic reflection profiling uses the same physical principles as an echo sounder, where an impulse of acoustic energy is generated close to the sea surface and the resulting wave front propagates towards the seafloor. At the seafloor, some acoustic energy returns to the surface as an echo and the remainder penetrates into the sediment to be further reflected by deeper sediment layers of contrasting physical properties. If successive echoes are detected and plotted as a seismic survey line progresses, a seismic section of the stratigraphy beneath the seafloor is assembled. To resolve closely spaced layers, a sharp pulse having a wide frequency bandwidth is required. Sound energy is attenuated (absorbed) as it propagates through sediments; however, lower frequency sound is less affected by this attenuation. To map deep layers, therefore, a higher energy source having a predominantly low frequency and wide bandwidth spectrum is required.

In the 1970s, geologists relied on various geophysical tools to understand the subsurface. Low frequency, high-energy sources, such as air gun- and sparker-based surface-towed seismic reflection systems provided information on sediment thickness, but lacked the resolution to provide detail about the character of sediments. Depth sounding was undertaken with relatively high frequency echo sounders such as the MS26B that provided internal detail in soft sediments, but did not penetrate harder sediments such as glacial till and gravel. Higher resolution surveys were undertaken with surface towed 'electrodynamic' sound sources such as boomers and sparkers with multi-element surface-towed hydrophone streamers (receivers) to detect the returning acoustic energy. These early profiling systems could perform satisfactorily in areas of soft sediments and when sea conditions were favourable; however, high acoustic noise and wave motion, typical of poor weather conditions encountered on continental shelf regions of eastern Canada, reduced the quality and quantity of data received. Larger surface-towed seismic systems of the era were also limited in that they could not resolve surficial sediment layers spaced <3-10 m apart. In part, to support offshore hydrocarbon exploration, there was a need for equipment with higher resolution and greater penetration to better define the surficial sediment stratigraphy and to understand relationships between various shallow sedimentary units.

FIRST STEPS: GOVERNMENT/PRIVATE SECTOR PARTNERSHIPS

The 'Unsolicited Proposal' program was a key element of the Government of Canada's 1972 'Make-or-Buy' policy in which major research initiatives were evaluated whether they would be cheaper and/or more efficacious to develop in-house or by contracting out. The objective was to encourage Canadian companies to apply for funding to develop devices and methods that would be of value to government departments and have potential for commercial application. These incentives encouraged R. Hutchins, president of Huntec '70 Limited, a Canadian company that designed and manufactured geoscientific instruments including seismic reflection systems for mapping seabed sediments, to meet with BIO scientists and explore options that might improve the resolution of existing seismic reflection systems without compromising seabed penetration. Huntec then formulated and presented a cooperative research and development plan to be carried out by them and two BIO agencies: the Atlantic Geoscience Centre (Energy, Mines and Resources Canada, now Natural Resources Canada) and the Metrology Division (Fisheries and Oceans Canada). The goal was to develop a deeply towed seismic system operable in open ocean (poor weather) conditions, and capable of achieving 0.2-m layer resolution and penetration of 200 to 300 m in clay sediments when towed at speeds up to 6 knots. The cost of the complete system was estimated to be $74,000 (in 1973) and the integrated system would offer attractive commercial possibilities worldwide. A key feature of the proposed system was the inclusion of a new high intensity electro-dynamic boomer acoustic source developed by Huntec. This novel source was pressure-equalized to maintain consistent output characteristics when towed down to 300 m. Towing closer to the seabed reduces the seismic footprint, giving greater horizontal resolution and corresponding reductions in both water-path signal loss and interference from surface noise sources. The repeatable output signatures from the boomer source would enable the use of advanced digital signal processing techniques for further data enhancement. The decision was taken by the Federal Government in 1974 to fund a significant portion of the work for concept design and the development and testing of the Huntec Deep Tow Seismic (DTS) system in two phases.

The first phase, described in detail in 'Operation Deep Thrust '74: A Program for the Evaluation of a new Seismic Source System' (Contract No. SV02.KF806-4-G061: 5 July 1974), proposed that Huntec would complete the development of a prototype DTS system, conduct sea trials to establish the dynamic characteristics of the towed body and cable, measure the acoustic characteristics of the source, and in collaboration with government scientists, evaluate the performance of the DTS system in an area of well-defined geology. Once these initial trials were completed, demonstrations of the system would be made to potential international customers. The second phase would be a full-scale multi-year research and development (R&D) program with clearly stated scientific, engineering, and commercial objectives that included the placement of a small R&D Huntec team at BIO.

In preparation for the initial trials, Huntec assembled the electrodynamic sound source (boomer), a high voltage Power Supply Unit (PSU), and an Energy Storage Unit (ESU) and merged them with existing proprietary seismic reflection receiving and display equipment. After successful tests of the 'boomer' source in Lake Ontario, Fathom Oceanology Limited was contracted to supply major components: the tow system comprising a towed body to contain the seismic source, the ESU and a single element hydrophone as a detector, a faired and armoured tow cable (with conductors for high voltage power, seismic and other signals including engineering data), an oceanographic winch (capable of handling rigid Flexnose fairing on the cable), and a crane and sheave block (for deploying and towing the device; Fig. 1).

For sea trials, an aged workboat, the MV *Survey Venture*, was chartered and arrived at BIO in August 1974. Once safety deficiencies on the vessel were rectified, BIO and Huntec staff installed the Fathom winch and towing system on the aft deck. The 6 kV high voltage power supply and seismic receiving and recording equipment were installed in a metal garden shed mounted on board (Fig. 1). A roll/pitch/depth sensor module was fitted in the DTS towed body to monitor tow fish position. The team finished all outstanding engineering work on the Huntec system and reinforced the garden-shed laboratory to withstand North Atlantic sea conditions.

Figure 1. Overall view of the after deck of MV *Survey Venture* showing the Huntec Deep Tow Seismic system: winch, cable with rigid Flexnose fairing, crane, sheave, block and towed body. The V-fin towed body on its side behind the Huntec towed body is associated with a Kelvin Hughes MS26B echo sounder.

Sea trials were conducted over both the Nova Scotia Research Foundation's (NSRF) 'Offshore' and 'Inshore' acoustic test ranges in Nova Scotia. The 'Offshore' range included the Sambro Moraine, Emerald Basin and Emerald Bank, where several geological formations including LaHave Clay, Scotian Shelf Drift, Emerald Silt, Sambro Sand, and various mixtures of Sable Island Sand and Gravel were known to exist. The 'Inshore' test range is located in Bedford Basin where the geology consists of a thin layer of mud covering sandy mud, and some gravel overlying Cambro-Ordovician bedrock.

During initial testing of the Huntec DTS, signal levels received were weak to non-existent. The newly installed roll/pitch/depth sensor showed that the tow body was at an extreme angle, and when trimmed to tow level, the seismic signal amplitude improved dramatically. In addition, the hydrophone receiver was mounted just below the acoustic source within the towed body to rigidly fix the hydrophone-source geometry, thereby improving system fidelity and substantially attenuating 'ghost' reflections received from the sea surface. This arrangement, however, resulted in the initial part of the reflected seismic signal being masked by acoustic 'ringing' of the towed body as it vibrated in response to firing of the 'boomer'. This problem was corrected by adding a second hydrophone towed about 5 m behind the 'fish'.

At the conclusion of sea trials, the DTS system was taken to the acoustic test barge of the Defence Research Establishment Atlantic (DREA) in Bedford Basin, for a detailed examination of its acoustic characteristics and reproducibility of the electro-dynamic 'boomer' transducer. A full description of the trials is reported in McKeown (1975).

The quality of seismic records obtained during these sea trials was outstanding and exceeded expectations of the evaluation team (Hutchins et al. 1976). The Huntec DTS system presented a significant improvement in high-resolution seismic survey capability. The fidelity of the boomer source was high with little variation in frequency content of the source signal as a function of input energy and tow depth (the spectral characteristics of the pressure signature was relatively flat over a frequency range from 800 Hz to 10 kHz). It was recommended that the system should immediately be incorporated into BIO's geophysical survey suite of equipment and a multi-year R&D program should be undertaken to further develop the system.

PROJECT SEABED I (1975-80)

A proposal was submitted by Huntec Limited in 1975 for a Federal Government-funded program to continue development of the Huntec DTS system for routine regional mapping off eastern Canada. The planned five-year program, given the title 'Project Seabed' (later named 'Project Seabed I'), was to begin in early 1975 involving Huntec and government scientists based at BIO and an acoustics group at the Oceans Engineering Department, Memorial University of Newfoundland (MUN), St. John's, Newfoundland. The principal goals were to develop the DTS system further as a seafloor mapping tool, to improve its overall effectiveness, and to support and extend the regional mapping programs planned by the Atlantic Geoscience Centre (AGC) at BIO. Special consideration was to be given to system calibration and high speed digital data acquisition to enable research into the characteristics of seafloor echoes as a method of remote sediment classification. The Seabed Program was not a scientific program but a technological development project to produce an improved tool to aid geological mapping (R.W. Hutchins, pers. comm. 1976).

Following funding of the proposal in April 1975, an upgraded Huntec DTS system was mobilized on CSS *Hudson* for a mission to the Grand Banks of Newfoundland to map bedrock and surficial geology. It was on this cruise (Hudson 75-009) that an effective heave-motion compensation system was introduced. The system used an accelerometer mounted in the deep-tow vehicle to provide a signal to a laboratory-based motion package that computed the heave component of the towed body. This heave estimate was subsequently used to reduce the effects of wave-induced motion on seismic profiles resulting in better 'shot-to-shot' coherency and more accurate seismic interpretation. In 1976, the addition of a pressure sensor component to the motion sensor package further improved the quality of seismic data (Hutchins 1980). An example of Huntec DTS real-time heave-motion-compensated data recorded on a flatbed graphic recorder during a 1979 expedition is shown in Figure 2. The image demonstrates high-resolution capabilities of the Huntec DTS system and shows the complex geological structure of Emerald Basin, an area of glacial and post-glacial sediments in the central region of the Scotian Shelf. Stronger reflections show as darker units and typically represent coarser sediments. Glacial till of the Scotian Shelf Drift is characterised by a highly reflective irregular upper surface, incoherent internal reflections, and loss of reflectivity beneath. Stratified or layered sediments overlie the till. These layered sediments consist of Emerald Silt Facies A represented by high amplitude coherent reflections, and Emerald Silt Facies B represented by medium amplitude reflections. At the top of the sedimentary section is a unit known as LaHave Clay, a postglacial muddy sediment that is mostly Holocene in age. Over most of the profile (Fig. 2), the upper surface of the LaHave Clay is the seafloor. These different acoustic units, or 'facies', can be followed for great distances, allowing geologists to map both the distribution of seabed sediments and the subsurface stratigraphy with precision.

Subsequent technological developments within the Project Seabed I program resulted in improved real-time display of high resolution seismic data along with computation and presentation of acoustic reflectivity estimates from the seafloor. Another profile of Emerald Basin, taken in 1980, is shown in Figure 3. At the top of the image are two graphs that represent quantification of the acoustic reflectivity (strength of the return signal) of the seabed profile. They were calculated in real-time by an 8-bit microprocessor unit called the Acoustic Reflectivity Module (ARM) and superimposed on the analogue data. The extracted parameter R1 is a measure of coherently reflected energy from the seabed. The width of the trace is an indication of the variance in the estimate of R1. Each of the scale lines represents a reflectivity increment of 10% of the incident acoustic energy at the seafloor. A second parameter, R2, is a measure of the scattered energy from the top metre of the seabed, where each of the scale lines represents 5% of the incident energy. The microprocessor tracked the seabed, performed the required calculations, and superimposed the display of R1 and R2 reflectivity on the analogue graphic record in real time. The microprocessor also placed a mark on the graphic record (labelled ARM) immediately above and paralleling the seabed to indicate the seafloor tracking trace.

The spatial resolution and dynamic range of the acoustic signals produced by the DTS system exceeded the display capabilities of existing flatbed graphic recorder technology when the system was developed. To overcome this limitation, an analogue signal processor, the Adaptive Signal Processor (ASP), was developed. On a shot-to-shot basis, the ASP tracked the seafloor, calculated its acoustic reflectivity, used these values to estimate the associated attenuation losses and adjusted an adaptive gain ramp to alter the displayed seismic signal accordingly. This gain ramp was also adjusted whenever a stronger reflection was encountered within the sediment column to compensate for stratification of an acoustically soft sediment such as clay overlying an acoustically hard sediment such as till or sand. A mark was made on the graphic record, labelled ASP in Figure 3, immediately above the seafloor to indicate that the ASP was correctly tracking it. This unit functioned independently of the ARM. The Huntec DTS system was the first profiling system to provide a real-time reflectivity display (ARM) and correction for reflection and attenuation losses (ASP). Entire industries providing real-time seafloor classification schemes are based on these technologies today.

High resolution characterization of seabed sediments allowed marine geologists to see, for the first time, features such as internal structure of large sand dunes, small scale bedding in hard indurated bedrock,

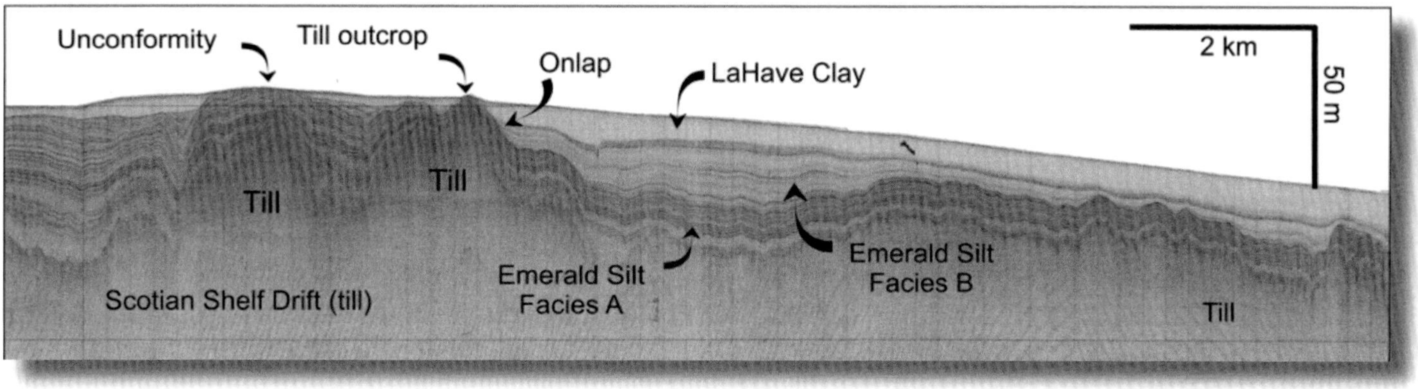

Figure 2. Huntec DTS profile from Expedition 79-011 (1979) on the Scotian Shelf. Heave compensation and a highly repeatable, broadband source provided unprecedented sub-bottom detail for geologic interpretation. The various geologic units from the Scotian Shelf are labelled (King and Fader 1986).

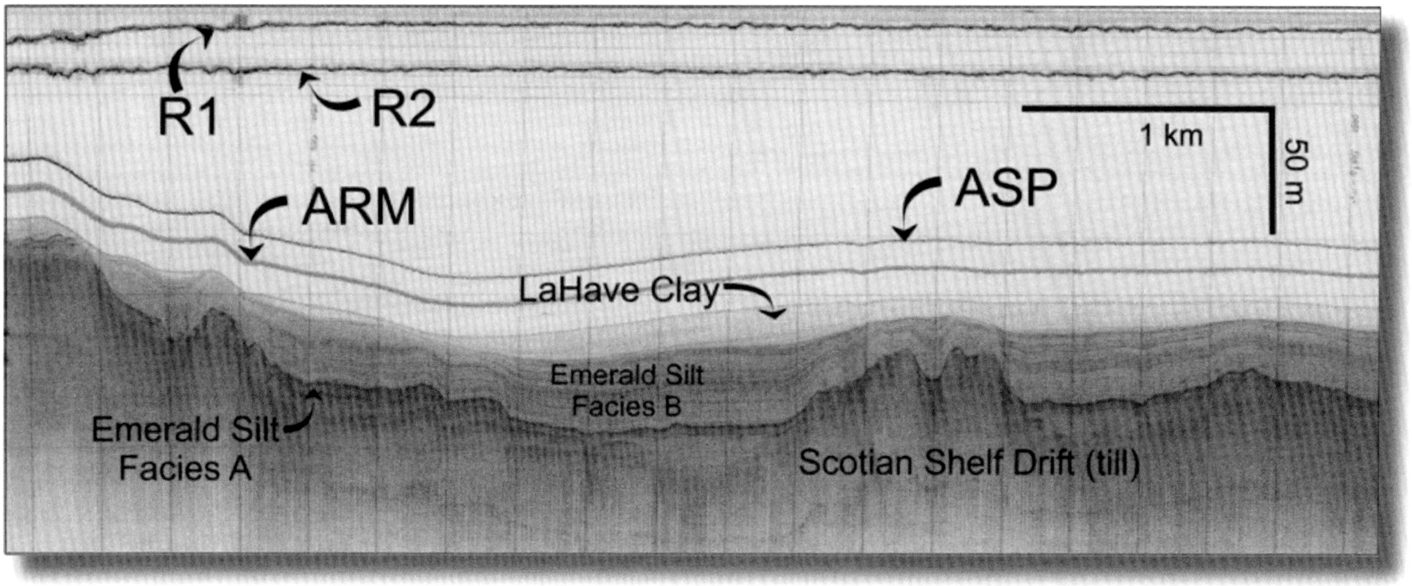

Figure 3. Huntec DTS profile from Expedition 80-010 (1980) showing a profile in Emerald Basin on the Scotian Shelf with reflectivity displays (R1 and R2), the first seafloor classification technology. ARM is the seafloor tracking trace of the Acoustic Reflectivity Module and ASP is the seafloor tracking trace of the Adaptive Signal Processor.

buried pockmarks within sediments, and multiple stacked tills providing evidence of varying glacial advances and retreats (King and Fader 1986). As a consequence of its outstanding ability to resolve stratigraphy, the Huntec DTS system made a major contribution to the success of surveys by enabling precise location of different stratigraphic units for sampling and ground truthing. This capability led to development of site survey investigation techniques for situating exploration drilling platforms (Hutchins 1980, King 1980). It was now feasible to identify the occurrence of bedrock within 6 m of the seabed surface, a requirement needed to select suitable sites for collecting cores with the BIO rock core drill (MacLean et al. 2014). In the past, locating suitable drilling sites was difficult due to poor resolution of air gun-based seismic systems and lack of penetration of echo sounders in thin gravel and till layers. Between 1975 and 1980, numerous (~100) suitable rock core drill sites were located using the Huntec DTS system. This combination of techniques eventually led to a much better understanding of the bedrock geology of the Grand Banks and adjacent Flemish Cap (King and Fader 1976, Fader and King 1981, King et al. 1985,) and subsequently influenced the selection of a gravity platform for production rather than a pipeline to shore in the development of the Hibernia oil field (King and Fader 1981).

From 1975 to 1980, many government offshore survey programs were supported by the Huntec DTS system. Areas of interest included the Bay of Fundy, Georges Bank, Sable Island Bank, the Grand Banks of Newfoundland, the Labrador Shelf, and Baffin Bay. During this period, a geophysicist and technician were provided by Huntec to support these activities.

Three Huntec scientists were based at BIO over a six-year period to work closely with AGC scientists in supporting Project Seabed I. Huntec DTS data were also provided to the underwater acoustics research group at the MUN Ocean Engineering Department where, from 1976 to 1980, a comprehensive research program was undertaken into the use of 'shot-to-shot' coherence as a means of sediment identification (Dunsiger and MacIsaac 1978, Cochrane and Dunsiger 1980). Software algorithms to map the transient acoustic field generated by the 'boomer' plate in the near- and far-field regions were also developed during this period (Simpkin 2005).

Some of the hardware/software developments undertaken between 1975 and 1980 for Project Seabed I included:

- Implementation of 12-bit digitization at 20 μs of Huntec profiler data, both on-line and from raw data recorded on analog tapes (Simpkin et al. 1976).
- Development and implementation of source and receiver calibration techniques to aid in maintaining consistent data quality.
- Development of a modular dual channel signal interface unit to provide consistent quality data recording and calibrated data playback.
- Implementation of a pressure (depth) component to the heave motion compensation system (Hutchins et al. 1976).
- Evaluation and adoption of SCR (Silicon Controlled Rectifiers) high voltage, high current switches to replace the original sparker discharge switch in the ESU.
- Development of software to characterize sediment types using frequency dependent sonogram analysis of the bottom echo (Dodds 1978).
- Development of a microprocessor controlled acoustic reflectivity module (ARM) to measure directly acoustic reflectivity of the seafloor and to present the data in 'real time' to the flatbed paper recording devices of the day (Parrott et al. 1980).

It is noteworthy that much of the computing activities were undertaken on mainframe or mini-computers of the 1970s, and the purchase of 32 Kbytes of memory was thought to be extravagant because it cost about $32,000!

Over the period of Project Seabed I, Huntec successfully brought the commercial version of the DTS to market with fully operational units being deployed in Canadian waters, the North Sea, and offshore Norway, Gulf of Mexico, and the Arctic and Antarctic oceans in programs supporting both academic and commercial interests.

PROJECT SEABED II (1981-85)

Following the success of Project Seabed I, a second, much larger, $5.5 million development program was initiated by Huntec'70 Limited with AGC scientists at BIO. This program, called 'Project Seabed II', utilized the knowledge and advances generated by Project Seabed I and added very deep tow (2,000 m) capabilities, a sidescan sonar, an advanced instrumentation and data transmission package, a second generation motion compensation system, a real-time reflectivity display, direct digital acquisition, and a 'sparker' source with increased power capabilities (Dodds and Fader 1987). Two test surveys of the new system were conducted in 1983 and 1984. The final testing of the 'Seabed II' system took place on the continental slope in the Verrill Canyon region with the system towed at depths of 2,000 m. The system performed flawlessly and produced the first high-resolution seismic profiles with over 200 m subbottom penetration showing escarpments, slump blocks, pockmarks, and debris flows down to 2,000 m water depth, and iceberg furrows in water depths of 640 m (Mosher et al. 1989, 1994). Unfortunately, budgetary constraints following the successful second trial in 1984 resulted in termination of the Seabed II program. Many of the advanced instrumentation units, however, were incorporated into the standard Huntec DTS system, and were utilized in deep tow packages of other institutions.

PRESENT STATUS (2012)

In 2012, the Huntec DTS system still plays a critical role in support of geologic mapping programs of Canadian offshore territories. The system is typically operated under contract with Geoforce Limited for most BIO missions and is available for contract worldwide. In excess of 180,000 line-km of Huntec DTS data have been acquired on BIO surveys up to and including the 2011 survey season. A further ~80,000 line-km of data have been acquired on Canada's west coast by the Geological Survey of Canada Pacific division at the Institute of Ocean Sciences, Sidney, British Columbia. The DTS system continues to provide high-resolution seismic profiles and quantitative geophysical information about the near-surface geology and is unmatched by more recently developed systems (see Mosher and Simpkin 1999 for comparisons). Between 1991 and 1993, processing power in desktop and portable computers reached a point that enabled Huntec DTS acoustic signals to be digitized at high sample rates and directly recorded in an industry standard format. This digitization allowed for post-processing and seismic interpretation using commercially available as well as customized software packages. These advances also enabled the integration of DTS data with georeferenced data available from multibeam bathymetric and other sonar systems. Between 2007 and 2010, digital modules replaced many of the DTS analogue hardware systems. Hardcopies produced by flatbed recorders are now optional, and 'real-time' data are normally displayed on computer terminals for quality control purposes during data acquisition. Wavelet compression techniques were developed at BIO to handle previously unmanageable volumes of digital data resulting from high-resolution sampling of Huntec DTS signals, and from high-resolution scanning of historical 'hardcopy' analogue datasets (Courtney 2007, 2013). All legacy and newly acquired Huntec profiles are now available for online download in these compressed formats.

The Project Seabed program is an excellent example of a true industry-government R&D project. Both parties worked closely together over several years to develop technology that met expectations and needs. The Huntec DTS system achieved international recognition as a cost-effective tool for offshore geological mapping under poor weather conditions, and is regularly viewed as a model success story of a joint industry/government scientific partnership lasting several decades, an arrangement that is ongoing. Several DTS systems were sold in the international market place for institutional and commercial use, several patents were issued to Huntec'70 Limited, and data collected by BIO have been interpreted and presented in many Geological Survey of Canada Atlantic papers, maps, and reports.

ACKNOWLEDGEMENTS

Although many people contributed to the creation of the Huntec DTS system, it would never have come to fruition without the vision, creativity, entrepreneurial spirit, and persistence of Roger Hutchins and Lewis King. We would also like to acknowledge and thank the many technicians and geoscientists from Huntec and BIO who contributed their skills and knowledge over the years to the development and operation of these complex systems.

REFERENCES

Cochrane, N.A. and A.D. Dunsiger. 1980. Sediment roughness characteristics measured by broadband spectral analysis of acoustic echoes. Pages 140-150 *in* Proceedings of First Canadian Conference on Marine Geotechnical Engineering (W.J. Eden, Ed.). Canadian Geotechnical Society, Richmond, BC.

Courtney, R.C. 2007. Storage and dissemination of SEGY Data in JPEG2000 format. Abstract IN51B-0402 *in* EOS Transactions American Geophysical Union 88 (52), Washington, DC.

Courtney, R.C. 2013. GEESE 2: Visualization of integrated marine geoscience data for Canadian and proximal waters. Geoscience Canada 40: 141-148.

Dodds, D.J. 1978. Application of pattern classification techniques to ocean-bottom echoes of broadband acoustic signals. Seabed Project Report H7807-04/ SB/DJD (April 1978). Unpubl. report to the Atlantic Geoscience Centre, Energy, Mines and Resources Canada, Bedford Institute of Oceanography, Dartmouth, NS.

Dodds, D.J. and G.B.J. Fader. 1987. A combined reflection profiler and sidescan sonar system for deep ocean geological surveys. Pages 169-180 *in* Progress in Underwater Acoustics (H.M. Merklinger, Ed.). Plenum Press, New York, NY.

Dunsiger, A.D. and R.R. Maclsaac. 1978. Broadband seismic data used for seafloor sediment classification. Pages 521-526 *in* Proceedings of Oceans'78, Marine Technology Society/Institute of Electrical and Electronic Engineers Fourth Annual Combined Conference. Marine Technology Society, Washington, DC.

Fader, G.B.J. and L.H. King. 1981. A reconnaissance study of the surficial geology of the Hibernia Discovery Area - Grand Banks of Newfoundland. Pages 45-46 *in* Current Research, Part A, Geological Survey of Canada Paper 81-1A. Energy, Mines and Resources Canada, Ottawa, ON.

Fader, G.B.J., T. Lynds, R.O. Miller, D.R. Parrott, S. Hynes, and A. Sherin. 2004. Scotian Shelf regional surficial geology compilation. Geological Survey of Canada, Open File 4671, Ottawa, ON. 1 CD-ROM. doi:10.4095/215682.

Hutchins, R.W., D.L. McKeown, and L.H. King. 1976. A deep tow high resolution seismic system for continental shelf mapping. Geoscience Canada 3: 95-100.

Hutchins, R.W. 1980. Development of new geophysical methods for site investigation studies. Pages 87-102 *in* Offshore Site Investigation (D.A. Ardus, Ed.). Graham and Trotman, London, England.

King, L. H. 1970. Surficial geology of the Halifax - Sable Island map area. Marine Science Paper 1, Marine Sciences Branch, Energy Mines and Resources Canada, Ottawa, ON.

King, L.H. 1980. Aspects of regional surficial geology related to site investigation requirements – Eastern Canadian Shelf. Pages 37-59 *in* Offshore Site Investigation (D.A. Ardus, Ed.). Graham and Trotman, London, England.

King, L.H. and G.B.J. Fader. 1976. Application of the Huntec Deep Tow High-Resolution Seismic System to surficial and bedrock studies – Grand Banks of Newfoundland. Pages 5-7 *in* Report of Activities Part C, Geological Survey of Canada, Paper 76-1C, Ottawa, ON.

King, L.H. and G.B.J. Fader. 1981. Seabed conditions east of the Avalon Peninsula to the Virgin Rocks - their relationship to the feasibility of a pipeline from Hibernia P-15 wellsite area to Newfoundland. Geological Survey of Canada, Open File No. 723, Ottawa, ON.

King, L H. and G.B.J. Fader. 1986. Wisconsinan glaciation of the Atlantic continental shelf of southeast Canada. Geological Survey of Canada, Bulletin 363, Ottawa, ON.

King, L.H., G.B.J. Fader, W.H. Poole, and R.K. Wanless. 1985. Geological setting and age of the Flemish Cap granodiorite, east of the Grand Banks of New foundland. Canadian Journal of Earth Sciences 22: 1,286-1,298.

MacLean, B., G.L. Williams, and G.A. Fowler. 2014. Bedrock studies of the Baffin Island Shelf and Hudson Strait: a technological and scientific adventure. Pages 331-336 *in* Voyage of Discovery: Fifty Years of Marine Research at Canada's Bedford Institute of Oceanography (D.N. Nettleship, D.C. Gordon, C.F.M. Lewis, and M.P. Latremouille, Eds.). Bedford Institute of Oceanography-Oceans Association, Dartmouth, NS.

McKeown, D. L. 1975. Evaluation of the Huntec ('70) Hydrosonde Deep Tow Seismic System. Bedford Institute of Oceanography Report Series BI-R-76-4, Dartmouth, NS.

Mosher, D.C., D.J.W. Piper, G.V. Vilks, A.E. Aksu, and G.B. Fader. 1989. Evidence for Wisconsinan glaciations in the Verrill Canyon Area, Scotian Slope. Quaternary Research 31: 27-40.

Mosher, D.C., K.M. Moran, and R.N. Hiscot. 1994. Late Quaternary sediment, sediment mass-flow processes and slope instability on the Scotian Slope. Sedimentology 41: 1,039-1,061.

Mosher, D.C. and P.G. Simpkin. 1999. Status and trends of marine high-resolution seismic reflection profiling: data acquisition. Geoscience Canada 26: 174-188.

Parrott, D.R., D.J. Dodds, L.H. King, and P.G. Simpkin. 1980. Measurement and evaluation of the acoustic reflectivity of the sea floor. Canadian Journal of Earth Sciences 17: 722-737.

Simpkin, P.G., D.R. Parrott, R. Hutchins, and D.I. Ross. 1976. Seabed '75 – Objectives and achievements. Bedford Institute of Oceanography Report Series BI-R-76-15, Dartmouth, NS.

Simpkin, P.G. 2005. The Boomer sound source as a tool for shallow water geophysical exploration. Marine Geophysical Researches 26: 171-181.

41. THE DEVELOPMENT OF ICYCLER AND SEACYCLER: ENERGY EFFICIENT PROFILERS FOR UPPER OCEAN OCEANOGRAPHIC MEASUREMENTS

George A. Fowler*, Greg R. Siddall, Brian D. Beanlands, Merle D. Pittman, and Simon J. Prinsenberg

SUMMARY

Responding to the scientific need for detailed oceanographic data from the ocean's surface layer for climate change research during the past 15 years, the Ocean Physics Group at the Bedford Institute of Oceanography has produced two novel upper ocean profiling platforms. These devices employ a patented energy conserving principle that permits deployments at sea for periods of a year or more. Depending on the power configuration, daily or multiple daily profiles are possible. Icycler is designed for operation under ice cover and can make measurements in the upper 50 m of the water column in water depths of 200-250 m. SeaCycler is designed for use in the open ocean and can make measurements in the top 150 m in water depths as great as 5,000 m. SeaCycler has an element that pierces the sea surface to send data ashore via an Iridium satellite link and receive commands from a shore operator to modify operational parameters. Recent cooperative work with the Woods Hole Oceanographic Institution and the Scripps Institution of Oceanography has shown that it is possible to make measurements and communicate data seamlessly from the surface to the seafloor in near real time. This paper describes the basic principle of operation, the challenges that were overcome during development, the innovations and engineering solutions that were accomplished, and presents some results from field operations.

Key words: profiler, upper-ocean physical properties, mooring, satellite.
***E-mail:** George.Fowler@dfo-mpo.gc.ca

Whether in open water or under ice cover, the surface layer of the ocean has significant impact on how the ocean interacts with the atmosphere and the resident biology. The interactive physical, chemical, and biological processes that occur here are highly complex and variable. As a consequence, their investigation can benefit significantly from measurements with high temporal and spatial resolution to reveal physical characteristics and vertical structure. However, making such measurements in the surface layer can be risky. Open water is highly energetic while areas of mobile ice cover can be swept by destructive ice keels. To avoid these problems, the concept of profiling, or the vertical movement of instruments through the water, is very appealing. Profiling becomes a highly attractive approach in situations where repetitive, high vertical resolution measurements must be made at a fixed geographic location and a permanent surface expression cannot be maintained. Rather than placing many sensors at numerous discrete depths, a single sensor suite can be profiled through the water to obtain sub-metre resolution. The concept has the additional advantage of 'parking' sensors at depth where they are protected from damaging effects of waves, ice, bio-fouling, and human interference. With profiling instrumentation, however, significant buoyancy is required to resist drag forces induced by ambient currents and to lift non-buoyant instrumentation from depth. To complete a profile cycle, the force exerted by this buoyancy must be overcome by expending energy to return that buoyancy to depth. The larger the buoyancy needed to accomplish the required 'lift', the greater is the energy needed to complete a profile. Since such a measurement scheme is only justifiable if multiple profiles can be accomplished over an extended period of time, energy consumption dominates its potential application.

System energy requirements for profiling instrumentation have been addressed at the Bedford Institute of Oceanography (BIO) by the development of a mechanism that employs a patented energy conservation technique (Fowler 2002). Instead of just allowing a buoyant instrumented package to rise freely in the water column and then overcome the force exerted by that buoyancy to sink it again, the mechanism recaptures a substantial portion of the potential energy 'lost' in the upward motion of the package. This is accomplished with the use of a winch with two drums mounted in a moored subsurface float having substantial buoyancy. The mooring line, connecting the system to the anchor, is wound on one drum (small diameter) while a cable running upward to a much less buoyant sensor float is wound in the opposite direction on the other drum (larger diameter). The different diameters are chosen so that, in concert with the different cable tensions and direction of wrap, the torque on one drum is balanced by torque on the other, resulting in essentially zero net torque on the drum assembly. When the drums are rotated, the smaller drum moves both floats a small distance while the larger drum moves only the small float a much greater distance. Since potential energy is the product of a force times a distance, the energy change of a large float moving a small distance can be balanced by that of a small float moving a large distance in the opposite direction. In operation, the system is analogous to an elevator which conserves energy by balancing the weight of the cage with a counterweight. Like an elevator, the only energy that must be provided to operate the system is that required to overcome system friction which would, in this case, also include hydrodynamic drag.

ICYCLER

The first operational application of this principle occurred in the Canadian high arctic. Scientists needed to assess the magnitude and timing of ice melt freshwater flux through the Arctic Archipelago as an indicator of climate change (Fowler et al. 2004). Acquiring this information was not possible with conventional mooring technology as lower density freshwater tends to concentrate at the top of the water column where dynamic seasonal ice cover has the potential to destroy any moored equipment. The nature of the measurement demanded *in situ*, daily sampling for a year which made an efficient profiling system, that could carry a conductivity, temperature, and depth recorder (CTD) into the danger zone and then return it to safe depth, an ideal choice. The mooring configuration of the Icycler, designed for deployment in Lancaster Sound (ca. 74° N) at a water depth of 200 m, consisted of a Sensor Float, a Mechanism Float, and anchoring components (including a descent slowing parachute and an acoustic release for recovery; Fig. 1). Buoyancies and required cable/line lengths were determined by J. Hamilton using BIO's mooring design model for the anticipated water current regime.

The Sensor Float was based on a BIO streamlined buoyancy package, with an internal buoyancy of 137 Newton (14 kg), which contained a SeaBird 19+ CTD with dissolved oxygen sensor plus a Wetlabs fluorometer and electronics package containing data storage and instrument control electronics (Fig. 2). The Sensor Float was also equipped with a miniature echo sounder to monitor depth below the ice/water interface as the profile progressed. This signal, plus instrument data, was multiplexed and routed through the electronics package to the Mechanism Float via a 4-conductor cable with a braided Vectran strength member.

The Mechanism Float, housing the drive, had a larger net buoyancy of 1,233 N (126 kg) and was secured to a braided Kevlar mooring line at a nominal depth of 50 m (Fig. 1). Both floats had a combined buoyancy of 1,370 N (140 kg). The two winch drums were geared together to give a torque/rotational relationship of 10:1 (Fig. 3). With the buoyancy of the Mechanism Float being nine times that of the Sensor Float, the Sensor Float drum winds out 10 times the line that the mooring drum winds

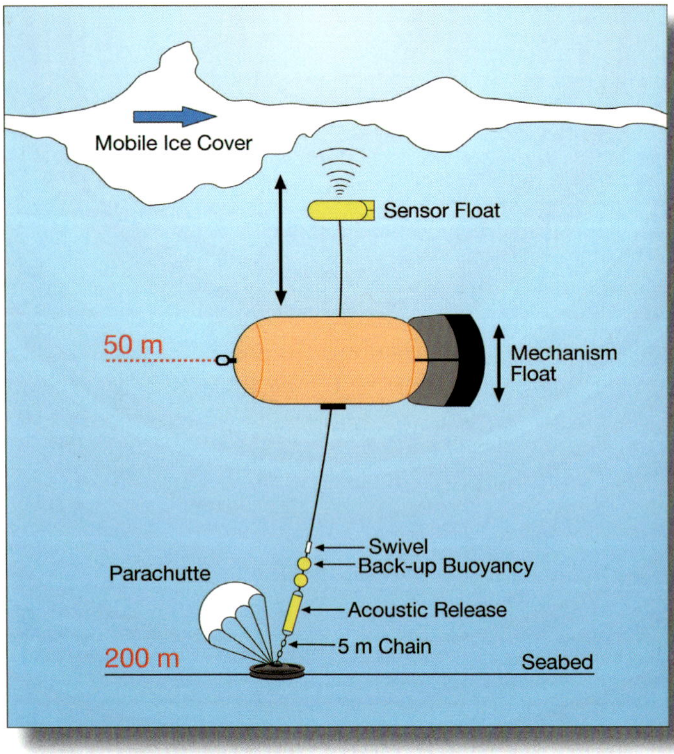

Figure 1. Icycler mooring configuration.

in, yielding a net upward motion ratio of nine. By using a lead screw to drive the winch assembly back and forth as cable and line is wound on or off, it was possible to eliminate the complexity and power loss involved in using powered spooling fairleads. Cable was laid on both drums in a single wrap to maintain a constant effective drum diameter to preserve torque and energy balance. The whole winch assembly was made neutrally buoyant so as not to upset float trim as the drums moved back and forth. Because of mooring knock-over imposed by water currents and the downward winching movement of the Mechanism Float, additional cable (16 m) was used to permit the Sensor Float to reach the surface or the underside of the ice.

The larger winch drum also functioned as the housing for the drive motor, batteries, and system electronics for both motor and instrument control and data storage. Because the cable from the Sensor Float was spooled directly onto this drum, no external slip rings were required. An innovative means of driving the drum, called the SeaMotor, was developed that needed no rotary seals, or underwater slip-rings (Fig. 4). The drive motor and battery pack are suspended together on an axial shaft within, and concentric with, the large drum to form a pendulum. A sprocket on the motor shaft engages an internal gear fixed to the pressure case end-cap of the large winch drum (Fig. 4) so that when the motor shaft turns,

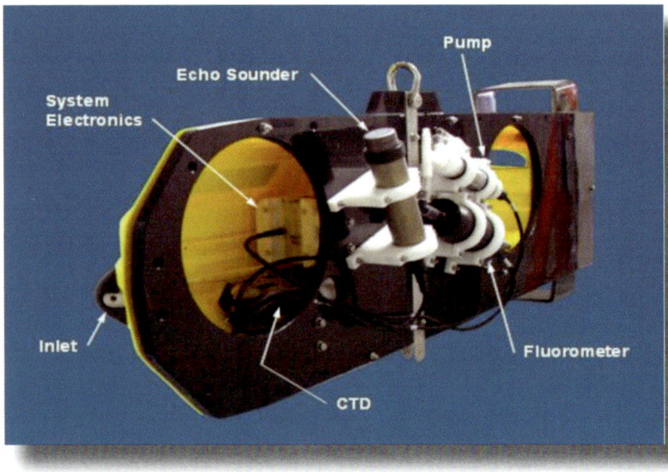

Figure 2. The Sensor Float for Icycler with one fairing and spherical buoyancy removed. The CTD and electronics package can just be seen on the far side of the bulkhead.

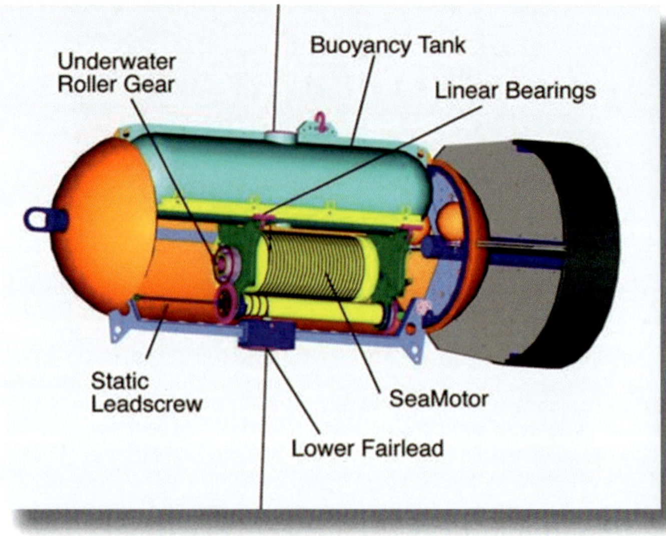

Figure 3. The Mechanism Float for Icycler with one fairing removed to show the winch drum/cable wrapping arrangement.

the outside drum rotates against the gravitational force on the pendulum like the interaction of a hamster on an exercise wheel. As torque requirements increase, the battery/pendulum rotates upward to meet the demand until gravity forces the pendulum weight downward and the winch drums rotate. At the start of a profile, the motor rotates the large drum to unwind cable allowing the Sensor Float to move upward, while the small drum winds in the mooring line to pull the Mechanism Float downward. When the Sensor Float has reached its surfacing depth, the motor

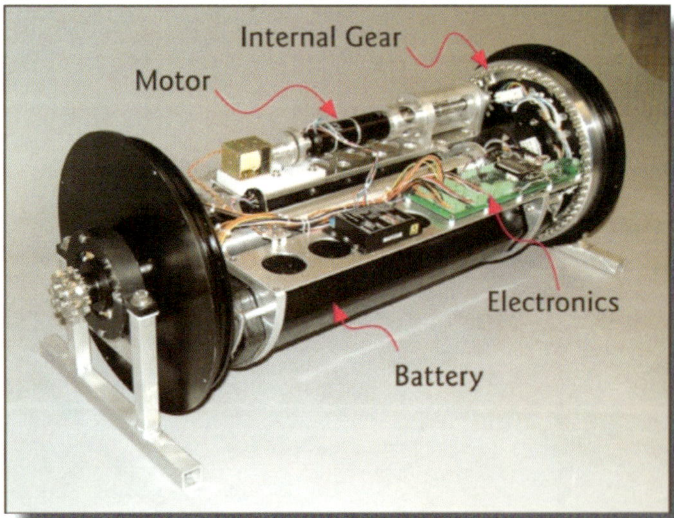

Figure 4. The SeaMotor for Icycler showing the shaft mounted battery/pendulum and motor assembly.

is reversed (Fig. 3) allowing the Mechanism Float to rise by unwinding line from the small drum which, in turn, winds in cable onto the large drum, to pull the Sensor Float back downward. This system proved to be exceptionally efficient, with an overall power consumption of just 23 watts while profiling. The fact that the motor/battery turns relative to the case means that a shaft mounted slip ring assembly was required, but that was not an issue since it could be housed inside the pressure case and thus operate in air.

The Icycler was successfully deployed in Lancaster Sound on two occasions in 2003-04 and 2006-07. In both cases, data were recovered for a full year (Hamilton et al. 2009). Interestingly, the initial goal of obtaining data on fresh water flow was met and satisfied project requirements, but the additional biological information gained with the fluorometer and oxygen sensor provided valuable and unprecedented insights into a high arctic ecosystem.

SEACYCLER

The early success with the Icycler led to international recognition that the system might be extended to more challenging applications. This interest was driven by the need for real-time data on the 'health' of the oceans and atmospheric-ocean interaction as it relates to the study of climate change. An international consortium was created to further develop the now-proven system (Siddall et al. 2012). The consortium consisted of BIO, the Scripps Institution of Oceanography (SIO) in La Jolla, California, the GEOMAR Helmholtz Centre for Ocean Research, Kiel and Bremen University in Germany, the National Institute of Oceanography in the United Kingdom, and Rolls Royce Canada Limited-Naval Marine in Dartmouth, Nova Scotia, as a commercial partner.

The envisioned scope and potential complexity of the project was greater than that of Icycler. Specifications called for deployments in water depths up to 5,000 m, the capability of profiling the top 150 m of the water column with a substantial sensor suite, and the capability of transferring data ashore via satellite. Operational conditions were also demanding with the accommodation of substantial mooring knock-over due to currents throughout a deep water column while still being able to transmit data ashore once per day for periods up to a year in wave heights up to 2 m. Later, other secondary objectives were incorporated such as the ability to acoustically receive operational commands, communicate inductively with other instruments located on the mooring line beneath the profiler, and increase the frequency of profiling. Two major challenges were tackled first since they would determine the project's ultimate success or failure.

The first challenge was to devise an approach that would permit the system to successfully offload data in the defined sea state. In any significant sea, wave forcing disrupts the stability of any structure on or near the surface. The normal way of resisting this instability is through an increase of size and/or buoyancy of a structure. However, both of these attributes have potentially negative impacts on the energy conserving drive system. A large body produces large wave-induced drag forces

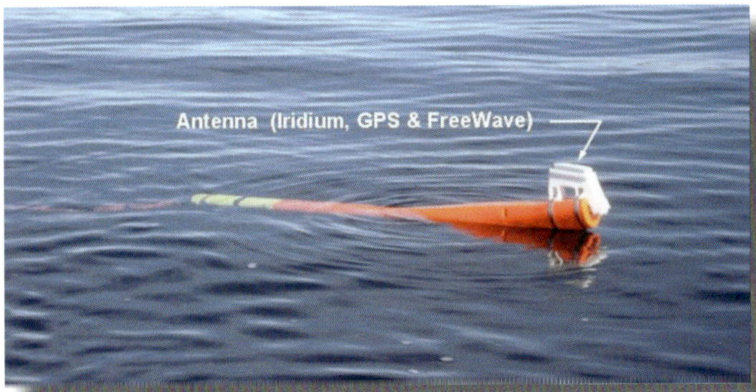

Figure 5. The Communication Float for SeaCycler with antenna clear of the water and showing the lead-in cable with attached, red buoyancy elements just visible beneath the surface. In a wave field, the Float rides the waves easily without dipping the antenna beneath the surface.

which upset system balance as the body approaches the surface. When a buoyant body surfaces, buoyancy is consumed to lift a portion of the body clear of the surface which again can upset the system's energy-balancing principle. Thus, to satisfy drive system constraints, the surfacing element had to be both small and possess little buoyancy, two characteristics that do not enhance stability.

An effective solution was eventually conceived that limited imbalance and thus the impact on system efficiency. A small 1.5 m long Communication Float, with 49N (5 kg) buoyancy, was designed to float near vertical when submerged to reduce vertical drag forces. When it reaches the surface, it flips to a near horizontal attitude with a counterweight 'keel' at the bottom end to ensure that an antenna assembly at the top remains clear of the water. A multi-conductor, double armoured steel cable connecting it to the rest of the mooring was rendered near buoyant by the addition of discrete buoyancy elements along its length to ensure that it had little impact on float attitude when surfaced. Since stability is a function of water plane area, the large surface area of the inclined cylinder relative to its size conferred surprisingly great stability to the assembly. The Communication Float's transmission capability consists of a FreeWave, UHF modem for local buoy to ship communication and Iridium satellite communication with integral GPS (Global Positioning System) for transmission to shore. These functions were accommodated with a submersible multi-function patch antenna mounted as shown in Figure 5. The Communication Float's performance dramatically exceeded the original specification with successful data transfer in waves up to 5.5 m in height.

The second major design challenge centred on scaling up the original Icycler design to meet the new project requirements. Modelling showed that it would require 1,078 N (110 kg) of buoyancy to lift a cable to the surface from the Mechanism Float in the anticipated currents compared to just 137 N (14 kg) of buoyancy for the Icycler. While the system would be moored with the Mechanism Float at a nominal depth of 150 m, the knock-over due to water currents on a 5,000 m mooring cable necessitated the storage and payout of 466 m of profiling cable to reach

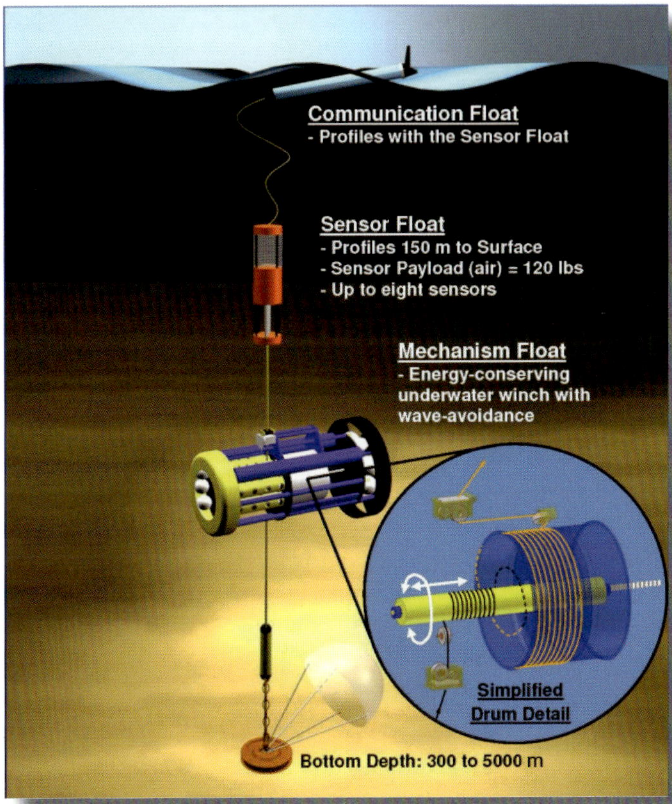

Figure 6. SeaCycler mooring configuration showing from top to bottom the Communication Float, Sensor Float, and Mechanism Float with inset showing a detail of the drum arrangement. The lead screw that drives the winch drums back and forth as cable is wound on or off is shown in white on the right of the Drum Detail.

the surface compared with the Icycler's profiling cable length of 66 m. It proved impossible to maintain Icycler's operating ratio of 10:1 because of the excessive torques that the required buoyancies would generate, so this ratio was reduced to 5:1 which did not have a dramatic effect on overall efficiency. While this reduced Mechanism Float buoyancy to 4,310 N (440 kg), additional in-line buoyancy could be inserted below it to regain mooring 'stiffness'. The lower operating ratio had the major benefit of simplifying the winch drum design. The assembly incorporated the two different drum diameters on a common shaft to dramatically increase efficiency due to fewer moving parts (Fig. 6 inset). Again, the cables were stored in a single layer to avoid any efficiency-destroying torque imbalance. To accommodate the required length of 6 mm diameter profiling cable, the drum had to be big, with the larger section having a diameter of 1.15 m and a length of 1 m (Fig. 6). As with the Icycler, cable spooling was accomplished with a lead screw to drive the winch drums back and forth under fixed fairleads as cable was wound on and off.

The drum configuration created a major challenge in the design of the drive motor since no submersible motors existed that could meet SeaCycler's massive torque requirements. While torques are balanced when running normally, wave forcing combines with the large torque arm of the drum to produce significant torsional loads. This was overcome by designing a variant of the SeaMotor, called the TorusMotor, which is mounted in the larger drum (Fig. 7). This motor works on the same principle as the SeaMotor with motor torque provided by gravitational force on a lead weight mounted eccentrically on a bearing-supported internal gear ring. The one major difference is that instead of the motor and pendulum weight being fixed together, a tiny motor is mounted on the pressure case driving the whole assembly around the gravity stabilized pendulum-ring. As torque output increases, the pendulum rotates upward just like the SeaMotor until gravity forces the winch drums to rotate. The distinctive feature of the TorusMotor is that it combines a large major diameter having considerable torque potential, with a much smaller diameter pressure housing which permits a thin-walled, and therefore lightweight, assembly. The TorusMotor/drum configuration confers multiple advantages. There is no need for slip rings at any point in the system and, because the large and small drums turn together, uninterrupted electrical connection exists between the cable above and below SeaCycler allowing seamless, whole-mooring communication. The large drum diameter provides adequate space to mount four battery packs and sufficient buoyancy, in the form of trawl floats and syntactic foam, to render the entire drum assembly neutrally buoyant. The major task of fabricating the TorusMotor housing, machined out of two pieces of solid 13 cm thick aluminum, was accomplished by our partners at SIO.

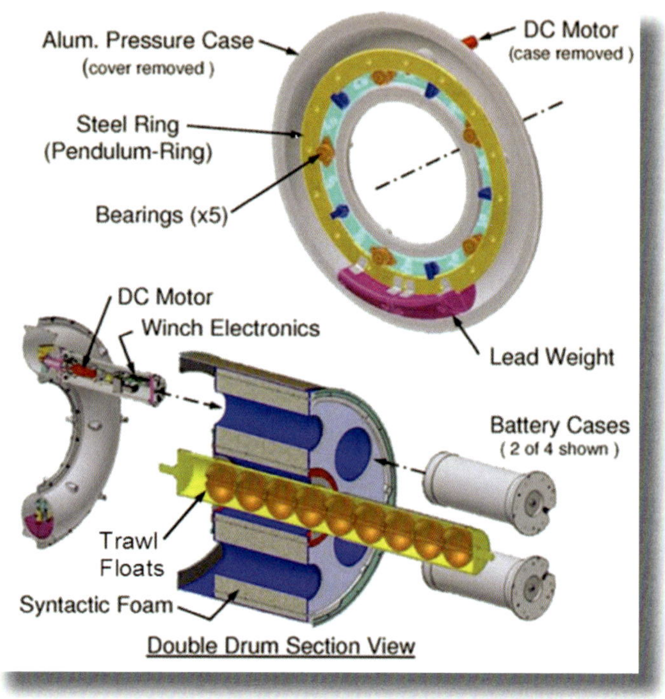

Figure 7. The layout of the SeaCycler winch drums showing the Torus Motor, the syntactic foam buoyancy contained within the larger drum, and two of the four main power battery packs.

It is the unique compliance of the drive system that allows the SeaCycler to work well when near the sea surface. Wave-driven loading would normally impose severe stresses on a system with a conventional fixed-frame drive by either overloading the motor as the cable to the surface elements is pulled taut by a passing wave crest or by producing slack in the trough that would give rise to snap loading at the next wave peak. With SeaCycler, however, these variations are accommodated by the rotationally elastic drive which gives up or takes back cable to smooth out the applied forcing and thus dramatically reduce the potential for damage from waves. This very large system operates with an average energy expenditure of just 15.3 watt-hours per 300 m round-trip profile including power for control and electronics.

Testing in BIO's wave tank revealed that the horizontal float configuration used in the original Icycler Sensor Float was totally inappropriate for exposure to waves. Since one of the scientific goals was to approach the surface in moderately severe weather conditions and modelling predicted that waves would be felt as deep as 45 m, a spar configuration was adopted instead (Fig. 6). The Sensor Float, which houses the substantial sensor suite identified to meet the scientific demands, the main system electronics, and the battery power for all instruments and communications, evolved into a 2 m long, 0.6 m diameter, and 250 kg mass structure. The design parameters for the Communication and Sensor floats were provided to the consortium's German partners who did the detailed design and fabrication for both of these components. However, the task of designing and building the electronics required to support the extensive sensor suite capability and effect system control remained the responsibility of BIO. The SeaCycler mooring configuration thus encompassed three components compared with Icycler's two (Figs. 1 and 6).

The Sensor Float electronics provide main data storage plus functional control of all subsystems including up to eight instruments, the winch on the Mechanism Float, and the two modes of communication, Iridium (worldwide) and FreeWave (local) on the Communication Float. The Communication Float is powered by the Sensor Float and assumes communication system control when energized. It interrogates the Sensor Float for data, controls the complete data transfer system, and is responsible for maintaining data integrity. Mission planning, including profiling interval and speed, sample stops, file transfer, and surfacing aggressiveness, resides in the Sensor Float. The Communication and Mechanism Floats each provide full deployment data back-up.

The Mechanism Float electronics also incorporate autonomous control features. For instance, it can perform 'internal' tasks like monitoring engineering parameters such as motor current to make the decision to abort a profile if wave loading becomes excessive. The Communication Float acts as the communications hub for the SeaCycler, capable of two way communication between a shore operator and the mooring. This communication link is provided via an Iridium-Internet connection which is established between the mooring and custom user software residing on a shore PC that issues commands to provide remote control, data collection, and archiving. The link between the Communication Float and the shore-based software also utilizes data compression techniques which greatly reduce data transmission times that result in reduced battery usage and time spent at the surface while conferring substantial airtime cost savings. The ability to control the system remotely improves system reliability by permitting the SeaCycler to remain submerged when major weather events pass through the deployment area.

Extensive field trials with SeaCycler have been conducted in local and offshore waters. The most significant of these occurred in the early spring of 2011 at a site on the edge of the continental shelf southeast of Halifax, Nova Scotia, in 1,100 m of water. The three components, just prior to deployment, are shown in Figure 8.

During this deployment, SeaCycler measured temperature, salinity, and dissolved oxygen on 644, 150 m deep profiles from 16 April through 26 May 2011 at Station 6 on the edge of the continental shelf directly south of Halifax. The data were recovered in real time and are summarized in Figure 9 (Send et al. 2013). Of particular note are the data describing ambient wave height recovered from a near-by wave-buoy operated by the United States National Data Buoy Centre (NDBC). Substantial waves were experienced during this deployment. Another 7 month deployment from 26 Sept 2011 to 11 April 2012, 200 nautical miles southeast of Cape Cod, Massachusetts, in 2,500 m of water was conducted with our partners at WHOI and SIO and demonstrated even greater system capability (Fig. 10). Data were returned not only from SeaCycler, but also from additional sensors mounted on the mooring cable below SeaCycler that sampled the deeper water column. These included a McLane crawling profiler and a Nortek AquaDopp acoustic doppler current meter. Data were brought to the surface through the SeaCycler components using inductive coupling and successfully transmitted to shore. This type of data collection and transmission represents a major technical achievement.

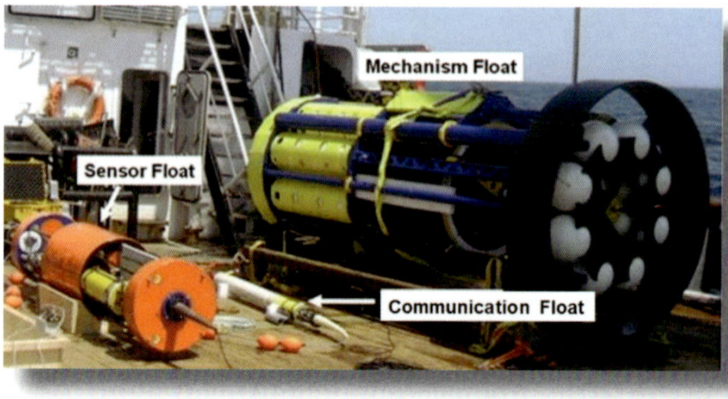

Figure 8. SeaCycler ready for deployment.

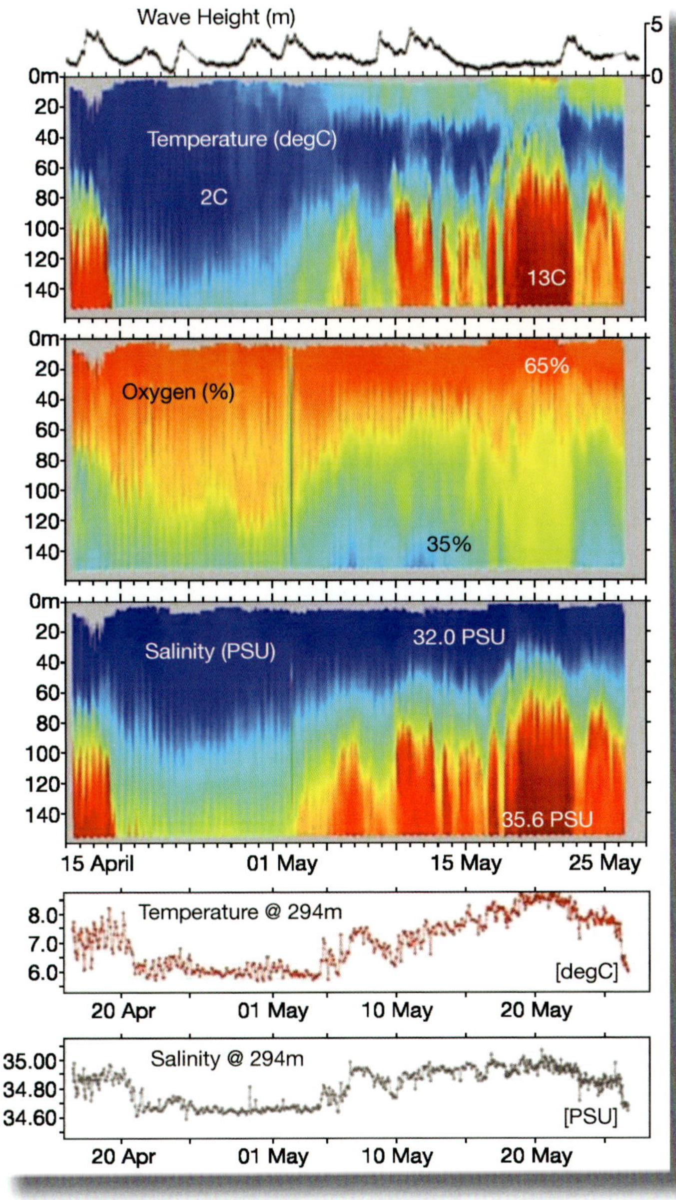

Figure 9. Time-series of surface layer profile data recovered in real time via Iridium satellite link from a mooring in 1,100 m water depth, 250 km southeast of Halifax, Nova Scotia, in April-May 2011. The top panel shows wave height obtained from a near-by United States National Data Buoy Centre (NDBC) buoy. The next three panels showing temperature, oxygen, and salinity data were obtained from sensors mounted on the profiling Sensor Float. Of particular note are the data shown in the two bottom panels that show data recovered inductively through the SeaCycler system from a SeaBird MicroCat CTD located on the mooring cable 130 m below the Mechanism Float.

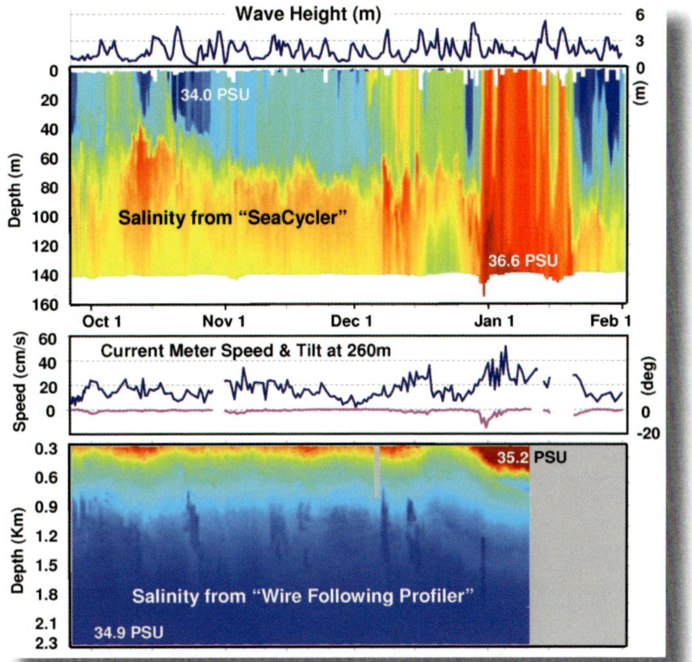

Figure 10. Data recovered in real time from a mooring 200 km southeast of Cape Cod, Massachusetts, in 2,500 m water depth from September 2011 to February 2012. The top panel shows wave height obtained from a near-by United States National Data Buoy Centre (NDBC) buoy. The second panel displays salinity recorded by the profiling Sensor Float. The third shows tilt and current meter data from an inductively coupled AquaDopp Acoustic Doppler Current Profiler and the bottom panel displays data from a CTD integral with a wire-mounted McLane crawling profiler.

CONCLUSION

These successful deployments clearly demonstrate the ability of Icycler and SeaCycler to obtain valuable information from the surface layer of the ocean and return it to researchers onshore in a rapid and usable form. The ability to perform a large number of profiles up to the sea surface in 'real-world' weather conditions is particularly significant. Recent work has shown that this profiling capability can be extended to the bottom of the ocean. The inductive coupling to instruments beneath the SeaCycler is one of the reasons why it is under active consideration by the Oceans Observatories Initiative as the primary platform for world-wide deep-water surface-piercing installations. The success of the energy efficient profiling systems pioneered at BIO is indeed gratifying and a vindication of the maintenance of significant technological capability over the fifty year history of the Institute.

ACKNOWLEDGEMENTS

We gratefully acknowledge funding from the Fisheries and Oceans Canada (DFO), the federal Panel on Energy Research and Development (Canada), the European Commission integrated project CARBO-OCEAN, Contract 511176, and from the (EU) NSF OCE Technology Grant OCE0501783 (United States). Many people gave generous support to the design team at BIO. Jim Hamilton provided mooring performance documentation that allowed us to properly establish the system's operational parameters. In many aspects of mechanical design and execution, Neil Mackinnon provided us with critical practical insights and execution, as did Randy King, Dan Moffatt, Dick Vine, and Scott Young, who came out of retirement to help us. Mechanically, much of the Icycler and SeaCycler was constructed within BIO, with dedication and skill demonstrated by the machine and welding shop personnel under the guidance of John Conrod. On the electronics side we were fortunate to have Mike Vining, Jeremy Lai, George States, and, in particular, Don Belliveau who, besides acting as an oft-consulted intellectual resource, was our mediator with management and the Canadian Coast Guard (CCG). Much of the project's invaluable testing was accomplished with ships generously provided by the CCG with Dave Morse as our constant advocate in procuring ship time. Deployment and recovery would not have been possible without the active participation of our Technical Operations group with Rick Boyce, Jason Burtch, and Jay Barthelotte. Administratively, and one cannot discount this important contribution, we were supported by Val Pattenden, Sandy Burtch, and Helen Dussault, with the division's manager Tim Milligan campaigning within the science community and upper management on our behalf. Many others at Scripps Institution of Oceanography, the University of Bremen Center for Marine Environmental Sciences, and GEOMAR Helmholtz Centre for Ocean Research Kiel helped the project to success. Early engineering support and guidance was provided by Lloyd Green of Scripps. The machine shops at Scripps Institution of Oceanography under supervision by Ken Duff took on the major and critical challenge of manufacturing the torus, with the help of Eric Slater, as well as many other components from drawings produced a continent away. In this endeavour, invaluable coordination and assistance were provided by Matt Moldovan of Scripps. Other components such as the Communication Float and the Sensor Float were constructed entirely in Germany in Kiel and Bremen by Andreas Pinck and Markus Bergenthal, and were successfully integrated with the assembly. Finally, the design team thanks the principal science investigators, Uwe Send (Scripps), Johannes Kartensen (Geomar), Christophe Waldmann (University of Bremmen) and Richard Lampitt (NOC) for their unfailing and patient support and encouragement throughout the life of the project. Even as we explored dead ends and encountered technical roadblocks they never wavered. It has been a rewarding experience to have worked with them.

REFERENCES

Fowler, G.A. 2002. A moored energy-conserving oceanographic profiler. Proceedings of Oceanology International 2002. Oceanology International, London, England.

Fowler, G.A., G.R. Siddall, and S.J. Prinsenberg. 2004. An energy conserving oceanographic profiler for use under mobile ice cover: ICYLER. International Journal of Offshore and Polar Engineering 14: 176-181.

Hamilton, J.M., K. Collins, and S. Prinsenberg. 2009. Temporal variability in arctic zooplankton and phytoplankton populations from moored ADCP and Icycler profiler measurements. International Council on Exploration of the Sea (ICES) Annual Science Meeting, CM 2009/I: 14. ICES, Copenhagen, DK.

Send, U., G.A. Fowler, G.R. Siddall, B.D. Beanlands, M.D. Pittman, C. Waldmann, J. Karstensen, and R. Lampitt. 2013. SeaCycler: A moored open-ocean profiler for the upper ocean in extended self-contained deployments. Journal of Atmospheric and Oceanic Technology 30: 1,555-1,565.

Siddall, G.R., G.A. Fowler, B.D. Beanlands, M.D. Pittman, U. Send, and A.R. Furlong. 2012. "SeaCycler": A deep ocean profiler with full mooring two-way satellite communication. Pages 493-501 *in* Proceedings of the Twenty-second (2012) International Offshore and Polar Engineering Conference (J.S. Chung and W.C. Kan, Eds.). International Society of Offshore and Polar Engineering, Cupertine, CA.

42. LORAN-C AT THE BEDFORD INSTITUTE OF OCEANOGRAPHY

Stephen T. Grant*, Nicholas Stuifbergen, and R. Michael Eaton

SUMMARY

In the 1970s, ship navigation in Atlantic coastal waters was done using the Decca Navigator system, a World War II radio navigation aid that had served well in the North Sea and English Channel. Over the much larger area of Atlantic Canada, however, Decca was severely limited at medium to long ranges by interference from its own sky-wave. Because the pulsed Loran-C system was unaffected by sky-wave interference, it was extended into Canadian waters from the United States. Loran-C signals emitted from shore-based transmitters travelled over land and water paths to radio receivers at sea. The signals travelled at different velocities depending on the terrain crossed along the propagating path, and these variations in propagation velocity had to be considered to avoid significant positioning errors. In order to improve positioning accuracy, the Navigation Group at the Bedford Institute of Oceanography (BIO) developed calibrated Loran-C lattices which were overprinted on nautical charts published by the Canadian Hydrographic Service. The rho-rho Loran passive-ranging measurement technique was enhanced by the Navigation Group for hydrographic and oceanographic positioning which contributed to the development of the BIO integrated navigation system called BIONAV.

Key words: Loran-C navigation system, hyperbolic and rho-rho radio-wave positioning, sky-wave interference, time-difference (TD), terrain propagation effects, additional secondary factor (ASF).

***E-mail**: Enci.Grant@gmail.com

Loran-C was the third in a series of radio-wave navigation systems used for ship positioning off the Canadian Atlantic coast. The first system, Decca Navigator System, was developed for the English Channel and North Sea and commercialized after World War II. It used continuous wave transmissions in the 70 to 130 kHz frequency band, provided positioning to a range of about 440 km in Canadian waters but was limited by interference with its sky-wave (Wells and Grant 2003). It was decommissioned in the mid-1980s. A second positioning system, Loran-A, was developed in the United States. It used higher frequency pulsed transmissions which provided positioning at longer ranges (up to 1,480 km), but with lower accuracy: 1.8 to 28 km compared with 0.03 to 1.2 km for Decca (Bowditch 1977, 1995). Loran-A receivers measured the time differences (TD) between pairs of pulsed shore based transmissions by superimposing the ground wave pulses which were relatively unaffected by the sky-wave that always arrived after the ground wave. The third system, Loran-C, also used pulsed radio-wave transmissions but with a lower frequency (100 kHz) to achieve greater range than Loran-A. Loran-C enjoyed the same advantage as Loran-A in that it was relatively unaffected by sky-waves, but achieved improved accuracy by making its TD measurement with respect to individual radio wave carrier cycles within the pulsed transmissions. Loran-C became operational off the United States Atlantic coast in 1957 and by 1977 was established in many areas, although a gap in its coverage between the northern United States and central Labrador prevented its use for shipping in Canadian Atlantic waters (Bowditch 1977; Fig. 1). This limitation was removed in 1984 when a Canadian east coast Loran-C chain became operational, the principal topic of this article. The Canadian and United States Loran-C chains were in operation until early 2010, by which time ground station radio-wave navigation systems were superseded by the satellite based Global Positioning System (GPS).

LORAN-C OPERATION

The transmitters of the low frequency (100 kHz) Loran-C radio navigation aid were configured geographically in chains of three or more transmitters at known locations arranged in a shallow 'V' with a master transmitter in the middle between the secondary transmitters. The master of the Canadian east coast chain was at Caribou in northern Maine, the X secondary was at Nantucket, Massachusetts, and the Y secondary was at Cape Race, Newfoundland. A third secondary transmitter, Z, was at Fox Harbour in Labrador (Fig. 2).

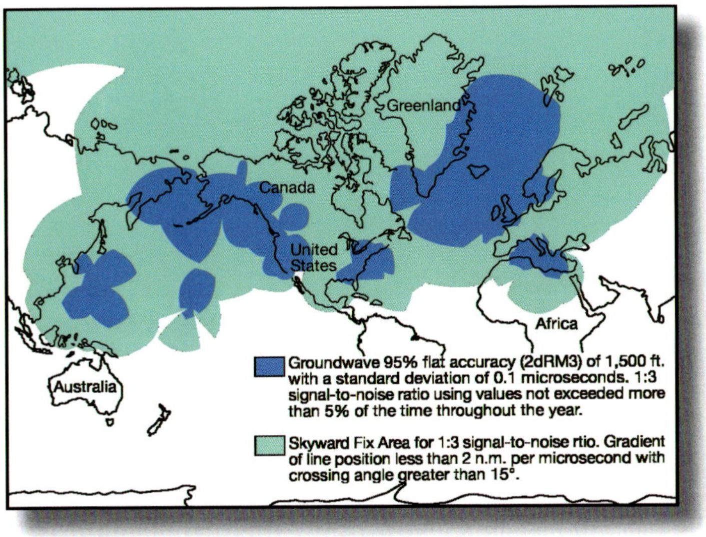

Figure 1. Hyperbolic Loran-C coverage diagram (after Bowditch 1977: Fig. 4340).

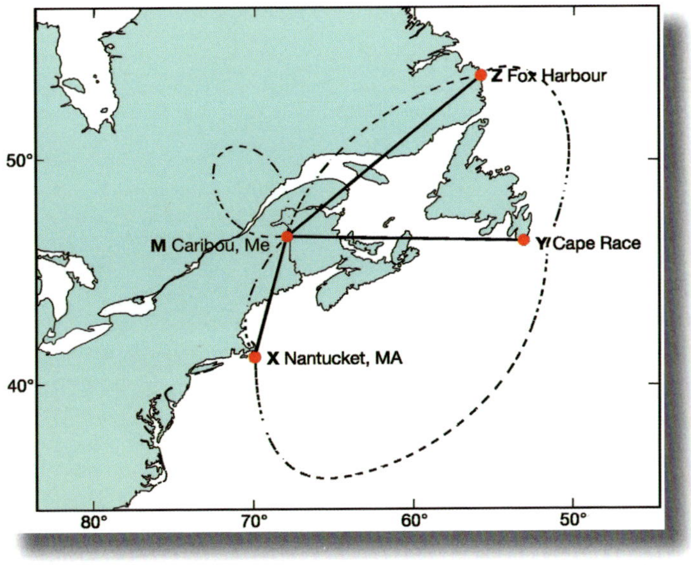

Figure 2. Loran-C Canadian East Coast chain using the Group Repetition Interval (GRI) of 5930.

In operation, the Master station first transmitted a burst of eight pulses plus one extra master identifier pulse (Fig. 3). On receiving this master pulse burst, secondary transmitter X waited a pre-determined identifying coding delay (CD) and then transmitted its eight pulses. Similarly, secondary transmitters Y and Z completed their longer pre-determined CDs before transmitting their eight pulses. Meanwhile the Master waited for a longer Group Repetition Interval (GRI) after its original transmission before initiating the next cycle of transmissions. The GRI of the Canadian east coast Chain was 59,300 micro-seconds, abbreviated to "5930" as the chain identifier.

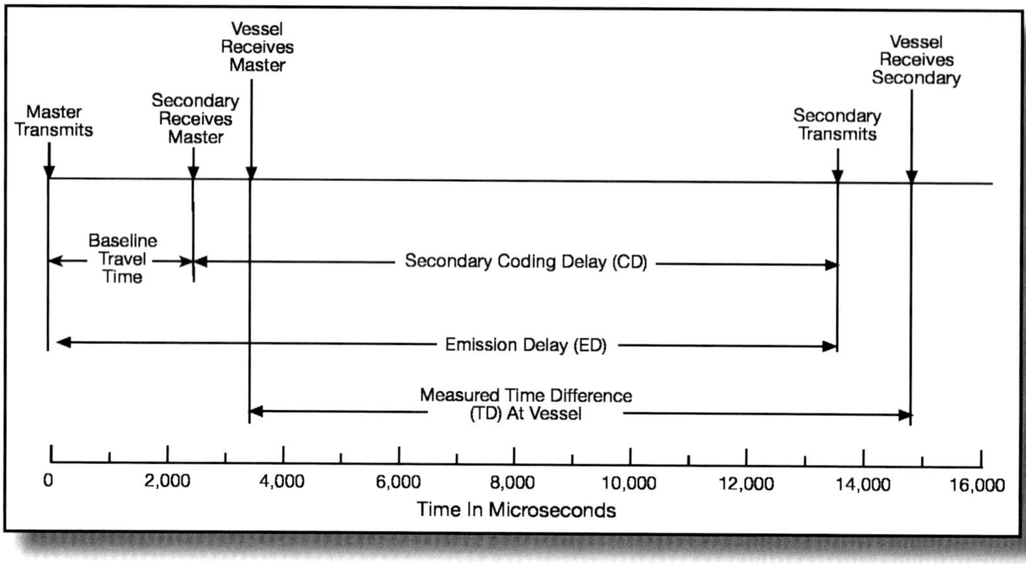

Figure 3. Diagram illustrating signal timing and time delays used in Loran-C radionavigation (modified after Bowditch 1995: Figure 1203b).

The standard Loran navigation receiver on a ship measured the time difference (TD) between the arrival of the Master signal and each Secondary transmission in turn and presented the TD measurements on its display. To find his position the mariner referred to his nautical chart on which lines of constant TD for each secondary station were overlaid, their intersections forming 'lattices'. The mariner found his position by locating the lattice lines corresponding to the readings on his receiver, and finding the point where they intersected. The TD lattice lines consisted of families of hyperbolic contours on the surface of the earth. Hence this and other time-difference systems were often referred to as 'hyperbolic positioning systems'.

Loran-C had two operating modes: (1) TD repeatability mode, and (2) geographic position mode. Using TD repeatability mode, a mariner could return to the same site of a previously recorded set of TDs from the same transmitters with an accuracy of about 0.2 microseconds or 60 m. This method was often used by fishermen to return to and locate moored gear. For this mode of operation, calibration was not needed. In its geographic positioning mode, a built-in micro-computer program, or co-ordinate converter, was used to calculate and display latitude and longitude. To yield true geographic positions, the computation adjusted TD receiver measurements with corrections for overland propagation delay, amounting to about 3.5 microseconds, or position errors up to a few km in Canadian Atlantic waters. Positioning in this mode required calibration of the system to evaluate the necessary TD corrections.

RHO-RHO LORAN NAVIGATION

In early Loran-C chains, parts of the chain could temporarily shut down if long range and radio interference interfered with the reception of the Master signal because secondary stations depended on receiving the master signal before starting their CD pause. To solve this problem the United States Coast Guard installed atomic clocks at each Loran-C station in the early 1970s to predict when the master signal should arrive. These installations opened the door for an innovative new use of Loran-C called rho-rho Loran-C (Eaton and Grant 1972) which enabled the Canadian Hydrographic Service (CHS) to more accurately calibrate the Loran-C lattices being printed on its nautical charts.

Rho-rho or passive ranging Loran-C receivers used their own atomic clock, first to predict when each of the Loran-C stations transmitted signals, and then to measure the travel time of the signals from the respective stations to the receiver. Using the radio-wave propagation velocity, corrected for propagation delays, it was an easy matter to calculate the range from the receiver to each of the Loran-C transmitters. The ranges generated range circles centred on the Loran-C stations and the receiver's position was found at the intersection of two or more of these circles. Rho-rho operation gave more accurate positions over a much larger area than the hyperbolic mode of operation and required only two shore stations for a fix instead of the three needed for hyperbolic operation.

In the early 1970s, CHS at Bedford Institute of Oceanography (BIO) purchased an Austron rho-rho Loran-C receiver which consisted of a specially designed radio receiver, a cesium atomic clock, and a Digital Equipment Corporation PDP8 mini-computer for data acquisition and computations. The PDP8 permitted the user to access the Loran-C rho-rho data and add custom programs to compute position, interface to digital displays, output to data loggers, and perform other tasks. The system was synchronized to the chain by locating the receiver at a known location (e.g., alongside the BIO jetty) and observing ranges to the Loran-C stations. The observed ranges were compared with actual ranges calculated between the known receiver and transmitter positions to derive Loran-C ranges corrected for propagation delays and a synchronization correction which was entered into the computer.

Unfortunately, the atomic clock times drifted, sometimes up to the equivalent of a few hundred metres per day. To correct for this at sea, a technique was developed using Transit Satellite passes (precursor of GPS), when available, in which the average Loran-C velocity during each typical 20-minute satellite pass was used in the Transit fix calculation and the Transit fixes were then used to calculate Loran-C ranges to the transmitters. By monitoring the receiver atomic clock over time, an accurate measure of its drift was determined and used to correct the Loran-C ranges to yield continuous positioning accurate to a few hundred metres. This technique was automated and extended in the Bedford Institute of Oceanography integrated navigation system (BIONAV) (Grant and Wells 2014).

LORAN-C LATTICE CALIBRATION

Loran-C position finding, both hyperbolic and rho-rho, suffered from the weakness that although the ground wave propagation velocity over water was known to a reasonable confidence, the velocity over land was significantly slower and variable, depending mainly on the ground conductivity and the terrain. The 5930 chain, with its long overland transmission paths from the Master at Caribou, Maine, was particularly susceptible to this problem. Virtually everywhere offshore there was much more land-path effect on the master signal than on either of the secondary station signals and this gave rise to systematic errors in the lattice.

The CHS decided to calibrate and then distort the charted lattice lines to account for these land path propagation delays. This meant that the mariner was able to plot the TDs straight from his Loran-C display instead of referring to special look-up tables and applying corrections before plotting his fix as was the case in some jurisdictions. The calibration procedure was quite simple in concept but was challenging to implement.

Working with the CHS Nautical Geodesy Group in Ottawa, procedures were developed for calibration observations, for processing the calibration, and for applying the results to adjust the Loran lattices on the CHS charts. Two approaches to calibration were used. The 'TD approach' used a typical hyperbolic TD receiver which had the advantage that the equipment was inexpensive and simple to deploy and operate, but the disadvantage that a fairly dense grid of calibration points was needed. The 'Rho-rho approach' on the other hand required an expensive rho-rho receiver which was difficult to deploy and operate, but which had the advantage that fewer calibration points were needed, and that information about the propagation velocities in over-land paths was obtained.

TD Calibration Approach

The TD approach involved recording the Loran-C TD readings at a large number of known points on land and at sea as determined by GPS when it was available (GPS was just coming on stream and its availability was limited), other positioning systems in nearshore areas such as microwave positioning, or government survey markers on land. The measured TD consisted of two parts: the difference between the travel times of the Loran-C signals from the master and secondary stations to the receiver plus time delays related to the fixed transmission delays built into each Loran-C chain, such as the coding delay (Fig. 3). The fixed delays were essentially constant and known, so the heart of the calibration was measurement of the range differences in microseconds which included differences from the nominal travel time at the speed of light induced by delays in travel time over land and water caused by their variable electrical properties. Since delays in radio-wave travel through the atmosphere and over water were well documented and essentially known, the main task of calibration was to determine values of over land radio-wave propagation delays, called the additional secondary factor (ASF) in Loran-C terminology. (The known delays caused by atmospheric effects and seawater effects were termed 'primary factor' and 'secondary factor', respectively.)

The overland time delays or ASFs were unique to specific land paths, and so differed for master and secondary signals. With the TD approach to calibration, it was impossible to separate the master and secondary contributions to the ASFs, each of which changed from point to point, so a dense distribution of calibration measurements was necessary. Calibration runs at sea were carried out in major cruises of the CSS *Baffin,* CSS *Maxwell,* CCGS *Bernier,* CCGS *Narwhal,* CCGS *Labrador,* and CCGS *Grenfell* using primarily GPS for reference, as well as a diversity of lines and sites near shore using small boats and microwave positioning.

Rho-rho Calibration Approach

The rho-rho approach to Loran-C calibration was done a little differently in that land-path delays were measured directly and calibration runs at sea were not required. The BIO Engineering Services Division outfitted a delivery van with a diesel generator and installed a work bench with a cesium atomic clock and an Austron rho-rho receiver. Before the first calibration trip, a local BIO reference point of known range readings was established by taking several sets of receiver readings at the reference point and at New Brunswick cadastral (land survey) control points close to the master transmitter at Caribou, Maine. The receiver was taken close enough to the transmitter to minimize errors in the calculated radio-wave travel time to the receiver, but far enough from it to avoid any near-transmitter field effects on the Loran readings.

At the start and end of each series of Loran calibration observation runs, the BIO reference point was used to check synchronization of the rho-rho receiver to the 5930 chain. The relative drift between the Loran chain and the calibration receiver atomic clock was also measured over two or more days. In order to make Loran calibration observations on land, the Austron receiver was located at one of the high quality government survey (cadastral) markers and used to compare the observed Loran range with that computed for the marker position. This procedure of setting up on known points and measuring individual ranges to the M, X, Y, and Z transmitters allowed the exact propagation velocity over that path to be determined. With these data collected over most of the chain coverage land area, it was possible to adjust the lattices over a large region with enhanced accuracy. Travel loops for calibration observations were made all along the Atlantic coastline from Saint John, New Brunswick, to St. John's, Newfoundland. M. Eaton, often assisted by an Engineering Services technician, drove around the country making observations at cadastral markers, while N. Stuifbergen made sense of the results by computing overland propagation delays, corrected for clock drift and other variables.

Computing and Applying ASF Corrections

The usual approach for computing corrections was to fit a bivariate polynomial surface to the calibration measurements. In places, the surface-fit method yielded unstable results, so an ASF prediction program was prepared with an added capability for accommodating ground-wave propagation over a non-homogeneous earth. This program essentially consisted of a simple mathematical model for overland phase lag as a function of distance estimated from a digital coastline file and earth and water surface conductivity (Millington 1949, 1950; Brunays 1976). The values of surface conductivity were adjusted to make the calculated delays fit the measurements. Predicted time delays were calculated at a fine spacing of 3-by-3 minutes for the entire Atlantic region.

Comparisons of the predicted and observed ASF values showed that the predicted values followed the variations of the observed ASF, but with a more or less constant offset. Thus, the ASF differences at calibration sites could be extrapolated and added to ASF predictions in a wider region (and offshore) to produce a dense file of ASF corrections at a grid spacing of 3-by-3 minutes. These ASF grid data files were used to tabulate hard copy print-outs for internal CHS use, create contour plots of ASF corrections for Department of Transport publications such as Radio Aids to Marine Navigation (RAMN), and adjust the Loran-C hyperbolic lattices on CHS published charts for overland propagation delays.

After analyzing the results and deriving averaged TD corrections, a special hyperbolic lattice drawing computer program was created that distorted the theoretical TD lines to account for the calibration measurements. The lattices were applied to charts of the Canadian Atlantic coast resulting in latticing accuracy of 0.25 micro-seconds (1 standard deviation), representing a multi-fold increase in positioning accuracy (Fig. 4; Eaton and Grant 1972, Wells and Grant 2003).

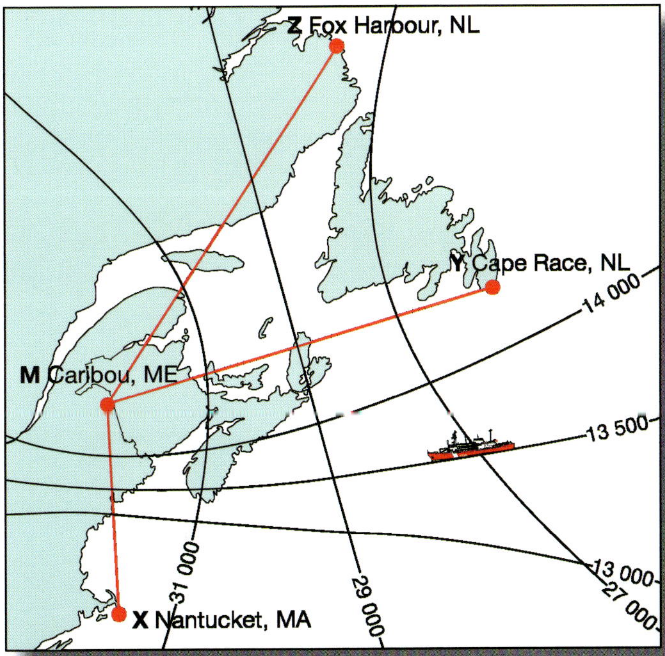

Figure 4. An example of positioning a ship at sea using the 5930 chain Loran-C time-difference (TD) lattices superimposed on CHS nautical charts. The observed shipboard TDs are 13,500 µs from the X transmitter at Nantucket, MA, and 27,000 µs for the Y transmitter at Cape Race, NL. The navigator then plotted the ship position on a chart at the intersection of the X = 13,500 µs and Y = 27,000 µs lattice lines.

RESULTS AND SIGNIFICANCE

CHS at BIO shared its expertise with Loran positioning through practical courses given to local fishermen and other mariners by S. Grant and M. Eaton. In addition, M. Eaton, owing to his experience with east coast Loran, worked with the Canadian Coast Guard in selecting the transmitter locations for the Canadian Pacific coast chain.

Important contributions of the BIO expertise were the enhanced hydrographic charts with Loran-C lattices produced for the Canadian Atlantic offshore (Fig. 4). With these charts, mariners were able to navigate under poor conditions. Instead of anchoring or delaying their estimated times of arrival until conditions improved, they were able to operate to tighter schedules with the consequent savings in operating costs. At the same time, their level of confidence was greatly improved with the knowledge that their positioning system was reliable and accurate, able to keep them clear of rocks and other obstructions. Mariners, scientists and surveyors were able, for the first time, to carry out more efficient operations. Hydrographers were able to run closely-spaced survey lines, for example, at the outer edges of the Grand Banks using calibrated Loran-C and not worry about losing the conventional Decca signal at sunrise and sunset and having to waste a day or more returning to nearshore to reset the Decca system. The overall spatial accuracy of hydrographic, geophysical, seabed, geological, and other oceanographic surveys was undoubtedly improved, recovery of moorings more successful, and ship operations were made more efficient due to the more accurate and improved reliability of Loran-C positioning.

ACKNOWLEDGEMENTS

This program would not have succeeded as well as it did without the assistance of many, many people from a number of agencies. The technicians and engineers of the BIO Engineering Services Division deserve special mention, not only for setting up the calibration van, but also for their ongoing support in the field as well as at BIO. The CHS National Nautical Geodesy Group helped enormously with the design of the calibration methods and the special calibration and latticing software. The officers and crew of the several Department of Fisheries and Oceans and Canadian Coast Guard vessels should be recognized for their help with the data collection and for their invaluable nautical advice. Finally, the numerous engineers, mariners and technical staff in the Canadian Department of Transport, the United States Coast Guard, and the Halifax Pilotage Authority should be recognized for their advice and assistance.

REFERENCES

Bowditch, N. 1977. Radionavigation systems, Chapter XLIII. Pages 967-1,018 *in* American Practical Navigator: An Epitome of Navigation, Vol. 1. Defense Mapping Agency Hydrographic Center, Washington, DC.

Bowditch, N. 1995. Hyperbolic systems — Loran C, Chapter 12. Pages 189-198 *in* American Practical Navigator: An Epitome of Navigation, Vol. 1. Defense Mapping Agency Hydrographic Center, Washington, DC. http://fer3.com/arc/imgx/bowditch1995/.

Brunays, P. 1976. Investigation of effects of inhomogeneous and irregular terrain on the groundwave propagation at 100 KHz. Unpubl. report, Canadian Hydrographic Service, Ottawa, ON.

Eaton, R.M. and S.T. Grant. 1972. Rho-rho Loran-C for offshore surveys. The Canadian Surveyor 26: 125-135.

Grant, S. and D. Wells. 2014. The Bedford Institute of Oceanography integrated navigation system (BIONAV). Pages 353-357 *in* Voyage of Discovery: Fifty Years of Marine Research at Canada's Bedford Institute of Oceanography (D.N. Nettleship, D.C. Gordon, C.F.M. Lewis, and M.P. Latremouille, Eds.). Bedford Institute of Oceanography-Oceans Association, Dartmouth, NS.

Millington, G. 1949. Ground-wave propagation over an inhomogeneous smooth earth. Proceedings of the Institute of Electrical Engineers - Part III: Radio and Communication Engineering 96(39): 53-64.

Millington, G.A. 1950. Ground-wave propagation over an inhomogeneous smooth earth, Part 2: Experimental evidence and practical implications. Proceedings of the Institute of Electrical Engineers - Part III: Radio and Communication Engineering 97(48): 209-221.

Wells, D. and S. Grant. 2003. Technical developments in depth measurement techniques and position determination from 1960 to 1980. GEBCO (General Bathymetry Chart of the Oceans) Centenary Conference Proceedings — Charting the Secret World of the Ocean Floor: The GEBCO Project 1903-2003. International Hydrographic Bureau, Monaco. http://www.gebco.net/about_us/presentations_and_publications/#centenary_conference/.

43. THE BEDFORD INSTITUTE OF OCEANOGRAPHY INTEGRATED NAVIGATION SYSTEM (BIONAV)

Stephen T. Grant* and David E. Wells

SUMMARY

In 1975, a survey of scientists, hydrographers, ships officers, and technical support staff at the Bedford Institute of Oceanography concluded that positioning accuracy and reliability on Institute ships could be improved by combining the outputs of the various onboard navigation systems in a computer-based system. As a result, the development of BIONAV began in 1975 and it was first used operationally in late 1978. In this paper, the unique BIONAV integration approach is described by comparing it with other integrated navigation approaches of the day. The method of using the strengths of one system to compensate for weaknesses in others to achieve improved accuracy and reliability is discussed. BIONAV gradually evolved over its 20-year lifespan before it was replaced by the Global Positioning System (GPS).

Key words: BIONAV, integrated navigation systems, GPS, Loran-C, Kalman filtering.
***E-mail:** Enci.Grant@gmail.com

Shiptime for marine scientific and hydrographic operations is very expensive. Therefore, it is important that no time be lost due to faulty or inaccurate navigation. In addition, accurate knowledge of position at sea is often important, for example, in hydrographic charting surveys. The development of the Bedford Institute of Oceanography (BIO) Integrated Navigation System (BIONAV) project started in 1975 when it was realized that, although BIO ships were equipped with numerous navigation instruments, only a small percentage of this equipment was being used at any given time. Navigators would simply 'choose the best and throw out the rest' when faced with time constraints and the need to select from so much data in so many forms.

The scientific exploration and survey work carried out by hydrographers, geoscientists, and oceanographers at BIO placed stringent and varied demands on the navigational requirements of BIO ships which have operated throughout the world, but work mainly off Canada's east coast and Arctic Canada. They are required to carry out many tasks such as running closely spaced survey lines, locating drill or sample sites to within a few tens of metres, maintaining station over sites for up to several hours, and deploying and recovering moored instrument packages. These tasks are carried out inshore as well as hundreds of kilometres offshore in depths of several kilometres. Frequently, all of these operations are carried out on a single cruise lasting a few weeks. BIO ships must also contend with ice, storms, and fog.

In the 1970s, all BIO ships were equipped with Transit satellite receivers, gyrocompasses, and Doppler or Pitot logs as well as Decca, Loran-A, and Loran-C receivers. Passive ranging or rho-rho Loran-C systems were also used routinely. These systems used atomic clocks to measure ranges to shore-based Loran-C transmitters (Grant et al. 2014). Occasionally Omega and VLF receivers were also carried. The radio navigation conditions varied from being able to receive Decca, Loran-A and C, Omega, and VLF signals in some areas off Newfoundland to only being able to receive Omega, VLF, and Loran-C sky wave signals in the Arctic. Acoustic techniques were used occasionally to position both the ship and towed underwater vehicles.

In 1975, a survey was conducted with about 80 users (geophysicists, oceanographers, hydrographers, ship's personnel, and technical support staff) to determine the existing status of and future needs for navigation in BIO ships. Their responses were as varied as their backgrounds, but the bottom line was that about 85% felt that a BIONAV type of navigation system was necessary.

Most people stressed that BIONAV should be reliable and simple to operate and that the navigation data should be made available when and where needed in the most convenient form for use by scientists and/or ship's officers (e.g., video displays and hard copy plotters). It was suggested that the following be provided: (1) real time Eötvös corrections, computed and filtered to match the damping in the gravimeter; (2) ocean current vector, estimated from comparisons between relative velocity (from log and gyro) and absolute velocity (from Loran-C); (3) all raw data logged along with the estimates of latitude, longitude; and (4) speed and/or distance travelled over the bottom in real time to devices such as side scan sonars, seismic profilers, and towed CTD (conductivity, temperature, depth) sensors.

As a consequence of discussions among users, key BIONAV design goals were established. These stipulated that the system should be reliable, simple to operate, compatible with independently functioning component navigation systems, and operated using existing equipment. It was also decided that the design should be capable of easily adding, deleting, and switching sensors, continually evolving but with annual changes small enough to avoid extensive retraining, and capable of being moved from one ship to another or into a standard-sized shipping container.

BIONAV continued to evolve throughout its 20-year lifespan in response to user feedback, changing requirements, and new technology (Wells and Grant 1981).

BIONAV INTEGRATION APPROACH

The generally accepted technique for optimally combining the outputs from dynamic systems, taking into account their differing error characteristics, was known as Kalman filtering (Kalman 1960). To set up a Kalman filter, it is necessary to specify a state vector (i.e., an array of position, velocity, and other need-to-know elements), a state transition model modelling the time variability of the state vector, and an observation model modelling the relationship between the system inputs (observations) and the state vector elements.

In early attempts at integrated navigation (Halamandaris and Ozdes 1970), a state vector was specified which contained all possible system error parameters (in one case as many as 45). However, the difficulties in assigning weights and correlations for all the elements of such a state vector prevented successful implementation of this approach which attempted to put too much physics into the Kalman filter. At the other extreme was the 'position-locked loop' technique (Clark et al. 1976) in which the state vector contained only positions and position biases. This approach was easier to implement, but ignored the physical reasons behind the position biases and was more easily degraded by changes in performance of component systems. Our approach fell between these two (Wells and Grant 1977). We wanted to use all the information at our disposal, including physical laws and causes, but we also wanted to keep the size of our state vectors to a minimum. We decided to restrict the elements of our state vectors to parameters with physical meaning and to 'modularize' our filtering by implementing several small Kalman filters rather than one large one. Each of our small filters was designed to handle one kind of error so that correlation between the filters could reasonably be ignored. Since the filter update intervals were considerably different for different kinds of errors, our several small filters were updated asynchronously. We also planned for the fact that the suite of navigation systems integrated by BIONAV would vary from cruise to cruise, or even during a cruise, and the addition or removal of individual systems could easily be accomplished by enabling or disabling the filter(s) used by that system.

BIONAV SOFTWARE STRUCTURE

During the decade prior to the start of BIONAV development, computer memory cost dropped by a factor of 20 while memory size increased by a factor of 50 (Wells and Grant 1977). The tools were changing and with that came new ideas about how to use them. The most expensive and most limiting resource was no longer the computer, but the programmer's time. Top-down approaches to software development were introduced that revolutionized the process of programming. It was realized that a complex problem was best handled by suitably abstracted terms and entities natural to the problem itself (e.g., instead of worrying about the technical details and correction models of a ship's log, it is more productive initially to just think of a device that measures ship's speed). This had two consequences for the development of BIONAV software. First, we should use the highest level language available to us and, second, we should first describe the problem macroscopically and then gradually refine our description of each aspect. Another rule of thumb during this period was that a computer program should be readable and that program readability would depend as much on style as structure. The most important guideline was simplicity: i.e., do not be unnecessarily clever or complicated nor worry about efficiency until you have to, and instead of trying to 'debug' bad code, simply rewrite it. The code should be self-documenting because, like flowcharts, external documentation most often described not what the code does but what the programmer thought it did at the time the flowcharts were drawn.

In applying these concepts to BIONAV, we decided to use standard FORTRAN IV as our programming language. Our choice was based on our familiarity with it and its portability between computers. We also knew that no matter how well-structured, modular, simply-written, self-documented, and easy-to-read our program was, it had to work reliably and be robust. It had to work not just on the easy or the most frequently-used applications, but all the time. It also had to defend itself against bad input data. Programs can be robust by being resistant to their own faults or additionally resistant to faults in their hardware environment. The more restricted robustness (in programs that resist faults in software only) is called anti-bugging or defensive programming. The more general robustness (in programs that resist faults in both software and hardware) is more important in real-time applications such as BIONAV than in data processing applications where hardware faults merely delay the job until they are fixed. Modules were designed to be mutually suspicious. All input data were checked. Debugging and error-checking statements were added from the start and were left in after the program was in production.

Because we were attempting to design BIONAV in a top-down fashion, we had to think carefully about its division into modules, not just between hardware elements but with ease of operation as well. The most serious problem we faced in structuring BIONAV was communication between independently scheduled modules. To make BIONAV robust, we built in primary modules and alternate modules for each critical task along with tests to determine whether the modules executed correctly. If so, then the secondary and even tertiary modules took over in succession. Any change in status was logged and listed on the operator's console and video displays.

During the 1970s, the trend towards 'smart' interfaces was well underway with some computations being moved from the central processor to independent pre-processors on the interface board or in the sensor itself. This trend was used extensively in BIONAV. The advantage of pre-processing and data logging outside the central processor was that the system was no longer totally dependent on the faultless operation of the central processor.

IMPLEMENTATION

The basic BIONAV system combined the outputs from the Transit satellite system, passive-ranging Loran-C, and ship's log and gyrocompass (Fig. 1). The strengths and weaknesses of these different systems are summarized in Table 1.

Transit Satellite Navigation (SATNAV)

Transit satellite navigation fixes were based on signals received from the overhead passage of a single satellite, unlike the present global positioning system (GPS) in which numerous satellites are available simultaneously. The Transit satellite fixes were referred to a well-understood, consistent coordinate system, were available anywhere in the world, and were free from time-dependent errors. They therefore provided an excellent framework of position fixes to which other navigation systems could be referred. However, only a few dozen Transit satellite point positions were provided per day, each requiring about 15 minutes or so of satellite tracking. The accuracy of these point positions was very sensitive to errors in the relative ship's track (which was provided by a complementary system) during these 15-minute periods. For example, Stansell (1978) estimated that for each knot of north-south velocity error, the resulting Transit point position would be in error by about 400 m. Due mainly to this sensitivity, the accuracy of an individual Transit fix was not as good as the repeatability of many other navigation systems. However, these Transit fix errors tended to cancel when averaged over several fixes. For example, the same velocity error operating on north-going and south-going satellite passes produced fix errors of equal but opposite sign (Eaton et al. 1976).

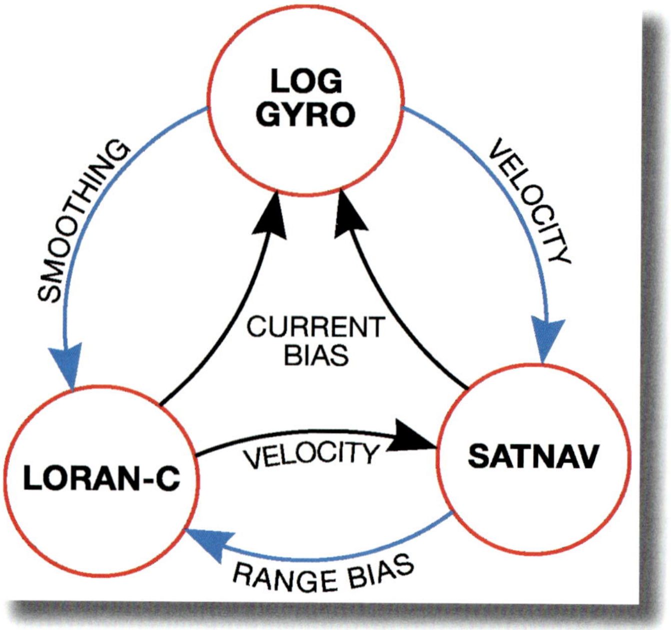

Figure 1. Schematic representation of the basic BIONAV system, showing interactions among the three components of BIONAV: ship's log and gyrocompass, Loran-C radio wave positioning, and Transit satellite (SATNAV) positioning.

Table 1. A comparison of the strengths and weaknesses of the basic BIONAV system components.

Component	Strengths	Weaknesses
SATNAV	geographic positions no long-term biases worldwide coverage	intermittent fixes velocity input needed
LORAN-C	geographic positions continuous medium-term accuracy	long-term drifts limited coverage short-term noise
LOG/GYRO	continuous worldwide coverage no short-term noise	log useless in ice, during rough weather, and on station

Loran-C

Rho-rho Loran-C (Grant et al. 2014) had a larger coverage area than hyperbolic Loran-C, because a minimum of two rather than three Loran-C transmitters had to be tracked. However, an atomic clock had to be carried on the ship and maintained in synchronization to the Loran-C transmitters. A clock synchronization error of 0.1 μs was equivalent to a range bias of 30 m. In addition, variations in the length and conductivity of the overland path between the transmitter and the ship introduced phase-lag variations which showed up as range biases of up to several hundred metres. To obtain the full benefit of rho-rho Loran-C, the receiver had to be capable of tracking ground wave signals at extreme ranges (we tracked one ground wave to 2,600 km from its transmitter) where the signal-to-noise ratio was sometimes less than 0.2. The Austron 5000 receiver, which was used on BIO ships, averaged or smoothed the noisy signals with an operator-selectable time constant that could be set to between 12.5 and 200 seconds. Hence, the response of the Loran-C ranges (and positions) to changes in ship's speed and course were delayed by some function of this time constant.

The BIONAV Loran-C fix program computed the average position from the intersections of up to four Loran-C ranges. Corrections to the Loran-C ranges were determined from comparisons with ranges computed from Transit fixes. However, since Transit fixes were only accurate to ± 100 m, Loran-C ranges only accurate to several tens of metres, and the range corrections tended to change with time due to the drift of the atomic clock, it was necessary to examine several Transit fixes to determine a trend and use this information to refine the Loran-C range corrections over time. The range errors were assumed to be uncorrelated. The program was flexible. For example, if the cesium clock failed in the Austron receiver, or the clock drift became very large, the Loran-C system could quickly and easily be converted from rho-rho to hyperbolic mode to make a hyperbolic fix calculation for which accurate times were not required.

Log/Gyro

Ship's tracks, determined by 'dead reckoning' (i.e., estimation of a new position based on known travel direction, ship's velocity, and elapsed time from a known initial position) from speed log and gyrocompass readings, were usually smoother over the short term than Loran-C tracks, due to the noise on the low level Loran-C signals, even when Loran-C was damped by the tracking loop. However, the log measures speed through the water, not over the ground, and its performance is degraded, sometimes to the point of being unusable, such as in rough weather, presence of ice, and when the ship is on station. A one-component Doppler log, as used on BIO ships, also only measured the component of speed in the fore-aft axis of the ship as determined by the gyrocompass. In the presence of crosswinds and during course changes, there was an offset between the fore-aft axis and the direction in which the ship was moving. Without a two-component log the amount of this offset could not be measured.

COMPLEMENTARY INTERACTIONS

Transit (SATNAV), Loran-C, and log/gyro interacted in several complementary ways in BIONAV (Fig. 1). Loran-C range biases (due to the clock synchronization error and non-modelled overland phase lag) were estimated from Transit position fixes (by means of a low pass filter). In the absence of winds and course changes, a comparison between Loran-C navigation and log/gyro dead reckoning provided a measure of the ocean-current/wind drift vector (current bias in Fig. 1). Loran-C corrected log/gyro velocities were used to describe the ship's motion during the 15-minute Transit satellite passes.

Due to its modular design, BIONAV introduced flexibility in these interactions. It was possible to reduce the noise of Loran-C at low signal levels by smoothing from log and gyrocompass. In the absence of Loran-C, the ocean-current vector could be estimated from a sequence of Transit fixes. In the absence of dead reckoning, relative ship's motion for Transit positioning could be provided by Loran-C. BIONAV was able to operate with any combination of the three basic inputs, including no inputs (in which case an operator had to enter course and speed changes manually). The remainder of this paper presents details of these interactions.

An early design decision in the development of BIONAV was, where possible, to determine the component observation errors either by comparing the observations with the output from other components (e.g., Loran-C clock bias from Transit fixes) or from self-contained deterministic models (e.g., overland phase lag). As a result, when there was a choice between implementing a particular interaction as either supplementary or complementary, the latter usually was chosen. Indeed, the only supplementary interaction in BIONAV was the combination of Loran-C and log/gyro positions described below.

The most obvious example of a complementary interaction in BIONAV was the combination of the log and gyro data to produce a relative ship's track from some initial position. A second example, was the Transit fix calculation, which required some external measure of the ship's relative motion during the satellite pass. The ship's relative motion was expressed as a table of ship's coordinates that came from either Loran-C or log/gyro. If the log/gyro data was used, the table of coordinates was used directly in the fix calculation. However, because of the noise in the Loran-C positions, if Loran-C data were used, quadratic functions of time were first fitted to both the latitudes and longitudes in the table of coordinates.

Phase-lag Bias

Actual radio waves travel more slowly, and therefore arrive later, than theoretical waves travelling at the vacuum velocity of light. The delay is known as phase lag and is a function of frequency, distance to the transmitter, atmospheric conditions, and the roughness and conductivity of the earth's surface. Phase lag corrections are usually separated into three parts: the primary phase lag (due to atmospheric effects), the secondary phase lag (due to the influence of an all salt water-covered earth's surface), and the so-called additional secondary factor (ASF; due to terrain effects). In BIONAV, the primary and secondary phase lags were computed for every fix. The overland phase lag changes more slowly and was therefore only updated every 15 minutes. The Loran-C overland phase lag model used a digital coastline file, a simple mathematical model for overland phase lag as a function of distance and conductivity developed by Brunays (1976), and the predictive technique called the Modified Millington's Method (Millington 1949). Every 15 minutes, the coastline file was scanned to identify the land-water segments of each ship to transmitter range and Millington's technique was used to update the prediction of the total overland phase lag. The model assumed the conductivity of the land to be the same everywhere. It gave good results at sea, but close inshore it had to be calibrated carefully. The observed overland phase lag and predicted phase lags for assumed conductivities of 3 and 1.5 milli-mho/m for the Nantucket Loran-C range to sites in Chedabucto Bay are shown in Figure 2. The phase lag routines developed for BIONAV were used as the basis of the method for accurately latticing the Canadian Loran-C charts (Grant et al. 2014).

Clock Bias

The accuracy of a Loran-C range measurement depended on accurately knowing the synchronization correction between the receiver atomic clock and the Loran-C transmitter clock. In BIONAV, accuracy was assured by comparing the observed Loran-C ranges with the 'theoretical' ranges computed from each Transit fix. Because the accuracy of a single-pass Transit fix (ca. 100 m) was much worse than the synchronization accuracy desired (ca. 10 m), BIONAV determined this synchronization correction by effectively averaging over many Transit fixes. Several averaging techniques, such as Kalman and other low-pass filters, were investigated before a hard-limited low-pass filter was adopted. From each Transit position fix (which met the acceptance criteria, such as maximum pass elevation greater than 10°, five or more 2-minute Doppler measurements and no major course alterations during the pass; see Wells 1980) a difference (D) between the 'theoretical' and measured range between Loran-C transmitter and ship was obtained. The synchronization for each range was updated by either D/5 or 30 m, whichever was smaller. All synchronization corrections were considered to be totally uncorrelated to avoid the problem of a noisy observation on one range introducing errors in the other ranges via the synchronization correction.

Current Bias

The log/gyro output was used three ways by BIONAV to estimate position by dead reckoning. In the first case, the dead-reckoned position was compared to the Loran-C position, typically every 10 minutes, and then reset to the Loran-C position for the next comparison. The difference between Loran-C and dead reckoning positions was assumed to be due to the ocean current and wind drift. In the second case, the current/wind drift measured from the previous 10-minute period was applied as a correction, but the dead-reckoned position was not reset. This provided a track without position discontinuities as was required for the table of relative positions used in the Transit fix calculation. In the third case, the ocean current/wind drift vector was also applied as a correction and the

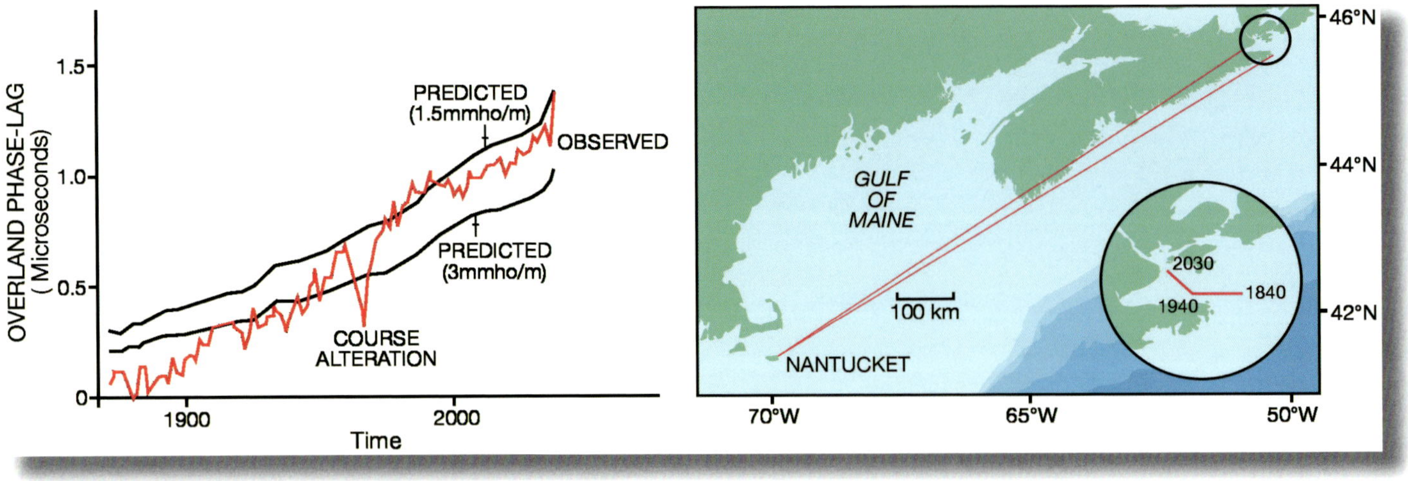

Figure 2. Loran-C phase lag example for a ship's course into Chedabucto Bay, Nova Scotia, from 1840 h to 2030 h. The observed and predicted overland phase lags (ASF) for the Nantucket Loran-C range increase (left) as the amount of land along the propagation path to the ship entering Chedabucto Bay increases (right). (Note: One microsecond of phase lag corresponds to 300 m in range.)

dead-reckoned position was shifted closer to the Loran-C track every 10 minutes by 10% of the Loran-C/dead-reckoned difference. This provided a track that was a compromise between being smooth and close to the absolute Loran-C track.

Log Smoothing

Flexibility in the BIONAV design permitted the nature of some of the complementary interactions to change smoothly as conditions dictated. For example, the scatter between successive Loran-C fixes due to radio noise could be several tens of metres and it was sometimes desirable to reduce this scatter (or smooth the Loran-C data) by combining it with the log/gyro data using a simplified form of the Loran-C least squares equations. Not only did this smooth the Loran-C positions but it also added the capability of combining a single Loran-C range (if that was all that was available) with log/gyro dead reckoning. This feature was essential in areas such as the mid-Atlantic Ridge near the Azores where only one Loran-C range could be received.

BIONAV OPERATIONS

The first routine in the BIONAV software package was written in March 1977 and it was used operationally for the first time during a Loran-C calibration cruise in November 1978. The success of its application led to the installation of BIONAV systems on CCGS *Narwhal*, CSS *Parizeau* (Pacific coast), CSS *Hudson*, CSS *Baffin*, and CSS *Dawson*. The most unusual achievement of BIONAV was its use near the North Pole in a hut during March-April 1979 as part of the Lomonosov Ridge Experiment (LOREX; Weber 1979). Over the years, numerous additional devices were interfaced to BIONAV including Decca, Hi-Fix, Mini-ranger, Omega, gravity meters, propeller rpm, rudder angle and GPS. BIONAV was ultimately replaced on BIO ships with GPS in the late 1990s.

BIONAV accuracy was always considered important and investigated (Wells et al. 1980, Grant 1980). BIONAV accuracy depended on many factors such as the range to the Loran-C transmitters (which affected the range measurement noise), the geometry (angles of cut) of the Loran-C ranges, and the smoothness of the vessel track (which affected the Transit Fix accuracy). The resultant accuracy ranged between 100 m under ideal conditions to as much as 700 m under poor conditions (both figures at 95% probability).

BIONAV'S CONTRIBUTION TO MARINE NAVIGATION

During its 20-year life, BIONAV was used on all three of Canada's seacoasts and enabled the scientists and hydrographers to conduct research and survey cruises at a quality level that would not have been possible otherwise. Indeed, some of this work would not have been possible without the accuracy and flexibility that BIONAV provided, and three decades later the surveys positioned using BIONAV are critical components in Canada's UNCLOS extended continental shelf submission (see Verhoef et al. 2014).

BIONAV consisted of about 150 programs, library routines, and procedures with a total length of about 30,000 lines of code, 95% of it written in FORTRAN. The BIONAV software and documentation was distributed freely to more than a dozen Canadian companies and institutions. Owing to the modular nature of the BIONAV software, they were able to use large blocks of programs even though their hardware configurations differed considerably from those at BIO.

ACKNOWLEDGEMENTS

BIONAV was very much a Bedford Institute of Oceanography project. Although we wrote the computer programs, the guidance and suggestions of the many scientists, surveyors, and engineers at BIO were a critical component of its success. The list of contributors is far too large to present here; they know who they are and also know how grateful we are for their contributions. Ideas like how to best compute the Eötvös corrections or match the course and speed filtering to the gravity meter damping came from BIO scientists; Loran-C phase lag computations involved staff from CHS headquarters, as well as Transport Canada; interfaces to various displays, plotters, loggers, and scientific instruments involved many engineers and technicians from the Engineering Services Division at BIO; and input from hydrographers helped with the design of special survey control functions. Consultations with staff from the University of New Brunswick, where we both earned degrees, helped with some of the more complex programming and lastly, but by far not least, is the major contribution by the editors and reviewers of this document who helped raise it to a much higher quality level.

REFERENCES

Brunays, P. 1976. Investigation of effects of inhomogeneous and irregular terrain on the groundwave propagation at 100 kHz. Internal Report, Canadian Hydrographic Service, Ottawa, ON.

Clark, J., P. Galyean, and R. Wanous. 1976. Recent developments in transit applications and integrated systems. Mahasagar Bulletin of the National Institute of Oceanography 9: 171-190.

Eaton, R.M., D.E. Wells, and N. Stuifbergen. 1976. Satellite navigation in hydrography. International Hydrographic Review 53: 99-116.

Grant, S.T. 1980. BIONAV - the Bedford Institute of Oceanography integrated navigation system. Pages 50-64 *in* Proceedings of the U.S. National Ocean Survey 7th Annual Hydrographic Survey Conference. National Oceanic and Atmospheric Administration, Gaithersburg, MD.

Grant, S.T., N. Stuifbergen, and R.M. Eaton. 2014. Loran-C at the Bedford Institute of Oceanography. Pages 349-352 *in* Voyage of Discovery: Fifty Years of Marine Research at Canada's Bedford Institute of Oceanography (D.N. Nettleship, D.C. Gordon, C.F.M. Lewis, and M.P. Latremouille, Eds.). Bedford Institute of Oceanography-Oceans Association, Dartmouth, NS.

Halimandaris, H. and D. Ozdes. 1970. A Kalman filter augmented marine navigation system. Pages 517-537 *in* Theory and Applications of Kalman

Filtering (C.T. Leondes, Ed.). NATO AGARDograph No. 139, North Atlantic Treaty Organization, London, England.

Kalman, R. E. 1960. A new approach to linear filtering and prediction problems. Journal of Basic Engineering 82: 35-45.

Millington, G. 1949. Groundwave propagation over an inhomogeneous smooth earth. Proceedings of the Institute of Electrical Engineers - Part III. Radio and Communication Engineering 96: 53-64.

Stansell, T.A. 1978. The Transit navigation satellite system. Magnavox Publication R-5933, Torrance, CA.

Verhoef, J., D.C. Mosher, and S.R. Forbes. 2014. Defining Canada's extended continental shelves. Pages 407-414 *in* Voyage of Discovery: Fifty Years of Marine Research at Canada's Bedford Institute of Oceanography (D.N. Nettleship, D.C. Gordon, C.F.M. Lewis, and M.P. Latremouille, Eds.). Bedford Institute of Oceanography-Oceans Association, Dartmouth, NS.

Weber, J.R. 1979. The Lomonosov Ridge Experiment: LOREX 79. Transactions of the American Geophysical Union 60: 715-720.

Wells, D.E. 1980. A new integrated navigation system: BIONAV. Proceedings of the Hydrographic Society Symposium on Position Fixing at Sea 18: 1-26.

Wells, D.E. and S.T. Grant. 1977. Reliable navigation through system integration. Pages 93-98 *in* Proceedings of the 16th Canadian Hydrographic Conference. Canadian Hydrographers' Association, Burlington, ON.

Wells, D.E. and S.T. Grant. 1981. An adaptable integrated navigation system: BIONAV. Pages 195-207 *in* Proceedings of Colloquium III on Petroleum Mapping and Surveys in the 80's. Canadian Petroleum Association, Calgary, AB.

Wells, D.E., S.T. Grant, and D.L. McKeown. 1980. Accuracy of BIONAV. Pages 43-52 *in* Proceedings of the 19th Canadian Hydrographic Conference. Canadian Hydrographic Service, Ottawa, ON.

Energy Developments

Sampling the benthic water layer at the Galaxy II drilling platform off Sable Island, Scotian Shelf, Nova Scotia

Energy Developments

44. THE IMPACTS OF OIL AND GAS ACTIVITIES ON THE MARINE ENVIRONMENT

Donald C. Gordon*, Kenneth Lee, Peter G. Wells, and Paul D. Keizer

SUMMARY

Since 1970, scientists at Bedford Institute of Oceanography (BIO) have conducted a wide range of research programs addressing the marine environmental implications of oil and gas activities in Canada. This research provided new insight into the behaviour and fate of spilled oil and its refined products in cold water environments, their ecological effects, and the rates at which different temperate ecosystems can recover from spills. It documented the distribution of both naturally-occurring and petroleum-derived hydrocarbons in the ocean over a large geographic area. It also investigated the toxic effects and environmental persistence of oil in the marine environment and the effectiveness and potential detrimental impacts associated with the use of oil dispersants. In addition, it contributed towards the development and evaluation of other alternative oil spill countermeasure technologies to minimize the impact of oil spills and to enhance the rates of habitat recovery. As a result of this research, Canada is much better prepared to respond quickly and effectively to oil spills. BIO research also addressed the behaviour, fate, and effects of operational wastes (drilling muds, cuttings, and produced water) discharged during offshore exploratory and development drilling off the east coast of Canada. These results have contributed to the improvement of regulations to minimize environmental impacts and the design of efficient environmental effects monitoring programs. While conducting this research, BIO scientists have played a major role in the international scientific community studying hydrocarbon impacts and in providing sound scientific advice to government managers, the oil and gas industry, and other clients.

Key words: oil spill effects, natural attenuation, bioremediation, oil-mineral aggregates, surf-washing, dispersants, particulate drilling wastes, produced water, environmental management.
***E-mail:** Donald.Gordon@ns.sympatico.ca

When the Bedford Institute of Oceanography (BIO) was founded in 1962, there was little global concern over marine pollution and the impacts of contaminants on marine ecosystems. This was the year that Rachel Carson's *Silent Spring* was published (Carson 1962) which marked the beginning of the environmental movement. Oceanographic research at the time was mainly focussed on determining the structure of the marine environment and understanding the fundamental physical, chemical, geological, and biological processes that shaped it.

All this has changed over the intervening fifty years. It is now clear that many human activities have profound impacts on the marine environment and must be carefully managed in order to avoid irreparable damage to marine ecosystems. The use of hydrocarbons in our society has increased markedly, and in Atlantic Canada we have developed a significant offshore oil and gas industry to help meet our energy demands (Lewis et al. 2014, Williams et al. 2014). In response to the growing need for scientific information to support the development of policies, guidelines, and regulations, over most of the history of BIO its scientists have conducted a wide variety of research programs in eastern Canada dealing with both oil spills and the regulated discharge of drilling wastes and produced water into the marine environment (Fig. 1). This paper highlights this fundamental and applied research and illustrates how the results have been used to provide sound management advice on oil and gas issues of importance to Canada.

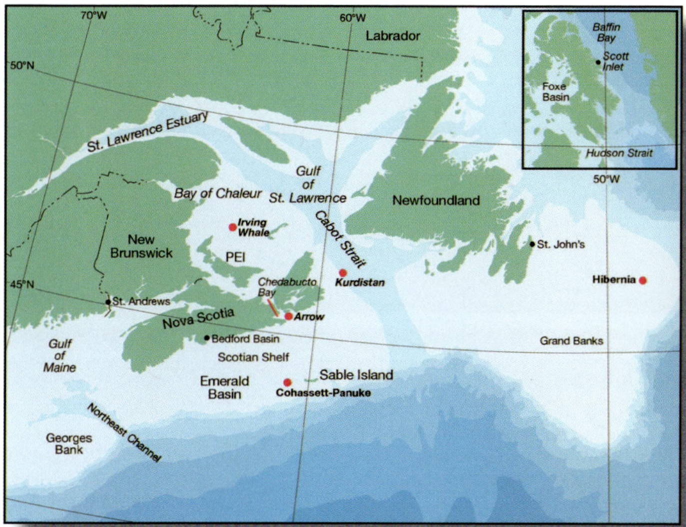

Figure 1. Map of major study areas in eastern Canada including sites of oil spills and offshore developments.

OIL SPILLS

World-wide concern about oil spills began to mount in the late 1960s because of major spills such as the *Torrey Canyon* in the English Channel (1967), the *Florida* in Buzzards Bay (1969), and the Santa Barbara Channel blowout (1969). These incidents received wide media coverage and subsequent scientific studies demonstrated significant environmental impacts. With increasing tanker traffic in Atlantic Canada, it was only a matter of time before a major oil spill disaster occurred close to home.

The BIO oil spill research program began almost overnight in February 1970 when the Liberian-registered tanker *Arrow* ran aground on Cerberus Rock in Chedabucto Bay, Nova Scotia, carrying a cargo of 14,700 tons of Bunker C fuel oil (Figs. 1, 2A). Immediate action was needed to handle this environmental emergency which was the first major oil spill in Canada. The Federal Minister of Transport appointed a three-person Task Force to oversea clean-up activities, an exercise named 'Operation Oil' and headed by Patrick McTaggart-Cowan of the Science Council of Canada (Fig. 2B). Following his appointment as Scientific Coordinator for the response operation, William Ford, Director of the Atlantic Oceanographic Laboratory at BIO, established a Scientific Coordination Team which was charged with coordinating projects being carried out by various federal agencies. Many existing research projects at BIO, as well as at the St. Andrews Biological Station (SABS), New Brunswick, were put on hold as scientists were commandeered overnight to provide support to 'Operation Oil'. No one at BIO had any previous experience working with oil spills, but staff of all disciplines immediately addressed the questions at hand, including creating new methods and tools to study the fate and effects of the spill. Research programs were quickly established using field crews, BIO ships, and Canadian Coast Guard (CCG) helicopters.

Figure 2. Dealing with oil spills: (A) tanker *Arrow* aground in Chedabucto Bay, Nova Scotia, in 1970; (B) physical removal of contaminated sediment from the shoreline of Chedabucto Bay during the 'Operation Oil' cleanup of the *Arrow* oil spill; (C) J. Vandermeulen surveying stranded oil in Chedabucto Bay six years after the *Arrow* spill; and (D) team of BIO scientists examining stranded oil on the shoreline of Bermuda in 1971.

Nearly two-thirds of the *Arrow's* cargo was released into the icy waters of Chedabucto Bay, much of which took the form of an oil-in-water emulsion (Operation Oil 1970). Floating oil subsequently stranded on approximately half the shoreline of the Bay with its behaviour dependent upon the kind of substrate (e.g., cobble, sand, marsh) and ice conditions. Some mortality of intertidal soft-shelled clams was observed, but there was no conclusive evidence of any significant damage to subtidal flora and fauna. Particles of oil were detected in the water column and observed to move out of the Bay and along the coast as far as Halifax, Nova Scotia. It was demonstrated that these particles could be ingested by zooplankton and excreted in fecal pellets. Stranded oil from the *Arrow* was observed as far away as Sable Island, approximately 160 km southeast of Chedabucto Bay.

Following 'Operation Oil', BIO scientists initiated a series of long-term research projects to address the recommendations for additional scientific information on the behaviour, fate, and effects of oil in cold water environments. Some of these projects were carried out in the Chemical Oceanography Division of the Atlantic Oceanographic Laboratory under the direction of E. Levy, while others were initiated in the new Environmental Quality Division of the Marine Ecology Laboratory led by D. Gordon (and later J. Vandermeulen). These were growing years for BIO. New staff was recruited, equipment was purchased, the BIO Fish Laboratory was expanded, and ample operating funds were provided to support the new program.

First, the chemical methodology needed to be improved for accurately determining the concentrations of complex mixtures of petroleum-derived hydrocarbons in water, sediment, and tissues. Concentrations in the environment are often very low (ppb range) and care must be taken to distinguish petroleum-derived hydrocarbons from naturally-occurring hydrocarbons which are widespread in the marine environment. Care also had to be taken to avoid contamination while sampling, especially when working on ships which use numerous hydrocarbon products such as fuel and hydraulic fluids. Fluorescence spectroscopy, which is quick and sensitive, was found to be a suitable method for estimating total petroleum-derived hydrocarbons (Keizer and Gordon 1973), while gas-liquid chromatography (at times coupled with mass spectrometry), a more expensive and time-consuming technique, was adopted to identify individual hydrocarbons (Keizer et al. 1977). This technique was particularly useful for distinguishing petroleum-derived hydrocarbons from naturally-occurring ones and for following changes in the composition of spilled oil due to natural weathering processes.

While the immediate impacts of the *Arrow* spill were evident, it was not known how long these impacts would continue. Therefore, BIO designed projects to investigate the long-term recovery of Chedabucto Bay from the spill. Measurements of petroleum-derived hydrocarbons in the water column were made on a series of cruises (Fig. 3A) and the results demonstrated that concentrations returned to pre-spill levels within a year (Levy 1972). However, stranded oil was found to persist much longer. Persistence was generally related to shoreline energy level (e.g., from waves, tides, and ice) with oil remaining longer in low energy shoreline areas (Owens 1978). It was also discovered that oil stranded near the high tide mark was not static, but was slowly released to intertidal and subtidal habitats where it could contaminate organisms such as soft-shelled clams and eel grass (Vandermeulen and Gordon 1976).

A field survey conducted in 1976, six years after the spill, identified some locations in Chedabucto Bay where oil still remained in intertidal and subtidal sediments (Fig. 2C), but results were confounded by the local chronic discharge of petroleum-derived hydrocarbons (Keizer et al. 1978a). Other studies demonstrated that certain deposit-feeding polychaetes had a high tolerance for living in sediments contaminated with *Arrow* oil and that their feeding activity accelerated the weathering rate of oil through various processes including bioturbation and digestion (Gordon et al. 1978a). Other intertidal organisms appeared to be more susceptible. For example, populations of soft-shelled clams in oiled sediments showed only limited recovery over six years with continued disruption of growth and abnormalities in young to adult ratios (Gilfillan and Vandermeulen 1978), thought to be due to the fact that soft-shelled clams do not possess the inducible mixed function oxidase (MFO) system for detoxification (Vandermeulen and Penrose 1978). Studies of intertidal communities revealed that significant differences still existed between oiled and control sites in 1976 (Thomas 1978). Chedabucto Bay was revisited twenty years after the *Arrow* spill (1990) and weathered oil was still found at some locations (Vandermeulen and Singh 1994). Further samples collected in 1993 and 1997 from Black Duck Cove, where oil from the *Arrow* spill was intentionally left untreated for scientific research, showed that a significant fraction of the remaining residual oil had undergone substantial biodegradation (Lee et al. 1999) and photo-oxidation (Prince et al. 2003). The environmental significance of these natural processes was assessed with a battery of microscale biotests including enzyme induction in winter flounder, amphipod survival, echinoid fertilization, grass shrimp embryo-larval toxicity, and bioluminescent bacterial tests (Wells et al. 1998). While a significant fraction of the residual oil remained in the sediment, biotests showed that it was of low toxicity and habitat recovery was evident from the degree of benthic diversity (Lee et al. 2003a).

The results of Canadian studies on the *Arrow* spill were compared with other oil spills at a symposium on oiled marine environments organized by BIO in 1977 (Vandermeulen 1978). Although immediate impacts can be severe, it was evident that recovery from oil spills is generally in the range of 5-15 years depending on factors such as the kind of oil, the local environmental conditions, and the resident biological communities. The most serious and lasting impacts were observed to occur in low energy coastal environments such as lagoons, estuaries, and marshes where stranded oil can persist for decades (Vandermeulen 1982).

In September 1970, the barge *Irving Whale*, loaded with 4,200 tons of Bunker C fuel oil, sank in the Gulf of St. Lawrence (Fig. 1). The *Irving Whale* was equipped with a heat exchange unit containing polychlorinated biphenyls (PCBs) and polychlorinated benzenes (PCBzs). Oil leaking from the barge created a slick which covered an estimated 400 km^2. Trajectory modelling indicated that the bulk of the oil released from the barge was likely carried by wind and currents through the Cabot Strait into the Atlantic Ocean. Over subsequent years, the barge continued to experience minor leakage and, assisted by BIO, the Canadian Coast Guard with the Canadian Wildlife Service made regular surveillance trips to document the extent of pollution and possible effects on seabirds. In 1996, twenty-six years after its sinking, it was decided to recover the barge with approximately 75% of its cargo remaining to avoid a potential major release of contaminants. BIO was involved in collecting background information and monitoring sediments, seawater, and snow crabs (*Chionoecetes opilio*) for contaminants around the wreck site during the salvage operation (King et al. 2003).

BIO scientists also responded to other oil spills. Advice was provided following the 1974 *Golden Robin* spill in the Bay of Chaleur (Gulf of St. Lawrence) and the 1976 *Argo Merchant* spill in United States waters off Nantucket, Massachusetts. In 1978, the *Amoco Cadiz* spill occurred along the Brittany Coast of France and a group of BIO scientists led by J. Vandermeulen was invited to visit the spill site and assist with the design of relevant post-spill studies. The team spent considerable time evaluating the burial process for oil in beaches and marshes (Vandermeulen et al. 1979) and advising on cleanup and recovery efforts. In 1979, the British tanker *Kurdistan* broke in two, spilling about 7,000 tons of Bunker C oil into the ice-infested waters of Cabot Strait (Fig. 1). This was Canada's first major oil-in-ice spill. The CSS *Hudson* was immediately diverted to the area to carry out observations and BIO staff conducted surveys of spilled oil along the adjacent shore of Nova Scotia. Other studies (Vandermeulen and Buckley 1985) included modelling potential drift trajectories, oil-in-ice interactions, and observations of seabird mortalities (Brown and Johnson 1980). The data were an important component of the litigation to recover millions of dollars in clean-up costs from the tanker owners.

In the 1970s, small-scale experiments were run in the BIO Fish Laboratory (Gordon et al. 1973) and outdoor tanks (Wells and Keizer 1975) to provide information on the concentrations and forms of petroleum hydrocarbons likely to occur in seawater under spill conditions (Fig. 4A). This knowledge was then used to design realistic biological effects studies. Experiments were also begun to investigate the weathering of stranded oil. Chemical changes in hydrocarbon condensate stranded on a low-energy sandy beach on the eastern shore of Nova Scotia demonstrated that volatile and soluble components can persist with little chemical change for many months (Strain 1986). Experiments were conducted on the weathering rates of buried oil using the Dalhousie University (Halifax, NS) Aquatron (Vandermeulen et al. 1994) and, consistent with the results of field studies following the *Arrow* spill, oil was found to persist well beyond 11 months under environmental conditions typical of low-energy, north-temperate conditions.

Figure 3. Collecting seawater samples for hydrocarbon analysis: (A) P. Vass deploying a Niskin bottle from the CNAV *Sackville* in Chedabucto Bay, NS; and (B) F. Zemlyak and E. Levy sampling sea surface hydrocarbons from a dory to avoid contamination from the research vessel.

Figure 4. Conducting experiments on the fate and effects of oil and drilling wastes: (A) D. Aldous, P. Keizer, and D. Gordon conducting oil spill experiments in outdoor tanks on the shore of Bedford Basin; (B) P. Wells conducting oil toxicity experiments with lobster larvae; (C) J. Vandermeulen conducting experiments with phytoplankton cultures.; (D) wave tank constructed at BIO to investigate the effectiveness and effects of oil dispersants; (E) P. Cranford dissecting a sea scallop; and (F) flume tanks constructed to study the effects of particulate drilling wastes on sea scallops.

DISTRIBUTION OF HYDROCARBONS IN THE MARINE ENVIRONMENT

In the early 1970s, BIO scientists began studying the distribution of hydrocarbons in the marine environment off eastern Canada. These background levels of hydrocarbons came from a variety of sources in addition to oil spills including shipping, fishing boats, ballast waters, atmospheric deposition, freshwater runoff, and natural seeps. This information was needed to assess the potential for significant environmental impacts and to provide baseline information for evaluating the impacts of future spills and offshore hydrocarbon exploration and development activities. Consequently, numerous surveys using BIO ships were run over a large geographic area to collect samples of water and sediments for analysis.

The highest concentrations of petroleum-derived hydrocarbons were found in Halifax Harbour and Bedford Basin while those in offshore waters between Nova Scotia and Bermuda were very low (Gordon et al. 1974). Hydrocarbon concentrations in Bedford Basin were found to be higher in winter and primarily anthropogenic in origin (Gordon et al. 1978b). Hydrocarbons in surficial sediments on the Scotian Shelf appeared to be primarily natural in origin, although there was some evidence of contamination at abandoned drilling sites (Keizer et al. 1978b).

Repetitive surveys in the Gulf of St. Lawrence over a ten-year period demonstrated that the major source of petroleum residues in the Gulf was Atlantic water entering through the Cabot Strait and that there was a substantial decline in these levels during the mid-1970s (Levy 1985; Fig. 3B). Levels in the early 1980s were similar to those of other unpolluted areas suggesting that atmospheric deposition exceeded input from accidental spills, deliberate discharges, and other point sources. Background levels of petroleum residues were measured during surveys of the Hudson Strait/Foxe Basin region and the Labrador Shelf in 1982 and 1983 (Levy 1986). Concentrations were found to be similar to other regions of the continental shelf off the east coast of Canada and well below those thought at the time to have adverse biological effects. In 1981, BIO undertook a baseline survey of volatile hydrocarbons and petroleum residues in the waters and sediments of the Grand Banks of Newfoundland (Levy 1983). While the levels were among the lowest found anywhere off eastern Canada, there was evidence that the exploration activities were having a detectable impact on background levels of hydrocarbons. A survey on Georges Bank found high concentrations of natural hydrocarbons in surficial sediments and it was proposed that bacterial processes involving methane and other low molecular weight hydrocarbons may contribute substantially to benthic production (Levy and Lee 1988).

BIO also investigated the distribution of tar balls floating on the sea surface. This phenomenon was first reported by Thor Heyerdahl while crossing the equatorial Atlantic on *Ra II* in 1970, and the fouling of beaches had become a major problem in Bermuda (Fig. 2D). For several years, oil tows using surface nets were conducted routinely by all BIO ships while at sea regardless of location. The compiled data demonstrated that tar balls in the western North Atlantic were predominantly associated with the Sargasso Sea and Gulf Stream system, and that regions to the north were essentially free from this form of oil contamination (Levy and Walton 1976). Other studies demonstrated that these tar balls were the result of oil tankers deliberately washing their tanks at sea and this problem was subsequently corrected by international regulations controlling the discharge of oily ballast wastes by tankers.

Hydrocarbon surveys were also conducted in Baffin Bay and the eastern Canadian arctic (Levy 1979a). During a geophysical survey in 1976, an oil slick was observed off Scott Inlet on the east coast of Baffin Island (Fig. 1). Follow-up studies indicated that this slick was a permanent feature and originated from natural seepage (MacLean et al. 1981). Direct visual examination of the seabed in the area using the submersible *Pisces IV* identified pockmarks (sedimentary features formed by gas seepage) and the presence of bacterial mats (Grant et al. 1986). Natural seepage was also discovered in nearby Buchan Gulf, Baffin Island (Levy and Ehrhardt 1981).

BIOLOGICAL EFFECTS OF HYDROCARBONS

Driven by the practical concerns of government, industry, and the scientific community to fully understand the potential biological impacts of marine oil spills, BIO scientists began to study the biological effects of petroleum hydrocarbons in the early 1970s. Studies on the effects of oil on the photosynthesis of natural phytoplankton assemblages collected in Bedford Basin and along a transect line between Halifax and Bermuda indicated that productivity could be significantly reduced at high concentrations, but that at low concentrations productivity could actually be enhanced (Gordon and Prouse 1973). It was concluded that petroleum hydrocarbon concentrations in Bedford Basin might be reducing photosynthesis by a few percent but that levels in the open ocean have no apparent deleterious effects. Similar results were obtained in laboratory experiments using unialgal marine phytoplankton cultures and it was concluded that, while oil concentrations in polluted water can affect phytoplankton growth, the effects seemed minor and short-lived (Prouse et al. 1976).

Some BIO-SABS studies examined the effects of crude oil on lobster larvae and post-larval stages, and demonstrated for the first time their high sensitivity to both dissolved and dispersed oil (Wells and Sprague 1976; Fig. 4B). Exposure to oil caused reduced feeding, interfered with development, and made larvae more sensitive during molting. To provide information for the development of oil refinery regulations and guidelines under the Canadian Fisheries Act, the toxicity of effluent from the Saint John Irving refinery in New Brunswick was determined using lobster larvae (Wells 1973). This led to further studies at BIO on oil refinery effluent toxicity.

Crabs exposed to seawater contaminated with crude oil had depressed levels of respiration, but returned to normal when the crabs were placed in clean water (Vandermeulen et al. 1980). The unicellular marine alga, *Palova lutheri*, was found to respond to petroleum hydrocarbons by changing its normal pattern of motility (Vandermeulen et al. 1983; Fig. 4C). Studies on the mutagenic potential of crude and refined oils on algae found that the concentrations capable of inducing mutations far exceeded concentrations observed under spill or pollution conditions (Vandermeulen and Lee 1986).

While numerous studies had been conducted by BIO scientists on the impacts of oil on organisms and some biological processes, little was known about how an oil spill might impact an entire marine ecosystem. Accordingly, BIO scientists constructed a numerical simulation model of the Grand Banks ecosystem and explored the indirect effects of different spill scenarios (Silvert 1985). This was the first attempt by BIO scientists to develop a quantitative model of a continental shelf ecosystem; the process was driven by a series of interactive workshops including external colleagues. The model had four large spatial compartments and the state variables (phytoplankton, zooplankton, and fish) were defined by size (Duplisea et al. 2014). The results suggested that the immediate impacts of an offshore spill would be short-lived and the affected populations would recover within a few months.

For many years, the Canadian Wildlife Service Seabird Research Unit at BIO conducted studies of the effects of oil spills on seabirds in the Arctic and off the east coast of Canada as part of their broader program described by Nettleship (2014). Swimming seabirds are the most conspicuous casualties of oil pollution (Evans and Nettleship 1985) and high levels of mortality from oil slicks have been observed off eastern Canada (Brown et al. 1973). The impacts of such mortalities on seabird populations have been assessed by Piatt et al. (1991).

DEVELOPMENT AND APPLICATION OF OIL SPILL RESPONSE TECHNOLOGIES

Different operational techniques to clean up oil spills have been developed around the world. The most common include booming and skimming, *in situ* burning, physical removal of stranded oil, bioremediation, and chemical dispersion. In response to the need for better understanding of the relative effectiveness of these different techniques, BIO scientists initiated a number of programs to study oil spill response technologies with a focus on bioremediation and chemical dispersion.

Collaborative studies with the Halifax Fisheries Research Board Laboratory immediately after the *Arrow* spill demonstrated that hydrocarbon-utilizing bacteria capable of degrading spilled oil are ubiquitous in seawater and sediments off eastern Canada (Mulkins-Phillips and Stewart 1974). These results demonstrated the considerable potential of the marine environment for self-cleansing following an oil spill and the concept of bioremediation was born whereby steps could be taken to accelerate the natural rates of bacterial degradation of the hydrocarbon constituents and reduce the overall concentration and toxicity of the spilled oil.

When K. Lee arrived at BIO in 1984, he began research to identify the factors limiting the natural rates of degradation for stranded crude oil. Initial laboratory work and small field experiments confirmed that adding ordinary garden fertilizer and tilling to enhance oxygen supply hastened the bacterial degradation process (Lee and Levy 1986). This early research on bioremediation strategies attracted international attention and was subsequently put to the test during the *Exxon Valdez* spill in Alaska where the addition of nutrients to stranded oil proved to be effective in enhancing both the rate and extent of oil degradation by natural bacteria (Boufadal et al. 2010).

The proven success of bioremediation led to the need for operational guidelines on oil spill bioremediation strategies that could be used to support decision making by the international oil spill response community (Lee and Merlin 1999). It was recognized that guidelines were best developed from the results of large-scale field trials. Accordingly, BIO scientists undertook a series of experiments exploring the effectiveness of different bioremediation techniques on oil stranded in a variety of coastal environments. These carefully-planned experiments were carried out in collaboration with other agencies and required extensive logistic support. These experiments included trials in sandy beaches in Long Cove, Nova Scotia (Lee et al. 1993), a sandy beach in Delaware (Venosa et al. 1996; Fig. 5A), freshwater wetlands along the shore of the St. Lawrence River (Venosa et al. 2002; Fig. 5B), and a salt marsh east of Halifax (Lee et al. 2002). Following the *Sea Empress* spill, additional collaborative field trials were conducted in the United Kingdom (Swannell et al. 1999), France (Merlin 1995), Svalbard, Norway (Lee et al. 2003b), and The Netherlands (Mitchell et al. 1997). As a result of these studies, standard protocols were established to measure the loss of contaminant hydrocarbons and the extent of habitat recovery (Haines et al. 2002). These studies identified the factors controlling the potential of various bioremediation techniques to increase the rate of natural oil degradation, cutting months or years from recovery time in vulnerable coastal environments (Lee and de Mora 1999).

BIO scientists were also active in developing new bioremediation strategies. Laboratory shaker-flask experiments demonstrated that the natural interaction between fine mineral particles and oil in seawater forms oil-mineral aggregates (OMA) which enhance both the rate and extent of oil degradation by stimulating bacterial activity (Lee 2003). This process was found to accelerate the natural self-cleaning of shorelines affected by oil spills. The significance of OMA formation on the fate of spilled oil was demonstrated following the release of oil from a pipeline into the Desaguadero River in Bolivia (Lee et al. 2001), as well as at the *Exxon Valdez* spill (Prince and Bragg 1997) and during the Baffin Island Oil Spill Project (Owens 1999). As a result of these studies, a cost effective shoreline clean-up procedure called 'surf-washing' was developed. Oil stranded in sediments at the high tide mark was mechanically relocated into the surf zone where wave action could stimulate the formation of OMA and thereby increase biodegradation of the oil (Owens and Lee 2003; Fig. 5C). The operational utility of surf-washing was validated at the Svalbard shoreline field trails in Norway (Guénette et al. 2003) and the *Sea Empress* oil spill in the United Kingdom (Lunel et al. 1997).

The risk of oil spills in Arctic Canada has increased because of increases in marine traffic associated with regional development and a longer open-water season for the Northwest Passage due to climate change. In response, BIO scientists initiated an active research program on the fate of oil spilled in ice-infested waters and the efficacy of various remediation technologies (Lee et al. 2011a). A field study conducted with a Canadian Coast Guard ice-breaker in the St. Lawrence River Estuary in the winter of 2007-08 evaluated a novel remediation technique by applying clay mineral particles to oil stranded on ice and in ice-covered waters and mixing with propeller-wash to promote the formation of OMA (Fig. 5D). The effectiveness of this technique was evaluated by monitoring the temporal and spatial changes of petroleum hydrocarbon concentrations in seawater as well as the rate and extent of biodegradation in laboratory microcosms. It was found that almost 60% of the total petroleum hydrocarbons were degraded after 56 days at an incubation temperature of 0.5°C (Lee et al. 2011b).

Chemical oil dispersants work by transferring oil from the sea surface into the water column as small droplets where they can be dispersed and then degraded more rapidly by naturally occurring microorganisms. Early formulations were used for the first time during the spill response operation following the *Torrey Canyon* incident. Observations of environmental impacts associated with their application clearly highlighted the need to understand the potential environmental impacts associated with chemical oil dispersant use and to ensure that only effective and environmentally 'safe' products were developed and used. Subsequently, experiments on the relative effectiveness and toxicities of chemical dispersants were initiated in the Environmental Protection Service toxicity laboratory (Environment Canada) at BIO (Wells and Doe 2014) to provide information required to make sound science-based decisions regarding the use of these products as operational oil spill countermeasures (Doe and Wells 1978). Detailed studies, conducted in collaboration with the University of Toronto and Exxon, identified the potential links between dispersant effectiveness and dispersed oil toxicity (Wells et al. 1982). In other experiments, Lee et al. (1985) observed that the dispersant Corexit 9527 stimulated bacterial production when mixed with crude oil and concluded that this biodegradation was more significant than abiotic processes in the loss of low volatility hydrocarbons. The results from these studies were used to establish guidelines for the selection of dispersants and their use by oil spill response teams. The results also contributed to a major review of the effectiveness of dispersants (National Research Council 1989).

To further study the environmental factors controlling the effectiveness of chemical oil dispersants and the potential effects of dispersed oil under realistic exposure conditions, a unique wave tank facility was constructed at BIO in 2004 in collaboration with the United States Environmental Protection Agency (King 2011). Using this facility (Fig. 4D), Li et al. (2010) studied the effects of temperature and wave energy on dispersion efficiency of crude oils. Measurements of droplet-size distributions were made using a laser *in situ* particle size analyzer during the evaluation of natural and chemical dispersion efficiency of crude oils under different wave and current conditions (Li et al. 2011). A new analytical method based on UV-fluorescence was also developed to monitor the effectiveness of chemical oil dispersants applied during response operations (Bugden et al. 2008). The wave tank facility was subsequently modified to be operated in both batch and flow-through modes to address concerns over the acute and chronic toxicity effects of dispersed oil expected at sea during operational activities. This work included experiments using herring embryos (Greer et al. 2012) and cod (Lyons et al. 2011). The results of these wave tank studies provided data for the development of improved fate and transport models for oil spill risk assessments and improved guidelines for using dispersants in spill cleanup operations.

In 2010, BIO scientists participated at the invitation of the United States Environmental Protection Agency in the oil spill response operations associated with the *Deepwater Horizon* blowout in the Gulf of Mexico (Lee et al. 2011c; Fig. 6A). This was the largest accidental oil spill

Figure 5. Oil spill response technologies: (A) bioremediation experiment on a sandy beach in Delaware, MD; (B) bioremediation experiment on freshwater wetlands along the shore of the St. Lawrence River, QC; (C) surf-washing field trials in Svalbard, Norway; and (D) bioremediation experiment using the CCGS *Martha Black* in the ice-covered St. Lawrence River Estuary, QC.

in the history of the petroleum industry, releasing 614,000 tons of crude oil before the wellhead, at a depth of 1,500 m, was capped. In addition to mechanical recovery techniques and *in situ* burning, oil dispersants were used in an attempt to prevent landfall of the oil. The BIO team monitored the efficacy of injecting chemical oil dispersants at the wellhead using a remotely-operated vehicle and tracked the plume of subsurface oil over a four month period (Fig. 6B). The results demonstrated that a substantial subsurface oil plume was created between 1,000 and 1,300 m, but that oil concentrations throughout the remainder of the water column were low. It was also observed that dissolved oxygen levels in the water column were depressed due to the microbial degradation of oil, but oxygen depletion did not reach hypoxic levels of environmental concern.

OPERATIONAL WASTES FROM OFFSHORE PLATFORMS

The first exploration wells were drilled in 1966 and 1967 on the Grand Banks of Newfoundland and Sable Island Bank, respectively, and substantial oil and gas reserves were subsequently found (Williams et al. 2014). With proven reserves and favourable economics, the eastern Canadian offshore oil and gas industry moved into the development phase in the 1980s.

In 1980, the Marine Environment and Ecosystems Subcommittee of the Canadian Atlantic Fishery Scientific Advisory Committee assessed the possible consequences of offshore oil production on the Scotian Shelf and Grand Banks to fish stocks and fishing. A physical oceanographic program, coordinated by J. Elliott, was established which focussed on topics of particular operational interest to the oil and gas industry such as currents, waves, and ice (Smith et al. 2014). Studies of seabed geohazards were also implemented (Lewis et al 2014).

With the resolution of the Georges Bank boundary dispute with the United States by the International Court of Justice in 1984, the oil and gas industry was able to proceed with exploration proposals. Texaco Canada Resources Limited applied to drill two wells in Canadian waters on the northeast tip of the Bank. This proposal met with very strong opposition from the fishing industry. Subsequently, BIO scientists were asked to carry out a scientific assessment of the possible environmental impacts of exploratory drilling on the fisheries resources of Georges Bank. This review (Gordon 1988) concluded that any impacts would most likely be short-lived and restricted to near the release site due to the highly dispersive nature of water circulation on Georges Bank. However, the assessment recommended that drilling proposals be reviewed on an individual basis and, if approved, proceed only under stringent regulations which reflected environmental and habitat concerns. Recommendations were also made to address the most serious knowledge gaps. This controversial issue was temporarily set aside by a twelve-year moratorium on oil and gas activity on Georges Bank established by the Governments of Nova Scotia and Canada in 1988 which gave BIO scientists time to address some of the important questions regarding the potential environmental impacts of offshore drilling. The United States also imposed a drilling moratorium on its portion of Georges Bank.

While the general circulation pattern of Georges Bank was well known, more information was needed on horizontal and vertical exchange processes, especially in the area of tidal fronts along the northern edge. Field studies provided a high-resolution description of circulation, hydrographic structure, and mixing in the frontal region (Loder et al. 1993). In collaboration with United States colleagues, BIO physical oceanographers developed a new three-dimensional, finite-element circulation model for the Gulf of Maine region including Georges Bank (Naimie et al. 1994). This model incorporated tides, winds, and density as driving forces and was able to track the trajectories of particles, such as drilling wastes, released into the water column at any location.

BIO also initiated a multidisciplinary research program to investigate the behaviour, fate, and biological effects of particulate drilling wastes (primarily muds and cuttings), which are routinely discharged at sea, and to estimate the spatial and temporal extent of potential impact zones around drilling rigs. The bottom-dwelling sea scallop (*Placopecten magellanicus*), a key resource species on Georges Bank, was chosen for biological effects studies (Fig. 4E). It was first observed that prolonged exposure to mineral oil-based drilling mud cuttings on the seabed increased mortality and reduced growth rates of scallops (Cranford and Gordon 1991). Laboratory experiments were then conducted in flume tanks (Fig. 4F) to examine the effects of suspended drilling muds on scallops. Multi-month experiments were run using dilute suspensions of bentonite, barite, water-based mud, and oil-based mud. Chronic intermittent exposure of scallops to dilute concentrations of these operational drilling wastes was found to affect the feeding, behaviour, growth, reproductive success, and survival of scallops (Cranford et al. 1999). Scallops were most sensitive to barite and oil-based mud and least sensitive to water-based mud. These effects were attributed to the addition of non-nutritious particles to the food supply, fine particle interference with the filter-feeding mechanism and, in some conditions, chemical toxicity. Subsequently, similar experiments examined the chronic effects of different synthetic drilling muds used by industry (Novaplus, IPAR-3, and Petrofree) and it was again found that the fine fraction of the drilling muds was the primary cause of observed impacts on scallop growth (Armsworthy et al. 2005).

Figure 6. Gulf of Mexico: (A) British Petroleum *Deepwater Horizon* blowout in 2010; and (B) BIO staff collecting seawater samples near the *Deepwater Horizon* blowout.

Laboratory studies demonstrated that drilling wastes rapidly form large, fast-sinking particle aggregates, or flocs. These flocs, along with cuttings, can settle rapidly to the seafloor where they are incorporated into the benthic boundary layer (BBL), the layer of water just off the bottom where suspension-feeding organisms such as scallops collect their food. New instruments were developed to sample suspended sediment in the BBL (Muschenheim et al. 1995) and a quantitative method was developed to estimate the concentration of drilling wastes in suspended sediment using particle size spectra (Milligan et al. 2005). These new sampling tools and analytical methods were applied to studies around active drilling sites on Sable Island Bank using BIO ships and industry supply vessels working in close collaboration with LASMO, the British oil company that was in the process of developing the Cohassett-Panuke light oil field. On one occasion, flocculated drilling wastes were readily observed in the BBL using video (Muschenheim and Milligan 1996) and particle size analysis confirmed that waste particles could be found in the BBL as far as 8 km from a drilling rig.

The results of studies of the physical behaviour and biological effects of particulate drilling wastes were integrated with those of physical oceanographic studies to develop numerical models to predict the impacts of different waste discharge scenarios on Georges Bank scallop populations. The first step was the development of a sediment transport model called 'bblt' (benthic boundary layer transport) which simulated the dispersion and transport of drilling wastes once they reached the BBL (Hannah et al. 1995). Using information provided by industry, a daily drilling waste discharge scenario was developed representing an exploration well using water-based mud over a three-month period. Driven by the 3-D finite-element circulation model for Georges Bank (Naimie et al. 1994), twenty-two applications were run for different locations, times of year and settling velocities for the flocculated mud. The predicted drilling waste concentrations in the BBL were interpreted in terms of potential impacts on scallop growth. Model results showed that impacts depended very much on the settling velocity of wastes and the location of the drill site on Georges Bank (Cranford et al. 2003). At high settling velocities, the greatest potential effects (up to 48 days of growth inhibition) occurred on the side of the Bank where dispersion is low. Potential effects in the shallow, well-mixed top of the Bank, where dispersion is high, were negligible. Impacts were less at lower settling velocities. The model proved to be a valuable quantitative tool for improving our understanding of the fate of drilling wastes in the BBL which could be used in environmental impact assessments, investigating mitigative measures, and designing environmental effects monitoring programs. Further refinements to the model captured the behaviour of fine-grained drilling wastes by varying the settling velocity based on the bottom stress (Hannah and Drozdowski 2005) and this version was used to explore drilling waste dispersion on Sable Island Bank and the Grand Banks, which have different environmental conditions than Georges Bank. Of the three locations studied, Georges Bank was the least likely to experience high accumulations of drilling wastes.

In 1996, the Georges Bank Review Panel was established to review the Georges Bank drilling issue and prepare recommendations for action when the moratorium expired at the end of 1999. Throughout the four-year review process, BIO scientists provided research results and advice. Using funding provided by the Review Panel, BIO scientists, in collaboration with colleagues at Dalhousie University, conducted experiments examining the impacts of drilling wastes on the larvae of haddock, lobster and sea scallop, important commercial species on Georges Bank (Cranford et al. 1998). Led by BIO, a peer-reviewed summary of the Georges Bank ecosystem and potential impacts from petroleum exploratory activities was carried out under Fisheries and Oceans Canada (DFO) Regional Advisory Process (Boudreau et al. 1999). In 1999, after considering all the available information, the Review Panel recommended that the drilling moratorium on Georges Bank should be continued until 2012. In 2009, BIO scientists led another assessment of the Georges Bank drilling issue, including the risk associated with hydrocarbon production activities (Fisheries and Oceans Canada 2011). In 2010, the Governments of Nova Scotia and Canada extended the drilling moratorium on Georges Bank until the end of 2015. The United States has also extended the drilling moratorium in its portion of Georges Bank.

In collaboration with R. Anderson and J. Payne of the DFO Northwest Atlantic Fisheries Centre in St. John's, Newfoundland, projects to observe the occurrence and distribution of drilling wastes around the Hibernia platform (Fig. 7A) were conducted in cooperation with the Hibernia Management and Development Corporation. In addition, new techniques were developed for environmental effects monitoring programs.

In 1995, an extensive survey of suspended particulate material and sediments (Fig. 7B) was made at Hibernia using CCGS *Parizeau* before the gravity-based structure was installed. The results showed low concentrations of naturally occurring suspended particulate material at all depths in the water column, including the BBL (Milligan et al. 1997). These observations were repeated for several years using CCGS *Hudson* after the gravity-based platform was installed in 1997 and drilling began. No significant differences were observed in suspended particulate material, in contrast to Sable Island Bank (Saunders et al. 1999).

Two environmental effects monitoring approaches using bivalves as sentinel organisms were designed and successfully tested at Hibernia (Cranford et al. 2005). Bivalve cages (Fig. 7C) containing Icelandic scallops, sea scallops (Fig. 7D), and blue mussels were moored on the sea bed at different distances from the platform and effects on growth and hydrocarbon body burden were used to assess the spatial extent of impacts from drilling activities. The second approach utilized an *in situ* biological effects monitoring system called Habitrap (Fig. 7E) that used Icelandic scallops to provide daily measurements of drilling waste exposure and bivalve deposition rate. While elevated levels of barium, an indicator of drilling wastes, were observed out to 2,500 m from the platform, no significant biological effects were observed with either of the two types of shellfish moorings. These new techniques, effective at Hibernia, could be valuable additions to environmental effects monitoring programs in general.

Produced water represents the largest volume of waste discharge associated with offshore oil and gas production activities. Produced water discharges occur throughout the production phase, and discharge rates generally increase over time. Studies were undertaken using samples collected at the Sable Offshore Energy Project and Hibernia to determine the potential impacts of produced water on fish and shellfish (Querbach et al. 2005), the marine bacterial community (Yeung et al. 2011), and the characteristics of seawater (Azetsu-Scott et al. 2007). Modelling investigations (Zhao et al. 2011) showed that a combination of near-field and far-field models was needed to predict the dispersion of produced water (Niu et al. 2011). The results of these studies showed that biological impacts from the current rates of discharge were largely limited to the near-field zone (<500 m). As a direct result of these studies, regulators did not demand re-injection of produced water from offshore facilities on the east coast of Canada.

INTERNATIONAL ACTIVITIES, COORDINATION, AND PROVISION OF ADVICE

BIO scientists have participated in numerous international activities, provided coordination to the wider scientific community, and supplied expert advice on a broad range of oil and gas issues to government and other organizations. In 1971, a team of BIO scientists led by W. Ford was invited to Bermuda to advise the government on how to deal with the problem of tar balls washing up on their beaches (Fig. 2D). In 1973, E. Levy, D. Gordon and J. Stewart (then at the Halifax Fisheries Research Board Laboratory) participated in a major review of the input, fates, and

Figure 7. Studies of drilling wastes on the Grand Banks of Newfoundland: (A) CCGS *Hudson* at the Hibernia platform; (B) processing Videograb samples collected at Hibernia: (l to r) K. Muschenheim, P. Vass, T. Milligan, and K. MacIsaac; (C) deploying bivalve cages at Hibernia; (D) S. Armsworthy preparing a panel of sea scallops for deployment; (E) deploying Habitrap at Hibernia; and (F) K. Lee at the *Terra Nova* floating platform storage and off-loading (FPSO) vessel near Hibernia.

effects of petroleum in the marine environment led by the United States National Academy of Sciences (National Academy of Sciences 1975). J. Vandermeulen and P. Wells participated in the update of this review ten years later (National Research Council 1985). Soon after, P. Wells contributed to the United States National Research Council review of the effectiveness of oil dispersants (National Research Council 1989). D. Gordon, J. Vandermeulen, and P. Wells were invited by Exxon to visit Prince William Sound in Alaska to review the results of clean-up efforts after the 1989 *Exxon Valdez* oil spill, after which P. Wells co-edited a book on the spill (Wells et al. 1995). For many years, P. Wells was active in the Group of Experts on Scientific Aspects of Marine Environmental Protection, an expert advisory body on marine pollution under the United Nations. One of its reports described all sources and annual amounts of oil pollution from sea-based activities and the global, spatial, and temporal trends in oil pollution (Wells 2007). E. Levy played a leading role in the Integrated Global Ocean Station System Pilot Project on Marine Pollution (Petroleum) Monitoring which synthesized data on the occurrence of oil in the ocean around the world (Levy 1979b).

BIO has hosted many committees, workshops, and conferences to facilitate the exchange of information within the scientific community and with external clients including the oil and gas industry, the fishing industry, and environmental organizations. In the 1970s, annual workshops were held with regional colleagues to discuss results and coordinate the planning of continuing research. In the late 1980s, recognizing that the impacts of oil and gas activities was a trans-boundary issue, a series of workshops were held to bring the Canadian and United States scientific communities together to review research on Georges Bank. BIO scientists also led committees that regularly reviewed the progress and plans of drilling waste programs with clients.

Owing to their experience, BIO scientists became a key resource for the review of environmental impact assessments for proposed offshore hydrocarbon developments within Canada and abroad. Furthermore, scientists at BIO provided input to the design and review of the environmental effects monitoring programs that were established by industry at the sites approved for development, including Cohasset-Panuke, the Sable Offshore Energy Project, Hibernia, and Terra Nova (Fig. 7F). BIO scientists also played a major role in the review and revision of drilling waste guidelines for the Canadian offshore oil and gas industry, an exercise led by the National Energy Board.

In 2000, a major workshop was organized in collaboration with the Sable Offshore Energy Environmental Effects Monitoring Advisory Group that reviewed the environmental effects of offshore hydrocarbon development using experience gained at Cohasset-Panuke, the Sable Offshore Energy Project, Hibernia, and Terra Nova (Gordon et al. 2000). In 2003, BIO scientists organized a major international conference that addressed the design of environmental effects monitoring programs for offshore oil and gas developments (Armsworthy et al. 2005). In 2006, BIO scientists organized an international conference to discuss the development and application of current and emerging technologies for oil spill response in the marine environment (Davidson et al. 2008). Practical methods used to deal with marine oil spills under a variety of environmental conditions were discussed and special attention was given to the evaluation of oil spill countermeasures for use under arctic conditions. BIO also helped organize a conference in 2007 which brought together scientists, regulators, industry, and non-governmental organizations to share their concerns, knowledge, and expertise on the discharge of produced water at sea (Lee and Neff 2011).

In 2002, building upon BIO's extensive expertise on the environmental impacts of oil and gas activities, DFO established the Centre for Offshore Oil, Gas and Energy Research (COOGER) at BIO with K. Lee as Executive Director (Fig. 7F). COOGER has built on existing regional expertise and infrastructure to coordinate national research on environmental and oceanographic issues associated with exploration, production, and transport of Canada's offshore oil and gas resources with a view to improving the quality of science, prioritizing research needs, and minimizing duplication by fostering collaboration with other government research agencies, universities, and industry partners. COOGER has been instrumental for the provision of facts for the development of science-based policies and regulations for frontier energy development in Canada. In response to emerging technological developments that will enable Canada to meet its future energy needs in an environmentally responsible manner, the mandate of COOGER was expanded in 2009 to include ocean renewable energy (i.e., tides, winds, and waves). COOGER also fosters collaboration at the international level to learn from the experiences of other countries to optimize the progress of Canadian research programs. Comprehensive, large-scale research projects can address global concerns through the sharing of expertise and resources in an international setting. For example, BIO is represented on working groups which are revising guidelines on the use of oil dispersants and bioremediation practices for oil spill responders, which includes a United States National Academy of Sciences committee (USNAS) that has assessed the impacts of the *Deepwater Horizon* oil spill on ecosystem services in the Gulf of Mexico. Furthermore, BIO scientists are participants on an American Petroleum Institute working group presently investigating the fate of the residual oil from the same spill, and a USNAS committee on 'Responding to Oil Spills in Arctic Environments'.

SYNTHESIS AND THE FUTURE

This long-term research program was driven by applied issues of understanding the environmental implications of oil spills and operational wastes from offshore hydrocarbon exploration, development, and production. BIO scientists responded to this need by carrying out projects providing critical information, developing new methods and instrumentation, developing predictive models, and providing sound scientific advice to a wide range of clients. The research provided new insight into the behaviour and fate of spilled oil, its ecological effects, and the rates at which different ecosystems can recover from spills. Chronic levels and sources of hydrocarbons in the marine environment of Atlantic Canada and the eastern Canadian arctic were investigated as well as the toxicity and effectiveness of oil dispersants. BIO scientists also improved existing technologies and developed new oil spill countermeasures embracing 'green technologies' based on the acceleration of natural remedial processes. The research also provided new insight into the behaviour and biological effects of operational wastes such as drilling muds and produced water which are routinely discharged from offshore hydrocarbon exploration and production platforms.

This program established BIO as a global leader in the international scientific community, especially in the development of effective oil spill countermeasures. As a result of this investment in research, Canada is much better prepared to respond quickly and effectively to future oil spills. It is also able to establish realistic regulations that minimize the environmental impacts of offshore drilling activities and design efficient environmental effects monitoring programs.

BIO scientists have played an active role in the international scientific community studying oil and gas issues which has often led to productive collaborative studies and exchange visits. Because of the targeted nature of this research, considerable attention was given to applying the results to questions raised on oil and gas issues by other government departments and agencies, the oil and gas industry, the fishing industry, and environmental organizations. These issues were often controversial and care was taken not to play an advocacy role but to be objective, and to provide the same information to all stakeholders.

The success of this research can be attributed primarily to the creativity and enthusiasm of the participating scientists. Another important factor was the presence of all marine scientific disciplines, including engineering support, under one roof at BIO which produced a creative research environment and encouraged the formation of unique multidisciplinary research teams, often with international collaborators and personnel in the oil and gas industry. For most of this research, resources (both internal and external) were available to hire new staff, purchase necessary instrumentation, and work effectively in the field.

Despite all that has been discovered, there are still major hydrocarbon-related questions that need further investigation. Owing to the recent *Deepwater Horizon* oil spill, the Canadian public is highly concerned over the potential impacts of a subsurface blowout as our frontier oil and gas operations off the east coast and in the Arctic Ocean move into deeper waters. In addition, there is demand for the development of improved oil spill cleanup technologies for use in the Canadian arctic which will see increasing ship traffic as ice continues to melt due to global warming. There are also environmental concerns related to potential spills from the transport of new hydrocarbon products such as biofuels, condensate, and synthetic oil from the tar sands. Whatever the future role of BIO in oil and gas research might be, the rich legacy of previous research achievements at BIO will form a sound basis for responding to future oil and gas emergencies and emerging issues.

ACKNOWLEDGEMENTS

The principal scientists involved in this research are identified as authors in the selected references listed below. We thank them all, and our many external colleagues, for their role in advancing the knowledge of oil and gas issues. In particular, we acknowledge the leadership and contributions made over the years by John Vandermeulen and Eric Levy. This research was also critically dependent upon the support of many other BIO staff who contributed behind the scenes by developing equipment, collecting and processing samples, processing data, and providing administrative and field support. The work at sea was critically dependent upon BIO research vessels and their expert crews. We thank the many BIO managers, funding agencies including the interdepartmental Panel on Energy Research and Development, the United States Environmental Protection Agency, and the oil and gas industry for their support in carrying out this research. We also thank Peter Cranford, John Loder, Tim Milligan, Brian Nicholls, and Gary Wohlgeschaffen for reviewing earlier drafts of this contribution. Cam Lirette kindly drafted Figure 1, and Claire MacIntyre and Kelly Bentham assisted in gathering the photos. And finally, we thank Mike Lewis and David Nettleship for their editorial assistance.

REFERENCES

Armsworthy, S.L., P.J. Cranford, and K. Lee. 2005. Offshore oil and gas environ mental effects monitoring: approaches and technologies. Battelle Press, Columbus, OH.

Azetsu-Scott, K., P. Yeats, G. Wohlgeschaffen, J. Dalziel, S. Niven, and K. Lee. 2007. Precipitation of heavy metals in produced water: influence on contami nant transport and toxicity. Marine Environmental Research 63: 146-167.

Boudreau, P.R. and 23 others. 1999. The possible environmental impacts of petroleum exploration activities on the Georges Bank ecosystem. Canadian Technical Report of Fisheries and Aquatic Sciences 2259, Fisheries and Oceans Canada, Dartmouth, NS.

Boufadel, M.C., Y. Sharifi, B. Van Aken, B. A. Wrenn, and K. Lee. 2010. Nutrient and oxygen concentrations within the sediments of an Alaskan beach polluted with the *Exxon Valdez* oil spill. Environmental Science and Technology 44: 7,418-7,424.

Brown, R.G.B., D.I. Gillespie, A.R. Lock, P.A. Pearce, and G.H. Watson. 1973. Bird mortality from oil slicks off Eastern Canada, February-April 1970. Canadian Field Naturalist 87: 225-234.

Brown, R.G.B. and B.C. Johnson. 1980. The effects of *Kurdistan* oil on seabirds. Pages 203-211 *in* Scientific Studies during the *Kurdistan* Tanker Incident: Proceedings of a Workshop (J. Vandermeulen, Ed.). Bedford Institute of Oceanography Report Series BI-R-80-3, Dartmouth, NS.

Bugden, J.B.C., C.W. Yeung, P.E. Kepkay, and K. Lee. 2008. Application of ultraviolet fluorometry and excitation–emission matrix spectroscopy (EEMS) to fingerprint oil and chemically dispersed oil in seawater. Marine Pollution Bulletin 56: 677-685.

Carson, R. 1962. Silent Spring. Houghton Mifflin, Boston, MA.

Cranford, P.J. and D.C. Gordon. 1991. Chronic sublethal impact of mineral oil-based drilling mud cuttings on adult sea scallops. Marine Pollution Bulletin 22: 339-344.

Cranford, P.J., K. Querbach, G. Maillet, K. Lee, J. Grant, and C. Taggart. 1998. Sensitivity of larvae to drilling wastes (Part A): Effects of water-based drilling mud on early life stages of haddock, lobster and sea scallop. Report of the Georges Bank Review Panel, Halifax, NS.

Cranford, P.J., D.C. Gordon, K. Lee, S.L. Armsworthy, and G.-H. Tremblay. 1999. Chronic toxicity and physical disturbance effects of water- and oil-based drilling fluids and some major constituents on adult sea scallops (*Placopecten magellanicus*). Marine Environmental Research 48: 225-256.

Cranford, P.J., D.C. Gordon, Jr., C.G. Hannah, J.W.Loder, T.G. Milligan, D.K. Muschenheim, and Y. Shen. 2003. Modelling potential effects of petroleum exploration drilling on northeastern Georges Bank scallop stocks. Ecological Modelling 166: 19-39.

Cranford, P,J., S.L. Armsworthy, S. McGee, T. King, and K. Lee. 2005. Scallops as sentinel organisms for offshore environmental effects monitoring. Pages 267-296 *in* Offshore Oil and Gas Environmental Effects Monitoring: Approaches and Technologies (S.L. Armsworthy, P.J. Cranford, and K. Lee, Eds.). Battelle Press, Columbus, OH.

Davidson, W. F., K. Lee, and A. Cogswell (Eds.). 2008. Oil Spill Response: A Global Perspective. NATO Science for Peace and Security Series C: Environmental Security, Springer, Dordrecht, The Netherlands.

Doe, K.G. and P.G. Wells. 1978. Acute aquatic toxicity and dispersing effectiveness of oil spill dispersants: results of a Canadian oil dispersant testing program (1973-1977). Pages 50-65 *in* Chemical Dispersants for the Control of Oil Spills (L.T. McCarthy, G.P Lindblom, and H.F. Walters, Eds.). American Society for Testing and Materials, STP 659, Philadelphia, PA.

Duplisea, D.E., P.R. Boudreau, and L.M. Dickie. 2014. The size-structured view of marine ecosystems. Pages 99-103 *in* Voyage of Discovery: Fifty Years of Marine Research at Canada's Bedford Institute of Oceanography (D.N. Nettleship, D.C. Gordon, C.F.M. Lewis, and M.P. Latremouille, Eds.). Bedford Institute of Oceanography-Oceans Association, Dartmouth, NS.

Evans, P.G.H. and D.N. Nettleship. 1985. Conservation of the Atlantic alcidae. Pages 427-488 *in* The Atlantic Alcidae: the Evolution, Distribution and Biology of the Auks Inhabiting the Atlantic Ocean and Adjacent Water Areas (D.N. Nettleship and T.R. Birkhead, Eds.). Academic Press, London, England.

Fisheries and Oceans Canada. 2011. The marine environment and fisheries of Georges Bank, Nova Scotia: consideration of the potential interactions associated with offshore petroleum activities. Canadian Technical Report of Fisheries and Aquatic Sciences 2945, Fisheries and Oceans Canada, Dartmouth, NS.

Gilfillan, E.S. and J.H. Vandermeulen. 1978. Alterations in growth and physiology in soft-shell clams *Mya arenaria* chronically oiled with Bunker C from Chedabucto Bay, Nova Scotia, 1970-1976. Journal of the Fisheries Research Board of Canada 35: 630-636.

Gordon, D.C., Jr., (Ed.). 1988. An assessment of the possible environmental impacts of exploratory drilling on Georges Bank fisheries resources. Canadian Technical Report of Fisheries and Aquatic Sciences 1633, Fisheries and Oceans Canada, Dartmouth, NS.

Gordon, D.C., Jr., and N.J. Prouse. 1973. The effects of three oils on marine phytoplankton photosynthesis. Marine Biology 22: 329-333.

Gordon, D.C., Jr., P.D. Keizer, and N.J. Prouse. 1973. Laboratory studies of the accommodation of some crude and residual fuel oils in sea water. Journal of the Fisheries Research Board of Canada 30: 1,611-1,618.

Gordon, D.C., Jr., P.D. Keizer, and J. Dale. 1974. Estimates using fluorescence spectrophotometry of the present state of petroleum hydrocarbon contamina tion in the water column of the northwest Atlantic Ocean. Marine Chemistry 2: 251-261.

Gordon, D.C., Jr., J. Dale, and P.D. Keizer. 1978a. Importance of sediment working by the deposit-feeding polychaete *Arenicola marina* on the weather ing rate of sediment-bound oil. Journal of the Fisheries Research Board of Canada 35: 591-603.

Gordon, D.C., Jr., P.D. Keizer, and J. Dale. 1978b. Temporal variations and probable origins of hydrocarbons in the water column of Bedford Basin, Nova Scotia. Estuarine and Coastal Marine Science 7: 243-256.

Gordon, D.C., Jr., L.D. Griffiths, G.V. Hurley, A. Muecke, D.K. Muschenheim, and P.G. Wells, (Eds.). 2000. Understanding the environmental effects of offshore hydrocarbon development. Canadian Technical Report of Fisheries and Aquatic Sciences 2311, Fisheries and Oceans Canada, Dartmouth, NS.

Grant, A.C., E.M. Levy, K. Lee, and J.D. Moffatt. 1986. PISCES IV research submersible finds oil on Baffin shelf. Pages 65-69 *in* Current Research, Part A, Geological Survey Canada Paper 86-1A, Ottawa, ON.

Greer, C.D., P.V. Hodson, Z. Li, T. King, and K. Lee. 2012. Toxicity of crude oil chemically dispersed in a wave tank to embryos of Atlantic Herring (*Clupea harengus*). Environmental Toxicology and Chemistry 31: 1-10.

Guénette, C.C., G.A. Sergy, E.H. Owens, R.C. Prince, and K. Lee. 2003. Experi mental design of the Svalbard shoreline field trials. Spill Science and Technology Bulletin 8: 245-256.

Haines, J.R., R. Herrmann, K. Lee, S. Cobanli, and C. Blaise. 2002. Microbial population analysis as a measure of ecosystem restoration. Bioremediation Journal 6: 283-296.

Hannah, C.G., Y. Shen, J.W. Loder, and D.K. Muschenheim. 1995. bblt: formula tion and exploratory applications of a benthic boundary layer transport model. Canadian Technical Report of Hydrography and Ocean Sciences 166, Fisheries and Oceans Canada, Dartmouth, NS.

Hannah, C.G. and A. Drozdowski. 2005. Characterizing the near-bottom dispersion of drilling mud on three Canadian offshore banks. Marine Pollution Bulletin 50: 1,433-1,456.

Keizer, P.D. and D.C. Gordon, Jr. 1973. Detection of trace amounts of oil in seawater by fluorescence spectroscopy. Journal of the Fisheries Research Board of Canada 30: 1,039-1,046.

Keizer, P.D., D.C. Gordon, Jr., and J. Dale. 1977. Hydrocarbons in eastern Canadian marine waters determined by fluorescence spectroscopy and gas-liquid chromatography. Journal of the Fisheries Research Board of Canada 34: 347-353.

Keizer, P.D., T.P. Ahern, J. Dale, and J.H. Vandermeulen. 1978a. Residues of Bunker C oil in Chedabucto Bay, Nova Scotia, 6 years after the *Arrow* spill. Journal of the Fisheries Research Board of Canada 35: 528-535.

Keizer, P.D., J. Dale, and D.C. Gordon, Jr. 1978b. Hydrocarbons in surficial sediments from the Scotian Shelf. Geochimica et Cosmochimica Acta 42: 165-172.

King, T. 2011. Surface films: do they influence the effectiveness of oil spill chemical dispersants as studied in a wave tank facility? M.Sc. thesis, Saint Mary's University, Halifax, NS.

King, T. L., K. Lee, P. Yeats, and R. Alexander. 2003. Chlorobenzenes in snow crab (*Chionoecetes opilio*): time-series monitoring following an accidental release. Bulletin of Environmental Contamination and Toxicology 71: 543-550.

Lee, K. 2003. Oil-particle interactions in aquatic environments: influence on the transport, fate, effect and remediation of oil spills. Spill Science and Technology Bulletin 8: 3-8.

Lee, K., C.S. Wong, W.J. Cretney, F.A. Whitney, T.R. Parsons, C.M. Lalli, and J. Wu. 1985. Microbial response to crude oil and Corexit 9527: SEAFLUXES enclosure study. Microbial Ecology 11: 337-351.

Lee, K. and E. Levy. 1986. Biodegradation of petroleum in the marine environ ment and its enhancement. Canadian Technical Report of Fisheries and Aquatic Sciences 1442, Fisheries and Oceans Canada, Dartmouth, NS.

Lee, K., G.H. Tremblay, and E.M. Levy. 1993. Bioremediation: application of slow-release fertilizers on low energy shorelines. Pages 449-454 *in* Proceedings of

the 1993 International Oil Spill Conference. American Petroleum Institute, Washington, DC.
Lee, K. and F.X. Merlin. 1999. Bioremediation of oil on shoreline environments: development of techniques and guidelines. Pure and Applied Chemistry 71: 161-171.
Lee, K. and S. de Mora. 1999. *In situ* bioremediation strategies for oiled shoreline environments. Environmental Technology 20: 783-794.
Lee, K., G.D. Wohlgeschaffen, G.H. Tremblay, J.H. Vandermeulen, D.C. Mossman, K.G. Doe, P.M. Jackman, J.E.H. Wilson, R.C. Prince, R.M. Garrett, and C.E. Haith. 1999. Natural recovery reduces impact of the 1970 *Arrow* oil spill. Pages 1,075-1,078 *in* Proceedings of the 1999 International Oil Spill Conference. American Petroleum Institute, Washington, DC.
Lee, K., P. Stoffyn-Egli, and E.H. Owens. 2001. Natural dispersion of oil in a freshwater ecosystem: Desaguadero pipeline spill, Bolivia. Pages 1,445-1,448 *in* Proceedings of the 2001 International Oil Spill Conference. American Petroleum Institute, Washington, DC.
Lee, K., A.D. Venosa, M.T. Suidan, C.W. Greer, G. Wohlgeschaffen, C. Cobanli, G.H. Tremblay, J. Gauthier, and K.G. Doe. 2002. Monitoring recovery of a crude oil-contaminated saltmarsh following *in-situ* remediation treatments. Pages 127-137 *in* Coastal Environment: Environmental Problems in Coastal Regions IV (C.A. Brebbia, Ed.). WIT Press, Southampton, England.
Lee, K., R.C. Prince, C.W. Greer, K.G. Doe, J.E.H. Wilson, S.E. Cobanli, G.D. Wohlgeschaffen, D. Alroumi, T. King, and G.H. Tremblay. 2003a. Composi tion and toxicity of residual Bunker C fuel oil in intertidal sediments after 30 years. Spill Science and Technology Bulletin 8: 187-199.
Lee, K., P. Stoffyn-Egli, G.H. Tremblay, E.H. Owens, G.A. Sergy, C.C. Guénette, and R.C. Prince. 2003b. Oil-mineral aggregate formation on oiled beaches: natural attenuation and sediment relocation. Spill Science and Technology Bulletin 8: 285-296.
Lee, K. and J. Neff (Eds.). 2011. Produced Water: Environmental Risks and Advances in Mitigation Technologies. Springer, New York, NY.
Lee, K. and others. 2011a. State of knowledge review of fate and effect of oil in the Arctic marine environment. A report prepared for the National Energy Board of Canada Arctic Roundtable, Ottawa, ON.
Lee, K., Z. Li, B. Robinson, P. Kepkay, B. Doyon, and M. Blouin. 2011b. Oil spill countermeasures in the Arctic. Pages 93-108 *in* Oil Spill Risk Management (N. Bellefontaine and O. Linden, Eds.). Proceedings of the International Conference on Oil Spill Risk Management: Preparedness, Response and Contingency Planning in the Shipping and Offshore Industries. World Mari time University Publications, Malmö, Sweden.
Lee, K., Z. Li, P. Kepkay, and S. Ryan. 2011c. Time-series monitoring the subsur face oil plume released from *Deepwater Horizon* MC252 in the Gulf of Mexico. Paper 2011-381 *in* Proceedings of the International Oil Spill Conference. IOSC, Portland, OR.
Levy, E.M. 1972. Evidence for the recovery of the waters off the east coast of Nova Scotia from the effects of a major oil spill. Water, Air and Soil Pollution 1: 144-148.
Levy, E.M. 1979a. Concentration of petroleum residues in the waters and sediments of Baffin Bay and Eastern Canadian Arctic – 1977. BIO Report Series BI-R-79, Fisheries and Oceans Canada, Dartmouth, NS.
Levy, E.M. 1979b. The IGOSS pilot project on marine pollution (petroleum) monitoring: its evolution and a personal viewpoint. Marine Pollution Bulletin 10: 5-11.
Levy, E.M. 1983. Baseline levels of volatile hydrocarbons and petroleum residues in the waters and sediments of the Grand Banks. Canadian Journal of Fisheries and Aquatic Sciences 40 (Suppl. 2). 23-33.
Levy, E.M. 1985. Background levels of dissolved/dispersed petroleum residues in the Gulf of St. Lawrence, 1970-1979. Canadian Journal of Fisheries and Aquatic Sciences 42: 544-555.
Levy, E.M. 1986. Background levels of petroleum residues in the waters and surficial bottom sediments of the Labrador Shelf and Hudson Strait/Foxe Basin regions. Canadian Journal of Fisheries and Aquatic Sciences 43: 536-547.
Levy, E.M. and A. Walton. 1976. High seas oil pollution: particulate petroleum residues in the North Atlantic. Journal of the Fisheries Research Board of Canada 33: 2,781-2,971.
Levy, E.M. and M. Ehrhardt. 1981. Natural seepage of petroleum at Buchan Gulf, Baffin Island. Marine Chemistry 10: 355-364.
Levy, E. M. and K. Lee. 1988. Potential contribution of natural hydrocarbon seepage to benthic productivity and the fisheries of Atlantic Canada. Canadian Journal of Fisheries and Aquatic Sciences 45: 349-352.
Lewis, C.F.M., S.M. Blasco, D.J.W. Piper, and G.V. Sonnichsen. 2014. Seabed geohazard knowledge for safe hydrocarbon development. Pages 383-394 *in* Voyage of Discovery: Fifty Years of Marine Research at Canada's Bedford Institute of Oceanography (D.N. Nettleship, D.C. Gordon, C.F.M. Lewis, and M.P. Latremouille, Eds.). Bedford Institute of Oceanography-Oceans Association, Dartmouth, NS.
Li, Z., K. Lee, T. King, M.C. Boufadel, and A.D. Venosa. 2010. Effects of tempera ture and wave conditions on dispersion efficacy of heavy fuel oil in an experi mental wave tank. Marine Pollution Bulletin 60: 1,550-1,559.
Li, Z., K. Lee, T. King, H. Niu, M.C. Boufadel, and A.D. Venosa. 2011. Application of entropy analysis of *in situ* droplet-size spectra in evaluation of oil chemical dispersion efficacy. Marine Pollution Bulletin 62: 2,129-2,136.
Loder, J.W., K.F. Drinkwater, N.S. Oakey, and E.P.W. Horne. 1993. Circulation, hydrographic structure and mixing at tidal fronts: the view from Georges Bank. Philosophical Transactions of the Royal Society of London 343: 447-460.
Lunel, T., R. Swannell, J. Rusin, P. Wood, N. Bailey, C. Halliwell, L. Davies, M. Sommerville, A. Dobie, D. Mitchell, M. McDonagh, and K. Lee. 1997. Monitoring the effectiveness of response operations during the *Sea Empress* incident: a key component of the successful counter-pollution response. Spill Science and Technology Bulletin 2: 99-112.
Lyons, M.C., D.L. Wong, I. Mulder, K. Lee, and L.E. Burridge. 2011. The influence of water temperature on induced liver EROD activity in Atlantic cod (*Gadus morhua*) exposed to crude oil and oil dispersants. Ecotoxicology and Environ mental Safety 74: 904-910.
MacLean, B., R.K.H. Falconer, and E.M. Levy. 1981. Geological, geophysical and chemical evidence for natural seepage of petroleum off the northeast coast of Baffin Island. Bulletin of Canadian Petroleum Geology 29: 75-95.
Merlin, F. X., A. Basseres, C. Chaumery, C. Dalmazzone, J. Ducreaux, K. Lee, J. Oudot, T. Reilly, and R.P.J. Swannell. 1995. Oil remediation: results of Landvennec field trials, France October 1993 - June 1994, Volume I. Technical Data Report R.95.38.1C, Centre de Documentation de Recherche et experimentations sur les Pollutions Accidentelles des Eaux (CEDRE), Plouzane, France.
Mitchell, D. J., R.P.J. Swannell, R.M. Dunn, H.H.V. Groenewoud, E. Foekema, M. Scholten, F. Merlin, S. Le Floch, K. Kersting, K. Lee, J.-F. Borseth, and R.C. Prince. 1997. A field evaluation of bioremediation strategies for mudflats. European Commission AEA Technology Report 1932, Abingdon, England.
Milligan, T.G., D.K. Muschenheim, K.S. Saunders, and A. Prior. 1997. Suspended particulate material observations at the Hibernia oil field development site, July 1995. Canadian Data Report of Fisheries and Aquatic Sciences 1009, Fisheries and Oceans Canada, Dartmouth, NS.
Milligan, T.G., T. Tedford, D.K. Muschenheim, and C. Hannah. 2005. Quantifying fine-grained drill waste in Scotian Shelf suspended sediments. Pages 201-226 *in* Offshore Oil and Gas Environmental Effects Monitoring: Approaches and Technologies (S.L. Armsworthy, P.J. Cranford, and K. Lee, Eds.). Battelle Press, Columbus, OH.
Mulkins-Phillips, G.J. and J.E. Stewart. 1974. Distribution of hydrocarbon utilizing bacteria in northwestern Atlantic water and coastal sediments. Canadian Journal of Microbiology 20: 955-962.
Muschenheim, D.K. and T.G. Milligan. 1996. Flocculation and accumulation of fine drilling waste particles on the Scotian Shelf (Canada). Marine Pollution Bulletin 32: 740-745.
Muschenheim, D.K., T.G. Milligan, and D.C. Gordon, Jr. 1995. New technology and suggested methodologies for monitoring particulate wastes discharged from offshore oil and gas platforms and their effects on the benthic boundary layer environment. Canadian Technical Report of Fisheries and Aquatic Sciences 2049, Fisheries and Oceans Canada, Dartmouth, NS.
Naimie, C.E., J.W. Loder, and D.R. Lynch. 1994. Seasonal variation of the three-dimensional residual circulation on Georges Bank. Journal of Geophysical Research 99: 15,967-15,989.
National Academy of Sciences. 1975. Petroleum in the Marine Environment. National Academy of Sciences, Washington, DC.
National Research Council. 1985. Oil in the sea: inputs, fates and effects. National Academy Press, Washington, DC.
National Research Council. 1989. Using oil dispersants on the sea. National Academy Press, Washington, DC.
Nettleship, D.N. 2014. The sea has wings: marine ornithology at the Bedford Institute of Oceanography, 1971-2000. Pages 123-135 *in* Voyage of Discovery: Fifty Years of Marine Research at Canada's Bedford Institute of Oceanography (D.N. Nettleship, D.C. Gordon, C.F.M. Lewis, and M.P. Latremouille, Eds.). Bedford Institute of Oceanography-Oceans Association, Dartmouth, NS.
Niu, H., K. Lee, T. Husain, B. Veitch, and N. Bose. 2011. A coupled model for simulating the dispersion of produced water in the marine environment. Pages 235-247 *in* Produced Water: Environmental Risks and Advances in Mitigation Technologies (K. Lee and J.M. Neff, Eds.). Springer, New York, NY.
Operation Oil. 1970. Report of the Task Force - Operation Oil to the Minister of Transport. Information Canada, Ottawa, ON.
Owens, E.H. 1978. Mechanical dispersion of oil stranded in the littoral zone. Journal of the Fisheries Research Board of Canada 35: 563-572.
Owens, E.H. 1999. The interaction of fine particles with stranded oil. Pure and Applied Chemistry 71: 83-93.
Owens, E.H. and K. Lee. 2003. Interaction of oil and mineral fines on shorelines: review and assessment. Marine Pollution Bulletin 47: 397-405.
Piatt, J.F., H.R. Carter, and D.N. Nettleship. 1991. Effects of oil pollution on marine bird populations. Pages 125-141 *in* The Effects of Oil on Wildlife: Research, Rehabilitation, and General Concerns (J. White, Ed.). Sheridan Press, Hanover, PA.
Prince, R.C. and J.R. Bragg. 1997. Shoreline bioremediation following the *Exxon Valdez* oil spill in Alaska. Bioremediation Journal 1: 97-104.
Prince, R.C., R.M. Garrett, R.E. Bare, M.J. Grossman, T. Townsend, J.M. Suflita, K. Lee, E.H. Owens, G.A. Sergy, J.F. Braddock, J.E. Lindstrom, and R.R. Lessard. 2003. The roles of photooxidation and biodegradation in long-term weathering of crude and heavy fuel oils. Spill Science and Technology Bulletin 8: 145-156.
Prouse, N.J., D.C. Gordon, Jr., and P.D. Keizer. 1976. Effects of low concentrations of oil accommodated in sea water on the growth of unialgal marine phytoplankton cultures. Journal of the Fisheries Research Board of Canada 33: 810-818.
Querbach, K., G. Maillet, P.J. Cranford, C. Taggart, K. Lee, and J. Grant. 2005. Potential effects of produced water discharges on the early life stages of three resource species. Pages 343-372 *in* Offshore Oil and Gas Environmental

Effects Monitoring: Approaches and Technologies (S.L. Armsworthy, P.J. Cranford, and K. Lee, Eds.). Battelle Press, Columbus, OH.

Saunders, K.S., S.E. Cobanli, R.R. Whalen, K. Lee, T.M. Schell, D.K. Muschenheim, T.G. Milligan, and M.R. Anderson. 1999. Observations at the Hibernia oil field site, October 1997. Canadian Data Report of Fisheries and Aquatic Sciences 1053, Fisheries and Oceans Canada, Dartmouth, NS.

Silvert, W. 1985. The Grand Banks modelling project. Pages 49-53 *in* BIO Review '85 (M.P. Latremouille, Ed.). Bedford Institute of Oceanography, Dartmouth, NS.

Smith, P.C., B.D. Petrie, J.A. Elliott, N.S. Oakey, and G.L. Bugden. 2014. Coastal ocean circulation studies. Pages 149-159 *in* Voyage of Discovery: Fifty Years of Marine Research at Canada's Bedford Institute of Oceanography (D.N. Nettleship, D.C. Gordon, C.F.M. Lewis, and M.P. Latremouille, Eds.). Bedford Institute of Oceanography-Oceans Association, Dartmouth, NS.

Strain, P.M. 1986. The persistence and mobility of a light crude oil in a sandy beach. Marine Environmental Research 19: 49-76.

Swannell, R.P.J., D. Mitchell, G. Lethbridge, D. Jones, D. Heath, M. Hagley, M. Jones, S. Petch, R. Milne, R. Croxford, and K. Lee. 1999. A field demonstration of the efficacy of bioremediation to treat oiled shorelines following the Sea Empress incident. Environmental Technology 20: 863-873.

Thomas, M.L.H. 1978. Comparison of oiled and unoiled intertidal communities in Chedabucto Bay, Nova Scotia. Journal of the Fisheries Research Board of Canada 35: 707-716.

Vandermeulen, J.H. 1978. Introduction to the Symposium on Recovery Potential of Oiled Marine Northern Environments. Journal of the Fisheries Research Board of Canada 35: 505-508.

Vandermeulen, J.H. 1982. Some conclusions regarding long-term biological effects of some major oil spills. Philisophical Transactions of the Royal Society of London B 297: 335-351.

Vandermeulen, J.H. and D.C. Gordon, Jr. 1976. Re-entry of 5-year-old stranded Bunker C fuel oil from a low-energy beach into the water, sediments and biota of Chedabucto Bay, Nova Scotia. Journal of the Fisheries Research Board of Canada 33: 2,002-2,010.

Vandermeulen, J.H. and W. Penrose. 1978. Absence of aryl hydrocarbon hydroxylase (AHH) in three marine bivalves. Journal of the Fisheries Research Board of Canada 35: 643-647.

Vandermeulen, J.H. and D.E. Buckley. 1985. The *Kurdistan* oil spill of March 16-17, 1979: activities and observations of the Bedford Institute of Oceanogra phy response team. Canadian Technical Report of Hydrography and Ocean Sciences 35, Fisheries and Oceans Canada, Dartmouth, NS.

Vandermeulen, J.H. and R.W. Lee. 1986. Lack of mutagenic activity of crude and refined oils in the unicellular alga *Chlamydomonas reinhardii*. Bulletin of Environmental Contamination and Toxicology 36: 250-253.

Vandermeulen, J.H. and J.G. Singh. 1994. *Arrow* oil spill, 1970-90: persistence of 20-yr weathered Bunker C fuel oil. Canadian Journal of Fisheries and Aquatic Sciences 51: 845-855.

Vandermeulen, J.H., D.E. Buckley, E.M. Levy, B.F.N. Long, P. McLaren, and P.G. Wells. 1979. Sediment penetrations of *Amoco Cadiz* oil, potential for future release and toxicity. Marine Pollution Bulletin 10: 222-227.

Vandermeulen, J.H., J. Hanrahan, and T. Hemsworth. 1980. Respiratory changes and stability of haemocyanin-O2 binding capacity in the crab *Cancer irroratus* exposed to Kuwait crude oil in seawater. Marine Environmental Research 3: 161-170.

Vandermeulen, J.H., W.L. Silvert, and A. Foda. 1983. Sublethal hydrocarbon phytotoxicity in the marine unicellular alga *Pavlova lutheri* Droop. Aquatic Toxicology 4: 31-49.

Vandermeulen, J.H., J.W. Thorpe, and K.E. Hellenbrand. 1994. Short-term weathering rates of buried oils in experimental sand columns over north-temperate temperature ranges. Bulletin of Environmental Contamination and Toxicology 53: 46-53.

Venosa, A.D., K. Lee, M.T. Suidan, S. Garcia-Blanco, S. Cobanli, M. Moteleb, J.R. Haines, G. Tremblay, and M. Hazelwood. 2002. Bioremediation and bioresto ration of a crude oil contaminated freshwater wetland on the St. Lawrence River. Bioremediation Journal 6: 261-281.

Venosa, A.D., M.T. Suidan, B.A. Wrenn, K.L. Strohmeier, J.R. Haines, B.L. Eberhart, D. King, and E. Holder. 1996. Bioremediation of an experimental oil spill on the shoreline of Delaware Bay. Environmental Science and Technology 30: 1,764-1,775.

Wells, P.G. 1973. Acute toxicity bioassay with an oil effluent and larvae of *Homarus americanus*. Pages 14-19 *in* A Toxicity Study of an Oil Refinery Effluent in Saint John, New Brunswick. Environmental Protection Surveillance Report, EPS 5 WP 73 1 (W.R. Parker, and R.P. Côté, Eds.). Environmental Protection Service, Environment Canada, Dartmouth, NS.

Wells, P.G. (Ed.). 2007. Estimates of oil entering the marine environment from sea-based activities. Joint Group of Experts on the Scientific Aspects of Marine Environmental Protection (GESAMP) Reports and Studies 75. International Maritime Organization (IMO), London, England.

Wells, P.G. and P.D. Keizer. 1975. Effectiveness and toxicity of an oil dispersant in large outdoor salt water tanks. Marine Pollution Bulletin 6: 153-157.

Wells, P.G. and J.B. Sprague. 1976. Effects of crude oil on American lobster (*Homarus americanus*) larvae in the laboratory. Journal of the Fisheries Research Board of Canada 33: 1,604-1,614.

Wells, P.G., S. Abernethy, and D. Mackay. 1982. Study of oil water partitioning of a chemical dispersant using an acute bioassay with marine crustaceans. Chemosphere 11: 1,071-1,086.

Wells, P.G., J.N. Butler, and J.S. Hughes (Eds.). 1995. *Exxon Valdez* oil spill: fate and effects in Alaskan waters. American Society for Testing and Materials, Special Technical Publication 1219, Philadelphia, PA.

Wells, P.G., K. Lee, and C. Blaise (Eds.). 1998. Microscale Testing in Aquatic Toxicology: Advances, Techniques and Practice. CRC Press, Boca Raton, FL.

Wells, P.G. and K.G. Doe. 2014. Applied aquatic toxicology: protecting the waters of Atlantic Canada. Pages 315-321 *in* Voyage of Discovery: Fifty Years of Marine Research at Canada's Bedford Institute of Oceanography (D.N. Nettleship, D.C. Gordon, C.F.M. Lewis, and M.P. Latremouille, Eds.). Bedford Institute of Oceanography-Oceans Association, Dartmouth, NS.

Williams, G.L., R.A. Fensome, and S.A. Dehler. 2014. Rocks of the deep: the subsurface geology of offshore eastern Canada. Pages 215-223 *in* Voyage of Discovery: Fifty Years of Marine Research at Canada's Bedford Institute of Oceanography (D.N. Nettleship, D.C. Gordon, C.F.M. Lewis, and M.P. Latremouille, Eds.). Bedford Institute of Oceanography-Oceans Association, Dartmouth, NS.

Yeung, C.W., B.A. Law, T.G. Milligan, K. Lee, L.G. Whyte, and C.W. Greer. 2011. Analysis of bacterial diversity and metals in produced water, seawater and sediments from an offshore oil and gas production platform. Marine Pollution Bulletin 62: 2,095-2,105.

Zhao, L., Z. Chen, and K. Lee. 2011. Modelling the dispersion of wastewater discharges from offshore outfalls: a review. Environmental Review 19: 107-120.

45. UNDERSTANDING THE MACROTIDAL ENVIRONMENT OF THE BAY OF FUNDY AND THE IMPACTS OF TIDAL POWER DEVELOPMENT

Donald C. Gordon*, Carl L. Amos, David A. Greenberg, Peter C. Smith, and Gordon B.J. Fader

SUMMARY

Engineers have long dreamed of harnessing energy from the tides in the Bay of Fundy which are the largest recorded in the world. Utilizing this renewable energy source could substantially reduce the dependence of Nova Scotia on fossil fuels for electrical power generation. Installing engineering works in this macrotidal region will alter important natural processes and create environmental impacts which must be assessed before any commitment is made to proceed with development. Over most of its history, the Bedford Institute of Oceanography has responded to this need by conducting research on various aspects of the Bay including the tides, physical oceanography, geology, sedimentology, chemistry, and ecology. This multidisciplinary program has been conducted in collaboration with other regional scientific establishments and has produced many exciting results which include developing tidal models, unravelling details of geological history and sediment dynamics, and determining the distribution, composition, and productivity of biological communities. These results have subsequently been applied to assessing the potential environmental impacts of different tidal power development scenarios, both earlier schemes based on building tidal barrages and current studies examining the use of in-stream turbines, and can help ensure that any tidal power development is carried out in an environmentally responsible manner. They have also been used to address other environmental issues in the Bay of Fundy.

Key words: Bay of Fundy, macrotidal estuaries, multidisciplinary environmental studies, tidal power development, environmental impact assessment.
***E-mail:** Donald.Gordon@ns.sympatico.ca

The Bay of Fundy (Fig. 1) is famous for having the highest recorded tidal range in the world (O'Reilly et al. 2005). In the upper Bay, the mean tidal range is about 11 m while the highest spring tides can reach 17 m (Fig. 2). Development of renewable energy from these tides could replace significant amounts of electricity generated by hydrocarbon combustion and is, therefore, a high priority. However, positioning energy-extracting devices in coastal waters will alter important natural processes and create environmental impacts so it is prudent to ensure that the long-term benefits gained outweigh any negative environmental consequences.

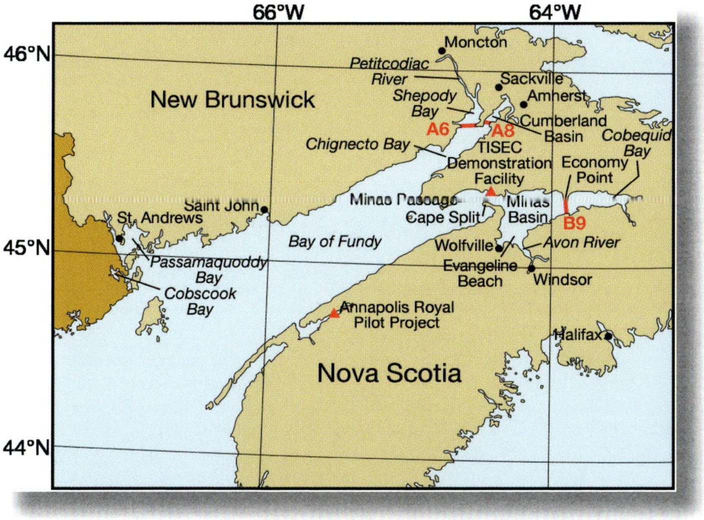

Figure 1. Map of the Bay of Fundy showing major geographic features and locations, and study sites referred to in the text. Sites A6, A8 and B9 identify the location of potential tidal power barrages recommended by the Atlantic Tidal Power Programming Board (1969).

For most of its 50-year history, the Bedford Institute of Oceanography (BIO) has been involved in studying the environmental characteristics of the Fundy macrotidal ecosystem and contributing to the understanding of potential environmental impacts of tidal power development. These studies have been a multidisciplinary effort involving BIO hydrographers, physical oceanographers, geologists, sedimentologists, chemists, and ecologists working closely with tidal power proponents, university colleagues, government regulators, and environmental organizations. This review summarizes the history of tidal power development proposals for the Bay and highlights the many important contributions of BIO to understanding the structure and functioning of this unique ecosystem and how it might be altered by the extraction of tidal energy.

EARLY TIDAL POWER STUDIES

Early proposals for tidal energy development were reviewed by Clark (1972). In 1919, Canadian and American engineers proposed a transboundary scheme involving the construction of tidal barrages in Passamaquoddy Bay and neighbouring Cobscook Bay on the United States side of the border (Fig. 1). This proposal stimulated a number of physical oceanographic and fisheries investigations by the nearby St. Andrews Biological Station (SABS). The results suggested that the environmental effects of the proposed project would be local (North American Council on Fisheries Investigations 1935). This proposal was subsequently dropped, but a smaller project entirely within Cobscook Bay, promoted by President Franklin Roosevelt, was started in 1935 but never completed.

In 1956, the Governments of Canada and the United States jointly referred further consideration of the Passamaquoddy Bay/Cobscook Bay proposal to the International Joint Commission (IJC) which in turn created International Engineering and Fisheries Boards to study the engineering and economic feasibility of the proposed barrage project and evaluate its possible effects on regional fisheries. The physical oceanographic studies (Trites 1961) yielded predictions of possible changes in tidal range, tidal and residual currents, temperature, salinity, stratification, and ice cover expected to be caused by barrage construction while the fisheries investigations (Hart and McKernan 1960) indicated that the overall impact of the proposed project on fisheries was unlikely to be important, except perhaps for changes in the relative abundance of some species. These results suggested that most environmental effects on fisheries would be localized near the barrage sites. However, this proposal was dropped in 1961 when the IJC concluded that the project was not economically feasible.

ENGINEERING STUDIES (1966-85)

During this period, extensive studies were carried out in the upper reaches of the Bay to examine the feasibility of extracting tidal energy by constructing large barrages, many kilometres in length, fitted with numerous turbines and sluices. These studies began in 1966 when the Governments

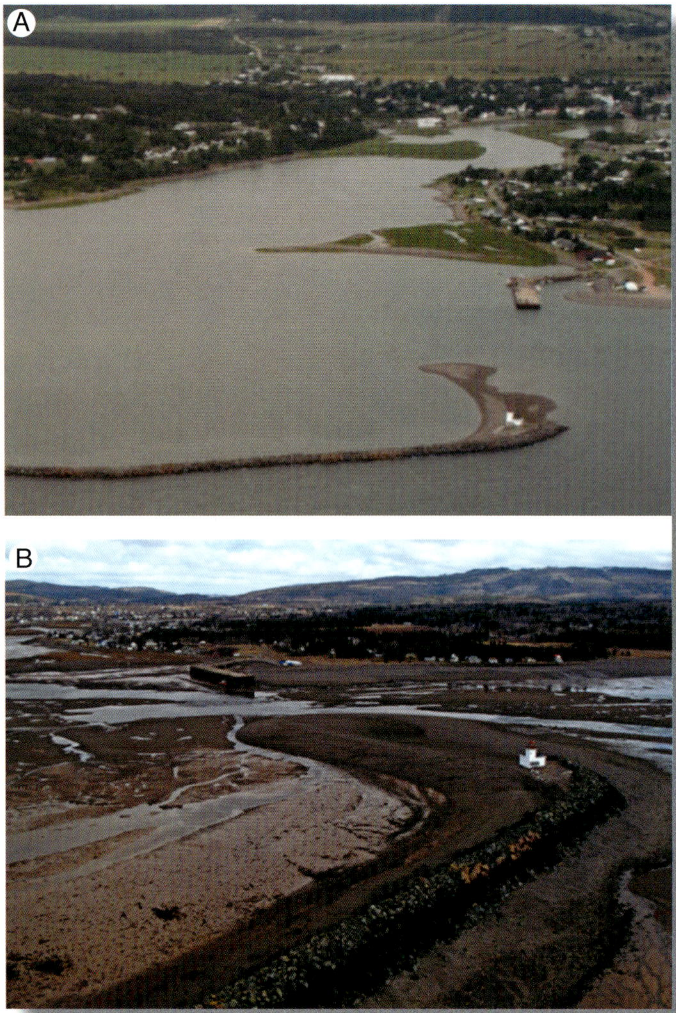

Figure 2. High and low water at Parrsboro, Nova Scotia, in the Minas Basin: (A) high tide, and (B) low tide (Photos: J.Woods, FORCE).

of Canada, New Brunswick, and Nova Scotia created the Atlantic Tidal Power Programming Board (ATPPB). This board initially assessed several dozen sites on both sides of the upper Bay and subsequently undertook comprehensive feasibility and limited environmental studies at the three most promising locations (Fig. 1): Shepody Bay (A6), Cumberland Basin (A8), and Cobequid Bay (B9). The ATPPB concluded that, although technically feasible, tidal power development was still not economically competitive with conventional power producing schemes (Atlantic Tidal Power Programming Board 1969).

Soon after, stimulated by the rapid escalation of fuel oil prices, the Governments of Canada, New Brunswick, and Nova Scotia jointly created the Bay of Fundy Tidal Power Review Board (BFTPRB) in 1972 to reassess the ATPPB conclusions. In 1974, the BFTPRB concluded that the economic feasibility of tidal power had improved considerably and a program of further investigation of tidal power feasibility was authorized (Bay of Fundy Tidal Power Review Board 1974), with one task area being a subcommittee to address potential environmental effects in which BIO participated. In response to the need for scientific advice, the federal Department of Environment (DOE), which included most of BIO at the time, created the Departmental Atlantic Region Fundy Working Group (DARFWG) to provide a mechanism for information flow at the working level between government scientists and the BFTPRB.

A workshop on Fundy tidal power development in 1976 (Daborn 1977), organized with the assistance of DOE and Acadia University (Wolfville, NS), brought together the regional scientific community to identify gaps in scientific understanding that later stimulated new research programs. The final BFTPRB report, which included tentative assessment of environmental issues, concluded that tidal power in the Bay of Fundy had finally become economically viable and recommended proceeding with the design of a single-effect tidal power development in the Cumberland Basin (Fig. 1:A8; Bay of Fundy Tidal Power Review Board 1977). However, soon after, the BFTPRB was dissolved and the recommended pre-commitment studies were not funded.

Nevertheless, the Province of Nova Scotia remained interested and in 1981 created the Nova Scotia Tidal Power Corporation (NSTPC). The NSTPC concluded that tidal power was now even more economically viable (Tidal Power Corporation 1982). The preferred projects at this time were Cobequid Bay (B9) alone or in combination with Cumberland Basin (A8) (Fig. 1). The report briefly addressed environmental concerns and acknowledged their importance in influencing the final design and operation of a possible project (Tidal Power Corporation 1985).

Funding to address these questions never materialized and, after many years of serious study supported by the federal and provincial governments, the concept of developing a tidal power project in the upper reaches of the Bay of Fundy, based on tidal barrage construction, came to an end. However, the Nova Scotia Power Corporation did proceed with the development of a pilot project at Annapolis Royal (Fig. 1) after undergoing a full environmental assessment. A single 20-megawatt STRAFLO turbine was placed in the existing Annapolis River causeway (Fig. 3A), the first such station in North America, and has operated successfully since 1984. It has provided the opportunity to investigate the impacts of turbines on the passage of anadromous fish (Dadswell et al. 1986), saline interactions with groundwater, and shoreline erosion.

BIO RESEARCH (1968–85)

A growing regional marine science community, stimulated by the engineering studies of tidal power development, suspected that constructing tidal barrages would cause major environmental impacts yet the underlying environmental properties and processes in the upper Bay of Fundy were poorly understood. With funding readily available, BIO was able to initiate a diverse research program which focussed on tides and physical oceanography, sedimentology, and ecology.

Tides and Physical Oceanography

A more complete understanding of tides and physical oceanography in the region was a high priority. It was clear from previous studies that the physical oceanography was greatly influenced by the tides, and that possible changes in tidal currents and water elevation could impact a multitude of physical, geological, chemical, and biological processes. Subsequently, BIO conducted a large number of studies on tidal dynamics in the Gulf of Maine which are reviewed by Smith et al. (2014).

In the late 1960s, D. Greenberg initiated a long-term program of developing numerical models of Fundy tides while a student (Greenberg 1969, 1975); subsequently he became a research scientist at BIO. In support of this work, D. DeWolfe of the Canadian Hydrographic Service (CHS) Tidal Section collected and analyzed additional tidal data for model calibration, verification, and refinement. This program, funded in part by the BFTPRB, installed tide gauges at a large number of locations within the Bay of Fundy and Gulf of Maine, including along the edge of the continental shelf. It was discovered with the aid of the numerical models that the exceptionally high tides in the Bay of Fundy were due to the forcing and near-resonant response of the combined Bay of Fundy and Gulf of Maine system, out to the edge of the continental shelf, where the natural resonant period of about 13 h is comparable to the M2 period of 12.42 h (Garrett 1972, Greenberg 1975). Owing to this unique property, it was essential to include the entire Gulf of Maine system, including Georges Bank, when assessing the impact of Fundy tidal power development on tidal properties (Ku et al. 1985).

The numerical tidal model (Greenberg 1977, 1979 and 1987; Fig. 4A) was calibrated by adjusting depths in the Gulf of Maine and the coefficient of friction to give the best agreement with observed tidal elevations. The complex current patterns were qualitatively reproduced and the residual currents agreed well with observation and independent models. Continued refinement of the model improved the accuracy even further and model results are accepted by the oceanographic and engineering communities with a high degree of confidence. The model was used by CHS to develop a tidal atlas of the hourly rate and direction of the major currents of the region for the use of mariners (Fig. 4B; Canadian Hydrographic Service 1981).

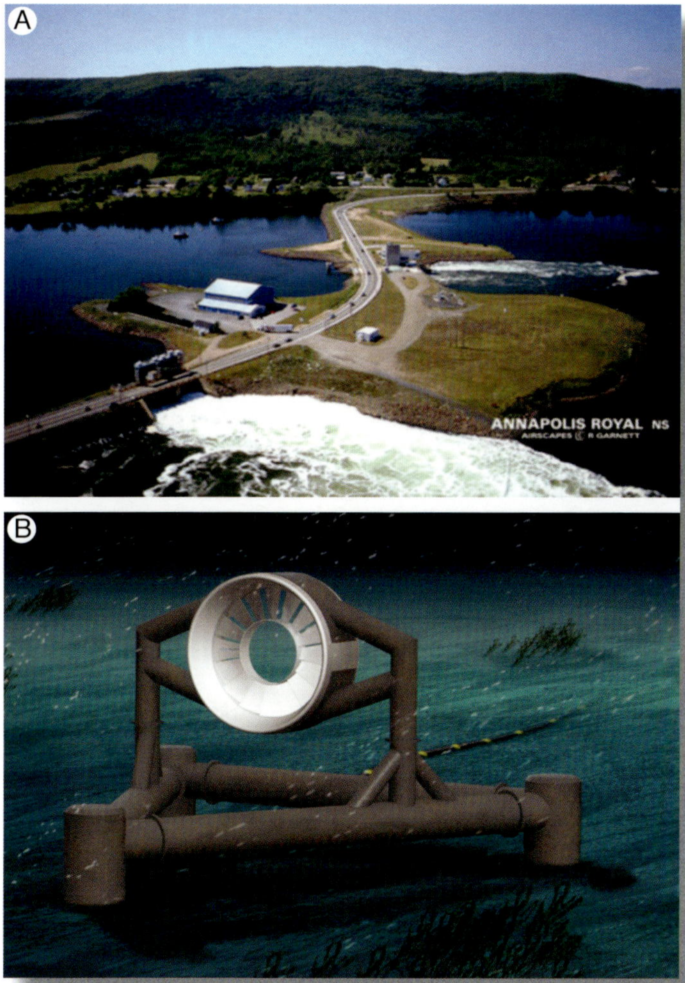

Figure 3. Tidal power projects: (A) Annapolis Royal, Nova Scotia, tidal power station built in 1984, the first in North America; (B) sketch of the OpenHydro experimental in-stream turbine deployed at the Minas Passage demonstration site in 2009-10.

In a parallel effort, K-T. Tee analyzed existing current meter observations in the upper Bay from the early 1960s and made additional measurements in 1974 in order to verify his numerical model estimates of the tide-induced residual current in the Minas Channel and Basin (Tee 1977). Soon after, circulation studies of Chignecto Bay using moored current meters were undertaken (Tee and Amos 1991) to interpret the overall tidal and residual current patterns along with concurrent measurements of temperature, salinity, and suspended sediment concentration. A strong two-layer circulation was observed at the entrance to the Bay with outflow in the upper layer and inflow in the lower layer.

Understanding the evolution of the macrotidal regime in the Bay has evolved over time. Using geophysical and sediment vibrocore data, Amos (1978) suggested that during the period 8,600-6,300 years ago, the Minas Basin appeared to be non-tidal and sedimentation occurred predominantly in the deeper parts. However, since then the tidal amplitude has been increasing, and sediment deposition became progressively more predominant in the marginal regions, developing the extensive sandflats, mudflats, and salt marshes visible today.

Using new sea-level data and the Greenberg tidal model, Scott and Greenberg (1983) came up with a different interpretation of tidal amplitude evolution in the Bay of Fundy. They concluded that tidal amplitude increased much more rapidly between 7,000 and 4,000 years ago than recently. Shaw et al. (2010) noted that the evolution of tidal amplitude in Minas Basin was delayed relative to that in Chignecto Bay until about 3,400 years ago. It was proposed that this delay was caused by a former sediment barrier in the Minas Passage and that, when it collapsed, the Minas Basin rapidly changed from a mesotidal to a macrotidal system with a concurrent drop in water temperature and increase in tidal currents and turbidity. The catastrophic breakdown of this barrier is reported in the legends of Glooscap showing that aboriginal peoples observed these rapid environmental changes and preserved an oral record of them for 3,400 years.

Sedimentology

After 1968-70, when causeways were built across the Petitcodiac River at Moncton, New Brunswick, and the Avon River at Windsor, Nova Scotia (Fig. 1), mud rapidly accumulated on their seaward sides (van Proosdij et al. 2009), and these observations emphasized the importance of understanding sediment dynamics before planning any tidal barrage construction. Therefore, a high research priority for the Atlantic Geoscience Centre (AGC) at BIO was investigation of sediment dynamics, bedform migration, suspended sediment mobility, ecological impacts on benthos, and geotechnical properties. This new initiative was initially spearheaded by D. Buckley who established collaborative research programs with G. Middleton and M. Risk at McMaster University (Hamilton, ON) to examine sediment bedforms and animal-sediment interactions in Minas Basin and Cobequid Bay (Middleton 1977, Risk et al. 1977). In the fall of 1974, C. Amos arrived as a postdoctoral fellow (PDF) from the United Kingdom and initiated research on sediment dynamics in the Minas Basin where B. Pelletier and M. McMullin had begun geological studies in the late 1960s (Pelletier and McMullin 1972). He was joined the following year by another PDF, B. Long, from France who focussed on the dynamics of sand transport. During this period, other AGC geologists mapped the surficial geology of the open Bay of Fundy (Fader et al. 1977).

C. Amos collaborated with the Canada Centre for Remote Sensing to explore applications for the new Multispectral Scanner (MSS) being flown on Landsat 1 and 2 satellites. During clear-sky satellite overpasses, samples of surface water were collected for developing an algorithm, the first of its kind, for transforming MSS radiance values from satellites to maps of suspended sediment concentration (Amos and Alfoldi 1979). Further calibrations were later derived for Nimbus 7 in Chignecto Bay using the same techniques (Amos and Topliss 1985).

A sediment budget for the Minas Basin (Amos 1977) showed that the major source was cliff erosion (average cliff retreat was 0.5 m/y) followed by input of suspended sediment from the open Bay through the Minas Passage. Inputs from rivers and erosion of subtidal sediments were found to be minimal. The residual movement of sediment, both as bed load and in suspension, was found to be headwards from the Minas Basin into Cobequid Bay and the Avon Estuary.

Owing to concerns that a mudflat might develop in front of a possible barrage at the B9 site in Minas Basin (Fig. 1), detailed field studies were conducted at the Windsor mudflat (Fig. 5A,B; Amos 1977). Accretion plates, installed to monitor the vertical growth of the flats, showed that the mudflat was accumulating soft, sticky mud at a rate of 14 cm/month. Under the federal Job Corps Program, and using a group of students, a more detailed sediment budget of Minas Basin was constructed which showed conclusively that both sand and fine-grained sediment were moving headwards into the inner parts of the southern Minas Basin (Amos and Joice 1977). In the late 1980s, the mudflat, now 6 m deep, became compacted and by the early 1990s, salt marsh vegetation began to colonize the surface. Growth since then has been rapid and by 2003 almost two-thirds of the mudflat was covered by salt marsh which is still growing and providing significant wildlife habitat. The far-field effects of causeway construction on sedimentation were investigated due to concerns that shoaling might interfere with the navigation of ships. At first it was thought that this was the case (Amos 1977), but more recent studies indicated that increased sedimentation from causeway construction extended just a few kilometres seaward of the causeway (van Proosdij et al. 2009).

The first sediment transport studies using radioactive sand in North America were conducted at the B9 site in Minas Basin (Fig. 6A) by B. Long who had carried out similar work with the developers of the technique in France. The experiments were preceded by an exhaustive risk analysis developed with the Atomic Energy Board of Canada and subsequently used in the development of more general guidelines for nuclear safety standards and risk (Long et al. 1978). In the first experiment, one kg of sand containing an isotope of gold with a half-life of 2.7 days was released and dispersion was measured by towing an iridium gamma counter behind an all-terrain tricycle until levels of activity dropped to background 16 days later. Innovative techniques were developed for photographing the study site using helium balloons. The second experiment used an isotope of neodinium with a half-life of 11.1 days. The combined

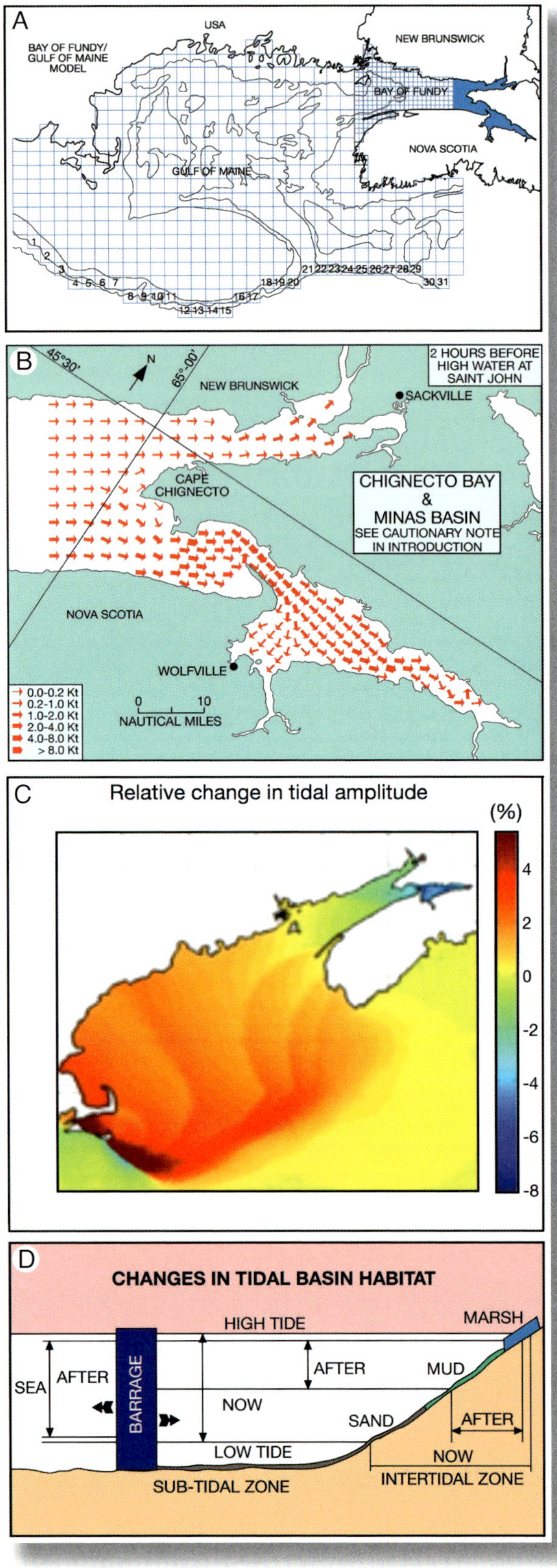

Figure 4. Understanding the tides of Fundy and impacts of tidal power development: (A) grid of the Greenberg numerical tidal model of the Bay of Fundy-Gulf of Maine system showing increasing resolution moving up the Bay of Fundy; (B) tidal currents predicted by the Greenberg tidal model in Minas Basin and Chignecto Bay (kt = knot; 1 kt = 0.5 m/s); (C) changes in tidal amplitude from barrage construction as predicted by the Greenberg tidal model (increases are depicted in red and decreases in blue); and (D) predicted changes in tidal amplitude immediately seaward and behind a hypothetical barrage (note the much smaller intertidal zone after construction).

Figure 5. Effects of causeway construction in the upper Bay of Fundy: (A, B) Windsor mudflat in the Avon Estuary before and after causeway construction; and (C) Moncton causeway in the Petitcodiac River showing the extensive mudflat that developed on the seaward side (right).

results clearly showed that intertidal sand was migrating eastwards at Economy Point at an average rate of 67 m per day which translated into a net movement of 460,000 m^3 of sand into Cobequid Bay each year (Long 1979).

Modelling the erosion, transport, and deposition of fine-grained sediment was hampered by the lack of reliable field data for defining important equations and constants. Therefore, the necessary calibration data were collected at the Windsor mudflat and Evangeline Beach (Fig. 1) as well as from a laboratory flume tank at BIO (Amos and Mosher 1985). Susceptibility of intertidal fine-grained sediment to erosion was found to be controlled largely by the degree of prior subaerial exposure and the consequent dehydration and compaction. The resistance of intertidal mud to erosion was found to be up to 80 times greater than its subtidal counterparts.

The multi-national Littoral Investigation of Sediment Properties (LISP) project, coordinated by G. Daborn of Acadia University, pioneered new thinking about the links between the plants, animals, and sediments (Daborn et al. 1993). As part of the innovation, an *in situ* benthic flume named Sea Carousel was developed and deployed in the field. In addition, H. Christian, a geotechnical engineer at BIO, developed an innovative *in situ* technique called INSIST to measure the shear strength of sediments.

In 1978, sedimentological studies were extended from the Minas Basin to determine the sediment budget and the seasonal variations in fluxes in the Chignecto Bay region where there was interest in constructing a barrage at the mouth of the Cumberland Basin (A8) (Fig. 1). It was found that the major sources of sediment were eroding cliffs (up to 1 m per year) while, in contrast to the Minas Basin, no appreciable sinks were identified (Amos and Tee 1989, Amos et al. 1991). Well-defined turbid ribbons were observed which meandered unpredictably through the sampling sites making estimates of sediment mass transport difficult.

Ecology

One of the major research gaps identified at the Acadia Workshop was understanding the structure and dynamics of intertidal and subtidal ecosystems in the upper Bay (Daborn 1977), information which was critical in understanding the potential impacts of tidal power development. The Marine Ecology Laboratory (MEL) at BIO subsequently began a new program coordinated by D. Gordon to address this gap. Others involved initially included B. Hargrave, G. Phillips, D. Peer, P. Keizer, N. Prouse, and J. Dale while P. Cranford and P. Schwinghamer joined the team a few years later. Funding included support for a series of PDFs including P. Neame, L. Cammen, F. Anderson, and C. Hawkins, all of whom made important contributions to the program. Program design was influenced by A. Longhurst who arrived at BIO in 1977 as the new director of MEL. Previously he had led an ecological program in the macrotidal Severn Estuary/Bristol Channel system in the United Kingdom which was also under consideration for tidal power development. The new ecological program was developed in close collaboration with the ongoing BIO physical oceanographic and sedimentological projects described earlier. In addition, collaboration was established with other new research projects, also stimulated by the Acadia Workshop, which were getting underway at other regional laboratories.

The BIO ecological program included extensive field operations to collect information at different spatial and temporal scales using a wide variety of platforms and equipment throughout the Bay. Most of these studies were carried out between 1978 and 1984 at all seasons. Fieldwork in the upper Bay presented a number of unique challenges including the large tidal range (Fig. 2), strong tidal currents (Fig. 4B), extensive mudflats (Fig. 6B), winter ice (Fig. 6C), and extensive salt marshes (Fig. 6D). New practices often had to be developed to work efficiently and safely in the field.

Physical, chemical, and biological data from the water column, and subtidal sediments along the axis of the open Bay were collected using the CSS *Dawson*. A series of anchor stations over complete tidal cycles was occupied in Minas Basin, Chignecto Bay, Shepody Bay, and Cumberland Basin using both the CSS *Dawson* and the charter vessel *Oran II*. In addition, in collaboration with D. Wildish of SABS, cruises on the CSS *Dawson* and CSS *J.L. Hart* examined subtidal benthic communities. Samples were collected using a new 0.5 m^2 Van Veen grab built at BIO specifically to improve recovery in gravel seabeds which are common in the Bay of Fundy.

Many physical, chemical, and biological variables and processes were also measured in the intertidal area. Sticky mud at some sites made this work difficult, a task that was more readily and rapidly accomplished over large areas using a Canadian Coast Guard helicopter. Ice dynamics in Cumberland Basin were studied with the assistance of C. Desplanque of the Maritime Resource Management Service (Gordon and Desplanque 1983).

This extensive field program produced a substantial database of key physical and chemical variables throughout the Bay of Fundy which illustrated important gradients and seasonal cycles (Keizer et al. 1984). Heavy metals in sediments were found to be at or near natural levels (Loring 1982). Nutrients in the upper reaches never fell to levels limiting to primary production and flux estimates suggested that there was a net export of dissolved nitrate and silicate from Cumberland Basin into Chignecto Bay (Keizer and Gordon 1985).

Because of light limitation caused by the increasing turbidity, phytoplankton production decreased up the Bay of Fundy, despite an abundance of nutrients (Prouse et al. 1984). Phytoplankton production of turbid water flooding the mudflats in Cumberland Basin was very low while that of benthic microalgae living on the mudflat surface exposed at low tide was moderate (Hargrave et al. 1983). Various aspects of the microbial ecology of the Bay were also investigated (Cammen 1984). The highest levels of primary production occurred in salt marshes around the edge of the Cumberland Basin (Gordon et al. 1985). Much of the salt marsh production, shown to have the greatest export potential of any salt marshes in the world, was exported as detritus and distributed widely throughout the estuary (Cranford et al. 1987, Gordon and Cranford 1994). It was determined that phytoplankton, salt marshes and benthic microalgae contributed 23%, 31%, and 46%, respectively, to the total annual primary production in Cumberland Basin.

In addition to the common Horse Mussel (*Modiolus modiolis*), which along with other suspension feeders accounted for 88% of production (Wildish and Peer 1983), 211 other subtidal benthic species lived in the lower Bay of Fundy while 137 and 126 species populated Chignecto Bay and Minas Basin, respectively (Peer et al. 1980, Wildish et al. 1983). It was concluded that tidal currents in the Bay of Fundy were a major determinant of the distribution and production of subtidal benthic communities.

Figure 6. Field work: (A) conducting sediment transport studies off Economy Point in the Minas Basin; (B) intertidal mudflats in the Cumberland Basin; (C) intertidal ice at Grande Pré in the Minas Basin; and (D) Tantramar salt marsh at the head of Cumberland Basin.

Following intertidal surveys in collaboration with P. Hicklin of the Canadian Wildlife Service (CWS), the production of the intertidal macrofauna community was estimated by Peer (1984). Other studies included population dynamics and production of the clam *Macoma balthica* (Cranford et al. 1985) and the amphipod *Corophium volutator* (Hawkins 1985, Peer et al. 1986). *Corophium* was found to be most abundant in the summer and provided a critical food source for migratory shorebirds (Hicklin et al. 1980).

In Pecks Cove, just inside Cumberland Basin, a study of mudflat food web dynamics with F. Tan using stable carbon isotope ratios showed that live marsh grass, fresh detritus and benthic diatoms were the major carbon sources for benthic consumers which was in agreement with the primary production results (Schwinghamer et al. 1983). Subsequently, experiments were carried out to examine the dynamics of marsh grass decomposition in intertidal sediments (Schwinghamer and Kepkay 1987). Monthly observations of benthic biomass spectra, never before measured in a benthic community, were used to estimate the production and respiration of bacteria, microalgae, meiofauna, and macrofauna from allometric equations (Schwinghamer et al. 1986). The results gave reasonable estimates of annual production and its distribution among size groups in the composite benthic community, information important for measuring ecological changes (Duplisea et al. 2014).

Other concurrent and collaborative studies of ecosystem components were important, including that of zooplankton communities by Acadia University (Daborn 1984), and those of fish by SABS which demonstrated that a large number of species utilize the upper reaches of the Bay of Fundy for part or all of their life cycle (Dadswell et al. 1984). Of particular note was the discovery that the summer run of American Shad (*Alosa sappidisima*) is composed of river populations from the entire Atlantic coast of North America (Dadswell et al. 1983). Detailed CWS studies of waterfowl, shorebirds, and seabirds in the Bay of Fundy (Hicklin and Smith 1984) highlighted the critical importance of the productive intertidal areas in the upper reaches as feeding grounds for migratory shorebirds, in particular the Semipalmated Sandpiper (*Calidris pusillus*) which feeds heavily on the amphipod *Corophium* during late summer to accumulate fat reserves before flying non-stop to South America.

The wealth of new information on the structure and dynamics of the ecosystems in the Bay led to development of a numerical simulation model of the Cumberland Basin ecosystem. This complex marine ecosystem model, the first of its kind in Canada, was conducted by a large team of BIO scientists and international colleagues (Keizer et al. 1987). The model demonstrated that the Cumberland Basin was a heterotrophic ecosystem with low primary production which requires imported organic carbon from salt marshes and Chignecto Bay to support the production and respiration of higher trophic levels (Gordon et al. 1987). The modelling process stimulated interdisciplinary discussion, identified important gaps in knowledge, and produced a quantitative tool which could be used to examine ecological hypotheses and determine critical environmental processes.

ENVIRONMENTAL ASSESSMENT OF TIDAL BARRAGES

In 1977, the Bay of Fundy Tidal Power Review Board referred the proposed barrage project to the Federal Environmental Assessment Review Office (FEARO) for formal environmental assessment which in turn established a joint federal-provincial Bay of Fundy Environmental Assessment Panel. The anticipated environmental assessment process and some of the potential environmental consequences were reviewed by Gordon and Longhurst (1979) who also emphasized the importance of considering the results of similar assessments being carried out in other regions. However, this assessment was never carried out since a tidal barrage project never came to fruition.

Tides and Physical Oceanography

The Greenberg tidal model (Fig. 4A) served as an excellent tool for investigating the potential impacts of different barrage scenarios. The general overall picture was a drop in tidal amplitude at and behind the barrage site and an increase away from the barrage as far away as the Gulf of Maine (Fig. 4C) (Greenberg 1977). Residual currents were noticeably reduced. In addition, the frictional dissipation and kinetic energy were drastically reduced in the headpond behind the barrage and in the channel in front of it while they were increased in the Gulf of Maine. It was also speculated that decreased mixing could increase ice formation. Changes in tidal regime from a barrage at the mouth of Shepody Bay (Fig. 1: A6) were less in magnitude but similar in pattern to those from a barrage in Minas Basin (Fig. 1: B9; Greenberg 1979).

Garrett et al. (1978) predicted the onset of stratification due to both solar radiation and freshwater input in previously well-mixed areas behind the projected barrages, changes that could have important consequences for biological processes and ice formation. Outside the barrages the changes were less dramatic. Garrett and Greenberg (1977) examined the assumption that the input tide at the open boundary of the model was unchanged by adding barrages and found that the error was small, on the order of 4% for a large tidal power development.

The predicted changes in tidal regime due to barrage construction were later updated and found to still hold true (Greenberg 1984). Barrages across the mouths of Shepody Bay (Fig. 1: A6) and Cumberland Basin (Fig. 1: A8) would give rise to similar changes in tidal regime. The M2 tidal amplitude would decrease at the barrage site and throughout the upper Bay of Fundy, but increase in the lower Bay and throughout the Gulf of Maine while a barrage at the mouth of Cobequid Bay (Fig. 1: B9) would lead to larger increases in tidal amplitude throughout the Bay and Gulf of Maine (Fig. 4C). The predictions of detectable changes in tidal amplitude in the Gulf of Maine prompted widespread concern in the United States scientific community. The Maine State Planning Office commissioned the Bigelow Laboratory for Ocean Sciences to explore potential impacts and their report concluded that a tidal power project in the upper reaches of the Bay of Fundy would have potentially important physical, geological, biological, and socio-economic consequences for coastal Maine (Larsen et al. 1984). Overall, predicted changes in tidal elevations and tidal currents were now well understood and accepted with a high level of confidence.

Sedimentology

The pronounced sedimentation associated with the construction of causeways at Windsor, Nova Scotia, and Moncton, New Brunswick, emphasized the concern for excess sedimentation at any of the proposed barrage sites. On the basis of the available information, it was initially speculated that a sand bar up to 600 m wide would develop on the seaward side of a barrage constructed in Minas Basin (Fig. 1: B9; Amos 1977, 1984). However, different results were obtained when more detailed quantitative studies were carried out using the Greenberg tidal model (Greenberg and Amos 1983). It was predicted that sedimentation could be expected in the intertidal area behind the barrage, but that suspended sediment would not inhibit the operation of a barrage. These results helped to alleviate concerns that mudflats would develop as they did at the Moncton and Windsor impermeable causeways. It was later found that sedimentation in the intertidal zone had been underestimated (Amos and Mosher 1985).

Ecology

Predictions of ecological impacts of barrage construction were based on the understanding that the highest spring tides would be excluded and the new mean high water level would be about 1 m lower while the new low tide level would be at about the present mean water level (Fig. 4D; Gordon and Dadswell 1984). As a result of these changes, approximately half of the present intertidal area would become subtidal. It was also understood that barrage construction would reduce tidal currents and energy levels and increase the potential for water column stratification.
Overall, it was suggested that there could be an increase in total primary production in the headpond area due to the anticipated drop in suspended sediment concentrations. There would be a pronounced decrease in the aerial extent of intertidal communities but also a complementary increase in the extent of subtidal communities. It was speculated that there would be major shifts in the properties and distribution of zooplankton and benthic communities which in turn could impact fisheries and shore birds. There was also concern raised about the potential of mortality to anadromous fish, such as shad, when passing through turbines. The ma-

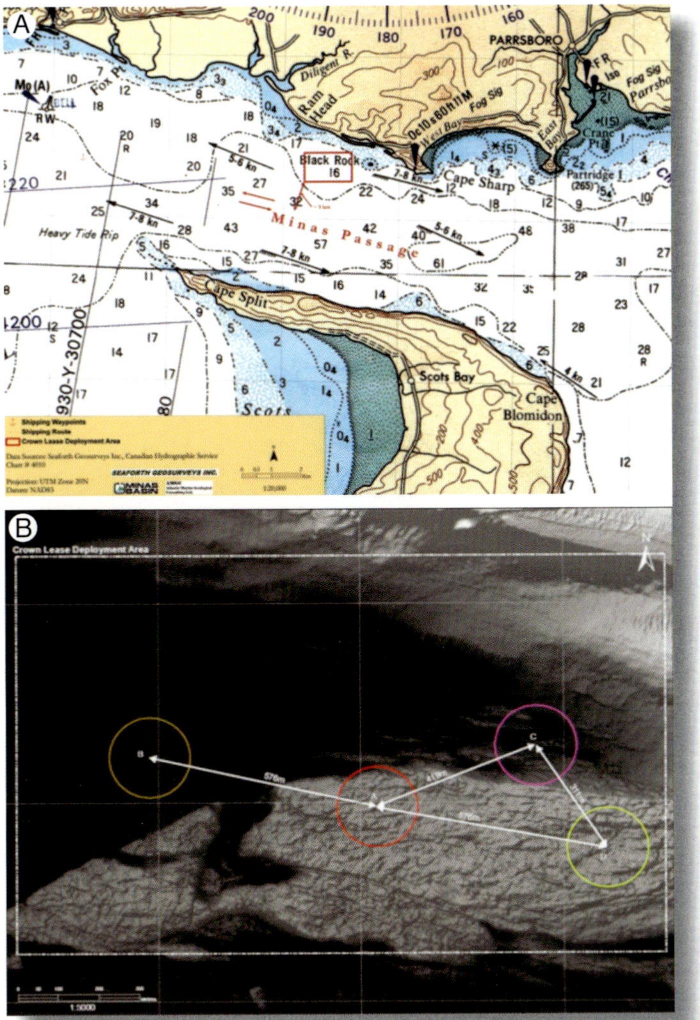

Figure 7. Tidal In-Stream Energy Converters (TISEC) demonstration site: (A) location along the northshore of Minas Passage (red rectangle); and (B) location of the four test berths overlain on an multibeam backscatter image of the seabed (courtesy: Atlantic Marine Geological Consulting and Seaforth Services).

jor changes expected in the intertidal area of the headpond behind a tidal barrage were summarized by Gordon (1994).

Wildish et al. (1986) coupled benthic production data with the Greenberg tidal model to explore possible seaward impacts of a barrage at the mouth of Cobequid Bay on subtidal communities through changes in tidal current speed, sediment type, and sediment bed stress. It was predicted that the production of suspension feeding organisms such as Horse Mussels in the lower Bay of Fundy would drop by 17%.

SCIENTIFIC COORDINATION

BIO staff were active in the coordination of Fundy environmental research, leading, for example, to the creation and operation of the Fundy Environmental Studies Committee under the Atlantic Provinces Council on the Sciences (APICS) which held regular and rotating workshops throughout the region to facilitate communication, review research results, and coordinate research planning. The Committee also undertook special projects, one of which was developing bibliographies on the Bay of Fundy and tidal power led by BIO Library staff (Moyse 1978, Plant 1985).

Other highlights of BIO coordination and involvement include the organization of the International Symposium on the Dynamics of Turbid Coastal Environments at BIO in 1981 (Gordon and Hourston 1983), a workshop on the environmental consequences of tidal power development at the University of Moncton, New Brunswick, in 1982 (Gordon and Dadswell 1984), and a workshop in 1996 in Wolfville, Nova Scotia, to review the broad range of environmental issues in the Bay of Fundy (Percy et al. 1997). Research results at the second event were captured in the award-winning book *Tidal Life* on the natural history of the Bay of Fundy (Thurston 1990). And concerns expressed at the third event led to the launching of the Bay of Fundy Ecosystem Partnership (BoFEP) which remains active today with BIO involvement (see www.bofep.org).

LULL PERIOD (1985-2005)

Although the concept of developing a large-scale tidal power project involving a tidal barrage in the upper reaches of the Bay of Fundy was dropped in the mid-1980s, some work in the Bay did continue under the lead of BIO, Environment Canada, and the Acadia Centre of Estuarine Research.

At BIO, geologists undertook an assessment of the marine aggregate potential of the Bay of Fundy focussing on the large sandwaves identified from the earlier mapping (Fader and Miller 1994), such as the Cape Split sand and gravel dunefield (Miller and Fader 1990). During this period, multibeam bathymetry was developed for detailed mapping of the seabed (Pickrill et al. 2014) and some of the first multibeam surveys were conducted in the Bay of Fundy by the Geological Survey of Canada-Atlantic (GSCA), the CHS, and the Ocean Mapping Group at the University of New Brunswick, Fredericton, New Brunswick (Todd and Shaw 2014). Studies of bedforms indicated long-term transport of sand toward the inner part of the Bay and helped increase understanding of the late glacial and sea-level history of the region (Fader 1997). Unique reefs of Horse Mussels were discovered covering large regions of the central and inner Bay (Wildish and Fader 1998), and large fields of gas-venting pockmarks were found in Passamaquoddy Bay (Pecore and Fader 1991).

In the late 1990s, BIO became involved in the controversial issue of the Moncton causeway, built across the highly turbid Petitcodiac River (Fig. 5C). There was immediate sedimentation of mud on the seaward side that extended more than 5 km down the estuary. Within a year of completion, the cross-sectional area of the Petitcodiac River at Moncton had been reduced by up to 80% which severely impacted shipping and hampered fish passage which led to a severe decline in anadromous fish such as salmon. Realizing the dearth of information available for the region, BIO, with T. Milligan in the lead, undertook to investigate the hydrodynamics and sediment dynamics in the Petitcodiac River system (Curran et al. 2004). Following an environmental impact assessment conducted in 2005, the causeway gates were opened in 2010 with a monitoring program initiated to observe changes and compare them to predictions made earlier. BIO scientists also contributed to a study comparing the responses of the Petitcodiac and Avon estuaries to causeway construction, which emphasized the need to include the entire estuarine system when evaluating the impacts of coastal engineering works (van Proosdij et al. 2009).

TIDAL IN-STREAM ENERGY CONVERTERS (2005-12)

Interest in developing tidal power resources in the Bay of Fundy reappeared in 2005. Earlier proposals for large tidal barrages would have extracted the *potential* energy of impounded water as it passed through turbines. However, by this time important advances had been made in the development of Tidal In-Stream Energy Converters (TISEC) which extract the kinetic energy of fast-flowing tidal currents. These turbines are normally mounted on the seafloor and can generate power on both ebb and flood currents. This approach offers many advantages including much lower costs and potentially fewer adverse environmental impacts. Also, if prototypes prove successful, additional units can be installed incrementally to form arrays or fields of turbines. In 2005, a study by the Electric Power Research Institute (EPRI) identified the Minas Passage (Fig. 1) as one of the most promising sites for TISEC development in North America (Hagerman et al. 2005). The Nova Scotia vision for proceeding with the new tidal power technology included choosing an optimal location, installing a small number of pilot demonstration turbines for engineering evaluation and then, if successful, expanding the site to commercial scale with a generating capacity on the order of 200-300 megawatts.

The regulatory process began in 2007 when the Nova Scotia Department of Energy commissioned a Strategic Environmental Assessment (SEA) on tidal energy development in the Bay of Fundy. Recommendations included: (1) restricting any commercial scale development until proponents have demonstrated that there will be no significant adverse effects on the fundamental environmental processes or key resources, (2) developing a collaborative research program to study marine renewable energy extraction from the Bay, and (3) establishing a demonstration facility to carefully test and evaluate some of the more promising tidal power technologies in the demanding Bay of Fundy environment before committing to any commercial development.

Meanwhile, the DFO Oceans, Habitat and Species-at-Risk Branch at BIO was requested to provide scientific advice on expected environmental impacts, mitigation measures, monitoring, and data requirements associated with TISEC development. It was concluded that four topics needed further investigation: changes to sediment dynamics both near and far field, impacts on the overall tidal forcing as a result of energy extraction, interactions between fish and turbines, and impacts of noise (Canadian Science Advisory Secretariat 2008). Current understanding of the environmental impacts of tidal and wave energy conversion projects was also reviewed at a DFO National Science Advisory Process meeting in 2009 (Canadian Science Advisory Secretariat 2009).

Following a request for proposals by the Province of Nova Scotia, Minas Basin Pulp and Power Limited was selected to develop the demonstration test facility and to conduct scientific studies of currents and the seabed, a mandate that has established working relationships with BIO scientists. The demonstration facility – the Fundy Ocean Research Centre for Energy (FORCE) – was created with federal, provincial, and corporate funding, and is sited along the northern shore of Minas Passage about 10 km west of Parrsboro (Fig. 7A) in 30 to 60 m water depths where 5-7 kt (9.3 to 13.0 km/h) tidal currents flow. The facility includes four test berths (Fig. 7B), submarine cables to shore, a visitor/observation/research facility, and connection to the local electricity grid, all of which have been environmentally assessed and approved.

Following the need of further research determined by the SEA, a BIO team (comprising P. Smith, G. Bugden, E. Horne, T. Milligan, B. Law, D. Greenberg, and Y. Wu), in collaboration with researchers at Acadia, Dalhousie, and St. Mary's universities (NS), is investigating tidal energy, current, and sedimentological issues. Currents have been measured at eight sites in Minas Passage, sedimentary processes have been observed on intertidal flats and in estuaries, and suspended sediment in surface water is being monitored using ocean-colour remote sensing. A sediment transport model has been developed (Wu et al. 2011) using grain size data collected during the 1970s. The grain size analysis is critical to the determination of the appropriate bottom stress parameters throughout the Bay of Fundy and greatly improves the validation of the model against tidal elevation and recent current data. In conjunction with the College of Geographic Sciences (Lawrencetown, NS), the intertidal area was also mapped using LiDAR (Light Detection And Ranging). Another project, led by G. Melvin of SABS and N. Cochrane of BIO, is developing acoustic methods for studying the behaviour of fish and marine mammals in the vicinity of active TISEC devices, an exceptionally difficult problem because of the strong, turbulent flow in the Minas Passage (Melvin and Cochrane 2012).

The first test turbine in the water (Fig. 3B), deployed by OpenHydro and Nova Scotia Power Corporation in November 2009, immediately experienced problems and when recovered a year later, all the blades had broken away but the gravity base did not move or affect the seabed (Fader 2011). This experience emphasized the strength of the currents in the Minas Passage and will contribute to the improvement of future turbine designs. Present plans call for the deployment of additional test turbines by other berth holders in 2014. Several retired BIO scientists currently serve on the Environmental Monitoring Advisory Committee that advises FORCE on the design and effectiveness of its environmental monitoring program.

Another proponent, Fundy Tidal Incorporated, is working to extract tidal energy using TISEC technology in Digby Gut and Petit Passage, and Grand Passage on Digby Neck, Nova Scotia. Other TISEC projects are also underway along the Maine coast.

SYNTHESIS AND THE FUTURE

Over its history, BIO has conducted a large number of research programs in the Bay of Fundy. These new programs were driven primarily by the applied issue of tidal power development, but there was also considerable motivation to unravel the mysteries of this unique macrotidal environment. These studies were conducted by teams of BIO hydrographers, physical oceanographers, geologists, sedimentologists, chemists, and ecologists who worked collaboratively with each other and numerous external partners. This research has provided a huge step forward in understanding the structure and dynamics of the Bay of Fundy environment.

BIO was ideally suited for this research because of its scientific and engineering expertise, equipment, and research vessels. Much of the work was conducted during the 1970s and 1980s when BIO was expanding and resources were plentiful. The importance and value of this research has been internationally recognized, and, as illustrated by the references provided, the many exciting new discoveries and tools have been well-documented in the scientific literature. BIO scientists have played a leading role in the international scientific community studying macrotidal ecosystems and tidal power development impacts, and foreign contacts often led to productive collaborative studies and exchange of valuable information.

As well as conducting research, BIO scientists have played a major role in coordinating regional scientific programs and providing objective advice on tidal power issues to various clients. Using the wealth of data and experience obtained, a concerted effort has been made to assess the potential environmental impacts of different development scenarios in order to provide sound and objective information for decision-making by both government and industry. At first, these predictions applied to tidal barrage construction, but now they concern the development of TISEC technology. Like all good research, the information, understanding, and tools developed can also be applied effectively to other environmental issues in the Bay of Fundy and adjacent regions.

The success of the Bay of Fundy program was due to several things. First and foremost was the creativity and enthusiasm of the participating scientists. Since its inception, BIO has provided a creative, stimulating and exciting research environment. Locating all oceanographic disciplines and support facilities from different government departments under one roof encouraged collaboration, plus BIO directors continually promoted the development of multidisciplinary research teams. For many years, research opportunities were virtually unlimited with ample personnel, funds, ships, and other essential support. Developing close collaborative links with other government agencies and laboratories, universities, tidal power proponents, and consultants also paid positive dividends, as did promoting open communication with local resource users and environmental groups. Results and issues were objectively discussed at regular workshops that were open to all interested stakeholders. The opportunity for BIO scientists to be part of the international scientific community through workshops, conferences, and joint projects was also a positive feature.

Looking to the future, the new Tidal In-Stream Energy Converter (TISEC) technology represents a major opportunity for Nova Scotia, not just for the generation of renewable energy, but also for the establishment of a new marine industry. Hopefully, BIO will be able to continue being a part of this promising venture by conducting needed research and providing sound scientific advice for good decision-making. However, present limitations may preclude study efforts on the scale of those conducted in the past. Extracting energy from the Bay of Fundy tides will cause environmental changes, and it is imperative that these be fully understood and considered as this potential industry develops.

The Bay of Fundy program serves as an excellent example as to why BIO was created. Making full use of the diversity of scientific and technical talent that resided under its roof, BIO staff of all disciplines carried out a long period of sustained research that produced results no single group of scientists or government department could have produced alone. In turn, these results are being used to help guide the potential development of an exciting new industry in Nova Scotia. The investments in BIO research over the years have paid, and continue to pay, healthy dividends to Canadians and the country as a whole.

ACKNOWLEDGEMENTS

We thank our many BIO colleagues as well as our many collaborators in other government laboratories, universities, and the consulting industry who contributed so much over the years to this multidisciplinary research program. Many of them are identified as authors in the references below. Many BIO staff contributed behind the scenes by developing equipment, collecting samples, processing data, and providing administrative support. Critical field support was provided by the BIO research vessel fleet and the Canadian Coast Guard. We thank the science managers of BIO and the various funding agencies for their support in carrying out this research. We also acknowledge the important contribution of numerous engineers and environmental managers to program design. We thank Graham Daborn, Barry Hargrave, Tim Milligan, Brian Nicholls, and Peter Wells for reviewing earlier drafts of this contribution. Cam Lirette kindly drafted Figure 1. And finally, we thank David Nettleship and Mike Lewis for their editorial assistance.

REFERENCES

Amos, C.L. 1977. Effects of tidal power structures on sediment transport and loading in the Bay of Fundy – Gulf of Maine system. Pages 233-253 *in* Fundy tidal power and the environment (G. R. Daborn, Ed.). Acadia University Institute Publication 28, Wolfville, NS.

Amos, C.L. 1978. The post glacial evolution of the Minas Basin, N.S.: a sedimentological interpretation. Journal of Sedimentary Petrology 48: 965-982.

Amos, C.L. 1984. The sedimentation effect of tidal power development in the Minas Basin, Bay of Fundy. Pages 385-402 *in* Update on the Marine Environmental Consequences of Tidal Power Development in the Upper Reaches of the Bay of Fundy (D.C. Gordon, Jr. and M.J. Dadswell, Eds.). Canadian Technical Report of Fisheries and Aquatic Sciences 1256, Dartmouth, NS, and St. Andrews, NB.

Amos, C.L. and G.H.E. Joice. 1977. The sediment budget of the Minas Basin, Bay of Fundy, N.S. Bedford Institute of Oceanography Data Series BI-D-77-3, Dartmouth, NS.

Amos, C.L. and T.T. Alfoldi. 1979. The determination of suspended sediment concentration in a macrotidal system using Landsat data. Journal of Sedimentary Petrology 49: 159-174.

Amos C.L. and D.C. Mosher. 1985. Erosion and deposition of fine-grained sediments from the Bay of Fundy. Sedimentology 32: 815-832.

Amos, C.L. and B.J. Topliss. 1985. Discrimination of suspended particulate matter in the Bay of Fundy using the Nimbus 7 Coastal Zone Color Scanner. Canadian Journal of Remote Sensing 11: 85-92.

Amos, C.L. and K.-T. Tee. 1989. Suspended sediment transport processes in Cumberland Basin, Bay of Fundy. Journal of Geophysical Research 94: 14,407-14,417.

Amos, C.L., K.-T. Tee, and B.A. Zaitlin. 1991. The post-glacial evolution of Chignecto Bay, Bay of Fundy, and its modern environment of deposition. Pages 59-90 *in* Clastic Tidal Sedimentology (D.G. Smith, G.E. Reinson, B.A. Zaitlin, and R.A. Rahmani, Eds.). Canadian Society of Petroleum Geologists, Memoir 16, Calgary, AB.

Atlantic Tidal Power Programming Board. 1969. Feasibility of tidal power development in the Bay of Fundy. Board Report and Committee Report, Atlantic Tidal Power Programming Board, Halifax, NS.

Bay of Fundy Tidal Power Review Board. 1974. Preliminary assessment of feasibility of tidal power development in the Bay of Fundy, Bay of Fundy Tidal Power Review Board, Ottawa, ON.

Bay of Fundy Tidal Power Review Board. 1977. Reassessment of Fundy tidal power, Bay of Fundy Tidal Power Review Board, Ottawa, ON.

Cammen, L.M. 1984. Microbial ecology of the Bay of Fundy. Pages 115-134 *in* Update on the Marine Environmental Consequences of Tidal Power Development in the Upper Reaches of the Bay of Fundy (D.C. Gordon, Jr. and M.J. Dadswell, Eds.). Canadian Technical Report of Fisheries and Aquatic Sciences 1256, Dartmouth, NS, and St. Andrews, NB.

Canadian Hydrographic Service. 1981. Atlas of tidal currents: Bay of Fundy and Gulf of Maine. Canadian Hydrographic Service, Ottawa, Ontario.

Canadian Science Advisory Secretariat. 2008. Potential impacts of, and mitigation strategies for, small-scale tidal generation projects on coastal marine ecosystems in the Bay of Fundy. Canadian Science Advisory Secretariat Science Response Report 2008/013, Dartmouth, NS.

Canadian Science Advisory Secretariat. 2009. Assessment of tidal and wave energy conversion technologies in Canada. Canadian Science Advisory Secretariat Science Advisory Report 2009/064, Dartmouth, NS.

Clark, R.H. 1972. Energy from Fundy tides. Canadian Geographic 85: 150-163.

Cranford, P.J., D.L. Peer, and D.C. Gordon, Jr. 1985. Population dynamics and production of *Macoma balthica* in Cumberland Basin and Shepody Bay, Bay of Fundy. Netherlands Journal of Sea Research 19: 135-146.

Cranford, P.J., P. Schwinghamer, and D.C. Gordon, Jr. 1987. Identification of microdetritus and its occurrence in the water column and intertidal sediments of Cumberland Basin. Estuaries 10: 108-117.

Curran, K.J., T.G. Milligan, G. Bugden, B. Law, and M. Scotney. 2004. Suspended sediment, water quality, and hydrodynamics of the Petitcodiac River Estuary, New Brunswick (2002-2003). Canadian Technical Report of Fisheries and Aquatic Sciences 2516, Dartmouth, NS.

Daborn, G.R. (Ed.). 1977. Fundy tidal power and the environment. Proceedings of a workshop on the environmental implications of Fundy tidal power. Acadia University Institute Report 28, Wolfville, NS.

Daborn, G.R. 1984. Zooplankton studies in the upper Bay of Fundy since 1976. Pages 135-162 *in* Update on the Marine Environmental Consequences of Tidal Power Development in the Upper Reaches of the Bay of Fundy (D.C. Gordon, Jr. and M.J. Dadswell, Eds.). Canadian Technical Report of Fisheries and Aquatic Sciences 1256, Dartmouth, NS, and St. Andrews, NB.

Daborn, G.R., C.L. Amos, M. Brylinsky, H. Christian, G. Drapeau, R.W. Faas, J. Grant, B. Long, D.M. Patterson, G.M.E. Perillo, and M.C. Piccolo. 1993. An ecological cascade effect: migratory birds affect stability of intertidal sediments. Limnology and Oceanography 38: 225-231.

Dadswell, M.J., G.D. Melvin, and P.J. Williams. 1983. Effect of turbidity on the temporal and spatial utilization on the inner Bay of Fundy by American shad (*Alosa sappidissima*) (Pisces: Clupeidae) and its relationship to local fisheries. Canadian Journal of Fisheries and Aquatic Sciences 40 (Suppl. 1): 322-330.

Dadswell, M.J., R. Bradford, A.H. Leim, D.J. Scarratt, G.D. Melvin, and R.G. Appy. 1984. A review of research on fishes and fisheries in the Bay of Fundy between 1976 and 1983 with particular reference to its upper reaches. Pages 163-294 *in* Update on the Marine Environmental Consequences of Tidal Power Development in the Upper Reaches of the Bay of Fundy (D.C. Gordon, Jr. and M.J. Dadswell, Eds.). Canadian Technical Report of Fisheries and Aquatic Sciences 1256, Dartmouth, NS, and St. Andrews, NB.

Dadswell, M.J., R.A. Rulifson, and G.R. Daborn. 1986. Potential impacts of large-scale tidal power developments in the upper reaches of the Bay of Fundy on fisheries resources of the northwest Atlantic. Fisheries 11: 26-35.

Duplisea, D.E., P.R. Boudreau, and L.M. Dickie. 2014. The size-structured view of marine ecosystems. Pages 99-103 *in* Voyage of Discovery: Fifty Years of Marine Research at Canada's Bedford Institute of Oceanography (D.N. Nettleship, D.C. Gordon, C.F.M. Lewis, and M.P. Latremouille, Eds.). Bedford Institute of Oceanography-Oceans Association, Dartmouth, NS.

Fader, G.B.J. 1997. Marine aggregate assessment and sediment transport. Pages 30-33 *in* Bay of Fundy issues: a scientific overview (J.A. Percy, P.G. Wells, and A.J. Evans, Eds.). Environment Canada Atlantic Region Occasional Report No. 8, Sackville, NB.

Fader, G.B.J. 2011. Environmental monitoring of seabed sediment stability, transport and benthic habitat at the reference site and the vicinity of the NSPI TISEC location in the Minas Passage. Atlantic Marine Geological Consulting Limited and Seaforth Geoservices Inc., Pages 1-42 *in* FORCE Environmental Effects Monitoring Report (Appendix J), Fundy Ocean Research Centre for Energy, Halifax, NS.

Fader, G.B.J. and R.O. Miller. 1994. A preliminary assessment of the aggregate potential of the Scotian Shelf and adjacent areas. Pages 230-262 *in* Coastal Zone Canada '94 (P.G. Wells and P.J. Ricketts, Eds.). Coastal Zone Canada Association, Dartmouth, NS.

Fader, G.B.J., L.H. King, and B. MacLean. 1977. Surficial geology of the eastern Gulf of Maine and Bay of Fundy. Marine Sciences Paper 19, Geological Survey of Canada Paper 76-17, Ottawa, ON.

Garrett, C.J.R. 1972. Tidal resonance in the Bay of Fundy and Gulf of Maine. Nature 238: 441-443.

Garrett, C.J.R. and D.A. Greenberg. 1977. Predicting changes in tidal regime: the open boundary problem. Journal of Physical Oceanography 7: 171-181.

Garrett, C.J.R., J.R. Keeley, and D.A. Greenberg. 1978. Tidal mixing versus thermal stratification in the Bay of Fundy and Gulf of Maine. Atmosphere-Ocean 16: 403-423.

Gordon, D.C., Jr. 1994. Intertidal ecology and potential tidal power impacts, Bay of Fundy, Canada. Biological Journal of the Linnaean Society 51: 17-23.

Gordon, D.C., Jr. and A.R. Longhurst. 1979. The environmental aspects of a tidal power project in the upper reaches of the Bay of Fundy. Marine Pollution Bulletin 10: 38-45.

Gordon, D.C., Jr. and C. Desplanque. 1983. Dynamics and environmental effects of ice in the Cumberland Basin of the Bay of Fundy. Canadian Journal of Fisheries and Aquatic Sciences 40: 1,331-1,342.

Gordon, D.C., Jr. and A.S. Hourston (Eds.). 1983. Proceedings of the Symposium of Turbid Coastal Environments. Canadian Journal of Fisheries and Aquatic Sciences 40 (Suppl. 1): 1-365.

Gordon, D.C., Jr. and M.J. Dadswell (Eds.). 1984. Update on the marine environmental consequences of tidal power development in the upper reaches of the Bay of Fundy. Canadian Technical Report of Fisheries and Aquatic Sciences 1256, Dartmouth, NS, and St. Andrews, NB.

Gordon, D.C., Jr. and P.J. Cranford. 1994. Export of organic matter from macrotidal salt marshes in the upper Bay of Fundy, Canada. Pages 257-264 *in* Global Wetlands: Old World and New (W.J. Mitsch, Ed.). Elsevier Science, Amsterdam, The Netherlands.

Gordon, D.C., Jr., P.J. Cranford, and C. Desplanque. 1985. Observations of the ecological importance of salt marshes in the Cumberland Basin, a macrotidal estuary in the Bay of Fundy. Estuarine Coastal and Shelf Science 20: 205-227.

Gordon, D.C., Jr., P.D. Keizer, P. Schwinghamer, and G.R. Daborn. 1987. Ecological evaluation of the Cumberland Basin ecosystem model. Continental Shelf Research 7: 1,477-1,482.

Greenberg, D.A. 1969. Modification of the M2 tide due to barriers in the Bay of Fundy. Journal of the Fisheries Research Board of Canada 26: 2,775-2,783.

Greenberg, D.A. 1975. Mathematical studies of tidal behaviour in the Bay of Fundy. Ph.D. thesis, University of Liverpool, Liverpool, England.

Greenberg, D.A. 1977. Effects of tidal power development on the physical oceanography of the Bay of Fundy and Gulf of Maine. Pages 200-232 *in* Fundy Tidal Power and the Environment (G. R. Daborn, Ed.). Acadia University Institute Publication 28, Wolfville, NS.

Greenberg, D.A. 1979. A numerical model investigation of tidal phenomena in the Bay of Fundy and Gulf of Maine. Marine Geodesy 2: 161-187.

Greenberg, D.A. 1984. The effects of tidal power development on the physical oceanography of the Bay of Fundy and the Gulf of Maine. Pages 349-370 *in* Update on the Marine Environmental Consequences of Tidal Power Development in the Upper Reaches of the Bay of Fundy (D.C. Gordon, Jr. and M.J. Dadswell, Eds.). Canadian Technical Report of Fisheries and Aquatic Sciences 1256, Dartmouth, NS, and St. Andrews, NB.

Greenberg, D.A. 1987. Modeling tidal power. Scientific American 257: 128-131.

Greenberg, D.A. and C.L. Amos. 1983. Suspended sediment transport and deposition modelling in the Bay of Fundy, Nova Scotia – a region of potential tidal power development. Canadian Journal of Fisheries and Aquatic Sciences 40 (Suppl.1): 20-34.

Hagerman, G., G. Fader, and R. Bedard. 2005. Nova Scotia tidal in-stream energy conversion survey and characterization of potential project sites. Electric Power Research Institute, Palo Alto, CA.

Hargrave, B.T., N.J. Prouse, G.A. Phillips, and P.A. Neame. 1983. Primary production and respiration in pelagic and benthic communities at two intertidal sites in the upper Bay of Fundy. Canadian Journal of Fisheries and Aquatic Sciences 40 (Suppl. 1): 229-243.

Hart, J.L. and D.L. MacKernan. 1960. International Passamaquoddy Fisheries Board Fisheries Investigations 1956-59, Introductory account. Journal of the Fisheries Research Board of Canada 17: 127-131.

Hawkins, C.M. 1985. Population carbon budgets and the importance of the amphipod *Corophium volutator* in the carbon transfer on a Cumberland Basin mudflat, upper Bay of Fundy, Canada. Netherlands Journal of Sea Research 19: 165-176.

Hicklin, P.W. and P.C. Smith. 1984. Studies of birds in the Bay of Fundy: a review. Pages 295-320 *in* Update on the Marine Environmental Consequences of Tidal Power Development in the Upper Reaches of the Bay of Fundy (D.C. Gordon, Jr. and M.J. Dadswell, Eds.). Canadian Technical Report of Fisheries and Aquatic Sciences 1256, Dartmouth, NS, and St. Andrews, NB.

Hicklin, P.W., L.E. Linkletter, and D.L. Peer. 1980. Distribution and abundance of *Corophium volutator* (Pallas), *Macoma balthica* (L.) and *Hetermastus filiformis* (Clarapede) in the intertidal zone of Cumberland Basin and Shepody Bay, Bay of Fundy. Canadian Technical Report of Fisheries and Aquatic Sciences 965, Dartmouth, NS.

Keizer, P.D, and D.C. Gordon. 1985. Nutrient dynamics in Cumberland Basin-Chignecto Bay, a turbid macrotidal estuary in the Bay of Fundy, Canada. Netherlands Journal of Sea Research 19: 193-205.

Keizer, P.D., D.C. Gordon, Jr., and E.R. Hayes. 1984. A brief overview of recent chemical research in the Bay of Fundy. Pages 46-63 *in* Update on the Marine Environmental Consequences of Tidal Power Development in the Upper Reaches of the Bay of Fundy (D.C. Gordon, Jr. and M.J. Dadswell, Eds.). Canadian Technical Report of Fisheries and Aquatic Sciences 1256, Dartmouth, NS, and St. Andrews, NB.

Keizer, P.D., D.C. Gordon, Jr., P. Schwinghamer, G.R. Daborn, and W. Ebenhoeh. 1987. Cumberland Basin ecosystem model: structure, performance and evaluation. Canadian Technical Report of Fisheries and Aquatic Sciences 1547, Dartmouth, NS.

Ku, L.F., D.A. Greenberg, C. Garrett, and F.W. Dobson. 1985. The nodal modulation of the M2 tide in the Bay of Fundy and Gulf of Maine. Science 230: 69-71.

Larsen, P.F., J.A. Topinka, A.L. Lerman, G.S. Geise, F.A. Anderson, R.W. Rudolph, and B.S. Timson. 1984. Fundy tidal power development; preliminary evaluation of its environmental consequences to the resources of the State of Maine. Technical Report No. 35, Bigelow Laboratory for Ocean Science, West Boothbay Harbor, ME.

Long, B.F.N. 1979. The nature of bottom sediments in the Minas Basin system, Bay of Fundy. Bedford Institute of Oceanography Data Series 79-4, Dartmouth, NS.

Long, B.F.N., N. Kulkarni, and G. Joice. 1978. Radioisotopes as sediment tracers: risks involved and proposed guidelines for use. Bedford Institute of Oceanography Report Series 78-3, Dartmouth, NS.

Loring, D.H. 1982. Geochemical factors controlling the accumulation and dispersion of heavy metals in the Bay of Fundy sediments. Canadian Journal of Earth Sciences 19: 930-944.

Melvin, G.D. and N.A. Cochrane. 2012. A preliminary investigation of fish distributions near an in-stream tidal turbine in Minas Passage, Bay of Fundy. Canadian Technical Report of Fisheries and Aquatic Sciences 3006, St. Andrews, NB.

Middleton, G.V. 1977. The sediment regime of the Bay of Fundy. Pages 125-130 *in* Fundy Tidal Power and the Environment (G. R. Daborn, Ed.). Acadia University Institute Publication 28, Wolfville, NS.

Miller, R.O. and G.B.J. Fader. 1990. Cruise Report C.S.S. *Navicula* 89-009, Phase C, The sand wave field-Scots Bay. Geological Survey of Canada, Open File Report 2298, Ottawa, ON.

Moyse, C.M. 1978. Bay of Fundy environmental and tidal power bibliography. Fisheries and Marine Service Technical Report 822, St. Andrews, NB and Dartmouth, NS.

North American Council on Fisheries Investigations. 1935. The effects of dams in Passamaquoddy Bay. Proceedings of the North American Council on Fisheries Investigations 1931/33, (2): 1-40.

O'Reilly, C.T., R. Solvason, and C. Solomon. 2005. Where are the world's largest tides? Pages 44–46 *in* Bedford Institute of Oceanography: 2004 in Review (J. Ryan, Ed.). Bedford Institute of Oceanography, Dartmouth, NS.

Pecore, S.S. and G.B.J. Fader. 1991. Surficial geology, pockmarks and associated neotectonic features of Passamaquoddy Bay, New Brunswick, Canada. Geological Survey of Canada, Open File Report No. 2213, Ottawa, ON.

Peer, D.L. 1984. A review of benthic macrofaunal production of the upper Bay of Fundy intertidal area. Pages 105-114 *in* Update on the Marine Environmental Consequences of Tidal Power Development in the Upper Reaches of the Bay of Fundy (D.C. Gordon, Jr. and M.J. Dadswell, Eds.). Canadian Technical Report of Fisheries and Aquatic Sciences 1256, Dartmouth, NS, and St. Andrews, NB.

Peer, D.L., D.J. Wildish, A.J. Wilson, J. Hines, and M.J. Dadswell. 1980. Sublittoral macrofauna of the lower Bay of Fundy. Canadian Technical Report of Fisheries and Aquatic Sciences 981, Dartmouth, NS.

Peer, D.L., L.E. Linkletter, and P.W. Hicklin. 1986. Life history and reproductive biology of *Corophium volutator* (Crustacea: Amphipoda) and the influence of shorebird predation on population structure in Chignecto Bay, Bay of Fundy, Canada. Netherlands Journal of Sea Research 20: 359-373.

Pelletier, B.R. and R.M. McMullin. 1972. Sedimentary patterns in the Bay of Fundy and Minas Basin. Pages 153-187 *in* Tidal Power (T.J. Gray and O.K. Gashus, Eds.). Plenum Press, New York, NY.

Percy, J.A., P.G. Wells, and A.J. Evans. 1997. Bay of Fundy issues: a scientific overview. Environment Canada Atlantic Region Occasional Report No. 8, Sackville, NB.

Pickrill, R.A., B.J. Todd, S.J. Smith, J.V. Barrie, and K.W. Conway. 2014. Marine habitat mapping in Canada's oceans. Pages 185-190 *in* Voyage of Discovery: Fifty Years of Marine Research at Canada's Bedford Institute of Oceanography (D.N. Nettleship, D.C. Gordon, C.F.M. Lewis, and M.P. Latremouille, Eds.). Bedford Institute of Oceanography-Oceans Association, Dartmouth, NS.

Plant, S. 1985. Bay of Fundy environmental and tidal power bibliography. Canadian Technical Report of Fisheries and Aquatic Sciences 1339, Dartmouth, NS.

Prouse, N.J., D.C. Gordon, Jr., B.T. Hargrave, C.J. Bird, J. McLachlan, J.S.S. Lakshminarayana, J. Sita Devi, and M.L.H. Thomas. 1984. Primary production: organic matter supply to ecosystems in the Bay of Fundy. Pages 65-95 *in* Update on the Marine Environmental Consequences of Tidal Power Development in the Upper Reaches of the Bay of Fundy (D.C. Gordon, Jr., and M.J. Dadswell, Eds.). Canadian Technical Report of Fisheries and Aquatic Sciences 1256, Dartmouth, NS, and St. Andrews, NB.

Risk, M.J., R.K. Yeo, and H.D. Craig. 1977. Aspects of the marine ecology of the Minas Basin relevant to tidal power development. Pages 164-179 *in* Fundy Tidal Power and the Environment (G. R. Daborn, Ed.). Acadia University Institute Publication 28, Wolfville, NS.

Schwinghamer, P. and P. Kepkay. 1987. Effects of experimental enrichment with *Spartina* detritus on sediment community biomass and metabolism. Biological Oceanography 4: 289-322.

Schwinghamer, P., F.C. Tan, and D.C. Gordon, Jr. 1983. Stable carbon isotope studies on the Pecks Cove mudflat ecosystem in the Cumberland Basin. Canadian Journal of Fisheries and Aquatic Sciences 40 (Suppl. 1): 262-272.

Schwinghamer, P., B. Hargrave, D. Peer, and C.M. Hawkins. 1986. Partitioning of production and respiration among size groups of organisms in an intertidal benthic community. Marine Ecology Progress Series 31: 131-142.

Scott, D.B, and D.A. Greenberg. 1983. Relative sea-level rise and tidal development in the Fundy tidal system. Canadian Journal of Earth Sciences 20: 1,554-1,564.

Shaw, J., C.L. Amos, D.A. Greenberg, C.T. O'Reilly, D.R. Parrott, and E. Patton. 2010. Catastrophic tidal expansion in the Bay of Fundy, Canada. Canadian Journal of Earth Sciences 47: 1,079-1,091.

Smith, P.C., B.D. Petrie, J.A. Elliott, N.S. Oakey, and G.L. Bugden. 2014. Coastal ocean circulation studies. Pages 149-159 *in* Voyage of Discovery: Fifty Years of Marine Research at Canada's Bedford Institute of Oceanography (D.N. Nettleship, D.C. Gordon, C.F.M. Lewis, and M.P. Latremouille, Eds.). Bedford Institute of Oceanography-Oceans Association, Dartmouth, NS.

Tee, K.-T. 1977. Tide-induced residual current – verification of a numerical model. Journal of Physical Oceanography 7: 396-402.

Tee, K.-T. and C.L. Amos. 1991. Tidal and buoyancy-driven currents in Chignecto Bay, Bay of Fundy. Journal of Geophysical Research 96: 15,197-15,216.

Tidal Power Corporation. 1982. Fundy tidal power update '82. Tidal Power Corporation, Halifax, NS.

Tidal Power Corporation. 1985. Fundy tidal power Stage 1. Tidal Power Corporation, Halifax, NS.

Thurston, H. 1990. Tidal life: a natural history of the Bay of Fundy. Camden House Publishing, Camden East, ON.

Todd, B.J. and J. Shaw. 2014. Discovering the seafloor of the Bay of Fundy. Pages 231-235 *in* Voyage of Discovery: Fifty Years of Marine Research at Canada's Bedford Institute of Oceanography (D.N. Nettleship, D.C. Gordon, C.F.M. Lewis, and M.P. Latremouille, Eds.). Bedford Institute of Oceanography-Oceans Association, Dartmouth, NS.

Trites, R.W. 1961. Probable effects of proposed Passamaquoddy power plant on oceanographic conditions. Journal of the Fisheries Research Board of Canada 18: 163-201.

van Proosdij, D., T. Milligan, G. Bugden, and K. Butler. 2009. A tale of two macrotidal estuaries: differential morphodynamic response of the intertidal zone to causeway construction. Journal of Coastal Research, Special Issue 56: 772-776.

Wildish, D.J. and D.L. Peer. 1983. Tidal current speed and production of benthic macrofauna in the lower Bay of Fundy. Canadian Journal of Fisheries and Aquatic Sciences 40 (Suppl. 1): 309-321.

Wildish, D.J. and G.B.J. Fader. 1998. Pelagic-benthic coupling in the Bay of Fundy. Hydrobiologia 375/376: 369-380.

Wildish, D.J., D.L. Peer, A.J. Wilson, J. Hines, L. Linkletter, and M.J. Dadswell. 1983. Sublittoral macrofauna of the upper Bay of Fundy. Canadian Technical Report of Fisheries and Aquatic Sciences 1194, St. Andrews, NB.

Wildish, D.J., D.L. Peer, and D.A. Greenberg. 1986. Benthic macrofaunal production in the Bay of Fundy and the possible effects of a tidal power barrage at Economy Point – Cape Tenny. Canadian Journal of Fisheries and Aquatic Sciences 43: 2,410-2,417.

Wu, Y., J. Chaffey, D.A. Greenberg, K. Colbo, and P.C. Smith. 2011. Tidally-induced sediment transport patterns in the upper Bay of Fundy: a numerical study. Continental Shelf Research 31: 2,041-2,053.

46. SEABED GEOHAZARD KNOWLEDGE FOR SAFE HYDROCARBON DEVELOPMENT

C.F. Michael Lewis*, Steve M. Blasco, David J.W. Piper, and Gary V. Sonnichsen

SUMMARY

Exploration and production of hydrocarbons from Canada's offshore sedimentary basins requires the seabed to support well heads, bottom-founded drilling and production platforms, anchoring systems, and pipelines, among other facilities. Knowledge of seabed and subsurface material properties, and the natural geologic processes that affect their stability is essential to avoid costly surprises, and to ensure safe and economical discovery and recovery of hydrocarbon resources. Evaluation of seabed geohazards has been a focus for geoscientists at Bedford Institute of Oceanography since the 1970s, shortly after offshore exploration drilling began in 1966. Seabed issues that were studied in the Atlantic offshore include the magnitude and frequency of dynamic geohazards such as iceberg scouring, wave and current modification of the seabed, as well as slope failure, and variability of foundation conditions. For the Beaufort Sea, hazards described include sea-ice scouring, seabed foundation conditions, subsea permafrost, pingo-like features, gas or fluid venting, and submarine landslides.

Key words: seabed stability, geohazards, offshore oil and gas exploration and production, Atlantic continental margin, Canadian Beaufort Sea.

***E-mail:** Michael.Lewis@NRCan-RNCan.gc.ca

Safe exploration drilling and installation of seafloor infrastructure for hydrocarbon production such as well head completion equipment and pipelines requires extensive seabed knowledge. A lack of understanding of seabed hazards or geohazards may lead to well and/or subsea pipeline failures or may result in economic costs because of over-engineering. These hazards are also a key factor in maintaining shallow hole stability in frontier exploration wells. These failures can lead to the uncontrolled release of hydrocarbons into the environment. The fate and effects of spilled oil are described by Gordon et al. (2014). Regulatory agencies use Bedford Institute of Oceanography (BIO) geohazard research results to help establish regulatory guidelines to ensure that the risk of hydrocarbon structure failure is minimized. Commonly, seabed hazards are first identified during regional geological mapping surveys, typically conducted by government agencies (Fader et al. 2014). Further understanding of hazards is acquired through targeted research programs, often in collaboration with the hydrocarbon industry and its consultants, and universities. BIO contributions to the acquisition of knowledge of seabed geohazards and their significance are subsequently described for the Atlantic continental margin, and the Beaufort Sea.

ATLANTIC CONTINENTAL MARGIN

Marine sedimentary basins with probable hydrocarbon resources underlie both the continental shelves and slopes of offshore eastern Canada (Fig. 1). Exploratory drilling for hydrocarbon resources began in 1966 and 1967 on the Newfoundland and Nova Scotia shelves, respectively, and in 1971 on the Labrador Shelf (Williams et al. 2014). Structures used for oil and gas exploration and production include jack-up drilling rigs, pile-supported structures, bottom-founded structures, well-conductor casings, pipelines, and anchoring systems for floating rigs and platforms. In addition to gravity loads of structures, the seabed must also support a component of the lateral loads imposed by environmental forces arising from currents, high waves, and icebergs (Lewis and Keen 1990, Sonnichsen et al. 1994). The principal geohazards of the Atlantic continental margin investigated by BIO geoscientists and described here consist of iceberg scouring, shelf erosion and sedimentation, slope stability, and variability of sub-seabed foundation conditions.

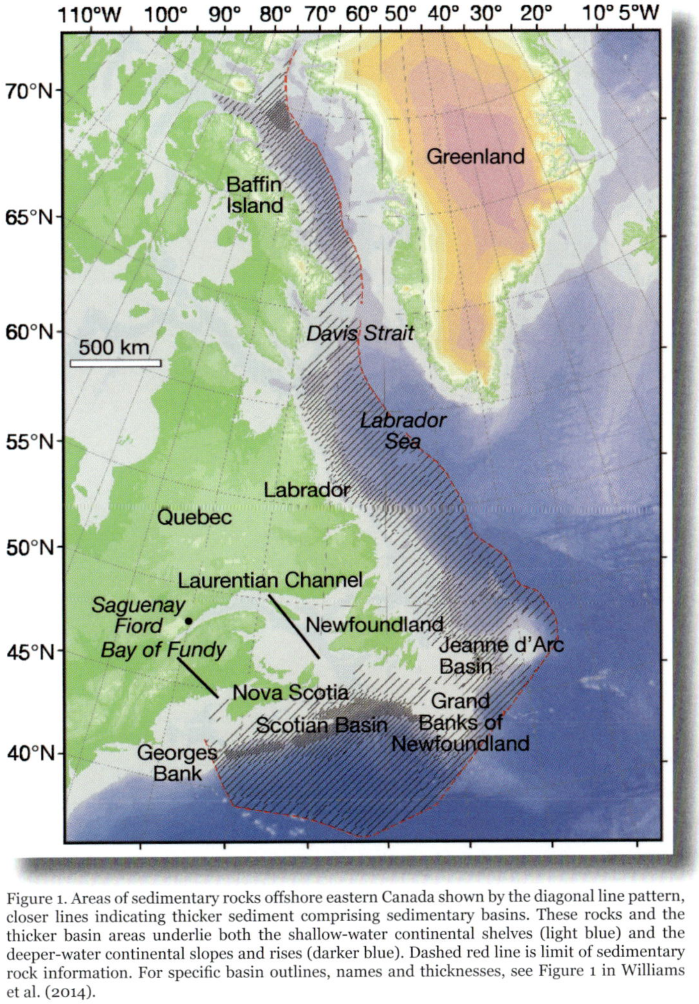

Figure 1. Areas of sedimentary rocks offshore eastern Canada shown by the diagonal line pattern, closer lines indicating thicker sediment comprising sedimentary basins. These rocks and the thicker basin areas underlie both the shallow-water continental shelves (light blue) and the deeper-water continental slopes and rises (darker blue). Dashed red line is limit of sedimentary rock information. For specific basin outlines, names and thicknesses, see Figure 1 in Williams et al. (2014).

Iceberg Scouring

The first operational records of the 70 kHz BIO sidescan sonar (Jollymore 1974) revealed cross-cutting furrows on the southern Labrador Shelf which Harris and Jollymore (1974) related to formation by bottom-dragging keels of icebergs. King (1976) later recognized abundant seabed iceberg furrows on the western Grand Banks and Laurentian Channel, areas where modern iceberg occurrence is rare. He attributed these 'relict scours' to the action of paleo-icebergs related to deglaciation of the last ice sheet, and suggested that a similar origin might apply to many of the furrows on the Labrador Shelf, rendering much of the iceberg scour record as benign with respect to concern for modern seabed disturbance.

Focussed research of the modern iceberg scouring process was conducted during the 1980s by BIO geoscientists, often in partnership with C-CORE at Memorial University of Newfoundland and industry. Results from these studies were discussed at workshops and compiled in proceedings volumes (Lewis et al. 1986, Lewis and Blasco 1990).

Grand Banks iceberg scouring – After the discovery of oil at Hibernia in 1979, and following extensive field work in 1980, Lewis and Barrie (1981) presented an overview of the then current knowledge of iceberg scour for the northeastern Grand Bank on behalf of members of the Hibernia Sediments Program comprising C. Amos, G. Fader, L. King, and M. Lewis (Atlantic Geoscience Centre, Geological Survey of Canada, at BIO) and V. Barrie (C-CORE). This overview was based on surficial geological reconnaissance using the BIO sidescan sonar and the new Huntec Deep Tow high-resolution seismic profiler (Fader and King 1981, McKeown et al. 2014), and on complementary data provided by Mobil Oil Canada Ltd. Collectively, these data provided evidence of a younger, sparse number of iceberg scours superimposed on a degraded relict network of iceberg furrows (Fig. 2).

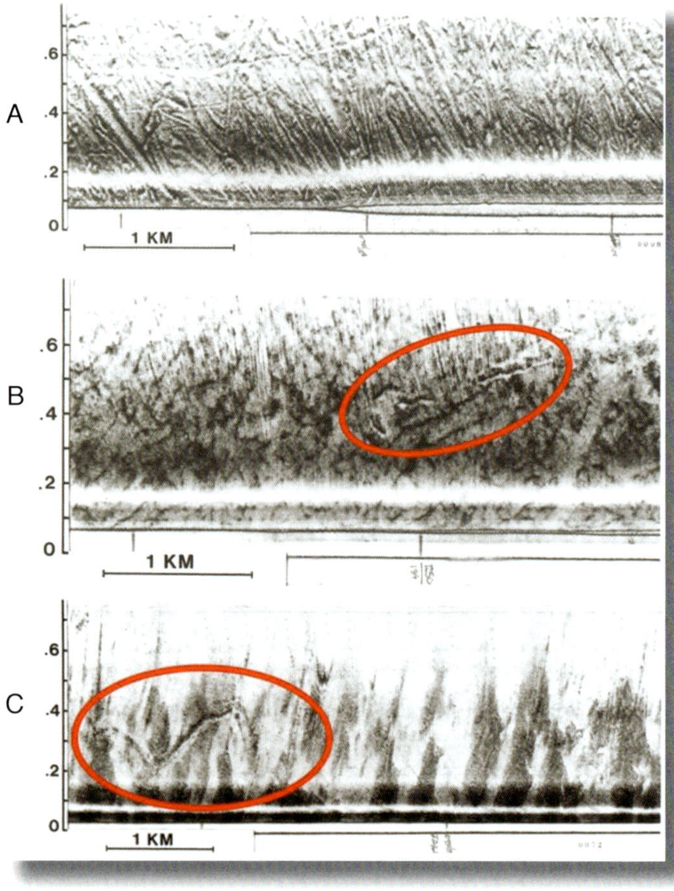

Figure 2. BIO sidescan sonar records (70 kHz) from 1980 showing ca. 0.7 km-wide swaths of seafloor on the northeastern Grand Banks of Newfoundland, and showing a transition in regimes of iceberg scouring from: (A) a dense network of paleo-iceberg scours at 172 m water depth, through (B) sparse occurrences of more recent iceberg scours (within red oval) superimposed on the paleo-scour network at 151 m water depth, to (C) continuation of recent iceberg scours (within red oval) over a degraded and partially sand-covered (light tones) paleo-scour network at 108 m water depth. The sand bodies at 108 m water depth (light-toned areas in C) developed by surf erosion during and following the last low sea-level stand about 21,000 years ago (Fader 1989, Shaw 2014).

Data for the younger population of iceberg scours provided insight into their regional distribution, which was reasonably attributed to the modern population of icebergs carried southward from Greenland and Arctic Canada glaciers in the Baffin and Labrador currents. At the time, the age of iceberg scours or duration of the scouring process were unknown, and no inferences about frequency or risk of iceberg-seabed contact could be made.

Later observations at known grounding sites provided useful information for input to engineering design of seabed structures. In 2000, a clear example of furrowing and pitting was obtained in which one iceberg produced a >2 m-wide upslope furrow with little change in scour depth (1.3 m maximum), which illustrates the ability of grounding icebergs to tilt and adjust to changes in bathymetry. The iceberg then stopped and developed a terminal pit 2.5 m deep (Sonnichsen et al. 2003). Cumulated and re-assessed data based on 1,100 'modern' scour features showed a maximum furrow width and depth of 157 m and 1.5 m, respectively, and maximum pit depths approaching 10 m (Sonnichsen and King 2005). Overall, the Geological Survey of Canada (GSC) at BIO has developed a comprehensive scour catalogue from government and industry surveys to assess the constraint posed by scouring icebergs on the Grand Banks.

Iceberg scouring on Labrador and Baffin Island shelves – The iceberg scouring hazard was considered more intense and urgent as exploratory drilling was undertaken farther north off Labrador and southeastern Baffin Island where iceberg flux was greater and seabed reconnaissance with sidescan sonars revealed a dense, widespread distribution of iceberg scours to 715 m water depth (Lewis et al. 1980, Praeg et al. 1987). Studies of iceberg scour morphologies during the 1980s began to yield clear evidence for differentiating relict and modern scouring events (Josenhans et al. 1986, Todd et al. 1988). Distinct changes in scour form, orientation and density at 220-250 m water depth were considered the limit of modern scouring, consistent with a maximum of 230 m found in a study of drafts of iceberg keels over the Labrador Shelf (Hotzel and Miller 1983).

A unique study of iceberg dynamics and iceberg-seabed interaction named the Dynamics of Iceberg Grounding and Scouring experiment (DIGS) was undertaken on the Labrador Shelf in 1985, led by scientists from BIO, C-CORE and Geonautics Ltd. (Hodgson et al. 1988; Fig. 3). Sidescan sonar and towed-camera transects, and submersible studies at sites of known iceberg groundings in association with DIGS, in addition to regional survey transects throughout the 1980s, provided a rich dataset of iceberg keel markings on the seabed (Josenhans and Barrie 1989, Woodworth-Lynas et al. 1991). Furrow orientations were seen to represent current and wind forces that propelled keel-dragging icebergs across the seabed, in places over bathymetry rises up to 25 m in areas of strong currents (Todd et al. 1988). Seafloor pits up to 10 m deep (Parrott et al. 1990, Barrie et al. 1992), in some places at the ends of furrows, were related to iceberg wallowing in response to ocean waves, swell, and tides (Clark and Landva 1988). Moving and bobbing icebergs may produce chains of pits (Bass and Woodworth-Lynas 1986). Pits may also be produced by large tabular bergs that split and intersect the seabed while rolling rapidly towards a new stable position. These pitting events were observed and verified during the DIGS experiment (Hodgson et al. 1988, Lever et al. 1989).

Frequency of iceberg-seabed contact – Although iceberg scour processes were becoming better known during the 1980s, determining the frequency and depth of iceberg scouring remained critical factors in assessing risk of iceberg-seabed contact at any site. Scour frequency was mainly estimated by repetitively mapping selected seabed areas after several years to detect scour additions in known time periods (Woodworth-Lynas and Barrie 1985, Lewis and Parrott 1987, Sonnichsen et al. 2009). In addition, probability theory was applied to the re-mapping results to estimate upper bounds of scour rate (Gaskill and Lewis 1988) and by modelling (e.g., interaction of iceberg flux, iceberg keel depth distribution, and known bathymetry: d'Apollonia and Lewis 1986, Lewis et al. 1988, King et al. 2003). The maximum annual scour rate was suggested to be about one scour in 100 to 1,000 km^2 of seabed in water depths >100 m on the exposed northern margin of the Grand Banks (Lewis et al. 1988, Lewis and Blasco 1990). This rate is generally acknowledged to represent low risk, but one that warranted continued monitoring. This low, but real risk of iceberg scouring, coupled with knowledge of thin sediment over bedrock (precluding safe burial depths) known from surficial geological mapping (Fader et al. 2014) led to early decisions to avoid pipelines to transport oil ashore from the Grand Banks. Instead, a gravity base structure with large storage volume was built at Hibernia to facilitate removal of produced oil by tanker ships. With new information, Sonnichsen and King (2005) proposed a lower annual scour frequency of about one scour in 10,000 km^2 of seabed for the general area surrounding Jeanne d'Arc Basin hydrocarbon discovery sites (for location, see Fig. 1).

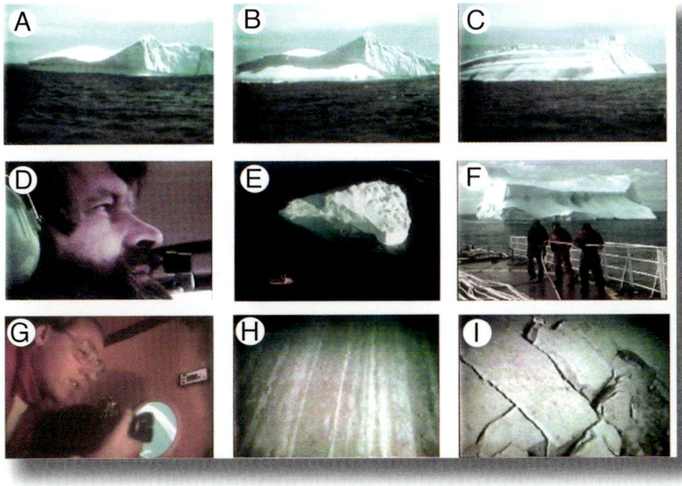

Figure 3. Dynamics of Iceberg Grounding and Scouring (DIGS) experiment on Labrador Shelf, August 1985: (A-C) rolling iceberg at 20-second intervals, previously grounded in 107 m water depth with a height of 35 m above water level; (D) M. Lewis in helicopter during iceberg reconnaissance; (E) aerial view of large tabular iceberg and 49.6-m long MV *Polar Circle*; (F) crew aboard MV *Polar Circle* positioning transponder rope in preparation for measuring large iceberg, 220 x 68 m above water and grounded in 170 m water depth; (G) H. Josenhans in *Pisces IV* submersible preparing to photograph an iceberg scour; (H) sediment lineations in trough of fresh iceberg furrow; and (I) fractured blocks of cohesive sediment displaced by moving iceberg keel onto side berm of fresh iceberg furrow. Note: width of view in (H) and (I) is ~1 m (from 1986 video 'New World Below' by Energy Mines and Resources Canada and National Film Board).

In 2006, BIO returned with multibeam sonar to remap three sites on the northern Labrador Shelf originally surveyed in 1979 and 1981. The comparison of survey data revealed a range in annual scour frequencies from one scour in 3,800 km^2 to one scour in 440 km^2 of seabed. These scour rates represent higher risk of iceberg-seabed contact than on the Grand Banks, but serve as upper bounds for risk on the central Labrador Shelf where hydrocarbon gas discoveries are known (Sonnichsen et al. 2009).

Iceberg scouring continues to be a hazard. Although scour rates are now known to be relatively low, they are sufficiently uncertain to require continued monitoring and review at intervals of several years, about 10 years on Grand Bank and 5 to 10 years on Labrador Shelf. In addition to natural variability not yet accounted for, some of the uncertainty arises from the progressive use of different survey technologies. Multibeam sonar is now the preferred survey tool for repetitive seabed mapping but its recent introduction has meant that its images have had to be compared with older sidescan sonar records and mosaics, with the result that new scour additions were identified with only moderate confidence (Sonnichsen et al. 2009, Sonnichsen and King 2011). Survey results at repetitive mapping sites with repeat multibeam surveys will provide more confident measures of scour additions and iceberg-seabed impact risk in future.

Shelf Erosion and Sedimentation

Erosion by surf action during rising postglacial sea level winnowed clay and silt from glacial deposits, but left behind sand and gravel in addition to glaciofluvial gravel deposited previously during low sea-level stands (Fig. 2). The sand fraction was observed on sidescan sonar records to be commonly organized into bedforms (i.e., flow-parallel sand ridges and ribbons, and flow-transverse sand waves and megaripples). This finding led to the inference that North Atlantic waves and currents could erode and transport sand-sized and finer particles on the southern continental shelves, a process that posed a geohazard for bottom-founded offshore structures. Jack-up rigs and gravity platforms could be undermined and destabilized by removal of underlying sediment by waves and currents, and pipeline support could be threatened by movement of bedforms (King 1980, Barrie 1990). On the Grand Banks, small features, such as ripples, megaripples, and sand waves, which had moved across recent fishing trawl marks on relict gravel surfaces, were recognized as bedforms responding to modern waves and currents (Barrie et al. 1984, Barrie and Collins 1989).

Sediment mobility was strongly evident on the shallower Sable Island Bank and Banquereau on the Scotian Shelf (Amos and Nadeau 1988). Sidescan recordings over Banquereau immediately after a storm revealed sand megaripples had degraded to a flat sand surface within hours. These and similar observations raised questions concerning the value of seeking these bedforms during summer ship surveys when the probability of seeing them was lowest (Amos and Dalrymple 1990). Advances in understanding sediment mobility were sought through the development of robust seabed-observing instruments including RALPH (Heffler 1984, Huntley and Amos 1990), and application of numerical models (SEDTRANS: Amos and Judge 1991) to estimate sediment transport on Canadian continental shelves.

Subsequent research focussed on technology for improved measurement of wave and current forces on the seabed, and bedform mobility, as well as refinements of sediment transport models, particularly for Sable Island Bank where offshore oil and gas development was in progress (Hodgins et al. 1986). It was here that the initial RALPH tripod was deployed in 1982 for bottom-boundary-layer monitoring (Heffler 1984). Over time the RALPH instrument was upgraded to a quadrapod with 23 sensors including suspended sediment concentration sensors, digital video camera, and sector-scanning sonar for measurement of bedform morphology and movement (Heffler 1996, Li and Heffler 2002a). Applications of this instrument produced several long-term datasets of boundary layer dynamics and bedform movement under storm conditions on Sable Island Bank (Li et al. 1997, 1999).

An important development was the advent of multibeam sonar bathymetric mapping with which seabed morphology, and bedform distribution, and regional patterns could be rapidly and accurately documented. Movement of large bedforms could now be established through repetitive mapping (Li and King 2007). The GSC SEDTRANS model was upgraded to apply combined wave-current bottom boundary layer theories to compute near-bed velocity profiles, combined-flow bed shear stresses, and bedload and suspended load sediment transport in coastal and shelf environments (Li and Amos 1995, 2001).

With application of these upgraded tools, bedform mobility and sediment transport were quantified and much better understood for the benefit of science and the engineering of seabed facilities for hydrocarbon development. A digital terrain model of Sable Island Bank revealed a wide distribution of large sand ridges (up to 14 m high with km-scale spacing), radiating from the shoreface of Sable Island (Fig. 4A). Repeat multibeam surveys in water depths <50 m revealed that these ridges and smaller superimposed sand waves (Fig. 4B) moved back and forth – up to 40 to 60 m per year, every year or two – but essentially remained in the same position over the long term, a pattern thought to result from the nearly equal number of major storms passing south and north of Sable Island so that the associated storm-driven currents affected the seabed equally (Li and King 2007). Serial sidescan sonar surveys showed that smaller bedforms associated with the major bedforms (Fig. 4C) were also active (Li et al. 2012).

The upgraded SEDTRANS model operated with wave, wind and tidal current input from other BIO studies (Lynch et al. 1992, Hannah et al. 2001, Dupont et al. 2002), and knowledge of seabed shear stresses and thresholds for sediment movement (Li and Heffler 2002b). Li et al. (2012) were then able to link sediment grain size and bedform distribution and mobility with magnitude and types of seabed disturbance based on the relative time percentages of exceedance of sediment movement thresholds by waves, wind-driven, currents, and tidal currents. Bedform zones with unique bedform association, energy level, and mobility characteristics were also defined (Li et al. 2012).

In an extension of the modelling approach from Sable Island Bank, regional sediment transport patterns were modeled for the entire Atlantic shelf for medium sand (Fig. 5A; Li et al. 2010, Shaw et al. in press). Zones of greatest sand mobilization are due to tidal forcing on southeast Baffin Shelf, in Davis Strait, on Georges Bank, and in Bay of Fundy (Fig. 5B). High rates of sand mobilization due to wave-dominant and mixed wave-current disturbance occur on the Grand Banks and Scotian Shelf (Fig. 5B). Knowledge and quantification of sediment mobility gained through collaborative BIO research during the last four decades is now providing meaningful constraints for seabed engineering to ensure safe offshore hydrocarbon development: for example, showing the probable limits of bedform movement for the design and construction of safe pipelines to transport natural gas across the Scotian Shelf.

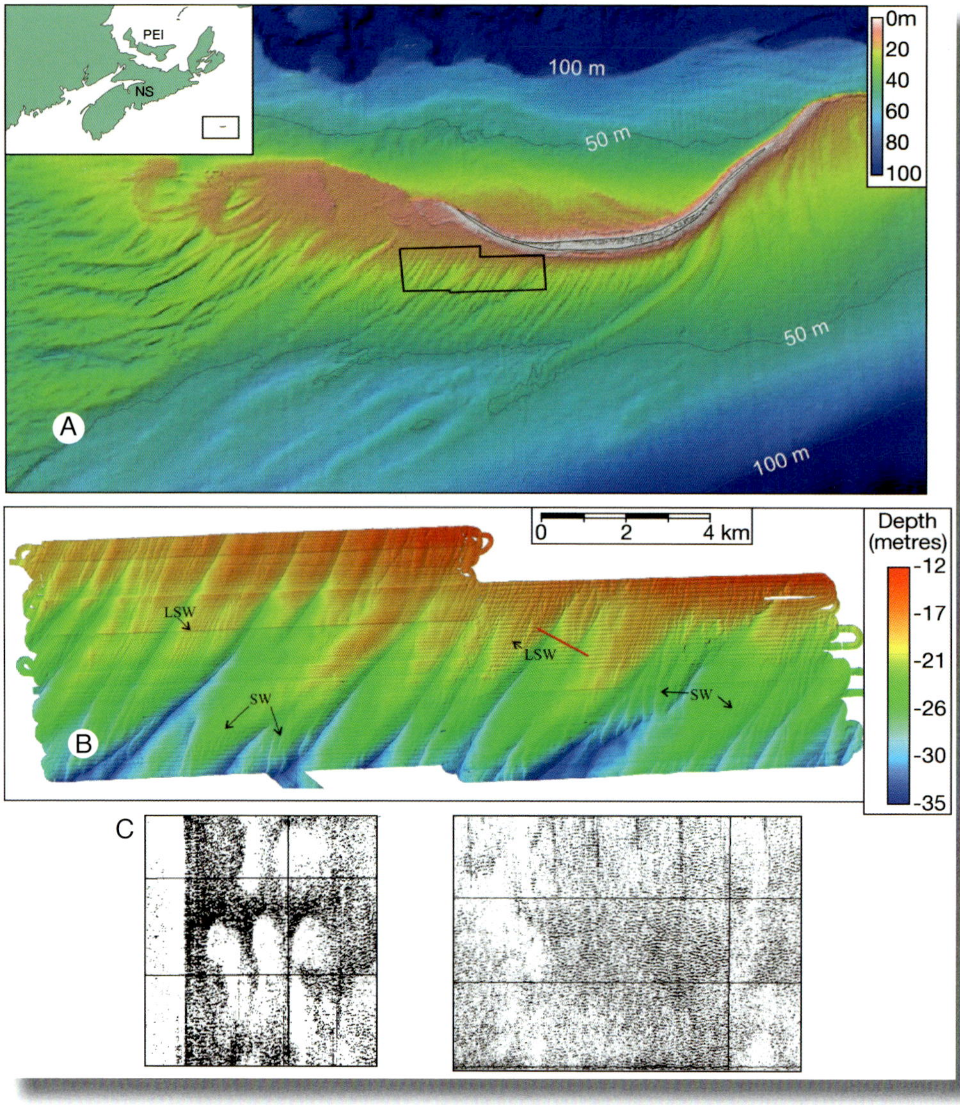

Figure 4. Sable Island Bank seabed morphology (from Li and King 2007, and Li et al. 2012): (A) shaded-relief bathymetry map (North at top) showing prominent NE–SW trending shoreface-connected and offshore sand ridges; (B) close-up multibeam map (12-36 m) of the area south of Sable Island (outlined in 'A') showing the large sand ridges (km-scale widths) with superposed sand waves (SW) and linear-crested sand waves (LSW); and (C) portions of a sidescan image along a sand ridge transect (location shown by red line in 'B') showing that megaripples and large wave ripples (linearly-organized specks), and sand ribbons (light tones) are associated with the larger bedforms (horizontal lines are 20 m apart).

Slope Stability

A first examination of the continental slopes off southeastern Canada reveals a complex landscape of countless failed and eroded sediment surfaces (Fig. 6). Downslope mass movement of sediment is an important geohazard in addition to powerful flows and boulder beds on the relatively steep continental slope and the lower gradient continental rise. Extensive regions of the sedimentary basins that potentially contain hydrocarbon resources underlie the continental slopes (Fig. 1; Williams et al. 2014), and areas prone to slope failure in these regions pose risks of foundation destabilization for structures placed upon them.

With the advent of deepwater exploration in the 1980s, it was recognized that much higher-resolution knowledge of the mechanisms and frequencies of sediment failures was needed for useful assessment of slope stability. Distinct progress toward these objectives was made at BIO after 1981 when D. Piper joined BIO staff at the Atlantic Geoscience Centre from Dalhousie University, Halifax, Nova Scotia. Also, the arrival of K. Moran and H. Christian in the 1980s provided needed expertise in geotechnical engineering for studies in both the Atlantic and Beaufort Sea regions.

During the 1980s, studies of the continental slope using high-resolution seismic profiling data connecting a few scattered exploratory wells began to show that the numerous features of sediment failure and erosion had occurred over a long period of time (Piper et al. 1987, Piper and Normark 1989). Significant slope dissection first occurred during the Late Pliocene about 3 million years ago when lowered global sea level allowed increased sediment discharge to the continental margin induced by increased rainfall and/or valley glaciation (Fig. 7A). Dissection increased with time, possibly because more sandy (erosive) sediment was being delivered to the shelf break during longer and more frequent sea level lowstands prior to about 2 million years ago (Fig. 7B). The style of slope sedimentation changed about 750 to 450 thousands of years ago (Fig. 7C), marked by the appearance of glacial sediments at the top of the slope, major shelf erosion such as Laurentian Channel and shelf basins, and channel reorganization on Laurentian Fan (Piper et al. 1994, Skene and Piper 2006).

Grand Banks earthquake and slope failure – The last and best-known event of sediment failure in this long sequence of slope development was related to the 1929 Grand Banks earthquake of magnitude 7.2 (Moran et al. 1990). The North Atlantic communication cables were broken instantaneously within 100 km of the epicentre, as indicated by widespread sediment slumping and sequential downslope movement up to 13.3 hours later by an inferred powerful turbidity current (Heezen and Ewing 1952, Heezen and Drake 1964; Fig. 8). Interpretations developed as the effects of past glacial and 1929 earthquake influences became better understood.

By considering evidence of previous sediment failures in their seismic reflection records, Piper and Normark (1982) estimated that failures on the scale of the 1929 event might only recur every few hundreds of thousands of years, although earthquakes with lesser, but still significant effects, could be considerably more common. Because the earliest known earthquake-triggered sediment failure in marine waters is the 1663 earthquake in the Saguenay Fiord area of Québec (Syvitski and Schafer 1996; for location, see Fig. 1), a long-term chronology of earthquake-induced and other slope failures could only be constructed from the sediment record itself.

More specific evidence of the 1929 slope failure was sought during the 1980s with observations obtained from medium range sidescan sonar surveys and submersible diving. With SEAMARC sidescan sonar (up to 5 km swath width) and associated sub-bottom profiles and cores, Piper et al. (1985) described surface sediment instability features in the area of the 1929 earthquake epicentre – shallow slumps and slides passing downslope into debris flows, arcuate slide scars, and an eroded seabed. *PISCES IV* submersible dives revealed large gravel megaripples, locally covered with debris flow deposits, on the unusually broad (25 km) Eastern Valley floor of Laurentian Fan (Fig. 6, lower left insert) with overlying sheets of coarse sand in its deeper parts (Hughes Clarke et al. 1989). As summarized by Piper et al. (1988), this spectrum of fresh-looking features was entirely attributed to failure and downslope movement of sediment during the Grand Banks earthquake. From these and additional studies using the deep-diving submersible DSRV *Alvin* (producing visual observations, higher resolution sidescan, sub-bottom profiler, and multibeam sonar surveys), failures were confirmed as not from a single major slump, but from widespread failures initiated on shallow (5-25 m) regional shear planes over local steep areas. The failures moved upslope as retrogressive slumping and the failed sediments passed downslope

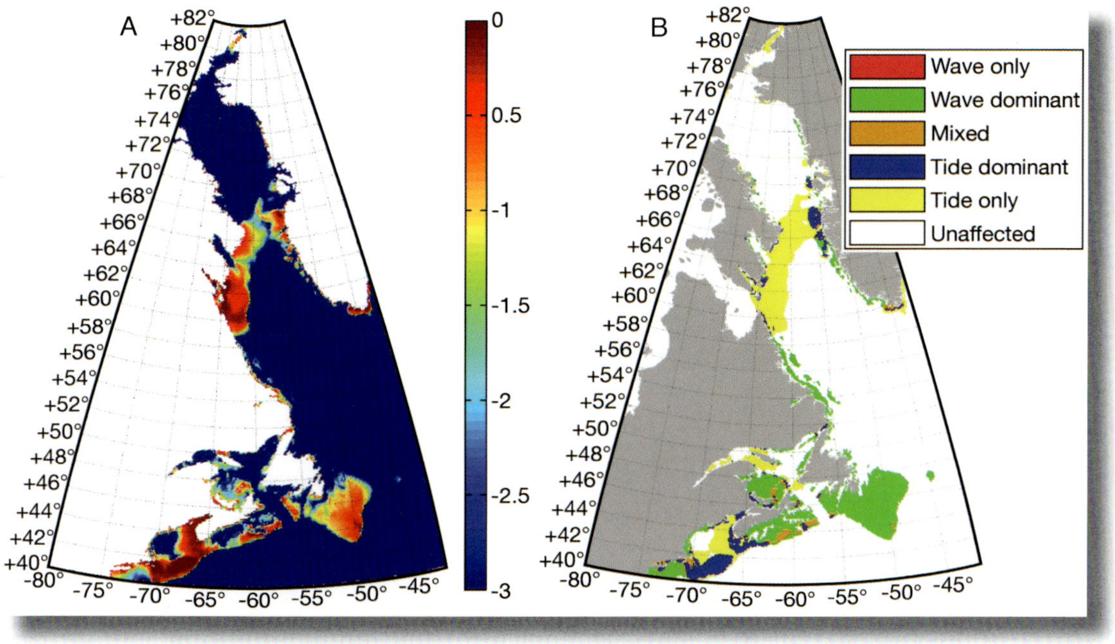

Figure 5. Maps of sediment mobility on the Atlantic shelf, SW Greenland and Eastern Canada (from Shaw et al. in press): (A) log frequency of percentage of time that medium sand is mobilized (red – most frequent, 10% of time; blue – least frequent, 0.001% of time); and (B) hydrodynamic disturbance type classification (red – wave only, green – wave dominant, brown – mixed, blue – tide dominant, yellow – tide only, white – unaffected).

into debris flows, and then, on steep parts of the slope, were transformed into turbidity currents which grew in volume by incorporating local water and sediment (Piper et al. 1999). These amplified currents were probably extended in duration by delayed retrogression of slumps upslope. It became apparent that relatively thin but widespread sediment failures could generate significant and fatal tsunamis as in 1929. By 2006, multibeam bathymetry coverage of the entire failure area provided a full appreciation of the scale and style of the sediment failure (Mosher and Piper 2007).

Studies in the 1990s and subsequent decade led to new insight that the wide valley deposits of gravel and possibly sand were not formed in 1929, but were inherited from earlier late-glacial events (Piper and MacDonald 2001). A major gullying event on the upper slope was dated about 19,000 years ago in accordance with the observation that this unusually wide valley was more akin to glacial spillways than valleys in non-glacial marine fans (Piper et al. 2007). This and other evidence led to the revised interpretation that the gravel bed on the floor of the abnormally wide valley originated from a catastrophic flow of meltwater and bedload from beneath a glacial margin at or near the shelf edge above the Laurentian Fan. The turbidity current originating from the 1929 Grand Banks sediment failures would have only reworked the surface of the gravel waves and sand bodies on the fan (Piper et al. 2007). Similar catastrophic flows have subsequently been recognized elsewhere on the eastern Canadian continental margin (Piper et al. 2012a) and have played an important role in sculpting margin geomorphology.

Scotian Slope failures – Mosher et al. (1989) showed that disturbed (failed) zones near Verrill Canyon (Fig. 6, upper left insert) were associated with the presence of glacial margins at the shelf edge which deposited till (sub-glacial sediment) and related glacial outwash and slumped sediment downslope to about 500–600 m in wedge-shaped deposits (till tongues); till tongues were first recognized on the flanks of shelf basins by King and Fader (1986). Later, a geotechnical analysis showed that most slopes were statically stable and probably required pre-conditioning (i.e., sediment weakening) and ground accelerations from a nearby earthquake to initiate failure (Mosher et al. 1994, 2004).

Mulder and Moran (1995), in exploring sediment failure and glaciation, showed that reduction of shearing resistance (i.e., sediment weakening) was related to ice and sediment loading with pore pressure buildup (i.e., underconsolidation) at the shelf break. Moving zones of high pore pressure and potential failure surfaces arising from these stresses may not be resisted at the seabed of the middle and lower slope, causing sediment failures there (i.e., bearing capacity failure). These analyses also suggested that major sediment failures likely occurred preferentially during glacial periods, which implies that the risk of slope failure during the present interglacial period is relatively low.

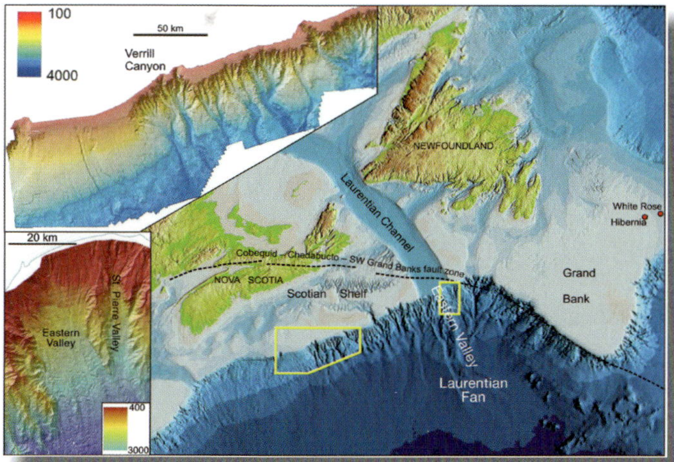

Figure 6. Digital elevation map image of southeastern Canada from Shaw et al. (2006) showing numerous gullies and canyons on the continental slope with more detailed multibeam bathymetry images for areas outlined in yellow shown as inset maps: upper (Verrill Canyon) from Mosher et al. (2004), and lower (Eastern Valley) from Mosher and Piper (2007); east-west dashed black lines show trend of Cobequid-Chedabucto and the SW Grand Banks transform faults. Locations of drilling operations (Hibernia, White Rose) on Grand Bank are shown.

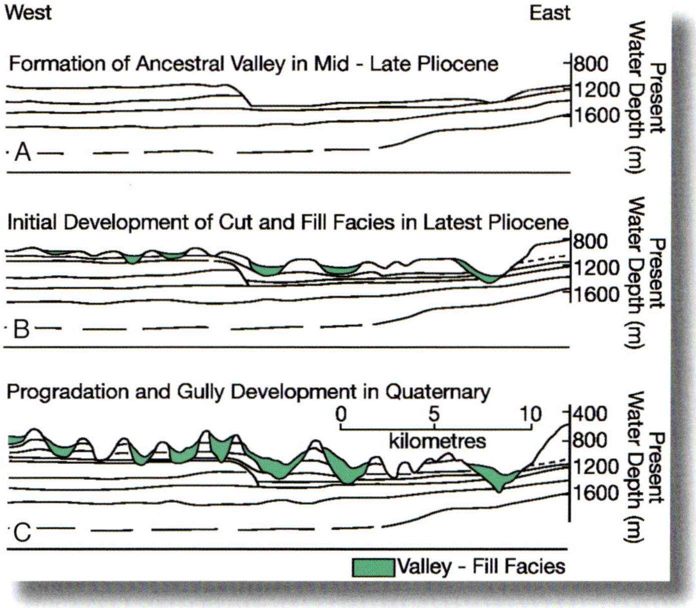

Figure 7. Schematic sections showing progressive increase (A to C) in dissection of the continental slope through the past ~3 million years (from Piper 1990).

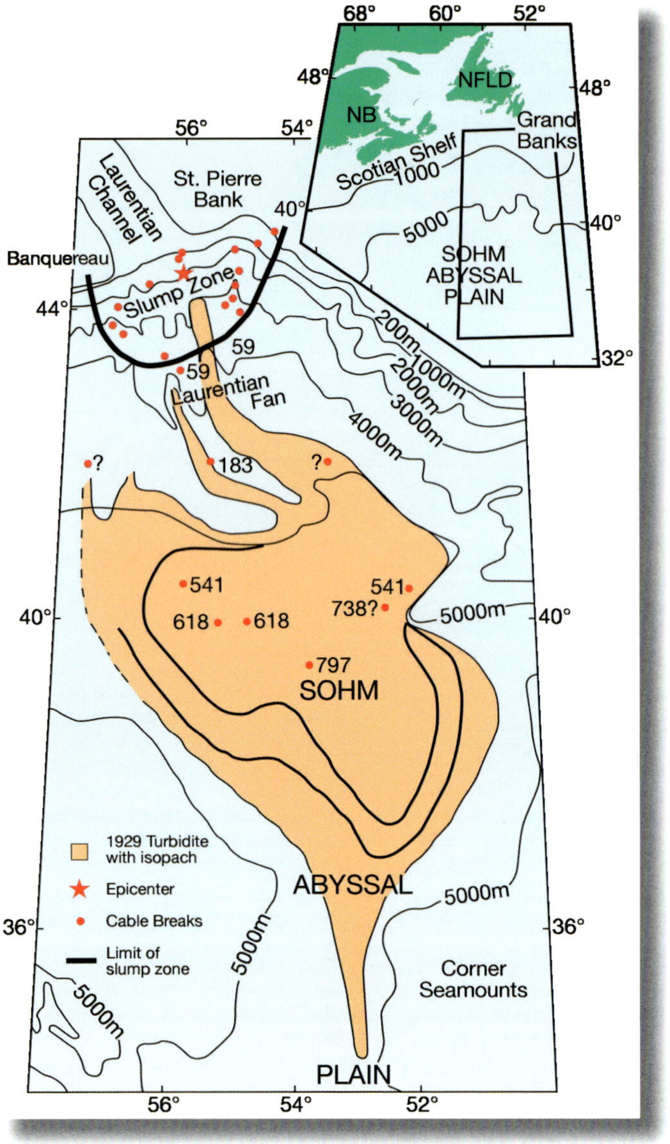

Figure 8. Map of Laurentian Channel and Fan, and Sohm Abyssal Plain showing epicentre of 1929 Grand Banks earthquake (red star), surrounding area of immediate cable breaks (red dots), downslope cable breaks with minutes of elapsed time (red dots with black numerals), and contours of sediment thickness deposited on Sohm Abyssal Plain (from Moran et al. 1990).

Continued study of the character and correlation of regional horizons in seismic reflection profiles and their meaning in the light of piston core sediment study has shown that the uppermost till-tongue reflection packet on the upper slope is a record of the last glaciation and its associated sediment failures and mass transport deposits (MTDs) (Piper et al. 1999, Campbell 2000). By carrying the correlation of horizons far offshore to sites where sediment layers are thinner and reachable by coring, seven such reflection packets were tied to the dated global marine isotope stratigraphy (Piper et al. 1994, 2002) showing that these cycles began to dominate slope sedimentation about 450,000 years ago (Fig. 9).

Fluid or gas venting and gas hydrates – Sidescan sonar records of undisturbed seabed in both the Grand Banks earthquake area and west of Verrill Canyon (for locations, see Fig. 6) revealed conical depressions called 'pockmarks' which are evidence of fluid or gas venting from the seabed, features that were discovered by BIO scientists in the 1970s (Fader et al. 2014).

Shallow gas or gas migrating upwards from dissociating (decomposing) gas hydrate zones can contribute to pore pressure buildup and loss of sediment strength (Mulder et al. 1997). Hydrate, a concentrated form of gas in solid phase, forms under conditions of high pressures and low temperatures which are found extensively throughout offshore regions of the Canadian continental margin (Mosher 2011). Changes in seabed pressure and temperature conditions may cause hydrate to dissociate and release gas, causing weakening within sedimentary layers, potentially leading to submarine landsliding. One sign of the presence of hydrate is a 'bottom simulating reflector' (BSR) on seismic reflection profiles which is caused by free gas trapped at the base of the hydrate stability zone. Hydrate without this free gas interface will not be readily detected, so hydrate can exist without being identified by seismic techniques. A margin-wide assessment of seismic profiles revealed BSRs at seven sites in water depths deeper than 620 m representing only 1 to 2 % of the theoretical hydrate stability zone along the Canadian Atlantic margin. This suggests that hydrate may be much more widespread than is evident on conventional seismic profiles. Within most sites the BSR lies in a sedimentary drift deposit or sediment wave field, indicating the likely control of grain sorting, potential porosity and permeability on its presence (Mosher 2011).

In general, gassy sediment and the presence of gas hydrates are considered factors of risk in assessing slope stability (Piper et al. 2012b), although most slope failures appear to be triggered by earthquakes (Tripsanas et al. 2008, Piper et al. 2012b).

Frequency of slope failures and hazard assessment – By 2005, large failures, mainly recognized from stacked MTDs on the rise and from buried scarps on the slope, were interpreted to largely result from major earthquakes with recurrence intervals in the range of 100,000 to 400,000 years. These large events should be expected all along the continental margin, probably on old basement lineaments (Piper et al. 2003, Piper and Campbell 2005). More frequent earthquake-triggered failures of about one every 50,000 years might be expected near the tectonic lineament of the Grand Banks transform and Cobequid-Chedabucto faults like the 1929 Grand Banks earthquake (Piper et al. 2005; Fig. 6). There is also a trend toward shorter recurrence times on steeper slopes. An apparently greater frequency of shallow continental slope failures during glacial periods was probably related to seismicity induced by glacial loading and unloading, and to underconsolidated sediment sequences from rapid sedimentation during deposition from glacial meltwater plumes (Piper and Campbell 2005). Other probable causes also applied, such as wave loading on the upper slope (<500 m), excess pore pressure related to ice and sediment loading (Mulder and Moran 1995) or possibly gas from gas hydrate dissociation (Mosher 2011), progressive creep failure, and toe erosion of canyon slopes by turbidity currents (Piper et al. 2003).

Critical factors that need to be assessed at specific wellhead and pipeline sites include seafloor morphology and slope angles, evidence of historic failures, steep slopes, weak sediment beds, and local *in situ* geotechnical properties such as pore pressure and slope stability (Mosher et al. 2004). Overall, the risk of natural sediment failures appears to be low, but quantitative slope stability analysis at specific sites is required (Piper and Campbell 2005). It was this knowledge of relatively low risk of sediment destabilization during the present interglacial interval that gave confidence to decisions by regulatory agencies to allow increased exploratory drilling on the slope in the late 1990s.

In recent years, multibeam bathymetry and 3D seismic (closely spaced seismic reflection profiles) technologies are being increasingly used in leading-edge industry-government collaborative surveys of the continental slope to obtain high-resolution seafloor measurements for geohazard assessment (Pickrill et al. 2001, Mosher et al. 2006). In addition, underwater autonomous vehicles have been developed and used for under-ice data acquisition (Verhoef et al. 2014), and these can provide cm-scale resolution regardless of the water depth. With these and conventional 2D seismic and coring technologies, BIO can be expected to continue effective research to understand slope stability geohazards to support safe exploration and development of hydrocarbon resources in frontier areas of the Canadian continental margin.

Variability of Seabed Foundation Conditions

Engineering of large heavy structures such as the Hibernia gravity platform, and other facilities, requires knowledge of sediment types and their geotechnical (engineering) properties to determine the strength, bearing capacity, and excavation potential of the seabed. These properties are measured from undisturbed samples obtained from boreholes drilled to depths of 100 m or more at hydrocarbon production sites, an expensive operation that is undertaken mainly by petroleum companies. The measured properties are valid at the borehole site and are assumed to apply to a considerable radius around the site,

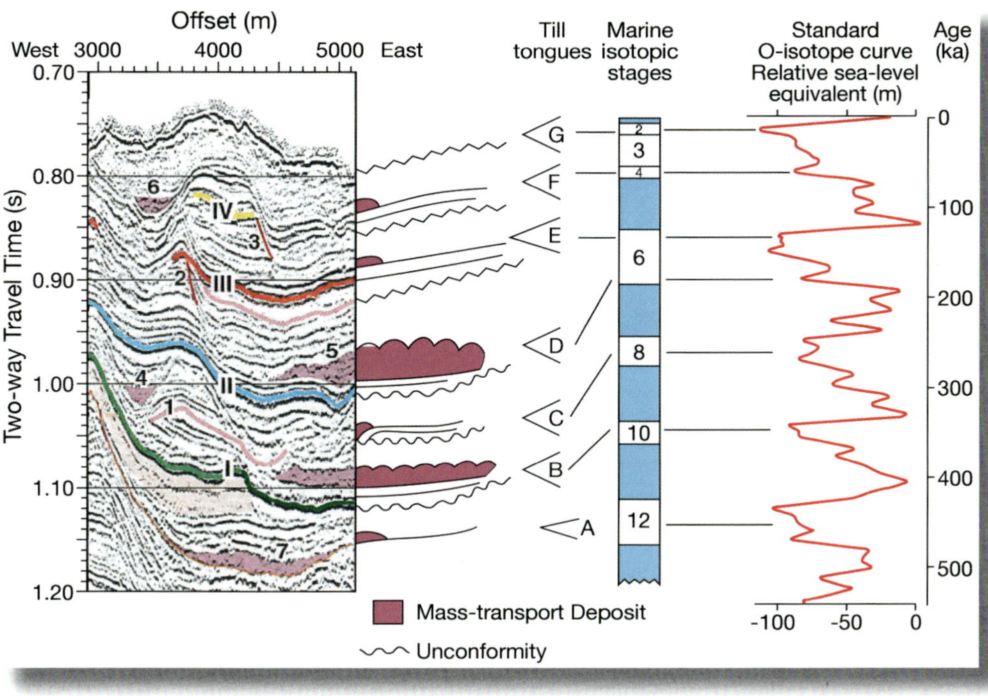

Figure 9. Seismic reflection profile (left) and correlation diagram of regional seismic reflection horizons showing the relationship of upper slope mass transport sedimentation to the last seven glacial cycles indicated by till tongues A to G, low sea level, and even-numbered marine O-isotopic stages 2 to 12 (ka = 1000s of years ago). I through IV are regional reflectors (i.e., commonly erosion surfaces or unconformities) used to correlate sediment sequences. Features 1, 2, 3 are erosion surfaces, 4, 5, 6 are Mass Transport Deposits, and 7 is a plume deposit (from Piper et al. 2002). Seismic profile is in 500-600 m water depth about 20 km northeast of Verrill Canyon (see Fig. 6, upper inset map).

or even to adjacent production sites. BIO scientists collaborated in almost all industry geotechnical investigations offshore eastern Canada, trading their geological expertise and analysis for access to geotechnical measurements and sediment samples.

BIO regional surveys have proven useful for constraining the range of borehole applicability. Data acquired from boreholes and seismic surveys have permitted BIO geoscientists to recognize at least four near-surface sequences of eastward-dipping strata that subcrop at a near-seabed unconformity on northeastern Grand Bank in the Jeanne d'Arc Basin hydrocarbon discovery area (Sonnichsen and King 2005; for location, see Fig. 1). During the period represented by deposition of these strata (~0.2-0.4 million years), several sea-level lowstands are thought to have provided intervals of subaerial (i.e., above water) exposure which would have induced surface weathering, drainage, and consolidation with associated changes in geotechnical strength properties. These dipping beds suggest that engineering properties would not be similar across the Jeanne d'Arc Basin through a zone 50 m below the seafloor, for example (Fig. 10). Similar rapid lateral changes may also occur at the boundaries of infilled glacial meltwater channels on both Grand Bank and the Scotian Shelf (King 1980). Seabed foundation conditions are important in deep-water as well, even for issues as seemingly mundane as anchoring of drilling vessels.

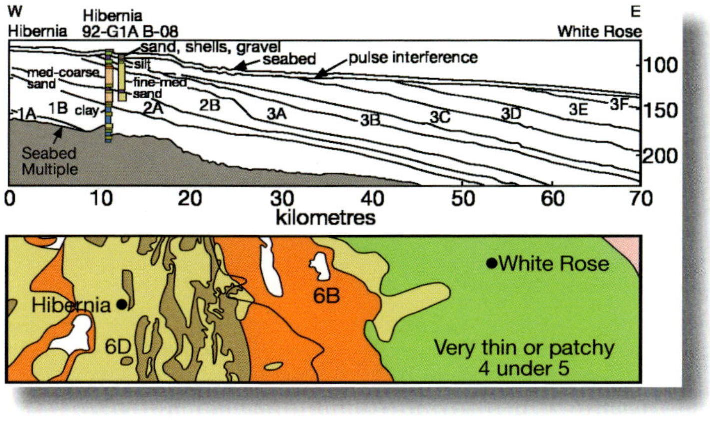

Figure 10. Cross-section (top, depth scale in m at right) of the sub-seabed strata between the Hibernia and White Rose discovery sites (for locations, see Fig. 6), northeastern Grand Banks, beneath surface sediments (bottom): pink - till (upper-right), brown and orange - gravel, yellow - sand, and green - thin sand over gravel (from Sonnichsen and King 2005).

CANADIAN BEAUFORT SEA

The history of Beaufort Sea seabed geohazard research is linked to industry hydrocarbon exploration which ramped up in 1970 and continued to 1990 (Clark et al. 1997). From 1990 through 2000 drilling declined, as did research. Exploration resumed on the shelf in 2001, along with increased seabed research, and in 2008, expanded to the outer shelf and upper slope in 50 to 1,500 m water depths (Fig. 11A).

BIO research has focussed on key seabed geohazards including scouring by ice keels, unstable foundation conditions, subsea permafrost, seabed instability features, submarine landslides, and even the fate of abandoned artificial exploration drilling islands. The first assessment of seabed geohazards was published by Pelletier (1979), and the most recent summary is provided by Blasco et al. (2013). Knowledge of the seabed geological history and processes (Fader et al. 2014) provides the geological framework for the assessment of seabed geohazards.

Seabed Scouring by Sea-ice Pressure Ridge Keels

Bathymetric data collected by the oil industry in 1970 showed the Beaufort seabed was not flat, but had an irregular, rough, microtopography. Convincing evidence of seabed disturbance by drift ice was acquired at the time of the *Hudson*-70 expedition in Beaufort Sea (see Wadhams 2014). J. Shearer aboard CSS *Richardson*, and B. Pelletier, chief scientist of CSS *Hudson*, recognized cross-cutting furrows in surficial sediment on sidescan sonar records which they termed 'ice scours', and correctly postulated that they were formed by bottom dragging keels of sea-ice pressure ridges and ice islands (Shearer 1971, Pelletier and Shearer 1972). Disruption of seabed sediments by the passage of keels of sea-ice pressure ridges locked into large ice floes poses a major threat to subsea pipelines. The interaction between ice keel and pipeline could lead to failure of the pipe and hence, the uncontrolled release of oil and gas into the marine environment.

During the mid-1970s Lewis (1978) was able to link the ice scouring process to sedimentation rates and, for the first time, estimate seabed re-scouring rates which became the benchmark by which the scouring process was understood for over a decade. Lewis and Blasco (1990) described the distribution of scour depths and re-scouring rates known at the time.

Selected sectors of seabed were mapped with sidescan sonar biennially from 1978 through 1990, and again from 2001 through 2008, to identify and count new and extreme scours (Fig. 11A,B), calculate the percent of seabed disturbance by scouring, and determine re-scouring rates. The results revealed that re-scouring rates peaked at 1.4 events per km per year in 24 m water depth (Blasco et al. 2013). After 100 years, 99 percent of the seabed would be re-scoured in the 4 to 25 m range of water depth (Fig. 11C, zone of darkest brown).

The distribution of extreme scour events is not shelf wide but geographically controlled by the sea-ice regime, bathymetry (Fig. 11A), and sediment strength (Blasco et al. 2011). Tracking the paths of extreme scours indicated that the depths of these features were limited by sediment strength and strength of the ice bond between keel and floe (Shearer et al. 1986, Myers et al. 1996). Once the ice keel lodged in sediment, the

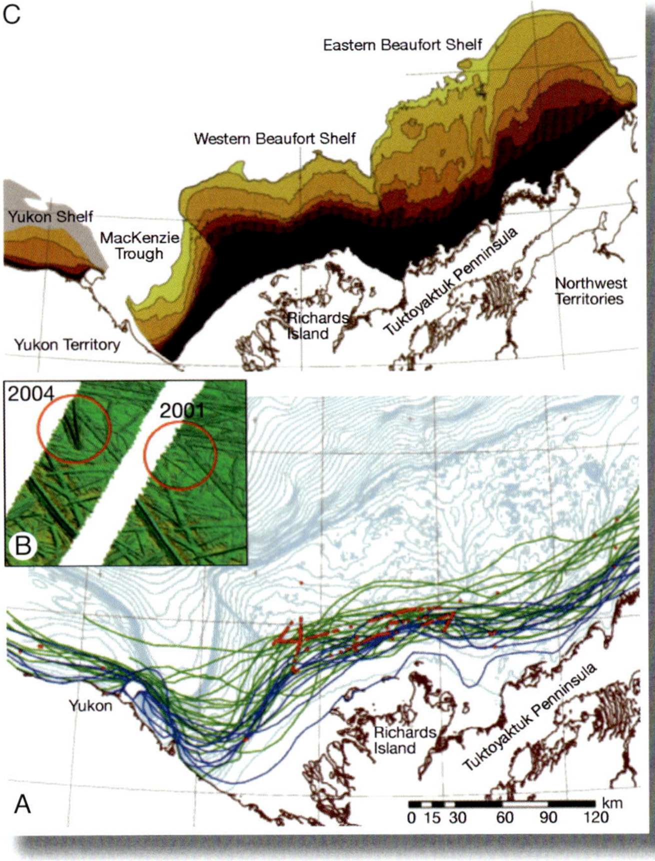

Figure 11. Bathymetry, ice, and ice scour in the Beaufort Sea (from Blasco et al. 2013): (A) bathymetry (5 m contour interval on shelf, e.g., to 120 km north of Richards Island, and 50 m contour interval north of shelf), edges of landfast ice in May 1982-2007 (green), in January 1989-1999 (blue), and extreme ice scour (2-5 m deep) positions (red); (B) multibeam sonar images in 24-27 m water depth showing new scours between 2001 and 2004; and (C) fraction of seabed re-scoured in 100 years ranging from <1% (yellow) to >99% (dark brown).

floe moved on, leaving the ice keel behind, thereby limiting the depth to which keels can incise the seabed (E. Carr, P. Campbell, and G. Gilbert, pers. comm. 2013). This process may also limit subscour deformation (Gilbert 1990).

Subsea Permafrost and Gas Hydrates

Ice-bearing sub-seabed sediments (Mackay 1972), subsequently found to 700 m below the sea surface, were puzzling and problematic (Fig. 12A). The concern was that heat from drilling or from hot oil and gas pumped from depth could lead to thawing of the ice, loss of casing support, well failure, and uncontrolled escape of oil and gas into the marine environment.

Subsea permafrost research by BIO scientists and colleagues showed that the ice-bearing sediments occurred in layered strata, and that the isotopic composition of the ice was that of meltwater from glaciers (Blasco 1995, Blasco et al. 2012). These facts suggested that during glacial cycles when sea level was 110-130 m below present, the Beaufort Shelf was subaerially exposed to very cold air temperatures which froze glacial outwash (freshwater) sediments during their deposition out to the shelf edge at 100 m present water depth. High sea level associated with subsequent interglacial cycles covered the shelf with low temperature (<0 °C) seawater which preserved the frozen outwash. Repeated glaciations allowed for the accumulation of multilayered ice-bearing sediments to a thickness of 700 m. The discovery that the ice encountered below seabed is of surficial terrestrial origin provided the means by which the quantity of ice in sub-seabed sediments could be estimated: i.e., by realizing that ice content at depth would be similar to that in recently aggraded ground ice. This knowledge allowed regulatory processes and engineering design to evaluate melting and potential loss of well-bore support, and to determine preventive procedures such as drilling with chilled circulating muds to prevent melting of sediment-bearing ice around the well bore.

Gas hydrates are likely present in the Beaufort Sea region due to its high hydrocarbon potential and extensive zone of suitable pressure and temperature conditions. Seismic data acquired in 2010 by BIO scientists for the Canadian and United States Law of the Sea programs (Verhoef et al. 2014) revealed at least one occurrence of a BSR in the Canadian Beaufort Sea; also, hydrate was recovered in a piston core from a seafloor mound on the Alaskan Beaufort Sea continental slope (Fig. 12B, Pohlman et al. 2011).

Seabed Foundation Conditions and Artificial Exploration Drilling Islands

Soft, muddy, surficial sediments were found to range from 0 m to >10 m thickness across the shelf, and sediment strength varied considerably depending on the amount of disturbance by repeated ice keel scouring (Blasco et al. 2013). As a result, weak sediments were excavated or sub-seabed structures were added to drilling platforms to enhance the resistance of the platforms to lateral movement by ice forces during winters.

During the first phase of hydrocarbon exploration, sediments were dredged from the seabed to form 37 temporary islands to support winter drilling before being abandoned in spring (Clark et al. 1997). With renewed exploration in 2001, multibeam sonar images showed that the islands had been eroded by wave action (Fig. 12C). The islands were moving southeastward and were then 3-5 m below sea-surface, which presented navigational hazards to vessels with drafts greater than 3 m (Blasco et al 2013).

Seabed Instability Features

The voyage of the SS *Manhattan* in 1969, the first transit of an oil tanker through the Northwest Passage, led to the unnerving discovery of a significant navigation hazard – a pinnacle jutting 30 m above the seabed. Shearer et al. (1971) hypothesized these features were seabed equivalents of onshore ice-cored conical mounds or pingos, and henceforth they were known as seabed pingo-like features. Later work has suggested a possible relationship to decomposing methane gas hydrates (Paull et al.

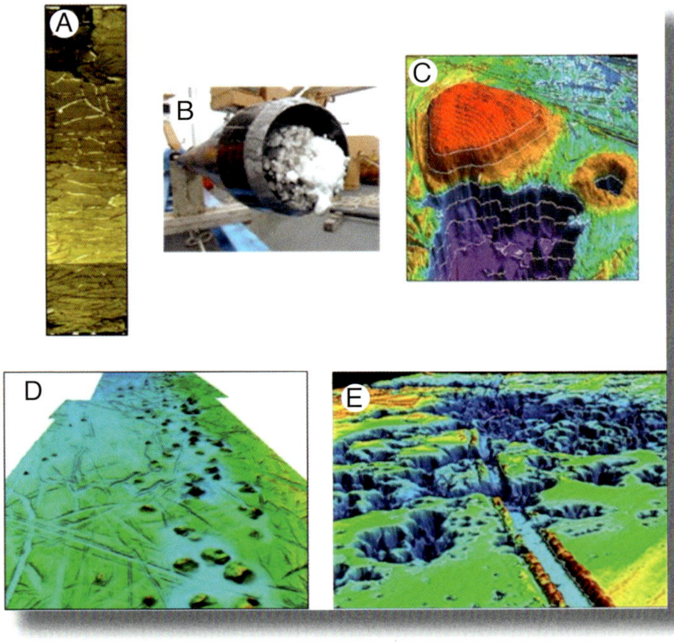

Figure 12. Seabed instability features (A,C,D,E from Blasco et al. 2013; B from D.C. Mosher): (A) sediment core section from within the upper 700 m of the Beaufort Shelf showing the distribution of ice veins (white zones), ice not visible to the naked eye also occurs in spaces between sand grains; (B) solid gas hydrate protruding from the end of a piston corer (10 cm diameter) recovered from the Alaskan Beaufort Sea slope by USCG *Healy*; (C) multibeam map view of an abandoned artificial island (red, about 500 m in diameter) located in 18 m water depth in the central Beaufort Shelf: original circular shape of the island has been elongated by wave action, the large depression in the foreground was formed by excavation of sand to build the island, and the small depression was a test pit; (D) multibeam image of pingo-like features along the ice-scoured eastern edge of Mackenzie Trough, interpreted as inactive mud volcanoes (50-300 m diameters and 16 m maximum relief); and (E) pockmarks indicating venting of fluids from Beaufort Shelf (also shows a long ice scour 23 m wide between berm crests).

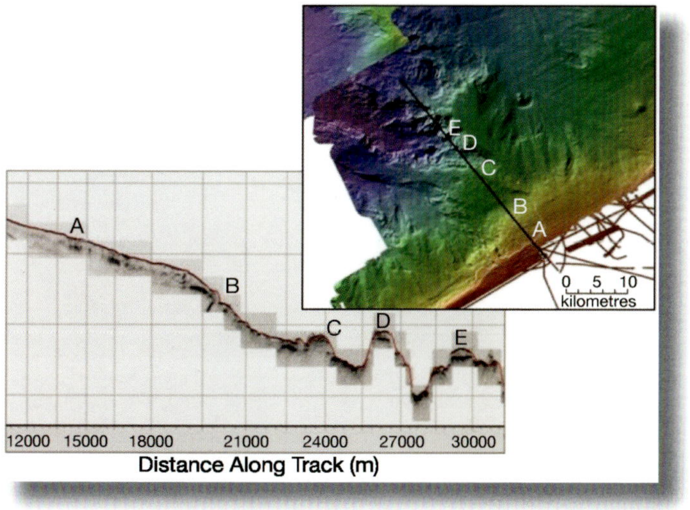

Figure 13. Multibeam image showing submarine landslides at 100 m depth (A-B) and 500 m depth (C-E) on the upper continental slope of the Beaufort Sea with sub-bottom profile along black line, equivalent points on profile and map image marked A-E (Blasco et al. 2013). Although the slide scars have not been infilled by sediment since failure and appear to be recent, their ages are unknown.

2007). Since their discovery, over 900 such features have been mapped on the seabed (Blasco et al. 2013). Many of the mounds appear to be mud 'volcanoes' (Pelletier 1979), some of which are actively discharging fluids today (Blasco et al. 2013). Along the edge of Mackenzie Trough, site of a glacially-eroded infilled channel (Shearer 1971), multibeam sonar imagery has revealed a linear array of over 130 such mud volcanoes (Fig. 12D). Seafloor pockmarks discovered elsewhere on the shelf in less well-organized groupings are attributed to venting of fluids (Fig. 12E).

Submarine Landslides

As exploration for hydrocarbons expands onto the Beaufort continental slope, the nature and risk of submarine landslides need to be understood to contribute advice towards the design of safe drilling and production facilities. Slides on the upper slope have been inferred from conventional bathymetric data (Pelletier 1979), and sedimentary creep folds recognized in seismic profiles (Hill et al. 1982) suggest incipient failures. Recent seismic surveys for UNCLOS investigations (Verhoef et al. 2014) have revealed thick sequences of turbidites and MTDs in the adjacent Canada Basin (Mosher et al. 2012), implying a significant geologic history of sediment failures on the Beaufort Slope for which recurrence intervals and triggering mechanisms still need to be established. In addition to earthquake ground acceleration, and variable permafrost thickness, the presence of *in situ* gas and possible gas hydrate will need to be taken into consideration in assessing the probability of submarine landsliding (Mosher et al. 2012). A geologically recent landslide 60 m thick that has failed along 9 km at the shelf edge has been imaged by multibeam sonar (Blasco et al. 2013; Fig. 13).

SIGNIFICANCE AND FUTURE

BIO geoscientists have built up a recognized reputation for shallow seabed investigations and knowledge of marine geohazards. BIO experts have published and presented their methods and results in international journals and as invited keynote speakers or as contributors to national scientific and engineering bodies in the United States, Norway, China, and Japan, for example. They participated and led international efforts in the study of marine geohazards such as the Can-COSTA program (Canadian part of the European program – Continental Slope Stability) and UNESCO IGCP (International Geological Correlation Program) and played a key role in making geohazards a principal component of the science plan of the international Integrated Ocean Drilling Program.

Lack of understanding of seabed instability conditions can lead to inappropriate regulations or their poor timing, and unsafe design and operation of facilities. It can also delay approvals, or unnecessarily drive up costs (due to conservative design principles being applied when knowledge of risk is lacking), and it can lead to unwanted oil spills. Overall, the BIO contributions have been essential for the current offshore oil and gas industry to develop in a safe and environmentally acceptable fashion

Examples where BIO seabed research has been a key input include:

- Industry decisions on the feasibility of shelf-crossing pipelines (positive for the Scotian Shelf due to better understanding of the seabed stability risks related to sediment transport; negative for offshore Newfoundland and Labrador where risk of iceberg scour and bedrock that cannot be trenched make pipelines uneconomic and environmentally unsafe).
- Regulatory approval to drill the first modern deepwater wells offshore Nova Scotia (Annapolis) based on advice and data from BIO scientists on the low risk of submarine landslides in certain seabed settings; BIO geoscientists have also advised engineers and industry consultants on the character of sediment into which wells were to be spudded.
- Seabed sediment types and distribution and their mobility have been important considerations in the design and evaluation of 'Environmental Effects Monitoring' programs for all the production projects (Gordon et al. 2014).
- Concern over disturbance of the seabed benthic community by bottom-founded drilling platforms in Beaufort Sea was alleviated when research showed that natural disturbance by ice scouring was far more extensive than would occur from the relatively small footprints of the platforms.
- A state of knowledge of Beaufort seabed geohazards (Arctic Drilling Review) was delivered in timely fashion in 2011 for regulatory agency (National Energy Board) public hearings and the establishment of guidelines for a decision to proceed with future exploratory drilling.

BIO geoscientists continue seabed geohazard research to inform regulatory agencies, engineering design, and decision-making processes in order to avoid surprises from the seabed environment, to contribute to current and future safe procedures for the search and recovery of energy resources, and to reduce the likelihood of oil spills. The work remains critically important for the future as the drive for new energy sources pushes the search into more extreme environments in deeper water and farther north from Baffin Bay to the arctic polar margin. In addition, there is increasing demand for research of geohazards to greater depths of several 100s of metres below the seafloor, for example the presence of overpressured sediments. Greater use of advances in technology will be needed to meet these future challenges, such as ice-breaking vessels, remotely-operated, under-ice vehicles, and instrumentation to acquire the equivalent of seafloor multibeam images at sub-seafloor depths, possibly by more collaborative research with industry and the analysis of 3D seismic survey data. We anticipate greater development of numerical models of geological settings and processes, and these will require careful calibration and testing from seabed observations.

ACKNOWLEDGEMENTS

We acknowledge input from colleagues Michael Li and David Mosher on the topics of shelf erosion and sedimentation, and gas hydrates, respectively. We thank David Frobel for deriving images from a video. We are grateful to Phil O'Regan and Alan Bateman for their design and construction of most of the figures. Finally, we thank David Mosher, Gordon Fader, Vaughn Barrie and the editors of the book '*Voyage of Discovery*' for their efforts in improving this review paper.

Many at BIO and in the consulting and university communities have contributed with the authors to seabed geohazard research, including Carl Amos, Eric Banke, Vaughn Barrie, Robbie Bennett, Gordon Cameron, Calvin Campbell, Harold Christian, Bill Collins, Steve d'Apollonia, Ed Davies, Gordon Fader, Herb Gaskill, Glen Gilbert, Bob Harmes, Dave Heffler, Phil Hill, Bud Hodgson, John Hughes Clarke, Kate Jarrett, Kim Jenner, Heiner Josenhans, Lew King, Ned King, Jim Lever, Michael Li, Kevin MacKillop, Brian MacLean, Bob Miller, Kate Moran, David Mosher, Russell Parrott, Bernie Pelletier, Jim Shearer, Roy Sparkes, Chris Woodworth-Lynas, John Zevenhuizen, and others, in addition to students, post-doctoral fellows, and visiting scientists. We acknowledge development of the SEISTEC system by Peter Simpkin for high-resolution, sub-bottom profiling in the Beaufort Sea. Extensive support and collaboration have been enjoyed over the decades from universities (e.g., C-CORE at Memorial University, St. John's, Newfoundland, ArcticNet, a network of universities and others conducting Arctic research, and University of Alberta, Edmonton, Alberta), oil and gas industries, and other government departments and agencies. We have also benefited from collaborative work with scientists and their equipment from IFREMER (France), Lamont-Doherty Geological Observatory

(United States), and TRAGSA (Spain). Collaboration and support, both within the Geological Survey of Canada Atlantic and other government departments in BIO were essential along with significant support by the Panel on Energy Research and Development, the Frontier Geoscience Program, the Northern Oil and Gas Action Plan, Northern Oil and Gas Science Research Initiative and the industry's Environmental Studies Research Funds for the acquisition and interpretation of the scientific data concerning seabed hazards. None of the research would have been possible without access to scientific vessels, including CSS *Baffin*, CCGS *Hudson*, CSS *Dawson*, CSS *Parizeau*, CCGS *Matthew*, CCGS *Nahidik*, CCGS *Amundsen*, MV *Pandora II* and the submersible *Pisces IV*, and several industry vessels, and especially the technical and marine crews skilled in the acquisition of marine scientific data who worked aboard all of the above vessels. This is contribution 20130209 of Earth Sciences Sector, Natural Resources Canada (© Her Majesty the Queen in Right of Canada 2014).

REFERENCES

Amos, C.L. and O.C. Nadeau. 1988. Surficial sediments of the outer banks, Scotian Shelf, Canada. Canadian Journal of Earth Sciences 25: 1,923-1,944.

Amos, C.L. and R.W. Dalrymple. 1990. Bedforms. Pages 626-628 *in* Geology of the Continental Margin of Eastern Canada (M.J. Keen, and G.L. Williams, Eds.). Geology of Canada No. 2, Geological Survey of Canada, Ottawa, ON.

Amos, C.L. and J.T. Judge. 1991. Sediment transport on the eastern Canadian continental shelf. Continental Shelf Research 11: 1,037-1,068.

Barrie, J.V. 1990. Erosion and sedimentation. Pages 784-785 *in* Geology of the Continental Margin of Eastern Canada (M.J. Keen, and G.L. Williams, Eds.). Geology of Canada No. 2, Geological Survey of Canada, Ottawa, ON.

Barrie, J.V. and M.B. Collins 1989. Sediment transport on the shelf margin of the Grand Banks of Newfoundland. Maritime Sediments and Atlantic Geology 25: 173-179.

Barrie, J.V., C.F.M. Lewis, G.B. Fader, and L.H. King. 1984. Seabed processes on the northeastern Grand Banks of Newfoundland; modern reworking of relict sediments. Marine Geology 57: 209-227.

Barrie, J.V., C.F.M. Lewis, D.R. Parrott, and W.T. Collins. 1992. Submersible observations of an iceberg pit and scour on the Grand Banks of Newfoundland. Geo-Marine Letters 12: 1-6.

Bass, D. and C. Woodworth-Lynas. 1986. Iceberg crater chains and scour up- and down-slope. Pages 122-128 *in* Ice Scour and Seabed Engineering, Proceedings of a Workshop on Ice Scour Research (C.F.M. Lewis, D.R. Parrott, P.G. Simpkin, and J.T. Buckley, Eds.). Environmental Studies Research Funds, Report No. 049, Ottawa, ON.

Blasco, S. 1995. Origin and engineering implications of deep ice-bearing permafrost, Canadian Beaufort Shelf. Pages 159-161 *in* Proceedings of the Oil and Gas Forum '95 – Energy from Sediments (J. Bell, T. Bird, T. Hillier, and P. Greener, Eds.). Geological Survey of Canada, Open File 3058, Ottawa, ON.

Blasco, S., E. Carr, P. Campbell, and J. Shearer. 2011. Impact of environmental factors on the distribution of extreme scouring (gouging) events, Canadian Beaufort Sea. Pages 1,402-1,411 *in* Proceedings of the 21st International Conference on Port and Ocean Engineering under Arctic Conditions Vol. 1, Montréal, QC. National Research Council of Canada, Ottawa, ON.

Blasco, S.M., K. Jenner, E. Davies, F. Michel, W. Pollard, C. Graham, and P. Ruffel. 2012. Origin and evolution of subsea ice-bearing permafrost on the Canadian Beaufort Shelf: implications of a 500 m deep borehole. Page 56 *in* Volume 4 of the Proceedings of the 10th International Conference on Permafrost, Salekhard, Russia (K.M. Hinkel, Ed.). Tyumen Oil and Gas University, Salekhard, Yamal-Nenets Autonomous District, Russia.

Blasco, S.M., and others. 2013. State of Knowledge: Beaufort Sea Seabed Geohazards Associated with Offshore Hydrocarbon Development. Geological Survey of Canada, Open File 6989, Ottawa, ON.

Campbell, D.C. 2000. Relationship of sediment properties to failure horizons for a small area of the Scotian Slope. Current Research 2000-D8, Geological Survey of Canada, Ottawa, ON.

Clark, J.I. and J. Landva. 1988. Geotechnical aspects of seabed pits in the Grand Banks area. Canadian Geotechnical Journal 25: 448-454.

Clark K., C. Hetherington, C. O'Neil, and J. Zavitz. 1997. Breaking Ice with Finesse: Oil & Gas Exploration in the Canadian Arctic. The Arctic Institute of North America, University of Calgary, Calgary, AB.

d'Appolonia, S.J. and C.F.M. Lewis. 1986. Numerical model for calculating spatial distribution and mean frequency of iceberg grounding events. Pages 221-232 *in* Ice Scour and Seabed Engineering, Proceedings of a Workshop on Ice Scour Research (C.F.M. Lewis, D.R. Parrott, P.G. Simpkin, and J.T. Buckley, Eds.). Environmental Studies Research Funds, Report No. 049, Ottawa, ON.

Dupont, F., C.G. Hannah, D.G. Greenberg, J.Y. Cherniawsky, and C.E. Naimie. 2002. Modelling system for tides. Canadian Technical Report for Hydrography and Ocean Sciences 221, Dartmouth, NS.

Fader, G.B.J. 1989. A late Pleistocene low sea-level stand of the southeast Canadian offshore. Pages 71-103 *in* Late Quaternary Sea-Level Correlation and Applications (D.B. Scott, P.A. Pirazolli, and C.A. Honig, Eds.). Kluwer Academic Publishers, Dordrecht, The Netherlands.

Fader, G.B. and L.H. King. 1981. A reconnaissance study of the surficial geology of the Grand Banks of Newfoundland. Pages 45-56 *in* Current Research Part A, Geological Survey of Canada, Paper 81-1A, Ottawa, ON.

Fader, G.B.J., B. MacLean, H.W. Josenhans, and S.M. Blasco. 2014. Seabed sediment mapping at the Bedford Institute of Oceanography: from single beam to multibeam. Pages 191-199 *in* Voyage of Discovery: Fifty Years of Marine Research at Canada's Bedford Institute of Oceanography (D.N. Nettleship, D.C. Gordon, C.F.M. Lewis, and M.P. Latremouille, Eds.). Bedford Institute of Oceanography-Oceans Association, Dartmouth, NS.

Gaskill, H. and C.F.M. Lewis. 1988. On the spatial frequency of linear ice scours on the seabed. Cold Regions Science and Technology 15: 107-130.

Gordon, D.C., K. Lee, P.G. Wells, and P.D. Keizer. 2014. The impacts of oil and gas activities on the marine environment. Pages 361-371 *in* Voyage of Discovery: Fifty Years of Marine Research at Canada's Bedford Institute of Oceanography (D.N. Nettleship, D.C. Gordon, C.F.M. Lewis, and M.P. Latremouille, Eds.). Bedford Institute of Oceanography-Oceans Association, Dartmouth, NS.

Gilbert G.R. 1990. Scour shape and sub-scour disturbance studies from the Canadian Beaufort Sea. Pages 127-144 *in* Proceedings of a Workshop on Ice Scouring and the Design of Offshore Pipelines, Calgary, AB. Canada Oil and Gas Lands Administration (COGLA) and Centre for Cold Ocean Engineering, Memorial University of Newfoundland (C-CORE). C-CORE, St. John's, NL.

Hannah, C.G., J.A. Shore, J.W. Loder, and C.E. Naimie. 2001. Seasonal circulation on the western and central Scotian Shelf. Journal of Physical Oceanography 31: 591-615.

Harris, I.M. and P.G. Jollymore. 1974. Iceberg furrow marks on the continental shelf northeast of Belle Isle, Newfoundland. Canadian Journal of Earth Sciences 11: 43-52.

Heffler, D.E. 1984. RALPH – An instrument to measure seabed sediments. Pages 47-52 *in* Current Research, Part B, Geological Survey of Canada, Paper 84-1B, Ottawa, ON.

Heffler, D.E. 1996. RALPH – A dynamic instrument for sediment dynamics. Pages 728-732 *in* Proceedings of Oceans '96 MTS (Marine Technology Society)/ IEEE (Institute of Electrical and Electronic Engineers): The Coastal Ocean – Prospects for the 21st Century, Fort Lauderdale, FA. IEEE, Piscataway, NJ.

Heezen, B.C. and M. Ewing. 1952. Turbidity currents and submarine slumps, and the 1929 Grand Banks earthquake. American Journal of Science 250: 849-873.

Heezen, B.C. and C.L. Drake. 1964. Grand Banks slump. American Association of Petroleum Geologists Bulletin 48: 221-225.

Hill P.R., K. Moran, and S.M. Blasco. 1982. Creep deformation of slope sediments in the Canadian Beaufort Sea. Geo-Marine Letters 2: 163-170.

Hodgins, D.O., D.A. Huntley, W.D.L. Finn, B. Long, G. Drapeau, and A.J. Bowen (Eds.). 1986. Bottom sediment transport – present knowledge and industry needs. Environmental Studies Research Funds, Report 027, Ottawa, ON.

Hodgson, G.J., J.H. Lever, C.M.T. Woodworth-Lynas, and C.F.M. Lewis, (Eds.). 1988. The Dynamics of Grounding and Scouring (DIGS) Experiment and Repetitive Mapping of the Eastern Canadian Continental Shelf. Environmental Studies Research Funds, Report No. 094, 2 vols. Ottawa, ON.

Hotzel, I.S. and J.D. Miller. 1983. Icebergs: their physical dimensions and the presentation and application of measured data. Annals of Glaciology 4: 116-123.

Hughes Clarke, J.E., L.A. Mayer, D.J.W. Piper, and A.N Shor. 1989. PISCES IV submersible observations in the epicentral region of the 1929 Grand Banks earthquake. Pages 57-69 *in* Submersible Observations off the East Coast of Canada (D.J.W. Piper, Ed.), Geological Survey of Canada, Paper 88-20, Ottawa, ON.

Huntley, D.A. and C.L. Amos. 1990. Instrumentation. Pages 628-631 *in* Geology of the Continental Margin of Eastern Canada (M.J. Keen and G.L. Williams, Eds.), Geology of Canada No. 2. Geological Survey of Canada, Ottawa, ON.

Jollymore, P.G. 1974. A medium range side-scan sonar for use in coastal waters; design criteria and operational experiences. Pages 108-114 *in* Oceans '74 Proceedings of the IEEE (Institute of Electrical and Electronic Engineers) International Conference on Engineering in the Ocean Environment Vol. II, Halifax, NS. IEEE, New York, NY.

Josenhans, H.W. and J.V. Barrie. 1989. Submersible observations on the Labrador Shelf, Hudson Strait and Baffin Shelf. Pages 41-56 *in* Submersible Observations off the East Coast of Canada (D.J.W. Piper, Ed.), Geological Survey of Canada, Paper 88-20, Ottawa, ON.

Josenhans, H.W., J. Zevenhuizen, and R.A. Klassen. 1986. The Quaternary geology of the Labrador Shelf. Canadian Journal of Earth Sciences 23: 1,190-1,213.

King, A.D., R.F. McKenna, I.J. Jordaan, and G.V. Sonnichsen. 2003. A model for predicting iceberg grounding rates on the seabed. Pages 679-688 *in* Proceedings of the 17th International Conference on Port and Ocean Engineering under Arctic Conditions (S. Løset, B. Bonnemaire, and M Bjerkås, Eds.), Norwegian University of Science and Technology, Trondheim, Norway.

King, L.H. 1976. Relict iceberg furrows on the Laurentian Channel and western Grand Banks. Canadian Journal of Earth Sciences 13: 1,082-1,092.

King, L.H. 1980. Aspects of regional surficial geology related to site investigation requirements – eastern Canadian Shelf. Pages 37-59 *in* Offshore Site Investigation (D.A. Ardus, Ed.). Graham and Trotman, London, England.

King, L.H. and G.B.J. Fader. 1986. Wisconsinan Glaciation on the continental shelf - southeast Atlantic Canada. Geological Survey of Canada, Bulletin 363, Ottawa, ON.

Lever, J.H., D.W. Bass, C.F.M. Lewis, K. Klein, and D. Diemand. 1989. Iceberg/ seabed interaction events observed during the DIGS experiment. Pages 205-220 *in* Proceedings of the Eighth International Conference on Offshore Mechanics and Arctic Engineering Vol. IV (N.K. Sinha, D.S. Sodhi, and J.S. Chung, Eds.), The Hague, The Netherlands, The American Society of

Mechanical Engineers, New York, NY.
Lewis, C.F.M. 1978. The frequency and magnitude of drift-ice groundings from ice scour tracks in the Canadian Beaufort Sea. Pages 568-579 *in* Proceedings of Fourth International Conference on Port and Ocean Engineering Under Arctic Conditions, Vol. I (D.B. Muggeridge, Ed.), Memorial University of Newfoundland, St. John's, NL.
Lewis, C.F.M. and J.V. Barrie. 1981. Geological evidence of iceberg groundings and related seafloor processes in the Hibernia discovery area of Grand Banks, Newfoundland. Pages 146-177 *in* Proceedings of the Symposium, Production and Transportation Systems for the Hibernia Discovery (W.E. Russell, and D.B. Muggeridge, Eds.), St. John's NL., Petroleum Directorate, Government of Newfoundland and Labrador, St. John's, NL.
Lewis, C.F.M. and D.R. Parrott. 1987. Iceberg scouring rate studies, Grand Banks of Newfoundland. Pages 825-833 *in* Current Research Part A, Geological Survey of Canada, Paper 87-1A, Ottawa, ON.
Lewis, C.F.M. and S.M. Blasco. 1990. Character and distribution of sea-ice and iceberg scours. Pages 57-101 *in* Proceedings of a Workshop on Ice Scouring and the Design of Offshore Pipelines, Calgary, AB. Canada Oil and Gas Lands Administration (COGLA) and Centre for Cold Ocean Engineering (C-CORE), Memorial University of Newfoundland. C-CORE, St. John's, NL.
Lewis, C.F.M. and M.J. Keen. 1990. Constraints to development, Chapter 14. Pages 743-823 *in* Geology of the Continental Margin of Eastern Canada (M.J. Keen, and G.L. Williams, Eds.), Geological Survey of Canada, Geology of Canada No. 2, Ottawa, ON.
Lewis, C.F.M., B. Maclean, and R.K.H. Falconer. 1980. Iceberg scour abundance in Labrador Sea and Baffin Bay; a reconnaissance of regional variability. Pages 79-94 *in* Proceedings First Canadian Conference on Marine Geotechnical Engineering, Calgary, AB., The Canadian Geotechnical Society (W.J. Eden, Ed.). BiTech Publishers Ltd., Richmond, BC.
Lewis, C.F.M., D.R. Parrott, P.G. Simpkin, and J.T. Buckley (Eds.). 1986. Ice Scour and Seabed Engineering. Proceedings of a Workshop on Ice Scour Research, Calgary, AB. Environmental Studies Research Funds, Report No. 049, Ottawa, ON.
Lewis, C.F.M., D.R. Parrott, S.J. D'Apollonia, H.S. Gaskill, and J.V. Barrie. 1988. Methods of estimating iceberg scouring rates on the Grand Banks of Newfoundland. Pages 229–254 *in* Proceedings of the 9th International Conference on Port and Ocean Engineering under Arctic Conditions, Vol. III (W.M. Sackinger, and M.O. Jeffries, Eds.). University of Alaska, Fairbanks, AK.
Li, M.Z. and C.L. Amos. 1995. SEDTRANS-92: a sediment transport model for continental shelves. Computers and Geosciences 21: 533-554.
Li, M.Z. and C.L. Amos. 2001. SEDTRANS-96: the upgraded and better calibrated sediment transport model for continental shelves. Computers and Geosciences 27: 619-645.
Li, M.Z. and D.E. Heffler. 2002a. Continental shelf sediment transport studies in Canada: theories and recent technology advances. Geoscience Canada 29: 35-48.
Li, M.Z. and D.E. Heffler. 2002b. Continental shelf sediment transport studies in Canada: principal scientific advances and future directions. Geoscience Canada 29: 53-68.
Li, M.Z. and E.L. King. 2007. Multibeam bathymetric investigations of the morphology of sand ridges and associated bedforms and their relation to storm processes, Sable Island Bank, Scotian Shelf. Marine Geology 243: 200-228.
Li, M.Z. C.L. Amos, and D.E. Heffler. 1997. Boundary layer dynamics and sediment transport under storm and non-storm conditions on the Scotian Shelf. Marine Geology 141: 157-181.
Li, M.Z., C.L. Amos, and D.E. Heffler. 1999. Hydrodynamics and seabed stability observations on Sable Island Bank: a summary of the data for 1996/97. Geological Survey of Canada, Open File Report 2997, Ottawa ON.
Li, M.Z., C. Hannah, C. Tang, W. Perrie, and R. Prescott. 2010. Modelling seabed disturbance and sediment mobility on the Canadian Atlantic shelf. Abstracts with Program, 18th International Sedimentological Congress (E. Schwarz, S. Georgieff, E.Piovano, and D. Ariztegui, Eds.), Mendoza, Argentina.
Li, M.Z., E.L. King, and R.H. Prescott. 2012. Seabed disturbance and bedform distribution and mobility on the storm-dominated Sable Island Bank, Scotian Shelf. Pages 197-228 *in* Sediments, Morphology and Sedimentary Processes on Continental Shelves (M.Z. Li, C. Sherwood, and P. Hill, Eds.). Special Publication 44, International Association of Sedimentologists. Blackwell Publishing , Berlin, Germany.
Lynch, D.R., F.E. Werner, D.A. Greenberg, and J.W. Loder. 1992. Diagnostic model for baroclinic, wind-driven and tidal circulation in shallow seas. Continental Shelf Research 12: 37-64.
MacKay, J.R. 1972. Offshore permafrost and ground ice, southern Beaufort Sea. Canadian Journal of Earth Sciences 9: 1,550-1,561.
McKeown, D.L., P.G. Simpkin, G.B.J. Fader, D.R. Parrott, and D.C. Mosher. 2014. The Huntec Deep Tow Seismic system: a revolution in high resolution profiling. Pages 337-341 *in* Voyage of Discovery: Fifty Years of Marine Research at Canada's Bedford Institute of Oceanography (D.N. Nettleship, D.C. Gordon, C.F.M. Lewis, and M.P. Latremouille, Eds.). Bedford Institute of Oceanography-Oceans Association, Dartmouth, N S.
Moran, K., M.J. Keen, D.J.W. Piper, and J. Adams. 1990. Slope stability. Pages 798-802 *in* Geology of the Continental Margin of Eastern Canada (M.J. Keen and G.L. Williams, Eds.). Geology of Canada No. 2, Geological Survey of Canada, Ottawa, ON.
Mosher, D.C. 2011. A margin-wide BSR gas hydrate assessment: Canada's Atlantic margin. Marine and Petroleum Geology 28: 1,540-1,553.
Mosher, D.C. and D.J.W. Piper. 2007. Analysis of multibeam seafloor imagery of the Laurentian Fan and the 1929 Grand Banks landslide area. Pages 77-88 *in* Submarine Mass Movements and Their Consequences III (V. Lykousis, D. Sakellariou, and J. Locat, Eds.). Springer, Dordrecht, The Netherlands.
Mosher, D.C., D.J.W. Piper, G. Vilks, A.E. Aksu, and G.B.J. Fader. 1989. Evidence for Wisconsinan glaciations in the Verrill Canyon area, Scotian Slope. Quaternary Research 31: 27-40.
Mosher, D.C., K. Moran, and R.N. Hiscott. 1994. Late Quaternary sediment, sediment mass-flow processes and slope stability on the Scotian Slope. Sedimentology 41: 1,039-1,061.
Mosher, D.C., D.J.W. Piper, D.C. Campbell, and K.A. Jenner. 2004 . Near-surface geology and sediment-failure geohazards of the central Scotian Slope. American Association of Petroleum Geologists Bulletin 88: 703-723.
Mosher, D.C., S. Bigg, and A. Lapierre. 2006. 3D seismic versus multibeam sonar seafloor surface renderings for geohazard assessment: case examples from the central Scotian Slope. The Leading Edge (December 2006): 1,484-1,494.
Mosher D.C., J. Shimeld, D. Hutchinson, N. Lebedeva-Ivanova, and C.B. Chapman. 2012. Submarine landslides in Arctic sedimentation: Canada Basin. Pages 147-157 *in* Submarine Mass Movements and their Consequences V (Y. Yamada, K. Kawamura, K. Ikehara, Y, Ogawa, R. Urgeles, D. Mosher, J. Chaytor, and M. Strasser, Eds.). Springer, Dordrecht, The Netherlands.
Mulder, T. and K. Moran. 1995. Relationship among submarine instabilities, sea level variations, and the presence of an ice sheet on the continental shelf: an example from the Verrill Canyon area, Scotian Shelf. Paleoceanography 10: 137-154.
Mulder, T., J.A. Berry, and D.J.W. Piper. 1997. Links between morphology and geotechnical characteristics of large debris flow deposits in the Albatross area on the Scotian Slope (SE Canada). Marine Georesources and Geotechnology 15: 253-281.
Myers R., S. Blasco, G. Gilbert, and J. Shearer. 1996. 1990 Beaufort Sea Ice Scour Repetitive Mapping Program. Environmental Studies Research Funds, Report No. 129, Ottawa, ON.
Parrott, D.R., C.F.M. Lewis, E. Banke, G.B.J. Fader, and G.V. Sonnischsen. 1990. Seabed disturbance by a recent (1989) iceberg grounding on the Grand Banks of Newfoundland. Pages 43-48 *in* Current Research Part B, Geological Survey of Canada, Paper 90-1B, Ottawa, ON.
Paull, C.K., W. Ussler, D.R. Dallimore, S.M. Blasco, T.D. Lorenson, H. Melling, B.E. Medioli, F.M. Nixon, and F.A. McLaughlin. 2007. Origin of pingo-like features on the Beaufort Sea shelf and their possible relationship to decomposing methane gas hydrates. Geophysical Research Letters 34: LO1603, 5 p.
Pelletier, B.R. 1979. Review of surficial geology and engineering hazards in the Canadian offshore. Maritime Sediments 15: 55-91.
Pelletier, B.R. and J.M. Shearer. 1972. Sea bottom scouring in the Beaufort Sea of the Arctic Ocean. Pages 251-261 *in* Section 8, Marine Geology and Geophysics (J.W. Murray, B.R. Pelletier, and J.R. Luternauer, Eds.), 24th International Geological Congress, Montreal, QC. 24th International Geological Congress, 601 Booth St., Ottawa, ON.
Pickrill, R., D.J.W. Piper, J. Collins, A. Kleiner, and L. Gee. 2001. Scotian Slope mapping project: the benefits of an integrated regional high-resolution multibeam survey. Paper OTC 12995, Offshore Technology Conference, Houston, TX.
Piper, D.J.W. 1990. Deepwater areas off southeastern Canada. Pages 529-536 *in* Geology of the Continental Margin of Eastern Canada (M.J. Keen, and G.L. Williams, Eds.). Geology of Canada No. 2, Geological Survey of Canada, Ottawa, ON.
Piper, D.J.W. and W.R. Normark. 1982. Acoustic interpretation of Quaternary sedimentation and erosion on the channeled upper Laurentian Fan, Atlantic margin of Canada. Canadian Journal of Earth Sciences 19: 1,974-1,984.
Piper, D.J.W. and W.R. Normark. 1989. Late Cenozoic sea-level changes and the onset of glaciation: impact on continental slope progradation off eastern Canada. Marine and Petroleum Geology 6: 336-347.
Piper, D.J.W. and A. MacDonald. 2001. Timing and position of Late Wisconsinan ice-margins on the upper slope seaward of Laurentian Channel. Géographie physique et Quaternaire 55: 131-140.
Piper, D.J.W. and D.C. Campbell. 2005. Quaternary geology of Flemish Pass and its application to geohazard evaluation for hydrocarbon development. Pages 29-43 *in* Petroleum Resources and Reservoirs of the Grand Banks, Eastern Canadian Margin (R.N. Hiscott, and A.J. Pulham, Eds.). Geological Association of Canada, Special Paper 43, St. John's, NL.
Piper, D.J.W., A.N. Shor, J.A. Farre, S. O'Connell, and R. Jacobi. 1985. Sediment slides and turbidity currents on the Laurentian Fan: sidescan sonar investigations near the epicenter of the 1929 Grand Banks earthquake. Geology 13: 538-541.
Piper, D.J.W., W.R. Normark, and R. Sparkes. 1987. Late Cenozoic stratigraphy of the central Scotian Slope, Eastern Canada. Bulletin of Canadian Petroleum Geology 35: 1-11.
Piper, D.J.W., A.N. Shor, and J.E. Hughes Clarke. 1988. The 1929 "Grand Banks" earthquake, slump, and turbidity current. Pages 77-92 *in* Sedimentological Consequences of Convulsive Geologic Events (H.E. Clifton, Ed.). Geological Society of America, Special Paper 229, Boulder CO.
Piper, D.J.W., A.E. Aksu, P.J. Mudie, and K.I. Skene. 1994. A 1 Ma record of sediment flux south of the Grand Banks. Quaternary Science Reviews 13: 23-37.
Piper, D.J.W., P. Cochonat, and M.L. Morrison. 1999. The sequence of events around the epicenter of the 1929 Grand Banks earthquake: initiation of debris

flows and turbidity current inferred from sidescan sonar. Sedimentology 46: 79-97.

Piper, D.J.W., D.C. Mosher, and S. Newton. 2002. Ice-margin seismic stratigraphy of the central Scotian Slope, eastern Canada. Current Research 2002-E16. Geological Survey of Canada, Ottawa, ON.

Piper, D.J.W., D.C. Mosher, B-J. Gauley, K. Jenner, and D.C. Campbell. 2003. The chronology and recurrence of submarine mass movements on the continental slope off southeastern Canada. Pages 299-306 *in* Submarine Mass Movements and Their Consequences I (J. Locat, J. Mienert, and L. Boisvert, Eds.). Springer, Dordrecht, The Netherlands.

Piper, D.J.W., A.W.A. Macdonald, S. Ingram, G.L. Williams, and C. McCall. 2005. Late Cenozoic architecture of the St. Pierre Slope. Canadian Journal of Earth Sciences 42: 1,987-2,000.

Piper, D.J.W., J. Shaw, and K.I. Skene. 2007. Stratigraphic and sedimentological evidence for late Wisconsinan sub-glacial outburst floods to Laurentian Fan. Palaeogeography, Palaeoclimatology, Palaeoecology 246: 101-119.

Piper, D.J.W., M.E. Deptuck, D.C. Mosher, J.E. Hughes Clarke, and S. Migeon. 2012a. Erosional and depositional features of glacial meltwater discharges on the eastern Canadian continental margin. Pages 61-80 *in* Application of Seismic Geomorphology Principles to Continental Slope and Base-of-slope Systems: Case Studies from Seafloor and Near-Seafloor Analogues (B.E. Prather, M.E. Deptuck, D.C. Mohrig, B. van Hoorn, and R.B. Wynn, Eds.). Society of Sedimentary Research (SEPM), Special Publication 99, Tulsa, OK.

Piper, D.J.W., D.C. Mosher, and D.C. Campbell. 2012b. Controls on the distribution of major types of submarine landslides, Chapter 9. Pages 95-107 *in* Landslides: Types, Mechanisms, and Modelling (J.J. Clague, and D. Stead, Eds.). Cambridge University Press, Cambridge, England.

Pohlman, J., T.D. Lorenson, P.E. Hart, C.D. Ruppel, C. Joseph, M.E.Torres, and B.D. Edwards, 2011. Evidence for freshwater discharge at a gas hydrate-bearing seafloor mound on the Beaufort Sea continental slope. Abstract GC41B-0813, American Geophysical Union, San Francisco, CA.

Praeg, D., B. MacLean, D.J.W. Piper, and A.N. Shor. 1987. Study of iceberg scours across the continental shelf and slope off southeast Baffin Island using the SEAMARC I midrange sidescan sonar. Pages 847-857 *in* Current Research Part A, Geological Survey of Canada, Paper 87-1A, Ottawa, ON.

Shaw, J. 2014. Deglaciation and postglacial sea-level changes in Atlantic Canada: science driven by technology. Pages 325-330 *in* Voyage of Discovery: Fifty Years of Marine Research at Canada's Bedford Institute of Oceanography (D.N. Nettleship, D.C. Gordon, C.F.M. Lewis, and M.P. Latremouille, Eds.). Bedford Institute of Oceanography-Oceans Association, Dartmouth, NS.

Shaw, J., D.J.W. Piper, G.B.J. Fader, E.L. King, B.J. Todd, T. Bell, M.J. Batterson, and D.G.E. Liverman. 2006. A conceptual model of the deglaciation of Atlantic Canada. Quaternary Science Reviews 25: 2,059-2,081.

Shaw, J., B.J. Todd, M.Z. Li, D.C. Mosher, and V.E. Kostylev. in press. Continental Shelves of Atlantic Canada. *in* Continental Shelves During Last Glacioeustatic Cycle: Shelves of the World (A.R. Chivas and F.L. Chiocci, Eds.). The Geological Society of London, London, England.

Shearer, J.M. 1971. Preliminary interpretation of shallow seismic reflection profiles from the west side of Mackenzie Bay, Beaufort Sea. Pages 13-138 *in* Paper 71-1, Part B, Geological Survey of Canada, Ottawa, ON.

Shearer, J.M., R.F. Macnab, B.R. Pelletier, and T.B. Smith. 1971. Submarine pingos in the Beaufort Sea. Science 174: 816-818.

Shearer, J., B. LaRoche, and G. Fortin. 1986. Canadian Beaufort Sea 1984 Repetitive Mapping of Ice Scour. Environmental Studies Research Funds, Report 032, Ottawa, ON.

Skene, K.I. and D.J.W. Piper. 2006. Late Cenozoic evolution of Laurentian Fan: development of a glacially-fed submarine fan. Marine Geology 227: 67-92.

Sonnichsen, G.V. and E.L. King. 2005. Grand Bank seabed and shallow subsurface geology in relation to subsea engineering design. Pages 11-27 *in* Petroleum Resources and Reservoirs of the Grand Banks, Eastern Canadian Margin (R.N. Hiscott, and A.J. Pulham, Eds.). Special Paper 43, Geological Association of Canada, St. John's, NL.

Sonnichsen, G.V. and T. King. 2011. 2004 Grand Banks iceberg scour survey. Pages 1,473-1,482 *in* Proceedings of the 21st International Conference on Port and Ocean Engineering under Arctic Conditions, Vol. 1, Montreal, Canada. National Research Council of Canada, Ottawa, ON.

Sonnichsen, G.V, K. Moran, C.F.M. Lewis, and G.B.J. Fader. 1994. Regional seabed geology and engineering considerations for Hibernia and surrounding areas. Energy Exploration and Exploitation 12: 325-345.

Sonnichsen, G., R. Meyers, K. Simpson, R. Brown, J. McClintock, T. Bullock, and P. Rudkin. 2003. Seabed surveys to document groundings from the 2000 Grand Bank iceberg season. Pages 655-666 *in* Proceedings of the 17th International Conference on Port and Ocean Engineering under Arctic Conditions (S. Løfset, B. Bonnemaire, and M. Bjerkås, Eds.). Norwegian University of Science and Technology, Trondheim, Norway.

Sonnichsen, G.V., C. Breton, E. Carr, P. Campbell, and T. King. 2009. Repetitive seabed mapping to constrain iceberg scour frequency estimates, offshore Labrador. Pages 653-662 *in* Proceedings of the 20th International Conference on Port and Ocean Engineering under Arctic Conditions, Luleå University of Technology, Luleå, Sweden.

Syvitski, J.P.M. and C.T. Schafer. 1996. Evidence of an earthquake-triggered basin collapse in Saguenay Fjord, Canada. Sedimentary Geology 104: 127-154.

Todd, B.J., C.F.M. Lewis, and P.J.C. Ryall. 1988. Comparison of trends of iceberg scour marks with iceberg trajectories and evidence of paleocurrent trends on Saglek Bank, northern Labrador Shelf. Canadian Journal of Earth Sciences 25: 1,374-1,383.

Tripsanas, E.K., D.J.W. Piper, and D.C. Campbell. 2008. Evolution and depositional structure of earthquake-induced mass movements and gravity flows: Southwest Orphan Basin, Labrador Sea. Marine and Petroleum Geology 25: 645-662.

Verhoef, J., D.C. Mosher, and S.R. Forbes. 2014. Defining Canada's extended continental shelves. Pages 407-414 *in* Voyage of Discovery: Fifty Years of Marine Research at Canada's Bedford Institute of Oceanography (D.N. Nettleship, D.C. Gordon, C.F.M. Lewis, and M.P. Latremouille, Eds.). Bedford Institute of Oceanography-Oceans Association, Dartmouth, NS.

Wadhams, P. 2014. The '*Hudson-70*' voyage of discovery: first circumnavigation of the Americas. Pages 21-28 *in* Voyage of Discovery: Fifty Years of Marine Research at Canada's Bedford Institute of Oceanography (D.N. Nettleship, D.C. Gordon, C.F.M. Lewis, and M.P. Latremouille, Eds.). Bedford Institute of Oceanography-Oceans Association, Dartmouth, NS.

Williams, G.L., R.A. Fensome, and S.A. Dehler. 2014. Rocks of the deep: the subsurface geology of offshore Eastern Canada. Pages 215-223 *in* Voyage of Discovery: Fifty Years of Marine Research at Canada's Bedford Institute of Oceanography (D.N. Nettleship, D.C. Gordon, C.F.M. Lewis, and M.P. Latremouille, Eds.). Bedford Institute of Oceanography-Oceans Association, Dartmouth, NS.

Woodworth-Lynas, C.M.T. and J.V. Barrie. 1985. Iceberg scouring frequencies and scour degradation on Canada's eastern shelf area using sidescan sonar mosaic techniques. Pages 419-442 *in* Proceedings 8th International Conference on Port and Ocean Engineering Under Arctic Conditions, Narssarssaq, Greenland. Danish Hydraulic Institute, Hørsholm, Denmark.

Woodworth-Lynas, C.M.T., H.W. Josenhans, J.V. Barrie, C.F.M. Lewis, and D.R. Parrott. 1991. The physical processes of seabed disturbance during iceberg grounding and scouring. Continental Shelf Research 11: 939-961.

Bedford Institute of Oceanography and the Law of the Sea

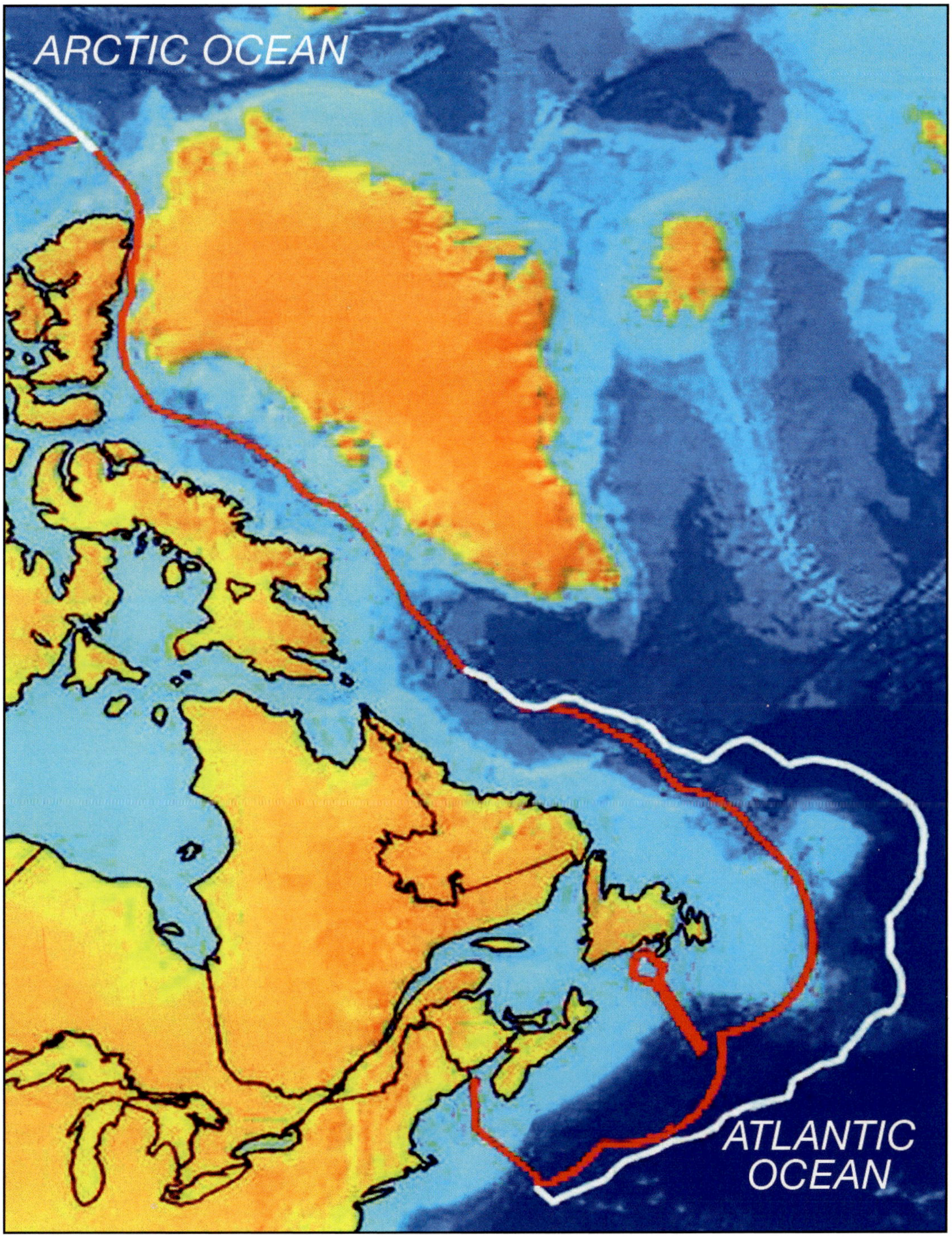

Current (red) and proposed (white) boundaries of Canadian jurisdiction in eastern Canada

BIO and the Law of the Sea

47. THE GULF OF MAINE BOUNDARY DISPUTE: THE ROLE OF THE BEDFORD INSTITUTE OF OCEANOGRAPHY

Michael M. Sinclair* and Robert N. O'Boyle

SUMMARY

Knowledge of the oceanographic, hydrographical, geological, and ecological features and processes off Atlantic Canada resulting from research and monitoring done between 1962 and 1984 was instrumental in defining the scientific grounds supporting Canada's case in its dispute with United States of America over the maritime boundary in the Gulf of Maine and across Georges Bank. Canada did well during the resolution of this dispute which was argued in 1984 at the International Court of Justice in The Hague. This paper summarizes the scientific information and knowledge provided by the staff of the Bedford Institute of Oceanography which played a significant role in the successful outcome for Canada. The sustainable fishery resources associated with the decision (particularly scallops and haddock) have generated considerable economic benefits for the Nova Scotia and New Brunswick fishing industries. Additionally, there are potential oil and gas reserves on Georges Bank.

Key words: Gulf of Maine, Georges Bank, Canada-United States boundary dispute, International Court of Justice.
***E-mail:** Michael.Sinclair@dfo-mpo.gc.ca

In 1964, following the Law of the Sea Conferences of 1958, 1960, and 1964, Canada began issuing oil and gas permits in the Gulf of Maine-Georges Bank area, using a median line between coastlines to delimit respective mineral rights. In 1969, the United States of America (US) informed Canada that it did not recognize Canadian permits for any part of Georges Bank, but did not make a specific claim. In 1974, the US granted permits for oil and gas exploration on the Canadian side of the median (or equidistance) line, to which Canada protested.

Diplomatic correspondence intensified in 1975 and 1976. The US adopted a so-called 'lobster line' (not shown) that included all of Georges Bank on the US side of the line. It defined their jurisdiction over the living organisms of the continental shelf and authorized exploratory drilling on the Canadian side of the equidistance line. The contentious tracts for the proposed sale of leases were withdrawn by the US following Canadian protests. In 1976, Canada and the US enacted legislation with specific overlapping boundary lines (not shown). Canada used a strict equidistance line while the US used a boundary line following the Northeast Channel.

After adoption of the 200-mile fishing zones (1 January 1977 for Canada and 7 March 1977 for the US), negotiations intensified further as the dispute expanded from mineral to fishing rights. Prime Minister Pierre Trudeau and President Jimmy Carter appointed Marcel Cadieux and Lloyd Cutler as lead negotiators, respectively. In the middle of these negotiations, based on the legal principles of the Anglo-French Continental Shelf award of 30 June 1977, Canada informed the US that they were disregarding Cape Cod and Nantucket Island as basepoints and extending their claim farther west in the Georges Bank area.

On 29 March 1979, as a result of negotiations, the parties signed two treaties: the 'Treaty to Submit to Binding Dispute Settlement the Delineation of the Maritime Boundary in the Gulf of Maine Area' and the 'Agreement on East Coast Fishery Resources'. The treaties were linked, one could not come into force without the other. The fishery agreement, which was linked to the dispute-settlement treaty, provided for permanent joint management and reciprocal access to the fishery resources of Georges Bank. However, by 1981, the US had not ratified the agreements and a bilateral negotiated settlement fell apart.

On 6 March 1981, President Ronald Reagan withdrew the Agreement on East Coast Fisheries Resources from the US Senate, and Canada accepted the severance of the two treaties. Later that year, a Special Agreement was filed by Canada and US in The Hague (The Netherlands) to submit the boundary dispute to a Specially Constituted Chamber of the International Court of Justice (ICJ).

The filing of the first written pleadings (memorials) occurred on 27 September 1981. The US memorial abandoned the 1976 'Northeast Channel line' and proposed an 'adjusted perpendicular line' (Fig. 1), claiming that the line was adjusted so as not to cross the land mass of Nova Scotia. Otherwise, Yarmouth, southwest Nova Scotia, would be on the US side of the line! The Canadian memorial proposed an 'equidistance line' that disregarded Cape Cod and Nantucket Island as baselines (Fig. 1). The second (counter memorials) and third (replies) written pleadings were filed on 28 June 1983 and 12 December 1983, respectively. Oral pleadings began on 2 April 1984, followed by the court's binding decision on 12 October 1984 (International Court of Justice 1984). The task of the ICJ was to determine the course of the US-Canada boundary from Point A (which was mutually agreed by both countries) to a point within the triangle enclosing the termini of the proposed boundaries (Fig. 1).

Léonard Legault from the Department of External Affairs led the Canadian team as agent for the case. Lawrence Herman, a lawyer in the private sector with the Ottawa firm of Burke-Robertson, Chadwick & Ritchie, led the case's scientific portion. As the workload increased, Ross Hornby of External Affairs was added to the team. In early 1984, after the US requested that a prominent marine science expert be cross-examined, the Canadian team decided to add Yves Fortier, a skilled trial lawyer with the Montreal firm of Ogilvy Renault, to the team. This small group of lawyers worked closely with Bedford Institute of Oceanography (BIO) staff from 1981 to 1984 (Fig. 2).

In 1981, a large and dedicated multidisciplinary team was formed at BIO to ensure that the scientific support work for the Canadian case was undertaken. BIO was involved at every step, from the definition of the scientific strategy in the Canadian submissions to the oral pleadings at the International Court of Justice. In the three sets of written pleadings, Canada submitted 6,000 pages of documentation, including 650 pages of argument, and deposited nearly 90,000 pages of supporting documents. The scientific strategy was a substantial part of this effort. Because all of the Institute's components were engaged in preparing material, the diverse individual contributions are not identified. It was a team effort, which included the staff of the Halifax Fisheries Research Laboratory (Halifax, NS) and the St. Andrews Biological Station (St. Andrews, NB).

CANADIAN AND UNITED STATES SCIENTIFIC STRATEGIES

Based on the lateral limits of the US 200-mile fishery conservation zone, it was clear that the US would build a case on geological, oceanographic, and fishery discontinuities defined by the Northeast Channel (Fig. 1).

The initial Canadian strategy was to emphasize the continuity of the ocean and seabed in the Gulf of Maine region and downplay the importance of the ecological distinction between Georges Bank and the Scotian Shelf. However, the BIO team pointed out that arguments could be made that the Great South Channel (Fig. 1) is as much a biological barrier as the Northeast Channel, thus demonstrating that Georges Bank is separate from areas both to the northeast off Canada's coast and southwest off the US coast and is part of the continuous continental shelf off North America. It was agreed that BIO would produce an outline demonstrating this approach, which was to become the core of the Canadian strategy for the scientific aspects of the case.

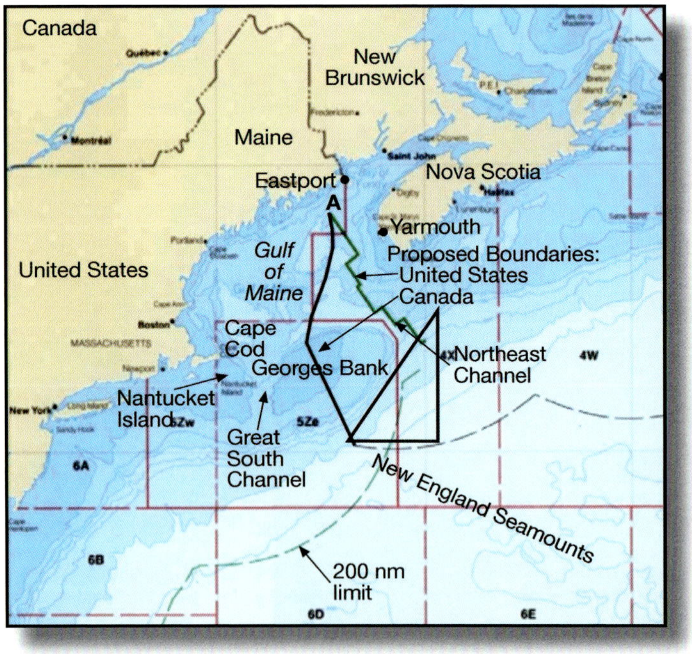

Figure 1. Boundaries proposed by Canada and the United States (US) at the start of the case dealing with the Gulf of Maine boundary dispute. The task of the International Court of Justice was to determine the course of the United States-Canada boundary from Point A to a point within the triangle enclosing the termini of the proposed boundaries. The red lines denote the NAFO fisheries management divisions. The dashed, curved lines are the 200-nautical mile limits of the United States and Canada.

By autumn 1981, BIO was galvanized by the case, which became its highest priority. Preparation for the case included: conducting aeromagnetic and seismic surveys, conducting directed hydrographic surveys and chart preparation, preparing summaries of the history of Canadian marine science in the Gulf of Maine and of International Commission for the Northwest Atlantic Fisheries (ICNAF) activities, analyzing US and Canadian groundfish surveys of the area, analyzing spatial distribution of catch statistics and Canadian/US fishing activities, and providing support for the general strategy's scientific arguments. In early 1982, a BIO steering committee was established to coordinate this work.

The overall Canadian strategy was to focus on the geographical features of the coastline and equitable distribution of renewable resources, undermining US geological, oceanographic, and ecological arguments. When the lawyers went beyond the information supporting this strategy, the BIO team pushed back to ensure scientific integrity.

THE MEMORIALS, COUNTER MEMORIALS AND REPLIES

Both countries presented their positions in the memorials. The boundary claimed by Canada was an equidistance line that disregarded Cape Cod and Nantucket Island as baselines (Fig. 1) on the grounds that they constitute a protrusion of the US coastline, one that would have had a disproportionate and inequitable influence. The Canadian proposal divided Georges Bank to reflect historical and contemporary fishing practices, arguing that US fishing had centred principally on the west side of the proposed Canadian line.

The US claimed a boundary based on a line perpendicular to the general direction of North America's east coast (Fig. 1), starting at Eastport, Maine, stating that it was entitled to jurisdiction of the maritime areas 'in front of' its coasts. The US claim argued that most of the Gulf of Maine lies in front of the primary coast of Maine, and so the southwest coast of Nova Scotia, characterized by the US as a 'secondary coast', should be granted a relatively small maritime area. It further argued that the Northeast Channel constitutes a 'single natural boundary', separating Georges Bank's ecological regime from that of the Scotian Shelf and that the proposed line would facilitate resource conservation and minimize bilateral disputes. In making its claim, the US contended that, historically, it had had 'complete dominance' over the Gulf of Maine area, e.g., fishing, charting and surveying, aids to navigation, and scientific research.

SCIENTIFIC ASPECTS OF THE CANADIAN MEMORIAL

Geology

The Canadian memorial made the case that the Northeast Channel is a minor feature and that other geological discontinuities in the Gulf of Maine area are of equal or greater importance. It described three physiographic provinces: a 'Georges Bank Province' separated from the 'US East Coast Shelf Province' by the Great South Channel, and from a 'Scotian Shelf Province' by the Northeast Channel. It demonstrated continuity of a passive margin from Nova Scotia to the Blake Plateau off Florida. Discontinuities in the geological features were shown not to be coincident with the Northeast Channel. Several major features were described: a linear trend in high magnetic intensity from Nova Scotia to the margin seaward of Florida, the Yarmouth Arch ridge of ancient basement rock extending southwest from Nova Scotia and plunging beneath Georges Bank in a direction transverse to the Northeast Channel, and the New England Seamount Chain in deep water trending southeast off Nantucket Island. None of these major geological features is coincident with the Northeast Channel (Fig. 3).

In summary, BIO geologists argued for a continuity of the Atlantic continental margin (shelf, slope, and rise) which constitutes the natural prolongation of the North American landmass into and under the sea. The topographic features etched into the surface of the seabed were geologically recent and not interruptions or discontinuities within the continental margin.

Oceanography and Biology

For the oceanographers and fishery scientists, the goal was threefold: to demonstrate the continuous oceanographic features off the North American Atlantic coast; to characterize Georges Bank as a productive ecosystem separated from both the United States and Canada by the Great South and the Northeast channels respectively; and to note that, to the degree that there are substantial ecological discontinuities in the relevant area, they lie to the southwest of Georges Bank.

The memorial portrayed the complex interaction of bottom topography, current patterns, and biological processes. On a broad scale, relatively cold currents from the Labrador and Scotian shelves flow through the Gulf of Maine area with recirculation occurring over banks and within basins. The gyre on Georges Bank was defined as separate from the gyres on Browns Bank and the Nantucket Shoals. It was noted that the topography of the Gulf of Maine generated great tidal energy and a single integrated tidal regime. The run-off from rivers flowing into the Gulf was also identified as being important to oceanographic processes, with approximately one-third of the run-off coming from Canadian rivers. These aggregate circulation and mixing features result in nutrient enrichment of surface waters throughout the year and high biological productivity, in particular on Georges Bank, which was identified as one of the world's richest fishing grounds.

The microorganisms in the Gulf of Maine area were identified as being similar to those on the Scotian Shelf and farther to the northeast. There was a similar pattern for benthic species. Those in the Gulf of Maine are similar to those on the Scotian Shelf, but less like those from the Cape Cod-Nantucket Shoals area and farther to the southwest. Emphasizing the coastal zone biogeographic perspective, the Canadian memorial noted that the Gulf of Maine is part of the 'Nova Scotian Province' with the faunal and floral boundary between this biogeographical province and the 'Virginian Province' being in the Cape Cod-Nantucket Shoals waters. Canadian lawyers noted the fortuitous names of these coastal zone 'provinces' with the Gulf of Maine coastal waters part of the 'Nova Scotian Province'.

Fishery Resources

In the Canadian memorial, the distribution of fishery resources was organized at three levels: species, stocks, and aggregate biomass. In terms of the distribution of species, it was demonstrated that Georges Bank is part of a larger oceanographic system, and to the degree that there are spatial discontinuities in the distribution of the range of species, they are to the southwest of the Great South Channel-Nantucket Shoals area. Three categories of species were identified: widely distributed, northerly, and southerly. It was highlighted that only two major species (Long-finned Squid *Loligo pealei* and Searobin *Prionotus carolinus*) have their northern distribution limit at the Northeast Channel. For all other

Figure 2. The Canadian team (heads circled) and other participants in the Chamber of the International Court of Justice constituted to settle the Gulf of Maine boundary dispute between Canada and the United States. The lawyers who addressed the science aspects of the case for Canada were: (1) L. Legault, (2) Y. Fortier, (3) L. Herman, and (4) R. Hornby; the Canadian marine science expert witness was (5) Dr. M.M. Sinclair.

northerly and southerly species, it was concluded that the discontinuity is at the Great South Channel-Nantucket Shoals area. Based on the combined coastal zone observations of species distributional ranges, the shelf seas larval distributions, and new shelf seas trawl survey analyses, it was concluded that, to the degree that the biogeographic province concept could be extended to the shelf seas, the Gulf of Maine area is within the Nova Scotia Province.

In terms of the distribution of stocks of fish and invertebrates, it was argued that a complex mix of species-specific stock structures exists. Some stocks cover a broad area, including the Gulf of Maine as a whole, whereas some are confined to Georges Bank, but with discontinuities both at the Northeast and the Great South channels (Fig. 4). It was highlighted that the distributions of marine mammals and seabirds did not provide evidence of the Northeast Channel being an important distributional feature. In terms of aggregate fishery-related biomass, based on the BIO trawl survey analyses, there is a relative evenness across Georges Bank and contiguous areas.

The conclusion of the memorial was that Georges Bank is to some degree a semi-discrete ecosystem, with both the Great South and Northeast channels separating it from contiguous areas. At the same

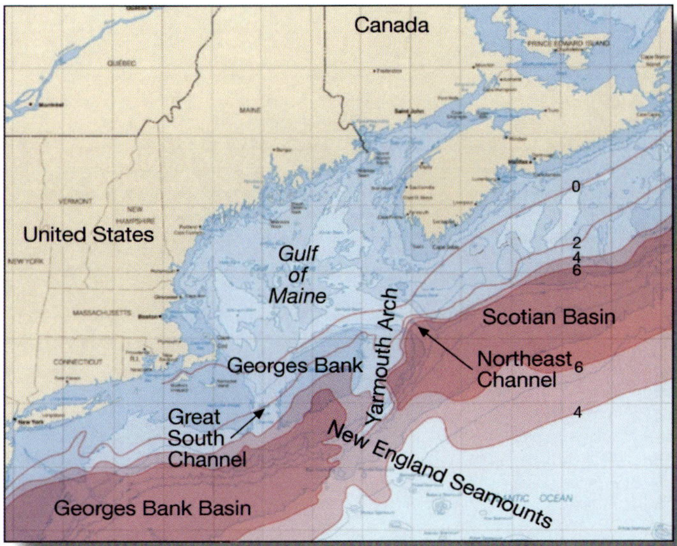

Figure 3. Location of the Yarmouth Arch and the New England Seamounts. The locations of the hydrocarbon-prone sedimentary rock basins, Scotian Basin, and Georges Bank Basin, are indicated by contours of rock thickness in kilometres.

time, it is part of a larger system with boreal features. To the extent that a major biogeographic discontinuity exists, it was argued to be southwest of Georges Bank and not at the Northeast Channel.

CANADIAN RESPONSE TO THE UNITED STATES MEMORIAL

There were some surprises in the US memorial. One was the identification of 'three ecological regimes' (Georges Bank, the inner Gulf of Maine basin, and the Scotian Shelf) divided by a 'single natural boundary'. By focussing on the putative existence of separate regimes in the disputed area, the US left itself vulnerable to criticism.

To respond to the US memorial, Canada quickly assembled the first critique of its scientific aspects and identified key issues for rebuttal. Research was initiated including: a request to the Newfoundland Region of Fisheries and Oceans Canada (DFO) for their trawl survey data to provide a broader spatial scale in the analyses of fish distributions. In addition, analyses were requested of the 1982 geophysical survey results, of superficial sedimentary deposits to prove the similarities between the Georges Bank and Scotian Shelf, and of historical data of benthic samples on the Scotian Shelf and Georges Bank.

The Canadian legal team directed the BIO team to integrate all results of scientific activities into a single document as an annex to the counter memorial. Based on the critique of the scientific aspects of the US memorial, Lawrence Herman stated that "… much excellent work had been done by the people at BIO" (letter from L. Herman to Dr. A.R. Longhurst, the Director-General of the Institute, dated 15 October 1982). The close working relationship between the lawyers and the BIO team was key to the tightness and credibility of the Canadian position.

SCIENTIFIC ASPECTS OF THE COUNTER MEMORIALS

Canadian Counter Memorial

The science sections of the Canadian counter memorial were assertive. BIO scientists had scoured the scientific literature for inconsistencies in the US arguments, and the Canadian strategy of describing Georges Bank as a semi-discrete 'topographical island' within a larger oceanographic system had been effective. There was no need for Canada to argue against the special features of this highly productive shelf sea bank. The original strategy of highlighting only the continuity in the oceanographic and ecological features of the relevant area could have put Canada on the defensive.

Geology — There were few points of disagreement about the geological characterizations. Canada did, however, contend that the US statement that the Northeast Channel is a major separation feature of the single continental shelf was an exaggeration. Maps were provided to illustrate that considerable vertical exaggeration was required to visualize the existence of the Great South and Northeast channels and that these features are shallower than other channels around the world that had been excluded as being significant to other maritime boundary delimitations.

Countering the US argument, Canada maintained that the most distinctive geological discontinuity was the New England Seamount Chain which extends southeast seaward off Cape Cod beyond the Great South Channel and the continental margin (Fig. 3). BIO research had revealed that the magnetic anomalies of the basement rock off Nova Scotia extend southwest across the Northeast Channel and beneath Georges Bank. Related to potential oil reserves, it was stated that there is no single hydrocarbon pool underlying the whole of Georges Bank, and that the US proposed line cut through the Yarmouth Arch (Fig. 3) and the Scotian Basin feature including the hydrocarbons they might contain, and concluded that the Northeast Channel is not a 'single natural boundary' from a geological and hydrocarbon standpoint. It was also concluded that spatial geological discontinuities, to the degree that they are significant, were to the southwest of Georges Bank, a shelf area that is non-glaciated compared with the glaciated continental shelf of the Gulf of Maine area and the Scotian Shelf.

The US statement that the glacial and fluvial deposits are thinner on Georges Bank than on the Scotian Shelf was indicated as being 'clearly wrong.' In Canada's view, the US had redefined the nature and extent of Georges Bank in a manner inconsistent with official US reports. In their memorial, the Great South Channel was not a feature that defined the

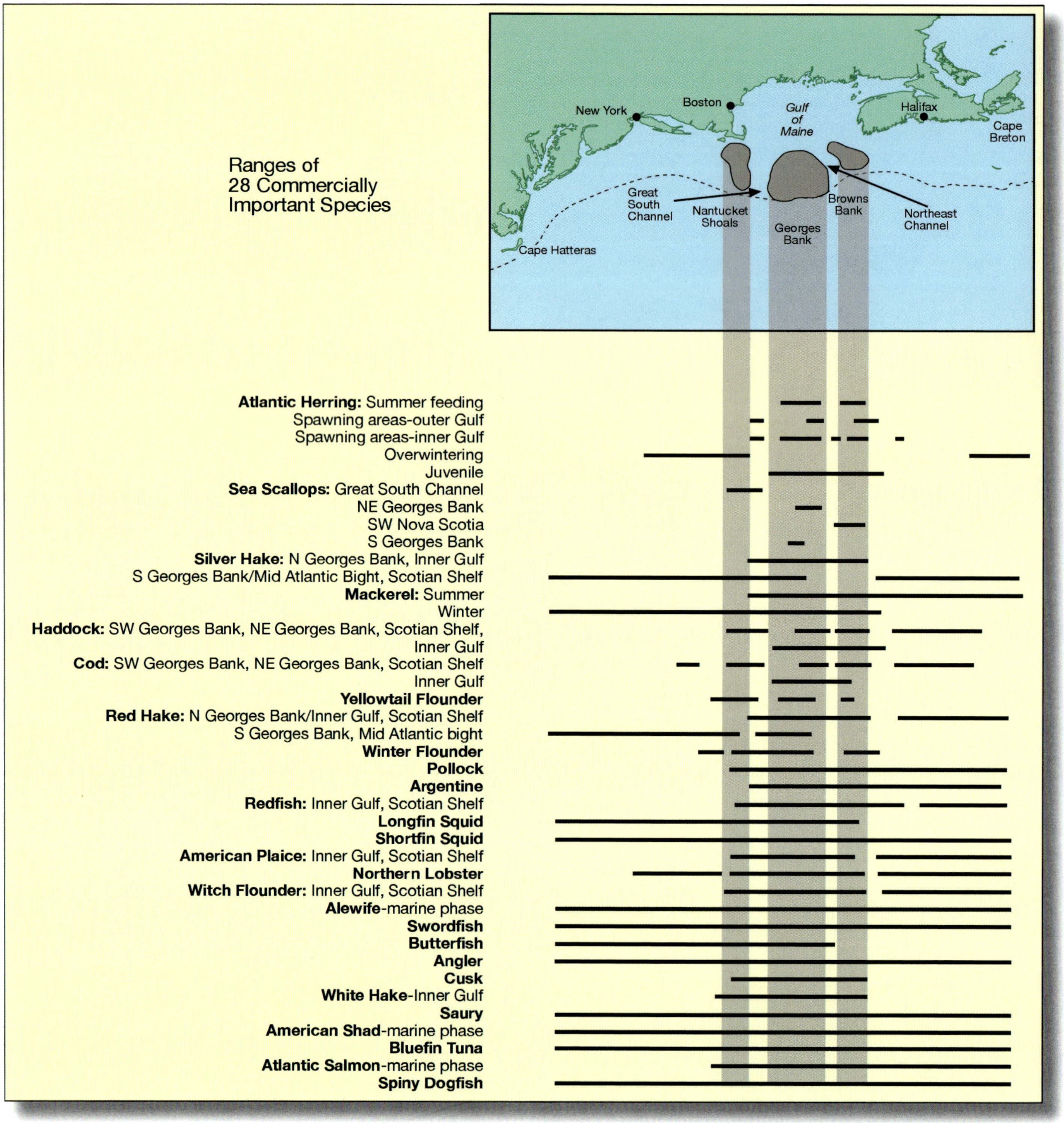

Figure 4. Ranges of stocks of 28 commercially important species (labelled in bold font) between Cape Hatteras (North Carolina), and Cape Breton (Nova Scotia) as summarized by Bedford Institute of Oceanography and presented in the Canadian Counter Memorial which criticized the US position that the fish stock data supported the view that three separate ecological regimes characterized ecosystems in the Brown's Bank (Scotian Shelf), Georges Bank, and Nantucket Shoals regions with distinct natural boundaries at Northeast Channel and Great South Channel.

Bank's western flank.

Oceanography and biology — The BIO team countered the US memorial statement that the salinity and temperature characteristics were different in each of the three ecological regimes. These geographic areas were argued to be similar, with the discontinuity being in the water characteristics that lie to the southwest of the Great South Channel. The single integrated tidal regime of Georges Bank, Gulf of Maine, and Bay of Fundy, which the US had not mentioned, was reiterated (Smith et al. 2014). Alternate interpretations were also identified in the general features and location of the putative frontal feature at the Northeast Channel.

The US memorial claimed that, according to oceanographic models, in the event of an oil spill on Georges Bank, oil would mostly pollute Georges Bank and Massachusetts coastal waters. The BIO team countered that southwest Nova Scotia would be most affected, implying that environmental issues associated with hydrocarbon exploitation on Georges Bank would have a greater impact on Canada's coastal waters than on the US.

The BIO team criticized an unsupported US assertion that phytoplankton on Georges Bank are generally larger than those on the Scotian Shelf. Further, it noted that most of the phytoplankton species on both the Bank and the Shelf are of a northern type (i.e., more typically Canadian). Satellite images of patterns of phytoplankton abundance, which tended to illustrate the separateness of Georges Bank from the Scotian Shelf, were characterized as misrepresenting the aggregate patterns. Canada also maintained, based on analyses, that the US was incorrect in stating that the zooplankton communities are different in the three ecological regimes. The benthic specialists at BIO had reanalyzed the data in an annex to the US memorial, and their results contradicted the conclusions that the three regimes are different and rather supported the Canadian characterization of the Gulf of Maine/Georges Bank/Scotian Shelf being 'part of an integrated ecosystem'.

Fishery resources — The Canadian memorial had summarized the fish distributional data at three levels (species, stock, and biomass). In the counter memorial, the same structure was used to advantage. The US characterization of the Northeast Channel as a 'single natural boundary' separating distributional limits of fish species was shown to be unsupported by the data. The BIO team had used the aggregate US/Canada trawl survey data to map the distributions of three categories of species (northern, southern, and wide-ranging). For many species, the southwestern limit of distribution is coincident with the transition of the Nova Scotian biogeographical province off Cape Cod, not the Northeast Channel. Georges Bank is dominated by northern and widely distributed fish species. Finally, to the degree that there is a discontinuity in the distribution of fish species, it is to the southwest of Georges Bank.

The line through the Northeast Channel as part of the ICNAF/NAFO statistical areas for reporting landings from diverse fisheries (Fig. 1), and in the delineation of management units (or stocks), was an important component of the US depiction of the 'single natural boundary' separating 'ecological regimes'. It was thus a vulnerable part of the Canadian position, requiring careful attention. The BIO team emphasized the nature of fishery management areas or fish stocks, i.e., stocks are spatial units for management that do not necessarily reflect the biological distributions of species populations. Canada argued further that the US memorial sought to force complex life history distributional observations into the three ecological regimes. The results of tagging data on fish and invertebrates were used to illustrate movements of diverse species throughout the Gulf of Maine, particularly back and forth across the Northeast Channel.

Canada criticized the US memorial for its handling of the distribution of the stocks of 16 commercial species. The BIO team provided a detailed literature review of these, as well as additional species that the US had not addressed. This review claimed to disprove the US position that the fish stock data and knowledge supported the three ecological regimes characterization. It was argued that only two species (Yellowtail Flounder *Limanda ferruginea* and Winter Flounder *Pseudopleuronectes americanus*) have stock structures reflecting the putative three ecological regimes (Fig. 4).

A special section was devoted to the migration of cod, herring, sea scallops, and lobster. Three key points were made. First, the presence on Georges Bank of more than one spawning area was considered to be inconsistent with the notion of Georges Bank being but one of three ecological regimes. Second, populations of all species on Georges Bank exhibit affinities with contiguous spawning populations in the broader Gulf of Maine and Scotian Shelf area with migrations across the Northeast Channel. It was concluded that, based on knowledge of fish stocks, the notion of three separate ecological regimes is not supported by the literature. As well, Georges Bank itself could not be considered to constitute a 'single stock regime'. Particular attention was paid to the inconsistency of the known ecology of cod, herring, scallops, and lobster with the US arguments. Third, the fish and invertebrate information on aggregate biomass required further analyses of the combined Canadian and US trawl survey data. The biomass spatial plots reflected neither the existence of three ecological regimes nor the Northeast Channel as a feature of discontinuity. A corollary of the US argument of the existence of the three ecological regimes in the Gulf of Maine, divided by the 'single natural boundary' at the Northeast Channel, was that single state management would be preferable to co-management by the two nations. BIO provided documentation demonstrating that extant co-management of Gulf of Maine fisheries by the US and Canada had been very effective.

The BIO team provided evidence of the Canadian fishing industry's historical presence in the entire Gulf of Maine, and specifically throughout Georges Bank, including high-resolution maps of the spatial distribution of landings of all species over time. This economic dependence on Georges Bank, Canada argued, was legally more relevant than putative oceanographic and ecological processes and patterns.

United States Counter Memorial

The US counter memorial included substantive criticism of the scientific aspects of Canada's memorial. It argued that Canada had misrepresented the scientific literature of current biogeographers, particularly in its assertion that Georges Bank was part of the Nova Scotia biogeographic province. A figure from a research article by Canadian scientists identified the Bank as being within a 'warm-water' province, with the separation between 'provinces' being at approximately the Northeast Channel. The US emphasized the Channel's influence on oceanographic circulation patterns, the spatial characteristics of seawater, the strength and patterns of tidal currents, and the separation of fish stocks. They denied that an oil spill on the bank would harm the Scotian Shelf and coastal Nova Scotia. The BIO team addressed these issues in the Canadian reply.

Conclusion of the Counter Memorial Phase

Canada argued that, if one were to use the US logic on natural discontinuities, all of Georges Bank is Canadian in nature as the major discontinuities are to the southwest of the Bank. However, Canada was claiming only half of the Bank, consistent with the Canadian characterization that the geological, oceanographic, and ecological discontinuities within the relevant area of the dispute are minor.

After reviewing both counter memorials, Canada felt that it was in a reasonable position to undermine the US scientific thesis of three ecological regimes separated by a single natural boundary. Lawrence Herman identified six key points for further work: Georges Bank is a detached offshore bank with affinities to the northeast, the Bay of Fundy is part of the Gulf of Maine, the Northeast Channel is not a 'natural boundary', Georges Bank is within the boreal (i.e., Nova Scotian) province, there are no 'separate and identifiable ecological regimes' in the Gulf of Maine area, and an oil spill on Georges Bank would seriously harm the Canadian environment. The BIO team began work on these issues for inclusion in the Canadian reply.

SCIENTIFIC ASPECTS OF THE REPLIES

Three broad topics in the Canadian reply required input from the BIO team, and are summarized below.

Continental Geography or the Geography of the Gulf of Maine Area?

The challenge in this issue was to critique the science basis of the US macro-geographical approach of defining the proposed boundary relative to the geographical features of the eastern coastline of North American continent as a whole. Under the US definition of the 'relevant area', Nova Scotia would be defined as a so-called 'secondary coast'. Canada contended that the relevant area was the Gulf of Maine proper, with Nova Scotia an integral part of its geographical context. BIO hydrographers provided innovative maps in which Nova Scotia was superimposed on those of France, Italy, the United Kingdom, and The Netherlands to illustrate that Nova Scotia is a large feature, not a 'secondary coastline', in the Gulf of Maine area. Coastlines of several of the judges' countries were shown, providing a personal sense of scale. The Canadian memorial line was central to each map, being located midway across the 'topographical island' of Georges Bank. These maps provided powerful and effective visual images supporting the Canadian arguments.

The Alleged 'Natural Boundary'

Geology — In a section entitled 'The Myth of the Natural Boundary' (i.e., the Northeast Channel), the Canadian reply was blunt: "the so-called discontinuities described by the United States have no basis in science" (page 65, paragraph 163 of the reply). Although both parties agreed that there is a 'single continental margin', Canada identified several important geological discontinuities that are more important than the Northeast Channel.

The US memorial and counter memorial maintained that it is "impossible to assign any direction to the extension of basement rock beneath Georges Bank and the Nova Scotia landmass." Canada called this assertion erroneous because the direction can be delineated by a combination of seismic reflection data, gravity, and aeromagnetic field observations. The US claim also denied that the Scotian Basin extended beneath the eastern part of Georges Bank. Canada cited recent geological research which countered this (Williams et al. 2014). A third geological argument of the US claim was the relevance of the New England Seamount Chain as a major structural boundary seaward of the

Great South Channel. The BIO team provided information supporting the geological significance of this feature, emphasizing, as it had in the Canadian memorial and counter memorial, that if there is a natural geological boundary at all it is to the southwest of Georges Bank.

The BIO team provided additional material demonstrating that the US counter memorial had erred in its assertion that the seabed of Georges Bank "differs substantially" from that both in the Gulf of Maine Basin and on the Scotian Shelf. It was argued by BIO that the scientific observations supported a geomorphologic change to the west and southwest of all these areas from glaciated to non-glaciated sediments, a shift from tidally-dominated to storm-dominated bedforms, and an end to the basin-bank system (from the Newfoundland Shelf to Georges Bank) at the Great South Channel.

Oil spills and biogeographic provinces — BIO oceanographers identified a weakness in the US claim that Nova Scotia would not be affected by an oil spill on Georges Bank. The US ocean current model focussed on the oil that would be within the water column (a relatively minor component of the total), rather than that transported by wind-driven surface currents (the major component). A BIO model of the same potential oil drift process used 23 years of wind and current data and effectively illustrated the Canadian perspective that Nova Scotia would indeed be impacted by an oil spill on Georges Bank.

The Canadian Reply further addressed the question of whether or not Georges Bank is part of the Nova Scotian biogeographic province using information provided by BIO fishery ecologists. The US counter memorial stated that "Canada misrepresents the work of current biogeographers". A detailed review of the literature countered this statement, resulting in a strong rebuttal that "Canada has not been able to find scientific studies of the Gulf of Maine area that support the suggestion that the Northeast Channel is a biogeographic boundary." Canada concluded that the published literature indicates that Georges Bank is boreal in its affinities, and that the transition from cold- to warm-water characteristics occurs in the vicinity of Cape Cod, not the Northeast Channel.

Oceanography and ecology — As to commercial fish species, Canada provided 'irrefutable evidence' that, contrary to the US characterization, Georges Bank is not a warm-water bank. More than 95% of the landings between 1962 and 1980 consisted of northern and widely distributed species. Canada countered the US argument for the segregation of fish and invertebrate stocks, based on the three ecological regimes, using an analysis of the material provided in an annex to the US counter memorial.

A section of the Canadian reply was devoted to what was considered an exaggeration by the US of the importance of the Northeast Channel, both morphologically and oceanographically. Technical points were countered, e.g., the use of temperature and salinity data to demonstrate the 'profound influence' of the flow of seawater through the channel on the features of the inner Gulf of Maine 'ecological regime'. It was argued that the data in the US annex did not support the US conclusion. This relatively minor point on spatial patterns of seawater characteristics illustrates the level of scrutiny that the BIO team applied to the scientific points in the US documents.

Considerable attention was paid to the effect of the Bay of Fundy on the so-called single Gulf of Maine area tidal regime, as seen from Canada's perspective. The inclusion of the Bay of Fundy in the relevant geographical area was important to Canada's case in the court's proportionality tests in which the area of the continental shelf for the two countries should be roughly in proportion to the respective extent of their coastlines in the relevant area. The US documentation suggested that the Bay of Fundy should not be included in the proportionality tests. BIO oceanographers had developed tidal models to illustrate the key role played by the Bay of Fundy in the tidal features of the Gulf as a whole, including Boston Harbor (Smith et al. 2014).

BIO ecologists critiqued the terms 'ecological regimes' and 'ecosystems' used in the US documents. The spatial definition of such areas largely depends on the research focus of the investigator, such that the Gulf of Maine area, or even the Northwest Atlantic shelf seas area, could be considered as a single ecosystem, or it could be divided into several smaller ecosystems, depending on the issues being investigated. Furthermore, the scientific literature makes no mention of 'three ecological regimes' in the Gulf of Maine area. The term was labelled an '*ad hoc* conception'. The Canadian reply concluded that the unity and complexity of the area are incompatible with the concept of a 'natural boundary' for the continental shelf and the water column resources of the Gulf of Maine area.

The Relevance and Reality of Southwest Nova Scotia's Dependence on Georges Bank

BIO input to this issue, although limited, was important. The US claim that the Canadian lines "disregard the only natural boundary in the Gulf of Maine area, the Northeast Channel" re-emphasized the importance of this claim to the US case, and how crucial it was for Canada to question it. It was certainly necessary to counter the contention in the US counter memorial that Georges Bank had been of little economic importance to Nova Scotia and Canada. This was done in part by eliminating the US landings from the Nantucket Shoals area which, from Canada's perspective, is not part of the Bank. High-resolution images of the spatial distribution of both countries' landings during the past several decades provided a strong visual representation of Nova Scotia's dependence on Georges Bank.

Significantly, the US Reply did not mention any of the geological features or biogeographic provinces supporting its claim, as it had earlier. Other than generally criticizing Canada's selective use of oceanographic data to obscure differences in the 'three ecological regimes', it concentrated mostly on geomorphology, satellite images of phytoplankton biomass, and especially the definition of fishery stock boundaries. It emphasized the Northeast Channel as the 'single natural boundary'. The US use of bathymetric maps of the Gulf of Maine area with increasingly smaller contour intervals in shallower water effectively illustrated that the Northeast Channel is considerably deeper than the Great South Channel. The seasonal satellite images of surface chlorophyll concentrations, which were perhaps the only new scientific data presented, countered the claim in Canada's counter memorial that the US had been selective in the representation of images that portrayed the Northeast Channel as a major distributional feature. Again, the data were well chosen by the US to visually emphasize the significance of the Northeast Channel as an ecological discontinuity

The final and most detailed issue considered in the US Reply was the stock divisions of 12 commercially important species at the Northeast Channel. The US alleged that Canada had attempted to confuse the issue of the Channel's role in stock management boundaries by portraying the Channel as unimportant to the distributional limits of species – as opposed to stocks – of commercial fish and invertebrate species, and by focussing on the lack of spatial discontinuities in aggregate fish biomass, again, as opposed to stocks.

They accused Canada of misrepresenting the exceptional nature of the few tagged lobsters that migrated across the Channel and of the transport of fish larvae. They accused Canada of being unreasonable for arguing that the Channel is not a natural boundary for fishery stocks, because Canada had used this feature to delineate stock boundaries for several decades. The US Reply concluded with six points demonstrating that the Northeast Channel is a natural boundary for stocks of 12 of the 16 commercial fisheries. This would emerge as a key point in the oral arguments.

ORAL ARGUMENTS IN THE HAGUE

On 8 February 1984, the US legal team had identified Dr. Robert Edwards as an expert witness who could potentially be made available for cross-examination. Calling a single witness who was a marine ecologist highlighted the importance of the case's scientific aspects, and indicated the US intention to use the cross-examination to strengthen this aspect of its case. Although Canada had not intended to cross-examine a scientist, to maintain balance, Dr. Michael Sinclair of BIO was identified as the Canadian scientific expert who could also potentially be a witness. During preparation for the oral argument phase of the case there was considerable discussion within the Canadian legal team over whether or not Canada should risk cross-examining Dr. Edwards, a widely respected, Harvard-trained marine scientist and senior US government administrator (former Director, Northeast Fisheries Center, NOAA, Woods Hole, MA). Most of Canada's legal experts strongly advised the Canadian Agent, Len Legault, not to pursue cross-examination, because of the perceived possibility that the expert could turn each Canadian question into an opportunity to reinforce the US case. It was felt that an articulate scientist, particularly within the restrictive rules of the International Court of Justice, could outmanoeuvre a trial lawyer.

The BIO team felt, however, that there was much to criticize in the US scientific arguments and that to not cross-examine Dr. Edwards might call into question key aspects of Canada's scientific arguments. A decision by the Canadian Agent was deferred, giving the BIO team an opportunity to devise a cross-examination strategy. The recommended strategy consisted of posing a series of questions assailing weak points in the US scientific documentation and for which there would be limited scope for lengthy answers. Each series of questions would underscore a contradiction between the expert's answer and a component of the US documentation. In preparation for the cross-examination, the BIO team read every paper that Dr. Edwards had written, making note of inconsistencies between his work and the US documentation. Fortunately, the Agent for Canada decided that Dr. Edwards would be cross-examined. Based on the material prepared by the BIO team, the lawyers prepared a series of questions about the Northeast Channel as a natural boundary for fishery stocks, a point central to the US scientific case. The oral arguments began on 2 April 1984.

At the start of the oral proceedings, the scientific aspects were presented by Yves Fortier and Ralph Lancaster, counsel for Canada and the US, respectively, both experienced trial lawyers. There were no surprises in these presentations. The drama, however, occurred during the cross-examination of Dr. Edwards by Yves Fortier.

Figure 5. The International Court in session in The Hague (The Netherlands) at the time of the cross-examination of Dr. R. Edwards, US Expert Witness (standing right) by Y. Fortier, the Canadian Counsel (standing left).

United States Cross-Examination

In his preamble to the cross-examination of Dr. Edwards, the US counsel provided the rationale for producing expert testimony, namely to develop the record on stock divisions and natural barriers in the Gulf of Maine, commonly accepted facts that the US believed Canada had evaded in the written phases of the case.

The first part of the cross-examination consisted of reading prepared answers to the US counsel's questions. The answers were intended for non-specialists, with illustrations on an easel for visual support, and using few technical terms. The aim of the cross-examination appeared to be to crystallize the evidence in support of the US claim's 'single natural boundary' and to counter Canadian criticisms of this concept. Significantly, as with the earlier US Reply, geology and biogeography, for which the Northeast Channel is not a major discontinuity, were not emphasized.

The US counsel then asked Dr. Edwards if he agreed with Canada's statement that "Unlike the land, the sea is not marked by geographic discontinuities or boundaries." He stated that he did not agree, stating that "There are geographically fixed discontinuities or boundaries in the sea, just as there are on land. In fact, in some cases, discontinuities or boundaries in the sea may be even more fixed than those on land." He further stated that climatic boundaries are "at least as precise and 'geographically fixed' in the sea as they are on land." He went on to elaborate: "Conditions in the ocean are such that boundaries can be more sharply defined and directly observable by eye or with instruments than those on land." The US counsel ended the cross-examination by asking Dr. Edwards if anything that he had heard at the Court would change his scientific opinion on the Northeast Channel as a natural boundary or barrier. He answered "No".

Canadian Cross-Examination

Canadian counsel Yves Fortier then cross-examined Dr. Edwards based on material provided by the BIO team (Fig. 5). He began his introduction in French, his maternal 'language of Molière'. This unsettled the unilingual witness who appeared to struggle to adjust his earphones to hear the translation. Just as he was set, Fortier switched to the 'language of Shakespeare' further unsettling Dr. Edwards who then had to remove his earphones. To each series of questions asked by Yves Fortier, the answer indicated an inconsistency between statements by Dr. Edwards and the scientific documentation provided by the US in their case. The themes included biogeographic provinces as well as the key US illustration indicating that 12 of 16 commercial species have stock discontinuities at the Northeast Channel. The overall result of the cross-examination was to call into question earlier testimony of Dr. Edwards on the 'single natural boundary'.

Near the end of the questioning, Yves Fortier returned to the more general discussion of the existence of geographically fixed boundaries in the sea and on land. He asked Dr. Edwards if he had always held the view that there are geographically-fixed boundaries in the sea, and if these boundaries are in some cases more clearly defined than land boundaries. Specifically, Yves Fortier asked Dr. Edwards if he remembered writing an article on recent changes in North Atlantic fisheries which had been published in the primary literature (Edwards 1976). Yves Fortier quoted a passage (page 306): "Terrestrial ecosystems are relatively stable in their geographic boundaries and in their persistence.... In the ocean, boundaries and distribution of ecosystems change constantly." Yves Fortier asked Dr. Edwards if this is what he believed in 1976. Dr. Edwards replied: "We have a famous saying, sir. At this point in time, given what we are dealing with, I could bite my tongue. I would have to read this carefully to try and recreate the ambiance in which that was written. May I find it and read it?" Yves Fortier passed Dr. Edwards the paper, providing the page number. Yves Fortier then completed his cross-examination by asking again "My question is a very simple one, whether in 1976 you believed that in the oceans, boundaries and distribution of ecosystems changed constantly." Dr. Edwards responded, "No, Sir, I do not. That is why I am trying to read it and understand exactly what it was I was intending to say." This apparently inconsistent testimony was followed by a brief silence, after which the President of the Court asked Dr. Edwards if he had anything more to say, to which he replied "No", and the hearing was adjourned for the day.

Yves Fortier, in masterful courtroom style, had undermined the credibility of the US expert in a little more than an hour of cross-examination. He had demonstrated that, given the opportunity and a good strategy, a talented trial lawyer can outsmart a talented and widely respected scientist, even under the ICJ's rules of conduct. The Canadian legal team then decided not to open its scientific expert to the same possible outcome. The US Counsel, Ralph Lancaster, was an equally talented courtroom lawyer and could also 'outsmart' the technical expert. The ICJ was informed that the Canadian expert would not be available for cross-examination and had returned to Canada.

The input to Dr. Edwards' cross-examination on 18 April 1984 was BIO's final contribution to the case. The only thing left to do was to wait until autumn for the judgement of the ICJ.

THE JUDGEMENT

This case was unusual and precedent-setting for two reasons. First, the ICJ had been requested to define the line itself, rather than provide guidelines for negotiations between the two countries about a boundary. Second, and more important from an international law perspective, this was the first time that delimitation of an international boundary related to both the continental shelf and exclusive fishing zones. The parties had requested that "the single line to be drawn should be applicable to all aspects of the jurisdiction of the coastal state." The Judgement, read to the Chamber on 12 October 1984, provides detailed analyses of all aspects of the case, highlighting the importance of the BIO contribution.

Scientific Aspects

The geological aspects of the US reply and the cross-examination of Dr. Edwards were weaknesses in the US case for the existence of a 'single natural boundary'. The Judgement noted that, although both parties had

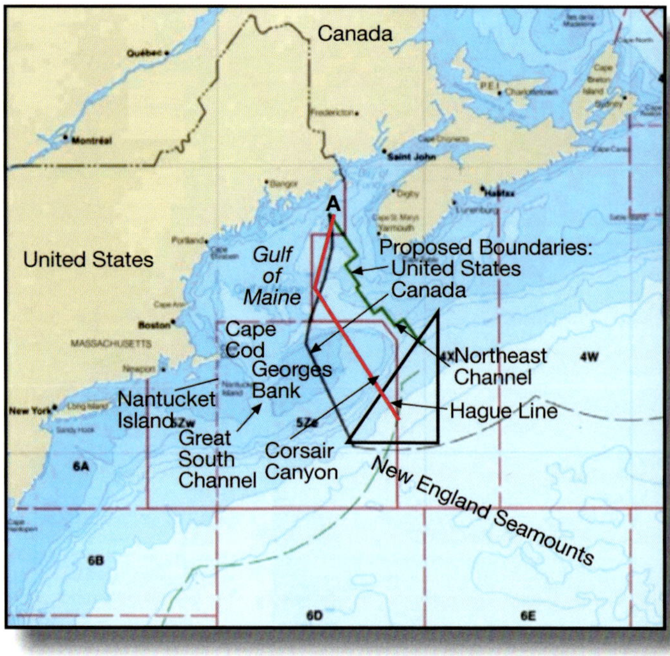

Figure 6. The Hague Line (red) as decided by the International Court of Justice in 1984. Also shown for comparison are the boundaries proposed by both the United States (US) and Canada at the start of the case.

pointed out geological affinities between Nova Scotia and Massachusetts, "the geological structure of the strata underlying the whole of the continental shelf of North America is essentially continuous." The Judgement is equally clear about geomorphology, about which the US had a stronger case for a 'single natural boundary'. It noted the unity and uniformity of the whole seabed, "even if here and there it features some secondary characteristics mainly from glacial and fluvial action," as described in the Canadian documentation. The Judgement affirmed that bathymetric features of the Gulf of Maine area were insignificant and could only be seen with the aid of considerable vertical exaggeration. Canada's emphasis on the visualization of these phenomena had worked well. The Judgement stated that the bathymetric differences between one spot and another "do not show any trace of natural differentiation," and a bit further "even the most accentuated feature, namely the Northeast Channel, does not have the characteristics of a real trough marking the dividing line between two geomorphologically distinct units." The visual aids depicting the comparative depths of channels globally, with the Northeast Channel as being relatively shallow, seemed to have worked well. The Chamber concluded that there is not a "natural separation in the seabed", and therefore the delimitation line need not consider factors of "natural separation of the continental shelf because no such factors exist."

An important aspect of this unique case noted by the ICJ's decision was the so-called 'water column' (i.e., the focus being on the seawater features, oceanographic and ecological, as well as the seafloor). Fish, rather than, or in addition to, minerals and hydrocarbons, were key and so the ICJ needed to focus on those aspects of the water column that were particularly relevant to fish and the ecosystem. During the reading of the decision, the Canadian Agent, Len Legault, passed a note to the BIO representative stating that the Institute's contribution had essentially won the scientific aspect of the case for Canada. This was undoubtedly an exaggeration, but was nevertheless well received! The enormous contribution of the BIO team to the overall scientific strategy and the memorial, counter memorial, and reply documents had convinced the Chamber of the dubious nature of the US assertions on the importance of natural boundaries in the sea. The joint effort by the legal and science teams had succeeded.

The overall strategy of characterizing Georges Bank as a topographical island within a continuous shelf sea, with the major biogeographical discontinuity being to the extreme west of the Gulf of Maine area, had also worked well. Essentially, the Chamber had agreed with Canada on every scientific point. It was clear that the Northeast Channel would not be a part of the boundary, and that Canada would have exclusive access to at least part of Georges Bank.

Other Aspects

The remainder of the Judgement dealt with the additional aspects of how the court's line was defined and the diverse tests of resulting equity. There were a few points about the equity tests for which the BIO input was important. The Bay of Fundy was included in the coastline comparisons for the equity tests because it was defined by the Chamber as being part of the Gulf of Maine area, an issue supported by BIO's Gulf of Maine tidal modelling. In considering the economic impacts of the line, the Chamber had paid careful attention to the illustrations of fishery landing information, both temporal and spatial. This was revealed by its remark that the line would preserve the major part of the Canadian scallop and offshore lobster fisheries. The information on the history of joint fishery management, to which the BIO team had contributed, led to the conclusion that no difficulties were expected in view of "a long tradition of friendly and fruitful co-operation in maritime matters." The Judgement's final sentence states: "The chamber may therefore confidently conclude that the delimitation effected in compliance with the governing principles and rules of law, applying equitable criteria and appropriate methods accordingly, has produced an equitable overall result."

The Outcome

The coordinates of the final boundary were read without a map displayed as a visual aid, leaving the Canadian team uncertain about the specific outcome of several years of exceptionally dedicated work. After the court closed, the team mustered in a backroom where a hydrographer plotted the coordinates on a chart (Fig. 6). A substantial part of Georges Bank, including Corsair Canyon, an important Canadian lobster fishing area, was on the Canadian side of the boundary which subsequently became known as the 'Hague Line', which was close to Canada's original proposal (Fig. 6). Canada had done well in the case.

It should be noted that the international border between Point A and the coastline has not yet been resolved and an area of 210 square nautical miles, including Machais Seal Island, is claimed by both countries.

THE JUDGEMENT'S FINANCIAL SIGNIFICANCE TO CANADA

When word of the decision spread, given that all of Georges Bank could have gone to the US, the Nova Scotia and New Brunswick governments responded positively, as did the east coast fishing industry. It is difficult to estimate the long-term value of the fisheries in the Canadian portion of Georges Bank because the relative abundance of the combined commercial species fluctuates year to year, owing to both natural conditions and conservation measures. It is possible, however, to estimate the importance of the Georges Bank fishery to the Canadian economy during the period before the decision.

The major species of interest to the Canadian fishery between the 1960s and early 1980s were scallops, groundfish, and offshore lobster. For scallops, the average annual landings during 1969-78 valued about $100 million. Owing to overfishing, scallop abundance was very low in the early 1980s, just before the ICJ case, with the 1983 landed value being down to about $30 million and the product value about $40 million. For groundfish, 1979-83 landed value was about $10 million with the product value about $25 million, while the offshore deep-water lobster fishery had a landed value of about $1 million. The minor fisheries, for which there was long-term potential for exploitation, included herring, mackerel, swordfish, squid, and argentine. The overall number of person-years involved in catching and processing landings from Georges Bank at the time of the decision was about 1,500. In 1980, Georges Bank generated more than $150 million in gross domestic product (GDP), about 15% of Nova Scotia's total GDP. These estimates give a rough idea of the importance of the Georges Bank fishery to Nova Scotia's economy just prior to the decision.

The decision gave Canada 1,352 square nautical miles of Georges Bank, about one-sixth of the Bank's total area. However, the northern portion of the Bank, which at that time contained the major part of the scallop fishing grounds, was of particular importance to the Canadian fishery. A detailed analysis of the fishing pattern in the decade before the decision revealed that there would be limited displacement of Canadian fishing effort as a result of the restriction of future fishing to east of the Hague Line.

In subsequent decades, the scallop resources on both sides of the line have increased substantially as a result of conservation measures, and the groundfish stocks on the Bank as a whole have fluctuated considerably.

Because of these fluctuations, it is difficult to assign an annual value of the Georges Bank fishery to Canada, but it was well in excess of $100 million GDP in 1980 dollars (and in perpetuity) or about $200 million in 2012 Canadian dollars. To date, neither country has begun further exploration of potential hydrocarbon resources because of drilling moratoria on both sides of the boundary.

SUMMARY OF BEDFORD INSTITUTE OF OCEANOGRAPHY'S ROLE

Why did Canada do well with the scientific aspects of the case? First, it was thanks to the outstanding leadership of the Department of External Affairs, in particular, the Canadian Agent for the case, Léonard Legault. He assembled a dedicated and talented legal team, including the three lawyers who focussed on the scientific part of the case: Lawrence Herman, Ross Hornby, and Yves Fortier. They built as strong a case as possible, given the constraints of the evidence. For each part of the case, there had to be technical advisors, and for the scientific aspects, Canada was fortunate to have BIO as a multidisciplinary federal institute to call upon for assistance. In essence, all of the marine science expertise required was housed at BIO (as well as the closely associated St. Andrews Biological Station and Halifax Fisheries Research Laboratory) and was accessible on a priority basis to the case. BIO staff had carried out important and relevant research and monitoring off Atlantic Canada during 1962-83. Equally important, they were cognizant of the broader international scientific literature relevant to all aspects of the science needed for the case.

The US has on aggregate considerably greater capacity and excellence in marine science through well-known organizations such as the Woods Hole Oceanographic Institute, Harvard University, the University of Maine, the University of Rhode Island, and several National Oceanic and Atmospheric Administration (NOAA) laboratories. However, other than within the NOAA laboratories, their outstanding expertise may have been harder to focus as a dedicated team given the dispersed nature of this expertise.

The strategy adopted by the US was high-risk and one that was tricky to deliver. Convincing the Chamber that there was a natural boundary in the water column generated by the Northeast Channel was an enormous challenge, as well as being potentially precedent setting. That said, the Canadian scientific team at BIO had to be up to the task of providing technical analyses to the Canadian lawyers on a priority basis. It had to be diligent to ensure that every aspect of the science could be backed up in a trial setting. BIO's scientific input was well-scrutinized and state-of-the-art. The knowledge of Canada's oceanographic, hydrographical, geological, and ecological features and processes off Atlantic Canada, resulting from BIO's research and monitoring, was instrumental in defining the scientific aspects of the case.

The Judgement may have influenced subsequent United Nations Convention on the Law of the Sea (UNCLOS) cases. Donald McRae, the Senior Legal Advisor to the Canadian Agent in the case, in a 1989 review article on the resolution of ocean management problems (McRae 1989), argued that: *"The Chamber's rejection in the Gulf of Maine Case of the United State's intriguing theory of single-state management of separate ecological regimes may have reduced the incentive for states to adopt a 'winner take all' approach to international litigation, thereby encouraging increased attempts to seek negotiated solutions."*

In a broader sense, the successful contribution of BIO to the case harkened back to the vision, and perhaps dream, of W.E. van Steenburgh for BIO, as articulated in his speech at Dalhousie University (Halifax, NS) in October 1962 (Mills 2014). The Institute had, in his words spoken 22 years before, *"contributed to the improvement of Canadian life"*, in this case, in perpetuity, particularly for those living in southwest Nova Scotia, who so depend on the sea and especially Georges Bank for their livelihood! Furthermore, van Steenburgh's philosophy of research, a good balance between pure and applied research, proved to be prescient. Both aspects of the research that took place at BIO between 1962 and 1983 proved relevant to the positive outcome for Canada in the Gulf of Maine case at the International Court of Justice.

ACKNOWLEDGEMENTS

The authors note that the scientific contribution to the dispute was in every sense a BIO team effort, with the able assistance of the staff from the St. Andrews Biological Station and the former Halifax Fisheries Research Laboratory. Furthermore, the lawyers, under the outstanding leadership of Len Legault, assured the necessary close collaboration that resulted in an effective preparation and presentation of the scientific aspects of the case.

REFERENCES

Edwards, R.L. 1976. Middle Atlantic fisheries: recent changes in populations and outlook. Pages 302-311 *in* Middle Atlantic Continental Shelf and the New York Bight (G. Gross, Ed.). American Society of Limnology and Oceanography, Special Symposium 2, Allen Press, Lawrence, KS.

International Court of Justice (ICJ). 1984. Delimitation of the Maritime Boundary in the Gulf of Maine Area, Judgement. Pages 246-352 *in* International Court of Justice Reports 1984. International Court of Justice, The Hague, The Netherlands. (www.icj-cij.org/docket/files/67/6369.pdf)

McRae, D. M. 1989. Approaches to the resolution of Atlantic and Pacific Ocean problems. Ecology Law Quarterly 16: 227-244.

Mills, E.L. 2014. Canadian marine science from before *Titanic* to the establishment of the Bedford Institute of Oceanography in 1962. Pages 3-11 *in* Voyage of Discovery: Fifty Years of Marine Research at Canada's Bedford Institute of Oceanography (D.N. Nettleship, D.C. Gordon, C.F.M. Lewis, and M.P. Latremouille, Eds.). Bedford Institute of Oceanography-Oceans Association, Dartmouth, NS.

Smith, P.C., B.D. Petrie, J.A. Elliott, N.S. Oakey, and G.L. Bugden. 2014. Coastal ocean circulation studies. Pages 149-159 *in* Voyage of Discovery: Fifty Years of Marine Research at Canada's Bedford Institute of Oceanography (D.N. Nettleship, D.C. Gordon, C.F.M. Lewis, and M.P. Latremouille, Eds.). Bedford Institute of Oceanography-Oceans Association, Dartmouth, NS.

Williams, G.L., R.A. Fensome, and S.A. Dehler. 2014. Rocks of the deep: the subsurface geology of offshore eastern Canada. Pages 215-223 *in* Voyage of Discovery: Fifty Years of Marine Research at Canada's Bedford Institute of Oceanography (D.N. Nettleship, D.C. Gordon, C.F.M. Lewis, and M.P. Latremouille, Eds.). Bedford Institute of Oceanography-Oceans Association, Dartmouth, NS.

48. DEFINING CANADA'S EXTENDED CONTINENTAL SHELVES

Jacob Verhoef*, David C. Mosher, and Stephen R. Forbes

SUMMARY

The determination of the outer limits of Canada's continental shelves in the Atlantic and Arctic oceans is one of the high profile recent science programs at the Bedford Institute of Oceanography. After ratification of the United Nations Convention on the Law of the Sea in 2003, Canada started a program to acquire and analyze the scientific data required for a submission to the Commission on the Limits of the Continental Shelf to define the outer limits of its extended continental shelf. This program, managed at the Institute through a close collaboration of the Canadian Hydrographic Service and the Geological Survey of Canada, will determine with precision the area beyond 200 nautical miles, where Canada may exercise its sovereign rights over the natural resources of the seabed. This article outlines the scope of that program and summarizes its scientific activities. By late 2012, the program was on schedule to meet the December 2013 deadline for submission to the Commission.

Key words: United Nations Convention Law of the Sea (UNCLOS), extended continental shelf (ECS) definition, Canadian ECS survey programs.

***E-mail:** JVerhoef@nrcan.gc.ca

Sinclair and O'Boyle (2014) outlined the role of the Bedford Institute of Oceanography (BIO) in defining the scientific aspects of the case in support of Canada's claim for the boundary between Canada and the United States (US) in the Gulf of Maine. They concluded that having BIO, a multidisciplinary federal institute, with all the required marine expertise under one roof, proved to be relevant to the positive outcome for Canada in the Gulf of Maine case. This paper builds on that concept and summarizes Canada's scientific activities in defining the outer limits of its continental shelf in the Atlantic and Arctic oceans under the provisions provided by the United Nations Convention on the Law of the Sea (UNCLOS or the Convention; United Nations 1982). The activities are for the most part led by scientists and technical staff at BIO, and as was the case in the Gulf of Maine dispute, it was the interaction among geoscience, hydrography, and technical innovation at BIO that has proven to be crucial for this program. By analyzing the existing large amount of oceanographic, hydrographic, and geoscientific information we were able to define, in the context of UNCLOS, where additional data were required, and to design and implement a cost-effective program to collect new data. Although the program to acquire and analyse the data to late 2012 had nearly finished, a submission to the United Nations Commission on the Limits of the Continental Shelf (the Commission) had not yet been made, so this contribution provides a status report, and refrains from speculating on the final outcome.

So what is required to define the outer limits of the continental shelf? A prerequisite is to outline the interesting and sometimes confusing interplay between the scientific concept of a continental margin and the legal definition of a continental shelf. In scientific terms, the continental margin is generally defined as the zone separating thin ocean crust from thick continental crust. The margin, including the continental shelf and slope, is viewed as the submerged prolongation (extension) of the continent. Geologists, however, understand that the geology and geomorphology of continental margins are diverse and reflect the various tectonic processes involved, including rifting, collision, and subsidence. In reality, therefore, the continental margin is often defined, in geological terms, as a zone with unclear boundaries, thereby making it unsuitable to be used in a legal definition of marine jurisdiction. It is in this context that UNCLOS, among its many provisions, provides a legal definition of the continental shelf.

UNCLOS AND ARTICLE 76

UNCLOS provides a comprehensive framework for the governance of the world's oceans. The Convention was adopted in 1982 and came into force in 1994 after ratification by sixty states. Canada ratified the Convention in 2003 and presently the Convention has been ratified by 161 states. The provisions of UNCLOS range from those on resource development to protection and preservation of the marine environment, marine scientific research to navigation, and conservation and management of living marine resources to settlement of disputes.

The Convention establishes several maritime zones (Fig. 1A), such as the territorial sea, the contiguous zone, the (juridical) continental shelf and the Area. All coastal states are entitled to a continental shelf of 200 nautical miles (nm) and states that meet certain criteria may have a shelf which extends beyond 200 nm. In its extended continental shelf beyond 200 nm, *"a coastal state has sovereign rights over natural resources which include mineral and other non-living resources of the seabed and subsoil, together with living organisms which either are immobile on, or under the seabed, or are in constant physical contact with the seabed or subsoil"* (United Nations 1982, Article 77). Only inside 200 nm does a coastal state have rights over the living resources in the water column. Sovereign rights over the extended continental shelf are exclusive and do not depend on occupation or proclamation. The seabed beyond the continental shelves is called the 'Area'; its natural seabed resources are considered the common heritage of mankind and are to be administered by the International Seabed Authority, as described in the Convention.

In case of an extended continental shelf beyond 200 nm, states are required to determine with precision the area in which they may exercise their sovereign rights. In Article 76, the Convention sets out a process by which a state can do this.

Article 76 (United Nations 1982)

In 617 words, Article 76 defines the juridical continental shelf of a coastal state by incorporating both legal and scientific terms (Fig. 1; Macnab and Haworth 2001). The continental shelf is defined legally as: "*... the natural prolongation of its land territory to the outer edge of the continental margin* (in the scientific sense)*, or to a distance of 200 nautical miles ... where the outer edge of the continental margin does not extend up to that distance.*" (Article 76, paragraph 1). This definition uses the continental margin as the 'yardstick', defined as: "*... the submerged prolongation of the land mass of the coastal State, and consists of the seabed and subsoil of the shelf, the slope and the rise* (i.e., in the scientific meaning of shelf, slope and rise). *It* (the scientific continental margin) *does not include the deep ocean floor with its oceanic ridges or the subsoil thereof*" (Article 76, Paragraph 3).

As mentioned before, there are significant differences between the scientific definition of the continental shelf (gently sloping submerged marginal zone of the continent extending from shore to an abrupt increase in bottom inclination) and the above legal definition, which includes the continental margin (scientific shelf, slope, and rise), and can include also parts of the deep ocean floor (Fig. 1). To avoid confusion, we will use the term 'shelf' to indicate the scientific continental shelf; the term 'continental shelf' will be used for the legal continental shelf.

In cases where a continental margin extends beyond 200 nm, the coastal state is required to demonstrate that the criteria of Article 76 are met and use geoscientific data (existing or newly acquired) to define its extended continental shelf. Article 76 provides formulae for measuring

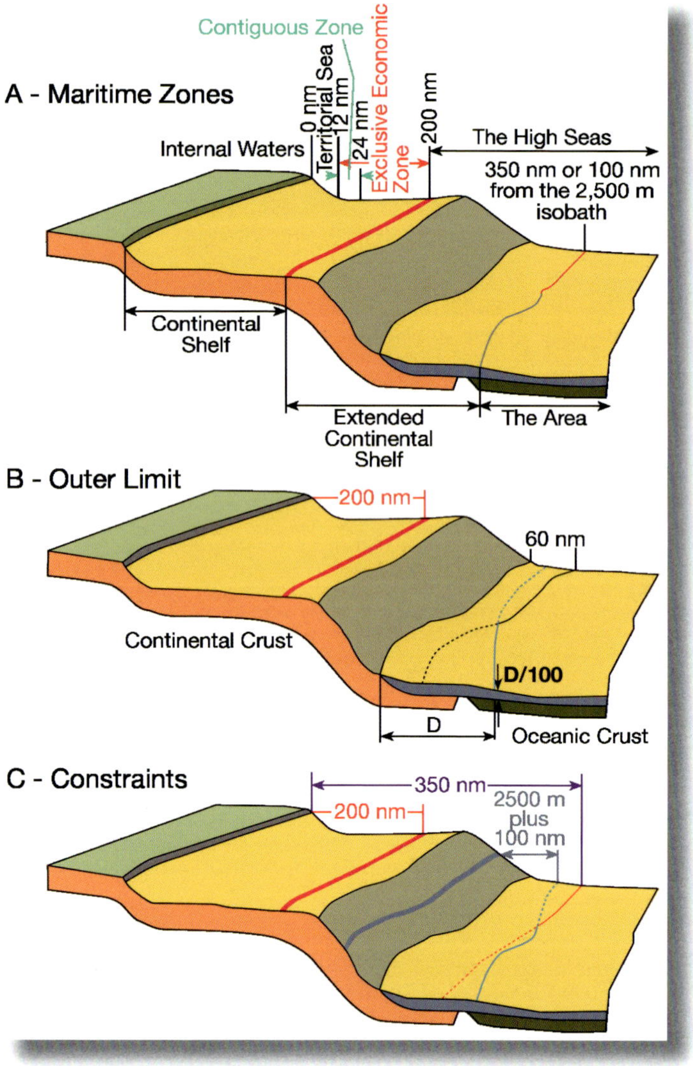

Figure 1. Schematic illustrations of the juridical UNCLOS zones, limits, and constraints: (A) The legal maritime zones as outlined by UNCLOS for the case in which the physiographic continental margin extends seaward of the Exclusive Economic Zone (EEZ); (B) Sketch of an idealized seafloor showing how the foot-of-the-slope (FOS)+60 nm line, and the D/100 (1%) sediment line (Gardiner line) are combined to form an outer limit; and (C) Sketch of an idealized seafloor showing how the 350-nm line, and the 2,500-m contour+100 nm line are combined to form the outer constraint.

the continental shelf seaward (Fig. 1B). The first step is to determine the location of the 'foot of the continental slope' (FOS), defined as the point of maximum change in the gradient at its base. Measuring from this point, the outer limit is then established either as a distance of 60 nm from the FOS, or the distance to a point where the thickness of the sedimentary layer is at least 1% of the shortest distance from such point to the FOS. Establishing a sediment thickness requires that travel times in seismic records be converted to depths, using measured seismic wave velocities. The line connecting the points where sediment thickness is 1% of the distance back to the FOS is often called the Gardiner line (Fig. 1B).

Article 76 also imposes constraints on the maximum extent of the continental shelf (Fig. 1C): the outer limit shall not exceed 350 nm from the baselines of the coastal state or extend beyond 100 nm from the 2500 m isobath. A coastal state can use a combination of the above criteria to determine the area of its continental shelf. The outer limit of the continental shelf beyond 200 nm is delineated by connecting the derived points with straight lines not exceeding 60 nm in length.

The next step in the process is for a coastal state to gather and analyze the scientific data and then prepare and file a submission to the Commission on the Limits of the Continental Shelf (CLCS; www.un.org/Dept/los/clcs_new/commission_purpose.htm). The role of the CLCS is to review a state's submission in light of Article 76 criteria and make recommendations to the state to ensure its submission meets the criteria. The members of the CLCS are elected by states parties to the Convention and are to be experts in the fields of geology, geophysics, or hydrography. To assist coastal states, the CLCS produced a set of technical guidelines outlining the information to be submitted (United Nations 1999). Only the coastal state can establish the outer limits of its shelf and if it does so based on recommendations of the CLCS, they are final and binding (Article 76, Paragraph 8). It is important to note that the CLCS has no mandate to resolve disputes between states and that the actions of the CLCS are without prejudice to the delimitation of boundaries between coastal states. Disputes must be resolved by the states involved through negotiation or a dispute settlement process.

States have ten years from the date they became party to the Convention to make their submission to the CLCS, though by virtue of decisions taken at meetings of states parties to UNCLOS, this deadline can now be satisfied through the filing of preliminary information about an intended submission. Since states became party to the Convention at different times, they have different deadlines. Canada became a party to the Convention in December 2003, so its deadline was December 2013.

THE CANADIAN SITUATION

Canada is surrounded by three oceans (Fig. 2), and its shelves and margins reflect a variety of origins and forms. The Atlantic margin is a passive margin formed by the opening of the North Atlantic Ocean. Rifting and subsequent seafloor spreading progressed from south (Scotian margin) to north (Labrador margin). The Scotian Shelf is more than 700 km long and at some places over 200 km wide. The Grand Banks shelf has a width that extends to 450 km and the Labrador Shelf is as wide as 300 km in some places (Keen and Piper 1990).

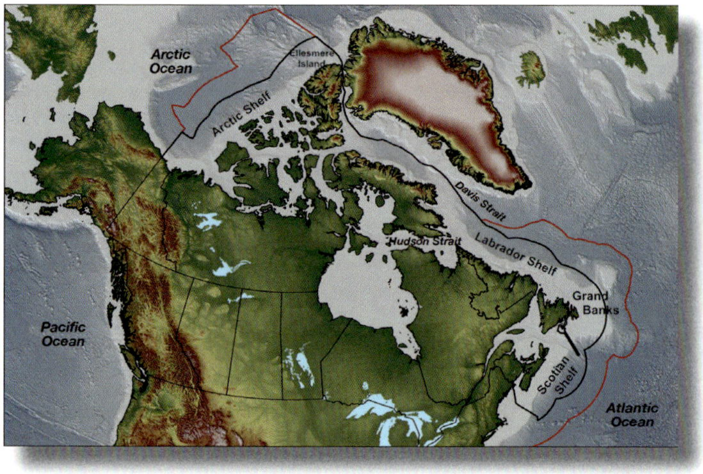

Figure 2. Canada's potential extended continental shelf based on a preliminary study in the mid-1990s. Black line denotes Canada's potential extended economic zone (EEZ) and the red line shows the preliminary outer limit of the extended shelf. The graphic is for illustrative purposes only.

The Canadian Arctic margin is poorly understood. Its western segment was formed during the opening of the Canada Basin, although the mechanism of formation of this basin is debated (Cochran et al. 2006). In the eastern Arctic, north of Ellesmere Island, the presence of the Alpha and Lomonosov ridges dominate the margin. The Arctic shelf varies in width from 65 to 180 km (Johnson et al. 1990).

The Canadian Pacific continental margin (Fig. 2) is an active subduction margin and occurs at the intersection of the North American, Pacific, Juan de Fuca, and Explorer tectonic plates (Hyndman and Rogers 2010). The margin has a narrow shelf, almost absent in places.

Over the years, scientists at BIO have acquired a significant amount of geoscientific and hydrographic data in Canada's offshore. These existing data sets were used in the mid-1990s to conduct a desktop study to determine a preliminary indication of Canada's extended continental shelves (Fig. 2). This analysis, applying the parameters and conditions set out in Article 76, demonstrated that Canada potentially has an extended continental shelf in both the Atlantic and Arctic oceans, which could be as large as the three Prairie Provinces. The narrow margin in the Pacific Ocean provided no clear prospects for an extended continental shelf (Macnab 1994). The desktop study did not include a full assessment of the resources in the extended continental shelf. However, it stated that some sedimentary basins on the Grand Banks extend beyond 200 nm offshore and are prospective for hydrocarbons. Information about resources in the Arctic regions beyond 200 nm was recognized as inadequate, but the outlook for gas hydrates in that area is promising (Macnab 1994).

THE CANADIAN PROGRAM

After Canada's ratification of UNCLOS in late 2003, work began to prepare a scientifically sound and defensible submission to the CLCS. Based on the analysis of existing data and recommendations of the aforementioned desktop study, survey programs were designed and focussed on the Atlantic and Arctic Oceans. Securing international recognition for the full extent of Canada's continental shelf was a priority for the Government of Canada, and as a result, the 2004 federal budget announced $69 million over ten years for the collection of bathymetric and seismic data. The 2008 budget announced an additional $40 million to cover increased data collection and logistics costs as well as legal costs for submission preparation.

Canada's Extended Continental Shelf (ECS) Program is the joint responsibility of Foreign Affairs and International Trade Canada (DFAIT); the Geological Survey of Canada (GSC), part of Natural Resources Canada; and the Canadian Hydrographic Service (CHS), part of Fisheries and Oceans Canada. DFAIT provided the legal expertise and advice, and is responsible for the overall preparation and presentation of the submission to the CLCS. The GSC and the CHS are responsible for the scientific and technical work necessary for the submission.

CANADA'S EXTENDED CONTINENTAL SHELF IN THE ATLANTIC

In offshore Eastern Canada, the acquisition of geologic and hydrographic data started in the mid-1960s with multi-parameter surveys, collecting bathymetric, seismic, gravity, and magnetic data (MacDougall 2014). The hydrocarbon exploration industry also collected over 1 million line-kilometres of seismic data in its search for resources in frontier sedimentary basins. A compilation of existing data showed that the focus of data collection had been on the shelf and that there were large information gaps in areas farther offshore (see Figs. 3 and 7). For example, little data existed for offshore Nova Scotia beyond 200 nm prior to the program (Fig. 3). Thus, the data were insufficient to define the outer limit of the continental shelf in that area using the 1% thickness-of-the-sedimentary-layer criterion (Fig. 1B).

The Scotian Margin Region and Slope Processes

The Scotian margin developed as a result of early Jurassic (~ 200 Ma or 200 million years ago) rifting and subsequent seafloor spreading between North America and North Africa. The margin includes a fairly narrow shelf, 125 to 225 km in width, and a steep narrow slope that extends from

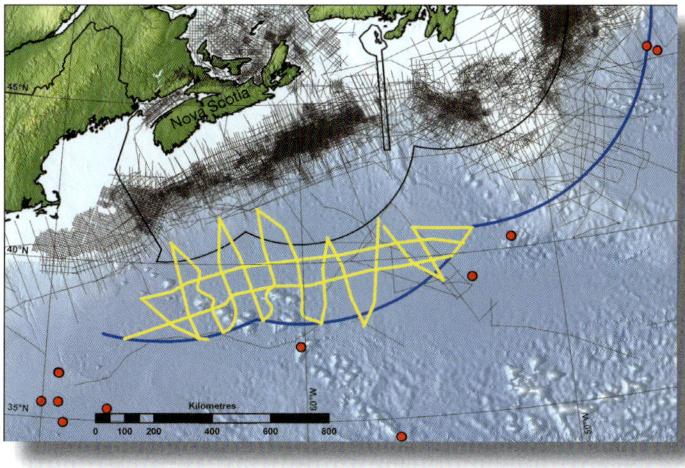

Figure 3. Existing industry seismic data on the Scotian margin (black lines) are mainly located on the shelf (light grey). In 2007, 6,900 km of multi-channel seismic data were acquired over the Sohm Abyssal Plain (yellow lines). Also shown are the 200 nm Exclusive Economic Zone limit (black), and 350 nm limit (blue), as well as the location of the Ocean Drilling Program (ODP) drill holes (black-ringed red circles).

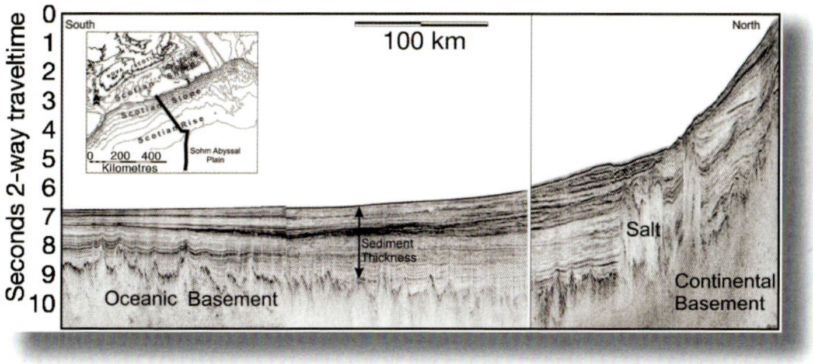

Figure 4. Example of a composite seismic line across the Scotian margin into the Sohm Abyssal Plain (see inset for location). This record clearly shows the large thickness of sediments, expressed as two-way travel times of reflected seismic waves, extending into the abyssal plain.

200 m to 4,000 m water depth into the Sohm Abyssal Plain. Underlying the slope region is the early Jurassic Scotian Basin, where the thickness of sediments in specific regions can exceed 16 km (Williams et al. 2014).

The Sohm Abyssal Plain (Fig. 3) generally has a thick sediment cover and estimates of thicknesses over 2 km were used in the desktop study (Macnab 1994). However, few seismic data exist in the area beyond 200 nm, and therefore 6,900 km of additional seismic data were collected in 2007 (Fig. 3). The survey was designed to cover the area from 200 nm offshore and the lines extended offshore 350 nm (the maximum possible outer limit). Seismic data show layers of sediment covering the abyssal plain (Fig. 4). With the seismic data and existing bathymetry profiles to define the FOS, preliminary 1% sediment thickness points have been identified. However, locating the FOS along this margin was complicated by salt diapirism within the sedimentary column (Shimeld 2004), and the

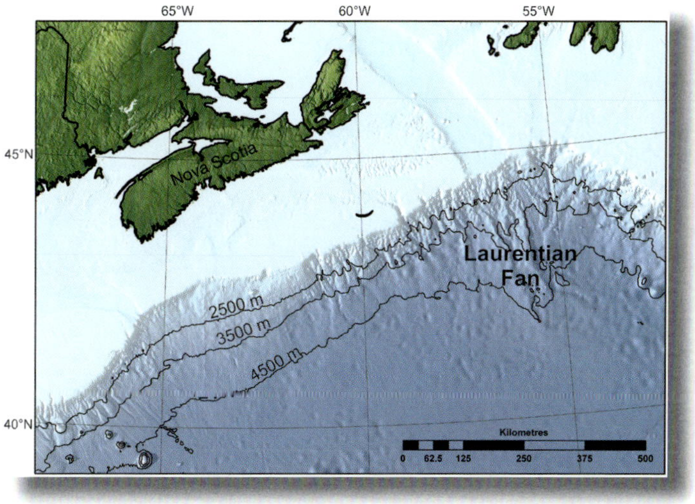

Figure 5. Bathymetry across the Scotian margin: contours clearly demonstrate the canyons as well as the Laurentian Fan.

presence of slope failures, and other downslope sedimentary processes.

Downslope processes, such as slope failures and erosion, along a continental margin can produce a complex lower slope. These processes are characteristic of slopes and not of rises. It is for that reason that the CLCS made a recent decision to consider slope processes as an integral part of the definition of the outer edge of the continental margin. This decision is an example of the evolving interpretation of Article 76, which benefits states that are still in the process of analyzing their data.

In areas of the Scotian margin, downslope processes clearly played a significant role in establishing its morphology (Lewis et al. 2014), and therefore are important for establishing FOS locations. The Scotian Slope has major submarine canyons (Fig. 5) that provide routes for sediment transport from the shelf and down the slope (Jenner et al. 2006). Outboard of the troughs and channels are sedimentary fans, the Laurentian Fan being the largest (Piper et al. 2007), extending the morphology of the slope offshore relative to the rest of the margin (Fig. 5). The slope along the Scotian margin was further modified by processes that cut into unconsolidated sediments and transported them to the lower slope and abyssal plain. For example, Mosher et al. (2010) studied a Plio-Pleistocene mass transport deposit from the central Scotian Slope that extends hundreds of kilometres from the shelf break of the margin to beneath the Sohm Abyssal Plain. Analyses show that the outer limit is located farther seaward than 200 nm, and that Canada will be able to define an extended continental shelf in this area.

Grand Banks Region

The Grand Banks, south and east of Newfoundland, constitute a broad platform, generally shallower than 100 m. This platform is underlain by Appalachian continental crust and its eastern parts extend beyond Canada's 200 nm limit (Fig. 2). The Grand Banks have a complex geological history that reflects their position between three spreading regimes. The southwestern edge of the Grand Banks is a transform margin associated with the rifting that separated Nova Scotia from Africa. The eastern Grand Banks margin formed as a result of rifting and early Cretaceous (~140 Ma) separation from the Iberian margin. The northern segment of the Grand Banks was formed as a result of the mid-Cretaceous (~100 Ma) separation of Europe from North America (Keen et al. 1990).

Much of the slope around the Grand Banks has canyons and gullies providing conduits for downslope transport of sediments. The southwestern Grand Banks slope shows evidence of mass transport processes moving sediment to the lower slope, rise and abyssal plain (Giles et al. 2010). Orphan Basin developed within the offshore extension of the Avalon zone (eastern part of the Appalachian continental crust) and is characterized by an extensive region of thinned continental crust. The basin floor largely consists of stacked mass transport deposits with interbedded turbidites (Tripsanas et al. 2008, Li et al. 2012), providing the sedimentary infill between the Grand Banks margin and Orphan Knoll (Fig. 6).

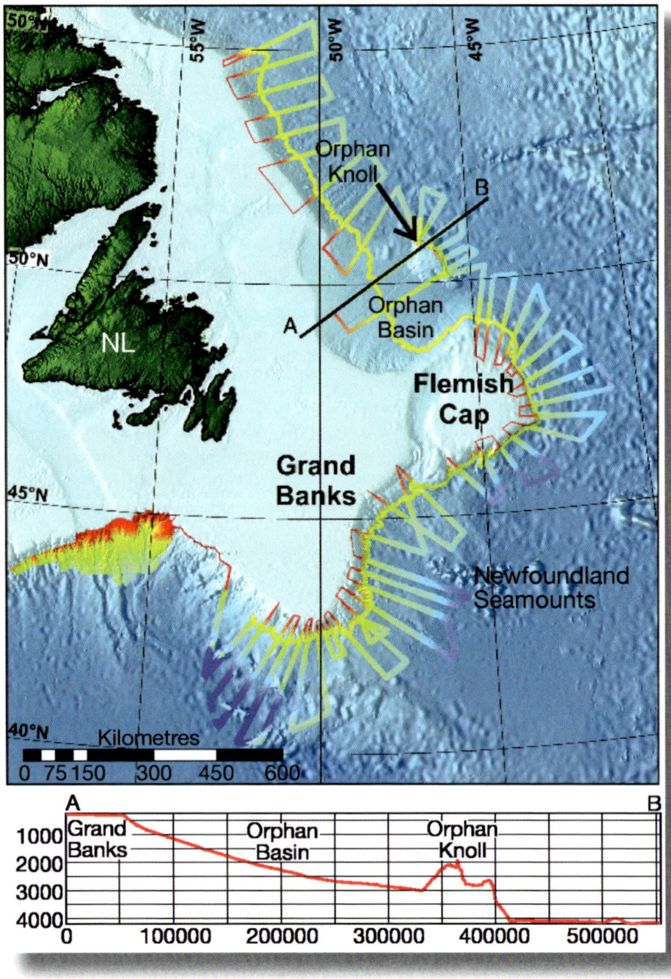

Figure 6. Location of the 2006 multibeam bathymetry profiles around the Grand Banks of Newfoundland. Together with existing bathymetry data in the area, these data provided locations for the 'foot of the slope'. The graph at bottom shows a bathymetric profile across Orphan Basin and Orphan Knoll, marked A and B on both map (upper) and graph (lower: x and y axes in m). The contour highlighted in yellow is the 2,500 m isobath.

For most of the Grand Banks margin, the most seaward outer constraints under Article 76 are based on the 'FOS+60 nm' and the '2,500 m isobath+100 nm' formulae. Therefore, around the Grand Banks a good definition of the FOS was important, as was the location of the 2,500 isobath. For this reason, a 2006 multibeam survey acquired bathymetry along profiles for a total of 18,500 line-km (Fig. 6).

Around the Grand Banks, there are several features that might complicate the determination of the outer limit, or offer an opportunity to further extend the limit (Fig. 6). Orphan Knoll is continental in origin, as was confirmed by drilling (Laughton et al. 1972). Orphan Basin links Orphan Knoll to the Grand Banks, and is underlain by thinned continental crust (Chian et al. 2001). Flemish Cap is a submarine knoll consisting of a central core of Hadrynian (neo-Proterozoic) rocks, associated with the Appalachian Avalon zone (King et al. 1985). The Newfoundland Seamounts are located east of the Grand Banks (Fig. 6). To consider each of these features part of the Grand Banks, it must be demonstrated that they fall inside the envelope of the FOS around the Grand Banks. The profile in Figure 6 shows an example of how this can be accomplished for Orphan Knoll: the bathymetric profile across Orphan Basin and Orphan Knoll clearly indicates that the deep ocean floor and the FOS, as defined under Article 76, are located on the seaward side of Orphan Knoll.

Labrador Sea Region

The Labrador Margin was created by the early Cretaceous rifting and subsequent break-up of the North Atlantic Precambrian craton (Keen et al. 1994). The exact timing of the onset of the seafloor spreading in this region is debated, highlighting the complication of the location and nature of the ocean-continent boundary. However, it is generally agreed that seafloor spreading occurred in the Paleocene to early Oligocene interval (ca. 65-30 Ma). The entire Labrador Sea seabed is covered with a thick sedimentary layer. From the shelf the thickness increases to 5 km or more near the Labrador continental margin, and generally decreases farther seaward to less than 2 km in the central part of the Labrador Sea.

Most of the Labrador margin's continental slope is incised by canyons, channels and gullies that coalesce downslope. These features run perpendicular to bathymetric contours over most of their lengths, but deviate towards the southeast as they reach the basin floor, following the change in direction of the slope gradient. At the northern limit of the Labrador Sea, Davis Strait and Hudson Strait (Fig. 2) provided a corridor for ice, water and sediment drainage from a significant portion of north-central and northeastern Canada. A result of high sediment input rates from these source areas directly to the ocean basin was the development of the Northwest Atlantic Mid-Ocean Channel (NAMOC), a meandering turbidite channel that runs down the axis of the Labrador Sea basin floor all the way south to the Sohm Abyssal Plain off Nova Scotia, a distance of over 3,000 km (Klaucke et al. 1998).

The initial analysis of the Labrador margin and possible locations of the FOS concluded that using the 'FOS+60 nm' option would define an outer limit of the continental shelf which is largely inside 200 nm (Macnab 1994). Thus, we reviewed existing seismic data to determine sediment thicknesses. The existing seismic data illustrated that several tracks crossed the entire Labrador Sea and both the Labrador and Greenland margins (Fig. 7; Hinz et al. 1979, Keen et al. 1994). Based on that review, it was decided to collect additional multi-channel seismic data (Fig. 7). In addition, significant evidence of downslope sedimentary processes was apparent along the Canadian side of the Labrador Sea margin, assisting in delimiting the FOS position. Denmark (on behalf of Greenland) was also in the process of defining the outer limit of its continental shelf in the Labrador Sea, for that purpose, they had acquired new multi-channel seismic data off the Greenland margin (Fig. 7). For several years, Canada collaborated with Denmark/Greenland in sharing and jointly analysing the seismic data in the Labrador Sea. This approach was beneficial to both countries: since the interpretation of the data from each side of the Labrador Sea is consistent and agrees, each country's submission is strengthened.

CANADA'S EXTENDED CONTINENTAL SHELF IN THE ARCTIC

The Arctic Ocean is one of the most understudied oceans in the world. It is unique with over 50% of its area consisting of shelf, generally shallower

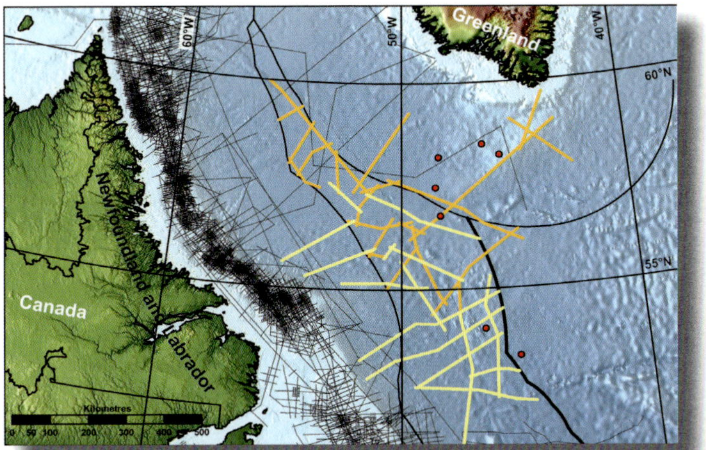

Figure 7. Existing seismic data across the Labrador margin (thin black lines) and the newly acquired multi-channel seismic data (yellow lines). Also shown are the seismic data acquired by the Danish Geological Survey (orange lines), and the 200 nm limits from Canada and Greenland (black lines), as well as the 350 nm limit from Canada (outer thick black line). The black-ringed red circles denote the location of the ODP drilling sites.

than 200 m (Jakobsson et al. 2003). The deeper seafloor is divided into two major basins: the Eurasian Basin and the Amerasian Basin separated by the Lomonosov Ridge (Fig. 8). A second range, the Alpha-Mendeleev ridge, subdivides the Amerasian Basin. These submarine features were unknown until the middle of the 20th century (Weber and Roots 1990). The Lomonosov Ridge is generally viewed as a continental sliver that stretches across the Arctic Ocean (Cochran et al. 2006). In contrast, the origin and structure of the Alpha-Mendeleev Ridge is still debated (Dove et al. 2010). The Eurasian Basin resulted from seafloor spreading about the Gakkel Ridge. The evolution of the Amerasian Basin and its sub-basin, the Canada Basin, is ambiguous, mainly as a result of complicated geology and insufficient data.

For the purpose of defining the outer limits of Canada's continental shelf, it was necessary to demonstrate that the Lomonosov and Alpha ridges are natural prolongations of its land territory, as defined in Article 76. Article 76 specifically excludes in the definition of a continental margin "*... the deep ocean floor with its oceanic ridges ...*" (paragraph 3). However, it includes "*... submarine elevations that are natural components of the continental margins, such as its plateaux, rises, caps, banks and spurs ...*" (paragraph 6). Submarine elevations that are not natural components of the continental margin are subject to a 350 nm cut-off; if they are a natural component, the continental shelf can extend beyond 350 nm, but shall not exceed 100 nm from the 2,500 m isobath. These 'ridge provisions' have become one of the most contentious and difficult aspects of applying Article 76. Their interpretation has evolved and the CLCS has recently summarized its views: "*... in cases where seafloor highs are enclosed by the FOS envelope, such highs are automatically regarded as an integral part of that continental margin ...*"

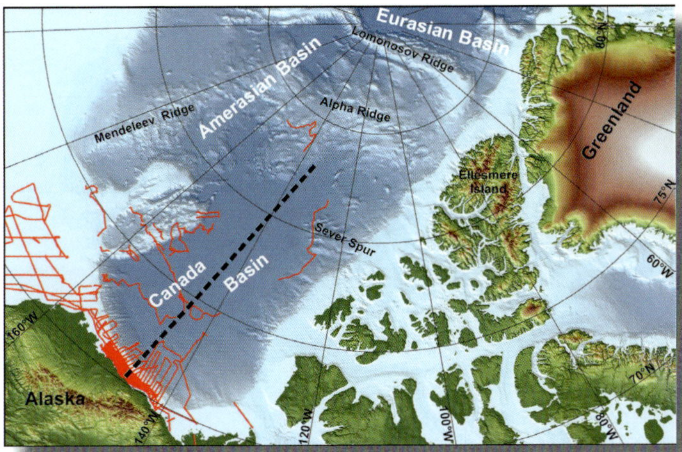

Figure 8. General bathymetry of the Arctic Ocean (based on the International Bathymetric Chart of the Arctic Ocean, Jakobsson et al. 2003). Also shown are the main structural features as well as seismic data (red lines) in and around the Canada Basin which were collected prior to Canada's ECS (extended continental shelf) surveys. The dashed black line gives the approximate location of the seismic profile shown in Figure 12.

A review of existing scientific data in the Arctic Ocean concluded that insufficient data existed to determine the outer limits of the continental shelf and, therefore, the acquisition of new data was a key component of the Canadian UNCLOS program. The acquisition of scientific data in that region is logistically and technologically challenging due to the remoteness of the area, the harsh environment, the unpredictable weather and ice conditions, and short field seasons. The survey program in Arctic Canada was designed with two main components. In the western arctic, in the Canada Basin, the sediment thickness was the key factor and to determine this, seismic surveys were required. Since ice conditions in the western arctic generally allow the use of heavy icebreakers to collect scientific data (Hutchinson et al. 2009), a data collection program was designed utilizing these vessels. In the eastern arctic where heavy ice conditions generally occur, especially in the region north of Ellesmere Island, icebreaker use is often difficult if not impossible (MacDougall et al. 2008). As a consequence, offshore ice camps were constructed in this region to use as base camps from which data were collected using helicopters, fixed-wing aircraft, and autonomous underwater vehicles (AUVs).

International Collaboration

The five Arctic Ocean coastal states (Canada, Russia, Norway, Denmark, and United States) are all in the process of defining their extended continental shelves, although they are at different stages. Since data acquisition in the Arctic is a challenging and expensive undertaking, Canada has explored and implemented international partnerships to collect data of mutual benefit. This cooperation mitigates the risks, reduces costs and environmental impacts while common data interpretation by neighbouring countries enhances the probability of a successful submission.

Since 2006, Canada conducted seven joint surveys, and undertook joint interpretation and publication of results with Denmark. With the United States, Canada has conducted four joint surveys in the western arctic (2008-11) using the Canadian icebreaker CCGS *Louis S. St-Laurent* and the United States icebreaker USCGC *Healy*. Since 2007, annual meetings have taken place between Canadian, Danish, and Russian officials to discuss the ongoing programs and results; these meetings also included officials from the United States (from 2009) and Norway (2010).

Canada's Eastern Arctic Program and Autonomous Underwater Vehicles

From the Canadian perspective, the eastern arctic continental margin is dominated by the Lomonosov and Alpha ridges (Fig. 8). A first step in determining the outer limits of the continental shelf in this region was to demonstrate that these features are natural prolongations of the continent. This determination was of interest to both Canada and Denmark (Greenland) for the Lomonosov Ridge, whereas Alpha Ridge was more important to Canada. However, bathymetry data showed a trough north of Ellesmere Island, seemingly separating the ridges from the mainland. To demonstrate the prolongation, it was necessary to image the crustal structure below the seafloor and to measure the crustal seismic velocities of the ridges in order to demonstrate their similarity to those on the adjacent continent.

The 2006 LOmonosov RIdge Test of Appurtenance (LORITA) project was a joint undertaking between Canada and Denmark to conduct seismic and bathymetric surveys on the Lomonosov Ridge. The Canadian Forces Station Alert (Fig. 9), northern Ellesmere Island, was used as the main base and a small ice camp was established about 100 km offshore. Despite losing 65-70% of the planned survey days to bad weather, the primary objective of collecting seismic refraction data was achieved along a 440 km-long north-south profile and a 110 km-long profile along the bathymetric trough (Fig. 9). The data were interpreted jointly with Denmark and the conclusion reached that there is continuity of the continental crust from the coast across the trough and onto the Lomonosov Ridge. The velocity structure in the trough suggests that no oceanic crust occurs there (Jackson et al. 2010). Additionally, much of the trough remains shallower than 2,500 m water depth. In the spring of 2008, a similar project named Alpha Ridge Test of Appurtenance (ARTA) was undertaken on Alpha Ridge, north of Ellesmere Island. For

Figure 9. Location of the two seismic refraction experiments (LORITA and ARTA) to investigate the deeper structures of the Alpha and Lomonosov Ridges. The green circles denote the approximate location of the ice camps and the green square denotes the ice camp which had to be evacuated in 2009. The black line denotes the Greenland-Canada boundary and the estimated position of the Canadian ECS in the Arctic Ocean.

this project, a large ice camp was constructed near the mouth of Nansen Sound as well as a small camp about 100 km farther offshore (Fig. 9). The seismic refraction experiment consisted of a 350 km-long line perpendicular to the margin and a 175-km-long cross line on the ridge (Funck et al. 2011). In 2009, a joint project with Denmark collected bathymetric data to measure the shape of the seafloor in the area between the Alpha and Lomonosov Ridges.

The three surveys in 2006, 2007, and 2009 were successful and collected a significant amount of new data. However, the construction of large ice camps in remote areas (Fig. 10A), which included flattening the area for runways to enable supply aircraft to land, was time-consuming and expensive. Moreover, unpredictable weather and ice conditions became a major concern. Open leads generated ice fog, preventing helicopters from flying, and ice floes broke up, leading to dangerous situations, once requiring an emergency evacuation of the small offshore camp in 2009 (Fig. 9). Moving farther offshore, as was planned for the last phase of the program, was deemed very risky and alternatives were investigated. In 2008, a joint project was initiated with Defence Research and Development Canada (DRDC) to use autonomous underwater vehicles (AUVs) to go under, rather than on, or through the ice to collect the requisite data.

The AUV survey started nearshore at the main camp, and then moved to a remote offshore camp (Fig. 10B) The AUVs were constructed by Vancouver-based International Submarine Engineering (ISE) Ltd. The vehicles are about 7 m long, battery-powered, carry a high resolution multibeam bathymetry system, and can dive to water depths of up to 5,000 m (Fig. 10C). After testing in ice conditions in 2009, the AUVs were deployed in April 2010 from a main ice camp near Borden Island (Fig. 10). A typical mission covered up to 400 km on one battery charge and took about 3 days to complete, during which time there was no communication with the AUV. The first deployments of the AUV were successful (Fig. 10C). In several deployments, it travelled over 1,000 km at water depths of over 3,300 m under the ice during an operating period of 10 days. During the missions, it completed about 500 km of bathymetric measurements in key areas. It also successfully homed in to the remote offshore ice camp, which was located on an ice floe that had drifted away from its original position by about 20 km over a 3-day period. Collectively these achievements represent a world record for under-ice AUV operations in the Arctic.

After evaluating the 2010 survey, however, it was decided that continuing with ice camps, which are more than 200 km offshore, was too dangerous. Therefore, the AUV program was modified and they were deployed from the icebreaker CCGS *Louis S. St-Laurent*. During the 2011 survey, the deployment was successful, and about 110 km of multibeam bathymetry was acquired in the Sever Spur region (Fig. 8), an area with heavy ice coverage (Mosher 2012).

Canada's Western Arctic Program

Prior to 2006, there existed only a few seismic lines crossing the Canada Basin (Fig. 8), constituting a 'serious knowledge gap' in producing a sediment thickness map of the Arctic (Jackson et al. 1990). Using the sparse data and existing gravity data, it was inferred that the Canada Basin

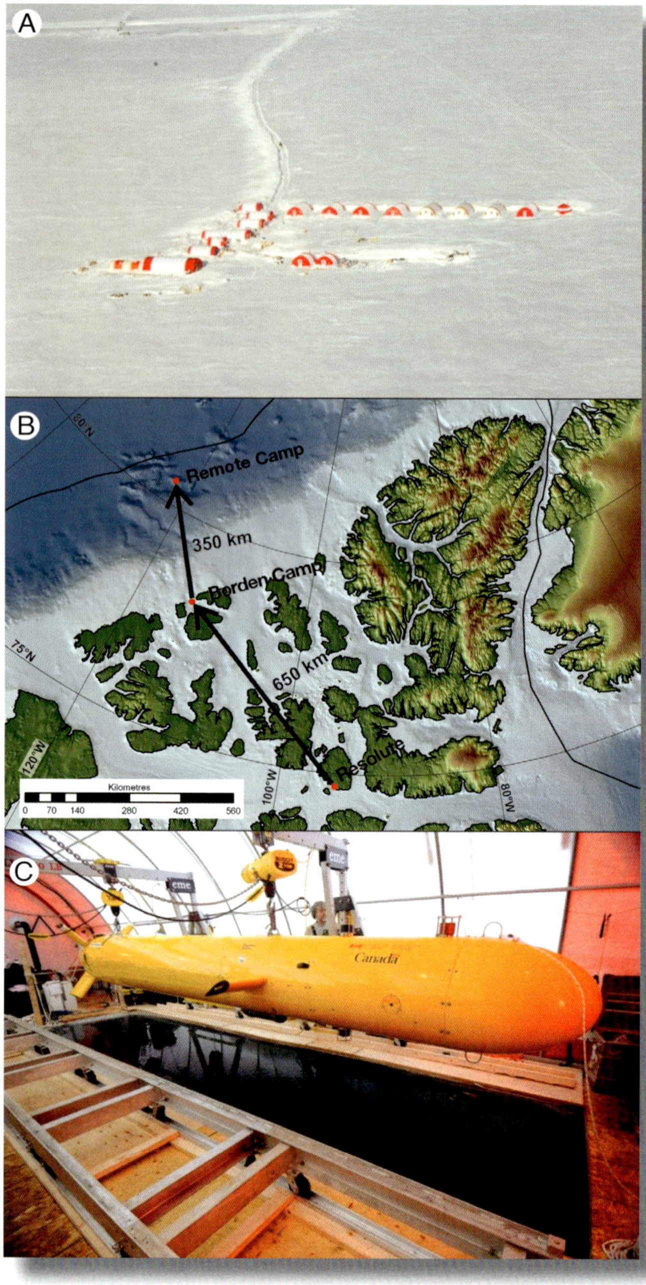

Figure 10. The autonomous underwater vehicle (AUV) survey. (A) The main Borden ice camp with 17 tents and a population of over 40 people. Also shown at the upper left is the runway (photo: J. Lang, DRDC). (B) Location of the main Borden ice camp and the offshore remote ice camp. All equipment was brought to Resolute, Cornwallis Island, and then flown to the two camps. (C) The AUV at the main Borden ice camp prior to being sent out on a mission. Also shown is the large hole that was created by removing over 30,000 kg of ice (photo: J. Lang, DRDC).

was covered by a thick sedimentary layer. However, the data density was inadequate to determine the 1% points. It was therefore decided to collect additional seismic data in the western Canadian arctic.

Collection of seismic data in the western Arctic was easier said than done, given prevailing difficult ice conditions. The potentially heavy ice conditions required that surveying be done with an icebreaker, but the noise emitted by its powerful engines can interfere with the seismic sound source. Moreover, the standard equipment for seismic data collection needs to be strengthened due to the presence of fragments of ice behind the icebreaker, which may interfere with the towing of the seismic sound sources and receiver. A test survey in 2006, on board the CCGS *Louis S. St-Laurent,* clearly demonstrated the difficulties and led to the development of a modified seismic system comprising a 1,150 cubic inch (18.8 litre) airgun array and a 16-channel digital hydrophone streamer (Mosher et al. 2009). To prevent interference of the source array with ice, it was towed at 11.5 m depth, below the keel depth of most sea ice. The hydrophone streamer (receiver) was towed from the rear of the source array, also to keep it deep beneath the ice. The length of the streamer (100 m) was short for operating in deep water, providing little move-out (i.e., reception of wide-angle reflections) for velocity analysis. Instead, velocity information was derived from wide-angle reflection and refraction data received on expendable sonobuoys, deployed at regular intervals.

In September 2007, a six-week seismic and bathymetric survey was conducted on board the CCGS *Louis S. St-Laurent* in the southern part of Canada Basin (Fig. 11). Ice conditions varied and heavier ice was generally encountered farther north and east, off the Canadian Archipelago. Upon reviewing the results and considering that future surveys would move farther north into heavier ice conditions, it was concluded that two icebreakers would be required in these regions. In 2008, the first joint survey with the United States was organized using both the CCGS *Louis S. St-Laurent* and the USCGC *Healy*. In areas where seismic data were important, the USCGC *Healy* broke ice and the CCGS *Louis S. St-Laurent* followed with its seismic system; in areas where the shape of the seafloor was determined to be important, the Canadian vessel broke ice and the American vessel followed with its high-resolution multibeam

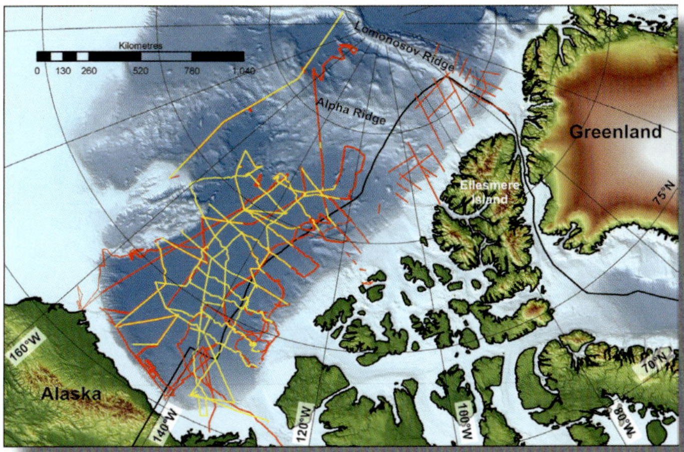

Figure 11. Overview of seismic (yellow) and key bathymetry (red) data collected over the period 2007-11 in the Canada Basin. A total of over 15,000 km of seismic and over 18,000 km of single-beam bathymetry data tripled data holdings in the Arctic Ocean.

bathymetry system. The advantage of this configuration was that since the following icebreaker did not have to break heavy ice, the quality of the data collected was significantly improved.

Five major surveys were completed in the western arctic (four joint with the United States) and they covered most of the area in which data were needed for establishing limits to the extended continental shelf (ECS) (Fig. 11). The survey activities were successfully completed in both the eastern and western arctic in 2011 with seismic data collected as far north as 88.23 degrees north latitude.

As a result of these surveys, the seismic data coverage in the western arctic has more than tripled. Over 15,000 km of high quality seismic data were collected, together with 18,000 km of multibeam bathymetry data and 38,000 km of single beam bathymetry data. A total of 171 sonobuoy deployments were made across the entire Canada Basin between Alaska and the Alpha Ridge to collect information about the velocity structure of the sediments to be used for conversion of seismic wave travel times to true depths and sediment thicknesses.

The analysis of these new data will significantly improve our knowledge of the region. As mentioned before, very little was known about the sediment thickness in the Canada Basin before the program started. An example of the new data, a 1,200 km seismic profile from the Alaskan margin towards the Alpha Ridge, is shown in Figure 12. The profile shows flat-lying sediments with thicknesses generally decreasing northward, from about 4.5 s (two-way travel time) and pinching out against the topographic highs associated with the Alpha Ridge (Shimeld et al. 2010, Mosher et al. 2011). In the context of defining the outer limits of Canada's continental shelf, the main finding is that the Canada Basin is generally covered by sediments of more than 4 km thickness, thinning to the north and to the west. Sedimentary processes also prove to be a significant element for defining FOS positions along the Canadian Archipelago (Mosher et al. 2012). These data support Canada's definition of a significant extended continental shelf in this region.

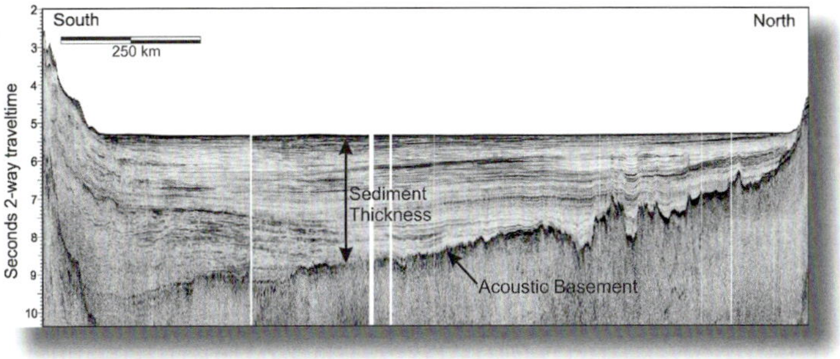

Figure 12. Example of a composite seismic record across the Canada Basin. The record covers about 1,200 km from the Alaskan margin in the south to Alpha Ridge in the north (for location, see dashed black line in Fig. 8).

NEXT STEPS

The main data collection phase in the Atlantic is complete and by the end of 2012 the data had been analysed to determine locations of the foot of the slope (FOS) and outer limits of the continental shelf. The program was on schedule to finalize the submission to CLCS by the deadline of December 2013. At the CLCS, the submission will be placed in the queue for review by the Commission. However, at the present pace of consideration it may be many years before it is reviewed and recommendations provided. The Arctic data are presently being analysed and an assessment is ongoing to determine whether more data are required to define the full extent of Canada's extended continental shelf.

CONCLUSIONS

By the end of 2012, Canada's Extended Continental Shelf Program had acquired all the planned scientific data in the Atlantic Ocean. The analysis of data was nearing completion and a submission was being prepared for the UN Commission on the Limits of the Continental Shelf.

The Arctic Canada component had proven challenging. The program successfully completed the main data acquisition phase, despite many risks and delays due to poor weather and significant ice conditions. The high quality of the Arctic Ocean data surpassed the initial hopes of the program. Acquiring these data necessitated several innovations, such as the development of a seismic system that worked in heavy ice conditions, and the use of automated underwater vehicles. Effective and continuing cooperation between Arctic Ocean coastal states was a key contributor to this achievement. In addition to providing strong support for Canada's submission to the Commission, the wealth of new data will, no doubt, lead to a better understanding of the origin and tectonic evolution of the Arctic Ocean.

The interaction between geoscience, hydrography, and technical innovation, all present at BIO, has proven to be instrumental in the success of this program. Using existing knowledge and data, a cost-effective program for the acquisition and analysis of needed new data was designed and implemented. As a result, Canada was close to a position to define outer limits of its extended continental shelf with substantiating information for a submission to the Commission by its deadline of December 2013 for the Atlantic and thereafter for the Arctic.

ACKNOWLEDGEMENTS

This program has involved many organizations and dedicated staff to collect and analyse the scientific data. We thank those who were involved in the earlier phases of the program: Ron Macnab, Richard Haworth, Dick MacDougall, and Julian Goodyear. We also thank all those who did the logistics for the ice camps (Polar Continental Shelf Program, Environment Canada, Canadian Ice Service, all the pilots and technical staff), those who were involved in the shipborne operations (Canadian Coast Guard, the Commanding Officers and crews of the CCGS *Louis S. St-Laurent*, the CCGS *Hudson*, and the USCGC *Healy*), and our staff and contractors who went out to ice camps and on board ships under rather difficult and sometimes dangerous situations to collect the data. We would also like to acknowledge our partners in the scientific work in Canada, the United States, and Denmark.

REFERENCES

Chian, D., I.D. Reid, and H.R. Jackson. 2001. Crustal structure beneath Orphan Basin and implications for non-volcanic continental rifting. Journal of Geophysical Research 106: 10,923-10,940.

Cochran, J.R., M.H. Edwards, and B.J. Coakley. 2006. Morphology and structure of the Lomonosov Ridge, Arctic Ocean. Geochemistry, Geophysics, Geosystems 7: 1-26.

Dove, D., B. Coakley, J. Hopper, Y. Kristoffersen, and the HLY0503 geophysics team. 2010. Bathymetry controlled source seismic and gravity observations of the Mendeleev ridge; implications for ridge structure, origin, and regional tectonics. Geophysical Journal International 183: 481-502.

Funck, T, H.R. Jackson, and J. Shimeld. 2011. The crustal structure of the Alpha Ridge at the transition to the Canadian Polar Margin. Journal of Geophysical Research 116: B12101. doi:10.1029/2011JB008411.

Giles, M.K., D.C. Mosher, D.J.W. Piper, and G.D. Wach. 2010. Mass transport deposits on the southwestern Newfoundland Slope. Pages 657-666 *in* Submarine Mass Movements and Their Consequences IV: Advances in Natural and Technological Hazards Research, Volume 28 (D.C. Mosher, C. Shipp, L. Moscardelli, J. Chaytor, C. Baxter, H. Lee, and R. Urgeles, Eds.). Springer Publishing, Dordrecht, The Netherlands.

Hinz, K., H.-U. Schluter, A.C. Grant, S.P. Srivastava, D. Umpleby, and J. Woodside. 1979. Geophysical transects of the Labrador Sea: Labrador to southwest Greenland. Tectonophysics 59: 151-183.

Hutchinson, D.R., H.R. Jackson, J.W. Shimeld, C.B. Chapman, J.R. Childs, T. Funck, and R.W. Rowland. 2009. Acquiring marine data in the Canada Basin, Arctic Ocean: EOS Transactions of the American Geophysical Union 90: 197-198.

Hyndman, R.D. and G.C. Rogers. 2010. Great earthquakes on Canada's west coast: a review. Canadian Journal of Earth Sciences 47: 801-820.

Jackson, H.R., D.A. Forsyth, J.K. Hall, and A. Overton. 1990. Seismic reflection and refraction. Pages 153-170 *in* The Arctic Region (A. Grantz, L. Johnson, and J.F. Sweeney, Eds.). The Geology of North America, Volume L. Geological Society of America, Boulder, CO.

Jackson, H.R., T. Dahl-Jensen, and the LORITA working group. 2010. Sedimentary and crustal structure from the Ellesmere Island and Greenland continental shelves onto the Lomonosov Ridge, Arctic Ocean. Geophysical Journal International 182: 11-35.

Jakobsson, M., A. Grantz, Y. Kristoffersen, and R. Macnab. 2003. Physiographic provinces of the Arctic Ocean seafloor. Geological Society of America Bulletin 115: 1,443-1,455.

Jenner, K.A., D.J.W. Piper, D.C. Campbell, and D.C. Mosher. 2006. Lithofacies and origin of late Quaternary mass transport deposits in submarine canyons, central Scotian Slope, Canada. Sedimentology 53: 1-20.

Johnson, G.L., A. Grantz, and J.R. Weber. 1990. Bathymetry and physiography. Pages 63-78 *in* The Arctic Region (A. Grantz, L. Johnson, and J.F. Sweeney, Eds.). The Geology of North America, Volume L. Geological Society of America, Boulder, CO.

Keen, M.J. and D.J.W. Piper. 1990. Geological and historical perspective. Pages 5-30 *in* Geology of the Continental Margin of Eastern Canada (M.J. Keen, and G.L. Williams, Eds.). Geology of Canada, No. 2. Geological Survey of Canada, Ottawa, ON.

Keen, C.E., B.D. Loncaravic, I. Reid, J. Woodside, R.T. Haworth, and H.Williams. 1990. Tectonic and geophysical overview. Pages 31-85 *in* Geology of the Continental Margin of Eastern Canada (M.J. Keen and G.L. Williams, Eds.). Geology of Canada, No. 2. Geological Survey of Canada, Ottawa, ON.

Keen, C.E., P. Potter, and S.P. Srivastava. 1994. Deep seismic reflection data across the conjugate margins of the Labrador Sea. Canadian Journal of Earth Sciences 31: 192-205.

King, L.H., G.B. Fader, W.H. Poole, and R.K. Wanless. 1985. Geological setting and age of the Flemish Cap granodiorite, east of the Grand Banks of Newfoundland. Canadian Journal of Earth Sciences 22: 1,286-1,298.

Klaucke, I., R. Hesse, and W.B.F. Ryan. 1998. Morphology and structure of a distal submarine trunk channel; the Northwest Atlantic Mid-Ocean Channel between 53°N and 44°30'N. Geological Society of America Bulletin 110: 22-34.

Laughton, A.S., and 20 others. 1972. Site 111. Pages 33-79 *in* Initial Reports of the Deep Sea Drilling Project, Volume XII (T.A. Davies, Ed.). US Government Printing Office, Washington, DC.

Lewis, C.F.M., S.M. Blasco, D.J.W. Piper, and G.V. Sonnichsen 2014. Seabed geohazard knowledge for safe hydrocarbon development. Pages 383-394 *in* Voyage of Discovery: Fifty Years of Marine Research at Canada's Bedford Institute of Oceanography (D.N. Nettleship, D.C. Gordon, C.F.M. Lewis, and M.P. Latremouille, Eds.). Bedford Institute of Oceanography-Oceans Association, Dartmouth, NS.

Li, G., D.C. Campbell, D.C. Mosher, and D.J.W. Piper. 2012. Comparison of Quaternary glaciogenic debris flows with blocky mass-transport deposits in Orphan Basin, offshore eastern Canada. Pages 723-734 *in* Submarine Mass Movements and Their Consequences V, Advances in Natural and Technological Hazards Research, Volume 31 (Y. Yamada, K. Kawamura, K. Ikehara, Y. Ogawa, R. Urgeles, D. Mosher, J. Chaytor, and M. Strasser, Eds.). Springer Publishing, Dordrecht, The Netherlands.

MacDougall, J.R. 2014. Hydrography: a foundation for multidisciplinary ocean science at the Bedford Institute of Oceanography, 1962-2012. Pages 169-180 *in* Voyage of Discovery: Fifty Years of Marine Research at Canada's Bedford Institute of Oceanography (D.N. Nettleship, D.C. Gordon, C.F.M. Lewis, and M.P. Latremouille, Eds.). Bedford Institute of Oceanography-Oceans Association, Dartmouth, NS.

MacDougall, J.R., J. Verhoef, W. Sanford, and C. Marcussen. 2008. Challenges of collecting data for Article 76 in ice-covered waters of the Canadian Arctic. 5th ABLOS (Advisory Board on the Law of the Sea) Conference 'Difficulties in Implementing the Provisions of UNCLOS', Monaco. www.gmat.unsw.edu.au/ablos/ABLOS08Folder/Session4-Paper1- Macdougall.

Macnab, R. (Ed.). 1994. Canada and Article 76 of the Law of the Sea, defining the limits of Canadian resource jurisdiction beyond 200 nautical miles in the Atlantic and Arctic Oceans. Geological Survey of Canada, Open File 3209, Ottawa, ON.

Macnab, R. and R. Haworth. 2001. Earth science and the Law of the Sea: key to Canada's offshore energy and mineral resources beyond 200 nautical miles. Geoscience Canada 28: 79-86.

Mosher, D.C. (Ed). 2012. 2011 Canadian high arctic seismic expedition: CCGS *Louis S. St-Laurent* expedition report. Geological Survey of Canada, Open File 7053, Ottawa, ON. doi:10.4095/290241

Mosher, D.C., J.W. Shimeld, and D.R. Hutchinson. 2009. 2009 Canada Basin seismic reflection and refraction survey, western Arctic Ocean: CCGS *Louis S. St-Laurent* expedition report. Geological Survey of Canada, Open File 6343, Ottawa, ON. doi: 10.4095/248208

Mosher, D.C., Z. Xu, and J. Shimeld. 2010. The Pliocene Shelburne mass-movement and consequent tsunami, western Scotian Slope. Pages 765-776 *in* Submarine Mass Movements and Their Consequences IV, Advances in Natural and Technological Hazards Research, Volume 28 (D.C. Mosher, C. Shipp, L. Moscardelli, J. Chaytor, C. Baxter, H. Lee, and R. Urgeles, Eds.). Springer Publishing, Dordrecht, The Netherlands.

Mosher, D.C., J. Shimeld, R. Jackson, D. Hutchinson, C.B. Chapman, D. Chian, J. Childs, L. Mayer, B. Edwards, and J. Verhoef. 2011. Sedimentation in Canada Basin. Geological Survey of Canada, Open File 6759, Ottawa, ON.

Mosher, D.C., J.W. Shimeld, D. Hutchinson, N. Lebedeva-Ivanova, and C.B. Chapman. 2012. Submarine landslides in arctic sedimentation: Canada Basin. Pages 147-158 *in* Submarine Mass Movements and Their Consequences V, Advances in Natural and Technological Hazards Research, Volume 31 (Y. Yamada, K. Kawamura, K. Ikehara, Y. Ogawa, R. Urgeles, D. Mosher, J. Chaytor, and M. Strasser, Eds.). Springer Publishing, Dordrecht, The Netherlands.

Piper, D.J.W., J. Shaw, and K.I. Skene. 2007. Stratigraphic and sedimentological evidence for late Wisconsinan sub-glacial outburst floods to Laurentian Fan. Palaeogeography, Palaeoclimatology, Palaeoecology 247: 101-119.

Shimeld, J. 2004. A comparison of salt tectonic subprovinces beneath the Scotian Slope and Laurentian Fan. Pages 502-532 *in* Salt Sediment Interactions and Hydrocarbon Prospectivity: Concepts, Applications, and Case Studies for the 21st Century, 24th Annual Bob F. Perkins Research Conference Proceedings Volume 24 (P.J. Post, D.L. Olson, K.T. Lyons, S.L. Palmes, P.F. Harrison, and N. Rosen, Eds.). Gulf Coast Section of the Society of Economic Paleontologists and Mineralogists, Houston, TX. doi:10.572/gcs.04.24.0502.

Shimeld, J.W., D. Chian, H.R. Jackson, D. Hutchinson, D.C. Mosher, J.A. Wade, and C.B. Chapman. 2010. Evidence for an important tectonographic seismic marker across Canada Basin and southern Alpha Ridge of the Arctic Ocean. Abstract T31A-2127, American Geophysical Union Fall Meeting, San Francisco, CA.

Sinclair, M.M. and R.N. O'Boyle. 2014. The Gulf of Maine boundary dispute: the role of the Bedford Institute of Oceanography. Pages 397-405 *in* Voyage of Discovery: Fifty Years of Marine Research at Canada's Bedford Institute of Oceanography (D.N. Nettleship, D.C. Gordon, C.F.M. Lewis, and M.P. Latremouille, Eds.). Bedford Institute of Oceanography-Oceans Association, Dartmouth, NS.

Tripsanas, E.K., D.J.W. Piper, and D.C. Campbell. 2008. Evolution and depositional structure of earthquake-induced mass movements and gravity flows, southwest Orphan Basin, Labrador Sea. Marine and Petroleum Geology 25: 645-662.

United Nations. 1982. The Law of the Sea – official text of the United Nations Convention on the Law of the Sea of 10 December 1982. United Nations, New York, NY.

United Nations. 1999. Scientific and technical guidelines of the Commission on the Limits of the Continental Shelf: Document CLCS/11. United Nations, New York, NY.

Weber, J.R. and E.F. Roots. 1990. Historical background: exploration, concepts, and observations. Pages 5-36 *in* The Arctic Region (A. Grantz, L. Johnson, and J.F. Sweeney, Eds.). The Geology of North America, Volume L. Geological Society of America, Boulder, CO.

Williams, G.L., R.A. Fensome, and S.A. Dehler. 2014. Rocks of the deep: the subsurface geology of offshore Eastern Canada. Pages 215-223 *in* Voyage of Discovery: Fifty Years of Marine Research at Canada's Bedford Institute of Oceanography (D.N. Nettleship, D.C. Gordon, C.F.M. Lewis, and M.P. Latremouille, Eds.). Bedford Institute of Oceanography-Oceans Association, Dartmouth, NS.

The BIO Experience
EPILOGUE

The Bedford Institute of Oceanography campus in 2012

THE BIO EXPERIENCE

EPILOGUE

BEDFORD INSTITUTE OF OCEANOGRAPHY

Past, Present, Future

Editorial Board

Canada borders three oceans and has the longest marine coastline of any country in the world. About 30% of its territory currently lies beneath the sea and this will likely increase as Canada extends its seabed territory under the United Nations Convention on the Law of the Sea (UNCLOS). The oceans matter for all Canadians and are an integral part of our national fabric. A strong marine science capacity is vital for sustaining Canada as a modern nation and responsible global citizen. Canada's oceans support human health, societal well-being, and the creation of wealth.

In establishing the Bedford Institute of Oceanography (BIO) in 1962, the federal government showed considerable foresight and provided an excellent opportunity for marine scientists to conduct oceanographic research for the betterment of all Canadians and humankind. Over the first 25 years, BIO developed into one of the world's major oceanographic research institutes with an international reputation as a centre of excellence in all fields of marine science. As shown in the preceding 48 papers that illustrate a representative collection of BIO's research accomplishments over the past fifty years, the Institute has fulfilled the vision and expectations of its founders and constituent federal government departments. Today, these departments are Fisheries and Oceans Canada, Natural Resources Canada, Environment Canada, and Department of National Defence. Collectively, the diverse contributions in this book document many of the scientific discoveries and technological developments that have increased our understanding of the structure and dynamics of the oceans, their shores, seabeds and subsurface geology, marine ecosystems, and renewable and non-renewable resources. BIO research has produced important and valuable long-term scientific, economic, and social dividends. This Epilogue briefly summarizes the general accomplishments and present status of BIO, and offers some perspective on the future.

ACCOMPLISHMENTS

The core of BIO research has comprised a wide variety of fundamental programs for the provision of advice on the 'health' of eastern and northern Canadian marine waters and seabeds, support sustainable resource management, and address the policy needs of Canada and the global community. These investigations have addressed the structure and function of the oceans and the seafloors beneath, through the basic disciplines of physics, chemistry, geoscience, and biology. Most programs have been multi-year, involved extensive fieldwork in all Canadian marine and some freshwater regions, and have been carried out in a multidisciplinary manner, often involving scientists from leading institutions and universities across Canada and throughout the world. Together, these programs increased Canada's fundamental understanding of the oceans and provided the essential foundation for addressing applied marine issues of high priority to the nation and its future. Most of these research activities have been reported in the annual and biennial reviews compiled and published by the Institute between 1962 and 2010 (Appendix 2). As part of the 50th anniversary festivities, Crystal Awards were given to outstanding team projects carried out by staff over the history of BIO (Appendix 8).

Application of Science

The boundary between fundamental and applied research is difficult to define. BIO has always conducted research for the 'public good' and applied the results from fundamental research to address practical issues of regional, national, and international significance in a timely, responsible, and cost-effective manner. Many of these issues involved the discovery and assessment of resources from the ocean and beneath the ocean floor, risks to human activities imposed by the marine environment, and impacts of human activities on marine species, ecosystems, and coastal and ocean processes. Not surprisingly, many applied research initiatives generated significant contributions to fundamental scientific concepts. In this way, the relationship between 'fundamental' and 'applied' research within the Institute is interwoven, and supports the long-held view that:

> *"There are no applied sciences, there are only applications of science and this is a very different matter"* (Louis Pasteur, 1871).

Provision of Scientific Advice

BIO scientific and technical staff, as public servants, have devoted considerable effort in providing sound, unbiased scientific advice for decision-making on a broad range of marine issues. This advice has been based on the results of BIO research as well as general knowledge gleaned from other marine institutions, universities, and collaboration with industry, with other colleagues involved in data acquisition, and through the scientific literature. Within the federal government, this advice has been provided primarily in support of federal legislative mandates for managing fisheries, marine reptiles, birds and mammals, hydrocarbon resources, the coastal zone, habitats, oceans, and threatened/endangered species. Externally, scientific advice has been provided to provincial, territorial, and municipal governments, industry, non-governmental organizations, and international agencies, among others. There has been close communication between research and operation components within BIO. In addition, the BIO research component has often served as a bridge between federal operational agencies and academic researchers.

Fisheries advice has dealt primarily with estimating the size of different commercial stocks and recommending harvesting quotas, information upon which fisheries management is based. Environmental advice has dealt with the impacts of human activities on aquatic ecosystems such as coastal engineering works, industrial effluents and chemicals, aquaculture, oil and gas developments, purposeful ocean fertilization, and fishing, as well as the effects of the environment on these activities and the conservation and protection of marine species. BIO staff has also reviewed numerous environmental impact assessments prepared by industry under the Canadian *Environmental Assessment Act*, as well as participating in panels and hearings, and serving as expert witnesses. Scientific advice has also been provided on the design of environmental monitoring programs, especially for offshore oil and gas development. In addition, BIO geologists have provided assessments of potential hydrocarbon content in the sedimentary basins of offshore eastern Canada. Through carefully integrated collaboration between Fisheries and Oceans Canada and Environment Canada, and related research by Natural Resources Canada, BIO research scientists have provided climate change information to federal and provincial policy-makers. BIO scientists participate regularly in special task forces, ranging from arctic oil and gas developments to local requirements such as the Halifax Harbour Task Force that developed recommendations for the design of a regional sewage treatment and disposal system. They also serve as members of panels charged with reviewing proposals for the construction of large coastal projects, such as petrochemical and marine terminal facilities.

Ocean Monitoring

Throughout its history, BIO has been active in ocean monitoring and data archiving to allow analyses of the temporal variability of coastal and offshore ecosystems. For example, the Canadian Hydrographic Service (and its predecessor organizations) has maintained a network of tide gauges since 1890 to measure sea-level changes at key locations throughout Canada. Shore profiles have been monitored in various coastal settings. Thermal effluent from the Point Lepreau nuclear power station was monitored in the Bay of Fundy for many years, as have persistent chemicals in mussels as part of the ongoing Gulfwatch program. Similarly, monitoring numbers and breeding performance of colonially-breeding seabirds at major nesting sites from high arctic to boreal oceanic water zones in Arctic and Eastern Canada have shown these top-trophic feeders to be sensitive bio-indicators of environmental change. Oceanographic data (e.g., temperature, salinity, oxygen) have been collected on a regular basis at numerous sites by various projects providing a solid baseline of environmental information. Most BIO ocean monitoring activities today are incorporated into the comprehensive Atlantic Zone Monitoring Program (AZMP) that collects and publishes hydrographic, biological, climatic, and meteorological data on a regular basis from important locations in Atlantic Canada. Related monitoring programs are also conducted in Bedford Basin and the Labrador Sea. Importantly, ocean monitoring today includes satellite remote sensing that yields quasi-synoptic spatial coverage of a few information-rich properties of the sea surface such as chlorophyll produced by phytoplankton.

On the international scale, BIO has been actively involved with Argo, a multi-national ocean climate-monitoring program. Since 2001, it has launched 340 Argo floats in the North Atlantic Ocean each of which is capable of obtaining up to 150 temperature and salinity profiles to depths of 2,000 m over a period of 4-5 years. Furthermore, beginning in 1978, BIO has collaborated with St. Andrews Biological Station, New Brunswick, in conducting multispecies surveys for fish and invertebrates which benefit stock assessments and the monitoring of important commercial and non-commercial species. The data generated from monitoring programs are used in global analyses of ecosystem change and recovery strategies for species at risk, and provides the basis for much academic and applied research inside and outside Canada.

Responding to Emergencies

A major strength of the Institute has been its capability to respond rapidly to marine-related emergencies. One of the first large-scale emergency responses came from the 1969 elemental phosphorous spill in Placentia Bay, Newfoundland. A short time later, BIO was called upon to respond to the 1970 *Arrow* oil spill in Chedabucto Bay, Nova Scotia, and the sinking of the oil-laden *Irving Whale* north of Prince Edward Island. In 1979, BIO responded to the breakup of the *Kurdistan* and subsequent oil spill in Cabot Strait, as well as the *Ocean Ranger* disaster on the Grand Bank in 1982. BIO also responded to the Prince Edward Island shellfish toxicity emergency of 1987 by helping to determine that the source of the contamination was domoic acid, a toxin produced by phytoplankton. In 1998, BIO played an important role in the federal government response to the Swiss Air Flight 111 tragedy off St. Margaret's Bay, Nova Scotia, by providing daily circulation maps of local currents, applying new multibeam sonar technology to map details of wreckage on the seafloor, and assisting in the recovery of wreckage.

BIO has also responded to emergencies at the request of other countries such as the 1978 *Amoco Cadiz* oil spill in France, the 1989 *Exxon Valdez* oil spill in Alaska, and the 2010 *Deepwater Horizon* blowout in the Gulf of Mexico. BIO is currently involved in tracing radioactive contaminants from the 2011 Fukushima Daiichi nuclear reactor disaster in Japan that have spread to Canada's Pacific coast. Over the years, BIO research vessels have responded regularly to 'search and rescue' calls at sea, some of which resulted in rescues and saving lives. These examples clearly demonstrate the benefits of having a well-equipped, multidisciplinary oceanographic institute with experienced scientific, engineering, and technical staff who have the flexibility to respond rapidly and effectively to environmental emergencies that pose a threat to Canadian coastal waters and ocean resources.

Products

The results of BIO research are available to scientists, resource managers and decision-makers, the public, and the world at large in a broad range of 'products'. These include peer-reviewed papers published in the scientific literature, technical and manuscript reports, books and monographs, advisory documents, new and revised hydrographic charts, numerous important databases, computerized storage and retrieval systems, and a broad spectrum of maps and atlases, in addition to oral presentations at conferences and other meetings. Many of the research findings by BIO staff are documented in the references presented in the 48 papers comprising this book. Detailed information is also available on federal government websites. For example, a partial bibliography of BIO publications is available on line at: http://www.mar.dfo-mpo.gc.ca/libraries-bibliotheques/bibliographies/home. Publications of the Earth Sciences Sector, Natural Resources Canada, can be obtained at: http://www.geoscan.nrcan.gc.ca. The BASIN database of Natural Resources Canada contains a wealth of geological, geophysical, and engineering information related to decades of petroleum exploration and is available at: http//www.basin.gdr.nrcan.gc.ca. Furthermore, the Canadian Science Advisory Secretariat of Fisheries and Oceans has a comprehensive repository for its research and advisory documents at: http://www.dfo-mpo.gc.ca/csas-sccs/index-eng.htm. A catalogue of Environment Canada publications can be found at: http://www.ec.gc.ca/Publications.

Technology Transfer

Considerable effort has been given to the transfer of ocean engineering technologies developed at BIO to private industry. In some cases, following development at BIO, industry assumed the manufacturing and marketing roles for instrumentation of commercial interest to the broader oceanographic community. Success stories abound and include the Huntec Deep Tow Seismic system, Ocean Bottom Seismometer, Batfish, Moving Vessel Profiler, Vessel Motion Sensor, Icycler, and SeaCycler. Numerous patents have been awarded to BIO engineers (Appendix 9). Institute personnel have also participated in numerous foreign aid projects in developing nations around the world.

National and International Scientific Communities

Much of the success of BIO stems from the interaction of its researchers with national and international scientific communities. This involvement, which takes various forms, ensures that BIO scientists are aware of the most recent developments in international marine science and how they can be applied to the Canadian situation. From 1962 onwards, BIO scientists and research managers have represented Canada on numerous committees and boards of international hydrographic, oceanographic, coastal, fisheries, and wildlife organizations. These have included the International Hydrographic Organization, Scientific Committee on Oceanic Research, Intergovernmental Oceanographic Commission, International Council for the Exploration of the Sea, Intergovernmental Panel on Climate Change, International Committee for the Coordination of Seabird Research, and Northwest Atlantic Fisheries Organization. BIO scientists have played leading roles in numerous international scientific programs including the World Ocean Climate Experiment, Argo, Ocean Drilling and International Ocean Drilling programs, Can-COSTA program, and various programs overseen by the International Geosphere Biosphere Program. Exchange visits have been most valuable for sharing knowledge, both BIO scientists working in foreign laboratories and scientists from outside Canada coming to BIO. Collaborative work at sea with foreign partners has often brought unique instrumentation to Canadian waters and helped BIO scientists contribute to or adopt international best practices. Participation in scientific conferences has been of vital importance in the exchange and transfer of the results of BIO research to the international scientific community, and learning details about the most current scientific developments in other countries. Moreover, most scientific staff are members of important national and international professional societies, with many elected to executive roles as presidents and/or editors of their scientific journals.

Economic Benefits to Canada

The results of BIO research and applications of marine science findings have provided significant economic benefits to Canada. Not surprisingly, due to the nature of research, many of these benefits were not envisioned when the studies were initiated. Brief summaries of representative examples follow:

Navigation – Hydrographic surveys, new and improved nautical charts (including electronic charts) of maritime highways, and navigation improvements have enhanced the safety of navigation and reduced marine disasters. The prime benefactor has been the Canadian public, owing to the economical transport of goods, and the many users of Canadian waters including commercial shipping; the fishing, petroleum, and mining industries; Department of National Defence; Canadian Coast Guard; and recreational boaters.

International boundaries – The resolution of the Gulf of Maine boundary dispute with the United States in 1984 awarded Canada a substantial portion of Georges Bank which supports a commercial fishery of great economic value to Canadian fishermen. Current efforts under the United Nations Convention on the Law of the Sea to determine the outer limits of Canadian jurisdiction beyond the 200-mile Exclusive Economic Zone off the east and Arctic coasts are expected to define the geographic extent of the juridical continental shelf where Canada has exclusive sovereign rights over seabed resources.

Oil and gas industry – Fundamental studies of offshore geology aided the description and evaluation of sedimentary basins for assessment of the oil and gas potential off eastern Canada for government information and public interest. Improved knowledge of seabed geotechnical processes, icebergs, currents, and waves has contributed to the safety of offshore exploration activities by industry including structures such as drilling platforms, well heads, and pipelines, and has significantly reduced costs by the avoidance of unnecessary precautionary engineering design. The development of improved procedures for combating oil spills has led to more effective and cost-efficient clean-up procedures, while a better understanding of the dispersal and consequences of discharged operational wastes has improved the efficiency of programs to monitor and limit environmental effects.

Fishing industry – The monitoring of fisheries resources, both vertebrate and invertebrate, has resulted in an improved understanding of the patterns of distribution, levels of abundance, and dynamics of important commercial species, as well as the identification of other species with potential for sustainable harvesting. Application of multibeam sonar mapping has increased the efficiency of the scallop fishery. Research on the effects of fishing on target species and their habitats has improved knowledge of human impacts on fisheries, while long-term physical oceanographic research has provided new insights into the effects of environmental variability on distribution and abundance of fish populations. This valuable information is factored into the fisheries management process to help maintain the long-term sustainability of commercial fisheries for the economic benefit of the industry and Canada as a whole.

Climate change – BIO researchers have made important contributions to global climate science programs that have quantified the ocean's role in our changing climate system. The long-term data sets generated by BIO research in the northwest Atlantic Ocean have illustrated the significant changes in important physical, chemical, and biological variables over the last five decades. Tidal monitoring and investigations of trends in relative sea level have demonstrated the sensitivity of the coastal zone to changing sea-levels and allow the prediction of future scenarios to assist coastal community adaptation. In addition to providing a postglacial perspective on paleoenvironmental conditions, arctic studies have documented recent changes in circulation and ice cover which will have an economic impact on communities in Arctic Canada, shipping, and future prospects of arctic ecosystems, and many marine species.

BIO Structure and Culture

BIO, a federal facility, was organized similarly to university-based oceanographic institutions such as the Scripps Institution of Oceanography (La Jolla, CA) and the Woods Hole Oceanographic Institution (Woods Hole, MA). The founders of BIO brought all the marine scientific disciplines at different locations, including engineering, together under the same roof. As a consequence, BIO quickly developed into a federal marine science centre comprising various agencies sharing common facilities and working in collaboration with other government laboratories, universities (both nationally and internationally), the private sector, and numerous other organizations. The establishment and support of a strong infrastructure (e.g., laboratories, equipment, research vessels, marine science library, computer centre and data management, machine shops, etc.) was essential to the success of the Institute.

Since its inception, BIO has provided a creative, collegial, and stimulating research environment. Collaboration among staff has been encouraged and many multidisciplinary research teams have been established across departmental lines to tackle important scientific questions. Working and living together in the field, often under arduous conditions, created strong bonds among staff. Opportunities for ground-breaking science were abundant. Owing to these attractants, BIO was able to recruit highly dedicated and motivated individuals who made the Institute a stimulating and rewarding place to work. The overall quality of BIO research is well demonstrated by the many major scientific awards bestowed upon its members (Appendix 6).

As an indication of the high degree of dedication to research and the BIO community, many retired scientists have continued to work as volunteers through emeritus programs. Moreover, in 1998, former employees established the BIO-Oceans Association, a not-for-profit organization comprising retired and current staff who share a desire to maintain BIO's history and spirit, and support outreach efforts to increase public understanding of the oceans that surround Canada. It is this enthusiasm that led to the development of the 50th anniversary commemorative book *'Voyage of Discovery'*. The BIO-Oceans Association also created the Beluga Award which is presented annually to an individual who has exhibited unselfish dedication to community spirit at BIO (Appendix 7).

Although the largest federal oceanographic institute in Canada, BIO is not alone in the aquatic science arena. It is one of a network of federal aquatic research institutes across the country that includes Northwest Atlantic Fisheries Centre (St. John's, NL), Gulf Fisheries Centre (Moncton, NB), St. Andrews Biological Station (St. Andrews, NB), Maurice Lamontagne Institute (Mont-Joli, QC), Canada Centre for Inland Waters (Burlington, ON), Freshwater Institute (Winnipeg, MB), Centre for Aquaculture and Environmental Research (West Vancouver, BC), Pacific Biological Station (Nanaimo, BC), and Institute of Ocean Sciences (Sidney, BC). Many joint projects have been conducted over the years with these closely allied federal research laboratories.

PERSPECTIVE ON THE FUTURE

Changing Conditions

The world has changed dramatically over the past fifty years, as has science in the federal government, with BIO no exception. The relative proportion of marine research conducted by universities and private laboratories has risen markedly compared to federal institutions. Beginning in the 1990s, a series of government-wide program review exercises led to substantially reduced outlays for federal science programs in order to help balance federal budgets. Policy for funding science has shifted from understanding ocean processes towards targeted funding tied to specific outcomes driven by socio-economic goals. For example, both financial pressures and policy thinking in Fisheries and Oceans Canada are leading to the co-location of federal management and science functions in the same facility. In Natural Resources Canada, program formulation has become increasingly formalized towards national goals and national projects with a more variable emphasis on marine geosciences than in the past, depending on the departmental priorities of the day.

These changes have had a profound impact on the Institute. However, despite these changes, BIO continues to be the largest oceanographic institute in Canada with highly competent and dedicated staff who maintain viable and important research programs. Although the BIO research effort has declined, it continues to be significant.

Challenges

The evolving working environments pose numerous challenges to BIO managers and scientists delivering science for conservation of the marine environment and the safety, economic benefit, and sovereign interests of Canadians. Budgetary and staff reductions make it increasingly difficult to carry out research programs. Considerable time and energy must now be devoted to finding alternative funding sources. Recruitment of new scientific staff at all levels is not keeping up with retirements. Reductions in funding have also made it more difficult to implement new programs and participate in relevant national and international scientific activities. BIO research staff, as well as university partners, require sea time with up-to-date equipment to collect new data for research projects and to maintain essential monitoring programs; but with a much reduced research fleet ship time is very limited. The CCGS *Hudson*, the only general purpose oceanographic vessel remaining in the fleet, delivered in 1963, is approaching the end of her lifespan. Planning is underway for a replacement, but it will be several years before the replacement research vessel will be available. This new vessel, as well as other novel sampling platforms, is essential for continuing research in ice-infested environments.

Parallel with the decrease in scientific program capability, there has been a corresponding increase in demand for scientific information and advice arising from more complex resource management regimes and new legislation. This makes it increasingly difficult to maintain a suitable balance between research and advisory activities. Additionally, the process for fisheries management advice is more difficult now that ecosystem effects are being considered. The species-stock status reports require input from more disciplines, and advice has become more complicated since the crisis of the groundfish collapse in the early 1990s. Free and timely release of research findings is essential to maintain the public trust and confidence that BIO has developed since its establishment in 1962. Similarly, BIO needs to maintain its scientific integrity and respect from the oceanographic, private sector, and environmental communities, as well as the public at large.

Continuing Role of BIO

The core of BIO research should continue to comprise a wide variety of fundamental ocean programs that contribute to the knowledge base necessary to safeguard the 'health' of Canada's marine waters and seabeds, support sustainable resource management, and address the policy needs of the country and global community. Federal government support for marine research is vitally important for Canada and Canadians, and their future welfare. The global ocean dictates conditions of weather, climate, pollution, and marine resources. Since there are many critical elements that universities and private sector operators are not interested in or capable of undertaking, government laboratories like BIO are needed, especially for programs that require long-term data gathering and stability, extensive ship time, database management, and other investigations directed by federal legislative mandates. Examples include renewable and non-renewable resource assessments; long-term monitoring programs to collect physical, chemical, geological and biological data; tracking marine biodiversity and threatened/endangered marine species; understanding the impact of human activities on marine ecosystems; assessing the impact of oceanic forces and geohazards on human activities; and ecosystem management. Federal institutes like BIO, and other marine research centres (federal and provincial) across the country, are needed to provide accurate scientific information and advice necessary for wise decision making by government in the development of policies benefiting Canadian interests and the wider global community in the future.

There is the need for BIO to take a role in organizing projects where federal, university, and private sector collaboration is essential for the attainment of common goals. In addition, the Institute needs to continue to provide one of the premier marine science libraries in Canada, be able to respond to environmental emergencies, and contribute to international obligations and collaborations.

As we ponder the future of BIO, it is useful to reflect on the content of Dr. William van Steenburgh's address given at Dalhousie University (Halifax, NS) on 24 October 1962, the day before the official opening of the Institute (van Steenburgh 1962). Highlighted was the vision to bring the marine expertise present in the Canadian Hydrographic Service, Fisheries Research Board of Canada, and Geological Survey of Canada together at a single location to form the nucleus for development of an oceanographic institute of international standing. He briefly outlined the marine issues facing Canada that BIO would attempt to address as part of its 'start-up' research program. These included navigation, water circulation, physical and chemical properties of seawater, ice, underwater sound transmission, submarine geology, marine geophysics, air-sea interactions, pollution, and biological productivity. Considerable focus would be directed towards the many unknowns in oceanography in Arctic Canada. He also recognized the emerging obligations arising from the 1958 Law of the Sea negotiations and the need to establish a national oceanographic data centre. He argued that these issues were best addressed by a balanced and coordinated partnership among the relevant federal departments (jointly housed at BIO), universities, and the private sector to ensure efficiency and encourage international collaboration.

Dr. van Steenburgh's vision reflected the needs of the time, but the world has changed profoundly between 1962 and 2012. The next 50 years will be quite different and BIO must adapt to the new conditions. Although many of the issues identified by Dr. van Steenburgh remain, there are many new ones facing the marine science community today. In 1962, most issues were regional or national in nature, and BIO research initially focussed on improving basic understanding of the structure and function of ocean waters, ocean basins, and shorelines. This was a time when there was limited understanding and focus on the impacts that human activities could have on the marine environment. Pollution studies were in their infancy, fisheries were healthy, threats to biodiversity went unnoticed, and monitoring of carbon dioxide in the atmosphere had only just begun. As is evident by the papers presented in this book, BIO has contributed extensively to the oceanographic 'information explosion' of the past fifty years. We now realize that human activities are having a huge impact on the global ocean. In the near future, we will be facing unprecedented challenges driven by the certainties of continued increase in numbers and expansion in range of the human population, and changes in climate that will affect all nations of the world. The levels of carbon dioxide and other greenhouse gases in the atmosphere will continue to increase. The oceans will become warmer and more acidic, sea level will increase, storm frequency and intensity will increase, biodiversity will decrease, and there will be more pollution and disruption to existing marine systems.

Looking forward fifty years, it is in Canada's interest to ensure that scientific and technical expertise is available to address these new and challenging global marine issues. Public understanding of the oceans will be essential for both 'evidence-based decisions' and associated changes in human behaviour. This will require the scientific community to play a more active role in applying research results to the development of public policy. Issues have indeed changed over five decades, but the answer Dr. van Steenburgh outlined for addressing them in 1962 remains the same today: i.e., a carefully balanced and integrated partnership among the relevant federal departments, universities, and the private sector.

Research Priorities

Details of proposed research priorities for ocean science in Canada are provided in two recent reports compiled by the marine science community and published by the Council of the Canadian Academies (CCA 2012, CCA 2013). These analyses are similar in approach to those conducted by Dr. van Steenburgh, albeit in more depth and focussed on current marine issues and problems. The first phase of the assessment of the state of ocean science in Canada addressed a large suite of research questions and is summarized as follows (CCA 2012):

"This report presents 40 priority questions that, if answered, would have the greatest impact on addressing future opportunities and challenges relating to ocean science in Canada ... The questions reflect a strong interest in increasing the fundamental understanding of the impacts of global change on the ocean, including climate change, acidification, and nutrient loading. Major knowledge gaps in areas such as the Arctic, deep water, and marine biodiversity are especially important in the context of global change, and are highlighted in several questions. Questions aimed at understanding global processes, as well as those addressing impacts of direct relevance to coastal communities and Canada's economy, reflect the multidisciplinary nature of ocean research and the need for improved international collaboration."

Phase two of the assessment evaluated, in general terms, Canada's present capacity to address the 40 research questions (CCA 2013). The results of the Council's analysis and key findings are particularly germane to the future directions of research and advisory services at BIO. In summary, the assessment indicates that an integrated federal government, university, and private sector research strategy is required to tackle the wide range of societal issues (e.g., ocean-climate interactions; biological, mineral and energy resources; human impacts on marine and coastal ecosystems; and natural hazards) associated with the conservation and multiple uses of Canada's three oceans within both a national and global context.

As was the case in the early 1960s, Canada needs an integrated ocean science research and advisory capacity applicable to our contemporary world. The two CCA reports clearly identify the key questions and, in general terms, the existing national research capacity relevant to the needs of the nation. Today's university research capacity is impressive, and owing largely to the leadership of the Canadian Consortium of Ocean Research Universities, there is a well-coordinated approach to both research infrastructure and programs. The university community is fully engaged in the identification of future research needs and the recruitment and training of new graduates capable of meeting the challenges ahead. The private sector is also well-coordinated at both the national and the international levels: e.g., the World Oceans Council and the international petroleum industry. As detailed in the next section, there is a need for a strong federal government marine research capacity to augment and synthesize marine outputs from academic and private sector organizations for the 'public good', particularly for the benefit of Canadians.

Another recent Canadian report pertinent to the future of BIO and marine science in Canada addresses the issue of marine biodiversity (Hutchings et al. 2012). Prepared by an expert panel of university scientists for the Royal Society of Canada (RSC), this report reviews current understanding of Canada's national and international obligations to sustain marine biodiversity. BIO has been involved in studies of biodiversity from the very beginning and much of the information reviewed in the report was collected by BIO scientists. The report evaluates past, present, and forecasted changes in the three prime stressors that affect marine biodiversity: climate change, fisheries, and aquaculture. It also describes how these three stressors have adversely affected, and likely to continue to affect, Canadian marine biodiversity. The report concludes by offering a number of broad, strategically-based recommendations, each accompanied by recommended key actions, to establish Canada as an international leader in stewardship of the oceans and marine conservation. These actions include establishing operational objectives to sustain marine biodiversity; maintaining and developing new long-term environmental monitoring programs, especially for the Arctic; developing a national program for mapping ocean habitat and its biological use; strengthening fundamental research on physical and biological oceanographic patterns, process, and function; and developing a comprehensive research program to forecast changes in Canadian marine biodiversity resulting from climate-related changes.

The Next Fifty Years

The conclusions and recommendations of the foregoing reports on the future of Canadian marine science, prepared by the academic community, offer much insight into the issues that challenge BIO today. Much of the needed research clearly falls within the mandates and experience of the federal agencies comprising BIO.

An adequate and sustainable federal science capacity is crucial to the future welfare of Canada's oceans and marine resources, particularly since federal leadership is essential for the implementation and maintenance of the *Fisheries Act*, *Environmental Assessment Act*, *Oceans Act*, *Migratory Birds Convention Act*, *Wildlife Act*, *Species at Risk Act*, and other legislation. Federal leadership is also required for the increasingly complex requirements for the management of the commercial fishing industry and the energy extraction industries in marine waters, and for infrastructure in support of long-term monitoring and ocean research (e.g., survey vessels, other observation platforms, technology development, and long-term data management and archiving). A vibrant BIO, as part of a comprehensive network of federal marine science laboratories and universities, is essential to complement bilateral arrangements with neighbouring countries and the Arctic Council, and the international groups that are addressing research questions of significance to the global ocean (e.g., the International Oceanographic Commission and International Council for the Exploration of the Sea).

In summary, Canada borders on three oceans and has the longest coastline of any country in the world. It is clearly in the national interest for BIO to rebuild its key roles of conducting oceanographic research and providing scientific advice. As during the first fifty years of BIO, an ongoing investment in federal marine research can be expected to continue paying important scientific, social, and economic dividends. The future of the oceans is not clear, but the expertise of BIO will be essential to steer us through the uncharted waters ahead, including the additional seabed that is expected to be added to Canada's area of jurisdiction under the United Nations Convention on the Law of the Sea.

We hope that decision makers will continue to appreciate the critical importance of oceanography to Canada and ensure that decisions in all aspects of ocean management are based on sound scientific evidence. This was the essence of the vision of Dr. van Steenburgh when BIO was established in 1962. With the strengths built over the years, and the quality and adaptiveness of its staff, we are hopeful that the Institute will continue conducting research for the 'public good' of all Canadians. However, how BIO will respond to the many challenges ahead and remain the dominant force it has been over the past 50 years is a story that has yet to be told. The hope is that the proud reputation and legacy from BIO's first 50 years, expressed in this commemorative book, will inspire existing and future staff during their 'voyage' of the next five decades to study and savour the wonders and rewards of ocean science.

ACKNOWLEDGEMENTS

This Epilogue was written by four retired marine scientists now somewhat removed from current events. To make sure it was factually correct and represented the general consensus of managers and scientific staff, earlier drafts were extensively reviewed by colleagues at BIO and the wider oceanographic community. We thank Don Bowen, Allyn Clarke, Bob Cook, Jim Elliott, Bob Fournier, Jeff Hutchings, John Lazier, Michel Latremouille, Bill Li, Alan Longhurst, Dick MacDougall, Eric Mills, Mike Murphy, Brian Nicholls, David Piper, Charles Schafer, Jim Stewart, Alain Vezina, Peter Wells, and Boris Worm for their insightful and constructive comments that vastly improved the final draft. We also gratefully acknowledge the many contributions made by all staff at BIO over the past 50 years to make the Institute such an outstanding scientific organization and stimulating place to work.

REFERENCES

Council of Canadian Academies (CCA). 2012. 40 priority research questions for ocean science in Canada: a priority-setting exercise by the Core Group on Ocean Science in Canada. Council of Canadian Academies, Ottawa, ON.

Council of Canadian Academies (CCA). 2013. Ocean science in Canada: meeting the challenge, seizing the opportunity. Council of Canadian Academies, Ottawa, ON.

Hutchings, J.A., I.M. Côté, J.J. Dodson, I.A. Fleming, S. Jennings, N.J. Mantua, R.M. Peterman, B.E. Riddell, A.J. Weaver, and D.L. VanderZwaag. 2012. Sustaining Canadian marine biodiversity: responding to the challenges posed by climate change, fisheries and aquaculture. Expert Panel Report prepared for the Royal Society of Canada, Ottawa, ON.

van Steenburgh, W.E. 1962. Address at the Special Convocation at Dalhousie University, Halifax, Nova Scotia, October 24, 1962 on the Occasion of the Official Opening of the Bedford Institute of Oceanography. BIO Library Archives, Dartmouth, NS.

APPENDICES

Page

APPENDIX 1

Bedford Institute of Oceanography

BIO TIME LINE

Noteworthy Historical Events
(25 October 1962 – 25 October 2012)

1962 Bedford Institute of Oceanography (BIO), Dartmouth, Nova Scotia, officially opened on 25 October. Founding organizations: Canadian Hydrographic Service (CHS), Atlantic Oceanographic Group (AOG) of the Fisheries Research Board of Canada (FRBC), and Marine Sciences Branch (MSB). [Notes: CHS and MSB were part of the Department of Mines and Technical Surveys (DMTS), and AOG was in the Department of Fisheries and Forestry (DFF).]

1963 Marine Geology Unit of the Geological Survey of Canada (GSC) transferred from Ottawa to BIO and became part of MSB. The Secretariat of the International Commission for the Northwest Atlantic Fisheries (ICNAF) was established.

1965 The Atlantic Oceanographic Group (AOG), previously part of the St. Andrews Biological Station, becomes an independent laboratory within FRBC.

1966 DMTS becomes the Department of Energy, Mines and Resources (DEMR).

1968 AOG becomes Marine Ecology Laboratory (MEL) and MSB at BIO becomes Atlantic Oceanographic Laboratory (AOL).

1970 A pollution research program is established in MEL. Other pollution studies are initiated by the Resource Development Branch of DFF. Resource Management and Conservation Branch (RMCB) of DEMR curates drilling samples and data collected by the oil and gas industry in the Argo Building.

1971 Federal Department of the Environment (DOE) is created and assumes most BIO activities except geoscience programs which remain with DEMR. Environmental Protection Service (EPS) created and establishes the Environmental Quality Laboratory. Canadian Wildlife Service (CWS) establishes its first seabird program for Arctic and Eastern Canada, and places one research scientist at BIO to study the pelagic ecology of marine birds. Eastern Petroleum Geology Section of GSC is established in the Argo Building.

1972 Geological and geophysical staff in DEMR, both MSB and GSC, combine to form the Atlantic Geoscience Centre (AGC) which became a division of GSC.

1973 FRBC dissolved. National Fisheries and Marine Service (FMS) created within DOE including MEL, AOL, and other ex-FRBC laboratories across the country.

1974 ICNAF Secretariat departs.

1975 A coal petrology labratory is relocated from the Geological Survey of Canada (GSC) in Calgary to the Atlantic Geoscience Centre at BIO.

1976 DOE renamed Department of Fisheries and Environment (DFE). Ocean and Aquatic Sciences (OAS) created to include AOL and MEL. Institute-wide technical services were incorporated into Institute Facilities and BIO Library designated the major Government of Canada oceanographic library. Entire Canadian Wildlife Service (CWS) Seabird Research Unit transferred from Ottawa to BIO.

1977 Extension of Canada's Extended Economic Zone (EEZ) to 200 nautical miles. Marine Fish Division established. Marked increase in use of BIO facilities by Canadian industry.

1978 Canadian Atlantic Fisheries Scientific Advisory Committee (CAFSAC) created with its Secretariat placed at BIO. Staff from GSC-Terrain Sciences Division in Ottawa join AGC.

1979 DFE divided into Department of Fisheries and Oceans (DFO) and the Department of Environment (DOE). OAS becomes Ocean Science and Surveys (OSS) and is incorporated into DFO. Other components of DFE join DOE. The AGC Eastern Petroleum Geology Subdivision moves into the Murray Building.

1980 Headquarters of the new Northwest Atlantic Fisheries Organization (NAFO), which replaced ICNAF, established at BIO. The A.G. Huntsman Award in marine science is created. The National Energy Program (NEP) is established and enhances the pace of offshore oil and gas exploration. Official opening of the new Strickland, Murray, and Holland buildings occurs. Offshore well samples and cores are moved to Murray Building repository.

1981 Marine Advisory and Industrial Liaison Office (BIOMAIL) is formed to serve as an entry point for anyone seeking information on Canadian oceanography and related topics. Atlantic Regional Office of Canada Oil and Gas Lands Administration (COGLA) is established, incorporating the Resource Management and Conservation Branch under DEMR.

1984 Resolution of the Gulf of Maine boundary dispute with the United States. AGC is mandated to assess oil and gas potential of offshore regions and to expand studies of the sedimentary basins.

1986 OSS is disbanded and integrated with the Fisheries Research Branch. Position of Director-General OSS terminated and replaced with lower level position of Regional Director of Science reporting to the DFO Regional Director-General. This change marked the end of direct reporting to Ottawa for BIO oceanography programs. DFO Fish Habitat Policy announced. National Energy Program (NEP) terminated. Canada-Newfoundland and Labrador Offshore Petroleum Board established.

1987 BIO celebrates its 25th anniversary. MEL is disbanded. Biological Sciences Branch (BSB) is created and includes scientists at Halifax Fisheries Research Laboratory and St. Andrews Biological Station. AOL becomes the Physical and Chemical Sciences Branch (PCSB). CHS becomes a separate branch under the Regional Director of Science. Sector management and formation of separate management branches is introduced. Marine Assessment and Liaison Division (MALD) is formed to facilitate interaction between DFO Science and Habitat Management.

1989 NAFO headquarters departs. Seabird Research Unit comes under the CWS Marine Wildlife Conservation Division. Transfer of Newfoundland core samples to the Canada-Newfoundland Offshore Petroleum Board core storage facility in St. John's, Newfoundland.

1990 Canada-Nova Scotia Offshore Petroleum Board established.

1991 COGLA departs from BIO. Remaining offshore well samples moved to core storage facility in Burnside Industrial Park.

1992 Public Works and Government Services Canada (PWGSC) assumes ownership, operation, and maintenance of BIO facilities. Burnside core storage facility is transferred to the Canada-Nova Scotia Offshore Petroleum Board.

1993 Department of National Defence (DND) establishes the Route Survey Office at BIO to provide detailed seafloor data for the Canadian Navy in support of surveillance and national security.

1994 Fishermen and Scientists Research Society (FSRS) is established and based at BIO.

1995 Canadian Coast Guard (CCG), previously with Transport Canada, is transferred to DFO and takes over operation of the BIO research vessel fleet. DEMR and the Department of Forestry merge to become Natural Resources Canada (NRCan).

1996 EPS Environmental Quality Laboratory of DOE moves to University of Moncton and CWS Marine Wildlife Conservation Division including the Seabird Research Unit moves to Queen Square in downtown Dartmouth. AGC becomes the Geological Survey of Canada - Atlantic (GSCA).

1997 The *Oceans Act* is approved and an Oceans Act Coordination Office (OACO) established at BIO. The Maritimes Region Regional Advisory Process Office (RAP) is formed and assumes responsibilities of CAFSAC.

1998 DFO Halifax Fisheries Research Laboratory is closed with staff transferred to BIO, St. Andrews Biological Station, or Gulf Fisheries Centre in Moncton, New Brunswick. The Bedford Institute of Oceanography-Oceans Association (BIO-OA) is created by retired and current staff.

1999 DFO Diadromous Fish and Habitat Management divisions move from the Maritime Centre in Halifax to BIO. OACO becomes the Oceans and Environment Branch (OEB) that includes the Environmental Sciences Division. The Maritimes Aquatic Species at Risk Office (MASARO) and Centre for Marine Biodiversity (CMB) are established at BIO.

2000 Canadian Coast Guard Technical Services and DFO Aquaculture Coordination Office are established.

2001 BIO-OA creates the Beluga Award.

2002 The *Species at Risk Act* is enacted. DFO National Centre for Offshore Oil and Gas Environmental Research (COOGER) is opened at BIO. The Institute celebrates its 40th anniversary and hosts a special two-day symposium on the *Future Challenges of Marine Sciences in Canada* and Symphony Nova Scotia performs an anniversary concert in the William Ford Auditorium at BIO.

2004 A United Nations Convention of the Law of the Sea (UNCLOS) office is established under NRCan to prepare technical material for Canada's claim for extended continental shelf jurisdiction. OEB becomes the Oceans and Habitat Branch (OHB).

2007 RAP is renamed the Centre for Science Advice (CSA).

2008 OHB becomes the Oceans, Habitat and Species at Risk Branch (OHSAR).

2010 BIO managers' 'Tuesday Club' renamed the 'BIO Campus Management Committee'. A separate BIO Science Management Committee is formed with membership from four science departments: DFO, NRCan, DOE, and DND. OHSAR is renamed the Ecosystem Management Branch.

2012 CCG base on Parker Street, Dartmouth, is closed with staff moving into the new Maritimes Headquarters building on the BIO campus. BIO celebrates its 50th anniversary on 25 October with an open house, climate change workshop, a 'Gala Celebration', and presentation of Crystal Awards to outstanding team projects over five decades.

APPENDIX 2

Bedford Institute of Oceanography

ANNUAL AND BIENNIAL REPORTS[1]

First Annual Report. 1962. B.I.O. Unpublished Manuscript 62-3, Bedford Institute of Oceanography, Dartmouth, NS. 52 pages.

Second Annual Report. 1963. B.I.O. Unpublished Manuscript 63-6, Bedford Institute of Oceanography, Dartmouth, NS. 57 pages.

Third Annual Report. 1964. B.I.O. 64-18, Bedford Institute of Oceanography, Dartmouth, NS. 103 pages.

Fourth Annual Report. 1965. BIO 65-17, Bedford Institute of Oceanography, Dartmouth, NS. 90 pages.

Fifth Annual Report. 1966. BIO 66-10, Bedford Institute of Oceanography, Dartmouth, NS. 103 pages.

Bedford Institute Biennial Review 1967-1968. 1968. Bedford Institute of Oceanography, Dartmouth, NS. 143 pages.

Bedford Institute Biennial Review 1969/70 (G. Elliott, Ed.). 1971. Bedford Institute of Oceanography, Dartmouth, NS. 283 pages.

Bedford Institute of Oceanography Biennial Review 1971/72 (B. Nicholls and G. Elliott, Eds.). 1972. Bedford Institute of Oceanography, Dartmouth, NS. 366 pages.

Bedford Institute of Oceanography Biennial Review 1973/74 (M.P. Latremouille, Ed.). 1974. Bedford Institute of Oceanography, Dartmouth, NS. 306 pages.

Bedford Institute of Oceanography Biennial Review 1975/76 (M.P. Latremouille, Ed.). 1976. Bedford Institute of Oceanography, Dartmouth, NS. 223 pages.

Bedford Institute of Oceanography Biennial Review 1977 & 1978 (M.P. Latremouille, Ed.). 1979. Bedford Institute of Oceanography, Dartmouth, NS. 249 pages.

BIO Review '81 (M.P. Latremouille, Ed.). 1981. Bedford Institute of Oceanography, Dartmouth, NS. 96 pages.

BIO Review '82 (M.P. Latremouille, Ed.). 1982. Bedford Institute of Oceanography, Dartmouth, NS. 96 pages.

BIO Review '83 (M.P. Latremouille, Ed.). 1983. Bedford Institute of Oceanography, Dartmouth, NS. 92 pages.

BIO Review '84 (M.P. Latremouille, Ed.). 1984. Bedford Institute of Oceanography, Dartmouth, NS. 67 pages.

BIO Review '85 (M.P. Latremouille, Ed.). 1985. Bedford Institute of Oceanography, Dartmouth, NS. 96 pages.

BIO Review '86 - 25th Anniversary Issue (B. Newman and M.P. Latremouille, Eds.). 1987. Bedford Institute of Oceanography, Dartmouth, NS. 98 pages.

Science Review 1987 (B. Bennett, Ed.). 1988. Department of Fisheries and Oceans, Scotia Fundy Region, Dartmouth, NS. 116 pages.

Science Review 1988 & '89 (T.E. Smith, Ed.). 1991. Department of Fisheries and Oceans, Scotia-Fundy Region, Dartmouth, NS. 142 pages.

Science Review 1990 & '91 (T.E. Smith and J. Cook, Eds.). 1992. Department of Fisheries and Oceans, Scotia-Fundy Region, Dartmouth, NS. 184 pages.

Science Review 1992 & '93 (A. Fiander, Ed.). 1994. Department of Fisheries and Oceans, Scotia-Fundy Region, Dartmouth, NS. 149 pages.

Science Review 1994 & '95 (A. Fiander, Ed.). 1996. Department of Fisheries and Oceans, Maritimes Region, Dartmouth, NS. 151 pages.

Science Review 1996 & '97 (A. Fiander, Ed.). 2000. Department of Fisheries and Oceans, Maritimes Region, Dartmouth, NS. 147 pages.

Bedford Institute of Oceanography 2000 (D. Geddes, Ed.). 2001. Fisheries and Oceans Canada and Natural Resources Canada, Dartmouth, NS. 88 pages.

Bedford Institute of Oceanography 2001 in Review (D. Geddes, Ed.). 2002. Fisheries and Oceans Canada and Natural Resources Canada, Dartmouth, NS. 84 pages.

Bedford Institute of Oceanography 2002 in Review – 40th Anniversary Edition (D. Geddes, Ed.). 2003. Fisheries and Oceans Canada and Natural Resources Canada, Dartmouth, NS. 108 pages.

Bedford Institute of Oceanography 2003 (D. Geddes and J. Ryan, Eds.). 2004. Fisheries and Oceans Canada and Natural Resources Canada, Dartmouth, NS. 92 pages.

Bedford Institute of Oceanography 2004 in Review (J. Ryan, Ed.). 2005. Fisheries and Oceans Canada and Natural Resources Canada, Dartmouth, NS. 88 pages.

Bedford Institute of Oceanography Annual Review 2005 (J. Ryan, Ed.). 2006. Natural Resources Canada and Fisheries and Oceans Canada, Dartmouth, NS. 92 pages.

Bedford Institute of Oceanography 2006 in Review (J. Ryan, Ed.). 2007. Natural Resources Canada and Fisheries and Oceans Canada, Dartmouth, NS. 92 pages.

Bedford Institute of Oceanography 2007 in Review (J. Ryan, Ed.). 2008. Natural Resources Canada and Fisheries and Oceans Canada, Dartmouth, NS. 96 pages.

Bedford Institute of Oceanography in Review - 2008 (J. Ryan, Ed.). 2009. Fisheries and Oceans Canada and Natural Resources Canada, Dartmouth, NS. 100 pages.

Bedford Institute of Oceanography 2009 in Review (J. Ryan, Ed.). 2010. Fisheries and Oceans Canada and Natural Resources Canada, Dartmouth, NS. 96 pages.

[1]These reports can be found on line at: http://www.dfo-mpo.gc.ca/libraries-bibliotheques/bio-iob-rev-eng.htm.

APPENDIX 3

Bedford Institute of Oceanography

SCIENCE DIRECTORS

BIO Science Directors between 1962 and 2012 showing their affiliation and duration of tenure.

Director	Organization	Tenure
*William H. English**	Marine Sciences Branch	1962-1964
G. W. LaCroix	Canadian Hydrographic Service	1962-1963
L.P. Murdock	Canadian Hydrographic Service	1963-1964
Russell Melanson	Canadian Hydrographic Service	1964-1979
*L.A. Earlston Doe**	Marine Sciences Branch	1964-1965
*William L. Ford**	Marine Sciences Branch	1965-1968
Lloyd M. Dickie	Atlantic Oceanographic Group	1965-1968
*William L. Ford**	Atlantic Oceanographic Laboratory	1968-1976
Lloyd M. Dickie	Marine Ecology Laboratory	1968-1974
Bosko D. Loncarevic	Atlantic Geoscience Centre	1972-1977
*William L. Ford**	Ocean and Aquatic Sciences	1976-1978
Cedric Mann	Atlantic Oceanographic Laboratory	1976-1978
Reginald L.G. Gilbert	Institute Facilities	1976-1987
*Cedric Mann**	Ocean and Aquatic Sciences	1978-1979
Michael J. Keen	Atlantic Geoscience Centre	1978-1989
George T. Needler	Atlantic Oceanographic Laboratory	1978-1984
Alan R. Longhurst	Marine Ecology Laboratory	1978-1979
*Alan R. Longhurst**	Ocean Science and Surveys	1979-1986
Adam Kerr	Canadian Hydrographic Service	1979-1988
Kenneth H. Mann	Marine Ecology Laboratory	1980-1987
James A. Elliott	Atlantic Oceanographic Laboratory	1984-1987
*Barry S. Muir**	Regional Director of Science	1986-1987
*Stephen B. MacPhee**	Regional Director of Science	1987-1995
James E. Stewart	Biological Sciences Branch	1987-1988
James A. Elliott	Physical and Chemical Sciences Branch	1987-1995
Paul Bellemare	Canadian Hydrographic Service	1988-1997
Michael M. Sinclair	Biological Sciences Branch	1988-1995
David I. Ross	Atlantic Geoscience Centre	1989-1992
David B. Prior	Atlantic Geoscience Centre	1992-1996
*James A. Elliott**	Regional Director of Science	1995-1996
*John S. Loch**	Regional Director of Science	1996-1999
Jacob Verhoef	Geological Survey of Canada-Atlantic	1996-2008
Faith Scattolon	Oceans Act Coordination Office	1997-1999
Laureen Kinney	Canadian Hydrographic Service	1997-1998
Charles Stirling	Canadian Hydrographic Service	1998-2000
Faith Scattolon	Oceans and Environment Branch	1999-2003
*Michael M. Sinclair**	Regional Director of Science	1999-2009
J. Richard MacDougall	Canadian Hydrographic Service	2000-2007
Carol Ann Rose	Oceans and Environment Branch	2003-2005
Carol Ann Rose	Oceans and Habitat Branch	2005-2007
J. Richard MacDougall	UNCLOS Program (CHS)	2007-2009
Stephen R. Forbes	Canadian Hydrographic Service	2007-2011
Michael Murphy	Oceans and Habitat Branch	2007-2008
Michael Murphy	Oceans, Habitat and Species at Risk	2008-2009
Jacob Verhoef	UNCLOS Program (NRCan)	2008-present
Stephen Locke	Geological Survey of Canada-Atlantic	2008-present
*Alain Vezina**	Regional Director of Science	2009-present
Julian E. Goodyear	UNCLOS Program (CHS)	2009-2011
David Millar	Ecosystem Management Branch	2010-present
Stephen R. Forbes	UNCLOS Program (CHS)	2011-2013
Michel Goguen	Canadian Hydrographic Service	2011-present

[1] List does not include Acting or Assistant Directors and includes Regional Hydrographers; asterisk denotes those who also served as Director-General or Director of BIO during their term in office.

[Notes: UNCLOS = United Nations Convention on the Law of the Sea, CHS = Canadian Hydrographic Service, NRCan = Natural Resources Canada.]

APPENDIX 4

Bedford Institute of Oceanography

DEVELOPMENT OF BIO CAMPUS

Development of BIO campus from 1962 to 2012 with name and year of initial construction of each facility. [Note: Most facilities were expanded and/or renovated over time; see below for layout.]

Year	Facility
1962	Main Building - later renamed van Steenburgh (north wing) and Polaris (south wing) buildings; Depot (later renamed the Vulcan Building); Jetty constructed.
1968	Fish Laboratory and Trailer Complex constructed.
1970	Argo Building and Sewage Treatment Plant (STP) constructed.
1978	Strickland and Murray Buildings constructed.
1979	Trailer Complex destroyed by fire.
1980	Holland Building constructed (comprises: W.L. Ford Auditorium, Library, and Cafeteria).
1988	Canadian Coast Guard Marine Communications and Traffic Services Building (MCTSB) constructed.
1998	Fish Laboratory closed owing to discovery of toxic mould; renovated and reopened 2000.
2002	Cooling Plant (CP) constructed.
2007	Katherine Ellis Building constructed.
2012	Canadian Coast Guard Maritimes Headquarters Building constructed.

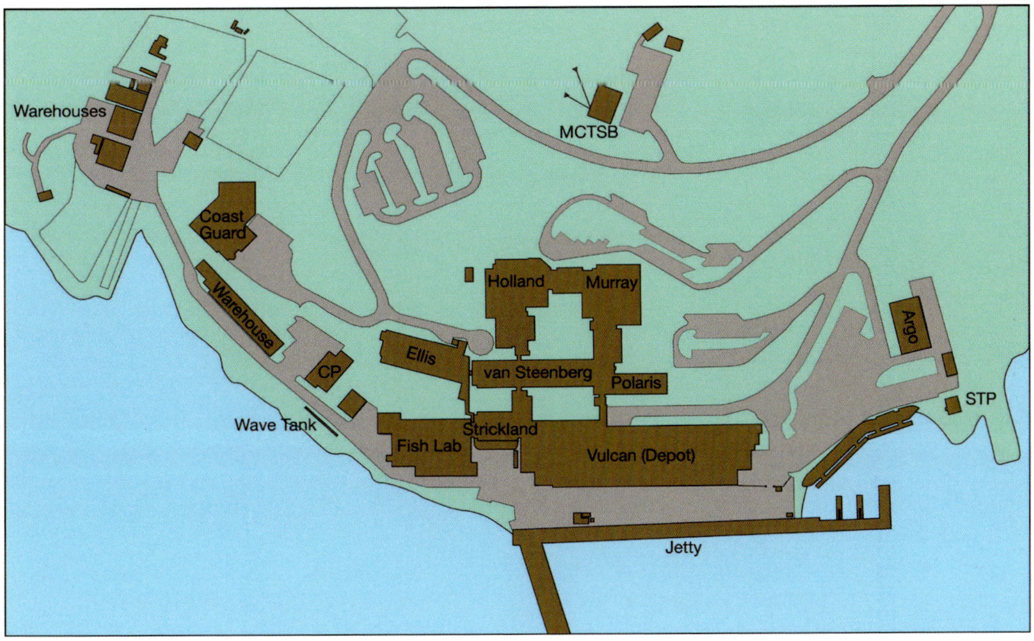

Sketch map of BIO campus showing location of major buildings. Light beige areas indicate roadways and parking lots.

APPENDIX 5

Bedford Institute of Oceanography

A.G. HUNTSMAN AWARD

The A.G. Huntsman Award (http://www.huntsmanaward.org) was established in 1980 by the Bedford Institute of Oceanography (BIO) on behalf of the Canadian marine science community to recognize excellence of research and outstanding contributions to marine sciences. The selection of awardees is made by a committee drawn from BIO, Dalhousie University, and other marine institutions across Canada. The award honours marine scientists of any nationality who have had and continue to have a significant influence on the course of marine scientific thought. It is presented annually by the Royal Society of Canada in one of three categories: marine geosciences (MG), physical/chemical oceanography (PC), and biological oceanography and fisheries science (BF). Awards were made in all three categories in the first year. In the twenty-fifth year, awards were made also in the three categories plus one in interdisciplinary marine science (IMS). The Award is named in honour of Archibald Gowanlock Huntsman (1883–1973), a pioneer Canadian oceanographer and fishery biologist.

A.G. Huntsman Medal

The A.G. Huntsman Award is administered by the A.G. Huntsman Foundation which is based at the Bedford Institute of Oceanography and organized as an independent, charitable, tax-free foundation. Business of the Foundation is conducted by a seven person Board of Directors assisted by a Coordinator and Treasurer. The Lieutenant Governor of Nova Scotia serves as honorary patron.

The Award was created in 1980 under the leadership of Dr. John Vandermeulen, Dr. James Elliott, and Dr. Bosko Loncarevic. It is now recognized as a major international oceanographic prize. The A.G. Huntsman Award is funded principally by interest earned on financial contributions received from Fisheries and Oceans Canada, Natural Resources Canada, Province of Nova Scotia, and Canadian Association of Petroleum Producers.

A.G. HUNTSMAN MEDAL WINNERS AND CATEGORIES[1]
1980-2012

1980 *Ramon Margalef*, University of Barcelona, Barcelona, Spain (BF).

1980 *Henry M. Stommel*, Woods Hole Oceanographic Institution, Woods Hole, MA, USA (PC).

1980 *Dan Peter McKenzie*, University of Cambridge, Cambridge, UK (MG).

1981 *J. Tuzo Wilson*, Ontario Science Centre, Toronto, ON, Canada (MG).

1982 *Christopher J.R. Garrett*, Dalhousie University, Halifax, NS, Canada (PC).

1983 *Reuben Lasker*, Southwest Fisheries Center, La Jolla, CA, USA (BF).

1984 *Wolfgang H. Berger*, University of California, San Diego, CA, USA (MG).

1985 *Wallace S. Broecker*, Columbia University, Palisades, NY, USA (PC).

1986 *Tom M. Fenchel*, University of Aarhus, Aarhus, Denmark (BF).

1987 *Xavier LePichon*, École normale supérieure, Paris, France (MG).

1988 *Carl Wunsch*, Massachusetts Institute of Technology, Cambridge, MA, USA (PC).

1989 *Lawrence R. Pomeroy*, University of Georgia, GA, USA (BF).

1990 *Nicholas J. Shackleton*, University of Cambridge, Cambridge, UK (MG).

1991 *Gabriel T. Csanady*, Old Dominion University, Norfolk, VA, USA (PC).

1992 *Trevor Platt*, Bedford Institute of Oceanography, Dartmouth, NS, Canada (BF).

1993 *Robert A. Berner*, Yale University, New Haven, CT, USA (MG).

1994 *Edward A. Boyle*, Massachusetts Institute of Technology, Cambridge, MA, USA (PC).

1995 *Victor S. Smetacek*, Alfred Wegener Institute, Bremerhaven, Germany (BF).

1996 *Robert Detrick*, Woods Hole Oceanographic Institution, Woods Hole, MA, USA (MG).

1997 *Russ E. Davis*, University of California, San Diego, CA, USA (PC).

1998 *Paul Falkowski*, Rutgers University, New Brunswick, NJ, USA (BF).

1999 *Nicholas McCave*, University of Cambridge, Cambridge, UK (MG).

2000 *William Jenkins*, Southampton Oceanography Centre, Southampton, UK (PC).

2001 *David Karl*, University of Hawaii, Honolulu, HI, USA (BF).

2002 *Donald W. Forsyth*, Brown University, Providence, RI, USA (MG).

2003 *Lynne Talley*, Scripps Institution of Oceanography, La Jolla, CA, USA (BF).

2004 No award

2005 *Trevor J. McDougall*, Commonwealth Scientific and Industrial Research Organization, Hobart, Australia (PC).

2005 *Edouard Bard*, Collège de France, Paris, France (MG).

2005 *Sallie W. Chisholm*, Massachusetts Institute of Technology, Cambridge, MA, USA (BF).

2005 *Robert Anderson*, Columbia University, Palisades, NY, USA (IMS).

2006 No award

2007 *Thomas Kiørboe*, Danish Institute for Fisheries Research, Charlottenlund, Denmark (BF).

2008 *Roger François*, University of British Columbia, Vancouver, BC, Canada (PC).

2009 *James P.M. Syvitski*, University of Colorado, Boulder, CO, USA (MG).

2010 *Curtis A. Suttle*, University of British Columbia, Vancouver, BC, Canada (BF).

2011 *Andrew J. Weaver*, University of Victoria, Victoria, BC, Canada (PC).

2012 *Katrina J. Edwards*, University of Southern California, Los Angeles, CA, USA (MG).

[1]See opening paragraph (p. 430) for definitions of categories given in parentheses: BF, IMS, MG, and PC.

APPENDIX 6

Bedford Institute of Oceanography

MAJOR REGIONAL, NATIONAL, AND INTERNATIONAL AWARDS[1]

BIO Scientists: 1962 - 2012

1962
William van Steenburgh, awarded an honorary doctorate degree by Dalhousie University, Halifax, NS.

1970
George Needler, named a Rossby Fellow by Woods Hole Oceanographic Institution, Woods Hole, MA.

1972
Cedric Mann, awarded an honorary doctorate degree by Nova Scotia Technical College, Halifax, NS.

1973
Lloyd Dickie, elected to the Royal Society of Canada, Ottawa, ON.

1974
Michael Keen, elected to the Royal Society of Canada, Ottawa, ON.

1975
Charlotte Keen, awarded the APICS/Fraser Young Scientist Medal (Science Atlantic), Dalhousie University, Halifax, NS.

1976
David Nettleship, named an Elected Member of the American Ornithologists' Union, New York, NY.

1978
Richard Brown, named an Elected Member of the American Ornithologists' Union, Madison, WI.
William Ford, awarded an honorary doctorate degree by University of New Brunswick, Fredericton, NB.

1979
William Ford, awarded an honorary Doctor of Laws degree by Dalhousie University, Halifax, NS.
Peter Hacquebard, awarded the Reinhard Thiesson Medal by the International Committee for Coal and Organic Petrology, Oviedo, Spain.
Peter Hacquebard, received the Gilbert H. Cady Award by the Geological Society of America, Boulder, CO.
Charlotte Keen, awarded the Past President's Medal by the Geological Association of Canada, St. John's, NL.

1980
Peter Hacquebard, received an honorary Doctor of Laws degree by Dalhousie University, Halifax, NS.
Charlotte Keen, elected to the Royal Society of Canada, Ottawa, ON.
Kenneth Mann, elected to the Royal Society of Canada, Ottawa, ON.

1981
Trevor Platt, awarded the APICS/Fraser Young Scientist Medal Medal (Science Atlantic), Dalhousie University, Halifax, NS.

1982
Norman Fenerty, received the William Gordon Memorial Award from the Biological Photographic Association, Hillsborough, NC.
David Nettleship, received the Distinguished Technical Communication Award (Books) from the Canadian Society for Technical Communication, Ottawa, ON.
David Nettleship, named Keynote Lecturer for the International Council for Bird Protection (BirdLife International) World Congress, Cambridge University, Cambridge, UK.
Eric Levy, presented a merit award for contributions to the Intergovernmental Oceanographic Commission's IGOSS Pilot Project on Marine Pollution (Petroleum) Monitoring, Paris, France.
*Daniel Ware**, named the 1982 J.C. Stevenson Lecturer, University of Windsor, Windsor, ON.

1983
Richard Brown, received the 1983 Outdoor Writing Award, Canadian Sportmen's Shows-Outdoor Writers of Canada, Toronto, ON.
Peter Hacquebard, awarded the Gold Medal of the Mining Society of Nova Scotia, Sydney, NS.
Peter Hacquebard, received the Distinguished Lecturer Award from the Canadian Institute of Mining and Metallurgy, Westmount, QC.

1984
Richard Brown, received the Science Journalism Award from the Canadian Science Writers' Association, Toronto, ON.
Robert Conover, Lloyd Dickie, and *Kenneth Mann*, received Citation Classic awards for research publications.
William Ford, awarded the J.P. Tully Medal in Oceanography by the Canadian Meteorological and Oceanographic Society, Ottawa, ON.
Michel Latremouille, received the Distinguished Technical Communication Award, Society for Technical Communication (Eastern Ontario Chapter), Ottawa, ON.

David Nettleship, named Chairman of the Standing Committee for Coordination of Seabird Research, International Ornithological Congress, Bielefeld, Germany.
David Nettleship, received a Service Award from the American Ornithologists' Union for exceptional assistance in the editing of the science journal *The Auk*, University of New Mexico, Albuquerque, NM.
Trevor Platt, awarded the Rosenstiel Award by the University of Miami, Miami, FL.

1985
George Needler, elected to the Royal Society of Canada, Ottawa, ON.
Raymond Sheldon, awarded Doctor of Science degree by the University of Manchester, Manchester, UK.

1986
*Kenneth Denman**, awarded the President's Prize by the Canadian Meteorological and Oceanographic Society, Ottawa, ON.
Charlotte Keen, elected a Fellow of the American Geophysical Union, Washington, DC.
Michael Keen, awarded the Logan Medal by the Geological Association of Canada, St. John's, NL.
William Li, awarded the APICS/Fraser Young Scientist Medal (Science Atlantic), Dalhousie University, Halifax, NS.
David Nettleship, named the Louis A. Fuertes Lecturer, Laboratory of Ornithology, Cornell University, Ithaca, NY.

1988
John Loder, named the 1988 J.C. Stevenson Lecturer, Canadian Conference for Fisheries Research, University of Windsor, Windsor, ON.
Alan Longhurst, elected to the Royal Society of Canada, Ottawa, ON.
Trevor Platt, awarded the Evelyn Hutchinson Award by the American Society of Limnology and Oceanography, Waco, TX.
Trevor Platt, national tour speaker for the Canadian Meteorological and Oceanographic Society, Ottawa, ON.

1989
David Nettleship, elected a Fellow of the American Ornithologists' Union, Pittsburgh, PA.

1990
Peta Mudie, elected to the Royal Society of Canada, Ottawa, ON.
Trevor Platt, elected to the Royal Society of Canada, Ottawa, ON.

1991
Lloyd Dickie, presented the Oscar Sette Memorial Award by the American Fisheries Society, Bethesda, MD.
Charlotte Keen, named the 1991 Rutherford Lecturer, The Royal Society, London, UK.
Alan Longhurst, awarded the Gold Medal by the Professional Institute of the Public Service of Canada, Ottawa, ON.
David Nettleship, named to the Executive Committee of 100, International Ornithological Congress, Christchurch, NZ.
Stuart Smith, awarded the 1991 American Meteorological Society's Editor's Award, Boston, MA.
Gus Vilks, awarded honorary membership, North American Micropalaeontology Section, Society of Economic Paleontologists and Mineralogists (Society for Sedimentary Geology), Tulsa, OK.
Daniel Wright, awarded the President's Prize by the Canadian Meteorological and Oceanographic Society, Ottawa, ON.
Daniel Wright, received the Excellence in Reviewing Award from Canadian Meteorological and Oceanographic Society, Ottawa, ON.

1992
Fred Dobson, awarded the J.P. Tully Medal in Oceanography by the Canadian Meteorological and Oceanographic Society, Ottawa, ON.
Kenneth Frank, named the 1992 J.C. Stevenson Lecturer, University of Windsor, Windsor, ON.
Lubomir Jansa, awarded the Professor Purkyne Medal by the Czechoslovakia Geological Survey, Prague, Czech Republic.
Charlotte Keen, awarded honorary membership in the Canadian Society of Exploration Geophysicists, Calgary, AB.
Michael Keen, honoured by the establishment of the Michael J. Keen Medal for contributions in marine and lacustrine geoscience by the Geological Association of Canada, St. John's, NL.
Trevor Platt, awarded the A.G. Huntsman Award, Bedford Institute of Oceanography, Dartmouth, NS.

1993
Rob Fensome and *Graham Williams*, received the Golden Trilobite Award from the Paleontological Association, Boulder, CO.
Charlotte Keen, awarded the Michael J. Keen Medal by the Marine Geosciences Division of the Geological Association of Canada, St. John's, NL.
Cedric Mann, awarded the J.P. Tully Medal in Oceanography by the Canadian Meteorological and Oceanographic Society, Ottawa, ON.

1994
Steven Campana, named the 1994 J.C. Stevenson Lecturer, Canadian Conference for Fisheries Research, University of Windsor, Windsor, ON.
Kenneth Drinkwater, awarded the François J. Saucier Prize in Applied Oceanography by the Canadian Meteorological and Oceanographic Society, Ottawa, ON.
Lubomir Jansa, awarded the Georgius Agricola Medal by the Technical University of Mining and Metallurgy, Ostrava, Czech Republic.
Lubomir Jansa, awarded the Masaryk Medal by Masaryk University, Brno, Czech Republic.
Peter Jones, awarded the degree of Doctor Honoris Causa by the University of Göteborg, Sweden.
Charlotte Keen, awarded the George P. Woollard Award by the Geological Society of America, Washington, DC.
Lewis King, awarded the Michael J. Keen Medal by the Marine Geosciences Division of the Geological Association of Canada, St. John's, NL.
John Lazier, national tour speaker for the Canadian Meteorological and Oceanographic Society, Ottawa, ON.
Kenneth Mann, received the first A.C. Redfield Lifetime Achievement Award presented by the American Society of Limnology and Oceanography, Waco, TX.

1995
Peter Hacquebard, first winner of the Walter Bell Silver Medal, from W.A. Bell Symposium on Euroamerican Carbonifierous Paleobotany & Coal Geology, Sydney, NS.
Peter Hacquebard, given the John Castano Honorary Membership Award, The Society for Organic Petrology, Reston, VA.

Charlotte Keen, presented the J. Tuzo Wilson Medal by the Canadian Geophysical Union, Calgary, AB.
Charlotte Keen, elected Fellow of the Geological Association of Canada, St. John's, NL.

1996
Stephen Blasco, received the H.G. Hamilton Award from Queen's University, Kingston, ON.
John Lazier, awarded the J.P. Tully Medal in Oceanography by the Canadian Meteorological and Oceanographic Society, Ottawa, ON.
Stuart Smith, awarded the President's Prize by the Canadian Meteorological and Oceanographic Society, Ottawa, ON.
Graham Williams, awarded the E.R. Ward Neale Medal of the Geological Association of Canada, St. John's, NL.
Graham Williams, awarded the American Association of Stratigraphic Palynology Medal for Scientific Excellence, Houston, TX.

1997
Alan Grant, awarded the Michael J. Keen Medal by the Marine Geosciences Division of the Geological Association of Canada, St. John's, NL.
Alan Longhurst, awarded the A.C. Redfield Lifetime Achievement Award by the American Society of Limnology and Oceanography, Waco, TX.

1998
Allyn Clarke, awarded the Government of Canada Award of Excellence by the President of the Treasury Board, Ottawa, ON.
Peter Hacquebard, honoured by the establishment of the Hacquebard Medal by the Canadian Society of Coal and Organic Petrology, Calgary, AB.
Lubomir Jansa, elected a Fellow of the Geological Society of America, Boulder, CO.
Neil Oakey, awarded the J.P. Tully Medal in Oceanography by the Canadian Meteorological and Oceanographic Society, Ottawa, ON.
David Nettleship, received the COSEWIC Service Award, Canadian Wildlife Directors Committee, Committee on the Status of Endangered Wildlife in Canada, Ottawa, ON.
Trevor Platt, elected to the Fellowship of the Royal Society of London, London, UK.
Peter Smith, David Greenberg, Donald Lawrence, Guoqi Han, Jennifer Shore, John Loder, Charles Hannah, Roger Pettipas, and *Brendon De Tracey*, awarded the François J. Saucier Prize in Applied Oceanography by the Canadian Meteorological and Oceanographic Society, Ottawa, ON.

1999
David Piper, awarded the Michael J. Keen Medal by the Marine Geosciences Division of the Geological Association of Canada, St. John's, NL.

2000
Richard Brown, received a Lifetime Achievement Award from the Pacific Seabird Group, Anchorage, AK.
David Piper, awarded the Gesner Medal by the Atlantic Geoscience Society, Wolfville, NS.
Peter Wells, elected a Fellow of the American Association for the Advancement of Science, New York, NY.

2001
Stephen Blasco, elected a member of the Order of Canada, Ottawa, ON.
Allyn Clarke, awarded the J.P. Tully Medal in Oceanography by the Canadian Meteorological and Oceanographic Society, Ottawa, ON.
Donald Gordon, presented the Government of Canada 5NR Science Award to Leaders in Sustainable Development, Ottawa, ON.
Richard Pickrill, *Leslie Burke*, *Richard McDougall*, *James Bradford,* and *Kate Moran*, presented an award by the Nova Scotia Federal Council for the SeaMap initiative, Halifax, NS.

2002
Jennifer Bates, Rob Fensome, and *Graham Williams*, received the Best Publication of the Year Award from the Association of Earth Science Editors, Pittsburg, PA.
Allyn Clarke, received Editor's Citation for Excellence in Reviewing from the American Geophysical Union, Washington, DC.
Rob Fensome and *Graham Williams*, received the Distinguished Service Award from the Atlantic Geoscience Society, Wolfville, NS.
Donald Forbes, received the Government of Canada 5NR Science Award to Leaders in Sustainable Development, Ottawa, ON.
René Lavoie, received the Honorary Lifetime Achievement Award from the Aquaculture Association of Canada, St. Andrews, NB.
Peta Mudie, awarded an Honorary Research Fellowship, University of Glasgow, Glasgow, Scotland, UK.

2003
Stephen Blasco, received Award of Excellence from Parks Canada, Ottawa, ON.
Charlotte Keen, awarded an honorary doctorate degree by the Department of Oceanography, Dalhousie University, Halifax, NS.
Kenneth Mann, presented the Gulf of Maine Council Visionary Award for Nova Scotia, Halifax, NS.
Graham Williams, received the Canpolar Sciences Communications Award (Science Atlantic), Dalhousie University, Halifax, NS.

2004
Steven Campana, presented with the Lifetime Achievement Award at the Third International Symposium on Fish Otolith Research and Application, Townsville, Australia.
Alan Grant, awarded the Gesner Medal by the Atlantic Geoscience Society, Wolfville, NS.
Kenneth Lee, received the Excellence in Technology Transfer Award from the Federal Partners in Technology Transfer, Ottawa, ON.
Brian Petrie, awarded the J.P. Tully Medal in Oceanography by the Canadian Meteorological and Oceanographic Society, Ottawa, ON.

2005
Michael Eaton, elected a member of the Order of Canada, Ottawa, ON.
Alan Grant, awarded the R.J.W. Douglas Medal by the Canadian Society of Petroleum Geologists, Calgary, AB.
*Daniel Ware**, received the Timothy R. Parsons Award, Fisheries and Oceans Canada, Ottawa, ON.

2006
Alan Grant, awarded an honorary doctorate by Dalhousie University, Halifax, NS.
Carl Myers, awarded the national Leadership and Excellence in Communications Award, Ottawa, ON.
David Nettleship, awarded a COSEWIC Certificate of Appreciation as a Founding Member of the Birds Specialist Subcommittee and for three decades of service, Committee on the Status of Endangered Wildlife in Canada, Ottawa, ON.

Trevor Platt and *Kenneth Denman**, received the Timothy R. Parsons Award, Fisheries and Oceans Canada, Ottawa, ON.
Graham Williams, awarded the J. Willis Ambrose Medal by the Geological Association of Canada, St. John's, NL.
Daniel Wright, national tour speaker for the Canadian Meteorological and Oceanographic Society, Ottawa, ON.

2007
Allyn Clarke, elected Fellow of the Canadian Meteorological and Oceanographic Society, Ottawa, ON.
Donald Forbes, Allyn Clarke, Trevor Platt, and *Igor Yashayaev*, honoured for contributions to the Fourth Assessment of the Intergovernmental Panel on Climate Change (shared the 2007 Nobel Peace Prize with former US Vice-President A. Gore), Oslo, Norway.
Erica Head, national tour speaker for the Canadian National Committee, Scientific Committee for Oceanic Research, Ottawa, ON.
Michael Lewis, awarded the Michael J. Keen Medal by the Marine Geosciences Division of the Geological Association of Canada, St. John's, NL.
David Piper, received a Special Award from the International Association of Sedimentologists, Ghent, Belgium.
Simon Prinsenberg, awarded the J.P. Tully Medal in Oceanography by the Canadian Meteorological and Oceanographic Society, Ottawa, ON.

2008
Gerard Costello, Michael Lamplugh, Bob Courtney, Vladimir Kostylev, Dick Pickrill, and *Brian Todd*, received the Excellence in Technology Transfer Award from the Federal Partners in Technology Transfer, Ottawa, ON.
Donald Gordon, awarded the Timothy R. Parsons Award, Fisheries and Oceans Canada, Ottawa, ON.

2009
*James Syvitski**, awarded the A.G. Huntsman Award, Bedford Institute of Oceanography, Dartmouth, NS.

2010
Stephen Blasco, received the Distinguished Merit Award from the Government of Canada for communicating science to northern communities, Ottawa, ON.
*Felix Gradstein**, awarded the Jean Baptiste Lamark Medal, European Geosciences Union, Munich, Germany.
Brian Petrie, awarded the Timothy R. Parsons Award, Fisheries and Oceans Canada, Ottawa, ON.
David Piper, awarded the Shepard Medal by the Society for Sedimentary Geology, Tulsa, OK.

2011
Stephen Blasco, received the Distinguished Merit Award from the Government of Canada for achievement in the synthesis of Beaufort Sea seabed geohazard research, Ottawa, ON.
Allyn Clarke, awarded an Intergovernmental Oceanographic Commission's 50th Anniversary Commemorative Medal, Paris, France.
Allyn Clarke, elected Guest of Honour at scientific symposium "Variability of the North Atlantic and its Marine Ecosystems during 2000-2009", International Council for the Exploration of the Sea and Northwest Atlantic Fisheries Organization, Copenhagen, DK.
Rob Fensome, received the Lifetime Achievement Award for work on dinoflagellates at the DINO9 meeting, University of Liverpool, Liverpool, UK.
Donald Forbes, received the Award for Geography in the Service of Government from the Canadian Association of Geographers, Montreal, QC.
Kenneth Lee, awarded the Discovery Centre Award for Professional Distinction, Halifax, NS.
John Loder, awarded the J.P. Tully Medal in Oceanography by the Canadian Meteorological and Oceanographic Society, Ottawa, ON.
Graham Williams, awarded the Billings Medal by the Geological Association of Canada, St. John's, NL.

2012
Kenneth Frank, elected national tour speaker for the Canadian National Committee for the Scientific Committee for Oceanic Research, Ottawa, ON.
David Piper, awarded an honorary degree by the University of Athens, Athens, Greece.

---

[1] List excludes internal departmental awards.
* Previous BIO employee.

APPENDIX 7

Bedford Institute of Oceanography

BELUGA AWARD

The Beluga Award recognizes employees who have exhibited unselfish dedication to community spirit at the Bedford Institute of Oceanography (BIO). The Award recognizes individuals in any professional or technical field, craft or skill who have made exceptional contributions to the success of BIO projects, initiatives or programs. These contributions exemplify unselfish effort that encourages cooperation and fosters the team-work approach of BIO. All present and past employees in any field or specialization are eligible. It is intended that this Award should recognize all professions including ship's crew, administrative personnel, technicians and scientists.

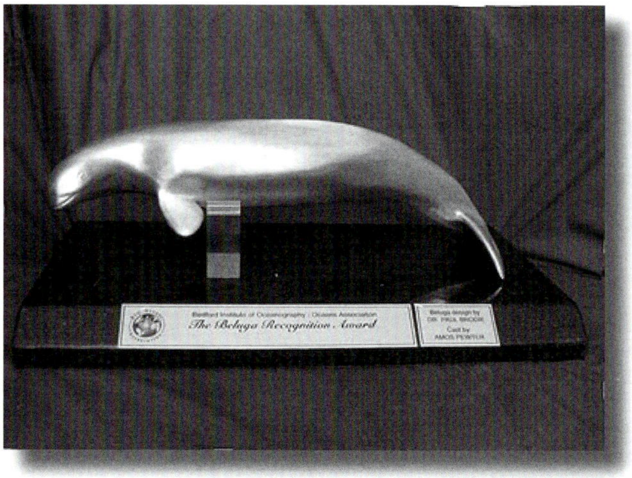

Beluga Award Sculpture

2001 *Roger Belanger*
2002 *Peter Vass*
2003 *Arthur Cosgrove*
2004 *David McKeown*
2005 *Jacqueline Dale*
2006 *Joseph Bray*
2007 *Murray Scotney*
2008 *Borden Chapman*
2009 *Bruce Anderson*
2010 *Sherry Niven*
2011 *Brian Beanlands*
2012 *Donald Gordon*

APPENDIX 8

Bedford Institute of Oceanography

CRYSTAL AWARDS[1]

The BIO 50th Anniversary Crystal Awards were presented on 25 October 2012 to commemorate outstanding and innovative accomplishments of scientific and technical staff during the first 50 years of BIO. The project teams were recognized by their peers for contributions that greatly expanded our knowledge and understanding of diverse ocean environments. [Note: names of project leaders are given in italics.]

1962-72

1. BIODAL and GEODAL
BIODAL and GEODAL are data acquisition systems, designed, and built at BIO during the pre-microprocessor era that enabled sea-going researchers to reliably record vast amounts of marine data for many applications.
Team members: *C. Mason*, D. Barrett, E. Bendell, A. Bennett, R. Cassivi, R. Gilbert, B. Loncarevic, S. MacPhee, W. Proctor, R. Vine, D. Wells.

2. Hudson-70 Expedition
This epic voyage, a collaborative effort of over 100 scientists and technicians, is the greatest single effort that Canada has made in oceanographic research, and marked the first circumnavigation of the Americas.
Team members: *C. Mann*, D. Barrett, P. Beamish, R. Belanger, R. Brown, J. Bruce, W. Cameron, B. Carson, V. Coady, R. Conover, A. Coote, T. Corbett, P. Corkum, T. Courtney, D. Druhan, I. Duedall, R. Eaton, T. Foote, K. Freeman, D. Garner, M. Gorveatt, A. Grant, W. Greifeneder, R. Haworth, H. Henderson, R. Hiltz, M. Hughes, L. Johnston, C. Keen, E. Lewis, B. Loncarevic, K. Manchester, C. Maunsell, S. McHughen, R. Melanson, F. Muise, J. Murray, J. Nielsen, M. Paranjape, B. Pelletier, J. Piechura, R. Pilote, A. Prakash, G. Purdy, R. Reiniger, D. Ross, C. Schafer, J. Shearer, R. Sheldon, K. Shih, R. Smith, P. Solowen, S. Srivastava, J. Steele, W. Sutcliffe, R. Taylor, A. Thomlinson, D. Tiffin, H. Toom, G. Vilks, P. Wadhams, F. Wagner, W. Whiteway, D. Winters, J. Woodside.

3. Hydrostatic Rock Core Drill
The hydrostatic rock core drill is an innovative sampling tool, powered by hydrostatic pressure, that was used successfully to collect rock core samples in water depths as deep as 1,600 metres on the Mid-Atlantic Ridge.
Team members: *R. Gilbert, J. Brooke*, G. Connolly, J-G. Dessureault, G. Fowler, D. Harvey, A. Johnson, P. Jollymore, P. Kingston, D. McKeown, R. Vine, S. Young.

1973-82

4. St. Georges Bay Program
Program scientists studied the interaction of physical, chemical, and biological factors controlling the dynamics of the growth and survival of larval mackerel and lobster in a coastal bay.
Team members: *D. Ware*, K. Beall, C. Bourbonais, M. Butler, R. Cunjak, A. Diepenbrock, D. Dobson, K. Drinkwater, G. Harding, B. Hargrave, G. Harrison, P. Harnish, B. Henriksen, T. Kenchington, T. Lambert, M. Lanctot, A. MacDonald, J. McRuer, B. Petrie, L. Petrie, G. Phillips, N. Prouse, D. Rutherford, R. Sheldon, G. Taylor, R. Trites, P. Vass, K. Watson.

5. Operation Oil
A multi-agency team that resolved a series of complex scientific and technical problems arising from the cleanup of the 1970 *Arrow* oil spill in Chedabucto Bay, Nova Scotia.
Team members: *W. Ford*, J. Allen, V. Asthana, T. Atkinson, G. Awalt, F. Barber, R. Belanger, J. Brooke, L. Brown, R. Brown, V. Carson, W. Carson, R. Conover, R. Cooke, A. Cosgrove, J-G. Dessureault, D. Dinn, D. Dobson, G. Drapeau, M. Falk, T. Foote, W. Forrester, S. Fowler, W. Gibson, J. Guilderson, D. Jamieson, D. Johnson, A. Hartling, K. Kranck, D. Lawrence, E. Levy, D. Loring, R. Loucks, S. MacPhee, M. Magill, K. Manchester, J. Marlowe, C. Mason, A. McLean, R. Mills, G. Mulkins-Phillips, J. Myrick, H. Neu, E. Owens, F. Payne, C. Peters, J. Pew, E. Puddington, O. Ros, D. Scarratt, C. Schafer, M. Scotney, D. Scott, N. Sellers, P. Seto, R. Sheldon, J. Simms, B. Smith, J. Sprague, J. Stewart, W. Sutcliffe, M. Thomas, R. Trites, P. Wells, S. Whiteway, D. Wiles, A. Wilson, K. Yuen, V. Zitko.

6. BATFISH
An innovative, undulating towed instrument designed to carry various oceanographic sensors for physical and biological oceanographic studies in offshore waters.
Team members: *J-G. Dessureault*, A. Bennett, W. Cooke, G. Dubois, R. Gilbert, C. Mason, T. Phillips, M. Stepanczak, P. Thorburn, S. Young.

7. Development of Ocean Bottom Seismometers
Ocean Bottom Seismometers were designed to detect shear and compressional seismic waves in the acoustically quiet seabed environment, a vast improvement over the sea-surface sonobuoys used previously.
Team members: *D. Heffler*, D. Barrett, B. Chapman, C. Keen, D. Locke, B. Loncarevic, K. Manchester.

8. Electric Rock Core Drill
Through the application of innovative engineering design concepts, the builders created a unique bedrock sampling device that contributed significantly to the mapping of shallow seafloor bedrock geology.
Team members: *G. Fowler*, T. Atkinson, E. Bendall, R. Cassivi, W. Cooke; F. Ewing, D. Harvey, P. Kingston, P. Ryall, W. Whiteway.

9. Mapping of the Surficial Sediments of Offshore Eastern Canada
The world's first surficial seafloor geologic mapping project of a continental shelf that became the framework for understanding seafloor geohazards and the development of ecosystem management based on seabed mapping.
Team members: *L. King*, D. Clattenburg, V. Coady, G. Drapeau, G. Fader, H. Josenhans, K. Kranck, D. Loring, B. MacLean, R. Miller.

10. Bay of Fundy Ecosystem Study
A multidisciplinary and multi-institutional study of tides and circulation, sediment dynamics, nutrient chemistry, biological productivity, shorebirds, and fish populations in the macrotidal Bay of Fundy ecosystem that enabled assessment of the environmental effects of tidal power development.
Team members: *D. Gordon, C. Amos, D. Greenberg*, P. Cranford, G. Daborn, M. Dadswell, J. Dale, B. Hargrave, P. Hicklin, P. Keizer, B. Long, D. Peer, G. Phillips, N. Prouse, P. Schwinghamer, W. Silvert, D. Wildish.

11. Geology and Geophysics of the Scotian Margin and Grand Banks
This ambitious geological and geophysical project, based on seismic data interpretation and well log and sample analysis, produced the first detailed synthesis of the subsurface geology of the Scotian Basin.
Team members: *B. Loncarevic, B. Sanford*, D. Barrett, S. Barss, A. Grant, G. Grant, I. Hardy, R. Haworth, D. Heffler, R. Howie, L. Jansa, C. Keen, M. Keen, L. King, B. MacLean, J. Wade, G. Williams.

1983-92

12. Radionuclide Studies in the Arctic Ocean
This suite of projects was designed to identify contaminant pathways and estimate transit times and mixing rates in the Arctic Ocean and to reveal changes associated with climate change and reduced sea ice cover.
Team members: *J. Smith*, J. Abriel, E. Carmack, K. Ellis, G. Folwarczna, P. Jones, R. Macdonald, F. McLaughlin, R. Moore, B. Moran, R. Nelson, L. Polyak.

13. Ocean Drilling Program
During the 1980s, Canada was a full partner in the international Ocean Drilling Program that contributed much valuable knowledge about the geologic history of the world's ocean basins and the composition of their oceanic crustal rocks.
Team members: *S. Srivastava, F. Gradstein, M. Salisbury*, R. Cranston, P. Hill, L. Jansa, M. Kaminski, K. MacKillop, J. Marsters, K. Moran, D. Mosher P. Mudie, G. Vilks, M. Williamson.

14. Optical Plankton Counter/Laser Optical Plankton Counter
Two projects that focused on the development of novel instruments to measure the size and concentration of zooplankton living at various depths in the ocean.
Team members: *A. Herman*, B. Beanlands, J. Conrod, T. Phillips, S. Young.

15. Canadian Ice Island
The 5-year Canadian Ice Island project, based on a tabular iceberg, carried out pioneering scientific studies of the Canadian polar margin which were critical for defining Canadian sovereignty and understanding the impact of climate change on Arctic Ocean biota.
Team members: *R. Jackson, P. Mudie, B. Hargrave, P. Jones*, J. Dabros, K. Ellis, M. Gorveatt, D. Heffler, M. Hughes, F. Jodrey, D. Locke, D. Mosher, R. Murphy, G. Sonnichsen, S. Thibaudeau, P. Vass, F. Zemlyak.

16. Geology of the Continental Margin of Eastern Canada
This project comprised a series of coordinated investigations and syntheses that defined the geological surficial and subsurface features of Canadian east coast continental shelf, slope, and rise geological environments for a book contribution to Geology of Canada and Decade of North American Geology.
Team members: *M. Keen, G. Williams*, J. Adams, A. Aksu, C. Amos, P. Ascoli, H. Balkwill, V. Barrie, S. Barss, C. Beaumont, J. Bell, M. Best, S. Blasco, G. Bonham Carter, D. Brown, D. Buckley, J. Bujak, G. Cameron, G. Campbell, B. D'Anglejan, R. Davidson-Arnott, E. Davies, P. Durling, G. Fader, R. Fensome, R. Gillie, F. Gradstein, A. Grant, P. Hale, I. Hardy, J. Harper, R. Haworth, P. Hill, D. Hodgson, R. Howie, D. Huntley, L. Jansa, A. Jennings, I. Jones, H. Josenhans, A. Judge, C. Keen, R. Klassen, M. Lewis, B. Loncarevic, B.C. MacLean, B. MacLean, R. Macnab, K. McAlpine, J. McMillan, K. Moran, P. Mudie, R. Myers, V. Noguera, G. Pe-Piper, B. Pelletier, D. Piper, C. Powell, D. Praeg, I. Reid, B. Sanford, C. Schafer, G. Sonnichsen, S. Srivastava, B. Stam, J. Syvitski, R. Taylor, J. Verhoef, G. Vilks, J.-S. Vincent, J. Wade, H. Williams, M. Williamson, J. Woodside, C. Woodworth-Lynas.

1993-2002

17. Physical, Chemical and Biological Oceanographic Variability in the Labrador Sea
This ocean climate and ecosystem multiyear observation program was conducted in one of the most important areas of the global ocean and is an excellent example of the type of world-class multidisciplinary science that BIO has been able to foster and support.
Team members: *J. Lazier, G. Harrison, P. Jones, A. Clarke*, J. Anning, C. Anstey, K. Azetsu-Scott, R. Boyce, J. Bugden, B. Carson, P. Clement, P. Dickie, R. Gershey, L. Harris, E. Head, R. Hendry, B. Irwin, A. Isenor, J. Jackson, P. Kepkay, W. Li, B. Ryan, M. Scotney, J. Smit, I. Yashayaev, F. Zemlyak.

18. Ecological Impacts of Mobile Fishing Gear on the Seabed
This interdepartmental and multidisciplinary study documented the environmental impacts of otter trawls, scallop rakes, and clam dredges on seabed habitats and communities off Atlantic Canada and described the extent of their post-impact recovery.
Team members: *D. Gordon, P. Schwinghamer, K. Gilkinson, E. Kenchington, T. Rowell*, K. Bentham, C. Bourbonnais-Boyce, A. Boyce, L. Buhl-Mortensen, B. Chapman, M. Chin-Yee, G. Fader, D. Hardy, M. Hawryluk, L-A. Henry, M. Hughes, B. MacEachern, K. MacIsaac, D. McKeown, R. Miller, P. Mortensen, D. Peer, J. Prena, D. Reimer, D. Roddick, G. Steeves, G. Sonnichsen, P. Vass, B. Wile, P. Woo, S. Young.

19. Fate and Effects of Particulate Wastes from Offshore Hydrocarbon Drilling
A multidisciplinary study of the fate and biological effects of particulate operational drilling wastes to assist regulators manage the use and disposal of drilling wastes off Canada's east coast.
Team members: *D. Gordon, K. Muschenheim, J. Loder, C. Hannah, P. Cranford*, S. Armsworthy, D. Belliveau, K. Bentham, A. Drozdowski, D. McKeown, T. Milligan, G. Morton, D. Reimer, Y. Shen, T. Tedford, P. Vass, Z. Xu.

20. Geological Survey of Canada (Atlantic) - Marine Geoscience Digital Initiative
This project transformed the GSC-Atlantic's analog seismic data collection to a digital format and replaced manual data processing methodologies with emerging digital systems-based technologies for collecting, processing and presenting marine geology data.
Team members: *R. Courtney*, R. Currie, D. Heffler, K. Manchester, B. Nicholls, R. Parrott, D. Prior.

21. Moving Vessel Profiler (MVP)
This BIO-designed instrument has been used extensively to collect fluorescence, sound velocity, and zooplankton abundance information in the upper part of the water column from research vessels while underway.
Team members: *J-G. Dessureau, B. Beanlands*, M. Chin-Yee, J. Conrod, R. King, D. McKeown, T. Phillips, G. States, S. Young.

22. BIO's Response to the Swissair 111 Tragedy
The BIO response to the 1998 crash of Swissair Flight 111 provided an excellent example of rapid mobilization capabilities of diverse types of marine expertise in response to a major disaster.
Team members: *LCdr J. Bradford*, Lt(N) S. Moody, CPO2 I. Stewart, PO2 R. Beckershoff, MS L. Guyomard, LS J. Foote, LS W. McMillan, GSC-Atlantic and DFO staff.

2003-12

23. Spatial Utilization of Seabed Habitat by Demersal Fish
This interdepartmental and multidisciplinary study defined the preferred seabed habitat and distribution for juvenile haddock on the Scotian Shelf to assist fisheries management in improving the long-term sustainability of haddock and other demersal fisheries.
Team members: *D. Gordon, J. Anderson*, R. Benjamin, K. Bentham, C. Bourbonnais-Boyce, A. Boyce, P. Clement, R. Courtney, E. Dalley, D. Davis, G. Evans, G. Fader, K. Gilkinson, B. Gregory, P. Hurley, E. Kenchington, C. Lang, J. Linehan, K. MacIsaac, D. McKeown, N. Ollerhead, D. Reimer, J. Simon, P. Vass.

24. Development and Application of Oil Spill Countermeasures
Scientists in this multiagency project improved existing and developed new 'green' oil spill countermeasure technologies used by the global oil spill response community for protecting the aquatic environment and its living resources.
Team members: *K. Lee*, B. Beanlands, D. Belliveau, M. Blouin, J. Budgen, L. Burridge, S. Cobanli, S. Courtenay, R. Doane, P. Kepkay, T. King, Z. Li, X. Ma, J. Mason, C. McIntyre, D. Moffatt, G. Morton, H. Niu, M. Pittman, B. Robinson, S. Ryan, P. Thamer, G. Wohlgeschaffen.

25. Discovery Science in Support of The Gully Marine Protected Area (MPA)
This comprehensive and multi-departmental investigation of The Gully exemplifies BIO's strengths in multidisciplinary science and their application to pressing matters of marine environmental policy.
Team members: *E. Kenchington, T. Worcester, P. Macnab*, K. Bentham, J. Black, D. Campbell, P. Clement, N. Cochrane, A. Cogswell, B. Greenan, E. Head, E. Horne, D. Fenton, S. Johnston, T. Kenchington, E. King, K. Lee, K. MacIsaac, H. Moors, C. Myers.

26. Ocean Profilers (SeaHorse, IceCycler, SeaCycler)
These engineering initiatives developed mooring systems for repetitive data collection over prolonged periods in ice-covered and deep waters while conserving energy by the innovative use of buoyancy forces.
Team members: *G. Fowler, J. Hamilton, G. Siddall*, J. Barthelott, B. Beanlands, D. Belliveau, J. Burtch, S. Burtch, R. Cassivi, Z. Chaisson, J. Conrod, H. Dussault, B. Ellis, A. Furlong, B. Julien, R. King, G. Lebans, N. MacKinnon, D. Moffatt, V. Pattenden, T. Peters, K. Phelan, M. Pittman, S. Prinsenberg, U. Send, G. States, L. Sutherby, D. Vine, M. Vining, B. Whiteway, S. Young.

27. Variability in the Structure and Functioning of the Scotian Shelf Ecosystem
Using a wide range of empirical and modelling approaches, BIO scientists interpreted causes of decadal changes in the structure and function of the Scotian Shelf ecosystem which increased understanding of trophic interactions within the marine environment.
Team members: *A. Bundy, A. Cook, K. Frank, R. Mohn, R. O'Boyle*, J. Araujo, D. Bowen, J. Choi, K. Drinkwater, P. Fanning, J. Fisher, C. Fu, T. Horsman, B. Leggett, R. Mahon, B. Petrie, D. Sameoto, N. Shackell, K. Trzcinskie, K. Zwanenburg.

28. Bedford Basin Monitoring Program
The Bedford Basin Monitoring Program revealed long-term ecological changes in a part of the ocean that is of significant scientific, socioeconomic, cultural, and historical importance to Canadians.
Team members: *W. Li*, J. Anning, C. Anstey, C. Caverhill, P. Dickie, G. Harrison, E. Head, E. Horne, B. Irwin, M. Kennedy, M. Landry, H. Maass, K. Pauley, T. Perry, C. Porter, M. Ringuette, J. Spry.

29. The Northern Labrador Charting Project
The eleven new charts produced by the Canadian Hydrographic Service signalled the end of a 75-year charting effort to ensure the safety of mariners transiting the treacherous coast of Labrador.
Team members: *S. Forbes, R. MacDougall*, B. Anderson, S. Akerman, A. Craft, F. Carmichael, M. Collins, C. Coolen, J. Cormier, G. Costello, L. Cuff, J. Griffin, H. Joyce, G. King, C. LeBlanc, M. Lamplugh, J. Manning, P. MacAulay, B. MacGowan, C. McCarthy, R. Morrison, M. Nickerson, S. Nunn, N. Palmer, R. Palmer, D. Regular, A. Roy, C. Rozon, K. Sabadash, J. Senay, D. Sinnott, G. Smith, D. Street, N. Stuifbergen, C. Zeller.

Multidecadal

30. BIO Mooring Technology
This project, an enduring effort for five decades, exemplifies teamwork that produced new and more reliable mooring designs, innovations in mooring recovery techniques, and modifications to ocean current meters that collectively resulted in significant improvements in data quality. Team members: *A. Hartling*, R. Boyce, T. Foote, G. Fowler, S. Glazebrook, J. Hamilton, R. Reiniger, M. Scotney.

---

[1] The Crystal Awards were created and organized by Claudia Currie and Charles Schafer with assistance from Sonya Dehler, Arnold Furlong, Donald Gordon, Michel Latremouille, Stephen Locke, Timothy Milligan, Thomas Sephton, Michael Sinclair, Alain Vezina, and the BIO-Oceans Association. Underlying the success of all projects was the crucial support provided by BIO's scientific and hydrographic survey vessels. All project leaders and participants gratefully acknowledge the dedicated services of ships' officers and crew over the past 50 years.

APPENDIX 9

Bedford Institute of Oceanography

PATENTS

Awarded to BIO staff

1967 *Reginald Gilbert* - Deep-water wave recorder (Canada Patent 768,793).

1969 *Reginald Gilbert* and *John Brooke* - A method and apparatus for energizing a prime mover at levels below the surface of a liquid (Canada Patent 822,351).

1972 *Jean-Guy Dessureault* - Gravity controlled stabilizer (Canada Patent 892,351).

1987 *George Fowler, Jim Hamilton,* and *Bill Whiteway* - Traction device for line handling equipment (United States Patent 4,678,132).

1988 *Alex Herman* - Optical measurement of marine conditions (Canada Patent 768,793).

1991 *John Brooke* - Underwater control system (United States Patent 4,996,673).

1993 *Mark Chin-Yee* - Recovery system for a submerged instrument (United States Patent 5,219,245).

1995 *John Brooke, Arnold Furlong* and *Geoff Lebans* - System for handling a remotely operated Vessel (United States Patent 5,378,851).

1996 *Jean-Guy Dessureault* - System for collecting oceanographic data from a moving vessel (Canada Patent 2,137,846; United States Patent 5,570,303).

1997 *George Fowler* - Wave-powered ocean profiler (United States Patent 5,644,077).

1998 *George Fowler* and *Jim Hamilton* - Streamlined buoyancy package for subsurface moorings (United States Patent 5,707,265).

2000 *George Fowler* - Energy conserving moored buoyant ocean profiler (United States Patent 6,463,800).

2000 *Herman Varma* - Method and apparatus for multidimensional database using binary hyperspatial code (United States Patent 6,161,105).

2004 *Alex Herman* Optical measurement of marine conditions (Canada Patent 1,233,665).

2011 *George Fowler, Greg Siddall,* and *Brian Beanlands* - Communications float (United States Patent 7,874,886).

APPENDIX 10

Bedford Institute of Oceanography

LIST OF AUTHORS[1]

(paper number, * sole/lead author;
for complete BIO address see footnote)

Dr. Richard F. Addison (36*)
1705 Eagle View Place
Duncan, BC, Canada V9L 6R1
E-mail: rfaddison@shaw.ca
Phone: (250) 597-1558

Dr. Carl L. Amos (45)
University of Southampton
National Oceanography Centre
Southampton S014 3ZH
Hampshire, United Kingdom
E-mail: cla8@noc.soton.ac.uk
Phone: 023-80596068

Dr. J. Vaughn Barrie (21)
Geological Survey of Canada (Pacific)
Natural Resources Canada
Institute of Ocean Sciences
9860 West Saanich Road (PO Box 6000)
Sidney, BC, Canada V8L 4B2
E-mail: Vaughn.Barrie@NRCan.gc.ca
Phone: (250) 363-6424

Mr. Brian D. Beanlands (6, 41)
6 Spinnaker Drive
Glen Haven, NS, Canada B3Z 2S7
E-mail: brianandcathy@eastlink.ca
Phone: (902) 823-3103

Mr. Steve M. Blasco (9, 22, 26, 46)
Geological Survey of Canada (Atlantic)
Natural Resources Canada
Bedford Institute of Oceanography
E-mail: Steve.Blasco@NRCan-RNCan.gc.ca
Phone: (902) 426-3932

Mr. Paul R. Boudreau (12)
60B Victoria Road
Dartmouth, NS, Canada B2Y 2V9
E-mail: paulboudreau@dal.ca
Phone: (902) 463-6191

Dr. W. Donald Bowen (14*)
Population Ecology Division
Fisheries and Oceans Canada
Bedford Institute of Oceanography
E-mail: don.bowen@dfo-mpo.gc.ca
Phone: (902) 426-8909

Mr. Dale E. Buckley (29*)
21 Dumbarton Avenue
Dartmouth, NS, Canada B2X 1Z7
E-mail: dbuckley@ns.sympatico.ca
Phone: (902) 434-5734

Mr. Gary L. Bugden (17)
Tritium Research
63 Union Street
Bedford, NS, Canada B4A 2B6
E-mail: gary.bugden@tritium-research.ca
Phone: (902) 835-5006

Mr. Gordon D.M. Cameron (26)
Geological Survey of Canada (Atlantic)
Natural Resources Canada
Bedford Institute of Oceanography
E-mail: gocamero@nrcan.gc.ca
Phone: (902) 426-7582

Dr. Jae S. Choi (32)
Fisheries and Oceans Canada
Bedford Institute of Oceanography
E-mail: Jae.Choi@dfo-mpo.gc.ca
Phone: (902) 426-1615

Dr. R. Allyn Clarke (16*)
5719 Southwood Drive
Halifax, NS, Canada B3H 1E6
E-mail: Allyn420@aol.com
Phone: (902) 420-0632

Dr. Ross R. Claytor (31)
Population Ecology Division
Fisheries and Oceans Canada
Bedford Institute of Oceanography
E-mail: Ross.Claytor@dfo-mpo.gc.ca
Phone: (902) 426-4721

Mr. Kim W. Conway (21)
Geological Survey of Canada (Pacific)
Natural Resources Canada
Institute of Ocean Sciences
9860 West Saanich Road (PO Box 6000)
Sidney, BC, Canada V8L 4B2
E-mail: Kim.Conway@NRCan.gc.ca
Phone: (250) 363-6400

Dr. Peter J. Cranford (33)
Fisheries and Oceans Canada
Bedford Institute of Oceanography,
E-mail: Peter.Cranford@dfo-mpo.gc.ca
Phone: (902) 426-3277

Dr. Sonya A. Dehler (25)
Geological Survey of Canada (Atlantic)
Natural Resources Canada
Bedford Institute of Oceanography
E-mail: sonya.dehler@nrcan.gc.ca
Phone: (902) 426-4289

Dr. Lloyd M. Dickie (12)
7 Lakewood Crescent
Dartmouth, NS, Canada B2X 2R6
Email: lloyddickie@eastlink.ca.
Phone: (902) 435-1545

Mr. Kenneth G. Doe (37)
74 Pinewood Drive,
Mount Uniacke, NS, Canada B0N 1Z0
E-mail: Kenneth.g.doe@gmail.com
Phone: (902) 866-3353

Dr. Kenneth F. Drinkwater (13)
Institute of Marine Research
Nordnesgaten 55 5005
5005 Bergen, Norway
E-mail: ken.drinkwater@imr.no
Phone: 47-462-50453

Mr. André J. Ducharme (30)
RR 3, Windsor Forks, NS
Canada B0N 2T0
E-mail: ducharme@eastlink.ca
Phone: (902) 792-1757

Dr. Daniel E. Duplisea (12*)
Fisheries and Oceans Canada
Institut Maurice-Lamontagne
Mont-Joli, QC, Canada G5H 3Z4
E-mail: daniel.duplisea@dfo-mpo.gc.ca
Phone: (418) 775-0881

Mr. R. Michael Eaton (20*, 42)
828 Bissett Road
Cole Harbour, NS, Canada B2V 2T8
E-mail: mikeeaton@eastlink.ca
Phone: (902) 434-1654

Dr. James A. Elliott (17)
90 Little Salmon River Drive
Dartmouth, NS, Canada B2Z 1H1
E-mail: eljgj@eastlink.ca
Phone: (902) 434-6072

Mr. Gordon B.J. Fader (22*, 40, 45)
Atlantic Marine Geological Consulting Ltd.
2901 Parkdale Avenue
Halifax, NS, Canada B3L 3Z2
E-mail: gordon.fader@ns.sympatico.ca
Phone: (902) 455-6100

Dr. Robert A. Fensome (25)
Geological Survey of Canada (Atlantic)
Natural Resources Canada
Bedford Institute of Oceanography
E-mail: rob.fensome@nrcan.gc.ca
Phone: (902) 426-2732

Dr. Donald L. Forbes (23, 26)
Geological Survey of Canada (Atlantic)
Natural Resources Canada
Bedford Institute of Oceanography
E-mail: DonaldL.Forbes@NRCan-RNCan.gc.ca
Phone: (902) 426-7737

Mr. Stephen R. Forbes (47)
604 Ketch Harbour Road
Portuguese Cove, NS, Canada B3L 1K1
E-mail: stephenforbes@eastlink.ca
Phone: (902) 868-2291

Mr. George A. Fowler (6, 39, 41*)
35 Lawson Ave.
Dartmouth, NS, Canada B2W 2Z2
E-mail: george.fowler@ns.sympatico.ca
Phone: (902) 462-5784

Mr. David Frobel (23)
14 MicMac Drive
Dartmouth, NS, Canada B2X 2H2
E-mail: Frobel@accesswave.ca
Phone: (902) 434-2844

Dr. Donald C. Gordon (2*, 11*, 34*, 44*,45*)
121 Crichton Avenue
Dartmouth, NS, Canada B3A 3R6
E-mail: donald.gordon@ns.sympatico.ca
Phone: (902) 469-2798

Mr. Stephen T. Grant (42*, 43*)
RPO Mic Mac Mall, Box 24026
Dartmouth, NS, Canada B3A 4T4
Phone: (902) 565-2501
E-mail: enci@ns.sympatico.ca

Dr. David A. Greenberg (45)
Coastal Ecosystem Science Division
Fisheries and Oceans Canada
Bedford Institute of Oceanography
E-mail: David.Greenberg@dfo-mpo.gc.ca
Phone: (902) 426-2431

Mr. Jim M. Hamilton (5)
Ocean and Ecosystem Sciences Division
Fisheries and Oceans Canada
Bedford Institute of Oceanography,
E-mail: Jim.Hamilton@dfo-mpo.gc.ca
Phone: (902) 426-3717

Dr. Barry T. Hargrave (11, 13, 33*, 36)
561 Balmy Beach Road
Owen Sound, ON, Canada N4K 5N4
E-mail: hargraveb@rogers.com
Phone: (591) 371-5908

Dr. Gareth C. Harding (13, 36)
2019 Bauer St.
Halifax, NS, Canada B3K 3W2
Email: Gareth.Harding@dfo-mpo.gc.ca
Phone: (902) 422-7115

Dr. J. Scott Holladay (6)
Geosensors Inc.
66 Mann Avenue
Toronto, ON, Canada M4S 2Y3
E-mail: Scott.Holladay@geosensors.com
Phone: (416) 486-6845

Dr. H. Ruth Jackson (8)
Geological Survey Canada (Atlantic)
Natural Resources Canada
Bedford Institute of Oceanography
E-mail: Ruth.Jackson@NRCAN-RNCAN.gc.ca
Phone: (902) 426-3791

Dr. E. Peter Jones (4*)
3 Lakeside Terrace
Dartmouth, NS, Canada B3A 2R1
E-mail: jones.peter@ns.sympatico.ca
Phone: (902) 469-6594

Mr. Heiner W. Josenhans (22)
1415 Second Peninsula Road, RR 3
Lunenburg, NS, Canada B0J2C0
E-mail: Josenhans@uniserve.com
Phone: (902) 634-8911

Mr. Paul D. Keizer (44)
20 Murray Hill Drive
Dartmouth, NS, Canada B2Y 3A8
E-mail: keizerp@gmail.com
Phone: (902) 466-7590

Dr. Ellen L.R. Kenchington (11, 34)
Ocean and Ecosystem Sciences Division
Fisheries and Oceans Canada
Bedford Institute of Oceanography
E-mail: Ellen.Kenchington@dfo-mpo.gc.ca
Phone: (902) 426-2030

Dr. Edward L. King (26)
Geological Survey of Canada (Atlantic)
Natural Resources Canada
Bedford Institute of Oceanography
E-mail: Edward.King@NRCan.gc.ca
Phone: (902) 426-7739

Mr. Peter A. Koeller (32)
445 Glen Arbour Way
Hammonds Plains, NS, Canada B4B 1N3
E-mail: pandalus@live.ca
Phone: (902) 835-3585

Mr. Louis A. Lalumiere (6)
Sensors by Design Ltd.
100 Peevers Crescent
Newmarket, ON, Canada L3Y 7T1
E-mail: Louis@sensorsbydesign.com

Mr. Timothy C. Lambert (13*)
Population Ecology Division,
Fisheries and Oceans Canada
Bedford Institute of Oceanography
E-mail: tim.lambert@dfo-mpo.gc.ca
Phone: (902) 426-3872

Mr. Michel P. Latremouille
48 Swanton Drive
Dartmouth, NS, Canada B2W 2C5
E-mail: Latremouille@accesswave.ca
Phone: (902) 434-4036

Dr. David Ledu (9)
1296 Rue de l'Escarpe
Sherbrooke, QC, Canada J1H 6P2
E-mail: david.ledu@yahoo.ca
Phone: (819) 347 1899

Dr. Kenneth Lee (44)
Australian Resources Research Centre
26 Dick Perry Avenue
Kensington, WA 6151, Australia
E-mail: ken.lee@csiro.au
Phone: 61-8-6436-8629

Dr. C.F. Michael Lewis (2, 26*, 46*)
Geological Survey of Canada (Atlantic)
Natural Resources Canada
Bedford Institute of Oceanography
E-mail: Michael.Lewis@NRCan.gc.ca
Phone: (902) 426-7738

Dr. William K. Li (10*)
Fisheries and Oceans Canada
Bedford Institute of Oceanography
E-mail: Bill.Li@dfo-mpo.gc.ca
Phone: (902) 426-6349

Mr. J. Richard MacDougall (19*)
38 Riverview Crescent
Bedford, NS, Canada B4A 2X4
E-mail: jrmacdougall@hotmail.com
Phone: (902) 832-3624

Mr. Brian MacLean (22, 39*)
Geological Survey of Canada (Atlantic)
Natural Resources Canada
Bedford Institute of Oceanography
E-mail: brimacle@NRCAN.gc.ca
Phone: (902) 426-3703

Mr. Paul A. Macnab (30)
Oceans and Coastal Management Division
Ecosystem Management Branch
Bedford Institute of Oceanography
E-mail: Paul.Macnab@dfo-mpo.gc.ca
Phone: (902) 426-6391

Dr. Gavin K. Manson (23)
Geological Survey of Canada (Atlantic)
Natural Resources Canada
Bedford Institute of Oceanography
E-mail: gmanson@nrcan.gc.ca
Phone: (902) 426-3144

Dr. David L. McKeown (40*)
6 Armshore Drive
Halifax, NS, Canada B3N 1M5
E-mail: davidmckeown@hfx.eastlink.ca
Phone: (902) 477-5887

Ms. Catherine B. Merriman (30)
Ecosystem Management Branch
Fisheries and Oceans Canada
Bedford Institute of Oceanography
E-mail: Catherine.Merriman@dfo-mpo.gc.ca
Phone: (902) 426-0518

Dr. Robert J. Miller (32)
Fisheries and Oceans Canada
Bedford Institute of Oceanography
E-mail: Robert.Miller@dfo-mpo.gc.ca
Phone: (902) 426-8108

Dr. Eric L. Mills (1*)
Department of Oceanography
Dalhousie University
1355 Oxford Street (PO Box 15000)
Halifax, NS, Canada B3H 4R2
E-mail: emills@dal.ca
Phone: (902) 422-4332

Dr. David C. Mosher (40, 47)
Geological Survey of Canada (Atlantic)
Natural Resources Canada
Bedford Institute of Oceanography
E-mail: dmosher@nrcan.gc.ca
Phone: (902) 426-3149

Dr. Peta J. Mudie (8*, 9)
Geological Survey Canada (Atlantic)
Natural Resources Canada
Bedford Institute of Oceanography
E-mail: pmudie@nrcan.gc.ca
Phone: (902) 426-8720

Ms. Odette C. Murphy (30*)
Fisheries and Oceans Canada
Bedford Institute of Oceanography
E-mail: Odette.Murphy@dfo-mpo.gc.ca
Phone: (902) 426-9734

Mr. Jason G. Naug (30)
Oceans and Coastal Management Division
Ecosystem Management Branch
Fisheries and Oceans Canada
Bedford Institute of Oceanography
E-mail: Jason.Naug@dfo-mpo.gc.ca
Phone: (902) 426-2574

Dr. David N. Nettleship (2, 15*)
Lundy Environmental Consulting
25 Tidewater Lane, Allen Heights
Head of St. Margaret's Bay, NS Canada B3Z 2G7
E-mail: dnnlundy@navnet.net
Phone: (902) 826-2360

Dr. Neil S. Oakey (17)
Ocean and Ecosystem Sciences Division
Fisheries and Oceans Canada
Bedford Institute of Oceanography
E-mail: Neil.Oakey@dfo-mpo.gc.ca
Phone: (902) 426-4163

Mr. Robert N. O'Boyle (31*, 48)
1042 Shore Drive
Bedford, NS, Canada B4A 2E5
E-mail: bcubed@accesswave.ca
Phone: (902) 835-6065

Mr. D. Russell Parrott (40)
5656 Highway 221
Woodville, Kings County, NS, Canada B0P 1V0
E-mail: d.russell.parrott@gmail.com
(902) 681-9838

Mr. Donald L. Peer (11)
PO Box 142
Hubbards, NS, Canada B0J 1T0
E-mail: d.peer@ns.sympatico.ca
Phone: (902) 857-9268

Ms. Ingrid K. Peterson (5*, 6)
Ocean and Ecosystem Sciences Division
Fisheries and Oceans Canada
Bedford Institute of Oceanography
E-mail: Ingrid.Peterson@dfo-mpo.gc.ca
Phone: (902) 426-6929

Dr. Brian D. Petrie (17)
Ocean and Ecosystem Sciences Division
Fisheries and Oceans Canada
Bedford Institute of Oceanography
E-mail: Brian.Petrie@dfo-mpo.gc.ca
Phone: (902) 426-2650

Mr. Roger G. Pettipas (5)
Ocean and Ecosystem Sciences Division
Fisheries and Oceans Canada
Bedford Institute of Oceanography
E-mail: Roger.Pettipas@dfo-mpo.gc.ca
Phone: (902) 426-4038

Dr. Richard A. Pickrill (21*)
4169 Highway 2
Wellington, NS, Canada B2T 1A3
E-mail: dpickrill@gmail.com
Phone: (902) 860-0692

Dr. David J.W. Piper (24*, 46)
Geological Survey of Canada (Atlantic)
Natural Resources Canada
Bedford Institute of Oceanography
E-mail: dpiper@nrcan.gc.ca
Phone: (902) 426-6580

Mr. Merle D. Pittman (41)
174 Meadowsweet Road
Middle Sackville, NS, Canada B4E 3J7
E-mail: merle@merlepittman.com
Phone: (902) 489-9900

Dr. Simon J. Prinsenberg (5, 6*, 41)
72 Douglas Drive,
Bedford, NS, Canada B4A 3A2
E-mail: prinsenberg.simon@gmail.com
Phone: (902) 835-6147

Dr. André Rochon (9*)
Institut des sciences de la mer de Rimouski
Université du Québec à Rimouski
310 allée des Ursulines
Rimouski, QC, Canada G5L 3A1
E-mail: andre_rochon@uqar.ca
Phone: (418) 723-1986, ext. 1742

Mr. Dale L. Roddick (32)
Fisheries and Oceans Canada
Bedford Institute of Oceanography
E-mail: Dale.Roddick@dfo-mpo.gc.ca
Phone: (902) 426-6643

Dr. Charles T. Schafer (28*)
1464 Waverley Road
Waverley, NS, Canada B2R 1W7
E-mail: charlestschafer@gmail.com
Phone: (902) 861-3145

Dr. John Shaw (23, 27, 38*)
Geological Survey of Canada (Atlantic)
Natural Resources Canada
Bedford Institute of Oceanography
E-mail: johnshaw@nrcan.gc.ca
Phone: (902) 426-6204

Mr. Greg R. Siddall (41)
3 Boundary Street
Dartmouth, NS, Canada B2Y 2K9
E-mail: Greg.Siddall@dfo-mpo.gc.ca
Phone: (902) 453-0040

Dr. Peter G. Simpkin (40)
1279 Old Sackville Road
Middle Sackville, NS, Canada B4E 3A6
E-mail: seistec@eastlink.ca
Phone: (902) 865-5971

Dr. Michael M. Sinclair (2, 31, 48*)
16 White Glove Terrace
Halifax, NS, Canada B3N 3L7
E-mail: michael.sinclair@dfo-mpo.gc.ca
Phone: (902) 431-3811

Dr. John N. Smith (7*)
Atlantic Environmental Radioactivity Unit
Fisheries and Oceans Canada
Bedford Institute of Oceanography
E-mail: john.smith@dfo-mpo.gc.ca
Phone: (902) 426-3865

Dr. Peter C. Smith (17*, 45)
Ocean and Ecosystem Sciences Division
Bedford Institute of Oceanography
E-mail: Peter.Smith@dfo-mpo.gc.ca
Phone: (902) 426-3474

Mr. Stephen J. Smith (21, 32)
Fisheries and Oceans Canada
Bedford Institute of Oceanography
E-mail: Stephen.Smith@dfo-mpo.gc.ca
Phone: (902) 426-3317

Mr. Gary V. Sonnichsen (46)
Geological Survey of Canada (Atlantic)
Natural Resources Canada
Bedford Institute of Oceanography
E-mail: gsonic@nrcan.gc.ca
Phone: (902) 426-4850

Dr. James E. Stewart (35*)
219 Glenwood Drive
Head of St. Margaret's Bay, NS, Canada B3Z 2E7
E-mail: jstewart@ns.sympatico.ca
Phone: (902) 826-2025

Mr. Nicholas Stuifbergen (42)
(deceased)

Mr. Robert B. Taylor (23*)
100 Pleasant Street
Dartmouth, NS, Canada B2Y 3P5
E-mail: taylorr@ns.sympatico.ca
Phone: (902) 469-4370

Dr. Brian J. Todd (21, 26, 27*)
Geological Survey of Canada (Atlantic)
Natural Resources Canada
Bedford Institute of Oceanography
E-mail: Brian.Todd@NRCan.gc.ca
Phone: (902) 426-3470

Dr. M. John Tremblay (32*)
Fisheries and Oceans Canada
Bedford Institute of Oceanography
E-mail: John.Tremblay@dfo-mpo.gc.ca
Phone: (902) 426-3986

Dr. Jacob Verhoef (47*)
Geological Survey of Canada (Atlantic)
Natural Resources Canada
Bedford Institute of Oceanography
E-mail: jverhoef@nrcan.gc.ca
Phone: (902) 426-3448

Dr. Peter Wadhams (3*)
Centre for Mathematical Sciences
University of Cambridge
Wilberforce Road
Cambridge CB3 0WA, United Kingdom
E-mail: p.wadhams@damtp.cam.ac.uk
Phone: 441-223-760372 or 576433

Dr. David E. Wells (43)
506 Squires Street
Fredericton, NB, Canada E3B 5A3
E-mail: dew@unb.ca
Phone: (506) 454-2650

Dr. Peter G. Wells (37*, 44)
International Ocean Institute
Dalhousie University
6414 Coburg Road (PO Box 15000)
Halifax, NS, Canada B3H 4R2
E-mail: oceans2@ns.sympatico.ca
Phone: (902) 237-0600

Dr. David J. Wildish (33)
Fisheries and Oceans Canada
531 Brandy Cove Road
St. Andrews, NB, Canada E5B 2L9
E-mail: wildishd@dfo-mpo.gc.ca
Phone: (506) 529-8854

Dr. Graham L. Williams (25*, 39)
Geological Survey of Canada (Atlantic)
Natural Resources Canada
Bedford Institute of Oceanography
E-mail: graham.williams@nrcan.gc.ca
Phone: (902) 426-5657

Dr. Philip A. Yeats (18*)
Fisheries and Oceans Canada
Bedford Institute of Oceanography
E-mail: Philip.Yeats@dfo-mpo.gc.ca
Phone: (902) 425-8674

---

[1] 1 Challenger Drive, Dartmouth, Nova Scotia Canada B2Y 4A2